# CANADIAN GOVERNMENT AND POLITICS

## Institutions and Processes

**McGraw-Hill Ryerson Series in Canadian Politics**

General Editor — Paul W. Fox

POLITICS: CANADA, Eighth Edition — Primis
   Paul W. Fox and Graham White

LOCAL GOVERNMENT IN CANADA, Fourth Edition
   C. Richard Tindal and Susan Nobes Tindal

POLITICAL PARTIES, LEADERS, AND IDEOLOGIES IN CANADA
   Colin Campbell and William Christian

THE REVISED CANADIAN CONSTITUTION: POLITICS AS LAW
   R. I. Cheffins and P. A. Johnson

FEDERAL CONDITIONS IN CANADA
   D. V. Smiley

THE JUDICIARY IN CANADA: THE THIRD BRANCH OF GOVERNMENT
   Peter H. Russell

POLITICS AND THE MEDIA IN CANADA, Second Edition (Forthcoming)
   Arthur Siegel

*Also available*

CANADIAN GOVERNMENT AND POLITICS: INSTITUTIONS AND
PROCESSES
   Michael S. Whittington and Richard J. Van Loon

MINDSCAPES: POLITICAL IDEOLOGIES TOWARDS THE TWENTY-FIRST
CENTURY
   Roger Gibbins and Loleen Youngman

# CANADIAN GOVERNMENT AND POLITICS

## Institutions and Processes

**MICHAEL S. WHITTINGTON**
*Carleton University*

**RICHARD J. VAN LOON**
*University of Ottawa*

**McGraw-Hill Ryerson Limited**

Toronto New York Auckland Bogotá Caracas
Lisbon London Madrid Mexico Milan New Delhi
San Juan Singapore Sydney Tokyo

## CANADIAN GOVERNMENT AND POLITICS: INSTITUTIONS AND PROCESSES

ISBN: 0-07-551102-9

1 2 3 4 5 6 7 8 9 10     BBM     5 4 3 2 1 0 9 8 7 6

Printed and bound in Canada

Sponsoring Editor: Gord Muschett
Supervising Editor: Margaret Henderson
Production Editor: Andrea Gallagher Ellis
Developmental Editor: Norma Christensen
Production Co-ordinator: Nicla Dattolico
Cover Design: Dianna Little
Cover Illustration/Photo: Corel Stock Photo Library
Typesetter: Computer Composition of Canada Inc.
Printer: Best Book Manufacturers

**Canadian Cataloguing in Publication Data**

Whittington, Michael S., 1942–
    Canadian government and politics

(McGraw-Hill Ryerson series in Canadian politics)
Includes bibliographical references and index.
ISBN 0-07-551102-9

1. Canada — Politics and government.   I. Van Loon, Richard J., 1940–    .   II. Title.   III. Series.

JL65 1995.W55 1995     320.971     C95-932398-8

*To Milt Trace and Max Van Loon*

# Contents

## Appendix

# Preface

When we first decided, in 1967, that Canadian government texts needed a new approach to the subject, we were still naive, if ambitious, graduate students. At the time we felt that the existing textbooks on Canadian government and politics were too "institutional." Excellent and influential classics such as Dawson's *The Government of Canada* focused on the formal structures of government but neglected to locate political and governmental institutions within the social, economic, psychological, and geographical contexts, which ultimately determine how such institutions actually work on a day-to-day basis. Heavily influenced by "behaviouralism" and the "systems approach," our first edition in 1971, entitled *The Canadian Political System: Environment, Structure and Process*, devoted three out of nineteen chapters to subjects such as the socio-economic context, political culture, political participation, political socialization, and political elites. By the time the fourth edition was completed, six out of nineteen chapters and more than one-third of the total text deal with "environmental" variables.

In 1994, when considering the daunting task of writing a fifth edition of *The Canadian Political System*, we concluded that the subject was in need of a new focus and a new approach. We felt that in attempting to deal comprehensively with the increasingly complex socio-economic and cultural environment of government, we and most of our competitors ended up with a choice between producing either a multi-volume edition or a single volume that would give even shorter shrift to the institutions and processes that are the ultimate focus of this textbook. Moreover, there are now many excellent articles and monographs that focus specifically upon the once neglected areas of political culture, political economy, and political sociology, and which can be used by instructors in conjunction with materials on institutions and processes of government.

This view, which was confirmed by discussions with various colleagues at Carleton, most notably Glen Williams, whose insights have been invaluable, led us to a decision to do a single volume that deals comprehensively with the institutions and processes of government and politics. While there are still two chapters that deal with society, economy, and culture as contexts within which the institutions operate, the aim of those chapters is to provide an overview of the relevant subject matter and to direct the student to other sources for more comprehensive coverage of the environmental variables that underlie and shape Canadian political life in the 1990s.

In focusing on institutions, we must emphasize that we have not reverted to an earlier style of institutional analysis that concentrated primarily on formal structure; rather, we have endeavoured to explain how Canada's political and governmental institutions interact with each other and with people and groups in Canadian society. In other words, our focus is upon the political and governmental *processes* within which the institutions operate. To reflect this change in emphasis, we also decided to retitle the book *Canadian Government and Politics: Institutions and Processes*. Aficionados of such things will also note that the authors' names are reversed for this edition. This reflects the fact that the Whittington part of the team took primary responsibility for the writing and preparation of the volume, since the Van Loon part of the team, in his current role in the federal bureaucracy, was not able to participate as fully.

As with any large academic project, we are indebted to the many people who have assisted us. We have already mentioned the encouragement and advice of a close friend and colleague, Glen Williams. We are also grateful to Carleton colleagues Professor Amy Bartholomew of the Law Department and Ph.D. candidate Patrick Gibson of the Political Science Department, who helped in researching the chapters on the judiciary and interest groups, respectively. Ron Gould of Elections Canada spent much of his valuable time in reading and commenting on the chapters on elections. Betty Whittington provided invaluable assistance in researching the chapters on the bureaucracy, and Pat Steenberg of the House of Commons staff provided up-to-date materials on parliamentary procedure. George Roseme read and critiqued many of the chapters — while we have decided "to boldly retain" a few split infinitives, his substantive suggestions and comments were mostly heeded. Phyllis Will of Statistics Canada is to be thanked heartily not only for digging up the "hard" social, demographic, and economic data in the earlier chapters, but also for her assistance in the conceptual development of many sections of the book.

We should also express our appreciation of the comments received in the pre-publication reviews commissioned by the publisher. While "to protect the innocent" we don't know who said what, Professor Jay Smith, Athabasca University; Professor P. W. Nesbitt-Larking, Huron College; Professor George Roseme, Carleton University; Professor C. R. Grondin, University of New Brunswick; Professor James Bickerton, St. Francis Xavier University; Professor William Matheson, Brock University; Professor David Stewart, University of Alberta; Professor E. Keenes, University of Victoria; Professor David Cameron, University of Toronto; Professor Brian Tanguay, Wilfrid Laurier University, are to be thanked for all their insightful comments, criticisms, and suggestions, which, we hope, greatly improved the end product.

Finally, we would like to acknowledge the contributions of Anne Louise Currie, Gord Muschett, Norma Christensen, and Margaret Henderson, all of McGraw-Hill Ryerson, in getting the book from the contract stage to the production stage. Special thanks go out to Andrea Gallagher Ellis whose editorial skills, patience, and sense of humour helped to convert a messy manuscript to a finished product. Any errors or omissions that remain, needless to say, can be blamed entirely on our computer software.

Mike Whittington
Carleton University
Ottawa

Richard Van Loon
Health Canada
Ottawa

# Introduction

*Chapter* 1

# Concepts and Approaches

Governments today are the dominant actors on the world's stage, and their activities constantly affect the economic, social, and psychological dimensions of our everyday lives. All societies[1] possess structures or institutions that we would recognize as governments. These ubiquitous entities provide myriad services ranging from the defence of our borders to the redistribution of income. They regulate industry, labour, and the professions; provide the roads we drive on, the water we drink, electrical power, national communications networks, public education, medical care, and low-cost housing; and even engage in commercial enterprises in competition with private corporations.

Beyond the provision of goods and services, the regulation of human behaviour, and the redistribution of wealth, governments also provide symbolic reference points for their citizens. They provide unifying national symbols such as flags and anthems, as well as leadership figures with whom we can identify or against whom we can vent our anger and frustration. Moreover, governments and the endless caravan of politicians crusading to control them are intrinsically interesting to the citizenry and add an entertaining and psychologically stimulating dimension to our lives.

---

1. By "society" we mean the network of social relationships that exists among individuals and is continuous through successive generations. This rather perfunctory definition is intended merely as a starting point for the reader, and will be elaborated upon as the discussion unfolds. See Marion J. Levy, *The Structure of Society* (Princeton: Princeton University Press, 1952), p. 113; and J. W. Vander Zanden, *Sociology* (New York: The Ronald Press, 1965), p. 153.

## ► A GENERIC DEFINITION

This book is about how government works at the national level in Canada. Virtually all Canadians have an intuitive sense of what government is about. We are all involved in the political process to varying degrees, we are all required to pay attention to and abide by the promulgations and decrees of our government, and, hence, we generally "know about" these things. However, it is still worth talking about **politics** and **government** as broader concepts in use in the modern world. While the form of government may differ widely from one nation to another, it seems logical to posit that all governments must fulfill some requirement or perform some "job" that is common to all societies, however disparate. If we can understand the *generic function*[2] performed by governments, wherever they may be, we will be better able to tackle the task of understanding how our Canadian system of government differs from that of other nations.

### Scarcity, Conflict, and Cooperation

There are three main factors that determine the existence and nature of the governmental or political function. First, human beings are *appetitive* creatures who have not only a multitude of primal needs that must be satisfied if the species is to survive, but also almost limitless desires and wants that must be at least minimally satisfied if people are to find individual happiness and live long and healthy lives.

Second, the human condition is a *social condition*. Human beings choose to live in societies not only because more can be accomplished through cooperation and joint effort than by individuals acting alone, but also because *homo sapiens* is naturally gregarious. Moreover, individuals also have social needs that can be satisfied only in a social context.

**Scarcity**    The third factor bearing on the human condition is that the material and non-material resources necessary for the satisfaction of individual human needs and wants must be extracted from a real-world environment that is finite or *limited*. Canadians are immensely lucky in terms of where they live. However, no matter how abundant our resources are relative to many other countries, no one would argue that even the Canadian economy produces enough material goods to completely satisfy every citizen. In fact, because human expectations tend to rise with the standard of living, the total elimination of material scarcity even in the wealthiest countries in the world remains an impossible dream.

But *material* scarcity is only one dimension of the limited environment. Even if there were no limit to the material resources of a society, there are

---

2.  Marion Levy defines the term as well as anybody: "A function is a condition or state of affairs resultant from the operation . . . of a structure through time. . . . A structure is a pattern, i.e., an observable uniformity of action or operation." Quoted in Roland Young, *Approaches to the Study of Politics* (Evanston: Northwestern, 1958), p. xv.

other situations where scarcity cannot be eliminated or even significantly reduced. Status,[3] prestige, honour, love, and recognition of individual accomplishments, for instance, are psychological needs that can be satisfied only relative to other people. Thus, one's status is high because that of others is relatively lower, and honour and prestige are also relative commodities that are socially defined. It is illogical, therefore, to speak of ever totally "eliminating" scarcity in such non-material commodities which are perpetually in high demand among our citizens. The inequality in the distribution of such psychological goods can be reduced only if people can be conditioned to need them less.

Finally, perhaps the most important and yet most misunderstood commodity in society is *individual freedom*. Freedom is a scarce resource because one individual's freedom limits the freedom of others. Simply by occupying space, an individual restricts the freedom of other individuals to occupy that same space. As well, in competing with other individuals for scarce resources the winners can't help but limit the freedom of the losers. As we will see in later chapters, governments moderate and manage conflict in society by making rules about human behaviour, all of which constitute limits on our individual freedom. Each piece of positive law imposes duties and responsibilities on us, which we accept because we prefer an ordered and peaceful society to chaos and unresolved conflict.

**Conflict** The triumvirate of boundless human wants, the social nature of the human condition, and limited or scarce resources combines to produce a situation where individuals or aggregations of individuals within societies must compete with others to maximize personal or group satisfaction. In other words, there exists a potential situation of virtually endless squabbling over who gets what, when, and how much of the available resources. This competition or **conflict** occurs at several levels. At one level, individuals may compete directly with other individuals, because, in spite of some halting evidence of changing values in North America, getting a promotion, finding a job in the first place, winning a scholarship, or having a nicer garden than the neighbour's are still central concerns of life.

But conflict often transcends the individual level. **Groups** of people with interests in common are also in competition with other groups. Labour unions compete with management and with each other, farmers compete with non-agricultural occupational groups, and dentists compete with denturists. Intergroup competition is a sort of bargaining game where the prize is the larger share of available but limited resources.

Moreover, competition among groups in society is transcended by even broader-based conflict among aggregations of groups or *sectors*. In our postindustrial society, some would argue that traditional interpersonal and inter-

---

3. Whether the need for status is biologically determined and common to other animals as well as humans or whether it is a culturally determined feature of human society is arguable. The key point here is that, for whatever reasons, most people in all cultures seem to have a need for status, and their political behaviour is influenced by this need. See Robert Ardrey, *The Social Contract* (New York: Delta, 1970).

group conflict is rivalled in importance by intersectoral conflict with big business, big labour, and big government as the main protagonists.[4] Moreover, in *federal systems* such as Canada's, intergovernmental conflict itself is an important dimension of the competition for the scarce resources of the federation.

Conflict within a nation state may also occur between and among large national, cultural, or regional groups. The French-English conflict that colours so much of Canadian politics or the growth of "Western alienation" are obvious examples of this, and the increasing demands of our aboriginal peoples for the settlement of land claims and recognition of their right to self-government might also be viewed in this way. But, at still another level, we see whole societies in conflict in the international arena, where sovereign states are the actors competing for global power and influence and where the ultimate manifestation of conflict is war.

Finally, it is also argued by some that the pre-eminent conflict in modern society is the direct and necessary product of fundamental structural flaws in our advanced capitalist system. Here the mainspring of political conflict and change is seen to be a struggle between broad-based groups called *classes*—working class versus capitalist class, proletariat versus bourgeoisie, or simply rich versus "not rich." The immediate cause of such conflict is held to be simply the unequal distribution of economic resources and opportunities among the members of society and the ultimate cause is seen to be capitalism whose market-based system makes such inequality inevitable and perpetual. We will return to the consideration of different levels of political conflict in later chapters.

**Cooperation** Conflict is inherently neither good nor bad, but simply an inevitable state of affairs that occurs when people's boundless appetites are loosed on a limited environment. However, it must be recognized that *cooperation* is as inevitable as conflict in society. The very fact that human beings *do* live in societies and not singly testifies to the fundamentally cooperative side of human nature. Cooperation would seem to be natural, because human beings are inherently sociable and gregarious and because they have social needs. Moreover, cooperating with others is *instrumental* because more can be accomplished through working together than by working alone. Within the context of a modern industrial society, this has led to highly developed systems of cooperation called **organizations**, which permit a high division of labour, greater cost efficiency, and an increased productive capacity, all of which help to minimize material scarcity.

Additionally, because most conflict in a society occurs between groups, organizations, or classes—in essence, among and between aggregations of individuals with similar interests—one of the direct results of such conflict is to encourage cooperative effort *within* the collectivity. The need to compete

---

4. This thesis is set forth most succinctly in J. K. Galbraith's *The New Industrial State* (Boston: Houghton Mifflin, 1969) and *Economics and the Public Purpose* (New York: Thomas Allen and Sons, 1973). For a different perspective, see articles in M. D. Hancock and G. Sjoberg, eds., *Politics in the Post-Welfare State* (New York: Columbia University Press, 1972), especially pp. 37–55.

effectively with other groups fosters group cohesiveness and coordination of organizational effort, both of which are important integrative mechanisms. Thus, conflict and cooperation are not only inevitable in human societies, but these apparently opposite forces, in fact, are mutually reinforcing in the real world.[5]

### The Governmental Function: Conflict Management

Governments appear to us as specialized social structures or complex organizations that exist in all societies. The function of these complex structures is to ensure that the conflicts among groups and individuals in society are managed in a peaceful and ordered manner. Without such a mechanism for the management of intra-societal conflicts, a society could likely not persist over any length of time. Hence, we can say that the underlying function of all governments is to *manage conflicts* that occur in society. Conflict in society is managed both by resolving specific disputes as they arise and by anticipating potential areas of conflict and then stepping in pre-emptively to halt their development. We will say more about the management of conlict when we look at the *instruments of conflict management* later in this section.

As a caution to the reader, we must emphasize that, in defining the function of government in terms of conflict, we have in no way assumed that conflict is the dominant dimension of human interaction in societies. While conflict often seems more interesting, more visible, and more newsworthy, the *cooperative* mechanisms and instincts that permit a society to come into existence in the first place are at least equally significant and form a "given" of all societies. In fact, the logical interrelatedness of the concepts of conflict and cooperation means that the role of governments can be seen either as conflict management or as the facilitation of cooperation.

We must remember, too, that governments are not the only societal mechanisms for managing conflict. Because people intrinsically enjoy and benefit from the companionship of other people, there is a natural inclination to share, to accommodate different individual needs, and to find informal ways of avoiding or moderating interpersonal conflict. The *family*, for instance, is able to resolve internal squabbles because there is an accepted division of labour based on biological and generational differentiation. The resources of the family, like the resources of the society, must be allocated among its members in a peaceful way if the family unit is to hang together.

Another important non-governmental conflict-management mechanism is the **market system.** Through a medium of exchange we call money and by a complex process of bargaining that we call a **price system**, the marketplace resolves many of the conflicts that arise over what material resources various individuals and groups will possess. While such informal mechanisms or systems that moderate conflict in societies are extremely important in helping to

5. When we come to analyze the societal bases of conflict and cooperation within Canadian society, we will use the terms *cleavage* and *consensus*. A *cleavage* is a line of conflict between two groups that are in competition for the same resources. Hence, for example, we will often speak of French-English cleavage, class cleavage, or regional cleavage. *Consensus* is a state of agreement among a group of people over the desirability of some end. Consensus is the foundation for cooperation among individuals, within groups, and within societies.

maintain social order, what differentiates them from government is that they are limited in their scope and are subordinate to government.[6]

**Legitimacy and Coercion** The trouble with "natural" mechanisms such as the family and the market system is that they do not always succeed in managing disputes, in which case the only fallback mechanism for resolving the conflict is brute force or voluntary withdrawal of some of the combatants. The resort to force or **coercion**, whether based on economic or physical power, can never sustain an ordered society for very long unless the use of such sanctions is accepted as legitimate by the members of the society. Government is the mechanism of conflict management that is distinguished by the fact that it enjoys a monopoly over the legitimate use of the collective coercive power of the society to back up its decisons.

By choosing to be a member of a given society, an individual has automatically agreed to live by the rules of that society as determined by its government. But while the exclusive power to employ coercion obviously lends a great deal of authority to governmental enactments, a system that relies only on coercion in order to make its decisions effective would be neither stable nor efficient. Too large a percentage of the available resources would be utilized in merely keeping the citizenry in line, and the slightest let-up in the use of force would leave the government vulnerable to overthrow or collapse. For a governmental system to persist, therefore, it must acquire **legitimacy**. The members of the society must accept the system not merely because they have to, but because they *choose* to—because there is agreement that the government is a "fair umpire" of societal conflict.

A system of government acquires legitimacy in many ways. Often it happens simply because people accept it out of habit or because it is easier to accept the existing regime than to rebel against it. But whatever the origins of a government's legitimacy, it can persist only if the values and norms according to which the government operates are acceptable to the society as a whole. The state must *continue* to be seen as the "fair umpire" and the citizens must abide by governmental decisions because they accept them as legitimate and not because they fear the imposition of coercive sanctions if they disobey.

**The "Master" System** Governments are the dominant mechanisms of conflict management in society, not only because they have the exclusive authority to use coercive sanctions, but also because they have *comprehensive* powers. They have jurisdiction over *all* aspects of our lives, and over *all* people in the society. A practical manifestation of the comprehensiveness of government's jurisdiction is that it is responsible for overseeing all other mechanisms of conflict management. For example, in most societies, parents will be permitted to discipline their children, but prohibited by laws enacted by government from abusing, killing, or abandoning them. Similarly, the operation of the economic system is limited by a host of laws prohibiting such things as misleading adver-

---

6. The examination of society as a group of systems and sub-systems has a history too long to be traced in a footnote. Most notably, the concept has been promoted by Talcott Parsons in most of his voluminous writings, and in political science by Gabriel Almond, David Easton, and Karl Deutsch, among others.

tising, undue restriction of competition, or unfair employment practices, and regulating matters as disparate as labour relations or the emission of pollutants into the environment.

However, there are reasons for not taking this description of the government as the *master* system too far. Governments in Canada may be formally omnipotent, but they are constrained by the distribution of economic power, the prevailing value system of the society, and the values and beliefs of the decision makers themselves.[7] As well, because Canada has a *federal* system with a constitutionally defined division of power, the federal and provincial governments constrain each other. While we will discuss in depth later the practical limitations on the exercise of governmental authority in Canada, we can still conclude at this point that governments are far and away the single most powerful, pervasive, and ubiquitous institutions in the modern world.

**Instruments of Conflict Management**  We have seen that the potential for conflict exists in societies because there is simply not enough of the things that people need and desire to go around. Government's job is to manage actual and potential conflict and it accomplishes this for the most part by forcing us to share the limited resources available with fellow members of society. If we accept the way in which the government has meted out or allocated the good things that we all want, actual conflict will be avoided or at least moderated. It is only as a last resort that government must step in and impose settlement of an active dispute.

There are a number of tools that the government has at its disposal for carrying out its responsibilities for the management of conflict. These **governing instruments** (Table 1.1) include a range of devices through which the government forces us to share the limited resources of our society. Bruce Doern and Richard Phidd see governing instruments as falling along a continuum according to the degree of coercion that must be employed by the state to carry them into effect.[8]

The governing instrument that is most familiar to us and the most coercive is **regulation**. Most laws passed by the government have the effect of regulating our behaviour. Regulation can range from outright **prohibition**, as with matters in the Criminal Code, to the setting of freight rates or air fares, or to requiring licences for engaging in certain kinds of enterprises. Regulation is more coercive than the instruments discussed up to this point because regulations are enforced in such a way that non-compliance can result in punitive sanctions such as revoking of a licence, fines, or even imprisonment.

**Taxation** is a governing instrument to the extent that the tax system can be employed to effect the distribution of wealth. *Who* pays taxes and *how much* they pay has as much a redistributive impact as explicit public-expenditure decisions. For instance, by allowing a large corporation a big tax write-off, the government can thereby encourage growth within such organizations or in

---

7. In Canada, governments have chosen to place limits on themselves both through simple restraint in areas where the intervention of the state is seen as illegitimate, and explicitly through the Constitution, which includes the Charter of Rights and Freedoms.

8. G. B. Doern and R. W. Phidd, *Canadian Public Policy: Ideas, Structure, Process* (Toronto: Methuen, 1983).

specific industries. Sometimes this style of governing instrument is referred to as **tax expenditure** because the net effect is that there is less money in the public coffers to go around. This instrument is no more or less coercive than simple expenditure of public moneys, but it is certainly less visible and hence it is a useful device if the government wishes to provide financial assistance to a particular industry, but would rather not let the average taxpayer know about it.

The next level of governing instrument in terms of coerciveness is **public expenditure**, the simple expenditure of public moneys. Expenditures can be either **distributive** or **redistributive**. The former are directed to the creation of a public good, through, for instance, the construction of a highway, the establishment of a national park, or the erection of a school, any of which are available for the use and benefit of all Canadians. Redistributive expenditures, by contrast, are measures such as old-age pensions or welfare programs, which have the effect of transferring wealth from all taxpayers to a special category of citizens deemed to be more needy than the rest of us. The instrument of public expenditure is thus

> only moderately coercive in that governments, when they spend, are distributing the funds as benefits or services. . . . Actual coercion occurs when the revenue is extracted, from the taxpayer, but when it is spent the coercive edge has disappeared.[9]

**State enterprise** or the direct involvement of the state in capitalist enterprise is a governing instrument that is especially characteristic of Canada. The vast number of crown corporations at both the federal and provincial levels in Canada provide ample examples of the use of this sort of governing instrument. While it is in most ways less coercive than regulation, public ownership does have an impact on a very wide range of Canadians as well as on private-sector individuals and corporations who must compete with the public enterprise. Moreover, in an integrated world economy the state capitalism device can also have impacts that cross our borders into the international economic community.

Finally, at the least coercive extreme is **exhortation** as a means of governing:

> To govern by exhortation is to engage in a whole series of potential acts of persuasion and voluntary appeals to the electorate as a whole or to particular parts of it. In this sense many would properly view exhortation as democratic government in its highest and most ideal form.[10]

Thus, exhortation is an instrument of governance that relies on the intrinsic merits of the policy goal and the legitimacy of the government to induce us to alter the patterns of our behaviour. Campaigns against smoking, drunk driving, or racism are examples of the use of exhortation in an attempt to alter our attitudes or behaviour directly or as a supplement to more coercive instruments.

---

9. Ibid., p. 24.
10. Ibid.

**TABLE 1.1**
Governing Instruments

| Level of Coercion | Policy Instrument | Examples |
|---|---|---|
| High | Prohibition | Criminal law, bans of products |
| | Regulation | Set fees/fares, standards; require registration or licensing |
| | Taxation | Differential rates and exemptions to be used as incentives and sanctions |
| | Public Expenditure—redistributive | Non-universal social-service and income-support programs |
| | Public Expenditure—distributive | Public works such as roads; services such as law enforcement, defence, and universal social programs |
| | State Enterprise—monopolistic | Atomic Energy of Canada, Canada Post |
| | State Enterprise—competitive | CBC, CNR, and other crown corporations with policy goals (many recently privatized) |
| Low | Exhortation—"anti" campaigns —"pro" campaigns | Anti-smoking and "Participaction" |

We will return to the discussion of these various types of governing instruments later in the book when we are dealing with the policy process. Thus far we have offered a "generic" *functional* definition of governments: they are *complex social structures that manage conflict within societies*. While we have discussed the tools of governance that are available to the state in performing its function, we have said very little specifically about our main focus which is the Government of Canada. To take this next step, and get on with the ultimate aim of the book, it would seem logical that we first outline our approach to the subject.

## ▶ THE STUDY OF CANADIAN GOVERNMENT AND POLITICS

In all textbooks in political science it is *de rigueur* to have an "approach." The problem we have found, however, is that there are likely as many approaches to the study of Canadian government as there are political scientists teaching it. Moreover, after teaching Canadian government and politics to university students for more than a quarter-century, be damned if we, ourselves, can agree on what our own "approach" is, let alone find the right label for it!

### A "No-Name" Approach
Given that we have already employed a generic description of the function of government the large grocery chains should not be offended if we use an

eclectic *no-name product* approach to the rest of the book. We will neither fully adopt nor fully reject any of the past or current approaches to the study of Canadian government; rather, we will sometimes ignore an approach completely and sometimes steal from it shamelessly, depending on whether it helps us to explain or clarify something. But one thing we must do is to explain what this volume is about, and the best place to start is with the concepts incorporated in its title: government, politics, institutions, and processes.

**Institutions and Processes**  **Institutions** are social structures that are contrived or purposive. They are set up deliberately and they are organized in such a way that will achieve a defined set of goals in society. Institutions are composed of **roles** (positions or jobs) that are configured in such a way that the real people who occupy the roles are able to work together to accomplish the institutional goals. Institutions may be highly structured as with formal organizations, in which every individual participating in the institution has a rigidly defined role to play. But they may also be loosely structured, as with voluntary associations or political parties, in which only a few "officers" have formally defined roles and all the rest are simply "members."

Once established, institutions may evolve through the actions of their participants. The definition of individual institutional roles can change, the relationships among the roles can change, and even the goals of the institution can change or be "displaced"[11] over time. The more highly structured the institution, the less likely it is to change and the more slowly any change that does come about will occur. Perhaps most important when looking at political and governmental institutions is the fact that institutions may come incidentally to perform new functions in the real world quite different from those that were originally intended.[12]

Institutions are structural phenomena. **Processes**, by contrast, are the activities or behaviours through which institutions accomplish their goals, purposes, or functions. In other words, a process is *how* an institution gets its job done. There are different categories of processes that institutions are engaged in. There are processes that allow the organization to accomplish its goals in the outside world but there are also processes internal to an organization that allow it to adapt to changes going on about it and to persist over time.

**Government and Politics**  We have already spoken of the *function* of governments—what they do and why they exist in all societies. But what *is* a government and, more importantly, what is *not* government? "The government," "the

---

11. While Roberto Michels is normally credited with originating the concept of *goal displacement*, there is a large body of literature that has developed the concept and applied it to specific organizations. This phenomenon is discussed briefly and clearly in A. Etzioni, *Modern Organizations* (Englewood Cliffs: Prentice-Hall, 1964), pp. 10–14. See also R. J. Merton, *Social Theory and Social Structure* (Glencoe: Free Press, 1957), pp. 197ff.; and P. Selznick, "An Approach to a Theory of Bureaucracy," *American Sociological Review*, vol. 8, no. 1 (1943), pp. 47–54.

12. Note here that there are some value limits beyond which an institution may not adapt without becoming a new institution entirely. In other words, whereas adaptation is a dynamic element in institutional change, *pattern maintenance* is the conservative element. The "raw material" of pattern maintenance can be found in the fundamental values of the members of the society, and/or in the "clientele" of the institution.

state," "the political system," and "the polity" are all used to describe the set of institutions that perform the governmental function in societies. All of these terms introduce the common notion that there is a boundary between government and "not-government." Hence, for example, we speak of government versus the people, the state versus society, the political system versus the environment, and polity versus economy and society. Moreover, all such dichotomies explicitly recognize that there are patterns of interaction, behaviours, or processes that link the government to its social, economic, and cultural context or environment (Fig. 1.1).

The terms *government* and *politics* are often used interchangeably and, in fact, they are so closely related in the real world that one virtually never exists without the other. However, we are going to make an *analytical* distinction between political processes and governmental processes that can help us to better understand two basic categories of activity in which our politicians and governmental officials engage.

**Figure 1.1**
Governmental and political processes.

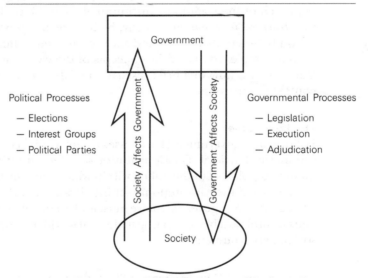

Governmental processes are characterized by the fact that they have a direct impact upon people in the real world outside government. While in practice these processes are interrelated and have reciprocal impacts one upon the other, it is possible to distinguish three basic sub-functions of government that are performed by three analytically discrete processes. The **legislative** process dominated by Cabinet and Parliament is one that results in the enactment of laws that are binding on all members of society. The **executive** or administrative process is one that implements and enforces the law and which is dominated by the Cabinet and the bureaucracy. Finally, the **adjudicative** process involves the interpretation of the law and the settlement of disputes that arise over its meaning and is dominated by the court system and the judiciary.

Political processes are those that permit people to have an effect on their government and thereby indirectly to influence the governmental processes. Interest-group politics is a political process in which organized interests in society attempt to influence the people in government to do or not to do things that will be beneficial to their members. Similarly, through the political party system and the electoral process, people in society are able to influence government not only by deciding *who* will form the government but also by expressing preferences for *what* party platforms they support.

Briefly then, the basic approach to the core chapters of this book will be first to look at a set of political or governmental *institutions* in terms of their functions, their origins, and what they *are* structurally. The next step will be to discuss the *processes* in which the institutions are engaged or *how* they perform their functions in Canadian society. Because we start with institutions, this approach clearly takes some inspiration from the "institutional school" of political analysis. However, by looking at the political and governmental *structures* in terms of their *functions* we have moved away from the more legalistic approach of the traditional institutionalists and have borrowed a page from the *structural-functionalists*. Finally, by looking at "process" in terms of interaction between institutions and society (the "environment" of government), we have employed one of the concepts of the *systems* approach. (Eclectic, eh?) But let's turn now to a brief discussion of the social, economic, and cultural context or environment.

### The Environment
Political and governmental processes occur within a context that is both institutional and societal. The Constitution sets the institutional context of government and politics but the milieu within which these processes operate is much broader than their institutional setting. If we are truly to understand the Canadian system of government we must look to the panoply of social, economic, and cultural variables operating in the real world outside those institutions—the societal **environment.**

**The Concept of "The Environment"**  In the widest conceptual sense, the environment of government includes everything that is "other" than the governmental institutions. However, this is far too broad a definition to be very useful in understanding what determines the nature and scope of politics in Canada. Clearly, in a technical sense, sunspots, quasars, black holes, and Halley's Comet are all part of the environment of Canadian government and politics but we can likely come to understand politics and government fairly well without much grounding in astrophysics. Nevertheless, as we move inwards from the outer ontological limits of this "universe" we can conceptualize the environment of government as a series of concentric rings, each of which includes variables of ascending relevance to the function of government.

**Figure 1.2**
The environment.

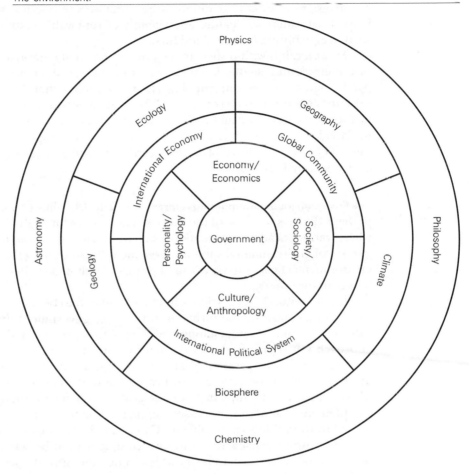

As can be seen from Fig. 1.2, each of these concentric rings tends to coincide with the research focus of a different academic discipline. One implication of this fact is that students of politics and government must acquire at least some familiarity with a number of sister disciplines in order to fully understand the phenomena that are the immediate concern of their research. Thus, while a political scientist can likely get by without a great deal of sophistication in the sciences of physics, chemistry, or microbiology, he or she may, from time to time, require some understanding of the basic concepts of geology, physical geography, macrobiology, and ecology.

Geology, for instance, can tell us about the location and commercial value of mineral resources, which can become the focus of issues in, for example, the intergovernmental arena, or in the development of a national industrial strategy. Similarly, physical geography may determine the nature and scope of regional conflicts in Canada, and the physical location of geographical features can become a determinant of political decisions. While the existence of a pingo in the Mackenzie Delta may not appear to have any intrinsic political relevance, it may acquire relevance if there is oil and gas underneath it or if it has spiritual significance to aboriginal people. Biology, ecology, and climate can similarly become significant considerations in political debate because such variables help to determine the nature and viability of renewable resource industries such as agriculture, fisheries, and furs.

However, it is with respect to the phenomena that comprise the *inner ring* of the environment—the disciplinary foci of the social-science disciplines of psychology, sociology, anthropology, and economics—that the political scientist must be most directly concerned.[13] Individual personality, socio-economic factors, and culture are all variables that set the agenda for political discourse in Canada. These variables are the determinants of the specific conflicts that the policy process must resolve—the "stuff" of Canadian politics, and the focus of the next chapter.

**The Environment and Competing Approaches**   The discipline of political science, perhaps the most eclectic of the social sciences, goes through phases or cycles where various academic practitioners come to champion the importance of one set of environmental variables over the others—arguing that some of the environmental factors have a "causal primacy" that makes them more important than the others.

In the 1950s, political science in Canada tended to be dominated by those who felt that knowing the formal institutions of government themselves was sufficient to gain an understanding of the political process. This **institutional approach** was supplanted in the 1960s by scholars in the discipline who espoused the view that psychological and sociological factors were the key determinants of politics, because, at root, institutions were important only as a venue within which various human actors behave. This **behavioural approach** was complemented and, in some cases, supplanted by the view that behaviour is caused by the attitudes and values of Canadians, both elite and non-elite. This **political culture approach** was in turn complemented by scholars who preferred to focus on the manner in which values and attitudes are acquired by individuals and transmitted from one generation to the next—the process of **political socialization**.

Since the 1970s political science has been dominated by the **political economy approach** which argues that the social and cultural variables are profoundly influenced by underlying economic variables. It is hard to disagree with the point that economic variables underlie and to a considerable extent determine our basic values and attitudes. For instance, it would be difficult to deny that the Canadian political culture is reflective of the values implicit in a capitalist economic system. Similarly, the uneven distribution of wealth among

---

13.  We have not explicitly mentioned the important discipline of human geography here simply because, like political science, it is not a discrete discipline but a hybrid that looks at culture, society, and economics within a specifically *spatial* context. Similarly, we have placed philosophy in the outer ring of our map of the environment because ultimately it is concerned with the nature of being and hence shares the ontological concerns of astrophysicists, who are exploring the limits of the universe. The specific field of *political philosophy* we see as the prescriptive branch of political science itself, and hence it forms part of the immediate ideational context of the political process.

regions, groups, and individuals in Canada is a critical determinant of the lines of conflict or **cleavages** in Canadian society and has an immediate impact on the political behaviour of voters, interest groups, and politicians. It is true also that the very institutions of government are the way they are in part because of certain structural givens in the Canadian economy.

It is also true, however, that our political culture, group loyalties, and personal value systems take on a life of their own and can have an effect on our political behaviour that is independent of economics. Thus, in our view, while economics can be looked upon as a sort of "primal ooze" of political life, environmental factors such as ethnicity, language, religion, culture, individual personality, and institutions all are independently important and in fact recip-rocally alter and attenuate the economic forces that underlie them. Hence, in discussing the environment of the political system in the next chapter, while we have identified economic factors as among the most important determi-nants of political conflict, we have avoided taking this to the deterministic extreme of suggesting that economic variables are the *only* variables.

Finally, **class analysis**,[14] a variant of the political-economy approach to Canadian government, is based on neo-marxist assumptions about the nature of state-society relationships in advanced capitalist societies. While the inevi-tability of class conflict in capitalist systems is a truism, we do have a complex *pluralist* society where class is not the only important determinant of conflict. Thus, class analysis can help us to better understand the battle lines of much of political discourse in Canada and it provides a critical tool for identifying many of the warts and flaws in the existing system, but it is not the *only* valid approach for understanding the workings of Canadian government and poli-tics.

To conclude, we think *all* of these sets of variables and therefore all of these approaches are important and that sub-disciplinary chauvinism, while fostering the development of new and expanded approaches to the study of the Canadian political process, can also serve to artificially narrow our under-standing of the subject. Hence, in keeping with our "generic" framework, we will consciously attempt to utilize whatever perspective best allows us to explain the subject matter and not feel bound to faithfully adhere to any one paradigm.

## ▶ THE STRUCTURE OF THE BOOK

The remainder of this book is broken down into twenty-three separate chap-ters. Each chapter can be read as a more or less independent module; hence, instructors using the text can assign readings in a sequence that suits their own course outline. However, while there is nothing sacred about the manner in which the chapters are ordered here, there is a conceptual thread that attempts to tie them all together. This thread is the relationship between the subject of each chapter and what the authors believe to be the central process of govern-

14. Leo Panitch, "Elites, Classes and Power in Canada," *in* M. S. Whittington and G. Williams, eds., *Canadian Politics in the 1990s* (Toronto: Nelson, 1994), pp. 152–75.

ment, **policy making**. In order to make this integrative thread explicit and specific, Chapter 2 provides an overview of the policy process, both conceptually and with specific reference to the Canadian experience.

Part One of the book is composed of two chapters that provide a brief discussion of the environment of Canadian government and politics. This environment generates the social, economic, cultural, and ideological variables that determine the basic lines of conflict, of cleavages, between and among groups and individuals in society. It is these conflicts and cleavages that define specific political issues, and, hence, set the agenda for policy decision-making. Chapter 3 discusses the geographical, economic, ethnic, and gender cleavages, which comprise the material context of political discourse in Canada. Chapter 4 talks about our political culture, which forms the value and attitudinal setting within which the political and governmental processes occur.

Part Two is comprised of three chapters which describe the constitutional matrix within which governments must operate. Chapter 5 sets out the basic functions of a constitution, provides a historical overview of constitutional development in Canada, and describes the component parts that make up what we call the *Constitution of Canada*. It also discusses the manner in which our Constitution evolves and can be adapted to new social and political circumstances, and, in particular, describes the process of constitutional amendment. Chapter 6 focuses on the component parts and substantive principles that are ensconced in our Constitution and that set the accepted limits of governmental activity and define the basic institutional components of our system of government. Chapter 7 zeroes in specifically on the constitutional relationship between the state and the individual in Canada, which is defined to a large extent today by the Charter of Rights and Freedoms.

Part Three is devoted to a discussion of the federal dimension of our system of government. While the imperatives of space and brevity preclude a detailed description of the governmental process of each province and territory, the complex relationship between the federal government and the provinces must be understood in order to comprehend Canadian government and politics. Chapter 8 places Canadian federalism in a historical, socio-economic, and constitutional context. Chapter 9 is devoted to a discussion of what has been a dominant concern throughout our history: the place of Quebec in the federation and the relationship of that province's distinct society to Canada as a whole. Chapters 10 and 11 look at the dynamics of intergovernmental relations, the latter focusing on what has come to be the "engine" of modern Canadian federalism, the complex system of federal-provincial fiscal relations.

Part Four focuses on the processes and institutions in our system that channel the wants, problems, concerns, and demands of Candians to the policy decision-makers in the government. Chapter 12 describes the electoral system, which, in a democracy, *is* the government. Chapters 13 and 14 deal with the phenomena of political parties and party systems, which are key actors in organizing and rationalizing political discourse and which make the electoral system work. Chapter 15 looks at parties and elections in a dynamic context by analyzing the manner in which parties have operated in general elections and by discussing the electoral behaviour of individual Canadian voters. Finally,

Chapters 16 and 17 look at the phenomenon of interest groups and how such collective entities influence the policy process.

Part Five is devoted to a discussion of the basic institutions and processes that we can generally describe as *government*. It is these institutions that generate policy and that bear the responsibility for implementing those policies in the real world. The first chapter in this part, Chapter 18, looks at the relationship between Parliament and the political executive in a governmental system founded on the constitutional principles of the supremacy of Parliament and responsible government. Chapter 19 shifts to a discussion of the structure and composition of the House of Commons and the procedures that govern the way in which this core institution of representative democracy actually works in Canada. Chapters 20 and 21 are focused on the locus of governmental power in Canada, the political executive, which includes the prime minister, the Cabinet, and the central agencies that provide policy support to the elected politicians. Chapters 22 and 23 look at the non-elected actors in government, the bureaucracy, and describe the role that bureaucratic agencies play in providing policy advice to the Cabinet and in implementing or applying policies outside government. Finally, Chapter 24 discusses the role of the judiciary in Canada, the nature of law in our system of government, and the way in which our system of courts applies and interprets the law.

*Chapter* **2**

# The Policy Process

The legislative, executive, and adjudicative activities of the government can be seen essentially as "what governments do." However, underlying and preceding the "doing" of something is a more complex process of "deciding" what to do. This is the process of **policy making** or the **policy process**, which, in a democratic system, is far and away the most important process in which governments are involved. The importance of the policy process is that it is the "bridge" between the political and governmental processes (see Fig. 2.1). Policies, on the one hand, determine what people in government must do and, on the other hand, are influenced by what people in society want government to do. Thus, while the policy process itself is essentially internal to government, the decisions taken not only have an effect on people outside of government but they are in turn affected by the circumstances in the society.

The policy process is, thus, at the heart of what we think of as government and politics and forms the dominant focus of this book. Our aim, when we look at political and governmental institutions and processes in Canada, will be in large part to explain their relationship to policy making and their place in the policy process.

### The Nature of Policy

A **policy** can best be defined as a decision of the government to exercise its legislative, executive, or adjudicative authority. We must recognize, however, that it is possible to think of policy and the process of policy making within the context of any organization and not just government. For example, it is quite reasonable to speak of "company policy" without implying any connection to the government or politics. However, unless otherwise specified, the term *policy*

**Figure 2.1**
Relationships among government, society, and policy.

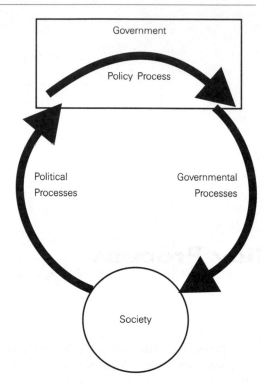

within the context of this book will refer only to governmental or "public" policy.

**Decision Making**  At the core of this definition of policy is the notion that the policy process consists of *decision-making* activity. Decision making is a complex process whereby a human mind perceives a problem, looks for alternative solutions to the problem, and then chooses one of the alternatives.[1] Because all decision making is, thus, in the end, the prerogative of individual minds, in order to understand the policy process completely it would be necessary to consider a wide range of individual psychological variables that are not practically available to us.

Hence, our focus here is on the more limited question of which people occupying which political and governmental roles have how much relative power in making or influencing policy decisions. On the one hand, we must

1.  Herbert Simon refers to these stages of decision making as "intelligence activity," "design activity," and "choice activity." See Herbert Simon, *The Scope of Automation: For Men and Management* (New York: Harper and Row, 1965), pp. 53–54. See also J. G. March and H. A. Simon, *Organizations* (New York: John Wiley and Sons, 1958), chs. 6–7.

look at how the political processes allow individuals and groups in society to influence the decisions of government policy makers. On the other hand, we must consider how the policy decisions are made within government and how they are put into effect through governmental processes.

**Law and Policy** Our notion of policy also recognizes that there is a distinction between policy and **law.** While the activities of government are always a reflection of decisions taken within the system, the leap from "deciding" to "doing" often requires formal steps to legitimize or render authoritative the internal decisions. For example, the policy decision to legislate something must first be passed by Parliament, assented to by the governor-general, proclaimed, and printed in the *Canada Gazette* before it becomes a binding enactment.

Because "being the government" in Canada to a large extent means having control over these formal legitimizing procedures, the transformation of government policy decisions to law is normally a fairly routine matter. Thus, while these formal steps that legitimize and implement policies are a necessary "last step" in the policy process, they are deployed virtually automatically and are not considered an important part of policy decision-making. As well, the choice of a governing *instrument* for implementing a given policy may be almost as important as the policy choice itself.

**The Primacy of Lawmaking** The three types of governmental processes are themselves very closely interrelated. Both the executive and adjudicative outputs depend upon the pre-existence of *laws*, with the former having the effect of implementing and the latter of interpreting them. Consequently, there is a certain *logical* primacy about legislation that has caused the lawmaking process to be viewed traditionally as the "master" sub-function of government. The principle of the supremacy of Parliament is a reflection of the *constitutional* primacy of lawmaking over other governmental functions in Canada. However, this should not allow us to minimize the importance of executive or judicial processes.

The effectiveness of government depends, as well, upon how the executive branch of government implements legislative enactments and upon the manner in which the vast tax revenues of government are allocated among various programs. Executive policy decisions, particularly those related to the preparation of the budget and the expenditure of public funds, are thus an increasingly important dimension of policy making. More than 90 per cent of the money appropriated to the Canadian government each year is spent on existing programs through executive and administrative decisions. Similarly, judicial decisions not only mediate the relationship between individuals and the state, but judicial interpretations also serve to shape our Constitution. However, while we recognize that judicial and bureaucratic policy decisions are important, our analytical departure point in the discussion of the policy process will continue to be the process whereby decisions about new legislation are taken.

**Politics and Administration** There have been many attempts to define policy in more restrictive terms than ours. For instance, policy decisions are frequently viewed as those more properly taken by politicians than by bureaucrats. In this view a distinction is made between "political" decisions, which involve "policy," and "administrative" decisions, which do not. While the distinction between policy making and policy implementation or between deciding and doing[2] may be analytically appealing, empirically the distinction very quickly breaks down. The decision to pass a piece of major legislation is clearly more important than the decision of a senior official who, in the course of implementing the law, sets guidelines as to when customs officers should use their discretionary authority to inspect someone's luggage. It must be recognized, however, that in each of these examples, a decision has been taken that affects people in the real world. To say that one process is policy and the other is not is to transform a difference of degree into a difference of kind.

While it is artificial to attempt to classify "political" decisions as policy and "administrative" decisions as some lower species, it is still useful to place policy decisions in different categories. The simplest categorization is to divide policy decisions into those that trigger legislative, executive/administrative, or judicial processes, respectively. In describing all such decisions by the common term *policy*, we can avoid a good deal of semantic debate about what is and is not a policy, while still being able to relate each type of decision to an analytically distinct governmental process.

### Policy Contexts

The theory of parliamentary democracy posits an ideal system of government in which legislative outputs prevail over all other outputs of the system and in which the power to legislate is vested in an elected parliament. Furthermore, the executive power in a classic parliamentary system resides with the prime minister and the cabinet, who are in turn responsible directly to parliament. Thus, in an ideal parliamentary democracy, ultimate power rests with the people who elect the parliament, which in turn controls the prime minister and the cabinet. The administrative arm of the government, the bureaucracy, is responsible directly to the cabinet, and indirectly, through the budgetary process, to parliament. While it is one of our political myths that there was a "golden age" of parliamentary democracy, it is unlikely that this vision of a supreme parliament sublimely presiding over the Canadian democratic system was ever a fact. However, even if we do not subscribe to this "Camelot hypothesis," we must recognize that the role of Parliament is much different today than it was in the 19th century. One major factor associated with this change in the nature of parliamentary democracy is *technological* advancement, although, in large part, it is not technology *per se* but the social and economic consequences of technological change that have altered the policy process most startlingly.

**The Expanding Role of Government** Technological advances in the 19th century precipitated industrialization, which has been the single most important vari-

---

2. Peter Drucker speaks of a split between the "deciders and the doers" in government and sees a clear delineation of these functions as a solution to some of the problems of the "age of discontinuity." See Peter Drucker, *The Age of Discontinuity* (New York: Harper and Row, 1969), p. 233. Also see the discussion about the ambiguity of the concept of "policy implementation" later in this chapter.

able in determining the nature of modern societies. The movement from a pre-industrial or agricultural society produced social discontinuities, which were so great that existing mechanisms of conflict management and social adaptation could not cope. Industrialization, for instance, created in Canada the phenomenon of the employable unemployed. The problem of welfare within the pre-industrial system had concerned the care of those unable to find employment because of physical or mental disability, a problem that could be dealt with by agencies such as the church and local charities. With the massive unemployment that resulted from economic fluctuations in industrial society, the traditional, private-sector "safety net" agencies were no longer capable of carrying the burden of welfare. By default, more than anything else, government was forced to step into the field of income redistribution and social insurance in order to alleviate the intense economic hardships of depression and unemployment.

Similarly, because an industrial society is complex and very sensitive to the activities of individuals who control large amounts of capital, economic stability can be maximized only if there is a degree of control and planning of the economy. Governments were the natural structures in society with sufficient resources and the ability to use coercion legitimately to step in and regulate the economic system, using such techniques as anti-combines and labour-relations legislation, legislated fair-employment practices, and fiscal and monetary policy. The "unseen hand" of Adam Smith did not effectively keep the economy in a state of equilibrium, and government stepped in to attempt to restore the balance.

Technology not only made industrialization possible in the first instance but, through developments in the field of economics, it also made possible the intervention of government as a planner and regulator of the industrial economy: "Even in the most conservative of the industrial states, technology has steadily expanded governmental activity in the fields once left exclusively to the private entrepreneurs."[3] Technology and industrialization thus stimulated an expansion in the role of the state. Where governments had once been very passive and negative, they assumed positive and active roles in society. Where the public attitude to the role of government had once been that "the best government is the one that governs least," government was now expected, as a matter of course, to perform broad regulatory and redistributive functions hitherto left to economic and social-conflict management mechanisms or not performed at all. Government as the passive guardian of peace and order had become "big government" in the mid 20th century.

**The Implications of Big Government** The immediate implications of this enlarged role of government for the nature of government were three. First, the activities of government increased numerically because there were simply a lot more things that government was expected to do. The linear increase in the amount of governmental activity means that the number of policy decisions in any given year will normally be greater than in the year before, with attendant strain on the attention span of our governmental leaders. Parliament no longer

---

3. E. G. Mesthene, *Technological Change* (Cambridge: Harvard University Press, 1970), pp. 64–65; and V. C. Ferkiss, *Technological Man* (New York: Braziller, 1969), p. 177.

could sit for a few months a year and still get through its agenda, and MPs could no longer be amateurs who could return to their law practices when the House was not sitting.

Second, the complexity of individual pieces of legislation also increased enormously during this period. The amount of detail required in a statute that spells out the procedures and formulae in a national pension plan, for instance, is much greater than that required in legislation to amend a Criminal Code provision, and an ever-increasing percentage of bills proceeding through Parliament deals with complicated subjects such as welfare schemes and medical-insurance programs.

Finally, not only have the policy decisions facing our political leaders increased in number and in the amount of detail they encompass, but their content has increased in technological sophistication as well. Policies dealing with subjects such as economic planning, scientific research, and taxation must of necessity be highly technical, reflecting as they do the most advanced levels of knowledge in the given field. All of this places greater burdens on our elected political leaders, who are still expected to make informed decisions despite the complexity of the issues before them.

**Technology, Bureaucracy, and Democracy** The combination of increased volume, complexity, and technological sophistication of governmental activity has made a high level of specialization and technical expertise necessary for effective policy making. This has had important consequences for the ideal of parliamentary democracy. In the first place, Parliament, being neither specialized nor highly expert, is often disqualified, in practical terms, from taking a central part in the policy process. The *de facto* lawmaking power in the Canadian system is concentrated in the political elites in the Cabinet. It is the political executive that has the authority to assume the leadership role and to set goals or establish priorities for governmental action. Through party discipline and through the Cabinet's access to the expertise within the various government departments, Cabinet members are placed in a position of considerable advantage over the backbench MP.

*Knowledge Elites* In part, however, the policy decision-making power has moved out of the Cabinet as well, and into the hands of the thousands of experts throughout the public service. These experts are formally entrusted with the responsibility to tender policy advice to their ministers. However, while the power to advise may seem a limited power, it becomes very significant power when the advice given is highly technical in nature and when the person being advised is not an expert. In Peter Drucker's terms, *knowledge has become power*; it is the "central capital" of modern society: "Scientists and scholars are no longer merely 'on tap,' they are 'on top.' . . . They largely determine what policies can be considered seriously in such crucial areas as defence or economics."[4]

While the power to decide policy still formally resides with political office holders such as the prime minister and the Cabinet, this is essentially **positional**

---

4. Drucker, *The Age of Discontinuity,* p. 372.

**power**. That is to say, it derives from the role or position an individual occupies and is only secondarily affected by the character and ability of the individual. Because rational decision making in a modern system necessitates the use of specialized and technical information that politicians do not possess, the actual power that accrues to them through their positions is significantly reduced. As E. G. Mesthene has pointed out:

> The task of the expert is to furnish the politician with information and estimates on which he can base a decision. . . . When the expert has effectively performed his task of pointing out the necessary ways and means, there is generally only one logical and admissible solution. The politician will then find himself obliged to choose between the technician's solution, which is the only reasonable one, and other solutions which he can indeed try out at his own peril, but which are not reasonable. . . . In fact, the politician no longer has any real choice; decision follows automatically from the preparatory technical labours.[5]

*Bureaucratic Elites*  Finally, it is also a fact of modern government that senior bureaucrats are the central contact point between the technocrats and the politicians. Lacking the political authority of the politician and the expertise of the technocrats, the senior public servants gain their power as the "managers" of expertise. They are the men and women who act as intermediaries between the political elites in Cabinet and the knowledge elites in the bureaucracy. They try to assemble and translate the technical information into terms the non-expert ministers can understand and to convey the political will of the Cabinet to the technocracy. Through this role, the senior bureaucratic elites have maintained a high level of power and influence in the policy process.

While the above generalizations likely apply fairly accurately to the Canadian situation, the fact remains that Cabinet will not infrequently make decisions that go contrary to the advice of its technical hired hands. Sometimes this happens because the politicians have sincere personal doubts about the validity of the expert advice from the bureaucracy or because they have found alternate sources of technical information outside the government whose conclusions conflict with those of their departmental officials. At other times, the political leaders will scuttle a policy proposal from the bureaucracy because they feel that non-technical or political considerations outweigh the technical merits of the policy. The point is that we should never lose sight of the fact that, whether because they have political antennae that give contrary signals or for more earthy reasons of political advantage or bonehead stubbornness, our political elites still possess the formal authority to make policy decisions that reject the "wise counsel" of the technocratic and senior bureaucratic elites.

*Administrative Discretion*  Public servants are also directly involved in making policy decisions through the instrument of **delegated power**. It is frequently necessary, because of the complexity of the matters being dealt with by government, for legislation to leave a great deal of discretionary authority in the hands of the public servants who implement it. Moreover, the power to work out the details of a particular government program, to establish regulations,

---

5.  Mesthene, *Technological Change,* pp. 64–65.

and to adjudicate disputes over the application of the regulations is often explicitly delegated to the administrative agency charged with the responsibility for implementing it. In such a way, instead of merely influencing policy decisions through offering expert advice, the administrators actually *become* law-makers and judges.

Such delegation of governmental powers to non-elected officials presents serious problems of control and accountability. The bureaucrats, unlike the politicians, are not subject to the periodic litmus test of the ballot. Although Parliament is supposed to review all instruments of delegated authority, there are so many of them that bad decisions are often missed unless an aggrieved citizen makes an explicit complaint through the courts. In the final analysis, perhaps the most effective way of preventing the abuse of delegated power today is through specialized judicial mechanisms—courts of *administrative law*—which provide civil remedies for individuals who are harmed by abuse or misuse of administrative power.

*Alternate Sources of Policy Advice* The outcome of the shift in policy-making power from those who occupy political authority roles to those who possess technical knowledge or information is that bureaucratic institutions that concentrate expertise will tend, in the long run, to dominate democratic institutions, such as Parliament, that do not have expertise. But, *prima facie*, there is no reason that concentrations of expertise in non-governmental locales such as industry, the universities, and pressure groups could not provide important alternative sources of policy influence to compete with the governmental bureaucracy. In some instances they do. However, two factors intervene to limit the practical use of sources of expertise outside government.

First, "the development and the application of technology seem necessarily to require large scale and complex social concentration,"[6] which occurs, at least with respect to social and economic policy, largely in government. Hence, there are relatively few non-governmental organizations that can control sufficient resources to generate technological information on a scale that would permit them to compete effectively with the governmental bureaucracy. Some of those that might, the multinational corporations, are so large and diversified that they must be analyzed as "proto-governments" rather than as private enterprise. The relationship between multinationals and government is more akin to the relationships among sovereign states than between a sovereign government and its domestic corporations. As such, a government is usually wiser to listen to the advice of its own bureaucracy, which is intended to operate in the national interest, than to heed the advice of multinational corporations, which are motivated by profit and the narrower interests of their own share-holders.

A second limitation on the ability of Cabinet to seek alternate sources of expert advice is the problem of information overload.[7] The number of sources

---

6. J. Ellul, *Technological Society* (New York: Alfred A. Knopf, 1965), pp. 258–59.
7. Victor Thompson speaks of "the knowledge explosion" and of "information affluence." See Victor Thompson, *Bureaucracy and Innovation* (Montgomery: University of Alabama, 1969), pp. 1–6.

of information that the harried political decision makers in Cabinet and in its executive support agencies can deal with is limited. There is simply not time to consider a larger number of alternative viewpoints. The political decision makers, therefore, must be satisfied with considering a limited number of possible alternatives and with making the decision on the basis of only partial information. Since it is the public service that performs the information "triage" or screening of the information flowing to ministers, it is its assessment of the relevance of information that still tends to determine what gets to the minister's desk.

### Policy Communities

We have seen that the agenda of political discourse is set by social and economic variables in Canadian society—in the environment. The actual resolution of the issues and conflicts generated by these environmental variables, however, occurs within a constellation of individual and organizational actors which together make up the **policy community** (Fig. 2.2).[8] The composition of a policy community will be determined by who the **stakeholders** are in the given policy area—by who has the most to gain and lose in the policy decision. Such stakeholders will include Cabinet ministers, the senior officials of the **lead agency** or sponsoring department, the leadership of key interest groups, journalists, MPs, and interested individuals.

The policy community can be visualized in the same way as the larger environment of politics, as a series of concentric rings. The most interested and influential groups and individuals will be concentrated near the centre of the policy community, with both interest and influence declining towards the outer reaches. At the extremities of the policy community we will find people who are only mildly interested in the outcome of the process because they do not feel that the decision will affect them very much, whatever the outcome.

It is important to recognize that a different policy community will evolve for each policy area. Moreover, a policy community will expand and contract over time as issues arise and fade away. Many individuals and interest groups will feel that they have a stake in the outcome of many policy deliberations and, as a result, will be involved in multiple policy communities. Hence, policy communities overlap to a significant extent, although the participants or stakeholders may move closer to the core of the community for some issues and retreat to the outer rings of the community where their interest is not as vital.

It is also clear that policy communities operate differently depending on the substance of the issue, the relative power and influence of the community members, and the personalities of the leaders of the various groups and organizations. Hence, in one policy community the decision-making process may be **state-centered** or dominated by the Cabinet and the bureaucracy, and in another, the process may be **pluralistic** with a more even distribution of influ-

8. For a more detailed discussion of the notion of policy communities in Canada, see M. Atkinson and W. Coleman, "Policy Networks, Policy Communities and the Problems of Governance," *Governance*, April 1992; and W. D. Coleman and Grace Skogstad, eds., *Policy Communities and Public Policy in Canada* (Toronto: Copp Clark Pitman, 1990).

**Figure 2.2**
A policy community. The central agencies are the Privy Council Office, the Treasury Board Secretariat, and the Prime Minister's Office.

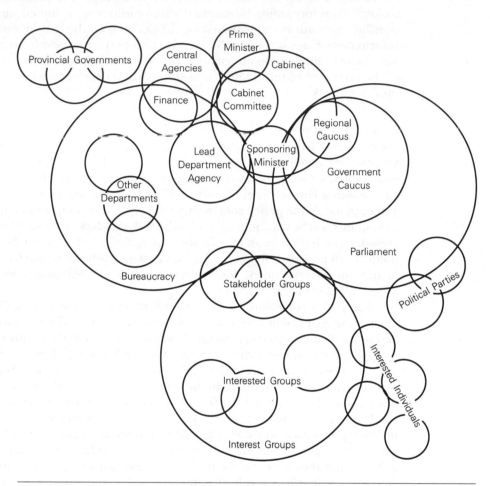

Source: Adapted from Paul Pross, "Pressure Groups: Talking Chameleons," *in* M.S. Whittington and G. Williams, *Canadian Politics in the 1990s* (Toronto: Nelson, 1994), p. 267.

ence among the various government agencies and interest groups. We will return to the concept of policy communities in later chapters when we discuss the role of interest groups, Cabinet, and the bureaucracy in the policy process.

**The Locus of Policy Power** The foregoing paints a picture quite different from the traditional one of a supreme parliament, responsible to an informed and active electorate, making policy on the basis of a grand concept of "national interest." Nevertheless, while the policy process in the positive state does not match our classical image of parliamentary democracy, the system does seem to work after a fashion. Furthermore, it is important to emphasize that there is no blame to be assigned for this shift in power within our system. Power has moved from Parliament to the Cabinet and from the Cabinet to the bureaucracy simply because the environment of the political system is such that experts in large information-gathering organizations are the ones most likely to find solutions to current problems. The bureaucrats and technocrats have not deliberately wrested policy-making power from the hands of our elected political leaders who should rightfully possess it. There has been no *coup d'état*; rather, suffice it to say that, in a technological society, those with technological know-how will inevitably wield power that exceeds what is implicit in their slot in an organization chart.

### Approaches to the Policy Process

There are a large number of analytical approaches to the study of public policy and, as with the approaches to the study of Canadian government in general, they all have merits and limitations. The notion of a policy community implies a multiplicity of actors or stakeholders involved in the policy process. While most paradigms basically incorporate this idea as a starting point, they diverge with respect to the locus of power within the policy community. All of the basic frameworks for analyzing the policy process focus on the question of what variables determine the outcomes of the process. In essence, all of these approaches are trying to determine the distribution of power and influence among the various stakeholders in the policy community and the manner in which these stakeholders exercise their power.

**Power and Influence in the Policy Community**  A **neo-marxist** approach to policy making assumes that policy outcomes are the product of deals made between the state, which has been "captured" by the ideology of capitalism, and the capitalist elites in large corporations. In this conceptualization of policy making, the other stakeholders in the policy community are influential only to the extent that their demands are either identical to, or at least not incompatible with, the interests of the capitalist classes. This approach takes the position that class persists as the only significant determinant of policy outcomes from one policy community to another and from one issue to the next over time.

**Public-choice theory** starts with the assumption that the stakeholders in the policy community are rational actors who make their choices on the basis of enlightened self interest. It is also assumed that the rational actors have sufficient information to be able to calculate the risks associated with different policy options in determining their strategy. In a manner analogous to the economic marketplace, the policy actors use their political and economic influence to "purchase" policy concessions from the other stakeholders, including the government. According to this model, the political communities will generally change kaleidoscopically from one issue to the next. However, even where the stakeholders remain the same over time in a given policy area, the locus of power within the policy community may shift according to the available bargaining capital of the actors.

**Liberal pluralism**, which assumes that the policy community includes a very large number of group actors, any of whom may influence policy outcomes, likely underlies most other paradigms, with the notable exception of neo-marxism. The pluralist vision of the policy process, however, can take either of two slightly different paths. Traditional pluralist thought assumes that the bargaining capital in the policy community is widely and fairly evenly distributed among the various stakeholders. The government is seen more as a passive arbiter presiding over the policy mêlée in a stern but impartial mien.

The other version of the pluralist approach sees the government actors as having the power to act independently of the other stakeholders in the policy community. The government, in this *state-centred* approach, can initiate policy and then sit back and let the other members of the policy community bargain for changes to the government's proposal. There is still a multiplicity of actors as in the more traditional pluralist paradigm, but in the state-centred model, the government plays a much more active and more dominant role in the policy process.

**Nobody's Perfect**  All of these approaches are useful and all of them provide different insights and perspectives when we come to look at the policy process in Canada. However, no one paradigm serves as an effective model in all instances of policy decision-making in Canada. Clearly the neo-marxist approach fails us in attempting to reduce all policy issues to questions of class and capitalist hegemony, and the traditional pluralist model errs in assuming far greater parity among interest groups competing for political advantage than occurs in reality.

The public-choice model depends upon the assumption of "rational actors" who are able to calculate the relative political risk of different policy outcomes. All too often the actors are not rational, being motivated by emotion and by oversimplifications of political reality that we call *myths*. Moreover, the strategic decisions that must be taken involve areas of stark *uncertainty*, where it is impossible to calculate the statistical odds, or relative risks, of multiple policy options.

The state-centred approach posits that the government actors tend to dominate policy communities. In fact, in the context of what we have said about the *de facto* power of the knowledge elites in the bureacracy, and in a world where public-opinion surveys are often very accurate indicators of Canadians' wants and needs, we have seen the role of government in the policy process become much more active, much more pre-emptive, and much more dominant. However, there are still too many instances where coalitions of interest groups, social movements, or amorphous but pervasive ground-swells of public sentiment stop the government locomotive, and derail the state-driven policy agenda.

**Elites and the Policy Process**  It should be obvious by now that your authors are unable to adopt, holus bolus, any single explanation of the policy process. Hence, as with our approach to Canadian government and politics in general, we will deal with the policy process by borrowing eclectically from whatever paradigm best suits the particular situation. However, while our approach will clearly end up a nameless hybrid of many others, it turns out that there may be a common but implicit assumption lurking in all of these paradigms. This conceptual "mole" that we feel has infiltrated most other paradigms, albeit to different degrees, is the acceptance of the dominant role of **elites** or leaders in the policy process.

There are many versions of **elite theory**, and each possesses both valuable insights and limitations in approaching political life. We recognize the folly of stating that elite theory provides us with a comprehensive analytical tool where all other approaches to the study of public policy fail. The point we wish to make here is much less grandiose: simply, that when we speak of "stakeholders" in the policy process we are really talking about stakeholder groups or "sub-communities" within the policy community. Each of these policy sub-communities has its internally generated leaders—its elites—who are the representatives or spokespersons for the group and are also the real "actors" in the policy process.

Hence, the actual state actors in the policy process are the political elites in the Cabinet, the bureaucratic elites from the ranks of the senior officials in the departments and agencies, and the technocratic or "knowledge" elites in the middle ranks of the bureaucracy. Interest groups participate in the policy community through the advocacy of their chosen leaders, and corporate interests are represented through the participation of CEOs, hired lobbyists, and the executives of business and industry associations. Even class-based interests in the policy process are articulated through union leaders, intellectual elites, and the political leaders of left-leaning parties such as the New Democratic Party (NDP).

Our conclusion here is that the actual bargaining process that results in a policy decision may be an insider-dominated process, one that often largely excludes the rank-and-file members of the stakeholder communities and is dominated by elites. This process has been described as **elite accommodation** and is likely a fairly accurate representation of much of the political discourse and self-interested horse-trading that surrounds the policy process in Canada.

**Democracy and Elite Accommodation**  By way of conclusion to this discussion of approaches to policy making in Canada it is necessary to say a few words about the political morality of a policy process in a democracy that is dominated by elites. *Prima facie*, elitism can be challenged convincingly on the grounds that it is undemocratic. If a small group of powerful people in society is able to prevail over the wishes of the mass public, the system, by definition, would be an *oligarchy* rather than a democracy. What makes the situation different in Canada is that our elites claim to *represent* the interests of a given segment of society rather than their own selfish needs.

In many cases the elites in Canada are indeed representative of groups in society. The executives of interest groups, union leaders, and our political leaders are all democratically elected. As long as these elected elites remember who made them important in the first place, and as long as their mass publics have an opportunity to reconsider their choice of leaders in periodic elections, our system can be said to be democratic. But one potential flaw in this system is that economic elites, such as corporate executives, are responsible only to their shareholders who are, in effect, an *elite class* to begin with and therefore have special interests that may conflict with the general interests of the Canadian people.

Thus, despite the fact that many of our elites are democratically accountable, some, such as the very powerful corporate elites, are not. As a result there is always the fear that policy outcomes may too often be biased towards a special, but very powerful, interest at the expense of the general interest. The "fuse box" that safeguards against such power imbalances is a policy process that is open to public scrutiny and accessible to multiple interest groups that counterbalance the dominance of any single special interest. As well, government still holds the critical trump cards—legitimacy and a monopoly over the use of coercion—that allow it to restore the balance in a policy community where any special interest has become too powerful.

Finally, perhaps the most important safeguard against unacceptable imbalances of power within policy communities is the fact that special interests in a liberal democracy such as Canada are only legitimate if they do not significantly impair the general interest. Special interests can compete with other special interests but, for the most part, the one that is perceived to be the most compatible with the national interest will prevail. Moreover, even the most strident special-interest chauvinists are sufficiently pragmatic to recognize that accommodating the general interest has to be an overriding concern. Corporations generally do not like taxes, welfare programs, government regulation, high interest rates, or government deficits, but they also understand that the indiscriminate reversal of such policies would have social and economic repercussions that might permanently maim even "corporate" Canada. In other words, there is a consensus that special interests are seldom served in the long run if the general interest is not served equally.

---

▶ **THE POLICY PROCESS: AN OVERVIEW**

The focus of this book is the political and governmental institutions and processes of Canada. The thread that ties the various chapters together is the relationship between the phenomena under discussion and the core process of government and politics which we see as policy making. Canadian society, economy, and culture are discussed in terms of determining policy issues and setting the agenda for policy decision-making. The Constitution sets the broadest ideological and institutional framework within which the policy process must occur, and our political institutions—parties, elections, and interest groups—link Canadian society to the policy makers in government. Finally, when we discuss the core institutions of government—Cabinet, Parliament, the bureaucracy, and the courts—the ultimate focus is upon the role of these bodies in policy making.

Before proceeding to the task of explaining the complexities of Canadian political life, we feel it is important to provide a brief overview of the policy process. This overview posits several stages in the policy process and outlines the core institutions involved at each stage. The aim here is to provide the reader with a "road map" that can be referenced from time to time in order to orient a given chapter or to act as a reminder of where we are going and where we have been.

### Policy Initiation

The policy process has been defined as internal to government. It is the process whereby persons inside the system decide what government should and should not do. But while the people working within government make the policy decisions, they do not do so on a random or whimsical basis. Rather, policy decisions are taken because a problem is identified that is deemed serious enough to merit government's attention and that is judged to be potentially solvable by the application of appropriate instruments of government. The policy process is *triggered* by information that brings such problems to the attention of the policy makers, and, with the exception of problems purely internal to government, such as those involving the organization and management of the bureaucracy, the origins of public policy lie in information about circumstances outside of government. The process whereby such information comes to the attention of the policy makers is the first stage in the formation of policy, **policy initiation.**

**Access**  The key problem facing groups or individuals in society who wish to influence policy decisions is to find channels through which their concerns can be brought to the attention of people occupying policy roles. Points of access occur naturally where people within the government are paying attention to what is going on outside. We encourage the continued attentiveness of our political elites by making them subject to periodic evaluation through elections. Institutions such as political parties and pressure groups also play a key role in articulating to government the wants and needs of their supporters. However, given the diversity and complexity of so many of the problems that exist in modern societies, and given the overall movement of decision-making power from the purely political institutions to the bureaucratic ones, channels of access to the policy process have evolved in government departments and agencies.

**Clientelism and Symbiosis**  Many government departments have as their organizational *raison d'être* a specific **clientele**. For instance, the Department of Agriculture exists to serve agricultural interests and to solve agricultural problems, and the Department of Veterans' Affairs exists to serve the interest of ex-servicemen. The survival and growth of these departments depends almost entirely on their success in representing the interest of their client-group. The more problems they can define and begin to solve, the greater will be their budgetary allocations and human resources establishment. Conversely, the stronger their rapport with their clientele, the more likely are they to be able to mobilize their public against reductions to their budgets when the time comes for expenditure cut-backs. Because departments and agencies must be ever attentive to the changing wants and needs of their clients, important channels of access to the policy process are always open not only at the ministerial level, but also at the level of the public service.

Today, all interest groups focus their attention on executive and bureaucratic channels. In fact, if there isn't already a department in existence that sees the members of the group as its clients, the group will press for the creation of one. Conversely, because of the internal bureaucratic clout a department acquires by having a well-organized clientele, departments often help their clients to set up an effective pressure group. Hence, the relationship between interest groups and clientele-oriented departments is a *symbiotic* one. Such relationships exist today, for instance, between organizations such as the Canadian Petroleum Association or the Canadian Manufacturers' Association and departments dealing with energy, industry, or corporate affairs.

Thus, while bureaucratic channels of access have not completely replaced the traditional ones, they are often more effective for policy initiation. Because so many agencies are clientele-oriented, and because they possess the expertise and experience in ferreting out problems among their clientele, the traditional political channels are increasingly in competition with the newer bureaucratic-based ones.

**State-Driven Policy** The thrust of our discussion of policy initiation to this point has been with respect to active policy advocacy on the part of groups and individuals outside the government. It must be recognized, however, that a great many policy initiatives are born within goverment circles. While the information that causes the policy decision-makers to decide that "something must be done" may come from outside government, the people likely to be affected by the problem may not yet have identified it themselves. In such cases the department may trigger the policy process indirectly, by informing its clients about the concern and getting them involved in advocating the necessary changes.

Another situation in which policy initiation can be *state-driven* rather than society-driven is in areas where the aggregate of specific interests in society is unwilling to advocate measures that are unpopular but objectively necessary in the long-term general public interest. Examples of this abound in the 1990s, where governments are forced to cope with generic problems such as large deficits and government debt loads that are expanding at alarming rates. Not surprisingly, initiatives to reduce expenditures on transfer payments to individuals, corporations, and provincial governments and to increase taxes have not come about as a result of widespread public advocacy. On the contrary, governments have been forced to develop such policies unilaterally and pre-emptively in a context of only lukewarm acquiescence, if not outright hostility, in many policy communities.

**Priority Determination**
We have seen that the flow of information to policy makers is a necessary condition for policy initiation. If that flow of information should cease for some reason, the policy process would grind to a halt. In Canada today, however, the central problem in determining policy priorities is not in garnering

information but in coping with the vast amounts of it. The problems of modern societies are so numerous and so complex that the greatest challenge to effective government may well be *information overload.*[9] The first internal step in the policy process, therefore, involves weeding out, reducing, and ordering in importance the vast quantity of information with which policy makers are constantly bombarded.

**Gatekeepers**  The core institutions involved in priority determination in the Canadian policy process are the federal and provincial cabinets. It is the political executive that possesses the formal authority and bears the ultimate responsibility for setting the broad directions of public policy. Because of the enormous number of wants and needs being articulated to government by groups and individuals in society, however, much of the initial reduction of policy demands and the preliminary weeding-out of information is performed elsewhere than in cabinet.

The non-governmental actors in the policy communities function as preliminary **gatekeepers** in filtering, integrating, and ordering policy information before bringing it to the attention of the policy decision-makers. Pressure groups, for instance, establish priorities among the various policy wants of their membership in order not to waste their influence on less important issues. Not all of the needs of the entire clientele of an interest group can be met simultaneously, so the organizational leaders must decide which policy objectives are most important and which, within a given time, are achievable.

Similarly, a clientele-oriented government department must limit and order the policy demands of its clientele. It is well known to the more savvy bureaucratic strategists that their minister has only a limited number of opportunities to get the attention of the prime minister and Cabinet. These opportunities must be "spent wisely" on the issues that are most important to the department and on policy proposals that have the best chance of gaining political approbation. In doing this, the bureaucracy as a whole reduces the number of choices ultimately facing the political executive.

At a point closer to the Cabinet and the prime minister, still more reduction and ordering of information occurs. The gatekeepers here are found among the advisory staff of the prime minister and Cabinet, located primarily in the Prime Minister's Office (PMO), the Privy Council Office (PCO), and, to a lesser extent, the political staffs in the offices of individual ministers. While the prime minister and the Cabinet can always bypass the PMO and PCO, most information coming both from the bureaucracy and from non-governmental actors in the policy community is, in fact, filtered through these offices.

By deciding which information is important enough to be passed on to their Cabinet masters, by summarizing information so as to brief ministers, and by helping to set the agenda for Cabinet and Cabinet committee meetings, the people in these central agencies play a significant role in determining what policy demands will even be considered by our political leaders. However, whether gleaned independently, or filtered through the various information gatekeepers, a great many policy ideas ultimately do come to the attention of

9. Thompson, *Beaureaucracy and Innovation,* pp. 1–6.

the Cabinet, and it is these that constitute the "raw material" of priority decisions.

**Feasibility Assessment**    The initial Cabinet-level decision in the process, and probably *the* most important decision at any stage of the policy process, is whether to reject a policy idea outright or to consider it further. For those ideas deemed important enough to be considered further, the Cabinet must then engage in a *triage* exercise to decide which should be dealt with first and which government agency should be given the responsibility for formulating specific operational options.

It is important to recognize that the rejection of a policy idea outright is as much a policy decision as the adoption of a policy proposal and can have equally damaging political repercussions for the government. Indeed, most policy decisions at this stage will inevitably be negative ones. Although the number of demands being made on government is potentially limitless, the resources available to meet those demands are severely limited. The human energy and financial resources must be parsimoniously allocated to those very few policy suggestions that are deemed most worthy.

While these Cabinet-level choices as to what should be done, and when, may seem relatively simple, given the reduction and ordering that has already taken place, they may not be so. Our political leaders may be able to make very broad decisions about the relative legitimacy or acceptability of policy proposals without the need for any expert advice. Such broad decisions are essentially normative and the individual ministers are able to deal with them on the basis of their own values and beliefs. Because of the complex and technical nature of most subjects of government concern today, however, other sources of information are usually necessary to supplement the minister's own knowledge.

The feasibility of a policy proposal will depend upon whether it is technically, financially, and constitutionally possible. In other words, a policy decision to put a person on Mars will be a bad decision if the technology is not available, if the costs would be prohibitive, or if space exploration is outside the constitutional jurisdiction of the sponsoring government. Hence, in making priority decisions, the political executive will seek technical advice from appropriate line departments, financial advice from the Department of Finance and the Treasury Board Secretariat, and legal advice from the Department of Justice.

**The Political Calculus**    Political considerations are likely the single most important determinants of priority decisions. Hence, information about the political viability or feasibility of a policy option must be brought to bear on the ultimate decision by the Cabinet. The criteria that must be employed in measuring the political advisability of a policy are determined by the nature of our political institutions themselves. Thus, in the Canadian system, which features elections with a universal franchise, the criterion is in large part how many votes a policy will ultimately win and lose for the current political office holders.

The main institutions tendering political advice to the Cabinet are the Prime Minister's Office and, to a lesser extent, the government party organization. By monitoring information flowing from political parties, pressure groups, the press, and the provincial governments, the people in the PMO keep themselves attuned to political developments across the country and prepared to tell the Cabinet the plusses and minuses of policy options. The bureaucracy also pays considerable attention to political information, for senior bureaucrats are well aware that there is no point in recommending policies, however sensible they may appear in objective terms, if they are politically unfeasible.

**Deciding: What, When, By Whom?**  Having obtained political, technical, legal, and financial information about the policy proposal under consideration, the Cabinet must ultimately decide whether to act at all. When there is conflicting advice, the Cabinet must make a choice. If the experts do not agree as to the feasibility of the policy suggestion, or if political exigencies conflict with substantive and technical concerns, it is a common response for the Cabinet simply not to act at all. The immediate effect here is the same as if a negative decision had been taken.

Another common response to conflicting technical information is for the Cabinet to refer the matter to a specialized body for further study. Royal commissions and task forces can often provide a vehicle through which difficult decisions can be postponed while new technical information is gathered. As well, it is becoming more and more commonplace for contentious policy issues to be handed over to parliamentary committees even before legislation is introduced. In this way the committee can study the proposals, hold public hearings, listen to the opinions of witnesses, and ultimately tender further recommendations to the government before the final decision has to be taken.

Perhaps the most common instances of conflicting advice at the level of priority setting are those between political and technical considerations. In private, technocrats are very quick to accuse the politicians of "playing politics" when their advice has been rejected. What often has happened in reality, of course, is that their technical advice has been rejected because of competing advice from the *political technocrats*. In that case, sometimes, as Jacques Ellul points out, "the conflict is not between politicians and technicians, but among technicians of differing categories."[10]

Once several policy proposals are adopted by the Cabinet, the next step is determining the order in which the policies should be tackled. As well, the decision must be made as to who will formulate the specific alternatives for putting the policy idea into effect. In other words, the Cabinet must decide which department or agency will take the responsibility for the next stage in the process, *policy formulation*.

### The Formulation of Policy
Until this stage, the concern has been with the broad directions of public policy rather than with the specifics. With **policy formulation**, the object is to narrow down the number of specific choices to a few "best" ones from which the final

---

10. Ellul, *Technological Society,* p. 257.

choice can be made. There are two analytically separate steps in the formulation of policy alternatives. First, the myriad experts within the public service must design a few workable schemes and come up with proposals as to the most effective *governing instrument* for bringing the programs into effect, and second, the political executive must choose the alternative that appears to be the best.

**Design activity** involves narrowing down the number of reasonable approaches to a workable few. This is to a large extent the responsibility of the more senior generalists in a department, who will have consulted other departments, central agencies, and possibly other levels of government as well. Then, those few viable choices must be fleshed out at the middle levels of the department through the participation of highly specialized policy officers. In Galbraith's terms: "Knowledge is brought to bear on the ultimate microfraction of the task; then on that in combination with some other fraction; then, on some further combination and thus on to final completion."[11]

In this sense, only very broad direction is given at the more senior bureaucratic and ministerial levels. The bulk of the responsibility for the ultimate detail of any policy usually resides with the many highly specialized technocrats at lower levels of the hierarchy. The end product is produced incrementally as many individuals make small technical decisions that are bundled together and integrated at higher levels of the department.

Given the incremental and aggregative nature of the process of policy design, the choice of the politician can be seriously curtailed. Departmental proposals have been produced through a hierarchy of decisions, beginning with the most highly specialized at the middle levels, and proceeding to ever more general ones at the higher levels. At each higher level of decision making, there is less choice than at the previous one, because there is proportionately less information transmitted with the proposals. By the time the politician, who is at the top of the hierarchy, comes to make the choice, it often will be simply to accept or reject the incrementally generated and monolithic conclusion of the department. The choice, in other words, will be determined largely through the design process itself.

Despite this, ministers sometimes *do* rebel against this process and reject a detailed policy proposal that has been meticulously crafted by the department. Normally, however, policies are significantly altered or rejected at this stage only because of new political circumstances that make implementation of the proposal risky to the party in power. But while a policy must continue to meet important political criteria, and while political or budgetary circumstances may temporarily stall the process, in most cases, once the formulation stage of the process has commenced, we can expect that some policy change will ultimately occur.

### The Legislative Stage

At the legislative stage in the policy process, the detailed policy proposal formulated by the bureaucracy and approved by the Cabinet must be translated into "legalese." The details of the policy proposal must be put into the language of legislation, a task which is performed by specialized legislative drafters in

---

11.  J. K. Galbraith, *The New Industrial State* (Boston: Houston Mifflin, 1969), p. 13.

the Department of Justice. After the draft is formally approved by the Cabinet, the bill is placed on the parliamentary agenda. The basic concern at this stage of the process is to ensure that the draft legislation accurately reflects the intentions of the policy makers and that there are no ambiguities in the bill that might lead to administrative problems in its implementation.

**Practical Limits on Parliament**  Because of party discipline the MP can have only limited impact on the substance of a policy once the legislation is introduced. The fact that the government of the day has approved and is sponsoring the draft legislation means the backbench MP faces a daunting task if he or she wishes to effect substantial changes. There has never been a piece of government legislation defeated by the House of Commons in a majority situation, and even with a minority government, government legislation has been defeated only on very rare occasions.

As well, because of the complex and technical nature of most legislation, the MP is usually confronted with a proposal that has taken years of full-time attention on the part of perhaps a few hundred specialists of different types. The overworked MPs who are not experts in the field in question, and who must deal with a large number of proposals per session, are unlikely to be able to mount substantive criticisms that cannot be countered by the government and its advisors.

**Refinement of Policy**  However, particularly at the committee stage of the legislative process, Parliament can have a limited impact on policy. It is at this stage that the MPs can propose amendments that are consistent with the "principle" of the bill that will have the effect of cleaning up or refining the legislation. This is a small but significant role, for the all-party vigilance at this stage provides a final check to ensure that the law as drafted actually accomplishes the policy aims of the government. Thus, while outright rejection of a piece of legislation at this stage is not possible, the MPs do participate actively in refining and clarifying the language of the end product.

**Obstruction and Delay**  Parliament does have some purely negative clout at this stage of the policy process. It is far from unknown for a government to withdraw legislation previously approved by Cabinet in the face of concerted opposition from members of its own caucus, and more than one significant piece of government legislation has been withdrawn or changed in the face of concerted opposition threats to obstruct the business of the House through procedural devices such as filibuster. However, while, as we shall see in later chapters, the opposition parties may stall government legislation temporarily because of their control over a considerable amount of time in the House of Commons, a determined government with a majority will always prevail in the long term.

Similarly, while the government caucus may occasionally be obstreperous, it will almost always, in the end, rally to the support of its leaders in Cabinet. Furthermore, even granting that a Parliament could, in legal terms, reject a government policy proposal, the power here is akin to a veto. The initiative to introduce legislation still resides with the Cabinet, and if a majority government is really determined that a piece of legislation will pass, it will indeed pass Parliament despite the most ardent efforts of its opponents.

### Policy Implementation

The term **policy implementation** can be seen in two distinct ways. Some models of the policy process in Canada posit a separate stage of "policy implementation" that ensues once a law or regulation is in place.[12] In this sense policy-making is seen narrowly as "lawmaking" and policy implementation involves "law application" or enforcement of the law in the real world outside government. The second approach is that policy decisions, by definition taken *internal* to government, can be "implemented" by legislative, executive, or adjudicative acts of the government. In this sense, policy implementation is seen as including more than simply the administrative process.

Obviously we do not disagree that policy decisions must be carried out in the world outside government. However, we prefer to take the more traditional approach that for the most part it is *law*, and not policy, that is applied or implemented through the administrative process. Hence, because our overall approach to Canadian government and politics distinguishes between a *policy* process and *governmental* processes, with the latter being triggered by the former, we will not deal with implementation as a separate "stage" in the policy process.[13] Policies are implemented by legislation, by executive or administrative actions, or by adjudication. Law, including statutes, regulations, and judicial decisions, is, in turn, given effect or implemented by bureaucratic and law-enforcement agencies, which are responsible for applying the law to real people in Canadian society.

---

12. See, for example, S. Brooks, *Public Policy in Canada: An Introduction* (Toronto: McClelland and Stewart, 1993), p. 109; and R. Dyck, *Canadian Politics: Critical Approaches* (Toronto: Nelson, 1993).
13. Clearly, there are *implementation policies*—policy decisions taken about *how* legislation should be implemented by the bureaucracy—but these are analytically separate decisions that establish guidelines for the officials who must actually *do* the implementing and not a separate "stage" in the policy process.

## ▶ FURTHER READING: INTRODUCTION

### General Concepts and Approaches

Almond, G. A., and G. B. Powell. *Comparative Politics*. Boston: Little-Brown, 1978.

Archer, Keith, R. Knopff, R. Gibbons, and Leslie Pal. *Parameters of Power: Canada's Political Institutions*. Scarborough: Nelson, 1995.

Atkinson, M. M. *Governing Canada: Institutions and Public Policy*. Toronto: Harcourt Brace Jovanovitch, 1993.

Brooks, Stephen. *Canadian Democracy: An Introduction*. Toronto: McClelland and Stewart, 1993.

Clement, Wallace, and Glen Williams. *The New Canadian Political Economy*. Montreal: McGill-Queen's University Press, 1989.

Dahl, R. *Democracy and Its Critics*. New Haven: Yale University Press, 1989.

Dyck, Rand. *Canadian Politics: Critical Approaches*. Scarborough: Nelson, 1993.

Easton, David. *A Systems Analysis of Political Life*. New York: John Wiley and Sons, 1965.

Gibbins, Roger. *Conflict and Unity: An Introduction to Canadian Political Life*. Scarborough: Nelson, 1994.

Jackson, Robert, and Doreen Jackson. *Contemporary Government and Politics: Democracy and Authoritarianism*. Scarborough: Prentice-Hall, 1993.

Jackson, Robert, and Doreen Jackson. *Politics in Canada: Culture, Institutions, Behaviour and Public Policy*. Scarborough: Prentice-Hall, 1994.

Panitch, Leo. *The Canadian State*. Toronto: University of Toronto Press, 1977.

Presthus, R. *Elite Accommodation in Canadian Politics*. Toronto: Macmillan, 1973.

Redekop, J. *Approaches to Canadian Politics*. Scarborough: Prentice-Hall, 1983.

Trebilcock, M., et al. *The Choice of Governing Instrument*. Ottawa: Economic Council of Canada, 1982.

Van Loon, Rick, and Mike Whittington. *The Canadian Political System: Environment, Structure and Process*. Toronto: McGraw-Hill Ryerson, 1987.

### The Policy Process

Atkinson, Mike, and Marsha Chandler. *The Politics of Canadian Public Policy*. Toronto: University of Toronto Press, 1983.

Brooks, Stephen. *Public Policy in Canada: An Introduction*. Toronto: McClelland and Stewart, 1989.

Doern, Bruce, and Peter Aucoin. *Public Policy in Canada*. Toronto: Macmillan, 1979.

Doern, Bruce, and Richard Phidd. *Canadian Public Policy: Ideas, Structure, Process*. Scarborough: Nelson, 1992.

Pal, Leslie. *Public Policy Analysis: An Introduction*. 2nd ed. Toronto: Methuen, 1987.

Pross, Paul. *Group Politics and Public Policy*. Toronto: Oxford University Press, 1986.

Wilson, Vince. *Canadian Public Policy and Administration: Theory and Environment*. Toronto: McGraw-Hill Ryerson, 1981.

## PART ONE

# The Environment: Society, Economy, and Culture

*Chapter* **3**

# The Social and Economic Context

It is now almost one hundred years ago that Prime Minister Sir Wilfrid Laurier optimistically predicted that the 20th century would belong to Canada. As we near the end of that period, while one must conclude that Sir Wilfrid was, perhaps, a tad overly optimistic, neither can we say that his comment was merely political hyperbole. A play-by-play announcer, recapping the century's highlights, would have to say that Canada has taken many significant strides since 1900.

## ▶ CANADA: GLOBAL CONTEXTS

In the first fifty years of the century, Canada did indeed come of age internationally. We earned our spurs on the bloody battlefields of two world wars and Canadian leaders were central players in the founding of the United Nations. The Dominion of Canada became an independent nation, freed completely from all but voluntary ties with Britain and the Commonwealth. As well, Canada emerged as a major trading nation, exporting natural resources and agricultural products to the industrial nations around the world. Depending on how one calculates the figures, Canada's economy, today, is consistently among the ten largest of the world's industrialized nations. Canadians have distinguished themselves individually in the international community with significant achievements in the arts, sciences, and medical research. Finally, our standard of living and quality of life have generally been recognized as among the highest in the world, a fact that has made Canada the country of choice of a large and diverse body of would-be immigrants.

## A Century of Growth

Other than the entry of Newfoundland and Labrador to the federation in 1949, the territorial integrity of Canada was essentially set by the year 1900. In 1905 the provinces of Alberta and Saskatchewan were carved out of federal territory, and the northern boundaries of many of the provinces were extended north into federal lands during the early years of the century. As well, by 1999, with the creation of Nunavut, Canada will have three separate territories north of the 60th parallel. While Canada has not changed significantly in terms of territorial jurisdiction, it has grown significantly in terms of population, from a sparse 5 million in 1900 to 30 million in 1995 (Table 3.1).

On the debit side of the ledger, it must be noted that the province of Quebec continues to flirt with the idea of secession from the federation and that aboriginal groups across the land feel that they have been dealt with less than fairly by successive governments. We have a high standard of living by global standards, but the wealth that is associated with that high standard is by no means evenly distributed. There are too many Canadians that can be classified as poor, and there are both "have" and "have-not" provinces in our federation. While economic growth figures in 1995 continue to be encouraging—we have the highest economic growth rate among the G-7 nations and inflation is low—our national unemployment rate rests at just under 10 per cent, and is not expected to decline significantly in the near future.

Perhaps the most serious problem Canadians face as we near the end of the millenium is a national debt (provincial and federal) of $700 billion, $280 billion of which is held by foreign lenders (see Fig. 3.1). The interest payments on the debt amount to more than $50 billion a year and the federal government's debt payments comprise approximately 30 per cent of its total annual budget. This indebtedness as a nation has created a fiscal crisis in the nineties,

**TABLE 3.1**

Population Growth

| Period | Population at end of Census Period (Thousands) | Period | Population at end of Census Period (Thousands) |
|--------|-----------------------------------------------|--------|-----------------------------------------------|
| 1851–1861 | 3,230 | 1956–1961 | 18,238 |
| 1861–1871 | 3,689 | 1961–1966 | 20,015 |
| 1871–1881 | 4,325 | 1966–1971 | 21,568 |
| 1881–1891 | 4,833 | 1971–1976 | 22,993 |
| 1891–1901 | 5,371 | 1976–1981 | 24,343 |
| 1901–1911 | 7,207 | 1981–1986 | 25,354 |
| 1911–1921 | 8,788 | 1986–1991 | 27,108 |
| 1921–1931 | 10,377 | 1993 | 28,753 |
| 1931–1941 | 11,507 | 1994 | 29,362 |
| 1941–1951[*] | 13,648 | 1995 (est.) | 30,000 |
| 1951–1956 | 16,081 | | |

[*] Includes Newfoundland after 1949.

Note: Readers wishing further information on data provided through the cooperation of Statistics Canada may obtain copies of related publications by mail from Publications Sales, Statistics Canada, Ottawa, Ontario K1A 0T6, or by calling 1-613-951-7277, or toll-free 1-800-267-6677. Readers may also facsimile orders by dialing 1-613-951-1584.

Source: Statistics to 1991 reproduced by authority of the Minister of Industry, 1995, Statistics Canada, *Canada Year Book, 1994*. Cat. 11-402E&F. Updated by the author.

which has increased the tax burden on Canadians and forced governments to cut back on the very programs that are intended to reduce the disparities in wealth among individuals and provinces. As indicated in Figure 3.1, the federal government continues to ring up significant annual deficits. Although the annual deficit is projected to decline, it will be many years before we can afford to begin repaying any of the principal of the national debt.

Hence, while there is reason to be mildly optimistic about our future, given high industrial production, steady job creation, and government efforts to reduce or eliminate deficits, uncertainties about our fiscal stability will continue to nag our collective consciousness into the next century. It is unlikely that anybody will say the 21st century belongs to Canada. However, as we shall see when we discuss Canada's role in the global community, it is unlikely that *any* single nation will ever again be able to dominate the international stage the way the USSR and the US did in the years after the Second World War.

### Canada As an International Actor

One of the reasons that Canada never became a dominant force in the global community during the 20th century was that the teams in the game of international politics had already been chosen by the time Canada wanted to join the game. The first half of the century was the era of the Great Power system of international relations, dominated by Britain, France, Germany, Russia, Japan, and the United States and their empires. The best Canada could hope for was to play a supporting role in one of the larger alliances of the great powers or to act as an intermediary between the United States and the United Kingdom in their often stormy relationship.

**Multilateralism and World Politics**  At the end of the Second World War, Canada emerged as a genuine world power, ranking about fourth among all nations in economic and military capability. This starring role was, not unexpectedly, shortlived as the war-ravaged nations of Europe and the Far East quickly recovered economically and reassumed much of their pre-war influence. The Canadian role was further obscured by the emergence of a large number of new nations, resulting from the decline of colonialism, and by the consequent dilution of any one nation's visibility on the world stage. Moreover, the onset of the Cold War signalled the beginning of the era of *bi-polarity* in world politics wherein even the erstwhile great powers were relegated to secondary status behind the Soviet Union and the United States. Most nations during this period were forced to align themselves militarily with either the US-led NATO (North Atlantic Treaty Organization) alliance or the Soviet-led Warsaw Pact, with a significant reduction in their freedom of independent action in world affairs.

*"Middle Powerism"*  Canada, during the Cold War, was forced to take the role of an influential **middle power** that was, clearly, close to the United States in its foreign and defence policy objectives but that could also act independently of its giant neighbour in international institutions. Throughout the Cold War era Canada pursued a foreign policy that was a mix of bilateral defence arrangements with the US, such as NORAD (North American Aerospace Defence Command) and multilateral associations such as NATO. In the post–Cold War

**Figure 3.1**
Annual federal deficits and debts.

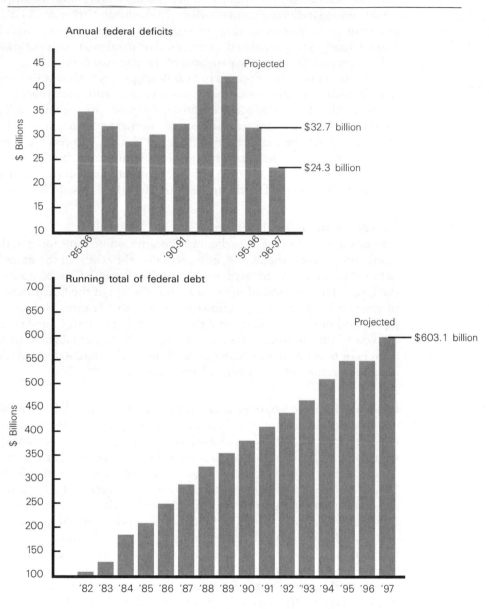

Source: Federal Budget, Feb., 1995, as reported in the *Ottawa Citizen*, Feb. 2, 1995.

period, these defence-related ties are being maintained but their roles are shifting both in importance and in emphasis. Canada is also a participant in UKUSA, the security and intelligence alliance that also includes Britain, the US, Australia, and New Zealand, although the significance of this highly secretive pact is likely to decline as the tensions of the Cold War era dissipate.

Canada also participates in non-military international organizations, such as the UN-sponsored Atomic Energy Commission; Educational, Scientific and Cultural Organization (UNESCO); Conference on Environment and Development (UNCED); and Relief and Rehabilitation Agency (UNRRA). Canada is active in the Organization for Economic Cooperation and Development (OECD) and is a member of the G-7, an annual summit of the seven most powerful industrialized nations. Finally, Canada has maintained its traditional ties with multilateral associations such as the Commonwealth, *la Francophonie*, and the Organization of American States (OAS).

Canada's middle power status has been enhanced by its leading role in founding and supporting the UN's **peacekeeping** capacity, and Canadian troops can be found in a dozen or more different trouble spots around the world at any given time (Fig. 3.2). As well as the Canadian Armed Forces participating in peacekeeping and peacemaking efforts around the world, Elections Canada officials have participated in overseeing and monitoring democratic elections in troubled regions such as Central America and South Africa, and the RCMP has been assigned the responsibility for training police forces in transitional societies such as Haiti. The role of "global referee" is one that Canada has taken on with pride and is a cornerstone of our foreign policy. Our participation is welcomed by other nations because we are seen as domestically stable and as capable of acting independently and neutrally in moderating conflict situations.

*Immigration Policy* Canada also plays a significant role in the international community through its immigration policies. Approximately one-quarter of a million new Canadians annually are accepted into our society (Table 3.2) and, in the 1990s, about 15 per cent of our total population is made up of immigrants. As a result of a liberalization of our immigration laws, refugees fleeing war or civil oppression were admitted to Canada in large numbers during the 1970s and 1980s. Where, in the early years, most of our immigrants came from Europe, today the largest numbers come from Third-World nations, particularly in Asia.

Canada has come to be recognized internationally for its generosity in providing a new home and a fresh start for victims of war and political strife, regardless of their race or country of origin. However, for most of its history Canada had immigration policies that discriminated against non-European applicants. This discrimination was sometimes *direct*, for instance, the "head taxes" or outright bans imposed on Chinese immigrants up until the 1940s; and sometimes it was *indirect*, for example, the granting of greater opportunities to those would-be immigrants who had capital assets or high educational or skill levels. Unhappily, the economic difficulties faced by Canada in the past decade, and shrinking domestic support for open immigration policies, have led to a partial return to more restrictive entry requirements. These include

**Figure 3.2**
Canada's peacekeeping role, 1949–1994.

| Location | Dates |
|---|---|
| India-Pakistan | 1949–1979, 1965–1966 |
| Korea | 1953– |
| Egypt, Israel, Lebanon, Syria | 1954– |
| Cambodia-Laos-Vietnam | 1954–1974 |
| Egypt-Israel | 1956–1967, 1973–1979 |
| Lebanon | 1958, 1978– |
| Congo (Zaire) | 1960–1964 |
| West New Guinea | 1962–1963 |
| Yemen | 1963–1964 |
| Cypress | 1964–1993 |
| Dominican Republic | 1905–1066 |
| Nigeria | 1968–1970 |
| Vietnam | 1973 |
| Israel-Syria (Golan) | 1974– |
| Egypt (Sinai) | 1986– |
| Afghanistan-Pakistan | 1988–1990 |
| Iran-Iraq | 1988–1991 |
| Namibia | 1989–1990 |
| Central America | 1989–1992, 1991– |
| Haiti | 1990–1991 |
| Angola | 1991– |
| Yugoslavia (Bosnia, Croatia) | 1991– |
| Western Sahara | 1991– |
| Persian Gulf, Kuwait | 1991 |
| Iraq-Kuwait | 1991– |
| Somalia | 1992–1993 |

Source: Adapted from *Peacekeeping: A Canadian Contribution to the World* (Ottawa: Department of National Defence, 1991–1992).

cutting the total number of immigrants admitted annually and charging each new Canadian an "admission fee" of $975, that, while not a large sum to North Americans, may effectively bar many otherwise deserving individuals from poorer countries.

*Trade and Globalization*   In the gradually "globalizing" world economy Canada consistently has been an active supporter of multinational trading associations. While we lay great emphasis on Canada's relationships with the United States, it is important also to recognize that the increasingly open nature of the global environment has meant the growth of multilateral trading institutions and the corresponding growth of Canada's participation in them. Much of the extensive growth of Canadian trade over the past two decades has occurred under the aegis of the General Agreement on Tariffs and Trade (GATT), a multicountry agreement with respect to tariff levels and trade patterns (Table 3.3).

**TABLE 3.2**

Immigrants Arriving, by Place of Birth

| | 1981 | | 1991 | |
|---|---|---|---|---|
| | Number | % | Number | % |
| Europe | 44,784 | 34.8 | 46,651 | 20.2 |
|   Great Britain | 18,912 | 14.7 | 6,383 | 2.8 |
|   Portugal | 3,292 | 2.6 | 5,837 | 2.5 |
|   France | 1,681 | 1.3 | 2,619 | 1.1 |
|   Greece | 924 | 0.7 | 618 | 0.3 |
|   Italy | 2,057 | 1.6 | 775 | 0.3 |
|   Poland | 4,093 | 3.2 | 15,737 | 6.8 |
|   Other | 13,825 | 10.7 | 14,682 | 6.4 |
| Africa | 5,901 | 4.6 | 16,530 | 7.2 |
| Asia | 50,759 | 39.5 | 122,228 | 53.0 |
|   Philippines | 5,978 | 4.6 | 12,626 | 5.5 |
|   India | 9,415 | 7.3 | 14,248 | 6.2 |
|   Hong Kong | 4,039 | 3.1 | 16,425 | 7.1 |
|   China | 9,798 | 7.6 | 20,621 | 8.9 |
|   The Middle East | 5,409 | 4.2 | 24,497 | 10.6 |
|   Other | 16,120 | 12.5 | 33,811 | 14.7 |
| North and Central America | 10,183 | 7.9 | 18,899 | 8.2 |
|   United States | 8,695 | 6.8 | 5,270 | 2.3 |
|   Other | 1,488 | 1.2 | 13,629 | 5.9 |
| The Caribbean and Bermuda | 8,797 | 6.8 | 13,046 | 5.7 |
| Australasia | 1,020 | 0.8 | 735 | 0.3 |
| South America | 6,114 | 4.8 | 10,468 | 4.5 |
| Oceania | 1,024 | 0.8 | 2,213 | 1.0 |
| Other | 36 | — | 11 | — |
| Total | 128,618 | 100.0 | 230,781 | 100.0 |

Source:  Statistics Canada, 1981 and 1991 Censuses of Canada.

Canada is the sixth-largest trading nation in the western world, ranking behind the United States, Germany, Great Britain, Japan, and France. About one-third of Canadian income is generated directly by exports. Given the lack of any permanent bilateral economic ties to any nations other than the US, the attention given by successive Canadian governments to the support of multilateral economic associations such as GATT and its heir apparent, the World Trade Organization (WTO), is understandable. Such multinational trading associations are seen, perhaps somewhat unrealistically, as giving Canada a fallback option in the event that relations with the US should sour. However, to understand Canada's role in the world today it is ultimately necessary to understand our close and complex relationship with our powerful and, thankfully, mostly friendly, neighbour to the south.

**TABLE 3.3**
Canada's Trading Partners, 1990, 1993

| Country | 1990 | | 1993 (3rd quarter) | |
|---|---|---|---|---|
| | Exports (%) | Imports (%) | Exports (%) | Imports (%) |
| USA | 75.1 | 68.7 | 80.2 | 73.2 |
| UK | 2.4 | 3.6 | 1.6 | 2.6 |
| Other EU | 5.9 | 7.4 | 4.5 | 5.5 |
| Japan | 5.4 | 6.0 | 4.5 | 4.9 |
| Other OECD | 2.4 | 3.6 | 1.7 | 2.7 |
| Others | 8.9 | 10.6 | 7.5 | 11.2 |

Source: Reproduced by authority of the Minister of Industry, 1995, Statistics Canada, *Canadian Economic Observer*, Jan., 1995. Cat. 11-010.

**Bilateralism: "Sleeping with the Elephant"** Whatever the assessment of Canada's potential influence in global affairs, its preoccupation with the United States is readily understandable. During a visit to Washington early in 1969, Pierre Trudeau said to his US audience: "Living next to you is in some ways like sleeping with an elephant. No matter how friendly and even-tempered is the beast, . . . one is affected by his every twitch and grunt."[1] The elephant in this case has a population ten times as large as Canada's and generates twelve times the gross national product. More than 90 per cent of Canadians live within 500 kilometres of the United States, and most live in a narrow strip within 160 kilometres of the border.

**Defence and Foreign Affairs** Sharing a continent with the United States has had significant consequences for Canada's military policy since the War of Independence. We have long ceased waging war on each other, but as recently as 1905 the Canadian military was taking substantial defence precautions against the United States. While fears of a direct attack from the south have finally vanished, Canada's proximity to the United States still shapes Canadian defence policy. During the Cold War, Canada was strategically "one target" with the United States. This led to the creation of NORAD. Under the terms of NORAD, the effective commander of Canadian air-defence forces in time of international crisis is the American NORAD commander.

While this does not mean that there is no room for independent manoeuvre in defence policy, it does mean that the room is sharply circumscribed. However, there are cases of Canada's refusal to toe the American line in defence matters. Diefenbaker in 1962 refused to arm Bomarc missiles on Canadian soil with nuclear warheads. The Mulroney government ultimately failed to approve the US "Star Wars" initiatives in the closing years of the Cold

---

1. Prime Minister Pierre Trudeau, in a speech to the Washington Press Club, Mar. 25, 1969.

War, a stance close to that of Canada's European allies. Canada has also been critical of recent US incursions into Panama, Granada, and Haiti. In the post–Cold War world, the *raison d'être* of NORAD is harder to justify, and the likelihood that Canada's defence initiatives will deviate from those of the US becomes much more probable.

**Trade Relations**  For many decades Canada and the United States have had by far the largest trading relationship of any two countries in the world. Periodically during the history of this trading relationship, the issue of freer trade between the two neighbours has been pushed to the forefront of political discourse in Canada. High points of Canadian interest in free trade with the US occurred in 1910–1911, immediately after the Second World War, and in the mid 1980s. Through various GATT agreements, signed by both Canada and the US, and through the bilateral *Autopact* of 1967, there were very few significant trade barriers left by 1985. This *de facto* situation was formalized through the *Canada–United States Free Trade Agreement* (FTA), which was signed in 1987; this agreement was extended to include Mexico in the *North American Free Trade Agreement* (NAFTA) in 1994. By the year 2003 it is expected that virtually all restrictions on trade and investment among the three countries will be eliminated, and it is likely that other western-hemisphere trading nations will gradually be incorporated into this vast trading bloc.

The proponents of free trade argue that the arrangement will open up new markets to Canadian producers, thus benefitting the Canadian economy, and the opponents counter that it is one more step in the direction of **continentalism** and the ultimate absorption of Canada into the American empire. It is true that in the period since the FTA was signed a number of Canadian manufacturing companies have failed and others, specifically, branch plants of American parent corporations, have been relocated to the US. However, it seems likely in retrospect that much of this economic hardship was due more to the broader economic woes faced by Canada in a period of serious recession. In the long run free trade will likely benefit Canada, even if there are some difficulties experienced in the transition period. In fact, since the FTA, Canada's trade with the US has increased to 80 per cent of our total international trade and our balance of payments with the US continues to be favourable.

Because Canada has only minimal trade with Mexico, the signing of NAFTA is unlikely to have much negative effect on our domestic economy, and in the long run the access to another 87 million consumers in Mexico can only prove advantageous to Canadian manufacturers. However, there are aspects of the economic relationship between Canada and the US in which the concerns of Canadian nationalists may have greater credence. These include concerns about *foreign ownership* of Canadian industry and the possibility of Canada's *cultural assimilation* into the American melting pot. Each of these bears further discussion.

*US Ownership of Canadian Industry*  In the late 1960s and throughout the 1970s, one of the dominant issues of Canadian politics was foreign ownership of Canadian industry. At the 1970 peak of the foreign-ownership phenomenon, almost 30 per cent of Canadian industry was controlled by American investors, and in the critical oil and gas, mining and smelting, and manufacturing sectors, US control exceeded 50 per cent. However, nationalist concerns about foreign ownership abated during the 1980s when the Government of Canada tended to define the problem as one of too little, rather than too much, foreign investment. That change was motivated in part by a concern to create jobs through investment in a period of relatively high unemployment, and in part because limits to and controls over foreign investment that were legislated during the l970s had significantly affected the flow of investment into and out of Canada.

Those who were alarmed by foreign, largely US, control of large segments of Canadian industry argued that foreign control might be undesirable for reasons related to both economic growth and economic stability.[2] To the extent that Canada depends on the investment decisions of foreign-controlled corporations, the economy and the jobs of Canadians are vulnerable to changes in the growth patterns of those firms. Those patterns will depend in turn on how the firms view their growth prospects elsewhere in the world. Since 1950 foreign corporations did, indeed, tend to concentrate much of their new investment (some of which was financed by the earnings of Canadian subsidiaries) in Europe and in developing areas such as Korea, Hong Kong, Singapore, and Taiwan, which have low labour costs.

Concern has also been expressed that foreign-owned firms carry out research and development activities in the home country rather than in Canada. Not only does this have the potential of denying Canadian scientists and engineers the opportunity of working in their chosen fields in Canada, but it may also place Canada and its industries in a situation of chronic technological dependency on the US. It is also argued that insufficient numbers of Canadians have access to the senior-management positions in the branch plants, that supplies are not purchased in Canada, and that the firms evade taxation by various subterfuges. Yet, it can be countered that, with regard to most of these activities, American affiliates are not in fact much different from Canadian-owned companies, which are equally motivated by profit rather than patriotism.

However, the problems posed by foreign subsidiaries cannot be understood or dealt with solely in terms of economic development. There are also issues of sovereignty and the control by a nation over its own economy, society, and territory. Perhaps the major political problem created by the more than ten thousand American-owned factories that were operating in Canada is that of **extra-territoriality**—the application of the laws of one nation within the boundaries of another. One American law that affects Canadian subsidiaries is antitrust legislation: Canadian subsidiaries are indirectly regulated through pressure imposed on the US parent. As well, Canadian branches of American corporations have often been precluded from selling their products to people in countries considered "enemies" of the US, such as China and Cuba, out of fear that the parent company would be penalized under the United States Treasury's *Foreign Assets Control Regulations* and the *Trading With the Enemy Act*.

---

2. See I. A. Litvak, C. J. Maule, and R. D. Robinson, *Dual Loyalty* (Toronto: McGraw-Hill Ryerson, 1971), p. 2.

Perhaps even more insidious, if not, strictly speaking, a case of extra-territoriality, is the common practice of having all exports to third countries channelled through the parent plant in the US. By company policy, goods manufactured in Canada by a branch plant of an American corporation are deemed to be "not for export." This practice severely restricts the competitiveness and growth potential of the subsidiary.[3]

*Cultural Domination*  Perhaps more important in the long run than the various economic, military, and foreign-policy ramifications of American proximity to Canada is the threat of cultural domination. A number of factors facilitate the impact of American culture on Canada. American television reaches almost everyone in Canada. English-Canadian stations carry a great deal of American programming, and virtually all Canadian viewers can receive US networks on cable and satellite systems. Of the more than forty channels available on a typical cable network, more than half will be American-based, and even the programming on Canadian networks during prime time is dominated by US shows. Moreover, studies of viewing habits conclude that Canadians opt overwhelmingly for the US-produced programs over the Canadian ones when they have a choice.

Children and adults alike pick up cultural images from television. John Meisel, at the time chairman of the Canadian Radio-television and Telecommunications Commission (CRTC), remarked in a speech in 1981 that television "has contributed significantly to the loss of regional and national identities" and to the "Americanization of Canada."[4] Quebec viewers, as one might expect, remain a partial exception to this trend. Fewer French Canadians watch American channels because of the language barrier, and the Canadian content of the French networks is much higher than that of the English networks. The language barrier has been instrumental in helping to insulate the French-Canadian culture from the overwhelming geographical proximity of the United States.

The problems of preserving a cultural identity in English-speaking Canada are compounded when the effects of magazines and other segments of the mass media are added. In 1969, 95 per cent of all magazines available in Canadian retail outlets were American imports. For decades, the two American giants, *Time* and *Reader's Digest*, took about 40 per cent of total magazine advertising in Canada. By the mid-1970s, *Reader's Digest* had a monthly circulation of 1.25 million, and *Time* of 550,000. In 1976, Canadian-content legislation brought about the demise of the Canadian edition of *Time*, at least temporarily, but many subscribers simply switched to the US edition, and so did the advertisers. Nonetheless, the situation did change somewhat during the 1980s. The circulation of *Reader's Digest* remained constant and that of *Time* magazine declined, while our home-grown *Maclean's* has risen steadily.

---

3. This issue receives extensive treatment in Glen Williams, *Not for Export* (Toronto: McClelland and Stewart, 1994). See also G. Williams, "Regions Within Regions: Continentalism Ascendant," *in* M. S. Whittington and G. Williams, eds., *Canadian Politics in the 1990s* (Toronto: Nelson, 1994), pp. 19–39.
4. Cited in F. J. Fletcher and Daphne Gottlieb Taras, "The Mass Media and Politics: An Overview," *in* M. S. Whittington and G. Williams, eds., *Canadian Politics in the 1980s* (Toronto: Methuen, 1984), pp. 292–319.

While cultural products are supposed to be exempted from the FTA, the US entertainment industry is strongly opposed to any attempts by the Canadian government to protect its cultural industries. Tariffs imposed on the Canadian edition of *Sports Illustrated* were met by strong objections from the US Congress and resulted in threats of countervailing measures against Canadian cultural exports to the US. Similarly, the decision of the CRTC to decertify a US country-music cable network and replace it with a Canadian clone caused an enormous uproar in the US industry and the expected threats of retaliation by the US. It is to be hoped that the FTA does not end up being a Trojan horse for the further US infiltration of our already overwhelmingly Americanized media of mass communications.

*Canada and the US: A Conclusion*  As a conclusion to this brief discussion of Canada's unique and complex relationship with its largest neighbour, we must start with the prosaic statement that neither nation has very much choice in the matter. The United States and Canada share a border several thousand kilometres long, similar historical roots, and English as a common language. Our economic trading relationship is mutually beneficial, and, in a world where protectionism is dying out and large trading blocs seem to be the norm, to suggest that Canada should limit its trade with the US is folly. Very few of even the most strident critics of the FTA would suggest today that Canada should extricate itself from the arrangement.

Canadians have always had an ambivalent attitude towards the US. In some fashion, the American way of life is very attractive, in terms of its affluence, its liberal values, and its democratic traditions, and, as with most nations around the globe, Canada tends to view the US as a model against which to measure its own success as a nation. On the other hand, while we aspire to some of the positive attributes of the most powerful nation in the world, we do not want to incorporate the more negative dimensions of America, such as extremely high violent-crime rates, racial conflict, and a much harsher and less forgiving brand of *laissez-faire* liberalism. The latter feature of American society denies the legitimacy of the social safety net, universal health care, and the tolerance of cultural diversity, all of which are cornerstones of Canadian political life.

Hence, while to some extent, as a nation, we emulate our southern neighbours, we do not want to *be* them. The Canadian way of doing things is significantly different from the American way, and we *like* the differences. The FTA and NAFTA have formalized the fact that we are part of a single continental *economy*, and that is unlikely to change. However, if we wish to preserve a somewhat different set of cultural values, we must remain a separate *society*. This is still achievable, by and large, because Canada is a separate sovereign nation, with a distinctive political culture and a healthy, if understated, national consciousness.

Moreover, the cultural incursions of American television and American publications that many elite observers fear will inevitably assimilate Canada do not give sufficient credence to the ability of non-elite Canadians to pick and choose from among the images of America that are portrayed to us. Canadians are subtle enough to recognize both the good things and the bad things about the US that are part of the message of the American media. In this sense, perhaps the images of American society that we receive through a continental mass-communications network are not so much instruments of cultural assimilation as reminders that we *are* different culturally, and better off for the differences. We will return to a discussion of the ideological differences between Canada and the US in the next chapter.

## ▶ CLEAVAGES IN CANADA

Having looked at Canada in a global and continental context, we must now turn to a discussion of the internal variables that form the *setting* of our politics and government. It is these internal variables that determine most of the issues addressed by our politicians and the conflicts that must be managed by our governments. Political issues arise because there are perceived differences among groups and individuals in society, which result in conflicting policy demands being articulated to government.

### The Concept of Cleavage

The politically relevant differences among various groups and individuals are called **cleavages.** These are based on a number of distinct but interrelated sets of objective variables that have the potential of generating political conflict. Before discussing the various types of cleavage that exist in Canada, we must point out that not all variables that differentiate individuals and groups are cleavages because they are unlikely ever to generate political conflict. For example, we can *differentiate* among people on the basis of eye colour, foot size, or hairstyle but the differences, so identified, are not cleavages because it is highly unlikely that public-policy decisions would ever result in unequal impacts based solely on such factors.

By contrast, variables such as race, level of income, or occupation identify differences that very often result in differential policy impacts and can therefore be seen as cleavages. Cleavages can be roughly classified as either vertical or horizontal. **Vertical cleavages** are based on essentially economic factors, such as level of income, social status, or class. Competing groups in this category square off in political conflicts according to their relative wealth or economic opportunity. **Horizontal cleavages** are based on non-economic factors, such as region, ethnicity, gender, and age, which can either cut across or coincide with economic factors.

It is important to recognize that cleavages are very rarely only one-dimensional factors. For example, ethnic, regional, cultural, and gender variables often coincide at least partially with economic lines of cleavage. This **coincidence of cleavage** deepens the conflict between groups and makes the conflict more difficult for government to manage. For example, racial conflict is made more severe if it is accompanied by a significant disparity in wealth or economic opportunity, and differences in employment opportunities between men and women can exacerbate gender cleavages.

However, cleavages also can be **crosscutting,** a phenomenon which has the effect of diffusing and weakening political conflicts. For example, if French-

and English-speaking workers belong to the same union, the *ethnic* conflict between them may be reduced because they are on the same side in an *economic* conflict. Thus, while the following discussion will focus on geographical, ethnic, and economic cleavages in turn, the reader must keep in mind that in the real world political conflicts always involve the interaction of many different variables that both coincide and crosscut.

▶ GEOGRAPHICAL CLEAVAGE: REGIONALISM

Where we live can be an important determinant of how we behave in political circumstances and, in a country as big and diverse as Canada, it is taken for granted that **regionalism** (or regional cleavage) plays a role in defining many of our political issues. In part, spatial variables such as regionalism have come to be a focus for political rallying cries because our political process is organized in spatial or territorial terms. Both federalism and our riding-based electoral system group Canadians together in territorially defined political units called provinces and constituencies, respectively. While this creates a consciousness of territorial identity, it may be somewhat superficial. On closer examination we discover that what is often more significant in causing different regions to express different political priorities is not geography *per se*, but the other variables that coincide with the regional boundaries.

In this sense, then, regions are better seen as *containers* within which the unique economic, cultural, and ethnic mix defines local political interests and makes a region politically unique. For example, Ontario and Quebec have a similar topographical, climatic, and geological mix and their economies are founded on broadly similar resource bases. We refer to them as separate regions because the ethno-cultural composition of their respective populations produces significantly different patterns of political behaviour. Similarly, the prairie provinces constitute a distinct region, not because the land is generally flatter than Ontario, but because of circumstances that have created a fundamentally different economic base and an economic relationship with central Canada that Westerners see as unfavourable to their interests. Let us now look further at some of these regional economic disparities and their causes.

**The Causes of Regional Economic Disparity**

Differences of terrain, climate, and the distribution of mineral and forest resources help to create regional disparities in Canada (Fig. 3.3). Of these three factors, climate is probably the least troublesome for, in spite of the overall harshness of the weather, there are fairly large areas of Canada where rainfall and mean temperatures are sufficient to grow productive crops, as long as the soil is fertile enough. Growing seasons vary greatly from region to region but if climate were the only determinant, regional disparities would not be as great as they are.

Distance, as well, can be a disadvantage for the regions of the Canadian hinterland. The cost of transportation of raw materials and agricultural prod-

**Figure 3.3**
Physiographic regions of Canada.

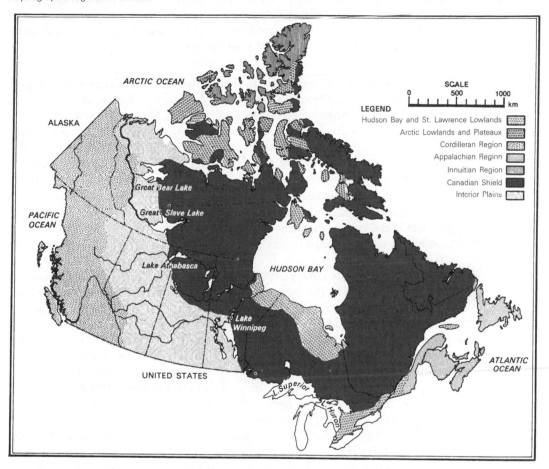

ucts to central Canada are much greater for producers in the West and in Atlantic Canada. Moreover, the fact that the biggest markets for manufactured products are in central Canada and the adjacent population centres in the United States has inhibited the growth of manufacturing outside the industrial heartland in the Great Lakes–St. Lawrence basin. The problems of distance become even more extreme in the case of Canada's far north, where, although there is vast potential for the development of primary industries, building the necessary transportation linkages, such as pipelines, roads, and railways, often involves cost-prohibitive mega projects.

Finally, Canada's topography combines with its size to create both economic and psychological barriers to national economic development. The Western Cordillera, the Canadian Shield, and the open water that separates the mainland from Newfoundland, Prince Edward Island, Vancouver Island, and the Arctic Archipelago not only make bulk shipping difficult but also make regions feel somewhat isolated from each other. The transportation and communications infrastructure that is a necessary precondition for trade among Canada's regions is so costly that our economic development can be seen as an unending series of "national dreams" in the form of construction mega projects. In sum, our national economy did not simply evolve, it had to be built, usually with the heavy involvement of government.

**Primary Resources**  Whatever the difficulties of climate, distance, and topography, Canada as a whole does have an abundance of at least four crucial resources—water, forests, petroleum, and minerals. Water has enabled Canada to generate large amounts of electricity inexpensively and has consequently made electrical energy one of its most plentiful commodities. Water has also provided the basis for one of Canada's largest industries—tourism—and has been talked about from time to time as an exportable commodity. Even if it did exacerbate regional economic disparities at the time, the concentration of oil and gas reserves in western Canada shielded our economy from the worst impacts of the energy shortages of the 1970s. Similar reserves off the east coast and in the far north may in the same way protect the Canadian economy in the future.

Canada's forests have made us the western world's largest producer of newsprint and one of the largest producers of lumber. Mineral deposits have made isolated areas of the Canadian Shield and the Cordillera pockets of prosperity. Coal production has periodically generated wealth in Canada and our uranium deposits have some potential to provide longer-term economic growth. Once an important primary product, Canada's fish stocks on both the Atlantic and Pacific coasts have been depleted to the point that the economic prospects in the fishery do not look promising for the near future.

One of the drawbacks here is that Canada's primary resources are not evenly distributed. Significant amounts of hydroelectric power can be generated only in large watersheds, mineralization occurs in isolated pockets in the rock, and the best forest stands are concentrated in only four provinces. Ontario, whose secondary industries are Canada's largest, also has the largest mineral production; British Columbia, with fertile interior valleys and a congenial climate, also has large deposits of minerals and the best timber stands; and Alberta, already agriculturally advanced, has the largest proven reserves of oil. The Atlantic provinces, with poor agricultural prospects, also lack the large mineral deposits, readily accessible petroleum reserves, stands of timber, and hydroelectric-power resources of central and western Canada. With the serious decline in the Atlantic ground fishery, Newfoundland and the Maritimes may see even more hardship in their already weak economies.

**Secondary Industry**  Part of the problem in poorer areas in Canada stems from the type of industry located there. Relative to the rest of Canada, the Atlantic provinces have less manufacturing and a higher concentration of primary industries such as mining, fishing, and forestry. Manufacturing industries are more beneficial to regional growth because they have a "multiplier" effect on the regional economy. Each step, from extracting minerals from the ground, through processing and manufacturing things out of the raw materials, and transporting the goods to market adds value to the end product. The number of jobs created and the amount of wealth generated by a secondary industry, such as manufacturing, is greater than for a primary industry, such as mining.

Approximately 80 per cent of Canada's manufacturing activity occurs in central Canada, partly because of the diversified economies of Ontario and Quebec, which have abundant raw materials, large labour forces, and a proximity to the lucrative markets of the eastern United States and partly because manufacturing developed first in these provinces. While Alberta, largely because of oil and gas reserves, and British Columbia, because of a strong forestry sector, a diversifying economy, and good emerging markets on the Pacific Rim, are "have" provinces, they are regional economies that are very sensitive to world fluctuations in prices (see Table 3.4). Moreover, a large percentage of the manufactured goods they require must be imported by the western provinces from central Canada or the US.

**Policy Discrimination** A case can be made that federal government policies *have* always favoured the central regions over the periphery. For instance, corporation tax collected from a firm whose head office is in Toronto is split

**TABLE 3.4**

Provincial Gross Domestic Product Per Capita Relative to Canadian Average (%)

|  | Nfld. | P.E.I. | N.S. | N.B. | Que. | Ont. |
|---|---|---|---|---|---|---|
| 1961 | 50.2 | 49.4 | 65.3 | 60.2 | 90.6 | 120.2 |
| 1971 | 56.0 | 51.5 | 67.6 | 64.3 | 90.1 | 117.8 |
| 1981 | 58.0 | 56.8 | 61.4 | 60.6 | 86.0 | 102.7 |
| 1986 | 60.0 | 59.5 | 75.1 | 71.3 | 90.3 | 111.9 |
| 1987 | 60.6 | 58.2 | 74.2 | 71.2 | 91.8 | 112.7 |
| 1988 | 60.3 | 59.0 | 73.0 | 70.8 | 91.5 | 114.5 |
| 1989 | 60.0 | 59.0 | 73.0 | 71.1 | 90.0 | 114.8 |
| 1990 | 61.4 | 60.7 | 75.5 | 72.7 | 90.7 | 111.4 |
| 1991 | 65.0 | 63.7 | 78.6 | 75.6 | 91.5 | 109.6 |

|  | Man. | Sask. | Alta. | B.C. | Y.T. and N.W.T. | Canada |
|---|---|---|---|---|---|---|
| 1961 | 90.1 | 78.0 | 108.7 | 111.4 | 107.6 | 100.0 |
| 1971 | 89.1 | 83.3 | 107.0 | 106.0 | 118.6 | 100.0 |
| 1981 | 87.4 | 103.0 | 157.2 | 112.7 | 141.3 | 100.0 |
| 1986 | 86.5 | 85.4 | 121.4 | 99.9 | 151.3 | 100.0 |
| 1987 | 84.3 | 79.1 | 116.9 | 100.3 | 154.5 | 100.0 |
| 1988 | 85.2 | 76.6 | 111.5 | 100.3 | 151.8 | 100.0 |
| 1989 | 85.4 | 78.8 | 109.7 | 102.4 | 153.2 | 100.0 |
| 1990 | 86.6 | 81.7 | 115.2 | 103.7 | 153.9 | 100.0 |
| 1991 | 85.7 | 80.8 | 115.1 | 105.3 | 151.0 | 100.0 |

Source: Reproduced by authority of the Minister of Industry, 1995, Statistics Canada, *Canada Year Book*, 1994, Cat. 11-402E&F.

only between the federal and Ontario governments, in spite of the fact that the earnings of the corporation may come from anywhere in Canada. The Atlantic provinces and the prairies claim, with considerable justification, that the tariff barriers that prevailed in Canada from the mid 19th century virtually until the 1980s protected industry in the central provinces but did nothing to protect the primary resources and agricultural production of the poorer areas from the fluctuations of world markets. Additionally, the consumers in the resource hinterlands of Canada had to pay higher, tariff-protected prices for the "tools of their trades" such as heavy equipment and farm machinery.

In order to ameliorate regional economic disparties, policy makers have adopted the policy of encouraging growth in less fortunate regions by infusions of capital. The *Agricultural and Rural Development Act* (ARDA), the Fund for Rural Economic Development, the Atlantic Development Board, the Area Development Agency, and, more recently, the Office of Western Diversification have all been directed at resolving economic disparities through capital expenditures but with uniformly disappointing long-term results. The most important of the federal initiatives, however, have been Equalization Payments to poorer provinces and regional redistribution of wealth through massive federal transfers to both individuals and provincial governments. Intergovernmental transfers are dealt with extensively in Chapter 11.

**The Human Cost** So far, we have spoken of economic disparities among the *regions* of Canada. However, perhaps more important in political terms is the impact of regional disparities upon the *people* who live in the various regions. Average family disposable income in 1992 varied from $35,000 in Newfoundland to $47,000 in Ontario, and only Ontario, Alberta, and British Columbia have an average family income at or above the national mean. Similarly, unemployment ranges from over 20 per cent in Newfoundland to a low of 6.1 per cent in Saskatchewan. Generally, from Ontario westward, the rate is below the national average and in Quebec and the Atlantic provinces it is above.

It is important to note here, however, that figures on what Statistics Canada calls the *low income cutoff* (LICO) and what those of a more polemical bent call the "poverty line" indicate that the regional differences in the incidence of low-income families are not all that significant. As can be seen from Table 3.6, 14.5 per cent of all families in Canada (1993) fall below the LICO. In the Atlantic provinces, the overall level is 13.5, with a high of 15.8 per cent in Newfoundland and a national low of 7.6 in Prince Edward Island. Quebec is the only region worse off than the national average, at 16.8 per cent of family incomes below the LICO. The more even distribution of low-income families across the country is partly due to much lower costs of living in the poorer regions. As well, poverty appears to be more evenly distributed because it is, to a large extent, a phenomenon of large urban centres that tend to be located more in the wealthier provinces.

**TABLE 3.5**
Provincial Unemployment Rates, 1995

|  | % |
|---|---|
| Canada | 9.6 |
| Newfoundland | 20.7 |
| Prince Edward Island | 15.0 |
| Nova Scotia | 12.3 |
| New Brunswick | 11.6 |
| Quebec | 12.1 |
| Ontario | 8.4 |
| Manitoba | 7.9 |
| Saskatchewan | 6.1 |
| Alberta | 7.6 |
| British Columbia | 8.4 |

Source: Statistics Canada, *Canadian Economic Observer*, Jan., 1995.

**TABLE 3.6**
Families below Low Income Cutoff (1992 base)

|  | 1983 % | 1984 % | 1985 % | 1986 % | 1987 % | 1988 % | 1989 % | 1990 % | 1991 % | 1992 % | 1993 % |
|---|---|---|---|---|---|---|---|---|---|---|---|
| Total | 15.1 | 15.5 | 14.2 | 13.3 | 12.8 | 12.0 | 10.9 | 12.0 | 12.9 | 13.3 | 14.5 |
| Atlantic Provinces | 19.9 | 18.1 | 16.4 | 15.7 | 14.8 | 13.1 | 12.3 | 12.6 | 13.3 | 13.8 | 13.5 |
| Newfoundland | 25.2 | 21.9 | 22.1 | 21.2 | 19.7 | 16.0 | 12.9 | 14.4 | 16.2 | 18.4 | 15.8 |
| Prince Edward Island | 10.8 | 12.4 | 11.7 | 9.6 | 10.5 | 10.9 | 9.8 | 10.2 | 10.6 | 7.2 | 7.6 |
| Nova Scotia | 17.2 | 15.8 | 14.2 | 14.3 | 11.9 | 11.6 | 12.2 | 11.8 | 12.8 | 13.8 | 14.4 |
| New Brunswick | 20.7 | 19.0 | 15.7 | 14.1 | 15.3 | 13.0 | 12.2 | 12.5 | 12.3 | 11.5 | 11.5 |
| Quebec | 17.9 | 18.6 | 16.6 | 16.3 | 16.0 | 15.8 | 12.8 | 14.7 | 15.4 | 14.8 | 16.8 |
| Ontario | 12.9 | 12.4 | 11.3 | 9.8 | 8.9 | 8.5 | 7.9 | 9.6 | 11.2 | 11.1 | 13.2 |
| Prairie Provinces | 14.1 | 15.4 | 13.8 | 13.8 | 13.9 | 13.1 | 12.9 | 13.5 | 14.1 | 15.2 | 14.6 |
| Manitoba | 15.8 | 14.5 | 14.6 | 15.9 | 14.2 | 13.2 | 13.0 | 14.4 | 17.4 | 14.2 | 14.3 |
| Saskatchewan | 14.6 | 15.4 | 14.7 | 15.9 | 12.7 | 13.8 | 12.8 | 13.8 | 13.6 | 13.8 | 13.5 |
| Alberta | 13.1 | 15.8 | 13.1 | 12.0 | 14.3 | 12.8 | 12.8 | 13.0 | 13.0 | 16.2 | 15.1 |
| British Columbia | 13.2 | 16.6 | 16.5 | 15.1 | 14.8 | 12.0 | 11.7 | 11.5 | 10.6 | 13.5 | 13.9 |

Source: Reproduced by authority of the Minister of Industry, 1995, Statistics Canada, *Canadian Economic Observer*, Jan., 1995. Cat. 11-010.

## ▶ RACIAL AND ETHNIC CLEAVAGES

At the most elementary level of analysis, ethnicity is simply an accident of one's birth—if our parents happen to be German or Chinese or Irish, then our ethnic origin will be, by definition, German or Chinese or Irish. However, what is most significant politically about ethnicity is not the simple genetic accident that links all of us to one or more national or cultural groups, but the various factors that are normally tied to ethnic origin. Hence, if an Anglo-Saxon child is adopted in infancy by a French-Canadian family, and brought up as a French Canadian, the genetic background will be virtually irrelevant in determining the patterns of behaviour, the cultural values, and the socio-economic status of the individual at maturity. Thus, the political relevance of ethnicity—its significance as a determinant of lines of cleavage in a society—is defined by the many non-hereditary factors that coincide with the inherited accident of birth (see Figs. 3.4, 3.5). These each must be considered in more detail.

### Geographical Concentration

We have already mentioned that Quebec is a distinct region because it comprises a geographical concentration of the vast majority of Canada's largest ethnic minority, the French Canadians. At this point we will not deal in any detail with French Canadians as an ethnic minority, nor will we elaborate extensively on the nature of French-English cleavage. Instead Chapter 9 is entirely devoted to a discussion of the origins and evolution of this fundamental and persistent source of political conflict within the Canadian federal system.

**Figure 3.4**
Ethnic composition of Canada's population, 1991.

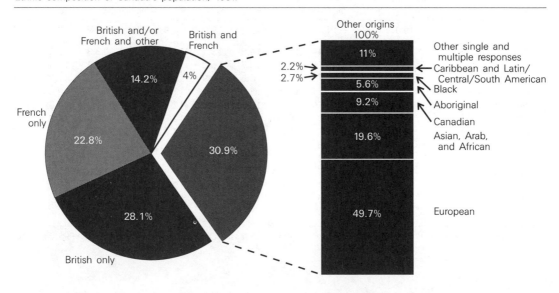

Source: Statistics Canada, 1991 Census of Canada. Reproduced by authority of the Minister of Industry, 1995, Statistics Canada, *Canadian Social Trends*, Autumn 1993. Cat 11-008E&F.

However, the geographical *concentration* of ethnic groups is significant in other cases as well. For example, Canada's Inuit are concentrated, for the most part, above the treeline in the Northwest Territories, in northern Quebec, and in Labrador. The Inuit of the NWT will soon be granted their own territory of Nunavut within which they will constitute more than 80 per cent of the population. Canadian Indians tend to be concentrated in the northern regions of the provinces, the Northwest Territories, and the Yukon; those in southern Canada are concentrated on reserves.

Similarly, although it is a manifestation of patterns of settlement and migration more than of historical residency, the phenomenon of *ghettoization*, the concentration of specific groups in specific urban districts or neighbourhoods, has also tended to exaggerate and reinforce social and ethnic differences. This has occurred particularly with respect to non-white or *visible minority* immigrant groups who tend to congregate in the large urban centres of Vancouver, Toronto, and Montreal.

Finally, it is also possible to identify some tendency for European ethnic groups to concentrate in certain regions of the country and in distinct districts or neighbourhoods in the cities and larger towns. However, while these settlement patterns often persist for several generations, so that it is possible, for example, to identify communities in western Canada that have high concentrations of German or Ukrainian Canadians, or districts in eastern Canadian cities that have high concentrations of people of Italian origin, generally, second- or third-generation European immigrants find little difficulty in moving out of their ethnic havens and integrating themselves into the so-called Canadian mainstream.

**Ethnicity, Culture, and Religion** Cultural diversity has been the hallmark of Canadian society, and while such diversity should not be allowed to manifest itself in the destruction of the federation, its existence enriches and stimulates Canadian political life. The pattern of values and attitudes, or the *culture* of an ethnic minority, is ultimately what makes the group different from other Canadians. It is not the colour of one's skin, the language spoken in the home, or the unique styles of dress but, rather, the beliefs of the group, and the behaviour patterns that reflect those beliefs, that make ethnic cleavage significant. We will return to this discussion in the next chapter when we look at the Canadian political culture.

Of particular importance in defining an ethnic group's culture is the group's religion (Table 3.7). Certainly, over two centuries, French-English conflict in Canada has been exacerbated by the coincident Protestant-Catholic religious cleavage, and, through long periods of Canada's early history, ethnic and linguistic cleavage was often overshadowed by religious differences. Irish immigrants of the 1840s transplanted much of the Protestant-Catholic strife from Ireland, and, for some fifty years afterwards, the predominant cleavage in many parts of Canada was Protestant-Catholic. Schools were denominational, as were hospitals, welfare institutions, newspapers, and many of the other institutions that connect citizens to society.

While the intensity of religious conflict has generally declined, there are still political issues that arise periodically to divide people along religious lines. Separate-school funding in Ontario has been an issue as recently as the 1985

**Figure 3.5**

Proportion of population reporting origins other than British or French, 1991.

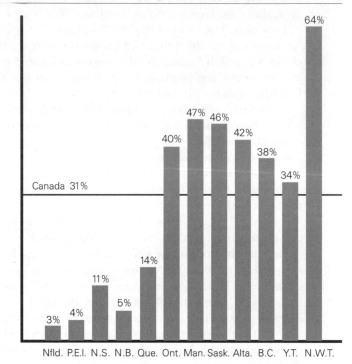

Source: Statistics Canada, 1991 Census of Canada. Reproduced by authority of the Minister of Industry, 1995, Statistics Canada, *Canadian Social Trends*, Autumn 1993. Cat. 11-008E&F.

provincial election, and in a 1995 referendum Newfoundlanders voted (by a narrow margin) to get rid of publicly funded denominational schools. As well, the rapid increase in the number of Canadians whose religious convictions are neither Catholic nor Protestant has increased the number and intensity of issues involving religious practice. Members of the Sikh religion have come into conflict with other groups over the wearing of turbans in the RCMP and in Legion Posts, and issues have arisen over Islamic students wearing the *chador* in highschool classrooms. Minority ethnic groups have also been active in attempting to extend the recognition of religious holidays in the workplace and schools to non-Christian celebrations.

While it is still possible to conclude that religious cleavage is not the most important manifestation of ethnic conflict in Canada, and while Canadians can take some solace in the fact that religious factions in this country do not generally resort to physical violence or acts of terrorism to make their points, religious issues do crop up from time to time on the agenda for political debate. Moreover, because lines of religious cleavage tend to coincide with ethnic ones, religious cleavage can help to reinforce and exacerbate ethno-cultural conflict in general.

**TABLE 3.7**
Religious Composition of Canada

| | Proportion of Population (%) | | | | | |
|---|---|---|---|---|---|---|
| | **1891** | **1911** | **1931** | **1951** | **1971** | **1991**[a] |
| Catholic | 41.6 | 39.4 | 41.3 | 44.7 | 47.3 | 45.7 |
|   Roman Catholic | 41.6 | 39.4 | 39.5 | 43.3 | 46.2 | 45.2 |
|   Ukrainian Catholic | — | — | 1.8 | 1.4 | 1.1 | 0.5 |
| Protestant | 56.5 | 55.9 | 54.4 | 50.9 | 44.4 | 36.2 |
|   United Church[b] | — | — | 19.5 | 20.5 | 17.5 | 11.5 |
|   Anglican | 13.7 | 14.5 | 15.8 | 14.7 | 11.8 | 8.1 |
|   Presbyterian[b] | 15.9 | 15.6 | 8.4 | 5.6 | 4.0 | 2.4 |
|   Lutheran | 1.4 | 3.2 | 3.8 | 3.2 | 3.3 | 2.4 |
|   Baptist | 6.4 | 5.3 | 4.3 | 3.7 | 3.1 | 2.5 |
|   Pentecostal | | — | 0.3 | 0.7 | 1.0 | 1.7 |
|   Other[c] | 19.1 | 17.3 | 2.3 | 2.5 | 3.7 | 7.9 |
| Eastern Orthodox | — | 1.2 | 1.0 | 1.2 | 1.5 | 1.5 |
| Jewish | 0.1 | 1.0 | 1.5 | 1.5 | 1.3 | 1.2 |
| No Religion[d] | — | 0.4 | 0.2 | 0.4 | 4.3 | 12.4 |
| Other[e] | 1.8 | 2.0 | 1.6 | 1.4 | 1.2 | 2.8 |

[a]  For 1991, inmates of institutions are excluded.
[b]  Between 1911 and 1931, the United Church denomination was formed through an amalgamation of the Methodists, Congregationalists, and about one-half of the Presbyterian group. For 1931 and thereafter, the figures for Presbyterian reflect the segment that did not amalgamate with the United Church.
[c]  Other Protestant denominations include Methodists and Congregationalists up to 1921, and other denominations such as Adventist, Churches of Christ, Disciples, and the Salvation Army. The "Other" group also includes a certain proportion of smaller Protestant denominations.
[d]  In 1891, "No Religion" is included in "Other." In 1971, the introduction of self-enumeration methodology may have been in part a cause of the larger increase in the proportion of the population reporting "No Religion." However, the 1971 and 1991 figures for this group are comparable.
[e]  In 1981, many of these smaller denominations were disaggregated and are counted in the "Other Protestant" category. The remainder of the "Other" group includes Eastern Non-Christian religious.

Source:  Reproduced by authority of the Minister of Industry, 1995, Statistics Canada, *Canada Year Book*, 1994. Cat. 11-402E&F.

## The Management of Ethnic Conflict: Problems and Dilemmas

Ethnic conflicts can be enhanced by economic disparity between an ethnic group and the society as a whole. The elimination of the wide disparities in wealth and economic opportunity among such groups is therefore an important strategy for managing ethnic conflict. However, as can be seen in Table 3.8, new Canadians actually fare quite well in Canada. Therefore, we must recognize that there are obstacles to the effective moderation of ethnic cleavage that go deeper than economic disparities. These must be dealt with directly and not only through economic redistributive measures.

**TABLE 3.8**
Canadian-born and Immigrant Income, 1993 Average

|  | Canadian-born Income ($) | Immigrant Income ($) |
|---|---|---|
| Individual | 24,295 | 24,860 |
| Man | 29,794 | 30,561 |
| Woman | 18,621 | 19,008 |
| Family | 52,946 | 55,565 |

Source: Reproduced by authority of the Minister of Industry, 1995, Statistics Canada, *Income Distributions by Size in Canada*, 1993. Cat. 13-207.

**Integration vs. Assimilation** It has become almost a cliché to refer to Canadian society as an ethnic or cultural **mosaic**—this to distinguish it from the United States, which is often likened to a **melting pot**—but what is implicit in this superficial distinction is that there are at least two analytical models that can explain how the various ethnic components of immigrant societies are bonded together. These models are **assimilation** and **integration**, and each requires elaboration in the interest of clarifying the nature of ethnic cleavage in Canada.

Assimilation is essentially the process whereby the various ethnic components of a political community become absorbed or dissolved by the majority or mainstream ethnic *mélange* and ultimately the component parts cease to be distinguishable. What is gained in this form of nation-building is a reduction or elimination of ethnic cleavage and a higher degree of consensus. But because culture is such an important reflection of ethnicity, what is lost is the richness of a truly multicultural society—one opts for a seafood purée and forgoes *bouillabaisse* because the former is easier to concoct and much more manageable at the table.

By contrast to assimilation, an integrative model recognizes the fact that minority cultures are in a state of siege that is imposed unconsciously and, often, with no malice by the majority or mainstream culture. As its starting point, this model takes the position that the many groups that make up a multi-ethnic or pluralist society have unique cultural characteristics that can often enhance and strengthen the national political community. The attractiveness of such a model of nation-building to the minority ethnic groups is that they are permitted to retain their cultural distinctiveness and at the same time participate fully in, enjoy the benefits of, and contribute to the shared experience of being Canadian.

Generally the model that has been employed in the building of the Canadian nation is an integrative or pluralist one. Our Constitution, as we shall see in later chapters, has reflected this from the outset. More recently, policies such as official bilingualism and multiculturalism, constitutional guarantees of aboriginal rights, and the equality provisions of the 1982 Charter of Rights and Freedoms are all indications of a continuing political will to foster cultural and ethnic diversity.

**Visible Minorities and Systemic Discrimination**  It is clear that **visible minorities** in Canada generally suffer from a slower rate of integration into Canadian society than do traditional immigrant groups from European countries. The reasons for this may include the existence of racist attitudes on the part of many individual Canadians. We will discuss this *psychological* dimension of ethnic relations in the next section of this chapter. However, visible minorities also face unintentional, institutionalized discrimination. This is what the 1984 Parliamentary Special Committee on Visible Minorities report calls **systemic discrimination** and, in terms of its effect, it is no less debilitating than the explicitly racist behaviour of individuals.

Perhaps the most important manifestation of systemic discrimination in Canada is in the employment markets, where many non-white ethnic groups are disproportionately excluded from participation in the labour force or, even more commonly, where such individuals are kept out of roles in sectors of the economy where these new Canadians would prefer to participate. They may not be disproportionately unemployed when compared with other groups, but they may be disproportionately *under-employed*.[5]

**Aboriginal People and Systemic Discrimination**  Aboriginal people continue to suffer from a wide range of discriminatory phenomena.[6] The *Indian Act* itself, while intended to protect aboriginal people from exploitation by the majority and to provide them with a broad range of social programs, including health care and education, stands as a monument to the notion of unintentional or systemic discrimination. As a vehicle for social integration, the Act has failed totally. Moreover, even in matters for which the Act was specifically designed, such as the delivery of health care, social services, housing, and education, the record is fairly dismal.

The litany of social and economic ills suffered by aboriginal people as a group is all too familiar by now. The completion rate for highschool, the rate of participation in the labour force, and the unemployment rate are all drastically worse for them than for other Canadians. Even among those who are employed, the average income is approximately two-thirds of the national average, and the proportion of aboriginal income in the form of transfers from government is twice that of non-aboriginal Canadians.

When one moves to a comparison of general social conditions, the picture for aboriginal Canadians on reserves is still more bleak. Aboriginal Canadians continue to suffer from extremely low standards of housing, with serious overcrowding and a disproportionately low level of facilities such as indoor plumbing, running water, and electricity. They have a higher rate of incarceration for criminal offences than other Canadians; life expectancy is lower and the rates of infant mortality, suicide, violent death, and admission to hospital are

5.  Canada, House of Commons, Special Committee on Visible Minorities in Canadian Society, *Equality Now!* (Ottawa: DSS, 1984). The committee points out, as well, that there are significant differences among the non-white ethnic groups. It was found, for instance, that West Indian blacks and South Asians particularly tend to have lower incomes and experience more unemployment than other Canadians, and that in such groups, the problem is exaggerated still more among young people aged fifteen to twenty-four.

6.  While in one sense the aboriginal people of Canada are racially "visible," they are significantly different from other non-white groups in that they cannot be considered an immigrant group (unless we go back at least seven thousand years!). The aboriginal people were here first and in fact should perhaps be recognized more as the "invisible charter group" than as a visible minority.

all much higher than for non-aboriginal Canadians. All in all, the standard of living and quality of life for Canada's aboriginal people is lower than for any other ethnic group, and there is little to indicate that there is any "quick fix" for this situation.

The important point to be made here is that a significant source of the problems of aboriginal people in Canada is systemic. Canadians are generally coming to appreciate the wrongs that have been done to aboriginal people in the past and to approve of the recognition and protection of aboriginal rights. However, our policies towards Indians, although probably well-meaning, have largely failed. Government initiatives have provided only for a level of *material* well-being and have not taken into account the psychological and cultural dimensions of the problem. Because the ultimate goal, historically, was to *assimilate* aboriginal communities into Canadian society, traditional community values, individual self-esteem, and traditional political practices all withered away as native people became "wards of the state." The main hope for reducing this trend would appear to be the more enlightened approach that seems to be emerging today in policy initiatives at the federal level. That approach is to phase out the custodial role of the Department of Indian Affairs and to allow aboriginal communities to asssume a large part of the responsibility for looking after themselves through the institution of aboriginal self-government and the settlement of land claims.

**Ethnicity and Ethnocentrism: A Conclusion**  As we shall see when we come to discuss the development of the franchise in the Canadian electoral system and when we discuss the machinery for the protection of civil liberties, Canada's record with respect to official racism is by no means unblemished. While Canada today is probably one of the least racially conscious nations of the world, federal and provincial legislation in the past has, by design, blatantly discriminated against sundry religious sects, non-white immigrant groups, aboriginal people, and even French Canadians. However, it is likely safe to state that today such deliberate and officially sanctioned discrimination is no longer tolerated and is effectively barred by human-rights legislation and the Charter of Rights and Freedoms.

The resolution of conflict between and among the various European ethnic groups that make up the Canadian mosaic, although admittedly difficult, has at least been possible. In the case of French-English cleavage, resolution came through institutional devices such as federalism and cultural, linguistic, religious, and educational guarantees to the smaller charter group. In the case of other European groups, resolution came through policies of multiculturalism that permit integration without total assimilation of the minority. However, many of the conflicts between visible-minority immigrant groups and the existing social system remain difficult to resolve. It is likely that part of the explanation for the persistence and pervasiveness of conflict between non-white ethnic groups and the majority racial group is the psychological phenomenon of **ethnocentrism**, which, in its uglier or more extreme manifestation, is often referred to as **racism**.

At the root of ethnocentrism is a seemingly natural tendency for national or ethnic groups to perceive the world in "we-they" terms. This consciousness of ethnic differences has historically facilitated the global growth of nation-states and has permitted cultural differentiation among the peoples of the world. While such differentiation may have benefits in organizing international politics, in fostering national integration, and in enriching the global cultural mosaic, it can have negative consequences, too. On the international level, ethnocentrism can lead to interstate conflicts, such as war, and within the context of a single nation-state it can be a serious disintegrative force.

While these broad systemic implications of ethnocentrism are important, perhaps the most serious result of this phenomenon within a single political community is the hardship and injustice it imposes on minority ethnic or racial groups. At the individual level, racism begins with prejudice, which is based on fear and suspicion and leads to the development of negative stereotypes of the minority ethnic groups. But racism is a two-way street. On the one hand, a kind of majority-culture chauvinism justifies the discrimination against the minority group, and on the other hand, the minority group will tend to respond defensively by withdrawing still more from the mainstream society. As described by a witness before the Special Committee on Visible Minorities, "the white Canadian . . . picks up on the fear and mistrust that the immigrant communicates—and communicates it right back."[7] Racism thus creates a vicious circle, which feeds on itself and becomes a self-perpetuating tragedy of human relationships.

There have also been increased incidents in Canada that would indicate a resurgence of one of the oldest and ugliest manifestations of ethnocentrism, anti-Semitism. The apparent rise in the number and activity of neo-Nazi and aryan-supremacist groups during the 1980s must cause grave concern in the minds of all Canadians who have long believed that such ethno-religious issues were disappearing anachronisms. While right-wing groups such as the Heritage Front cannot in any way be seen as representing the mainstream attitudes of Canadians, it is sad that they persist, despite the lessons of history.

Time and the political will to do so can ultimately eliminate systemic discrimination in Canada, but the psychological dimension of such discrimination—racial intolerance on the part of average Canadians—still remains the most critical barrier to the fuller integration and participation of visible minorities in the Canadian community. As the Special Committee on Visible Minorities stated in 1985:

> We are a flawed society. Research has shown that as many as 15 per cent of the population exhibit blatantly racist attitudes, while another 20–25 per cent have some racist tendencies. Moreover, even those individuals who are very tolerant can, with the best of intentions, engage in racism without knowing it or meaning to do so.[8]

Thus, while it may be possible to eliminate systemic discrimination against Canada's visible minorities, and while it is also possible to find public policy solutions to problems such as discrimination in the workplace, the ultimate means of reducing racial intolerance must be found with attitudinal changes

7.  Canada, *Equality Now!*
8.  Ibid.

on the part of individual Canadians. The integration of non-whites into the community can be achieved only if whites learn to accept ethnic and social differences without prejudice and only if our educational institutions, communications media, and public policies actively foster the goal of greater understanding among the various ethnic groups that make up the Canadian cultural mosaic.

## ▶ GENDER CLEAVAGE

As with ethnic conflict, gender cleavages are generated both by structural or systemic discrimination and by prejudice. As we shall see in later chapters, women in Canada couldn't even vote until 1920, and, even today, females are under-represented in virtually all positions of authority in society. As well, discrimination against women happens because of "gendercentric" or **sexist** attitudes that persist in our society. The beliefs that women are temperamentally unsuited to some occupations, that they should not be paid as much as males because they are likely to let childbearing interrupt their careers, and that "a woman's place is in the home" are still widely held and function to restrict women's economic opportunities.

### The Salience of Gender

One of the reasons such apparently male-chauvinist attitudes persist is that a fairly significant number of women hold them as well. Thus, gender cleavage is somewhat different from, for instance, racial cleavage. Whereas no member of a racial minority would approve a racial stereotype, many women seem to tolerate or even approve of at least some sexual stereotypes. Gender cleavage is also different from other types of cleavages because so many categoric groups with identifiable political interests include roughly equal numbers of men and women. Finally, perhaps gender cleavage is more difficult to define because men and women generally have a wide range of political interests in common. In the context of the family unit, for instance, men and women usually take similar positions on political issues that affect the family as a whole.

Where gender cleavages become salient is with respect to the differential treatment of women *within* families, labour unions, occupational groups, ethnic communities, or other types of organizations. To a significant extent, this sort of gender discrimination translates directly into economic disparities between males and females. Women tend to be over-represented in lower-income and lower-prestige occupations and they are still rarely to be found in significant numbers in corporate boardrooms. As we shall see in the next section, female-headed households are also far more likely to fall below the poverty line than are male-headed families.

Finally, male-female cleavages may also become relevant in certain non-economic areas of conflict. So-called women's issues arise with respect to broad social problems that happen to affect women more profoundly or directly than men. Examples of the latter would include matters such as spousal assault and sexual harassment. While both men and women will grant that such phenomena are "bad," women, through the women's movement and issue-specific interest groups, have generally been the ones who force such issues onto the political agenda.

### Gender and Economic Disparity

The economic differences between men and women are ultimately rooted in historical views about the appropriate roles for females in the family and in society. A woman's role in the traditional division of labour was seen as child-rearing and care-giving and not in the labour force outside the home. While times have changed, and women do find employment in the non-domestic workplace, a residual effect of the more traditional values is that women today still have a lower level of participation in the labour force, 57 per cent as opposed to about 75 per cent for men. While the discrepancy remains, female participation in the labour force is on the increase as more and more women seek employment outside the home. The norm today is for family income to be based on both husband and wife working at least some of the time.

Women tend to be concentrated in certain occupations such as clerical and secretarial work and primary-school teaching. By contrast there are very few women in fields such as physics, engineering, and forestry. Moreover, despite the steady increase of women as a percentage of the total labour force, on the whole, women make less money than men do. Full-time female workers earn an average of 72 per cent of what male workers earn (Fig. 3.6). On the positive side, this ratio has been steadily improving and, in certain categoric groups, women have actually caught up to their male counterparts. For instance, single women earn as much as single men, and, in the under-twenty-five category, women's salaries are over 90 per cent of men's. When level of education and the rate of participation in the labour force are taken into account, these discrepancies shrink even more.

While discrimination against women in the workplace and in the labour market is declining, a more troubling statistic is that single-parent, female-headed families are much more likely to fall below the low-income-cutoff line. Almost 60 per cent of single-parent families headed by a female fall below the LICO and, what is more disturbing, this trend is not declining. This phenomenon spills over directly to what has been described as "child poverty." In 1993, 21.3 per cent of children under 18 years of age fell below the LICO and this trend has been increasing throughout the 1980s and 1990s (Table 3.9). At the other end of the age spectrum, single persons over 65 years have the highest low-income rates of any group, 51 per cent, and women are the vast majority of people in this category.

While it is not a justification for ignoring the remaining instances of economic disadvantage suffered by women in Canada, there are signs that the situation is generally improving. One reason for the improvement is that women are more and more motivated to enter the labour force and both societal values and the attitudes of employers have changed to accommodate this trend. Affirmative action, pay equity, and sexual-harassment policies have all contributed to making equal female participation in the workplace possible. As well, trends indicate that women are catching up to men in acquiring the

**Figure 3.6**
Female-to-male earning ratios for full-year, full-time workers.

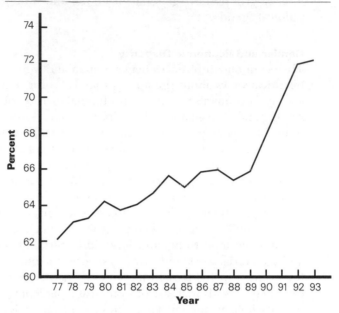

Source: Reproduced by authority of the Minister of Industry, 1995,
Statistics Canada, *Earnings of Men and Women*, 1993. Cat. 13-217.

education and training necessary to allow them to compete equally for the
available jobs in a widening range of occupations and professions.

Women now receive well over 50 per cent of all bachelor's degrees, almost
50 per cent of Master's degrees, and 32 per cent of Ph.Ds. Women are roughly
equally represented in law schools and they are even moving into traditionally
male-dominated fields such as journalism, commerce, medicine, and political
science, where they now comprise about one-half of the graduates. While there
are still very few women in engineering, and while women still dominate fields
such as education and nursing, the overall conclusion has to be that the inroads
women are making into traditionally male occupations will continue to change
the dynamics of the Canadian labour market well into the future.

To conclude this section on gender cleavage, we should emphasize that
male-female issues are a fairly recent phenomenon in Canada. One obvious
reason for this is that until recently women were effectively shut out of positions
of political and economic influence. Issues of special concern to women seldom
got on the agenda of political discourse because the politicians were all men.
However, the number of women in positions of political authority has increased to the point where women's concerns *do* get addressed. Furthermore,
even today, pure "gender" conflicts, with males lined up on one side and
females on the other, are extremely rare. Gender issues are not purely conflicts
between two competing self-interested groups but involve societal values and

**TABLE 3.9**
Persons with Income below the Low-Income Cutoff (LICO) or "Poverty Line"

|  | 1981 (%) | 1986 (%) | 1991 (%) | 1993 (%) |
|---|---|---|---|---|
| All persons | 15.7 | 16.4 | 16.5 | 17.9 |
| Men | 13.8 | 14.7 | 14.7 | 15.8 |
| Women | 17.6 | 18.1 | 18.2 | 19.9 |
| Children under 18 | 16.0 | 17.3 | 18.8 | 21.3 |
| Elderly over 65 | 33.1 | 26.5 | 21.7 | 22.3 |
| Others 18–65 | 13.0 | 14.4 | 14.6 | 15.8 |
| All Persons in Families | 12.5 | 13.0 | 12.9 | 14.5 |
| Children | 16.0 | 17.3 | 18.8 | 21.3 |
| Elderly | 17.4 | 12.4 | 7.7 | 8.2 |
| Others | 10.3 | 11.1 | 11.0 | 12.3 |
| All Unattached Individuals | 42.6 | 42.1 | 40.0 | 40.8 |
| Elderly | 66.3 | 58.1 | 50.8 | 51.1 |
| Others | 33.1 | 36.1 | 35.8 | 36.6 |

Source: Reproduced by authority of the Minister of Industry, 1995, Statistics Canada, *Income Distributions by Size in Canada*, 1993. Cat. 13-207.

different visions of social organization that are not cleanly divided between men and women. Moreover, there appears to be a growing acceptance of the importance and legitimacy of resolving gender-related issues on the part of both men and women in Canada today.

## ▶ ECONOMIC CLEAVAGE

The focus of this section is on the economic variables that lead to political conflicts. We have already looked at economic disparities as they relate to specific groups in society, but here we will look at the phenomenon of class and stratification as it affects our society as a whole. First, however, we must provide an overview of the Canadian economy in terms of the sectoral balance, the nature of the labour force, and the distribution of income.

### The Canadian Economy

**The Sectoral Balance** The Canadian economy can be broken down into two broad sectors, the **goods sector** and the **services sector**. The goods sector includes **primary industries**, such as agriculture, fishing, forestry, mining, and oil and gas, and **secondary industries**, such as manufacturing and construction.

The services sector includes the transportation industry; the federal, provincial, and municipal public services; banking and finance; and business and personal services. The services sector accounts for 75 per cent of employment in Canada and it is growing more rapidly than the goods sector (Table 3.10).

Canada has always been thought of as an exporter of primary products or staples, and up until recently that image was accurate. Many of Canada's larger industrial complexes are still in the primary sector of the economy, in industries such as mining or pulpwood production. In terms of numbers of workers, secondary and service industries far outrank primary industries, but Canadian exports have always included a high proportion of primary and semi-manufactured goods (see Table 3.11). In 1984, 58 per cent of Canadian exports were agricultural, raw, or semi-manufactured goods, while only 34 per cent of its imports were in that category. However, this situation has been changing rapidly. By 1993, Canada's exports of manufactured goods had surpassed the exports of primary products. This is, in part, a result of declining oil and gas exports and declining prices for crude oil and of increased exports of manufactured goods, such as high-tech hardware, particularly to the US.

The increased export trade in manufactured products is very good for our economy, not only because manufacturing creates more jobs, but also because the prices of manufactured products do not fluctuate as much as the prices of raw materials. Exports of primary goods may be suddenly and drastically affected by unpredictable factors, such as rainfall in Russia and China or the discovery of nickel deposits in New Caledonia. The most recent recession was deeper in Canada than in the United States, in large part because it was accompanied by the falling value of Canadian resource exports, the prices of which are set in world markets beyond Canadian control (see Figs. 3.7, 3.8).

**The Labour Force** Until 1960, the rate of growth of the labour force approximately paralleled that of the population. Since that time, the rapid influx of women into the labour force has created labour-force growth that has been very rapid by historical standards. In 1951, 23 per cent of Canadian women were in the labour force and in 1991 that figure had risen to 58 per cent. The years from the mid 1960s to the late 1970s were characterized by particularly rapid labour-force growth as the baby boomers entered the labour force at the same time as the participation rates of women continued to increase. From 1971 to 1981, our labour force grew by 3.3 million workers to a total of 11.9 million. Since then the growth has tapered off, but in 1995 there are approximately 14 million in our labour force. Unfortunately, our economy still faces an unemployment rate of over 9 per cent.

Paralleling these changes in labour-force composition were two other broad sets of changes. One was in the composition of employment by type of industry. The three decades since 1960 saw a massive shift from blue-collar to white-collar employment and from primary and secondary industrial employment to tertiary or service-sector employment. As can be seen in Table 3.10, more than half of the jobs in Canada today are in the service, trade, and manufacturing industries. This has meant that there is a greater requirement for training and education than there was when the labour force was more focused on primary production. As Table 3.14 indicates, more than one-third

**TABLE 3.10**

Employment by Industry, Annual Average (Thousands)

| Industry | 1951 | 1961 | 1971[a] | 1981 | 1991 |
|---|---|---|---|---|---|
| Agriculture | 939 | 681 | 514 | 488 | 488 |
| Other Primary Industries | 224 | 184 | 221 | 321 | 280 |
| Manufacturing | 1,350 | 1,452 | 1,766 | 2,124 | 1,865 |
| Construction | 348 | 376 | 489 | 651 | 695 |
| Transportation, Communication, and Other Utilities | 449 | 563 | 707 | 911 | 916 |
| Trade | 718 | 1,025 | 1,335 | 1,884 | 2,169 |
| Finance, Insurance, and Real Estate | 154 | 239 | 399 | 594 | 760 |
| Service | 916[b] | 1,178 | 2,128 | 3,262 | 4,376 |
| Public Administration | | 356 | 545 | 767 | 832 |

[a]  Population aged 15 and over from 1966. Data prior to 1966 are based on population aged 14 and over.
[b]  Includes public administration.

Source:  Reproduced by authority of the Minister of Industry, 1995, Statistics Canada, *Canada Year Book,* 1994. Cat. 11-402E&F.

**TABLE 3.11**

Trade Figures by Industry, October, 1994

| Industry | Exports | | Imports | | Trade Balance |
|---|---|---|---|---|---|
| | $ Billions | % | $ Billions | % | $ Billions |
| Agriculture and Fish | 1,613 | 8.3 | 1,089 | 6.15 | 524 |
| Energy | 1,601 | 8.2 | 610 | 3.45 | 991 |
| Forest Products | 2,644 | 13.6 | 167 | .94 | 2,477 |
| Industrial Goods | 3,618 | 18.6 | 3,328 | 18.8 | 290 |
| Machinery, Equipment | 4,024 | 20.7 | 5,804 | 32.79 | (1780) |
| Automobile Products | 4,986 | 25.6 | 4,125 | 23.31 | 861 |
| Consumer Goods | 580 | 3.0 | 2,035 | 11.50 | (1455) |
| Total | 19,447 | | 17,700 | | 1,908 |

Source:  Reproduced by authority of the Minister of Industry, 1995, Statistics Canada, *Canadian Economic Observer,* Jan., 1995. Cat. 11-010.

**Figure 3.7**
Canada's trade balance.

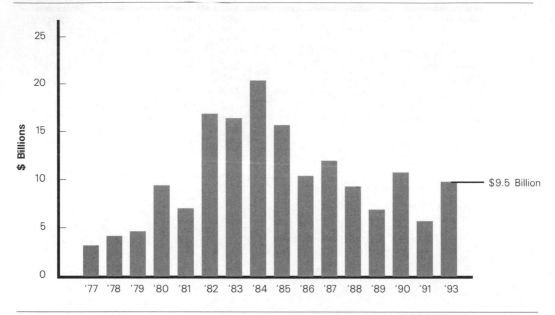

Source: Reproduced by authority of the Minister of Industry, 1995, Statistics Canada, *Canada Year Book*, 1994. Cat. 11-402E&F.

**Figure 3.8**
Canada's trade balance by sector.

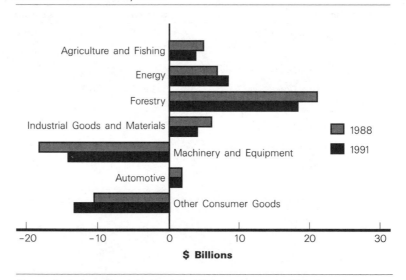

Source: Reproduced by authority of the Minister of Industry, 1995, Statistics Canada, *Canada Year Book*, 1994. Cat. 11-402E&F.

of Canadians of working age today have a post-secondary certificate, diploma, or degree, and current enrolments would indicate that the trend is continuing.

Another factor affecting the nature of the labour force is in the proportion of workers that are organized into collective bargaining units (Table 3.15). In 1971, 26.6 per cent of the civilian labour force was unionized. That figure rose to 31.2 per cent by 1978, but since then the rate of unionization has declined and is currently at just over 29 per cent. Among the largest unions in Canada today are those such as CUPE and the Public Service Alliance that represent public-sector employees. Overall, the power of unions appears to be declining. Through the recession of the late 1980s, rising unemployment and falling inflation made the right to strike almost unusable, and in the deficit-focused 1990s, public-sector unions' powers have been overridden by legislation on a number of occasions. As the economic recovery gains momentum, however, it is to be expected that the unions will recover their strength also.

**Income Distribution** The average family income in 1995 is approximately $55,000. However, income is not evenly distributed among Canadians. If families are divided into ten equal groups or *deciles* on the basis of total income, it

**TABLE 3.12**
Rate of Participation in the Labour Force by Gender and Age, 1995

|  | Total (%) | Men (%) | Women (%) |
|---|---|---|---|
| Total | 64.9 | 72.8 | 57.3 |
| 15–25 Years | 62.0 | 64.3 | 59.6 |
| 25 Years and Older | 65.4 | 74.7 | 56.8 |

Source: Statistics Canada, *Canadian Economic Observer*, Jan., 1995. Cat. 11-010.

**TABLE 3.13**
Unemployment Rates by Gender and Age, 1995

|  | Unemployment Rate (%)[a] |
|---|---|
| Total | 9.6 |
| Men | 10.0 |
| Women | 9.0 |
| 15–25 years | 15.7 |
| 25 years and older | 8.4 |

[a] The unemployed as a percentage of the labour force.
Source: Statistics Canada, *Canadian Economic Observer*, Jan., 1995. Cat. 11-010.

can be seen that the wealthiest 10 per cent of families earned 22 per cent of the total income earned by Canadians and the lowest 10 per cent earned only 2.9 per cent. However, while the egalitarians among us might be morally outraged at the income range in our society, of greater concern is the number of Canadian families who are below the so-called poverty line (see Table 3.9).

This line is called the Low Income Cutoff (LICO) by Statistics Canada and varies across the country depending on the cost of living in the community and region in which a family resides. The LICO is then established at the point where approximately 55 per cent of family income must be spent on food, shelter, and clothing. In 1993, a total of 14.5 per cent of families were below this line and, while the good news is that more than 85 per cent of families are *not* poor, there are some disturbing trends in the way in which poverty is concentrated in certain sectors of the population. Twenty-one per cent of children under the age of eighteen, 56 per cent of single-parent, female-headed

**TABLE 3.14**
Educational Attainment, 1993

| | Percentage of the Working-Age Population | | | | | | | | | | |
|---|---|---|---|---|---|---|---|---|---|---|---|
| | Nfld. | P.E.I. | N.S. | N.B. | Que. | Ont. | Man. | Sask. | Alta. | B.C. | Canada |
| Post-Secondary | 31.2 | 33.0 | 37.7 | 31.8 | 35.9 | 35.4 | 30.6 | 31.4 | 38.8 | 36.5 | 35.5 |
| Secondary | 23.7 | 26.0 | 23.3 | 28.6 | 25.1 | 32.2 | 30.2 | 29.9 | 32.3 | 37.1 | 30.2 |
| No Secondary | 45.2 | 41.0 | 38.9 | 39.8 | 39.0 | 32.4 | 39.3 | 38.5 | 28.9 | 26.5 | 34.2 |

Notes: *Post-secondary:* post-secondary certificate, diploma, or degree. *Secondary:* highschool or incomplete post-secondary. *No secondary:* incomplete highschool or less. No data available for Yukon and Northwest Territories.
Source: Reproduced by authority of the Ministry of Industry, 1995, Statistics Canada, *Canada at a Glance,* 1994.

**TABLE 3.15**
Union Membership

| Year | Union Membership (Thousands) | Non-Agricultural Paid Workers (Thousands) | Union Membership as a Percentage of Civilian Labour Force | Union Membership as a Percentage of Non-Agricultural Paid Workers |
|---|---|---|---|---|
| 1971 | 2,231 | 6,880 | 26.6 | 32.4 |
| 1976 | 3,042 | 8,238 | 30.5 | 36.9 |
| 1981 | 3,487 | 9,495 | 30.1 | 36.7 |
| 1986 | 3,730 | 9,888 | 29.8 | 37.7 |
| 1987 | 3,782 | 10,219 | 29.7 | 37.0 |
| 1988 | 3,841 | 10,519 | 29.5 | 36.5 |
| 1989 | 3,944 | 10,891 | 29.7 | 36.2 |
| 1990 | 4,031 | 11,147 | 29.9 | 36.2 |
| 1991 | 4,068 | 11,195 | 29.7 | 36.3 |
| 1992 | 4,089 | 10,931 | 29.7 | 37.4 |

Source: Reproduced by authority of the Ministry of Industry, 1995, Statistics Canada, *Canada Year Book,* 1994. Cat. 11-402E&F.

families, and 51 per cent of elderly people living alone are below the poverty line in Canada.

### Class and Stratification in Canada

Having discussed a number of statistical findings with respect to the distribution of *income* in Canada, we are still left with an only partial picture of vertical cleavage in this country. There is more to vertical cleavage than annual family income or numbers of families and individuals below the Low Income Cutoff. **Class**, in most of its conceptual manifestations, is, similarly, a less than satisfactory categorization for discussing vertical cleavage in Canada. Canada, for instance, does not have a "class system" like that of the UK, where individuals are, to some extent, born to a level of social status and where, while upward mobility is possible through education and financial success, individuals remain conscious of and sensitive to their class roots, in spite of life's successes and failures.

Marxist class analysis similarly provides a less than complete framework for discussing vertical cleavage in Canada. Canada does not have a stratum that is analogous to a *proletariat*, nor are very many Canadians conscious of class. While Canadians are aware of relative levels of economic affluence and deprivation, and of differential levels of **empowerment** in both politics and economics, very few people actually think of themselves as "oppressed" and almost all eschew "class struggle." Instead, even the less fortunate Canadians cling to their liberal-pluralist optimism and believe, perhaps naively, that "things are going to get better someday." Moreover, although it is possible to identify people who are poor and people who are very rich, the vast majority of Canadians are "middle class" and think of themselves that way.

**A Hybrid Concept of Class**  As an alternative to squeezing the phenomenon of stratification into a ready-made paradigm, it is perhaps more fruitful to attempt a more subjective and impressionistic description of what we might still want, loosely, to call "class" in Canada. The key components of this hybrid concept of class are income, security, satisfaction, independence, and hope. The relative presence or absence of these components in the aggregate allows us to place Canadians into several class groupings. But first let's make sure we understand what each of these components comprises.

**Income** means, simply, the amount of money an individual earns. The more money we make, generally, the higher up in the class system we find ourselves. However, the advantage of high income may be reduced if our level of **security** is low. Generally, by security, we mean job security, or the certainty that our level of income will not be interrupted by layoff or dismissal, and that when retirement comes we will continue to enjoy an acceptable level of income. However, security can also be achieved through **wealth** in the sense that investing our income wisely can put us in a position where a job loss or retirement will not significantly affect our lifestyle.

While some people might enjoy a high salary for its own sake, most people require other kinds of **satisfaction** to be truly content. Job satisfaction can be related to the nature of the workplace, the relationships with fellow employees, or a sense that the job is important in a broader social context. Thus, if an occupation is "just a living" it will not be as attractive as if it gives a worker pride and a sense of self-esteem to be doing it. Some people might well forego a higher salary to work in a job that they feel is more meaningful.

Having a job of any sort is itself an important determinant of an individual's sense of **independence**. Without a job, or with a job that is part-time, temporary, or of insecure tenure, an individual is placed in a situation of **dependency**. This can involve dependency on a working spouse, on parents or children, or, more commonly in an age of social safety nets, on the state. Dependency can generate feelings of low self-esteem, depression, and despair, and while dependent individuals may have enough to eat and be fairly comfortable in material terms, they are not usually very happy. Finally, even the negative concomitants of dependency can be offset if there is **hope** of upward mobility. Dependency is most destructive both to individuals and to the societies of which they are a part if hope is replaced by **despair** and despondency and a sense that things will never get any better.

**The Canadian "Class System"**  Based on the variables mentioned above, it is now possible to make some generalizations about class in Canada. While we have defined several distinct groups, it should be recognized that the boundaries between the groups are blurred and that there is mobility within and between the various levels. The conclusions here are not intended to be statistically accurate, but to provide an overview of stratification in our society (Table 3.16).

*The Very Wealthy*  At the very top of the heap in Canada, and in all societies, is a very small percentage of people who can be classed as the very wealthy. These individuals, who constitute less than one per cent of the population, include business "tycoons," bank presidents, the CEOs of large corporations, senior partners in law firms, and entertainment celebrities such as professional athletes, rock musicians, and movie stars. These individuals have six- and seven-figure incomes, the security that comes from wealth, the satisfaction that comes from high status, fame, or celebrity, and influence and power that places them above economic dependency on other individuals or the state. While Conrad Black, Wayne Gretzky, and Bryan Adams are not above the government in the sense that they can disobey the law, they don't need the government to provide amenities such as unemployment insurance!

*The Upper Middle Class*  The next level is the closest thing Canada has to an upper class but, to avoid confusion with the British sense of the term, we should probably refer to this group as the **upper middle class**. This stratum of our society is composed of Canadians who have "made it"—professionals, engineers, technical and scientific personnel, senior managers, and senior bureaucrats. Their family incomes range from $75,000 a year upward and their security is based on guaranteed pensions, investments, and the ability to move easily from job to job. This group is a "knowledge elite," with high levels of formal education and high levels of job satisfaction. Predominantly white, middle-aged, and male, this group comprises about 20 per cent of the popu-

**TABLE 3.16**
Families by Income Group and "Class," 1993

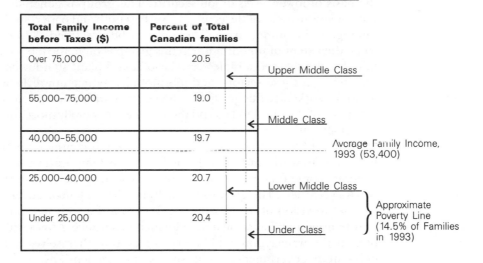

| Total Family Income before Taxes ($) | Percent of Total Canadian families |
|---|---|
| Over 75,000 | 20.5 |
| 55,000–75,000 | 19.0 |
| 40,000–55,000 | 19.7 |
| 25,000–40,000 | 20.7 |
| Under 25,000 | 20.4 |

Upper Middle Class

Middle Class

Average Family Income, 1993 (53,400)

Lower Middle Class

Under Class

Approximate Poverty Line (14.5% of Families in 1993)

Note that the "class" designations are the authors' approximations only, and have no statistical validity. The dotted lines indicate the effect of non-monetary variables such as security, satisfaction, independence, and potential upward mobility. Because the poverty line varies significantly depending upon family size and from region to region we cannot draw a "line" on the table.

Source: Figures taken from Statistics Canada, *Income Distribution by Size*, 1993.

lation. The upper middle class is generally conservative politically, not needing government as much as the rest of society, but likely active in politics and concerned with issues such as deficit reduction and taxes.

*The Middle Class*  The **middle class** in Canada includes about 40 per cent of the population, whose family incomes range from about $40,000 to $70,000 a year. There are at least two sub-groups within this category that can be differentiated on the basis not of income, but of job security and job satisfaction. At the upper end, the **salaried middle class** is comprised of employees, usually in unionized, white-collar occupations such as teaching, middle management, or public service. As well, workers in the service and high-tech "new industry" sectors of our economy would be included in this middle-class sub-group. The salaried middle class enjoys security based on tenured employment, union contracts, and attractive pension plans. Workers in this category generally have some post-secondary education and a level of job satisfaction based on a comfortable workplace and a degree of discretionary authority in the performance of their jobs. While this category is generally still upwardly mobile, recent trends, such as public-service cutbacks, may have reduced the overall job security of this segment of the middle class.

The **wage-earning middle class** includes employees with family incomes which overlap with those of the salaried middle class but is differentiated on the basis of lower levels of job security. This group is generally employed in the "old industries" of the economy, such as pulp and paper, steel production, mining, and manufacturing. The jobs can be described as blue collar, and, while the extent of unionization in this group is high, the job security is lower than for the salaried middle class. Layoffs and plant shutdowns are always a possibility in these sectors, and job mobility, either upwards or laterally, is limited. Workers in this group have lower levels of formal education than other segments of the middle class and their jobs are generally more routine and less personally satisfying.

For the Canadian middle class as a whole, it is common for both adults in the family to work, and, while being laid off or temporarily unemployed may generate some financial difficulty, there is security in the fact that there are two wage earners. This group is normally not dependent on government except for the provision of universal services, such as health care and periodic but only temporary reliance on unemployment insurance. After retirement, members of the wage-earning middle class may find themselves much more dependent on government benefits such as old-age pensions.

*The Lower Middle Class: Dependency* The **lower middle class** in Canada can be distinguished from the middle class by the degree of dependency individuals and families experience. Families in this group usually have incomes above the Low Income Cutoff, but their jobs are not secure, they have low employment mobility, and they have low levels of education. Jobs in this category are low-skilled and often seasonal, and, if both spouses work, it is not unusual for one to be part-time. This group is, all in all, more diverse than the middle class. It includes individuals who are either unemployed or underemployed for reasons of economic fluctuations beyond their control. Fishermen, loggers, and unskilled construction workers face constant layoffs because of market shifts and are therefore heavily reliant on the social safety net for their survival.

As well, this class includes young people, such as students who are dependent on their families or the government, but who still have high hopes of completing their schooling, entering the labour force, and moving up into a higher stratum of society. Working people who have retired may fall down into this class if they become permanently dependent on fixed pensions and government old-age security payments for survival. It is hard to estimate the size of this category accurately because of the high mobility, both upward and downward, and because there is considerable overlap between the upper segments of this group and the lower segments of the wage-earning class. However, we can guess that it ranges generally from 15 to 25 per cent of the population, depending on the state of the economy.

*The "Under Class": Poverty, Dependency, and Despair* At the bottom of the Canadian social structure is what can be referred to as the **under class** or the very poor. This group, comprising 15 per cent to 20 per cent of the population, is uneducated, chronically unemployed, and, when working, employed in unskilled, low-paying, menial labour. There is no job security for these individuals and little hope of escaping the cycle of economic dependency. Ultimately what distinguishes this group from the lowest levels of the lower middle class is the lack of any hope of improvement. Individuals in this category have essentially given up. This group is dependent on government or private charity for subsistence and includes disproportionate numbers of young people who have never had a job, single-parent females, and the elderly.

Superficially, the greatest handicap the poor face in modern society is simply low income. The problem goes deeper, however, for poverty creates a sub-culture within the larger Canadian culture—a sub-culture with its own norms and values. Some of these norms, such as a lack of belief in the value of education, make it extremely difficult for the poor to escape their situation. Poverty leads, as well, to crime, disease, and low productivity and constitutes a vast waste of potential talent within Canadian society. It is morally unacceptable for an affluent democracy such as ours to tolerate any amount of poverty at all.

**Class and Empowerment** One final dimension of the concept of economic stratification or class in Canada is empowerment. Ultimately, the higher one is in our social structure, the greater one's political power. The economic elites are very powerful politically because of the close relationship between economic and political power, and the upper middle class is empowered because of its knowledge and expertise. The power of the middle class is in numbers and in its ability to organize politically. The political weakness of the lower middle class is, in part, that individuals in this group are too busy trying to make ends meet to devote much time and energy to political organization. Those in the under class, while most in need of governmental assistance, have lost any faith they might have had in the political system as a vehicle for generating the policy changes necessary to improve their lot.

Thus, while 30 to 40 per cent of Canadians find themselves in situations of economic difficulty or outright despondency, what sets them apart from the rest of our society is as much their lack of political empowerment as it is their relative economic deprivation. The converse of this is that the answers to the plight of the working poor, the chronically unemployed, and the economic "outsiders" of our society must be found in increased political awareness and political mobilization of the disadvantaged strata of society.

*Chapter* **4**

# Political Culture and Ideology

Having looked at the socio-economic and international context within which our system of government is set, we must now look at the other major set of variables that determine the agenda of political discourse in Canada. These variables are attitudinal rather than material, and, while they are difficult to discover without burrowing into the minds of individual Canadians, they are at least as important as socio-economic cleavages in defining the conflicts that our governmental system must manage.

▶ THE CONCEPT OF POLITICAL CULTURE

A nation's **political culture** is composed of the values, attitudes, and beliefs of its citizens with respect to political objects and phenomena. To understand the concept, a few basic characteristics must be clarified.

### Societal Culture and Political Culture

In the first place, the *political* culture is but one dimension of the total culture of a society. Hence, the Canadian culture is a montage of our religious beliefs, our artistic or aesthetic preferences, our social norms and mores, our ethical values, and our philosophies of life. As well, however, our culture includes the basic values we share about the role of government in society and the limits that should be placed on its activities. Because our political culture is a sub-set of our broader societal culture, our political values will be congruent with the non-political things that we believe in.

Thus, for example, the Canadian culture is largely rooted in the Judaeo-Christian tradition which, because each of us is said to be "created in God's image," places a high value on the individual. Hence, it should not be surprising that some of our most fundamental *political* values include popular sovereignty, political equality, justice, and political freedom, all of which flow from the ultimate sanctity of the individual. As we shall see in Chapter 6, these basic political values are operationalized in our liberal democratic system of government and are entrenched in our Constitution.

### Political Culture and Political Behaviour

The determinants of political discourse and governmental activity can be logically reduced to two main groups of variables, those that are internal, or *of the mind*, and those that are external, or *of the world*. Values and attitudes, which are the stuff of political culture, exist in our minds rather than in the real world. Hence, we must be careful to distinguish between human behaviour, which, while obviously affected by our values and attitudes, is external and observable to others, and political culture, which by contrast is *what we think*, not *what we do*.

What makes people behave the way they do is, in part, circumstances, conditions, events, and stimulae in the world around them. In other words, things that happen in our lives, and not in our heads, directly affect the way we behave or react. However, there is a close two-way relationship between external stimulae and our political values and attitudes. What we experience in the real world can affect the way we think about politics and can either change or reinforce our basic values and attitudes. Conversely, how we see the world around us is determined, in part, by our basic political values, which provide a *conceptual screen* through which we filter, interpret, and categorize real-world political phenomena.

### Culture and Socialization

We are not born with a ready-made set of political values and attitudes; rather, we must acquire them from our experiences. Moreover, how we think about politics and government, is not, in the first instance, acquired through independent observation of political events in the real world. Instead, we learn our political values from others who are influential in our early lives and who either explicitly *teach* us about politics, or at least "cue" us as to how we should respond to political stimulae.

The process whereby individuals acquire the basic values of the culture into which they are born is called **socialization**. Through this process individuals become full members of society morally, ethically, and aesthetically. The process whereby we acquire our *political* values is, logically enough, referred to as **political socialization.** Political socialization is *developmental* in that we acquire more knowledge about politics as we grow older and, as well, our intellectual sophistication about political phenomena increases as we mature.

Finally, the process of political socialization never stops until we die, and our accumulated political experiences can both reinforce our earliest political beliefs and, at the same time, cause us to change how we think about political phenomena. Moreover, as we get older, the number of **agents of socialization** to which we are exposed widens and diversifies. In childhood, the primary agents of political socialization are parents and teachers; as we reach adulthood, our political information is gleaned from the media, books we read, our peers' and colleagues' opinions, organizations we belong to, and "significant others" whom we admire and respect.[1]

### Values and Attitudes

Political **values** can be distinguished from political **attitudes** because they are more fundamental. By this we mean that they are more closely derivative of the broader social values of our culture as a whole and therefore more stable and less likely to change over our lifetimes. Political values set the broadest limits of legitimate political behaviour, beyond which no responsible citizen would venture. By contrast, while our political attitudes must be consistent with our political values, they are not formulated in our minds as abstract or universal principles but are oriented towards specific **political objects.**

Political objects towards which we develop attitudes can include *conceptual* abstractions (social justice, equality of opportunity, Canada as a political community), *symbols* (the flag, the national anthem, the Monarchy, the Constitution), *institutions* (Parliament, federalism, the bureaucracy), and individual politicians, bureaucrats, or judges. Our attitudes towards such objects can range from simple, neutral awareness of them, to approval or disapproval, to outright love or hatred. Because they are related directly to real-world objects, political attitudes are likely more important as immediate determinants of behaviour. Thus, for example, not only are individual attitudes to a particular political party likely to vary widely, but they are more likely to stimulate political action than would a basic value such as popular sovereignty.

### Political Culture and Sub-Cultures

While the stuff of our political culture is *individual* values and attitudes, the concept is really useful to us only if we can generalize about those values and attitudes. Hence, political culture is the *aggregate* of political values and attitudes of individual Canadians at any point in time. While for the most part there is a consensus among Canadians about the basic values, such as popular sovereignty and political equality, there is less than unanimity when it comes to values such as free enterprise, and major disagreement when it comes to attitudes to political objects such as parties or leaders. Thus, while we can speak of a "Canadian political culture" at one level of analysis, except with respect to the most elemental political beliefs it is very difficult to accurately generalize about 30 million people.

It is possible to challenge the assumption that generalizations about political culture at the national level are meaningful at all. Some would argue that it is better to focus on *regional* political sub-cultures, which together comprise

---

1. For more detail on political socialization in Canada see J. Pammett and M. S. Whittington, *The Foundations of Political Culture: Political Socialization in Canada* (Toronto: Macmillan, 1976); and Rick Van Loon and Mike Whittington, *The Canadian Political System: Environment, Structure and Process* (Toronto, McGraw-Hill Ryerson, 1987), ch. 5

a sort of patchwork "Canadian political culture."[2] But even regional or provincial variations in political attitudes represent only one dimension of the complexity of the Canadian political culture. Political sub-cultures may be based on religion, race, ethnicity, or class, as well as around an ideology. Recent immigrants, the visible minorities, and aboriginal peoples could all be singled out as sub-cultures whose values and attitudes differ from those of the dominant groups in Canadian society.

On the other hand, it is not that much easier to generalize, for instance, about the political culture of Ontario, or *the* political culture of the aboriginal people, or a discrete working-class culture, than it is to generalize about a national political culture. The problem is simply one of deciding, arbitrarily, the level of aggregation that is desired, with the realization that the more inclusive and the more sociologically complex the unit of analysis, the more general and more qualified will be the conclusions. Given that the focus of this book is Canada's *national* government and politics, it is our intention, ultimately, to summarize, in general terms, what we have discovered about the Canadian political culture as an aggregate concept.

### Elite and Non-Elite Political Values

The political culture of Canada is the values and attitudes of *all* Canadians, not just those of the most powerful or influential individuals or classes in the political community. Because our political values and attitudes help to determine our political behaviour, and because mass political behaviour in democratic institutions, such as elections, determines the fate of political elites, the political beliefs of the average Canadian are very important. Hence, in describing the Canadian political culture, we are concerned, not just with the attitudes of politicians, senior bureaucrats, or the leaders of the largest interest groups, but with the man on the street or the woman in the middle row of a community-association meeting.

However, it is important to point out that most of the values and attitudes described in this section are shared, to a large extent, by elites and non-elites alike. Indeed, it is this sharing of values that does a great deal to stabilize and integrate the Canadian political community, both vertically and horizontally, and to ensure that, in spite of the barriers the ordinary man or woman may encounter when trying to participate in politics, governmental decision-makers *do* take into account many of the average person's attitudes. Moreover, they very often discover that their attitudes are the same or at least very similar.

### Ideology and Political Culture

An **ideology** can be defined as a system of political values, attitudes, and beliefs. Political culture is also comprised of political values, attitudes, and beliefs, but

2. See Stephen Ullman, "Regional Political Culture in Canada, Part I: A Theoretical and Conceptual Introduction," *American Review of Canadian Studies*, Autumn 1977, pp. 1–22; and Ullman, "Regional Political Cultures in Canada, Part II"; *American Review of Canadian Studies*, Autumn 1978, pp. 70–101; D. Bell and L. Tepperman, *The Roots of Disunity: A Look at Canadian Political Culture* (Toronto: McClelland and Stewart, 1979), ch. 6; R. Simeon and D. Elkins, "Regional Political Cultures," and J. Wilson, "The Canadian Political Cultures," both in *Canadian Journal of Political Science*, September 1974, pp. 397–484; A. Gregg and M. Whittington, "Regional Variation in Children's Political Attitudes," *in* David Bellamy, J. Pammett, and D. C. Rowat, *The Provincial Political Systems* (Toronto: Methuen, 1976), p. 76.

it is distinguishable from ideology in three ways. First, ideology is a less inclusive category than political culture, and a political culture may host more than one ideological component. Second, an ideology is a *system of beliefs* which is cobbled together to form a coherent world view. Political culture, by contrast, is not contrived, but is simply the aggregate of the dominant values and attitudes of society, and may contain internal ideological inconsistencies. Finally, ideologies are action-oriented sets of doctrines that purport to offer solutions to the various ills of society. An ideology doesn't just happen to people, it must be embraced by a conscious act of commitment. In this way, an ideology is a "secular religion," whose adherents often display the sort of devotion, commitment, and fervour we normally associate with religious fundamentalism. The dominant ideologies in Canada are liberalism, conservatism, and socialism, but as we shall see, they are so loosely defined and so casually adhered to that they may not be "true" ideologies in the sense that, for instance, Marxist-Leninism is (or was).

### Approaches to Political Culture

As we pointed out earlier, political culture is of the mind rather than of behaviour. Since we cannot read people's minds we must discover other methods for uncovering the basic values of our society. In essence, these methods come down to five approaches, each of which must be considered briefly.

The simplest approach is an *attitudinal* survey. It is possible to take a stab at establishing what attitudes and values make up a culture simply by asking a scientifically selected sample of individuals a set of carefully designed questions that add up to "What are your values and attitudes?" A second approach is to speculate about the predominant attitudes of a political culture by observing the patterns of political *behaviour* that are typical of the citizenry. The researcher then works backwards, inductively guessing at what attitudinal patterns likely underlie the observed behavioural patterns.

The third approach is *institutional* in its focus. Here the presumption is that we can discover something about the long-run value preferences of a society by investigating the legal and institutional framework within which politics occurs. For example, the existence of parliamentary institutions likely reflects a deep-seated commitment to the values of popular sovereignty and representative democracy in the Canadian political culture. We will say more about the basic political values of Canada later in this chapter and when we discuss the Constitution in Chapter 6.

These three approaches to the study of political culture all focus on the need to discover the actual stuff of political culture—the attitudes and values that make it up. A fourth approach is to view political culture as the *result* of political socialization. This mode of analysis, which has not been very fruitful, assumes that discovering the nascent political values and attitudes of children may help us to understand the political culture by seeing it as a part of the process of individual development.

The fifth approach, and the one that has generated the most interesting academic discussion, starts not from an analysis of individual development, but from the perspective of the historical development of the nation and the society. This approach eschews the quantitative tools and hard data of survey research, employing instead the softer and more impressionistic or intuitive techniques of historical analysis. We must now look at our political culture within the context of its historical development.

## ▶ THE SOCIO-HISTORICAL ROOTS OF POLITICAL CULTURE

The historical approach to the development of the Canadian political culture is, in fact, several approaches, each characterized by a different perspective on history. In examining these approaches and the particular insights to be drawn from each, we must point out that the focus has traditionally been exclusively upon the values and attitudes of the European settlers that came to what is now Canada after about 1600. In discussing this, we must not lose sight of the fact that there were peoples living in North America many thousands of years before the first Europeans arrived and that these peoples had well-developed cultures, which included values and attitudes about the best ways of managing conflict in their communities. In other words, the pre-contact aboriginal people had political values and political institutions when the Europeans arrived, but until recently these have languished in the shadow of the political values of the dominant culture.

### Fragments and Formative Events

One of the most enduring interpretations of the origins of the Canadian political culture begins with the assumption that the earliest European immigrants to this country imported with them, as part of their intellectual baggage, the values and attitudes of the mother country. As authors such as Louis Hartz, Ken McRae, and Gad Horowitz have concluded, North American society is composed of **fragments** of the European countries that provided the 17th- and 18th-century feedstock for the New World colonies.[3]

While these writers differ as to the exact nature of the fragment that was transported to the New World, and also as to why Canada and the United States have ended up with similar but yet quite distinctive patterns of political values, they would generally agree that the differences between French- and English-Canadian society are in large part reflective of the differences between 17th-century France and England. As well, it is now generally accepted that at least part of the difference and much of the similarity between the political cultures of the United States and English Canada can be explained by the fact that the United Empire Loyalists (a counter-revolutionary element in American society) formed the largest portion of the earliest non-French settlers to British North America.

Here, however, the "fragment" school has been challenged and enlarged upon by a second genre of interpretation of the origins of political culture.

---

3. While Louis Hartz, Kenneth McRae, Gad Horowitz, and Seymour Martin Lipset are the best-known proponents of a historical approach to Canadian political culture, a 1977 article by Reg Whitaker breaks new ground, extending the usefulness of this approach. See R. Whitaker, "Images of the State in Canada," in Leo Panitch, ed., *The Canadian State: Political Economy and Political Power* (Toronto: University of Toronto Press, 1977). See also David Bell, *The Roots of Disunity: A Study of Canadian Political Culture* (Toronto: Oxford University Press, 1992).

This approach, largely the creation of Seymour Martin Lipset, posits that the importation of cultural traits from the mother country is less significant than the **formative events** that shape its historical experience: "The variations between Canada and the United States stem from the founding *event* which gave birth to them both, the American Revolution."[4] Thus, the United States is seen as influenced by a liberal revolutionary tradition, and Canada by the counter-revolutionary values of the Loyalists.

Similarly, the formative-events approach can also help us to explain the political culture of French Canada, except that here the key event was not the American War of Independence, but the "conquest" of New France by the British. The sense of betrayal by France, coupled with the fear of assimilation by the English after the Loyalist migration, has obviously coloured French-Canadian political attitudes to the present time. The development of Quebec as a distinct society and as a homeland for Canada's francophone minority will be discussed in greater detail in Chapter 9.

The fragment and the formative-events interpretations together help us to better understand the historical roots of our political culture. They focus on the same phenomena, the Loyalist migration and the conquest, and, in so doing have helped to focus the debate about the nature of ideology in Canada:

> Both Hartz's "fragment theory" and Lipset's "formative events" notion focus attention on the Loyalist experience as a major source of English Canada's political culture. Yet the cultural consequences of the Loyalist migration are a subject of considerable controversy among historians and social scientists. Much of the debate has turned on defining the ideological outlook of the Loyalists. The main issue has been to what extent the Loyalists presented an "organic conservative" alternative to the "liberal" world view of the revolutionaries who expelled them and shaped the political institutions and culture of the new United States.[5]

However, despite the usefulness of these two approaches in better understanding the origins of the Canadian political culture, even in combination they offer only an incomplete picture. Their limitations lie in their failure to incorporate economic variables in tracing the path of Canadian cultural development.[6] It is here that a third set of interpretations, based on what David Bell refers to as the "structural" or "material" bases of political culture,[7] can be employed as a complement to the more idealistic paradigms of Hartz and Lipset.

### Materialistic Interpretations

The materialistic or non-idealistic interpretations of the historical underpinnings of our political values are, in turn, rooted in two quite divergent intellec-

---

4. S. M. Lipset, "Canada and the United States: The Cultural Dimension," *in* C. F. Doran and J. H. Sigler, eds., *Canada and the United States: Enduring Friendship, Persistent Stress* (Englewood Cliffs: Prentice Hall, 1985), p. 110.
5. David Bell, "Political Culture in Canada," *in* M. S. Whittington and G. Williams, *Canadian Politics in the 1990s* (Toronto: Nelson, 1994) pp. 105–28.
6. In fact, in his most recent work, Lipset has incorporated much of the political-economy approach in his analysis. See Lipset, "Canada and the United States."
7. Bell, "Political Culture in Canada."

tual traditions. The first of these, epitomized by the works of Harold Innis and Donald Creighton, argues that political culture is the product of economic factors, such as the structure of the means of production and the technology of transportation and communication. According to this **staples theory**, our political culture is a reflection of the fact that our international economic role has been as a resource **hinterland**, supplying raw materials to the industrial **heartland** of first Britain and more recently the United States. This means, in the more macroscopic context, that we rest inextricably in a situation of economic dependency on the United States.

On the sub-national level, this pattern of economic dependency has meant that the Canadian economy is regionalized, with the resource hinterlands of the West, the far north, and the Atlantic provinces being dependent upon the central Canadian industrial heartland in the St. Lawrence–Great Lakes basin. In terms of policy outcomes, this hegemony of central Canada has meant that the process of nation building has been characterized by a series of national dreams, each a reflection of the transportation and communications technologies of the times. Railways, canals, pipelines, microwave systems, satellite communications, and programs fostering cultural nationalism have been the technological "fixes" both for consolidating our independence from the United States and for healing the inter-regional rifts within the country. Thus, the long-standing debates about whether Canada has one or many political cultures and whether Canada has a political culture different from that of the United States have arisen, at least in part, as a product of the economic and technological circumstances of our cultural development.

### Class-Analysis Interpretations

The second type of non-idealistic approach to explaining the roots of the Canadian political culture finds its inspiration in Marxist and neo-Marxist paradigms. At the simplest level of analysis, one can assert that Canada is a capitalist country, and as such it will exhibit a characteristic pattern of relationships among the various classes and class fragments in society. In other words, the structure of the economy differentially affects the material circumstances of individuals, and those differences, in turn, colour the way Canadians of various class groupings see the world. More specifically, the neo-Marxist interpretations of Canadian society argue that the role of the state in Canada, as in all capitalist systems, is to facilitate the accumulation of capital by the capitalist class. This is alleged to ensure that the underdog classes remain underdogs. To the extent that people are aware of this class bias on the part of the political elites, it will colour their sense of efficacy and of the legitimacy of the political system as a whole.

Finally, the neo-Marxists also have an interpretation of the significance of economic dependency that differs from that of more traditional political economists such as Innis. One interpretation is that Canada's slowness compared to Britain and the United States to develop a solid industrial base was in part deliberately fostered by the mercantile class fragment that made its fortunes, not on the production of goods, but on the *exchange* of raw materials for export and manufactured goods for import.

Whether this resulted from a deliberate conspiracy involving, variously, the mercantilists, the Canadian state, and foreign capitalists, is a moot point. The fact remains that the neo-Marxists agree with the more traditional political-economy school, that the Canadian economy is largely dependent upon that of the United States, and that this has the potential of undermining, indirectly, both our cultural and our social uniqueness vis-à-vis our neighbour to the south. As an example of the impact of such material circumstances on attitudes and opinions in Canada, we need look no further than the frequent disputes arising over cultural exemptions from the Canada–US Free Trade Agreement.

To conclude this section, we can say only that no single approach to explaining the historical roots of our political values, attitudes, and opinions can suffice. Rather, to effectively explain where our political culture comes from, we must look to the "ideological DNA" that our ancestors imported to North America, to the significant events that shaped our history, and to the economic and technological forces that formed the material matrix of nation building.

## ▶ POLITICAL VALUES IN CANADA

As we stated earlier, basic political values underlie people's attitudes towards specific political objects and also set the broadest limits of political behaviour in a society. Because they are *basic* they are seldom consciously articulated. Nevertheless, they form the guiding principles for the operation of our political and governmental institutions and modify the behaviour of individuals in political circumstances. In other words, our political values not only influence the behaviour of citizens and governmental officals but they are also reflected in the operative principles of the Constitution. At the most fundamental level, the values held by Canadians are rooted in the Judaeo-Christian religious tradition and in 18th- and 19th-century principles of liberalism and democracy, all modified and tempered by the traditions and events of the 20th century.

### Democratic Values

These basic values include a commitment to popular sovereignty, political equality, majoritarianism, and individualism. They form a set of unstated premises that underlie attitudes more directly related to the day-to-day workings of political institutions and are the bedrock of consensus in our political community.

**Popular Sovereignty**  Canadian political values are traditionally broadly described as **democratic**. Democracy may be viewed as a set of ultimate values, but we prefer to view it primarily as a set of operational procedures for realizing certain broad societal goals. Stated as a theoretical abstraction, the democratic aim or the ultimate democratic value is the common good or the common interest. Democracy, as a means of realizing the common good, is a system of government designed to reflect the will of the people as a whole rather than the will of any one individual, special interest, or elite. The limitations of democracy, as stated in such ethereal terms as these, follow from the fact that there is likely to be imperfect agreement as to what the common good is. In many cases the common good will conflict directly with the particular short-run demands put forward by individuals and groups within the society. Therefore, democracy is perhaps best viewed as a form of government that attempts to maximize or optimize the common good by establishing operational rules that will satisfy the needs of as many people as possible. This attempt is expressed in the principle of popular control or **popular sovereignty**.

Direct democracy, or the actual involvement of all of the members of a society in the policy process, is not possible in a large nation-state such as Canada. The complex and technical policies being dealt with by governments today do not encourage direct participation in government by all of the people. Indeed, the thought of passing even non-technical legislation in a legislature of thirty million is plainly ludicrous. Some indirect means must be found, therefore, to give effect to popular sovereignty, and the most common method of achieving this in a modern democracy is through elected representatives. Thus, as in most modern democracies, the Canadian people do not govern; rather, they choose their governors.

**Political Equality** Popular sovereignty is usually institutionalized through a system of periodic elections, which, in turn, presumes certain secondary values. The secondary values have been referred to collectively as the principles of **political equality**: every adult should have the right to vote; each person should have one vote; no person's vote should be weighted differently from another person's vote; and representation should be at least roughly proportional to population.

Political equality, however, means more than "one man, one vote," for a further assumption behind democratic elections is that the voter has real alternatives from which to choose, and that the voter can make a choice freely. Thus, the political freedoms—freedom of assembly, association, conscience, and expression—are fundamental values tied up inextricably with democracy as a governmental form. The institutional guarantees of these basic freedoms are to be found in devices such as the secret ballot, and in legal documents such as the federal and provincial election acts and the 1982 Charter of Rights and Freedoms.

**Majoritarianism** Majority rule, or **majoritarianism**, is a key operational principle of democratic government. The term means two things. First, it applies to the electoral process itself, in that the candidate who gets the largest number of votes, or a *plurality*, in an election becomes the representative for a geographical unit. Second, it applies when the representatives make policy decisions. In cases where there is not unanimous agreement as to what should be done, the alternative preferred by the largest number of representatives is the one implemented. However, the majoritarian principle is not absolute; there are limits placed on the majority. For instance, if a majority decided to abolish one of the basic freedoms, such as freedom of association, the system would cease to be democratic. Such tampering with democratic values, even by the majority, is normally considered to be unacceptable in democratic regimes. Thus, while majority rule is a very important principle of democracy, it is seldom, if ever, deemed to be absolute.

A corollary of the limitation on the principle of majority rule is that the minority will accept decisions of the majority as long as the majority does not violate other democratic values, such as political equality. Should a dissident minority refuse to abide by a policy decision of the majority, or should the majority take an extreme measure to suppress the legitimate rights of the minority, the system would be in danger either of breaking up or of ceasing to be democratic.

**Individualism and Collectivism**  As we shall see in the next section, the Canadian political culture can be broadly described as "liberal-pluralist." Classical liberalism includes a commitment to **individualism** and to individual liberties, a closely related commitment to the principles of individual private property and individual property rights, and a commitment to economic free enterprise and capitalism. As we shall see in the chapter on the Charter of Rights and Freedoms, the protection of the rights of the individual from unreasonable interference by the government is still an important cornerstone of our constitutional practice.

While individualism is a dominant political value in Canada, because of the way in which Canada was founded, the *dualism* of Canada is a value reflected both in our political culture and in our Constitution. Because the *Constitution Act*, 1867, explicitly recognizes and affirms the special place of French Canada in the federation, through the sections dealing with language rights and denominational schools, our Constitution can be said to be more tolerant of **collectivism** or to the principle of *community rights* than the more purely liberal constitution of the United States.

Given that the notion of vesting rights in collectivities, rather than individuals, is anathema to classical liberal values, it is perhaps remarkable that the most liberal of our constitutional components, the Charter of Rights and Freedoms, entrenches the collective rights of linguistic groups. The Charter also states explicitly that its provisions cannot be construed so as to abrogate or derogate from aboriginal or treaty rights. This has the effect of placing collective or communal rights—those of aboriginal peoples—above the rights of the individuals that make up the aboriginal communities.

It can be concluded that Canadian political values always have reflected and continue to reflect an accommodation of collective rights alongside individual rights. The existence of this collectivist or communalist component of our basically liberal-individualist society is an important difference between Canada and its neighbour, the United States, whose culture does not have the communalist idiosyncracies of Canada's.

### Liberal Values and Canadian Democracy

Many Canadians have come to identify democratic values with the somewhat more specific principles embodied in liberal democracy. **Liberalism**, as we have seen, incorporates a commitment to individualism, individual liberties, private property, and free enterprise. These may very well be important values held by a majority of people in the western democracies, particularly in the United States and Canada, but they are not necessary to a system of *democratic* politics.

**Canadian Liberalism**   Liberalism is not a "true" or typical ideology. It might be better referred to as a *semi-ideology* because it is much less coherent and certainly far less explicit to its adherents than, for instance, Marxism. In fact, it seems inarguable that liberal values in Canada have been gradually diluted by at least partial acceptance of competing ideological tenets such as economic equality, social and economic planning, and increased intervention of government in our everyday lives.

*The Pervasiveness of Liberal Values*   While we call liberalism a semi-ideology, largely because its principles, although widely held, are seldom made explicit by those who hold them, the basic values of liberalism are nevertheless a dominant influence in Canadian political life. Values such as individualism, competition, private property, and a laissez-faire relationship of the state to the individual, pervasively and persistently dominate the collective mind-set of Canadians. The pervasiveness can be seen in the extent to which liberal values are institutionalized in our Constitution, mouthed by our politicians, crusaded for by our media, and staunchly believed in by average Canadians.

Even the "left" in Canada, while attempting to explicitly reject and supplant liberalism, never quite seems to succeed because bits and pieces of liberal values remain as part of their unconscious or at least unarticulated intellectual baggage. Marxist intellectuals in Canada reject individualism at one level but embrace the fight for the protection of individual rights from the interference of the state at another. As well, left-leaning political parties in Canada speak of controlling and limiting capitalism but never of replacing it with a radically different social and political order.

*The Persistence of Liberal Myths*   The pervasiveness of liberalism in the Canadian political culture is only part of the mystery. The still more puzzling phenomenon of liberalism is the dogged *persistence* of liberal values. This persistence is probably made easier because liberalism is not codified as "Our Ideology" but remains a set of vague principles. In this sense, liberalism persists because it is too vague to be a clear target for criticism.

Liberalism remains strong in Canada, even in the face of factual evidence and hard experience that tell us that many liberal "truths" are only illusions. Many of our cherished liberal values are, in fact, **myths** or abstract ideals, which bear little relationship to modern realities. Nevertheless, even when confronted with strong evidence of the fraudulence of these values when they are taken literally, we tend to explain away the contradictions and cling to the myths.

As an example of this, let us look at the notion of *equal opportunity* in the economic system. This liberal notion is that all individuals possess the same opportunity to become millionaires or, at least, to be treated by the economic system in consonance with their contribution to it. But our experience tells us that there are relatively few Horatio Algers today, and few of us seriously believe that we will ever actually get rich. There is widespread evidence of the persistent disadvantages faced by women, aboriginal people, and visible-minority groups in the workplace, but our political culture still nurtures and cherishes the myth of equal opportunity.

*Legitimation of Liberal Values*  The persistence of this sort of false consciousness can in part be explained through the blurring of class distinctions in liberal societies and by the policy steps governments take to mitigate at least the worst evils of the untrammelled workings of the free-market economy. Even though, as we have seen, there are wide disparities in the distribution of income, the better-off individuals in society are willing to inoculate themselves against radical change in the economic structure by paying for, through their taxes (or, all too often, through deficit financing!) the high costs of social programs such as universal welfare benefits, income security, and health care. The lot of the have-nots in Canadian society is thus kept at a level far below that of the middle class but well above the level where material deprivation or psychological disgruntlement might be translated into working-class unrest or class revolution. Despite the social safety net, and the liberal vision of self-generated upward mobilty, however, the best hope for the average Canadian who hopes to "make it" still remains with a government-sponsored lottery ticket.

The overall point to be made here is that, while liberalism is difficult to deal with as a true ideology, there *is* a set of political values that we call liberal, and those values are so deep-rooted in our political culture that they colour the thinking of even explicitly anti-liberal critics of our system. We are concluding, then, that ours is basically a liberal society whose liberal values have been diluted (or polluted) by principles such as toryism, socialism, and corporatism. In the next section of this chapter we intend to analyze the influence of those non-liberal political values on the structure and content of the Canadian political culture.

**The Hybridization of Liberalism**  While all of the English-speaking democracies have in common a commitment to the values of popular sovereignty, political equality, and majoritarianism, it is the relative purity of their commitment to liberalism that ultimately distinguishes their political cultures one from the other. Hence, it can be generally concluded that the political culture of the United States of America is the most purely liberal, and that the political culture of the United Kingdom is the most diluted by strains of toryism. Canada, Australia, and New Zealand it seems, stand somewhere in the middle.

*The Tory Streak*  While the fragment theorists differ substantially on several points concerning the differences between Canadian and American value systems, they essentially agree that the English-Canadian political culture is more conservative, or **tory**, than that of the United States.[8] They conclude that the

---

8.  For more recent material on the difference between Horowitz and McRae, see Gad Horowitz, "Notes on 'Conservatism, Liberalism, and Socialism in Canada,' " *Canadian Journal of Political Science*, June 1978, p. 383; K. D. McRae, "Le Concept de la société fragmentaire de Louis Hartz: Son application à l'exemple canadien," *Canadian Journal of Political and Social Theory*, Fall 1979, p. 69.

values of collectivism, corporatism, and an organic view of the state have made Canadian liberalism far more a *hybrid ideology* than American liberalism:

> Canadian political society has thus stressed order, loyalty, and deference to government more than popular assent. Rather than "life, liberty, and the pursuit of happiness," the need has been peace, order, and good government. Social equality is desired but with less fervour than in America. Hierarchy in all spheres of life is taken for granted.[9]

Paradoxically, it is pointed out by one of the fragmentists, Gad Horowitz, that it is the tory streak in the Canadian political culture that supports collectivist tendencies.[10] Because the tory tradition is rooted in **feudalism**, which is ultimately a system featuring an organic or collectivist relationship of the individual to the state, the "tory-tinged" Canadian state has been far more willing to invest in social-egalitarian health and income-security programs than has that of the United States. In the same sense that the feudal landlord feels responsible for the well-being of his tenants or serfs and their families, the Canadian tory feels a *noblesse oblige* towards the less fortunate classes of society.

By contrast, the pure classical liberal assumes that all people are born free, but with different abilities and potential. The legitimate role of the state is seen to be limited to ensuring that the individual is free to pursue the maximization of his or her "God-given" potential. All the state must do is eliminate artificial barriers to equal opportunity and social justice will be automatically served. The classical tory, on the other hand, assumes that all people are *not* equal and never will be, so that the state must look after the "genetically inferior" classes of society. The modern tory achieves this, not through the institutions of feudalism, but by providing redistributive social programs.

*Socialism and Red Toryism*  **Red toryism** refers to the phenomenon of a "Tory with a social conscience." Many conservative politicians in Canada have been willing to initiate social programs that one might expect to be more exclusively championed by socialists. Conservative prime ministers R. B. Bennett, John Diefenbaker, and Joe Clark all took pro-active roles in attempting to introduce social-security legislation (although Bennett would certainly have balked at being called a *red* tory!). Moreover, as Horowitz has argued, this red tory streak in our political culture has made possible the emergence and survival of "an influential and legitimate socialist movement in English Canada as contrasted with the illegitimacy and early death of American socialism."[11]

Thus, English Canadian liberal values have been hybridized to the extent that Canada accepts wide class divergences, yet is amenable to some of the norms of economic egalitarianism and to the use of state power to implement those norms. By contrast, the United States is, in principle, committed to social equality, but more opposed to imposing limits on the laissez-faire operation of

9.  Erwin Hargrove, "Popular Leadership in Anglo-American Democracies," *in* Lewis Edinger, ed., *Popular Leadership in Industrial Societies* (New York: John Wiley and Sons, 1966), p. 147.

10.  Gad Horowitz, "Conservatism, Liberalism and Socialism in Canada: An Interpretation," *Canadian Journal of Economics and Political Science*, vol. 32, no. 2, May 1966, pp. 143–71. Note that "small-t toryism" and "small-l liberalism" cannot always be equated with the parties of the same names. As we point out frequently in this text, each of the two major Canadian parties contains bits and pieces of the full spectrum of ideological components.

11.  Gad Horowitz, *Canadian Labour in Politics* (Toronto: University of Toronto Press, 1968), p. 9.

the economy that would be necessary to achieve more than extremely modest steps in the direction of economic egalitarianism. This contrast is underscored by Lipset, who used a broader framework, which includes Australia, Britain, Canada, and the United States, to make political cultural comparisons. Lipset used survey data to show that Canadians generally evince more of a collective orientation than do Americans, and less than the British. Lipset also concludes on the basis of his data that Canadians are both more elitist and more ascriptive in their attitudes than Americans, but, again, less so than the British.[12]

The points Lipset makes are corroborated by many Canadian historical scholars.[13] Moreover, Lipset and those same Canadian historians are also in agreement that another reason for Canadian-American differences revolves around the relatively tame style of Canada's westward expansion, the relative dominance of Anglican and Roman Catholic, rather than Calvinist and fundamentalist, religious traditions in Canada, and the non-revolutionary nature of Canada's achievement of nationhood.

*The Corporatist Streak*  One part of Canada in which liberal values are not as dominant a dimension of the political culture is Quebec. Here, as Ken McRae has pointed out in his adaptation of the Hartzian model to Canada, we have a *feudal fragment*, which forms a stark contrast to the rest of the country. Canada, according to McRae, is a "dual fragment," and although he tends to understate the tory dilution of English-Canadian liberalism emphasized by Horowitz, he is most astute in his description of the non-liberal value system of French Canada, which he sees as a legacy of the *ancien régime* in *La Nouvelle France*. One of the most significant non-liberal components of the value system in French Canada, and one that may be present to some extent in the rest of the country, is the political value system called **corporatism**. The corporatist component of our political culture conceives of society as an aggregation of large *groups* rather than individuals. It challenges the legitimacy of individual rights and demands unless the individual puts forward his or her claims on government as a part of a group.

Hartz, Horowitz, and McRae all agree that corporatism was imported into Canada partly by the earliest French settlers, who brought with them a feudal concept of society.[14] In fact, it is only in Quebec that corporatist values have ever had an impact on political and governmental processes. As we shall see

---

12. For an updated version of Lipset's views, see S. M. Lipset, "Canada and the United States: The Cultural Dimension," *in* C. F. Doran and J. Sigler, eds., *Canada and the United States: Enduring Friendship, Persistent Stress* (Englewood Cliffs, N.J.: Prentice Hall, 1985).

13. See, for example, W. L. Morton, *The Canadian Identity* (Madison: University of Wisconsin Press, 1961), pp. 84–87; Chester P. Martin, *The Foundation of Canadian Nationhood* (Toronto: University of Toronto Press, 1955); A. R. M. Lower, *Colony to Nation: A History of Canada* (Toronto: Longmans Green, 1946); J. Porter, *The Vertical Mosaic* (Toronto: University of Toronto Press, 1965); Erwin C. Hargrove, "Notes on American and Canadian Political Culture," *Canadian Journal of Economics and Political Science*, vol. 33, February 1967, pp. 21–29; and George Grant, *Lament for a Nation* (Princeton: Van Nostrand, 1967).

14. Louis Hartz, ed., *The Founding of New Societies* (New York: Harcourt Brace, 1964); K. D. McRae, "The Structure of Canadian History," *in* Hartz, *The Founding of New Societies* ; and Horowitz, "Conservatism, Liberalism, and Socialism." It might be worthwhile to suggest a reinterpretation of their views of French-Canadian society as a "feudal fragment" to take account of the prevailing view of French-Canadian sociologists and historians that the earliest French society in North America had a predominantly mercantile value system, and that it was only after the conquest that the mercantile elements of that value system disappeared, leaving the corporatist feudal fragment.

in Chapter 9, Quebec remained partially feudal well into the 20th century. Quebec society was dominated by the church and the state elites who worked out an accommodation with the English business and mercantile elites. This elite domination retarded the development of unionism in the province, but interestingly, when Quebec workers finally did succeed in organizing, the union movement in that province took on some corporatist trappings. The relationship among state elites, union leaders, and the corporate sector still has elements of corporatism in it today.

Corporatism was also a small component of the type of conservatism the Loyalist element brought from the Thirteen Colonies after the American Revolution. Corporatism, while never a dominant force in English Canada, has been widely celebrated from time to time, first by the church, and later by a few leading intellectuals. Mackenzie King was a strong advocate of what was essentially a system of corporatism, where labour, business, and government leaders were supposed to cooperate in a *tripartite* governing coalition, but this idea was never acted upon. In the 1970s there was another spate of calls for tripartism to cope with the then-prevailing economic malady of inflation, but again, other than a few conferences, nothing ever came of it.

Leo Panitch, who has preferred to define corporatism as a "political form" and not as an ideology, admits that there is an ideological basis for corporatism in Canada. He argues that while corporatist values were inherited from the Loyalist tory streak in English Canada, and from the pre–French Revolution feudal streak in French Canada, and while these values have sporadically reappeared in Canadian liberalism, French-Canadian Catholicism, and agrarian populism, the values have never given birth to corporatist political forms.[15] It is only in Quebec, where liberal values are less compelling to begin with, that corporatist ideas have been significant in terms of the governmental process, and even there such values are not dominant. Generally, as with conservatism and socialism, corporatism has been permitted only to tinge our political culture and to qualify and dilute the dominant liberal value system, without replacing it.

*Liberal Pluralism*  As a result of the anti-individualist thrust of corporatism, Robert Presthus has concluded that corporatism may have broader implications for the way in which the Canadian political system operates:

> These components of Canadian political culture culminate, in turn, in a national political process that may be called one of elite accommodation. Essentially, . . . this is a system in which the major decisions regarding national socioeconomic policy are worked out through interactions between governmental (i.e., legislative and bureaucratic) elites and interest group elites.[16]

This sounds more like a description of **pluralism** than of corporatism. What, then, is the difference?

The difference between corporatism and pluralism is that the former recognizes fewer functional groups. The corporatist collectivities are limited to

---

15. Leo Panitch, "Corporatism in Canada," *Studies in Political Economy,* Spring 1979, p. 46. See also Leo Panitch, "The Development of Corporatism in Liberal Democracies," *Comparative Political Studies,* April 1977, p. 61.
16. R. Presthus, *Elite Accommodation in Canadian Politics* (Toronto: Macmillan, 1963), pp. 20–21.

three or four major sectoral groups, such as labour, industry, government, and agriculture. As well, corporatism features a more rigidly structured set of relationships both among the sectoral groups and between each of the sectors and the state. Pluralism, by contrast, sees society as a vast network of groups interacting both within and between the major sectors of society. Another difference is that the corporatist ideal requires that all individuals *must* belong to one of the groups and *only* one. There are no overlapping group member-ships in the corporatist model and only the group is empowered to represent individuals' interests in the interaction with the state.

In contrast to this highly structured and rigidly organic conception of society, pluralism is rooted in liberal individualism. Large numbers of interest groups compete with each other, and their relationships to each other and to the state are left to float according to the vagaries of group leadership, social and economic conditions, and widely disparate bargaining power. Individuals belong to as many groups as they choose, and multiple, overlapping member-ships tend to be the rule rather than the exception. Individuals also have legitimate rights of their own, separate from their group identities. We will revisit the concept of **liberal pluralism** when we discuss interest groups in later chapters.

*The Communalist Streak*   Quebec is a distinct society because its political cul-ture is different from that of the rest of Canada. However, the very existence of a culturally distinctive French-Canadian minority is itself a major influence on our political culture and on the overall nature of Canadian political life. It is an essential concomitant of liberalism that legal *rights and freedoms* are vested in individuals rather than in collectivities, such as communities, sectors, groups, or classes. However, because of the way in which Canada was founded, and because of the "French fact," the duality of the Canadian nation is reflected both in our institutions and in our political values. Our Constitution recognizes and affirms the special place of French Canada in the federation, particularly through the sections dealing with language rights and minority religious-edu-cation rights.

Logically, within the liberal ideological context, the granting of special rights to a group of people on the basis of ethnic origin should be anath-ema—for by creating a group of citizens with rights that exceed those of the majority, we create a class of "citizens-plus." As Raymond Breton has argued with respect to special rights for visible minorities, the extension of this con-clusion may well be that the rest of us are "citizens-minus."

> Changes to accommodate visible minorities are sometimes interpreted by other groups as a decrease of their importance in the eyes of public authorities. Some feel resentment about being considered "invisible."[17]

This argument is also made with respect to granting special educational rights to Roman Catholics but not to other religious minorities, and to granting special status to the French language in Canada when other minority languages are given no protection at all.

---

17.  R. Breton, "Multiculturalism and Canadian Nationbuilding." Research paper prepared for the Royal Commission on the Economic Union and Development Prospects for Canada (The Macdonald Commis-sion), 1985, p. 50.

Despite these complaints, neither politicians nor, as it seems, the general public in Canada, have been willing to move from simple bitching and belly-aching to an out-and-out demand for the removal of such special-status provisions from the statute books and the Constitution. The conclusion must be that, generally, Canadians either have been willing to accept or are grudgingly resigned to such qualifications of the unitary nature of Canadian citizenship. This general acceptance of the principle of minority rights and special status for collectivities in Canada has more recently been reflected in the provisions of the Charter of Rights and Freedoms, which entrench the principles of minority language and education rights. Moreover, the *Constitution Act, 1982,* defines another group of Canadians, the aboriginal peoples, as having a special status.

Thus, the Canadian political culture has always accepted the principle of collective rights, which serves to moderate and adapt our basic liberal values. Moreover, there are indications, since the Second World War, of a growing significance of group rights in the development of various public policies relating to, for instance, bilingualism, multiculturalism, affirmative action for visible minorities and women, and self-government for First Nations. This significant collectivist streak in our basically individualist value set has been described by Bernard Blishen as a form of **communalism** whereby the society accepts the legitimacy of group rights along with those of the individual.[18]

The communalist or collectivist streak in our political culture is important in comparing Canada with its fellow democracies, the United States and Britain. Canadians are more willing than Americans or Britons to tolerate the vesting of special status or privileges in the hands of collectivities or minority groups. However, there are indications, such as the upsurge in the popularity of the right-wing Reform Party, that this tolerance of minorities in Canada may be declining. If the Reform Party were to come to power, the institutional mandate for ethnic diversity could be expected to change quite radically. That party has indicated an opposition to aboriginal rights, open immigration policies, official bilingualism, and multiculturalism, which might lead us to conclude that Reform represents a political sub-culture in Canada that incorporates a "rawer" and more American form of liberalism. Certainly, the 1995 images of Preston Manning "cozying up" to Newt Gingrich and the American Republican Party must have made many Canadian liberals cringe just a little.

### Aboriginal Political Culture

Perhaps one of the purest forms of collectivist values can be found in the political culture of Canadian aboriginal people. While it is difficult to generalize about literally hundreds of different First Nations, multiple languages, and disparate tribal traditions, there are certain political values that are common to most aboriginal groups. Aboriginal political values are more collectivist because they grew out of a hunting- and- gathering economy and social structure. In such societies, the rights of the individual must be secondary to the needs of the collectivity if the community is to survive.

---

18. B. Blishen, "Continuity and Change in Canadian Values." Research paper prepared for the Macdonald Commission, 1985.

Aboriginal political values in Canada are thus much more reflective of an organic conception of community than are the predominantly liberal values of our political culture as a whole. The patterns of political decision making are consensual and not majoritarian, and traditional leadership is diffuse rather than monolithic. Political influence rests with different leaders depending on what the decision is about, so that, for example, the female elders may resolve conflicts over family matters while the best hunter may decide where to set up a hunting camp.[19]

In the far north, many of these aboriginal values are being reincorporated into political and governmental systems. The current Northwest Territories legislature, for instance, has remained a non-partisan, consensual decision-making structure since it became fully elected almost twenty years ago.[20] The new territory of Nunavut, which will come into existence in 1999, will feature a constitution that is a reflection of traditional Inuit culture, and the remaining part of the NWT, in the Mackenzie Valley–Great Slave Lake region, is looking at adopting a highly decentralized, community-based system of government. The First-Nation self-government agreements being put in place in the Yukon feature constitutions that are developed by each individual First Nation to blend the unique values and traditions of the specific community with the core values of liberal democracy.

Thus, while it cannot be said that the aboriginal sub-cultures have greatly influenced our doggedly liberal mainstream political values, neither has liberalism pervaded the aboriginal communities to the extent it has elsewhere in the country. The aboriginal political cultures have survived and will in all likelihood persist and develop into the future. The particular mix of our liberal democratric values and the strong collectivist-consensual tradition of the aboriginal cultures might, in the long run, prove to be one of the most interesting sub-cultural hybrids in the Canadian political culture.

### Political Negativism

It is obviously not possible in a text focusing primarily on institutions and processes to catalogue all of the attitudes that Canadians hold with respect to political objects. However, one generalization that can be made is that Canadians are on the whole remarkably *negative* in their feelings about government in general and about politicians in particular. A major piece of survey research in the 1970s, conducted by Clarke, Jenson, Leduc, and Pammett, uncovered this phenomenon, and since that time the Canadian public has become, if anything, even more cynical and jaded about government, politics, and politicians.[21]

While it is difficult to make accurate comparisons across time, it seems fair to say that this **negativism** described by Clarke et al. is a fairly recent phenom-

19. See M. S. Whittington, "Aboriginal Self-Government in Canada," *in* Whittington and Williams, *Canadian Politics in the 1990s*, p. 3.
20. See M. S. Whittington, "Canada's North in the 1990s," *in* Whittington and Williams, *Canadian Politics in the 1990s*, p. 23.
21. H. Clarke, J. Jenson, L. Leduc, and J. Pammett, *Political Choice in Canada* (Toronto: McGraw-Hill Ryerson, 1980) and *Absent Mandate: The Politics of Discontent in Canada* (Toronto: Gage, 1984), p. 183.

enon in Canadian politics. It was first identified in the seventies and can likely be explained, in part, in terms of the events, issues, and personalities of that period in Canadian history. In the first place, the decade of the seventies was dominated by major social and economic problems for which our political leaders were not able to provide solutions. Inflation ran at 8 to 10 per cent per annum, unemployment rates steadily climbed, and resources were considered to be not only finite, but virtually depleted as well. It is no wonder that Canadians began to be a little cynical about politics, given the apparent failure of the system to solve the major problems facing it.

A second possible cause for this negativism might be related to a perceived general decline in our international status. During the decade of the seventies, Canadians came to feel that we were not a very important power in international affairs and would never play more than a minor supporting role to the United States on the global stage. During the 1970s and 1980s, rather than accepting with dignity Canada's middle-power status, most of our political leaders persisted in making a pretence of having great influence on the superpowers and often ended up looking like "great-power groupies."

Linked closely to this is the third probable cause of negativism among the Canadian public, the general failure of our national leaders to live up to our expectations domestically. The dominant figure in the seventies was clearly Pierre Trudeau, who came in on a wave of support not paralleled since the Diefenbaker landslide of 1958. Trudeau was the new breed of leader, the man for the future. He combined personal charisma and "style" with intelligence and imagination. But, while two of his three children were born on Christmas Day, he could neither walk on water nor turn it into wine.

Nor did the Progressive Conservative government of Brian Mulroney fare much better. While the first few months—the honeymoon—after the Tory landslide in 1984 were characterized by favourable media reports and high public confidence in the opinion polls, after a year in office, the shiny new government had begun to develop some rust spots. Late-night trips to strip joints, rancid tuna fish, allegations of nepotism and of political interference in the justice system, and a multitude of opposition claims of mismanagement and bungling led to ministerial resignations and demotions. It did not take long for the public to wake up to the fact that the new guys were not necessarily very different from the ones we had just dumped. By the end of his second term, Mulroney's popularity had dropped to an unprecedented low for a prime minister, and he was essentially forced to quit.

In the nineties, there is little to indicate that this negativism has declined. While Canadians continue to feel positive about our democratic system, and while United Nations reports indicate that Canada is the number-one place in the world to live, the public still does not hold politicans or political parties in very high regard. Moreover, the nineties is a time to bite bullets and take bitter pills (and mix metaphors!). Governments are forced by economic circumstances to undertake various unpopular measures, none of which cause the citizenry to do anything more than tolerate their politicians.

## ▶ PROTEST, CIVIL DISOBEDIENCE, AND POLITICAL VIOLENCE

We will discuss the manner and extent to which Canadians participate in the grand spectacles of politics—elections—in later chapters. However, it is important to say a bit here about the place of less conventional political activities in our political culture. When considering tactics of exerting political influence we must recognize that such activities range from legitimate and peaceful forms of protest to non-legitimate and even violent manifestations of political dissent, such as riots, the deliberate destruction of property, political assassination, and terrorism.

### The Peaceable Kingdom

We generally think of Canada as the "peaceable kingdom," committed to the principles of peace, order, and good government, and exhibiting a definite preference for change that is gradual, evolutionary, and according to the rules of parliamentary democracy. However, the period of the 1960s was characterized by an increase everywhere in the amount of less conventional and non-conventional political activity, particularly in the United States, and that trend spilled over to some extent to peaceable, conservative, and law-abiding Canada. As indicated in Table 4.1, there is, today, generally a high rate of approval of mild forms of less-conventional political activity, such as signing petitions, but a decreasing rate of approval for the more radical forms of protest, such as illegal strikes and marches. It is perhaps significant that more than 10 per cent of those questioned in the survey even approved of demonstrations with a chance of violence, at least in some circumstances.

**TABLE 4.1**

Political Protest Activities: Attitudes and Participation

| Activity | Approve of the Activity (%) 1983 | Think the Activity is Effective (%) 1983 | Participate in the Activity (%) 1983 | 1988 |
|---|---|---|---|---|
| Signing of Petitions | 85 | 71 | 68 | 68 |
| Boycott of Goods or Services | 64 | 61 | 38 | 38 |
| March or Rally | 53 | 52 | 20 | 24 |
| Sit-in | 26 | 35 | 5 | 8 |
| Potentially Violent Demonstration | 11 | 23 | 4 | 8 |

Note: Weighted national samples, 1983 N-2117, 1988 N-2215, missing data removed.

Source: Harold Clarke and William Mischler, "Political Participation in Canada," in M. S. Whittington and G. Williams, eds., Canadian Politics in the 1990s (Scarborough: Nelson, 1994), p. 136.

### Political Violence in Canada

Canada has a long history of political violence, surprising as that may be, but such activity has never been widespread, nor has it ever been viewed as legitimate by most Canadians. The assassination of D'Arcy McGee shortly after Confederation was an early and rare example of political assassination in Canada. Similarly, there were a number of confrontations involving the labour movement in the period leading up to the First World War, and the Winnipeg General Strike, in 1919, stands as a distinct blot on our record. The irony with the General Strike and with various confrontations during the Depression years (such as the so-called Regina Riots) is that it is a toss-up whether the ensuing violence was caused by the protesters or by the military and police authorities who were called upon by the governments of the day to "restore order."

In the 1950s there were few incidents of political violence, and the majority of those reported in that decade involved the Sons of Freedom Doukhobors in western Canada. The Doukhobors, who had immigrated to Canada from Russia earlier in the century, but wished to return to their homeland, seemed to have a peculiar antipathy towards electric transmission towers, which they dynamited with alarming regularity. As well, they employed the rather unusual terrorist tactic of conducting mass protest marches in the nude. However, other than damage to property and to the moral sensibilities of rural Albertans and British Columbians, the Doukhobors did not do a terrible amount of harm.

In the 1960s, there was a definite turn in the direction of greater violence when a number of small French-Canadian nationalist groups, such as the FLQ, became involved in incidents ranging from demonstrations and defacing property to bombings and kidnappings. Several of these incidents resulted in personal injury and loss of life. The culmination of this period of violent protest was the kidnapping of a British diplomat, James Cross, and the murder of a Quebec Cabinet minister, Pierre Laporte, which precipitated the October Crisis of 1970. However, since 1970 the tendency in Quebec has been for the nationalist movement to use primarily conventional and legitimate forms of political participation. It is likely that historians will be able to say that this brief, nasty period in the late sixties and early seventies was only an aberration.

Through the 1980s, while there were various protests, sit-ins, mass demonstrations, and marches (and even a hunger strike by a senator), the number and intensity of such activities did not increase significantly. Moreover, such protests and marches were for the most part well-organized, peaceful, and law-abiding. Where there was a greater cause for concern in Canada in the eighties was in the increased incidence of extremely violent acts of terrorism and assassination by immigrant groups who have brought some of their historic political hatreds and grudges with them to Canada. The most serious of these incidents, the bombing of an Air India 747 and the assassinations and attempted assassinations of Turkish diplomats, were not directed at Canada, the Canadian government, or Canadians directly. However, Canadian citizens did lose their lives in these incidents, and certainly the possible implications for the nature of political life in Canada are deeply disturbing. However legitimate the causes being espoused by groups such as the Armenians or the Sikhs living in Canada may be, acts of terrorism committed in Canada simply cannot be tolerated.

Sadly, too, one of the inevitable consequences of such violence is that it comes to reflect negatively upon the entire immigrant community involved, thus seeming to justify and reinforcing whatever racist and discriminatory attitudes may exist in the Canadian social mainstream. One of the better examples of this sort of negative backlash occurred in the context of the standoff between the Mohawks and the authorities at Oka, Quebec. An officer of the Sureté de Québec was killed in the initial confrontation, although it is quite possible that the fatal shooting was accidental. The situation got nastier when non-natives, who were upset by a Mohawk blockade at the Pont Mercier, hurled rocks and racial epithets at automobiles moving some of the Kanawake elders out of the nearby reserve. Somehow, to those of us watching this on television, it didn't quite seem like Canada.

There is no indication that aboriginal unrest is going to go away in the near future. The summer of 1995 witnessed a number of armed confrontations between aboriginal groups and the authorities, most notably at Ipperwash, Ontario, Gustafson Lake, Alberta, and in the interior of British Columbia. These incidents all ended, but not before one person was fatally injured at Ipperwash. While most First Nations are committed to working out their differences with governments in a peaceful manner, it appears that a growing minority of individuals in the aboriginal community are willing to engage in confrontational tactics to press for change. Unhappily, the immediate consequence of this would seem to be a hardening of non-aboriginal Canadians' attitudes towards even the most legitimate claims and grievances of aboriginal peoples.

### The *Relatively* Peaceable Kingdom

While it is alarming to discover that our peaceable kingdom is not as orderly as our national myths would have it, we are still significantly more peaceable than Britain and the United States, the countries with which Canadians most frequently compare themselves. Moreover, very few individual Canadians ever actually participate in riots, demonstrations, political strikes, and other more violent forms of political protest. As Bill Mishler put it, "despite the frequency of political protest in Canada, it is reasonable to estimate that the number of Canadians participating in the most extreme forms of political protest has never exceeded ten percent and probably has averaged less than one percent."[22]

## ▶ CONCLUSION: THE CANADIAN POLITICAL CULTURE

With the material in this chapter entered and noted, what can we say about the Canadian political culture by way of summary? First, from the evidence of history and from the study of Canadian political institutions, we can safely say that the Canadian political culture includes a commitment to democratic values

---

22. William Mishler, *Political Participation in Canada* (Toronto: Macmillan, 1979), p. 43.

such as popular sovereignty, majoritarianism, and the political rights and freedoms associated with representative government. Second, again, it is the evidence of history and of our political, economic, and legal institutions that tells us we have a political culture dominated by the pervasive and persistent ideological blend that is Canadian liberalism. While we have seen that our liberal values are qualified by streaks or strains of toryism, socialism, corporatism, and communalism, the fact remains that, for all regions, ethnic groups, and social classes in Canada, liberal values dominate.

Third, when we come to look at Canadians' attitudes and orientations towards specific political objects, we do not have enough information to generalize effectively. On the basis of the few surveys there are, we do know that such attitudes vary widely with different regions, ethnic groups, and social classes, and that the only general impression is one of a growing cynicism or negativism towards politics, which emerged in the late sixties and early seventies and is still with us in the nineties. Finally, while every decade sees a measure of unconventional political activity, that kind of behaviour does not appear to be growing from decade to decade. While we have experienced periodic and usually tragic incidents of political violence, it is likely still safe to conclude that these are strictly aberrant cases and in no way reflective of Canada's political culture as a whole.

▶ FURTHER READING: PART ONE
THE ENVIRONMENT: SOCIETY, ECONOMY, AND
CULTURE

### Economic Cleavages

Brodie, Janine. *The Political Economy of Canadian Regionalism.* Toronto: Harcourt Brace, 1990.

Carroll, William. *Corporate Power and Canadian Capitalism.* Vancouver: University of British Columbia Press, 1986.

Clement, W., and Glen Williams. *The New Canadian Political Economy.* Montreal: McGill-Queen's University Press, 1989.

Coates K., and J. Powell. *The Modern North.* Toronto: Lorimer, 1989.

Curtis, J., Edward Grabb, Neil Guppy, and Sid Gilbert. *Social Inequality in Canada: Patterns, Problems, Policies.* Scarborough: Prentice-Hall, 1988.

Gibbins, R. *Conflict and Unity.* Scarborough: Nelson, 1990.

Gifford, C. G. *Canada's Fighting Seniors.* Toronto: Lorimer, 1991.

Hunter, A. A. *Class Tells: On Social Inequality in Canada.* Toronto: Butterworths, 1986.

McDaniel, Susan. *Canada's Aging Population.* Toronto: Butterworths, 1986.

Sarlo, C. *Poverty in Canada.* Vancouver: Fraser Institute, 1992.

Savoie, Donald. *The Canadian Economy: A Regional Perspective.* Toronto: Carswell, 1986.

Whittington, M. S., and G. Williams, eds. *Canadian Politics in the 1990s.* Scarborough: Nelson, 1990. Part I: "The Regions in National Perspective," pp. 3–133.

Williams, Glen. "Regions Within Regions: Continentalism Ascendant," *in* Whittington and Williams, eds. *Canadian Politics in the 1990s.* Scarborough: Nelson, 1994, pp. 19–39.

### Ethnic Cleavages

Abu-Laban, Yasmeen, and D. Stasiulis. "Ethnic Pluralism Under Seige: Popular and Partisan Opposition to Multiculturalism." *Canadian Public Policy*, vol. 18, no. 4, p. 365.

Asch, Michael. *Home and Native Land.* Toronto: Methuen, 1984.

Boldt, Menno. *Surviving Indians: The Challenge of Self Government.* Toronto: University of Toronto Press, 1993.

Elliot, J. L., and A. Fleras. *Unequal Relations: An Introduction to Race and Ethnic Dynamics in Canada.* Scarborough: Prentice-Hall, 1991.

Frideres, J. *Native People in Canada: Contemporary Conflict.* Scarborough: Prentice-Hall, 1988.

Megyery, K. *Ethnocultural Groups and Visible Minorities in Canadian Politics: The Question of Access.* Toronto: Dundurn Press, 1991.

Stasiulis, Daiva, " 'Deep Diversity': Race and Ethnicity in Canadian Politics," *in* M. S. Whittington and G. Williams, eds., *Canadian Politics in the 1990s.* Scarborough: Nelson, 1994, pp. 191–219.

Tennant, Paul. *Aboriginal Peoples and Politics.* Vancouver: University of British Columbia Press, 1990.

Whittington, M. "Aboriginal Self Government in Canada," *in* M. S. Whittington and G. Williams, eds., *Canadian Politics in the 1990s.* Scarborough: Nelson, 1994, pp. 3–18.

**Gender Cleavage**

Bashevkin, Sylvia. *Toeing the Lines.* Toronto: University of Toronto Press, 1985.

Begin, M. *Some of Us: Women in Canada in Power and Politics.* Mississauga: Random House, 1991.

Brodie, Janine. *Women and Politics in Canada.* Toronto: McGraw-Hill Ryerson, 1985.

Burt, Sandra. "Rethinking Canadian Politics: The Impact of Gender," *in* M. S. Whittington and G. Williams, eds., *Canadian Politics in the 1990s.* Scarborough: Nelson, 1994, pp. 176–90.

Burt, Sandra, Lorraine Cade, and Lindsay Dorney. *Changing Patterns: Women in Canada.* Toronto: McClelland and Stewart, 1993.

Canadian Advisory Council on the Status of Women. *Women and Labour Market Poverty.* Ottawa: DSS, 1990.

Kealy, Linda, and Joan Sangster. *Beyond the Vote: Canadian Women and Politics.* Toronto: University of Toronto Press, 1989.

Megyery, K. *Women in Canadian Politics: Toward Equity in Representation.* Toronto: Dundurn Press, 1991.

Vickers, Jill, C. Appelle, and P. Rankin. *Politics As If Women Mattered.* Toronto: University of Toronto Press, 1993.

**Political Culture**

Bell, David. *The Roots of Disunity: A Study of Canadian Political Culture.* Toronto: Oxford University Press, 1992.

Bell, David. "Political Culture in Canada," *in* M. S. Whittington and G. Williams. *Canadian Politics in the 1990s.* Scarborough: Nelson, 1994.

Blair R. S., and J. T. McLeod. *The Canadian Political Tradition: Basic Readings.* Scarborough: Nelson, 1993. Part 2.

Byrum, R. J., and Bonnie Fox. *From Culture to Power: The Sociology of English Canada.* Toronto: Oxford University Press, 1989.

Franks, Ned. *Dissent and the State.* Toronto: Oxford University Press, 1989.

Hartz, Louis, ed. *The Founding of New Societies.* New York, Harcourt Brace, 1964.

Lipset, S. M. *Continental Divide.* New York: Routledge, 1990.

Mishler, William. *Political Participation in Canada: Prospects for Democratic Citizenship.* Toronto: Macmillan, 1979.

Nevitte, N., and Roger Gibbins. *New Elites in New States: Ideologies in the Anglo-American Democracies.* Toronto: Oxford University Press, 1991.

Pammett, Jon, and M. S. Whittington. *The Foundations of Political Culture: Political Socialization in Canada.* Toronto: Macmillan, 1976.

## PART TWO

# The Constitution

*Chapter* **5**

# The Constitution: Functions, Origins, Evolution

A constitution is a body of fundamental laws and principles that define the relationship between a society and its government, and the manner in which the government must operate. From the point of view of a student of politics, the constitution of any political system is of interest for two main reasons. First, it is a prescriptive device that is intended to set limits on the behaviour of individuals who are in positions of governmental authority. In this sense, a constitution determines the nature of the political and governmental processes. Second, a constitution is a reflection of basic societal values. In this sense, it is itself a product of the history and political culture of a nation and of the social and economic forces that have shaped that nation. In studying the Canadian Constitution, therefore, we not only come to understand the legal and normative limits on our government's authority, but we also find out a lot about the fundamental values of our political community.

It is the aim of this chapter to look first at the Constitution in functional terms, that is, to attempt to explain what the Constitution *does* in the Canadian political and governmental processes. Second, we will describe the origins of our Constitution, that is, the historical events and forces that shaped it up until 1867. Finally, we will look at two of the basic themes or preoccupations of our constitutional development since 1867.

## ▶ FUNCTIONS

All institutions of a political system must be both stable and flexible. On the one hand, stability is necessary if the citizenry is to be able to learn about the basic values of the regime and the "rules of the game" of politics. The most fundamental of our political values must stand still long enough for us to come to know, understand, and appreciate them. It is because the political process is seen as stable and predictable that we, the citizens, come to accept its laws and policies as legitimate. On the other hand, because social and economic conditions are continually changing, both domestically and globally, the regime must be flexible enough to react and adapt fairly quickly to new circumstances and to relieve the related institutional stresses.

In the Canadian system, most of our basic political institutions are fairly flexible. Political parties and pressure groups are generated and modified by changing social forces and issues, and for the most part they don't even have a statutory foundation. As well, even more formal institutions such as Parliament, the Cabinet, and the bureaucracy can be restructured to meet new circumstances fairly easily. All of these core institutions of our system, therefore, have sufficient flexibility to be able to react directly and immediately to rapid changes. The Constitution, because it can be changed only through complicated processes of formal amendment, or gradually, through the evolution of new conventions and practices, provides the system with its needed stability and predictability over time.

Thus, in the widest sense, the function of a constitution is to provide the system with a backbone — to set the ultimate limits on the adaptive behaviour of the more flexible political institutions and to give the governmental system the overall structural integrity that allows it to persist over time. But constitutions have more immediate and more specific functions to perform, which are often unique to the individual political system and to the particular form of government in operation. These we consider next.

### Constitutionalism and the Rule of Law

A constitution, in the most general terms, simply defines the relationship between the citizen and the state. In this sense, therefore, every country, even the most despotic dictatorship, can be said to have some form of constitution. This is the principle of **constitutionalism**, and most modern regimes, however autocratic, at least pay lip-service to the principle. However, this is too general a concept to be of much value in helping us to understand the Canadian setting. What is key in the notion of constitutionalism in Canada, is the way in which we operationalize the principle of the **rule of law**.

The rule of law means simply that the authority of the state must be exercised only through legal processes. Having a constitution, or, in other words, *a supreme body of law*, is a necessary condition for achieving the rule of law. The rule of law in the British and Canadian traditions asserts that any interference with the rights and freedoms of any individual may be imposed only according to the legal process and carried out by legitimate authorities. No one is exempt from the law, neither citizens nor officials of the government; there is *equality* before the law for all members of our political community.

The rule of law is a doctrine we in Canada have inherited from the English Constitution. It was transported to Canada during the colonial period and constitutionally implanted here through the BNA Act (or the *Constitution Act,*

1867), whose preamble states that Canada is to have a "Constitution similar in principle to that of the United Kingdom," that is, among other things, founded on the rule of law. In Britain, the doctrine of the rule of law dates from 1215, when the Magna Carta was signed (albeit under some duress) by King John, affirming that the king would henceforth rule *per legem terrae* — according to the law of the land. The principle has been expanded and refined since that auspicious occasion in history, and was explicitly entrenched in the Constitution of Canada through the 1982 Charter of Rights and Freedoms, whose preamble states that Canada is founded upon (among other things) the rule of law.

Given that the Constitution of Canada is built on the principle of the rule of law, how does the rule of law benefit us on a practical level? The function of the rule of law on a day-to-day basis is, stated briefly, to protect us from the arbitrary interference of government, or of government officials, in our everyday lives. The law is **knowable**; that is, in principle, we can become aware, through the law, of the standards of behaviour that are expected of us as Canadians. The law is **impartial**; that is, we are to be treated fairly by the system regardless of our individual characteristics, beliefs, and idiosyncrasies. The law is **predictable**; that is, it is applied to us as individuals in a consistent manner over time. By contrast, the rule of the most benevolent of dictators could conceivably deteriorate to rule by whim and caprice. The law does not get out of bed on the wrong side, have quarrels with its spouse, get cranky because of pressures at work, or have "bad hair days." Laws, unlike people, are impersonal, impartial, predictable, and coldly rational, rather than emotional or moody.

### Defining the Limits on Government

The rule of law, as we have seen, is desirable in a society that values the principle of an impartial and predictable relationship between the citizens and their government. The constitutional entrenchment of the principle of the rule of law, however, is not in itself sufficient to secure the kind of constitutional order we desire. The inherent weakness of the rule of law is the fact that laws are made, applied, and interpreted by *people* — and people are not always impersonal, predictable, and rational. Thus, in order to prevent unjust laws from being passed and to guard against the unjust or inequitable application of laws, a constitution must go beyond the mere recognition of the rule of law; it must also set limits on the kinds of laws that can be made.

Our Constitution defines very broadly the area of legitimate lawmaking by giving us a body of fundamental principles to which all public policy must conform. These principles are the most elemental norms of the system, and they define the boundary between matters in which the state can legitimately impose legal constraints on individual behaviour and matters in which individual freedoms are so important that even the authority of a democratically elected parliament must be limited. Many of these basic limits on the legitimate role of the state are defined by constitutional conventions inherited from Britain and reflective of the dominant political values of our political culture. While their limits have been explicitly defined, recognized, and entrenched in the 1982 Charter of Rights and Freedoms, their guarantee still rests most importantly in the continued commitment to them on the part of the government and the governed alike.

### Defining the Regime: Operative Principles

Not only does the Canadian Constitution set the limits within which governments must operate — the legitimate *ends* of the state — but it also defines the form of government, or the **regime**. The Canadian Constitution defines the operational structure of the political system, and it also defines the relationships among parts of the system. In J. A. Corry's words, "The constitution is the frame or chassis in which the working engine of government is set."[1] In this sense, for instance, the *Constitution Act* of 1867 gives us, among other things, a federal system, representative democracy, a parliamentary system, and an independent judiciary — the institutional features that characterize our system.

Further, the Canadian Constitution defines many of the rules of the game of politics. It broadly defines the tactics and the *means* that are acceptable within the governmental process, and it describes formal procedures that must be followed in order to implement policy decisions. The Canadian Constitution, in other words, sets formal limits on *how* our government performs its basic responsibilities. It does not matter what the ends are, or how popular the ends may be; the Constitution sets limits on the means that can be legitimately employed to achieve them. An example of these rules of the game of politics in Canada is the principle that there should be ample time provided in the House of Commons for the opposition to criticize government policy. No matter how urgent the government policy may seem at the time, the opposition is always guaranteed at least some opportunity to debate any issue. Although the Constitution does not specify exactly how much time, even in the cases where government has the power to limit debate, the opposition must still be given a substantial opportunity to make its views known in Parliament.

### Symbolic Functions

A constitution is, or should be, a source of pride and a unifying influence within a political community. Generally this is the case, and certainly it applies to the Constitution of the United States and to the unwritten constitution of Britain. In each of these systems, the constitution, for widely differing reasons, has become a symbol of the society's particular brand of democracy, and, indeed, an object of national pride. In Canada, however, our Constitution has sometimes been maligned. Rooted as it is in English law, it has been, from time to time, a disintegrative symbol for those Canadians who are not of British ancestry.

While it is still too early to come to a firm conclusion, it would appear that at least parts of the 1982 made-in-Canada constitutional reforms, such as the Charter, have come to have important positive symbolic value to most Canadians. As a formal, documentary codification of many constitutional principles

---

1. J. A. Corry and J. E. Hodgetts, *Democratic Government and Politics* (Toronto: University of Toronto Press, 1959), p. 85.

that were previously "unwritten," the 1982 Charter can act as an important *educative* device in teaching new Canadians and young Canadians the basic political values of our system.

On the other side of the coin, however, the decade of "constitutionalizing" since l982 has produced significant negative feelings, not only with respect to the failed *process* of constitutional reform, but also with respect to the *substance* of the Constitution itself. Even though they ended in failure, the Meech Lake and Charlottetown rounds opened up the Constitution to possible improvements, and virtually every Canadian was able to find at least something wrong with it. Our Constitution will never be perfect in the eyes of any specific interest or group, and, far from being a flaw, this is its greatest virtue. Until Canadians accept their Constitution as a reflection of compromise, accommodation, and mutual tolerance over centuries, and embrace that tradition of tolerance and accommodation as one of our most important political values, the Canadian Constitution will never be the unifying national symbol that it should be.

## ▶ ORIGINS

It is the aim of this section to look at the Canadian Constitution as a body of written laws and unwritten principles that are themselves products of our national origins and subsequent patterns of development. As we shall see, the Constitution is a living organism which has been and continues to be shaped by the forces of both heredity and environment.

### Representative and Responsible Government

While the Dominion of Canada formally came into existence with the proclamation of the *British North America Act* on July 1, l867, two of the most important defining principles of our Constitution were already in place in the constitutional practice of the pre-Confederation colonies: **representative government** and **responsible government**. The former means that the legislative branch of government must be representative of its citizenry or *democratic*; the latter means that the executive branch of government can function only with the majority support or *confidence* of the legislature.

These principles had been firmly established in English constitutional practice at least since the 17th century (albeit in more rudimentary forms than are familiar to us today), and it was natural that British colonists would wish to import the best features of the British system to their new homelands.

**The Origins of Canadian Democracy**  The earliest representative institutions in the British colonies of the New World were established first in Virginia and Plymouth in what is now the United States and in Bermuda. These legislatures, each at least partially elected, were put in place in the 1620s with the general support and approbation of the Crown, and by the end of the 17th century British settlements in the American colonies and the West Indies generally enjoyed some form of representative government.

Unfortunately, the importation of English constitutional practice was not achieved as smoothly in the colonies that were to become parts of Canada. The British courts had determined that, in colonies established by peaceful settlement, the colonists were deemed to have taken all of their rights as British subjects with them, including the right to representative institutions of governance. However, the problem with the "Canadian" colonies was that most of them had been acquired by conquest, and as such, said the courts, the English common law did not apply. While the imperial government, as a matter of policy, did promise to extend representative government to the colonies acquired through conquest, the nature and extent of such powers not only varied a great deal from colony to colony but, as well, the colonists themselves had little control over the timing.

While aboriginal people in all parts of Canada point out correctly that they had representative political institutions long before Europeans arrived on these shores, the first representative legislature in colonial Canada was summoned by the governor of Nova Scotia in 1758. Prince Edward Island got its representative assembly in 1773, and New Brunswick, after being split from Nova Scotia in 1784 , was granted its own assembly as well.

Democracy did not come as quickly or as easily to the parts of pre-Confederation Canada that are now Ontario and Quebec. Initially, although Quebec was clearly a conquered territory, the governor of the new colony was instructed by the Proclamation of 1763 to establish a legislative assembly as soon as practicable. However, there were a number of practical obstacles to implementing representative institutions immediately in Quebec. Most importantly, in the population centres such as Montreal, the English-Protestant commercial interests were reluctant to put themselves at the mercy of the recently conquered French-Catholic majority; and there is no indication that the French Canadians themselves, with no tradition of democracy, were even very interested in representative institutions at this time.

In any event, before the governor of the colony could be forced to act on his instructions, the British Parliament enacted the *Quebec Act* of 1774, which revoked the promise of self-government contained in the Proclamation of 1763. The Quebec territory was expanded at this time to include the southern portion of what is now Ontario, much of upstate New York, and Ohio. While the *Quebec Act* was an important recognition of the rights of French Canadians to their own religion and civil law, it also expressed the view that to grant power over such a vast domain to a legislature that would be dominated by the concentration of people in the St. Lawrence Valley would be "inexpedient."

It was the American Revolution that ultimately paved the way for democratic institutions in what is now Ontario and Quebec. The revolution brought a large influx of Loyalists from the American colonies to southern Quebec and to the region north of Lake Ontario and Lake Erie. These new arrivals were long accustomed to self-government and were unwilling to tolerate the status quo under the *Quebec Act*. In 1791, with the passage of the *Constitutional Act*, the portion of the Quebec territory that remained British was divided into Upper and Lower Canada and each was given its own governor and elected assembly.

With the exceptions of Vancouver Island, which had a small elected assembly from 1856, and Newfoundland, which was granted an assembly in 1832, the institutions of British-style representative democracy were not extended to the rest of modern-day Canada until after 1867. However, by 1791 it could be said that representative government was firmly established in those colonies that would ultimately be united as the Dominion of Canada in 1867.

**The Evolution of Responsible Government**  While the institution of representative government in Canada was by any measure a significant accomplishment, it did not go far enough to satisfy the colonists' appetite for full self-government. The problem was that while elected assemblies were in place, they were forced to share their authority with the governor and an appointed executive council. During this period, the cornerstone of the authority of the elected assemblies was, as it is today, their power to levy taxes on the citizenry and to appropriate such revenues to the governor and council. However, the crown at this time did have independent revenue sources, such as income from the disposition of crown land, so it was not always easy for the legislature to force its will on the executive if the governor and his advisors were determined to resist.

Part of the logic for leaving significant authority in the hands of the governor was that he was expected to act on the instructions of the Colonial Office in imperial matters. But the division of powers between the imperial and colonial governments was not clearcut in the real world of colonial politics. Often the priorities of the mother country could overlap and be at odds with the wishes of the assembly in matters of local concern. It appeared that many of the grievances that had triggered the revolt of the American colonies in the 18th century were being replicated in British North America during the first half of the 19th century.

The solution was obvious to the colonial representatives, because that solution had been developed many years before in England: the executive had to be made responsible to the legislature and the appointed executive council could be permitted to function only if it enjoyed the *confidence* of the assembly. In other words, the institutions of representative government had to be complemented by the practices of responsible government.

The fight for responsible government in Canada was essentially unsuccessful until the Rebellions of 1837 in the Canadas. While these uprisings had elements of tragedy, individual courage, and comic opera, the outcome was never in doubt, and the rebels were routed. However, the British government got the message and appointed Lord Durham as a sort of "Super Governor" of all of the British North American colonies. While his famous *Report* presented an extremely broad set of recommendations, many of them still controversial today, the critical recommendation for our purposes here is that he unequivocally advocated responsible government for the colonies.

Many of the recommendations of the *Durham Report* were implemented immediately through statutes such as the *Act of Union* of 1840, which reunited Upper and Lower Canada. However, because responsible government in Britain was and is purely a constitutional practice or *convention*, it was not legislated into effect in Canada either, but left to evolve naturally. There ensued a brief transitional period in which various governors in the colonies gradually accepted incremental steps towards responsible government. But the final step in achieving full-fledged responsible government in Canada was made possible by a change in government in Britain, in 1846, which brought the liberal-minded Earl Grey to the Colonial Office. Grey made it clear to his colonial governors in North America that they should give their full support to the implementation of responsible government.

Responsible government as we know it today was officially launched in Nova Scotia in 1848, where, after a general election, the assembly voted non-confidence in the Executive Council, and the governor of the day asked the leader of the majority party to "form a government." The assemblies in Canada and New Brunswick achieved the same result later the same year.

### Federal Government

We have seen that two of the most important principles of our Constitution, representative and responsible government, trace their origins directly to practices that evolved in Britain. Another cornerstone of our system of government is the institution of federalism, whose roots are not to be found in our English constitutional genes but in our historical experiences in the New World.

**The Historical Causes of Confederation**  In the mid-19th century, as today, perhaps the single most significant factor affecting Canadian political life was the proximity of the United States of America. In the 1860s, people in the British North American colonies were not only faced with an increased protectionist mood in the US but also had cause to fear direct military invasion from the south.

*The Military Threat*  At the conclusion of the Civil War, the Union Army was the most powerful and advanced fighting machine in the world. Furthermore, incidents during the war — for example, the St. Alban's raid in 1864 and the activities of the British-built Confederate cruiser *Alabama* — had incurred the displeasure of the United States. At the conclusion of the war, some of the American press and a few jingoistic congressmen were advocating the outright invasion of Canada, and there was a great fear in Canada that the newspapers would arouse sufficient public pressure to convince Congress and the president that invasion was, indeed, a good idea.

The sense of danger was heightened by the militant activities of the American wing of an Irish nationalist organization called the Fenian Brotherhood. The Fenians attracted large numbers of Irish veterans of the Civil War who were happy to re-enlist in this unofficial army to free Ireland from "English tyranny." One of the ways in which they hoped to achieve this was by conquering Canada. Their sundry pronouncements and the publicity they gained were received with trepidation in Canada. The subsequent "invasions" of British North America by the Fenians were, in retrospect, more farcical than threatening, and all were repulsed without difficulty. But while the menace the Fenians presented to Canada was exaggerated, when added to the existing evidence of an American predisposition to continental imperialism, it did reinforce Canadian perceptions of a military threat from the south.

While Canadians grew increasingly alarmed at the sabre rattling in the United States, the British, who had formerly taken much of the responsibility for defending their North American colonies, began to give every indication that they were no longer willing to go very far in that enterprise. Politicians in Britain began to speak of the desirability of shifting the responsibility for colonial defence to the colonies, and the British Cabinet was not overly generous in its budgeting for such things as the fortifications of Quebec. Thus, while Canadians were looking apprehensively at the military might of the United States, there was little evidence that Britain either shared our concern or was willing to exert very much energy in our defence.

*American Protectionism*   Economic factors also helped in setting the stage for Confederation. Again, the United States played a starring role in our worst nightmares. The immediate economic problems of the British North American colonies actually dated back to 1846, when the Navigation Laws, which gave preferential treatment to colonial trade, were repealed by Britain. However, the negative effect of the repeal had been offset somewhat, at the time, by a **reciprocity agreement** with the United States, which allowed Canadian primary products duty-free access to US markets. In the 1860s, partly because of generally bad British-American relations, and partly because of new domestic economic pressures, the US served notice of its intention to terminate the reciprocity agreement. Reciprocity was finally terminated in 1866, at a time when Britain seemed more committed than ever to eliminating colonial trade preferences. Excluded from the American market, and forced to compete with more advanced economies in the open British market, the British North American colonies looked, perhaps as a last resort, to each other:

> If preferences in Britain and the United States were not to be had, the colonies could at least give preference to each other. Commercial union of the British American provinces would weld them into a single vast trading area within which products might be freely exchanged. If the markets of all the provinces could be opened to the industries of each, an economic system would be created, which, by lessening dependence on external markets, would offer greater stability than the economies of the separate provinces could hope for, and which, because of the diversity and complementarity of its resources, would have a potential for growth.[2]

Technological changes probably helped to accelerate the movement towards Confederation, because the colonial economies were strained by the costs of taking full advantage of new transportation technologies. The shift from sail to steam and from canals to railways, for instance, forced the colonies, especially the Maritimes, to incur large provincial debts:

> By incurring debts to build the railways which they so earnestly desired, the Maritime provinces had, as it were, given hostages to fortune. By increasing the burden of fixed charges on their revenues, they had curtailed their ability to withstand adversity.[3]

2.  W. T. Easterbrook and H. G. J. Aitken, *Canadian Economic History* (Toronto: Macmillan, 1965), p. 251; see also D. Creighton, *British North America at Confederation* (Ottawa: Queen's Printer, 1963).
3.  Easterbrook and Aitken, *Canadian Economic History*, p. 250. Reprinted by permission of Macmillan of Canada, a Division of Canada Publishing Corporation.

*The Intercolonial Railway* A commercial union offered Nova Scotia and New Brunswick not merely the hope of new markets in the Canadas, but also the promise of a share of national revenues, which would ease the burden of their debts. To ensure that the Maritimes would, in fact, gain markets in central Canada, a very specific and, for a constitution, unusual provision promising the construction of the Intercolonial Railway was written directly into the BNA Act:

> It shall be the duty of the Parliament of Canada to provide for the commencement within six months after the Union of a railway connecting the River St. Lawrence with the city of Halifax in Nova Scotia and for the construction thereof without intermission, and the completion thereof with all practicable speed.[4]

While the promise of the Intercolonial Railway looks very much like simply a bribe to entice the Maritimes into the federation, it can be argued that the Canadas also could anticipate certain advantages from the railway. As well as facilitating interprovincial trade, the Intercolonial Railway would provide exporters in Ontario and Quebec with an ice-free port in the winter months, when Quebec City and Montreal were normally closed. This was an important consideration, for Canadian business and mercantile interests feared that the termination of reciprocity by the United States might lead to Canadian exporters' being denied access to the winter ports on the US eastern seaboard. Certainly Maritimers welcomed the jobs handling the transshipment of Canadian goods, in the winter months, through the ports of Halifax and Saint John.

*Reluctant Unity* Political factors also pushed the colonies towards Confederation. The *Act of Union* of 1840 had joined Upper and Lower Canada in an uneasy political marriage that was no longer working. The *Act of Union* had guaranteed equal representation in the colonial legislature to Canada East and Canada West, but by the 1860s the population of Canada West (now Ontario), which was originally smaller than that of Canada East (now Quebec), had been greatly increased by an influx of immigrants. Once the people of Canada West realized that the guarantee of equal representation was working against them, they began to agitate for "representation by population." The French Canadians of Canada East countered with demands for guarantees of their rights as a linguistic, religious, and ethnic minority. The colonial government was left in a constantly shifting but unbreakable deadlock. Hence, Confederation, whatever its faults, offered an immediate solution to the stalemate by providing for the separation of the Canadas once more into two provinces within the larger union.

When we view the history of the Confederation period in Canada, it becomes clear that the section of North America that was to become the province of Ontario had more to gain from union than any other:

> The complicated compromise which was finally embodied in the British North America Act reflected in large part the aspirations and interests of that populous, prosperous and dynamic region [Upper Canada], with such concessions to Lower

---

4. Ibid.

Canada and the Maritimes as were necessary to gain the support of their leaders for union.[5]

The Maritimes saw certain economic advantages in Confederation, but a large proportion of the people living in New Brunswick and Nova Scotia were fervently opposed to any agreement that tied them to Canada. It can even be argued that the Maritimes were never really in favour of Confederation, and were railroaded into it, literally, by the promise of a railway, and ultimately by the complicated political manoeuvring and the silver tongue of Sir John A. Macdonald. French-Canadian politicians saw Confederation as a way of safeguarding their language and religious rights and, on the whole, as a lesser evil than the Union of 1840. Generally, it can be concluded that there was little common purpose, no vision of greatness, and no noble cause that united Canada initially. Perhaps, as Professor Smiley points out,

> the underlying agreement among colonial politicians which made Confederation possible was that the continuance of monarchial and parliamentary institutions and of the British connection was infinitely preferable to absorption into the U.S.[6]

This seems a very negative motivation for national unity, and it must be asked whether fear of invasion can ever produce any lasting unity among people once the threat has dissipated.

To return to the original query as to what motivated the British colonies in North America to seek a union of some kind, one finds a generally negative and unstable set of attitudes towards Confederation in 1867. Apparently abandoned by the mother country and left prey to the military and economic might of the war-torn but brawny United States, the British North American colonies turned, in desperation, to each other.

**The Genesis of Federal Union**  Having described the hesitant and uncertain way in which the colonies finally reached a reluctant agreement that some form of union was desirable for British North America, let us deal with the forces and events that influenced the decision that the union should be *federal* in form. The social, economic, and ethnic diversity of the colonies made a **unitary** form of government, or legislative union as it was then called, completely unacceptable to the Maritimes and Quebec, although evidence indicates that Macdonald and many of his Upper Canadian colleagues preferred this alternative. Quebec wished to preserve its unique linguistic, religious, and cultural character, and the Maritimes wished to ensure that the peculiar economic needs of their region be provided for. All provinces wished to retain control over matters that would allow them to preserve their local character and institutions. Provincial autonomy, therefore, had to be guaranteed before the Maritimes and Quebec would agree to a union.

Given the obvious differences that existed among the founding provinces, the Fathers of Confederation realized that a legislative union was not a viable

---

5.  D. V. Smiley, *The Canadian Political Nationality* (Toronto: Methuen, 1967), pp. 13–14.
6.  *Ibid.,* p. 2.

alternative for British North America. Furthermore, it was hoped that Prince Edward Island, British Columbia, Newfoundland, and the Northwest could subsequently be lured into the union, in which case the regional and economic diversity of Canada would increase rather than diminish. Even Macdonald recognized that there could be no union *a mare usque ad mare* unless the provinces retained some degree of local autonomy:

> Macdonald argued the case for a legislative rather than a federal union, yet geography, provincial identities and Quebec separateness united to confound his principle. He was deftly persuaded from his folly.[7]

*Military and Trade Alliance*  The alternative of an economic and military **alliance** of the British North American colonies was initially considered as a form of union that would go a long way towards solving the immediate problems of the 1860s. At both the Charlottetown and Quebec conferences, a British North American customs union, or *Zollverein*, was suggested — in effect, a form of free trade that would leave the sovereignty of the members intact. The main problem here was that neither a customs union nor a military alliance would provide a permanent central decision-making body or a central enforcement mechanism. Since there would be no derogation of the sovereignty of the signatories of the treaty or alliance, the alliance itself would be powerless to enforce its own provisions.

A second problem with such a loose form of union is that it would have been ineffectual in financing the joint defence or economic programs of the union. A project such as the Intercolonial Railway, for instance, would have been out of the question. Macdonald recognized the inadvisability of a customs union and suggested that, because of the potential economic conflicts between the colonies, it would not always be congenial to all its members: "It is impossible to have a *Zollverein*. We must continue to have hostile tariffs unless we have a political union."[8]

A third major disadvantage of any form of less-than-political union was that it would lack permanence. Members would have the right to withdraw from it at any time if they felt that its terms were no longer advantageous. It was obvious that if the economic and military problems of British North America were to be solved, they would have to be dealt with continuously over a long period of time. It was not possible to find immediate cures for the ills of the colonies; therefore, a form of union that was not for keeps would not be acceptable.

The fourth drawback of a simple alliance of the British North American colonies was that an alliance is *functionally specific*. In other words, the terms of reference or functions of the alliance are set very specifically at the outset, in such a way that new needs of the members of the alliance cannot be addressed without renegotiating the original agreement. In a rapidly changing world, a form of union that could adapt itself quickly to the performance of new functions was viewed as imperative.

---

7.  Rod Preece, "The Political Wisdom of Sir John A. Macdonald," *Canadian Journal of Political Science*, September 1984, p. 479.
8.  G. P. Browne, ed., *Documents on the Confederation of British North America* (Toronto: McClelland and Stewart, 1969), p. 96.

**TABLE 5.1**

Forms of Political Asssociation

| Form | Locus of Power | Structural Arrangements | Examples | Level of Political Integration |
|------|----------------|-------------------------|----------|-------------------------------|
| Unitary state | undivided sovereignty | single level of government | UK, Sweden, France | highest |
| Centralized federation | divided sovereignty; division of powers; *de facto* residuary power with central government | two sovereign orders of government; dispute settlement by judicial review | US, Germany, Canada in 1867 | high |
| Decentralized federation | same as above but *de facto* residuary power with states/provinces | same as above; many non-binding intergovernmental pacts | Canada, Switzerland | medium high |
| Confederation | sovereignty with member states; powers of congress only delegated | non-sovereign central congress; laws of congress not binding | US before 1789, European Union in the 1990s | low; voluntary participation in the union |
| Common market, free trade area | member states remain sovereign | non-binding dispute resolution | EEC (at first), FTA, NAFTA | economic integration only |
| Military alliance, specific treaty | no derogation of sovereignty | summit meetings; may be an assembly | NATO, SEATO, North Atlantic Fisheries Organization (NAFO) | none |

There were other objections to a non-political union: a mere alliance would not satisfy the need for Canada East and Canada West to be politically separated, and the colonies within the British Empire were not sovereign and therefore could not enter into alliances unilaterally, even with sister colonies. These objections were secondary, however, and could have been overcome had the notion of an economic and military alliance been otherwise acceptable.

*The Confederation Option*   A **confederal** union was also an alternative for the British North American colonies, but when this form of union was subjected to scrutiny, it was recognized that a confederation[9] would provide only a slightly higher level of political integration than an alliance. A confederation is a union of sovereign states that features a permanent central decision-making body, or congress, to which the members of the confederation send delegates. In terms of the matters with which it deals, a confederation is considerably broader than an alliance, for the central congress is empowered to make decisions concerning a very wide range of subjects.

The weakness of a confederation is that, as with an alliance, there is no transfer of sovereignty from the member states to the central congress. While empowered to make decisions, the congress is given no power to enforce them,

---

9. "The term 'Confederation,' when applied to the Canadian union of 1867, is a misnomer, for the form of government set up by the BNA Act is definitely not 'confederal.' 'Confederation,' a word normally associated with the absence of a strong federal government, was deliberately misused by those who, in fact, intended to create one in an effort to confuse those who might find such a project alarming." Garth Stevenson, *Unfulfilled Union: Canadian Federalism and Canadian Unity* (Toronto: Gage, 1987), p. 9.

and the members of the confederation can, if they choose, refuse to comply with any decision with which they disagree. The parties to a confederal agreement also have the right to secede from the union if they feel that its terms of reference no longer provide sufficient benefits.

Thus, while the confederal form of union is functionally more diffuse than an alliance, it suffers from many of the same faults. Furthermore, the historical lesson of the United States under the Articles of Confederation in the 1780s, with the chaotic and unpredictable conditions that prevailed during that period, gave the Fathers of Confederation ample cause for avoiding that particular form of union.

*Federalism* A **federal** form of union was ultimately decided upon by the Fathers of Confederation because, unlike either an alliance or a confederal union, it vests real powers in the hands of a central legislature, the federal Parliament. In a federal system, sovereignty is distributed among provincial and federal governments, and the exercise of legislative and executive powers is limited to subject matters allotted to each level or order of government by the constitution. A federal system is also an unbreakable and permanent union, in the sense that the member states or provinces do not have the constitutional right to withdraw unilaterally from the union. While this prohibition might prove *practically* unenforceable if the people of a member state or province were determined to secede, in *law* a federal state is indivisible.

The constitution of a federal system must distribute legislative authority between the provincial and federal orders of government, and the division of power is intended to be *exhaustive*; that is, *all* matters of legislative authority are parcelled out and must fall within the jurisdiction of one of the two orders of government. The only exception to this principle of **exhaustiveness** in Canada is that under the Charter of Rights and Freedoms, some matters are deemed to be so important in terms of individual rights and freedoms that they are placed beyond the reach of *all* governments. In a confederal union, on the other hand, it is simply assumed that the state or provincial governments have the responsibility for everything except a few matters that are specifically the responsibility of the confederation.

To explain this in another way, in the case of a confederation, the **residual power** is always left with the states, and constitutes a very large area of jurisdiction. By contrast, in a federal system, the jurisdiction of the two levels of government is parcelled out more comprehensively and the residual power can be left with either the provinces or the federal government. In either case, the residual area of jurisdiction is intended to be very small. The advantage of such a comprehensive definition of the powers and responsibilities of government is that the element of uncertainty is eliminated. The federal government and the provincial or state governments are each in possession of exclusive and sovereign powers that cannot be encroached upon by the other level of government. Unlike the central congress in a confederal union, the national government in a federal system has the authority to make a range of decisions that are binding on the citizens of the member states, and furthermore, it is granted the power to enforce them.

**The Confederation Bargain**  The constitutional arrangement that emerged from the Confederation period was very much the product of a complex process of **elite accommodation.** In the first instance, the Confederation agreement was the result of a deal worked out between colonial and imperial elites, which allocated powers and responsibilities between the new Dominion and the mother country. Secondly, the overall thrust of the new arrangement was to protect the existing commercial and mercantile interests in the new Dominion and those of its major trading partner, Britain.

Certainly the *people* of the British North American colonies had little to say about the deal that was struck in 1867. The colonial economic and political elites of the time were either "interlocking" or they worked together very closely to maximize and consolidate their mutual advantage. The Fathers of Confederation (it is significant but not surprising, for the time, that there were no "Mothers of Confederation") may have had different views about the appropriate balance between federal and provincial powers, but they were in complete agreement that the Canadian union should be based upon "peace, order, and good government" rather than upon the American heresy, "life, liberty and the pursuit of happiness."

While we do not wish to go so far as some American textbooks, which refer to that country's founding fathers as "godlike men" who were "divinely inspired,"[10] we perhaps should not be too hard on the men who forged the Confederation agreement. A federal form of government was adopted by the Fathers of Confederation because they hoped to create a union that would eventually become more than a marriage of economic expedience and military convenience. People like Sir John A. Macdonald wished to create a new political community in North America, and it is largely to their credit that Canada has evolved as more than a merely temporary association of friendly but independent neighbours.

The actual shape of our federal system, and the idiosyncracies that make Canadian federalism a genre apart, also bear the stamp of Macdonald's strong personality and vision — not to mention political ambition — and of his view of the ideal relationship that should exist between the provinces and the national government in a federal system. Having in mind the then-recent and tragic experiences of the Civil War in the United States, Macdonald wanted to see as centralized a federal system as the provinces would accept: "We should concentrate the power in the federal government and not adopt the decentralization of the United States."[11]

There is some evidence that Macdonald viewed federalism somewhat cynically — as a temporary arrangement to secure initial unity — and that he fully expected provincial governments to wither away from lack of exercise, leaving a basically unitary system in place in Canada. Indeed, some aspects of the BNA Act, 1867, indicate that the intention of the drafters of the Act was to leave the

---

10.  Theodore Lowi, *American Government,* 2nd ed., (New York: W. W. Norton, 1994), pp. 27, 59.
11.  Browne, *Documents on the Confederation,* p. 124.

preponderance of legislative power with Ottawa.[12] But in spite of these biases, the *British North America Act* does vest some significant legislative power in the provinces. As one eminent political scientist once asserted: "The provinces are of equal constitutional power and status, and they operate without any serious interference from the Dominion. . . . Provincial powers are as full and complete as those of the Dominion within the areas allotted by the BNA Act."[13]

Thus, the federal component of our Constitution was not inherited from the English constitutional tradition; rather, it was a product of forces unique to Canada in the pre-Confederation period. The original impetus for some kind of political union was a perceived threat from the United States and a belief on the part of the colonial elites that there were benefits to having a free-trade arrangement among the British North American colonies. The fact that the ultimate form of union agreed to was *federal* was the result of a fundamental tension between those who believed in a dominant central government and those who preferred the sovereign powers to rest with the provinces. A confederal union was unacceptable to the former and a unitary state was unacceptable to the latter, so that a federal union was the compromise option. As we shall see in later chapters, these same centrifugal and centripetal forces have continued to shape the federal aspects of our Constitution to the present day.

---

### ▶ CONSTITUTIONAL DEVELOPMENT

The development of the Canadian Constitution from Confederation to the present day can be analyzed in terms of at least four distinct themes. The first theme focuses on the quest for a clarification of the distribution of legislative jurisdiction between the provinces and the federal government. This we will address in Chapter 8. A second theme, which emerged in the period after the Second World War, focuses on providing for more adequate protection of individual rights and freedoms and for the rights of minorities. This will be addressed in Chapter 7. The other two themes, the quest for an acceptable amending formula, which would allow for the patriation of the Constitution, a process that began in earnest in the 1940s, and the search in the 1980s for a "once and for all" accommodation of the needs of Quebec within the Constitution, we shall deal with in this section.

#### The Search for an Amending Formula: 1867–1982

The stimulus for the constitutional quest for an amending formula was the fact that the core document of our Constitution, the BNA Act, contained no general provision for its amendment when it was passed in 1867. Since it was a statute of the Parliament of Britain, it seemed obvious at the time that it could and would be amended by ordinary British legislation. At Confederation,

---

12. W. L. Morton describes the union as "a scheme of legislative union in a federal guise." See W. L. Morton, *The Critical Years* (Toronto: McClelland and Stewart, 1964), p. 68. See also R. C. Vipond, "Constitutional Politics and the Legacy of the Provincial Rights Movement in Canada," *Canadian Journal of Political Science*, June 1985, pp. 271–75.
13. R. MacGregor Dawson, *The Government of Canada* (Toronto: University of Toronto Press, 1970), p. 78.

Canada was subordinate to the supreme British Parliament, and our evolution to the independent status that we enjoy today was not foreseen by the British Parliament or even by the Fathers of Confederation.

**The Problem**   The inability of the Dominion of Canada to amend the BNA Act soon became a problem for the young country, growing rapidly both in political autonomy and in population, and faced with a growing number of responsibilities due to the increasing involvement of government generally in matters such as education, welfare, and public works. In response to demands for formal change of the BNA Act, a method that involved various conventional procedures for amendment was gradually developed.

_Amendment by Joint Address_   At the core of the procedure for amendment of the BNA Act were four conventions or practices that defined the respective roles of the provincial legislatures, the federal Parliament, and the Parliament of Britain. The earliest of these to evolve was that the Parliament of Britain would not amend the BNA Act without an express request by Canada. This convention, recognized before the turn of the century, was affirmed by the Statute of Westminster in 1931:

> No act of Parliament of the United Kingdom passed after the commencement of this act shall extend or be deemed to extend, to a Dominion as part of the law of that Dominion, unless it is expressly declared in that act that the Dominion has requested, and consented to, the enactment thereof.

The second convention was that a request for amendment must be by the Canadian *Parliament* and not by the executive. Thus, the standard means that emerged for requesting British legislative action was a joint address or "resolution" of the House of Commons and the Senate. The resolution was presented to the Queen in the form of a draft amendment with an attached request to place it on the agenda of the UK Parliament. The third convention was the positive aspect of the first: that is, that the British Parliament *would act* to amend the BNA Act if requested to do so by a joint address of the Canadian Parliament. While this convention was never given statutory expression, there were no cases from 1867 to 1982 in which the British Parliament refused to meet the request of the Dominion with regard to amendment of the BNA Act.

The fourth convention was far more complicated than either of the first two, for it involved the extent to which the consultation and consent of the provinces should be sought by the federal government prior to petitioning Britain by a joint address. There are some facts that will guide us to a better understanding of the practice that evolved in this area. First, the British Parliament never amended the BNA Act on the request of a province or of any number of the provinces, unless the provinces' wishes happened to be expressed in a joint address by both Houses of the Canadian Parliament. Second, the British Parliament never turned down a request for amendment by the federal government because the amendment was opposed by the provinces or by any particular province.[14] However, by the 1960s and 1970s the provinces

---

14.  For details on past practice, see Canada, *The Canadian Constitution and Constitutional Amendment* (Ottawa: Federal Provincial Relations Office, 1978), p. 13. This paper comprises a useful survey of practice in four other federations, a historical summary, and a proposal for alternatives.

had become so powerful politically that it was generally agreed in Canada that it would not be legitimate for the Parliament of Canada to request an amendment that might affect provincial powers without obtaining the agreement of the provinces.

The original argument for the participation of the provinces in the amendment of the BNA Act stems from a theory of confederation that has become known as the **compact theory**. The compact theory of the Canadian federal system states that the Act of 1867 was, in effect, a treaty or a *compact* among equal political entities in existence before Confederation. It followed that any changes to the original agreement could be made only with the consent of all the original participants. Despite the fact that the compact theory had little historical validity,[15] the custom of consulting the provinces whenever an amendment under contemplation involved their rights did evolve over the years. This practice was sanctified by the Supreme Court of Canada in its decision regarding the constitutionality of the federal move to unilaterally patriate the Constitution in 1981. Here the judgement of a majority of the court was that a federal request to Britain for significant amendments to the BNA Act required, by convention, the "substantial agreement" of the provinces.

*Parliamentary Amendment: 1949–1982*  In 1949, by a joint address of the Canadian Parliament, an amendment to the BNA Act was secured, which gave the federal Parliament the power to amend, by simple act of Parliament, the "Constitution of Canada," with the exception of provisions that dealt with the guarantees of minority-language and education rights, the rights of the provinces, the provision regarding the five-year limit on the life of a Parliament, and the requirement that the federal Parliament meet at least once a year. The weakness of this provision, section 91(1), was that virtually any amendment to the Constitution could be construed as affecting provincial powers. In fact, the only judicial test of the scope of 91(1) came in a 1980 reference case, when federal draft legislation to alter the structure and appointment procedure of the Senate was declared *ultra vires* the Parliament of Canada. The basic reasoning was that the Senate provides for representation of provincial interests, and to alter the system of appointment or to abolish the Senate entirely would constitute an abrogation of provincial rights. Hence, the court held that it was a matter explicitly excluded from the scope of section 91(1).[16]

In the end, the amending power of section 91(1) was used only five times before the 1982 amending formula replaced it, and three of these instances involved redistribution of seats in the House of Commons. The other two altered the rules of the Senate (compulsory retirement at age seventy-five, in 1965, and granting representatives to the Northwest Territories and the Yukon,

---

15.  Dawson, *The Government of Canada*, p. 124. See also N. M. Rogers, "The Compact Theory of Confederation," in *Proceedings of the Canadian Political Science Association*, 1931, pp. 205–30; and G. F. G. Stanley, "Act or Pact? Another Look at Confederation," C.H.A. *Annual Report* (Ottawa: Canadian Historical Association, 1956).

16.  *Reference Re: Legislative Authority of Parliament to Alter or Replace the Senate* (1980), 1 SCR. 54. Note that while this indicated a willingness on the part of the Supreme Court to interpret the scope of section 91(1) narrowly, it did not deal expressly with the question of whether the *Supreme Court Act* should be considered a part of the "Constitution of Canada."

in 1974), but not in a manner that seriously affected the interests of the provinces. The effect of this unilateral amending power was therefore insignificant, particularly when combined with the practical political limits on federal interference with the provinces. By 1980, most of the Constitution of Canada was, in effect, unamendable, and the only resolution of this stalemate lay in securing federal-provincial agreement on a formal amending formula.

**Early Efforts to Find a Formula** The question of how to deal with the amendment of those parts of the Constitution of Canada that were explicitly excluded from 91(1) and, by convention, were precluded from change by joint address unless there was substantial agreement of the provinces, was the subject of much debate from 1950 to 1982. In fact, dating back to 1927, there were many federal-provincial conferences devoted almost entirely to discussions of how the procedure for the amendment of the BNA Act could be completely "Canadianized," that is, how it could be changed so that the Canadian Parliament would no longer have to petition Britain's Parliament in order to get the Act amended.

We must remember that Britain's Parliament never did particularly cherish the function it was called upon, from time to time, to perform on our behalf, and, in fact, at the time of the passage of the Statute of Westminster in 1931, Britain attempted to give the Parliament of Canada the unilateral power to amend the BNA Act in its entirety. Canada refused because of pressures from the provinces. The problem in finding a satisfactory all-Canadian amending scheme was that we in Canada could not agree which legislatures should have the power to amend which parts of the BNA Act. Several schemes were proposed, the most promising of which involved a detailed breakdown of the various clauses of the BNA Act into categories, according to the relative extent of federal and provincial participation required.

The Fulton-Favreau Formula of 1964[17] was rejected by Quebec because the requirement for unanimity to change the federal-provincial distribution of powers would inhibit Quebec's push to *expand* its own powers through bilateral deals with the federal government. The successor to the Fulton-Favreau Formula was the Victoria Charter of June 1971. This document, agreed to by all federal and provincial representatives, was similar in many respects to the one that was ultimately implemented in 1982, but it was subsequently rejected by the premier of Quebec after some apparent scolding from his cabinet colleagues. The problem was not with the amending formula, which gave Quebec a veto, but with an obscure section of the agreement that could have had the result of permanently entrenching or even expanding federal powers in the area of social policy.

In June, 1978, the efforts to secure an agreement again heated up, largely in response to the election of a separatist government in Quebec. The federal government published two white papers: *A Time for Action*, which set out general principles for "constitutional renewal," and *The Canadian Constitution and Constitutional Amendment*, which suggested alternative formal means for constitutional amendment, but did not choose among them. The Senate was

---

17. This version came to be known as the Fulton-Favreau Formula after the two federal justice ministers who held office while it was being drafted.

to be abolished and replaced by a "House of the Federation" with significantly increased powers; the size of and method of appointment to the Supreme Court was to be altered; and there was to be a constitutional requirement for an annual first ministers' meeting. Among various other provisions, a Charter of Rights and Freedoms was to be entrenched in the Constitution. As to the process of formal constitutional amendment, the federal proposals were similar to those included in the Fulton-Favreau Formula and the Victoria Charter, but with the added twist of possible ratification by referendum.

Like their predecessors, the constitutional talks of the late seventies did not bear fruit; indeed, the discussions did not progress far beyond early skirmishing over the proposals for changes to federal institutions. Several provinces were suspicious that the more effective representation of regional interests in the Senate would greatly strengthen the *national* institutions of "intrastate federalism" at the expense of provincial governments. Many premiers felt that institutions such as a House of the Federation would weaken their legitimacy as provincial spokespersons at first ministers conferences. In some ways, the 1978 proposals failed because they tried to do too many things through a single initiative instead of concentrating on finding an amending formula. In a manner sadly prophetic of what was to happen to the Charlottetown Accord, the 1978 constitutional reform proposals collapsed under their own weight and complexity.

**1982: "Substantial Agreement"**   In September, 1980, Prime Minister Trudeau made one final attempt to reach a consensus with the premiers. Although some agreement was reached on a few issues, the sought-after consensus failed to materialize, and on October 2, 1980, Trudeau announced the intention of the federal government to go it alone and unilaterally seek patriation through a joint address. Although the federal initiative was strongly opposed by eight of the provinces (Ontario and New Brunswick supported the proposal), the federal government pressed on, and on November 6, 1980, a special joint committee of the House of Commons and the Senate commenced hearings on the constitutional resolution.

Finally, after a stormy passage of the resolution through both houses of Parliament, and after the Supreme Court of Canada declared that the unilateral action of the federal government was "legal" (but in violation of a convention that required "substantial provincial agreement"), the provinces agreed to a last-ditch effort to reach a consensus. A compromise constitutional accord between the federal government and all of the provinces but Quebec was signed on November 4, 1981, and the necessary amendments were passed by Parliament on December 8. The "Canada Bill" was given final approval by the British House of Lords in March, 1982, and was proclaimed as the *Constitution Act*, 1982, on 17 April, 1982. As we shall see in Chapter 7, the *Constitution Act* of 1982 does somewhat more than simply achieve the patriation of the BNA Act with an amending procedure, for it also provides an entrenched Charter of Rights and Freedoms. However, the "success" of 1982 without the agreement of Quebec was to trigger the next ten years of constitutionalizing in Canada.

### Constitutional Renewal: "The Quebec Round," 1982–1995

The 1982 amending formula has been used infrequently, and in the few instances that it was employed, it dealt with fairly routine "process" issues or tidying the wording of the 1982 Act to clarify the intent. Hence, sections were added in 1983 that committed the governments of Canada and the provinces to hold a series of first ministers conferences on aboriginal self-government. These conferences were held and ended in stalemate, and the enabling amendment automatically lapsed.

Other amendments that were also proclaimed in 1983 clarified the definition of aboriginal *treaty* rights to include "modern treaties or land claims agreements." As well, section 35.1 was added to guarantee that before any amendment affecting aboriginal rights — that is, section 91(24) of the *Constitution Act*, 1867, or sections 25 and 35 of the *Constitution Act*, 1982 — there had to be a constitutional conference to which the representatives of the aboriginal peoples of Canada would be invited. Finally, a clause was added to section 35 guaranteeing aboriginal rights equally to men and women.

**The Meech Lake and Charlottetown Accords**   That there have been but few amendments to the Constitution from 1982 to the present is not for lack of trying. As mentioned above, an "aboriginal round" of constitutional conferences, which would have put provisions respecting aboriginal self-government into the Constitution, ended in March, 1987, without agreement. The only significant outcome of these conferences was that for the first time aboriginal leaders and territorial first ministers sat at the table with the prime minister and the premiers. That this apparent precedent was ignored in the subsequent Meech Lake process may have played a role in ultimately dooming that effort to failure.

*Meech Lake*   The Meech Lake Accord was the end product of what has been referred to as the "Quebec round" of constitutional conferences. It was motivated by a desire on the part of the prime minister and the premier of Quebec to secure amendments to the *Constitution Act*, 1982, that would allow Quebec to "sign on." While it is important to emphasize that the 1982 Act applies to Quebec despite the fact that Quebec did not consent to it, Brian Mulroney and Robert Bourassa, particularly, felt it was important to find a constitutional accommodation between the interests of Quebec and the rest of Canada. Many of the rest of the premiers more or less went along with the process in hopes that some of their particular constitutional hobby horses, such as Senate reform, might be dealt with as part of the package, or as part of a package in a later round.

While the accord was originally negotiated at private meetings at Meech Lake, it was renegotiated and fine tuned in a number of subsequent sessions. In its final form the accord met most of Quebec's bottom-line demands but was acceptable to the rest of the premiers only because they also got what Quebec got. Hence, where Quebec had demanded a veto over a wider range of constitutional amendments, this was achieved by increasing the list of matters that required the unanimous consent of the provinces. Similarly, the provinces were to be given the right to nominate Supreme Court judges and sena-

8 PART Two: The Constitution

tors, all provinces were to be given the right to opt out of federal programs in provincial areas of jurisdiction with compensation if they had programs "consistent with national objectives," and the provinces were to be given the right to negotiate constitutionally entrenched agreements with the federal government on immigration. The "distinct society clause," which recognizes the distinctive nature of Quebec society, was a bit more problematic because it could not be granted to all of the provinces. However, agreement was finally reached on wording that was acceptable to all governments.

The Meech Lake Accord was a remarkable achievement in that it was unanimously endorsed by all of the premiers and the prime minister — a rare consensus on constitutional matters. However, the subsequent process of ratification by the legislatures and Parliament ultimately ran aground, with fatal consequences for the accord.

One of the tragic flaws in the ratification process was that it simply took too long to accomplish. Flushed with the successful negotiation of a deal, our political leaders failed to put in place any sort of timetable for completing the process of ratification. As a result, the only deadline for completion was the three-year time limit that is written into the amending formula itself. Only Quebec recognized the importance of finishing the job before the bloom was off the rose, and its National Assembly ratified immediately. Most of the other provinces and the federal government apparently felt that there was no rush, and even proceeded to hold public hearings on the accord before putting it before the legislatures. This not only allowed time for the forces of opposition to gear up, but also made it inevitable that several provincial elections would have to be held before final approval. In the end, four of the premiers who had signed the accord lost elections and were replaced with leaders from other parties, many of whom had actually campaigned on an anti-Meech platform.

Meanwhile, the public hearings being held by the various governments did not bode well for the agreement either, with each hearing process culminating in a long list of things that were wrong with the package of reforms. The catch here was that Quebec had already ratified, stating that the provisions of the accord represented a "bottom-line" bare minimum for that province, and that nothing could be reopened in the current round. Hence, many governments were faced with the awkward situation of holding hearings, with much pious speechifying about the importance of public participation, and then explaining that no matter what came out of the hearings, nothing could be changed.

Besides the fact that the *process* was seriously flawed, the substantive critiques of the accord were indeed compelling to a lot of Canadians. Women's groups were angry that there were no protections for their rights in the accord and they mobilized nationally to oppose ratification. Aboriginal peoples, angry that their concerns were ignored in this round of constitutionalizing, were also insulted that Quebec was recognized as a "distinct society" while Canada's original peoples were to be treated as just another interest group. Finally, although amounting to fewer than a hundred thousand, the residents of the northern territories deeply resented the fact that their aspirations for provincehood at some point in the future had been dashed by the provision that the creation of new provinces out of federal territories could now be vetoed by a single province.

The already lukewarm reception of the accord in English Canada and particularly in the West was cooled still more by the sequence of events in Quebec that culminated in the Bourassa government's reinstating the English-only sign laws by using the *non-obstante* clause after the Supreme Court of Canada had declared the law to be contrary to the Charter. If this was what the "distinct society" clause was all about, then perhaps English Canadians should be extremely wary of its implications for the rights and freedoms of non-French speakers in the province of Quebec.

In the end, despite the eleventh-hour conclusion of a "companion agreement" to the Meech Lake Accord, which promised a new constitutional round to deal with the smorgasbord of concerns not yet addressed, the accord was doomed. Canadians will long remember the lonely battle of Elijah Harper in the Manitoba legislature, the clumsy efforts of the Mulroney government to salvage the deal, and Clyde Wells' ultimate withdrawal of the ratification resolution in the Newfoundland legislative assembly. Three years after the euphoric orgy of mutual backslapping and self-congratulation on the part of our first ministers, the Meech Lake Accord was dead.

*Charlottetown*  Faced with a new upsurge of nationalism in Quebec and with strong signs of growing aboriginal discontent such as the armed confrontation at Oka, a new round of constitutionalizing began almost immediately after the demise of Meech. Having learned some lessons from the Meech Lake debacle, governments decided to take the novel approach of holding the public consultation *before* the reform package was negotiated by the first ministers. Quebec produced the Belanger-Campeau Report, Canada set up both the "Citizens Forum" chaired by Keith Spicer and the Beaudoin-Edwards parliamentary committee, and all of the provinces and territories had their own public consultations.

The federal government unveiled its constitutional proposals in September, 1991, in a booklet entitled *Shaping Canada's Future Together* and then set up another parliamentary committee to hold public hearings on its contents. This Beaudoin-Dobbie committee, after months of hearings and a rough reception in many parts of Canada, produced a report entitled *A Renewed Canada* at the end of February, 1992. This was the set of proposals that the federal government took to the constitutional conferences that led to the signing of the Charlottetown Accord at the end of August.

If the Meech Lake Accord was complex, its successor, the Charlottetown Accord, was positively Byzantine. This agreement included most of what had been contained in the Meech Lake Accord, but in addition it had extensive provisions on matters such as recognizing an inherent right to aboriginal self-government, an elected and reconstituted Senate, gender equality, guaranteed representation in the House of Commons, a statement on the Social and Economic Union, and elimination of the federal powers of reservation and disallowance. As spice to this already aromatic constitutional soup were added specific provisions allowing the federal government to create new provinces out of federal territories but with the participation of the resident northerners, guaranteed representation of aboriginal people in the Senate, guaranteed participation of aboriginal people and territorial governments in annual first-ministers conferences, and much more.

The process leading to Charlottetown was very different from the process of Meech Lake. Not only were the negotiations preceded by extensive public consultation, but the representation at the actual bargaining sessions was expanded to include representatives of four national aboriginal organizations and the first ministers of the Northwest Territories and the Yukon. While the negotiations themselves were held behind closed doors, the process was far more inclusive than the talks that led to Meech Lake, and the closed doors themselves were distinctly porous.

Moreover, the outcome, unanimous agreement among seventeen political leaders representing very diverse interests, on some sixty individual proposals, was an incredible accomplishment. Unfortunately for the accord and for the seventeen sets of political elites that laboured so hard and so effectively to reach an accommodation among themselves, the decision had already been taken in most jurisdictions to submit the package to the test of public approval in a referendum before proceeding to formal ratification in the legislature. As we now know, 55 per cent of those Canadians casting a ballot voted no to the agreement and it was suddenly as dead as its predecessor, Meech Lake.

The explanation for the large "no" vote in the referendum is, at the most simplistic level, that Québécois thought it did not give them enough and the rest of Canada thought it gave Quebec too much. However, it also may have signalled a general disillusionment of Canadians from all parts of the country, including aboriginal Canadians, with their leaders. In other words, Canadians may have been rejecting the politicians who negotiated the deal as much as the deal itself. Finally, a lesson of the no vote to those who would engage in constitutional renewal in the future is that the question must be more specific and more understandable. If sixty complex sets of provisions are tied together to be either approved or rejected by the people, everyone will be able to find something that he or she understands but does not like, and much that is incomprehensible — but darkly suspicious!

### The Future of Constitutional Change

While little of substance was changed, the implications of the past decade of constitutionalizing on the process of constitutional change are many, and some of them may not yet be apparent. Among the most important of these is that it is now likely a convention of our Constitution that major amendments will have to be referred to the people for approval before going before the legislature for formal ratification. While such referenda would not be formally binding on the legislatures, no legislature could afford politically to ignore the outcome of such canvasses of public opinion.

A second implication is that the classical "executive federalism" model of constitutional conferences, with meetings of the ten premiers and the prime minister held in secret, is no longer acceptable. In its place is a process that requires a lot of public consultation before the first meetings are held, a much less secretive kind of bargaining, and a more inclusive list of invitees, including aboriginal leaders and the first ministers of the territories.

Finally, it has become clear that the "big bang" theory of constitutional politics does not work. Problems will have to be dealt with piecemeal and modes of constitutional change less dramatic and more informal than "unan-imous-consent-type" amendments will have to be employed. Constitutional conflicts can still be resolved by bilateral arrangements between the federal government and Quebec or any other province. Aboriginal people can be given self-government through negotiated treaties as they already have in northern Quebec, the Yukon, and Nunavut, or they can simply assert that an *inherent* right already exists in section 35 of the *Constitution Act*, 1982, and take steps to exercise it. As well, we have the example of New Brunswick, which entrenched the rights of the English and French languages in the province through an amendment to section 43(b), which required only the ratification of the federal Parliament and the New Brunswick Legislative Assembly.

It is clear that average Canadians and even most of our politicians are, in general, fed up with the high cost, in terms of money and political angst, of comprehensive constitutional reform. The only circumstances that could con-ceivably trigger another round of such talks would be a vote for independence in the province of Quebec.

*Chapter* **6**

# The Constitution Today: Component Parts and Operative Principles

In the previous chapter we examined the Constitution in terms of what it is supposed to do, how it came into being, and how it has developed and evolved. The aim of this chapter is to look at the substance of our Constitution today and what it means in terms of the actual **operation** of our governmental institutions. However, before moving to a discussion of the **operative principles**, it is appropriate to say a few words about the Constitution's component parts.

## ▶ COMPONENTS: WRITTEN AND UNWRITTEN

It has become a tradition of political science, when making comparisons between the political systems of the United Kingdom and the United States, to state that the former has an unwritten constitution and the latter a written one. This distinction is a relative rather than a categoric one, which places constitutions, for the purposes of comparison, on a continuum ranging between the hypothetical extremes of "purely written" and "purely unwritten." Upon examination, it rapidly becomes apparent that the constitutions of the two largest English-speaking democracies are neither purely written nor purely unwritten. The American Constitution, which started with the impressive document of 1789, has been filled out by conventions, judicial decisions, and statutes that express "fundamental" principles. Similarly, Britain's Constitution, while consisting largely of principles embodied in the common law, has, at its core, written documents such as the Magna Carta and the Petition of Right. The Canadian Constitution, which consists of a hodgepodge of written documents, judicial interpretations, and unwritten conventions, falls on the continuum somewhere between the constitutions of Britain and the United States.

Constitutions that are primarily either written or unwritten may have different impacts on nation-building and political integration. It would seem obvious that a written constitution will be more effective as an instrument for teaching citizens about their national heritage and thereby helping to foster a sense of national pride. On the other hand, a sense of national pride is not absent in Britain, where the Constitution, by any criterion, is basically unwritten. Also, a written constitution may be more effective in inculcating the norms of the regime to children and newcomers, for the values of the society, being written, are more visible and, hence, more knowable. Let us now turn to a discussion of the written and unwritten components of our Constitution.

### The Written Constitution

**The *Constitution Act*, 1867**   The *Constitution Act*, 1867 (the *British North America Act*, 1867), and its amendments over the years, form the core of the Canadian Constitution. It was a statute of the British Parliament, and its contents were based almost entirely on resolutions drawn up at two colonial conferences, one in Quebec and one in London, by the representatives of the original four provinces. The legal-historical significance of the Act is that it created a federal union, the Dominion of Canada, out of Upper and Lower Canada and the Maritime provinces of New Brunswick and Nova Scotia. Because, at the time of Confederation, the Canadas were united, the *Constitution Act*, 1867, also created the provinces of Ontario and Quebec.

The 1867 Act is not a comprehensive document like the Constitution of the United States. Rather, it deals with certain broad topics such as the division of legislative authority between the federal and provincial governments and the relationship between the Crown in Britain and the new Dominion. The Act defines the general structure of the national government and the executive power of the lieutenant governors in the provinces, and it provides a basic constitutional framework for the newly created provinces of Quebec and Ontario.

However, the 1867 Act does not go very far in defining basic political values or the legitimate role of government vis-à-vis individual rights. As we shall see in the next chapter, this was no accident of omission. One of the basic principles of English democracy from which the BNA Act was derived, was that Parliament was supreme and could not be fettered in the exercise of its powers in the way that Congress is by the US Constitution.

However, the BNA Act did not leave the Canadian Parliament totally free to do as it chose. Sections 96–101 operationalize the principle of judicial independence, section 93 provides some protection for denominational schools, and section 133 guarantees the right to use either French or English in Parliament and in the legislature of Quebec. Beyond these specific provisions, the preamble of the Act states that Canada is to have "a Constitution similar in Principle to that of the United Kingdom." This would imply that, in the absence of explicit provisions to the contrary in the Act, all of the basic political values and principles in the Constitution of the UK were to be incorporated into the Constitution of Canada.

**TABLE 6.1**
Components of the Canadian Constitution

| Component | Examples |
|---|---|
| Core documents | • *Constitution Act,* 1982<br>• *Constitution Act,* 1867 (BNA Act before 1982)<br>• Charter of Rights and Freedoms |
| UK Statutes | • *British North America Act,* 1867, as amended to 1982<br>• Statute of Westminster, 1931<br>• *Newfoundland Terms of Union Act,* 1949 |
| UK Orders in Council | • 1870 Order ceding Rupert's Land to Canada<br>• 1880 Order ceding Arctic Archipelago to Canada<br>• orders admitting B.C., 1871, and P.E.I., 1873 |
| Statutes of Canada | • "organic laws" such as *Supreme Court Act*<br>• *Manitoba Act,* 1870<br>• *Alberta Act* and *Saskatchewan Act,* 1905 |
| Provincial constitutions | • Ont., Que., N.B. and N.S. set up in the BNA Act<br>• Alta., Sask., and Man. set up by federal statute<br>• Nfld., P.E.I., and B.C. established by UK statutes and Orders in Council |
| Aboriginal treaties, land-claims settlements | • James Bay and Northern Quebec Agreement<br>• Inuvialuit Final Agreement<br>• Gwitchin, Sahtu, and Nunavut Agreements in the N.W.T.<br>• Yukon First Nations Final Agreements<br>• Treaties 1 to 11 |
| Judicial decisions | • cases dealing with sections 91 and 92 (see Chapter 8)<br>• Charter cases (see Chapter 7) |
| Conventions | • responsible government<br>• exercise of royal prerogatives |

In sum, as a constitution, the BNA Act was limited from the beginning. It was never intended to be the omnicompetent document that the Constitution of the United States is, and, in fact, much of what must be included as part of "the Constitution of Canada" is to be found elsewhere.

**The *Constitution Act,* 1982** The *Constitution Act,* 1982, brought the BNA Act and its subsequent amendments under the exclusive control of the Parliament of Canada and the provincial legislatures, and provided a comprehensive amending formula for the Canadian Constitution. Schedule I of the 1982 Act lists, and in most cases renames, the statutory components of the Canadian Constitution; hence, for instance, the BNA Act itself is now formally called the "*Constitution Act,* 1867" and the subsequent amendments to that Act, from 1867 to 1982, are each renamed "Constitution Act" (of the appropriate year.)

The various acts of the British Parliament and British Orders-in-Council that admitted new provinces into the federation after 1867 and which now form the core documents of those provincial constitutions, are also renamed to reflect their purpose, and are listed in Schedule I. Hence, for example, the Order-in-Council admitting Prince Edward Island is renamed the "Prince Edward Island Terms of Union." and the BNA Act of 1949 is renamed the *Newfoundland Act.* Schedule I of the *Constitution Act, 1982,* also lists British statutes that apply to Canada, such as the Statute of Westminster, 1931, thus affirming them as written components of our Constitution. Similarly, Schedule I includes British Orders-in-Council, such as those ceding Rupert's Land and the Northwestern Territories in 1870 and the Arctic Archipelago in 1880 to the Dominion.

**Canadian Constitutional Statutes** Some statutes of the Canadian Parliament, such as the *Alberta* and *Saskatchewan Acts* of 1905, which created the provinces of Alberta and Saskatchewan out of the Northwest Territories, are also listed in Schedule I as constitutional components. These particular Canadian acts are unique in that they are no longer amendable by the legislature that originally enacted them. Since the *Alberta* and *Saskatchewan Acts* form the constitutions of those provinces, they can be amended only by the provincial legislatures except for matters affecting the office of the lieutenant governor.

Other federal statutes that can be included in an inventory of the written components of the Canadian Constitution are classed by R. M. Dawson as **organic laws.**[1] These statutes, although legally amendable by a simple act of Parliament, deal with fundamental principles of a constitutional nature. One such organic law, the *Supreme Court Act,* has been *entrenched,* or given formal written constitutional protection, in its most important aspects by sections 41(d) and 42(d) of the *Constitution Act, 1982.* Still another, the Canadian Bill of Rights, has in part been superseded by the 1982 Charter of Rights and Freedoms. Thus, while a number of organic laws have been given formal constitutional protection by the 1982 Act, others such as the *Canada Elections Act,* the *Citizenship Act,* and perhaps the *Indian Act* allow us to continue to use the concept. While Parliament may from time to time change some of the provisions of such legislation, the fundamental principles are so important that it would be politically unacceptable for Parliament to do so without the substantial consent of the provinces and of the groups or individuals affected.

Section 45 of the *Constitution Act, 1982,* gives the provinces the power to amend their constitutions, excepting the sections dealing with the office of the lieutenant governor. Any provincial statutes that amend the provincial constitutions, therefore, must, like the British or Canadian enactments that originally set them up, be considered a part of the Canadian Constitution. The *Constitution Act, 1982,* has affirmed that the provincial constitutions are indeed component parts of the written Constitution by listing them in Schedule I.

**Aboriginal Treaties and Land Claims** Although most works on the Canadian Constitution would not accord "constitutional" status to aboriginal treaties and land-claims agreements, there is a strong case to be made that such docu-

---

1. R. MacGregor Dawson, *The Government of Canada* (Toronto: University of Toronto Press, 1970), p. 63.

ments are significant enough to be included as components of our written Constitution. Section 35 of the *Constitution Act, 1982,* "recognizes and affirms" the existing aboriginal and treaty rights of the aboriginal peoples of Canada. The section goes on to state that modern treaties or land-claims agreements, whether already in place in 1982 or concluded in the future, are "treaties." While "recognition and affirmation" likely does not entrench these rights and treaties, it gives them a level of constitutional importance at least equal to that of the organic statutes discussed above. They are often referred to as constitutionally "protected" if not entrenched.

While the jurisprudence to date dealing with aboriginal and treaty rights is incomplete, it is clear that Parliament can abrogate aboriginal treaties only for extremely good cause, such as an overriding national concern or matters of public health and safety. Even then, the Crown must meet a number of rigorous legal tests in order to legitimize its action. Treaties and land-claims agreements are entered into in good faith by all parties. The land-claims agreements that have been negotiated since 1982 all have explicit provisions to the effect that the agreements can be amended only with the consent of the parties that negotiated them, and, by implication, the many treaties that existed before have to be seen in the same way. Certainly, aboriginal treaties and land-claims agreements and the legislation that gives them effect have a higher status than either ordinary statutes or simple *contracts* with the Crown. They are solemn covenants entered into in such a manner that the honour of the Crown is at stake if they are ever to be abrogated or amended unilaterally. Whether aboriginal treaties are components of the Canadian Constitution is thus a moot question; whatever the answer, it is clear that they should be treated as if they are.

### The Unwritten Constitution

**Judicial Precedents** We have asserted that constitutions are more formal and more difficult to change than simple statutes. Nevertheless, constitutions still do consist, in large part, of laws or collections of laws, which means that they are general prescriptions that, in practice, must be applied to specific cases. The application of constitutional principles to specific cases involves the interpretation of the Constitution, which, in our system, is one of the most important functions of the judiciary. As the courts apply the constitutional principles to many different cases, a body of judicial decisions is built up, which elaborates and fleshes out the Constitution. The judicial decisions that interpret the Constitution must thus must be viewed as component parts of it.

In Canada, because our legal system is based on the English common-law tradition, and because the BNA Act states in the preamble that we are to have a form of government similar in principle to that of Britain, precedents established in British common law can also be used in interpreting our Constitution. As well, the interpretation of the BNA Act itself by the Judicial Committee of the Privy Council, which was the final court of appeal for Canada until 1949, built a large body of decisions that elaborate and clarify the Act. These judicial decisions, plus those of the Supreme Court of Canada since 1949, are a most important component of the Constitution of Canada, especially as they have helped to interpret and clarify the federal dimension of our Constitution.

**Convention and Custom** The Canadian Constitution includes a number of important but unwritten principles, such as *responsible government*. These **conventions** are not set down explicitly in any constitutional document, yet they are as much a part of the Constitution as the BNA Act itself. The only sanction that effectively enforces the principle of responsible government, for instance, is the weight of public opinion, which places a high value on it.[2]

A few of the customary and conventional parts of our Constitution have been written down in some form and have therefore acquired the support of legal or quasi-legal sanction. For instance, the rules and many of the privileges of Parliament are explicitly set down in the Standing Orders of the House of Commons. Generally, however, while conventions and customs involve some of the most important principles of the Constitution, they exist as implicit, imprecise, and unwritten "understandings" rather than as explicit, precise, and legally enforceable written instruments.

**Basic Political Values** Finally, a constitution can be considered to contain a number of principles or values that form the normative basis of the regime. These are difficult to pin down, for they exist largely as tacit assumptions or understandings in the minds of the members of the political community and they are passed on from generation to generation in very subtle ways through the process of political socialization. There is perhaps some argument whether such values should be considered a component part of the constitution or as simply principles that underlie it. However, within the context of this treatment of the Canadian Constitution the more important point is that these values, discussed in Chapter 4, are rooted in our political culture and are *implicit* in both the written and unwritten components of our Constitution.

Thus, we have seen that the Canadian Constitution is a mix of written and unwritten components. The written part of our Constitution includes British, Canadian, and provincial statutes, as well as a number of British orders-in-council. The unwritten part of our Constitution includes Canadian judicial decisions, a number of conventions, practices, and usages, as well as the underlying societal norms and values that define what is acceptable behaviour in our political community.

▶ THE OPERATIVE PRINCIPLES OF THE
CONSTITUTION

It has already been established that all forms of constitutional government are rooted in the principle of the rule of law. But if law is to "rule" us, it is going to need a lot of help from the people who occupy positions of authority in our political institutions. Laws must be made by somebody, and they must be carried into effect by somebody. As a result, the substance of a constitution is

---

2. As well, it can be argued that the prerogatives of the Crown in Canada as exercised by the governor-general and the lieutenant governors of the provinces include the power to overrule the political executive (the prime minister and the Cabinet) in cases where there is a clear abrogation of these important conventions.

fundamentally concerned with three sets of institutions performing the three basic "jobs" of government: the *legislative, executive*, and *adjudicative* functions. In most political systems, it is possible to make at least some distinction among these three functions, and usually it is possible to distinguish among the organs or branches of the government to which the constitution assigns the responsibility for the performance of each function. However, the constitutional relationship among these branches can vary a great deal from one country to another.

It must be recognized that the three functions of government in Canada are performed not by one but by several governments, each of which is sovereign within its sphere of jurisdiction. The legislative, the executive, and, to a certain extent, the adjudicative functions of government are performed by both federal and provincial governments in Canada. This operative principle of the Constitution is *divided sovereignty*, which adds greatly to the complexity of the political process in Canada. Finally, constitutions must not be too rigid; rather, they must be adaptable to changing circumstances. In the final section of this chapter we will look briefly at this dynamic dimension of the Constitution, the ways in which it can evolve and develop, and the manner in which it can be formally amended.

### The Supremacy of Parliament: The Legislative Function

The function of the legislature is to pass statute laws. In Canada, as in the United Kingdom where the origins of our democratic institutions are to be found, the legislative branch is intended to be representative of the population. Parliament and the provincial legislatures have the power to pass laws and are *supreme* in the sense that they control the executive branch through the convention of responsible government. The only limit on the exclusive legislative authority of legislatures in Canada is that all legislation must be consistent with the Charter of Rights and must receive *royal assent* and be *proclaimed* by the executive-in-council.

**Bicameralism**   There is one more feature of our legislative institutions that we share with both the US and the UK — **bicameralism.** Bicameralism means that the legislature is composed not of a single deliberative body, but of two chambers. In Britain, the **upper house** or upper chamber, the House of Lords, is made up of the *peers of the realm*. It is not elected; rather, membership is determined by heredity or, in the case of *life peerages*, individuals may gain membership for life through attaining knighthood. Because it is not popularly elected, the House of Lords lacks the political legitimacy of the **lower house**, the popularly elected House of Commons.

Taking its lead from the British tradition, the Constitution of the United States originally provided that the Congress be made up of a democratically elected House of Representatives, and an appointed Senate. The composition of the US Senate was to be two senators from each of the states appointed every six years by the state legislatures. While term of office and composition is the same today, the Senate was converted from a state-appointed to an elected body by an amendment to the US Constitution in 1913. Most of the state constitutions provide for elected upper houses as well.

The BNA Act, 1867, followed the US and UK tradition by providing for an elected House of Commons and an appointed Senate. The Senate is roughly representative of the various regions of the country and senators are appointed, in effect, by the prime minister. Originally, the appointment was for life, but since 1965, senators are appointed only until age seventy-five. More will be said about the functions of the Senate in Chapter 18. While the provincial legislatures were originally bicameral as well, with appointed upper houses, all provincial senates have been abolished.

**Parliamentary Supremacy and Canadian Federalism**  As noted earlier, the preamble of the *Constitution Act*, 1867, states that Canada is to have "a Constitution similar in principle to that of the United Kingdom." This means, *prima facie*, that the supremacy of Parliament is a substantive principle of the Canadian Constitution. Our Constitution, however, goes beyond this broad statement of intent, and the extent to which the Canadian Parliament is really supreme must be examined in light of other provisions in the Constitution that explicitly limit the power of Parliament.[3]

At the most elemental level, the Parliament of Canada is restricted by the provisions of the *Constitution Act*, 1982, which set down formulae for amending the Constitution. Those formulae require the participation of at least some or even all of the provincial legislatures for all matters except those having to do with federal government institutions. We will discuss the amending formula in detail in a later chapter.

The second and perhaps the most important limitation on the supremacy of the Canadian Parliament is found in the federal distribution of legislative powers, set out mainly in sections 91–95 of the *Constitution Act*, 1867. Because of these sections of the Act, the courts in Canada, unlike the courts in Britain, have the power to declare acts of the federal Parliament unconstitutional if they are judged to be beyond the legislative jurisdiction assigned to the federal level by the 1867 Act. Many pieces of legislation passed by the Canadian Parliament have been declared invalid on these grounds, and in fact, the interpretation of the federal legislative competence by the judiciary has played a significant role in remodeling Canadian federalism since 1867.

The important point here is that the judicial branch in Canada has the power to declare laws passed by either the federal Parliament or the legislatures of the provinces to be *ultra vires* and therefore invalid. In sum, legislative authority in Canada is divided among two separate types of legislative bodies: the Parliament of Canada, and the legislatures of the ten provinces, with the judiciary deciding any jurisdictional disputes.

**Exhaustiveness**  An additional question concerning the extent to which the doctrine of the supremacy of Parliament obtains in Canada is whether the combination of these two levels of legislatures, taken together, possesses leg-

---

3.  In fact, the preamble itself also specifies that Canada's Constitution is *federal*, which implies a different form of parliamentary supremacy from the unitary form of Britain's Parliament.

islative supremacy. In other words, is the legislative authority of ten provincial parliaments and the federal Parliament **exhaustive**?

At Confederation, the combined authority of the legislatures in Canada was limited by residual powers left in the hands of the British Parliament. The conduct of foreign affairs and matters of imperial concern were not given up by Britain until the Statute of Westminster came into effect in 1931, and all other residual imperial powers, such as the amendment of the BNA Act, were transferred to Canada with the *Constitution Act*, 1982. However, while eliminating the last *imperial* limits on the exhaustiveness of legislative power of Canadian legislatures, the 1982 Act may have simultaneously imposed some new, domestic ones.

**The Supremacy of Parliament and the Charter**   In the United States, there are some matters that are beyond the legislative competence of all levels and branches of government. These principles are considered to be so fundamental that no government should be able to interfere with them and are therefore entrenched in the Constitution. In Canada before 1982, judicial opinion generally supported the doctrine of exhaustiveness, giving to the provinces and the federal Parliament, collectively, full sovereign authority.

However, the 1982 Charter of Rights and Freedoms may have altered the situation by guaranteeing a wide range of rights and freedoms to Canadian citizens. The implication of the Charter is that its provisions supersede the enactments of both the federal Parliament and the provincial legislatures. However, certain provisions of the Charter may limit the extent to which the ultimate power of the eleven legislatures has been restricted in actuality.

In the first place, the Charter is filled with qualifiers that, depending upon subsequent judicial clarification, may take some force out of the guarantees. Most notably, section 1 of the Charter states that it operates "subject only to such reasonable limits prescribed by law as can be demonstrably justified in a free and democratic society." As we shall see in the next chapter, the courts have only begun to define what these "reasonable limits" include, and it doesn't appear as if a large number of laws will be declared *ultra vires* for imposing unreasonable limits on our rights.

Throughout the Charter there are specific qualifiers that could potentially weaken the impact of the Charter on federal and provincial legislation, but, even more significant than these, is the ***non-obstante*** provision in section 33 that permits Parliament or a legislature to declare that a given act is intended to "operate notwithstanding the Charter." However, certain important guarantees are not subject to the *non-obstante* gambit. Most significantly, these include the right to vote, the five-year term of a legislature, the requirement for an annual session of the legislature, and the complex official-languages and minority-language educational-rights provisions.

The immunity from the Charter provisions that is given to a law by a "notwithstanding" clause has a five-year "sunset," but may be renewed for further five-year periods. Its effect is to allow governments to override key sections of the Charter at will, but to force the politicians who wish to do so to "own up" to what they are doing by having to publicly "redo the dirty deed" every five years.

Thus, the supremacy of Parliament has been limited, at least in the sense that the courts can challenge laws on the basis that they are inconsistent with provisions of the Charter. But Parliament and the legislatures are still the only institutions with the authority to define the changing values and norms of our society over time. The body of dynamic law that Canadian society gradually creates for itself, as its needs evolve, continues to flow, at the very highest level, from legislation enacted by Parliament and the legislatures of the provinces.[4]

On a final note, it is interesting that the preamble to the Charter of Rights and Freedoms states that Canada is founded on principles that recognize the supremacy of God and the rule of law," but fails to mention the supremacy of Parliament. Nobody could dispute the fact that our Constitution incorporates the latter principle, but the recognition of the "supremacy of God" seems peculiar in a constitutional democracy. Fortunately the preamble is not justiciable and can be used only as a guide to interpretation. It is to be hoped that the *will of God*, as interpreted by some pious judge, is never deemed to supersede the *will of the people*, for history has demonstrated that democracy works infinitely better than theocracy.

**Parliamentary Supremacy Today**   To conclude, then, while the principle of the supremacy of Parliament is definitely still an integral part of the Constitution of Canada, and while the form it takes is not as unambiguous as it is in Britain, its implications remain significant. Unlike the Constitution of the United States, which has always put some matters beyond the grasp of *all* legislative bodies, the Constitution of Canada has historically vested exhaustive legislative authority in the collectivity of federal and provincial legislatures. While the Charter of Rights and Freedoms does impose some *prima facie* limits on the legislative authority of Parliament and the legislatures of the provinces, these have to be seen in the limited context within which they must operate. We have already spoken of the specific qualifiers in the Charter itself, but at a more elemental level, the power of the courts to override legislation is still only a *passive* power. The courts, in other words, are limited to a sort of veto, and even then, they may exercise it only when some other agency or individual has brought the matter before the court.

Finally, the nature of the amending formulae set down in the *Constitution Act*, 1982, may give back the *de jure* supremacy of the eleven legislatures. This will be discussed at greater length, but the fact remains that all parts of the Constitution are technically amendable through the combined intervention of the eleven (or fewer) legislatures. Our Constitution cannot yet be changed by *referendum*, nor can it be amended by executive or judicial action. In this sense, despite some *practical* obstacles, the constitutional *principle* of legislative supremacy can be said to remain strong and healthy in Canada.

---

4.  Henri Brun, "The Canadian Charter of Rights . . .," *in* C. Beckton and W. Mackay, *The Courts and the Charter* (Toronto: University of Toronto Press, 1985), p. 6.

### The Crown and Cabinet Government: The Executive Function

The executive function of a political system is to put the laws enacted by the legislature into effect — to carry out or to *execute* acts of Parliament. In Canada, the executive power, which includes the power to assent to legislation, is defined by section 9 of the BNA Act: "the Executive Government and Authority of and over Canada is hereby declared to continue and be vested in the Queen." Formally, therefore, the executive function in Canada is performed by the Queen. Our Constitution has evolved to the point that while, technically, we can be said to have a *monarchical* form of government, the monarch of the day has no actual power. The most significant implication of our formal ties to the British monarchy is the consequent transferral of all *prerogative rights* of the Crown in Britain to the Crown in respect of Canada. This statement, however, requires some explanation, particularly regarding the terms *Crown* and *prerogative rights*.

**The Crown and Prerogative Rights**   The term **the Crown** is used to describe the collectivity of executive powers that, in a monarchy, are exercised by or in the name of the sovereign. These executive powers, vested by the Constitution in the person of the reigning monarch, flow from the historic common-law rights and privileges of the Crown in England. These are referred to, collectively, as the **royal prerogative**. Prerogative rights exist primarily because they always have, and not because they have been created at some point in time by statute. The prerogative rights and privileges of the Crown are the residue of authority left over from an age when the power of the reigning monarch was absolute. This absolute power has been whittled away bit by bit, by both statute and convention, until today only a few remnants of it remain.

It is important to emphasize here that prerogative rights cannot be created by statute. If a statute were to extend the power of the Crown, the effect would be to create a new *statutory* power of the Crown but not a prerogative power. On the other hand, a prerogative right can be eliminated or restricted by statute. An example of this is in Crown liability legislation which limits the prerogative right of the Crown not to be held liable in tort for damages resulting from acts committed by public officials in the service of the Crown. This prerogative can never be returned as a prerogative right, although a future parliament could return it as a statutory right. Hence, the royal prerogative is slowly shrinking, and in Canada it is being replaced by both constitutional conventions and statutory provisions that define the limits of executive authority.

While the royal prerogative is not what it used to be, there are still some significant executive powers based on it. Among these are the right of the monarch to all ownerless property, hence, *Crown land*; the right of the government to priority as a creditor in the settlement of bankruptcies; and the rights to summon, prorogue, and dissolve Parliament. Because of the convention that these powers are all exercised "on the advice" of the ministers of the Crown — the prime minister and Cabinet — they are exercised, in reality, by our elected government.

**The Governor-General** In Britain, the formal **head-of-state** functions of the executive branch are performed personally by the Queen. In Canada, while the Queen can still be called "Queen of Canada," most of the monarchical functions are performed, in her name, by the governor-general at the national level and by the lieutenant governors at the provincial level. The appointment of the governor-general was originally the responsibility of the monarch, acting on the advice of the government of Britain. This made the governor-general effectively independent of the Canadian prime minister and Cabinet. Since the Imperial Conferences of 1926 and 1930, however, the governor-general has been independent of the British government. While the appointment of the governor-general is, formally, a function of the Queen, in fact it is always made today on the instructions or "advice" of the Canadian prime minister. Also, while the normal term of office of the Canadian governor-general is now five years, the term can be shortened or stretched according to the wishes of the government of the day.

The *Constitution Act*, 1867, continued the authority of the pre-Confederation colonial governors and identified the governor-general as the Crown's representative at the federal level. The actual office of the governor-general was created by letters patent issued to the first governor-general, Viscount Monck, in 1867. The governor-general's current "job description" and the specific powers of the office are set down in the letters patent of 1947, in which the governor-general is empowered to exercise "all powers and authorities," both statutory and prerogative, of the **Crown in right of Canada**. The letters patent also state that the powers of the governor-general are to be exercised on the advice of the "Queen's Privy Council for Canada." Among the exectuive powers specified by the letters patent are the use of the Great Seal of Canada; the appointment of judges, commissioners, diplomats, ministers of the Crown, and sundry other officials, along with the power to dismiss or suspend them; and the prerogative powers to summon, prorogue, and dissolve Parliament.

There are certain other powers ceded to the governor-general by the *Constitution Act*, 1867. Among these are the authority to appoint senators and the Speaker of the Senate; the exclusive right to recommend legislation involving the spending of public money or the imposition of a tax; and the right, formally, to prevent a bill from becoming law by withholding assent or by *reserving* the bill "for the signification of the Queen's pleasure."[5]

The governor-general also has the power, stated in section 56 of the 1867 Act, to "disallow" any provincial legislation of which he or she disapproves. The real significance of the **disallowance power** is that it gives the federal government a potential veto over all provincial acts. While it has not been used since 1943, it remains in the Constitution as a reminder that the Fathers of Confederation viewed the provincial legislatures as subordinate to the federal government.

**The Lieutenant Governors** The office of lieutenant governor was created by section 58 of the BNA Act. The holder of the office in each province is appointed by the governor-general-in-council, and the salary is set by the Cana-

---

5. Canada, *Constitution Act, 1867*, section 55.

dian Parliament. Furthermore, the lieutenant governors are removable "for cause" by the governor-general-in-council. This means that, in some respects, the lieutenant governors are officers of the federal government who are responsible to the governor-general.

On the other hand, however, the courts have decided that, in fact, the lieutenant governors are representatives of the Crown directly, despite the fact that the appointments and salaries are controlled directly by the executive branch of the Government of Canada. In an important constitutional case in 1892, the Judicial Committee of the Privy Council held that the lieutenant governor was a representative of the Queen directly, and therefore could exercise the same prerogative powers on behalf of the Crown in right of the province that the governor-general exercises in the name of the Crown in right of Canada.[6] The significance of this is that the lieutenant governor, while in some respects the subordinate of the governor-general, is in other respects an equal. In turn, this has the effect of making the provincial governments, which are personified in the lieutenant governors, more important than they would otherwise be. The BNA Act provides that the lieutenant governor of the province has the power to assent to or to refuse to assent to acts of the provincial legislature, and furthermore, by the *Constitution Act*, 1867, is given the power to **reserve** a bill for the signification of the governor-general's pleasure. In sum, the lieutenant governor in each province has powers that are analogous to and commensurate with the powers of the governor-general at the federal level.

### The Privy Council

The *Constitution Act*, 1867, provides for a body of advisors to assist the governor-general in performing the onerous burden of executive responsibilities that come from the same Act, and from the letters patent of 1947. Section 11 of the 1867 Act states that

> there shall be a Council to aid and advise in the Government of Canada, to be styled the Queen's Privy Council for Canada; and the Persons who are to be Members of the Council shall be from time to time chosen and summoned by the Governor General and sworn in as Privy Councillors, and Members thereof may be from time to time removed by the Governor General.

The **Queen's Privy Council for Canada** is made up of individuals recommended by the prime minister, and appointed and sworn in, normally for life, by the governor general. For the most part, Canadian privy councillors are either ministers of the Crown or, because the appointment is for life, anyone still alive who has ever been in the Cabinet in the past. As well, the Privy Council includes other notables such as the chief justice of the Supreme Court (who is also the deputy governor-general), provincial premiers, the leader of the opposition, retired governors-general, and a number of people who have been made Privy Councillors as a gesture in honour of their achievements. The Privy Council never meets as a deliberative body, although, rarely, all living privy councillors may be brought together for important ceremonial events, such as a coronation or to give their collective godfatherly blessing to a royal wedding.

---

6.  *The Liquidators of the Maritime Bank v. the Receiver General of New Brunswick* (1892).

There is no financial reward for being a privy councillor, but (some would say despite the fact that most of them are politicians) each member is entitled to be referred to as "The Honourable" with the initials "P.C." after his or her name. Canadian prime ministers become "Right Honourable," signifying that they are *ex-officio* members of the Queen's Privy Council in Britain, as well. This is a convention that allows the prime minister of Canada to advise the monarch directly on the few personal powers she still retains under the Canadian Constitution, the most important of which is the authority to name or dismiss the governor general. (The *Privy Council Office* is an important central agency which provides policy support for the Cabinet. It is made up largely of career public servants and, with the exception of administrative duties related to orders-in-council, it has nothing to do with the Privy Council. It will be discussed in detail in a later chapter.)

**Cabinet Government**   Up until now we have been speaking in rather formal and legalistic terms about the powers of the governor-general and the lieutenant governors. The intention has been to clarify the strict constitutional nature of the executive function in Canada. Now, however, it is necessary to bring the discussion of the executive function down from this rarified atmosphere and to deal with the constitutional realities of the executive function in Canada.

The 1867 Act does not state that the governor-general has to take the advice of the Privy Council but, in fact, even at the time of Confederation there was a well-established convention that the governor of the colony would, in almost all cases, act purely on the advice of the government of the day. The **Cabinet**, which is not mentioned at all in the Constitution, is really a committee of privy councillors, chosen by the leader of the majority party in the House of Commons from among supporters in Parliament. Formally, all executive acts are performed by the **governor-in-council** or governor-general-in-council, through instruments called **orders-in-council**. But, in reality, executive decisions are made by the prime minister and Cabinet, and merely affirmed or assented to by the governor-general.

While convention requires that the governor-general accept the advice of the Cabinet when exercising both statutory and prerogative powers, there remains a small area of executive power where the governor-general can still exercise his or her own discretion. The most significant of these discretionary powers is the selection of a prime minister. While the electorate normally makes the decision for the governor-general, in cases of close elections, where no party has a clear majority, the governor-general may or may not take the advice of the outgoing Cabinet when deciding which party leader to ask to form a government. As well, if the prime minister were to die in office, the governor-general would likely ask the governing party to suggest an interim replacement. In the event that the members could not agree, the governor-general would have to take his or her own counsel to ensure that there is a government in place.

There is also a small but potentially very important **reserve-power** of the governor-general, which could be exercised in certain crisis situations. Such situations are not clearly defined, but a good example, while unlikely to occur, would be a prime minister's refusal either to resign or to ask for a dissolution of Parliament after a defeat in the House in a non-confidence motion. In such a case it would be appropriate for the governor-general to dismiss the intransigent prime minister and either call an election or ask the leader of another party to form a government.

Another example of the potential use of the reserve power of the governor-general occurs when a prime minister, having been defeated in a general election, refuses to face the House, instead asking the governor-general to dissolve Parliament so there can be another election immediately. This was the situation in 1926, the last time a governor-general went directly against the advice of the prime minister. Mackenzie King's Liberals had been defeated in the 1925 election but had refused to resign, instead forming a government with the support of the Progressive Party. During a debate the following year that was clearly going to conclude with the defeat of King's government on a non-confidence motion, King tried to force another election by requesting Governor-General Lord Byng to dissolve Parliament. Byng refused, instead asking Arthur Meighen, the leader of the party with a plurality in the House, to form a government. The result was a general outcry, led by Mackenzie King, against the "undemocratic" action of the governor-general and the defeat of the Meighen government (in the House after a mere three days, and at the polls in the subsequent election.)[7]

It could also be argued that, faced with a government that attempted to pass legislation violating a fundamental value of our Constitution, such as freedom of the press, the governor-general could step in and refuse royal assent. The problem here would be that, however well intentioned, in refusing assent, the governor-general would be violating another fundamental norm of our system of government, by claiming to represent the public interest better than the public's elected representatives. To say that a governor-general would never dare to oppose the will of the prime minister is pure speculation. But the fact remains that the norm of popular sovereignty, at the core of the Canadian Constitution, imposes severe political limitations on the actual powers of the Queen's representative.

**Cabinet Government in the Provinces**   The relationship between the lieutenant governor of a province and the provincial premier is almost identical to that between the prime minister of Canada and the governor-general, and the BNA Act provides that each lieutenant governor must act with the advice of the **executive council** of the province. The executive council is, in fact, the provincial Cabinet, which is chosen by the premier. All provincial executive decisions are made by the premier and Cabinet, and the lieutenant governor, as with his or her federal counterpart, more or less rubber-stamps them.

As with the governor-general, the one time a lieutenant governor might be called upon to exercise some discretionary authority is in the case of the death in office of the leader of the government, where the successor is not obvious. Clearly, the lieutenant governor must seek the advice of the Cabinet ministers, but in some cases their advice might not be unanimous. In such a

---

7.  See E. A. Forsey, *The Royal Power of Dissolution of Parliament in the British Commonwealth* (Toronto: Oxford University Press, 1968), ch. 5.

situation, the lieutenant governor must decide whose advice to take, on the basis of personal discretion and political acumen, for, above all else, the lieutenant governor must ensure that there *is* a government.

Such a situation appeared to develop in Quebec at the death of Premier Maurice Duplessis in 1959, and of his successor, Paul Sauvé, a few months later. In neither case was the Cabinet solidly united behind a single choice of successor. While the Cabinet managed eventually to achieve a consensus by itself, and the lieutenant governor was able to make the decision on the basis of their advice, the incident makes it clear that there is a potentially important political role to be played by the formal executive in such rare, but conceivable, circumstances.

To conclude, the formal executive power in Canada is vested in the Crown and, in a very formal sense, Canada can be said to have a monarchical form of government. The governor-general exercises all of the prerogative and statutory rights and privileges of the Queen in right of Canada, but the constitutional doctrine of popular sovereignty has reduced the *de facto* role of the governor-general to that of a figurehead. The real power is exercised, as it should be in a democracy, by the prime minister and the Cabinet, who obtain their legitimacy from the fact that they are responsible to a legislature that is elected by the people of Canada.

### Judicial Independence: The Adjudicative Function

The adjudicative function is the hardest to distinguish of the three basic output functions of the political system. In fact, it can be argued that there are only two basic functions — making law and applying it — because both the judiciary and the executive can be perceived as applying the law to specific cases, albeit in slightly different fashions. There are two reasons, however, for shying away from that twofold method of classification. First, the *Constitution Act*, 1867, makes very definite distinctions among the *executive* and *legislative* powers, and the *judicature*. Second, even if a functional distinction is difficult, the judicial branch in Canada can be clearly distinguished through the principle of **judicial independence**, which insulates the judiciary from any direct responsibility to either of the other two branches. The independence of the judiciary is one of the essential principles of our system of government, and, as such, it merits a longer look.

**Judicial Independence**  The historical roots of the principle of judicial independence[8] lie in the English common-law tradition, and it is from that source that Canada has inherited the doctrine. The principle was adopted formally in Britain through the *Act of Settlement* of 1701, where the security of tenure and salary and the independence from royal whim were legally guaranteed. British North American colonies were finally granted the privilege of an independent judiciary in the middle of the 19th century, and the doctrine was set down explicitly in the *Constitution Act*, 1867.

In Canada, the constitutional affirmation of the principle of judicial independence can be found in sections 96–101 of the 1867 Act. Section 99 states

---

8.  W. R. Lederman, "The Independence of the Judiciary," *Canadian Bar Review*, 1956, p. 769ff.

that superior court judges shall hold office *during good behaviour* up to the age of seventy-five, implying that a judge cannot be dismissed for incompetence or laziness but only for a criminal offence. Section 99 also provides that a judge is removable only by the governor-general on a joint resolution by the Senate and the House of Commons. This means that the executive can remove a judge only at the request of both houses of the Canadian Parliament, and the practice has evolved that even this is undertaken only after a judicial inquiry into the judge's alleged wrongdoings.

The salary of a judge is set by statute, so that it is not possible for the judge to become involved in bargaining with the executive for salary increments, nor is it possible for the executive to pressure a judge by controlling his or her livelihood. Every effort is made to ensure that the judge is protected from influences that might affect objectivity in coming to decisions. As R. M. Dawson has said,

> the judge is placed in a position where he has nothing to lose by doing what is right, and little to gain by doing what is wrong, and there is, therefore, every reason to hope that his best efforts will be devoted to the conscientious performance of his duty.[9]

Moreover, judicial independence is a two-way street. Judges are expected to act in a manner that is impartial and apolitical in all aspects of their lives, personal and professional. They were not even permitted to vote in general elections until recently, nor are they permitted to comment publicly on general social or political issues.

Further to the guarantees of the *personal* independence of the judge is the guarantee of jurisdictional integrity, which is given to the superior courts in Canada. A common assumption is that any government official will attempt to widen the scope of his or her jurisdiction — a practice often referred to disapprovingly as "empire-building." Limits must be placed on this sort of activity, usually by the intervention of other officials. However, the independence of the judiciary is perceived as such an important value of our system that the danger of judicial empire-building is ignored. Instead, a remarkable faith in the honesty and level-headedness of our judges is indicated by allowing superior courts to decide not only their own jurisdiction, but the jurisdiction of other governmental officials as well. In effect, this means that the legislative branch could not vest superior-court jurisdiction in a judicial body other than a superior court without first securing amendments to sections 96–101 of the *Constitution Act*, 1867.

**Judicial Review** *Judicial review* has been cited already as a possible limitation on the supremacy of Parliament in Canada. Now it is necessary to consider to what extent the principle of judicial review is, itself, an operative principle of our Constitution. Judicial review is essentially the power of superior courts to review the decisions or actions of governmental officials, administrative boards or tribunals, other courts, and even Parliament itself.

The significance of judicial review in **administrative law** is that no official of government, an administrative agency, a quasi-judicial board or tribunal, or

---

9.  Dawson, *The Government of Canada*, p. 409.

an executive body is above or outside the law of the land. Its significance in **constitutional law** is that the courts can declare acts of Parliament or of provincial legislatures unconstitutional, or *ultra vires*, and therefore void. In a broader sense, judicial review includes the ability of the courts to slow, or brake, the legislative branch by imposing a narrow interpretation of the law. It is in this broader sense that constitutional judicial review might be said to exist even in political systems such as Britain, where, strictly speaking, no act of a *supreme* parliament can ever be *ultra vires*. Hence, when we speak of judicial review of legislation, we must keep in mind that there are two forms or levels at which the process operates. J. E. McWhinney refers to these two levels of judicial review as *direct* and *indirect* forms of judicial authority.[10]

*Direct Judicial Review*  **Direct judicial review** is the kind exercised by, for example, the United States Supreme Court. In the US the Supreme Court has the power to declare acts of Congress and acts of the state legislatures unconstitutional, and therefore void. This direct form of judicial review is exercised by Canadian courts as well. Our judiciary has the authority to interpret the federal distribution of powers and to determine the applicability of the Charter of Rights and Freedoms to both provincial and federal legislation.

The constitutional origins of direct judicial review in Canada, however, are not clear. The right to declare acts of Parliament *ultra vires* certainly does not flow from the English common law, which recognizes the principle of parliamentary supremacy. Nor is this judicial power specifically vested in the courts by the *Constitution Act, 1867*. We can speculate, however, that the practice of direct judicial review in Canada evolved simply out of pragmatic considerations, as it did in the United States. The principle is likely implicit in the principle of federalism,[11] which is a key substantive component of our Constitution. As evidence of this, direct judicial review of legislation in Canada evolved almost exclusively with respect to the distribution of powers between the federal Parliament and the provincial legislatures. It is only since the Charter, by which time judicial review had been constitutionally legitimized, that the courts have been permitted to place certain matters beyond the legislative competence of government generally.

*Indirect Judicial Review*  **Indirect judicial review** is described by McWhinney:

> A court, either not having the power to annul or override enactments of the legislature as "unconstitutional" or else simply choosing not to exert that power in the instant case, says in effect in the process of interpretation of a statute, that the legislature may or may not have the claimed legislative power, but it has not in the language it has used in the enactment now in question employed that power.[12]

This form of judicial review will naturally be more significant in countries like Britain, where the Constitution is extremely flexible and without clear bound-

---

10.  See Edward McWhinney, *Judicial Review* (Toronto: University of Toronto Press, 1969), p. 13; and J. Smith, "The Origins of Judicial Review in Canada," *Canadian Journal of Political Science*, March 1983, p. 115.

11.  The predominant view, as set forth in the United States, in *Marbury v. Madison* (1803), is that the power to review acts of Congress is "implicit" in the federal Constitution.

12.  McWhinney, *Judicial Review*, p. 13.

aries, but such judicial braking will be used occasionally in countries like the United States and Canada, where direct judicial review is also an appropriate judicial alternative. The reason for a court's choosing indirect rather than direct review might be that the facts of the case are not clear enough to justify setting a precedent that may preclude legislative enactments in that area in the future. Or it may be a more practical reason: the court does not wish to become embroiled in the political hassle that could ensue if popular legislation were to be rendered completely void by a judicial decision.

Indirect judicial review is achieved by a set of *presumptions*, which the courts make in the interpretation of a piece of legislation. For example, they will assume, unless the legislation states specifically to the contrary, that Parliament does not intend laws to have retroactive effect; or they will refuse to interpret any statute in such a way as to take away a citizen's right to a fair hearing. The effect is to slow up, or brake, the legislative branch when the judiciary feels it has overstepped the bounds of constitutional propriety, even though it may still be within the limits of *de jure* constitutionality. The courts in this sense are functioning more like the conscience of the state than as a stern arbiter.

The constitutional basis for the exercise of indirect judicial review in Canada is the English common law. The limitation on this type of judicial review is that it is merely a stalling technique. Parliament can always, in theory, rework the legislation so that there is no ambiguity, thus bypassing the judiciary's "assumptions." On the other hand, the courts will have forced the legislature to publicly redefend a position that may be politically sensitive, and in so doing will have allowed time for a (hopefully) sober second thought.

*The Rule of Precedent*   A final possible limitation on the power of judicial review may be imposed by the principle of **stare decisis**, which means that courts are bound by previous decisions when deciding current cases. While lower courts are clearly bound by previous decisions of higher courts within the same hierarchy, this aspect of the principle of *stare decisis* does not affect the longer-term constitutional implications of judicial review.

The more important question is whether precedents established by the final court of appeal in the past are binding on the same court today. While such precedents are usually found to be very persuasive and are usually adhered to by the Canadian judiciary, this is done by choice and not by constitutional prescription. We will discuss many of these issues in greater detail when we describe the judicial system in Chapter 24.

### The Federal Principle: Divided Sovereignty

In international law, the concept of **sovereignty** means that a nation-state is independent of all other states and possesses the totality of political power within its own boundaries. In a federal system, the nation-state is, indeed, independent from its neighbours in the international community, but the totality of political power within its boundaries is shared by two levels or orders of government. **Divided sovereignty** means simply that the powers and responsibilities of government are divided between the federal and provincial authorities. In the Canadian Constitution, which is characterized by the supremacy of Parliament, this is accomplished by listing the *legislative* jurisdiction of the federal Parliament and the provincial legislatures.

While we often refer to the federal and provincial *levels* of government, within their specified areas of jurisdiction there exists no superior-subordinate relationship. The legislatures of the provinces and the Parliament of Canada have constitutionally distinct functions, and neither can trench upon the constitutional authority of the other. The term **orders of government** has increasingly come into use to emphasize that the provinces and the federal government are constitutional equals, simply operating in different spheres of jurisdiction.

**The Federal Function** The operative principle of divided sovereignty is ensconced in the *Constitution Act*, 1867, and represents an intention on the part of the drafters of that Act to establish a federal system of government in Canada. There have been many definitions of federalism and many approaches to its study.

The most important modern contribution to the study of federalism has been that of K. C. Wheare. Since the 1946 publication of Wheare's classic, *Federal Government*, theoretical writings on the concept of federalism have added relatively little except qualifications and interesting changes in emphasis. Wheare's analysis is institutional in the sense that he views federalism as a *form of government* that embodies what he calls *the federal principle*: a method of dividing governmental powers so that the general and regional governments are each, within a sphere of jurisdiction, "coordinate and independent."[13]

A federal system of government is most appropriate when a number of preconditions exist. First, there must be pre-existing communities or territories that see some mutual advantage in cooperating with neighbour communities on a long-term basis. Second, the communities must be different enough and sufficiently committed to protecting their uniqueness that the option of full legislative union or a unitary system of government is not acceptable. Third, the diversity among the communities must coincide with spatial or geographical lines of cleavage. Finally, there must exist the political will within the member communities to surrender some of their local powers to a central authority in the interest of providing a greater overall benefit. In Wheare's words,

> to begin with, the communities or states concerned must desire to be under a single independent government for some purposes. . . . They must desire at the same time to retain or establish independent regional governments in some matters at least.[14]

Thus, in functional terms, a federal system reconciles a desire for overall *unity* with a desire for local or regional *diversity*.

**The Federal System** In structural terms, a federal system is seen as having independent national and regional governments, each operating in a hypo-

---

13. K. C. Wheare, *Federal Government*, 2nd ed. (Toronto: Oxford University Press, 1961), p. 11.
14. Ibid., p. 33.

thetically distinct jurisdictional compartment, which is entrenched in the constitution so that neither order of government can destroy the other. As well, the federal system requires the empowerment of a judiciary that can function as an impartial arbiter or *referee* in settling jurisdictional disputes. The federal process, or "how federal government actually works," will vary from federation to federation, but as long as the federal function is being performed and the basic structural characteristics of federalism are present, the system can be called federal.

There is no question that Canada is regionally diverse and has remained united for 128 years. The Canadian system features two levels or orders of government, each is independent of the other in constitutionally specified jurisdictional bailiwicks, and we have an independent judiciary that has been kept busy throughout our history clarifying the jurisdictional boundaries. Hence, we clearly have a federal system of government. The evolution of the Canadian federal system and the idiosyncracies of our particular brand of federalism will be discussed in later chapters. The fact that four separate chapters are to be devoted to the federal aspects of the Canadian political system indicates the importance that must be attached to federalism as an operative principle of the Constitution.

## ▶ THE PROCESSES OF CONSTITUTIONAL CHANGE

Having looked at the component parts and substantive principles of the Canadian Constitution, it is now necessary to put that information within a more dynamic setting by looking at the processes of constitutional change. We take the analytical position that the relationship between the individual and the state is reciprocal, for constitutional change not only *reflects* changes in a political culture, but also *induces* change in the values, attitudes, and behaviour patterns that characterize a political culture.

In the long run, a constitution must reflect the values of society. If it does not, the laws and policies of the government will gradually cease to be accepted as legitimate and the entire system could collapse. Hence, while it is true that the constitution provides the regime with necessary rigidity, the constitution must also have the capacity for change; it must not be so rigid that it cannot be adjusted to meet new needs and priorities in the society. The most obvious way in which a constitution can change, although one that seldom succeeds in Canada, is through deliberate use of the **formal amendment** process, which is itself a part of the written constitution. The nature of that process will be determined by the society's basic political values and, in particular, will indicate a society's preference for the relative balance between constitutional rigidity and flexibility — between constitutional conservatism and progressivism.

While the most visible type of constitutional change occurs through the process of formal amendment, there are several other, and perhaps more important, ways in which the Canadian Constitution can be changed. As we have seen in earlier chapters, different component parts of the Constitution evolved in different ways, and the manner in which they continue to evolve varies depending upon whether they are formal or informal, written or unwritten, explicit or implicit. Before turning to an examination of the process of formal amendment, it is useful to look at the other, less formal, types of constitutional change that adapt and modify our fundamental law.

### Evolutionary Change

The Canadian Constitution, as we have seen, is composed of underlying fundamental values, conventions and customs, judicial precedents, organic laws, and the "core documents" of our written Constitution, the *Constitution Acts* of 1867 and 1982. The latter can be changed only through the deliberate and explicit enactment of a formal amendment. The unwritten parts of the Constitution can, for the most part, be changed by formal amendment too — by entrenching them explicitly or by stating explicitly, in a formal amendment, that they either are no longer operative or are altered in their effect. However, for the most part, they continue to change gradually and informally as they have in the past.

**Political Socialization and Constitutional Change** As we have seen in our discussion of the process or processes of political socialization, broad historical forces and factors provide the political value "set" of our society. Too often, political socialization is viewed as an essentially conservative force that ensures value consistency over time in a political community — as a force that freezes current values and thus inhibits constitutional development. But political socialization can engender change as well as consistency over time, not only from one generation to the next, but also through ongoing intellectual and moral development throughout the lifespan of an individual.

To take some examples, attitudes towards racial discrimination have, in the past fifty years, changed quite markedly throughout North America. Policies that, for instance, provided for educational segregation were once either accepted as legitimate or even actively supported by the general population. Today, however, such policies are held by the vast majority to be non-legitimate and have been replaced by policies that instead actively foster integration and seek to make up for past discrimination through devices such as affirmative action. The formal parts of our Constitution now include explicit provisions on non-discrimination that reflect the changing attitudes.

Similarly, attitudes towards aboriginal rights have changed significantly in Canada, even within the last decade. While the recognition of aboriginal rights in the *Constitution Act*, 1982, reflected growing acceptance of such rights by non-aboriginal Canadians, the incorporation of such principles in the Constitution has further enhanced our awareness and sensitivity to aboriginal issues. In this sense the causal links work both ways — the shift in values triggered explicit changes in the Constitution and the symbolic and educative impact of the constitutional changes has been to alter further our political values.

The phenomenon that societal values change during an individual's lifetime, and the more macroscopic phenomenon that one generation takes on a set of values different from the previous one, testify to the fact that the process of socialization can indeed alter the values that underlie our Constitution. Such changes in our political culture may well come to be explicitly recognized in our Constitution, but they can also give us clues to why certain of our other values do *not* change, even over long historical periods.

**Customary and Conventional Change**  As pointed out earlier, conventions and customs[15] are important components of our Constitution. These are rules and principles that, while important, are not written down anywhere. They are said to bind the government and the governed alike, but only insofar as people choose to adhere to them. If a convention or a custom ceases to be congruent with the basic values of the political culture, eventually it will be abrogated or ignored and ultimately forgotten. In a sense, we can say simply that the customs and conventions of our Constitution can be changed in the same way they originated — by the estsablishment of a precedent and the subsequent adherence to that precedent.

The origins of the customary and conventional components of the Canadian Constitution lie in the misty labyrinths of English constitutional history, imported into our system as part of the ideological baggage of the earliest British settlers. English constitutional practice is explicitly incorporated into the Canadian Constitution by the preamble to the *Constitution Act*, 1867, which grants Canada a "constitution similar in principle to that of the U.K." The problem with constitutional principles that are manifested only in their practice is that disputes frequently arise over which practice applies to the specific case, to what extent it applies, and how binding it is in the current circumstances.

If there is a dispute about whether and to what extent a convention applies in Canada, and if there there are no statutory provisions that make the rule explicit, we may be able to seek an answer in the *practice* in Britain. However, there are uniquely Canadian conventions as well, whose existence and applicability can be clarified only by the citation of precedents in our own constitutional practice.

The settlement of such disputes is rarely referred to the courts, but more often, the effective arbiters may be academics or constitutional experts who, while learned, may be totally outside the governmental process. It is not uncommon, in disputes over what the convention is in a given circumstance, for the parties to the dispute to quote Bagehot's or Jennings' writings on the English Constitution, and in Canada, it has sometimes been that our unwritten Constitution is effectively what the late Eugene Forsey said it was!

However, it must be reiterated that the interpretations of the accepted practice in the past, the citing of precedents, and the wisdom of the constitutional experts are still more *persuasive* than legally binding. If we wish a constitutional convention to change, all it takes is the political will to abrogate it. If the new precedent is consistent with current political norms and values, it will be accepted, and if it is not, the perpetrators of the change will face the political music at the next election. Ultimately, governments may replace conventions

---

15.  Dawson, *The Government of Canada*, p. 65n: "No attempt has been made to distinguish between custom, usage and convention. A common distinction is to treat custom and usage as synonymous terms, and convention as a usage which has acquired obligatory force." See also D. V. Smiley, *Constitutional Adaptation and Federalism Since 1945*, Royal Commission on Bilingualism and Biculturalism Study No. 16 (Ottawa: Queen's Printer, 1970).

with explicit enactments such as statutes or formal amendments to the Constitution. In other words, the unwritten convention can be transformed into a written component of our Constitution.

We shall see in the discussion of the pre-Charter protection of civil liberties that the courts will sometimes use convention as grounds for striking down legislation. The best examples of this involved the use of the "Duff doctrine" by which provincial laws affecting freedom of expression and freedom of the press were overturned on the grounds that they violated conventions implicit in the preamble to the 1867 Act. More recently, the courts were called upon to clarify the conventions that surrounded the process for seeking amendments to the BNA Act by the British Parliament. Having failed to gain the unanimous support of the provinces, the Trudeau government indicated its intention to proceed unilaterally.

When the issue was referred to the Supreme Court,[16] the court concluded that it was *legal* for the federal government to unilaterally request that the British Parliament amend the BNA Act. However, the court went on to say that such unilateral action was *unconstitutional*, because there existed a convention that amendment of the Constitution required the "substantial agreement" of the provinces. As we have seen, the federal government and a "substantial" number of the provinces — nine — did arrive at an eleventh-hour agreement, and the request for amendment went to Britain with provincial support. However, had the agreement not been forthcoming, the Parliament of Canada could still have gone ahead with its unilateral request. In so doing, had Britain agreed to the federal request, as it likely would have, the convention would have been, at least temporarily, inoperative.

Conventional change can also be brought about by *desuetude* or the disuse of a given constitutional provision. The best example of this is the disallowance power of the federal government, which has not been used since 1943. Despite the fact that recent constitutional reform initiatives, which would have explicitly removed these provisions from the Constitution, failed to be ratified, the use of such powers by the federal government would be unacceptable in our federal system today. The reason it has ceased to be a viable constitutional device is related to the reality of power distribution in Canada today, which is, in turn, related to the coming of age of the provinces. Indeed, it is possible that if the federal government had continued to make a habit of disallowing provincial acts, the provinces might never have come of age.

Customary and conventional change is occurring constantly through the use and desuetude of various constitutional practices. It is a significant form of evolutionary constitutional change but difficult to see while it is happening. It is only through the passage of time that we are able to judge the force of convention in constitutional practice, which is why, throughout this section, we have used phrases such as "appears to have" changed, or "may have been" rendered inoperative.

**Judicial Change** Judicial decisions fill out the bare bones of the Constitution by interpreting it and by applying it to specific cases. In Chapter 8 we will consider such things as, for example, the way in which the federal legislative

---

16. See *Reference re Amendment of the Constitution of Canada* (1981) 1 SCR 754.

powers under the BNA Act were significantly curtailed by the Judicial Committee of the Privy Council. We will see, for instance, that the Judicial Committee chose to interpret section 91(2) to mean the regulation of *interprovincial and international* trade but not intra-provincial trade. Similarly, the "Peace, Order and Good Government" clause was interpreted in such a way that it became merely an emergency power or a federal residuary power. In this way, the judiciary effectively redefined the nature of Canadian federalism through the interpretation of our Constitution. As we will discuss in the next chapter, the courts are also assuming a very active role in the fine-tuning of the Charter of Rights and Freedoms and in defining the nature and extent of aboriginal rights.

Constitutional change through judicial review has certain built-in limitations, however, particularly because the courts do not review all legislation automatically. It is important to recognize that the courts can interpret a law only when its interpretation becomes central to deciding a case. In other words, the courts have to wait until, in the normal course of litigation, some citizen brings a case before them and questions the validity of a given statute before they can rule on its constitutionality.

The only exception to this rule is a unique device available to Canadian governments known as a **constitutional reference**. A reference case occurs when a government refers a matter to the highest court in its jurisdicition for a judgement regarding its constitutionality. The device was created originally by a section of the *Supreme Court Act* and had the effect of allowing the federal government to test the constitutionality of a law in the highest court of the land before attempting to implement it. The provinces liked the idea and legislated the right to submit reference cases to their highest courts as well. Ultimately, the decision on a provincial reference can be appealed to the Supreme Court of Canada.

While governments like the device of setting up such test cases for their policy proposals, the judges generally do not. The problem with the constitutional reference as a method of judicial change is that the judges are forced to judge the legislation not merely within the context of the facts of a single case, but within all conceivable contexts in which it can be employed. Because we will discuss a number of specific constitutional references in Chapter 8, at this time we merely wish to reiterate that the reference case is one way in which the judiciary can have the opportunity to change or shape the Constitution through the interpretation of federal and provincial laws.

**Legislative Change** The forms of constitutional change that have been discussed thus far are all rather haphazard, informal, and unpredictable. The outcomes of such changes are difficult for our political decision-makers to plan for or to control. This is not the case with **legislative constitutional change**, for its essence is that it is deliberate and contrived, and formal regime mechanisms are employed to produce it. There are two broad types of legislative change in the Canadian political system, not including formal amendment, which will be discussed separately.

The first type of legislative change is the kind of amendment of the BNA Act that is authorized originally by the Act itself. Examples are provided by a whole class of clauses of the Act that are prefaced by the words "until the

Parliament of Canada otherwise provides." These provisions of the Act were intended to provide interim measures, at the time of Confederation, until Parliament could get around to setting up more permanent ones. Most of these clauses are now defunct or irrelevant, having been replaced by statutes soon after Confederation or superseded by the 1982 amending formula.

The second type of legislative constitutional change that has been employed in Canada involves the alteration of *organic laws* through acts of Parliament. An example of this kind of constitutional change would be an amendment to the Canadian Bill of Rights. Here, while the subject matter can be considered constitutional, the method of changing it would be by a simple act of Parliament. The impediment to the repeal or amendment of organic laws is the force of public opinion that views them as sacrosanct. Moreover, we may be seeing a convention evolving to the effect that organic laws can be changed, even by the legislature that passed them, only if there has been prior consultation and substantial agreement on the part of provinces, territories, groups, and individuals affected by the proposed changes.

### Formal Amendment

The basic formula for the amendment of the Canadian Constitution is set down in section 38(1) of the *Constitution Act*, 1982, and provides that changes to most parts of our Constitution can be achieved with the agreement of both houses of Parliament and the legislative assemblies of two-thirds of the provinces containing at least 50 per cent of the population of Canada. Significantly, the formula does not give a veto to any specific province, but, through section 38(3), it provides any province that might disagree with such an amendment the power to exclude itself from its provisions. This provision of **dissent**, while facilitating a system where no province has a veto over an amendment, was opposed by Prime Minister Trudeau at the time, on the grounds that it could result in a "checkerboard Canada." In the end, however, a federal acquiescence to the opting-out provision was likely essential to obtain the agreement of the nine provinces in November, 1981. As well as permitting as many as three provinces to opt out of an amendment, the formula also provides that, where financial benefits would accrue to the provinces as a result of an amendment respecting education or culture, dissenting or opting-out provinces are to be awarded equivalent compensation (section 40).

There are also some types of amendment that are attainable through the general procedure but for which the right to dissent does not apply. These include such constitutional matters as changes to national institutions, the creation of new provinces, and the extension of existing provinces into the territories. Significantly, as well, there is no provision for obtaining the agreement of the legislative assemblies of the Northwest Territories or the Yukon, either on questions of provincehood or on the extension of existing provincial boundaries northward, a point the territorial governments, understandably, find alarming.

Certain constitutional matters deemed especially important cannot be amended by the basic formula, but require the **unanimous consent** of all provinces and the federal Parliament. These matters include the following (from section 41):

(a)   the office of the Queen, the Governor-General, and the Lieutenant Governor of a province;

(b)   the right of a province to the number of members in the House of Commons not less than a number of senators by which the province is entitled to be represented at the time this part comes into force;

(c)   subject to section 43, the use of the English or French language;

(d)   the composition of the Supreme Court of Canada;

(e)   and, an amendment to this part.

Finally, the amending procedure also provides that constitutional matters such as the adjustment of interprovincial boundaries require only the consent of the provinces directly involved and the federal Parliament, and that the amendment of provincial constitutions remains exclusively in the hands of the individual provincial legislatures. The Act specifies as well that, subject to other provisions of the *Constitution Act*, the Parliament of Canada can, by section 44, unilaterally make changes to federal institutions. However, because of the integrated nature of our federal system, and the manifestations of the federal principle even in national institutions, the unilateral amending power of the Parliament of Canada may not include much.

The verdict about the 1982 amending formula after more than a decade in operation can only be very tentative because it has not been used very much. Some would agree that the very fact that agreement on the amending formula itself took some fifty years, and even then it required the threat of unilateral federal action and was still not unanimous, likely indicates that unanimity, or even two-thirds assent of the provinces, will occur only rarely. The irony is that, having finally approved an amending formula for the Constitution, it may, in practical terms, turn out to be virtually unamendable.

# Chapter 7

# The Constitution Today: Rights and Freedoms

When the *Constitution Act*, 1982, was proclaimed, the Charter of Rights and Freedoms became part of our fundamental law. While the entrenchment of such rights and freedoms constituted a significant symbolic act, it must be recognized that we did not thereby acquire any *new* rights or freedoms. These rights have been a part of our Constitution since the beginning and are reflective of the basic values that underlie it. The Charter must be seen as a codification of these rights, or as a transformation of part of our unwritten Constitution into written form. Hence, before turning to a discussion of the Charter and its effect on Canadian political life, we must look at the pre-Charter status of our rights and freedoms, which forms the legal and normative base upon which the Charter must function today.

## ▶ RIGHTS, FREEDOMS, AND LIBERTIES

The terms **civil liberties** and **fundamental freedoms** may be different in very subtle ways, but for the most part they are used synonymously. We will follow that practice here. However, it is not as easy to dismiss distinctions between the terms *right* and *liberty*. In Canada, the term **civil rights**, as used in section 92(13) of the *Constitution Act*, 1867, and as modified through extensive judicial interpretation, is closely connected, not just with the rights of individuals, but, specifically, with rights that accrue through *property* and through *contract*. The original significance of this clause was that it permitted Quebec to have its own system of property and contract law based on the French system of a *code civile* rather than the English common law.

The term *civil liberties* is properly used in the Canadian context to refer to our fundamental freedoms. The vocabulary is somewhat different in the United States. There the term *civil rights* means more or less what we in Canada would call civil liberties. The American term derives from the fact that the first ten amendments to the US Constitution, which set out what we would call civil liberties or fundamental freedoms, are referred to as the Bill of Rights.

In 1953, while delivering a judgement on a case involving the principle of religious freedom, Canadian Supreme Court Justice Ivan C. Rand attempted to clarify the distinction between civil rights and civil liberties. He explained that every individual, simply by virtue of being a person, is born with a total area of freedom, the limits of which are defined only by his or her physical strength, mental capacity, and other personal characteristics. However, we each give up a certain percentage of our absolute, or original, freedom and allow the government to regulate and limit everybody's behaviour in return for the predictability, order, and safety of a civil society.

Each piece of positive law, therefore, takes away some of our freedom but replaces it with both *rights* and *obligations*. For example, a law prohibiting patricide creates an obligation in all children not to kill their fathers, thus restricting the absolute freedom of children. At the same time, such a law creates a right in all fathers not to be killed by their sons and daughters. The positive law thus creates rights and obligations out of the existing area of absolute freedom.

To return to our definitions, then, *rights*, in the purest sense of the term, are created through the enactment of positive laws, while *liberties* are the residual area of freedom left to an individual after the totality of the positive law is subtracted from it. However, as Walter Tarnopolsky has pointed out, most fundamental freedoms are, in fact, beefed up by the positive law. By way of example, he cites religious freedom:

> We speak of "freedom of worship," but only as defined by law, and not including such practices as human sacrifice, for example. Such freedoms can also be protected by law, for instance, by forbidding unlawful interference with the conduct of a religious service.[1]

Finally, to torture our innocent readers one bit more, it should be noted that a partial distinction can be made *empirically* between civil rights and civil liberties. The former tend to be associated with the civil rights movement in the United States which focused on the elimination of discrimination on the basis of race by both government and private businesses dealing with the public. The Bill of Rights in the US deals with both public and private discriminatory practices. Civil liberties, on the other hand, tend to be concerned more exclusively with individual-to-state relationships. Civil liberties are thus viewed as freedom *from* interference or restriction by the government.

---

1. See W. S. Tarnopolsky, *The Canadian Bill of Rights* (Toronto: McClelland and Stewart, 1975), p. 2.

## ▶ RIGHTS AND FREEDOMS IN CANADA

Several implications derive from the fact that the BNA Act, 1867, gives Canada a constitution similar in principle to that of Britain. Because Britain's Constitution reflects, or did reflect in 1867, a set of principles that includes individual freedoms and democratic rights, Canada directly inherited a body of unwritten constitutional principles that protected our basic rights and freedoms from the beginning.

### Democratic Rights and Freedoms

These include both substantive freedoms and political rights, and are implicit in and necessary to a democratic system of government. The democratic freedoms are instrumental in realizing the basic democratic values of popular sovereignty and political equality, and they function both by setting limits on governmental interference with the individual and by providing specific political rights.

The substantive **democratic freedoms** in Canada include freedom of association, freedom of assembly, freedom of expression, freedom of conscience, and freedom of the press. Collectively, these freedoms allow individuals to engage freely in the sort of discourse that is essential if free elections are to be effective in controlling the behaviour of our elected representatives. An election would be a meaningless exercise if the voters, parties, and candidates were not allowed to assemble and discuss the issues of the day free from interference by the current government. These democratic freedoms were only implicit in our Constitution until 1982 when they were set down explicitly in sections 2–5 of the Charter.

The basic **political rights** of Canadians start with the right to vote and to seek candidacy in an election. Again, such rights are necessarily implicit in an electoral democracy and were set down originally by the provincial and federal election acts. More will be said in Chapter 12 about the evolution of the right to vote and in Chapter 15 about the extension of the franchise. The right to vote is now stated explicitly in section 3 of the Charter.

A corollary of the right to vote is that in order to ensure fair and effective representation, each ballot should be weighted roughly equally. This has never been easy to achieve, in practical terms, for shifting populations have meant that the sizes of constituencies vary a great deal over time. As well, it was felt in the pre-electronic era that transportation and communication difficulties, not to mention a historical belief in the moral superiority of those who lived and worked on the land, justified an over-representation of rural and remote constituencies. Nevertheless, the principle that each vote should be roughly equal is an important — albeit yet to be attained — goal of truly representative democracy.

The *British North America Act* originally included two clauses that define our basic political rights. Section 20 specified that there must be a session of Parliament and of each provincial legislature at least once a year. This is to ensure that the executive branch, which exercises the prerogative power to *summon* Parliament, does not avoid a non-confidence vote in the House by simply not summoning it. This clause has been deleted from the *Constitution Act*, 1867, and replaced by section 5 of the Charter.

Section 50 of the *Constitution Act*, 1867, provides that the life of a Parliament or legislature shall not exceed five years. This clause is intended to ensure that our right to express our political will through periodic elections is not thwarted by the device of simply not calling any. Again, it is intended to protect us from an unscrupulous executive branch, which having secured majority support in the House, might simply decline to exercise the prerogative power of dissolution, as a means of staying in power. This principle is now set down in the Charter as section 4, which also provides that in national emergencies, the five-year limit can be extended by a two-thirds vote of the legislature.

### Procedural Rights (Legal Rights)

Procedural rights primarily involve criminal proceedings and include protection from arbitrary arrest, the right to a fair hearing, the right to counsel, and the right of *habeas corpus*. Moreover, they have come to include the rules of evidence that, in criminal judicial proceedings, determine the admissibility of evidence. As technologies have evolved, these procedural rights have been expanded to include protection from invasions of privacy through, for instance, wire-tapping or electronic eavesdropping. These procedural rights institutionalize the rule of law in the British sense of the term. They ensure *equality before the law* for all individuals and corporations and prevent arbitrariness and discrimination on the part of governmental officials or the police. These procedural rights, or **legal rights**, were traditionally protected by convention, by the common law, and by the provisions of the Criminal Code dealing with procedure and rules of evidence. Since 1982, our legal rights have been entrenched in sections 7–14 of the Charter.

### Liberal Rights and Freedoms

Certain of our fundamental rights and freedoms are implicit in the values of liberalism, but not necessarily in the values of democracy. In large part, these **liberal freedoms** deal with an individual's rights in regard to property and contract. They include the right to own property, the right not to be deprived thereof except through due process of law, and the freedom to enter into private contracts. These rights and freedoms are rooted in the English common law, but the Canadian Bill of Rights of 1960 explicitly recognizes the right to "the enjoyment of property" unless deprived thereof by due process of law.

Twenty years later, the Charter omitted any mention of a right to private property, and despite extensive lobbying to that end, the Charlottetown Accord of 1992 also omitted any such clause. This might be a reflection of the fact that our political culture is gradually shifing away from classical liberal values, but it seems more likely that such values are so deeply ingrained that there is simply no need to reiterate them.

While it is difficult to separate liberal freedoms from democratic freedoms in a country whose values are liberal-democratic, a possible distinction is that the former are very closely tied up with the economic system of capitalism. The liberal freedoms are, therefore, more important in achieving the ostensible liberal goal of *equal opportunity* within a free-market economy than they are in achieving the democratic goals of popular sovereignty and political equality. Two aspects of these liberal rights, the freedom of movement and the right to earn a livelihood, are entrenched separately in section 6 of the Charter as **mobility rights.**

### Egalitarian Rights

Egalitarian rights or **equality rights** are the so-called *human rights*, which are instrumental in achieving the goals of social and economic equality. Stated in the extreme, liberal and egalitarian values tend to conflict with each other, although, in fact, in Canada, there is gradual acceptance of limitations on the liberal freedoms, in order to promote human rights and to combat discrimination. While the egalitarian rights would certainly limit governmental discrimination against various classes of individuals, they also involve private-sector relationships, and include freedom from discrimination in employment, accommodation, transportation, and other such areas by reason of race, religion, gender, ethnic origin, or nationality.

Most Canadians would agree that these are, indeed, fundamental human rights, and egalitarianism and non-discrimination are becoming more and more important values in Canadian society. By now, all of the provinces and the federal government have human-rights legislation, which guarantees protection from discrimination by government agencies and private corporations alike. The Canadian Human Rights Commission, created in 1977, has as its mandate the investigation and resolution of claims of discrimination made against federal government agencies and federally incorporated companies. The Commission has been very active since its creation and has likely accomplished a great deal in discouraging discrimination in employment.

Section 15 of the Charter of Rights and Freedoms, guarantees equality rights, although it does not directly protect individuals from discrimination in the private sector. In fact, it can be argued convincingly that, in the long run, the only effective way to eliminate discrimination is to eliminate the personal prejudice, stereotyping, sexism, ethnocentrism, and racism that underlie all acts of discrimination. In other words, legislation can only affect *acts* of discrimination, whereas it is the predisposition to discriminate or the discriminatory *attitudes* of Canadians that must ultimately be conquered if we are to eliminate the problem.

### Privacy

It bears mention here that a positive individual right may be evolving in Canada in the area of *privacy*. The foundation of a **right to privacy** likely lies in in the common law (a man's home is his castle) and in some criminal provisions such as "peeping Tom" laws. Violations of privacy on the part of private individuals are viewed as trespassing; and encroachments, even by governmental officials such as the police, require significant justification and some level of judicial involvement, such as a warrant. However, most of the original tenets of a common-law right to privacy involve only the physical or *territorial* dimension of privacy, which is related to the law of property.

Modern electronic technology has created a situation where *information* concerning an individual can be gathered, collated, and retrieved with frightening efficiency. It has been recognized that the common-law protections of the right to territorial privacy have to be backed up by legislation to protect the informational privacy of individuals from unscrupulous business enterprises and governmental agencies, as well. The positive law response to this recent threat to individual freedom has been legislation that limits the operation of consumer credit ratings, and that imposes strict limits on the use of electronic surveillance devices, by both public and private organizations. The result is that a previously unrecognized and thought-to-be unnecessary *right to privacy* is being defined incrementally, through a series of positive law enactments.

The 1977 Canadian *Human Rights Act* provides for one of the members of the Commission to act as a "privacy commissioner." The job of this official is to investigate complaints arising out of part 4 of the *Human Rights Act*. This part of the Act requires the federal government to publicize the existence of the various information banks within the bureaucracy, to provide some access to this information on the part of the individual concerned, and to limit the use to which the information can be put. In the latter case, for instance, the federal government is restricted in the extent to which information gathered for one purpose and by one agency can be used by other agencies of the government or by other governments.

While this legislation was a step in the right direction, it will likely be necessary for a future government to introduce more comprehensive legislation dealing with privacy. Ultimately, similar legislation will have to be introduced in each of the provinces, so that comprehensive protection of the right to privacy can be attained for all Canadians in dealings with all governmental information-gathering institutions.

Finally, there is some indication that the courts may be willing to interpret sections 7 and 8 of the Charter as providing a right to privacy. Section 7 grants the right to "liberty and security of the person" and a violation of an individual's privacy by officals of the state could be construed, in some circumstances, as unreasonable. Similarly, the Supreme Court has stated specifically that the protection against "unreasonable search" in section 8 amounts to a privacy guarantee when it is the government that is snooping.[2]

### Emergency Powers and Rights and Freedoms

Virtually all governments have the authority to suspend fundamental rights and freedoms in emergency situations. Whether such emergency procedures should be tolerated in a democratic society depends on how they are used. Great injustices were done to Canadians of Japanese extraction during the Second World War simply because Canada was at war with Japan, and to Ukrainian immigrants during the First World War because of their suspected allegiance to the Kaiser. In retrospect, this seems a shameful blot on the civil liberties record of Canada, although, at the time, the government's action

---

2. *Hunter v. Southam Inc.* (1984) 2 SCR 145.

under the *War Measures Act* was probably condoned by nearly everyone except the victims themselves.[3]

A similar interpretation appears to have developed with respect to the invoking of the *War Measures Act* in the fall of 1970 because of an "apparent insurrection" in the province of Quebec. While in retrospect it does not appear that the Quebec situation was indeed an insurrection, at the time, a sizable proportion of the Canadian population agreed with the governments involved that such drastic measures were justified. Now that the "crisis" has long faded, many Canadians, including many who, at the time, supported the actions of federal and Quebec authorities, look back on the October Crisis with something of the same sense of shamefacedness with which we regard the treatment of the Japanese Canadians in 1942. The only conclusion to which one can come in this regard is that, if a comprehensive emergency power is to be vested in the government, and if that emergency power is to be exercised unilaterally at the discretion of the government, the public must be aware of the potential for abuses in such procedures. Certainly, any government which does exercise its emergency powers must be prepared to submit to the harsh judgement of future generations which will see the impact of the legislation without feeling the pressure and anxiety of the time.

The more fundamental question here, however, is whether a political system can permit legislation such as the *War Measures Act* and still remain a liberal democracy. If it is possible to conceive of *any* circumstances in which fundamental freedoms may be legitimately abrogated, then perhaps those freedoms are not so fundamental after all. Possibly, even in societies deeply committed to individual rights and freedoms, the stability and survival of the system becomes a more fundamental value than the substantive values implicit in the regime. Liberal-democratic systems are thus caught in a dilemma: on the one hand, if they do not take severe and arbitrary measures under certain circumstances, they might be overthrown and replaced by an authoritarian regime; on the other hand, by taking such measures, they will be, *ipso facto,* more authoritarian themselves.

There is no easy answer to this problem, but it is critical to an appraisal of the protection of rights and freedoms in Canada to ask the question. It is also telling that the 1982 Charter, although not explicitly stating (as did the Bill of Rights) that the Charter itself is inoperative when the government has declared an emergency, is silent on this point. It would seem likely that the *Emergencies Act*, 1988, which replaced the *War Measures Act*, will be interpreted as valid by virtue of the fact that the limits it temporarily imposes on our rights and freedoms are "reasonable limits" in the event of a genuine state of emergency.

### Aboriginal Rights

The *Constitution Act*, 1982, is associated in the public mind with the Charter of Rights and the amending formula for the Constitution. Another major impact of the 1982 Act, however, is that section 35(i) states that "the existing aboriginal

---

3.  While many Canadians, particularly the CCF party, consistently opposed the treatment of the Japanese Canadians, they were definitely in the minority.

and treaty rights of the Aboriginal peoples of Canada are hereby recognized and affirmed." **Aboriginal rights** are rights that the Indians, Inuit, and Métis possess by virtue of their ancestors' use and occupancy of North America before European contact. These rights have continued to exist despite the fact that the continent has come to be populated by large numbers of "newcomers."

**The Status of Aboriginal Rights**  As affirmed by the Canadian courts, and consistent with international law, aboriginal rights may be extinguished only by conquest, by treaty, or by an explicit act of the Parliament of Canada. Moreover, the courts have determined that, since the affirmation of those rights in 1982, even Parliament may not enact legislation that affects aboriginal rights unless it follows certain rules. The status of aboriginal rights flows from the fact that aboriginal people are deemed to be in a **fiduciary** relationship with the Crown, whereby all of their rights and titles are held in trust for them by the Crown in right of Canada. The Crown can extinguish or limit those rights and titles only through an act of Parliament in an *honourable* and just manner.

Following precepts set out in a 1990 Supreme Court of Canada decision,[4] the government can tamper with aboriginal rights only for fairly limited valid policy objectives, such as an overriding national interest, public health and safety, or conservation concerns. Even if there is a valid objective, the government must consult with the affected people, must limit the infringement to what is absolutely necessary to achieve the objective, and must provide compensation. The provincial governments likely have no authority to infringe aboriginal rights, and they do not have authority to enter into treaties with First Nations if the treaties involve the surrender of aboriginal rights or titles.

**Constitutional Protection**  Aboriginal rights were originally incorporated into what would become our Constitution through the *Proclamation of 1763*, which recognized the existence of the Indian nations, and provided that their lands or rights could not be taken away except according to the fundamental principles of British justice — in effect, by negotiated treaty. The obligations under the Proclamation were automatically transferred to the Government of Canada by the *Constitution Act*, 1867, and, by section 91 (24) of that Act, it is only the *federal* government that has the legislative authority to accept the surrender of any aboriginal rights.

As we have seen, the *Constitution Act*, 1982, affirms aboriginal rights without defining them, and section 25 of the Charter provides that its provisions cannot be construed so as to abrogate aboriginal or treaty rights. Hence, the Constitution of Canada explicitly recognizes the existence of aboriginal rights and provides protection for those rights but does not tell us what those rights are, nor whether they might have been surrendered or extinguished at some time in the past.

**The Land**  Since aboriginal rights derive from the occupancy and use of North America before European contact, one way of attempting to define the nature

4. *R. v. Sparrow* (1990) 70 DLR (4th) 385.

and extent of aboriginal rights is to ask what were the traditional or pre-colonial patterns of use and occupancy of the **land**. Indeed, because traditional aboriginal societies were based primarily upon hunting and gathering and, to a lesser extent, simple agriculture, the relationship of the aboriginal community to the land defines the aboriginal economy, culture, and society. But the aboriginal concept of land is very different from the European one. Where our system is based on the notion of private property, aboriginal societies base their system on the notion of shared *use* of the land. The rights to the land belong to everyone living today and to the unborn generations of the future. While, often, there were informal understandings among communities or tribal groups that recognized each others' more-or-less exclusive use of certain territories for purposes of hunting and fishing, the land was owned only by the Creator who put it there for the use of *all* people.

Thus, while aboriginal rights have not been exhaustively defined by the Constitution, statutes, or the common law, it is generally agreed that, at a minimum, such rights include the rights to hunt and fish and to harvest plants, and the necessarily incidental rights of access to and occupancy of the land upon which such resources are found. Hence, unless there has been an explicit surrender of rights through a previous treaty or land-claim agreement, governments, both federal and provincial, are constitutionally bound to protect or compensate the aboriginal interests in the land before they can sell it or otherwise grant interests that affect it to third parties.

The courts have indicated a willingness to find in favour of aboriginal-rights claimants in recent years and as a result, governments, both federal and provincial, have speeded up their attempts to negotiate comprehensive land-claims agreements in parts of Canada where there are no treaties. Such agreements are intended, in the government's vocabulary, to "exchange" the undefined aboriginal rights for a set of defined rights incorporated in a claims agreement or treaty. The aboriginal people are more likely to describe the process as one which simply "defines" aboriginal rights in a modern context, but the vernacular discrepencies have not prevented the negotiation of several major claims agreements. As well, even where there are treaties in place, the courts are broadening the definition of "treaty obligations," forcing governments to live up to these obligations and providing compensation where there have been breaches.

It is clear that aboriginal rights include at least a set of **usufructuary** rights associated with the use and occupancy of the land and that these rights remain alive and in effect until such time as they have been surrendered. The question that has not been answered by the courts is whether there is an aboriginal right to self-government. Whatever the verdict on this issue, the federal and several provincial and territorial governments have indicated a willingness to assume that there *is* such a right and to negotiate agreements with the various First Nations as to how aboriginal nations will relate politically, administratively, and constitutionally to other governments in Canada. We will deal with the issues of aboriginal self-government in Chapter 10.

## ▶ PRE-CHARTER PROTECTION OF RIGHTS AND FREEDOMS

Before the enactment of the Charter, the legal protection of our civil liberties was left, at first, for the courts to "discover," implicit within existing constitutional provisions and, later, in federal and provincial statutory guarantees of rights and freedoms.

### Federalism and Civil Liberties: 1867–1960

In the period up to the enactment of the Bill of Rights in 1960, the federal division of powers was the main tool used to find oppressive or discriminatory legislation *ultra vires*. For example, some laws in British Columbia, which discriminated against Canadians of oriental or East Indian descent, were declared invalid because they interfered with the federal government's exclusive power to pass laws regarding "naturalization and aliens."[5] Similarly, as recently as the 1950s, provincial laws in Quebec that interfered with freedom of expression were declared invalid because they encroached on the federal government's exclusive authority over the criminal law.

A potential breakthrough in broadening the power of the courts to protect civil liberties occurred in the 1930s when several Alberta laws were thrown out on the basis of a clever interpretation by the Chief Justice of the Supreme Court, Sir Lyman Duff. This interpretation, which is known as **the Duff Doctrine** is based on the preamble to the *Constitution Act*, 1867, which states that Canada shall have a system similar in principle to that of Great Britain. Duff argued that this statement implied parliamentary democracy, which "contemplates a parliament working under the influence of public opinion, and public discussion,"[6] and, in effect, accepts as axiomatic that "the right to free public discussion of public affairs, notwithstanding its incidental mischiefs, is the breath of life for parliamentary institutions."[7] Consequently, Duff argued,

> the parliament of Canada possesses authority to legislate for the protection of this right. . . . That authority rests upon the principle that the powers requisite for the protection of the constitution itself are, by necessity, implications from the BNA Act as a whole (Fort Frances Case, [1923] A.C. 695) and since the subject matter in relation to which the power is exercised is not exclusively a provincial matter, it is necessarily vested in Parliament.[8]

However, while Duff concluded that any interference with a fundamental democratic freedom was beyond the competence of the provinces, he did not

---

5. *Union Colliery Company v. Bryden* (1899) A.C. 580. However, the Judicial Committee found that the *British Columbia Elections Act* which denied the vote to orientals was valid because it involved purely provincial matters. At this time, there was no separate federal franchise and, hence, the British Columbia election legislation barred orientals from voting in federal elections as well. More about this in Chapter 13. See *Cunningham v. Tomey Homma* (1903) A.C. 151, and *Quong Wing v. King* (1916) 49 SCR 440.
6. *Reference re Alberta Statutes* (1938) 2 SCR 133.
7. Ibid.
8. Ibid., p. 134.

suggest that such matters were beyond the competence of the federal Parliament as well.[9]

Thus, through a number of cases dealing with restrictive provincial laws, the courts began to sort out the federal-provincial distribution of legislative power with regard to civil liberties. However, up until 1960, decisions relating to civil liberties were viewed almost entirely in terms of deciding *which* level of government had the power to interfere with them, and never whether *any* government should in fact have such power. This *passivist* or literalist approach to judicial interpretation has haunted Canadian constitutional development throughout our history, and it has been particularly restrictive in the area of civil liberties. As J. R. Mallory has put it,

> this is not a very elevating way of looking at our much cherished liberties of speech, conscience and religion. . . . Before the enactment of the Charter, the dialogue — in constitutional terms — about basic political and civil rights was essentially confined to the narrow issue of jurisdiction.[10]

On the more positive side, long before the passage of the Charter in 1982, things did get better. A general agreement emerged in all provinces that certain rights and freedoms are too fundamental to be tampered with by any level of government, and legislative abrogation of substantive freedoms by the provinces has been rare since the late 1950s.

## The Canadian Bill of Rights: 1960–1982

The Canadian Bill of Rights, enacted in 1960, sets out our basic rights and freedoms in much the same way that the Charter does. The list includes most of the things in the Charter, but the difference is that the Bill is only a federal statute and, hence, does not apply to the provincial legislatures. When this inherent limitation was combined with the fact that the Supreme Court's interpretation of the Bill was very inconsistent, it is not difficult to understand why many Canadians wished to see a constitutionally entrenched Charter. While it did supply "grist to the judicial mills"[11] throughout the 1970s, and although Mr. Justice (Chief Justice by 1975) Bora Laskin consistently presented articulate dissenting opinions, the court essentially stuck to a fairly restrictive application of the Bill of Rights.[12] With very few exceptions, such as the Drybones case in 1970,[13] which declared portions of the *Indian Act* to be invalid, the Bill of Rights did not substantially add to the *legal* protection of our fundamental freedoms in Canada.

---

9.  The Duff Doctrine is still alive in Canada. It was used in a decision of the Supreme Court of Canada in 1987, *OPSEU v. A-G Ontario* (1987) 2 SCR 2.

10.  See J. R. Mallory, "Evolving Canadian Constitutionalism." Research paper prepared for the Royal Commission on the Economic Union and Development Prospects for Canada (MacDonald Commission) (Toronto: University of Toronto Press, 1985), pp. 5–6.

11.  *A-G. Canada v. Lavell and Bédard* (1974) SCR 1349. For those interested in the detailed arguments presented in this case, both the majority judgement delivered by Mr. Justice Ritchie and a lengthy dissent delivered by Mr. Justice Bora Laskin bear careful reading.

12.  See, for instance, *Burnshire Case* (1975) 1 SCR 693; *Canard Case* (1976) 1 SCR 170; *Bliss Case* (1979) 1 SCR 183; and *Prata Case* (1976) 1 SCR 376.

13.  *The Queen v. Drybones* (1970) SCR 282.

The overall effect of the Bill of Rights and corresponding provincial enactments was still beneficial in that such explicit statements of our political
values have symbolic and educative utility. Their function is as much to educate
as it is to provide binding *de jure* protection for our rights and freedoms.[14]
Moreover, before moving to a discussion of the Charter, it is necessary to point
out that any written guarantees of rights and freedoms may provide merely
illusory protection. If the norms and values reflected in the constitutional,
statutory, and common-law provisions defining our rights and freedoms are
not congruent with the prevalent modes of thought and attitudes in the society
at large, such laws will have little real effect on our substantive freedom. The
best guarantee of fundamental freedom in any society, therefore, is a consensus
among the members of the society as to what those freedoms comprise.

## ▶ THE CHARTER OF RIGHTS AND FREEDOMS

Perhaps the most significant component of the 1982 *Constitution Act* is the
entrenchment in the Canadian Constitution of a Charter of Rights and Freedoms. While the sorts of rights and freedoms so protected are not all that
different from those listed in the Bill of Rights, the Charter is an improvement
over the Bill because the Charter applies equally to the provinces and the
federal government, and is, in fact, entrenched in the sense that it can be
altered only by all of the provinces and the Parliament of Canada through the
constitutional-amendment process. The **entrenchment** of basic rights and freedoms is a major departure from previous constitutional practice in Canada,
and likely should be considered a new *operative principle* of the Constitution
along with parliamentary supremacy, responsible government, judicial independence, and divided sovereignty.

### The Charter: Substantive Provisions

Section 2 of the Charter guarantees fundamental freedoms such as freedom
of conscience, thought, belief, expression, assembly, and association. It also
guarantees freedom of religion, despite the fact that the preamble recognizes
the "supremacy of God." Although there is no jurisprudence yet to clarify this
apparent inconsistency, we might guess that Canadians can worship as they
choose — but that they *must* worship!

Sections 3–5 identify the **democratic rights**: the right to vote; the five-year
limit on the life of a Parliament or legislature; and the requirement for at least
one annual meeting of all legislatures. Where the Charter deviates a bit from
the substance of pre-1982 rights is in the area of **mobility rights.** The deviation
is not, however, in the inclusion of the right of free movement of Canadian
citizens, and of the corollary freedom to seek employment in any part of
Canada — for such rights already existed, both implicitly, in the structure of
the *Constitution Act*, 1867, and explicitly, in common-law jurisprudence — but

---

14. While the 1960 Bill of Rights has been largely eclipsed in the public mind by the Charter, it is still
in full effect and complements the provisions of the 1982 document. See *Singh v. Minister of Immigration*
(1985) 1 SCR 177.

in the qualifier that laws creating "local preferences" in hiring practices are exempt from this provision if unemployment in that province is above the national average.

Sections 7–14 guarantee **legal rights**, or procedural rights, most of which were already protected by the Canadian Bill of Rights, the Criminal Code, and the British common-law precedents. The only distinctive provision with respect to legal rights is the "enforcement" section of the Charter, section 24(2), which states that the admissibility of evidence obtained illegally will depend upon whether the court feels that "having regard to all circumstances, the admission of it in the proceedings would bring the administration of justice into disrepute."

Section 15 provides for **equality rights.** No individual can be discriminated against by reason of race, religion, gender, age, or disability. However, affirmative-action programs are acceptable where circumstances warrant. Official-language rights are protected in sections 16–22, although there is little here that was not already in effect before 1982. Finally, section 23 provides for the rights of linguistic minorities to have their children educated in the language of choice (French or English), out of public funds, "where numbers warrant."

### Explicit Limits on the Charter's Applicability

While there are many qualifiers and exceptions written into the specific clauses of the Charter, a few sections have been and will continue to be critical in determining the scope and impact of the Charter on Canadian society. We have already encountered these in the context of the supremacy of Parliament, but each deserves more detailed consideration.

**The Legislative Override**  The *legislative override* or ***non-obstante*** provision in section 33 permits Parliament or a provincial legislature to pass legislation that is to operate "notwithstanding a provision included in section 2 or sections 7 to 15." The Charter limits the applicability of such an override to five years, after which time the legislature must re-enact it. The impact of section 33 will ultimately depend upon the political determination of legislators to utilize this power, and their willingness to suffer the potential public criticism and embarrassment of having to re-enact it every five years.

The main use of this provision was by the *Parti Québécois* government of Quebec, which passed blanket legislation exempting all of Quebec's pre-1982 laws from the relevant sections of the Charter. From 1982 until their defeat in 1984, the *Parti Québécois* government routinely put a notwithstanding clause in all new legislation as well. This was partly a symbolic gesture to disassociate the Quebec government from a constitutional evocation it did not agree to in the first place, and not as a way of rejecting the basic principles entrenched in the Charter. In fact, Quebec has its own charter, which essentially guarantees all of the rights and freedoms enumerated in the Canadian Charter.

The exception to this was with respect to the French-only provisions in the Quebec language laws, which banned the use of English on commercial signs throughout the province. The courts, in 1988, determined that these provisions of the language legislation were *ultra vires* on the grounds that they infringed freedom of expression.[15] The Government of Quebec re-enacted the law with a *non-obstante* clause to get around the Charter. Saskatchewan also used the *non-obstante* clause in 1986 in passing back-to-work legislation to end a public-service strike, but subsequent decisions of the courts have ruled that the right to strike can be limited. The use of the override provision was, in this case, unnecessary.

**Reasonable Limits Prescribed by Law**   The second clause of the Charter that has been extremely important in determining its scope is section 1, which states that the Canadian Charter of Rights and Freedoms guarantees those rights and freedoms set out in it "subject only to such reasonable limits, prescribed by law, as can be demonstrably justified in a free and democratic society." By contrast to section 33, which allows the *legislature* to affect the scope of the Charter, section 1 is an interpretation clause that allows the *judiciary* to endorse limits on the scope of the Charter so long as those limits are 1) reasonable, 2) prescribed by law, and 3) demonstrably justified in a free and democratic society.

Faced with a Charter case, the courts ask first that the claimant demonstrate to the court's satisfaction that an impugned law does indeed place a limit on an entrenched right or freedom. If the claimant can demonstrate that there is a *prima facie* abrogation of the Charter, then the court assumes that the legislation being challenged is unconstitutional. To escape this fate, the government's lawyers must demonstrate that the *prima facie* abrogation is *reasonable* within the terms of section 1. The clause *demonstrably justifiable* has been interpreted by the courts to mean that the burden of proof is with the government, which must demonstrate that the limit placed on the right is reasonable. In other words, the courts have not allowed the presumption that, because an abrogation is enacted by a democratically elected legislature, it is automatically "reasonable" in a free and democratic society.

The test of reasonableness was established by the Supreme Court of Canada in a 1986 decision, *R. v. Oakes*.[16] The court stated that, first, the objective of the legislation must be important enough in terms of the interests of society to justify limiting the right or freedom. Second, the government measure cannot be in excess of what is minimally required in order to accomplish the objective. Thus, it should not be arbitrary or capricious; it should limit the right as little as possible and still accomplish the valid objective; and the effect of the limit must be in proportion to the societal problem being tackled, that is, the treatment cannot be so severe that it kills the patient. The other qualifier in section 1 of the Charter, that the limit be *prescribed by law*, has turned out not to be a problem because for the most part the only measures that have been challenged have been laws or actions taken by officials pursuant to laws.

**Interpretation Clauses**   While sections 1 and 33 place the most important limits on the operation of the Charter, sections 24–32 limit the operation of the Charter by providing direction to the courts in the interpretation of its substantive provisions. Section 24(1) grants *standing* before the courts to any

15.  *Ford v. A-G Quebec* (1988) 2 SCR 712; and *Devine v. A-G Quebec* (1988) 2 SCR 790.
16.  *Queen v. Oakes* (1986) 1 SCR 103.

individual whose rights or freedoms under the Charter have been infringed. This is important because it allows any individual to directly and immediately challenge government enactments or the actions of governmental agencies and officials. The other side of the coin is found in section 32, which provides that the Charter applies to *all* governments, government agencies, and government officials in Canada. The significant point here is that the Charter does *not* apply to private-sector individuals or corporations.

Section 24(2) deals with the admissibility of evidence. It states that, in determining the admissibility of evidence that was obtained in a manner contrary to a provision of the Charter, the court may exclude it if it determines that to admit it would "bring the administration of justice into disrepute." The significance of this clause is that illegally obtained evidence is not necessarily excluded, as has been the case in the United States. Rather, it allows the *court* to decide to admit the evidence even when it is clear that the evidence was obtained illegally. This is intended to avoid the situation in criminal procedure in the US, where the courts must sometimes toss out a case on a minor technicality even if the individual is clearly guilty. On the other hand, if the breach of the Charter is not a minor one, such as a confession extracted by torture, the judge can still exclude it as evidence.

Other interpretation clauses that may, to some extent, limit the operation of the Charter include provisions that the Charter must be applied equally to men and women and that it should be interpreted in a manner consistent with the "multicultural heritage of Canadians." As well, the Charter is not intended to limit rights and freedoms set down elsewhere such as in statutory bills of rights and human-rights legislation, nor is it intended to *expand* the existing powers of governments. With the exception of section 25, which provides that the Charter should not be construed so as to limit aboriginal rights, these interpretation clauses are important mainly as symbolic affirmations of "good things" in our political culture and have not cropped up to any significant extent in the Charter cases to date. Section 25 will be discussed further in the section on aboriginal rights later in the chapter.

## The Impact of the Charter

One fact has emerged uncontested in the experience of the first dozen years of the Charter's existence, and that is that the Charter has been raised in a very large number of cases. In the first three years, Peter Russell estimated that the Charter was raised at a rate of about 50 cases per month.[17] While most of these early cases were in the lower provincial courts, and while the flood of cases has abated significantly since the first few years, the Supreme Court of Canada has brought down over 200 decisions dealing with Charter issues since 1982. Today, about 20 per cent of the total decisions of the Supreme Court involve Charter arguments.

We cannot deal with all of these cases, nor can we devote a lot of time to explaining the complex legal arguments surrounding the decisions in an already very large textbook. However, in the following pages we will outline, in

---

17. See P. Russell, "The First Three Years in Charterland," *CPA*, Fall 1985, p. 369. See also F. L. Morton, "Charting the Charter — Year One: A Statistical Analysis," a paper presented at Canadian Political Science Association Conference, June 1984.

general terms, the substantive impacts of the most important cases, the overall impact of having an entrenched Charter on Canadian political life, and the impact on the political process, "writ large."

**Important Cases: 1982–1994** The most general conclusion about Charter challenges in the courts is that most of them fail in the lower courts and are never appealed to the Supreme Court of Canada. While there were a number of successful challenges in the first few years, many of these involved violations of procedural rights by individual police officers and government officials. Where statutory provisions have been overturned by the Supreme Court of Canada, most of them involved relatively minor procedural flaws rather than issues of substance.

Since the first few years, the overall success rate of Charter cases has been around 15 per cent.[18] On appeals to the Supreme Court of Canada, approximately one-third of the Charter claimants have been successful. A second general conclusion about Charter cases is that most of the deft legal thrusts and parries are concentrated on section 1 arguments to justify rights infringements as "reasonable" limits. The low success rate of Charter challenges to legislation has to do with the relatively high success rate of government lawyers in convincing lower court judges that the legislative infringements on Charter rights and freedoms are reasonable.

*Fundamental Freedoms* With respect to laws infringing on our fundamental freedoms as set down in section 2 of the Charter, the Supreme Court of Canada declared the *Lord's Day Act ultra vires* because it infringed upon the religious freedom of non-Christians.[19] On the other hand, Ontario Sunday-closing legislation was declared valid because its purpose was to provide workers with a day of rest and not explicitly to recognize the Christian sabbath. The court ruled that the infringment of religious freedom was a reasonable limit in this case.[20]

The freedom of thought and expression clause of the Charter has been upheld in a number of cases. In a case in Ontario in 1983, the powers of the Ontario Board of Censors were challenged, and the Ontario Court of Appeal upheld the decision of the lower court that the board, as then constituted, interfered with freedom of expression.[21] The case was never appealed to the Supreme Court of Canada because the provincial government changed the legislation to bring the operation of the board in line with the provisions of the Charter. Unreasonable interference with freedom of expression was also the court's rationale in declaring *ultra vires* the French-only sign provisions of Quebec's Bill 101.[22] As discussed above, the Quebec legislature re-enacted the provisions with a section 33 notwithstanding clause. Provisions of the federal *Public Service Employment Act*, which restricted the political activity of public

18. See Radha Jhappan, "The Charter and the Courts," *in* M. S. Whittington and G. Williams, *Canadian Politics in the 1990s* (Toronto: Nelson, 1994), pp. 335–59.
19. *R. v. Big M Drug Mart* (1985) 1 SCR 351.
20. *R. v. Edwards Books and Art* (1986) 2 SCR 713.
21. *Ontario Film and Video Appreciation Society v. Ontario Board of Censors* (1983) 147 DLR (3d) 58.
22. See *Ford v. A-G Quebec*.

servants, were shot down by the Supreme Court in 1991, again as an unreasonable limit on the freedom of expression.[23]

On the other side of the ledger, various pieces of legislation that place a *prima facie* limit on freedom of expression have been upheld as constituting reasonable limits under section 1. These include mostly criminal-law provisions dealing with pornography, hate literature, publication bans in sexual assault cases, and prostitution.

Unions have generally not fared well in their attempts to define the scope of freedom of association. While the right to picket was upheld as an extension of freedom of expression,[24] the courts have determined that the right to strike is not a fundamental freedom flowing out of the freedom to associate. Hence, back-to-work legislation and laws prohibiting strikes by certain groups of employees have been deemed to be reasonable. As well, challenges to legislation capping public-sector wages have all failed.[25]

*Legal Rights*  There has been a lot of Charter litigation with respect to section 7 which guarantees "the right to life, liberty and security of the person and the right not to be deprived thereof except in accordance with the principles of fundamental justice." In a very early Charter case, *Queen v. Operation Dismantle Inc.*,[26] a peace group argued that the testing of the cruise missile in Canadian airspace violated our "security of the person," and the Cabinet's decision to allow the testing of the missile was therefore unconstitutional. While the Supreme Court agreed that nuclear war would, indeed, be bad for our health, they rejected this argument.

However, in the Morgentaler case in 1988,[27] the Supreme Court struck down the section of the Criminal Code dealing with abortion on the grounds that section 7 of the Charter included a woman's right to terminate an unwanted pregnancy. In the Borowski case,[28] the counter argument, that a *fetus* has the right to life, liberty and the security of the person was rejected in the following year as moot in light of the Morgentaler decision. In 1993, in the Rodriguez case, the Supreme Court rejected the argument that section 7 included an individual's right to a physician-assisted suicide and upheld the relevant sections of the Criminal Code.[29]

Finally, perhaps the most significant decision involving section 7 was brought down in the Singh case of 1985.[30] Here, provisions of the *Immigration Act* were invalidated because the court agreed that to deny refugee claimants a fair hearing before deportation was a denial of "fundamental justice." What was a new departure in this decision was that the court stated that the Charter provisions protect Canadian citizens, landed immigrants, and visitors, whether here legally or illegally.

---

23. *Osborne v. Canada* (1991) 2 SCR 69.
24. *Dolphin Case* (1986) 2 SCR 573.
25. See *Re Public Service Employees Relations Act* (1987) 1 SCR 313; *RWDSU v. Saskatchewan* (1987) 1 SCR 460; and *PSAC v. Canada* (1987) 1 SCR 424.
26. *Queen v. Operation Dismantle Inc.* (1985) 1 SCR 441.
27. *Morgentaler v. The Queen* (1988) 2 SCR 30.
28. *Borowski v. A-G Canada* (1989) 1 SCR 342.
29. *Rodriguez v. A-G British Columbia* (1993) 3 SCR 519.
30. *Singh v. Minister of Immigration* (1985) 1 SCR 177.

The other sections of the Charter dealing with "legal rights" have been invoked many times and some have resulted in favourable judgements. In *Hunter v. Southam*,[31] the search and seizure practices of the Combines Investigation Branch were declared to be unreasonable, and had to be modified to bring them into line with section 8 of the Charter. Writs of assistance, which were open-ended warrants issued to police officers in the past, have been struck down as unreasonable; strip searches, while not unreasonable per se, can only be conducted if the individual is given the opportunity to retain counsel; and blood samples cannot be taken without legal authorization. On the other side of the coin, the court decided that it is not unreasonable for a police officer to demand to see an individual's driver's licence during a highway spot check.

In sum, one of the fears of the early critics of the Charter was that Canada could end up with a situation similar to the one in the United States, where obviously guilty criminals may elude conviction because of technical violations of the rights of the accused. It would appear that, for the most part, these fears were unfounded, for while there have been some successful challenges of criminal procedure on the basis of the Charter, judges have generally taken a fairly generous view of what is reasonable in such cases. With respect to the admissibility of evidence, judges have tended to shift the burden of proof, under section 24 challenges, from the Crown to the accused. In other words, the *defence* must show that to admit the impugned evidence would "bring the administration of justice into disrepute."[32]

*Equality Rights* The jurisprudence generated by the section of the Charter dealing with equality rights has not produced any startling results. Sections of the *Unemployment Insurance Act* that discriminated on the basis of gender and age were struck down,[33] and a provision of the Ontario Human Rights Code that exempted sports teams from its gender-discrimination provisions was declared invalid.[34] However, in other cases that invoked section 15 provisions, the courts have found that compulsory retirement laws, while *prima facie* discriminatory, were reasonable in a free and democratic society.[35]

In *Andrews v. The Law Society of British Columbia*, in 1989,[36] the Supreme Court of Canada ruled that discrimination on the basis of citizenship was not constitutional. Radha Jhappan finds it ironic that the Andrews case, while one of the more important of the decisions involving the non-discrimination section of the Charter, "upheld the equality rights of a healthy, wealthy, white male of British origin, rather than a member of a group that has been historically disadvantaged."[37]

*Democratic Rights* The only cases in which the courts have been asked to use the democratic-rights section of the Charter have involved the section 3 guarantee of the right to vote, and the only successful decisions have been those

---

31. *Hunter v. Southam Inc.*
32. Russell, "The First Three Years," p. 392.
33. *Brooks v. Canada Safeway* (1978) 1 SCR 1219; *Tetreault-Gadoury v. Canada* (1991) 2 SCR 22.
34. *Blainey v. Ontario Hockey Association* (1986) 54 OR (2nd) 513.
35. *McKinney v. University of Guelph* (1990) 3 SCR 229.
36. *Andrews v. The Law Society of British Columbia* (1989) 3 SCR 22.
37. Jhappan, *The Charter and the Courts.*

that struck down provisions of elections acts disfranchising prisoners and people in mental institutions. In general, while the courts have agreed that there can be reasonable limits placed on peoples' voting rights, the blanket exclusions in many election laws were deemed to be excessive. In the same way, the courts have determined that the right to vote in a provincial election can require a certain period of residency in the province, but that the period must be reasonable.[38]

As discussed above, limits on the political activities of public servants can be imposed in order to ensure a neutral public service, but the limits must not be greater than what is necessary to achieve that goal. Blanket provisions have thus been declared unconstitutional, not because they run up against section 3, but because they unreasonably restrict freedom of expression.

An important successful Charter challenge was the National Citizen's Coalition case in 1984. This involved a section of the *Canada Elections Act*, which made it an offence for private citizens and organizations to advertise independently for or against candidates or parties during a campaign. The Alberta Supreme Court held that such a restriction was not a "reasonable limit" because it could not be demonstrated that such independent participation in campaigns would damage the democratic election process.[39] This was not appealed to the Supreme Court of Canada. Amendments to the law that would bring it into line with the Charter have been enacted, but have not yet been tested in court.

Finally, in 1991 the Supreme Court dealt with a challenge based on section 3 that could have rendered inoperative every elections act in Canada, federal and provicial. The argument was made that section 3 implied *fair and effective* representation and that the variations in the size of rural and urban constituencies denied this right. The court decided that representation could be fair and effective without being *equal* and that, therefore, a reasonable discrepency between urban and rural ridings is acceptable.[40]

**The Charter and Canadian Political Life**  The above discussion of the Charter is intended to provide an overview and does not pretend to explain the full complexity or all of the subtleties in the court interpretations of this important component of our Constitution. However, at the broadest level of generalization, it can be concluded that the Charter has not yet had a very great impact either on our system of government or on the multitude of statutes currently on the books. Thirteen years' experience with the judiciary's interpretation of the scope of the Charter indicate that the courts will not tolerate far-fetched attempts to overturn a wide range of policies of our elected governments. But neither have the courts taken the approach that because something is enacted by a sovereign democratic legislature it is automatically reasonable in a free and democratic society:

> Generally Canadian judges have not taken the easy way out of giving the legislature the benefit of the doubt and presuming the legislation to be reasonable and there-

38.  See Ian Greene, *The Charter of Rights* (Toronto: Lorimer, 1989), pp. 110–25.
39.  *National Citizens' Coalition Inc. v. A-G Canada* (1984) 11 DLR (4th) 48.
40.  See R. Knopff and F. L. Morton, *Charter Politics* (Scarborough: Nelson, 1992), pp. 332–73.

fore constitutional. On the contrary they have, in effect, required the government to assume the burden of demonstrating the reasonableness of legislative limits on rights.[41]

By way of summary, the Charter has turned out to be neither as bad as its detractors feared nor as wonderful as its proponents hoped. It is clear, as well, that in the cases decided since 1982 we can see that the Charter has had and will continue to have a much greater influence on the way Canada is governed than did the 1960 Bill of Rights.[42] We will say more about the Charter and the changing role of the judiciary, particularly the Supreme Court of Canada, in Chapter 24.

## ▶ CONCLUSION

While the *direct* impact of the Charter through its application by the courts may not be as extensive as expected, it has undoubtedly had an impact on the attitudes of the lawmakers themselves. Because it exists, and because it is being applied by the courts, legislators are wary of possible court challenges. Governments not only screen all new policy proposals to ensure that they fall within the boundaries defined by the Charter, but they have also had to go back and "audit" exisiting laws in order to bring them in line with Charter decisions.

At another level, the values and attitudes of governmental officials dealing directly with the public, particularly police and security officers, are critical in determining the actual extent of our rights and freedoms and the quality of life in Canada. Given the wide discretionary powers that we have traditionally vested in members of the law-enforcement community, it is essential that such people understand and respect our basic political values. While we must certainly pay more attention to the recruitment and training of police and security officials to ensure that people with deep prejudices, closed minds, or little tolerance are not placed in positions of such power, it is also clear that the Charter, and the manner in which it has been interpreted, serves as a constant reminder to these officials of the enormous responsibility with which we have entrusted them.

Finally, as a general conclusion to this discussion of rights and freedoms in Canada, it is necessary to point out that the constitutional guarantees provided by legal instruments such as the Charter cannot in and of themselves protect our liberties. While such institutional guarantees do deter those who would try to abuse our freedoms, their more important role is as symbolic and educative devices. They teach Canadians about the importance of our rights and freedoms and about the importance of non-discrimination. In the final

---

41. Russell, "The First Three Years," p. 376.
42. Perhaps, in the first few years, the area in which the effect of the Charter on legislation was the most profound was that of language-education rights. Key sections of the Quebec Charter of the French Language were thrown out because they violated the rights of English Canadians under section 23 of the Charter of Rights (*A.G. Quebec v. Quebec Association of Protestant School Boards* [1984] 10 DLR [4th]) 321). In another case, the Ontario Court of Appeal upheld the rights of Franco-Ontarians to education in their own language (*Re Education Act of Ontario* [1984] 10 DLR [4th] 491). However, the early successes with respect to this section have not generated a lot of new decisions since.

analysis, it is the deep-rooted values and attitudes of Canadians that determine the kind of society we are going to live in. The symbolic role that formal statements and guarantees of rights and freedoms play in the process of political socialization may be more important than the positive-law remedies that are provided in them, for, in the long run, the most important sanction against repressive laws is a public opinion that is opposed to them. The danger lies either in the public's ceasing to pay much attention to the government, thus letting repressive legislation slip by unnoticed, or in the majority's uncritical acceptance of laws that suppress the freedoms of minorities.

▶ FURTHER READING: PART TWO
THE CONSTITUTION

### General
Cairns, A. C. *Constitution, Government and Society in Canada.* Toronto: McClelland and Stewart, 1988.

Cheffins, Ron, and P. A. Johnson. *The Revised Canadian Constitution: Politics or Law.* Toronto: McGraw-Hill Ryerson, 1986.

Heard, Andrew. *Canadian Constitutional Conventions.* Toronto: Oxford University Press, 1991.

Hogg, Peter. *Constitutional Law of Canada.* Toronto: Carswell, 1993.

MacKinnon, F. *The Crown in Canada.* Calgary: McClelland and Stewart West, 1976.

Milne, D. *The Canadian Constitution.* Toronto: Lorimer, 1991.

Reesor, B. *The Canadian Constitution in Historical Perspective.* Scarborough: Prentice-Hall, 1992.

Slattery, B. "First Nations and the Constitution," *in* R. S. Blair and J. T. McLeod, *The Canadian Political Tradition: Basic Readings.* Scarborough: Nelson, 1993, p. 112.

Ward, Norman. *Dawson's The Government of Canada.* Toronto: University of Toronto Press, 1987.


### Constitutional Change
Beck, S., and Ivan Bernier. *Canada and the New Constitution.* Montreal: Institute for Research and Public Policy, 1984.

Beheils, M. *The Meech Lake Primer: Conflicting Views on the 1987 Constitutional Accord.* Ottawa: University of Ottawa Press, 1989.

Cairns, A. C. *Disruptions: Constitutional Struggles.* Toronto: McClelland and Stewart, 1991.

Gibbins, Roger. *Meech Lake and Canada: Perspective from the West.* Edmonton: Academic Publishing, 1988.

Gibbins, Roger. "Constitutional Turmoil and Frustration: From Trudeau to Mulroney," *in* M. S. Whittington and G. Williams, eds., *Canadian Politics in the 1990s.* Scarborough: Nelson, 1994, pp. 323–34.

Russell, Peter. *Constitutional Odyssey.* Toronto: University of Toronto Press, 1992.


### The Charter of Rights
Bayefsky, A., and M. Eberts. *Equality and the Canadian Charter of Rights and Freedoms.* Toronto: Carswell, 1990.

Berger, T. *Fragile Freedoms: Human Rights and Dissent in Canada.* Agincourt: The Book Society, 1983.

Borovoy, A. *When Freedoms Collide: The Case for Our Civil Liberties.* Toronto: Lester and Orpen Dennys, 1988.

Greene, Ian. *The Charter of Rights.* Toronto: Lorimer, 1989.

Jhappan, Radha. "The Charter and the Courts," *in* M. S. Whittington and G. Williams, eds., *Canadian Politics in the 1990s.* Scarborough: Nelson, 1994, pp. 335–59.

Knopff, R., and F. L. Morton. *Charter Politics*. Scarborough: Nelson, 1992.

Mandel, M. *The Charter of Rights and the Legalization of Politics in Canada*. Toronto: Wall and Thompson, 1993.

Russell, Peter, R. Knopff, and F. L. Morton. *Federalism and the Charter*. Ottawa: Carleton University Press, 1989.

Schmeiser, D. A. *Civil Liberties in Canada*. London: Oxford University Press, 1975.

## PART THREE

# Federalism

*Chapter* **8**

# Constitutional Development and Canadian Federalism

The Dominion of Canada came into existence in 1867 with the passage of the *British North America Act* by the Parliament of the United Kingdom. The BNA Act was passed at the request of the British North American colonies and was based on resolutions that had been worked out jointly by the colonies themselves. As discussed in Chapter 5, the deliberations had originally included all of the British North American colonies. However, Newfoundland and Prince Edward Island soon lost their enthusiasm, and it was left to the remaining colonies, Upper and Lower Canada, New Brunswick, and Nova Scotia, to come to a negotiated agreement on the terms of the union. Once the agreement had been thrashed out, it was a relatively simple matter for Britain's Parliament to put it into the form of a statute, which came into effect on July 1, 1867.

## ▶ THE DISTRIBUTION OF POWERS IN 1867

### Sections 91 and 92

The federal-provincial division of authority was set down in some detail in the BNA Act. The powers of the federal Parliament are, for the most part, defined in section 91. Section 91 is in two parts. The first part was a broad and general grant of power, giving Parliament the authority to make laws for "the Peace, Order, and Good Government of Canada in relation to all Matters not coming within the Classes of Subjects by this Act assigned exclusively to the Legislatures of the Provinces." The second part of section 91 was an enumeration of twenty-nine subject matters, such as "the Public Debt and Property," "the Regulation of Trade and Commerce," "the Raising of Money by any Mode or System of

Taxation," and "the Criminal Law." These were set down "for greater Certainty, but not so as to restrict the Generality" of the **peace, order, and good-government clause**.

The legislative powers of the provinces were, for the most part, set out in section 92 of the BNA Act. Section 92 does not begin with any comprehensive grant of power to the provinces, but simply states that, within each province, "the Legislature may exclusively make Laws in relation to Matters coming within the Classes of Subjects next herein-after enumerated," and then proceeds to list sixteen subject matters, such as "Direct Taxation within the Province," "the Solemnization of Marriage," "Property and Civil Rights," and "Generally all Matters of a merely local or private Nature." Thus, when sections 91 and 92 are read together, it is clear that the intention was to give the federal government a comprehensive power to make law and then to exempt from this general grant certain carefully specified powers, which were to be retained exclusively by the provinces.

### Shared Jurisdiction: Sections 93 and 95

The subject of education is normally considered to rest within the exclusive jurisdiction of the provincial legislatures by section 93 of the BNA Act. However, section 93 places certain limitations and conditions on the exercise of this power by the provinces. First, it states that no provincial law shall "prejudicially affect any right or privilege with respect to denominational schools" that existed at the time of Confederation. Second, it states that the rights of Catholic separate schools in Upper Canada and Protestant separate schools in Lower Canada shall continue after the union. Third, it establishes a right of appeal to the governor-general-in-council if the education rights of a Protestant or Catholic minority are abrogated by a provincial legislature. Finally, in the event that the province does not respond positively to an appeal that is allowed by the governor-general-in-council, provision is made for the Parliament of Canada to "make remedial Laws for the due Execution of the Provisions of this Section."

The significance of this section of the BNA Act is that it makes the federal government a policeman, with the power and the responsibility to protect the education rights of religious minorities from encroachment by the provinces. This has proved an awkward burden for the federal government to bear, for by intervening to protect the rights of a religious minority, the federal government would be forced to interfere with provincial autonomy. Faced with a "damned if it does and damned if it doesn't" dilemma, the federal government has never used this remedial power.

Section 95 established **concurrent** federal-provincial powers in matters of agriculture and immigration. While both levels of government may enact laws in these two areas, section 95 establishes federal **paramountcy** in the case of a conflict between provisions of a federal and provincial law:

> Any Law of the Legislature of a Province relative to Agriculture or to Immigration shall have effect in and for the Province as long and as far only as it is not repugnant to any Act of the Parliament of Canada.

### Special Provisions: Sections 109, 121, and 132

By section 109, the provinces are granted full title to "all Lands, Mines, Minerals, and Royalties" within their boundaries, a concession that was not viewed as very important in the pre-petroleum era. Title to crown lands was retained by the federal Crown at the time the Western provinces came into the federation, but provincial pressures forced Ottawa to give them up in 1930. This control over **crown land**, and therefore over both renewable and non-renewable natural resources, has proven to be one of the major foundations of province-building in the 20th century and has been a major source of provincial power since the Second World War.

Another important provision that certainly limits the provinces and would appear, at first glance, to limit the federal power as well, is section 121, which states that there may not be any interprovincial trade restrictions. The aim of this clause was to make explicit the Confederation goal of a common market within British North America, but as we shall see, it has not always been able to prevent interprovincial trade restrictions.

A specific grant of federal legislative competence is specified by section 132, which states that the Parliament of Canada

> shall have all Powers necessary or proper for performing the Obligations of Canada or any Province thereof as Part of the British Empire towards Foreign Countries arising under Treaties between the Empire and such Foreign Countries.

This **treaty power** and the manner in which the courts have interpreted it will be discussed later.

### Reservation and Disallowance

Finally, to round out this snapshot of Canadian federalism at the time of Confederation, the federal government's power over the legislatures of the provinces contained in the **reservation** and **disallowance** provisions of the BNA Act must be mentioned. The power formally vested in the central government by these provisions amounts to a federal veto that may be applied to any act of a provincial legislature. These devices reflect the fundamentally *centralist* character of the union that was envisaged by the Fathers of Confederation.

The reservation provision gives the lieutenant governor of a province the power to *reserve* a bill for the "pleasure of the Governor General in Council," after which, if no positive action is taken by the federal official, the bill dies. In the case of the disallowance power, the federal government can unilaterally invalidate any provincial law within a year of its passage. These powers — the reservation and the disallowance — were used extensively before the turn of the century, and then intermittently until the forties, when the last disallowance was recorded. As we have seen earlier, by convention they have become vestigial appendages in a federal system that has become decentralized to an extent that such heavy-handed centralist devices are no longer acceptable.

### The Centralist "Spirit" of 1867

The Canadian federal system at Confederation gave the lion's share of the legislative power to the federal government, established the principle of federal paramountcy in areas of concurrent jurisdiction, set up the federal government as a policeman in the area of the education rights of religious minorities, and, just to make sure nothing had been missed, gave the federal government a discretionary veto over all provincial enactments.

Had the centralist spirit of the BNA Act of 1867 been upheld in subsequent judicial decisions, our federal system today would look very different than it does. However, for a variety of reasons, this centralist spirit did not captivate the courts. To see the results of this on our Constitution, let us trace the evolution of Canadian federalism from its beginnings as a highly centralized form of union to the more decentralized form it takes today.

## ▶ THE EVOLUTION OF CANADIAN FEDERALISM

The division of powers has evolved to some extent through deliberate modifications implemented through formal amendment. For example, in 1940, a clause was added to section 91, giving the federal government the exclusive authority over unemployment insurance. As well, section 94A, which was

**Figure 8.1**
Boundaries of Canada, 1867.

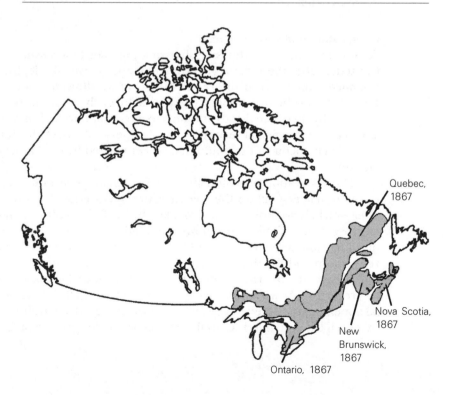

Quebec, 1867

Nova Scotia, 1867

New Brunswick, 1867

Ontario, 1867

**Figure 8.2**
Boundaries of Canada, 1873.

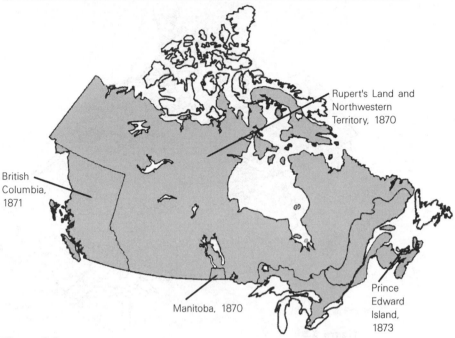

**Figure 8.3**
Boundaries of Canada, 1905.

**Figure 8.4**
Boundaries of Canada, 1912.

Manitoba, Ontario,
and Quebec
expanded, 1912

**Figure 8.5**
Boundaries of Canada, 1949.

Newfoundland,
1949

Source: Figs. 8.1–5 adapted from Department of the Secretary of State of Canada. *Symbols of Nationhood* (Ottawa: Supply and Services, 1991), p. 16.

added in 1951 and modified in 1964, gives the Parliament of Canada the power to pass laws in relation to old-age pensions, subject to provincial paramountcy in the event of any conflict between federal and provincial legislation. Finally, section 92A was added in 1982, giving the provinces the authority to pass laws in relation to the export of resources and to levy indirect taxes with respect to electricity generation, forestry, and non-renewable resources, all subject to federal paramountcy. However, by far the greatest changes in our federal Constitution from 1867 to the present have come through the process of **judicial review**.

The literature of Canadian constitutional law is replete with articles on the interpretation of sections 91 and 92 of the BNA Act by the **Judicial Committee of the Privy Council**. Some commentators approve and others strongly disapprove,[1] but virtually all are agreed that, in the process of interpreting the Act, the Judicial Committee significantly altered its effect. Taking to heart the statement in the preamble of the BNA Act that our Constitution was intended to be *federal*, their lordships transformed the Act from the highly centralist document of 1867 into a more truly federal constitution, leaving meaningful legislative authority in the hands of the provinces. All of this was accomplished through the incremental process of judicial review whereby the British "law lords" defended provincial authority, albeit at some cost to the language of the BNA Act, which often had to be "bent" to fit their views.

### The Judicial Committee and the Erosion of the Federal Power

The Judicial Committee of the Privy Council is technically not a court at all. Rather, it is made up of judges who are appointed to the Queen's Privy Council in Britain and who are mandated to advise the monarch on the disposition of appeals from the common-law courts. The Judicial Committee was responsible for ensuring that the laws enacted by the colonial legislatures were not repugnant to the laws of Britain. Because the BNA Act was a British statute, the Judicial Committee had to ensure that the laws passed by the provincial legislatures and the Parliament of Canada were consistent with its provisions.

While this august body was called upon to interpret the meaning of most of the clauses in sections 91 and 92 of the BNA Act, we will focus here on the most important cases only, most of which involved the opening words of section 91, the trade-and-commerce power (s. 91[2]) and the criminal-law power (s. 91[27]) of that section, and the property and civil-rights clause of section 92.

**Peace, Order, and Good Government**  The thin edge of the wedge that opened the way for a more provincialist interpretation of sections 91 and 92 was the series of opinions that *separated* the peace, order, and good-government clause of section 91 from the twenty-nine enumerated subheadings of that section.

---

1. See, for instance, W. P. M. Kennedy, "Interpretation of the BNA Act," *Cambridge Law Journal*, vol. 8, p. 146; V. C. Macdonald, "The Constitution in a Changing World," *Canadian Bar Review*, vol. 26, 1948, p. 21; *Report to the Senate of Canada on the BNA Act*, "The O'Connor Report," annex 1, p. 25, 1939; Bora Laskin, "Peace, Order and Good Government Reexamined," *in* W. R. Lederman, *The Courts and the Canadian Constitution* (Toronto: McClelland and Stewart, 1964), p. 66n. The best single article on the subject for political scientists is Alan Cairns, "The Judicial Committee and Its Critics," *Canadian Journal of Political Science*, vol. 4, September 1971, pp. 301–45.

This principle was initially conceived by Sir Montague Smith in the Parsons case in 1881,[2] and consolidated by Lord Watson in the Local Prohibition case in 1896.[3] Lord Watson went a step further, by interpreting the opening words of section 91 as secondary and subordinate to the enumerated subheads of both sections 91 and 92:

> The exercise of legislative power by the parliament of Canada, in regard to all matters not enumerated in s. 91, ought to be strictly confined to such matters as are unquestionably of Canadian interest and importance, and ought not to trench upon provincial legislation with respect to any of the classes of subjects enumerated in s. 92. To attach any other construction to the general power which in supplement of its enumerated powers is conferred upon the parliament of Canada by s. 91 would, in their Lordships' opinion, not only be contrary to the intendment of the act but would practically destroy the autonomy of the provinces. If it were once conceded that the parliament of Canada has authority to make laws applicable to the whole Dominion in relation to matters which in each province are substantially of local or private interest, upon the assumption that these matters also concern the peace, order and good government of the Dominion, there is hardly a subject enumerated in s. 92 upon which it might not legislate to the exclusion of the provincial legislatures.[4]

Thus, by 1896, the Judicial Committee held that the peace, order, and good-government clause gave no powers to the federal parliament, except as a **residuary clause**, that is, when the matter in question was of "unquestionably Canadian importance" and could be found neither in the enumerated subheads of section 91 nor in section 92. The federal Parliament was granted *prima facie* exclusive jurisdiction only with regard to matters that came under one of the enumerated subheads of section 91, despite the fact that the drafters of the BNA Act had intended that the general grant of authority at the beginning of section 91 would leave the largest share of responsibilities of government in the hands of the central Parliament.

This narrow construction of "peace, order, and good government" evolved in spite of the fact that there had been earlier decisions that upheld a more generous view of this clause. In *Russell v. the Queen*, in 1882, federal legislation that provided for local prohibition, subject to local option, was upheld by the Judicial Committee on the grounds that liquor control was a subject matter not enumerated in section 92, and, therefore, the federal Parliament had jurisdiction through the peace, order, and good-government clause. Had the principles of interpretation employed in this case been followed in subsequent decisions, the federal power under the opening words of section 91 might have developed more along the lines anticipated by the Fathers of Confederation. However, this was not to be.

In *Hodge v. the Queen*, in 1883, the Judicial Committee enunciated a "canon of interpretation," which has come to be known as the **aspect doctrine**. In the case in point, the appellant was fined under an Ontario act that regulated

2. *Citizens Insurance Company of Canada v. Parsons* (1881) 7 AC 96.
3. *Attorney-General for Ontario v. Attorney-General of Canada* (1896) AC 348; also known as "the Local Prohibition case."
4. Ibid., p. 360.

liquor traffic in the province. He argued that the conviction was invalid because this was an exclusively federal matter, affecting the peace, order, and good government of Canada, and he cited the Russell case as a precedent. In delivering the judgement, Lord Fitzgerald held that the Ontario act was *intra vires* because it involved matters, such as "property and civil rights," that are clearly enumerated in section 92. He went on to state that the federal legislation that was validated in the Russell case involved another "aspect" of the regulation of the liquor traffic: "Subjects which in one aspect and for one purpose fall within section 92, may in another purpose fall within section 91."[5] In this way, the interpretation given the peace, order, and good-government clause in the Russell case was narrowed significantly, and was never again given as broad a meaning.

The Judicial Committee of the Privy Council continued to whittle away at the introductory words of section 91 and to reduce further the significance of the Russell decision. In a 1916 case, Viscount Haldane, who was to become renowned for his championing of provincial rights and for his imaginative interpretations of section 91, attempted to summarize the relevance of the peace, order, and good-government clause at that time:

> It must be taken to be now settled that the general authority to make laws for the peace, order and good government of Canada, which the initial part of Section 91 of the BNA Act confers, does not, unless the subject matter of legislation falls within some one of the enumerated heads which follow, enable the Dominion Parliament to trench on the subject matters entrusted to the provincial legislatures by the enumeration in s. 92. There is only one case outside the heads enumerated in s. 91 which the Dominion Parliament can legislate effectively as regards a province and that is where the subject matter lies outside all of the subject matters enumeratively entrusted to the province under s. 92. *Russell v. the Queen* is an instance of such a case.[6]

Haldane continued to narrow the meaning of the opening words of section 91 in a series of cases in the 1920s. In the Board of Commerce case in 1922, he admitted that the peace, order, and good-government clause might be used as a justification for federal encroachments on matters enumerated in section 92, but only in extreme circumstances: "Circumstances are conceivable, such as those of war or famine, when the peace, order and good government of the Dominion might be imperilled."[7] A year later, Haldane reinterpreted the peace, order, and good-government clause as only an **emergency power**, to be used in times of national crisis: "In a sufficiently great emergency such as that arising out of war, there is implied the power to deal adequately with that emergency for the safety of the Dominion as a whole."[8]

Utilizing this narrow interpretation of the peace, order, and good-government clause as an emergency power, Viscount Haldane went on to dispatch the precedent of the Russell case once and for all, in what is one of the most imaginative judicial *dicta* in Canadian constitutional law:

5. *Hodge v. the Queen* (1883) 9 AC 117.
6. *Attorney-General for Canada v. Attorney-General for Alberta* (1916) IAC 588; 26 DLR 288.
7. In *Re: the Board of Commerce Act and the Combines and Fair Prices Act, 1919* (1922) DLR 513.
8. *Fort Frances Pulp and Power Co. Ltd. v. Manitoba Free Press Co. Ltd.* (1923) 3 DLR 629.

Their Lordships think that the decision in *Russell v. the Queen* can only be supported today . . . on the assumption of the Board, apparently made at the time of deciding the case of *Russell v. the Queen*, that the evil of intemperance at that time amounted to one so great and so general that, at least for the period, it was a menace to the national life of Canada, so serious and pressing that the Parliament of Canada was called upon to intervene to protect the nation from disaster. An *epidemic of pestilence* might conceivably have been regarded as analogous.[9]

To summarize, having severely limited the scope of the peace, order, and good-government clause in cases before the 1920s, the Judicial Committee then reconstructed it as an emergency power. According to three decisions in the 1920s — the Board of Commerce case, the Fort Frances case, and the Snider case — the federal government could make laws for the peace, order, and good government of Canada with regard to matters that would come *prima facie* within the powers of the provincial legislatures, but only if a national emergency required it.

In the Fort Frances case, the Judicial Committee had allowed that the federal government should be given the full benefit of the doubt in determining when a national emergency exists and when the state of emergency has passed. This power was extended to the federal government during both world wars, when Parliament vested significant powers in the federal executive through the *War Measures Act*. The Judicial Committee was not so generous, however, when the federal Parliament attempted to implement a series of welfare measures, usually referred to as "the Bennett New Deal," during the Great Depression. In the reference case that tested the validity of the *Unemployment and Social Insurance Act*,[10] their lordships refused to agree that the economic hardships of the Depression constituted a national emergency, largely because the laws were not purely temporary measures and because the federal government, for political reasons, had not explicitly declared that an emergency existed. All of the important legislation of the Bennett New Deal was declared *ultra vires* the federal Parliament on similar grounds.

Thus, after approximately fifty years of interpretation by the Judicial Committee of the Privy Council, the opening words of section 91 had been transformed from a general and comprehensive grant of legislative competence to the federal Parliament, to a grant of exclusive, but temporary, federal power only in times of a declared national emergency. Furthermore, in fifty years of judicial review, their lordships had construed only two events as national emergencies: the First World War and a "pestilential epidemic of intemperance" in the 1870s.

**The Regulation of Trade and Commerce**  At a very early point in the evolution of Canadian federalism, it became clear that the Judicial Committee of the

---

9. *Toronto Electric Commissioners v. Snider* (1925) 2 DLR 5; in defence of Haldane, it is possible that Canadian consumption of firewater in the 1870s was alarmingly high; *O. J. Firestone, Canadian Economic Development 1867–1953* (London: Bowes and Bowes, 1955) cites the per-capita consumption of spirits as 1.58 gallons in 1871 and only 0.59 gallons in abstemious 1951. See also J. Robinson, "Lord Haldane and the BNA Act," *University of Toronto Law Journal*, vol. 20, 1970, pp. 55–69; vol. 21, 1971, pp. 175–251.
10. *Attorney-General for Canada v. Attorney-General for Ontario (Reference Re Unemployment and Social Insurance Act)* (1937) AC 355.

Privy Council was willing to admit exclusive federal powers with regard only to the **enumerated matters** in section 91. Accepting this setback, the federal authorities proceeded to try to find justification for federal legislation within the various subheads of that section of the BNA Act. The one that seemed most comprehensive, and which the federal authorities hoped might replace some of the legislative power lost with the narrowing of the peace, order, and good-government clause, was section 91(2), "the Regulation of Trade and Commerce." In two early judgements in the Supreme Court of Canada,[11] section 91(2) was interpreted not only as a very broad but also as an exclusive power of the Dominion. The Canadian judges, at least at the outset, seemed willing to view the regulation of trade and commerce as a comprehensive grant of power that might extend even to the regulation of a trade carried on within the boundaries of one province. In *Citizen's Insurance Co. v. Parsons*, however, both the Supreme Court of Canada and, on appeal, the Judicial Committee of the Privy Council placed a far more limited construction on the federal trade and commerce power:

> The words "regulation of trade and commerce" in their unlimited sense are suffi-
> ciently wide, if uncontrolled by the context and other parts of the act, to include
> every regulation of trade ranging from political arrangements in regard to trade
> with foreign governments, requiring the sanction of Parliament, down to minute
> rules for regulating particular trades. But a consideration of the act shows that the
> words were not used in this unlimited sense. In the first place the *collocation* of No.
> 2 with classes of subjects of national and general concern affords an indication that
> regulations relating to general trade and commerce were in the mind of the legis-
> lature when conferring this power on the Dominion Parliament. If the words had
> been intended to have the full scope of which in their literal meaning they are
> susceptible, the specific mention of several of the other classes of subjects enu-
> merated in Section 91 would have been unnecessary; as, 15, banking; 17, weights
> and measures; 18, bills of exchange and promissory notes; 19, interest; and even
> 21, bankruptcy and insolvency.[12]

Briefly, therefore, the federal trade and commerce power was construed so as not to interfere with the provinces' power under 92(13), property and civil rights, to "regulate contracts of a particular business or trade such as the business of fire insurance in a single province."

In *Montreal v. Montreal Street Railway* (1912), Lord Atkinson argued against a broader interpretation of the federal trade and commerce power on the grounds that, "taken in their widest sense, these words would authorize legis- lation by the Parliament of Canada in respect of several of the matters specif- ically enumerated in s. 92 and would seriously encroach upon the autonomy of the province."[13] This is notable partly because it is the same argument used by Lord Watson to justify his restrictive interpretation of the peace, order, and good-government clause in the Local Prohibition case. While both the *colloca- tion* argument and the provincial autonomy argument produced inflexibility in determining the scope of the federal trade and commerce power, it took

---

11. *Severn v. The Queen* (1878) SCR 70; *Fredericton v. The Queen* (1880) 3 SCR 505.
12. *Citizen's Insurance Company v. Parsons* (1881) 7 AC 96.
13. *Montreal v. Montreal Street Railway* (1912) 1 DLR 681, p. 687.

the imagination of Viscount Haldane in the Board of Commerce case and the Snider case to dismantle completely the federal power. In the former decision, Haldane queried:

> Must not it be taken that since the 1896 case, at all events, perhaps earlier, sub-s. 2 of s. 91 must be taken as containing merely ancillary powers? A power that can be exercised so as to interfere with a provincial right only if there is some paramount Dominion purpose as to which they are applicable.[14]

And, in the Snider case, he summed up the position of the trade and commerce power, concluding that

> it must now be taken that the authority to legislate for the regulation of trade and commerce does not extend to the regulation, for instance, by a licensing system, of a particular trade in which Canadians would otherwise be free to engage in the provinces. It is, in their Lordships' opinion, now clear that, excepting as far as the power can be invoked in aid of capacity conferred independently under other words in s. 91, the power to regulate trade and commerce cannot be relied on as enabling the Dominion Parliament to regulate civil rights in the province.[15]

In this fashion, Haldane reduced the federal trade and commerce power to a "merely ancillary" power that was only relevant "in aid of" some other subhead of section 91. Furthermore, it seems that the only aspect of trade and commerce that could be regulated by the federal government was international or interprovincial trade. As with the federal peace, order, and good-government power, the trade and commerce power had been reduced, courtesy of Viscount Haldane, to a mere shadow of what the Fathers of Confederation had intended it to be.

**Holding the Line** In the decade after the Snider case, there was a partial retreat from the restrictive view of both these parts of section 91. In *Proprietary Articles Trade Association v. Attorney-General for Canada* (the PATA case), Lord Atkin gave back some respectability to the trade and commerce clause by disassociating their lordships from the decision in the Board of Commerce case:

> Their Lordships merely propose to disassociate themselves from the construction suggested in argument from a passage in the Judgment of the Board of Commerce case, 1922 1 A.C. 191, 198, under which it was contended that the power to regulate trade and commerce could be invoked only in furtherance of a general power which Parliament possessed independently of it. No such restriction is properly to be inferred from that judgement.[16]

In 1946, an appellant asked the Judicial Committee to find that the Russell case had been wrongly decided. But Viscount Simon held that the decision in the Russell case should stand, and he was also severely critical of the emergency power interpretation of the peace, order, and good-government clause in the

---

14. *Re: the Board of Commerce Act and the Combines and Fair Prices Act, 1919* (1922) DLR 513.
15. *Toronto Electric Commissioners v. Snider* (1925) 2 DLR 5.
16. *Proprietary Articles Trade Association v. Attorney-General for Canada* (1931) 2 DLR 1; AC 310.

Board of Commerce, Fort Frances, and Snider cases.[17] Despite these decisions, however, the damage had been done, and while, as we shall see later, other cases, particularly since the abolition of appeals to the Judicial Committee of the Privy Council in 1949, may indicate the possibility of a slightly less restrictive interpretation of the federal power in the future, the constitutional ground rules of Canadian federalism were likely fairly firmly established by 1925.

**Section 92(13): The *De Facto* Residuary Clause**  If, as we have seen, much of the power that the Fathers of Confederation conceived as federal was taken away from the federal Parliament, it is time to consider where that power was transferred. Section 92(13) reads "Property and Civil Rights in the Province," and it was intended as merely one of the sixteen subheads of section 92. The Judicial Committee of the Privy Council, however, chose to interpret the words of this subhead in their widest possible connotation. They were deemed to include such things as contracts, property rights, and "civil rights" in its broadest meaning, that is, almost every aspect of all subject matters that are not specifically interprovincial or international in their scope.

By construing section 92(13) in its widest sense, and by strictly limiting the interpretation of the more general sections of section 91, the Judicial Committee transformed the **property and civil rights clause** into the *de facto* residuary clause of the BNA Act. Thus, the general grant of power in the opening words of section 91 was severely restricted and its substance was rediscovered in 92(13), with the result that, fifty years after Confederation, the face of the federal union would have been unrecognizable to the men who created it.

**The Criminal Law Power**  One enumerated federal power that was permitted to encroach upon subject matters that are *prima facie* covered by this wide interpretation of section 92(13) is section 91(27), the federal **criminal law power**. The competence of the federal Parliament to encroach upon the area of property and civil rights when legislating with regard to criminal law was at first questioned, particularly by Viscount Haldane, who argued that the Dominion could not create a crime where the subject matter did not by its very nature belong to "the domain of criminal jurisprudence." In the PATA case, mentioned above, the Judicial Committee of the Privy Council disassociated itself from Haldane's restrictive interpretation and admitted that the federal government could, in fact, declare an act to be criminal even if it had not in the past been considered so.

The main limitation on this federal power to declare a certain act or category of acts criminal is the condition that Parliament may not in the guise of enacting criminal legislation in substance encroach on any of the classes of subjects enumerated in section 92. This is referred to as the doctrine of **colourability**. Thus, the federal Parliament, may not "disguise" as criminal legislation that is in pith and substance provincial simply to gain access to the field of jurisdiction. However, the courts have conceded that the federal government can validly encroach upon *prima facie* powers of the provincial legisla-

---

17. *Attorney-General for Ontario v. Canada Temperance Federation* (1946) 2 DLR 1.

tures, if such an encroachment is clearly *necessarily incidental* to the achievement of a genuine federal purpose.

**The Treaty Power**  Section 132 defines the federal treaty-making power. Essentially, in the implementation of British Empire treaties to which Canada is a signatory, the federal Parliament possesses the authority to encroach on provincial jurisdiction to the extent necessary to give effect to the treaty. In the Aeronautics case of 1932,[18] the Judicial Committee held that federal legislation dealing with the regulation and control of aeronautics was *intra vires* because it had been passed to implement the provisions of a treaty that Canada had signed as a member of the British Empire. Lord Sankey, who delivered the verdict, went on to say, in an *obiter dictum*, that the legislation dealt with matters that had attained "such dimensions so as to affect the body politic of the nation." He concluded that, even if it had not been passed to implement an Empire treaty, the legislation would have been *intra vires* the federal Parliament anyway through the peace, order, and good-government clause.

The force of this federal power did not come into question until Canada gained the right to enter into treaties with foreign countries, not as a member of the Empire but as an independent signatory. The federal authorities felt that the evolution of Canada's independent role in foreign relations could not have been foreseen by the Fathers of Confederation, and that, as a result, the full power that the federal Parliament had possessed with regard to the implementation of Empire treaties should continue with regard to the implementation of treaties signed by Canada in her new international role.

The first real test of this came with the Radio Reference case of 1932. Here the decision of the Judicial Committee of the Privy Council, as delivered by Viscount Dunedin, basically supported the view of the federal government, namely, that although federal legislation to regulate and control radio communication was passed to implement a treaty that Canada had signed as a sovereign nation and not as a member of the Empire, it amounted to the same thing: "In fine, though agreeing that the convention was not a treaty as is defined in s. 132, their lordships think that *it comes to the same thing.*"[19] The reasoning of the Judicial Committee was that the matter of treaty implementation was not enumerated in either section 91 or section 92, and that therefore the federal Parliament should have the authority to implement Canadian treaties through the opening words of section 91 as a *residuary* clause. In other words, it didn't matter what the treaty was about; if it *were a treaty*, the federal government could implement it no matter what impact it might have on provincial powers.

The decisions of the Radio and Aeronautics cases seemed to augur well for a broader interpretation of the federal power in the area of treaty implementation, and even gave a glimmer of hope that the Judicial Committee might be willing to broaden the scope of the general power in section 91. However, in a 1937 case dealing with federal legislation purporting to implement labour conventions that Canada had agreed to as a member of the International

---

18.  *Re: Regulation and Control of Aeronautics in Canada* (1932) AC 54.
19.  *Re: Regulation and Control of Radio Communications in Canada* (1932) AC 304, p. 313.

Labour Organization(ILO), Lord Atkin effectively reversed the judgement of Viscount Dunedin in the Radio case.

That the Government of Canada possessed the exclusive executive power to *make* treaties with foreign countries was never seriously questioned. However, their lordships held that the power to enter into such treaties does not give the federal Parliament the unfettered right to implement them in Canada:

> There is no existing constitutional ground for stretching the competence of the Dominion Parliament that it becomes enlarged to keep pace with enlarged functions of the Dominion executive. . . . The Dominion cannot, merely by making promises to foreign countries, clothe itself with legislative authority inconsistent with the constitution which gave it birth.[20]

In other words, it seems that the Judicial Committee was afraid that, if they granted Canada a broad power to implement treaties, the federal government would use the power *colourably* as a device for invading areas of otherwise exclusive provincial authority.

The Judicial Committee went on to point out that "in totality of legislative powers," the provincial legislatures and the federal Parliament can, together, pass laws implementing any treaty signed by the Government of Canada. However, that the legislation happens to be necessary to implement a treaty does not alter the constitutional distribution of powers in sections 91 and 92. Lord Atkin, obviously a closet poet, went on to state that, "while the ship of state now sails on larger ventures and into foreign waters she still retains the watertight compartments which are an essential part of her original structure." To blushingly pursue this dreadful judicial hyperbole, it is good that the Judicial Committee gave our ship of state "watertight compartments" because they had unwittingly removed her helm.

**The Judicial Committee and Canadian Federalism: The Verdict**  It can be seen, from what has been said in the past several pages, that the interpretation of the BNA Act, specifically the interpretation of sections 91 and 92, had achieved a major alteration in the relationship of the provinces to the federal Parliament, up to the time when appeals to the Judicial Committee were abolished in 1949. The clear intention of the Fathers of Confederation had been to leave the provinces as relatively insignificant entities, in the possession of relatively modest legislative powers. The Judicial Committee of the Privy Council, however, according to the tradition of the British legal system, had little regard for either the intentions of the men who had drafted it or current political opinion.

Based on a literal reading of the BNA Act, and a general feeling that the Act *had* intended our federal union to be federal, the law lords interpreted our Constitution in such a way that the provinces ended up with the lion's share of the legislative powers that must be exercised by a modern government. The centralist instrument that the BNA Act was in 1867 had been transformed into a charter of provincial rights, the basic rules of which can be summarized.

First of all, if a provision of a piece of legislation came *prima facie* under one of the subheads of section 91, then without question it was within the

---

20. *The Labour Conventions Case* (1937) AC 327.

exclusive jurisdiction of the Dominion Parliament. Second, if the subject matter came under one of the subheads of section 92, the federal Parliament was still the paramount authority, as long as the subject was also covered by one of the enumerated subheads in section 91. If the jurisdiction was *shared*, either government could legislate, with the provision that if both levels of government occupied the *same* jurisdictional space, the federal laws would be unquestionably *paramount*.

Third, the provincial authority to make laws with respect to property and civil rights in the province was construed very broadly, while the federal enumerated powers were, for the most part, construed narrowly, with the result that even matters that had a clear *national aspect* were more often than not given over to the provinces. The only exception to this rule was deemed to exist in times of national emergency, when the federal power to make laws for the peace, order, and good government of Canada might permit federal encroachments on normally provincial matters. Finally, if a subject matter could not be located either among the enumerated subheads of section 91 or within section 92, then it came within the jurisdiction of the federal Parliament through the peace, order, and good-government clause as a *residuary* power.

It is tempting, at this point in our analysis of the evolution of the federal-provincial distribution of powers, to pass judgement on the manner in which the Judicial Committee of the Privy Council rewrote our Constitution. However, in order to come to any verdict as to the culpability of their lordships, it would be necessary to assume that the BNA Act, as drafted in 1867, was itself beyond criticism. Clearly this is not the case, for sections 91 and 92 contain especially ambiguous phrases that lend themselves to various and often conflicting constructions.

Several questions come to mind: If the Fathers of Confederation saw the peace, order, and good-government clause as a truly comprehensive grant of power, why did they confuse the issue by adding twenty-nine "examples"? If they viewed the trade and commerce power as a broad grant of authority to the federal Parliament, why did they proceed to collocate other subheads that related to trade and commerce? If they wanted the provinces to have a modest role in the government of Canada, why did they give them the ambiguous and potentially vast power over property and civil rights in the province?

The purpose of this discussion is not to praise or blame the Judicial Committee of the Privy Council for altering the intention of the BNA Act. Certainly, one can maintain that some of Viscount Haldane's judgements are puzzling if not arcane, and that Lord Atkin might well have been more suited to writing sonnets or country music. But it must also be admitted that the Act itself is contradictory and ambiguous and that the "watertight compartments" that separate federal and provincial jurisdictions clearly leak badly. We turn now to a discussion of the extent to which the Supreme Court of Canada imposed its own stamp on the federal system after it became the final court of appeal in 1949.

### The Supreme Court of Canada and the Division of Powers Since 1949

Three things must be remembered in looking at the interpretation of the BNA Act since the abolition of appeals to the Judicial Committee of the Privy Council. First, it is often held, mistakenly, that the Judicial Committee's decisions regularly overturned the decisions of the Supreme Court of Canada; while that *did* happen, particularly in the very early years, in many cases the Judicial Committee confirmed the decision of the Supreme Court. This was in part because the Supreme Court of Canada as a lower court in the hierarchy was bound by the precedents established by the Judicial Committee and in part because approximately one-half of the cases that went to the final court of appeal bypassed the Supreme Court of Canada entirely, jumping directly from the court of appeal in the province to the Judicial Committee. As in the later years, it was not uncommon for the Judicial Committee to invite judges from the Commonwealth dominions, such as Mr. Justice Sir Lyman Duff from the Supreme Court of Canada, to sit with them.

Second, it must be recognized that it is difficult to be a creative jurist in an area of law that has been picked over and poked at by judges for something approaching eighty years. There are a lot of givens, a lot of deeply entrenched canons of interpretation, that severely hinder the lawmaking space of our more recent Supreme Court judges. Moreover, our judges are a part of the same legal culture as the British law lords and they are imbued with the same respect for the stability and predictability that adherence to precedent lends to the system of jurisprudence.

Finally, because the Judicial Committee was technically only offering *advice* to the British monarch "in council," its decisions were always unanimous. While there must have been many dissenting opinions among the members of the Judicial Committee over the years, those opinions were not reported, and as a result the Supreme Court couldn't use them as a guide to developing new precedents.

Thus, it would have been naive to expect the Supreme Court of Canada to immediately begin the dismantling of the house that Watson, Haldane, et al. built. While there have been discernibly different trends since 1949 that bear elaboration, we could in no way have expected immediate and radical reversals of the basic interpretive doctrines that were the legacy of the Judicial Committee of the Privy Council.

**The Peace, Order, and Good-Government Clause** As we have seen, the Judicial Committee had limited the force of the opening words of section 91 to three possible situations: first, and least equivocally, when there exists a national emergency; second, where it is used as a residuary power; and, third, rarely, where a matter has attained a national dimension. In a 1952 decision, the Supreme Court of Canada in essentially reaffirming the decision in the Aeronautics Reference case of thirty years earlier, had the opportunity to reinterpret the force of the peace, order, and good-government clause. The issue was whether, in the course of zoning, a municipality might make regulations affecting airports.[21]

The court decided that the subject matter involved was aeronautics and aerial navigation, and that the federal government has exclusive jurisdiction over such matters. What is important is that the Supreme Court went beyond

---

21. *Johannesson v. West St. Paul* (1952) 1 SCR 292.

the "Empire treaty" justification and a majority of the court looked to Lord Sankey's *obiter dictum* in the Aeronautics Reference of 1932, that the subject of aeronautics and aerial navigation was of *national importance* and therefore within the exclusive domain of the federal Parliament to make laws for the peace, order, and good government of Canada. They held that even if such legislation incidentally interfered with areas of provincial jurisdiction, such as civil rights and municipal institutions, the subject matter went beyond merely local or provincial concerns.

The same **national dimension** or "national concern" interpretation of the peace, order, and good-government clause of section 91 was used again in 1956, by the Supreme Court of Ontario, to give the federal Parliament exclusive jurisdiction to make laws with respect to labour relations in the uranium industry.[22] The court was unanimous in affirming that the uranium industry is a matter that, by its very nature, went beyond matters of merely local concern, and therefore was within the exclusive domain of Parliament.

In *Munro v. National Capital Commission*,[23] in 1966, the right of the federally established NCC to expropriate land in the Ottawa area to create a green belt around the national capital was challenged on the grounds that the federal Parliament did not have the legislative jurisdiction to grant the NCC the power to expropriate. The Supreme Court reasoned that the matter of the National Capital Region was, in fact, a matter that went beyond local or provincial concerns; but instead of relying on the national-dimension aspect of the general power to give the federal Parliament the jurisdiction, the court went on to state that the matter of a national capital was not enumerated within either section 91 or 92, and that, therefore, the subject came within the *residuary* power of the federal Parliament to make laws for the peace, order, and good government of Canada.

In the following year, however, in a case regarding the jurisdiction over offshore minerals, the Supreme Court of Canada did not rely on the residuary power in the peace, order, and good-government clause, but held that the Parliament of Canada had jurisdiction because such matters go beyond local or provincial concerns and affect Canada as a whole.[24] The court, in this instance also, distanced itself from the decision of Lord Atkin in the Labour Conventions case by stating that Canada's full sovereignty in international affairs had given the country expanded legislative powers that could be expected to puncture the "watertight compartments" of the ship of state.

Finally, in recent years an expanded interpretation of the national-dimension aspect of the opening words to section 91 may be emerging. In a 1982 case which the federal government lost, Mr. Justice Brian Dickson developed the concept that the federal government could acquire jurisdiction over matters that might be *prima facie* provincial if such matters could not be dealt with effectively by the provinces. This has come to called the **provincial inability test**[25] and contemplates situations where the federal government can acquire jurisdiction because there is no guarantee that the provinces acting cooperatively can do the job. This argument was used by Mr. Justice Le Dain in the

---

22. *Pronto Uranium Mines v. OLRB* (1956) 5 DLR (2d) 342.
23. *Munro v. National Capital Commission* (1966) SCR 663.
24. *Reference Re: The Offshore Mineral Rights of British Columbia* (1967) SCR 792.
25. *Schneider v. The Queen* (1982) 1 SCR 112.

Crown Zellerbach case (1988)[26] to uphold federal legislation dealing with marine dumping of waste even if the waters affected were entirely within a province.

The force of the peace, order, and good-government clause as a residuary power has not really been expanded since 1949, but the Supreme Court of Canada has been willing to use it more readily than the Judicial Committee. As mentioned above, it was the main reason for deciding that federal legislation dealing with the National Capital Region was *intra vires*. Similarly, in a 1974 case that involved the validity of the *Official Languages Act*,[27] the Supreme Court held that all aspects of the subject of official languages not covered by section 91(1) and section 133 were within the federal Parliament's jurisdiction because of the residuary power implied by the opening words of section 91.

As well, while the national-dimension doctrine was not used in deciding jurisdiction over the Hibernia offshore oil-and-gas field, the court did grant full legislative authority to the Government of Canada because it involved *extraterritorial jurisdiction*, which was a subject matter not contemplated in the 1867 division of powers and, hence, fell to the federal government by the residuary power of the opening words of section 91.[28]

The peace, order, and good-government clause as a residuary power was used in another case involving the authority of federal crown attorneys to prosecute offenders under the *Narcotics Act*. The court decided that the *Narcotics Act* was not "criminal law" and that it involved matters not enumerated in either section 91 or section 92 and hence federal because of the residuary power. However, this was a device used by the court to sidestep the broader question of whether federal involvement in *criminal* prosecutions was *ultra vires* because section 92(14) gives the provinces control over the administration of justice.[29] The authority of the federal government to pass the narcotics-control legislation was not challenged at all. More will be said about the evolution of the federal prosecutorial power later in the chapter.

In what one author at the time called "probably the Court's most heralded decision since it became Canada's final court of appeal,"[30] the federal government's controversial *Anti-Inflation Act* was held to be *intra vires*.[31] According to Peter Russell, the Anti-Inflation Board (AIB) case was

> the first clear test of whether the Supreme Court would "liberate" the Federal Parliament's general power to make laws for the "peace, order, and good government of Canada" from the shackles placed upon it by the Privy Council's jurisprudence and thereby provide the constitutional underpinnings for a revolutionary readjustment of the balance of power in Canadian federalism.[32]

However, the court's verdict was, all in all, pretty tame. While the federal *Anti-Inflation Act* was upheld by a seven-to-two decision in the Supreme Court, the *rationale* of the case was Haldane's "emergency doctrine," and the jurisdiction

---

26. *The Queen v. Crown Zellerbach Canada* (1988) 1 SCR 401.
27. *Jones v. A.G. Canada* (1974) 45 DLR (3d) 583.
28. *Reference Re Continental Shelf Offshore Newfoundland* (1984) 1 SCR 792.
29. *Regina v. Hauser* (1979) 1 SCR 984.
30. Peter Russell, "The Anti-Inflation Case: The Anatomy of a Constitutional Decision," *Canadian Public Administration,* Winter 1977, p. 632.
31. *Reference Re: Anti-Inflation Act* (1976) 2 SCR 373.
32. Russell, "The Anti-Inflation Case," p. 632.

of the federal Parliament was seen as temporary — to last only as long as the economic crisis of inflation continued to plague us. While a minority of the court felt that the legislation could be upheld permanently by utilizing the national-dimension interpretation of the peace, order, and good-government clause, a majority of the court either rejected this view or declined to comment on the point at all.

The only substantive gain for the centralist perspective in the AIB case, therefore, was the admission of the court that the federal Parliament does not have to *proclaim* the existence of a national emergency to justify legislation under the emergency doctrine. According to this test, Bennett's New Deal legislation of the 1930s, which was rejected by the courts at that time, might now be *intra vires* the federal Parliament. As Peter Russell put it,

> temporary federal legislation may be upheld on emergency grounds if federal lawyers can persuade the Court that there is not enough evidence to conclude that it would have been unreasonable for parliament to have regarded a matter as an urgent national crisis at the time it passed the legislation. Given the probable deference of most Supreme Court Justices to the judgment of Parliament, this is at least a small gain for federal authority.[33]

Thus, we can conclude that the Supreme Court of Canada has generally been more sympathetic to the general power of section 91 than the Judicial Committee. While the justices have not been willing to abandon the key precedents established by the Judicial Committee, they have been willing to pick and choose among their lordships' differing approaches to the opening words of section 91. The most important manifestation of this has been an increased willingness to employ the national-dimension view of peace, order, and good government, which was first enunciated by Lord Watson in 1896, but was generally ignored in subsequent Judicial Committee decisons. Moreover, the trend today may indicate a willingness on the part of the Supreme Court of Canada to extend the meaning of the national-dimension doctrine with the development of the provincial inability test in some cases in the 1980s.

**The Regulation of Trade and Commerce** The generally cautious approach of the courts with respect to the peace, order, and good-government clause has been maintained with respect to the federal trade-and-commerce power as well. However, the Supreme Court has gone beyond the narrow black-and-white distinction between matters of interprovincial and international trade on the one hand, and matters of intra-provincial trade, on the other.

In the fifties, the Supreme Court of Canada clarified the distinction without significantly altering the balance of power between the federal government and the provinces. In *Reference Re: Farm Products Marketing Act (Ont.)*,[34] for instance, the court reiterated the necessity for federal-provincial cooperation in marketing schemes because of the extent to which interprovincial and intra-provincial trade are intertwined. But in this case, the court also recognized that even though a "transaction" is entirely intra-provincial, the regulation and control of the transaction is not necessarily an exclusively provincial matter. If

---

33. Ibid., p. 662.
34. *Reference Re: Farm Products Marketing Act (Ont.)* (1957) SCR 198.

the industry or business as a whole has significant international and interprovincial dimensions, the federal government may have jurisdiction as well.

In *Murphy v. CPR*[35] the *Canadian Wheat Board Act* was declared to be *intra vires* the federal Parliament because it concerned international and interprovincial trade; and in *R. v. Klassen*,[36] the Court of Appeal of Manitoba took the next step and affirmed the right of the Wheat Board to regulate intra-provincial transactions, as being *necessarily incidental* to the regulation of the interprovincial and international aspects of marketing grain. This approach was reaffirmed in a 1971 case dealing with federal regulations implementing the national oil policy. The true character of the National Energy Board regulations involved the control of imports, and the incidental interference with local trade was acceptable.[37]

These decisions had the effect of clarifying the boundaries between the federal power and the provincial authority over purely intra-provincial trade. It is the *object* of the impugned legislation that determines the extent to which it can interfere with the other level of government's power and it works in both directions. In the 1968 Carnation case,[38] Quebec legislation setting the price of milk within the province was declared to be *intra vires* the province because the intention of the legislation was clearly intra-provincial and the interprovincial ramifications were only incidental.

The object of the legislation also became the critical variable in determining the scope of provincial authority over marketing in the *Chicken and Egg Reference* of 1971.[39] Here, provincial legislation was declared *ultra vires* because purportedly local marketing schemes had, as their primary object, the protection of local producers through the restriction of imports from other provinces. By 1975, the court had indicated clearly that it was going to take a very narrow view of the extent to which provincial marketing schemes would be permitted to interfere with interprovincial trade if the main aim of the regulations was to protect local producers from competition from producers in other provinces.

It is important to point out here that while these issues primarily involve the scope of the federal trade and commerce power, they also involve the "common market" provision in section 121 of the *Constitution Act, 1867*. There is no question that provincial legislation runs directly contrary to that provision and could likely have been declared *ultra vires* on those grounds alone. However, the federal and provincial governments subsequently utilized the instruments of cooperative federalism to effectively delegate to the provinces the power to regulate interprovincial trade.

This was accomplished, in the case of egg marketing, by the federal government setting up the Canadian Egg Marketing Agency to coordinate the provincial marketing boards. The Supreme Court found in the *Agricultural Products Marketing Reference* (1978)[40] that while provinces were precluded from unilateral interference with interprovincial trade, the federal government was

---

35.  *Murphy v. CPR* (1958) SCR 626.
36.  *R. v. Klassen* (1959) 20 DLR (2d) 406.
37.  *Caloil Inc. v. Canada* (1971) SCR 543.
38.  *Carnation Co. Ltd. v. Quebec Agricultural Marketing Board* (1968) SCR 238.
39.  *AG Manitoba v. Manitoba Egg and Poultry Association et al.* (1971) SCR 689.
40.  *Reference Re: Agricultural Products Marketing Act* (1978) 2 SCR 1198.

not. The implication here is that the power to regulate trade and commerce allows the federal government to supersede section 121 in order to implement national marketing schemes.

As if to consciously balance their pro-federal decisions in the *marketing* cases, the Supreme Court indicated that they might not take a favourable view of the federal trade and commerce power in other areas such as trademarks and consumer protection. In *Macdonald v. Vapour Canada* (1976)[41] for instance, the Supreme Court found a section of the federal *Trade Marks Act ultra vires* because it was intended to regulate the conduct of local trades and to establish standards of fair competition in local business ventures. In deciding the case, the Supreme Court reiterated the dictum of the Judicial Committee in the Parsons case of 1881 to reaffirm the point that section 91(2) does not extend to the regulation of individual trades entirely within a single province. Similarly, in the Labatt case[42] in 1980, the court held that federal regulations under the *Food and Drugs Act* were not supportable under the trade-and-commerce clause insofar as they had nothing to do with interprovincial trade.

This apparent tendency to balance decisions favouring one level of government with decisions going the other way was seen in a series of cases in the late 1970s and early 1980s in which provincial legislation restricting interprovincial and international trade were struck down. In the CIGOL case,[43] the Supreme Court placed limits on the provinces' power to levy an export tax on natural resources. The main argument was that the Saskatchewan tax was indirect and therefore exclusively federal. However, the court also argued that the subject matter affected international and interprovincial trade, which was an exclusive federal matter.

The Supreme Court also denied Saskatchewan's right to manage the international aspects of that province's important potash industry because its interference with the federal trade-and-commerce power was more than simply incidental to a provincial object.[44] This problem for the provinces was subsequently remedied by an amendment to the *Constitution Act*, 1867, section 92A, which gives the provinces a wider range of powers including indirect taxation over certain natural-resource matters.

At first glance it could be concluded that the interpretation of the trade-and-commerce power has not greatly expanded beyond where the Judicial Committee left it. However, the Supreme Court has indicated that the federal power includes the power to regulate international and interprovincial trade, even where there is a *prima facie* impairment of the provincial power over local trade matters. The test is whether the federal legislation has a valid interprovincial or international objective and whether the interference with provincial powers is limited to whatever is necessary to give effect to the federal objective.

On the other side of the coin, the Supreme Court has also indicated that it is going to take a restrictive view of the extent to which provincial marketing acts can interfere with international and interprovincial matters. In fact, since 1949, there have been a lot more provincial than federal enactments in this

---

41. *Macdonald v. Vapour Canada* (1976), 66 DLR (3d) 1.
42. *Labatt v. A.G. Canada* (1980) 1 SCR 914.
43. *Canadian Industrial Gas and Oil Ltd. v. Government of Saskatchewan* (1978) 2 SCR 545.
44. *Central Canada Potash Co. v. Government of Saskatchewan* (1979) 1 SCR 42.

area struck down by the Supreme Court, particularly in the area of natural-products marketing.

Finally, in the Parsons case in 1881, the Judicial Committee had stated that the federal trade-and-commerce power might extend to "the general regulation of trade affecting the whole dominion." This dictum has been ignored in the arguments of constitutional jurists since, including the justices of the Supreme Court. However, in a decision in 1983, which involved the prosecutorial powers of the federal Crown in cases involving anti-combines legislation, Mr. Justice Dickson used this "general trade" construction of section 91(2) in concurring with the majority of the court. While it is impossible to predict how this will be viewed in the future, it is possible that a future court could use this interpretation of section 91(2) as a sort of economic *national-dimension* doctrine that would enable the federal government to pass far-reaching laws to implement national economic policies even if the matters affected were *prima facie* within the provincial bailiwick.

**The Criminal Law Power**  The scope of the criminal-law power of the federal government, section 91(27), has not altered significantly since 1949. In 1949, in a case that involved a piece of legislation prohibiting the manufacture and sale of margarine and other butter substitutes, which the federal government was trying to justify as being within the scope of its criminal-law power, Mr. Justice Rand attempted to establish a test for the legitimate scope of criminal law:

> A crime is an act which the law, with appropriate penal sanctions, forbids; but as prohibitions are not enacted in a vacuum, we can properly look for some evil or injurious or undesirable effect upon the public against which the law is directed. That effect may be in relation to social, economic or political interests; and the legislature has in mind to suppress the evil or to safeguard the interest threatened.

Then, later in the same case, Rand applied his test:

> Is the prohibition then enacted with a view to a public purpose which can support it as being in relation to criminal law? Public peace, order, security, health, morality: these are the ordinary though not exclusive ends served by that [criminal] law but they do not appear to be the object of the parliamentary action here. That object, as I must find it, is economic.[45]

Mr. Justice Rand concluded that the federal legislation, under the guise of creating a new crime, was, in fact, merely trying to protect the dairy producers from competition from the butter-substitute producers. The Supreme Court of Canada found the federal legislation to be *ultra vires*.

While the existing balance between federal and provincial powers in the area of criminal justice may not have altered, there have been a number of cases that may have changed the composition of that balance. On the one hand, the exclusiveness of the federal power under section 91(27) to determine what is criminal has been undermined to some extent by decisions in the late 1970s

---

45. *Reference Re Validity of Section 5(a) of the Dairy Industry Act* (1949) SCR 1 (the "Margarine Case").

that allow a greater provincial role in determining the scope of what is "criminal."[46]

Section 92(15) gives each province the power to impose penal sanctions to enforce its laws. In areas such as highway traffic, censorship, and the regulation of public behaviour in streets and other public places, the courts have affirmed a provincial power to enforce prohibitions with sanctions identical to those in the Criminal Code. Such provincial "criminal" law is *intra vires* the province as long as it does not directly conflict with the federal laws, in which case the provincial legislation would be inoperative to the extent that it is **repugnant** to the federal enactment. Hence, in practice, the criminal-law power in Canada is actually *concurrent* and shared by the two orders of government.

On the other hand, the federal role with respect to the *administration* of criminal justice appears to have been expanded significantly, reducing the once generally accepted exclusivity of the provincial authority in that area under section 92(14) of the BNA Act. As we have already seen in the Hauser case, the Supreme Court ruled that the federal government had the power to prosecute offenders under statutes other than the Criminal Code, in this case, the *Narcotics Act.*

However, later the same year, in the C. N. Transportation case,[47] a majority of the court held that the federal government could prosecute offenders under all of its laws including the Criminal Code. The chief justice stated, in rendering the decision, that provincial attorneys-general have conducted criminal prosecutions since 1867 by *delegation* from Canada and not because they have the exclusive constitutional authority. In this instance, the court probably went further than the Government of Canada would have liked, and the practice of the past century and a quarter has continued as usual.

To conclude this section, it cannot be said that the Supreme Court of Canada has put the legacy of Watson, Haldane, and Atkin away in mothballs since it became the final court of appeal. It would have been difficult for the Supreme Court of Canada, steeped in the basically conservative legal tradition that we share with Britain, to strike off immediately in radically new and different directions. The provincial governments and Canadians in general have become accustomed to our federal system the way it has evolved and would not accept the idea of the judiciary arrogating to itself the job of remodelling the division of powers. Moreover, as we shall see in Chapter 10, the Canadian federal system has developed in such a way that the givens of the constitutional division of powers are only the starting point for a panoply of cooperative mechanisms that allow the provinces and the federal government to carry out their responsibilities despite the "watertight compartments."

The Supreme Court of Canada is now in its fifth decade as the final court of appeal and it has built its own extensive body of precedent. We should not be surprised that current Canadian constitutional jurisprudence still carries the genetic material of the Judicial Committee decisons. So many of the questions being asked in the period up to the mid 1970s had been asked so many

---

46.  See *Nova Scotia Board of Censors v. McNeil* (1978) 2 SCR 152; and *A-G Canada and Dupond v. Montreal* (1978) 2 SCR 770.
47.  *A-G Canada v. Canadian National Transportation Ltd.* (1983).

times before that there simply was not a very great opportunity for the judges to be particularly innovative as long as the issues were the scope of the peace, order, and good-government clause, sections 91(2) and 91(27), and section 92(13). Since then, however, the constitutional division of powers has come to be far more reflective of the legal thinking of our own judges and of the practical accommodations that have been struck in the intergovernmental forums of our political process.

## Chapter 9
# Quebec and Canadian Federalism

Since the colony of New France was formally ceded to Britain in 1763, the agenda of political discourse in the northern half of North America has always included French-English relations. The intensity of these issues has varied over time, and Canada's political and constitutional history has been characterized by episodic spasms of Quebec nationalism followed by periods of mutual accommodation among the elites of English and French Canada. The most recent nationalist upsurge in Quebec was triggered by the demise of the Meech Lake Accord and culminated in the sovereignty referendum of October, 1995. Although the time-tested processes of accommodation continue to moderate the conflict, demands from certain segments of Quebec society for a totally new constitutional order are unlikey to go away.

Our Constitution, as we have seen, is itself an accommodation between French and English interests. It acknowledges, implicitly at least, that French Canada is a **distinct society** and that Quebec is a province not like all of the others. But our Constitution also assumes that accommodation is always possible and does not explicitly provide for constitutional change of the magnitude contemplated by some of the *indépendantiste* or sovereigntist leaders in that province. The formal amending formula does not provide specifically for the separation or secession of a province from the federation, and it is difficult to see how the informal means of constitutional change could ever operate to achieve a fully sovereign Quebec. If, at some time in the future, the demands from Quebec to part company with Canada should reach a critical mass, Quebec and the rest of Canada would have to negotiate a totally new relationship, one that would radically alter the constitutions of both Canada and Quebec.

To better understand the nature of Quebec's nationalist aspirations and in an attempt to prepare ourselves for the unhappy possibility of having to negotiate Quebec's independence in the future, we must look at the historical roots of discontent in Quebec and the nature of nationalist demands in the last decade of the 20th century. As we shall see, there is nothing very new about the *crisis* of French-English relations in the 1990s.

---

▶ FRENCH-ENGLISH RELATIONS IN CANADA

Our history is both *about* the fundamental cleavages that exist between French and English groups in Canada as well as being one of the *causes* of those rifts. Thus, the events described in the following section can be seen as the direct result of deep-seated differences between the two charter groups but, in turn, each of these "crises" comes to be remembered by French Canada as yet one more piece of evidence to justify its feelings of injustice at the hands of the English.

### The Colonial Period: *La Survivance*
The basic thrust in early attempts at accommodation between the French and English, whether through constitutional or policy changes, was to protect the semi-feudal, Roman Catholic, and extremely conservative society of French Canada from encroachments or "contamination" by British power and influence. French-Canadian nationalism throughout this period was essentially inward-looking and defensive, and the deals worked out between the traditional elites of French Canada and the British set the tone of French-English relations well into the second half of the 20th century.

**The Cession of New France**  New France at the time of the Seven Years' War between England and France was a feudal society, with no democratic institutions. The Catholic Church dominated virtually all aspects of society and the King of France granted trade monopolies to mercantilists who accumulated great wealth based on the export of furs. This wealth, naturally, did not stay in New France, but was all amassed in the mother country. After the Treaty of Paris in 1763, which ended the Seven Years' War, France ceded New France to Britain. The British chose to leave things pretty much as they were, except that the trade monopolies either ceased to apply, or they were now exercised by British rather than French merchants. The seigneurial system was left essentially intact but, because many of the seigneurs returned to France, their holdings were sold to English merchants who continued the system, not as feudal barons, but as absentee landlords.

With much of the French petty nobility gone back to France and the middle class, such as it was, replaced by English merchants, the Catholic Church became even more dominant in the community of French Canada. The key interest of the Catholic Church was to continue its dominance and to ensure the survival (*la survivance*) of the rural-agricultural and Catholic society. The church hierarchy and the British governor achieved the first accommodation between English and French Canada. The hegemony of the church in Quebec society and the hegemony of the English merchants in the Quebec economy became the governing principle of English-French relations, and remained essentially intact until the 1950s.

**The Rebellion of 1837**  All in all, the so-called conquest changed very little in the day-to-day life of French Canada. If anything, things might have been even somewhat of an improvement over the benevolent neglect of the King of France, and in 1791 the people of Quebec (Lower Canada) actually got representative government. The Rebellion of 1837, while reflective of the same political reformist ideals in both Upper and Lower Canada, was in part a *nationalist* revolt in Lower Canada. Here, Louis Joseph Papineau, unlike William Lyon Mackenzie in Upper Canada, was motivated by deep resentment of the racist and assimilationist sentiments of English officialdom which threatened *la survivance* and by colonial land policies which ensured the domination of the English landowners in the rural countryside where most French Canadians lived.

As we have seen in an earlier chapter, the ultimate resolution of this crisis was to grant responsible government. In the short term, however, utilizing the *Durham Report* as a blueprint, Britain attempted to resolve the problem of growing French-Canadian nationalism by creating in 1840 the United Province of Canada. In this way, it was hoped that French-English conflict could be resolved by simply assimilating French Canada. (Nobody except the French Canadians seems to have been able to understand why French Canadians wouldn't naturally prefer to be British!) In Quebec, this spasm of nationalism was calmed by the fact that under responsible government the Province of Canada evolved, by convention, to a "double-majority" system where Canada East and Canada West possessed equal shares of governmental power.

**Confederation**  As has been discussed earlier, the Confederation agreement was itself an accommodation between French and English Canada. It has even been argued, mostly by French Canadians, that Confederation was a *deux nations* compact; a compact, not among provinces but between two founding "races" or language groups. The basic premise of this version of the **compact theory** would appear to have some historical justification, in that the Confederation agreement did recognize cultural duality in Canada. The BNA Act itself contained guarantees of language and religion and the continued use of a very different system of civil law in the province. All of these features were obviously intended to protect the rights of the French-Canadian minority.

From the perspective of the Quebec elites at the time of Confederation, the key to the deal was that Quebec would be separated from the growing population of Upper Canada and given legislative authority over matters such as civil law, health, education, language, culture, and religion. As well, the status quo with respect to denominational schools at the time of Confederation was frozen in time. All of these provisons satisfied the concerns of the Catholic Church and the traditional elites in professions such as law and medicine. It accomplished the isolation of Quebec from the rest of North American society, the insulation of her culture from the encroachments of modernization, and the continuation of *la survivance*. What the Confederation agreement did not accomplish was any attenuation of the complete dominance of English capital in the Quebec economy, which would ultimately spawn the economic nationalism of the Quiet Revolution in the 1960s.

### Quebec and French Canada: 1867–1917

With the continued survival of French-Canadian culture secured by the BNA Act, and the dominance of the Catholic Church within Quebec assured through collusion with English corporate interests and, ultimately, with the *Parti bleu*, French-English conflict within the province was virtually nil. The two language groups were left to their "two solitudes" and had little direct *contact*, let alone conflict. However, in the post-Confederation period, Quebec came to assume the role of protector of all things French and *fidei defensor* of Catholic schools elsewhere in Canada.

**The Riel Rebellion**  The period immediately following Confederation could be called a honeymoon period in ethnic relations in Canada. Upper Canadians had achieved their goal of "representation by population" and French Canadians had a government in Quebec that they felt they could call their own. The coalition of John A. Macdonald and George-É. Cartier seemed to be working well at the federal level, and the two ethnic groups seemed more concerned with internal than external problems. There had been a brief uprising of the Métis people in Manitoba in 1870, in which an Ontario Orangeman died, but Louis Riel, the leader of the rebellion, fled to the United States and little more was heard of the incident. Riel, however, returned to Canada in 1885, and Canada's first major post-Confederation ethnic quarrel broke around him.

On his return, Louis Riel regrouped his Métis and Indian forces and led them in a second rebellion. Troops were sent from Ontario to put down the insurrection; Riel was captured with several of his followers and sentenced to death for treason. He became a symbol, in Quebec, of the struggle to maintain the French language and the Catholic faith. To Ontarians, he was a traitor and a murderer, and to the powerful bigots of the Orange Lodge he typified all that was undesirable about "popery." Despite pleas from French Canada for a pardon or clemency, Riel was executed.

The Riel Rebellion controversy illustrates a number of important aspects of ethnic conflict in Canada. In this case, the conflict was caused by the symbolic importance of the issue to various religious and ethnic organizations, and the political elites of both major parties urged moderation. Macdonald tried to delay Riel's execution, but was forced to give in to pressure from Ontario, particularly from that most potent of forces in early Ontario politics, the Orange Lodge. The French-Canadian members of Macdonald's Cabinet, while privately opposed to the execution, refused to break with Macdonald and urged calm in Quebec. Sir Wilfrid Laurier, then Leader of the Opposition, opposed the government's handling of the matter, but urged his countrymen to adopt a moderate approach. The higher clergy of the Catholic Church also played a moderating role, and Bishop Taché even urged French-Canadian Conservative MPs not to vote against their own party.

Another set of leaders, however, acted to foster and exacerbate the conflict. In Ontario, the Orange Lodge and other Protestant groups played an important role in condemning the French-Canadian "papists." The Ontario press also played on ethnic hostilities. For example, the Toronto *Mail and Empire* declared: "As Britons, we believe that the conquest will have to be fought over again. Lower Canada may depend on it, there will be no new treaty of 1763. The victors will not capitulate the next time."

In Quebec, on the other hand, the "out" political leaders seized this opportunity to overthrow and virtually destroy the provincial Conservative Party. Playing on the same sort of ethnic hostility as that used by Ontario's Orangemen, Honoré Mercier led a resurgence of the *Parti national*, which was aimed at uniting all French Canadians in all provinces into a single party. The *Parti national* was never successful at the federal level, but it did gain power provincially in spite of the fact that it was opposed both by the church hierarchy (though not necessarily the lower clergy) and by the incumbent political leaders.

A pattern can be discerned here that has recurred frequently in French-English conflict. The incumbent governmental elites may act to minimize intergroup conflict, and may be assisted in this by non-governmental leaders, such as the clergy, who have an interest in stability. However, other leaders, currently out of power, may use the inherent intolerance and ethnic hostility opportunistically, to build their base of popular support. The "outs" may attempt to use the crisis to gain political power, while the "ins" prefer to maintain the *status quo*. Hence, the opportunities for rabble rousing that are always present in a democracy, combined with the fact that the "outs" will not be overly scrupulous in their efforts to become "ins," vitiate the capacity of elite accommodation to resolve ethnic conflict.

It is of interest that the death of Riel is no longer the symbol it once was of French-English conflict, largely because Riel himself has become a heroic symbol of the Métis Nation. In retrospect, it seems puzzling that his cause was appropriated so readily by French-Canadian nationalists, when he wasn't Québécois and likely didn't even think of himself as French.

**The Manitoba Schools Question**  In 1890, Manitoba passed a law establishing a completely non-sectarian educational system, replacing a system in which Catholic schools had received provincial funding. The bitter debate that ensued placed the opponents of the legislation, most of whom were French, Roman Catholic, and from Quebec, in an anomalous position. To oppose Manitoba's school law was to demand that the federal government use its power under section 93 of the BNA Act to disallow the provincial legislation. However, this would mean advocating federal interference in provincial matters, something that Quebec was opposed to first and foremost.

Provincial politicians in Quebec squirmed uncomfortably while the Catholic Church hierarchy pressured the federal government to disallow the legislation. Sir Wilfrid Laurier, as Leader of the Opposition in Parliament, took his stand on the side of provincial rights. The courts declared the Manitoba legislation to be within provincial powers, but affirmed that the federal government could use its power to disallow it, and the Conservative government finally did introduce a bill to invalidate the law. However, an election intervened and the subsequent campaign, fought largely on the school issue, resulted in a national Liberal victory.

Laurier did not respond to the schools question in Manitoba by exercising the federal override power. Rather, he negotiated a compromise with the

Manitoba premier, which left the legislation basically unaltered. This crisis in French-English relations was able to be resolved partly because Laurier's opponents, the Quebec elites, were split over whether the issue was about separate schools or provincial rights, and it disappeared, in part, because, for the first time, the prime minister was a French Canadian. Laurier's election represented a very significant accommodation in and of itself.

**Regulation Seventeen** In the early part of the 20th century, several nationalist movements appeared in French Canada. The most important of these was led by Henri Bourassa. Bourassa's nationalism demanded more power for the province in cultural matters and more independence of Canada from Britain. Although Bourassa did not go so far as to advocate outright separation, the movement posed a threat to Laurier, because the nationalist demands generally ran counter to the Liberal policy of moderation, compromise, and accommodation.

The early nationalist movements were, in part, a response to defeats on the issues of language and education elsewhere in Canada, and it was another such issue that triggered the next crisis in French-English relations. In 1913, Ontario introduced Regulation Seventeen, which limited the use of French in its schools, and while the political elites struggled to find a resolution, the population of Quebec became incensed. There were frequent mass rallies and demonstrations in the province. Quebec schoolchildren and school boards contributed money to maintain the French schools in Ontario, as did many municipal governments in Quebec. A petition asking for use of the disallowance power, signed by six hundred thousand people, was presented to the federal government. Virtually all elements of the Quebec population supported the attack on Ontario's Regulation Seventeen.

As in previous conflicts, the population was spurred on by non-governmental agencies and by intemperate editorializing. As *Le Soleil*, a Quebec City newspaper, put it, "the hour of mobilization of the French race has come." In Ontario, the Orange Lodge, predictably, demanded an end to *all* teaching of French in Ontario schools, and English-Canadian newspapers presented the issue as a question of "papist" domination and a French-Canadian conspiracy to dominate English Canada. Said one overwrought (and undoubtedly unilingual) member of Parliament: "Never shall we let the French Canadians plant in Ontario the disgusting speech they use." Fortunately, he never made it to the Cabinet![1]

### *La Survivance* under Siege: 1917–1959

It was during the First World War that the first encroachments of the federal power were felt within Quebec. Issues that directly threatened the rights of the Québécois within their own province now became salient. It was to become more and more difficult for Quebec to continue with the isolationist posture that had kept the influences of the rest of the world at bay. Global war and the belated coming of the industrial revolution to Quebec soon rendered the

---

1. See J. Schull, *Laurier* (Toronto: Macmillan, 1965), for an excellent and balanced discussion of the pre–First World War period.

traditional instruments of *la survivance* ineffectual in stemming the tides of modernity and a resurgent federal government.

**Conscription: 1917**  It was in an already tense atmosphere that the conscription crisis arose. At first, all elements of the population had enthusiastically supported Canadian participation in the war, though some nationalist leaders, such as Henri Bourassa, advocated only limited activity. As the war went on, however, enlistments from Quebec, which had never been numerous, dwindled. There were many reasons for this besides the obvious one, that if you go to war there will be a lot of unpleasant people trying to kill you. In the first place, French Canadians did not appreciate the overwhelmingly English character of the armed forces, the lack of French-speaking units, and the failure to give French Canadians equal opportunities for promotion. Moreover, most Québécois, who had been cut off from Europe completely since 1759, felt no loyalty to France or England, whereas English Canadians, many of whom had only recently arrived from England, retained a deep sense of duty to the mother country.

As Canadian casualties in Europe mounted, the need became more and more urgent for new recruits to maintain Canada's commitments. In efforts to stave off the possibility of conscription, political leaders like Wilfrid Laurier, and even the church hierarchy, campaigned for French Canadians to volunteer. Outside of Quebec, there was widespread resentment on the part of those who felt that the Québécois were not pulling their weight, while soldiers from the rest of the country were dying in the trenches of France. Finally, in 1917, after a visit to the troops in Europe, Robert Borden became convinced that conscription was indeed necessary and announced in May that selective conscription would soon be introduced.

The Quebec reaction included riots, attacks on pro-government newspapers, and mass demonstrations. Laurier, still playing the mediator role, warned that if the Liberals agreed to conscription, they would, in effect, be handing Quebec over to the nationalists. He pointed out that the Liberals were the only political representatives of the majority in a province that was both pro-Canadian and anti-conscription, and Laurier judged that anti-conscription feelings were stronger than pro-Canadian sentiment. Conscription would, he said, "create a line of cleavage within the population, the consequence of which I know too well, and for which I will not be responsible."[2]

Having said his piece, Laurier also signified his loyalty to Canada by asserting that, if the majority passed a conscription law, he would still attempt to secure Quebec's compliance. All but one French-Canadian Cabinet minister resigned from Borden's Conservative government, as did the deputy speaker and the chief government whip, who also were from Quebec. One Quebec MP warned that conscription might mean civil war and the end of Confederation. When the vote on conscription came, party lines were crossed and ethnic lines maintained: most English-speaking Liberals supported it; virtually all French-speaking Conservatives voted against it.

The extreme polarization of the electorate was revealed in the bitter election fight that followed passage of the conscription bill, and there was a serious

---

2.  Ibid.

threat of civil disobedience in Quebec. English Liberals united with the Conservatives to form the Union Government, which ran Union candidates in the 1917 election. The French-Canadian nationalists this time supported the Laurier Liberals in Quebec, and the Laurier followers won 84 per cent of the vote and 62 of the 65 seats in the province. Outside Quebec, the split in popular vote was not so glaring, as the Laurier Liberals won 35 per cent, which translated into only 20 seats. In terms of parliamentary seats, a united Quebec faced a united English Canada across a seemingly unbridgeable chasm.

The traditional mechanisms of elite accommodation had broken down and the French-English rift Laurier had always feared, and which he had worked all his life to avoid, had become a reality. Wilfrid Laurier, however, remained personally strongly committed to a united Canada and continued to preach the virtues of moderation. Fortunately, the war ended soon thereafter. Few people were ever actually drafted and the conscription crisis blew over, but the bitterness remained.

**Nationalism and the Duplessis Years**  During the 1920s and 1930s nationalist agitation grew in Quebec, partly as a result of the wartime hostility and partly in response to economic factors. Nationalist sentiment gained strength under the impact of the Depression and found expression in the rise of a new Quebec provincial party, the *Union Nationale*, led by Maurice Duplessis. Duplessis was elected in 1936 on a program of provincial rights and opposition to the federal government. With one exception, during the Second World War, this sort of appeal led Duplessis to victory in every election until his death in 1959.

Under his leadership, conflict between the Quebec and federal governments often took the form of provincial protests against alleged federal encroachments on provincial jurisdiction, especially federal anti-Depression measures. The conflict was thus institutionalized as an accommodative process between Quebec and Canadian governmental elites, and this process moderated French-English relations during most of the Duplessis period. Moreover, non-elite French and English Canadians suffered equally from the ravages of the Depression.

**Conscription: The Sequel**  The Duplessis years could be characterized as an era in which ethnic conflicts were papered over, but not resolved. However, there was one serious ethnic crisis and that involved, once again, the issue of conscription. When Canada entered the Second World War in 1939, the Mackenzie King government, understandably afraid of a recurrence of the bitter and divisive crisis of 1917, promised not to institute conscription for overseas service. But, just as in the previous world war, the demands of total war soon outran voluntary enlistment, and the Conservative opposition, as well as other elements in English Canada and the military, began to demand compulsory military service.

Mackenzie King, seeing no hope of an accommodation at the elite level, held a national referendum to legitimize breaking his promise to French Canada. The referendum was as divisive as the formation of the Union Government in 1917 had been. French-Canadian groups such as *La Ligue pour la défense du*

*Canada*, supported by much of the lower clergy, campaigned for a *non* vote. In the eight English-speaking provinces, the vote went 80 per cent in favour of conscription; in Quebec it was 72 per cent against, and among French Canadians in Quebec the *non* vote rose to 85 per cent. Opposition to the war in Quebec was polarized by the campaign and statements on each side grew more bitter. *La Ligue* grew stronger and became a political party, the *Bloc populaire canadien*.

The government avoided imposing conscription until 1944, when it finally appeared that King could no longer walk a tightrope between the English and French sections of his party and of the country. In the final parliamentary vote on conscription, King lost the support of thirty-four French-Canadian Liberals, although they continued to support him as prime minister. King's dismissal of his pro-conscription defence minister, J. L. Ralston, and the decision that conscripts were not to be sent overseas, allayed some French-Canadian suspicion, but once again, as is so often the case in government, it was simply the passage of time that saved the day.

Fortunately, the war was, by then, near conclusion, and none of the conscripts was ever used in battle. In any event, most French-Canadian leaders appeared to realize that it was better to have an attenuated form of conscription under King than full conscription under the English-dominated Conservative government that would replace him should he fall. King's political skill and the end of the war avoided a conscription crisis of anything like the magnitude of the earlier one, but again, the residue of mistrust had thickened.

### The Quiet Revolution and the Rise of Separatism: 1960–1981

The postwar period was a time of apparent calm in Quebec, and except for the occasional railings of Maurice Duplessis against the federal government, there was relatively little interaction between the two solitudes of English and French societies. The calm was more apparent than real, however, for the rapid urbanization and industrialization of Quebec, combined with the unbroken economic hegemony of the English corporate elites, were sowing the seeds for the next paroxysm of Quebec nationalism. As well, the control of the church was beginning to slip as a generation moved off the land to work in the mines, mills, and factories of the new Quebec.

**The Causes of the Quiet Revolution**  While Duplessis could be criticized for the iron-fisted manner in which he ran Quebec for most of three decades, he did, in fact, bring the Quebec economy into the 20th century. He accomplished this, however, by seeking new accommodations with the English and multinational elites and by maintaining the traditional alliance of the Quebec state with the Catholic Church. He gained the support of the corporate elites by suppressing unionism in the province, and he retained the backing of the church by not secularizing or otherwise reforming the educational system. In so doing, he was unintentionally creating the preconditions for a social and economic revolution in Quebec society.

Change eventually came about because by the late 1950s the pressures for social and economic reform could be suppressed no longer. There was an increased consciousness and resentment of the fact that Québécois *worked* in the industries of Quebec but the English *owned* and managed them. Moreover, to keep a decent job in a Quebec that was 80 per cent French-speaking, French Canadians had to learn English because the bosses had never bothered to learn any French. On top of this travesty, even if a young Québécois did learn English, it was difficult to compete for the best jobs because the classical educational system did not offer programs in management, business, public administation, engineering, or technology — the function of the *collèges classiques* was to turn out literate Catholics, not bureaucrats and technocrats. Finally, the wages and working conditions in the workplaces of Quebec were worse than in other parts of Canada where the legitimacy of unionism and collective bargaining had long been accepted (albeit reluctantly.)

If this "time bomb" had been built and armed by Duplessis, it was his death that ultimately detonated the device. When he died in office in 1959, his successors in the *Union Nationale* were unable to maintain the tight control he had had over Quebec's political life. In the following year, the Liberals, led by Jean Lesage, defeated the *Union Nationale*. It is difficult to know just how seriously many of the Lesage Liberals took their slogan of the 1960s, "*maître chez nous*," but it seems likely, in retrospect, that some, such as René Lévesque, took it very seriously indeed. It was in this period, often referred to as the **Quiet Revolution**, that a growing number of politically active Quebeckers began to advocate a separate Quebec.

**The Legacy of the Quiet Revolution**  The Quiet Revolution in Quebec can be seen both as a reflection of the political will to leave behind the "dark age of Duplessis" and as the immediate forebear of the separatist movement of the 1970s. Basically, Duplessis had left education, social services, and health care to the church, and economic development to the English and the multinational corporations. The people of Quebec had become disgruntled with this state of affairs and demanded both a bigger role in the economy of the province and a higher level of social services, education, and health care. The Lesage government moved to provide all of these things.

In the area of education, for example, the new government very quickly took the responsibility for higher education out of the hands of the church and established the first secular department of education in the province since 1875. The thrust of the educational system shifted from the traditional emphasis on the old professions — law, medicine, and theology — to an emphasis on science, engineering, business administration, and the social sciences. This resulted, in a very few years, in a large number of young Québécois entering the labour force with skills and academic credentials that should have secured them good jobs in the booming economy of the sixties. The problem was that the private-sector economy and the labour market that it created was still English dominated, and the good jobs were already occupied. The new, well-trained graduates of the revamped education system were simply not being absorbed fast enough.

This circumstance not only generated high levels of dissatisfaction among young, well-educated, and politically aware Québécois, it also triggered a period of rapid change in the provincial economy. Because the private sector either could not or would not adapt quickly enough to the new Quebec, the government was forced to take extensive measures to stimulate and restructure the economy. One result was a rapid growth of government and direct state participation in the private sector, the most important symbol of this being the nationalization of Hydro-Quebec. While the *economic* components of the Quiet Revolution were the most immediate and most visible, the new economic confidence of the province also helped to stimulate a new **ethnic consciousness** among French Canadians in the province. As well, a new awareness of the special place of Quebec in Canada led to the appointment of the Royal Commission on Bilingualism and Biculturalism, which spent several years preparing a report on the options open to the federal government in recognizing and accommodating the "French fact" in Canada. As well, the leaders of the Quiet Revolution pressed for more powers from the federal government — in areas such as health, social services, training, immigration, and communications — and a commensurately greater share of tax revenues to pay for the exercise of its expanded powers.

So, it is true that the Quiet Revolution began as an economic phenomenon, but it quickly expanded to produce fundamental changes in all aspects of Quebec society. It is also true that it began as a demand that Quebeckers become masters within their own house but it expanded to incorporate demands for a new constitutional relationship with the rest of Canada as well. Finally, and perhaps most importantly, the Quiet Revolution became a state of mind among young Quebeckers. It was that new state of mind, a new consciousness not just of French Canadian ethnicity but of Quebec *nationhood*, that was the intellectual trigger of the separatist movement.

**Separatism**  The movement began quietly enough, with the publication of a number of pamphlets such as one called *Pourquois je suis séparatiste* by Marcel Chaput, who was a disaffected scientist with the federal Defence Research Board, but escalated through a wave of bombings of federal installations in the 1960s. Although there were a number of fractious groups engaging in such non-legitimate tactics of political change, the primary group was the *Front de libération du Québec* (FLQ). The FLQ, whose membership was never greater than a couple of hundred, gained international notoriety in October, 1970. when two of its cells kidnapped and murdered Quebec Cabinet minister Pierre Laporte and kidnapped James Cross, a British diplomat. While the government's response, the invocation of the *War Measures Act*, was, in retrospect, likely an overreaction, there was widespread public revulsion to the terrorist acts, and the violent side of the separatist movement went dormant.

On the legitimate side of Quebec politics, manifestations of separatist strength had grown quietly and steadily during the sixties and seventies. This growth was consolidated when René Lévesque left the Liberals, formally joined the separatist cause, and united the movement's various legitimate factions under the *Parti Québécois* (PQ) banner. From the time of its formation in 1968, the PQ gained steadily in popular vote support. In the 1966 Quebec election, when the *Union Nationale* was returned to power, 8 per cent of Quebec voters had supported one of the PQ's predecessors, the RIN (*Rassemblement pour l'indépendance nationale*). In 1970, while the PQ won only seven seats, some 23 per cent of all Quebeckers and 33 per cent of French-speaking Quebeckers supported the party. Its representation in the National Assembly fell to six after the 1973 election, in spite of the fact that its share of the popular vote rose to 30 per cent. Finally, in the provincial election of November 15, 1976, the *Parti Québécois* actually took power, gaining seventy-one of the seats in the Quebec National Assembly.

It is difficult to evaluate how many PQ voters were actually *separatist*. Clearly, many supported Lévesque the man or the democratic socialism that at least one faction of the party espoused, and many voters were simply seeking an alternative to the Bourassa Liberals. However, the PQ came to power with 41 per cent of the popular vote and with an overwhelming majority of seats. Surveys taken at the time of the election indicated that only 49 per cent of PQ voters supported independence in 1976.[3] The level of popular support for independence fluctuated around 20 per cent throughout the 1970s and did not change significantly after the PQ took power.

The PQ victory in 1976, then, can likely be attributed to a feeling that it could provide a "good-government" alternative to the Liberals, who were widely felt to have mismanaged the economy and to have pursued policies that created a hostile environment for labour relations, particularly in the public sector. The *Parti Québécois* succeeded in maximizing its support by virtue of the now-familiar strategy, adopted at its 1974 convention, of separating the independence issue from the election by declaring that, after the election, a referendum on separatism would be held. Moreover, the rhetoric of PQ policy statements moved away from the terms **separatism** or *independence*, and invented the softer concept of **sovereignty association**, which implied an ongoing relationship with Canada.

The concept of sovereignty association espoused by the *Parti Québécois* in the 1970s was in some respects consistent with the *deux-nations* compact-theory tradition. According to the PQ white paper on sovereignty association, and strikingly similar to the 1995 sovereignty position, a pact would be negotiated between a sovereign Quebec and "the rest of Canada" covering areas of joint jurisdiction, such as tariffs and monetary policy, with both parties to the agreement retaining an effective veto power. The "compact" in this case would be a confederal one between two new sovereign entities.

Since support, even for the more moderate sovereignty-association option, did not seem to be growing, the referendum was put off for almost four years. It was finally held on May 20, 1980, after a fairly brief but intensive campaign. The Lévesque government did not want to scare off Quebeckers who wanted change but were not sure about how much change, so the referendum question was softened still more by asking only for the right "to negotiate" sovereignty association, and the PQ promised that no action would be taken on the results of such negotiations until a further referendum was held. However, despite the cautious and conciliatory wording on the referendum ballot, the result was a rejection of the PQ proposal. Approximately 83 per cent of Quebeckers turned out, and the final tally was 59.5 per cent *non* and 40.5 per cent *oui*. In

---

3. Maurice Pinard and Richard Hamilton, "The Parti Québécois Comes to Power," *Canadian Journal of Political Science*, vol. 11, no. 4, December 1978, p. 745.

fact, when we take into account that more than 90 per cent of the non-French residents of Quebec supported the *non* side, the result indicates that French-Canadian Québécois were split almost evenly on the question as posed.

In summary, the "crisis" of the 1960s and 1970s in Quebec arose from demands for significant changes in the direction of greater provincial autonomy. What makes this period more significant, however, is that the level at which change was to be achieved had escalated. Where, in the past, Quebec nationalism, whether defensive, focusing on *la survivance* of an insular and conservative Quebec society, or, with the coming of the Quiet Revolution, aggressive and expansionist, the nationalist goals could still be achieved at the level of policy changes and negotiated intergovernmental arrangements. By the 1980s, however, the aspirations of Quebec could be realized only at the level of *constitutional* change. While the demands ran the gamut from the outright separation of Quebec, through recognition of a "special status" for Quebec, to changes in the financial structure of Canadian federalism, none could be achieved by the time-worn mechanisms of intergovernmental agreements and administrative arrangements.

## ▶ THE FAILURE OF NATIONAL RECONCILIATION AND CONSTITUTIONAL RENEWAL

We have already looked in detail at the efforts to put together comprehensive constitutional-reform packages from 1987 to 1993. Now we examine these events more narrowly, as attempts by our political elites to once again find an accommodation between Quebec and the rest of Canada. In this case, the instrument of accommodation was not to be federal-provincial agreement or policy development, but formal amendment to the Constitution.

### National Reconciliation: 1985–1990

Despite the "betrayal" of Quebec by the rest of the premiers and the prime minister in securing the patriation of the Constitution in 1982, over the objections of the PQ government, French-English relations were somehow calmer during the eighties. Even the separatist or *indépendantiste* sentiments that appeared to be gaining strength rapidly in the late seventies were on the wane. The *Parti Québécois* reversed its decision to campaign in the 1985 election on the issue of sovereignty association and ultimately dropped independence from the party rhetoric entirely. Despite all of these efforts, the PQ still lost the election by a landslide to the solidly federalist Liberal Party. By 1988, only 16 per cent of Quebeckers supported independence and fully 75 per cent opposed it.[4]

But perhaps the more peaceful and less strident face of French-Canadian nationalism in this period should not have surprised us. The conflict was no

---

4. Maurice Pinard, "The Secessionist Option and Quebec Public Opinion, 1968–1993," Council for Canadian Unity, *Newsletter,* June 1994, p. 1.

longer French vs. English, or even Quebec vs. the rest of Canada; rather, it was a conflict between differing opinions among French Canadians about what direction Quebec should take in the future. The referendum result of 1981, with French-speaking Québécois virtually evenly divided, suggests that the cleavage was more between two sets of attitudes in Quebec than between Quebec and Canada.

The reasons for this new reconciliation between Quebec and Canada were many. At the most elementary level, it was difficult for Québécois to claim that being a part of Canada disempowers the province when, for most of the period beginning in 1968, the prime minister, a significant percentage of the Cabinet ministers, and the majority of the government caucus in the House of Commons have been Québécois. The government of Canada, for most of three decades, has been as much "of the people of Quebec" as the governments in Quebec City.

At another level, the cooling down of nationalist fervour during this period may simply reflect the fact that many of the goals of an independent Quebec were accomplished without separation:

> The generation which came of age at the time of the Quiet Revolution has moved through a historic alteration in the old pattern of unequal accommodation between the two language groups. The generation coming of age in the 1980s faces fewer of the blatant aggravations which galvanised an earlier generation into militant indépendantiste politics.[5]

Some of these "aggravations," such as unequal opportunity to seek jobs in the federal public service, the inability to feel confident that one could receive services from federal institutions in the official language of choice, and the general feeling that French Canadians could not feel at home in any part of Canada but Quebec, had been removed by a combination of federal policies, a new consciousness of the "French fact" in other parts of Canada, and, in the case of New Brunswick, the declaration of official bilingualism in the Constitution. Ironically, although the then-separatist government of Quebec refused to ratify it, the constitutional reform passed in 1982, most notably the Charter of Rights and Freedoms, firmly entrenches French-language and educational rights and affirms again the principle of bilingualism originally enunciated in the BNA Act.

Within Quebec as well there were many changes during the Lévesque years that redressed the grievances and assuaged the fears of francophones within the province. French has clearly become the language of the workplace throughout the province, and while a few stodgy anglophones may have fled the province rather than learn a second language, those who remain have accepted the status quo of the new Quebec and many, if not most, have become bilingual. The French language is alive and well, and the number of unilingual francophones has actually increased.

Ironically, the success in making Quebec a province where people can live and work without the once-compulsory fluency in English may turn out to be

5. R. Whitaker, "The Quebec Cauldron," in M. S. Whittington and G. Williams, eds., *Canadian Politics in the 1980s* (Toronto: Methuen, 1984), p. 53.

a Pyrrhic victory to francophones. French may well be the language of the workplace in Quebec, but most of the higher-paying and higher-status jobs in government and in the private sector still require personnel who can function in English as well. This is increasingly the case in the wake of the Canada–US Free Trade Agreement and NAFTA.

In the area of education, too, provincial legislation has secured the position of French as the language of instruction throughout the province. Bill 101, the controversial Quebec Charter of the French Language, originally provided that only children with one parent educated in Quebec in English would be permitted to attend English-language schools. While the courts have said that section 23 of the Canadian Charter of Rights and Freedoms effectively extends that right to all English-speaking Canadians, this legislation and subsequent reforms to the Quebec educational system have, indeed, guaranteed the continuing pre-eminence of the French language in the province's educational system.

However, it was the relentless imperatives of economics that most significantly cooled the seductiveness of separatism during much of the 1980s. At one level, this can be seen in terms of the global economic and fiscal crisis of the seventies and eighties. Quebec was affected by the recession of 1981–1983 as much as or even more than many other parts of Canada, and the preoccupation with nationalist issues simply became a luxury that politicians in both Canada and Quebec could no longer afford. Attention had to be turned to the more immediate and pressing concerns of the economy.

As well, economic variables diminished the salience of ethnic conflict in a more positive way. The fact is that, during the seventies and eighties, the relative deprivation of francophones vis-à-vis anglophones within Quebec was either significantly reduced or eliminated. To a large extent, as a result both of the rapid growth of the role of the Quebec state in the economy and of parallel changes in the education system in the province, French Canadians have been able to secure the best jobs in Quebec. French Canadians are now paid as well or even better than English Canadians in the province,[6] and the end result of this phenomenon has been the enormous growth of the francophone middle class in the province. The new middle class was, at least temporarily, content to sit back and enjoy the fruits of its economic success and tended to be more conservative and more hesitant to embark on nationalist adventures that might threaten the newly acquired affluence:

> Some of the most flagrant abuses and injustices — which had sparked a generation of middle class Québécois to lead a nationalist movement — have dissipated. The middle classes now turn their energies elsewhere.[7]

Nor should one assume that this new middle class in Quebec was made up only of employees of the Quebec state and state enterprise. There is growing evidence that French Canadians are increasingly successful as capitalists within Quebec, in Canada, and even in the multinational marketplace. The traditional

---

6. See Whitaker, "The Quebec Cauldron," pp. 52–53; and R. Lacroix and F. Vaillancourt, *Les Revenus et la langue au Québec* (Quebec: Government of Quebec, 1981).

7. J. Sher, "Québec and the Parti Québécois," *Canadian Dimension*, December 1985, p. 19.

perspectives on Canadian capitalism that see the upper class as predominantly Anglo-Saxon are simply no longer accurate.

Thus, in the latter half of the eighties, it was possible to conclude that the level and intensity of French-English conflict had declined. The material disparities that traditionally existed between individuals from the two charter groups had been eliminated or reduced significantly. The aggravations and problems that traditionally nurtured French-Canadian nationalism had been salved, if not solved. The threat of separatism appeared to have faded from the agenda of both Quebec and national political discourse during the decade of the 1980s.

### The Sovereignty Movement: Quebec in the 1990s

Ironically, the brief period of reconciliation during the 1980s ended because it ultimately went too far. Spurred by the vision and political ambition of two native sons of Quebec, Robert Bourassa and Brian Mulroney, Canada set out to fix what wasn't really "broken," embarking on a round of constitutional renewal that was to have ended "once and for all" the threat of separatism. The Meech Lake Accord, which was signed by all of the premiers and the prime minister in 1987, was the outcome of these discussions, and it was seen at the time of its signing as the ultimate step in the process of national reconciliation. Unfortuately, when it failed to be ratified in 1990, it became exactly the opposite: a symbol to many in Quebec of the ultimate incompatibility of Quebec's interests and those of the rest of Canada.

The failure of the Meech Lake Accord to be ratified was seen by Quebeckers as a rejection of them and of the legitimacy of their aspirations by the rest of Canada, and it was the spark that ignited a new wave of separatism. Within a few days, a number of Conservative and Liberal MPs from Quebec quit their respective caucuses to form the *Bloc Québécois* (BQ). Led by the high-profile, disaffected Tory Cabinet minister Lucien Bouchard, the BQ stated its intention to work relentlessly for the separation of Quebec from Canada. Unlike earlier separatist movements, the *Bloc* took the position that the only option for Quebec was full sovereignty. Support for independence ballooned from 17 per cent in 1985 and 18 per cent in 1988 to 50 per cent immediately after the Accord was rejected. Support for the putatively "softer" option of sovereignty rose to 58 per cent of those polled (see Fig. 9.1).

Although, as we have seen in the previous chapter, there was an energetic attempt to salvage the key components of the Meech Lake Accord with the Charlottetown agreement, this second package was rejected both in Quebec and in the rest of Canada in a national referendum. The *Bloc Québécois* and the Quebec opposition, the *Parti Québécois*, campaigned vigorously for its defeat in Quebec, as did high-profile federalists, such as Pierre Trudeau and the Western-based Reform Party. It was a noble attempt, but in the end, in trying to satisfy everybody, it failed to satisfy anybody.

The Charlottetown agreement was aimed at healing the wounds sustained by the body politic over the failure of Meech Lake, but, if anything, it inflicted new ones. The tone of the referendum "no" campaign, particularly the one waged by the Reform Party in western Canada, was calculated to stir up the deep-seated antipathy to French Canada and to Quebec. Intemperate state-

**Figure 9.1**

Support for sovereignty within Quebec.

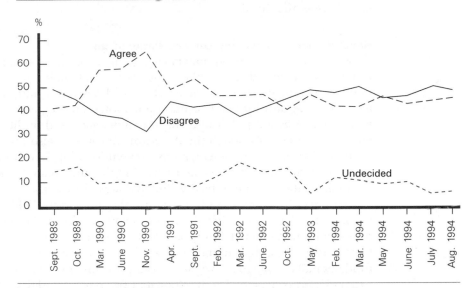

Source: *Toronto Globe and Mail*, Sept. 13, 1994.

ments by the "no" forces, many of them nothing less than racist, were given a high profile in Quebec. The unhappiest outcome of this episode was not so much the defeat of the Accord, which was itself not without flaws, but that the message to Quebec was that the rest of Canada was essentially no longer willing to even attempt to accommodate Quebec's constitutional interests. Many Québécois who had hitherto clung to the hope that a new constitutional order within Canadian federalism was "doable" now reluctantly embraced Quebec sovereignty as the only viable option.

## ▶ WHAT IF: THE CONSTITUTION AND QUEBEC INDEPENDENCE

Quebeckers voted in October 1995 to remain a part of Canada, but by the narrowest of margins (*Non* — 50.6 per cent, *Oui* — 49.4 per cent). So there is still a distinct possibility that Quebec may attempt to form an independent, sovereign nation at some time in the future. It is therefore worthwhile to consider how Quebec independence could come about and what the repercussions might be. As to the form of constitution Quebec might adopt in the event of separation, we must leave that for the Quebec people to decide. We can conclude, however, that because Quebec is a liberal democracy currently, it will continue to be so with or without separation.

It is clear that the separation of Quebec would have a profound effect on Canada and that our Constitution has never contemplated, even implicitly, the possibility that a province might wish to leave the federal union. Hence, in attempting to assess the means of achieving sovereignty for Quebec, we must consider what extra-constitutional processes might be applicable. We will begin by looking at the concept of revolutionary change and how it is achieved elsewhere in the world.

### Revolutionary Change and Quebec Nationalism

By way of definition, revolutionary change in any political system can be said to have occurred if there is either a significant change in the *regime* or in the definition of the *political community*. Thus, the French Revolution can be called a *revolution* because the repressive absolute-monarchist regime of the Bourbons was replaced by a republican form of democracy based on liberty, equality, and brotherhood. Although the American Revolution also involved changes to the structure of government, it was a revolution more because it altered the political community that was the British Empire and created a new and independent political community, the United States of America.

However it is important to recognize that to warrant being called "revolution," the change to either the political community or the regime must be drastic and fundamental. For instance, the abolition of the Senate, while perhaps drastic to the supernumerary "pols" sitting there, would not constitute a fundamental change to the regime of our government. Similarly, adjustments to a nation's borders, such as the transfer of Rupert's Land to Canada in 1870, are not significant enough changes to the political community of Canada to be called revolutionary.

Finally, in attempting to define revolutionary change, the pace of change and the perceived urgency of achieving it are also important variables. Revolutions not only involve change that is radical and fundamental, but also, they involve grievances that have usually festered for a long time. By the time revolutionary change is being advocated seriously, there is usually considerable urgency. Hence, revolutions, by definition, do not *evolve*; rather, they *happen*, and usually quite suddenly.

**The Revolutionary Process: Legality, Legitimacy, Violence** Constitutions generally do not explicitly provide a process for achieving revolutionary change, particularly if that change involves their own dismemberment, and the Canadian Constitution is no exception. If revolutionary change is to occur, therefore, the process or the instruments for achieving that change will usually have to be non-constitutional or extra-legal. For instance, radical *regime* changes may occur through a "palace coup," or through a takeover of the government by dissident forces, which happened in the latter days of the Soviet Union. Similarly, fundamental changes to the *political community* may occur if a dissident region or colony simply makes a unilateral declaration of independence. This happened in Rhodesia in the 1970s when the colony broke with the mother country and became an independent country.

Perhaps more important than the question of the legality of revolutionary constitutional change is the question of **legitimacy**. The military takeover of Haiti and the removal of democratically elected President Aristide was illegal, but it was also illegitimate because it did not enjoy popular support. On the other hand, the fall of the Soviet communist regime in Russia and the subsequent secession of Soviet republics such as Latvia and Estonia were legitimate because they were supported by the vast majority of the citizenry. In international law, there is by now a general acceptance of the principle of **national self-determination**, which recognizes the legitimacy of independence movements in colonial empires. As well, there is a general international acceptance, supported by the United Nations, that the overthrow of undemocratic regimes by popular movements is legitimate, whereas the overthrow of democracies by dictators is not.

Finally, if we take a global perspective in discussing the means of achieving revolutionary change, it must be recognized that such change is not only non-legal in the context of the existing system, but it is usually achieved with some amount of violence. Most *coups d'état* are not bloodless, most colonized peoples break away from the imperial power through wars of independence, and most revolutions are violent upheavals. The violence occurs because there is never unanimous agreement that the radical changes are a good idea. There are always vested interests in the status quo, and very often, at least in the beginning stages of a revolution, the powers that be still control the coercive instruments of the state. Hence, the insurrection, however legitimate in terms of morality, is usually resisted by the forces of counter-insurgency, and bloodshed becomes inevitable.

### The Quebec "Revolution"

The likelihood of revolutionary political change in Canada has always been fairly slim for the simple reason that the social and political issues that divide us are usually moderated by a deep-seated consensus on basic values. Even in instances, such as the conscription crisis of 1917, where our political differences have become so divisive that the *substantive consensus* has started to break down, there has remained a **procedural consensus**. In other words, there is still an agreement as to the rules of the game of political and constitutional change, and a willingness to accept even very unpopular government decisions, because the government that promulgated them is itself seen as *legitimate*. This all may have changed in the nineties with a significant number of people in Quebec challenging the very legitimacy of the exisiting political community.

The nature of the constitutional change required to put in place an independent Quebec can likely be described as revolutionary because it will fundamentally alter the Canadian political community. As we have seen, cultural dualism is of the essence of our Constitution, and one of the things that differentiates us from other nations is the existence of Quebec's distinct society within the larger cultural mosaic that is the Canadian federation. The separation of Quebec would thus leave Canada a fundamentally different and, in more than simply geographical terms, a significantly diminished political community.

**Legality**  The Canadian Constitution does not provide a mechanism for the seccession of a province from the federal union. However, it might be possible to use the existing amending formula to redefine the Canadian political community as excluding Quebec. A problem arises immediately here in that an "independence amendment" would likely be subject to a veto by any one of the provinces. Quebec independence would affect the composition of the Supreme Court, the use of the French and English languages in Quebec, and the office of the lieutenant governor of Quebec. Moreover, having nine provinces rather than ten would affect the amending formula itself. By the existing amending procedure, an amendment affecting these matters would require the approval of all of the provinces and the federal government.

While a sovereigntist government of Quebec would prefer to negotiate a bilateral agreement with the federal government, permitting the province to leave the federation, any federal legislation giving effect to the agreement would be *ultra vires*. Hence, if Quebec wishes to leave the federation legally, it will have to work out a complicated divorce settlement with the other nine provinces as well as with the federal government. And even if unanimous agreement to the independence amendment is achieved, the document itself would be extremely complicated and in many cases very difficult for the rest of Canada to stomach. For one thing, the amendment would have to exclude citizens of Quebec from the protection of the Charter, and for another, the guarantees of aboriginal rights in section 35 of the 1982 Act would have to be repealed to exclude aboriginal peoples in Quebec.

The conclusion here must be that a complicated amendment would have to be negotiated and the federal Parliament and all of the provinces, including Quebec, would be required to ratify it. If our differences cannot be accommodated without a "divorce," this would be the preferred way of allowing Quebec to separate. It is to be hoped, as well, that a separate Quebec would agree to provide the equivalent protections of rights and freedoms that Quebeckers currently enjoy as Canadians and that the aboriginal people of Quebec would be guaranteed the same rights in an independent Quebec that they now enjoy as Canadians.

**Legitimacy** While questions of legitimacy, conscience, and political morality will likely play a big part in determining whether the other provinces will agree to an independence amendment, if unanimous agreement is achieved, the separation of Quebec can be achieved legally and constitutionally. If an independence amendment is not ratified unanimously, however, the issue of legitimacy will become extremely important.

If Quebec were to seek separation through the device of a **unilateral declaration**, such an action would be, strictly speaking, illegal, or *ultra vires* the provincial government. However, separation could almost certainly be achieved successfully if it could be demonstrated that the action had the consent of the people of Quebec. It would be justified, or legitimate, in terms of the international principle of national self-determination. Furthermore, the mere fact that the breakaway province had gained its independence "illegally" might well be ignored, by Canadians, in the need to establish friendly diplomatic and economic relations with a neighbour.

A more important question that might arise concerns the internal legitimacy of the change, and the measures, such as referenda or public opinion polls, that the rest of Canada would be willing to accept as proof of support for the change by the people of Quebec. Certainly, it would be necessary to demonstrate at least majority support, and the closer to unanimity, the stronger the case for the internal legitimacy of a unilateral declaration of independence.

Another challenge to the legitimacy of unilateral secession might occur if groups or regions within Quebec asserted their own rights to self-determination and attempted to separate from Quebec. It is likely that English enclaves, for instance, the western part of Montreal Island, would not be accorded much sympathy in the international community were they to declare their independence from Quebec. Such communities are in parts of Quebec that were originally settled by France and were part of Quebec at the time of Confederation.

A a more serious challenge to the legitimacy of unilateral secession might occur if the First Nations of northern Quebec attempted to assert their right to national self-determination by remaining in Canada. Northern Quebec has been the traditional homeland of Inuit, Cree, Naskapi, Montagnais, Attikamek, Algonquin, Huron, and several smaller tribes since long before the first French settlers showed up in the St. Lawrence valley. Moreover, the land that they occupy was historically a part of Rupert's Land, ceded to Canada in 1870, and turned over to Quebec only in 1912.

The legitimacy of the claim to the right of self-determination on the part of the aboriginal people would be based on a number of important facts. First, they currently live in the region, they are the majority of the population in the region, and they have their own distinct languages and cultures. More importantly, they have lived on these lands "since time immemorial," whereas the French-speaking Québécois came as subjects of a colonial power and never did effectively occupy many of the regions in question. Viewed in these terms, it is entirely possible that the international community would recognize that the right to self-determination of the aboriginal peoples is stronger than that of the French Canadians, who became British subjects by an internationally recognized treaty, and became Canadian citizens by the Confederation agreement to which their leaders consented.

It has been suggested by the *Parti Québécois* that the Cree and the Inuit of northern Quebec gave up their rights when they signed a land-claim agreement in 1976. While it is true that they gave up some aboriginal *land* rights in return for a package of treaty rights, the land-claim "treaty" itself is far more than a bilateral agreeement with Quebec. Canada is a signatory as well, and the treaty rights are protected by the Canadian Constitution, not by the provincial constitution. The Province of Quebec, acting alone within its jurisdiction, could not have completed a treaty involving the surrender of aboriginal rights of any kind.

The aboriginal people of Quebec will argue, with reason, that Canada cannot morally or legally duck its constitutional obligation to them by transferring authority over them and over their lands to an independent Quebec, unless they consent. Finally, any existing aboriginal peoples' right to national self-determination is not affected by land-claims treaties any more than Quebec's right to self-determination is affected by the Treaty of Paris of 1763.

Presumably Quebec would make every effort to negotiate agreements with and secure the consent of the Quebec First Nations before taking the action to declare independence unilaterally. Quebec would also have to make every effort to assuage the fears of non-francophone Quebeckers and anti-separatist francophones to prevent the rise of "internal separatist" movements in regions such as the West Island, the Outouais, and western Quebec, even though such groups would lack the legitimacy of the Cree or the Inuit. But what if these efforts fail, and aboriginal groups or anti-separatist regions declare their independence from a sovereign Quebec? Is there a possibility of violence if Quebec uses the coercive power of the state to thwart these actions?

### The Not-So-Quiet Revolution?

In a nation such as Canada it would be unthinkable for our government to use military force to prevent any region from leaving the federation if it were clear that the people of that region wished to do so. Similarly, it would be unthinkable for Quebec or any other region to force the issue of independence through violent means. It should be easy to conclude, on this basis, that, after some inevitably lively negotiations on difficult questions such as Quebec's share of the national debt and the disposition of federal property in Quebec, Canada would say, "Wayward sister, go in peace." Unfortunately, there remain some unpredictable variables that make the probability of peaceful separation less than a hundred per cent.

**Political Violence and Quebec**  As we have seen in Chapter 4, the Canadian political culture is relatively non-violent when compared to other countries in the world. But it must be recognized that violence, as a tactic of political change, is always a possibility. It takes but one deviant individual to assassinate a political leader, plant an explosive device in a public place, or hijack an aircraft, so that, while the dominant values of a political system may be basically non-violent, isolated violent events may periodically occur. While generally speaking the evidence of our history has backed up the contention that Canada is a "peaceable kingdom," isolated events, such as FLQ terrorist activities of October, 1970, have lent some credence to the idea that perhaps even in Canada there is a tiny minority of deviant individuals ever willing to engage in non-legitimate tactics to attempt to induce political change[8] or redress grievances. The virtual impossibility of successfully achieving political change by this approach in Canada will not be a significant deterrent to such individuals, and political violence, however isolated and episodic, will force governments to counter with the use of the coercive power of the state.

The decade of the seventies did not witness an escalation of the kind of political violence that marred its first year, partly because of effective (and sometimes questionable) counter-measures by the police and the Canadian Security Service, and, more importantly, partly because the rapid ascension to power of the separatist *Parti Québécois* in the 1970s gave real hope for the possibility that Quebec could achieve independence legitimately and non-violently. It seems that even the most extremist factions of the independence movement were willing to draw in their claws and wait to see if the PQ could succeed.

---

8. Pinard, "The Secessionist Option," p. 2.

What could be viewed as a harbinger of what might happen if Quebec secedes from Canada, with or without the approval of the rest of Canada, was the standoff at Oka, Quebec, that occurred in the summer of 1990. In a dispute over land claimed both by the Kanesetake Mohawks and the municipal golf course, an officer of the *Sureté de Quebec* was killed in an abortive attempt to storm the roadblock set up by the aboriginal people. The Mohawks set up barricades and Canadian Armed Forces troops were brought in to oversee the tense situation. Fortunately, while there were some dicey moments, there were no more serious casualties and the standoff ended when the people inside the barricade finally decided to come out.

The Oka crisis sent a message to Canadians, both inside and outside Quebec, that the potential for armed insurrection on the part of Canada's aboriginal peoples is not insignificant. Aboriginal groups staged blockades and demonstrations right across Canada in support of the people of Kanesetake, and their Mohawk brothers and sisters at Kanawake closed the Mercier Bridge for several weeks. What is more alarming about this incident is that the Mohawks were "armed to the teeth" with extremely sophisticated weapons of modern warfare, and were willing to use those weapons to defend what they believe to be their land.

**Thinking the Unthinkable**   It is likely safe to conclude that, however disgruntled they may be by the thought of living in a separate Quebec, anglophones and "allophones" likely will not resort to acts of terrorism or armed insurrection. Either they will learn to live with the inevitable and seek accommodation of their interests through the democratic process in Quebec, or they will leave. If the response of any dissident groups in Quebec were to be violent acts of terrorism, the law-enforcement agencies of the new nation-state would have to deal with the problem in the same way any civilized nation deals with such atrocities. The rest of Canada and the international community would view such action on the part of the dissidents as unacceptable and the response of the state as legitimate.

It is not safe to conclude that the same holds true for aboriginal people in the province. If they were to engage in acts of terrorism, their actions would be generally condemned and the response through force by the government would be seen as tragic and sad, but completely legitimate. But the legitimacy might shift if a First Nation simply declared its independence from Quebec and peacefully resisted the authority of the new regime by banning Quebec government officials and law-enforcement agencies from its community. The aboriginal community would assert an inherent aboriginal right to self-government and pass and enforce its own laws within its own territory. The government of Quebec would have to respond sooner or later, for no state can long tolerate the blatant defiance of its authority within its boundaries without eventually losing its legitimacy in the eyes of its citizens. What would ensue would be a "conflict of legitimacies."

The most extreme response for Quebec would be to use military or armed police intervention to force such a breakaway First Nation to obey Quebec law. This would inevitably lead to blood shed and, because of superiority of numbers, most of the blood shed would be aboriginal. It is possible that the Government of Canada itself would feel at least morally obliged to step in, in order to protect the lives and the rights of people who under Canadian law would still be Canadian citizens. It is also quite possible that the United Nations would be asked to intervene on behalf of the aboriginal people. Similarly, if Quebec were to besiege or cut off the rebellious communty from supplies and services, either Canada or the UN would feel obliged to intervene to bring in food and supplies to the blockaded community.

In sum, this sort of response, particularly if it involved the use of force, would be a no-win situation for all involved. The conclusion is that Quebec has very little real choice if there is widespread opposition to independence on the part of aboriginal communities. Quebec must negotiate deals with the aboriginal communities guaranteeing, for instance, semi-sovereign status within the new state, a wide range of law-making powers, exclusive aboriginal control over large tracts of land, and/or significant financial compensation. Failing a negotiated agreement with the aboriginal peoples, the other option is for Quebec to agree that "what's good for the goose is good for the gander" and allow each of the First Nations in the province to choose its own destiny. Perhaps best of all options is that Quebec remain a part of Canada and that Canada continue its historical tradition of political and constitutional accommodation, which has, all in all, worked quite effectively for more than two hundred years.

*Chapter* **10**

# Intergovernmental Relations: The Federal Process

We have seen in earlier chapters that governmental decision-making in Canada is divided between the provinces and the federal government, each of which is sovereign in its own jurisdictional sphere. We have also looked at the manner in which the Supreme Court of Canada, and, before it, the Judicial Committee of the Privy Council, have been called upon to resolve the jurisdictional disputes that have arisen between the federal government and the provinces, and how those judicial pronouncements altered the balance of power in the federation. But so far the focus has been upon the formal structures of the federal system as defined in the Constitution and refined by the courts. This chapter will look at how the federal system actually works in the real world of Canadian politics.

In the ethereal world of constitutional theory, the federal and provincial governments are intended to operate in completely separate and self-contained jurisdictional spheres. If the constitutional division of powers is defined concisely in the Constitution, the two levels or orders of government will operate entirely within their respective bailiwicks with the only direct intergovernmental interaction occurring when the two orders must face off across the courtroom to obtain a clarification of jurisdictional boundaries. However, as we shall see, the Canadian federal system, like federal systems around the world, does not work this neatly in practice, and it is necessary to develop ancillary mechanisms of intergovernmental accommodation to complement the formal process of judicial conflict resolution.

▶ THE PROBLEM: JURISDICTIONAL OVERLAP

That there is a need for the resolution of intergovernmental conflict in Canada is not difficult to establish, for the very *raison d'être* of a federal form of union is the existence of regional diversity. The cultural and economic variance among the regions of our federation produces wide differences in policy priorities, not only among the provinces, but between the provinces and the federation. If all policy issues docilely conformed to the rigid jurisdictional boundaries established by the BNA Act and its judicial interpreters, the priorities of the various governments in Canada would not come into conflict. The federal government would operate within its sphere to implement national priorities, and the provinces would operate within their respective spheres to give effect to regional priorities. Unfortunately, even after all of the judicial fine-tuning of our Constitution, the boundaries between federal and provincial jurisdictions are still very blurred.

### The Causes of Jurisdictional Overlap

Perhaps in a simpler world, in an earlier period, the "watertight compartments" might have held, but the social and economic context within which the Fathers of Confederation innocently divided up the responsiblities of the two orders of government in 1867 was to change more in the following half century than it had in the previous two hundred years.

First, the Fathers of Confederation felt that they had dealt exhaustively with the division of jurisdiction over transportation and communications by assigning federal and provincial powers in respect of public works such as roads, bridges, harbours, railways, canals, and telegraph lines, which had been leading-edge technologies in 1867. However, revolutionary *technological* advances in the areas of transportation and communication made it necessary for governments to get into the business of regulating radio transmissions, telecommunications, and air transportation, and of developing highway systems that could cope with the long-term consequences of the unbridled success of the internal combustion engine. All of the new matters of governmental concern turned out to have local, national, and international dimensions, and it was virtually impossible to assign them exclusively to either the federal or the provincial governments.

Second, the *industrialization* of Canada's economy created hitherto unheard-of policy concerns in the areas of public health, welfare, labour relations, and economic regulation of business and marketing. Urbanization, a concomitant of industrialization, also created a host of new problems that had to be dealt with by governments. While most of these matters were clearly within the jurisdiction of the provinces, they had attained magnitudes, both in terms of sheer volume and in terms of complexity, such that the limited revenue resources of most provinces precluded an effective response at the purely local level. Again, the international and interprovincial aspects of the 20th-century economy were inextricably intertwined with strictly local concerns and required both levels of government to become involved if comprehensive policy solutions were to be found.

Changes in technology and in the structure of the ecomony also had profound effects on the role of education in Canada. Far from the "three Rs" education of the mid 19th century, the business of education had become a very large and expensive responsibility of government. The provinces, with the exclusive legislative responsibility for providing education, found their technological resources, not to mention their treasuries, strained to the breaking point.

A final problem in the 1867 constitutional arrangements, which is inexorably linked to all of the above, was that the distribution of revenue sources among the various governments had not anticipated either the overall increase in the role of the state, nor the extent to which those new burdens of government would fall disproportionately to the provinces. The question of federal-provincial financial relations, and in particular the sharing of the tax revenues of the federation, will be discussed in some detail in Chapter 11.

In summary, it was not long after Confederation that the carefully negotiated distribution of federal and provincial powers in the BNA Act proved to be obsolete. While the creative jurisprudence of the Judicial Committee was turned to the task of placing the square pegs of 20th-century policy concerns into the round holes of the 19th-century division of powers, this exercise was, in and of itself, insufficient. For the federation to work there would have to be mechanisms developed that would allow the *direct* interaction of the two orders of government and that would foster the accommodation of competing federal and provincial priorities in policy areas that sprawl untidily across jurisdictional boundaries.

### Interjurisdictional Conflict Resolution: Traditional Mechanisms

As we have already pointed out, the drafters of the BNA Act anticipated that the division of powers would turn out to be fairly cut and dried. They expected that there would be little need for instruments of federal-provincial coordination and that most conflicts could be settled by the process of judicial review. However, there are some mechanisms of dispute resolution and intergovernmental accommodation, other then judicial review, that were built into the system in 1867. These mechanisms, which are built directly into the national government, are sometimes referred to as institutions of **intra-state federalism.**[1]

**Formal Mechanisms**   First, through the reservation power, or its equally homely sibling, the dissallowance power, federal-provincial conflicts can be resolved through the rather draconian device of federal executive veto over provincial enactments that the national government doesn't like. As well, if there is conflict between federal and provincial laws in areas of *concurrent* jurisdiction such as agriculture and immigration, the conflict is resolved by the principle of federal **paramountcy.**

The Senate was also designed, in part, as an institution of intra-state federalism to accommodate the interests of the regions and provinces in the national Parliament. The Senate has largely failed as an effective forum for the expression of provincial interests because it has largely failed to maintain the

---

1.  D. V. Smiley and R. L. Watts, *Intrastate Federalism in Canada* (Toronto: University of Toronto Press, 1986). Research paper prepared for the Royal Commission on the Economic Union and Development Prospects for Canada (Macdonald Commission), vol. 36.

constitutional legitimacy or political authority of the elected House of Commons; that is, the Senate doesn't effectively represent *provincial* interests because it doesn't effectively represent *any* interests at all.

The House of Commons, on the other hand, has been able to play at least some role in the accommodation of regional interests. While a vote against a government bill by a government backbencher would be exceedingly rare, there have always been strong **regional caucuses** within the parties in the House. Any government policy that impacts heavily on a particular region must be, by custom, cleared with the regional caucus by the sponsoring minister, and it is not unusual for a measure to be blocked or delayed if there is strong regional dissent.

However, the House has not fully succeeded in representing regional interests largely because of the system of responsible government and the concomitant tradition of party discipline. The MPs, particularly on the government side of the House, are expected to vote with the party, and not to act independently on behalf of the region or province they hail from. Moreover, they are elected to the *national* legislature and are expected to think about the national interest and national priorities while representing their constituents.

**Informal Mechanisms**  At the less formal level, the Cabinet has evolved as an institution that, by custom, is representative of the various provinces. In the discussion of policy items in Cabinet, individual ministers often speak out on behalf of their regions as well as on behalf of their portfolios. The wise minister, when introducing an item with potentially negative consequences for a region, must always touch base with the Cabinet "lieutenant" for that region, and if there is strong opposition from the region, the proposal may be killed. However, Cabinet ministers are still expected to act publicly as members of the federal executive *team*. Within the inner sanctum of the Cabinet chamber, ministers will speak out on behalf of their regions or provinces, but for the most part, even *in camera*, the national priorities should and do take precedence over the sub-national ones when decisions are taken.

In the United States, the interests of the individual states can often be accommodated through the machinations of the party system. By being members of the same political party, state and national political elites may be able to work out mutually acceptable accommodations with "behind-the-scenes" trade-offs and "logrolling." This informal backroom deal-making is possible at both the executive and legislative levels and is a consequence of the political leaders at both levels of government being members of and benefitting from a single party machine. Moreover, the "separation-of-powers" system, in contrast to the system of responsible government, allows legislators to operate without the fetters of party discipline and to enter into political contracts with counterparts at the other level of government.

The party system in Canada has been much less effective than the American party system in providing the same sort of forum for intergovernmental deal-making. In the first place, Canada has not very often in its history had a true two-party system, and it is not unusual for a party in power at one level of government to not even exist at the other level. It is the rule rather than the exception that voters will elect a government at the provincial level of a different political stripe than the one in Ottawa. Moreover, the provincial and federal party systems are separate to the extent that even parties that operate at both levels are separate organizations federally and provincially. Despite overlapping memberships between federal and provincial organizations, the lack of an integrated two-party system in Canada has made it much more difficult for political parties to nurture intergovernmental accommodative measures to any extent at all.

**Conclusion**  The formal institutions of federal-provincial conflict resolution have never been adequate to the task of mediating intergovernmental differences, and the informal mechanisms, such as intra-party elite accommodation, failed to evolve in that direction in Canada. The problem, in part, is that the federal government was elected to represent the *national* interest, which, at any given time, inevitably "fit" better with the priorities of some regions or provinces than of others. As well, the occurrence of same-party regimes at two levels of government, which would facilitate intra-party elite accommodation, has always been spotty and unpredictable. At any given moment in history, the party in power at one level would be mirrored at the other level in only a few of the ten provinces.

Finally, we must make a distinction between the representation of regional *interests* in federal institutions and the representation of provincial *governments*. The fact is that the provincial government elites, then as now, often earned their political *kudos* by "bearding the federal lion." They were understandably jealous of the quiet accommodation of their province's interests within federal institutions because they would not get the credit. The provincial political elites would prefer that the accommodation be worked out *intergovernmentally*, between themselves and the national political leadership, where they can be seen by their electorates to be fighting the good fight on behalf of the province's interests.

Hence, there has always been an ongoing need for federal and provincial governments to coordinate their policy efforts if the responsibilities of government to its citizens are to be carried out effectively. Let us now turn to a consideration of how interjurisdictional policy coordination has been achieved in the past and how it has evolved up to the last few years of the 20th century.

## ▶ THE EVOLUTION OF INTERJURISDICTIONAL COORDINATION: 1867–1990

The process of intergovernmental relations has evolved gradually since 1867. While the changes that have occurred were often triggered by events that had global repercussions as well, many of them resulted entirely from the idiosyncracies of our experience here in Canada. Hence, in breaking the history of this evolutionary process into historical periods or eras, the dates are intended only as rough guides, and are in no way cast in stone. Moreover, in looking at the various eras in the history of federal-provincial relations we have taken some licence in referring to a generalized "mood," "attitude," or "spirit" that dominated intergovernmental interaction in the period under discussion. In fact, these are inductive conclusions, which, while likely fairly accurate, are not based on first-hand empirical evidence as to which first ministers were particularly ebullient, affectionate, manic, or grumpy in dealings with their colleagues.

### Federal Hegemony: 1867–1890

In the earliest days of the federation, the dominant feature of federal-provincial coordination was the political and constitutional **hegemony** of the Dominion. Despite widespread anti-Confederation sentiments, especially in the Maritimes, the dominance of the federal government in all matters of public policy was virtually unchallenged. This was in part a reflection of the "capture" by the national political parties of many of the most prominent regional political figures of the pre-Confederation era. However unpalatable they might have found it, Canadian politicians at all levels resigned themselves to the fact that the major functions of government would be performed by the Dominion. Some provincial leaders, such as Joseph Howe of Nova Scotia, who had been strong opponents of Confederation were enticed into the Cabinet of Sir John A. Macdonald, for the most part because Ottawa was where the "action" was in the latter part of the 19th century.

This era of intergovernmental coordination by federal fiat, while it did not last very long, featured frequent use of the reservation and disallowance powers. While some strong premiers such as Taschereau in Quebec and Mowat in Ontario objected strongly, the federal government repeatedly used the power to pass laws for the "peace, order, and good government of Canada" to encroach upon areas of provincial jurisdiction. But it did not take long, once the first few cases were decided in their favour, for the provinces to begin to assert their sovereign rights to establish their own priorities in a wide range of policy areas. The provincial governments matured during the 1870s and 1880s and were increasingly successful in recruiting and keeping capable political leaders at the provincial level.

### Classical Federalism: 1890–1914

Encouraged by the favourable decisions of the Judicial Committee and with the emergence of effective leaders such as Oliver Mowat of Ontario, the provinces soon acquired the confidence and the political legitimacy to challenge the policy priorities of the federal government when those touched upon matters within the legislative jurisdiction of the provinces. The dominant mechanism of interjurisdictional conflict resolution during this period of **classical federalism** was the arbitration of jurisdictional disputes by the judiciary. This era was characterized by an absence of any interest in face-to-face consultation, because both the federal government and the provinces believed that all matters of governmental concern could be parcelled out once and for all to one or the other of the orders of government. Thus, any apparent overlap in jurisdiction was simply a cue to ask the courts to refine their interpretations with a new pronouncement.

That this combative attitude to federal-provincial relations continued well into the 20th century was due to the essentially uncomplicated nature of the issues facing the policy makers of the day, the practical limitations of travel and communication, and the competing goals of nation-building and province-building. While it goes without saying that the two orders of government had different policy priorities, during this period the kinds of policy alternatives being considered were usually straightforward enough that they could be introduced and administered by one level of government acting alone.

### From *Classical* to *Cooperative* Federalism: 1919–1945

What ultimately precipitated the end of the era of classical federalism was the oubreak of the First World War when the federal government used its *national emergency* powers to supersede provincial jurisdiction in all areas of government. Under the authority of the *War Measures Act*, the federal government reassumed the position of hegemony that had prevailed in the immediate post-Confederation period, and from 1914 to 1919 the provinces were forced to once again take a back seat in the affairs of the nation. While one might have expected a return to the system of classical federalism at the end of the war, this was not to be the case.

The change in the style of intergovernmental relations can be traced to changing social and economic conditions in the postwar period. In the first place, where the ability to make policy had once depended primarily upon the constitutional jurisdiction to do so, the expanding scope and complexity of the problems facing governments in the twenties and thirties dictated that the costs of implementing the programs would become an even more serious constraint. Often it was the case that the provinces, while possessing the constitutional authority to initiate policies in areas such as welfare, unemployment relief, the regulation of labour relations, and manpower training, often lacked the revenue base to pay for them. The federal government, on the other hand, possessed the necessary resources, but all too often lacked the jurisdiction.

The second factor precipitating the decline of the combative style of federal-provincial relations was the untidiness of contemporary problems. Policy makers began to recognize that most issues facing them were interrelated, and that it was impossible for a single level of government to produce a policy that would deal comprehensively with major problems that crossed jurisdictional boundaries. It was a combination of the growing financial crisis facing the provinces and the realization that either level of government, acting alone, lacked the full jurisdiction to deal adequately with many policy matters, that led to the adoption of a coordinative mechanism based on true **interjurisdictional bargaining**.

Through the thirties, the mood of federal-provincial relations remained basically combative; however, the desperate economic circumstances of the period forced genuine federal-provincial accommodation. Differences in priorities among the various governments were resolved through consultation and the negotiation of piecemeal and temporary intergovernmental agreements to meet specific problems. The goal was to solve specific policy problems and not to develop a comprehensive blueprint for interjurisdictional coordination. The attitude was that federal-provincial collaboration was a necessary evil for the time being, and the most common policy manifestations of these collaborative efforts were shared-cost programs or conditional grants from the federal government to the nearly bankrupt provinces.

While not an integrated system of conflict resolution, the piecemeal co-ordinative efforts of the thirties flowed from a genuine *bargaining* situation; the bargaining "capital" or "currency" used in the negotiations was jurisdiction and tax revenues. The provinces, for the most part, would promise to legislate temporary social programs such as unemployment relief in return for which the federal government would pay all or a percentage of the operating costs. While, naturally, some provinces were financially better off than others and could therefore afford to hold out for better offers from the feds, by and large, because the provinces possessed equal jurisdictional clout, all nine could take an active part in periodic negotiations.

### Cooperative Federalism: 1945–1965

The process of Canadian federalism changed yet again during the Second World War. As with the previous wartime period, the federal government used its emergency powers to invade all significant fields of provincial jurisdiction and particularly to take over complete control of all major tax fields. At the war's end the provinces were initially resigned to the fact that, for a while at least, the federal government would be in the driver's seat. Having provided both substantive and psychic leadership during the war, the federal government would continue to assume that role in the public eye for the period of postwar economic reconstruction. The federal government maintained this comprehensive leadership role in policy making into the fifties, setting many of the priorities for the provinces through the traditional instrument of conditional grants and subsidies, which the provinces could not politically afford to reject.

However, as the war became merely tragic history, and as the Canadian economy continued to grow despite minor setbacks, the federal government began to fade in the eyes of the public as the government that necessarily could and should set all our political goals. The initiative began to shift again to the provinces, who could now afford to get back to the business of province-building. Moreover, the public focus and public expectations turned to matters such as social programs and highway construction, both of which lay in provincial spheres of jurisdiction.

Also, towards the end of this period, Quebec was involved in the Quiet Revolution, with the result that the passive and defensive nationalism that had characterized the province's posture towards federalism in the past became aggressive and assertive. The government of Quebec began to demand a sufficient share of the tax dollars to be able to run its *own* programs, instead of merely sharing the costs and administrative responsibilities for those that were federally sponsored. Taking the lead from Quebec, the other provinces also began to assert themselves, reflecting the new confidence inspired by an economic and administrative coming-of-age and a dissatisfaction with the implicit paternalism of the conditional grant-in-aid device.

The rejuvenated political muscles of the provinces did not, however, precipitate a return to the federalism of the thirties. Not only had the mood of federal-provincial relations become more cooperative and less combative, but the interjurisdictional bargaining ceased to be purely piecemeal, pragmatic, and problem-oriented. There was by now a tendency to seek more completely integrated programs, such as the comprehensive tax-sharing system. Moreover, the provinces were growing very important with respect to their effect on the Canadian economy as a whole, and it was becoming clear that any meaningful control over economic fluctuations would have to be exercised through joint federal-provincial action.

In order to restrain or stimulate the Canadian economy, it is no longer sufficient for the federal government to undertake an austerity program or to grant tax incentives to certain industries. Unilateral action by the federal government will make only a small dent in the economic status quo, for the provinces themselves control, directly or through their municipalities, more than half the public-sector expenditures. The provinces are in a position to strongly affect the working of the economy through economic and fiscal measures that are constitutionally within their exclusive jurisdiction. The regulation of the Canadian economy, which had traditionally been considered one of the prerogatives of the central government, now had to be achieved through federal-provincial cooperation. Thus, where this system of **cooperative federalism** was originally characterized by the federal government's sharing the responsibility for provincial matters with the provinces, the tables were turned, and by 1975 cooperative federalism included the additional sharing of federal matters with the provinces. The federal system was by this time highly integrated, with the federal government and the provinces meeting on a regular basis to coordinate the exercise of their respective jurisdictional powers.

### Integrated Federalism: 1965–1990

As intergovernmental policy coordination became broader in focus, the bargaining process became a regular, indeed a constant, activity for the eleven governments. It is obvious that this could tax the resources of the smaller provinces more than those of the big ones, but the introduction in the 1960s of unconditional federal subsidies for the poorer provinces, in the form of equalization grants, helped the provinces to bear the growing costs of government in the era of **integrated federalism**.

Hence, despite the new administrative burdens of interjurisdictional coordination, possession of the basic bargaining capital of jurisdiction over social programs permitted all the provinces to participate actively if not equally in the negotiations. Coordination was ultimately achieved where it was necessary to integrate federal and provincial programs, and mutual compromise and accommodation in the interest of solving Canada's problems was made easier by a basic mood of cooperation and a sense that "we are all in this mess together." As we have seen, this was all to change with the Quebec round of constitutional renewal and with the stark realities of national and provincial debt loads.

## ▶ INTERGOVERNMENTAL STRUCTURES

As we have seen in earlier chapters, the failure of the Meech Lake and Charlottetown Accords likely marked a significant turning point in our constitutional development. While we should hesitate to designate this point in history as the beginning of the breakup of Canada, it does seem that we have reached a point where the balance between integrative and disintegrative forces tips towards the latter. In the l990s, Western provinces are again grumbling about the domination of Ontario in the Canadian economy, Quebec has a separatist government, and deficits and the debt have become priorities on the national agenda.

In sum, the accommodation of federal and provincial interests through bargains struck among governmental elites simply does not work the way it once did. For the system to persist as we know it we will have to develop new mechanisms of interjurisdictional cooperation that are less exclusive and more open to the scrutiny of the Canadian public. But before moving to a consideration of the current trends in federal-provincial relations in Canada, it is necessary to describe the institutional devices that have evolved to facilitate the almost constant process of interjurisdictional bargaining.

### The Structures of Interjurisdictional Coordination

In the early years of federal-provincial relations, meetings of federal and provincial officials occurred in an *ad hoc* manner, and at fairly senior levels in the governmental hierarchies. The first intergovernmental conference of a formal nature was a meeting of the provincial premiers held in 1887. The focus here was not to coordinate policy initiatives but to develop strategies to attack the government of Sir John A. Macdonald. The first formal federal-provincial conference was held in 1906 when Prime Minister Laurier invited all of the premiers to Ottawa to discuss proposed amendments to the BNA Act in order to revise the structure of subsidies to the provinces. Meetings of the premiers and the prime minister continued be called at irregular intervals, usually at the initiative of the federal government, to discuss specific problems of concern to all jurisdictions.

In the thirties, the ravages of the Depression nearly bankrupted several of the provinces and generated an almost constant if not regularized process of intergovernmental interaction to deal with the national economic woes. By this time it was becoming clear to all governments in Canada that the interrelatedness of policy areas made it essential for the provinces and the federal government to meet on a regular basis. The report of the Rowell-Sirois Royal Commission, in fact, recommended that first ministers conferences be institutionalized and held on a regular basis and that a permanent intergovernmental-relations secretariat be set up and staffed at the federal level.

While the recommendations of the Rowell–Sirois Commission were never acted upon, in part, at least, because the Second World War intervened, the wartime period itself stimulated a new level of federal-provincial cooperation to choreograph Canada's war effort in areas of largely provincial jurisdiction. When the war ended, many of the interjurisidictional committees that had been established to deal with the national emergency were retained to form the core of the enormous intergovernmental infrastructure that we see today.

## Intergovernmental Institutions

In an article published in 1965, Edgar Gallant (then a deputy secretary to the Cabinet) remarked that "the number of [federal-provincial] conferences and committees doubled over eight years."[2] In absolute terms, the number of such committees had risen from 64 in 1957 to 125 in 1965, which by most standards is indeed a remarkable rate of growth. However, the *Inventory of Federal Provincial Committees* compiled in 1972 concluded that the number of permanent interjurisdictional institutions in existence at the time could be established at more than 400.[3] Today, the total number of interjurisdictional committees numbers somewhere around a thousand and this does not include the countless informal or *ad hoc* meetings and conference calls that occur among officials on a daily basis. There are, as well, a great many areas of joint federal-provincial concern where there are no explicit joint programs and no formal committees but where ongoing liaison is maintained at the operational levels of federal and provincial bureaucracies.

The number and frequency of federal-provincial meetings is another indicator of the extent of intergovernmental activity in Canada. One researcher identified only 158 interjurisdictional bodies in 1977, but cited 335 recorded meetings of those joint bodies.[4] In the same year another researcher stated that 500 was likely a more realistic number of actual meetings,[5] and, again, this did not take into account the countless informal meetings among federal and provincial officials that happen as a day-to-day part of their jobs. Today, the volume and frequency of intergovernmental meetings and the number of formally constituted intergovernmental bodies is still growing. One need only board an aircraft for a domestic flight in Canada to recognize that many of the seats (senior bureaucrats and ministers in executive class, operational-level public servants in "steerage") are filled by federal and provincial officials travelling to each others' capitals to meet. Moreover, the face-to-face meetings are only the tip of the iceberg, for less formal contacts, such as meetings, lunch dates, telephone calls, E-mail, and documentary correspondence, are almost constant.

**Intergovernmental Institutions by Policy Area** The heaviest concentration of intergovernmental interaction has traditionally been in the policy areas of the environment, health, social assistance, finance, and regional development. The reason for this is partly the contemporary political relevance of such issues in Canadian society, and partly the degree of jurisdictional untidiness, or overlap, that characterizes the fields.

---

2. Edgar Gallant, "The Machinery of Federal Provincial Relations," *Canadian Public Administration,* December 1965, p. 515.
3. Canada, *Inventory of Federal Provincial Committees,* 2 vols. (Ottawa: PCO, 1972).
4. G. Veilleux, "L'évolution des mécanismes de liaison intergouvernementale," *in* R. Simeon, ed., *Confrontation and Collaboration* (Toronto: IPAC, 1979), p. 35.
5. Gordon Robertson, "The Role of Interministerial Conferences in the Decision-Making Process," *in* Simeon, *Confrontation and Collaboration,* p. 79.

However, it does not necessarily follow that where the jurisdiction is clear and settled there will automatically be less intergovernmental contact. Where the matter is clearly within the legislative jurisdiction of the federal government, such as veterans affairs or national defence, there is very little federal-provincial interaction. On the other hand, in primarily provincial areas, such as housing, health, highways, and education, it is common to see intergovernmental committees struck to coordinate the activities of the several governments involved and to negotiate the amount and disposition of federal transfer payments.

It is the federal government's **spending power** that gives it a powerful bargaining lever even in policy areas totally within the jurisdiction of the provinces. The federal spending power is, simply, the power of the federal government to spend money on any matter it chooses, provided it does not pass legislation that is *ultra vires*. Unfortunately for those of a centralist bent, however, the federal spending power is far more significant when dealing with the have-not provinces than it is when dealing with the wealthier provinces. The bargaining process at the root of cooperative federalism is not only one-sided in favour of the federal level, but it is also quite asymmetrical in its effect on the various provinces.

**Intergovernmental Institutions by Decision-Making Level**  The level at which intergovernmental interaction occurs can be categorized initially according to whether the individuals involved are political or bureaucratic, and secondarily, if they are bureaucrats, by their organizational rank in the governmental hierarchy. For clarity and ease of discussion, we have defined four decision-making levels at which interjurisdictional committees operate in Canada: the **political**, the **senior bureaucratic** (including deputy ministers and assistant deputy ministers), the **technocratic** or professional, and the **operational**. It must be noted that operational and technical committees (while functionally distinct) may include personnel at approximately the same level and that the senior bureaucratic level meetings often involve more junior officials who are filling in for their busy bosses. The operational committees tend to be involved directly in the actual implementation of joint federal-provincial programs, while the technical committees and working groups tend to be more concerned with policy analysis, intergovernmental liaison, and joint research projects. Similarly, at the political level, we must distinguish between *specialized* ministerial conferences (such as those held by ministers of agriculture, ministers of finance, provincial treasurers, and health ministers) and the **First Ministers Conference (FMC)**, which have a more *generalist* role over time. As well, in recent years we have come to distinguish between the annual FMCs and the more specialized constitutional conferences that may be expanded to include territorial leaders and representatives of the First Nations.

The actual distribution of committees among these decision-making levels in Canada is uneven. For the most part, there will be only one political-level committee in each policy area, and it will be composed of appropriate federal and provincial Cabinet ministers. On the other hand, more than two-thirds of all the committees in any given policy area will be at the technical and operational levels. One can thus conclude that the most common form of federal-provincial interaction occurs below the ministerial level, and in practice most are even below the senior bureaucratic level.

Analysis of federal-provincial committees in the context of their numerical distribution by decision-making level does not take into account comparative measures of their impact on policy outputs. For instance, perhaps the most important interjurisdictional committee in operation in Canada today (with the possible exception of the First Ministers' Conference) is the Continuing Committee on Fiscal and Economic Matters. This is a senior-bureaucratic-level committee composed mainly of the deputy ministers of finance or the deputy provincial treasurers. Its responsibility on paper is to provide technical advice and support for the Conference of the Ministers of Finance. However, the fact that this body meets more frequently than its political-level parent committee, and the fact that the committee membership is more constant than that of the political-level bodies, gives it a great deal of *de facto* power. As well, the fact that it is composed mainly of highly skilled professionals in key administrative roles who are plugged in directly to the extensive expertise of their departments, places this committee in a position of great influence over the country's broad fiscal priorities and over the coordination of measures designed to cope with economic difficulties.

Finally, in terms of the actual frequency of meetings, perhaps the greatest increase in intergovernmental activity in recent years has been at the level of the FMCs, which proliferated through the 1970s and early 1980s, and peaked with the constitutional renewal process of 1987–1992. While some of this increase in first-ministerial interaction can be explained by the unique circumstances of the period, such as the constitutional reform process, it was also reflective of a new style of federal-provincial "summitry," which the Mulroney government attempted to institutionalize by holding an annual FMC at a fixed time of the year. While the recent constitutional renewal soap opera apparently either has ended or is in a lengthy commercial break there is no indication that the Chrétien government or the current covey of premiers is about to scale down the frequency of their meetings.

**The Composition of Intergovernmental Institutions**  Federal-provincial committees can also be classified according to the number of governments included in their membership. Because of the amount of attention paid to the political-level conferences by the media, one might get the impression that interjurisdictional committees are for the most part **omnilateral**, or composed of representatives of all eleven governments. This is far from the case, for more than half of all intergovernmental activity is **bilateral**, or composed of representatives of the federal government and one province only. Less exclusive than the bilateral committees, and yet more inclusive than the omnilateral committees, are **multilateral** committees, composed of the federal government and at least two but not all of the provinces. Major exceptions to the general rule about the predominance of bilateral committees are in the areas of finance, fiscal relations, and constitutional reform, where almost all of the active committees are not only omnilateral but may be expanded still more to include aboriginal leaders and territorial governments.

An important development in intergovernmental relations that emerged in the 1980s was the increased participation of the Yukon and the Northwest Territories in federal-provincial deliberations. Partly this is because of the role of those governments in matters relating to aboriginal rights, but there is also a growing recognition that the territorial governments are coming of age. While not technically sovereign, they have fully elected legislatures, responsible government, and delegated responsibility within their boundaries for most of the matters under provincial jurisdiction in the rest of Canada. As such, while they are not provinces, they are being included in most intergovernmental forums from which they used to be excluded.

The overall distribution of interjurisdictional committees by decision-making level and by inclusiveness is charted in Table 10.1. The political-level committees tend to be omnilateral or multilateral for three reasons. First, the ministers are less likely than their bureaucratic and technical staff to be able to deal with the nitty-gritty negotiations that often occur at the bilateral level. Second, it is at the political level that the final agreement on priorities affecting the federation as a whole must be reached. While often the political-level meetings only confirm agreements hacked out by lower-level officials, formal agreements must ultimately be ratified at the ministerial level. Third, the ministers at the federal level tend to be too busy to devote the time needed to haggle individually with the provinces. They prefer to meet only after some general agreement has been worked out at lower levels through bilateral and multilateral talks.

By contrast, almost all of the operational-level committees are bilateral and the technical policy committees are either bilateral or multilateral. While some of the technical-level committees in the area of finance involve representatives of all of the provinces and the federal government, for the most part the role of the technical people is more specific — not only in terms of subject matter but in terms of geography as well. Finally, and again this is specific to the emerging political systems in the North, there are a large number of federal-territorial committees at the technical and operational levels. Most of these are bilateral, but a few are trilateral, including representatives of both territories and the federal government.

**TABLE 10.1**

Inclusiveness of Committees

| Decision-Making Level of Committees | Omnilateral | Multilateral | Bilateral |
|---|---|---|---|
| Technical and operational | few | some | many |
| Senior bureaucratic | most | some | some |
| Political | most | very few | few |

**Interprovincial Institutions** Up until now we have spoken only of federal-provincial committees. While such committees make up by far the largest percentage of interjurisdictional bodies in Canada, there are other organizational forms. The **interprovincial committees** are bodies that exclude the federal government, although in many cases a federal observer is invited.

As with the federal-provincial bodies, the interprovincial ones can be classified as omnilateral (for instance, the annual Premiers' Conference, which includes all of the premiers and the territorial leaders), multilateral, or bilateral. They also vary as to the decision-making level in the same way the federal-provincial committees do, and for the most part the generalizations about the distribution of such bodies by level and inclusiveness apply to the interprovincial arena as well. While it has been suggested that some political-level, multilateral interprovincial bodies, such as the Council of the Maritime Premiers and the Western Premiers' Conference, are "proto-coalitions" and will ultimately strengthen the federal-provincial bargaining power of individual regions, there has been little hard evidence that this trend is evolving very rapidly. For the most part, the provinces will squabble among themselves as much as or more than they currently do with the federal government; moreover, informal and *ad hoc* collusion among groups of provinces tends to be a better way of maximizing the provincial bargaining position on any particular issue. Thus, while we can conclude that there is a great latent potential in interprovincial relations, particularly in the rare instances where most or many of the provinces find themselves united in their opposition to a federal proposal, it is unlikely that this process can be formalized to any great extent. The provinces and territories are simply too diverse and their interests shift too quickly for interprovincial institutions to function consistently as instruments of national policy.

Finally, a trend appeared to be emerging in the 1970s where the federal and provincial governments held **trilateral conferences**, in which municipalities were included. However, because municipal affairs is a purely provincial matter, the federal role here has declined and the provinces choose instead to deal with their municipal governments on a bilateral basis. Today, while municipal officials might be invited to attend federal-provincial meetings that affect urban problems, they do so as members of the provincial delegation and their interaction with the federal level is indirect.

**Non-Governmental Participation** Until now, our focus has been on interjurisdictional coordinative bodies, which are purely governmental in composition. But some committees that operate in the intergovernmental arena have non-governmental members as well. Perhaps the best traditional examples of this are committees that deal with the interests and problems of specific industries within specific regions, such as the series of committees and sub-committees established to deal with the Atlantic fishery, which are composed of relevant governmental representatives as well as commercial fishermen and even local anglers' associations.

More recently, the inclusion of non-governmental actors in federal-provincial bodies became fairly common in the area of aboriginal rights and the Constitution. Here, even at the level of first ministers, the leaders of major aboriginal organizations participated as full members of conferences convened to deal with issues of direct concern to their constituents. At the level of officials (as distinct from politicians), federal and provincial public servants interact directly with aboriginal groups in the context of negotiating land-claims settlements and self-government agreements.

This combined private-public type of committee has become more commonplace in the growing area of government–private-sector joint enterprises, and with the increased tendency to involve the private sector directly in national economic conferences. There are advantages to such organizational forms. On the one hand, intergovernmental bargaining must occur under the scrutiny of representatives of the private sector, which helps to keep government honest. On the other hand, by including members of public-interest groups in the early stages of policy development, policy ideas can be pre-sold or legitimized before they enter the political arena through co-opting of non-governmental organizations. However, during the Mulroney years this type of interaction actually declined because of broad federal initiatives to *privatize* governmental enterprises and to *deregulate* many industries.

Finally, during the seventies, federal and provincial governments became directly involved in enterprises along with private-sector corporate actors. An early example of this trend was the Syncrude project, in which the federal, Alberta, and Ontario governments launched an oil-sands recovery venture along with private-sector partners including Esso Resources, Gulf Canada, and Canada Cities Service.[6] The motivation for moving into such ventures is usually to bail out a failing industry, to subsidize research-and-development activities, or to defray the start-up costs of large capital projects such as Syncrude. Again, with increased privatization, the tendency has been for the federal government to get out of such enterprises and to leave them to the private sector.

### Intergovernmental Bureaucracy

While we have indicated that interjurisdictional coordination has become institutionalized and less *ad hoc* than it once was, the same is less true of the support staff for the committees. Generally, the provision of secretariat services to intergovernmental committees, even today, is still primarily *ad hoc*, worked out informally by the members of the particular committee. The most common arrangement has been for the necessary support staff to be provided by the government whose representative chairs the particular committee. This meant, in the past, that federal departments often provided support services for federal-provincial committees, a convenient arrangement, since Ottawa had the financial and personnel resources to be able to afford it.

However, this trend was reversed during the seventies. It became normal practice for provincial ministers to co-chair federal-provincial committees, and a number of the provinces now possessed the resources to provide support staff. They were also increasingly suspicious of support services domiciled in the federal bureaucracy. In the case of interprovincial committees, the secretariat is normally part-time, composed of temporarily seconded officials of the government that chairs the meetings. As the chairing of interprovincial com-

---

6. See Larry Pratt, *The Tar Sands: Syncrude and the Politics of Oil* (Edmonton: Hurtig, 1976).

mittees often rotates, this means that the secretariat to the committee is located in a different provincial capital each year. Underlying all of this discussion is the fact that the individual federal and provincial delegations all draw heavily on the technical and administrative briefings from within their own governmental hierarchies.

**Permanent Secretariats** The strengths of permanent secretariats are that they provide continuity and a level of expert advice that the committee could not achieve with annually rotating secondments. However, the great potential weakness of the examples we cited is obviously that the host government may come to dominate the setting of the committee agenda, the briefing of conferees, and, to an extent, the conduct of the meetings themselves. While provinces have the opportunity to bring their own advisors to meetings, some smaller provinces either can ill afford the expense or do not have expert advisors in the same numbers and quality as the federal government. In addition to the fairly obvious advantage to the federal government of having the committee on payroll, the legitimacy of the secretariat may be questioned by provincial officials who come to feel that the support staff is "in Ottawa's pocket."

Finally, mention should be made here of the Canadian Intergovernmental Conference Secretariat, which is domiciled in Ottawa but staffed by federal and provincial bureaucrats who are seconded to it by their home governments. Its role is not substantive in policy terms; rather, it is to choreograph and "cater" the innumerable intergovernmental conferences, to maintain an intergovernmental documents centre, and to look after all of the administrative arrangements that are necessary if the conferees are to be able to concentrate on the substantive discussions. By all counts the Secretariat works to the satisfaction of all governments and might point the way to an institutional form that could work effectively in a wide range of relatively uncontroversial areas of federal-provincial-territorial cooperation.

**Intergovernmental Affairs: Central Agencies** During the heyday of cooperative federalism in the fifties, the departments of government most involved in intergovernmental negotiations set up separate federal-provincial relations divisions or branches to coordinate such negotiations. Portfolios such as Health, Welfare, Agriculture, and Finance at both the federal and provincial levels took the lead role in developing such specialized intergovernmental units whose function was to ensure the reasonably smooth conduct of intergovernmental relations in their respective policy areas.

However, as our system moved from the cooperative mode back to a more confrontational one in the sixties and seventies, the power of the specialized intergovernmental divisions within departments was reduced with the establishment of omnibus central agencies that could coordinate intergovernmental affairs across the bureaucracy. The Quebec Department of Federal-Provincial Relations was the prototype of this kind of agency, and was set up originally in 1961 by the Lesage government. In the 1970s the wealthier provinces, Ontario, Alberta, and Saskatchewan, set up corresponding departments, and most of the other provinces followed suit soon after.

At the federal level, the Trudeau government set up a federal-provincial relations division of the PCO in the late 1960s, which became a separate body, the Federal Provincial Relations Office (FPRO), in 1975. From time to time since that period, depending on the intensity of intergovernmental interaction at the time, the FPRO has alternated between separate institutional status and temporary demotion to a branch of the PCO. The same alternation in the importance of intergovernmental affairs central agencies has occurred at the provincial level in response to the ebb and flow of interjurisdictional interaction.

In the 1980s the power of the intergovernmental central agencies grew with the designation of separate ministers of "Intergovernmental Affairs" in most governments. This trend peaked in 1992 and the number of separate intergovernmental ministries shrank dramatically with the collapse of the constitutional renewal process. In 1995, all provincial intergovernmental affairs offices, with the exception of Quebec's, report to the premier rather than to a separate minister, and in the majority of the provinces, the intergovernmental affairs bureaucracy is attached to another central agency. At the federal level, Prime Minister Chrétien reinstated the separate ministry format in 1993, designating Marcel Masse as the minister responsible, but since then the FPRO has once again been absorbed into the PCO.

Central-agency intergovernmental *diplomats* evolved as important power brokers within both federal and provincial bureaucracies during the 1980s, but their clout has been reduced, at least for the time being, in the mid nineties with the shift in intergovernmental politics away from the grandiose notions of constitutional renewal and back to the more specialized intergovernmental relationships that are best managed by non-political professionals and technocrats toiling faithfully in the bowels of the line departments. We will revisit the significance of the central-agency approach to the *intra*-governmental coordination of *inter*governmental relations in the next section.

---

## ▶ THE INTERGOVERNMENTAL PROCESS IN THE 1990s

Having looked at the evolution of intergovernmental relations from 1867 to the present, and having described the basic structures involved in the process of negotiating and coordinating interjurisdictional policy initiatives, we now turn to a more generalized discussion of the main characteristics of the intergovernmental process in Canada today. These include, on the one hand, current tendencies of the process such as *executive*, *bureaucratic*, and *asymmetrical* federalism and, on the other hand, emerging trends such as the more *inclusive* process of constitutional reform and the evolution of an aboriginal *third order* of government.

### Executive Federalism

No one today would question that the interdependence of most social and economic problems requires ongoing federal-provincial consultation and cooperation. Moreover, while the growth in the number and compexity of inter-governmental institutions may have levelled off in the 1990s, the current level of activity is likely to continue. Even radical changes to the structure of the fedcration such as the possible separation of Quebec would not reduce the amount of intergovernmental interaction at all. New international structures would have to be developed to facilitate the new Quebec-Canada relationship, and the remaining nine provinces would likely continue to participate in the same number of relationships with the federal government as they do today. In sum, the critical policy decisions of the federation will continue to be re-ferred to the federal and provincial representatives who meet at intergovern-mental conferences, and there is little to indicate that either federal or provin-cial institutions, operating unilaterally, are capable of taking over these interjurisdictional coordinative functions.

There is a startling lack of involvement of either Parliament or the provin-cial legislatures in matters of intergovernmental affairs. There are no intergov-ernmental committees composed of legislators, and there is very little even informal contact among legislators of the two orders of government. Certainly, members of the opposition parties in the legislatures are completely locked out of the intergovernmental process. Donald Smiley dubbed this phenome-non **executive federalism**[7] for the obvious reason that the ulimate policy de-cisions in the federation are taken by committees made up exclusively of political executives and their closest bureaucratic advisors.

On the one hand, this has contributed to the continued shrinking of the role of Parliament and the provincial legislatures in the policy process in gen-eral, which we discuss elsewhere in the book. On the other hand, however, the causal links are likely in the reverse direction as well; that is, the evolution of executive federalism is a symptom of the general impotence of legislative institutions vis-à-vis the executive branch at all levels of government in Canada. While, in a formal sense, the prime minister and the premiers must still get legislative ratification of their agreements "back home," this becomes an au-tomatic step in a process featuring responsible government and strict party discipline. The legislature does not exercise day-to-day control over "its" del-egates to intergovernmental conferences; rather, it functions as an electoral college, giving tacit assent to the choice of who will represent the government in the particular interjurisdictional arena.

A further problem of executive federalism is that, while it fosters decen-tralization and may exaggerate the centrifugal forces in the federation, it does not result in any decentralization of political power in the system as a whole. Rather, the heavy concentration of decision-making power in the hands of a very tiny political elite may shift governmental power *geographically* from the centre to the periphery, but it prevents any shift in the locus of power to the Canadian people. Certainly, where the key priority decisions are made by committees of eleven (or as high as seventeen recently) at intergovernmental conferences, democratic control is more difficult than in a system where such decisions are approved by a Parliament of 295 men and women from all parts of Canada, and by provincial legislatures comprising hundreds more.

---

7. See D. V. Smiley, *Canada in Question* (Toronto: McGraw-Hill Ryerson, 1976), ch. 4.

Thus, while the dominance of any one government is being reduced as power is dispersed among several, the power of the state in general becomes more concentrated and elitist through the phenomenon of executive federalism. We are left overall with a diminished governmental accountability and responsiveness to the public. The process of executive federalism not only reflects but contributes to the general trend of increasing executive domination in the policy process.

### Bureaucratic Federalism

Executive federalism, as we have seen, has contributed to concentration of power in the Canadian system. However, we have also identified a general tendency for policy making in the modern world to depend heavily upon technical inputs from various non-elected officers of government residing in the federal and provincial bureaucracies. When these two trends are viewed together with the fact of the increased number of interjurisdictional committees operating at the senior bureaucratic, technical, and operational levels of government, one cannot avoid the conclusion that bureaucratic executives are as important as political executives in the day-to-day practice of contemporary Canadian federalism. This is **bureaucratic federalism**.

While the direct formal accountability of government agencies to Cabinet ministers enhances the power of the political executive vis-à-vis the legislative branch of government, which does not have access to such expert advice, the political executive may end up being less powerful overall. In the first place, where the decisions to be taken involve complex issues and problems, the advice of knowledgeable bureaucratic specialists may be unchallengeable by the non-expert politicians or even the most senior bureaucrats. There may be little real choice left to the politicians when faced with a consensus as to what should be done among the bureaucratic policy advisors.

It is fairly clear generally that in the *formulation* of detailed policy options after a governmental priority has been set, and in the *implementation* of policy, the *de facto* power of the bureaucracy over its political masters is greatest. From another angle, when the focus of *intergovernmental* policy deliberations is upon formulation or implementation of policy, the ministerial-level committees tend to go along with the joint recommendations of their officials in bureaucratic and technical working groups.

It is more difficult, however, to maintain that bureaucrats dominate *priority determination*, for despite the technical merit of a policy idea, the broad policy direction taken by the government must ultimately be justified politically. As with the *intra*-governmental policy process, in the *inter*governmental priority-determination process, the bureaucratic and technical recommendations, while often *prima facie* appealing, may be overturned at the ministerial level for political reasons. Or, what is more likely, the officials themselves may be unable to reach a consensus because each government's representative will be sensitive to the political priorities "back home" and, like all good bureaucrats, each would know that one does not cause one's minister to be embarrassed publicly.

Nevertheless, we have seen that a very large percentage of total intergovernmental activity occurs at the bureaucratic level. The proof of this is that the number of interjurisdictional committees and the frequency of meetings at this level far exceed those at the ministerial level. Given that there is almost constant interaction among non-elected officials, given that politically success-ful programs will often be contingent upon implementability and technical feasibility, and given that smart bureaucrats will have a good sense of what will fly politically, policy ideas generated by senior bureaucratic and technical com-mittees will very often be consistent with political priorities and for that reason will be adopted as priority items by the ministers.

A positive result of bureaucratic federalism is that intergovernmental co-ordination is probably improved. In the first place, as the frequency of inter-action has increased at the non-elected levels of government, the people in-volved in the bargaining process actually come to know each other personally and professionally. They often supplement more formal exchanges at com-mittee meetings with informal contact through telephone calls, correspon-dence, and E-mail. The members of the committee often develop a sense of pride in their joint accomplishments and acquire a sense of ownership over the recommendations they are taking back to their respective governments. They may go so far as to attempt to sell the product of their committee's deliberations to their dubious superiors back home.

Second, because the bureaucratic part of the intergovernmental process does not take place in public, the officials do not have to be as concerned as the politicians with faithfully advocating the interests of a particular region — there is greater freedom for compromise. For instance, if forestry officials are meeting to set up a program for combatting a spruce-budworm epidemic, they are usually more concerned with "lickin' the worm" than with defending pro-vincial or partisan priorities or pandering to special-interest groups.

The combination of shared professional interests, personal ties, such as friendships, which grow through long-standing formal and informal contact, and a non-partisan milieu tends to facilitate coordination at the bureaucratic level. As advisors to the ministers, the bureaucrats can, through their personal and professional relationships with each other, help to moderate the more conflictual public and political dimension of federal-provincial bargaining, and contribute to an overall environment within which interjurisdictional compro-mise and cooperation is possible. In this sense, federalism works in large part because of networks or trust relationships among senior officials, program officers, and technocrats at both levels of government, who work together to solve common problems and achieve common program goals.

### Central-Agency Federalism

We have already spoken about the growth and subsequent decline of federal-provincial central agencies in the various government bureaucracies. This is, in fact, a different manifestation of bureaucratic federalism and one that per-haps should cause us to qualify the conclusion that this aspect of the process facilitates intergovernmental cooperation. It is likely that the coordination of the intergovernmental activities of the various departments and agencies within individual governments is improved by having a central clearing house such as the FPRO. This institutional arrangement ensures that agencies within a single government are all pointed in the same direction when dealing with

another level of government and permits the development of integrated negotiation strategies in the intergovernmental arena. However, the efforts of
such central agencies may, in fact, run counter to the accommodative and
integrative effect of bureaucratic federalism described above.

What happened was that this **central-agency federalism** spawned a new
breed of specialized officials, analogous to the foreign-service officers who
represent Canada in international relations. These central-agency types are not
directly involved with specific programs, but have influence over a wide range
of policy areas that have an intergovernmental component. They tend to be
less problem-oriented and focused more either on "winning" the interjurisdictional skirmishes with the other levels of government or, occasionally, in
avoiding skirmishes altogether in order to avoid bad press. As a result, the
shared professional interests and the low-key practical focus on solving common policy problems that characterize cooperative federalism are sometimes
supplanted by a more highly politicized and often more combative attitude to
intergovernmental relations.

Moreover, coincident with this trend towards greater centralization of the
intergovernmental role within the participating governments during the 1980s
was the evolution of a more "institutionalized" Cabinet committee structure.[8]
This both encourages the hegemony of central agencies and breaks down the
functional autonomy of the individual ministers and their departmental officials in dealing with their counterparts in other governments. Thus, while
federal-provincial relations could still be deemed "bureaucratic," increasingly
the interaction was between central agencies rather than program departments. Similarly, even at the political level, it was *governments* dealing with other
governments rather than individual functional ministers dealing with each
other in often long-established relationships of mutual trust and understanding.

Another aspect of this change in the intra-governmental balance of bureaucratic power is that the process may tend to reward conflict rather than
the resolution of it. As Richard Simeon has put it,

> the process, far from being an effective mechanism for the resolution of conflict,
> in fact, exacerbates it. Indeed, it is even suggested that the emergence of larger
> ministries of intergovernmental affairs — an internal diplomatic corps — creates a
> group whose sole *raison d'être* is to look out for and promote their government's
> interest and for whom the federal-provincial game is an end in itself. The process
> engages institutional rivalries, not real policy disputes.[9]

Thus, not only does intra-governmental centralization attenuate the positive
trust relationships among federal and provincial program officials; it actually
can foster more combative relations between and among the governments
involved.

To conclude this section, while its importance waxes and wanes, the central-agency style of intergovernmental diplomacy is here to stay and it both

---

8. J. S. Dupré, "Reflections on the Workability of Executive Federalism," *in* R. Simeon, ed., *Intergovernmental Relations* (Toronto: University of Toronto Press, 1985), p. 4.
9. R. Simeon, "Intergovernmental Relations and the Challenges to Canadian Federalism," *Canadian
Public Administration,* Spring 1980, p. 23.

helps and hinders the process of intergovernmental conflict resolution. However, with the foundering of the most recent spate of constitutional renewal, we have seen a trend away from any dominant role for such agencies in virtually all governments in Canada. As the focus of intergovernmental affairs shifts from the high-profile "summitry" of constitutional FMCs and returns to the more normal, low-key, and less visible process of intergovernmental interaction in specific policy areas, there is a more comfortable balance between the roles of central-agency diplomats and departmental technocrats.

### Bilateral Federalism

We have seen that a very large percentage of interjurisdictional committees in Canada are bilateral; that is, they involve the federal government and one of the provinces or territories. This tendency towards bilateral committees can be explained, in part, by the need for federal-provincial coordination in the *implementation* of many joint programs. A large percentage of the bilateral committees are, in fact, at the operational level, and are bilateral in their composition simply because the particular program being administered involves only two governments.

However, this tendency towards bilateral rather than multilateral or omnilateral interaction may reflect more complex trends in the nature of federal-provincial bargaining. The omnilateral meetings, particularly at the ministerial level, do not appear to be particularly effective as forums for intergovernmental bargaining because they are too public and too dominated by partisan posturing. In bilateral relations, the extensive media coverage that inevitably surrounds and, some say, undermines formal omnilateral meetings may be avoided. The federal government, particularly, recognizes this, given the time-worn tradition of provincial politicians' using omnilateral ministerial conferences exclusively as opportunities for "fed bashing."

At the more-or-less annual First Ministers' Conference, the "mother of all intergovernmental committees," it is not uncommon for each government to put forward a different set of policy priorities as a bargaining position. In this way the FMC is not used for negotiation but as a podium for "pitching" the voters back home. Moreover, the number of combinations of positions possible as compromise solutions in a multiple-stakeholder situation is, in any event, so great that serious negotiation is virtually impossible. Most importantly, the attending delegations have difficulty *identifying* the range of options open to them, let alone *choosing* the accommodation that achieves agreement at the least cost to the position of their government. Hence, the provincial premiers are often hesitant about making deals in multilateral or omnilateral situations, simply for fear of "blowing it" in public. They instead do what is safest, and simply state and restate the position they started with.

Given the difficulty of bargaining in a highly complex omnilateral conference, and given the evidence of much bilateral interaction in operational and technical committees, one might hypothesize that there is, in fact, a lot of bilateral interaction at the more senior levels as well. This, however, will not be manifested by the existence of many formal or permanent bilateral committees, for the ministers and senior bureaucrats are simply too busy to be involved in regular meetings. However, informal bilateral meetings or telephone conversations between a federal minister and a provincial counterpart occur frequently so that the ministers can discuss specific policy questions. In such a setting, with only two governments present, and only two positions to accommodate, bargaining is a much simpler process. Moreover, as such sessions are informal and *ad hoc*, they will not be publicized to any great extent, and because they are held behind closed doors, the horse trading can go on candidly and frankly with no motivation for provincial ministers to champion their electorate in ritualistic combat with the feds.

It has been suggested that **bilateral federalism** not only facilitates accommodation, but that it also may be used by the federal government to control the bargaining process. On a one-to-one basis, the federal government can often dominate a bargaining situation, whereas on a one-to-ten basis, the provinces hold sway. In this sense, by consummating sequential deals in several bilateral situations the federal government may be able to divide and conquer, accomplishing piecemeal what it could not in the multi- or omnilateral forums. However, to counter this strategy, the provinces can make deals among themselves, establishing united bargaining positions before facing the feds in a bilateral situation. While such temporary interprovincial coalitions can offset the potential bullying by the national government, the bargaining positions of the provinces are often too far apart for them to reach agreement among themselves.

Finally, some provinces are sufficiently powerful and influential in the intergovernmental arena that they do not fear the bilateral bargaining process. Provinces such as Alberta, which has had real clout from time to time because of its oil reserves, prefer to bargain one-to-one with Ottawa, for the simple reason that, in an omnilateral meeting, Ottawa will have strong allies in the ranks of the energy-consuming provinces such as Ontario. Ontario, because of its sheer size in terms of population and economic wealth, always is able to deal as an equal with the federal government. Similarly, Quebec, because of its special status in the federation, has been enormously successful in negotiating bilateral accords with Canada and will continue to be so.

### Asymmetrical Federalism

We have seen that interjurisdictional coordination in the Canadian federal system is achieved essentially through a process of negotiation among governments. The traditional bargaining capital in our system is determined by the fact that the provinces have something the federal government wants and vice versa. The provinces will offer to trade a share of their jurisdiction in key policy areas such as health, welfare, and economic regulation where the federal government wishes to establish *national* programs and standards, in return for a greater share of the federal government's large revenue base and spending power. However, while these trade-offs are at the core of the process, intergovernmental negotiations are more complicated in practice.

Intergovernmental relations in Canada have always been **asymmetrical**. The BNA Act established principles that necessitated different kinds of relationships among the various governmental actors. Quebec is the most obvious example, because, as the homeland to most of Canada's second charter group, it enjoys a special constitutional status in areas such as the use of the French language, the *Code civile*, and denominational schools. This special constitutional status has given Quebec's claims for special privileges vis-à-vis the other provinces a higher order of legitimacy than similar demands from other provinces or regions would ever enjoy. Moreover, in recent years, Quebec has learned that it can also influence negotiations in its favour by playing its "threat-to-separate" trump card.

In another way, special bargaining relationships have evolved with, for instance, the Maritime provinces. Because of the federal jurisdiction over fisheries, and because the fishery has been a principal economic concern of the Atlantic region since Confederation, continual coordination among the governments involved is required to develop joint programs in that industry. As well, accidents of geography and geology have determined that certain provinces and regions will be much wealthier than others. For instance, Alberta with its gas and oil, Quebec with its hydro-electric generation potential, and Ontario with its large population and stable industrial sector, have sources of economic wealth that enhance their bargaining strength at intergovernmental meetings.

However, while provinces such as Alberta and Ontario have extraordinary bargaining power because their economies are so important to the economic health of the federation as a whole, the secondary bargaining strength of wealthier provinces flows from their considerable tax revenues. The wealthy provinces can enhance their bargaining clout by being able to buy the very best professional and technical help to buttress their team at intergovernmental negotiating sessions. The ability to field a highly competent negotiating team can enhance the bargaining power of a given province considerably in an era when governmental decisions generally depend more and more upon the input of technical advice.

Policy decisions should be made on the basis of full knowledge of present public demands, projections identifying future needs, a full awareness of all present policy options, and a careful analysis of the relative costs and benefits of each policy option. The determination of the policies that should be implemented must then be made, with a view to maximizing long-range benefits and minimizing political and financial costs. The ability to bargain effectively in the intergovernmental arena is linked to whether a government's policy priorities are organized and articulated in comprehensive terms. The ability to bargain in this fashion is, in turn, linked to the number and quality of human resources that a particular government can bring to the table.

That the federal government and the wealthier provinces can afford to buy the commitment of high-priced technocrats and policy planners is beyond question. However, the have-not provinces are less able to pay for such high-priced help and may be reduced to accepting on faith the kinds of policy alternatives articulated by the wealthier provinces and the federal government. In this sense, a new lever or capital with which to bargain successfully in the interjurisdictional sphere is the possession of expert human resources; governments lacking this resource may be effectively disenfranchised when it comes to federal-provincial bargaining.

One possible way to offset the tendency in interjurisdictional relations towards a virtually permanent oligarchy of the have provinces and the federal government is for the federal government to increase unconditional grants to the poorer provinces in absolute rather than per-capita terms. This would increase the financial ability of the have-not provinces to hire the necessary technocratic support to make their negotiating teams more competitive. Unfortunately, in a time of fiscal restraint and frighteningly large federal deficits, it is unlikely that the larger provinces, who have their own debt problems, would be very happy with such a measure. In the absence of a remedy, intergovernmental relations will continue to be asymmetrical, with a select few provinces and the federal government dominating centre stage and determining the major policy priorities into the next century.

Finally, the Canadian federal system is also asymmetrical in terms of the *results* of the intergovernmental bargaining process. As examples, we can cite the fact that for the most part all provinces and territories except Ontario and Quebec contract their policing responsibilities out to the RCMP; Ontario, Alberta, and Quebec collect their own corporation income tax; Quebec has opted out of most shared-cost programs; and Quebec has entered into agreements with the federal government having to do with federal assistance to municipalities and the financing of provincial employment-training programs. However, while asymmetrical federalism can be viewed as negative in that it enhances the gap between the have and have-not provinces, Ken McRoberts points out that the asymmetry is *inevitable* in a diverse society:

> Asymmetrical federalism would seem to be tailor made for a political system such as Canada's in which the accommodation of societal diversity has been an endemic problem. It should not be surprising then that asymmetry has emerged in so many areas as governments have sought to reconcile competing objectives and concerns.[10]

On the other hand, the constitutional entrenchment of asymmetrical provisions such as the "distinct-society" clause was offered up as a possible means of accommodating the concerns of Quebec in the federation. That Canadians do not generally approve of **asymmetrical federalism** is one of the obvious conclusions to be drawn from the results of the referendum on the Charlottetown Accord.

---

▶ CONCLUSION: CANADIAN FEDERALISM INTO
THE NEXT CENTURY

When the Liberals were returned to power in 1980 after the short-lived Clark interregnum, the government served notice very quickly that it was going to assert the federal presence in the federation to a much greater extent than before. This was a reaction to the "community-of-communities" image of Canada that had been espoused by Joe Clark, and a belief that Canadians had to decide "whether to have a country not." Prime Minister Pierre Trudeau declared in 1981 that it was

---

10. K. McRoberts, "Unilateralism, Bilateralism, and Multilateralism," *in* Simeon, *Intergovernmental Relations,* p. 79.

time to reassert in our national policies that Canada is one country which must be capable of moving with unity of spirit and purpose towards shared goals. If Canada is, indeed, to be a nation, there must be a national will which is something more than the lowest common denominator among the desires of the provincial governments.[11]

The Liberal government then embarked on a period of fairly remarkable unilateral initiatives that challenged the right of the provincial governments to speak (even collectively) for Canada as a whole. Trudeau, never famed for his understatement, declared that cooperative federalism was effectively dead:

> The old type of federalism where they [the provinces] kick us in the teeth because they didn't get enough . . . is finished. The pendulum would keep swinging until we end up with a community of communities . . . a confederation of shopping centres . . . and that is not my view of Canada. I thought we could build a strong Canada through cooperation. I have been disillusioned.[12]

The Liberals were true to their word from 1980 to 1984. The *Constitution Act, 1982*, was achieved largely because of the unilateral initiative of the federal government; the National Energy Program, which included measures deeply resented by the oil-producing provinces, was imposed without consultation with the provinces; the *Canada Health Act* was used to force provinces to outlaw extra billing; and amendments to certain parts of the Established Programs Financing legislation that directly affected provincial income from transfer payments went through with very little consultation, and over the unanimous objections of the provinces.

Whether related to their flirtation with unilateralism or not, the Liberals saw themselves humiliated in the 1984 election at the hands of the Progressive Conservatives, led by Brian Mulroney. Buoyed by his enormous national mandate and reassured by the presence of so many provincial Conservative governments, during this period Mulroney served notice that we were about to embark on a new era of cooperation in intergovernmental relations. True to *his* word, the new prime minister quickly worked out essentially bilateral accords with Newfoundland, Alberta, and the two northern territories with respect to the exploration, development, production, and taxing of petroleum resources.

However, it is likely that the Mulroney years will be remembered more for the orgy of intergovernmental summitry that the country engaged in from 1985 to 1992. The 1985 and 1987 First Ministers' Conferences on aboriginal self-government ended in deadlock, but established the convention that the aboriginal people and the territorial governments must be involved in constitutional discussions that affect aboriginal rights. The many behind-closed-doors FMCs that led to the Meech Lake Accord in 1987 demonstrated that the old-fashioned processes of elite accommodation through executive federalism could still be made to work. But the subsequent "dying on the vine" of the

---

11. Cited in S. Dunn, "Federalism, Constitutional Reform and the Economy," *Publius*, Winter 1984, p. 134.

12. Brooke Jeffrey, "A New Era in Intergovernmental Relations," *in* Library of Parliament, *Machinery of Government in Transition* (Research Branch, Library of Parliament, December 1984), p. 131.

Accord in 1991 demonstrated that this kind of decision making was no longer acceptable to a large number of Canadians, in particular, to the aboriginal peoples.

Thus, it would seem that the central institution of the integrated federal system that had evolved by the eighties, the First Ministers' Conference, has undergone important changes. No longer are the "eleven white men" able to successfully accommodate the competing interests of the federal government and the various provinces without having to meet the test of public approval. And the exclusive FMC "club" now admits women members, and has been forced to invite aboriginal and territorial government leaders to participate in its deliberations.

The Charlottetown Accord, signed in 1992, showed us that elite accommodation could still be made to work but that the elite "executive federalism club" had to expand its membership to include First Nations representatives and territorial leaders. The resounding rejection of this Accord in a referendum showed us that the "elite club" was still too exclusive and far too private for the Canadian people. The most important message here seems to be that, at least with repect to constitutional matters, the time-worn and tattered practices of executive federalism were being complemented if not supplanted by an emerging trend towards **populist federalism**, where the conduct of constitutional negotiations is more public and the outcomes of the process must be subjected to direct public approval by referendum.

One further result of the Charlottetown process was that the evolution of a **third order of government** representing the peoples of the First Nations seems virtually inevitable. While it is not to be expected overnight, the creation of many First Nations governments, which will have to be accommodated within the intergovernmental arena, will increase the complexity of the process of interjurisdictional coordination enormously. Coupled with the creation of a separate Inuit territory, Nunavut, by 1999 and the possibility of a new relationship with Quebec, our federal system may be unrecognizable by the year 2000.

This concludes our discussion of intergovernmental relations in Canada. Much of this final section has been speculative and, at time of writing, it is still impossible to say very much about whether the Chrétien government will impose a new stamp on the face of the federation. Certainly, it is hoped that the constitutional spleen-venting of the eighties has sated our national appetite for angst and that we and our governments can get down to the business of addressing more prosaic problems such as the national debt, economic recovery, and the social and economic inequalities that continue to plague us.

All that can be said in conclusion is that Canadian federalism is today, and always has been, in a state of flux; it has evolved from what it was in 1867 to what it is today through constant adaptation to new social, economic, and political circumstances. It is, today, a very tightly integrated network of intergovernmental consultative bodies at various governmental levels. There is a constantly changing relationship among the stakeholders as each of the provinces and territories and the federal government attempts to maximize its bargaining advantages vis-à-vis the others. Moreover, as aboriginal governments, new territories, and, possibly, new provinces evolve, there will be many more governments entering the fray and many more interjurisdictional bodies created.

We have seen that intergovernmental conflict is inevitable in a diverse society such as ours. We must also recognize, however, that the conflicts can be resolved only if the active process of self-interested horse-trading is tempered with some fundamental consensus. There must be some mutual feelings of good will, a basic agreement on very fundamental values, and, most importantly, the shared acceptance of Canada as a legitimate political community. These attitudes form the pedestal upon which the machinery of intergovernmental conflict-resolution is mounted and, despite the dissaffection of some Québécois, for the most part, there remains, under the coverlet of constant conflict, a willingness to seek agreement, to compromise, and to continue to bargain.

# Chapter 11
# Federal-Provincial Fiscal Relations

In the previous chapter we discussed the *machinery* of intergovernmental relations. In this chapter we will discuss the *engine* that drives that machinery, the complex system of federal-provincial fiscal relations. At the root of Canadian federal-provincial relations in general is an *imbalance* which was unintentionally built into the original Confederation settlement and increased by the passage of time and the expanding role of government. The pre-eminent ability to raise money was vested in the federal government because the Fathers of Confederation expected the Dominion to perform the lion's share of governmental responsibilities. However, as we have seen in earlier chapters, through social and economic change and jurisprudential evolution, the major expenditure burden shifted to the provincial governments, which are responsible today for the delivery of costly but essential services such as health care, education, and social programs. Unfortunately, the provinces' ability to raise revenues has not grown commensurately with the growth of their program responsibilities.

The correction of this imbalance would appear, at first glance, to be a fairly simple matter involving one of two options. Either the federal government could transfer its excess tax revenues to the provinces who would then be able to afford to carry out their expanded responsibilities, or the provinces could transfer their legislative authority to the federal government, which already has the revenues required to do the job. The latter option is precluded by the Constitution, which does not permit the delegation of legislative power from one level of government to the other and because, even if the constitutional obstacles could be overcome, provincial governments are extremely jealous of their constitutional powers. Moreover, many Canadians believe that in normal times the responsibilities currently exercised by the provinces can, indeed, be carried out more effectively regionally than nationally.

However, the former option is not an easy solution either. For the political decision-makers in any government, the essence of popularity and, hence, political survival is to be able to spend money lavishly delivering popular programs to the voting public. Unfortunately, in order to spend the money, it must first be raised and this means engaging in the patently unpopular business of levying and collecting taxes from that same voting public. So, to solve the problem by having the federal government levy the taxes and the provincial governments spend the revenues is, understandably, not a happy solution to the federal politicians. As a result, the dominant focus of intergovernmental relations in Canada since the 19th century has been upon the ongoing attempts of our federal and provincial political elites to deal with the imbalance in the distribution of program responsibilities and revenues between the two orders of government.

## ▶ THE FISCAL "BALANCE" IN THE 19TH CENTURY

The most fundamental rules of the game of federal-provincial fiscal arrangements are established by the Constitution, which divides legislative jurisdiction over both program responsibilities and revenue sources. However, as important as the formal, legal rules of the game is the changing social and economic context within which government is set. In order to understand the interrelationship among these factors we must begin with a look at the manner in which the fiscal arrangements established in the 19th century evolved and adapted to a rapidly changing world.

### The "Fiscal Blueprint"

The nature and content of any system of public finance depends largely upon the role that government, in general, is expected to play in the lives of its citizens. In 1867, the role of government was perceived in terms of rugged individualism, and the best government was judged to be that which governed least. Government was expected to confine itself mainly to the provision of national security, including defence, to the administration of justice, and to promoting national economic development through "big ticket" public works such as railways.

Thus, at the time of Confederation, the most important and costly functions of the state were placed in the hands of the federal government. As well, because the provinces were expected to operate on fairly limited revenues, the burden of the pre-Confederation debts of the provinces were to be assumed by the national government. The provinces, by contrast, were to take on matters of a merely "local or private nature" such as education, public welfare, and public works within the province. These provincial powers were thought to be relatively minor when compared to the federal responsibilities, and consequently it was anticipated that the provinces would require commensurately minor sources of revenue.

This fiscal blueprint was based on the fact that expenditures for health, education, and welfare in 1866 amounted to only 14 per cent of total governmental outlays in 1866 (compared to almost two-thirds in 1995). Similarly, the largest revenue sources at Confederation were customs and excise duties, which accounted for approximately 80 per cent of the total revenues of the colonies of Nova Scotia and New Brunswick, and 66 per cent of the revenues of Upper and Lower Canada.[1] It was felt that sufficient provincial revenue could be generated from real property taxes, various types of fees and permits, provincial licensing systems, and timber royalties.

Because the BNA Act vested the legislative authority over the "great functions of government" in the federal Parliament, and because the Dominion was to assume responsibility for the existing debts, the major sources of revenue at that time were given to the Dominion. The federal tax power, as specified in section 91(3), thus gives the Parliament of Canada the authority over "the Raising of Money by *any* Mode or System of Taxation." The provinces, on the other hand, were limited by section 92(2) to *direct* taxation within the province.

**Direct and Indirect Taxation**  The area of direct taxation was viewed as a sort of residual source of provincial revenue and was not intended to be used extensively. "Direct taxes were extremely unpopular: they had never been levied by the provinces and . . . the nature of the economy made the administration of direct taxation, except by the municipalities, very difficult."[2] Thus, the modern direct taxes such as personal income tax were undreamt of, except perhaps in nightmares, and the indirect tax fields were expected to continue to be the most lucrative revenue sources.

The terms **direct taxation** and **indirect taxation** require some clarification. Sections 91 and 92 of the BNA Act do not make any clear distinction between these two terms, and it was not until a decision of the Judicial Committee in 1887 that a working definition was set down. The distinction made then has stood the test of time, and remains even today the basic rule for determining the validity of provincial tax measures. The Judicial Committee took a definition from the writing of John Stuart Mill and stated:

> Taxes are either direct or indirect. A direct tax is one that is demanded from the very persons who it is intended or desired should pay it. Indirect taxes are those that are demanded from one person in the expectation and intention that he shall indemnify himself at the expense of another. Such are the excise or customs. . . . He shall recover the amount by means of an advance in price.[3]

Direct taxes thus include such things as personal income tax, corporate income tax, real property tax, and succession duties or inheritance tax, while indirect taxes include such levies as customs duties and excise taxes.

The courts have tended to emphasize the *intention* of a provincial tax measure as the crucial determinant of its validity, and have not too seriously limited the tax power of the provincial legislatures, merely because one of the incidental *effects* of a tax measure might be indirect. In the case of corporation income taxes, for instance, it is quite likely that corporations *do* attempt to indemnify themselves at the expense of the consumer, but the courts have

---

1.  Canada, *Report of the Royal Commission on Dominion-Provincial Relations* (Ottawa: King's Printer, 1940), Book 1, p. 131. Subsequent references are to *The Rowell-Sirois Report,* or *Rowell-Sirois.*
2.  Ibid., p. 44.
3.  *Bank of Toronto v. Lambe* (1887) 12 AC 575. See also *Rowell-Sirois,* 1, p. 59.

judged such a provincial tax valid because the intention is that it is to be paid directly by the corporation.

In the case of retail sales tax, which is a very important provincial revenue source today, the provinces have been able to collect a revenue from the retailer, which is in fact passed on to the customer through a legal fiction. The retailer is assumed to be the *agent* of the government for the purposes of administering this tax. Thus, when store clerks punch up the *price* of your purchase, they are functioning on behalf of the retailer, but when they calculate and add the sales tax to the total, they are functioning as tax collectors for the province. By deeming each retailer to be a provincial tax collector, and by requiring that the tax be calculated separately from the before-tax price, the sales tax can technically pass as a direct tax on the consumer. If the sales tax were to be included in the prices of retail goods (a much simpler arrangement for all concerned!) and collected from the store, it would be *indirect*, because the retailer would be "indemnifying himself at the expense of the customer" by increasing the retail price of the goods.

**Sharing Direct Taxation**   While the provinces were given the power to levy direct taxes, and the interpretation of the scope of "direct taxation within the province" has been fairly broad, this tax power has not been deemed to be *exclusive* to the provinces. It has been felt by the courts that the terms of section 91(3) are general, and that they therefore give the federal Parliament the power to impose both indirect and direct tax measures. Conversely, section 92(2) is very specific, and it therefore must be construed only to *limit* the provincial legislatures to the raising of revenues by direct taxation, and not to reserve the direct tax fields to the exclusive use of the provinces. The constitutional authority to levy indirect taxes therefore rests exclusively with the Parliament of Canada, and the authority to levy direct taxes is shared by the provinces and the federal government.

In retrospect, the way in which sources of revenue were distributed between the provinces and the federal government could be considered shortsighted. The drafters of the BNA Act assumed that there would be no change in the distribution of the costs of government that each would bear. Furthermore, they assumed that the major revenue sources would continue to be indirect — customs and excise — after 1867. While both of these assumptions were eventually to prove incorrect, it would be unfair to criticize the Fathers of Confederation too harshly for their lack of foresight. The changes in the economy and in Canadian society since 1867 could not have been foreseen except through the gift of clairvoyance.

### The Statutory Subsidies

It was clear to the Fathers of Confederation, however, that the provincial revenue sources provided in 1867 were not sufficient to meet the expenditure needs of the provincial legislatures, at least for a transitional period. In recognition of this, provisions for federal subsidies, or **transfer payments**, to the provinces were written directly into the BNA Act. Section 118 gave the provinces three broad types of federal grants: annual grants to support provincial governments and legislatures; per-capita grants; and payments on debt allowances.

**Grants in Support of Provincial Governments**  The grants in support of the provincial governments were intergovernmental transfers based on the population of the province at the 1861 census and were to be paid to the provinces annually. These were intended to assist the provinces in the initial setting up and operation of their governments and legislatures in the first few years after Confederation. Such an annual grant was to be given to the provinces in perpetuity, but no provision was made for population growth.

While a general revision of the federal subsidies to the provinces took place in 1907, and this grant was raised for all the provinces, by comparison with total federal subsidies, the grants to support the provincial governments and legislatures amounted to a mere pittance, ranging from $100,000 for Prince Edward Island to $240,000 for Ontario. These provisions regarding grants to provincial governments were ultimately repealed in 1950 and the actual payment amounts were rolled into the broader system of intergovernmental transfers.

**Per-Capita Grants**  The second subsidy, the per-capita grant, was intended to be the major assistance that the federal government would render to the provinces. Based on the 1861 census, the provinces were to be given eighty cents per capita per annum in perpetuity, although the per-capita grants to New Brunswick and Nova Scotia were to increase with population up to 400,000 people. The per-capita grant was manipulated, from time to time, through the device of estimating the population of the province generously in order to entice new provinces into the federation and to meet the special needs of one province or another. For instance, when British Columbia came into Confederation in 1871, her population was estimated at 60,000, when in fact it was only 34,000; Manitoba was given the fictitious population of 17,000 when it had only 12,200.[4]

While these grants were to be fixed at the figure established at the time of Confederation, the 1907 revisions of the subsidies allowed the eighty-cents-per-capita grant to increase up to 2.5 million people, and sixty cents a head was provided for any number over that figure. In 1950, these grants were discontinued and the paltry amounts involved were simply incorporated into the current fiscal arrangements package.

**Payments on "Debt Allowances"**  Finally, while the federal government had accepted the responsibility for all of the debts of the provinces at Confederation, it was felt that the provinces with smaller debts should be rewarded, in order to equalize the benefits that each province would reap from the union. Each province was allocated a *debt allowance*, based on approximately $25 a

---

4.  R. MacGregor Dawson, *The Government of Canada* (Toronto: University of Toronto Press, 1970), p. 102.

head according to the 1861 census.[5] If the actual debt of a province amounted to less than this figure, that province was to receive 5 per cent of the difference as a grant from the federal government, annually and in perpetuity. If the debt of the province was higher than the debt allowance, the province would be required to pay the federal government a figure equal to 5 per cent of the difference between the actual debt and the amount allowed by the Confederation agreement.

According to this scheme, while New Brunswick and Nova Scotia gained a little from the Dominion, Ontario and Quebec had debts that were far in excess of the debt allowance. However, only half of this arrangement was ever implemented, and the "profligate" provinces were never required to pay their share, partly because of the difficulty of assessing how much Ontario and Quebec should each pay on a debt they incurred jointly as the united colony of Canada. To get around this difficulty, and to further appease Nova Scotia, the debt allowance was raised so that Ontario and Quebec broke even and New Brunswick and Nova Scotia got an even larger payment from the Dominion.

As other provinces came into the federation, they also were given generous debt allowances. What is somewhat curious is that even the provinces of Alberta and Saskatchewan, which had been federal territories before their coming of age, and so therefore obviously had no debt, received an annual payment based on the difference between their "debt allowance" and their non-existent debt.

**Special Subsidies** In addition to the three basic subsidies, ever since Confederation there have been a number of special federal grants to various provinces and regions in order to meet special needs. New Brunswick, for example, received a grant for ten years after Confederation, and Newfoundland received a healthy subsidy on entering Confederation in 1949. Special grants were given to Saskatchewan and Alberta on entering Confederation in 1905, as compensation for the Dominion's retaining its rights to their natural resources. Even after the Dominion gave the natural resources of the prairies back to Saskatchewan and Alberta, the compensation grant was continued.

Thus, while it was assumed that the arrangements concluded at Confederation would be permanent and unalterable, in fact, the federal subsidies to the provinces began to undergo almost constant revision from the day of their inception. Despite these constant adjustments, the statutory subsidies today have been incorporated into the unconditional transfers to the provinces, and in 1994/95 they amounted to but $40 million out of a total of $41.9 billion.

▶ THE FISCAL IMBALANCE OF THE 20TH CENTURY

By the turn of the century, the federal-provincial financial structure had begun what would become a startling metamorphosis. Following a period of economic

---

5. Ibid., p. 100.

stagnation when provincial expenditures did not increase markedly, the wheat boom, among other things, stimulated an immense growth in overall government expenditures. The prosperity of the period generated the extra revenues, and all levels of government — federal, provincial, and municipal — began to spend large sums of money on urban development, public works, and economic expansion. From 1896 to 1913, total expenditures by all governments quadrupled.[6]

### The Failure of the "Fiscal Blueprint"

Initially, at least, the costs of this rapid expansion of the role and responsibilities of government were matched by corresponding increases in federal revenue, as customs and excise receipts, which at this time accounted for more than 90 per cent of all federal revenues, produced large budget surpluses during most of the years between 1900 and the First World War.[7] While provincial revenues from traditional tax sources also increased, provincial expenditures grew still more rapidly, so that the traditional tax bases of the provinces began to be squeezed dry. The inelasticity of federal subsidies and the inability of existing provincial revenue sources to cope with the rising costs of delivering government services was a harbinger of the fiscal woes that would plague the provinces in the future.

**The Fiscal Crisis of the 1930s** After the war, welfare expenditures increased by 130 per cent, and three-quarters of this burden fell upon the provincial governments and the municipalities.[8] Federal outlays in this period were limited largely to grants to the provinces through the first of Canada's major shared-cost social programs, in support of provincial old-age pension schemes and unemployment relief. Meanwhile, the costs of the traditional provincial and municipal responsibilities for roads and highways grew rapidly. The coming of the automobile increased the need not only for interurban highways, but for better roads and street systems within the cities and in suburban areas.[9]

While the costs of provincial government soared, provincial revenues increased rapidly as well. The automobile, for instance, brought in large additional revenues through taxes on gasoline and motor-vehicle licences. Indeed, provincial revenues doubled from 1921 to 1930, and two-thirds of this increase was due to additional tax yields in the three fields of motor-vehicle licences, gasoline taxes, and liquor control. However, at this time, there were also growing disparities in provincial revenues with more than 80 per cent of total direct-tax revenues collected in the provinces of Ontario and Quebec. The cause of this inequity was the growing number of national companies with head offices in Toronto or Montreal. Provincial corporation taxes were (and still are) imposed at the head office of a corporation — profits earned by corporations right across Canada were taxed almost exclusively by the governments of On-

---

6. *Rowell-Sirois,* 1, p. 80.
7. Ibid., p. 81.
8. Ibid., p. 128.
9. Ibid., p. 129.

tario and Quebec. This has been an important factor in the serious regional disparities in provincial revenues to the present day.[10]

With the onslaught of the Great Depression, the tax base in many provinces virtually collapsed. The provinces relied heavily on revenues from tax fields such as liquor control and automobile licences, which tend to be very sensitive to economic fluctuations of a general nature. Similarly, the municipalities relied entirely on real-property tax revenues, which declined when the value of real estate dropped during the Depression. On the other hand, the provinces' expenses increased enormously. Total government expenditures on *relief* grew nearly tenfold, from $18.4 million in 1930 to $172.9 million in 1935. Since the constitutional responsibility for such matters lies with the provinces, who were essentially "broke," the federal government, having been denied the power to intervene directly by the Judicial Committee of the Privy Council, was forced to transfer large portions of its revenue to the provinces to help pay for their unemployment-relief programs.

Thus, by the mid thirties, Canadian federalism was faced with a financial crisis. The traditional functions of government had grown far beyond the expectations of the Fathers of Confederation, and the bulk of this growth involved great increases in provincial expenditures. As well, new responsibilities of government, such as unemployment relief, which had not even been conceived of in 1867, had emerged. At the same time, the revenue structure of the Canadian federal system provided the provincial governments with an inadequate tax base from which to raise the revenues needed to meet their expanded responsiblities. The Depression also exaggerated the already serious disparities in wealth among the various regions of Canada and produced alarming inequalities in the standards of governmental service from one province to the next. By 1936 the federation was facing a fiscal crisis, and there was little reason to hope that the day would be saved by an early end to the Depression.

One major response to the fiscal crisis was the appointment, in 1937, of the Royal Commission on Dominion-Provincial Relations (Rowell-Sirois Commission), which was charged with undertaking "a reexamination of the economic and financial basis of Confederation and of the distribution of legislative powers in the light of the social and economic developments of the last seventy years."[11] The findings and recommendations were finally reported in May 1940. The Rowell-Sirois Commission recommended an extensive shift of both governmental functions and tax powers, and as a solution for the latter, it recommended a permanent system of unconditional **equalization payments** from the federal treasury to the needy provinces and a fully integrated tax system. The outbreak of war in Europe effectively pre-empted any action on the Rowell-Sirois recommendations.

**Fiscal Federalism: 1947–1962** The outbreak of war had given the federal authorities the moral justification and the legal authority under the emergency

---

10. Ibid., p. 131.
11. Ibid., p. 9.

powers of the *War Measures Act* to suspend the major direct-taxation powers of the provinces. Through the Wartime Tax Agreements of 1941, the provinces ceased to levy personal income taxes, corporation income taxes, and all other corporation taxes. While these fiscal arrangements are euphemistically referred to as "agreements," the fact was that, in 1941, the provinces had no choice but to do what the federal authorities wished. The essence of the wartime system was that, in return for the revenue that would be lost to them by giving up these fields of taxation to the Dominion, the provinces were to be paid a "rent" or a **tax rental payment**.

After the war, the federal government proposed that the integrated direct-taxation system be continued. In the so-called Green Book proposals of 1945 the provinces would have handed over to the federal government the exclusive power to levy what came to be known as the three **standard taxes**, personal income taxes, corporate income taxes, and succession duties, in return for a series of cost-matching federal **conditional grants**.[12] The provinces rejected these proposals because they felt, correctly, that conditional grants effectively transferred major policy initiatives in provincial areas of jurisdiction to the federal government.

However, all of the provinces except Quebec and Ontario did agree to continue the *tax rental* system of the war years. There ensued, for fifteen years, a series of five-year federal-provincial tax-rental or **tax-sharing agreements** in which all of the provinces except Quebec participated in whole or in part. A significant incentive for the provinces to participate was that the federal government assumed the responsibility and the full cost of collecting income taxes. Not only was this a significant cost saver for the provinces, but, since the role of tax collector is something the vast majority of politicians seek to avoid, the offer by the federal government to act as the "heavy" was one that most provincial governments couldn't refuse. While the terminology of the federal-provincial agreements has gradually changed to make it more clear to the taxpayers that the federal government is only "hired" by the provinces to collect provincial revenues, it is doubtful that most Canadians understand this.

While the provincial share of the tax collected by Revenue Canada gradually increased throughout this period, there were other important innovations. The system of unconditional equalization payments has become the institutional core of the more decentralized federalism that we have today. The equalization system is implemented through a transfer of funds from the federal treasury which raises the per-capita revenue of the poorer provinces to some national standard. While the formula for calculating the payment has changed over time, the basic principle is the same in 1995 as it was at its inception in 1957. Another device that evolved was the ability of the provinces to **opt out** of shared-cost programs without financial penalty. When a province opts out of a shared-cost program, the province receives an additional share of tax revenue in lieu of the matching grant from the federal government.

---

12.   D. V. Smiley, "Public Administration and Canadian Federalism," *Canadian Public Administration*, vol. 7, no. 3, September 1964, pp. 371–88.

## ► THE EMERGENCE OF CONTEMPORARY
FINANCIAL ARRANGEMENTS

By the time the federal and provincial governments were negotiating the financial relationship that was to prevail from 1962 onwards, it was clear that the basic bargaining chips had been defined. One cornerstone of the arrangement was to be a continuation of the practice of sharing the key areas of taxation that was begun in the immediate postwar period. The changes in the financial relationship between the two levels of government had introduced a second cornerstone, intergovernmental transfers. Before discussing the specific arrangements that have operated since 1962, we must say a few words about the core principles that underlie them.

### Federal Transfer Payments: The Basic Principles
There are three basic sets of options that apply differentially to the various federal transfers to the provinces and territories in Canada: they may be conditional or unconditional; they may be cost-matching or block-funded; and they may be in the form of cash payments or "tax room."

**Conditional or Unconditional**  In a **conditional grant** arrangement, federal legislation defines the terms, standards, or conditions that must be met by the provincial program if the program costs are to eligible for the federal grant. Thus, for example, the *Canada Health Act* states that if provinces are to receive federal transfers to cover hospital and medical services, their programs must provide universal coverage of their population, must be available to everyone under equal terms and conditions, and must be free of any barriers to access, such as extra-billing by doctors. As well, the provincial health insurance must be portable from province to province, must be publicly administered, and must cover a comprehensive range of services.

By contrast, transfers may also be **unconditional**. The money is transferred to the province with no strings attached and the receiving government may spend the money however it chooses without penalty. The most important of these transfers in Canada is the fiscal equalization program, the principle of which is now entrenched in the Constitution. The Statutory Subsidies, discussed in an earlier section, are also unconditional as are the Formula Financing grants to the Northwest Territories and the Yukon.

Conditional grants permit the federal government to set spending priorities even in fields that are constitutionally beyond its legislative competence. The basic source of this federal influence is the **spending power** by which the central government is free to spend its tax dollars in any way it sees fit. By offering to make transfers provided that provincial governments supply programs that meet certain national standards, Ottawa can usually convince the provinces to implement programs that, constitutionally, the federal government could not undertake itself.

On the positive side, this federal intervention in matters of provincial jurisdiction may allow poorer provinces to implement programs they might otherwise be unable to provide, and it encourages *national standards* of service that might not be attainable if the provinces were acting alone. There seems little doubt, however, that such grants can also be characterized as federal meddling in areas otherwise outside its jurisdiction. Generally, the poorer provinces are more favourably disposed to such grants than are the wealthy ones, but all provinces, naturally, would prefer simply to be given the money without any conditions attached.

Another criticism of conditional grants is that once the money has been transferred to a province, there is no sure procedure by which the federal authorities can ensure that all of the funds transferred have been spent for the purposes specified, or that all conditions are being met. Attached to all conditional grants are information and audit requirements, but as time goes on, there is a tendency for provinces to attempt to maximize receipt of funds while minimizing compliance with the terms of the agreement. The only recourse for the federal government would be to refuse to support the province in future joint projects, a tactic that might prove politically unwise, since the people of the provinces also vote in federal elections.

**Cost-Matching or Block-Funded**  Some transfers are structured so that the amount transferred by the federal government depends upon the level of provincial government expenditures on particular programs. Such grants may be described as **cost-matching**. In order to qualify for them, a provincial government must spend money to deliver the program and then submit an account to the federal government, describing how the money was spent. The federal government then reimburses the provincial government for some fixed portion of the expenditures, usually 50 per cent.

That kind of arrangement, used, for example under the Canada Assistance Plan (CAP), to cover social-assistance and social-services programs, can be contrasted with **block-funded** programs, where the federal transfer is not directly related to current provincial expenditures. The Established Programs Financing (EPF) arrangements, which are discussed in detail below and which cover post-secondary education and health-insurance programs, make grants based on the provincial population and the historical costs of those programs, escalated according to some indicator of overall economic growth.

A problem with cost-matched programs is that the provinces may be enticed into spending money that they don't have. A province may be forced, by political expediency, to commit its limited resources to programs partially funded by the federal government, because such programs appear to be such a "bargain." In the 1990s the largest of the cost-matching grants have been those provided under the Canada Assistance Plan. While those program areas have not, in recent years, been popular areas for provincial governments to spend money, much of the ballooning provincial debts of the 1980s can be traced to the proliferation of cost-matched social programs in the "high-living" 1960s and 1970s, as well as to the reluctance of governments to raise taxes to balance budgets.

For the federal government, there is a similar basic problem inherent in the cost-matching mechanism. Typically, under its terms, the federal treasury agrees to match, according to whatever proportion is specified in the agreement, the *actual* program costs incurred by provincial governments. This means that the size of federal disbursements is actually under provincial control, a situation fraught with terror for federal finance ministers. The recognition of these problems helps to explain why no major cost-matching programs have been implemented since 1968. That recognition also led to the replacement of a number of cost-matching programs, such as health insurance and the support for provincial second-language education, with block funding.

Block funding has three major advantages. First, it makes total expenditures more knowable in advance to all involved. Second — a feature particularly appealing to provincial treasurers — block grants ensure a level of funding for the province without imposing a requirement that they spend an equal amount of their own money. Finally, block grants are simple to administer, avoiding the complex auditing and reporting procedures inherent in cost-matching grants.

Block-funding programs are not, however, problem-free. They do encourage provincial governments to save money, but one way in which money may be saved is through reducing standards of service and accessibility — a problem we see being exacerbated today because of financial restraint measures. Moreover, while the programs often retain the rhetoric of conditionality, they largely eliminate the financial terms that could permit the federal government to ensure that the conditions are being met. The very nature of block grants means that accountability of the federal government to Parliament and the taxpayers for the expenditure of federal tax dollars is extremely difficult to achieve.

There is, thus, a conflict that has not been resolved by any of the current payment mechanisms. The conflict is between the need for accountability for expenditure within the federal government (both in the strict accounting sense, of assuring that the dollars are spent where they are intended to be spent, and in the broad policy sense, of assuring that the desired outcomes occur) and the problems created by federal interference in an area of provincial jurisdiction such as health. Starkly stated, neither accountability nor national program standards are possible without interference. Yet such interference also hampers the full exercise of provincial jurisdiction in areas that might be better managed according to local priorities and standards rather than national ones.

**Cash or Tax Transfers**   Finally, transfers can be made in the form of cash or tax. **Cash transfers** are exactly what the term implies. **Tax transfers** involve one order of government reducing the amount of income tax it collects, thus allowing the other order of government more "tax room" to collect more tax itself. For example, the EPF arrangements involve not only a cash transfer, but also a tax transfer, in which the federal government forgoes 13.5 per cent of personal income tax and 1 per cent of corporate income, allowing provincial governments the room to increase their own tax take.

A benefit of the tax-transfer device is that political accountability can be better assured. By the complete transfer of sufficient taxing power to the provinces to allow them to raise all the money necessary to finance all the programs in their jurisdiction, the governments levying the taxes would be the governments actually spending the money. However, federal transfers to the provinces comprise such a large portion of total government expenditure in Canada that, if all cash transfer payments were converted to tax transfers the federal government would lose much of the revenue-raising clout it now possesses.

It is generally agreed in Canada, even among the most fervent supporters of provincial autonomy, that a pre-eminent role of the federal government is to manage the national economy. Given that one of the two major tools available to it in accomplishing this task is the ability to tax and to spend the proceeds, such large-scale transfers of tax powers would significantly weaken the national government's economic planning function. Thus, not only are the concepts of national service standards and provincial autonomy in conflict, but so are the concepts of provincial fiscal accountability and national economic management. None of the mechanisms for intergovernmental transfers so far developed have been able to resolve this dilemma.

It is important to note, in conclusion, that any particular intergovernmental transfer will be characterized by a mix of the principles discussed above. For example, EPF, the largest, most complex, and most recent of the major transfer programs, has a conditional component for health, the conditions being stated in the *Canada Health Act*, and an unconditional component for post-secondary education. The transfer is partly cash and partly tax. It is, however, pure in one sense — it is entirely block-funded; the amount of the federal transfer is unrelated to current provincial expenditures in the fields the transfer nominally covers.

### Federal-Provincal "Fiscal Arrangements": 1962–Present

Until 1962, the federal-provincial tax agreements were based on the principle that the federal government should levy the taxes and collect the revenue, and then pass over a percentage of the take to the provinces participating in the agreement. The federal government believed, correctly, that the ability to tax (or not) is crucial to effecting its macro-economic policies. Hence, if the federal government could convince the provinces to give up at least some of their tax powers, it would enhance its own role in the management of the national economy. As we have stated before, the down side of this situation is that the federal government takes the "hit" as the tax collector, while the provinces garner the kudos as the governments that *deliver* programs and services.

**"Tax Room" for the Provinces**  Reflecting the federal view that the provinces should share some of the blame for increasingly higher taxes along with the revenues from those taxes, the *Federal-Provincial Fiscal Arrangements Act* (1961) set out a tax-sharing plan that was different in form from its predecessor. According to the Act, the federal government would undertake to provide **tax room** by completely withdrawing from a percentage of each of the fields it had previously shared with the participating provinces. These withdrawals by the federal government worked in much the same way as the tax abatements had worked for non-participating provinces in the previous tax agreement. Thus, the federal government, in 1962, actually withdrew from the corporation income-tax field to the extent of 9 per cent of corporate profits, from the personal income-tax field by 16 per cent of the federal tax, and in 1963, by 75 per cent of the succession duties.

While the intention of the federal government in undertaking to withdraw from the shared-tax fields was to distribute the political responsibility for taxes among the governments that were spending the revenues, it did not wish to penalize the provinces financially, and it did wish to maintain a uniform tax system throughout Canada. Hence, under the *Fiscal Arrangements Act*, the federal government offered to continue to collect provincial income tax and corporation income tax, free of charge, provided the provinces utilized the same tax base as that defined by the federal *Income Tax Act*. As a result, the provinces all passed their own tax laws consistent with the federal Act, and all except Quebec, which had long had its own collection machinery, signed collection agreements with the federal government. Ontario continued, as it does to this day, to collect its own corporate income tax.

Perhaps the most significant result of this new approach to the sharing of the standard tax fields was that the provinces were now free to increase the tax burden on their citizens if they were willing to take the political heat for doing so. Thus, for example, by 1966 the federal government was withdrawing from the personal income-tax field by 24 per cent. However, a province could choose to levy a tax on its citizens that was greater than the 24 per cent of "tax room" made available by the federal withdrawal. As long as the increased provincial tax was based on the federal tax *base*, Revenue Canada would collect the extra tax assessment for the provinces. Since this system was implemented, we can see a significant variation in the amount of income tax individuals and corporations pay from province to province (see Table 11.1).

**Established Programs (Interim Arrangements)**  In 1965, the federal government passed the *Established Programs (Interim Arrangements) Act*, by which provinces were permitted, without any financial penalty, to opt out of a significant number of federal-provincial shared-cost programs. For each program the province chose to opt out of, the federal government allowed either more tax room in the field of personal income tax or a cash transfer payment in lieu of the amount of the federal share of the cost of the program, had the province participated. Provinces wishing to take advantage of the opting-out provisions were still required to continue the program along the same lines as the federal program for a certain specified interim period. During this interim period, the participating provinces had to agree to a sort of audit by the federal authorities, to ensure provincial compliance with the terms of the Act.

Only the province of Quebec exercised its opting-out privilege under this Act, gaining an additional 20 per cent of room in the field of personal income tax. When this was added to the 24 per cent of income-tax room that applied to all of the provinces by 1966, Quebec ended up with a total abatement of 44 per cent of personal income tax. Quebec's choice was probably determined by the high level of nationalist feeling within the province, and by the desire of the provincial authorities to focus the loyalties of Québécois on Quebec rather than on Canada. The rest of the provinces decided to stay in the joint programs for reasons of economic efficiency — it was simply less expensive for them to

**TABLE 11.1**
Provincial Income-Tax Rates, 1995

| | Tax Rate (% of basic federal tax) | Surtax, Flat Tax, and/or Tax on Net Income |
|---|---|---|
| Newfoundland | 69.0 | yes |
| Prince Edward Island | 59.5 | yes |
| Nova Scotia | 59.5 | no |
| New Brunswick | 64.0 | yes |
| Quebec | rate based upon taxable income calculated on provincial return | yes |
| Ontario | 58.0 | yes |
| Manitoba | 52.0 | yes |
| Saskatchewan | 50.0 | yes |
| Alberta | 45.5 | yes |
| British Columbia | 52.5 | yes |
| Yukon Territory | 50.0 | yes |
| Northwest Territories | 45.0 | no |
| Non-resident surtax | 52.0 | no |

Source:  Canada, Department of Finance.

continue to use the federal machinery and procedures already in place than to create completely new provincial ones.

**The Canada Assistance Plan**  In 1966, the Canada Assistance Plan (CAP) was established as a means of consolidating and improving the federal transfer payments to the provinces in respect of a wide range of provincial welfare and social-assistance programs. The CAP provided for a fifty-fifty sharing of the costs of provincially established and administered programs aimed at alleviating the plight of the needy. There was to be no upper limit to the amount of the transfer to each province and as a result the distribution of the CAP transfers has varied a great deal from province to province. The initiative for a CAP program lies with the provincial government and the trigger mechanism was (and is) a negotiated bilateral federal-provincial agreement that outlines the details of the proposed provincial program.

Conditions were established in the enabling legislation: first, the province was required to set up the program and initially bear the full cost; then, if the program was consistent with the terms of the federal-provincial agreement, the government of Canada would match the eligible provincial expenditures. As well, the provinces were required to provide unrestricted access to the jointly funded program and were not permitted to, for instance, impose a period of residency in the province as a condition of eligibility.

**Figure 11.1**
Canada Assistance Plan transfers, 1983/84–1994/95.

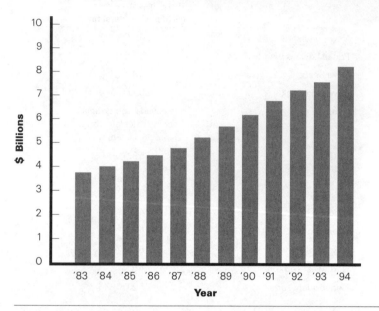

Source: Canada, Department of Finance, *Federal Transfers to the Provinces*, Apr., 1994 (p. 25).

**Figure 11.2**
Canada Assistance Plan transfers to the provinces, 1994/95.

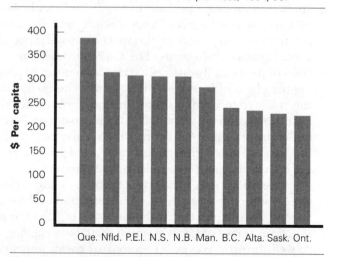

Source: Canada, Department of Finance, *Federal Transfers to the Provinces*, Apr., 1994 (p. 25).

**Figure 11.3**

Provincial shares of Canada Assistance Plan transfers, 1994/95.
Total CAP transfers = $8.2 billion.

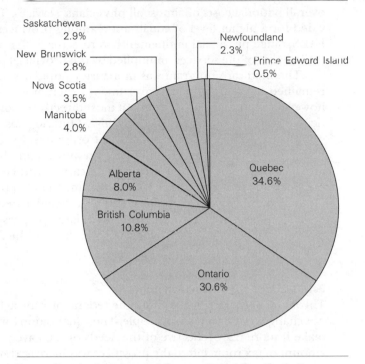

Source: Canada, Department of Finance, *Federal Transfers to the Provinces*, Apr., 1994 (p. 26).

**Health Transfers**  The year 1957 had seen the inception of the *first* of the huge postwar federal cost-matching conditional-grant programs, in the form of the *Hospital Insurance and Diagnostic Services Act* (HIDS).[13] Paradoxically, given the drawbacks of conditional-grant programs from the provincial point of view, HIDS was negotiated primarily at the behest of several provincial governments, including Ontario. Several provinces, led by Saskatchewan, already had hospital insurance, and most that did not were eager to implement it but could afford to do so only with federal assistance. That assistance was originally negotiated at a series of federal-provincial meetings in 1956 and 1957, and the new federal Conservative government of John Diefenbaker went ahead, in 1957, and implemented the program negotiated by its predecessor.

---

13.  Unlike CAP, which was a pure cost-matching program with the federal government exactly matching individual provincial expenditures, HIDS had a moderately equalizing effect. By its formula, the federal government reimbursed 25 per cent of actual provincial expenditures and added 25 per cent of the national per-capita average expenditures multiplied by provincial populations. For details on HIDS and medicare, see Malcolm Taylor, *Health Insurance and Canadian Public Policy* (Montreal: McGill-Queen's University Press, 1978). Taylor's work combines a thorough policy analysis with an excellent set of examples of the real workings of fiscal federalism.

The next fiscal decade saw the establishment of the last of the major federal shared-cost social programs — **medicare.** The *Medical Care Act,* passed by the federal government in 1967, provided for 50 per cent federal funding of the overall national costs of almost all physicians' services. The formula also provided for a higher level of equalization among provinces than either CAP or HIDS, since provincial entitlements were actually the national-average, per-capita costs of the services, multiplied by the provincial population.

The medicare program was immensely popular with the public and has remained the most popular government program in Canada. Paradoxically, however, the provincial government most directly responsible for federal participation in hospital insurance in 1957, Ontario, was by 1967 vehemently opposed to any new federal shared-cost programs. Its opposition, plus Quebec's resentment of this federal intrusion into yet another area of provincial jurisdiction, combined to ensure that medicare was the last of the major federal-provincial shared-cost programs. This continued unhappiness, combined with federal concern over the rapid increases in health-care (and post-secondary-education) costs in the early 1970s, was in large part responsible for the next major initiative in federal-provincial fiscal relations, the Established Programs Financing arrangements.

### Established Programs Financing

Through the sixties and seventies the federal-provincial fiscal agreements did not change significantly in principle. The equalization formula was adjusted to make it more truly reflective of the needs of the have-not provinces, and the amount of tax room left to the provinces was increased steadily, but there was an underlying consistency from one five-year agreement to the next. As well, the entire system was adjusted to incorporate the very significant reforms in the 1972 *Income Tax Act.* There was, however, a major change in the 1977 arrangements, the inclusion of a measure called **Established Programs Financing (EPF).** This was a set of arrangements enshrined in legislation with a formidable title, the *Federal Provincial Fiscal Arrangements and Established Programs Financing Act* (1977).

The EPF arrangements were intended to replace the older cost-sharing arrangements for provincial health-care programs and for post-secondary education with a combination of more tax room for the provinces and a block-funding formula. As well, there was to be a continuing tax abatement and cash payment, nominally for the financing of post-secondary education. The formula was complex, but since the amounts involved have been by far the largest of the intergovernmental transfers, they merit some more detailed attention.

**Block Funding** The first part of the EPF arrangement was a partly conditional block transfer payment, amounting to about one-half of the former federal contribution for health insurance, based on 1975/76 per-capita payments and escalated annually according to population and GNP increases. This block grant was conditional because it was payable only if the province continued to meet the federally established program standards. Since it amounted to about one-quarter of the full program costs, and since the programs were very pop-

**Figure 11.4**
Established Programs Financing, payments to provinces, 1994/95.

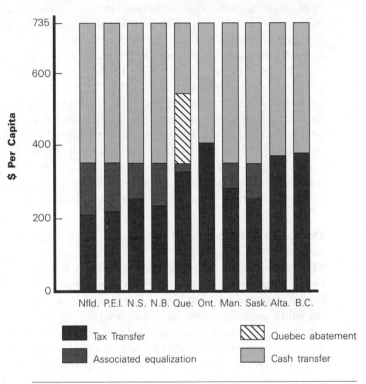

Source: Canada, Department of Finance, *Federal Transfers to the Provinces*, Apr., 1994 (p. 21).

ular, the federal government felt reasonably sure that provinces would continue to meet those conditions, which were fairly broadly stated.

**More Provincial "Tax Room"**  Second, the federal government agreed to provide 13.5 percentage points more room in the personal income-tax field and one additional percentage point of corporate income tax, and to equalize the yield from these sources according to the same formula used to calculate the unconditional equalization payments. As well, a $20 per-capita annual payment was to be provided, escalated annually in the same way as the basic block payment. This payment was intended to provide funding "in respect of extended health care services," such as home nursing or ambulatory services. These presumably lower-cost alternatives to the use of acute-care hospital beds were not covered by earlier cost-sharing legislation.

**Transitional Adjustment Payment**  Finally, there was a **transitional adjustment payment**, intended to ensure that provinces did not suffer financially as a result of the changes. The transitional adjustment payment was intended to guarantee that provinces would receive adequate funding even if something should happen to make the rate of increase in the revenue yield of the new tax room decline to less than the yield of the block transfer. In that eventuality, the federal government would undertake to make up the difference, although federal officials never expected such payments to become very significant.

However, because of a 1975 federal decision to index the value of personal income-tax exemptions to the rate of inflation, the revenues from the extra tax room did not rise as quickly as inflation. The result was a boon to provincial treasuries and a major headache for the federal government. The federal government had to make good on its transitional adjustment guarantee, to the tune of $1 billion extra per year in the early 1980s. This was an unexpected turn of events for the federal government, and its impact was particularly onerous during the 1982–1983 recession, when even larger transitional payments had to be made from a shrinking federal tax base.

**The *Canada Health Act*** Obviously the provinces were very happy with this serendipitous outcome and they certainly put the extra money to good use. The federal government, on the other hand, was not happy at all, but put on a brave, if crabby, face and honoured the agreement it had signed. However, a further twist was added by the fact that the provinces received the EPF cash transfers pursuant only to rather vaguely defined program conditions for health services, such as portability from province to province and equal access. These imprecise conditions provided provinces with an opportunity to reduce health-program costs in order to free up the money guaranteed by federal payments for other things, such as keeping a lid on provincial taxes and deficits.

In the extreme, however, some provinces in the late 1970s and early 1980s seemed determined to reduce health-care expenditures as far as they possibly could without either forcing the federal government to suspend payment or inciting the wrath of their voters to the point where they might be turfed out of office. Some provinces' cost saving began to be associated with the passing on to the public of some of the hitherto insured costs of health care, as doctors were permitted to opt out of the system or "extra-bill" their patients, and hospitals introduced various forms of user fees. The federal government was paying more, but Canada's universal health-care system appeared to be deteriorating.

The federal response to this was a change to the *Hospital Insurance and Medical Care Acts*, which set out the terms under which the EPF transfers for health programs are made. In 1984, in response to a considerable degree of public concern about extra-billing by doctors and user fees in hospitals, the *Canada Health Act* was passed by Parliament. It stipulated that the federal transfers to a province were to be reduced, dollar for dollar, for any province allowing extra-billing or user fees. The Act was the subject of very considerable federal-provincial controversy at the time it was passed, but by 1987 all provinces had ceased allowing either user fees or extra-billing. While enforcement is a growing problem in financially stringent 1995, it is still possible for the federal government to unilaterally impose conditions on provincial programs partially funded by intergovernmental transfers.

**The Federal Deficit and EPF**  In 1985, as part of a package of deficit-reduction measures, the federal minister of finance announced that intergovernmental transfers would be reduced by up to $2 billion per year by 1990/91. In theory, the reductions could come from any intergovernmental transfer program. In a time of recession, the cuts could not be brought to bear on equalization, which supports poorer provinces, or on the Canada Assistance Plan, which supports poorer people. The reductions were therefore taken from EPF. The average growth of EPF transfers from 1983 to 1995 was 4.2 per cent per year and in 1994/95 it was only 1.3 per cent. By contrast, in 1994/95 equalization payments and CAP transfers grew by 6.3 per cent and 5.4 per cent, respectively. We will say more about the effect of federal deficit-reduction initiatives in the concluding section of the chapter.

## ▶ FISCAL FEDERALISM IN THE 1990s

We have seen how Canada's system of intergovernmental financial relations has evolved, and we have highlighted the major innovations that have emerged over the years. Now it is appropriate to provide a snapshot of the current situation of fiscal federalism and its prospects as we approach the next century. We shall begin by outlining the functions that federal-provincial fiscal arrangements perform for our country as a whole and then move to a description of the intergovernmental transfers that are the foundation of fiscal federalism today.

### The Functions of Federal-Provincial Fiscal Arrangements

The functions performed by our current federal-provincial fiscal arrangements can be placed in two broad categories. The first includes functions related to the **provision of interprovincial equity**; the second includes functions having to do with the overall **management of the national economy**. Each must be considered in greater detail.

**Interprovincial Equity**  It was anticipated even at the time of Confederation that the provinces in the federation were not going to be equal partners in terms of population, social complexity, and economic wealth. The Fathers of Confederation were accurate in this case: we do indeed have a country with very severe regional disparities and with very different sorts of internal problems from province to province. While the provinces will never all be equal, the use of intergovernmental transfer payments can ensure that they each have a minimum per-capita revenue base from which to operate.

One effect of such transfers to the poorer provinces is to provide citizens of Canada, wherever they may live, with a comparable level and quality of government services. This is a good thing in terms of our basic values of fairness and equal opportunity. As well, however, transfer payments help to maintain a quality of life at or around the national average for most regions. This helps to offset the tendency, which might otherwise prevail to a greater extent than it does, for people to migrate, within Canada, from the poor provinces to the wealthy ones. To the extent that such migration does occur, it is more a result of a quest for better economic opportunities than of a search for a better social safety net (see Fig. 11.5).

Through the device of conditional transfers, it is also possible for the national government to set **national standards** of services and to ensure the **portability** of benefits from one province to another within Canada. Similarly, transfer payments can serve to offset what have been referred to as **interprovincial spillovers**, which occur because of the mobility of Canadians. For example, if Prince Edward Island pays for the training or education of an individual and that individual then takes a job in Toronto, the educational investment benefits Canada as a whole but is, in effect, lost to the province. Transfer payments help to offset this by sharing the national wealth with the less fortunate provinces in return for their contributions to the national good.

**National Economic Management** One of the key jobs of national governments throughout the world is the management and planning of the economy. Monetary and fiscal policy are important tools for a national government in stabilizing its economy. The arrangements for federal-provincial sharing of the major tax fields leave the Canadian government the ability to stabilize the economy by controlling the tax base. The economy of Canada can be stimulated or slowed down through changes to the income-tax system, which is controlled by the federal government. In Canada this works because all of the provinces have agreed to base their own income-tax systems on the federal one. Even

**Figure 11.5**
Major federal transfers as a share of provincial revenues, 1994/95.

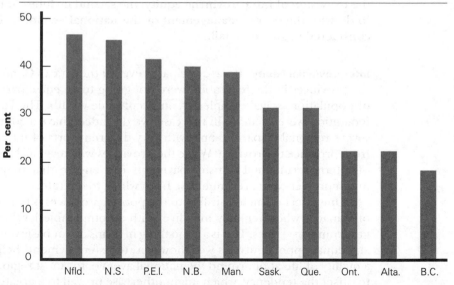

Source: Canada, Department of Finance, *Federal Transfers to the Provinces*, Apr., 1994 (p. 25).

Quebec, which has its own income-tax act, has, for the most part, voluntarily kept its tax base in harmony with the federal one.

Finally, we have spoken of the interprovincial equity that is fostered by transfer payments, but such transfers also function to *stabilize* provincial economies. Through the use of transfer payments the federal government can to some extent level the playing field for the less fortunate provinces and can moderate year-to-year fluctuations in provincial revenues. The economic fluctuations that occur cyclically may affect different provinces at different times because they are at different stages of the cycle. The integrated fiscal arrangements that we have in Canada allow us to pool the risk across the country and to even out the cyclical impacts of economic growth and stagnation in the regional economies.

### Federal-Provincial Transfers in 1995

In total, federal transfers to the provinces and territories amounted to $42 billion in 1994/95 (see Fig. 11.6). This makes up approximately 24 per cent of federal-government program spending and the federal transfers themselves account for as much as 46 per cent (Newfoundland) and as little as 19 per cent (British Columbia) of provincial revenues (see Fig. 11.5). The tax room left to the provinces has not changed since 1977 when EPF was put in place. Today, the basic tax room for the provinces is 24 per cent of personal income tax and 9 per cent of corporate income, although, as we have seen, most of the provinces have opted to occupy a bit more room than what is vacated by the federal government.

**EPF and CAP** We have already discussed the transfers through Established Programs Finanacing and the Canada Assistance Plan. The former is intended to assist the provinces in carrying out their responsibilities for post-secondary education (PSE) and health insurance, and the latter provides matching federal grants to help the provinces pay for social assistance. These have not changed significantly since the 1970s except for the conditions placed on the EPF health transfers by the *Canada Health Act* in 1984. The PSE component of EPF is completely unconditional.

For the moment, EPF is composed of a cash block transfer to the provinces which is escalated according to the overall growth of the Canadian economy. EPF also provides for an additional tax transfer amounting to 13.5 per cent more room in the personal income-tax field and an additional 1 per cent of corporate income. The tax-transfer component of EPF is equalized to ensure that the poorer provinces are able to provide a level of health care comparable to that of the wealthier ones. Quebec, which prefers to completely opt out of most federal-provincial programs, receives an additional 8.5 per cent of income tax in lieu of the cash component of EPF, 5 per cent in lieu of CAP cash transfers, and 3 per cent in lieu of cash transfers in other shared-cost programs (see Table 11.2). In total, the tax room left to Quebec in the area of personal income tax is now 48 per cent.

However, since 1986, the federal governmment has attempted to reduce its burden under both CAP and EPF. The escalator provision tied to the block-

**Figure 11.6**

Federal transfers to provinces 1994/95. Note: Equalization associated with the tax transfers under EPF is included in both EPF and Equalization. The transfers total has been adjusted to avoid double-counting the Associated Equalization.

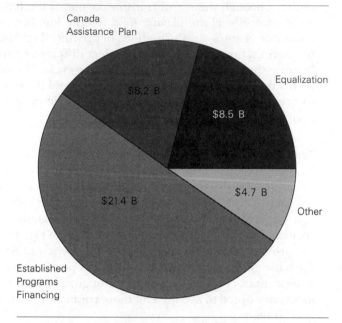

Source: Canada, Department of Finance, *Federal Transfers to the Provinces*, Apr., 1994 (p. 7).

funded component of EPF has been kept below the rate of gross national product (GNP) growth and as part of the 1991 Expenditure Control Plan, the per-capita entitlement of each province was frozen at 1989/90 levels. The Expenditure Control Plan also set a 5 per cent ceiling on the growth of CAP transfers to the three wealthiest provinces and in 1994 the CAP entitlements for all provinces was frozen at 1994/95 levels until the Social Security Review is completed. Finally, the 1995 federal budget essentially signalled an end to the current era of federal-provincial transfers. By the 1997/98 fiscal year, more than $7 billion will be cut from EPF and CAP, and, effective in 1996, those two programs will be rolled into a single **Canada Social Transfer (CST)** (see Table 11.3). In return for the cuts, there will be fewer federal standards imposed, thus giving the provinces greater flexibility in how they spend the money.

**Equalization** The major unconditional federal transfer to the provinces is the **equalization** payment. Equalization is based on the notion that despite accidents of history and geography, which have created regional disparities in Canada, the wealthier provinces will share their financial good fortune with the less fortunate regions of the country. The principle of equalization is so

**TABLE 11.2**
Other Transfers, 1994/95

|  | $ Millions |
|---|---|
| Territorial Financing | 1,193 |
| Infrastructure | 687 |
| Gross Revenue Insurance Plan | 487 |
| Grants in Lieu of Property Taxes | 435 |
| Other | 351 |
| Miscellaneous Health and Welfare | 310 |
| Transportation | 260 |
| Official Languages Education | 255 |
| Public Utilities Income-Tax Transfer | 237 |
| Young Offenders | 158 |
| Preferred-Share Dividend Taxes | 150 |
| Justice | 93 |
| Statutory Subsidies | 40 |
| Total | 4,656 |

Source: Canada, Department of Finance, *Federal Transfers to the Provinces*, Apr., 1994 (p. 27).

important to the basic values underlying the federation that it was incorporated into the Constitution in 1982. Section 36(2) of the *Constitution Act*, 1982, states:

> Parliament and the Government of Canada are committed to the principle of making Equalization payments to ensure that provincial governments have sufficient revenues to provide reasonably comparable levels of public services at reasonably comparable levels of taxation.

In 1994/95 all provinces received equalization except for Alberta, British Columbia, and Ontario; the total equalization payments made amounted to nearly $8.5 billion (see Figs. 11.7–8).

Equalization transfers are calculated on the basis of the **fiscal capacity** of the provinces, which is established by estimating the revenue that each province would be able to raise if all provinces were levying the same taxes at roughly the same rates — the **Representative Tax System**. The reason that the formula is based upon the *capacity* to raise revenues and not the actual amount raised is that each province is expected to make the same effort to raise revenues. If a province should decide, for instance, not to have a sales tax in order to increase its political popularity, it is not permitted to recover the forgone revenue out of the federal coffers because it did not make the same **tax effort** as its sister provinces.

When equalization was first introduced in 1957 it was based on the estimated yields of the provinces in the three standard taxes — personal income,

**TABLE 11.3**
Projected Federal Transfers to Provinces, 1994/95, 1996/97

| | 1994/95 ($ Millions) | 1996/97 ($ Millions) | Change (%) |
|---|---|---|---|
| Newfoundland | 1,484 | 1,512 | +1.9 |
| Prince Edward Island | 316 | 323 | +2.2 |
| Nova Scotia | 1,932 | 1,949 | +0.9 |
| New Brunswick | 1,610 | 1,632 | +1.4 |
| Quebec | 11,446 | 11,096 | −3.1 |
| Ontario | 10,530 | 9,653 | −8.3 |
| Manitoba | 2,039 | 2,032 | −0.3 |
| Saskatchewan | 1,411 | 1,450 | +2.8 |
| Alberta | 2,525 | 2,313 | −8.4 |
| British Columbia | 3,573 | 3,291 | −7.9 |
| Northwest Territories | 74 | 68 | −8.1 |
| Yukon | 34 | 32 | −5.9 |
| Total | 36,974 | 35,351 | −4.4 |

Figures for 1994/95 include Equalization, Established Programs Financing, and Canada Assistance Plan payments. Figures for 1996/97 include Canada Social Transfer and Equalization payments.
Source: *Maclean's*, Mar. 31, 1995 (p. 25).

corporate income, and succession duties. Today, the Representative Tax System is estimated on all provincial and municipal revenue sources, which are broken down into thirty-three categories. The total fiscal capacity for the province is then established by assuming a national average rate of taxation for each of the thirty-three tax categories. On the basis of this the total potential revenue for each province is estimated, and this figure is divided by the population of the province to establish the per-capita fiscal capacity of each province.

The equalization payment to each province was originally calculated so that the transfer would bring the per-capita revenues of each province up to the average per-capita revenue of the two richest provinces. This was ultimately felt to be too expensive because it meant that all provinces except the richest one would get an equalization payment. The payment was then calculated on the average per-capita revenue of *all* provinces and this formula seemed to work until Alberta's revenues from oil and gas royalties soared in the 1970s. During this period, Alberta's per-capita revenue potential was so high that it skewed the national average upwards to a point where by the 1980s even Ontario was eligible for equalization.

Ontario never did receive any equalization payments because the province agreed, in the short term, to allow its own fiscal capacity to be the standard to which other provinces would be equalized, and in the subsequent fiscal arrangements the formula was changed once more. Today the equalization pay-

**Figure 11.7**
Equalization transfers, 1994/95.

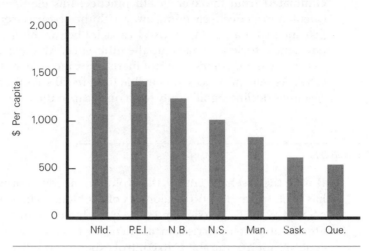

Source: Canada, Department of Finance, *Federal Transfers to the Provinces*, Apr., 1994 (p. 14).

**Figure 11.8**
Provincial shares of Equalization, 1994/95. Total Equalization transfers = $8.5 billion.

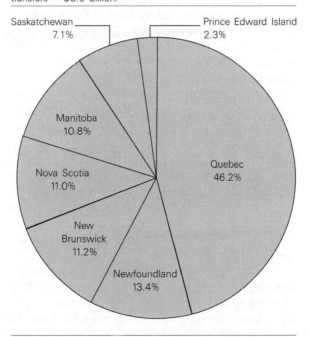

Source: Canada, Department of Finance, *Federal Transfers to the Provinces*, Apr., 1994 (p. 14).

ment to which a province is entitled is based on the average per-capita fiscal capacity of five provinces — the wealthiest and the four poorest provinces are eliminated from the average. In practice, this eliminates Alberta from the calculations, effectively doing away with the resource-revenue problem. Each province with a per-capita fiscal capacity below the average is given a cash payment sufficient to make up the difference. An **escalator ceiling** is applied to the payments, so they cannot increase by more than the rate of increase of GNP. As well, provinces are eligible for a **fiscal stabilization payment** if their revenues decline significantly from one year to the next.

## ▶ CONCLUSION

During the past half-century, the evolution of federal-provincial fiscal relations has been spurred by two major sets of problems. The first was the fiscal crisis created by the Depression and subsequently altered by the Second World War. One solution to that crisis, in an era of Keynesian economics, was a significant centralization of the ability to control expenditures through the federal spending power. The spending power of the federal government stems from the fact that while Canada cannot pass *laws* in areas of provincial jurisdiction it can spend money on anything it wants. Thus, by offering to pay all or a percentage of their costs, the government of Canada was able to induce the provinces to increase their levels of expenditure on social programs. That the programs also often met federal priorities and standards permitted an extension of federal influence into areas outside its formal jurisdiction.

The second solution to this first "fiscal crisis of the federation," also in the Keynesian tradition, was the further centralization of the ability to raise money. This was initially driven by the federal government's wartime emergency powers, and subsequently by the arrangement whereby Revenue Canada collected the taxes for both levels of government and then reimbursed the provinces for their share of the take.

Paradoxically, the centralizing solution to the first crisis contained within it some of the seeds of the second problem, which has been referred to as the "fiscal crisis of the 1980s" (and 1990s) — the extremely large and growing national debt and the seemingly intractable federal deficit. The excessive centralization of the period up to 1968, characterized by enormous growth in social-program costs in the provinces, crested like a wave and then collapsed. The current fiscal crisis is, together with other economic and social factors, based on the fact that the provinces are locked into many expensive programs and the federal government is less and less able to bear the costs. The provinces are as strapped for cash as the national government and the provincial debts are growing at alarming rates.

The very large size of federal transfer payments makes them a very attractive target in a time when federal ministers of finance are struggling to reduce the deficit. As we have seen, EPF has been targeted for significant reductions in its rate of growth since 1986, there has been a ceiling on the annual growth rate of equalization payments, and CAP has been frozen at 1995 levels. Moreover, the 1995 budget introduced even further cuts and announced the replacement of both CAP and EPF with a single Canada Social Transfer by 1996. The other side of the equation can be seen in Figure 11.5, which indicates that intergovernmental transfers account for between 19 and 46 per cent of provincial revenues. Thus, while the federal government has a very great desire to reduce the transfers, the provincial governments have at least as great a desire to keep them up — hardly a situation calculated to improve federal-provincial harmony.

Fiscal federalism in the mid 1990s is badly in need of reform and restructuring, and the solutions are unlikely to be found at a single level of government. Current initiatives to engage the provincial governments in a dialogue to try to find a cure for the ills of the federation include federal proposals for an even more integrated tax system that would see the provinces share indirect as well as direct tax revenues and proposals for a major overhaul of social programs. Such large and important adjustments are not going to be placid, but because both levels of government agree they are necessary, we can expect that they will eventually be worked out.

► FURTHER READING: PART THREE FEDERALISM

### General

Bakvis, Herman, and W. M. Chandler. *Federalism and the Role of the State*. Toronto: University of Toronto Press, 1987.

Banting, K. *The Welfare State and Canadian Federalism*. Kingston: McGill-Queen's University Press, 1987.

Beckton, C.F. and A. W. MacKay. *Recurring Issues in Canadian Federalism*. Toronto: University of Toronto Press, 1985.

Black, E. R. *Divided Loyalties: Canadian Concepts of Federalism*. Montreal: McGill-Queen's University Press, 1975.

Cairns, Alan. "The Judicial Committee and Its Critics." *Canadian Journal of Political Science*, September 1971, p. 301.

Leslie, Peter. *Federal State, National Economy*. Kingston: McGill-Queen's University Press, 1987.

Oling, R. D., and M. Westmacott. *Perspectives on Canadian Federalism*. Scarborough: Prentice-Hall, 1988.

Riker, W. H. *Federalism: Origin, Operation, Significance*. Boston: Little Brown, 1964.

Simeon, Richard. *Federal Provincial Diplomacy*. Toronto: University of Toronto Press, 1972.

Simeon, Richard. *The Political Economy of Canadian Federalism 1940–1984*. Toronto: University of Toronto Press, 1985.

Smiley, D. V. *The Federal Condition in Canada*. Toronto: McGraw-Hill Ryerson, 1987.

Stevenson, Garth. *Unfulfilled Union: Canadian Federalism and Canadian Unity*. Toronto: Gage, 1987.

Stevenson, Garth. *Federalism in Canada*. Toronto: McClelland and Stewart, 1989.

Stevenson, Garth. "Federalism and Intergovernmental Relations," *in* M. S. Whittington and G. Williams, eds., *Canadian Politics in the 1990s*. Scarborough: Nelson, 1994, pp. 402–23.

Wheare, K. C. *Federal Government*. London: Oxford University Press, 1963.

Whittington, M. *The North*. Toronto: University of Toronto Press, 1985.

### Quebec

Beheils, M. *Quebec Since 1945: Selected Readings*. Toronto: Copp Clark Pitman, 1987.

Coleman, W. *The Independence Movement in Quebec: 1945–1980*. Toronto: University of Toronto Press, 1984.

Dodge, William. *Boundaries of Identity: A Quebec Reader*. Toronto: Lester, 1992.

Gagnon, Alain, and Mary Beth Montcalm. *Quebec: Beyond the Quiet Revolution*. Scarborough: Nelson, 1990.

Gagnon, Alain. *Quebec: State and Society*. Scarborough: Nelson, 1993.

Lachapelle, Guy, G. Bernier, Daniel Salee, and Luc Bernier. *The Quebec Democracy: Structures, Processes and Policies*. Toronto: McGraw-Hill Ryerson, 1993.

McRoberts, Ken. *Quebec: Social Change and Political Crisis*. Toronto: McClelland and Stewart, 1993.

McRoberts, Ken. "Quebec: Province, Nation or 'Distinct Society'," *in* M. S. Whittington and G. Williams, *Canadian Politics in the 1990s*. Scarborough: Nelson, 1994, pp. 80–103.

Whitaker, Reg. "The Quebec Cauldron," *in* M. S. Whittington and G. Williams, *Canadian Politics in the 1980s*. Toronto: Methuen, 1984.


## Intergovernmental Relations

Canadian Tax Foundation. *The National Finances, 1994*. Toronto: CTF, 1994.

Courchene, Tom, D. Conklin, and Gail Cook. *Ottawa and the Provinces: The Distribution of Money and Power*. Toronto: Ontario Economic Council, 1985.

"Fiscal Federalism: Debating Canada's Future," *Policy Options*, December, 1993 (articles by several authors).

Gillespie, Irwin. *Tax, Borrow and Spend: Financing Federal Spending in Canada*. Ottawa: Carleton University Press, 1991.

Krasnick, Mark. *Fiscal Federalism*. Toronto: University of Toronto Press, 1985.

Simeon, R. *Intergovernmental Relations*. Toronto: University of Toronto Press, 1985.

## PART FOUR

# Politics

*Chapter* **12**

# The Electoral System

Elections are the formal institutional mechanisms for giving effect to the constitutional principle of popular sovereignty. Democracy, as we know it, is operationalized through periodic votes that allow Canadians to select their representatives and ultimately to choose their governments at the federal, provincial, territorial, and local levels. While this may seem to be obvious and unremarkable, we must keep in mind that many political systems do not provide such procedures for review and peaceful change of the political leadership.

Moreover, we must remember, even in some systems that *do* provide an electoral system, we find that it is adhered to in form but not in spirit. The citizens are called upon to vote from time to time, but informal restrictions on candidacy and rather unsubtle discouragement of those who would dare to oppose the existing regime ensure that there is never a real choice on the ballot. In Canada, however, elections are real contests, we do have the freedom to make our choice as individuals, without interference, and we are given real choices when we go to the polls.

## ▶ REPRESENTATIVE VS. DIRECT DEMOCRACY

Canadian democracy is **representative democracy**. By this we mean that individual citizens to not directly participate in the legislative process; rather, they elect men and women to act on their behalf within the positions of political authority in the government. **Direct democracy** is possible only in very small communities where all of the citizens can be brought together in an *assembly* or *town meeting*. The classic examples of direct democracy in action are Athens at the time of Pericles and the New England town meeting. In the former case, direct democracy was possible because only a small percentage of the male population of Athens was deemed to be "citizens." The majority of the population of the city-state, including women, slaves, artisans, and traders, were disfranchised because they were not considered to be citizens. The town meeting persists to this day in a few small communities in the United States, but in practice it only complements elected municipal councils.

Canadians do not have to go to ancient Athens or to New England's small towns and villages to find examples of direct democracy. The aboriginal people of Canada have always practiced forms of direct democracy. Despite the imposition of elected band-council systems of government through the *Indian Act*, many First Nations today still use mechanisms such as general assemblies, clan assemblies, councils of elders, and councils of clan mothers. These bodies arrive at a community *consensus* and then "instruct" the elected band council to pass a resolution or by-law to put the consensus decision into effect. As aboriginal self-government is restored in Canada, we will inevitably see the First Nations developing their own constitutions that formally recognize these traditional ways of coming to community decisions through the direct participation of all citizens.

### "Quasi-Direct" Democracy

Unfortunately, Canada as a whole, the provinces and territories individually, and even most municipalities are simply too big for a general assembly or a town meeting. However, there are a few **quasi-direct** mechanisms of public involvement that have been tried from time to time in Canada and elsewhere. We refer to these devices as quasi-direct because while the citizenry are permitted to overrule their elected representatives, they do so by "remote control." Hence, the *referendum*, the *initiative*, and the *recall* are all devices that allow citizens to instruct their representatives but they must do so by ballot and not directly.

**Initiative and Recall**  The **initiative** is a device that is used in a number of the American states and in a few democracies around the world. It allows the citizenry to trigger the legislative process directly through a petition containing the names of a certain percentage of the population. While we often see *petitions* being read into Hansard in the House of Commons or being presented to ministers by groups of citizens who want to see action on some issue or other, they are not in any way binding on the legislators. They may well persuade our political leaders to pay attention to an issue that they have hitherto been unaware of or ignored, but the impact of the petition comes from the number of signatures it contains and the *prima facie* merit of the proposal, not from force of law. A true initiative system obligates the legislators to deal with it by introducing legislation or by submitting the question to referendum.

The **recall** is similar to the initiative except that the effect of the petition is a vote of non-confidence in a sitting member. If a number of constituents, usually a fairly large percentage of the eligible voters in the previous election, sign a petition "recalling" their representative, a by-election must be held in the constituency. While the member recalled may run in the by-election, this device is seen as a way of keeping representatives more directly accountable to their electors between general elections.

**Referenda**   The initiative and the recall have never been used in Canada, but both the United Farmers and the Social Credit governments in Alberta flirted with such devices in the 1920s and 1930s until the courts decided such populist devices violated the principle of the supremacy of Parliament. The **binding referendum** met the same fate before the courts, but non-binding referenda, or **plebiscites**, have been used periodically in Canada. At the provincial level there have been numerous referenda, particularly on issues involving the consumption of booze. Newfoundland held two referenda in 1948 on whether to become part of Canada, and Quebec held referenda in 1981 and 1995 on whether to cease to be part of Canada. Municipalities in Canada hold referenda relatively frequently on a wide range of local issues.

The first national referendum was held in 1898 on prohibition. The "drys" won narrowly but the turnout was less than 50 per cent of the eligible voters, and the Cabinet of the day, most of whom were at least moderate imbibers, used the poor turnout as an excuse not to introduce the necessary legislation. The second national referendum was held in 1942 on the issue of conscription and although the outcome was a 65 per cent vote nationally in favour of compulsory military service, three-quarters of the voters in Quebec opposed it. Hence, far from legitimizing the government's position, as Mackenzie King had hoped, it seriously divided the country and the Liberal Cabinet and caucus along ethnic lines.

The third national referendum, which we have discussed elsewhere, was the 1993 vote on the Charlottetown Accord. Fifty-four per cent of the voters rejected the package but it did make Canadians think about the referendum device itself as a possible means of ratifying all constitutional amendments. While, under our current Constitution, it is not possible to make a referendum legally binding on our legislatures, if a government chooses to hold one, and if the result is conclusive, it would be virtual political suicide for the government to ignore it. Hence, in this sense, it likely doesn't matter if the referendum is legally binding: the governments will be bound by the result in practical terms.

The best thing about referenda is that the people are permitted to directly determine government policies. The worst thing is that the people are permitted to directly determine government policies! Policy questions are very often too complex and technical for even our elected governments to deal with without significant help from expert advisors in the bureaucracy. The average Canadian would be at an even greater disadvantage if such complex policy issues were routinely submitted to the people for a verdict. Hence, one does not have to be an anti-democratic elitist to conclude that many policy issues are simply not resolvable through the instrument of a referendum.

However, some issues may be suitable for resolution by referendum. In the first place, it must be possible to state the referendum question in terms simple enough that people without a lot of expertise are able to understand the issue. Moreover, the question posed must be answerable by a simple "yes" or "no." The 1993 referendum required nineteen million "non-constitutional experts" to say "yes" or "no" to a complex document containing some sixty separate provisions, each of which had many subtle implications internally — all of this while the Blue Jays were winning the World Series! It would seem that the ratification of the Charlottetown Accord was precisely the sort of thing that should *not* be submitted to a referendum.

It is often suggested that policy issues that involve questions of community standards or morality, such as abortion, capital punishment, or prohibition, lend themselves more naturally to resolution by referendum. Indeed, most people at least understand such issues and they are able to intelligently decide on a yes-or-no basis. However, the problem with these sorts of issues is that the outcome can have a devastating effect on minorities. The danger of utilizing the referendum to deal with issues of conscience is that there is no possibility of a compromise; rather, the process becomes a "zero-sum" game where there are only winners and losers. The tyranny of the majority, which we escape under our current system of parliamentary democracy, intergroup accommodation, and constitutional protection of individual and group rights, could become a frightening possibility if referenda were to be used indiscriminately.

The conclusion here must be that since democracy is a good thing, the more meaningful participation of the *demos* is something to strive for. However, the referendum device has many implications for the way in which our system works, and, at least at the national level, it should be used only cautiously until we can better understand it. Conversely, it would seem that referenda work better in smaller and more limited jurisdictions, such as municipalities, for popular votes on issues such as Sunday closing, tavern hours, and whether a local arena or community hall should be built. Finally, Canadians will likely have to resign themselves to periodic referenda on Quebec sovereignty until either Quebec leaves Canada or the Quebec voters stop electing separatist governments.

## ▶ THE FUNCTIONS OF THE ELECTORAL SYSTEM

Elections, to the majority of Canadians, are the most visible and the most intrinsically interesting events of the political process. Moreover, voting is the commonest and in some ways the easiest form of political participation. Between 70 and 80 per cent of the eligible population will show up at the polls on the day of a federal election, and the campaign leading to that election is, of all political phenomena in Canada, the most widely covered by the media and the most closely watched by the public. However, the electoral system performs many functions, both for our political system and for individual Canadians, which are ancillary to operationalizing representative democracy.

### Recruitment and Selection
The primary function of the electoral system in Canada is to provide for an orderly and democratic succession from one set of political authorities to another. It permits the citizens of Canada a periodic review of the performance of their political leaders and allows them to pass judgement as to whether the

government of the day should be permitted to continue or should be replaced by a new set of representatives.

When we think of the electoral process we normally zero in upon the campaign hoopla and the moment of truth when each of us must actually mark a ballot in the lonely isolation of the polling booth. However, it is important not to forget that there are really two separate steps involved in electing our representatives. The first is the recruitment of *candidates*. To be a candidate, all that is formally required is the desire to run, the signatures of 100 eligible voters in the constituency, and a deposit of $1000. However, it is extremely rare for such self-recruited or *independent* candidates to actually succeed in the subsequent election.

The recruitment of candidates is, in practical terms, dominated by the political parties, which choose individuals in each of the constituencies to run for election under the party banner. The parties have developed a number of different techniques for weeding out the would-be candidates in a constituency, but most come down to holding a "pre-election election," where the members of the party's constituency association choose among those seeking the nomination. Hence, the electoral system not only performs the function of **selection of representatives** through the actual election, but also provides for the pre-election **recruitment of candidates** through the nomination process.

### Policy Functions

While an interstellar traveller observing a Canadian election campaign might come to the conclusion that our politics is entirely about personalities, images of leaders and parties, scandal and corruption, and tiresome rhetoric, elections *do* provide, at least, the *opportunity* for the articulation of policy proposals and the public airing of issues. There are, however, a number of flaws in the idea that political parties and candidates, ever vigilant for the vote, can use the electoral process to form a vital link between the citizen and the policy-making apparatus of the modern state. The most important flaw, one we have already considered, is that many, if not most, policy decisions in Canada are made on the basis of extensive input from experts in the bureaucracy. Thus, high-minded policy proposals articulated during a campaign are often modified, abandoned, or conveniently forgotten when the new government is briefed by the bureaucracy as to what the ultimate costs and the problems of implementation are likely to be.

Moreover, party platforms and the policies parties suggest during elections are, for the most part, extremely nebulous. They usually promise something for everyone but often cannot meet the practical test of having to put their policies into effect at reasonable cost. Hence, in most elections, the parties that have a realistic shot at forming the government all tend to stick to vague platforms that include planks such as a healthy economy, reduced unemployment, better social and health services, reduced crime, lower interest rates, less corruption in government, a reduced deficit, free ice-cream, and blah, blah, blah. The only differences among the platforms of the various parties competing for our votes are subtle variations in emphasis on the various promises. And the incumbent party, for obvious reasons, does not talk much about reducing corruption in government!

While most parties seek to identify themselves with issue positions that will appeal to as many voters as possible and alienate as few as possible, they do, from time to time, take firm positions in an election campaign. Elections have been fought over single issues such as wage-and-price controls, free trade, and the goods and services tax. Furthermore, during a campaign, parties search high and low for votes, and this search may lead them to articulate very specific policy ideas that appeal to various groups in the population that might otherwise remain in the background. Finally, since approximately half a million Canadians are working for the political parties during a national election campaign, most of them at the constituency level, if an issue is of special importance in a particular constituency, it may be aired and debated locally, even if it is not part of the national platform.

Hence, while it cannot be said that initiating policy is a key function of the electoral system, election campaigns nevertheless address issues and at a minimum they raise the awareness of the electorate as to what is politically important. In this sense, the electoral process sets an agenda for political discussion and cues us as to what we should be thinking about. This is part of the overall process of political education that teaches us about the multitude of possible policy options. It may stimulate us, at some time in the future, to put pressure on government to give a particular policy idea more serious consideration.

### Systemic Functions: Legitimation and Integration

Another important function of the electoral system is the generation of support for our political system as a whole. It is obvious that elections elicit direct support for a specific group of candidates, that is, the winners!. This electoral result becomes the mandate to govern, if not to implement a particular set of policies, and gives the government of the day the legitimacy to lead the country until the next election.

Elections also help to establish the **legitimacy** of the system as a whole. This broader **systemic function** results from the fact that the election forces people to become interested and even directly involved in the democratic process. They learn about the rules of the game of politics and are presented with a very practical demonstration of the nature and extent of the power of the mass public in a democratic election. Because elections do produce changes in the occupants of the elected offices of our political system, they serve to remind even the most cynical citizen that, while democracy sometimes works in strange ways, it still works.

A broad measure of support for the **political community** is also generated by the fact that, during the eight weeks of a national or general election campaign, all those Canadians who pay any attention to public affairs focus on a single national event. For a brief period, national issues supersede most local issues and, in this manner, elections function as agents of **national integration**, reaffirming, at least for a day, that East and West, francophone and anglophone, ultimately, we are all in the same boat. Provincial elections on the other hand are often determined by which party most effectively and creatively "bashes the feds," an exercise not likely to generate much national integration. More specifically, recent provincial elections in Quebec have been fought over the issue of whether to separate from Canada, which certainly does not reinforce the legitimacy of Canada as a political community.

Thus, elections force us to think about more than the specific issues and the personalities of the candidates and party leaders. They function also as instruments of political socialization, teaching us about the importance of democratic institutions, fundamental values such as freedom of expression and political equality, and in general the many blessings and benefits of being a Canadian.

### Social and Psychological Functions

There are three other non-political functions of the electoral process. First, elections have a **sociability function**. In other words, many participants in the electoral process are there because they enjoy the social interaction with others during the campaign and because being involved is very satisfying personally. Others participate simply because the campaign itself is fun — they are drawn to the high-spirited, euphoric, party atmosphere. Surveys of party activitists generally confirm this, and indeed, for many party workers, the election may be the high point of social and organizational life for a four-year period.

Second, federal general elections are the grand spectator events of Canadian politics. Whatever effect election campaigns have on the final outcome, they are great theatre, with leaders dashing to and fro trying to establish their images and sell their party platforms. The leaders are accompanied by faithful retinues of weary (and often, so it's said, beery) reporters who fill our television screens with carefully staged two-minute clips of leaders in action, and the newspapers with all manner of fact, fancy, rumour, and comment on the race.

Then there is the thrill of the race itself, with public-opinion polls and assorted pundits giving us a week-by-week picture of the positions of the various parties. At the local level, coffee parties and all-candidates' meetings abound, and, for eight weeks at a stretch, local television producers are spared any anxiety about how to fill up prime time, and local newspapers are spared any anxiety about what to use to fill the space between advertisements. It is difficult, during an election campaign, for even the most apolitical and cynical Canadian not to become interested as election day draws near.

Finally there is the drama of election night itself. Because of Canada's time zones, election night is more dramatic the further east one lives. While Newfoundland viewers can enjoy the unfolding of the results from eight o'clock local time, for the people of British Columbia, the outcome is usually already decided by the time their polls close four and a half hours later. Nevertheless, as the polls close in the various time zones, and the results come in, very few of us can pull ourselves away from the election-night TV coverage, even to watch "Roseanne" or "Baywatch." When we turn off the TV and retire for the night, we may not be sure what it all means or even if it really matters a whole lot, but we have certainly been entertained for the evening.

## ▶ THE ELECTORAL SYSTEM

While elections are held at all levels of government in Canada as well as in the selection of school boards, hospital boards, and other minor bodies with specific local responsibilities, the focus of this section will be primarily upon the federal level. The most important electoral event at the federal level is, of course, the **general election**, where all seats in the House of Commons are up for grabs. **By-elections** are held in specific constituencies to fill vacancies that occur from time to time between general elections due to the death or resignation of the incumbent. Before proceeding to an examination of the federal electoral system however, it is necessary to describe in the broadest terms the basic structure of our system of representation.

### Systems of Representation

We have already discussed the differences between representative democracy and direct democracy. In giving effect to representative democracy through the device of an election, there are a number of different ways in which the electorate may be represented. The most common is by geographic area, where individuals are elected to represent all of the people in a specific constituency, district, ward, or riding. Representation also can be based on non-geographic criteria such as each party's proportion of the popular vote nationally or regionally. Moreover, within the basic system of representation by geographical area, it is possible to have a single candidate or several elected in each constituency. Finally, election outcomes can be determined by absolute majority or by a simple plurality of votes cast.

**Plurality Systems** The national electoral system in Canada is based on the **single-member plurality** system of representation which has three main characteristics. First, representation is by **constituency** or **riding**. Second, we elect a single member for each constituency. And, third, the representative is elected by **plurality** or "first past the post" and not by a full majority. In other words, the candidate who receives the most votes is declared the winner and there is no requirement for an *absolute* majority of 50 per cent plus one.

A variation of this system is the **multiple-member plurality** system in which two or more representatives are elected in each constituency. Up until 1965 there were a few two-member federal ridings in which the two candidates with the most votes were declared elected. It is interesting to note that in these two-member constituencies it was not unusual for the two winners to be from different parties, an outcome that might have indicated either that the electors were voting for the candidates as individuals and not for the party or that they were hedging their bets to ensure a bit of patronage for the constituency whatever party formed the government. Today, only Prince Edward Island uses the multiple plurality system, having sixteen two-member constituencies in its provincial system of representation.

**Majority Systems**  Another system that has been tried at the provincial level in Canada is the **single-member majority** system, where the voter indicates which candidates are the best alternatives if the first choice does not succeed. The ballots cast for the candidate who places last are then distributed to the remaining candidates according to the second choice indicated, and so on, until one candidate gets an absolute majority. Also referred to as the **alternative-vote** system, this method of election was used briefly in British Columbia during the 1950s, and in both Manitoba and Alberta it was introduced in the 1920s for rural constituencies. It was last used in Canada in Alberta, where it was finally abandoned in 1959.

**Proportional Systems**  **Proportional representation** (PR) is a system used in many other parts of the world and has been tried at the provincial level in both Manitoba and Alberta. The most common form of PR provides representation for political parties on the basis of their percentage of the popular vote in a geographic area. In the end, the aim of the system is to ensure that the percentage of the total vote is roughly equal to the percentage of seats gained in the legislature or Parliament, something that, as we shall see, is quite rare in single-member plurality systems.

In the simplest form of PR, each party lists its candidates in order of the party's preference. Then, based on its percentage of the total votes cast the party is allocated the same percentage of seats which are doled out to the top candidates on the list. This **party-list system** is common in Europe, but it has never been tried in Canada. The weakness of this system would seem to lie in the amount of power placed in the hands of the party elites who can "play god" with their rank-and-file candidates by being able to arbitrarily determine their order on the list.

Another variety of proportional representation is based on a **single transferable vote** system, which is similar to the alternate-vote system discussed above, where voters rank the candidates from first to last. A certain number of votes or a quota is required to be elected; a successful candidate's votes in excess of the quota are then redistributed to the second choices, and so on, until the number of seats at stake are all allocated. If, after the votes in excess of the quota are distributed, there are still seats to be filled, the last-place candidate is eliminated and those votes transferred to the second choice until all the available seats are distributed. This system was used at the provincial level in Alberta until 1959 (for Edmonton and Calgary), and in Manitoba until 1953 (for the city of Winnipeg), but has never been tried at the federal level.

**The Single-Member Plurality System: Pros and Cons**
In spite of all the positive attributes of the Canadian electoral system, it has been widely argued that its basic structural feature, the single-member plurality system, creates problems. One of the traditional defences of the present electoral system in Canada has been that it provides us with majority governments, and consequently with greater governmental stability and predictability. While the present system does, to some degree, increase the likelihood of majority government, it does so by consistently giving the party with a plurality of the

popular vote a larger percentage of the seats than its percentage share of the vote. As an example, the Liberal Party in 1993 gained 60 per cent of the seats in the House of Commons while winning only 41 per cent of the popular vote nationally.

Moreover, the system encourages minor parties, such as the Social Credit and the *Créditistes* in the past, and more recently the Reform and the *Bloc Québécois* (BQ), with regional bases of support while damaging minority national parties such as the NDP, whose support is spread evenly over the country. The 1993 election provides a glaring example of this anomaly of our system of representation. The BQ concentrated its support in Quebec and won 18 per cent of the seats with only 14 per cent of the popular vote, and the Reform Party netted 18 per cent of the seats with 19 per cent of the vote. By contrast, the Progressive Conservatives, who enjoyed a majority government at dissolution, won 16 per cent of the popular vote which translated into less than 1 per cent of the seats. Similarly, the NDP won 7 per cent of the vote but only 3 per cent of the seats.

The results of the 1979 election demonstrated the potential for a different kind of imbalance in representation. The Liberals, with 40 per cent of the vote, did get 40 per cent of the seats, but the PCs, with only 35.9 per cent of the vote, won 48 per cent of the seats. The NDP, with 17.8 per cent of the vote but only 9 per cent of the seats, had half the electoral support of the Conservatives but just one-fifth the number of seats. The PCs formed a minority government with just a little more than one-third of the voters. In 1984 the Conservatives captured 75 per cent of the seats in the House of Commons with only 50 per cent of the national vote, the Liberals garnered just 14 per cent of the seats with 28 per cent of the vote, and the NDP gained 11 per cent of the seats with 19 per cent of the vote.

As these results indicate, the peculiar arithmetic of the single-member constituency system works differently for large than for small parties. A large party will gain the maximum number of seats if its support is widely dispersed, while a small party will obtain the maximum number of seats if its support is concentrated in a few areas. Moreover, the system favours parties with a regional base over parties that attempt to mobilize support nationally on the basis of cleavages such as class which cut across regional boundaries. Alan Cairns points out part of the problem:

> Sectionalism has been rendered highly visible because the electoral system makes it a fruitful basis on which to organize electoral support. Divisions cutting through sections, particularly those based on the class system, have been much less salient because the possibility of pay-offs in terms of representation has been minimal.[1]

Cairns concludes that the electoral system in Canada has a detrimental effect on national unity:

---

1. A. C. Cairns, "The Electoral and the Party System in Canada, 1921–65," *Canadian Journal of Political Science*, vol. 1, no. 1, March 1968, p. 62. See also the critique of Cairn's ideas in J. A. A. Lovink, "On Analyzing the Impact of the Party System in Canada," *Canadian Journal of Political Science*, vol. 3, no. 4, pp. 497–516, and Cairn's reply, pp. 517–21 in the same issue.

Sectional politics (which are exacerbated by the electoral system) has an inherent tendency to call into question the very nature of the political system and its legitimacy. Classes, unlike sections, cannot secede from the political system and are consequently more prone to accept its legitimacy.[2]

We need not agree entirely with this analysis, but it does force us to ask whether Canadian unity suffers from the divisive effects of an electoral system that highlights and exaggerates our regional cleavage. If regional cleavages are explicitly sanctioned by the federal system and only slightly counterbalanced by the brokerage activities of the national political parties, then we have a serious problem indeed. Certainly this message is being driven home clearly by the success of the regional/separatist BQ at the federal level and the *Parti Québécois* at the provincial level in Quebec.

---

## ▶ THE PARTICIPANTS

Because they are such complex events, elections cannot be understood if viewed from a single vantage point. Therefore, we will look at the Canadian electoral system as a number of separate but interrelated sub-processes with a wide variety of participants or actors. However, before moving to the discussion of these sub-processes, it is necessary to provide a *dramatis personae* of the spectacle of a federal general election in Canada.

### The Voters

The most numerous and, ultimately, the most important players in an election are the voters. Who votes and who does not is determined partly by the psychological and motivational characteristics of the Canadian electorate, and partly by the formal rules that set down the qualifications for voting, or the franchise. The former are the complex determinants of electoral participation, which will be discussed at length in Chapter 15. It is the formal rules with which we are concerned here.

**The *Canada Elections Act***   The **franchise**, or the rules about who can and cannot vote in a national election, is defined by the *Canada Elections Act*. The basic rule today is that any Canadian citizen eighteen years of age or older has the right to vote in a general election or in a by-election being held in the constituency in which the voter resides. An elector must vote in the constituency in which his or her name appears on the **electoral list**, although there are special provisions for members of the armed forces and for Canadians living abroad or within Canada but temporarily absent from their home constituency. Voters may cast one ballot and may vote only for a candidate whose name appears on the ballot. There are no **write-in** votes in the Canadian system, except under the **Special Voting Rules**, where members of the military, non-resident elec-

---

2. Cairns, "The Electoral and the Party System," p. 62.

tors, and absentee voters must write in the name of their candidate of choice, but the ballot will be counted only if the name written in is that of an official candidate.

The *Canada Elections Act* excludes certain classes of individuals. Those disqualified from voting are the chief electoral officer and the assistant chief electoral officer; the returning officers in each constituency (except in the case of a tie, when the returning officer must cast the deciding vote); inmates of correctional institutions serving terms of more than two years; and persons convicted of offences under the *Canada Elections Act*.

### The History of the Franchise

The Canadian electoral system today features **universal adult suffrage**. However, what seems to be an obvious criterion for a liberal democratic regime has not always been accepted so fully in Canada. For much of the period between 1867 and 1920, when a major revision of the *Dominion Elections Act* was passed, the federal franchise was determined by the provincial elections acts. This meant that the franchise in national elections was not consistent across the country and that the qualifications and the basis for disqualification of voters in federal elections varied with the whim and prejudice of provincial governments.

Many provinces originally had a property qualification for voting, a reflection of a basically elitist attitude to the responsibilities of choosing a government. The feeling was that people who owned property had a stake in the community and would be more responsible in casting a ballot. However, there are no property qualifications today. Women were generally excluded from voting until 1918, and could not stand as candidates until 1919. In Quebec, women remained disfranchised in provincial elections until 1940. Other unusual and blatantly discriminatory provisions that disqualified Canadian citizens who were of Oriental or Hindu descent were in the *British Columbia Elections Act* up to 1945. Because provincial rules determined the federal franchise until 1920, Oriental Canadians in British Columbia were automatically disqualified from voting in federal elections as well.

Some provinces have also had literacy requirements for voting. The requirement of being able to read either French or English was subject to abuse by the people administering the test, who could exclude new Canadians who might be very well educated in their native tongue, Canadians who simply did not get the benefit of enough schooling, or speakers of an aboriginal language. These requirements have all disappeared by now, however, and the Charter effectively guarantees that all citizens shall have the right to vote. Despite the rather tarnished history of provincial franchises, today the provincial elections acts define an eligible voter in a manner close to identical to that of the *Canada Elections Act*.

Lest we appear too hard on the provinces, we must recognize that the federal franchise has not always been "as universal" as it is today. Women became universally enfranchised only in 1920, but perhaps the most enduring injustices have been in the treatment of aboriginal peoples. The Inuit ("Esquimau person" in the 1934 Act) were explicitly excluded until 1950, because there were no federal electoral districts in the territorial regions of Keewatin and Franklin, where most Inuit reside. It was not until the creation of the constituency of the Northwest Territories, after the 1961 Census, that most Inuit were able to vote for the first time. Indians living on reserves were also explicitly excluded from the franchise until 1960, when such discriminatory provisions were removed from the *Canada Elections Act*.

### The Candidates

The qualifications and disqualifications for candidacy in a federal election are set down in the *Canada Elections Act*. The basic rule is that candidates must be eligible to vote in a Canadian election and must be formally nominated. Disqualified persons include those found guilty of corrupt election practices; legal officers of the Crown such as sheriffs, clerks of the peace, crown attorneys, and federally appointed judges; members of a provincial legislature or a territorial assembly; and the chief and assistant chief electoral officers, the returning officers, and other election officials.

In the distant past, candidates in federal elections were required to own a certain amount of property, but this stipulation was abolished soon after Confederation. To be a candidate in a federal election, the individual must reside in Canada. There is no legal requirement that candidates be residents of the constituencies in which they are running, although candidates who are **parachuted** into a riding by the party leadership are sometimes spurned at the polls by the local party faithful. In provincial elections acts, residence in the province is a requirement of being a candidate, although, as with the federal Act, there is no requirement that the candidate be a resident of the constituency in which he or she runs.

### The Political Parties

We will discuss the partisan campaign in the next chapters, but it is necessary at this juncture to deal briefly with the formal aspects of the role of political parties in the election system.

**Registration**  The *Canada Elections Act* sets out the conditions and procedures for *registration* of a political party. Registration gives the party's candidates the right to have the party name listed beside theirs on the ballot paper. It is the responsibility of the chief electoral officer to maintain a **registry of political parties** and to determine which applications for registration meet the stipulations set down in the Act. To be registered, the party must field at least fifty candidates in an election, and to maintain continuous registration and qualify for ongoing financial support, the party must have twelve seats in the House of Commons at dissolution.

Restrictions on registration also include sundry formal requirements having to do with information about the party's address, the names of the party executive, the chief party agent, and the party auditor; as well, the name of the party must not be the same or even too similar to the name of an already registered party. This latter requirement is to prevent a marginal group from calling itself, for instance, the Conservative Progressive Party or the NPD and thereby picking up gratuitous support from a careless minority, who thought they were voting for a major political party. Despite these provisions, in Canada's 1993 general election, there were fourteen registered parties, one of which called itself the Libertarian Party. Although this label might have been deemed rather close to another, more prominent, party in Canadian politics, the results of the election indicate that very few Liberal voters were fooled by the similarity in name. How many Libertarians might have voted Liberal by mistake is impossible to estimate.

**Official Agents**  As mentioned above, the registered parties must name an individual to be the **chief agent** of the party and each candidate names an **official agent** as well. The responsibilities of the chief agent are to a large extent associated with the management of the finances of the party. The rules regarding campaign expenditures, which will be discussed in more detail in later chapters, require that party donations and expenditures be channelled through the chief agent who is required to submit a full report on the financing of the campaign after the election. As well, each party must name a **party auditor** who is to operate at arm's length from the party organization and who must have full access to all of the party's records in conducting the audit at the end of the election.

The official agents of the candidates play a similar role for the parties at the level of the constituency. Perhaps most importantly for the candidate, it is the receipt of the report of the official agent by the chief electoral officer that triggers the mechanism for candidates to be reimbursed for 50 per cent of their deposit. The incentive for filing expeditious and complete reports is, thus, high for all party candidates, and for those who also received at least 15 per cent of the vote it is higher because they are reimbursed the full $1000 of their deposit.

### Election Officials

There are a number of offices created and defined by the *Canada Elections Act*. Some of these are at the national office of Elections Canada, and others are in the constituencies. While the key jobs at the national level are permanent positions, a great many of the people appointed to administer a general election are at the constituency level and work only during an election.

**The Chief Electoral Officer**  The most important position in the electoral process is that of the **chief electoral officer** (CEO), who is appointed by special resolution of the House of Commons, with the effective rank of deputy minister. The CEO's term is until age sixty-five and he or she can be removed only for "cause" (i.e., conviction of heinous crimes or failure to perform duties) following a joint address of both houses of Parliament. There have been only five CEOs since the office was founded in 1920. The salary of the CEO is equal to that of a judge of the federal court and the office is given an independence from the government of the day that is analogous to that of a superior court judge. The costs of the office and support staff are provided directly from the consolidated revenue fund without approval of the Cabinet. The office of the chief electoral officer is now referred to as **Elections Canada**. The responsibilities of this office are to oversee the conduct of federal elections and referenda and generally to carry out the responsibilities set down in the *Canada Elections Act*. The CEO is also granted very broad discretionary powers to adapt the election process in the event of unusual or unforeseen circumstances.

Prior to 1966, the primary responsibility of the office was simply to see that enumeration and vote counting took place according to the rules set forth by Parliament. Since 1966, however, a steady expansion of the office's functions has taken place, with the addition of responsibilities for representation and redistribution, the registration of political parties, and the administration of election-expenses legislation. As well, in recent years, Elections Canada officials have participated internationally in helping to set up new electoral systems in other parts of the world such as Central America and South Africa, assisting local authorities and monitoring the transition to democratic politics. The job has become administratively very complex, and the Act provides that the CEO is to be backed up by an **assistant chief electoral officer**, who is appointed by the governor-general-in-council, and such other personnel, appointed under the *Public Service Employment Act*, as required to effectively carry out the duties of the office.

**Returning Officers** For each electoral district in Canada, the governor-general-in-council appoints a **returning officer** (RO). The RO, who actually reports to the CEO, is appointed until age sixty-five, and the requirements of tenure are that the RO remain a resident of the constituency for which the appointment is made, maintain a non-partisan stance in the performance of duties, and, in general, do the job defined by the *Canada Elections Act*. The RO's responsibilities are to manage the election process in the constituency, to appoint enumerators, to appoint at least one **assistant returning officer** (ARO) for the constituency, and, once the election is called, to appoint a deputy returning officer (DRO) and poll clerk for each of the polls within the constituency.

The RO must maintain an office in the constituency from the time the election writs are issued, and either the RO or the ARO must be on duty in the office during the hours the polls are open throughout the election period. The job was once considered a patronage "plum," but now it is more often than not difficult to find someone both able and willing to perform the task, since it involves intense effort under considerable pressure for a fifty-day period and it does not pay particularly well.

**Deputy returning officers** are minor officials who hold office at the pleasure of the RO in the electoral district during the election period and can be removed by the RO at any time. The roles of the DRO are to administer the election process at the level of the individual polling station and to oversee the balloting and unofficial count in the poll. To assist in these duties, the returning officer is also required by the Act to appoint a **poll clerk**. There is one DRO and one poll clerk appointed for each of the polling divisions in a riding. The Act provides that DROs must be appointed from a list submitted by the political party holding the seat at dissolution, and the poll clerks are appointed from a list prepared by the political party that placed second in the last election.

**Enumerators** As mentioned above, the returning officer of each constituency must appoint **enumerators**, who are charged with the responsibility for preparing the preliminary voters' lists in each polling division. Generally, two enumerators are appointed for each poll, and the *Canada Elections Act* requires that the RO select them on the basis of bipartisan representation. Essentially, the RO asks the registered parties that placed first and second in the previous election to provide a list of qualified individuals and appoints half from each list. The same practice applies to the process of appointing **revising officers** and **revising agents** who, in effect, hear appeals from people left off the voters list in the initial enumeration.

A minor benefit of this system, from a partisan standpoint, is that the local candidates of the two most successful parties in the previous election may be able to dole out a bit of patronage in return for a little volunteer work later on in the campaign. However, as with the ROs, it has become increasingly difficult to find people willing to do the work of enumerators for the small amount of money involved. In fact, one of the bigger administrative problems surrounding elections is to find, within ten days of an election call, more than one hundred thousand qualified people who will work very hard for several days for a few hundred dollars. The quality of those applying is not always high, and applications have been received in the recent past for positions as "remunerators" and "eliminators."

**Broadcasting Arbitrator** A **broadcasting arbitrator** is appointed by the CEO to settle disputes arising over the allocation of both free time and purchased advertising on radio and television during the campaign. After each election an arbitrator is selected by a panel of representatives of all of the official parties in the House of Commons. If this panel is unanimous on the selection, the CEO makes the formal appointment. If the panel is unable to reach a consensus, the CEO is empowered to make the appointment unilaterally. The term of office of the broadcasting arbitrator expires six months after the following general election, although there is no barrier to reappointment for the next term.

The role of the broadcasting arbitrator is not large in the interelection period. He or she is required to convene and chair a meeting of representatives of the political parties annually, to review the entitlement of the parties to broadcast time. However, when a general election is called, the broadcasting arbitrator has the very onerous responsibility for settling disputes among the parties and between the parties and the broadcasters over the allocation of broadcasting time. While the arbitrator must first seek to achieve consensus among the parties, failing agreement, he or she has the power to make the decisions unilaterally. We will say more about the role of the broadcasting arbitrator when we discuss the regulation of campaign advertising in the following chapters.

There are other minor officials and functionaries who, while bit players in the complex theatre that is a Canadian general election, are important in maintaining checks and balances among partisan interests and in keeping the process honest. These include the scrutineers and party officials, who are present in each polling station on election day and who make sure that here are no irregularities in the conduct of the poll. Their roles will become apparent as we move to a discussion of the election process itself.

---

▶ THE ELECTORAL PROCESS

The electoral process in Canada is, in fact, a complex set of sub-processes. Each of these sub-processes must be considered in turn, starting with the distribution of ridings among the provinces and the drawing of constituency boundaries. We will be focusing on the conduct of national *general elections*, although students must remember that there are also *by-elections* that must be held from time to time to fill vacancies in individual constituencies between general elections. The same basic formal rules apply for by-elections and general elections. However, by-elections have a generally lower turnout, they do not normally affect the fate of a government, and each by-election must be seen as an essentially idiosyncratic event.

### Redistribution

The purpose of **redistribution** is simply to ensure that the distribution of constituencies across the country and within each province is such that Canadians are more or less equally represented in the House of Commons. The general rule is that the number of people represented by one member of Parliament should be roughly equal from constituency to constituency.

**Over-representation**   The principle of equal representation must be adjusted a bit in a country as vast and diverse as Canada. For instance, it has generally been agreed that rural constituencies and remote constituencies can be based on a smaller population size than a geographically compact but densely populated urban district. While the logic of this was that such constituencies were harder to represent effectively because of difficulties of travel, such disparities are more difficult to justify in an era of modern communications technology. Nevertheless, at the time of the 1993 election, the constituency of Nunatsiaq in the Northwest Territories had a total population of less than 20,000, whereas many of the Metropolitan Toronto ridings had populations in excess of 200,000.

It is also considered important in a federal system that there should be minimum guarantees of representation for each of the provinces. As a minor step towards achieving this goal, the BNA Act was amended in 1915 to provide that a province's seats in the House of Commons should not fall below the number of Senate seats allocated to that province. As a result of this provision Prince Edward Island and New Brunswick are guaranteed, in perpetuity, four and ten seats, respectively, despite their declining population relative to the rest of Canada. As well, it has always been considered important that a province's share of the seats not fall significantly from one redistribution to the next. Hence, section 51 of the BNA Act provided that the number of seats allocated to a province should not drop by more than 5 per cent from one census to the next, and the *Representation Act* of 1985, which is still in effect in 1995,[3] through a **grandfather clause,** pegs minimum provincial representation at the 1976 level.

**Allocation of Seats** It has been recognized since Confederation that there would have to be a regular redistribution of seats among the provinces to take into account rapid population shifts in a growing nation. Section 51 of the BNA Act provides that there must be a redistribution after each decennial census. The number of seats per province is established by a complicated formula, which operates as follows:

1. Assign 2 seats to the Northwest Territories and one to Yukon (3 seats).
2. Use 279 seats and the census population (except the Northwest Territories and Yukon) to establish a *national electoral quotient*, representing the average number of voters per seat for Canada.
3. Calculate number of seats per province based on the quotient.
4. Add seats to provinces pursuant to the *Senate clause* in the Constitution and the *grandfather clause* in the 1985 formula.
5. Add seats to adjust for provincial population increases.

It is the responsibility of the chief electoral officer to calculate each province's entitlement of seats by applying the formula to the census data as soon as the chief statistician of Canada gives the CEO the required information. Having made these calculations, the CEO then instructs the electoral boundaries commissions to assign the new seats and redraw the constituency boundaries within their respective provinces and territories.

**Drawing the Constituency Boundaries** At one time, the changes in electoral boundaries were the prerogative of the House of Commons. This meant that the government of the day was always in a position to be able to adjust the ridings in such a way as to maximize its own electoral success. This often led to distortion in the way in which constituency boundaries were drawn, referred to as **gerrymandering**. However, since 1964, Canada has had a system of electoral-boundary adjustments based on the principles that existing political boundaries such as those of municipalities should be adhered to as closely as possible, that communities of interest should be kept intact, and that historically recognized constituency boundaries should be maintained. These principles are backed up by an all-party acceptance of the need for a less partisan and more impartial system of redistribution.

The current system of federal redistribution in Canada is based on eleven impartial **electoral boundaries commissions**, one for each province and one for the Yukon and the Northwest Territories. These are made up of a judge from the province or territories, who is appointed by the chief justice of the provincial Supreme Court, and two other members, who are appointed by the Speaker of the House of Commons, one of whom is often the Speaker of the provincial legislature. The base from which these electoral-boundaries com-

---

3. At the time or writing, the new electoral-boundaries legislation was still being held up in Parliament.

missions begins is the number of seats assigned to their province according to the formula and to the *Electoral Boundaries Readjustment Act*, which determines how boundaries are drawn within each province. The boundaries commissions have considerable leeway to set boundaries, in keeping with factors such as physical features (roads and rivers) and community borders or population concentrations, and it is thus very important that they be viewed as impartial. The *Canada Elections Act* specifies that the size of any electoral district within a province should not deviate from the quotient by more than plus or minus 25 per cent. This is, however, only a target, and exceptions are permitted on reasonable grounds.

The preliminary reports of the commissions are open to public scrutiny and comment within the province, and, after any changes brought about at this stage are completed, the completed report of the commission is sent on to the CEO. The Speaker then tables all of the reports of the electoral boundaries commissions in the House of Commons. The House has thirty days to examine the reports, and objections signed by ten members can be filed with the Speaker. These are then debated, and the results of the debate, along with the appropriate copies of Hansard, are sent back to the relevant commission for reconsideration. However, the commissions are free to implement or disregard these recommendations at their discretion.

The ultimate step in the process of redistribution is the drafting of a representation order by the chief electoral officer. This document sets down in detail the names and boundary descriptions of the constituencies established by the commissions and is given effect by the governor-general-in-council. Given the complicated nature of this process, not to mention the inevitable delays in getting census data out, the process is not a short one. The 1993 election, for example, was carried out under the distributions determined by the 1981 census, and the redistribution based on the 1991 census still has not been passed in 1995.

---

▶ CALLING THE ELECTION

Barring the defeat of a government in the legislature and with the exception of the constitutional provision that the life of a Parliament is limited to five years, the timing of an election in Canada is wholly the prerogative of the prime minister or premier. Customarily, if the government in power has a majority, elections will occur at about four-year intervals, although the maximum allowable term is five years. A government will not wait out the full five years unless it is in trouble, and then, because the government takes on the unsightly appearance of clinging desperately to power, the results are not likely to be propitious. As evidence of this, the 1979, 1984, and 1993 elections were all held in the fifth year and all resulted in the defeat of the government.

While elections are always held on a Monday, the prime minister decides which Monday. Moreover, while the conventional wisdom is that elections should not normally be held in the heat of the summer or in the dead of winter, the timing is still up to the government. The prime minister will make the decision about election timing on the basis of information from the party about its state of preparedness, from the Cabinet about how any current policy initiatives are progressing, and, particularly, from public-opinion polls. This information is all interpreted by personal advisors, the party "brain trust," and sundry party "gurus" and pollsters who attempt to divine the likelihood of electoral victory. Depending on his or her temperament, the prime minister may also feel moved to take long walks in a blizzard, to look at horoscopes, tea leaves, or the entrails of pigeons, or to consult a long-dead mother or doggy, for the timing of an election is, in the end, an inexact science.

Once a decision on timing has been made, the prime minister visits the governor-general, who has the formal power to dissolve Parliament and call an election. (In the provinces, the premier visits the lieutenant governor, who has a similar formal power with regard to provincial elections.) The chief electoral officer then issues the **election writs** and transmits them to the returning officers in each of the electoral districts and the electoral machinery is put into motion.

### Enumeration

To be eligible to vote, a person must have his or her name appear on a voters' list. In Canada and in all provinces except British Columbia, lists are prepared anew for each election. At the federal level, if two elections fall within one year, the final list from the previous election may be used as the preliminary list for the second one at the discretion of the CEO. The list of electors is prepared through a two-step process of **enumeration** and **revision**. As soon as the writs are issued, the returning officer appoints two enumerators for each poll in the constituency and gives them their instructions. Then, enumerators, travelling in pairs, visit each residence in the poll at least twice (if necessary), and determine the names of all eligible voters residing there. The returning officer is responsible for seeing that preliminary voters' lists are prepared and that everyone whose name appears on the list is notified by a postcard which also informs the voter of the location of the poll, the times for voting, and the times and procedures for advance polls. Each candidate also receives copies of the preliminary lists and may use these to inform their potential supporters if they are not on the list. Simultaneously, notices appear in the media informing those who do not receive postcards that, if they wish to vote, they must appeal, following the steps set out in the notices.

The returning officer is also required to group polling divisions together into **revisal districts** and to set up a **revisal office** in each district. For each revisal district there is a supervisory **revising officer** and several **revising agents** who work in pairs to amend and update the preliminary lists, adding persons left off and deleting those incorrectly included in the first stage of the enumeration. Based on the revised lists, the returning officer then prepares the **Final List of Electors** which determines one's eligibility to cast a ballot on election day. Finally, even if an elector is left off the voters' list, the Act provides that he or she may still vote by providing proof of eligibility at the poll on election day.

## Nominations

The formal rules for the nomination of candidates are set down in the *Canada Elections Act*. While most candidates will already have been selected by the party organization in the constituency by the time the election is called, the formal nomination must occur after the issuance of the writs and by the Monday four weeks before the vote. The nomination requires the signature of at least one hundred eligible voters in the constituency, a deposit of $1000, and, if the candidate is representing a registered party, the endorsement of the party leader. Fifty per cent of the deposit is refundable if the candidate files the necessary returns with the CEO, and the remaining 50 per cent is refunded if the candidate receives at least 15 per cent of the valid votes cast. Otherwise, all of the deposits are forfeited to "Her Majesty".

The selection of candidates by the party riding associations will usually have taken place some time before the campaign begins, but in some ridings the announcement of the election date will find one or more parties so ill-prepared that no candidate is available. In others, parties may have delayed nomination meetings to take advantage of the publicity they generate. Nomination procedures vary from party to party and from riding to riding. At the one extreme are completely open conventions where anyone who has paid nominal party membership dues may vote, while at the other extreme are carefully controlled nominating conventions where all the candidates are hand-picked by the party executive to avoid any unfortunate "errors."

In practice, most nominating conventions lie somewhere between the two extremes. In some ridings, "perennial bridesmaid" parties are as likely to be embarrassed by a lack of potential nominees as by an excess, and, at every election, constituency executives face the unpleasant task of searching frantically for a suitable party candidate. If all else fails, a member of the party executive will accept a draft and carry the party's colours into the local campaign. We shall say more about the process of nomination in Chapter 15.

## Polling the Electors

**Polling stations** in the past were often located in the houses of supporters of the "right party," and the owners were paid for the use of their premises. While this used to be a fairly significant bit of patronage, today the remuneration is hardly worth the inconvenience of a stampede through one's house, so churches, schools, and other public buildings as well as rented commercial premises tend to be used more and more as polling stations. The polling station contains tables or desks for the use of the poll clerk and the party scrutineers, and a **polling booth** where the voters can mark their ballots in privacy. The principle of the **secret ballot** is a long-standing requirement of truly free elections, and the *Canada Elections Act* very carefully specifies the procedures for protecting this right.

There are also provisions in the Act for ensuring that the poll is accessible to handicapped persons, that special templates are provided for blind electors, and that an elector who requires physical assistance or who requires translation services is accompanied by another individual, if necessary, even in the voting booth itself. **Advance polls** are established for those who must be out of town on voting day, and those who cannot vote on either election day or advance-polling day may vote in the office of the returning officer up to three weeks before polling day. As well, there are Special Voting Rules for armed forces personnel, non-residents, and absentee voters. The votes from advance polls are not counted until after the close of regular polls.

The *Canada Elections Act* also contains provisions respecting the maintenance of "peace and order" on election day. For example, the use of loud-speakers within earshot of the polling station is prohibited, as is campaigning or displaying posters, signs, emblems, or any other party advertising within the immediate vicinity of the station. The long-standing rule that bars and liquor stores had to close during the time that the polls were open has recently been repealed. One might speculate that this happened either because it no longer seems relevant in the sober 1990s or because, given the quality of the choices facing voters in recent elections, most of us need a good stiff drink before casting our ballot for the lesser of evils. Perhaps the provision in the Act, that employers must allow their employees a period of four consecutive hours in order to vote, is related to this!

### Counting the Vote

After the regular polls close on voting day, the deputy returning officers and poll clerks at each poll, including advance polls, count the ballots under the watchful eyes of the party agents or scrutineers. This is an entirely unofficial count, tabulated in newsrooms and party headquarters, but it is what produces the excitement on election night. The ballot boxes are sealed and delivered to the returning officer after the unofficial count, and the RO then has the responsibility of keeping them until the official count, which legally may not be sooner than seven days after the election. By this time, of course, the excitement is over in all but ridings that were very close, where candidates bite their nails as the armed-services vote and ballots cast under special voting rules, such as voters who are in prison, institutionalized, bedridden, or outside their electoral districts, are added to the final totals.

In the case of close elections, or if irregularities are alleged in the conduct of the election, either the returning officer or one of the candidates may apply for a **judicial recount**. (A recount is automatic if the difference is less than twenty-five votes). The recount is performed by a judge in the presence of the candidates or their agents. In the case of a tie even after a recount, the returning officer must cast the deciding vote in the constituency. When all of this is done, the returning officer then returns the election writ, declaring the candidate with the most votes the winner, to the chief electoral officer. The CEO is required to keep, as potential evidence, all of the ballots and ancillary documentation for one year after the election returns are in.

## ▶ REGULATION OF ELECTION EXPENSES

Party finance can obviously be open to gross abuse, and the whole question of campaign finance in Canada has been a constant target for reformers. In the

1960s the Committee on Election Expenses did extensive research and made a series of recommendations in its report published in 1966. These recommendations were finally acted upon after further study by the House of Commons, and, in 1974, Parliament passed a series of sweeping reforms, which have done much to change the face of campaign financing in Canada. The legislation, now incorporated into the *Canada Election Act*, requires the identification of donors, sets ceilings on both party and candidate campaign expenditures, and provides a reporting and accountability requirement with the onus on the party or the candidate as the case may be.

### Disclosure and Tax Credits

The *Canada Elections Act*, as amended, requires disclosure and publication of the names of all donors who donate more than $100 and of the amounts of all donations of more than $100 to a party, or to an individual candidate. This requirement is intended to prevent a government or an MP from favouring specific corporate interests or the interests of the corporate classes at the expense of average Canadians. The belief is that if it is publicly known that a party is indebted to a corporation, the party must be extraordinarily careful not to appear to be returning favours, for instance, by awarding government contracts to major contributors.

As well, the *Income Tax Act* has been amended to provide tax credits to the donors on a sliding scale, up to $500. The reason for the relatively low ceiling on the amount that is tax deductible is to encourage the parties to fund their activities from a wide base of supporters and not to rely solely on the donations of large corporations. In the past, the reliance on corporate donations not only gave the two establishment parties a big edge, but it also created the potential that the corporate interests were making donations on a *quid pro quo* basis. Whether or not campaign contributions actually influence the policy decisions of the government in favour of the corporate elites, the situation certainly gives the appearance that the wealthy corporations "buy" political favour with campaign contributions. Even the appearance of such influence might serve to delegitimize the system as a whole in the eyes of the citizenry.

### Expenditure Limits

While the *Canada Elections Act* does not place a limit on the amount an individual, corporation, or labour union can kick in to the party coffers, it does place a ceiling on the total spending by national parties on the campaign. The ceiling is set according to a simple formula based on 30 cents for each elector in all constituencies where the party has candidates. This figure is then adjusted according to an escalator or fraction established by the chief electoral officer and based on the Consumer Price Index. The total was $10.5 million for each of the Conservatives, Liberals, and NDP in the 1993 campaign.

The Act also limits the amounts that can be spent by individual candidates to $1.00 for each of the first 15,000 voters on the list, 50 cents for each of the next 10,000 voters, and 25 cents for each of the remaining voters. The maximum allowable expenditure for a candidate in a riding of 50,000 electors in 1993 was, therefore, $26,250. The individual candidates' ceilings are also adjusted according to the CEO's fraction. As well, there are provisions that apply to sparsely populated and physically large constituencies, where the allowable expenses are increased by 15 cents per square kilometre.

### Government Campaign Subsidies

Parties, through their registered agents, must provide full audited accounts to the CEO, detailing all money spent and received, and any *gifts of service* which must be declared both as donations and as part of overall expenditures. If a registered party meets the reporting requirements, and if its expenditures are at least 10 per cent of the spending ceiling, it is eligible for reimbursement of 22.5 per cent of its total expenditures from the Consolidated Revenue Fund.

The *Canada Elections Act* also provides a subsidy to each candidate who meets a set of criteria. Any candidate who gets 15 per cent of the vote, and who has submitted, through the official agent, the required *return* to the CEO, detailing the donations and expenditures during the campaign, will be reimbursed for 15 per cent of the expenditure ceiling, out of the Consolidated Revenue Fund.

Most local expenses are covered by local donors, membership fees, or transfers from the national office. Transfers from the national party to help defray a candidate's expenses are not considered a campaign expense to the party. But when the moneys so transferred are spent, they must come within the limit established for the candidate. As well, money spent by the candidate on personal expenses during the campaign are exempt from the spending ceilings, the logic being that candidates have to eat dinner regardless of whether they are embroiled in an election campaign. We will say more about the enforcement of election-finance regulations when we deal with party finance in Chapter 15.

---

▶ DÉNOUEMENT

When the hullabaloo is over, the work is just beginning for some of the election actors. The CEO must file a report with the Speaker of the House of Commons, detailing the results by constituency as well as the outcomes of recounts and reported irregularities. The chief party agents and the official agents of the candidates must also make their reports, detailing what money was spent and where it came from, and the auditors of the parties must also submit their audits. While these are all important parts of the process, the fun is over by the time they are carried out and they go largely unnoticed by the public and unreported by the media.

# Chapter 13

# Political Parties: Functions and Structures

For many Canadians, politics *is* political parties. Political reporting by the media concentrates on party leaders' statements about the issues of the day and on the performance of the government and opposition parties in the House of Commons. At election time, the focus of the media is even more exclusively and more intensively on the party leaders and on the partisan race in which the victors will win not just the election, but governmental power as well. The best-selling books on Canadian politics are not, alas, textbooks, but those that give us the inside dope and the juiciest gossip about partisan politics and its stars and celebrities.

But, while parties clearly pique our curiosity and entertain us in our leisure hours, this is not their main role in Canadian political life. In this chapter, we will examine the functions that political parties perform in our system of governance, and we will describe their basic structural features. In Chapter 14 we will look at how they originated and evolved to the present day.

## ▶ THE FUNCTIONS OF POLITICAL PARTIES

### A Functional Definition

Perhaps the simplest way to begin our examination of political parties in Canada is to look at their primary objective, which is, quite simply, to bring together likeminded people in an attempt to maximize their control and influence over the governmental process. A party, if it is in opposition, will seek to influence governmental policy decisions on an issue-by-issue basis, but the "jackpot" for a political party is to win enough seats in a general election to be able to form the government.[1]

---

1. For a classic comparative statement of party functions, see Anthony King, "Political Parties in Western Democracies: Some Skeptical Reflections," *Polity*, vol. 2, no. 2, 1969, pp. 111–41.

**"Proto-Parties"** Political parties evolved in the Westminster tradition as *ad hoc* coalitions of Parliamentarians who worked together in order to support or oppose specific legislative enactments or to maintain a majority in the House of Commons, thereby to control the government over some period of time. Initially such coalitions were extremely unstable, and the various factions in the legislature would shift kaleidoscopically from one coalition to another, sometimes giving the government a majority and other times combining to defeat it. Most importantly, these **proto-parties** were purely temporary accommodations worked out in the corridors and lobbies of the legislative chambers. The representatives did not seek election under a party banner; rather, they remained independent until after the election, when they would selectively enter into coalitions to secure maximum advantage personally and for their electors.

Modern political parties emerged only as the franchise was broadened and as the politicians gradually realized that it was possible not just to control or influence the government but to *be* the government if the electorate could be convinced to vote for a full slate of party candidates. Belatedly, the electors also came to realize that partisan elections ultimately gave them the power to elect or turf out not just individual MPs, but whole governments. As a result, while the ultimate goal of the political party was still to become the government, this could happen only if the party was first successful in the electoral process. Hence, whereas the *immediate* goal of political parties today is success in the electoral process, their ultimate goal is either to form the government or to have some control or influence over the governmental process.

**Parties and "Quasi-Parties"** Naturally, each party would prefer to win a sufficient number of seats to be able to form the government. However, there will be only *one* prime minister, and only one party will form the government. Hence, even parties that realize they do not have a very good chance of winning a majority of seats in the House of Commons may enter the election fray because, by having even a few of their candidates elected, they are given a podium from which to publicly criticize the government and to communicate to the Canadian people their party's policy preferences. As well, the second- and third-place parties usually hold on to the hope that, in the future, the political tide will turn in their favour, and that they may be looked upon as an alternative "government party."

Finally, as we noted in the previous chapter, there were fourteen registered parties in the 1993 general election, and only five or six of these had a chance of electing even a single candidate. This tells us that many of the organizations that enter the competition for elected office, and even become officially registered as parties under the *Canada Elections Act*, don't actually expect to get anybody elected. Instead, these organizations have opted to use the election campaign itself as a national soap box from which to publicize their doctrines and policy "wish lists." Because of the intensive media focus on the campaign, such fringe groups, or **quasi-parties** can attract media attention and perhaps, through the consequent public exposure, enhance the political legitimacy of their causes.

What distinguishes political parties, in the broadest sense of the term, from other organizations is that they sponsor candidates in the electoral process. When we speak of political parties in the context of the **party system**, however, we must narrow our focus to those few **true parties** that have a realistic chance of electing at least a few of their candidates. In this sense the *raison d'etre* or manifest function of political parties is to *get people elected* and not just to participate in the electoral contest. As by products of the effort to get people elected, political parties perform a number of other important functions for our political system, each of which bears elaboration.

### Parties and the Electoral Process

In Chapter 12 we discussed the functions of the electoral system. Most of those functions, while technically performed by the electoral system, are in fact performed largely by the political parties operating within the system. While it is true that independent candidates can and do get elected from time to time, it does not take a very sophisticated observer to conclude that 99 per cent of the electoral process happens through the machinery of party politics. Political parties recruit the gladiators who duel in the electoral arena, they mobilize and educate the voters, and, with a bit of help from the receiver-general, they finance the election campaign.

**The Staffing Function: Recruitment, Selection, and Training**  Political parties are the **recruitment** agencies that fill the political jobs of prime minister, Cabinet ministers, and members of Parliament. This process of recruitment involves not only the **selection of local candidates** for elected office through constituency nominating meetings, but also the **selection of party leaders** through the national conventions. Similarly, the **training** for a career in politics is often provided through party organizations at the constituency, provincial, and national levels.

Because parties are organizations themselves, they must also recruit people to fill positions in their various constituency, provincial, and national wings. The party organization must expand and contract like an accordion to match the ebb and flow of political activity. During an election, the organization must recruit and train, on the job, thousands of volunteers to do the many chores that have to be done during the campaign. Even between elections, when the party machinery goes into virtual hibernation, the constituency organizations must nurture the ember of partisan loyalty and enthusiasm so it can be fanned into life as the next election nears. This means holding periodic meetings of the local party membership and more frequent meetings of the party executive. At the national and provincial levels, the parties continue to be active in fundraising and in the organization of annual party conventions that serve to keep the rank and file interested and feeling (perhaps falsely) efficacious.

An important incidental by-product of this organizational activity is that many Canadians get a closer look at the political process and learn about how it operates. The experience may lead them personally to become more involved in Canadian political life and to convince others to become involved too. Unless there is a steady flow of young recruits into the party organizations, the partisan campaign in the constituency could be completely lost in the media circus of leadership debates and the national campaign. As well, without political involvement at the grassroots level, it would be more difficult to find people willing to take on even the small but important official positions in the process, such as scrutineers and enumerators.

**Mobilization of the Voters** At election time, and to a lesser extent between elections, political parties provide political stimuli to which people can respond: publicity for the issues around which political attitudes can be shaped, and symbols with which people can identify. It would be extremely difficult for average citizens to make voting decisions on the basis of independent personal knowledge of all the issues. They can, however, use parties as convenient surrogates to which they can attach their allegiance and with which they can simplify the complex realities of politics.

In this sense it can be said that Canadian political parties "organize" the election campaign so that the voters are better able to understand what it is about. Canadians are made aware that they are electing an MP and choosing a prime minister, all through making a single mark on a single ballot. The fact that we are electing a prime minister and a government by casting a ballot for a local candidate is driven home by explicitly linking the candidates in the constituency to the national parties. In turn, it is the function of the national partisan campaigns to tell us about the leaders and about the parties' positions on the issues.

Each party's national campaign must first of all get our attention. The campaign must therefore be designed first to attract a maximum of media attention and second to ensure that the media reportage portrays the party in a positive light. The national campaigns thus set the issue agenda for the election and thereby cue the media as to what they should be reporting to a, hopefully, rapt electorate. The old-fashioned tactics, such as door-to-door canvassing and defiling the landscape with lawn signs, posters, and billboard ads, are still used by the parties with uncertain effect. The parties persist in these kinds of activities "just in case" they might help and because all of the other parties are doing it too. As well, the publication and distribution of campaign literature — pamphlets, candidate profiles, and various elaborate and pretentious "bluebooks," redbooks," and "pucebooks" — are all aimed at educating us and influencing our voting choice. However, the ultimate outcome of a national election today is determined by and large by what we read in the papers, what we hear on the radio, and, most important by far, what we see on the television.

In recent elections, televised leadership debates have become the flagship media events of the campaign, and it is the political parties that organize and stage these with the eager collaboration of the television networks. As well, more traditional tactics of getting the attention of the media are carefully staged appearances of the leaders at partisan rallies as well as riskier media events such as **mainstreeting** — shaking hands, kissing babies, and mugging for the TV cameras — in key constituencies across the country. While the media are the information conduits through which we learn about the election, we must appreciate that it is the political parties collectively that provide the "stuff" that gets reported.

**Articulation and Aggregation of Interests**  Political parties in Canada attempt to mobilize electoral support through four types of electoral strategies. First, they may seek to define or articulate issues in such a way that they mobilize support by *differentiating* themselves from other parties, and their supporters from other voters. When they do so they are usually described as performing the function of **interest articulation**. A second strategy is to put together packages of positions, sometimes in the shape of formal electoral platforms, which, rather than seeking to maximize the differences among the voters, seek to maximize the common ground across the largest possible coalition of supporters. When parties do this they are usually described as performing the function of **interest aggregation**.

Third, parties may essentially avoid specific issues, concentrating instead on the record of the previous government. Naturally, the party currently in power will focus on the positive aspects of its record, while the opposition parties will zero in on its failings, emphasizing the unredressed grievances of the electorate. Finally, the parties may avoid or de-emphasize substantive debate over issues to focus instead on the party leaders. In this context, each party simply attempts to convince the voters that its leader is the better qualified to steer the ship of state.

A moment's consideration will lead to the conclusion that these four strategic styles are neither mutually exclusive nor exhaustive. Most party campaigns will employ a mix of strategies, and what differentiates the parties' campaign styles is often the relative emphasis on leadership, past performance, interest articulation, and interest aggregation. The two older parties, the Liberals and the Conservatives, concentrate more on aggregation and leadership. The NDP and, more recently, the Reform Party concentrate more on attempting to articulate the interests of the little guy against the dominant elites, although these two parties approach politics from radically different ideological positions. The *Bloc Québécois*, while attempting to aggregate the interests of all Québécois, and while effectively exploiting the charismatic appeal of its leader, Lucien Bouchard, is, in effect, a single-issue party, attempting to articulate what it sees as the interest of Quebec vis à vis the rest of Canada. We will deal with the differences among the political parties, and the manner in which they help to finance the electoral process, in more detail in Chapter 14.

**Parties and the Governmental Process**
We have seen how it is that political parties function to organize the electoral process in Canada. However, they also play an important role in the governmental process in the periods between elections. It is the political parties that organize the conduct of affairs within Parliament, both providing stability and predictability in our system of responsible government, and organizing and moderating government-opposition conflict in Parliament. While we will return to the discussion of the manner in which the government operates when

we consider the policy process in future chapters, at this juncture we must outline the basic governmental functions of political parties.

**Organizing the Government** Given that the manifest function of "true" parties as opposed to "quasi-parties" is to get people elected in order either to form or to influence the government, it is not surprising that the functioning of government once elected reflects the role of parties. In the first instance, in choosing party leaders and nominating candidates, the successful parties are also selecting the people who will become our governmental leaders in the ministry and occupy the seats in the House of Commons. The leaders of the party that forms the government become the leaders of the country, representing all Canadians both domestically and in the international community.

Because we have a system of government based on the constitutional principle of responsible government, governments fall if they lose the support of a majority in the House of Commons. It is the governing political party, through the instrument of **party discipline**, that allows the government to maintain the confidence of the House over time. This lends a predictability and a stability to our system of governance whereby the prime minister and the Cabinet can embark on comprehensive sets of policy initiatives rather than having to take their chances of surviving a vote of confidence with each piece of legislation they introduce.

**Organizing the Opposition** The converse of making stable government possible is making the opposition to government effective and meaningful; the structure and the process of opposition in the House of Commons is also reflective of the party system. While the rules of the House recognize that individual backbench MPs should have some right to participate, it is presumed that it is the *organized* opposition to the govenment of the day, provided by the non-government parties in the House, that really keeps the government honest. As a result, the conduct of oral question period, the rules regarding participation in debates on the throne speech and the budget speech, and the opportunities for introducing non-confidence motions are all built around the fact that it is the leaders of the opposition *parties* and their front-bench co-stars who will occupy centre stage during such events.

As evidence of this prima ballerina role for parties in Parliament, we can see that the business of the House is choreographed on a weekly basis by meetings among the party *house leaders* and *whips*. As we shall see in Chapter 19, these party officers cooperate to ensure that the business of the House is carried on in an expeditious fashion, permitting a balance between the desire of the government to get on with business, and the desire of the opposition parties to have sufficient time to debate the issues and criticize the government's legislative initiatives. In this way, the political parties perfom the very important function of structuring government-opposition conflict in the legislative process.

**Inter-Party Accommodation** The function of organizing and structuring the interparty conflicts in the House is more visible to Canadians because *conflict* is intrinsically interesting and therefore newsworthy. But, while the conflictual aspect of party relations in Parliament is more faithfully reported by the media, we must not overlook the fact that a lot of the work of Parliament is accomplished through interparty cooperation and accommodation. We have seen, for instance, how the parties manage the interparty conflict on the floor of the House of Commons through agreement among their respective house leaders.

However, this agreement as to how to disagree is taken a step further in the conduct of the committees of the House. Here the debates are less structured, less formal, and for the most part carried on without media scrutiny. The atmosphere generally tends to be amiable, and while the committees are structured to ensure the government still has a majority, the focus is on attempting to work together to improve on the legislation being considered in a non-partisan manner. Cooperation is easier because a bill has usually already been approved in principle by the full House at second reading before it goes to committee, where the emphasis is on the details.

In many parliamentary committees there is a still greater opportunity to build all-party agreement in that there is no requirement to *decide* anything. Rather, many committees are set up to conduct hearings, to study problem areas, and to come up with recommendations to the government, even before a bill is introduced formally. As the use of these pre-legislative, task-force-type committees has increased, so has intra-party cooperation and the likelihood of all-party consensus in the findings reported back to the House. The role of committees in the policy process will be discussed further in Chapter 19.

**Staffing Government**  A staffing function of parties in Canada, secondary to the role parties play in recruiting candidates, leaders, and political activists, is the selection and recruitment of people to fill appointed positions in the government. Although such **patronage** appointments are often vehemently criticized — usually by those out of office and therefore without access to them — Canadian parties do continue to recruit people for a large number of positions, ranging from minor electoral officers, such as enumerators, to the presidencies of crown corporations and superior court judges. As well, not only is the upper house of our Parliament, the Senate, staffed by patronage appointments by whoever happens to be prime minister when the vacancy occurs, but it also plays an active and partisan role in the legislative process.

While, as it should be, the power of the Senate is small by comparison to that of the elected House of Commons, if the opposition controls the Senate, it may use its majority there either to delay the passage of legislation or, at least, to attract media attention to its concerns. In the period since the 1993 election, the Conservative majority in the Senate has posed a somewhat more threatening spectre to the Liberal government, because for the Tories, having been reduced to two seats in the lower house, the Senate is the only game in town.

We will consider the issues surrounding patronage appointments when we discuss the public service, Parliament, and the judiciary in Part Five. It may, however, be at least suggested here that, for some types of public positions, it is as appropriate to base selection on party service as on other types of past experience. We shall see, too, that patronage in the past performed important functions in consolidating the party organizations themselves. Meanwhile, we should note that nothing is more certain in Canadian politics than that parties will decry patronage when out of office, and then enthusiastically make use of it when in.

**Municipal Party Politics**  The discussion of party functions up to this point has been primarily focused at the federal level, with passing reference to the provincial level, and with no mention of the realm of municipal politics. In 1969, the Liberals and the NDP did enter municipal politics in Toronto. However, the success of this foray of national parties into city politics was relatively limited, and both the Liberals and the NDP, after a fairly intensive effort in 1970, agreed to keep a low profile in 1972, and have abstained from conducting city-wide campaigns since then.[2] The same can be said with respect to the national parties in municipal elections in other Canadian cities.

Even the specifically *municipal* parties such as the Civic Party in Toronto, which had considerable success in 1970, disintegrated in 1972 when three of its leaders decided to run against each other for mayor. In Montreal, Mayor Jean Drapeau led a municipal political party of sorts, but it was really a personal machine rather than a real political party and did not survive his disappearance from the scene. Municipal politicians are very often known by their national or provincial party allegiances, and the people who knock on doors for them in municipal campaigns will often be predominantly from one or another political party. However, as far as overt electoral activity by political parties is concerned, there is very little of it at the municipal level in Canada.

### Linkage Functions

While they are closely related to the functions political parties perform for the governmental process, the **linkage** functions of parties are important enough to be given discrete consideration. Linkage functions provide channels for information flow between the state and society — between government and the people. On the one hand, the political parties are among the institutions that can articulate the wants and needs of people in society to the policy makers in government. On the other hand, political parties are also able to communicate information about government and its policies to Canadians outside government. While these two functions are closely interrelated, for greater clarity we will consider them separately.

**Information IN: Policy Functions**  We have seen that, in the electoral process, political parties set the issue agenda for the campaign and that they *do* take positions on issues and offer their policy proposals as solutions to Canada's various problems. However, parties as organisms seeking power and influence through being elected, transform into wholly different critters once in office. To retain credibility, the government party must deliver on a modicum of its campaign promises. However, once a party is elected, the task of governing

---

2.  Stephen Clarkson, "Barriers to the Entry of Parties in Toronto Area Politics," *in* L. Axworthy and James M. Gillies, eds., *The City: Canada's Prospects, Canada's Problems* (Toronto: Butterworths, 1973).

becomes far more focused on dealing with problems that pop up while in office and less on single-mindedly pursuing a policy blueprint (or Red Book in the case of the 1993 Liberals) created in the pre-election period. Governing, as we shall see in later chapters, is more about responding to new concerns than about keeping past promises.

A second problem is that it is easier to make extravagant promises on the hustings than it is to keep them when faced with the practical realities of cost, implementability, and the opposition of organized interests. Once in office, the prime minister and Cabinet have the benefit of the high-priced expert advice in the bureaucracy; they are faced with numerous interest groups and lobbyists who can marshall excellent evidence that what was promised is unwise practically and politically; and they are overwhelmed with a multitude of other, apparently more urgent, demands on their time. As a result, the parties in power are much more likely to be involved in affirming and giving effect to policy initiatives developed elsewhere, than in initiating policies themselves.

A third reason why the party platform is often left far behind once in office is that the political signposts are no longer to be found in the party. There was a time when the government of the day could consult its caucus about the relative political advisability of sundry policy options. The individual back-bench MPs would be in touch with influential party supporters and opinion leaders in the constituency and could, in fact, offer cogent advice as to whether the policy would "sell back home." Today, however, the party caucus has been supplanted by much more accurate measures of public opinion such as scientific public-opinion surveys. The polls have to a very large extent replaced the "pols" as a source of advice on what is politically sexy and what is not.

It is possible to be much more sanguine, however, when we consider the policy role of the political parties who are in opposition. Here, as in the election campaign, the party representatives in the House of Commons are not called upon to actually give effect to their policy preferences. In criticizing the government, it is not inconceivable that the wishes of the party rank and file might be reflected in the antigovernment positions taken by the opposition parties. Moreover, an opposition party does not have to compete with the bureaucracy for the attentions of its parliamentary wing. Rather, an opposition party often needs all the help it can get, and suggestions from the extra-parliamentary party are welcome.

To summarize, a number of reasons for the decline in the influence of parties in the policy process can be suggested. The increasing complexity of issues and the rise of the executive-bureaucratic state are interconnected, "chicken-and-egg" phenomena. However, regardless of which came first, increasing technical complexity does tend to make substantive policy issues extremely difficult to handle for organizations that are primarily electoral machines. The increasing role of interest groups and the increasingly symbiotic relationships between them and clientele-oriented departments that speak the same technical language, has also been significant in diminishing party influence. Nevertheless, despite the fact that this function of parties is somewhat attenuated, parties continue to operate at the boundary between society and government, and they continue to function as a conduit through which the concerns of individual electors can reach the policy machinery of government.

**Information OUT: Communications Functions** Canadian parties, like their counterparts throughout the world, keep in touch with their supporters between elections. Since issues are what politicians must ostensibly concentrate upon between elections, in their struggle to present themselves in the best possible light, much of the flow of information to Canadians is simply a by-product of the struggle for partisan advantage. Hence, the parliamentary wings of the parties maintain a steady flow of information to the public, all of which is coloured in a manner calculated to show themselves in a favourable light. This is done not so much as a public service as in the hope of increasing the levels of partisan support at the next election.

Clearly, the government parties have an edge in this respect, for they have at their disposal all of the departmental information services and communications units that are spread throughout the bureaucracy. While these agencies are expected to inform us objectively and dispassionately about government programs and policy initiatives, without the taint of partisan bias, the government party can't help but benefit from information touting the government's accomplishments. As well, the media-relations staff in ministers' offices and press secretariats in the central agencies are paid to operate in a frankly partisan fashion. The official press releases from ministers' offices and from the Prime Minister's Office, and the frequent ministerial press conferences, allow the government party to bask in the positive light of "official" government pronouncements that are, in fact, thinly veiled partisan horn-tooting. While the opposition parties do not have access to the bureacratic communications machinery, their leaders nevertheless have their own media-relations staff who attempt to counter the government party's effusion of self-congratulatory information with effusions of their own.

Most of the communications functions of political parties between elections are performed by parties that had at least some electoral success at previous elections. Moreover, it is the parliamentary branches of the parties rather than the extra-parliamentary organization that dominate the limelight between elections. The reason for this is that generating information is not in and of itself sufficient to communicate with the public, for there is no direct communications link between political parties and their target audiences. Rather, the parties must rely on the media to transmit the information they generate for the intended target groups. Because what will be reported by the media must be deemed by them to be newsworthy, the anonymous outputs of the extra-parliamentary branches of the parties, or the occasional whimperings from the fringe parties, simply don't get much media attention.

Some types of issues are much more suited to discussion in the media than others. While the print media can handle complex issues, television, the dominant medium of today, is far better suited to simple, or even simple-minded, treatment of issues or to human-interest stories about individual politicians, their spouses, children, or paramours. Thus, despite the efforts of the parties to paint themselves in a favourable light and to focus on substance, the media often fail to respond to the cues. The Mulroney years, which in this respect were not remarkable in our history, saw several Cabinet ministers forced to resign over "media-hyped" scandals.[3] The prime minister himself was pilloried for his wife's expensive tastes in carpeting (and recarpeting) 24 Sussex, and for the number of pairs of Gucci loafers alleged to be lurking in his own closet. The unfortunate fact is that tainted tuna, visits to foreign (or even domestic) strip joints, careless management of personal financial affairs, and immigration scandals play better on TV than free trade or tax reform, even though the latter have a great deal more to do with how well we are governed. This is a universal propensity in Western democracies, and accounts, in part, for the tendency of parties to concentrate on simple and even frivolous issues, and for their serious communications efforts to fall short much of the time.

Finally, some of the communications activity of political parties is designed to test their specific policy positions or to get a better picture of how the public feels about them in general terms. They disseminate information to the public in the form of "trial balloons" in order to generate feedback as to the effectiveness of their proposed policies and about the general political climate. A party in power must have accurate information in order to assess public attitudes to its record, and the opposition parties must know the public's perception of the relative weaknesses of government, and of themselves, in order to launch a credible campaign at the time of the next election. Like most of the functions described so far, this **feedback function** is not performed particularly well by Canada's parties, nor are they alone in performing it.

To conclude, the rise of the electronic media has pre-empted much of the direct political communication role of political parties. In so doing, it may have created a new partisan role that involves the recruitment of media stars, the casting and staging of media events (such as leadership conventions) to launch and lionize those stars, and the unending quest for scandal and dirt with which to discredit one's opponents. In a related vein, the rise of investigative journalism may have usurped some of the opposition parties' role in uncovering government improprieties and in scandal mongering, although it can be countered that there has been media muckraking and its more respectable euphemistic cousin, investigative journalism, as long as there has been journalism at all.

## Parties and Society: Systemic Functions

The functions performed by political parties in Canada all derive from their single-minded quest for partisan advantage in either forming the government or attempting to influence its decisions. We have seen that the electoral and governmental processes as we know them could not operate without the contribution of political parties. Similarly, in the course of pursuing their partisan self-interest, political parties in the aggregate, or the **party system,** incidentally perform important functions for the political system as a whole. These include political socialization and political education, the generation of support for our system of government, and the integration of our political community. Each of these must be dealt with in turn, keeping in mind that they are inter-

---

3. See Sharon Sutherland, "The Canadian Federal Goverment," *in* John Langford and Alan Tupper, eds., *Corruption, Character and Conduct* (Toronto: Oxford University Press, 1993), p. 113.

related functions and that they overlap significantly with the functions parties perform in the electoral and governmental processes.

**Political Socialization** Political education and socialization are functional spin-offs from a more elemental party function, that of mobilizing the mass electorate. By now, virtually all citizens of developed nations are accustomed to the universal franchise, and we therefore tend to forget what a massive effort it must have taken to bring into the mainstream of political life the millions of electors enfranchised during the latter half of the 19th century and the early years of the 20th. Political parties as we know them developed at that time, and their major early function was to bring the new voters into democratic political life, albeit on the side of the right set of partisan political leaders!

In the course of seeking to convince voters to vote for their candidates, political parties also teach us about politics and define the issue choices and leadership choices we must make at the polls. In this sense, the parties stimulate the development of a more aware and more responsible electorate by educating voters about the issues of the day and their relative significance. While the aim of the individual parties' campaign hyperbole is to create and nurture highly committed partisan voters, political parties as a collective contribute to an increased awareness and political sophistication among the citizenry as a whole. An aware and sophisticated *demos* is a necessary precondition for a healthy democracy, so by teaching about political issues, the party system further strengthens Canadian democracy.

Moreover, simply by involving us in the democratic process and by educating us about the relevant issues of the day, the parties are also teaching us about the democratic cornerstones of our political culture. They are telling us about the benefits of voting and the significance of the choices we are able to make because we are fortunate enough to live in a healthy democracy. In this sense the political parties are functioning as agents of political socialization, clarifying and reinforcing our commitment to the basic values inherent in our constitutional system.

**Legitimacy and Systemic Support** Citizen support for the Canadian system of government or for specific aspects of it is often stimulated by political parties. At the lowest level, this fostering of support can take the form of providing the opportunity for wider public involvement in the political process, through, for instance, working for a party or actively campaigning in an election. When people get involved in the process, it becomes their process, not something that is outside; thus the system becomes more legitimate to the citizenry.

It was suggested in the previous chapter that many Canadians participate in electoral politics primarily because they find it an interesting social activity. The parties provide much of the campaign pyrotechnics, which, around election time, attract attention to politics. A party attempts to create support for its candidates by selling people on its policies, its leaders, and, if it has one, its ideology. By creating support for itself, the party also incidentally creates support for the regime of which it is a part. This **diffuse support**, derived from general confidence and faith in the system, and simply from efficacious involvement in its processes, is important for the stability of the regime.

Diffuse or generalized support for the system can also be created directly through certain campaign tactics of the political parties. In the attempt to get their candidates elected, parties try to give themselves added legitimacy by identifying themselves with such values of the regime as justice, freedom, equality, opportunity, and democracy. As well, although it is more common in the United States, Canadian political leaders will sometimes "wrap themselves in the flag," attempting to identify their narrow partisan interests with the interests of the country as a whole. An important incidental effect of such tactics is to remind people that the Canadian system is a very good one and to create in them a basically supportive orientation towards it.

In other cases, however, support for a party may not be transferable to the system. Thus, support for the neo-Nazis is hardly an indication of support for our liberal democratic regime, and support for the *Parti Québécois* or the BQ, both of which seek to take Quebec out of the federation, can be interpreted as a lack of support for the Canadian political community. Paradoxically, even parties that would delegitimize the regime or the political community may be functional for the existing system in that they provide a legitimate and peaceful channel for the expression of dissent. Were this dissent to be expressed through rioting, bombing, and kidnapping, the effect would be devastating. Furthermore, by providing focal points for dissent, fringe parties like the Greens, the Abolitionists, and the Marxist-Leninists make us aware of the fact that certain segments of society have serious real or imagined grievances that must be dealt with, if not accommodated. Thus, oddly enough, even parties whose major goal is the overthrow of the existing political community may unintentionally perform useful functions for the system to which they are opposed.

**National Integration**  Undoubtedly the most significant systemic function of political parties is **national integration**. If parties seek to mobilize support by emphasizing or articulating interests, such as class, that cut across regional cleavages, then the threat of territorial divisiveness is likely to be reduced. Conversely, if parties seek to mobilize electoral support by emphasizing regional cleavages, territorial conflict will increase and class conflict will be reduced in importance.

The party may also simply ignore long-term societal cleavages, emphasizing instead leadership and leadership-style issues. This tactic is risky, for it might generate national integration or it might be extremely divisive, depending on what stance the leader adopts and on his or her personal appeal. However, if a party can succeed in aggregating a wide range of long-standing interests that cut across both regional and class cleavages, then not only will the electoral success of that party be enhanced, but overall national integration will be greatly strengthened as well.

In Canada, the potential for territorial integration inherent in the articulation of class as opposed to regional interests has never been realized. Some analysts would claim that the Canadian political culture has not yet attained a sufficient degree of "maturity" for this to happen, although most have given up waiting for that millenium. The fact remains that, while class-based politics might have served at one time to weaken regional loyalties, Canada has never had a significant level of class consciousness among its citizens. Hence, class-based appeals do not elect national governments, and, therefore, successful national parties have been those that ignored or downplayed class in their campaigns.

Some political scientists have suggested that, in the absence of class-based politics, political parties could still play a major role in fostering national integration if they were to succeed in aggregating the full range of non-class, non-regional interests sufficiently across all regions of the nation. Brian Mulroney's Conservatives came as close as any political party to achieving this from l984 to 1992. Unfortunately, due to a combination of the failure of the Meech Lake Accord and the widespread public dissatisfaction with Mulroney's leadership style, the wheels seem to have fallen off the Tory wagon.

**Brokerage Politics**  By accomplishing a multifaceted national accommodation, political parties would be heralded as the grand brokers and mediators of a fractious society, which otherwise is assumed to have a very great tendency to come apart at the seams. The suggestion that parties could, should, and frequently do try to play this role is referred to as the **brokerage theory** of Canadian politics.[4] The examination and re-examination of that theory, and the decrying of the frequent failure of Canadian parties to build a unified Canada, have been dominant themes in the academic analysis of the Canadian party system. The characteristics of brokerage and non-brokerage systems are summarized in Table 13.1.

**TABLE 13.1**
Characteristics of Brokerage and Non-Brokerage Party Systems

| Non-Brokerage Systems | Brokerage Systems |
| --- | --- |
| • Electoral coalitions that are recreated each election | • Well-defined, stable electoral support |
| • Competition for same policy space and voters | • Clear policy differences reflected in electoral support |
| • Parties that multiply cleavages but minimize effects of each | • Parties that seek to minimize number of cleavages while maximizing political effects of them |
| • Appeals to many narrow interests based on short-term views of specific issues | • Appeals to "world views" |
| • Lack of consistency in policies caused by search for electorally successful positions | • Fairly consistent follow-through on policies adopted in the past |
| • Organization based on leaders | • Organization based on principles and ideologies |

Source:  Adapted from Harold Clarke, Jane Jenson, Lawrence Leduc, and Jon Pammett, *Absent Mandate* (Toronto: Gage Publishing, 1984), p. 10.

4.  The original expressions of this "broker-mediator" function are found in H. Clokie, *Canadian Government and Politics* (Toronto: Longmans Green, 1944), pp. 81–83.

The consensus of Canadian political scientists is that our political parties have generally tried to operate on brokerage principles, and while these efforts have often translated into electoral success, they have not functioned to secure national integration. This putative failure is often held to account for the elusiveness of national unity in Canada. This failure of brokerage politics has occurred either because the parties have failed as brokers or because, even when they have succeeded in accommodating a wide range of interests, the consensus that they built was based on resolving the wrong political conflicts; that is, the successful political parties have consistently failed to accommodate *regional* interests in their electoral coalitions. While national unity can survive a certain amount of class cleavage or ethnic cleavage, cleavages based on geography are more difficult to accommodate, especially when they coincide with economic or ethnic divisions, as they do in Quebec.

Part of the reason for the persistence of regional cleavages is that the drastic option of physical separation or secession of the dissident region is always visible as an obvious ultimate solution to the conflict. The fact remains that however severe class conflict or racial strife may be, unless the dissident classes or races are neatly concentrated in one geographical "container," secession is not a viable solution. However, in Canada, regional cleavages do coincide, to some extent, with other lines of cleavage. Quebec is the most obvious example of this phenomenon, but western Canada is a region that can also be differentiated from the rest of Canada by more than simply geographical factors. The West has always had a different kind of economic system, which suffers from the exploitative relationship with central Canada. Even the most successful brokerage parties cannot be expected to provide political integration in a nation that has major territorial cleavages, provincial governments that reinforce those territorial cleavages, and an electoral system that rewards regional voting patterns with electoral success.

In sum, while brokerage politics has proven a good way for a political party to achieve electoral success at the national level, it has not gone the extra mile in securing a unified Canada. The reasons are, as we have seen, the absence of class politics, the single-member plurality system, and a very decentralized federal system. As well, as we shall see in the next section, the structure of the national political parties is highly decentralized. On the one hand, this can enhance regional loyalties at the grassroots level. On the other hand, the local party apparatus tends to disappear between elections, and the party leadership in Parliament, having little direct input from the regions, tends to ignore them in favour of an excessively centralist perspective on policy issues.

**Conclusion: Party Functions**

While the many functions of parties or party systems are clearly important in Canada as well as in other Western democracies, we must remind ourselves that most important functions are shared and carried out simultaneously by various other structures in the system such as the bureaucracy or interest groups. Indeed, it is important to make this point because there is a tendency among those who study political parties to assume that if the parties do not adequately perform some important systemic function, the whole system must be at risk.

While parties are important, and Canadian democracy would be very different without them, they need not flawlessly perform every function ascribed to them for democratic government to survive and prosper.[5] Indeed, as we have pointed out, with a few minor exceptions, democracy thrives without political parties at the municipal level in Canada (sometimes in governments much larger than provincial governments). As well, both the electoral process and the governmental process in the Northwest Territories operate quite effectively on a consensus-based rather than a party-based model.

## ▶ CANADIAN PARTY STRUCTURES

In the next chapters, we will look at the origins of political parties and how they have evolved to the present time. We will look at the electoral performance of parties historically and provide a snapshot of the party system in the mid-1990s. As well, we will look in more detail at the party roles in the processes of candidate nomination, election campaigning, and election finance. However, before moving to that set of discussions we must look at the structure of the party system and at individual party organizations.

### Party Systems

While so far we have considered the functions performed for the political system by the individual parties, we must recognize that the parties operate in opposition to one another. The interests articulated and aggregated successfully by one party place practical limits on the amount of room left over for the other parties to occupy. By capturing and occupying different segments of the total territory of political discourse the parties profoundly affect each others' strategies and tactics in the battle for electoral victory. Because our political parties must constantly react to each other, we often speak of a **party system** within which interparty *interaction* occurs. This interaction among the parties may well be as important to the Canadian political process as the independent behaviour of the individual party organizations.

**Functions of Party Systems**  Perhaps the most obvious effect of our party system is that, because several parties are competing for political office at election time, the voters are presented with a real *choice*. It matters little whether that choice is made according to perceived differences in the parties' ideologies, leadership, policies, or campaign style, as long as the voter is indeed given choice, for this is of the essence of a true democratic system.

A second result of interparty competition is that, through this mechanism, our political leaders can be held accountable. We can vote to "throw the rascals out" because there are clear lines, drawn by the party system, between rascals and non-rascals. As we shall see when we discuss the governmental process in

5. Paul G. Thomas, "The Role of National Party Caucuses," *in* Peter Aucoin, ed., *Party Government and Regional Representation* (Ottawa: Royal Commission on the Economic Union and Development Prospects for Canada, Research Volume 36, 1985) points out that Canadian parties have been particularly weak at integration of the political system, the aggregation of interests, and the making of public policy.

Part Five, while this accountability is of a very general nature, it remains a *sine qua non* to the workings of the Canadian democratic system. The voters are thus able to express dissatisfaction with the performance of one party's team, secure in the knowledge that another team is sitting on the bench, eagerly waiting to be put into the game.

A further critical function of the party system is to provide the electorate with a definition of what politics is all about. The party system helps to set the agenda for political discourse, for, as Janine Brodie and Jane Jenson state, the party system

> shapes the interpretation of what aspects of politics should be considered political, how politics should be conducted, what the boundaries of political discussion most properly may be and what kinds of conflicts can be resolved through the political process.[6]

Brodie and Jenson argue critically that it is through this process of defining "the political" that the Canadian party system has given us an agenda for political discourse that focuses on regionalism and ethnicity rather than on class. One result, as we saw in the previous section, may be the frailty of the bonds of national unity in Canada.

**Types of Party Systems**  One of the favourite exercises of political scientists has been the attempt to characterize and differentiate among the party systems of various nations. The most widely accepted, if not particularly imaginative, taxonomy has been based on the number of parties participating in the electoral process. At the most simplistic level of comparison, party systems can be classified as **one-party**, **two-party**, or **multiparty**. The Peoples' Republic of China, Cuba, and Franco's Spain could all be described as one-party systems; the United States and most of the Scandinavian countries are essentially two-party systems; and France, Italy, and Israel are multiparty systems.

Unfortunately, this system of classification doesn't help us very much in differentiating among political systems around the world. The one-party systems are not "systems" at all because only one party is permitted to exist and the so-called two-party systems such as the United States sometimes have third parties competing. Hence, a second criterion, that of the relative *competitiveness* of the party systems, is usually applied to complement the simple numerical classification. According to this system of classification, party systems are grouped according to how many of the parties in the system have a realistic chance of winning power. Mexico has a number of political parties but because only one of them, the PRI, has any chance of success, the system is usually dubbed **one-party dominant.** Britain can be classified as essentially a two-party system because although four or five parties may elect some MPs, only the Conservatives and Labour have any realistic chance of forming the government. True multiparty systems exist in France and Italy, where no single party ever elects a majority, and where forming a government requires forging a coalition among two or more parties.

6.  Janine Brodie and Jane Jenson, *Crisis, Challenge and Change: Class and Party in Canada* (Toronto: Methuen, 1980), p. 67.

However, to be able to understand how Canada's party system compares with systems elsewhere, we have to plug in yet one more criterion. Because Canada is a federal system, with elections happening at two levels of government, it is difficult to compare us directly with unitary systems such as Britain. However, even to compare us with other *federal* systems, such as the United States and Australia, the extent of the *integration vs. regionalization* of the parties must be taken into account. In the US, and to a large extent in Australia, the same political parties compete at both levels, and the party organizations are integrated. By contrast, Canada's parties are usually completely different organizations provincially and federally, with very loose ties, if any.

One reason for the regionalization of our party system is that, unlike state and federal elections, which occur simultaneously in the US, our federal and provincial elections never occur at the same time. If we were electing both national and provincial governments in a single election, there might be some incentive to "piggyback" the two campaigns, given that it is the same electorate that has to make both decisions. Another reason that the federal and provincial party systems are separate is that electoral success for a provincial party may be based on the campaign strategy of "fed-bashing," even if the party in power in Ottawa bears the same name. The provincial parties want to be free to criticize the federal government and not to feel bound by partisan loyalties. Finally, it may be that the regional diversity of Canada and the decentralized nature of our federal system make it impossible for parties at the two levels to find any common policy ground from which to operate in the first place.

In the light of the above considerations and criteria we can conclude that, at the national level, Canada basically has a two-party system. However, we must qualify this by recognizing that since the 1921 election, there have always been third parties seeking to elect MPs, albeit with little hope of forming the government. The CCF and its offspring, the NDP, has been a persistent and prominent competitor since 1940, but has never come close to forming a government at the national level. Moreover, for much our history, one or the other of the two major parties has dominated: the Tories from 1867 to 1896 and 1984 to 1993, and the Liberals from 1896 to 1911 and 1935 to 1984.

As well, we must conclude that our political parties are so regionalized that there are effectively separate party systems at the federal level and in the provinces. While the two-party systems in the Atlantic provinces look a lot like the national party system, the provincial party organizations are completely autonomous entities. Moreover, as we move westward, we find that the provincial party systems bear less and less resemblance to the federal party system, often featuring governments formed by parties that are either non-existent or totally uncompetitive at the national level. Finally, many of the provincial party systems have functioned as sequential one-party dominant systems, in which election outcomes are seldom in doubt and there is almost no opposition representation in the legislature. We will say more about this phenomenon in Chapter 14.

### Parties as Organizations

Before looking at the way in which Canadian political parties are organized internally, it is useful to look at the manner in which party organizations are classified comparatively. These typologies are based upon three main criteria: the locus of power within the party organization, the extent of centralization-decentralization, and the substantive style of the party's campaign strategy.

**Mass and Cadre Parties** The most durable typology of party structures is the one first suggested by the French political scientist Maurice Duverger. He suggested that political parties could be broadly typified as being **mass parties** or **cadre parties**.[7] Mass parties are characterized by extra-parliamentary origins and by the fact that the grassroots support of the organization has a significant degree of control over the legislative branch in policy determination. The British Labour Party, continental social democratic parties, and, perhaps, the NDP or the Reform Party in Canada are occasionally adduced as examples of mass parties. The Progressives, the early CCF, and the Social Credit in Alberta are other Canadian examples of grassroots political movements that transformed themselves into electoral machines.

However, an important qualification must be entered. Roberto Michels, writing early in the 20th century, noticed that the social democratic parties in Europe showed a discouraging tendency to be controlled by small cliques within either the legislature or the party executive.[8] His "iron law of oligarchy" posits that large organizations — no matter how democratic their origins and ideology — will end up being controlled by a relatively small group of people at the top. This will limit the extent to which any political party can be controlled by its mass membership. At a certain point, the requirements of efficiency appear to override the requirements of democracy. This malady has afflicted all of Canada's mass parties, and whenever mass parties have formed a provincial government, the iron law becomes tempered steel.

Cadre parties are different from mass parties because they usually originate as coalitions of factions within legislatures that subsequently become electoral machines. The grassroots support of the cadre party is recruited into the organization to support the party elite's efforts to get elected. Thus, in a cadre party, a relatively small group of parliamentary elites, or a "cadre," dominates the party. Both the Liberal and the Conservative parties are of this type, and even the NDP has come to function primarily as a cadre party. Certainly, NDP *governments* in the provinces have, without exception, transformed their extra-parliamentary organizations into powerless fan clubs for the elected front benchers.

---

7. M. Duverger, *Political Parties* (New York: John Wiley and Son, 1963), first published in 1951. Frederick Engleman and Mildred Schwartz have modified this typology to fit Canada in *Political Parties and the Canadian Social Structure*, 2nd ed. (Toronto: Prentice-Hall, 1975). Note that Duverger cites a third category of party, the *militia party*. These are parties that have a tightly organized central core with highly dedicated supporters. In mass and cadre parties, the party is a relatively minor part of the life of most members, but in a militia party the party is virtually everything. The militia party is essentially an organizational weapon to be used to overthrow an existing political system or to maintain a totalitarian one. The Canadian Communist Party would like to be a militia party, but is too weak to be properly categorized as such. The *Front de libération du Québec* is the closest thing to a recent Canadian example, although it never took the step of running candidates in elections and so cannot be called a "party" at all. The Communist Party of the Soviet Union and the Chinese Communist Party have been the classic examples of militia parties.
8. Roberto Michels, *Political Parties* (Glencoe: Free Press, 1949).

**Hierarchy and Stratarchy**  Within cadre parties, a further structural differentiation can be suggested. A cadre party may take the form of a hierarchy, a
stratarchy, an alliance of sub-coalitions, or a combination of these.[9] A *hierarchical* structure is pyramidal, with a single leader at the top and a chain of
command running through successive levels to the bottom, as in a traditionally
organized bureaucracy. While within the national headquarters of Canadian
cadre parties, for instance, there is a hierarchical chain of command, the rest
of the organization may be more diffuse. The lines of communication and
control between and among the parliamentary leaders, the caucus, the national
headquarters, provincial organizations, and constituency associations are generally very weak. Moreover, while the party elites can dominate the party's
decision-making machinery in blithe ignorance of the wishes of the extra-
parliamentary organization, not to mention the rank-and-file membership, the
leaders have virtually no direct control over party members either. As a result,
the grassroots followers may make statements and act in ways that are not at
all in line with what the party elites might like.

As a reflection of this, it has been suggested that large political parties,
such as the Liberals and Conservatives, are better described as **stratarchies**.[10]
A stratarchy is basically an organization that, on the surface, appears to be
hierarchical, but in which the lines of vertical authority between levels are
rather weak. In Canada, the local elites within the constituency association
executive often have only the faintest idea of what the national party is doing,
and even when they do know, they may deliberately espouse positions that run
counter to national or provincial party policy. More important, the provincial
organizations of Canadian parties operate virtually autonomously and certainly
are in no way subordinate to the national organizations or to the parliamentary
wing in Ottawa, as might be expected in a classical hierarchical structure.

**Party Style: Brokerage, Doctrinaire, Single Issue**  Canadian parties can also be
categorized in terms of the substantive content of their pitch to the electors.
According to this method of categorization, most political parties in Canada
can be classified as **brokerage** parties. They seek to maximize their electoral
support by taking a pragmatic, middle-of-the-road position, avoiding deeply
divisive issues and emphasizing policy positions that are attractive or at least
acceptable to a wide segment of the electorate. At any given election the
brokerage parties may complement their brokerage approach by taking a firm
stand on a few important issues such as free trade, but the specific issue stance
is constructed on the foundation of a platform that is still resolutely middle of
the road.

The principal way for the voter to differentiate over time between the
classic brokerage parties — the Conservatives and the Liberals — is according
to the different styles or images of the party leaders or by divining subtle
differences in the shades of emphasis in their platforms. The 1993 election,
for instance, was partly about leadership, but the campaign demonstrated that

---

9.  See S. Eldersveld, *Political Parties* (Chicago: Rand McNally, 1964), pp. 47–178, where this classification was first suggested.
10.  Eldersveld, *Political Parties*, pp. 98–117.

while both parties wished to reduce the deficit and create jobs, the Liberals were identified as placing a slightly higher priority on the latter. As the Conservatives discovered to their dismay, the electorate was obviously more concerned with job creation than with deficit reduction.

The obverse of the brokerage party is the **doctrinaire party**, which is based on fairly strict adherence to a consistent body of principles, or an ideology. Here, a party such as the NDP (and its predecessor, the CCF) has consistently based its substantive pitch to the electors on the principles of social democracy. However, the NDP is best described as "flexibly doctrinaire" rather than "rigidly doctrinaire" because its leaders have been forced to broaden their appeal in order to succeed at the polls. In forming governments at the provincial level and in seeking to challenge the Liberal and Conservative domination of the federal Parliament, the NDP has been forced to compromise its strict adherence to social democracy and to become simply a left-leaning brokerage party.

Finally, there are parties that can only be described as **single-issue parties** because they forgo the quest for broad-based electoral support in order to articulate a position on a single issue. While most single-issue parties are unsuccessful in Canada, with, for instance, the Green Party and the Prohibition Party never coming close to electing even a single MP, the *Bloc Québécois* did elect a majority of the seats in Quebec in the 1993 federal election by running on the single issue of Quebec sovereignty.

**Alliances of Sub-Coalitions** Specific issues aside, political parties in Canada may also tend to build stable bases of support over time among a range of interests or groups in society.[11] While this phenomenon is a necessary concomitant of the brokerage approach, it has long-term effects on the party organizations, particularly at the regional and constituency levels. The party structure becomes an **alliance of sub-coalitions**, binding together a miscellany of groups and interests, each fairly cohesive in itself and bound loosely to the other sub-coalitions in the party organization. Individuals are loyal to the party only indirectly, by virtue of their attachment to a sub-coalition that has linked its fortune to the party.

This structural variant of the brokerage party is most visible in the large urban constituencies where the local association is a melange of ethnic and religious groups, unions, trade associations, and community organizations initially coming together in an attempt to maximize their political influence. In some local organizations of the NDP, for instance, union locals and labour councils may be allied with community associations and women's groups, and the Liberal Party is known for building local coalitions among new Canadians and ethnic communities in its urban constituencies. The Reform Party has recently built its base of support on a populist coalition of small-town, small-"c" conservative interests, fundamentalist Protestant religious groups, and far-right fringe groups that are variously anti-immigrant, anti-French, anti-aboriginal, and even white supremacist in their beliefs.

Finally, in order to build coalitions and act as brokers or aggregators of interests, party organizations must be *open*. A party, to be successful, must be

11. Ibid., pp. 73–97.

extremely flexible with respect to membership. The openness allows the party to expand to take in new sub-coalitions, for instance, newly arrived immigrant groups. The down side of organizational openness can be seen in the growing pains of the Reform Party. While Preston Manning may take right-of-centre positions on most issues, he has clearly been embarrassed from time to time by the intemperate statements of some of his candidates and caucus members. Hence, we have seen the Reform Party attempting to purge itself of its more extremist right-wing elements and reaching out even to French Canada in an attempt to build a broader base of support and legitimacy that might make the party viable as an alternative government party.

The openness of the party organizations also permits them to be used as an avenue of upward mobility and social integration for their members. Ever since the original development of the major parties in Canada, at a time of rapid growth of the electorate, through both an expanding franchise and successive waves of immigration, all Canadian parties have from time to time performed this function. The increasing number of Liberal, NDP, and Conservative candidates who come from non-charter ethnic groups provides persuasive evidence of the effectiveness of party organizations as instruments of upward mobility.

## Internal Party Structures

While the typologies and categorizations discussed above may help us to differentiate among party structures as a whole, they do not provide a full inside picture of how Canada's main political parties are actually organized. There are many similarities and there are some noticeable differences among the organizations. Party constitutions and the formal organization charts don't tell the whole story.

**Constituency Associations**  The basic organizational unit of the political party is the constituency or riding association. The association is made up of the members of the party in the constituency but the active part of the local party organization is the *riding executive*, which is elected by the membership. In Canada there are separate constituency associations for the federal and provincial wings of the party. One structural explanation for this is that the federal and provincial constituencies boundaries do not coincide. However, because of the relatively weak links between the federal and provincial parties at all levels, the differentiation would likely persist even if the riding boundaries were the same.

As we have already mentioned, at all levels below national or provincial offices, the party structures virtually cease to exist between elections. The local strategists and election workers retire to their rotary clubs, community associations, union halls, or skidoo clubs. Except for the local MP and his or her staff, and a few political junkies on the riding executive, the party disappears at the local level until the next election looms on the horizon. At that time, the party again expands to take on campaign workers, volunteers, and various party activists, fundraisers, and strategists.

**Figure 13.1**

Schematic organization chart, Progressive Conservative Party of Canada
(1989 constitution).

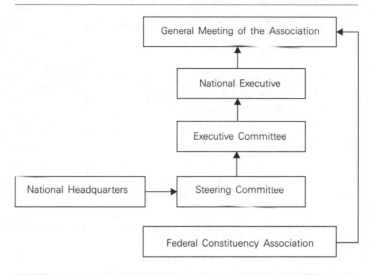

Source: Royal Commission on Electoral Reform and Party Financing,
Research Studies, vol. 13 (Toronto: Dundurn Press, 1991).

**Figure 13.2**

Schematic organization chart, New Democratic Party of Canada (1989 constitution).

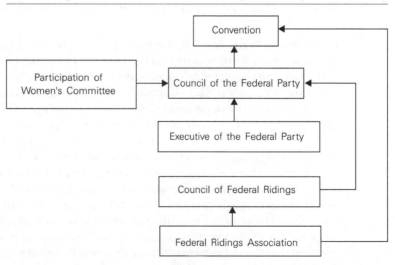

Source: Royal Commission on Electoral Reform and Party Financing, Research
Studies, vol. 13 (Toronto: Dundurn Press, 1991).

**Figure 13.3**

Schematic organization chart, Liberal Party of Canada (1990 constitution).

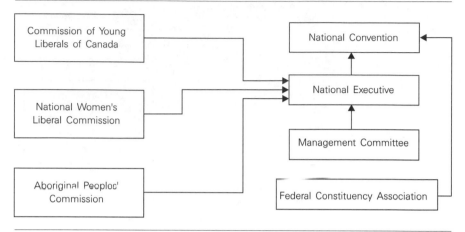

Source: Royal Commission on Electoral Reform and Party Financing, Research Studies, vol. 13 (Toronto: Dundurn Press, 1991).

The lines of communication between the national or provincial offices and the constituency associations are surprisingly weak. The problem derives partly from the lack of work to do in a party organization between elections, but what is more surprising is that these lines of communication do not always become strong even during election campaigns. The torrent of directives, literature, and local campaign kits that flows from provincial or national headquarters at election time is sometimes totally ignored by the local candidates and strategists, who feel that focusing on local issues, on which they are better informed than the national party gurus, gives them a better chance of winning the seat.

**The National Party** Even at the level of the national party organization, the pace and intensity of activity and the number of people directly involved ebbs and flows with the electoral cycle. Between elections, only the *national executive*, a few party bag men who continue to solicit financial donations from party supporters, and the permanent staff of the *national office* and the *caucus research office* are active. The party, in the interelection period, is dominated by the parliamentary caucus and the office of the leader. The same is true of the provincial organizations between provincial elections.

Hence, while the national and provincial executives and the headquarters staff continue to function between elections, the lines of communication between the extra-parliamentary wing and the parliamentary wing are often inoperative. The national executive meets at least annually, and, while MPs are often on the executive, the caucus and the parliamentary leadership take the position that the national executive exists only to administer the party electoral machinery and not to meddle in party policy. Indeed, members of legislatures are the most visible part of the party between elections, and what they say and do is what the media report and what the public picks up about the party.

**Figure 13.4**
Schematic organization chart, Reform Party of Canada.

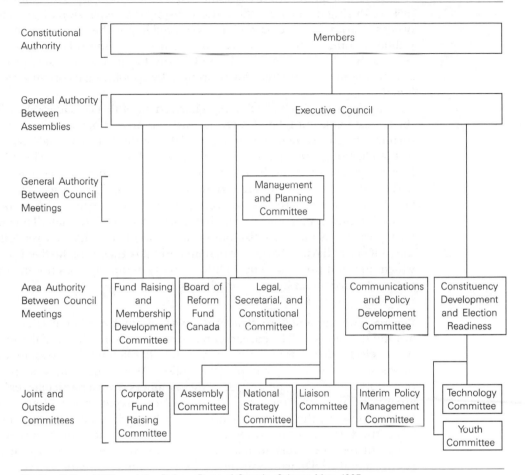

Source: National Office of the Reform Party of Canada, Calgary, May, 1995.

The extra-parliamentary party executives are thus virtually automatically relegated to a minor role in party policy making. Moreover, perhaps ironically, the extra-parliamentary wing of the party is far less active and less influential in intra-party affairs if the party *wins* the election. A party leader who becomes prime minister unfortunately has more to think about than the concerns and interests of the organization that helped get him or her the job, on top of which there is a lot of high-quality, non-partisan policy advice generated by the bureaucracy. Thus, despite the fact that winning the election may constitute a mixed blessing for party activists, they still loyally beaver on, never considering throwing an election just to stay relevant!

Attached to the executive of most provincial and national parties is a permanent party office under the direction of an executive director. Until the mid 1970s, a typical national party office might contain, between elections, a chief party organizer, an executive secretary for the party, two or three party researchers or administrative assistants, a public-relations person, and a typist or two. During the eighties there was considerable expansion of the national offices of both the Liberals and the NDP, made possible in part by the direct public funding of the caucus research offices and the offices of the party leaders. In addition, the party in power, the Progressive Conservatives, was able to augment its organizational strength by appointing its organizers to the Senate.

However, the 1993 election has changed all of this considerably. Clearly, the almost bankrupt Liberal Party has vastly improved prospects as a result of forming the government, but both the NDP and the Tories, virtually wiped out in the election, have had to drastically cut back on their staff. The NDP, although it won more seats than the Conservatives, is particularly hard up, having had to lay off most of its staff and even to sell its national office. The Tories are able to maintain a reduced presence, in part because they still have personnel and resources that flow from their majority status in the Senate. The Reform Party, which has made a fetish out of appearing frugal, has not yet followed the practice of having a large permanent national office, and the *Bloc Québécois*, which does not pretend to be a national party, naturally does not maintain a national office—at least not a Canadian national office.

**Caucus**  The parliamentary structure of virtually all Canadian parties revolves around the **caucus**.[12] The parliamentary caucus is essentially a regular meeting of the elected legislators of the party. While Parliament is in session, caucus meets at least once a week in plenary session. As well, there may be meetings of regional caucuses consisting of all the members from a particular region. In an opposition party, caucus meetings can often be quite lively. Almost all MPs feel free to have their say; consequently, policy debates can become heated. Since the 1993 election, however, the Tory caucus, with only two members, does not require a very formal or complex structure (nor a large meeting room), and the NDP with only nine MPs is in a similar situation.

The Reform Party came to power taking the populist position that the constituency organizations and the rank-and-file members of the party should prevail over the caucus. The individual Reform MPs were expected to take their instructions from their constituents; hence, the parliamentary party could operate in an *ad hoc* manner, without any need for a highly structured caucus. However, in the first six months, the Reform Party performed extremely ineffectually in Parliament, and thereafter took steps to organize its parliamentary wing. For each of the government portfolios, the party has now designated specific MPs as party critics who collectively operate as a sort of shadow cabinet much in the style of traditional opposition parties.

In the caucus of a governing party, the situation is different. There are clearly recognized party leaders — the prime minister and the Cabinet — and party backbenchers must support the policies put forward by the leaders. The

12. There is a thorough and excellent discussion of the structures and role of the parliamentary caucus in Paul G. Thomas, "The Role of National Party Caucuses," *in* Aucoin, *Party Government and Regional Representation.* We also consider the role of caucus in Chapter 19.

Cabinet has access to considerable expertise from the public service and from its political technocrats in the Prime Minister's Office, and it is often more inclined to listen to them than to its own non-expert backbenchers on matters of policy.

This is not to say that the government caucus has no influence on priority determination or policy formulation. Backbench government MPs take their representational roles seriously, and while they virtually always will support their leaders in public, they may well disagree with them in caucus, particularly on issues that deeply affect their regions. They may, in particular, be able to influence the priority ordering that Cabinet assigns to issues, and they may even on occasion succeed in convincing the government to withdraw proposed legislation they consider politically unwise. Minimally, they may convince the Cabinet to make minor amendments to bring policy enactments more in line with what they believe to be acceptable to the average voter in Wawa, Antigonish, Trois-Rivières, or metropolitan Vancouver.

**The National Convention**  The national convention or, in the case of the Tories, the "general meeting," is made up of delegates named by the constituency organization, all MPs, party officials, and, in the case of some parties, representatives of the provincial wing of the party. It is generally held biennially to discuss policy matters. As well, the party convention may be convened for special purposes such as the selection of a new leader. The rules on delegate selection vary from party to party and even from constituency to constituency within the parties.

The general picture of Canadian political parties (see Figs. 13.2–13.5) places the **convention** near the top of the party structure, but in reality it is rather difficult to fit into the picture. Until the 1960s, conventions were not a regular feature of Canadian politics. In the two older parties they were held whenever there was a need to elect a new leader, and only sporadically at other times. Currently, the Liberals, the Conservatives, and the New Democrats are all committed to holding a mass gathering of the party faithful every two years. The Reform Party, in keeping with its populist principles, holds national meetings more frequently. As might be expected in organizations as heavily dependent for electoral success on their leaders as Canadian parties, the real nature of the party convention will depend on its leadership-related activities. There is an automatic leadership review at each NDP convention, whereas the Liberals and Conservatives hold a leadership review once between elections. The leadership review, effectively a vote of confidence in the party leader, is accomplished by a vote on whether a **leadership convention** should be held.

For all three parties, the routine policy convention performs similar functions, related more to improving levels of participation, maintaining group solidarity, and garnering free publicity via press and television coverage than to the establishment of party policy. The national NDP convention has considerably more influence over party policy than the Liberal and Conservative counterparts, although it is not as likely to have to deliver on its convention statements because it has never formed a government nationally. Similarly, the Reform Party is committed to acting on the policy recommendations of its extra-parliamentary organization, but it is too soon to assess how well the Reform MPs live up to this noble principle.

The *Bloc Québécois*, being closely tied in with the provincial *Parti Québécois* organization, has not organized itself as formally as the other parties operating on the federal level. Because its goal is to render itself irrelevant at the national level, by securing the separation of Quebec, there is no need for national conventions, and the party operates, in the purest sense, as a cadre party in the federal party system. We will say more about this in the next section.

**Federal and Provincial Organizations** Perhaps one of the most curious features of Canadian political parties is the general absence of formal ties between federal and provincial party organizations. Federal and provincial leaders frequently disagree, or simply fail to communicate. The national and provincial executives and offices are often formally unconnected, and the national and provincial conventions, except for having some members in common, are also separate and independent entities. Since the major Canadian national parties are, in effect, loose *confederations* of provincial units, the provincial organizations may at times dominate the national organizations, particularly when the national party is out of power.[13]

Since there are only a limited number of local strategists and activists available, there is some overlap between federal and provincial memberships at the constituency level, and coordination of sorts may be achieved in that way. For the NDP, membership in either a provincial or a federal association automatically grants membership in the other organization. At the very bottom of the hierarchy of participation, the voters, there may again be considerable differentiation between federal and provincial parties, for Canadian voters frequently vote for different parties at the federal and provincial levels. Approximately one-third of Canadian voters show different long-term partisan loyalties at the federal and provincial levels of government.[14]

The structural differentiation between federal and provincial parties has stubbornly resisted sporadic efforts by federal-level parties to change it. Attempts to impose federal control over provincial parties inevitably cause a furor in the provincial organization, with the result that the federal party must either retreat or watch the provincial party sever its ties with the national party. Thus, Canadian federalism is extremely decentralized and the party system reflects the same tendencies.

The most extreme examples of the independence of provincial parties are in Quebec. Here, the federal and provincial Liberal Party organizations are completely separate. There is no provincial Conservative Party in Quebec, and the Quebec NDP has split from the national party, and functions as a left-of-centre fringe separatist party in provincial elections. The Reform Party is at-

---

13. See Joseph Wearing, *The L-Shaped Party: The Liberal Party of Canada 1958–1980* (Toronto: McGraw-Hill Ryerson, 1981).

14. Harold Clarke, Jane Jenson, Larry Leduc, and Jon Pammett, *Political Choice in Canada* (Toronto: McGraw-Hill Ryerson, 1980), p. 141, indicates that only 44 per cent of Canadians studied in 1974 showed consistent patterns of identification (in both direction and intensity) across the two levels of government. For more recent data, see H. D. Clarke, J. Jenson, L. Leduc, and J. Pammett, *Absent Mandate* (Toronto: Gage, 1984). Consistency did not increase between the 1974 and the 1980 elections.

tempting to set up a Quebec wing of the federal party, but it is unlikely that it will garner much support in the province. The aberrant case in Quebec is the *Bloc Québécois*, which has no permanent constituency organizations of its own in the province, and instead relies on close cooperation with the *Party Québécois* machine to fight its constituency campaigns.

### Conclusion: Party Structure

Whatever organizational chart we use to describe their structure, we must remember that political parties, perhaps even more than most human organizations, operate on networks, contacts, friendships, enmities, and personal judgements about people. Canadian parties thus can be analytically described as stratarchical-cadre structures, as alliances of sub-coalitions, and as pragmatic brokerage mechanisms, but most of all they are networks of *people* scheming together, and sometimes separately, in the quest for the Holy Grail of elected office. We will examine the successes and failures of that quest in the next chapter.

# Chapter 14

# Political Parties: Origins, Evolution, Electoral Performance

Having discussed the overall role of political parties in the Canadian political process, we turn in this chapter to a more detailed examination of Canada's party system. We will consider the origins of our party system, the subsequent historical evolution of today's political parties, and the electoral performance of our national political parties up to the 1993 general election. While our focus will be on parties at the national level, we will also make reference to the provincial party systems which, in many cases, have been the calving grounds for third parties that have participated at the federal level.

## ► THE ORIGINS OF THE PARTY SYSTEM

The origins of the present-day party system in Canada can be traced to the legislature of the United Provinces of Upper and Lower Canada following the *Act of Union* of 1840.[1] The early years of the Union government were characterized by a series of coalitions among various factions in the legislative assembly. While the factions, which coalesced around strong leaders, were themselves quite stable, the coalitions of factions that constituted the embryonic political parties were at first quite unstable. However, in the pre-Confederation period, the coalition that was to become the Conservative Party of Canada began to gel under the joint leadership of John A. Macdonald and George-Étienne Cartier, whose "Liberal-Conservative" alliance not only successfully promoted Confederation, but survived after it.

---

1. E. M. Reid, "The Rise of National Parties in Canada," in *Papers and Proceedings of the Canadian Political Science Association,* vol. 4, 1932; Peter Aucoin, "Regionalism, Party and National Government," David E. Smith, "Party Government, Representation and National Integration in Canada," and Paul G. Thomas, "The Role of National Party Caucuses," all *in* Peter Aucoin, ed., *Party Government and Regional Representation in Canada* (Ottawa: Royal Commission on the Economic Union and Development Prospects for Canada, Research Volume 36, 1985), pp. 1–68 and 69–128.

The basic roots of **party government** were thus already in place at the time of Confederation, and the dominant leaders in the new Parliament of Canada understood the importance of stable partisan institutions in making responsible government work. Stable parties are the critical mechanisms, not only for sustaining a legislative majority, but also for organizing and moderating the role of Her Majesty's Loyal Opposition in the House of Commons. As well, it was hoped that an integrated federal-provincial party system could enable national *and* regional interests to be accommodated both within the Cabinet and through the electoral system.

### The Evolution of the Two-Party System: 1867–1896

The gradual evolution of factional coalitions, which had begun in the pre-Confederation era, continued after 1867. Between 1867 and 1873, the government of Macdonald and Cartier still consisted of a loose alliance of many of the elements that had initially favoured Confederation, buttressed by the cooptation of some anti-Confederation Tories such as Joseph Howe from Nova Scotia. Their party unity, such as it was, arose out of a common desire to build a nation, to keep it together, and, naturally, to stay in power.

**The "One-and-a-Half" Party System** John A. Macdonald may have been the prime minister and official leader of the coalition, but several of his ministers had their own personal followings in both the House of Commons and the country. Building a government consisted of keeping enough of these factions together to form a voting bloc in Parliament. Within the first House of Commons there were Tory and Grit factions from Ontario and *Bleus* and *Rouges* from Quebec, but there were, as well, other kinds of groupings. On the government side sat Cabinet members, their personal supporters, and assorted "loose fish" or **ministerialists**, who had been elected by their constituents for the express purpose of supporting any government coalition in hopes of gaining favours for their constituencies. The existence of ministerialists was made possible by a system of non-simultaneous elections, whereby the party in power could call an election in safe seats first, and then gradually work to less favourable ridings. In addition to giving the party in power a great advantage by allowing it to create its own bandwagon, this system also eliminated any guesswork on the part of electors who wanted to ensure their riding's share of patronage by electing a loose fish.

However, even by 1867 there were beginning to emerge some consistent patterns to the Liberal-Conservative governing coalition and to their Liberal opponents. The former comprised Cartier's *Bleus*, which consisted of the French-Canadian majority blessed by the Church establishment, Macdonald's Ontario Tories, big-business interests from Montreal arrayed around Alexander Galt, and various supporters of the Grand Trunk Railway. Their orientation was firmly protectionist, expansionist, pro-railroad, and pro-business.

The Liberal opposition was an even looser coalition consisting of Ontario Clear Grits — agrarian reformers loosely tied to George Brown and his newspaper, the *Globe* — plus the *Parti rouge* — radical anti-clerical reformers from Quebec. The Liberals' orientation was anti-railroad, anti-protectionist, and pro-agrarian. Maritime members, with the exception of a group of Nova Scotia MPs associated with Joseph Howe and initially opposed to Confederation, made what alliances they could to ensure patronage for their region. For another ten years, individual MPs would move back and forth from one faction to another, or even from government to opposition, but factional elements *per se* and their leaders remained relatively stable.

Patronage pervaded the system during this period and it was an accepted way for governments to do business. The distribution of patronage was controlled directly by the party leadership, with the prime minister naturally playing the lead role. However, even a political culture that accepted the principle of the pork barrel still had basic rules about what was acceptable and what was excessive. In 1872, the Macdonald government broke the rules of the game. They made the mistake of getting caught accepting rather large kickbacks (under the guise of election-fund contributions) from the promoters of the Canadian Pacific Railway, and, although they won the election of 1872, Macdonald and his supporters were forced to resign shortly thereafter, when the dimensions of the "Pacific Scandal" became known.[2]

The Liberals who replaced Macdonald's government held power from 1873 to 1878 under Alexander Mackenzie. This government had little new or different to offer in the way of policy and lacked a cohesive party organization — indeed, in 1873 the Liberals were not even absolutely certain who their leader was. Mackenzie had to fight a continual battle with Edward Blake, who was apparently unable to decide whether he really wanted to lead the party, but who nonetheless retained great personal popularity. As well, Prime Minister Mackenzie truly did have moral and ethical concerns about the practice of patronage and refused to dole out the spoils of office to the government's supporters. Partly because of this aversion to the patronage system that was so essential to consolidating party unity, and partly because of the persisting leadership question, after five years in power the Liberals were defeated by the better-organized Conservatives.

**The Emergence of the Two-Party System**  The first ten years of Confederation, thus, were characterized by growing patronage-based party cohesion in the dominant Conservative coalition, with a much slower consolidation of the Liberal opposition. The lack of simultaneous elections and of the secret ballot made party organization in the years before 1878 a rather different problem than it is today. However, by 1878 there were simultaneous elections by secret ballot at least in eastern Canada, so that it became necessary for candidates to choose party lines before, not during or after, an election. This emergence of a modern electoral system encouraged much firmer partisan loyalty.

From 1878 to 1891 there evolved a stable consolidation of the Conservative Party under Macdonald's strong leadership and around his *National Policy*, which included commitments to railway construction, westward expansion, and protective tariffs. The Liberal Party in this period was characterized by aimlessness and lack of organization under the leadership of Mackenzie and

---

2. The "Pacific Scandal," as it was called, is described thoroughly by Pierre Berton in *The National Dream* (Toronto: McClelland and Stewart, 1970), pp. 90–134.

his successor, Blake. However, the simple motive of shared opposition to the Tories and the desire for power gradually united the disparate factions making up the opposition, and, by 1891, under the leadership of Wilfrid Laurier, the Liberal Party of Canada had become a stable and well-organized government-in-waiting.

We should not, however, exaggerate the strength of our early parties. While the parties had matured and consolidated organizationally, at the same time helping to structure the political life of the growing and expanding nation, they still did not control the business of the House of Commons as they do today. A modern-day Canadian would have noticed some very considerable differences on stepping out of a time machine into the visitors' gallery in 1880:

> In the first two or three decades after Confederation, the Canadian party system was not fully developed or truly national in scope. Individuals were recruited and supported in elections to the House of Commons by local elites and were more responsive to them than to the national party leadership.
>
> Party discipline was weak within the House of Commons. J. D. Edgar, who served during the 1870s as the informal whip in the House of Commons for the Liberal party, described the House as a contest of undisciplined factions, each laced through with a high proportion of members who did not take kindly to whipping.[3]

Thus, it is not surprising that during the first four sessions of the first Parliament, Macdonald was defeated six times on minor bills, twice on resolutions preceding bills, and twice on supply votes. In that Parliament, MPs on all sides of the House failed to vote with their party 20 per cent of the time, compared to less than 1 per cent in the 1980s and 1990s.

**Western Canada**  The practice of non-partisan and ministerialist politics persisted much longer in western Canada than it did in the rest of the country. The primary concern of Westerners was to ensure that the transcontinental railway was completed to the Pacific. They would have supported any ministry that promised to get the job done, and in practice that meant Macdonald's Conservatives. The non-partisan tradition was given additional impetus during this period because the introduction of simultaneous elections was limited to the provinces of eastern Canada.

Not only did the practice of non-simultaneous elections encourage ministerialist politics, but it also may account, in part, for the fact that strong two-party traditions have never developed at the provincial level west of Ontario. Early provincial governments in Manitoba and British Columbia, and after 1905 in Saskatchewan and Alberta, did follow the standard Liberal and Conservative Party labels. However, the elections tended to be non-competitive, with one or other party usually winning an overwhelming majority, and governing with little or no opposition in the legislature. This lack of strong bipartisan competition both in elections and in the legislature led to hegemonic and non-combative **administrative government** rather than to true parliamentary

---

3. Thomas, "The Role of National Party Caucuses," pp. 61–62. Reproduced with permission of the Minister of Supply and Services Canada.

government, and, as we shall see, ultimately made it easier for third-party movements to emerge in the 1920s and 1930s.

**The Golden Age of Two-Party Politics: 1896–1917** The post-Macdonald years from 1896 to 1917 could perhaps be characterized as the golden age of two-party politics in Canada. The Conservative and Liberal parties, led by Robert Borden and Wilfrid Laurier, had well-organized electoral machines and well-disciplined parliamentary wings. No other political parties of any significance had yet emerged, and regional discontent had not yet made a strong impression on Parliament or the party system. The strong leadership of Laurier, a native son of Quebec, helped to moderate French-English cleavage for the time being, and the rural-urban cleavage that was to spawn the Progressive movement of the 1920s had not yet become important. Economic prosperity helped to minimize class conflict, and those who were discontented could always move West to start again.

The two-party system was able to successfully accommodate most conflicting interests because the job was, for the first time, doable. The need for patronage and pork-barrel politics to cement the party organization faded as the party leadership began to forge programmatic consensus by aggregating a wide range of interests. The new cement of party unity in this period was successful intra-party accommodations along the most severe lines of cleavage and the ability of Laurier and Borden to articulate credible alternative national visions of Canada.

The emergence of a truly national two-party system may have been the result of conscious efforts by Laurier and Borden to overcome the parochial orientation of Canadian politics and to use parties as more than pragmatic instruments of electoral success. Parties became more than simply opportunistic coalitions of ambitious politicians united by their lust for political power and by the bonds of patronage, and emerged as instruments of political progress and national vision. Both Borden and Laurier felt that "parties should offer alternative definitions of the national interest and should bind their elected members to implement such broad programs once in office."[4]

In order to achieve this, a number of structural reforms were undertaken by both parties, including a move to separate party financing from the leader and to eliminate, or at least greatly reduce, patronage in civil-service appointments.[5] Laurier and Borden also sought to strengthen ties with the provincial wings of their parties, and to reflect regional interests in national party platforms and in Cabinet. But the integrated national two-party system that was the dream of Laurier and Borden did not survive the First World War.

**The Collapse of the Two-Party System**
Although Laurier and the Liberal Party were defeated in 1911, the equilibrium of the two-party system persisted until 1917. The First World War, the conscription crisis of 1917, and the formation of the Union Government ended

---

4. Ibid., p. 82.
5. John English, *The Decline of Politics: The Conservatives and the Party System 1901–1920* (Toronto: University of Toronto Press, 1977), p. 15ff.

those days. Some three years after the outbreak of the war, it became necessary, in Prime Minister Borden's view, to institute conscription in order to keep up the size of Canada's forces in Europe. We have seen in Chapter 9 that French Canadians, particularly those living in Quebec, felt that the war had little relevance to their lives. This attitude, combined with evidence of inhospitable treatment received by any francophone Canadians who did join the armed forces, ensured the opposition of French Canada to conscription.

In an effort to unite Canadian opinion, the Conservative prime minister, Robert Borden, formed the Union Government, which was a coalition supported by most English-speaking Liberals and opposed by practically all French-speaking Liberals. The election that followed all but isolated French Canada, and temporarily destroyed the Liberal Party coalition between French Canada and the West that Laurier had so carefully forged. In addition, it spelled the end, for nearly forty years, of any strong support for the Conservative Party in Quebec.

Although the immediate cause of the collapse of the two-party system was the conscription crisis and the formation of the Union Government, a number of more fundamental causes lay in the background. Despite the honest efforts of the party leaders to make their organizations truly national, the Conservative Party structure had become overcentralized in eastern Canada, particularly in Ontario, while the Liberals had become too strongly identified with French Canada. Attempts to overcome these divisive imbalances, which were recognized and deplored by both Laurier and Borden, had failed. The sense of not really belonging in either of the national parties combined with the absence of a strong two-party tradition in the West was shortly to result in the sudden emergence of the Progressives at both the federal and provincial levels.

## ▶ "THIRD PARTIES" IN CANADA

Under the leadership of Mackenzie King and Meighen the Liberals and the Conservatives both made the mistake of trying to win the first postwar election by playing on the still-raw French-English rift that was the legacy of the conscription crisis and the Union Government. However, it is likely that party strategists intended to use this approach only temporarily, feeling confident that if they could win the election by exploiting ethnic conflict in 1921, they could immediately turn their governmental power to the task of rebuilding the prewar multidimensional coalitions.

Then, as now, an excessive emphasis on ethnic cleavages was an extremely risky business and the result was that the ethnic conflict between French and English Canada grew still deeper and less resolvable. As well, by essentially ignoring the growing urban-rural, regional, and economic cleavages, both older parties moved out of touch with important elements of the electorate and lost the broadly based support needed to maintain a two-party system. The next twenty-five years witnessed the rise of several third parties, and the Canadian party system was changed forever.

## The Progressive Movement

While the emergence of new political *movements* that made the transition to electoral politics is normally associated, correctly, with western Canada, ironically, the first non-establishment party to achieve electoral success did so in the heartland of central Canada. In November of 1919 there was a provincial election in Ontario, and, when the smoke had cleared, the largest single group in the legislature and the backbone of the new coalition government was the **United Farmers' of Ontario**,[6] the Ontario wing of a mainly Western movement whose political arm came to be known nationally as the Progressive Party.

The movement was already well established in the West, and in 1921 the **United Farmers of Alberta** were swept to power in the provincial election of that year. Also in 1921, any notion that Canada still had a two-party system was shattered when sixty-five Progressive MPs were elected in the national election, twenty-four of them in rural Ontario. They were the second-largest group in the House of Commons, with fifteen more seats than the Conservative Party.[7]

Compared to other Canadian parties, the Progressives relied upon relatively homogeneous electoral support. Aside from a few small-business interests from Manitoba, the group's support was almost entirely rural. In general, the more agricultural the economy of a province, the more likely it was to return Progressives. Even New Brunswick, which virtually never breaks with older party lines, returned a Progressive MP from a rural constituency in 1921, and Nova Scotia gave the Progressives 15 per cent of the vote, although the group won no seats there.

The Progressives were a populist party and consequently concentrated much of their criticism on the elitist, caucus-dominated structure of the older parties. As they pointed out, the agrarian-dominated Western regional caucuses of the Liberals and Conservatives were inevitably out-voted by the parties' Eastern interests. They therefore surmised that the only way to make themselves heard in Parliament was to abandon the old parties and attempt to achieve their ends through the process of interparty competition in the electoral process.

Structurally, the Progressive Party was an alliance of regionally-based farmers' organizations. The only acknowledged national leader in the movement was T. A. Crerar, a dissident Liberal, but he broke with the movement in 1922 and subsequently returned to the Liberal fold. What overall national cohesion existed was provided by adherence to a few common principles expressed in "The Farmers' Platform." The most important of these was simply opposition to the old party system and to Eastern business interests. There was considerable emphasis among Progressives on grassroots democracy, but the opinions about how to best achieve it varied widely from one regional sub-coalition to another. Thus, the Manitoba farmers' Progressive government and the United Farmers of Alberta experimented with legislation to provide for the recall of

---

6. The other party in the coalition was the small Independent Labour Party.
7. The words "movement" and "party" are both used in political-science literature to describe the Progressives. There are a number of excellent studies of the group. Two are W. L. Morton, *The Progressive Party in Canada* (Toronto: University of Toronto Press, 1948); and C. B. Macpherson, *Democracy in Alberta* (Toronto: University of Toronto Press, 1954), pp. 62–92. Macpherson's book deals with the Alberta wing of the party.

MPs to face their constituents in a by-election if a specified proportion of the voters in a riding requested it. Other wings of the Progressive Party toyed with various forms of the referendum and the initiative, but the parliamentary system precludes such measures constitutionally, and as a result the populist planks in their platforms both federally and provincially were ultimately abandoned.

The Progressive movement perished of its own structural deficiencies. Its populist principles got in the way of any consolidation of power in the parliamentary caucus, and the regionally based factions found it more and more difficult to find common ground on national issues. By the mid 1920s, the Progressive Party had lost most of its importance in Canadian national politics, with many of its supporters and many of its agricultural policies absorbed into the brokerage sponge that was Mackenzie King's Liberal Party. However, it continued to be important in provincial governments in the West, where the United Farmers remained in power in Alberta until the Social Credit sweep in 1935, and in Manitoba, where the Progressives held power in one form or another for some thirty years. The Progressive era in Manitoba ended when its leader, Premier John Bracken, was lured to the leadership of the national Conservative Party in 1942 on the condition that the Tories change the name of the party to the *Progressive* Conservatives.

## Social Credit

Strictly speaking, **social credit** is a financial theory developed by Major C. H. Douglas, a retired British army engineer, although it contains elements of a broader view of society as well. The root of the theory is the *A plus B theorem*, which essentially advocates creating more purchasing power by printing more money. Social credit also featured a populist critique of parliamentary democracy, pointing out that control over members of Parliament had escaped the little person and now rested with large financial interests. Since the large financial and banking interests were depicted as part of a purported Jewish conspiracy to control the world, anti-Semitism was also prominent in the early rhetoric of the movement.

At first glance, the success of the Social Credit Party is a highly complex phenomenon. The party held power in two provinces and had a significant presence in the House of Commons. Yet the federal and provincial segments of the party were frequently scarcely on speaking terms, and the ties among the various branches of the party have never been strong. The Quebec-based wing of the party, the ***Ralliement des créditistes***, was basically nationalist in orientation, and its real presence was felt only in federal politics during the 1960s. Thus, Social Credit was never a single political party at all; rather, it was a set of at least three separate parties, operating largely independently of each other in quite different venues. While there are common threads, it is probably best to treat the three major segments, in Alberta, Quebec, and British Columbia, separately.

**Alberta** By the end of the third decade of this century, the Progressive movement no longer acted as an effective vehicle for protest in the West. Yet the

Depression and the prolonged drought on the prairies in the early 1930s served, if anything, to emphasize still further the differences between eastern and western Canada. As a result, by 1935, a new grassroots protest movement had established itself in Alberta provincial politics, and Alberta voters, never known for excessive caution, eliminated all United Farmers of Alberta members and filled fifty-six of the sixty-three seats in their legislature with followers of Social Credit.[8]

While the peculiar and simplistic ideology of social credit offered a panacea for all Alberta's problems, the sudden ascendency of the Social Credit Party of Alberta was due primarily to the coincidence of the Depression of the 1930s with the organizational and histrionic abilities of William Aberhart. Aberhart began his working life as a schoolteacher and preacher. After moving to Alberta as a young man, he founded the Prophetic Bible Institute. Given the fire of his evangelical preaching and the limited range of alternative Sunday-afternoon activities in Alberta in the early 1930s, Aberhart's religious radio broadcasts soon enjoyed tremendous popularity.

Aberhart gradually began to use his radio persona to present the ideas of social credit in 1932, and his broadcasts, together with an excellent grassroots political organization, swept him into power in 1935. After a few half-hearted attempts to apply social credit principles through legislation, the Alberta Social Credit movement, thwarted by the realities of the Constitution and the economic system, became a government cadre party of more-or-less standard form. The Alberta Social Credit Party consolidated itself as an electoral and governmental machine and successfully ran the province for thirty-six years.

The party was born of the historical confluence of the social disruption of the Depression, the alienation of Westerners from Eastern institutions, the conservative entrepreneurial ethic of Alberta, and the particular genius of William Aberhart. It survived through the ability of his successor, E. C. Manning, to run a successful administration, and through the fortuitous prosperity ushered in by the discovery of oil in 1947. It perished essentially of old age and the voters' desire for change soon after Manning's retirement. The Social Credit Party effectively disappeared from the provincial scene in 1971, when a resurgent provincial Conservative Party led by Peter Lougheed captured the province's government.

**Quebec** The *Ralliement des créditistes*, the Quebec-based wing of the Social Credit movement,[9] was characterized by the same pragmatism and leadership orientation that had allowed it to exploit regional-cultural characteristics in

---

8. There are three major academic accounts of the Social Credit Movement in Alberta: C. B. Macpherson, *Democracy in Alberta*; J. A. Irving, *The Social Credit Movement in Alberta* (Toronto: University of Toronto Press, 1959); and J. R. Mallory, *Social Credit and the Federal Power in Canada* (Toronto: University of Toronto Press, 1954).

9. The *Ralliement des créditistes* has also been extensively studied. See, particularly, Maurice Pinard, *The Rise of a Third Party* (Englewood Cliffs: Prentice-Hall, 1971); and Michael Stein, *The Dynamics of Right Wing Protest: A Political Analysis of Social Credit in Quebec* (Toronto: University of Toronto Press, 1973); Graham White, "One-Party Dominance and Third Parties"; André Blais, "Third Parties in Canadian Provincial Politics"; and Maurice Pinard, "Third Parties in Canada Re-Visited"; all in *Canadian Journal of Political Science*, September 1973, vol. 6, pp. 439–60. Although the major success of the *Ralliement* has been in federal elections, it is realistic to treat it as a Quebec party, in accord with its electoral base.

Alberta, and it showed a similar vulnerability to decline once the strong leader disappeared. The *Créditistes* started life as a protest movement, although much later than the Alberta party, and they were mildly successful in Quebec in the 1960s largely because rural Quebeckers did not find the federal Conservative Party a credible alternative to the governing Liberals, whom they felt had ceased to look after their interests.

In the 1962 federal election, the *Créditistes*, led by the fiery Réal Caouette, won twenty-six seats in rural Quebec and captured 26 per cent of the Quebec vote. Until 1974 they earned more than 18 per cent of the federal vote in Quebec and won never fewer than nine seats. For a time after the 1962 election, they were, outside of Montreal, the dominant federal electoral force in the province.

While in 1970 the *Créditistes* also entered provincial politics and won thirteen seats in the National Assembly, they were unable to build on this. They were crushed in the *Parti Québécois* victory of 1976. Federally, the fortunes of the *Ralliement des créditistes* declined precipitously with Caouette's death and the party was completely eliminated in the 1980 election.

**British Columbia** The British Columbia Social Credit Party, or the Socreds, won a minority victory in the provincial election of 1952. Here again, the movement had some things in common with its origins in Quebec and Alberta. Economic conditions in British Columbia were not nearly as bad as they were in Alberta in 1935 or in rural Quebec in 1962, but the British Columbia government in 1952 was a tired and disintegrating coalition of Conservatives and Liberals. Neither of the older parties had much in the way of provincial organization, and the CCF was too far left for the conservative electors of British Columbia. The only credible alternative that emerged was the Social Credit Party.

The 1952 Socred campaign was run with considerable help from Alberta, but without a leader; W. A. C. Bennett, a dissident former Conservative, did not become leader until after the election. Social Credit was helped in the election by the two older parties, who had enacted an "alternative-vote" electoral scheme, intended to shut out the socialist hordes of the CCF — a scheme that aided significantly in their own demise but left the CCF essentially as before. Bennett, surmising correctly that a proportional representation system rarely works to the advantage of a party in power, promptly (and cynically) eliminated it after the election.

In British Columbia, Social Credit fell rather than charged into power, but a prosperous economy and an ebullient, if not overly polished, party image kept it there for all of forty years, with one brief interregnum by Dave Barrett's NDP from 1972 to 1975. During that time, the various antics and policy peregrinations of W. A. C. Bennett, who defined social credit as simply "the opposite of socialism," served to create an image of British Columbia politics as low comedy. Bennett was succeeded as leader and premier by his son, Bill. Under Bill Bennett, British Columbia's Social Credit Party effectively retained a base of middle-class and small-entrepreneurial support. It also remained moderately right-wing in orientation.

Following the 1983 election, the party moved somewhat further to the right, imposing a fairly Draconian (by Canadian standards) set of expenditure restraints. Any remnant of social credit theory had, however, long since disappeared from its repertoire, and Bennett's successor, William Vander Zalm, returned the party to power in 1986 on a campaign based on middle-of-the-road policy proposals. In 1991, amidst much internal strife and allegations of financial improprieties, the party lost power to Mike Harcourt and the NDP.

As in Alberta, the British Columbia Socreds were successful because they managed to find consistent support within their respective provinces by articulating the right-of-centre, anti-Ottawa views of the electorate. The Conservative Party ceased to function at the provincial level during the Social Credit hegemony in both provinces, and the ideological ground normally occupied by the Tories was "easy pickins" for any right-of-centre, regionally based party. In each case the Socreds died as a result of the decline of leadership dynasties, internal bickering, and organizational old age.

### Socialism in Canada: CCF and NDP

Since 1921, J. S. Woodsworth had led a tiny group of Socialist MPs in the federal Parliament. By 1932, in the depths of the Depression, Woodsworth helped to bring together a loose coalition of disempowered groups in Canadian society who had in common the shared hardships of the Depression. Western farmers who had been active in the cooperative movement, labour leaders, and academics oriented towards democratic socialist principles got together to draft a statement of political principles called the **Regina Manifesto**. This was the catalyst that led to the founding convention of the **Cooperative Commonwealth Federation** (CCF) in Regina in 1933.[10] The CCF and its successor, the **New Democratic Party** (NDP), have remained a constant part of the national and most provincial party systems since 1932, with varying levels of success.

**Ideological Evolution** The *Regina Manifesto*, the declaration of principles passed at the first annual convention of the Cooperative Commonwealth Federation in Regina in 1933, was high-minded, idealistic, and, perhaps, just a little naive to us cynical denizens of the 1990s. However, it clearly placed the infant political party well to the left of the Tories and the Liberals.

> We aim to replace the present capitalistic system, with its inherent injustice and inhumanity, by a social order from which the domination and exploitation of one class by another will be eliminated, in which economic planning will supersede unregulated private enterprise and competition and in which genuine democratic self-government based upon equality will be possible.

The CCF held to its doctrinaire socialist platform and populist style of politics for the first twenty years of its life, but by 1956 it had begun to change its ideological face. While it continued to call for an egalitarian and classless society, the party began to shift towards the ideological centre in Canadian politics. In response to the fact that its national electoral support appeared to have peaked in 1944–1945 without moving the party into national power or

---

10. The best study of the CCF is W. D. Young, *The Anatomy of a Party: The National CCF 1932–61* (Toronto: University of Toronto Press, 1969).

moving the electorate significantly to the left, the CCF backed away from some of its more doctrinaire proposals such as wholesale nationalization of industry and the eradication of capitalism. Its new, more pragmatic ideology was expressed in the **Winnipeg Declaration** of 1956 and called for

> the application of social planning. Investment of available funds must be channeled into socially desirable projects; financial and credit resources must be used to help maintain full employment and to control inflation and deflation.

This was a set of principles that both the Liberals and the Progressive Conservatives could have happily endorsed. However, in the 1958 general election, the party fell victim to the Diefenbaker landslide victory and was reduced to a mere eight seats and 9 per cent of the popular vote. It was clear that to survive, the CCF was going to have to change its image and broaden its base of support.

**The Birth of the New Democratic Party**  Meanwhile, organized labour in Canada, particularly the Canadian Labour Congress (CLC) had begun to take an interest in openly linking itself to a political party, and the logical choice was the CCF. The result was a dissolution of the CCF and the formation of the New Democratic Party in 1961.[11] For the most part, NDP activists included many of the same people who had supported the CCF but they were strengthened by the addition of people from the labour movement and the urban middle class. However, the NDP has become less a populist party than the CCF, and has moved away from its mass party roots to a more conventional, centralized, cadre-style organization.

The NDP has proven willing to modify its principles from time to time to keep itself relevant to a wider range of Canadian voters. The NDP leadership since 1961 has been moderately social-democratic rather than doctrinaire in its ideological stance, and, as with many social-democratic parties, it has drifted closer to the centre as the structure of capitalist society as a whole has drifted to the left. This ideological drift has not been without some severe organizational stresses. One of these was caused by the strongly nationalistic and more radically left-wing Waffle group, which in the 1970s sought a return to more doctrinaire socialist principles and greater domestic control of Canadian industry. In tones reminiscent of the *Regina Manifesto* but also reflective of neo-Marxist paradigms, the Waffle declared, "Capitalism must be replaced by socialism, by national planning of investment and by public ownership of the means of production in the interests of the Canadian people as a whole."[12]

The Waffle group became sufficiently strong that, in the 1971 national leadership convention, their candidate ran a fairly close second to the winner, David Lewis. However, the conservative trade-union wing of the party and the almost equally conservative (for a socialist party) parliamentary caucus were able to force the expulsion of the group from the Ontario party in 1973. The

---

11. For the post-1961 period, see Desmond Morton, *NDP: The Dream of Power* (Toronto: Hakkert, 1974).

12. Robert Hackett, "The Waffle Conflict in the NDP," *in* H. G. Thorburn, *Party Politics in Canada*, 1972, differentiates between the democratic-socialism position and the social-democrat position. The former is much more militantly left-wing, favouring broader government control and more public ownership than the latter. The latter is the establishment position in the party.

group's direct influence has vanished since then, although there can still be found strong traces of its views among many supporters of the party.

What has been said about the shift away from socialist ideological orthodoxy in the NDP, however, should not be interpreted to mean that the party is identical to the older parties. The NDP remains more committed to economic equality than the older parties. While wholesale state ownership of the means of production is no longer a central plank in its platform, it is a somewhat stronger advocate than the Liberals and far to the left of the Conservatives on questions of public enterprise. The NDP has also tended to be more nationalistic and in some cases more isolationist than either of the older parties, opposing strongly any trend towards the closer economic integration of North America. Thus, along with the union movement that sometimes supports it, the party opposed FTA and NAFTA and has, since 1969, opposed Canadian participation in military alliances such as NATO and NORAD.

It has often been suggested that the CCF/NDP, while never close to gaining power at the federal level, can take solace in the fact that they have fostered policy innovation in Canadian politics. The Liberals, especially, have often been accused of (or praised for) appropriating policy ideas espoused by the NDP, taking the credit and the political kudos for being so progressive. This phenomenon of "contagion from the left"[13] has been greatest with respect to health and social-welfare policy areas where the NDP has traditionally been most vocal. As well, at the provincial level, where the party has had the opportunity to form governments, the party has championed policies such as rent control and strict occupational health-and-safety regulations.

**Electoral Performance** There are some substantial differences in the base of support between the NDP and the older parties. The NDP has traditionally drawn disproportionately from union voters, but for a party that is based on a coalition that includes organized labour and that appeals directly to the union vote, it is remarkable that the party has not done better. The NDP has never garnered more than 40 per cent of the union vote nationally and in certain regions, such as Quebec, it runs a distant third in terms of labour support. The profile of NDP supporters suggests that, while Canadian politics in general is not class-based, support for the NDP to some extent is. Thus, we have the phenomenon of a somewhat class-based party in what is not a class-based voting system, which may go a long way to explain the failure of the party to make a significant breakthrough at the national level.

*Brokerage Socialism* The combination of an attempt to mobilize and hold labour support and a failure to articulate and sell a view of Canadian politics much different from that of the older brokerage parties has created difficulties for the NDP. Once the party became determined to pursue the essentially conservative union movement in Canada as its major organizational building block, it had to eschew much of the class-based rhetoric of its earlier years.

---

13. William M. Chandler, "Canadian Socialism and Policy Impact: Contagion from the Left?" *Canadian Journal of Political Science*, vol. 10, no. 4, December 1977, pp. 755–80, and C. Caplan, *The Dilemma of Canadian Socialism: The CCF in Ontario* (Toronto: McClelland and Stewart, 1973).

After all, Canadian workers, blue or white collar, public or private sector, almost uniformly view themselves as middle class, not working class. The mainspring of NDP ideology after 1956 became increasingly accepting of Keynesian orthodoxy combined with large social safety nets, a position only slightly to the left of that held by the Liberals.

Not only did the attempt to mobilize organized labour lead to internal ideological problems for the NDP, the effort also did not add much in the way of electoral support. The NDP-CLC alliance was mainly an accommodation among elites or, as Brodie and Jenson put it, "a marriage of notables."[14] The membership of the union movement displayed an active hostility to any idea of a radical transformation of a society that had delivered high wages and affluence to them. Even job insecurity, engendered by high unemployment rates during the 1980s, had little effect in convincing the mainstream membership of organized labour to support left-wing alternatives. Instead it, too, tended to support the "new" economic orthodoxy, which was that neo-conservative and business-driven rather than state-driven solutions would provide the best hope of renewed economic and employment growth.

With no political vernacular of its own, with no solid working-class support, and attached at the elite level to a largely conservative labour movement, the NDP has had increasing difficulty offering a world view that will clearly differentiate it from the Liberals. It has thus increasingly had to represent itself as essentially a Liberal party "with a soul." As evidence that this is an unlikely base from which to move towards major party status in the 1990s, the NDP support plummeted nationally in the 1993 election.

*Regional Socialism*  While the NDP can be described as a national party, there has always been a strong regional bias to NDP support. The CCF was born in Saskatchewan, and formed the government there first in 1944. Both the CCF and its successor, the NDP, have been strong there ever since, forming the provincial government a number of times and consistently electing a respectable number of MPs at the federal level. Even the 1993 disaster saw the NDP win 27 per cent of the vote in Saskatchewan. Support has also been strong in Manitoba, producing NDP victories in the 1969, 1973, 1982, and 1986 provincial elections and consistently sending MPs to Ottawa, particularly from the Winnipeg area.

There is also sufficient support centred in the powerful West-Coast trade-union movement to have enabled the NDP to consistently elect a bloc of MPs and to capture British Columbia's provincial government in 1972 and 1991. As well, the party formed the government in the Yukon through two elections in the late 1980s, and the Yukon MP, Audrey McLaughlin, became the leader of the national party in 1989. However, the NDP has never garnered much support in Quebec or the Atlantic region, or in large sections of Ontario outside the metropolitan areas. Although it was swept to power in Ontario in the September 1990 provincial election it was also decisively swept out of power in 1995. We will say more about the current trials and tribulations of the NDP in the conclusion to this chapter.

---

14. M. Janine Brodie and Jane Jenson, "The Party System," *in* M. S. Whittington and G. Williams, *Canadian Politics in the 1980s* (Toronto: Methuen, 1984), p. 264.

## The Reform Party

The Reform Party was founded in 1987, it won no seats at all in the 1988 federal election, and it came, apparently out of nowhere, to take fifty-two seats in 1993. As with many other third-party movements, the Reform Party grew out of Western allienation and a sense that the exisiting parties had failed to adequately articulate the interests of rural and small-town Canadians.

**Origins**  The Reform Party began as a mass movement based on a grassroots coalition of anti-Eastern, far right, rural, and small-town interests in western Canada. It was nurtured and spurred on through the enthusiastic campaigning of its founder and leader, Preston Manning, who used his own political roots and political experiences to identify and articulate the interests that had kept his father, E. C. Manning, in power as the Social Credit premier of Alberta for so many years. The Reform Party is the right-wing populist successor to the Progressives and the Social Credit, and its electoral success has been constructed on the same ideological foundations and electoral base as those earlier political movements.

The Reform Party first loomed in the national consciousness through its opposition to the Charlottetown Accord in the 1992 referendum. Although the *Bloc Québécois* also took an anti-Accord position in the referendum campaign, Reform stood alone among the national federal parties in its opposition to the Accord, and its campaign drew public attention to the party and its leader. While the party's popular support in the polls did not increase immediately as a result of its referendum exposure, it became a known commodity to the voters, some of whom came to view Reform as a viable right-wing alternative when the Conservatives' 1993 campaign collapsed.

**Platform**  The initial policy positions of the Reform Party were developed at its 1991 assembly in Saskatoon. At the core of the party's platform was opposition to bilingualism and multiculturalism, and more restrictive immigration policies. As well, the party was opposed to the conditions placed on federal transfers to the provinces under the *Canada Health Act*, feeling that the provinces should be free to permit extra-billing by doctors and whatever other cost-saving mechanisms they felt appropriate as a means of balancing provincial budgets. As well, the party keeps the populist faith by advocating the extensive use of the devices of quasi-direct democracy such as the referendum, the initiative, the recall, and the creation of an elected Senate.

In the 1993 election campaign, Reform took the position that deficit reduction should be the highest priority and that the federal deficit should be eliminated entirely within three years. Most interesting, if not very credible, is the party's contention that this could be accomplished without tax increases. The thrust of the Reform proposals was that the deficit should be reduced by drastically cutting federal transfers to individuals and, even more drastically, cutting transfers to the provinces. The latter perhaps goes some way to explaining why the party continues to take the positon that it should not participate in provincial elections! As well, the party did not fare well in Newfoundland, partially as a reflection of the fact that Manning advocated the elimination of federal support for the Hibernia offshore drilling project but also because of the inherent traditionalism of the Atlantic provinces.

As mentioned briefly in the previous chapter, Preston Manning has been plagued by the public pledges of support from groups that are overtly white supremacist, anti-Semitic, anti-aboriginal, anti-French, and even neo-Nazi. A Reform candidate was dumped during the 1993 election campaign for racist statements, and some Reform MPs have since caused embarrassment to Manning. In one case, derogatory remarks about aboriginal people made in June 1994 by Reform MPs in Parliament had to be disclaimed by the party leadership. One interpretation is that Preston Manning must shake his head from time to time and say "with friends like this who needs enemies?" However, the other, more disturbing interpretation is that the reason for the success of the Reform Party may be that a lot of Canadians actually share such extreme right positions.

### Bloc Québécois

The newest political party on the Canadian political scene has in many ways been around in varying forms for decades. The *Bloc Québécois* is a strictly regional party based in Quebec with a single-issue agenda. That a party committed to the breakup of the federation is Her Majesty's Loyal Opposition may leave some constitutional experts with bemused expressions on their sombre visages, but it does not alter the fact that the Canadian party system has a new and, at least temporarily, important actor.

**Origins** Unlike the Reform Party whose origins are outside of Parliament, the BQ was formed out of a coalition of Quebec MPs who left their Liberal and Conservative caucuses to work for the independence of Quebec. While minor parties have sprung up from time to time to run federal candidates on the platform of Quebec independence, none of them ever succeeded in electing any MPs. The *Bloc populaire* ran candidates unsuccessfully in the 1945 general election, and the *Union populaire* ran candidates in both 1979 and 1980 elections, again without success. Part of the failure of separatist parties in federal politics in recent years has been the hesitancy of the provincial *Parti Québécois* to support them out of fear that participating in federal politics may tend to legitimize the federal system they are trying to destroy.

With the failure of the Meech Lake Accord, the polls indicated that the support for sovereignty had surged to 60 per cent in the province. The defection of prominent members of the Tory caucus, including the high-profile minister of the Environment, Lucien Bouchard, provided an instant base for separatist advocacy within the federal Parliament. When that base was extended as a few Liberal MPs crossed the floor to join the growing bloc of sovereigntists, the PQ began to see the advantages of a second front in their war on federalism. The PQ tested the waters in a federal by-election in 1991 where they threw the full support of the provincial organization behind the *Bloc Québécois* candidate. The PQ-Bloc effort won easily and the decision was taken to run a full slate of independentist candidates in Quebec in the next federal election.

While the PQ had come to believe that the march to independence ulti-mately could be speeded up by having separatists in Parliament, the immediate goal of the PQ was really to prevent the hated federal Liberals under the equally hated Jean Chrétien from occupying the vacuum left by the evaporation of Tory support in the province. The PQ organization became the *Bloc Québécois* campaign machine in the 1993 election; the Bloc captured 49 per cent of the popular vote and fifty-four of the seventy-five seats in the province and ended up as the official Opposition in Parliament.

**Platform and Organization**  The *Bloc Québécois* platform is simple — to fight for Quebec sovereignty within the federal government. While it could be argued that the party is slightly left leaning in its social and ecomomic policy positions, it is difficult to prove this, given that, with a few exceptions, the Bloc MPs have been very quiet as the official Opposition. As well, the Bloc is a coaltion that includes right-leaning ex-PCs and ex-*Créditistes* who are a long way from being social democrats ideologically. Finally, the Bloc originated as a classic cadre party dominated by its leadership in the House — and its extra-parliamentary party is the PQ *government* of the province of Quebec! Maurice Duverger certainly would have difficulty fitting this organizational arrangement into his mass-cadre typology.

We will return to our discussion of the *Bloc Québécois* in the national party system after we have looked at the two traditional parties, the Conservatives and the Liberals. However, before moving to that discussion it is useful to attempt a few generalizations about third parties in the Canadian system.

## Conclusion: Third Parties in Canada

We have seen that there is much in common among various third-party move-ments in Canadian politics, even when they have ideological stances as widely disparate as the Reform Party and the NDP. They have all expressed discontent with Canada's central political and economic institutions, they all have had regional bases of support, and none of them has ever come close to forming a government at the national level. Let us now look at some of the reasons third parties have sprung up in our system.

First, because of the necessity of maintaining cohesive parliamentary vot-ing blocs in a system based on the principle of responsible government, party discipline must be strict. In the United States, very loose party discipline allows sectionalism, protest, and dissident factions to emerge and persist within the Democratic and Republican parties, so the formation of separate third parties is seldom necessary. In Canada, by contrast, if radical dissent is to be heard at all, it must be heard outside the confines of our two older brokerage-style parties.

Second, the Canadian federal system may have provided some encourage-ment to would-be third parties. Even if it isn't possible to win a national election, the minor party may have a fair chance of winning power in a province and, in fact, every province west of New Brunswick has at some time had a third-party government. Moreover, in our decentralized federal system, success at the provincial level is not a political prize to take lightly. There is real power to be exercised and often, because of the importance of intergovernmental relations, a dissident region may even acquire a degree of influence at the national level by being the government provincially.

Third, the coincidence of social and economic cleavage with some provincial or regional boundaries, and the relative homogeneity of most provinces, have been important in fostering third-party movements. It would be difficult to imagine much success for the *Union Nationale*, the *Parti Québécois* or the Bloc in a Quebec that was 50 per cent English. Similarly, C. B. MacPherson attributes much of the early success of third-party movements in Alberta to the relative social homogeneity of that province, and S. M. Lipset suggests that the CCF may have succeeded in Saskatchewan at least partially for the same reason.[15] Of course, this does not explain the election of an NDP government in socio-economically diverse Ontario in 1990.

A fourth possible reason for the rise of third parties in Canada has been suggested by Maurice Pinard.[16] Canadian electoral politics, both nationally and provincially, has been characterized often by long periods of one-party dominance. For example, at the provincial level in Alberta in 1935, there had been no effective opposition to the United Farmers government for fifteen years. Hence, when the Social Credit emerged, they succeeded by filling the vacuum and providing an opportunity for Alberta voters to express their pent-up discontent with the UFA government.

At the federal level, looking specifically at the rise of the *Créditistes* in Quebec, Pinard hypothesized that the long period of Liberal Party dominance in federal politics in rural Quebec led to a perception on the part of Quebeckers that the Conservative Party was not a legitimate alternative. They voted Progressive Conservative in 1958 so as not to be cut off politically from the party in power, but they shortly discovered that the Conservatives under Diefenbaker did not pay any attention to them. If they were still not satisfied — and rural Quebec has had a great deal to be dissatisfied about — their only legitimate outlet for protest was through a third party, and the *Ralliement des créditistes* provided this outlet. Similarly, it was the demise of the dominant Tories after the failure of the Meech Lake Accord and the inability of the federal Liberals to offer a credible alternative that led to the success of the *Bloc Québécois* in 1993.

Many of these arguments can be seen to apply with respect to the rise of the Reform Party. The brokerage parties, striving to build coalitions that included Quebec and immigrant groups, were simply unable to articulate the right-of-centre, anti-French, and anti-immigration sentiments of the segments of the electorate that voted for Reform. Moreover, the long-time domination of the Conservative Party in federal politics in the West and the perception of the Liberals as an unacceptable alternative when the Tories stumbled, left a vacuum that the Reform Party was extremely effective in filling. Finally, the sense of alienation from national political institutions and the perceived failure

---

15. MacPherson, *Democracy in Alberta*, and S. M. Lipset, *Agrarian Socialism* (Berkeley: University of California Press, 1950).
16. Pinard, *The Rise of a Third Party*. See also the discussion of this theory in the *Canadian Journal of Political Science*, vol. 6, no. 3, September 1973, pp. 439–60.

of traditional parliamentary representation to redress Western concerns made the populist Reform Party, which advocated more direct accountability of MPs to their constituencies, a very attractive alternative to the old brokerage parties.

Undoubtedly, all these explanations have some validity. It is in the coincidence of two or more such factors, which happened with the emergence of the Reform Party, that we find the most fertile soil for the germination of third-party movements. However we account for their emergence and persistence, we must still conclude that third parties, at both federal and provincial levels, have done much to give the Canadian party systems their distinctive complexion.

▶ THE "BROKERS" AND THE PARTY SYSTEM

Since 1867, only two political parties have ever formed the government at the national level in Canada. While the Tories called themselves the Liberal-Conservatives in the 19th century and the Progressive Conservatives since 1942, they are still the "grand old party" of John A. Macdonald. Although, with only two MPs after the 1993 election, they are, at least temporarily, more old than grand, the Conservatives have alternated with the Liberals as the government party in Canada.

These parties have succeeded where third parties have not because they have been effective brokers and accommodators of a wide range of political interests. They can form governments because they are able to assemble coalitions of disparate factions within the electorate that are broad enough to produce majorities. Earlier in this chapter we looked at the origins of Canada's major parties; now we must consider their evolution to the present day.

**The Liberal Party of Canada**

In 1921 the Liberal Party of Canada was elected under the leadership of a most unlikely man, William Lyon Mackenzie King. Historians have not always treated King kindly, and his biographers have made of him a less than heroic figure.[17] Yet in some ways King can be viewed as a hero, even if an unprepossessing one. He took over a party decimated by the events of the previous decade and rebuilt it into Canada's most successful brokerage party. The legacy of King's rumpled genius was that for more than half a century, the Liberal Party dominated Canadian electoral politics at the federal level. That King accomplished this by equivocation, occasional deceit, and large doses of compromise, is merely testimony to his consummate skill as a broker and an accommodator of elites. That, as it is said, he also managed all of this with the

17. There are a number of biographies of King. The best is undoubtedly the series of volumes begun by R. MacGregor Dawson and continued by Blair Neatby, *William Lyon Mackenzie King: A Political Biography* (Toronto: University of Toronto Press, 1958 and 1963). See also J. W. Pickersgill, *The Mackenzie King Record*, vol. 1, 1939–1944, and vol. 2, 1944–1948 (Toronto: University of Toronto Press, 1960 and 1970). Many of King's diaries became available in 1975, and they provide a fascinating picture of the man and his view of Canadian politics in his era. The diaries are in the National Archives in Ottawa.

spiritual guidance and comfort of his departed mother and his dog, Pat (who was also deceased!), is perhaps as much a comment on Canadian politics as it is on the man himself.

**Party Structure** The party King and his advisors, dead and alive, constructed is a cadre party in most of the senses described by Maurice Duverger in his original analysis of party structures, but it has other structural features as well. First, it was, and remains, a stratarchy. There are nominal lines of authority and communication between the leader and the provincial and constituency levels, but in practice these lines of authority remain weak. In contrast to the highly centralized Conservative Party under Bennett in the thirties, the Liberals showed considerable decentralization both in financial structure and in policy matters.[18]

Second, since 1921 the national Liberal Party has been the party most *open* to the incorporation of new groups, interests, and sub-coalitions into the Liberal family. It was able to swallow up and absorb the Progressives and much of the Western agrarian protest in the 1920s and 1930s, because King and his party were primarily oriented towards electoral success and not overly fussy about "principles." Unlike the somewhat more dogmatic Conservatives under Arthur Meighen and R. B. Bennett, the Liberals were willing to make room in their party leadership and on their platform to accommodate such discontent.

Similarly, many groups of new Canadians in the 1950s, and later a portion of the unrest that characterized Quebec in the 1960s and 1970s, were absorbed and accommodated within the Liberal coalition. The party's lower-profile commitment to our British-Empire ties made them a more comfortable domicile for immigrants who were neither British nor French, and who came to Canada in the post-1945 period. Later, under Pearson, the party was also able to accommodate at least some of the Quebec unrest by allowing the Quebec provincial Liberal Party to become a completely separate entity, and by recruiting prominent spokesmen for reform in Quebec, such as Pierre Trudeau, Jean Marchand, and Gérard Pelletier.

Having been clobbered by the Tories in 1984 and 1988, the Liberals have re-emerged in the 1990s as the only party with a claim to being genuinely national. In the tradition of Mackenzie King, the Liberals forged an electoral victory without charismatic leadership, without any national vision, and with a mostly vague policy platform. The party succeeded in 1993 by exploiting the weaknesses of its opponents and, in true brokerage fashion, by occupying the middle ground in an extremely fractious and acrimonious campaign.

---

18. Reginald Whitaker, *The Government Party: Organizing and Financing the Liberal Party of Canada 1930–1958* (Toronto: University of Toronto Press, 1977), is perhaps the definitive study of the Liberal Party during much of its period of dominance. Joseph Wearing, *The L-Shaped Party* (Toronto: McGraw-Hill Ryerson, 1980), provides a valuable source of information. Christina McCall-Newman, *Grits: An Intimate Portrait of the Liberal Party* (Toronto: Macmillan, 1982), provides a highly readable account of that part of the Liberal Party in the 1970s represented by its Ottawa establishment. Because it focuses on Ottawa and on a few key personalities, it provides a somewhat less than complete picture of the Liberal Party of Canada.

**Party Support**  No picture of a political party would be complete without some view of its supporters over time. However, two cautionary comments are in order at the outset. First, probably only about 30 per cent of Canadian voters can be described as strong, stable supporters of any party. As we shall see in the next chapter, almost half of even these people are "flexible partisans" who will occasionally cross party lines in a given election. Second, there is relatively little difference in the socio-economic base of support for the major political parties in Canada. While we can make statements of tendency, given the ephemeral nature of Canadian party support, virtually all of the correlations we express below are really rather weak generalizations

With these caveats in mind, the Liberal base of support can be said to be both broad and narrow. It is broad in the sense that no other Canadian party can claim to draw support consistently from such a broad social spectrum. On the other hand, its support has been narrow regionally. This can be seen, for instance, in its electoral dependency, until 1984, on the Quebec vote, and in its major weakness in the West that persists to this day. There is also strong support for the Liberals from French minorities outside of Quebec. Franco-Ontarians and Acadians have supported the federal (and provincial) Liberals in overwhelming proportions, and there was little evidence, even in the Conservative electoral sweeps of 1984 and 1988, that this support is evaporating.

Liberal voters have been drawn somewhat disproportionately from the upper socio-economic stratum, while Western farmers and small-business interests have tended to avoid the party. Rural, small-town, and farmer support for the Liberals is also generally somewhat lower than the proportion of those groups in the population. In spite of strong efforts by all other parties, the Liberals have consistently held greater appeal for minority groups, ranging from the large English and non-French minorities in Quebec to new Canadians—immigrants who have arrived since 1945. The party also has been better supported by younger voters than by older ones.

**The Government Party**  Reginald Whitaker has suggested in his study of the Liberals that the explanation of the long period of Liberal dominance in Canadian federal politics is that the Liberal Party is the "government party."[19] The Liberals have utilized the apparatus of the federal government as a virtual extension of the party organization. The down side of this, leaving questions of ethics and political morality aside, is that the extra-parliamentary party is marginalized. The locus of power within the party lies very obviously with the prime minister and the Cabinet who control the government bureaucracy. Instead of looking to the party structure at large for ideas, the elites of the party either formulate policy themselves or rely upon the bureaucracy for innovation. The party outside the governmental executive is thus reduced to functioning as an election-machine-in-waiting and its policy ideas are neither listened to nor appreciated.

---

19. Whitaker, *The Government Party*, particularly pp. 401ff. The same theme dominates in Wearing, *The L-Shaped Party*, and in Christina McCall-Newman, *Grits*.

Under the Liberal version of this system, individual Cabinet ministers are expected to use their departmental organizations not just to perform the functions of the modern state, but also to provide the rewards necessary to motivate party workers and to ensure electoral support. The most powerful of them also operate as power brokers in order to consolidate support in the regions and to represent those regional interests at the centre. In general, all of this is a satisfactory situation as long as the party holds office. However, as we saw with respect to the Liberals during the Mulroney years, the organizational structure of a cadre party operating in a federal system, with heavy reliance on the public service as the source of many of its ideas, is particularly vulnerable once it has lost office.

As well, a federal cadre party, out of office, cannot even fall back on the autonomous provincial parties as a base of support in its hour of organizational need. Part of the reason for this problem is that the party's provincial wings may not even be on the same wavelength as the national party. As we have seen, the provincial parties have different electorates, very different policy concerns, many of which compete head-on with those of the national party, and even different sources of party funding. Thus, lacking an organizational base outside the government structure, when the Liberal Party loses office it is faced with the daunting task of rebuilding an extra-parliamentary organization to help it regain power. In 1993, it was more the self-destruction of the Conservative Party than a rejuvenated Liberal organization that allowed the Liberals to come back to power after the Conservative electoral victories of 1984 and 1988.

### The Progressive Conservatives

While Mackenzie King set the tone of party organization and tactics for the Liberals from 1921 on, it may be a proper description of the Progressive Conservatives up to the mid 1980s to suggest that no leader has succeeded in putting any very permanent stamp on the party. Since 1917, instability has been its most prominent characteristic. If the Liberals have tended to become the government party, the Conservatives have tended to suffer their own particular disease, the **Tory syndrome**, leaving them perpetually in opposition, with brief periods of "remission" during which they form the government. The most recent period of remission lasted from 1984 to 1993, and for a while it looked like the Tory syndrome had been cured for good. But with only two members elected in 1993, the Tories are not officially a *party* at all, let alone the official Opposition party. Thus, while we might conclude that the Conservatives have at last dodged the label of "perpetual opposition party," it is unlikely that the few remaining party faithful will take much solace from that!

**The "Perpetual Opposition"**  Arthur Meighen, who succeeded Sir Robert Borden as leader of the Conservative Party in 1920, was claimed by some to be a brilliant intellectual, but he was competely unable to develop the common touch. This, combined with total lack of support in Quebec and the ability of the Liberals to absorb dissident populist factions, marks the onset of the Tory syndrome.[20] R. B. Bennett, who succeeded Meighen, won the 1930 election, and this first period of remission lasted from 1930 to 1935. Bennett completely dominated the party organization while in power, in large part because he was its largest financial backer. In this sense he led the party because he "owned" it and his leadership was "a benefit which his party scarcely survived."[21]

As well, the party's "misfortune" of being the government party during the worst years of the Depression ensured that it would fail electorally in 1935 and that the Tory syndrome would recur. It seems doubtful that any government or party could have successfully resolved the deep cleavages and crises caused by the Depression, but the Conservatives had developed an over-centralized, elite-dominated structure that was singularly inappropriate for even attempting the task.

Bennett's departure from the leadership was followed by a period in Conservative Party history that could most charitably be called a prolonged interregnum. One leader after another failed to lead the party out of the electoral wilderness. Between 1940 and 1956, the Conservative Party went through four leaders, and even sponsored an abortive comeback attempt by Arthur Meighen.[22] Finally, in the 1957 and 1958 elections, the perpetual leadership crisis seemed to be resolved when the messianic John Diefenbaker led the party to electoral victories.

However, Diefenbaker's leadership ended in 1967 after electoral defeats in 1963 and 1965, leaving the party deeply and acrimoniously divided. His successor, Robert Stanfield, saddled with the vindictive former prime minister in his caucus, never did succeed in completely reuniting the party during the eight years he was leader. Moreover, despite the fact that he was exceptionally competent and one of the genuinely "nice" people in politics, Stanfield's term of office coincided with the reign of Pierre Trudeau as the absolute monarch of the Liberals. Stanfield's successor, Joe Clark, initially succeeded in getting the various warring factions within the party to work together in harness, winning a minority victory in the 1979 general election. However, the Tory syndrome failed to go into remission and Clark's minority government was defeated after less than a year in office. Clark resigned in 1983 following his failure to gain at least two-thirds support for his leadership at the party convention that year. Clark did run to succeed himself as leader, just as Diefenbaker had, and, while he did not suffer the ignominious defeat incurred by his predecessor, he nonetheless lost on the last ballot to Brian Mulroney.

**Out of the Wilderness** While Clark was somewhat identified with the left wing of the Tory party, Mulroney appealed directly to the centre and right. He came originally from a working-class background and had made an early reputation in labour law, but he was more generally identified, by the time of his victory, with the Eastern establishment. His objective was to hold the party's strength in the West and to build an electoral coalition that included the former Liberal

---

20. George Perlin, *The Tory Syndrome* (Montreal: McGill-Queen's University Press, 1980).
21. K. Z. Paltiel, *Political Party Financing in Canada* (Toronto: McGraw-Hill Ryerson, 1970), p. 17.
22. See J. L. Granatstein, *The Politics of Survival 1939–1945* (Toronto: University of Toronto Press, 1967).

bastion of Quebec. Mulroney generally avoided any unequivocal policy positions, attempting instead to find the middle ground and emphasizing his own leadership qualities. He was, in 1984, an attractive, youthful leader with the sort of charismatic appeal that comes across so well on television. Particularly important to his appeal was the fact that he came from Quebec and spoke French perfectly — and with an accent not acquired at Berlitz. He was, simply, more marketable to the public than either his predecessor or his Liberal opponent, John Turner.

Electoral victory is what parties want most, and in that respect Mulroney delivered. In September 1984 his campaign led the party to the largest electoral sweep in Canadian history, taking 211 of the 282 seats in the House of Commons and winning more than 50 per cent of the national vote. At least as important as the absolute size was the breadth of the mandate obtained. The Conservatives won a plurality of votes in every province and an absolute majority in six. The most significant aspect of this support was the Conservative sweep in Quebec where the Tories gained fifty-eight of seventy-five seats, obliterating the Liberals in their one-time feifdom.

When the Tories repeated in 1988 after initially trailing the Liberals in the polls, it seemed that the Tory syndrome had at last been left behind. Although the victory left the government with a reduced majority, the support was spread across all regions of the country. It appeared in this period in the late 1980s that one of the brokerage parties had at last emerged as a truly national party and that, none too soon, the much-maligned party system could begin to perform the function of national integration. As we all now know, this was not to be the case.

**Party Structure**  The basic structure of the Conservative Party in the past half-century has been, like the Liberals, essentially that of a stratarchical-cadre party. But the Conservative Party has never been as successful as the Liberals in the incorporation of new groups and interests into the party organization. The formal organization of the Conservative Party is rather similar to that of the Liberals, and there are also many similarities in the two parties' informal structures. Like the Liberals, the Conservatives have a permanent staff at a national party headquarters, and several regional offices with permanent staff. Like the Liberal structure, a vital component of Conservative party structure is the voluntary part that magically appears just before each election.

It takes little sophistication to recognize that the Conservative Party is no less centralized and controlled by its parliamentary wing than is the Liberal Party. Both are clear examples of a cadre-party structure and, in power, the reins of office are held as tightly by a Conservative prime minister as by a Liberal one. The sole exception, and this is true for both Liberals and Conservatives, is that the national president is elected by the convention, and the convention does not always select the candidate favoured by the leader, even when the leader is the prime minister. Of course, in a cadre party, any resulting tension redounds as much or more to the disadvantage of the extra-parliamentary party as to the parliamentary wing.

**Party Support** We have already pointed out that, over time, individual Canadian voters are very flexible in their partisanship. Hence, the generalizations about Conservative Party support should be read in the context of the fact that most Canadians will vote for more than one party over their lifetimes. In a very general way, it can also be said that the support for the Liberals and the support for the Conservatives are inversions of each other. For example, the statement that the Liberals draw support disproportionately from Catholic voters can be read to mean that the Tories draw disproportionately from non-Catholics. Similarly, the Tories have greater success with rural voters and the Liberals are much more the party of urban electors, and Conservative voters also are more likely than Liberals to be middle-aged or older.

In the Atlantic provinces these tendencies are often reversed: the PCs draw more heavily than the Liberals from urban voters, possibly as a legacy of the years when maritimer Robert Stanfield was the party leader. In the West, in part because of the residual appeal of John Diefenbaker, reinforced by the antipathy felt towards the Liberal prime minister, Pierre Trudeau, in the 1970s, the voters consistently opted for the Tories until the 1993 election. Such stable regional patterns of personal appeal or antipathy have been common in Canadian politics, often persisting for decades, and the suggestion has sometimes been made that this pattern is the Canadian counterpart of the more strongly persistent and less flexible partisanship of United States voters.

The Conservatives have occasionally tried to expand their organization by recruiting other groups. In the 1940s they attempted to co-opt Progressive support from the West by choosing as their leader the former Progressive premier of Manitoba, John Bracken, and by adding the name "Progressive" to their party masthead. Unfortunately for the Conservatives, Mackenzie King had already co-opted most Western Progressive support some twenty years previously. Similarly, under Diefenbaker, the Conservatives tried to become the party of the "other" ethnic groups of Canada by emphasizing "unhyphenated" Canadianism. But in this attempt they alienated as many new Canadians as they attracted by calling attention to the differences in their cultural backgrounds. At any rate the Liberals continue to be far more successful than the Tories in building a stable base of support among immigrant groups.

While the older patterns could still be detected, they were considerably attenuated during the 1980s, and the massive Conservative electoral victory of 1984 was so broadly based that it seems likely the patterns of support for the Tories in the mid 1980s had become much like the patterns of Liberal support in the mid 1970s. The real key to this, however, was that the Tories were finally successful in broadening their base of support in Quebec, luring the voters away from the Liberals so successfully that party loyalists dared to hope that the sixty-year curse of the Tory syndrome had been lifted.

## ► CONCLUSION: PARTIES AND THE PARTY SYSTEM IN THE NINETIES

When Canadians woke up one Tuesday morning in November of 1988 they found that the Mulroney Conservatives had been returned to power with a solid majority. The Tories had apparently consolidated their position as the new government party in Canada, with broad-based support in all regions of Canada. The coalition of electoral support assembled by Mulroney and the Progressive Conservative Party was genuinely national in its composition, and there was reason for Canadians to be optimistic about forging a new and stable national consensus in an economy that was slowly but surely on the road to recovery.

### 1988: A Three-Party System?

The Liberals, as a party, had a lot less to be optimistic about. They had been in a neck-and-neck race with the Tories as the 1988 election drew near, but they (and their leader, John Turner) had blown it in the latter days of the campaign. While the Liberals were still the official Opposition with eighty-three seats, the party that had once automatically assumed that forming the national government was their organizational karma, had fared well only in the Atlantic provinces. The party won but twelve seats in its one-time bastion of Quebec and had not made the hoped-for breakthrough in the West, winning only eight seats west of Ontario, five of which were in Manitoba, two in the Northwest Territories, and Turner's own seat in British Columbia. The once-proud party of Laurier, King, and Trudeau was in disarray.

The NDP was generally pleased with their result in 1988, increasing their seats to forty-three from the thirty they had held in the previous Parliament. Although they had taken no seats east of Ontario, and only ten seats in that highly unionized province, their support appeared to be growing. Ed Broadbent resigned the leadership of the party despite the electoral gains, and the party elected Audrey McLaughlin, the first woman to lead a national party in Canada, at the national convention in 1989. The NDP appeared to be gaining credibility by mounting a more effective opposition in the House of Commons than the demoralized and leaderless Liberals.

When, in 1990, the Liberals chose "yesterday's man", Jean Chrétien, to succeed John Turner, it did not significantly enhance their standings in the polls, and for a time the NDP support nationally was actually higher than either of the two older parties.

The NDP was on a roll and the overall mood of optimism was given an enormous boost by the stunning 1990 NDP victory in Ontario and in the expected but nevertheless encouraging electoral wins in British Columbia and Saskatchewan in the following year. It appeared that at last the NDP's time had come and the party strategists were looking forward to the next national election with eager anticipation. There was just a possibility that our two-party cocktail with an NDP chaser could well emerge as a competitive three-party system for the first time in our history.

## The "Revolution" of 1993

The polls had been indicating a lot of voter volatility in the two years leading up to the 1993 election. The support for the Tories had been as low as 11 per cent in early 1992 and as high as 36 per cent after the election of Kim Campbell as the successor to Mulroney. While the Liberals generally led the polls they did not do so decisively, to a large exent because of the low profile maintained by Jean Chrétien. The NDP, which had so much reason to be optimistic in 1991, had faded badly in the polls by the date of the election call, sitting at a mere 8 per cent nationally. Initially, it seemed that the more things changed the more they remained the same, and there was a strong possibility that the Tories could pull it off again, as they did in 1988.

On the other hand, the two newcomers, the BQ and Reform, had established substantial support and increased it as the campaign went along. The Bloc enjoyed approximately 40 per cent of support in Quebec in 1991 and that figure continued to increase up to election day; the Reform Party's support in the polls had been as high as 19 per cent nationally in 1991 but was less than 10 per cent when the election was called. However, support for Reform in Alberta was almost 40 per cent, so there was reason to predict some success for the party, at least regionally. Still, while conceding some regional wins for the two new parties, many pundits were not counting out a Tory victory when the writs were issued.

**The Tory Meltdown**  While Canadians might have recognized that the Tories' prospects had declined during the 1993 campaign, very few were prepared for the catastrophic meltdown that occurred on election day. Only Jean Charest, the runner-up to Campbell in the leadership contest, and Elsie Wayne, a novice to federal politics but a popular mayor of Saint John, won their seats. The party's share of the popular vote had dropped from 43 per cent in 1988 to 16 per cent and its seats had dropped from 169 to 2. The party of John A. Macdonald ceased even to have the official status of a political party in the House of Commons. Canada's first female prime minister, Kim Campbell, lost her own seat in Vancouver and quickly resigned as leader, leaving Jean Charest as the "interim leader" — of Elsie Wayne!

*The Mulroney Legacy*  The Tories had begun to slip in the polls immediately after being sworn in as the government in 1988. Much of the slide was linked to Mulroney's growing personal unpopularity, but there were substantive problems as well. While the economy appeared to be recovering, the pace of recovery was slow, and there was no indication that the unemployment situation was going to improve.

This "jobless recovery" could be blamed in part on structural changes in the economy such as "high-tech" innovations in industrial production that were less labour-intensive. However, some of the blame could be placed on the free trade agreement negotiated by the Mulroney government that led to the relocation of Canadian branch plants to the United States. This likely did cost the economy jobs, and the government votes, in heavily industrialized Ontario. Moreover, the anticipated benefits of free trade to primary producers in resource-rich economies such as Alberta and British Columbia did not immediately translate into larger trade surpluses in, for instance, the oil-and-gas and softwood-lumber sectors.

Finally, policies such as the GST and the single-minded obsession of the Mulroney government with reducing the deficit (as it turned out, without any success) did not sit well with Canadians who were out of work or facing wage cuts. What was worse was that the government and Mulroney himself went about all this in a way that made them seem coldhearted and out of touch with working people who had to bear not only the brunt of the recession but also the full impact of Tory fiscal restraint and its collateral damage. Both the Liberals, who explicitly promised to replace the GST, and the populist Reformers, who simply promised to stay in touch with the little guy, stood to benefit from the Tories' forgetting who helped put them in power in the first place.

The other area of dissatisfaction with the Mulroney government was that they had kept the country focused on constitutional renewal for several years. When the smoke cleared, they were seen to have failed totally, leaving the country more bitterly divided than ever before. Many Westerners felt that Quebec was offered far too much in both the Meech Lake and Charlottetown Accords. Most Quebeckers, on the other hand, felt that they were being forced to accept far less than they wanted, and even then the constitutional proposals were rejected by the rest of Canada. These bitter regionally based feelings created fertile soil for a crop of anti-Tory protest votes, which were reaped by the Bloc in Quebec and the Reformers in the West.

However, despite the uphill fight the Tories would have to wage in order to overcome the handicap of the Mulroney legacy, they appeared initially to have pulled it off. The election of a woman to lead the party was a clear indication that the party was willing to change, and the emergence in the leadership race of the youthful, but very attractive, Jean Charest as the Quebec lieutenant and leader-in-waiting indicated that the party was still committed to the base of support it had developed in that province. In the summer before the election, the polls showed a remarkable recovery of the popularity of the Conservatives under new management and by the time the election was called, they were in a dead heat with the Liberals. With an unimpressive Liberal opposition it seemed quite possible that the Tories could pull off yet another victory.

*The Botched Campaign* When the 1993 election was called, the Conservative Party campaign strategists didn't seem to be able to get anything right from the start. The campaign stumbled out of the gate and kept stumbling and the election battle became a Tory rout. Part of the problem was that Prime Minister Campbell was still a rookie in the political big leagues. She had her own views about how to deal with the press and how to run a national campaign, which were often at odds with the strategies developed by her campaign braintrust. That she was new and inexperienced could have been an asset in helping to distance herself from the Mulroney legacy, and the party campaign team wanted to emphasize her personality and the fact that she was going to "do politics differently," avoiding anything that might remind the voters of Brian Mulroney.

The strategy failed in part because Kim Campbell couldn't stick to the script and kept the press focused on her gaffe of the week rather than on her personality and the freshness of her approach to politics. On the day the election was called Campbell stated that Canada would face high unemployment until the turn of the century and that we should all focus on eliminating the deficit as a way of speeding up the economic recovery. This was not what the voters wanted to hear. A couple of weeks later, Campbell told voters that social policy issues were too complicated to be dealt with in an election campaign, and that Canadians should in effect just "trust" her to do the right thing after she was elected. Finally, remarks she made that were critical of some Quebec ministers, including Jean Charest, caused a major rift in the Quebec wing of the party, which worked to the advantage of the *Bloc Québécois*.

While her "handlers" might complain that Campbell wasn't "coachable," some of the blame for the failure of the campaign must be laid at the feet of her campaign committee. The most glaring and damaging tactical error was the decision to use negative advertising against Jean Chrétien. The TV ads, which showed the Liberal leader in various unflattering poses, were seen as attempting to exploit a facial defect that he had had since a child. The exploitation of his physical handicap completely backfired, gaining sympathy for Chrétien and making the Tories appear heartless and insensitive to those less fortunate. The ads were withdrawn almost immediately but the damage was done.

Finally, the campaign was likely doomed from the start, at least in part because Kim Campbell really wasn't all that different in political style from her predecessor. The campaign showed her as more suited to the elite accommodation *modus operandi* that characterized the Mulroney years rather than to the more people-oriented politics that Canadians want today. Her dialogues with voters all too often turned out to be stern scholarly lectures on economics and her attempts to relate to average Canadians came off as patronizing and condescending rather than genuine. In this sense, she failed to convince us that she would do politics differently because she *couldn't* do them differently.

**Canadian Socialism on the Rocks** While the Tories were reduced to a paltry two seats in 1993, they did get 16 per cent of the national vote and had no lower than 11 per cent in any province. The situation of the NDP, while superficially better than that of the Tories, is likely much more serious. The NDP won nine seats, but that was because of regional concentrations of support in Saskatchewan (26.5%), British Columbia (15.5%), and Manitoba (16.5%). The national support for the NDP was less than 7 per cent, and much lower than that in seven of the ten provinces, and there is some question as to whether the party can ever recover at the national level.

*The Causes of the NDP Collapse* The reasons for the steep decline in the fortunes of Canada's only social-democratic party cannot be explained away in terms of weak leadership or a failed campaign. Rather, the NDP was declining as a political force throughout the 1990s and had lost the election of 1993 before the writs were even issued. While the leadership of Audrey McLaughlin was not as strong as it might have been, it is unlikely that even Moses could have turned things around for the party, given its enfeebled state in 1993. McLaughlin probably worked harder and demonstrated a higher level of personal commitment than any of the other leaders during the campaign. She did the noble thing after the election by resigning as leader, and was succeeded in 1995 by Nova Scotian Alexa McDonough.

In attempting to move to the political centre in order to become a credible alternative to Canadians who were unhappy with the exisiting parties, but unwilling to radically alter the economic system itself, the NDP lost its identity. The NDP lost, to the Reform Party, the protest vote, which had ensured a significant bloc of support in every past election, at the same time failing to lure any middle-of-the-road voters away from the Liberals. Most of its innovative policy positions were long ago adopted by the main parties, so that in the eyes of the public the NDP had become simply another and less effectual party of the status quo. The party "fell between two stools" and may not be able to regain its feet.

Another cause of the NDP decline, perhaps ironically, was its remarkable success in the 1990s at the provincial level. Initially this translated into increased popularity for the national party in the public-opinion polls. However, when faced with being the government, the provincial parties discovered that it was not always easy to live up to the promises made while in opposition. Particularly in Ontario, where Bob Rae's government inherited a large provincial deficit, it was very difficult to implement socialist policies while at the same time trying to reduce the annual deficit. The Rae government had to do what any government, socialist or not, would have had to do — reduce the deficit.

This brought the party into conflict with many supporters, in particular, the provincial public servants, who were forced to take cuts in pay as a part of the so-called social contract. In fact, the social contract was not a contract at all because the provincial unions refused to go along with it and the Rae government was forced to impose its provisions unilaterally through legislation. This ultimately led to the defection of the Ontario Federation of Labour from the NDP, and a disastrous, if not fatal, spillover effect on the support for Audrey McLaughlin and the national party. In 1995, Ontario voters emphatically rejected the Rae government and elected the conservatives led by Mike Harris.

The Harcourt and Romanow governments in British Columbia and Saskatchewan have not experienced the same degree of internal strife as the Rae government in Ontario, but, again, *being* the government forces the NDP to *act* like a government. This means having sometimes to implement policies and take decisions that are not popular. In British Columbia, for instance, the government has taken decisions in the area of timber harvesting that have put it into conflict both with environmental groups who feel its policies are not "green" enough and with the loggers' unions who see jobs lost to appease the tree-huggers. As in Ontario, the dissaffection with the provincial party translates directly into reduced support for the national party.

*The NDP Dilemma*   The electoral success of the NDP at the provincial level in the 1990s has driven home two points. First, it is difficult for the NDP to be as socialist in power as it is in opposition, and second, it may be totally impossible to be a socialist government at the national level in this country. Most of the key planks in the NDP platform involve matters such as social policy, health, education, daycare, and housing, all of which are provincial responsibilities. Hence, even if the NDP were to form a government at the national level, it would be unable to do very much because of the federal distribution of powers.

The strategists in the national party must be plagued by the difficulty of developing a platform of policy promises that, on the one hand, can be kept if the party forms a government, and that on the other hand, sufficiently differentiates the NDP from the Liberals. While the voters may not even be conscious of the jurisdictional limits on the federal party, they were unimpressed by the 1993 election platform that, compared to the Liberals', was little more than "me too, but with more feeling."

**Populism, Protest, and *Indépendantisme*: Reform and BQ** The 1993 election resulted in the decimation of two of our traditional parties, the NDP and the Conservatives, but it also resulted in the emergence of two parties new to the national scene. The Reform Party and the *Bloc Québécois*, each of which won significant regional support, were the direct beneficiaries of the demise of the Conservatives and the NDP.

*The Bloc Québécois*  The *Bloc Québécois* had never before run candidates in a general election although the party did successfully contest a by-election in Quebec in 1991 with the support of the *Parti Québécois* organization. The Bloc held eight seats at dissolution, but seven of these were as the result of defections by separatist MPs who had been elected under the banner of either the Conservatives or the Liberals. The Bloc, under the strong leadership of Lucien Bouchard, won fifty-four seats and 49 per cent of the popular vote in Quebec in the 1993 election and, perhaps unexpectedly, even to the party leadership, assumed the role of official Opposition in the House of Commons.

The BQ makes no pretense of being a national party, running in no constituencies outside of Quebec. While the party did enunciate broad, middle-of-the-road positions on non-nationalist issues during the election, their only unequivocal promise was to fight single-mindedly for the independence of Quebec. The party has no extra-parliamentary organization, and it functions simply as the federal wing of the *Parti Québécois*, whose organization serves the Bloc by providing the organization for contesting elections and raising campaign funds. The Bloc caucus maintains close and constant ties to the provincial party leadership, which now happens to be the provincial Cabinet.

The future of the *Bloc Québécois* is very uncertain. They take the official position that their job as a political party at the federal level is time-limited. The "best-before" date on the party is the day Quebec sovereignty is achieved, at which time there will no longer be a need for a separatist voice in Parliament. However, the full independence of Quebec cannot happen overnight even if there is general agreement between Canada and Quebec that it is the best thing. The divorce would have to be phased in with intense negotiations at all stages, and, during this period of transition, the Bloc would try to play the somewhat anomolous role of representing Quebec's interests in the Canadian Parliament.

As well, if the split were not total and if Quebec and Canada were to continue to share an infrastructure that includes, for instance, currency, the banking system, the armed forces, and the postal service, there may have to be some form of ongoing representation for Quebec in Parliament whenever matters of shared jurisdiction are being discussed. The *Bloc Québécois* could continue to exist as one of the Quebec parties vying for such part-time seats in the Canadian Parliament, although its platform would have to focus on issues *within* Quebec as well as issues between Canada and Quebec, after separation.

Even without separation, there can conceivably be an ongoing *raison d'etre* for the Bloc, as a voice for Quebec in Parliament. In fact, it is likely that many of the voters who supported the BQ in 1993 did expect it to be that voice. However, such a strictly regionally based party could never hope to form the government, and the influence of a minor opposition party in the House of Commons is extremely limited. The Quebec voters have always tended to vote nationally as a bloc for the government party, thus giving the province a significant, if not a majority, voice in the government caucus and representation in the Cabinet. On the basis of this historical trend, it seems likely that in the absence of separation, the Quebec electorate would reject a strictly regional party such as the Bloc, even with a popular leader, choosing instead to support a national political party that has a chance of forming the government.

*The Reform Party*  The Reform Party, as we have already seen, emerged as a grassroots movement in western Canada. Its initial foray into electoral politics was in the 1988 election, where it ran a few candidates and picked up 15 per cent of the vote, but no seats, in Alberta. The Reform Party won a by-election in Alberta in 1989 and tested its national campaign organization in its fight against the Charlottetown Accord in the 1992 referendum. In the 1993 election, Reform ran full slates of candidates in all of the Western provinces and ran some candidates in all provinces but Quebec. The result was fifty-two seats and 19 per cent of the popular vote nationally, which placed it second to the Liberals — and without any candidates in Quebec.

However, electoral support for the Reform Party is still essentially regional, and outside Alberta its strength is based in rural rather than metropolitan constituencies. In Alberta, Reform won twenty-two of twenty-six seats with 52 per cent of the vote, and in British Columbia, they won twenty-four of thirty-two seats with 36 per cent of the vote. In each of Ontario and Manitoba Reform won a single seat and took, respectively, 20 and 22 per cent of the popular vote. The future of the Reform Party depends upon the broadening of its national base to other provinces and building on the support it received in 1993.

There is some evidence that this might prove difficult unless the Conservative Party really is defunct as a right-of-centre alternative to the Liberals. Fully 52 per cent of the Reform vote came from people who had voted Conservative in 1988, and only time will tell whether this was a one-time protest vote, spanking the Tories for their naughtiness while in office, or a permanent shift of a large bloc of Canadian voters further to the right. Past experience tells us that Western-based populist and protest movements, such as the Progressives and Social Credit, do from time to time enjoy success in national elections, but quickly fade away or become absorbed into one of the two brokerage parties.

**TABLE 14.1**

Federal Election Results, 1878–1993.

| Election Year | Party Forming Government | Total Seats | Conservative Seats | Conservative Votes (%) | Liberal Seats | Liberal Votes (%) | Progressive Seats | Progressive Votes (%) | CCF/NDP Seats | CCF/NDP Votes (%) | Social Credit/Créditiste Seats | Social Credit/Créditiste Votes (%) | Bloc Québécois Seats | Bloc Québécois Votes (%) | Reform Seats | Reform Votes (%) | Other Seats | Other Votes (%) |
|---|---|---|---|---|---|---|---|---|---|---|---|---|---|---|---|---|---|---|
| 1878 | C | 206 | 140 | 53 | 65 | 45 | | | | | | | | | | | 1 | 2 |
| 1882 | C | 211 | 138 | 53 | 73 | 47 | | | | | | | | | | | | |
| 1887 | C | 215 | 128 | 51 | 87 | 49 | | | | | | | | | | | | |
| 1891 | C | 215 | 122 | 52 | 91 | 46 | | | | | | | | | | | 2 | 2 |
| 1896 | L | 213 | 88 | 46 | 118 | 45 | | | | | | | | | | | 7 | 9 |
| 1900 | L | 213 | 81 | 47 | 132 | 52 | | | | | | | | | | | | 1 |
| 1904 | L | 214 | 75 | 47 | 139 | 52 | | | | | | | | | | | | 1 |
| 1908 | L | 221 | 85 | 47 | 135 | 51 | | | | | | | | | | | 1 | 2 |
| 1911 | C | 221 | 134 | 51 | 87 | 48 | | | | | | | | | | | | 1 |
| 1917 | C | 235 | 153 | 57 | 82 | 40 | | | | | | | | | | | | 3 |
| 1921 | L | 235 | 50 | 30 | 116 | 41 | 65 | 23 | | | | | | | | | 4 | 6 |
| 1925 | L | 245 | 116 | 46 | 99 | 40 | 24 | 9 | | | | | | | | | 6 | 5 |
| 1926 | L | 245 | 91 | 45 | 128 | 46 | 20 | 5 | | | | | | | | | 6 | 4 |
| 1930 | C | 245 | 137 | 49 | 91 | 45 | 12 | 3 | | | | | | | | | 5 | 3 |
| 1935 | L | 245 | 40 | 30 | 173 | 45 | | | 7 | 9 | 17 | 4 | | | | | 8 | 12 |
| 1940 | L | 245 | 40 | 31 | 181 | 51 | | | 8 | 8 | 10 | 3 | | | | | 6 | 7 |
| 1945 | L | 245 | 67 | 27 | 125 | 41 | | | 28 | 16 | 13 | 4 | | | | | 12 | 12 |
| 1949 | L | 262 | 41 | 30 | 193 | 49 | | | 13 | 13 | 10 | 4 | | | | | 5 | 4 |
| 1953 | L | 265 | 51 | 31 | 171 | 49 | | | 23 | 11 | 15 | 5 | | | | | 5 | 4 |
| 1957 | C | 265 | 112 | 39 | 105 | 41 | | | 25 | 11 | 19 | 7 | | | | | 4 | 2 |
| 1958 | C | 265 | 208 | 54 | 49 | 34 | | | 8 | 9 | 0 | 2 | | | | | | 1 |
| 1962 | C | 265 | 116 | 37 | 100 | 37 | | | 19 | 14 | 30 | 12 | | | | | | 1 |
| 1963 | L | 265 | 95 | 33 | 129 | 42 | | | 17 | 13 | 24 | 12 | | | | | | 1 |
| 1965 | L | 265 | 97 | 32 | 131 | 40 | | | 21 | 18 | 14 | 9 | | | | | 2 | 1 |
| 1968 | L | 264 | 72 | 31 | 155 | 45 | | | 22 | 17 | 14 | 6 | | | | | 1 | 1 |
| 1972 | L | 264 | 107 | 35 | 109 | 38 | | | 31 | 18 | 15 | 8 | | | | | 2 | 1 |
| 1974 | L | 264 | 95 | 35 | 141 | 43 | | | 16 | 15 | 11 | 5 | | | | | 1 | 1 |
| 1979 | C | 282 | 136 | 36 | 114 | 40 | | | 26 | 18 | 6 | 5 | | | | | | 1 |
| 1980 | L | 282 | 103 | 33 | 146 | 44 | | | 32 | 20 | 0 | 1 | | | | | 1 | 2 |
| 1984 | C | 282 | 211 | 50 | 40 | 28 | | | 30 | 19 | | | | | | | 1 | 2 |
| 1988 | C | 295 | 169 | 43 | 83 | 32 | | | 43 | 20 | | | | | | | | 4 |
| 1993 | L | 295 | 2 | 16 | 177 | 41 | | | 9 | 7 | | | 54 | 13 | 52 | 19 | 1 | 4 |

C = Conservative. L = Liberal.

Source: Hugh Thorburn, Party Politics in Canada, 6th ed. (Scarborough: Prentice-Hall, 1991) p. 533. Used with permission. Updated by the author.

▶ THE FUTURE OF THE PARTY SYSTEM

Up until now, we have not said very much about the Liberal Party and its tremendous success in the 1993 election. In fact, it can be said that the Liberals did not so much "win" the contest as the Tories and the NDP "lost" it, and the Reform and the BQ split the voters who could not bring themselves to vote Liberal. The Liberal campaign was not particularly brilliant, and the campaign *persona* of Jean Chrétien was anything but charismatic. However, the party strategists didn't make any mistakes, they effectively exploited the mistakes made by the other parties, and in general they gave us a picture of boring but workmanlike competence and honesty.

Perhaps the 1993 election result was not as much a watershed in our party system as it might appear from a quick glance at the results. In the first place, the "true" government party is back in power, with a solid majority and with representation from all regions of the country. There are two new parties sharing the opposition benches, but are they really that new? Western protest movements have always occurred episodically in Canada, and the emergence of a party in Quebec based on an appeal to nationalist sentiments is hardly a precedent. However, what makes the 1993 election result appear to be different is the collapse of the Tories and the NDP, and the verdict on whether this was a historical blip or a revolution must be reserved until we can see the outcome of the next election.

The NDP and the Conservatives are definitely down, but they have not disappeared from the Canadian political landscape. The NDP currently is the government party in two provinces, and the Tories hold power in three. As well, the Tories or the NDP are the official Opposition in many of the provinces where they are not the government. Given the solid provincial base, either the Conservatives or the NDP could mount a resurgence in national politics, although, for reasons cited earlier, the NDP has a tougher row to hoe. Even insiders in the NDP have questioned whether the party should back out of national electoral competition entirely and function instead as a "political movement" nationally, remaining a political party only at the provincial level. At the national level, the lack of an alternative to the left of the Liberals might induce erstwhile NDP supporters to ally themselves with the Liberals in the hope of driving that party at least a bit further to the left.

One possibility for the Conservatives nationally might be to forge an alliance with the Reform Party and thus emerge once more as a right-of-centre alternative to the Liberals. The obstacle to this might be that the Reform activists are too far right in their political convictions to be able to accept the more moderately conservative positions of the Tories. Another complication in attempting to form a new coalition of the right in Canada could arise if the Reform enters the provincial arenas. In British Columbia there is considerable movement in that direction, and while Preston Manning is officially opposed to direct involvement at the provincial level, there is not much he or the party can do about it if Reform supporters are determined to go ahead.

Hence, our party system in the mid 1990s may not be dead, but it is at least temporarily in a deep coma. In fact it might be argued that for the first time in our history we do not really have a party *system* as such, because there is no viable alternative government sitting in the opposition benches. With their strictly regional bases of support, the Bloc and Reform are not truly *national* parties; disintegrative tendencies may be winning the battle against Canadian unity. The evolution of the party system from this point, as with the survival of the federal system, will depend much on events in Quebec; in the meantime, the only vehicle of national integration is the Liberal Party and its historical success as a broker of diverse interests.

*Chapter* **15**

# The Dynamics of the Electoral Process: Parties and Voters

The world of politics has changed considerably since Stephen Leacock described the aftermath of the dissolution of Parliament in Mariposa shortly after the turn of the century. But it has not changed with respect to the excitement general elections still generate:

> The whole town and country is a hive of politics, and people who have only witnessed gatherings such as the House of Commons at Westminster and the Senate at Washington and never seen a Conservative Convention at Tecumseh Corners or a Liberal Rally at the Concession Schoolhouse, don't know what politics means.
>
> So you may imagine the excitement in Mariposa when it became known that King George had dissolved the Parliament of Canada and had sent out a writ or command for Missinaba County to elect for him some other person than John Henry Bagshaw because he no longer had confidence in him.[1]

In this chapter we are going to take a closer look at what the people in Mariposa and other towns and cities across Canada get so excited about.

The goal of this chapter is to explain the electoral process itself as a dynamic set of interrelated activities or sub-processes. In previous chapters we have looked at the functions and formal structures of the electoral system and at the functions and organization of the political parties, which are so important in the workings of the electoral process. We have also looked at the history and evolution of our party system, and the relative success of individual political parties in the electoral process over time. However, to fully understand the workings of Canadian electoral democracy, we must look beyond the formal structures and institutions and consider how they operate in practice. First, we will focus on the election-related activity of the political parties, and second,

---

1. From Stephen Leacock, *Sunshine Sketches of a Little Town* (Toronto: McClelland and Stewart, 1912), Reprinted by permission of McClelland and Stewart Limited.

we will attempt to explain the electoral behaviour of the individual voters, all the time recognizing that it is the media in a modern election that provide the communication linkages between the parties and the voters before, during, and after the campaign.

## ▶ PARTIES AND THE ELECTORAL PROCESS

While, as we have seen, political parties perform functions other than those associated with the electoral process, the most visible and the most interesting party activities to the average Canadian are those related to elections. These party activities, or *sub-processes* of the electoral process, can be broken down into two broad types — interelection activities and campaign activities.

### Interelection Activities

The activities of political parties between elections are dominated by the elected representatives in caucus and the parliamentary leadership. Neverthe-less, the party organization continues to exist, and the executives of the extra-parliamentary party set the party electoral machine on slow idle until the next election draws near. There are four categories of interelection party activity however, that do bear directly on the election outcome — periodic leadership reviews, the selection of a new party leader, the selection of candidates in the constituencies, and the raising of funds to finance the election campaign. Each of these must be considered in turn.

**Leadership Review** Periodically, the party will hold a **policy convention** be-tween elections and from time to time the party will be called upon to choose a new leader to carry the party banner in the next election. As might be expected because leadership is so salient in determining the electoral success of political parties, conventions that focus on questions of leadership are more important than those that do not.

All political parties in Canada conduct periodic **leadership reviews** and these are normally routine votes of confidence in the incumbent. However, when the party has faced a recent defeat in an election, the review may be a genuine vote of confidence or non-confidence in the leader. There is no firm rule about when a leader is assumed to have lost the confidence of the party, but usually it is fairly obvious when it is time for a change and the leader will simply resign without facing the convention.

Ed Broadbent resigned after the NDP didn't fare as well as the party faithful had hoped in the 1988 election, and his successor, Audrey McLaughlin, also resigned after the party's humiliation in 1993. Pierre Trudeau actually resigned twice. The first time was after the defeat at the hands of Joe Clark and the Tories in 1979, but when the Clark government lost a non-confidence vote before the Liberals could hold their leadership convention, Trudeau was lured out of retirement to lead the party to a victory in the 1980 election. He resigned again in 1984 and this time it "took." Trudeau's successor, John Turner, lost the subsequent election badly, but was given an 80 per cent vote of confidence at the next scheduled leadership review in 1986. However, after failing to bring the party to power in 1988, Turner resigned without having to face a review that, in all likelihood, would have been embarrassing personally and divisive for the party.

Where it would seem to be the practice at Liberal leadership-review conventions to close ranks and support the incumbent by tradition, Conservatives have been more likely to eat their defeated leaders alive. As James Lightbody put it, it is an "article of faith that Liberals support their leaders uncritically, unlike Conservatives who customarily initiate leaderly cannibalism (apparently a necessary party ritual spawned by the vernal equinox)."[2]

Diefenbaker was forced out of the leadership through a review, and although he ran for his own job in the 1967 leadership convention, he was badly embarrassed by the outcome, which saw him fall completely out of contention and be succeeded by Robert Stanfield.

Joe Clark resigned the leadership of the Conservatives in 1983 after barely failing to carry a two-thirds majority in a leadership review, believing that the party could only be united by having an open airing of grievances at a leadership convention. As we know, Clark was narrowly defeated by Brian Mulroney in the 1983 convention, but his principled decision to view anything less than two-thirds support at the leadership review as a rejection helped lead to a united party and nine years in government.

**The Conduct of Leadership Conventions**  The Liberals since 1919 and the Tories since 1927 have selected their leaders through the instrument of a **national leadership convention**. The NDP and its predecessor the CCF have chosen leaders through the convention method since the founding of the CCF in 1933. The *Bloc Québécois* and the Reform Party also used a party convention or congress to select their current leaders, although both Lucien Bouchard and Preston Manning ran unopposed in their respective leadership bids.

While the leadership conventions of the major national political parties may ultimately provide the short list of prime-ministerial job applicants, the process of leadership selection by the parties is completely unregulated by government. The only rules regarding the conduct of leadership conventions are established by the party constitutions and party by-laws, and party activists generally oppose the idea of governmental regulation of what they see as an internal affair.[3]

*Delegate Selection*  Perhaps the key component of the convention method of leadership choice is the selection of delegates. Many delegates to the Tory and Liberal conventions are *ex officio*, and include MPs, candidates, members of provincial legislatures, and party executive officers. The NDP convention has fewer *ex officio* delegates but does provide for its labour-union affiliates to name

---

2. James Lightbody,"Dancing with Dinosaurs: Alberta Politics in 1986," *Canadian Forum*, January 1986, p. 11
3. See George Perlin, "Attitudes of Liberal Convention Delegates Toward Proposals for Reform of the Process of Leadership Selection," and Keith Archer, "Leadership Selection in the New Democratic Party," *in* H. Bakvis, ed., *Canadian Political Parties: Leaders, Candidates and Organization* (Toronto: Dundurn Press, 1991), pp. 57–96, 3–56.

a significant number of delegates. The parties also allocate delegates to various youth groups, womens associations, and university clubs. For all parties, however, the largest percentage of the delegates are selected by the constituency associations, usually by a vote at a delegate-selection meeting in the riding.

The NDP generally regulates the process of delegate choice in the constituency more closely than either the Liberals or the Conservatives. One flaw in the NDP process is that the number of delegates to be selected by a constituency is determined by the number of party members in the local organization. This has tended to skew the representation at NDP leadership conventions in favour of regions where the party's membership is strong. For instance, in the 1989 leadership convention, Quebec's constituency delegates made up only 2.6 per cent of the total whereas Ontario had 20 per cent and Saskatchewan 14 per cent.[4]

The Liberals and the Conservatives assign an equal number of delegate positions to each constituency across the country, so the convention is more regionally representative than that of the NDP. However, the two older parties have faced another problem in recent conventions, which is a by-product of the openness of the riding organizations. Because the national parties set no cutoff dates or residency requirements for eligibility to vote in a constituency delegate-selection meeting, there have been many cases of packing the meetings with "instant Tories" or "instant Liberals" who are recruited simply in order to allow the supporters of a particular leadership candidate to get their chosen people to the convention. The delegate-selection processes for both the 1990 Liberal leadership convention and the 1993 Conservative convention were marred by numerous instances of packing the local selection meetings. Neither party's image benefits from this unseemly spectacle of an open democratic process gone wrong, and the Liberals have introduced reforms to take effect whenever a successor to the current leader, Jean Chrétien, is to be chosen. The basic model for delegate selection will be based on a sort of **primary** vote in the constituency. All of the party members in the riding will vote directly for one of the leadership candidates and the riding delegates will be selected according to the proportion of the vote from slates of declared supporters of the leadership hopefuls.

The NDP has not suffered the same problems with respect to packing delegate-selection meetings, in part because the party places very strict spending limits on leadership campaigns that preclude buying new members at the last minute. As well, unlike the Tories or the Liberals, the NDP requires that to vote in a nomination meeting or delegate-selection meeting, one must have been a party member for at least 120 days, which precludes last-minute recruitment of instant partisans. However, the NDP, facing a time of reconsideration and, hopefully, renewal, implemented a system of non-binding primaries in its 1995 leadership convention.

*The Convention Vote*  Leadership conventions in Canada today are major media events, carefully planned months in advance, preceded by highly visible campaigns, and played out in a circus atmosphere. In this sense they look more

---

4. Bakvis, *Canadian Political Parties*, p. 8.

and more like their counterpart events in the US. However, the similarity is in reality quite superficial. Because of the *primary system*, whereby registered party members vote directly for presidential hopefuls, and because of the "unit rule," which means that states, not individual delegates, select the party's presidential nominee, US conventions are more ritual than contest. Canadian leadership conventions are usually exciting because, despite the usual spate of public-opinion polling, the result is not always predictable.

One reason for the unpredictability of Canadian party-leadership races is that many delegates do not declare themselves for a particular candidate before the convention. More than half of the delegates to recent Liberal and Tory leadership conventions were not committed publicly to supporting any particular candidate. Moreover, many delegates who do declare for a candidate are only committed for one ballot and may switch their support on subsequent ballots. Finally, because Canadian leadership conventions utilize the secret ballot, there is nothing to ensure that declared delegates maintain their commitments even on the first ballot.

All of the parties select their leaders through a multiple-ballot majority system. With a few small variations, the basic system is that the candidate with the fewest votes on each vote is dropped from the ballot for the next vote until one candidate has a clear majority. Candidates who place better than last, but who recognize that they don't have a chance of winning, will often withdraw from the race in order to throw their support behind a likely winner in the hopes of earning some favours from the new leader in the future. The difficulty here is that very few candidates can actually deliver their delegates on a subsequent ballot.

Whatever the subtle dynamics of the process, leadership conventions are as exciting as elections and draw almost as much media attention. The Liberal convention of 1990 may have been the exception to this, for the party selected Chrétien on the first ballot. Similarly, the selections of Manning and Bouchard as the first leaders of their respective parties were little more than coronations, given that they had founded their respective parties and were both unopposed and acclaimed as leaders. However, the 1989 NDP convention narrowly chose Audrey McLaughlin after four exciting ballots, and the 1983 Conservative convention saw Brian Mulroney, after trailing on the first three ballots, come from behind to edge out Joe Clark on the fourth. An interesting twist in the 1995 NDP convention saw Svend Robinson, who was *leading* after the first ballot, withdraw from the race, conceding the victory to the second-place candidate, Alexa McDonough.

*Financing Leadership Selection* Financing party-leadership contests is merely a subset of general party financing but, unlike the parties' election expenditures, the costs incurred for leadership campaigns are unregulated by the state. A leadership convention is a very expensive undertaking for a national political party, which must pay for the actual convention and for many of the expenses of the thousands of delegates who will attend. It is expensive as well for the individual candidates if they are to conduct credible campaigns. Each individual leadership hopeful must find the funds to pay not only for his or her campaign, but also for the convention-week hospitality suites (with open bars!)

and for the banners, bunting, placards, posters, and Dixieland bands that are now felt to be a necessary part of the fabricated hoopla on the convention floor.

In order to prevent candidates from buying the party leadership and to discourage candidates from incurring obligations to corporate donors who might attempt to call in markers at some future date, all of the parties attempt to limit the amount each leadership candidate spends on the campaign and the convention-floor mayhem. Because donations to leadership contenders are tax deductible in the same way as election contributions, it is hoped that the necessary funds will come more and more from small individual donations rather than from the cynical largesse of big corporations. However, the parties also require that all significant donors be identified specifically, which may limit their influence over the party if it becomes the government.

By contrast, the Liberals set a spending limit of $1.7 million in 1990 and the Tories attempted, unsuccessfully, to limit the budgets of leadership hopefuls in 1993 to $900,000. While all the parties have such rules, there are no penalties specified for breaking the rules. It is also likely that the self-imposed limits on money spent on leadership races will never be enforced very stringently. The fact remains that the money spent translates directly to positive exposure for the party as a whole and the convention media-hype often provides a running start to the party's next election campaign. We will say more about party finance in general in the next section of this chapter.

*Conclusion*  A leadership convention is bigger, noisier, and more exciting than a policy convention, and it gets the party vast amounts of free publicity, which helps in its attempts to get elected. While the shifts in policy direction produced by a change in leadership have usually been small, for the party activists and the public alike, leadership races within parties carry much of the excitement of elections. They focus attention on the party, just as elections focus attention on the political system, and they provide a game party activists can play and the public can watch. While everyone would like to see the leader of his or her choice win, the contest has fun value in itself.

But leadership races are, for some, high-stakes games, and the most active participants, particularly in the teams of the candidates who come close to winning, are not always quick to accept the outcome. Thus, a leadership convention is welcomed because it showcases the party's talent and enhances its visibility to the public. However, the inevitable down side to such events is that they are often acrimoniously fought battles, with the losers bearing grudges and the winners "getting even" and with the party possibly entering the next election campaign less than completely united. There is a fine line between the positive effects of media exposure for the party notables and the negative effects of what may become a family squabble in public.

**Candidate Selection**  While the *Canada Elections Act* sets the formal requirements of candidacy in a national election, the **nominating process** is essentially unregulated by law. The parties control the process entirely, and for the most part, within the parties it is the local constituency associations, rather than the national organization, that make the rules for candidate selection in each riding. Although this local control over the process of candidate selection might lead one to expect a wide variation in the practice from one constituency to another and among the parties, there is a surprising consistency in the way in which candidates are selected in Canada.

_Membership Rules_  Without exception, the selection of local candidates is by a vote of the party _membership_ in the riding association. What varies are the rules regarding who is permitted to be a party member for purposes of voting in a nomination meeting. The Liberals and the NDP have a rule that their members may not be members of another political party, although the rule is impossible to enforce. Moreover, while we are certain that some individuals do hold simultaneous memberships in more than one political party, there is no evidence that members of one party have ever been able to affect the outcome of a rival party's nomination process by packing the rival organization with their own members.

Residency in the constituency is a requirement for membership in some constituencies, but none of the national party constitutions require it of the local association. More than half of the local organizations of the three traditional parties have indicated that they have non-resident members, but in no case do the non-residents amount to a significant percentage of the total.[5] Some flexibility in such matters is necessary because constituency boundaries do change regularly, and, when a riding in which the party has a chance of winning is located adjacent to a "hopeless" riding, the party activists in the general region might wish to become involved in a constituency where their participation is meaningful.

_Voting at Nomination Meetings_  As we saw in the discussion of the selection of constituency delegates for leadership conventions, one of the problems with the openness of the local selection process is the phenomenon of the **instant partisan** as a device used to pack a meeting. The same problem exists with respect to the eligibilty to vote at nomination meetings. The majority of riding associations in all parties require individuals who wish to vote at a nomination meeting to be members for more than one week but not more than a month. At the extreme, some ridings require several months and others permit same-day sign-ups to participate. The concern with such time limits on effective membership increases with the likelihood of winning the coming election, and in hopeless ridings the local organization will accept anybody who comes up with the five to ten bucks right up to the opening of the meeting.

Finally, most constituency associations do not require party members to be eligible voters. This is quite important in that people who are too young to vote may be able to participate in the selection of the candidate. In ridings where the party is almost certain to win, the nomination meeting, in effect, is electing an MP, because the election itself is a forgone conclusion. As a result, in some ridings, party members who are as young as fourteen are given _de facto_ enfranchisement through the nomination process. While concern has been

5.  R. K. Carty and Lynda Erickson, "Candidate Nomination in Canada's National Political Parties," _in_ Bakvis, _Canadian Political Parties,_ pp. 97–189.

expressed that this thwarts the intention of the *Canada Elections Act*, there is little indication that under-age party members are ever a significant percentage of the total participants at a nomination meeting.

*Competitiveness* The timing, tone, and outcome of nomination meetings is determined by a number of variables, many of which are the same variables that will determine the outcome of the election itself. However, two variables stand out as especially important in determining the competitiveness of the nomination process within the constituency; the first is the likelihood of the local party winning the coming election and the second is whether there is an incumbent MP currently holding the seat for the party.

Generally speaking, the more safe the seat for the party, the more competitive the nomination process. For obvious reasons, serious would-be candidates are going to be much more interested in winning a nomination in a safe riding than in a riding where there is no hope of a victory for the party. As a result, there will be a correlation between the number and quality of candidates seeking the nomination in a riding and the likelihood of electoral victory. The exception to this is the case of the local candidate who is the sitting MP and wishes to run again.

Where the local association is lucky enough to have the incumbent seeking a renomination, it is unlikely that a serious rival candidate will contest the nomination and even less likely that the challenge will be successful. Incumbents, then, are almost always renominated and, although the constituency will wish to hold a *pro forma* nomination meeting to affirm the choice, such meetings seldom become real contests. Moreover, where there is a rare challenge to a sitting member, it is most likely to occur if the party is in opposition and almost never if the incumbent is a member of the government caucus. Needless to say, ministers and party leaders never face serious challenges at their nomination meetings.

The opposite extreme to very competitive nominations happens when the party has virtually no chance of winning the seat. Here it is often necessary to draft a member of the local executive to be a sacrificial lamb in showing the party colours in a hopeless cause. In some cases, in elections that are not competitive, or where there are no appropriate volunteer aspirants to the party's nomination in a constituency, the riding executive will establish a **search committee** to find a suitable individual and then convince that individual to act as the party standard-bearer in the election.

Search committees are also used in ridings where the nomination is highly desirable but where there is neither an incumbent nor an obviously acceptable local aspirant. Here the search committee will look for appropriate candidates, often prodded by the national party, which might be seeking a safe seat into which to **parachute** a high-profile "star" candidate. In the 1993 election the Liberal Party national campaign committee broke with the long-standing tradition of local autonomy in the nomination process and essentially appointed a number of high-profile candidates over the objections of the constituency associations. Among other things, this was done in order to increase the number of female candidates on the Liberal ticket. In cases where a good candidate is being touted by the national party, the search committee may also be called upon to convince other, less attractive, hopefuls to withdraw their candidacies.

Candidate spending on attempts to get nominated is for the most part insignificant, and as a result the parties have not attempted to set expenditure ceilings on individuals seeking a nomination. Even in hard-fought nomination races in constituencies where the party has a high likelihood of success, individual candidate expenditures usually amount to no more than a few thousand dollars, although there are exceptions.[6] However, it is clear that the more competitive the contest, the higher the price tag on winning the nomination. Generally, because the NDP has fewer safe seats, the party's nominations are less hotly contested, and generally less money is spent.

Finally, the *timing* of nomination meetings is also affected by the desirability of the nomination. The vast majority of nominations has usually been determined by the time the election writs are issued. Again, where there is an incumbent, the meetings are likely to be held fairly early on, and where the likelihood of success is low, the local party associations will often wait until after the election is called to find a candidate who is willing to be embarrassed on voting day in order, at least, to bravely show the party flag during the campaign.

**Party Finance**  Political parties need money not only to fight elections, but also to maintain their organizations between elections. The money for the latter is more likely today to be raised from sales of memberships and individual donations than from large corporations. In fact, during the Mulroney years, the Liberal Party ran large deficits because corporate donations, once the cornerstone of the "government party's" budget, essentially dried up. The party out of power is more and more forced to rely on public money provided to the Leader of the Opposition's Office (the "LOO") and money provided for caucus research by the House of Commons.

While in some sense it is clear that parties are always campaigning, even between elections, the parties' expenses soar when they are fighting an election campaign. To conduct an effective campaign in this era of media politics and elaborate tours by the national leaders, millions of dollars must be raised by the party in an election year and even during the campaign itself. In Chapter 12 we described the provisions of the *Canada Elections Act* that deal with election expenses, but little has been said about how parties and candidates raise money and what they specifically spend it on during the election campaign.

*Raising Money*  One of the problems political parties face in attempting to raise money is that they do not have a "product" that they can legitimately "sell" to a consuming public. If they do have a product to sell, it is a leader, a platform, and a share of the influence that parties have over the policy process, particularly if the party is fortunate enough to form the government. Clearly, such "influence peddling" is not only contrary to the ethics of democratic politics where the government is expected to serve the general public rather than any special interests, but it is also an offence under the Criminal Code.

---

6. Ibid., p. 125.

Hence, money must be raised with "no strings attached" and corporations and individuals must be induced to contribute to the party out of an altruistic sense of public service, general commitment to the democratic process, or loyalty to the party.

Traditionally, the Liberal and Conservative parties' most important sources of funds have been large corporations. However, because a profitable "bottom line" and altruism are not often compatible motives, the financial ties between banks, big business, and private industry on the one hand, and government on the other, are always suspect. In fact, in the past, the suspicions have often been borne out in that overly close financial ties between parties and the corporate elites led to episodes such as the Pacific Scandal in 1872, which precipitated the defeat of Macdonald's government, and the Beauharnois scandal in the late 1930s, which almost toppled the governing Liberals.

Such scandals are not only costly politically to the party so implicated but also create crises in the legitimacy of the democratic process. The appearance of being above corruption is as important as the reality in terms of the legitimacy of the system. It was this, coupled with the fact that third-party movements, lacking the corporate sources of funds, are forced to fight elections on an uneven playing field, that led ultimately to the introduction of election-expenses regulations in 1974. As we have seen, the *Canada Elections Act* limits the amount a party can spend on elections, makes public the sources of all donations, and provides cash subsidies to parties and candidates.

The fund-raising structures of the two older parties are still geared to tracking down corporate donors but the corporate donors are not quite as willing to kick into the party campaign fund when their "generosity" is subject to public scrutiny. The **bag-men**, as the party fundraisers have come to be known, are generally well-to-do business people or lawyers who have good connections with corporation heads. The "first-string" bag-men — to whom the many other collectors report — are located in the major cities of Canada, where business interests are concentrated.

Many of the large corporate donors in the past hedged their bets by giving money to both the older parties, 60 per cent to the one in power, 40 per cent to the one in opposition, or, if the race appeared close, 50 per cent to each. This had the effect of being "on side" with whichever party won the election and, more importantly, helped to ensure that the "socialist hordes" represented by the NDP were kept out of office. However, there are indications that the tradition of corporate bet-hedging as a means of maintaining a good business climate broke down during the Mulroney years because the neo-conservative rhetoric of the government was so much more attractive to the business community than the alleged "near left" social-policy approaches of the Liberals under Trudeau. Nevertheless, when it appeared that the Tories were headed for defeat in the 1993 campaign, the fickle corporate donors unceremoniously dumped their one-time pals and began to support the likely winners. The Liberals have recovered their financial solvency once more and today it is the Tories, with only two seats in the House, who are deeply in debt.

It was, for years, traditional for party leaders to disclaim all knowledge of the sources of their party's campaign funds, and hence to be above any temptation to reward the benevolent for their generosity. To suspicious minds, such "leaderly innocence" always seemed unlikely. However, the election-expenses laws make this claim more plausible because all donations are made through the party's official agent who in turn must file a return with the chief electoral officer listing the names of all donors who have given more than $100. This means that because the information is public, the leader cannot deny knowledge of major donors. However, anyone else who is interested will know as well.

The NDP, not surprisingly, gets virtually nothing in the way of corporate sponsorship but, because of its special relationship to organized labour, it receives a significant amount of its total budget from unions. While this party has never had the huge purse that the Tories and Liberals have to work with, it has still been able to wage competitive election campaigns. As well, all parties are more and more raising funds from small individual donors who are given a tax credit for their contributions. Finally, the parties all raise funds during the campaign by charging admission fees or asking for donations from attendees at official appearances of their leaders. The Liberals may have taken this a bit far in the 1993 campaign when they held a $1000-a-plate dinner in Montreal for supporters to meet the leader. It almost backfired because the media portrayed it as the wealthy being able to "buy access" to Mr. Chrétien. Fortunately for the Liberals, it was quickly replaced on the front pages with coverage of still more Conservative campaign bloopers.

*Spending the Money*  Even while the campaign is underway, the funds are being raised. Indeed, payments for campaign costs are usually made on the instalment plan as donations are received. Locally, the party's structures and activities often vary greatly from one constituency to another, reflecting the local candidate's own idiosyncrasies. Some control over individual constituency campaigns is exercised by the national parties through "strings attached" to their financial contributions to the local campaign chests, although many riding associations raise more funds locally than they can spend legally and deliver the surplus to a grateful party HQ.

In addition to the money spent by the parties, corporations often make substantial donations "in kind," or *gifts of services*. This is particularly true of public-relations firms, advertising agencies, and public-opinion research groups, which may donate their services and the use of their human resources to the two older parties. While most corporations, as we have seen, make contributions with no expectation of immediate payoff, ad agencies and pollsters may well benefit directly and immediately. If the horse they back wins the race, they will have an edge on their competitors when it comes to the allocation of government contracts for tourism promotion, publicizing new programs, and conducting surveys of public opinion.

*The Impact of Election-Expenses Regulations*  Election-expenses legislation is rigorously enforced by the chief electoral officer and, with the exception of slowness in reporting on the part of some local candidates, non-reporting by some fringe candidates, and some difficulty in defining provisions with respect to the gratuitous provision of services to candidates, it is fairly well observed. While the legislation goes a long way to reducing abuses of the electoral system, there are still some problems. One was removed in 1983 when the levels of allowable expenditures were indexed to inflation (previously, they had been frozen at 1974 levels).

While a significant percentage of campaign expenses is not covered by government, the proportion paid out of the public purse is still not sufficient to fund the partisan campaign. Therefore, parties still must engage in substantial outside money-raising activities. The tax-credit system has made it more attractive for individual donors to give money, while disclosure rules have made some corporations more shy. The result, up to 1993, was an evening out of the amounts available to parties, with the NDP being the biggest relative winner and the Liberals, out of office and out of favour, the biggest loser. It has also meant that individual donors, especially those making contributions in the $100 to $1000 range, are now a more important source of money for Canadian parties than are large corporate donors, particularly in non-election years.[7]

The tax-credit system has also made local and provincial organizations far less dependent on the national organization; in fact, the system often reverses the situation where most funds flowed into the national treasury and then were distributed across the country.

> Now that the taxpayer is helping to fund political parties and their election campaigns, the parties have become more like corporations. Politics is a multi-million dollar business, and raising money has become, to an increasing degree, the achievement of sure-fire techniques of direct mail; the computer has made the bagman a lesser figure in the system.[8]

The system as it now exists also makes it easier for new parties to enter the fray and compete on a relatively level playing field. While the Liberals and the Tories have had an edge because of their corporate donations, and the NDP has a built-in guarantee of at least some financial assistance from union dues, the imbalance is not what it was before the introduction of disclosure, spending ceilings, and subsidies from the public purse.

The Reform Party receives very little financial support beyond the government subsidies, and virtually all of the additional contributions to the campaign came from membership dues. Despite this, the party was able to be competitive in the 1993 election and apparently ended up with a surplus in the party coffers (see Table 15.1). The *Bloc Québécois*, while unable to count on corporate donations, was able to succeed, albeit within one province, through the public moneys, private contributions, and the help of the *Parti Québécois* organization.

**Campaign Activity**

By the time the prime minister visits the governor-general to ask for a dissolution, political parties will already have undergone the long process of waking up from their deep sleep of the previous few years, oiling and polishing their electoral machines, nominating candidates, and reactivating their national,

---

7. Joseph Wearing, *The L-Shaped Party* (Toronto: McGraw Hill Ryerson, 1980), pp. 58–64.
8. Dalton Camp, *Points of Departure* (Toronto: Deneau, 1979), pp. 140–41. Reprinted by permission of Deneau Publishers and Company Ltd., Toronto.

**TABLE 15.1**

Election Expenses of Registered Political Parties, 35th Federal General Election, 1993

| Registered Political Party | Number of Candidates | Indexed Election Expenses Limits | Election Expenses Reported |
|---|---|---|---|
| *Progressive Conservative Party of Canada | 295 | $10,531,510.37 | $10,398,901.00 |
| *Liberal Party of Canada | 295 | $10,531,510.37 | $9,913,190.00 |
| *New Democratic Party | 294 | $10,499,279.67 | $7,447,564.93 |
| *Natural Law Party of Canada | 231 | $8,575,543.97 | $3,398,879.22 |
| *Reform Party of Canada | 207 | $7,519,795.68 | $1,465,379.44 |
| *National Party of Canada | 171 | $6,357,586.72 | $2,092,689.00 |
| Abolitionist Party of Canada | 80 | $2,994,660.03 | $72,176.00 |
| *The Green Party of Canada | 79 | $2,998,643.35 | $974,490.30 |
| *Bloc Québécois | 75 | $2,718,745.48 | $1,896,136.62 |
| Christian Heritage Party of Canada | 59 | $2,201,170.52 | $37,021.79 |
| Party for the Commonwealth of Canada | 59 | $2,290,296.62 | $141,456.00 |
| Canada Party | 56 | $1,939,125.77 | $172.72 |
| Libertarian Party of Canada | 52 | $2,106,015.86 | $20,963.43 |
| Marxist-Leninist Party of Canada | 51 | $1,851,489.07 | $1,000.00 |

Political parties eligible for a reimbursement are indicated with an asterisk (*).
Source:   Elections Canada news release, Apr. 28, 1994.

provincial, and riding organizations. The actual setting of the election date is rather like the firing of the starter's pistol.

At **national campaign headquarters,** a number of things will be happening. Schedules for speaking tours by the leaders will be set up for the whole campaign. An avalanche of party literature, speakers' handbooks, and so on, will descend on the local constituency associations. Party fund-raising activities will redouble, and budgetary priorities will be set. New staff and volunteers will be taken on, and press releases and speeches ground out by the yard. National polls will be commissioned in order to divine the major issues — which are invariably the deficit, unemployment, and national unity.

**National Campaign Structures**   During election campaigns, the parties' extra-parliamentary structures expand as the skeleton of full-time workers is fleshed out with hundreds of volunteers. The key national structure during a campaign is a **national campaign committee**, which for most parties consists of a national campaign chairman, a national treasurer (both appointed by the party leader), and representatives from each of the ten provincial campaign committees, chosen in consultation with the provincial associations. The national campaign committee arranges for national advertising including radio and television productions, plans the leader's tour and big special events, and hires or drafts volunteers to fill the the extra staff positions needed at national headquarters.

The provincial committees help to coordinate the leader's tour in their provinces and provide advice and information to individual candidates. In provinces other than Quebec the national party more or less dominates the provincial party office for the duration of the campaign. Since it is many of the same people who are involved, this is not too difficult to do, nor is it met by much opposition by local party officials. The exception to this, particularly with respect to the Liberals, is that the Quebec campaign committee of the federal wing of the party traditionally has exercised considerable autonomy in both planning and fund-raising, and runs its own campaign. To ensure coordination between the Quebec and the national campaign, both the Liberals and the Conservatives have employed the device of appointing the Quebec chairman as an *ex-officio* co-chairman of the national committee.

The national campaign committee not only plans and directs the general strategy of the campaign, it also consults with advertising experts and pollsters, and makes any mid-campaign adjustments that are required. In recent elections, instead of hiring one advertising agency, the parties have tended to draw together several media experts to form a **communications group** or media committee attached to the national committee. This group not only advises the national committee on its advertising program, but also deals directly with each provincial campaign executive, to help adapt the national advertising campaign to each province's specific needs. Finally, since the 1980 campaign, the Liberals have had a **platform committee**, which begins its work long before the election is called and is backed by the expertise of the party leader's staff. The Conservatives did not follow suit, preferring a more regionally managed campaign, until 1992 when they established their National Platform Planning Committee.

In the 1980s the Conservatives under Brian Mulroney developed a strongly decentralized form of national campaign organization, but they seemed to reverse this trend in the 1993 election when the control of the campaign was dominated by a few powerful individuals, most notably Alan Gregg and John Tory, who had direct access to Kim Campbell. The Liberals, as in the past, continued to operate a largely centralized national campaign, the exception being that the Quebec campaign operated parallel to and largely independent of the rest of the national campaign. Both parties have tended, at the national level, to rely more and more on professionals, either paid or volunteer, and less on the loyal party amateurs who reappear at election time to work for the cause.

The NDP structure is somewhat different again. With a broader membership based on committed local activists, it depends more directly than do the older parties on constituency volunteers. NDP workers are well known in Canadian electoral politics for their ability to mobilize supporters by direct door-to-door canvassing techniques. The large membership base of the NDP is, to some degree, a substitute for money, and the rather more ideological nature of the commitment of its organizers seems to act as a substitute for the patronage that organizers of the older parties come to anticipate.

The Reform Party has a two-tier organization, lacking the provincial level of organization of the other national parties. Both the conduct of the campaign and the fundraising activities of the party occur within this framework. Membership in a Reform Party constituency association gives automatic membership in the national party and the membership fees are divided evenly between the two tiers. The national campaign organization is headed up by the Campaign Managment Committee, which is chaired by the leader. In 1993 the campaign was run from the party's Calgary headquarters and supported by the national party staff. The national and constituency campaigns are coordinated by a candidate liason group.

**The Constituency Organizations** At the local level, events can be much more variable. Some local election machines are highly efficient; others are very much less so. Ideally, the earliest stages of an election campaign will see the establishment of a careful schedule of activities, which peaks on election day. Local workers are recruited and fundraising efforts are stepped up. **Poll captains** must be appointed to coordinate party efforts in given neighbourhoods. Door-to-door canvassing begins, rising in intensity as the great day approaches, and mail and telephone campaigns are conducted to reach as many voters as the party workers can find. On voting day the poll captain will arrange for the transportation of any known supporters who cannot otherwise make it to the polls, and scrutineers will sit in the polling station to ensure that irregularities do not occur.

In practice, it may be difficult to find willing party workers, and parties can always use more people. Canvassing itself is often a hit-and-miss affair, with large sections of the city, especially in lower-class areas, left untouched, and phone campaigns are also usually rather uneven. In many homes, the candidates' literature is thoughtfully filed in the garbage can. Meanwhile, communication flows back and forth between the constituencies and provincial and national headquarters and, as befits a stratarchical structure, many of the national directives get lost, ignored, or creatively misinterpreted at the local level. Leaders criss-cross the country, visiting key constituencies, and giving encouragement to the local candidates and their workers.

**Campaign Advertising and the Media** In part to reduce the overall cost of elections, the time between the issuing of the writs and polling day, the **campaign**, can be no longer than forty-nine days and no less than forty. As well, considerations of cost were likely a factor in establishing a **blackout period** on all paid advertising from the issuance of the writs until the twenty-ninth day before the election. Mercifully, this limits the **broadcasting period** during which Canadians are bombarded with television, radio, and newspaper ads promoting parties and candidates to the last four weeks of the campaign.

The ads in the media may not be broadcast or published after the Saturday before the election, and the results of public-opinion surveys may not be published or reported by the media after midnight on the last Friday of the campaign. There are other rules regarding the conduct of the campaign that are to ensure fair play. For instance, defacing or removing the campaign posters, lawn signs, or other advertising of the parties and candidates is prohibited. As well, every poster, sign, or advertisement, must identify who sponsored or paid for it.

*Limits on Media Advertising*   There are no limits on the number or length of ads that parties and candidates may purchase during the four-week broadcasting period except that the amount spent must not exceed the spending ceiling established pursuant to the election-expenses rules. However, there are special provisions with respect to radio and television advertising because of the pervasive power of the broadcast media in influencing the voters.

The *Canada Elections Act* sets up a process for the allocation of **paid broadcast time** among the registered political parties. Radio and TV stations are required (subject to the *Broadcasting Act* and CRTC regulations) to make available for purchase, by all political parties, a total of six and a half hours of prime time. Representatives of all of the registered parties are then brought together to negotiate an allocation of the available time among themselves. If the parties cannot reach a unanimous agreement among themselves, the *broadcasting arbitrator* has the authority to impose an allocation taking into account the number of seats the party held at dissolution and the percentage of the popular vote received in the previous election. New parties each must be given at least some of the available time, to a minumum of six minutes, and no party may be allocated more than 50 per cent of the available time.

The *Canada Elections Act* also provides that additional time, up to a total of thirty-nine minutes, must be made available to the parties for straight announcements and information about, for instance, nominating meetings. While such "neutral" broadcasting may be exempt from the limits on election expenses, the costs of the *paid-time* ads of the parties and candidates must be within the expenditure ceilings. There are also provisions in the Act to ensure that the broadcasters do not change their advertising rates during an election campaign. They are permitted neither to give reduced rates to their political friends nor to gouge their political enemies.

The *Canada Elections Act* makes provision for **free broadcasting time** to be allocated among the registered political parties by the radio and television networks. The allocation among the parties is to be in the same proportions as the allocation of paid time, to a minimum of two minutes to every registered party. The parties and the networks must get together to decide when and how the party's allocated time will be used, and any disputes between the networks and the parties are subject to arbitration by the broadcasting arbitrator.

Naturally, all of the provisions regarding free-time political advertising are subject to the *Broadcasting Act*, the *Criminal Code*, and the *Canada Elections Act*. However, beyond this qualifier, the parties may use the time available as they see fit, and can pitch their ads to focus on whatever aspects of the campaign they feel are most important. The networks must ensure that the free-time political broadcasts are identified as such, and must indicate which political party is the author of the material. As well, the networks may not give extra free time to any political party. The free-time broadcasts, unlike the paid ads, are not to be counted as part of the parties' campaign expenses for purposes of the spending ceilings.

*Advertising by Private Individuals and Corporations*  The regulations described above all have to do with the campaign advertising by registered political parties and candidates. However, the *Canada Elections Act* is intended also to place restrictions on the ability of private individuals and corporations to purchase their own unsolicited advertising on behalf of candidates or political parties. In 1979 the CEO reported twenty-one complaints arising out of incidents where persons other than the parties and candidates themselves disseminated information that effectively supported or opposed policies clearly identifiable with one of the political parties. In response to this, Bill C-169, an amendment to the Act passed in November 1983, explicitly prohibited all organizations and individuals other than registered political parties from spending money during elections to promote or support a candidate or party.

When the CEO attempted to enforce the legislation it was promptly challenged by the Citizen's Coalition as conflicting with provisions for freedom of expression in the Charter of Rights and Freedoms. As we saw in an earlier chapter, the appeal was upheld by the Alberta Supreme Court. The federal government did not contest that decision, and when the *Canada Elections Act* was changed to limit the amount that non-partisan groups could spend on such ads to $1000, it was again successfully challenged. The CEO did not attempt to enforce the impugned legislation in 1993 and new proposed amendments to the *Canada Elections Act* that would reinstate these provisions have not yet been enacted. As a result, the issue of the extent to which and the manner in which private organizations or individuals may directly spend money to support parties, thus effectively raising the spending limits of the parties during elections, remains an open one.

*Leaders' Debates*  The media give millions of dollars of free publicity to the parties, and the parties spend millions of dollars sponsoring events for the electorate to watch and the media to report, but the key event in most modern elections is the leaders' television debates. The first leaders' debate in Canada was held during the 1968 election campaign, and today the practice has become institutionalized to the extent that there have been proposals to provide for and regulate such debates through amendments to the *Canada Elections Act*.

That the TV debates have become so important is a direct result of the focus on leadership in modern elections and the power of the television medium in influencing voting choice. The tradition began in the 1960 US presidential campaign and since has become an established practice in presidential campaigns. Sometimes the debates have an impact on the outcome of the election, but more often than not, the debate is judged to be a draw. The important thing for the leaders is to avoid a serious gaffe during the debate rather than to hope to "win" the contest.

The debates in Canada are held in both official languages, which has the effect of affirming the unspoken requirement that a national leader must be fluently bilingual. It has also evolved that the debates are more important to new leaders rather than long-established individuals or incumbent prime ministers. The public exposure in the national debates gives new leaders and new parties an opportunity to create new images in the minds of the electorate, whereas the more experienced leaders will focus more on appearing "prime ministerial."

In the 1993 leaders' debates the format was such that each of the partici- pants made brief opening and closing statements and then responded to ques- tions posed by journalists. In the two debates held in this campaign, there was also an opportunity for members of a carefully selected "studio audience" to ask questions of the candidates, but the experiment did not come off very well because the questions generally were not well formulated and the exchanges between the leaders and the audience made for pretty boring television. The verdict in the 1993 debates was that leaders may have reinforced people's existing predilections and that the outcome of the election was not significantly altered by the leaders' performance.

_Advertising vs. "News"_ The significance of the media, especially television, cannot be over-emphasized. The only contact that individual voters have with the parties and the leaders both between and during election campaigns is through the media. The "spin" that reporters put on campaign events can have a significant effect on our perceptions of the leaders during the campaign. For instance, how the media judge winners and losers in leaders' debates is far more important than what people actually see watching the debate itself. In this sense, we wait for the media to cue us as to how to react to what we have seen with our own eyes.

The significance of media interpretation of campaign events has created difficulties in the enforcement of provisions of the _Canada Elections Act_ that prohibit campaign advertising during the blackout periods. The legislation does not prevent the media from dealing with public affairs, from reporting the activities of the party leaders, and even from interviewing the candidates on the day of the election. Similarly, the parties get lots of free publicity, which is not formally advertising, through news reporting in the period before the broadcasting period.

Numerous allegations of partisan reporting by the media have been raised with Elections Canada, but no prosecutions have ever resulted. The difficulty is that attempts to eliminate bias in media reporting would come into direct conflict with freedom of the press. Ultimately, it would seem, again, that the only real control possible here is the good faith and the cooperation of the media, the parties, and the candidates in ensuring that the spirit of the legis- lation is maintained.

## ▶ VOTERS AND THE ELECTORAL PROCESS

Having described the activity of political parties as organizations in the electoral process, we must now look at the participation of individual voters in elections. However, since electoral activity is only one of several forms of participation in the political process, first it is perhaps useful to situate that specific form of political activity within the broader context of **political participation**.

### Non-Electoral Participation

The level and intensity of non-electoral participation in the Canadian political process is more difficult to substantiate than the political activity related to elections. We know the turn-out of the electorate and the success or failure of the political parties and individual candidates because the result of the election is publicly reported. Moreover, for the most part, survey research in Canada has tended to focus far more on the activities related to elections than on other dimensions of political participation. Nevertheless, there have been a few studies that have made a start in attempting to uncover the nature and extent of citizen involvement in non-electoral political activities.[9]

**Group Activity**   It is estimated that between 50 and 60 per cent of Canadians belong to at least one voluntary association. Such associations would include professional organizations, labour unions, community groups, service clubs, and church organizations, any of which are from time to time involved in attempting to influence governmental decisions. This makes us a "country of joiners" when compared to almost any other country in the world except the United States. One might be tempted to conclude from this that Canadians are very active in terms of non-electoral political behaviour, but unfortunately there is no necessary relationship between *belonging* to a group and being *active* in the political efforts of the group. In fact, the intensity of the involvement of most members of voluntary associations is likely extremely low.

Very few of us will ever serve as executive members of an association, and even if we did, such involvement in the organization may not be in any way related to its political or lobbying functions. Bill Mishler has concluded that less than 25 per cent of members of such organizations are ever active in the group, and fewer still ever become involved in the specifically political activities of the group.[10] Instead, either they belong to the group because they intrinsically enjoy the psychological or social benefits of belonging, or they join up for professional reasons.

**Individual Activity**   Another indicator of the extent of non-electoral participation in Canada has been the response to survey questions asking about individuals' attempts to contact MPs and government officials. As many as one in four Canadians will indicate that they have contacted public officials or members of Parliament at some time.[11] However, surveys of MPs themselves indicate that a great many of the letters from constituents do not concern problems that can be classed as political. Personal problems, requests for jobs, or assistance in dealing with administrative agencies of government are far more

9.   William Mishler, *Political Participation in Canada* (Toronto: Macmillan, 1979); see also A. Kornberg, I. Smith, and H. Clarke, *Citizen Politicians — Canada* (Durham: Carolina Press, 1979), pp. 58–61; and W. Mishler and H. Clarke, "Political Participation in Canada," *in* M. S. Whittington and G. Williams, eds., *Canadian Politics in the 1990s* (Toronto: Nelson 1994), p. 129.

10.   Mishler, *Political Participation in Canada*, p. 51.

11.   H. Clarke, J. Jenson, L. Leduc, and J. Pammett, *Political Choice in Canada* (Toronto: McGraw Hill Ryerson, 1979), and *Absent Mandate* (Toronto: Gage, 1984). Much of the data used in the preparation of this section on voting behaviour is drawn from these two books.

frequent than genuine policy-related demands.[12] Hence, if fewer than one-quarter of our citizens choose to avail themselves of even this low-intensity form of involvement in the political process, and if a large percentage of those who do are not concerned with political issues at all, we must conclude that such involvement is not a very significant component of individual political participation in Canada.

**Protest Activity** Finally, as discussed in Chapter 4, political violence is not a significant component of our political culture. However, many Canadians do go beyond the traditional forms of participation in politics to engage in various behaviours that can be described collectively as **political protest**. William Mishler and Harold Clarke have reported that more than two-thirds of Canadians have signed petitions at one time or another, and more than a third have participated in a boycott.[13]

The rate of participation in more active forms of political protests such as marches, rallies, and demonstrations is lower. As many as 25 per cent of Canadians have participated in a march or rally, and less than 10 per cent have ever been involved in a sit-in. Strike activity is something that very many Canadians have been involved in as members of a union, but such activity, while it may have political implications, is not, strictly speaking, "political." Very few Canadians have ever been involved in more violent activities, although incidents of stone-throwing, forceful occupation of legislatures or government offices, and confrontations, such as those that occurred at Kanesatake in 1990, Davis Inlet in 1994, and Ipperwash and Gustafson Lake in 1995, do seem to be on the rise.

### Electoral Participation

Electoral behaviour, or participation in the electoral process, includes a wide range of activities, from actually running for elected office to simply voting for a candidate. Figure 15.1 posits three broad levels of political activity, dividing participants into **gladiators**, **activists**, and **spectator**s. People who participate at any particular level of activity will likely participate in all or most of the activities *below* that level, for our categorization is a *hierarchy* of electoral participation.

Thus, virtually every person who holds a political office has also engaged in a variety of lower-intensity political activities, including voting, campaigning either on one's own behalf or for someone else, and participating in political strategy meetings. Similarly, a person who participates in strategy meetings will certainly vote and be an active party member as well.

The higher up the hierarchy, the fewer participants there are. Probably less than 5 per cent of Canadians ever participate at the gladiatorial level, while fewer than 25 per cent can be classified as activists. The most common of the activist behaviours are attending a political rally or all-candidates meeting, and attempting to convince friends and co-workers how to vote. The latter category of participation, however, is getting fairly close to the spectator level of involve-

12. A. Kornberg and W. Mishler, *Influence in Parliament* (Durham: Duke Press, 1976).
13. Mishler and Clarke, "Political Participation in Canada."

**Figure 15.1**

A hierarchy of electoral participation.

| | |
|---|---|
| Gladiators | • Office holders |
| | • Candidates |
| | • Party officials |
| | • Fundraisers and ''bag-men'' |
| | • Members of campaign committees, etc. |
| | • Convention delegates |
| | |
| Activists | • Financial contributors |
| | • Volunteer campaign workers |
| | • Participants at meetings or rallies |
| | • Party advocates (influence other voters) |
| | • Party members |
| | |
| Spectators | • Those interested in politics |
| | • Those who follow political events |
| | • Those who initiate political discussions |
| | • Voters |

Source:   Adapted from Lester Milbrath, *Political Participation* (Chicago: Rand McNally, 1965), p. 18.

ment. While such discussion is likely motivated more by interest than by deep commitment, even in simply discussing politics casually with friends, one inevitably expresses a point of view and tries to sway the opinion of others.[14]

Finally, at the spectator level of activity, participation rates are generally very high. Fewer than 5 per cent of the respondents in election studies since 1965 report never having voted in a federal election, and between 80 per cent and 90 per cent of respondents consistently indicate that they follow the campaigns and discuss the issues informally with friends. Since 1945, the average voter turn-out at federal general elections is about 74 per cent with the highs approaching 80 per cent and a low of 67 per cent in 1953.

**The Determinants of Electoral Participation**   There are two broad sets of determinants of people's participation in the political process — systemic and nonsystemic. The more elementary of these is related to the system of government itself. As we have seen in earlier chapters, our Constitution is a democratic one that provides and guarantees the opportunities for the citizenry to be involved in the democratic process. There are positive guarantees of our rights to vote and to run for elected office and there are, as well, provisions that prohibit the interference by government in freedom of expression, freedom of the press, and freedom to organize collectively. But the provision of legal and constitutional opportunities to participate does not necessarily mean that people will be motivated to take advantage of them.

Given that our system of government does provide a wide range of formal opportunities for participation in the political process, there are three subsets

14.  Mishler, *Political Participation in Canada*, p. 43; and Mishler and Clarke, ''Political Participation in Canada.''

**TABLE 15.2**

Participation in the 1993 Federal Election Campaign

| | % |
|---|---|
| Those who voted in 1993 Federal Election | 71 |
| Those who "often" or "sometimes" | |
| — discussed politics with others | 81 |
| — watched TV programs about the election campaign | 80 |
| — read about the election campaign in newspapers | 79 |
| — listened to radio programs about the election campaign | 51 |
| — tried to influence friends' vote | 23 |
| — attended political meeting or rally | 12 |
| — worked for political party or candidate | 7 |
| Those who were | |
| — very interested in 1993 federal election | 52 |
| — fairly interested | 31 |
| — slightly interested | 14 |
| — not at all interested | 3 |

Source: William Mishler and Harold Clarke, "Political Participation," *in* M. S. Whittington and G. Williams, *Canadian Politics in the 1990s* (Toronto: Nelson, 1994) p. 134. By permission of Harold D. Clarke.

of non-systemic determinants of the extent to which we will take advantage of them. The first of these is the sum of the individual's *socio-economic resources*. These resources include the amount of free time and money available to be spent on political activity. How much one can afford to invest will depend in part upon one's occupation and income and upon the non-political activities, such as earning a living, that compete for one's time.

A second and vital set of determinants is the individual's *social context*. Political participation at the more intense levels of involvement has social costs and requires social resources. These social resources are determined by a range of demographic variables such as ethnicity, religion, geography, age, and gender, all of which will predispose people differently with respect to their interest and activity in political life.

The third set of determinants are the *personality resources* of the individual who wishes to participate in politics. People who have more social aplomb and self-assurance are more likely to participate in politics than less outgoing people. As well, the more confident individuals are that their political involvement will matter, the higher the level of political activity in which they will engage. The feeling that one can have a meaningful role in politics, and that the system will respond, is termed a sense of **political efficacy**. We must now attempt some generalizations as to who participates in the Canadian electoral process by examining the socio-economic, demographic, and psychological correlates of participation.

**Socio-Economic and Demographic Variables** One of the most consistent correlates of political participation, not only in Canada but throughout the Western democracies, is the socio-economic status (SES) of the individual. Whether

**TABLE 15.3**
Turn-out Rates in Federal Elections.

| Election Year | % Voting |
|---|---|
| 1945 | 75 |
| 1949 | 74 |
| 1953 | 67 |
| 1957 | 74 |
| 1958 | 79 |
| 1962 | 79 |
| 1963 | 79 |
| 1965 | 75 |
| 1968 | 76 |
| 1972 | 77 |
| 1974 | 71 |
| 1979 | 76 |
| 1980 | 69 |
| 1984 | 76 |
| 1988 | 75 |
| 1993 | 71 |

we utilize subjective criteria of class (self-classification through direct questions such as "What class do you think of yourself belonging to?") or objective criteria such as income, occupation, or education, it is clear that lower SES correlates positively with lower levels of political participation.

*Income, Occupation, and Education*   The general rule that SES and level of participation are positively related has a few exceptions. While high *income* is a good predictor of participation at the gladiatorial level in elections or in non-electoral activities such as approaching government officials and MPs, wealthier people are not appreciably more likely to vote or participate in partisan campaigns than even the poorest citizens. Similarly, while *occupation* is a good predictor of gladiatorial participation, with members of the professions and business people occupying a disproportionate percentage (75%) of elected offices in Canada, professional people are likely to be less concerned with participation in local campaigns and are not significantly more likely to vote than members of lower-status occupational groups.[15] This may reflect the fact that higher-status groups perceive their opportunities to influence the political process to be greater if they deal directly with the elected officials of government, or if they actually become one themselves, than if they simply exercise their franchise or work in somebody's campaign.

The influence of *education* reflects a pattern similar to that of occupation. Levels of participation increase with education up to the highschool level, but university-educated people are no more likely to vote than highschool gradu-

---

15.   Mishler and Clarke, "Political Participation in Canada," p. 126.

ates. Similarly, people with a university education are more likely to attempt to influence the political process through direct involvement as gladiators, or in lobbying government officials, either as individuals or as active members of an interest group. That the distribution of participants is similar to that demonstrated by higher-status occupations is hardly startling, given that there is a direct relationship between higher levels of education and the professional occupations.

*Ethnicity and Language*  Language, ethnicity, and religion are all fairly closely related variables, and as a combination of coincident cleavages they can affect both the opportunities for and the propensity towards political participation. However, if we expected a dramatic difference between ethnic groups, we would be very disappointed. While French Canadians are marginally less likely than English Canadians to become involved in non-electoral activities such as contacting an MP or belonging to a community association, they are slightly more likely to become party activists in the electoral process.

French Canadians have been historically less likely than anglophones to vote in federal elections. However, when we look to French-Canadian participation in provincial politics, we find that the discrepancy virtually disappears. Essentially it seems that, compared to anglophones, French Canadians view themselves as relatively more efficacious at the provincial level than at the federal level. They are, therefore, more likely to vote in provincial elections, and more likely to approach provincial government officials than federal ones.[16]

Non-English, non-French Canadians are different in that they are disproportionally under-represented at the gladiatorial levels of electoral participation. The "non-charter" groups are only beginning to make inroads to elected office or even to candidacy in Canada, although the 1993 election saw a significant increase in the number of candidates from other ethnic groups running for office, many of them successfully.[17]

While many small differences in political activity do correlate with variables such as ethnicity, religion, and language, for the most part these differences disappear if we control for socio-economic status. It is true, for instance, that aboriginal people are less likely to vote in national elections. However, the determining variables are not ethnicity or culture *per se*; rather, they are the lower levels of income and education in aboriginal communities. As well, many aboriginal people in Canada may have opted to involve themselves more in their internal political affairs where they feel they can have a more significant impact in the community.

*Regionalism and Geography*  Much has been written in Canada about the influence of geography on patterns of political behaviour. While there are clear differences in partisan choice from one region to the next, attempts to demonstrate regional variations in the level and intensity of political participation have not been particularly successful. Overall differences in levels of partici-

16. Mishler, *Political Participation in Canada*, p. 99.
17. Ibid., p. 100.

pation by province are more likely affected by particular local political conditions than by regional cleavages. As we saw with respect to ethnicity, any consistent regional differences are quite readily attributable to differing levels of education or income, with poorer and less well educated regions showing slightly lower levels of most types of participation.

The level of activity in a province may be temporarily increased by a heightened level of political party competition, by a particularly exciting political leader, or by the emergence of a new political movement.[18] For instance, the generally high voter turn-out and heightened levels of participation in Quebec and Alberta during the 1993 election can be explained in part by the emergence of the *Bloc Québécois* and the Reform Party, respectively. Overall, however, we feel fairly safe in dismissing regional variations in the patterns of political participation as idiosyncratic and usually temporary.

*Urban-rural* differences in political participation in Canada are fairly significant, although the patterns of variation are unlike those characteristic of the other socio-economic and demographic determinants of participation. According to the 1974 and 1980 election survey results, the relationship between urbanization and political participation was found to be *curvilinear*.[19] The frequency of voting is highest in the large urban areas and in the rural or farm communities, and lowest in the medium-sized cities and towns. The same curvilinear pattern applies with respect to non-electoral participation, such as contacting MPs, but participation in local or community activities increases linearly with the smaller size of community.

Likely these differential patterns of political participation by community size can be explained in two ways. The higher levels of participation in the cities will generally be a reflection of higher SES, income, and education, coupled with the fact that cities simply afford more opportunities for participation. On the other side, the high participation in rural communities might be explained by the fact that involvement in community affairs is a result of a more genuine sense of community than prevails in larger urban centres. The involvement in local matters, of which politics is one aspect, is generally higher because people know each other, deal with each other regularly, and are thus more interested in being active in community affairs.

*Age* Age is a variable that profoundly affects individual participation in both electoral and non-electoral politics. Unlike many other demographic variables, the determining effect of age on political participation does not completely disappear when we control for socio-economic status. One obvious reason for this is that our system explicitly discriminates against people aged under eighteen by denying them the franchise. While some age limitation on the right to vote is legitimate and likely necessary, the fact is that younger people have lower rates of participation because they are not *permitted* to participate directly in the electoral process.

Moreover, younger people — those between ages eighteen and twenty-five — are also likely affected by what Clarke and Mishler refer to as the "start-up

---

18. S. M. Lipset, *Agrarian Socialism* (Berkeley: University of California Press, 1950).
19. Clarke et al., *Absent Mandate* and *Political Choice in Canada*; and Mishler, *Political Participation in Canada*, pp. 72–74.

effect."[20] They are preoccupied with finishing their education, finding jobs, and starting a family. They simply lack the resources such as the free time to be able to devote much effort to being "political." As well, younger people may not be as active at the gladiatorial levels of participation simply because experience is an asset that correlates with age and is an important determinant of the electibility of a candidate.

Age is also a determinant of levels of political activity at the other end of the scale. The elderly are less likely to be active in politics, and the level at which they participate is likely to be lower, despite the fact that the individual may be in a high SES group and have time available. The reason for this is in part the obvious problem of declining health, but it may also be explained by the fact that the older people of today had fewer opportunities to get an education when they were younger.

The conclusion here is that both the level and intensity of political activity increases as we get older up until late middle age, after which it declines gradually — until, for obvious reasons, it stops completely! While there are many individual exceptions of gladiators who stay active in politics until they are quite elderly, and we also have the somewhat embarrassing exception of the Senate, there is little question that electoral participation at all levels of our hierarchy is highest from age thirty to age sixty.

**Gender and Electoral Participation**   Historically, politics has been more or less the exclusive domain of males, and that tradition was institutionalized in Canada until quite recently. Women did not win the right to vote in federal elections until 1918, and at the provincial level the last holdout was Quebec, which gave the vote to females only in 1940. Today in Canada women have the same political rights as men and discrimination against women is prohibited by the Charter. However, this has not translated into anything approaching equality on a practical level in society, and while gender inequalities are decreasing gradually in most areas, we are nowhere near the goal of a gender-equal political community.

*Gender Inequality*   Much of the disadvantaged status of women in our political process can be explained by discriminatory patterns in the social and economic processes that underlie and determine political participation. Under-representation of women among the university educated, in the labour force, and in the national and provincial elites stubbornly persists despite efforts to alleviate the problem through policies of pay equity, affirmative action, quotas in post-secondary institutions, and extremely active advocacy by high-profile women's organizations.

But even if we take into account the socio-economic variables, the differences between men and women in the political process remain significant. Well-educated women in high-status occupations still continue to be under-represented at the higher levels of participation in government and politics. Women remain under-represented in federal and provincial cabinets, in leg-

---

20.   Mishler and Clarke, "Political Participation in Canada."

islatures, among candidates in elections, in party organizations, and among senior public servants, labour leaders, business elites, and judicial appointments.

We have discussed the socialization process in Chapter 4 and it is clear that the roles young females come to see as appropriate for themselves in their adult lives are different from those aspired to by their male cohorts. Moreover, even if women overcome the societal biases lurking in the socialization process and actively vie with males for jobs in traditional male bastions, they are still not competing on a level playing field. In part this is because males tend to be the "gatekeepers" who control access to the most sought-after jobs, and males have been socialized to believe that women are more suited to the nursery than to the corporate boardroom or the political backroom. While such attitudes are likely changing, they are changing over generations rather than over years, and even the most enlightened anti-discrimination legislation cannot change attitudes in the short run.

*Female Participation in Elections*   Despite the underlying structural and attitudinal discrimination against women in society, there have been significant gains in the representation of women in all categories of electoral participation. Female voter turn-out is virtually the same as male turn-out, and any slight differences that might appear wash out if we control for socio-economic factors. Similarly, at the *activist* levels of participation, women are just as likely to work in election campaigns, be members of a political party, read about and discuss politics, and attempt to influence other people's voting choice.[21]

Where gender differences persist in electoral participation is at the *gladiatorial* levels. Women are active in party organizations, but primarily at the lower levels. They are less likely to be constituency-association presidents or senior policy advisors and more likely to be riding secretaries, although during the 1993 Liberal campaign, the high-profile Chaviva Hosek was the party's director of policy research, and Sheila Copps was the co-chair of the platform committee.

Women are less likely to be convention delegates, even though most parties explicitly provide that a certain number of constituency delegates must be female. In the case of the NDP, whose efforts in respect of pushing for male-female parity have been admirable, women remain in a minority situation at national conventions because the large union-appointed share of the delegates is overwhelmingly male-dominated.

Although women make up a growing percentage of candidates for office, they are still firmly in a minority situation. The NDP came close to achieving the target of a fifty-fifty gender distribution of candidates in the 1993 election, and both the Liberals and the Tories nominated more females than in previous elections. The Liberals went so far as to impose "star" female candidates in some constituencies, although not without some opposition from the local associations. However, while the situation is improving, and women are increasing their share of total candidacy, they are still more likely to be nominated

---

21. Ibid., p. 141.

in ridings where the party has a low chance of winning. Both the Reform Party and the *Bloc Québécois* had significantly lower percentages of female candidates than the three older parties.

*Women in Elected Office*   In 1980, only fourteen women were elected to the House of Commons, but that number has increased steadily since, and when the smoke had cleared from election night 1993, fifty-three women had won seats. The fact that similar increases in female represention in legislatures can be cited at the provincial level can lead us to be mildly optimistic about the prospects for gender parity in elected office. Similarly, women have been party leaders and leaders of the opposition in a number of provinces, and we have had two female premiers. In the 1993 federal election, two of the national party leaders were women, one of whom was the incumbent prime minister.

However, it would be a mistake for women to rejoice or for liberal-minded men to pat themselves on the back because the number of female MPs has "increased by 500 per cent since 1980." Our optimism about achieving gender equality in elected office must be tempered by the fact that women are still significantly under-represented as candidates, as legislators, and in the cabinets at both levels of government. Both men and women must attempt to build on the gains that have been made and to eliminate the structural and attitudinal discrimination that underlies the persistence of gender inequality.

**Psychological Correlates of Participation**   Even a cursory glance is enough to indicate that socio-economic and demographic factors alone are not sufficient to explain why people are motivated to participate in politics. There are still many people who have all the necessary resources but pay no attention to politics. Many voting-age Canadians are middle class or working class, with enough education to give them many of the necessary resources to participate. Whether they will participate depends on a number of psychological and attitudinal variables as well.

*Interest and Awareness*   *Interest* in politics, as might be expected, is an important attitudinal trait distinguishing participants and non-participants in Canada. Generally speaking, Canadians are only mildly interested in politics with about 20 per cent of individuals polled indicating that they actually pay attention to political events on a day-to-day basis. But the level and intensity of that interest waxes and wanes with changing circumstances. Politics must be seen to matter to our day-to-day lives if we are to become interested and hence involved. Ironically, when things are going well and there is full employment, healthy economic growth, and no profoundly divisive issues, Canadian politics can be pretty boring stuff to the average citizen. In boring political times, our interest in politics is often spurred only if the politicians themselves and their personal lives become intrinsically entertaining or if a close election race stimulates our involvement.

Recently, Canadians have come to perceive politics as important because the country is faced with high unemployment, wage cuts or freezes, and yet another chapter in our national unity saga. Over 80 per cent of people surveyed indicated that they were "very interested" or "fairly interested" in the 1993 election although this only translated into a surprisingly low 71 per cent turnout at the polls (see Table 15.2).

Closely related to interest is knowledge or awareness of politics and government. The people who are the most interested in politics also tend to know more about government and the issues of the day. Moreover, as might be expected, respondents in opinion surveys who score high on "political information" tests also tend to participate more frequently and at higher levels in electoral activities. However, what is disturbing here is the generally low level of cognitive sophistication among most Canadians. A 1974 study showed that almost half of the respondents could not score 50 per cent on a series of fairly straightforward questions about the powers of the federal and provincial governments. While the level of knowledge about the system seems to be higher among individuals in the 1980s and 1990s than it was in the 1960s and 1970s, very few Canadians truly understand the complexities and subtleties of the critical economic and social policy issues that face the country today.

*Partisanship and Ideology*   Partisan loyalty, or the psychological phenomenon of identifying with a political party, is a good predictor of higher levels and intensity of political participation. The findings of election studies since 1965 have shown that there is a consistently strong relationship between partisanship and participation, and that the intensity of party loyalty correlates positively with the intensity of political participation. It should not surprise us that it is the most committed partisans who become involved directly in the partisan election campaign, who donate money and time to the party, and who are the most likely to become involved at the gladiatorial level in an election.

But while party loyalty generally correlates with higher levels of participation in politics, election studies have also revealed consistently that Canadians are not very loyal in their commitment to a political party — fewer than 40 per cent could be described as **durable partisans**.[22] As well, there generally are not significant differences in levels of electoral participation among even the durable supporters of the various political parties on the Canadian scene. The exception here is that supporters of the NDP traditionally seem to be more likely to become involved at the gladiatorial and activist levels than do supporters of the two traditional parties. The reason for this may be that the NDP generally has fewer supporters than the Liberals or Conservatives or it may reflect that NDP partisanship is more *ideologically* based relative to PC or Liberal partisanship.

The literature in the United States indicates that very few citizens are genuinely ideological, and there have been no studies to indicate that Canadians who support the Liberals or the Tories are any different. However, when at least one of the political parties, even a minor one such as the NDP, the *Bloc Québécois*, or Reform, takes an ideologically distinguishable position on the political spectrum, it encourages more intense electoral participation. Hence, while *ideologues* do not comprise a very large percentage of the Canadian citizenry, ideological *commitment* is likely related both to the intensity of partisanship and to the level and frequency of political participation.

---

22. See Clarke et al., *Absent Mandate*.

*Political Efficacy*  **Political efficacy** is the feeling or perception of one's ability to have an impact on the political process. Our motivation to participate depends to a large extent on how much impact we believe we are capable of having. Generally it can be stated that the levels of political efficacy in Canada are lower than those present in the other Anglo-American democracies. Moreover, since 1965, the levels of efficacy have generally declined in Canada, as have the general levels of *trust* in the authorities of the political system. In 1993, almost 75 per cent of Canadians surveyed indicated that they felt that governments "don't care" and MPs "lose touch" (Fig. 15.2), and 60 per cent stated that average Canadians "have no say" in political decisions (Fig. 15.3).

Political efficacy is a good predictor of the levels and intensity of political participation. Although the relationship is not strong with respect to voting, for other levels of electoral participation and for non-electoral categories of political participation, the propensity to participate declines with the level of political efficacy. A possible explanation of the fact that a relatively large percentage of respondents *do* vote, despite general feelings of political inefficacy, is that exercising the franchise is seen as an important symbolic affirmation of the democratic process. In other words, people may vote out of a sense of civic duty rather than out of any faith that they can actually have an impact on policy outputs. It is also possible that the act of voting is a cathartic experience, allowing people to "get even" with the "scoundrels" in power by sacking them — even if it is only to replace them with a new set of scoundrels!

**Figure 15.2**

Response to the statement that MPs lose touch and government doesn't care, 1965–1993.

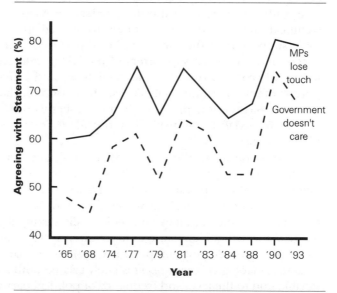

Source: William Mishler and Harold Clarke, "Political Participation in Canada," *in* M. S. Whittington and G. Williams, *Canadian Politics in the 1990s* (Toronto: Nelson, 1994), p. 146.

**Figure 15.3**
Response to the statement that politics is too complicated and
that average Canadians have no say, 1965–1993.

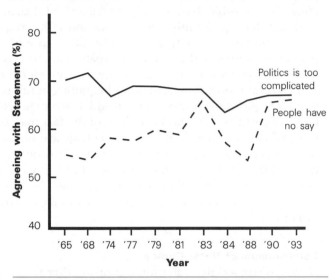

Source: William Mishler and Harold Clarke, "Political Participation in
Canada," *in* M. S. Whittington and G. Williams, *Canadian Politics in
the 1990s* (Toronto: Nelson, 1994), p. 146.

People may also become involved at the activist levels of the electoral
process, such as campaigns, because such activities are of psychological value
to them. Thus, it is possible that political participation in group activities
provides positive psychological reinforcement to individuals that has nothing
to do with their political needs. Consistent with this is the converse finding,
that the non-political aspects of one's personality can have some impact on the
motivation to become involved in politics. The gregariousness of an individual
generally, or the extent to which one is outgoing, may be important in motivating people to become involved in political parties and election campaigns.

*Participation and Complacency* Finally, we must conclude this very brief discussion of the relationship between efficacy and participation in Canadian
politics with a cautionary note. While we have been able to cite a strong correlation between the two sets of variables, we have not been able to determine
the *direction* of the causal links. It is normally assumed that efficacy determines
the level of participation, that the attitudes determine the behaviour. We would
like to suggest that the reverse be considered as a possible explanation of the
empirical findings in this area, that is, that people believe voting to be important
because they have done it a lot and it has proven to be an easy, interesting, and
psychologically satisfying experience.

Similarly, people who do not get involved at higher levels of electoral
participation may give, as a reason, their conviction that such involvement is

not worth their while, that it will not produce any positive results, and therefore that it is a waste of their valuable time. Thus, while a sense of civic duty motivates people to engage in activities such as voting, which do not take much time or effort, it is possible that, out of complacency and laziness, they are unwilling to invest the significantly greater time and effort required to participate in higher-order political activities. As a result, a sense of "civic guilt" may cause people to rationalize their non-participation in terms of cynicism, negativism, and inefficacious statements about the higher orders of political behaviour.

To return to what we said in the beginning of this section, participation in politics requires resources, some of which are time and psychic energy. Low levels of participation may be a result of the fact that, underneath the expressions of cynicism and inefficacy, Canadians are not willing to devote much time or energy to political activity because it is not as important to them as many of the other things in their lives. Although we should not rejoice in the fact, it is quite possible that, despite their "bitching," a majority of Canadians are actually quite satisfied and — perhaps mistakenly — complacent about their situations.

### Determinants of Voter Choice

Having discussed the determinants of whether Canadians will participate in elections, we must now turn to a consideration of the variables affecting the decisions taken by the largest group of electoral participants — the voters. Given that an individual has made the decision to participate in the election by casting a ballot, what determines the elector's voting decision?

The ultimate target of all election-campaign activities is the Canadian voter and we can conclude tentatively that campaigns do indeed have an effect. Almost half the Canadian electorate claims to make up its mind during the campaign, and in many elections voters have claimed they decided in the last week.[23] A lot of the reason for this is that as we have seen in the last section, most Canadians do not simply vote according to party loyalty over long periods of time.

**Flexible Partisanship**  In *Absent Mandate*, their study of the 1980 election, Harold Clarke and his co-authors demonstrated that only 37 per cent of Canadian voters could be categorized as durable partisans — voters who show consistent, stable, and strong patterns of support for a particular party.[24] The other 63 per cent of Canadian voters are **flexible partisans** — unstable in their partisanship over time, inconsistent between the federal and provincial levels of the Canadian political system, or weak in their intensity of partisanship. Nothing has changed since this study except that, if anything, Canadian partisans are even more fickle in their loyalty. Only 30 per cent of 1993 voters indicated that they voted for the same party in 1988, and fully 40 per cent indicated they were "switchers."

Given the high degree of flexibility of the Canadian voter, we should not be surprised at the kind of large electoral swing that allowed the Conservatives

---

23. Jon Pammett, "Elections," in Whittington and Williams, *Canadian Politics in the 1990s*, pp. 238–51.

24. Clarke et al., *Absent Mandate*.

to move from 33 per cent of the popular vote and 103 seats in 1980 to 50 per cent of the vote and 211 seats in 1984, and then to move from 169 seats and 43 per cent of the vote in 1988 to 2 seats and 16 per cent of the vote in 1993. It also makes possible the kind of situation described earlier, in which an apparently perpetual provincial dynasty in Alberta or Quebec can fall from pre-eminence to almost instant oblivion in a single election.

Earlier, in discussions of the individual parties, we indicated something of the socio-economic and demographic composition of party voting. However, while the aggregate impact of these variables does add up to some seemingly consistent patterns of interparty differences, the ability of these variables to predict the voting behaviour of individual Canadians is relatively limited. What appeared at first to be consistent patterns, and what struck pioneering political scientists in the field of election studies as constituting rather good explanations of the voting behaviour of individual Canadians, turned out on closer examination to explain only the behaviour of a minority of voters who are durable partisans. Most Canadians' voting decisions are made on the basis of shorter-term variables.

Clarke found the most appropriate explanation for the short-term orientation of voters to be party leadership, party positions on issues, and, to a lesser extent, individual candidates. In 1974, these short-term factors, combined with attitudes towards local candidates, were crucial determinants for 62 per cent of the voters, and studies since have revealed the same result.

**Leadership** It is a truism of political analysis that Canadians are highly leadership-oriented when they come to make their voting decisions. Survey results indicate that orientations towards the leader *do* make a considerable difference, but the significance of leadership as the most important determinant of voter choice has declined from 30 per cent in 1984 to 22 per cent in 1993. Similar results are seen for the supporters of all parties.

**TABLE 15.4**

Most Important Factor in Voting, Voter Response, Federal Elections

| | Voters Ranking the Factor as Most Important (%) | | |
|---|---|---|---|
| Factor | 1993 | 1988 | 1984 |
| Party Leaders | 22 | 20 | 30 |
| Issue Basis | 62 | 71 | 56 |
| Personal Qualities | 38 | 29 | 44 |
| Local Candidates | 21 | 27 | 21 |
| Issue Basis | 52 | 57 | 46 |
| Personal Qualities | 48 | 43 | 54 |
| Party as a Whole | 57 | 53 | 49 |
| Issue Basis | 54 | 57 | 37 |
| General Approach | 46 | 43 | 63 |

Note: Population weights have been applied.
Source: 1993 Insight Canada Research post-election survey; 1984 National Election Study; 1988 reinterview of 1984 National Election. Cited in J. Pammett, "Elections," *in* M. S. Whittington and G. Williams, eds., *Canadian Politics in the 1990s* (Toronto: Nelson, 1994), p. 241.

This suggests that even in highly leadership-oriented contests, independent perceptions of parties and their positions on issues do exist and are important determinants of voting choice. Contrary to popular wisdom, then, in Canada, the party and the leader are not synonymous to the voter. This is, perhaps, fortunate for the political system as a whole, since all leaders have declined in esteem in the eyes of the public and the media since the 1970s. In fact, in the 1993 election, voters surveyed indicated that they were much more likely to switch their vote from one party to another on the basis of negative feelings about a leader. Hence, voters who decide on the basis of leadership are more often voting *against* a leader they dislike rather than for a leader they find attractive.[25]

**Issues** The impact of issues on the voting decision is concentrated mainly among the one-third of the electorate characterized as flexible partisans with high levels of interest in politics. The impact of issues is considerably lower among the durable partisans, no matter what their level of interest in politics. The problem faced by parties with respect to issues is that, to have a significant net effect on electoral results, there must be a significant "skewness" — that is, one party must be perceived much more favourably than another with respect to some key issue. Because most issues lack this skewness, and because there are so many possible issues, their overall effect tends to wash out in aggregate electoral results.

At times, of course, one issue can tend to dominate in an election. If this should happen and if one party can establish a unique and positive position with respect to that issue, it may win considerable support. As an example, after the election of the *Parti Québécois*, and intermittently though the 1970s, national unity was just such an issue for the federal Liberals. In more recent elections economic issues such as unemployment, free trade, and the deficit have been the major issues, but no party was able to take a unique enough position in dealing with them until 1993. In this election, the Liberals were able to capture a significant number of supporters because of their identification with job creation.

### A Non-Conclusion

In spite of the fact that a significant group of voters does claim to be concerned with issues, the evidence still points to the conclusion that the significance of issues is closely tied to the individual voter's feelings about the political parties and leaders espousing the issue positions. Moreover, we must be careful with responses to survey questions about which of issues, leader, or party is the most important factor in the voting decision. Respondents will tend to cite issues as more important because it is the more intelligent, more rational, and more socially accepted basis on which to make the voting decison. No one will readily admit voting for a leader because he or she is "cute" or for a political party because grandma and grandpa did.

The conclusion here is that what we can say about voter choices in elections is all very tentative. Individual voting decisions are extremely complex and the

---

25. Jon Pammett, "Tracking the Votes," *in* Alan Frizzell, Jon Pammett, and Anthony Westell, *The Canadian General Election of 1993* (Ottawa: Carleton University Press, 1994), pp. 143–60.

survey instruments that we have developed to explore the reasons for how people vote are still imperfect. In fact, part of the problem is that the individual voter may not even be aware of what perceptions, feelings, or loyalties went into the choice. When we attempt to explain the aggregate outcome of an election — "voters voted for free trade in 1988," "Canadians rejected the Mulroney legacy in 1993" — we are on even thinner ice. Political scientists and pollsters are better at predicting the outcomes of elections than they are at explaining them.

# Chapter 16

# Interest Groups: Functions and Structures

Interest groups or pressure groups are active everywhere in Canadian politics. They represent the "interests" of groups of Canadians with like-minded policy concerns by attempting to influence or "pressure" the people in government who have the power to make policy decisions. The terms **interest group** and **pressure group** are used synonymously in Canadian politics, but it is possible to distinguish between essentially non-political organizations that periodically attempt to pressure governments and "true" interest groups whose organizational *raison d'être* is to represent the political interests of their membership. It is important, however, to recognize that at the core of this discussion is the fact that we are dealing with *groups* rather than with individuals, so first we must explore the concept of group.

## ▶ GROUPS AND COLLECTIVE ACTION

We have spoken in earlier chapters of the importance of the individual in a political culture and a constitutional system that bears the stamp of liberalism. However, while the individual is the basic unit of political analysis in a liberal society, it should be obvious that isolated individuals rarely have very much influence over the outcomes of political conflicts, and even elites, who are by definition "important individuals," have little influence except when they are acting in concert with other elites or when they are representing a significant aggregation of supporters. In sum, **collective action** is more likely to have an impact on policy decision-making than individual action.

### Concept of the Group
In the simplest sense, a *group* can be defined as any two or more individuals. However, two strangers standing on a streetcorner waiting for a bus do not

**Figure 16.1**

Groups and collective action.

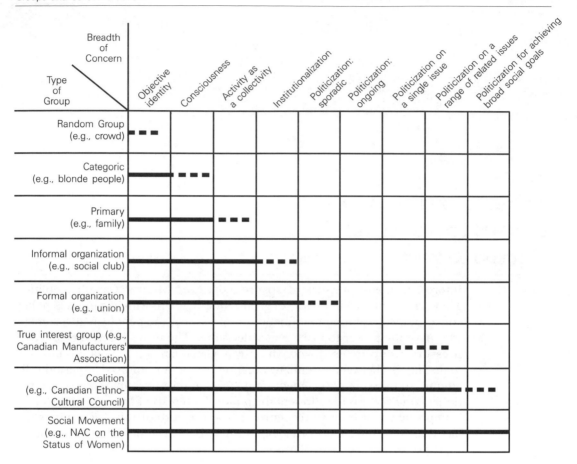

constitute a group. The concept of a group is more complex and implies more than a random association among its members

**Categoric Groups** At the most elementary level, it is possible to describe a collectivity as a group if all members of the collectivity have a common identifiable characteristic. This is a **categoric** group and allows us to classify individuals according to a wide range of individual characteristics. For instance, individuals with blue eyes, large noses, crooked teeth, or athlete's foot can be grouped together in a category with other individuals who share the same physical characteristic. Similarly, people who believe that the earth is flat, the moon is made of green cheese, or Elvis is still alive can be placed in categoric groups because of beliefs or ideas that they share with others.

**Consciousness and Group Activity: Informal Groups** Categoric groups, while interesting to the taxonomists among us, are really only important in society if belonging to a categoric group generates consistent patterns of activity or behaviour among the members of the group. Thus, for instance, while bald men may tend to wear hats, and "flat earthers" may eschew long ocean voyages, as students of politics and government, such behavioural patterns are not particularly relevant. For a categoric group to become politically relevant, the members of the group must engage in collective activity that can potentially affect individuals in society who are *not* members of that group.

Moreover, we must recognize that there is a difference between the random behaviours of individual members of categoric groups and what we may call **group activity**. If individual bald men took to robbing hat stores, for instance, it would be of concern to us but we could not describe such aberrant individual behaviour as group activity. Group behaviour requires, first, **consciousness** on the part of the individual members that they are part of a group, and second, some deliberate attempt on the part of the group members to organize themselves so that they can act in concert.

Consciousness or self-awareness in a group is a necessary condition for the members to do things together, and the initiative of the informal leaders of the group is required to organize the members. Bridge clubs, neighbourhood house parties, family reunions, or even the regulars at the local pub can be seen as groups in the sense that the same set of individuals is conscious of itself as an informal group; it interacts, at least irregularly, over time; and informal leaders emerge who may attempt to organize group events. However, we are still talking about very informal organizations in which membership in the group is casual rather than institutionalized.

Finally, it should be mentioned that there are basic groups in society that are much more socially relevant than mere categoric groups, but which are, like categoric groups, largely passive. These social structures are called **primary groups.** They are natural collectivites that occur in all societies and are an important component of social organization. Such groups include families, neighbourhoods, communities, and religious denominations. The members of a primary group are, to varying degrees, conscious of themselves as a collectivity, and they do interact within the group. However, if primary groups become engaged in collective action, or if they become institutionalized, they may become relevant to politics and government, but then, by definition, they will have ceased to be primary groups.

**Institutionalization and Leadership: Formal Organizations** Groups begin to be **institutionalized** when the informal collectivity becomes a formal **association,** and membership requires the positive act of *joining* on the part of the individual members. Associations usually require a greater commitment on the part of the group membership than informal social groups, with membership dues, regular meetings, elected officers, and even rules governing the behaviour of the members. However, such associations are voluntary, and the members participate because they gain some personal benefit from belonging to the association. These organizations are referred to in the literature of sociology and political science generically as **voluntary associations**, **secondary groups**, or **secondary associations**.

Another important manifestation of group dynamics is that as they mature organizationally, groups generate their own internal *elites*. These elites are both a cause and an effect of group institutionalization. It requires informal leaders to take the organizational step to becoming a formal institution or association in the first place, and once the formal organization is in place, the group must institutionalize its leadership by electing an executive. In most cases it will be the informal elites that end up being selected initially as the formal group leaders.

**Politicization of Groups** Neighbourhood-improvement associations, cinema clubs, birdwatching groups, and Girl Guide troops are often well organized and extremely active, and in some cases, for instance, community curling clubs, they may have sizable budgets and significant capital assets. However, the membership of most such organizations is motivated by social and psychological needs, not by any political agenda. What is ultimately of interest to us here is groups that not only have become institutionalized but also have, as part of their organizational *raison d'être*, at least some political goals.

Thus, the curling club may become involved in lobbying Sport Canada to support the inclusion of curling as an olympic sport, the cinema club may have strong views respecting provincial censorship of films, and the birdwatchers' group may attempt to convince governments to protect more wetlands, to restrict the hunting of migratory birds, or to reduce the sales taxes on binoculars. Hence, despite the fact that an organization's major function is to provide an organizational milieu for like-minded people to pursue a common passion and opportunities for social interaction, when it attempts to influence government policy, it is functioning as a pressure group. This political function may be a small percentage of the overall activity of the group, and many of the members may not be very interested in such matters at all, but nevertheless the group can be classified loosely as a **sporadic pressure group.**

**"True" Interest Groups** There are large numbers of organizations and associations in Canada that, while their manifest role is non-political, occasionally attempt to influence political decisions. The more important group actors in the political and governmental process are the **true interest groups**. These groups are set up deliberately to represent the political interests of the membership through attempting to collectively put pressure on the policy makers in government. While such organizations do facilitate the exchange of views and the sharing of common concerns, and while the members may find the social interaction of the group personally satisfying, their manifest function is still to articulate the interests of the membership to the government.

The true interest groups are central actors or stakeholders in the political process and they can clearly have profound influence on policy decisions. Classic examples of such organizations at the national level include the Canadian Manufacturers Association, the Canadian Chamber of Commerce, the Canadian Federation of Agriculture, the Canadian Labour Congress, the Canadian Medical Association, and the Canadian Bar Association. While all of these organizations perform a range of services for their membership, it is clear that their manifest functions are all related to providing a voice for their interests in the political process.

Having attempted to make a distinction between groups that are only incidentally and sporadically involved in political activities and those that exist primarily as vehicles of political influence, we must caution that there exists no clear line of demarcation. When looking at groups or organizations that are involved in political activity, we must recognize only that they can be placed on a continuum ranging from groups whose goals are purely political to those that are rarely political. Most interest groups are multifunctional, lying somewhere on the continuum between the two poles. Organized groups that become involved in an ongoing way in interacting with government are also often referred to as **non-government organizations** or simply NGOs.

While most interest groups will tend to focus fairly narrowly on pursuing the specific interests of their membership, it is becoming more common for groups with similar concerns in a broad policy sector to form coalitions or alliances in order to enhance their collective influence with government. These **group coalitions** may spring up to support or oppose a specific policy initiative but they frequently stay together if the specific interests of the groups making up the coalition do not come into direct conflict. The Canadian Ethnocultural Council (CEC) is an example of a group coalition. It is composed of nearly forty different ethnic associations and is active on a wide range of issues that are of concern to Canada's minority ethnic communities.

**Social Movements**  New **social movements** provide for the expression of broadly based interests that have been effectively frozen out of the mainstream political process:

> [Since] the 1960s, new social movements throughout the western world have contested the established parameters of valid political discourse, and have changed societal conceptions of legitimate politics. In Canada, the feminist, gay rights, animal rights, ecological, and peace movements (to name a few) have altered the way in which we think, not just about political issues, but about the political in general.[1]

Social movements can thus be distinguished from both traditional interest groups and political parties by the fact that, in terms of structure, they are not "organizations."[2] They are informal networks of interaction among a large number of often diverse individuals and groups that have a shared collective identity and that are conscious of themselves as having interests that are not being served by the status quo in society.

As an example, the Canadian environmental *movement* is made up of a constellation of individual and organizational actors who have in common concerns on a very wide range of environmental issues. There may be hundreds of individual environmental interest groups in the movement, and the network includes many other groups and individuals that, among their other concerns, see environmental issues as very important. Thus, the environmental move-

---

1.  C. Galipeau, "Political Parties, Interest Groups and New Social Movements," *in* Alain Gagnon and Brian Tanguay, eds.,*Canadian Parties in Transition* (Toronto: Nelson, 1989).
2.  M. Diani, "The Concept of Social Movement," *The Sociological Review,* vol. 40, no. 1, 1992, pp. 13–14.

ment in Canada not only includes a multitude of single-issue organizations centred around specific "green" concerns such as logging in Clayoquot Sound, but also includes students, public-health officers, cottage owners, anglers and hunters, aboriginal communities, unions, community groups, and professional associations both organized and unorganized.

Social movements can become institutionalized through umbrella organizations known as **social-movement groups**, which are composed of a number of organizations that think of themselves as part of the given social-movement network. The best example of such an organization is the National Action Committee on the Status of Women, (NAC) which has over 500 affiliates, including groups as disparate as prostitutes' rights organizations, church groups, unions, and professional associations. NAC speaks out publicly on a very wide range of issues that are generally of concern to women, and while it appears to be experiencing some internal conflict today, it has managed to hold together since the early 1970s.

### Interest Groups and Political Parties

We have attempted above to define a threshold whereby we can distinguish between institutionalized groups in general and organizations we can call interest groups or pressure groups. We must now look at the threshold between pressure groups and political parties. After all, political parties are groups to the extent that party members display consistent patterns of behaviour, they are conscious of themselves as a group, and party associations or organizations are highly institutionalized. Moreover, political parties, particularly at the level of the riding association, may satisfy a wide range of social and psychological needs for their members in much the same way as non-party organizations do for theirs.

However, while we have seen that the difference between purely political organizations and non-political organizations that periodically get involved in politics is a difference of degree only, the difference between a political party and an interest group is clearer. Even true interest groups, which are exclusively political, differ qualitatively from political parties in that they do not actively seek to elect slates of candidates to political office. While they share with political parties the desire to effectively articulate the interests of their membership, they do not run candidates or attempt directly to control the apparatus of government.

Finally, we can also distinguish between political parties and interest groups in terms of the inclusiveness of their respective memberships. Political parties, to be successful, must **aggregate** a wider range of interests than an interest group, which can focus on the **articulation** of the more narrow concerns of its membership. In the next section we will look in more detail at the political functions of interest groups, and the functional differentiation between political parties and interest groups will become still more evident.

► THE FUNCTIONS OF INTEREST GROUPS

There are literally tens of thousands of organizations in Canada that become involved at least some of the time in activities that would allow us to place them in the broad category of interest groups. All of these groups perform non-political functions, meeting various social and psychological needs of their membership. However, what is of interest in a textbook on Canadian government and politics is their *political* functions. These political functions include a primary or manifest function and a number of secondary functions that are performed incidentally in the course of pursuing the groups' primary goals.

**Political Functions**

An early student of interest groups in the United States, Gabriel Almond, stated that the function of interest groups was to **articulate the interests** of the group membership to the authorities of the political system with the ultimate aim of having an effect on policy outcomes.[3] The current *éminence grise* on the subject of Canadian pressure groups, Paul Pross, states that the primary function of such groups is **communication**.[4] We can generally agree with both approaches except that when interest groups or pressure groups are sited within the context of democratic government and politics, we feel that, at the most elemental level, their primary function is really **representation**. Articulating interests, communicating, or lobbying political and bureaucratic influentials are all simply the means through which the group carries out its representative function.

**Representation**   Along with political parties and the electoral system, interest groups complement the democratic processes by providing alternate means whereby Canadians are represented. We say that interest groups "complement" the representative functions performed by parties and elections because the ways in which they represent us is different. In the first place, political parties and elections perform a representative function that is at the level of the entire political community — the entire *demos*. Through instruments such as voting and majoritarianism the electoral process allows us to choose representatives who will govern in the *general interest* or on behalf of all Canadians. By contrast, interest groups are able to represent the more *specific interests* of identifiable groups within the larger political community.

Second, as we have seen in previous chapters, parties functioning within the electoral process allow us to express our preferences through *periodic* votes that determine which set of political leaders will take the governmental helm for the next few years. By contrast, interest groups have an ongoing rather than

3. Gabriel Almond, "Interest Groups and the Political Process," *in* R. C. Macridis and B. E. Brown, *Comparative Politics* (Homewood: Dorsey Press, 1964), pp. 132–33.
4. See Paul Pross, "Pressure Groups: Talking Chameleons," *in* M. S. Whittington and G. Williams, *Canadian Politics in the 1990s* (Toronto: Nelson, 1994); see also Paul Pross, "Pressure Groups: Adaptive Instruments of Political Communication," *in* Paul Pross, *Pressure Group Behaviour in Canadian Politics* (Toronto: McGraw-Hill Ryerson, 1975); and Paul Pross, *Group Politics and Public Policy* (Toronto: Oxford University Press, 1992).

a periodic role, operating between elections to bring the interests of their membership to the attention of our elected governmental "helmsmen."

Thirdly, unlike parties and elections, which provide for representation on a riding-based or *territorial* framework, interest groups can represent groups of individuals across geographical boundaries. Interest groups represent Canadians on the basis of economic, religious, ethnic, and moral interests, regardless of whether their members happen to be concentrated in a single territorial unit. The members of the group may live in many different constituencies and many different regions of the country because their common "interest" is not geographically specific.

Finally, the representation provided by parties and elections is formal, and highly institutionalized, and has statutory sanction. The electoral system is the most explicit and formal regime mechanism for democratic representation, and as such it is less flexible and less adaptable in the short term. By contrast, interest groups can emerge and fade away or evolve and adapt as their objectives change and as political circumstances shift over time. As we shall see later in the chapter, as the world changes, groups are able to change not only their strategy and tactics but their ultimate objectives as well. To quote Paul Pross, they are truly "chameleons" among our political institutions.[5]

**Communication** An interest group represents its membership by acting as a communications link between the group and the officials in the state apparatus who have the power to make the policy decisions desired by the group. This communications function is performed through the leaders of the interest group's articulating the group's interests to government, albeit slanted in such a way that the appropriate authorities will be convinced that the group's particular demands are worthy of consideration. When the message being communicated is delivered in private and directly to the political decision-makers of government, this process is also referred to as **lobbying**.

It is through this communication activity that interest groups can become important *diagnostic* tools for government, helping them to identify the most important issues in our society and to find appropriate policy "cures." Because interest groups are such valuable sources of **policy intelligence**, governments will frequently actively solicit the participation of major interests with the intention of ensuring that they haven't missed anything when considering policy options.

Most academic discourse on interest groups focuses on this "information-in" aspect of their communications role. Interest groups, however, also communicate messages from governments to their members. Almost as important as the communication of policy demands from society to the government is the *dissemination* of information about government policies to people in society. As we have seen in earlier chapters, people cannot obey the law unless they know what the law is, and they cannot take advantage of government programs unless they know about them. It is interest groups that often provide these necessary state-society linkages, which ensure that government's pronouncements are heard out in the real world. Virtually every trade association, union,

---

5. Pross, "Pressure Groups: Adaptive Instruments," p. 6.

or promotional group at least publishes a newsletter, and much of the work of the head offices of interest groups consists of determining which government activities are pertinent to the particular group's interests and then informing members about those activities.

Interest groups also play an important role by providing the political decision-makers in government with *feedback* about the effectiveness of their policies. Interest groups monitor the manner in which programs are delivered to the public and are in a position to identify problems encountered by their members in the process of program implementation. Such information is extremely useful to government officials in adapting and fine-tuning their program delivery and in anticipating policy demands that might be generated in the future.

**Legitimation**  Among their political functions, second only to communication is the role interest groups play in the **legitimizing** of policy. Organized interests provide an effective vehicle for disgruntled individuals to get their concerns listened to by government. They also help to ensure that various stakeholders with conflicting demands all have an opportunity to be heard. Even policies that have been opposed by a group or policies that do not go far enough in meeting the demands of the group are more likely to be accepted if there is a sense that everybody has had a "day in court" and that all interested groups have had an opportunity to state their case.

Governments also use interest groups to help "sell" their ultimate decisions to an often sceptical public. The government can **pre-legitimize** its policy decisions by making it clear that it is simply responding to public opinion as reflected by group pressure. If the governmental actions are in line with the interests of important groups in society, the organizations representing those interests will often participate actively by praising the government for its "courage and clear-headedness" in doing something the groups were demanding. However, in this regard, it must be noted that client groups are not shy about "biting the hand that feeds them" if they are not happy with a policy decision.

**Interest Aggregation**  Because groups of any kind are, by definition, aggregations of individuals, interest groups can be seen as performing an aggregative function in our society. Interest groups bring together individuals with common concerns about government policy at least in part because, by acting in combination, those individuals can have a greater impact on government. There is indeed strength in numbers and in a democratic society the more votes an organization can claim to represent, the more clout that organization will have in influencing policy-makers.

In attempting to maximize its political influence by **aggregating interests**, a pressure group also performs a useful function for the government of the day. If the government were faced only with demands from individuals acting alone, it would be very difficult to sort out the types of policy responses that would be acceptable to the widest number of individuals. By speaking on behalf of large categoric groups of individuals in society who have interests in common, interest groups help to rationalize and hence reduce the total number of policy demands the government is forced to deal with at any given time.

Some organizations, which are in fact coalitions or confederations of various groups having similar goals, or having different but compatible goals, take this aggregative role even further. By prioritizing related issues among several organizations concerned with a given policy area before making a demand on government, such coalitions of groups can reduce still further the number of options the government has to consider. The aggregation of interests by pressure groups, and by coalitions of groups, is thus beneficial both in increasing the influence of the group over government and in helping the government to screen policy demands and reduce the complexity of the policy agenda.

### Administrative Functions

Interest groups also participate directly in the administration of programs for governments. In part they do this by the communication function mentioned earlier. For example, if a program of subsidies for a particular industry were established, the industry's trade association would likely wish to "blow its own horn" by publicizing to its membership its success in convincing the government to favour the group's interests. The organization would also communicate, in a more neutral tone, the actual details of the program, and may even gather and coordinate applications from its members who wish to avail themselves of the new program opportunities. However, for groups to be drawn into assisting departments in the administrative process, they must be somewhat happy with the programs being delivered.

Interest groups may also perform more direct administrative functions for the government. For instance, medical associations determine the division of government-provided fees among various medical specialties, and hospital associations gather data that governments use in allocating funds among medical institutions. In a similar way, grain-elevator cooperatives and farmers' associations participate in many aspects of government farm-price-support programs; environmental non-government organizations (NGOs) provide informal inspection services and warn government agencies of emerging environmental problems; and universities administer student-aid programs subject to advice, in some cases, by student associations.

**Self-Regulation** One of the most important administrative functions of many groups, and certainly the most cherished by the groups themselves, is **self-regulation**. For example, society agrees that it would be undesirable to have a large number of unqualified people claiming to be doctors, dentists, lawyers, engineers, or architects. Accordingly, by delegation from governments, law societies determine who is qualified to become a lawyer, and provincial colleges of physicians and surgeons are largely responsible for the regulation and certification of the medical profession in each province.

This self-accreditation and self-regulatory mechanism extends far in Canadian society, for not only are professions controlled in this way, but so also are trades and crafts. The function extends beyond the mere definition of who is qualified to practice, and may provide guidelines as to what constitutes ethical or fair practices and appropriate fee structures. Similar mechanisms have also evolved in the business community, through better business bureaus and other voluntary self-monitoring business associations. Were it not for the self-regulatory functions of many interest groups in society, the governmental structure in Canada would have to be considerably larger than it is now.

Conversely, the self-regulatory function is particularly valuable to groups because of the monopoly position it gives group members in the provision of services — and, of course, in receiving the rewards therefrom. The right to restrict numbers of practitioners of a trade is crucial in maintaining the incomes of the members of the trade, so it is guarded jealously by the association holding that right. Moreover, by doing it themselves, these organizations keep government out of what they view to be their own internal affairs, inoculating themselves against the dreaded epidemic of public regulation. In sum, these activities cannot be viewed as anything but part of a *symbiotic* relationship between certain interest groups and the government.

### Systemic Functions

We have already discussed a number of functions that pressure groups perform for the governmental system in the course of seeking to maximize their own political influence. Organized interests assist in the policy process by providing important linkages between the government and groups in society, and by providing better and more effective access to the decision-makers of the state. We have also seen that interest groups assist in the legitimizing of specific policies and in reducing the length of the policy agenda by aggregating interests. However, interest groups also perform functions for the Canadian system as a whole, lending political stability and legitimacy to the regime and fostering the integration of the political community.

**Legitimacy**  Pressure groups make it easier for individuals who, acting alone, might be ignored, to get the attention of the people in government. By being part of a group and, hence, representing a group of potential votes, individual Canadians enhance their personal influence over the policy process. While group pressure often does have some impact on policy outcomes, when a group is not successful in its pressure tactics, it is often because competing groups with a different set of priorities have been more persuasive. In this way, people see that working collectively with other like-minded individuals does have an impact, even if another group's campaign happened to be more effective in any particular instance. Thus, participating in an interest group can enhance the individual's feelings of *political efficacy*, and in so doing reinforces the legitmacy of the regime as a whole as well as the legitimacy of the specific policy decision.

Participating in interest groups can indeed **empower** individuals, just as becoming politically active can empower an existing categoric group. The enhanced sense of being able to get the attention of the government through acting collectively also reduces the generalized frustration individuals often feel when faced with the distant, monolithic, and apparently inattentive government. Participation in groups with political goals gives individuals a feeling of empowerment even if the group is not always successful in its lobbying efforts. This buttresses the legitimacy of the system and encourages the active participation of citizens in the political life of the country even between elections.

**Social Movements and Systemic Change** Social movements, unlike interest groups, often have broader goals of systemic change as well as specific policy concerns. They arise to represent ideas and approaches that have been ignored or shunned in mainstream politics, and they are centred around new collective identities based on gender, sexual orientation, or a broadly based world view or counter-cultural set of values. They can also be understood as reflecting new ways of thinking about political reality and as new ways of fostering social and political change.

The ideas fostered by new social movements circulate not only in the world outside of government but, as well, within the corridors of power — in Cabinet, Parliament, and the bureaucracy. Although there is always resistance to the sorts of change they advocate, social movements in Canada and elsewhere around the world have indeed generated shifts in social values and in the agenda and *modus operandi* of political and governmental institutions.

**Pluralism and Political Integration** Interest groups also reinforce the system as a whole by providing a vehicle that helps to connect the individual to the state. As sociologist Émile Durkheim put it:

> The state is too remote from individuals, its relations with them too external and intermittent to penetrate deeply within individual consciences and socialize them within. When the state is the only environment in which men can live communal lives, they inevitably lose contact, become detached and society disintegrates. A nation can be maintained only if, between the state and the individual, there is intercalated a whole series of secondary groups near enough to the individuals to attract them strongly to their sphere of action and drag them, in this way, into the general torrent of social life.[6]

There is by no means unanimity that the pervasiveness of interest groups and their close relationship to government is a desirable feature of modern society. In particular, the belief that older and more legitimate institutions of government, particularly Parliament and political parties, are being supplemented or even supplanted by an alliance between the executive level of government and the constellation of interest groups that make up a policy community is a very disquieting one for many political scientists.[7] However, it is a reasonable hypothesis to go along with Durkheim and suggest that in general, organizations or *secondary associations*, including interest groups, do act as a buffer between

---

6. From Émile Durkheim, *The Division of Labour in Society*, translated by George Simpson (New York: The Free Press, 1964).

7. A wide sampling of such views is to be found in *Canadian Public Administration*, vol. 25, no. 2, Summer 1982, in a report on the Institute of Public Administration of Canada 1981 annual seminars entitled "Governing Under Pressure." The most extreme version, in which the state is hypothesized to have created groups as a means by which to control and manipulate society, is in Dominique Clift, "L'état et les groups d'intérêts: perspectives d'avenir," pp. 265–78.

the individual and the state in modern mass societies, *integrating* the individual into the nation.

In the absence of smaller organizational entities through which individuals can deal *indirectly* with the state, the individual in society would be forced to identify directly with the state or with symbols of the state. The psychological effect would be to leave the individual feeling hopelessly inefficacious with at least two possible outcomes. On the one hand the individual might become totally alienated from the state and simply withdraw into an apolitical and apathetic isolation. On the other hand the individual might come to identify completely and unquestioningly with state symbols such as a messianic dictator or an official ideology. Neither of these possibilities is compatible over time with democratic politics as we know it.

The existence of large numbers of secondary associations, and in particular the presence of organized interest groups, is characteristic of what some theorists call *pluralist* societies. **Pluralism** is thought to be a form of social organization that allows individuals to integrate into society as members of multiple groups and organizations, which in turn represent the individual in dealings with the monolithic and impersonal modern government. Through even passive membership in various groups, the individual doesn't feel so alone and is better able to cope psychologically with the awesome size and power of modern government.

**Pluralism and Elitism**   As well as the social implications of pluralism in modern nations there is also an *instrumental* effect of organized interest groups on the general nature of political and governmental processes. Most significantly, **interest-group pluralism** implies that the various organizations we call interest groups will interact with each other and with governments. This interaction does not occur to any significant extent at the level of the individual rank-and-file members but between and among the leaders of the organizations. These leaders, or elites, are chosen by the members through processes that are essentially internal democratic elections; the group elites can therefore be said to *represent* the group members. Nevertheless we must remember when analyzing the role of interest groups in Canada that it is the interest-group elites and not the members that dominate the process.

We have already discussed the process of elite accommodation as the dominant conflict-resolution mechanism in constitutional development, French-English relations, and intergovernmental relations. Now we must add **pressure-group politics** to the list of political and governmental processes that operate, at least in part, through elite accommodation. The leaders of various groups bargain among themselves, forming long-term coalitions and short-term alliances of convenience in order to increase their effectiveness in lobbying government. These accommodations among the elites of interest groups help to integrate disparate groups and, at least temporarily, to reduce intergroup conflict and increase intergroup cooperation.

The elites of the most powerful interest groups also interact on a regular basis with the elites in the Cabinet and the bureaucracy, forming alliances and forging coalitions to pursue mutually acceptable policy goals. On the positive side, this sort of elite interaction between the leaders of interest groups and the leaders of government facilitates the machinery of policy decision-making and "gets things done." However, the down side is that there is always a possiblity that if the interaction among the elites gets too cosy, the leaders in government and the leaders of the major interest groups may come to make deals in their own personal interest and not in the interest of the people who elected them. Moreover, the interaction among elites, being essentially a be-hind-closed-doors process, is not subject either to the moderating effect of public scrutiny or even to the approbation of the people that the elites purport to represent.

Since the late 1960s, broadly based social unrest and economic instability have challenged the assumption of interest-group politics that elite accom-modation can effectively broker all conflicting public demands. Despite gov-ernmental rhetoric encouraging public participation, and despite efforts to include a wider spectrum of the population in policy debate, there are signifi-cant sectors of the population who remain excluded from the mainstream of interest-group pluralism. The failures of the brokerage system have led to the rise of new social movements that challenge not only the policies of the status quo but the policy system itself.

### Group Survival and Adaptation

One of the major preoccupations of any organization is self-preservation. The leaders of interest groups are, quite naturally, interested in keeping their jobs and in ensuring the survival of the organization within which they work. Min-imally, this means that the leaders of the organization must keep in touch with the rank and file and must generally pursue goals that are compatible with the desires of the membership. It is this need to keep their own constituency happy that to some extent counters the tendency for the organizational elites to act in a purely self-serving manner. **Intra-group democracy** with periodic elections may not be any more effective than the national or provincial election pro-cesses, but it does keep the leadership honest and aware that they owe some-thing to the people who elected them.

The organizational survival instinct occasionally leads to a situation where the greatest enemy of an interest group is another interest group pursuing the same goal, for both are competing for the allegiance of the same clientele and for the recognition of the same governmental agencies. For instance, labour unions are often in direct competition through certification battles even though the workers they seek to represent have the same basic needs. Similarly, the Canadian Federation of Agriculture and the National Farmers Union often find themselves implacably opposed, even though one would expect their goals to be similar.

Finally, one of the most serious problems a group can face is, ironically, too much success. If a group organized to achieve a specific goal is successful in achieving that goal, logically there is no longer any need for the organization. However, it is not unusual for a successful group to take on a new *raison d'être*, and to opt to pursue a new "worthy cause" in order to justify its continued existence. This phenomenon is referred to as **goal displacement**.[8] Thus, for

---

8. While Roberto Michels is normally credited with originating the concept of *goal displacement*, there

interest groups no less than for other large organizations, the survival of the organization itself may supersede the substantive interests of the membership as the primary organizational goal.

## ▶ CLASSIFICATION OF INTEREST GROUPS

To make sense out of the political activities of the literally thousands of interest groups in Canada, it would be useful if they could be classified or categorized in some way. Unfortunately, most attempts to provide such a taxonomy have not proven very successful because in some ways each group is *sui generis*. Each interest group has its own unique structure, clientele, *raison d'être*, and *modus operandi*, and generalizations do not help very much in understanding how the myriad organizations deal with government, their membership, or other groups. Having in mind the limitations of such systems of classification however, it is still worth mentioning some of them to familiarize students with the terms and concepts found in the academic literature. Moreover, while they may not be very effective taxonomies, they do provide insights as to the range and diversity of species we are dealing with.

### Dichotomies

One typology divides interest groups into economic and non-economic groups. The economic groups are, in turn, subdivided into agriculture, labour, and business groups; the non-economic groups are divided into nine sub-types.[9] Such a scheme, however, tells us relatively little about the activities of a group or about its orientation towards government, and it is, after all, the *process* of interest-group politics that ultimately interests us here.

A more interesting if only marginally more useful taxonomy classifies groups according to a number of paired-opposite categories.[10] The paired opposites are:

compulsory vs. voluntary
temporary vs. permanent
economic vs. instrumental
mass vs. selective
producer vs. consumer
local-provincial vs. federal
federated vs. unitary
oligarchical vs. participative
private vs. public

is a large body of literature that has developed the concept and applied it to specific organizations. This phenomenon is discussed briefly and clearly in A. Etzioni, *Modern Organizations* (Englewood Cliffs: Prentice-Hall, 1964), pp. 10–14. See also R. J. Merton, *Social Theory and Social Structure* (Glencoe: Free Press, 1957), p. 197ff.; and P. Selznick, "An Approach to a Theory of Bureaucracy," *American Sociological Review*, vol. 8, no. 1 (1943), pp. 47–54.

9. Frederick Englemann and Mildred Schwartz, *Political Parties and the Canadian Social Structure* (Toronto: Prentice-Hall, 1975), pp. 95–96.

10. R. Presthus, *Elite Accommodation in Canadian Politics*, (Toronto: Macmillan, 1973), p. 67.

The problem with this elaborate system of nine dichotomies is that we have hypothetically eighty-one different categories of groups, which is a little unwieldy. The purpose of this exercise is, after all, to simplify reality, not to make it more complicated. Moreover, the taxonomic matrix that this system would generate would be still more complex because a variable such as "temporary vs. permanent" is, in fact, a continuum, not a dichotomy. Nevertheless, when examining the case of a given interest group, the nine paired variables form a useful checklist for ensuring comprehensiveness in making comparisons with other organizations.

Another dichotomy used to classify interest groups differentiates between **special-interest** groups and **public-interest** groups.[11] The former include groups that seek to further the narrow interests of their membership, particularly in monetary or economic terms. They are frankly self-interested and often fairly exclusive in their membership. The best examples of special-interest groups are business and industry associations. Public-interest groups, by contrast, advocate policies that are held to be in the broader interests of society as a whole rather than in the interest of the group activists. Such organizations tend to broader based, more inclusive in their membership, and focused on social and political concerns rather than pecuniary ones. Environmental groups are a good example of public-interest organizations.

The main problem with this dichotomy is that nobody is certain what the *public interest* is. Self-styled public-interest groups may be pursuing diametrically opposed policy goals, as is the case with the groups on opposite sides of the abortion issue. Both sides claim to be acting in the public interest rather than narrow self-interest. Part of the problem may be a failure to recognize that a group can be self-interested and yet be advocating policy positions that affect broad societal concerns and issues of ethics and morality. Moreover, self-interest does not have to be tied to economic or pecuniary gain. Anti-smoking lobbies can be as passionate and as single-minded as business associations, even though what they stand to gain is psychological and emotional satisfaction rather than monetary advantage.

Where the public-interest/special-interest dichotomy provides a useful distinction is in the area of the inclusiveness of the organization. If we think of *public* interest-groups instead of *public-interest* groups, such organizations can be set apart because of their openness and inclusiveness. In this sense, the dichotomy contrasts special-interest groups, which are narrow and exclusive, with public groups, which involve a much wider membership.[12] Whether the goals being pursued are in the "public interest" is no longer the main criterion for the dichotomy. As with other dichotomy approaches to the classification of interest groups, however, this one has only limited utility.

### Continua

A classification scheme developed by Paul Pross suggests that groups can be classified according to what he calls a **continuum framework**.[13] This framework

11. W. T. Stanbury, "A Sceptic's Guide to the Claims of So-called Public Interest Groups," and Susan D. Phillips, "Of Public Interest Groups and Sceptics: A Realist's Reply to Professor Stanbury," both in *Canadian Public Administration*, vol. 36, no. 4, Winter 1993.
12. Phillips, "Of Public Interest Groups and Sceptics."
13. Pross, "Pressure Groups: Talking Chameleons."

views groups in a *developmental* context evolving from **nascent**, to **fledgling,** to **mature**, and ultimately graduating to **institutionalized**. As the group evolves, its objectives become increasingly complex and more broadly based and it grows in organizational complexity and sophistication. While this is an interesting system, it suffers from being overly complicated — there are too many cells in the matrix — and from the fact that many of the categories are not mutually exclusive. It is most useful in that it presents a series of broad generalizations about how interest groups usually evolve and how their strategies shift as they climb ever closer to the summit of group development, *institutionalization.*[14]

Any criticism of our colleagues' brave attempts to classify interest groups must, however, be seen in the light of our own folly! In *The Canadian Political System*, we attempted to categorize interest groups in Canada along four continua.[15] The first continuum suggests that the activities of interest groups can tend towards either the **self-interested** or the **promotional**.[16] Self-interested groups tend to look towards the direct material advantage of their membership, whereas promotional groups are interested in doing things for what they perceive to be the betterment of society.

This distinction is similar to the one between special-interest groups and public-interest groups in the previous section. The difference is that, in this case, we do not see the distinction as dichotomous. For example, the Canadian Manufacturers' Association, the Canadian Labour Congress, or the Canadian Federation of Agriculture are self-interested in that they are in varying degrees concerned with securing policies that are advantageous to their members. The John Howard Society is a promotional group because it "promotes" penal reform and prisoner rehabilitation, despite the fact that few of its members are prisoners or ex-prisoners. Similarly, animal-rights groups promote the interests of sea mammals despite the fact that they do not have many seals or whales attending their meetings.

A second continuum, based in part on Paul Pross's typology, is between fledgling and institutionalized groups. The latter type tends to have a formal and permanent structure, a stable and cohesive membership, and institutionalized access to the government. While such groups have concrete operational objectives, generally the survival of the organization itself and its continuing privileged access to decision-makers is more important than any single issue, and such groups are successful because they virtually become part of the elite establishment. Fledgling groups, by contrast, are usually concerned with only one or two issues and their life expectancy is usually tied to the life of those issues. Their structural characteristics are almost completely opposite to those of institutionalized groups. However, since some issues remain in the forefront of political discourse over extended periods, some single-issue groups actually achieve considerable permanence and gradually develop many of the organizational characteristics of institutionalized groups.

A third continuum is between groups that have been primarily responsible for their own creation and maintenance, and groups that have been either

14. Pross, "Pressure Groups: Talking Chameleons" provides an elaboration of this typology.
15. Rick Van Loon and Mike Whittington, *The Canadian Political System: Environment, Structure and Process* (Toronto: McGraw-Hill Ryerson, 1987), pp. 402–34.
16. S. E. Finer, *Anonymous Empire* (London: Pall Mall, 1958).

created or strongly encouraged by government itself. The former type we call **autonomous** pressure groups and the latter are called **reverse** groups. Reverse pressure groups may be created because political decision-makers are anxious to have all the inputs they can get before they set out to make policy, and because they wish to create generalized support or legitimacy for their policy proposals. In addition to this function of creating or mobilizing a clientele, government-sponsored organizations may also be used for communication with an otherwise poorly organized portion of the public, or even to administer some aspects of an agency's program. Alternatively, government may attempt to reinforce and co-opt existing organizations by providing financial support and privileged access to the policy decision-makers.

At one time or another, at least half of all federal government departments have created such groups. The modern aboriginal peoples' associations were initially promoted by the federal government and are still essentially dependent on it for "core" funding. Another example was the Eastern Fishermen's Federation, which was encouraged and supported by the federal and provincial governments and became a major source of communication to and from the fishermen. However, as these examples testify, reverse groups do not always become the domestic pets of government, and far from becoming co-opted, once created, they may thrive as thorns in the side of their creator.

Finally, groups may be placed on a continuum according to whether they are **active** or **categoric** groups.[17] This continuum assumes that there are latent interest groups in society that may become active only if a pressing issue presents itself. For example, practising Christians can hardly be viewed as a single cohesive interest group, yet, if the political system threatened to outlaw religious practices, this categoric group would soon become active. Canadians older than sixty-five have been a largely dormant categoric group, but, as we have often seen, whenever governments threaten their pensions, they awaken very quickly to become an active special-interest group with very great political power.

We must conclude that all such attempts at classifying and categorizing interest groups are flawed because the categories are neither exhaustive nor mutually exclusive, because the taxonomies are often more complicated than the reality they attempt to simplify, and because they are an incompatible mix of dichotomies and continua. However, these attempts to classify groups are still useful because they provide us with lists of characteristics to look for when we analyze any specific interest group.

---

## ▶ CONCLUSION

It is clear that groups are an important part of the fabric of Canadian society. The liberal component of our political culture, which places a great deal of

---

17. See D. B. Truman, *The Governmental Process* (New York: Alfred A. Knopf, 1965), pp. 23–26. Truman makes a distinction, similar to our own, between *categoric* and *institutionalized* groups.

importance on the individual, is tempered in part because a majority of Canadians do in fact belong to one or more organizations that engage in pressure-group activity. Our social structure is, thus, liberal-pluralist[18] in form and, as we shall see in the next chapter, our political process is characterized by the widespread and intensive involvement of literally tens of thousands of interest groups.

18.  See T. Lowi, *The End of Liberalism* (Chicago: Norton, 1979).

*Chapter* **17**

# Interest Groups:
# Access and Influence

The aim of any interest group is to have influence over policy decisions that affect the interests of its members. The aim of this section is to examine the points of access to the policy process that are available to organized interests in Canada. It is *a sine qua non* of interest-group strategy that the leaders or spokespersons for the organization must be heard by the policy makers of government if they are to be able to even attempt to affect policy outcomes. Thus, while **access** is a necessary condition for an organization to have any influence on policy decisions, we must keep in mind that access is not in itself sufficient to give the group power. The **influence** or power of groups that enjoy equal access to the core decision-makers may still vary depending on a number of other circumstances that determine their relative influence. These we will consider in the next section of the chapter.

The access points available to a group will be determined by a number of factors, including the position of the group within the particular **policy community.** As described in Chapter 2, a policy community operating in an area of federal jurisdiction will have at its *core* the federal Cabinet and a lead agency or department. Surrounding this decision-making core are "concentric rings" of other policy actors and institutions whose influence increases with their proximity to the core. The rings include MPs, other departments and agencies, provincial governments, the media, and a cluster of non-government organizations, groups, and individuals that are interested in and attentive to that particular policy area. The most influential interest groups in any given policy area likely will have direct, institutionalized access to the policy core, and the influence of other groups will be determined by how far they can worm their way into the heart of the policy community.

## ▶ DIRECT ACCESS TO GOVERNMENT

Interest groups in Canada face two essential facts about our system of government: it is both federal and parliamentary in structure. The former means that power is widely dispersed geographically. The latter means that, within each of the capital cities, the lion's share of decision-making authority is concentrated in the Cabinet and the bureaucracy rather than in the legislature.

### Federalism and Group Tactics

Shared and overlapping jurisdiction in the Canadian federal system frequently makes it necessary for groups to employ a strategy of exerting pressure at both federal and provincial levels of government. Under our highly integrated system of federalism, policy decisions are often taken at both levels of government simultaneously. Thus, if a group wants to influence policy outcomes, it may find that it is necessary to divide its organizational energies and to wage separate pressure campaigns on many fronts. For instance, hospitals and related institutions seeking to maintain a regulatory framework sympathetic to their interests have been obliged to press their case not only with the federal government, which regulates some aspects of the health-care system, but also with the provincial and territorial governments, which actually control the health-insurance programs across the country.

While having to divide its efforts and resources may be inconvenient and inefficient for an interest group, the federal system of government may provide additional opportunities for both access and influence. Not only does divided jurisdiction provide additional points of access to the system, it also allows a group to play one government off against the other in pressing its case. For example, in opposing tax reforms, mining and oil-and-gas companies find it an effective tactic to first convince provincial governments, in "producing" provinces, of the alleged detrimental impact of higher taxes on investment and employment opportunities in those provinces. Provincial treasurers then ally themselves with the industry moguls in pressuring the government in Ottawa to back off on its reform proposals. Multiple access points are most valuable to a group trying to block government initiatives since it is always easier to convince governments *not* to do something.

Most large Canadian interest groups are themselves federations, and the provincial bodies that make up these federations are often, in turn, coalitions of local groups. Frequently, the local and provincial organizations are more powerful than the national structure, as is the case with the Canadian Hospital Association. The CHA has a small national headquarters staff and modest office quarters in Ottawa, whereas the Ontario Hospital Association has a far larger staff and owns a large office complex in Toronto. In such organizations, it is sometimes difficult to arrive at any consistent national viewpoint, for that requires the finding of common ground among provincial organizations, which may have widely disparate interests. The national director or president may find himself or herself contradicted by some provincial group whenever a point is being made, and this dilutes the group's strength in dealing with government. Moreover, very often there are no direct dues-paying members of the national organization. National headquarters thus exists on funds provided by the provincial associations, with the inevitable result that the central office is almost certain to find itself underfunded.

All these factors will have some influence on the ways groups make contact with governments. While the Canadian Hospital Association works with the federal government, its provincial affiliates are usually relatively more influential in their own provinces. The Canadian Chamber of Commerce has a general role in Ottawa, as spokesman for a segment of the business community, but it is at the local level that the Chamber's power is greatest. On the other hand, a few interest groups, some of them not formal federations, have become highly centralized and highly focused on federal government agencies. The Consumers' Association of Canada does most of its governmental work from Ottawa, as does the Canadian Manufacturers' Association. In such cases, contact between the federal government and the national organization is much stronger than that between the provincial governments and provincial affiliates.

### Parliament and Group Access

Since modern government in Canada concentrates the bulk of power in the Cabinet and the bureaucracy, Parliament is not the primary focus for interest-group activity. As one experienced lobbyist once said, "When I see Members of Parliament being lobbied, it's a sure sign to me that the lobby lost its fight in the civil service and the cabinet."[1] While the group lobbying MPs may occasionally gain *indirect* access to the Cabinet through their concerns being raised in caucus, its chances of success in the longer run are slight unless the group can convince some Cabinet ministers as well. The following list,[2] although based on fairly old data, is still an accurate reflection of the relative priority (ordered from most important to least important) that Canadian pressure groups place on the various potential points of access to the federal system.

RELATIVE IMPORTANCE OF ACCESS POINTS

Interaction with Senior-Level Public Servants
Interaction with Cabinet Ministers
Participation on Joint Business-Government Committees
Interaction with Junior or Mid-Level Civil Servants
Contact with Central Agencies
Appearances before Parliamentary Committees
Interaction with Government MPs
Interaction with Opposition MPs

The list indicates that opposition MPs are the least desirable access points, but even here there are exceptions. Immediately after an election, when the opposition is some years away from any opportunity to gain power, groups will

---

1. Quoted in Frederick Englemann and Mildred Schwartz, *Political Parties and the Canadian Social Structure* (Toronto: Prentice-Hall, 1975), p. 105. Similar quotes appear in much of the literature on interest groups.
2. Adapted from T. A. Litvak, "National Trade Associations," *Business Quarterly,* Autumn 1982, p. 39.

be most likely to ignore them. However, as an election looms larger and as the government's popularity wanes, interest groups may begin to pay more and more attention to the opposition MPs in the hope that they may soon be on the government benches or even in the Cabinet. The relative desirability of access to the minister or the public servants will depend on the magnitude and political significance of the issue — the more political the issue the more important it is to get the minister on side. Conversely, if the issue is highly technical in nature, it will be more important for the group to bend the ear of the bureaucrats.

There are, of course, exceptions to the rule that the parliamentary arena is a bad one for interest groups to play in. For instance, in a minority-government situation, the Cabinet tends to pay a great deal more attention to Parliament than during majority governments. From 1972 to 1974, any group that could enlist NDP members to support its cause was in a very powerful position, since the government of the day was dependent upon the NDP for its survival.

**Parliamentary Committees**  The presentation of briefs to the committees of the House of Commons is a tactic that, in the past, has seldom proven very effective by itself. Indeed, it could not be expected to be very effective, since the committee stage normally follows second reading of a bill, which constitutes "approval in principle" of the bill's major measures. However, ministers and their officials do tend to seize upon briefs favourable to their position as tangible evidence of wide support for their policies. Not unexpectedly, the government will tend to ignore briefs that go against them.

Even when there is little hope of blocking legislation that has the support of the Cabinet, sometimes simply delaying a piece of legislation in committee is worthwhile to a group, because the delay buys time during which the group can possibly marshall suffcient public support to get the Cabinet to change its mind. There have certainly been exceptions where group pressure at the committee stage of the parliamentary process has been successful. In a minority situation, for instance, parliamentary committees do not have a majority of government members, so the possibility of achieving significant amendments in committee is increased. However, even in the fairly rare circumstances where interest groups are able to convince the government to make changes to the legislation, such exceptions may well be evidence of only limited government commitment in the first place.

Given that the role of parliamentary committees has been broadened in recent years, it may be that interest groups will pay rather more attention to Parliament in future. As we will see when we consider recent changes to parliamentary rules, parliamentary task forces, standing committees, and even individual backbenchers may have considerably more influence in the 1990s than they did before. Certainly interest groups will continue to pay close attention to the activities of special House committees working in areas of concern to them as a complement to their efforts to directly influence the executive. As well, more private member's bills will actually come to a vote in the House of Commons in future, making the backbench sponsors of the bills a potential target for group pressure. However, we must still conclude that interest groups lobby Parliament mostly when they have not been successful in their efforts with the Cabinet and the bureaucracy.

### Cabinet and Group Access

As we shall see in the next chapter, the Cabinet is at the centre of the policy process in Canada because it is the Cabinet that has the responsibility for establishing the broad policy priorities of government. As a result, interest groups have always sought to develop points of access with Cabinet ministers and in fact history shows us that the relationship between individual ministers and interest groups can be very close. Meetings between Cabinet ministers and interest-group leaders go on constantly, and it would be a rare week indeed when a minister's schedule did not provide for several such meetings. Ministers often use groups as a counterweight to the advice of their bureaucratic officials, and certainly if a group can succeed in convincing a strong minister of the rightness of its cause, its chances of success are greatly enhanced.

One highly structured technique of dealing with Cabinet that is well publicized but probably not very effective is the **annual briefing**. Several large national groups, such as the Canadian Labour Congress, the Canadian Chamber of Commerce, and the Canadian Manufacturers' Association, present an annual brief to the whole Cabinet, with much attendant fanfare. Such briefs are generally filled with pious generalization and self-serving hyperbole but they may tell the Cabinet something about the mood of an important sector of the economy. However, such institutionalized interaction between the leaders of a national organization and the leaders of the government do not normally result in the resolution of any specific policy issues. They may be significant in strengthening Cabinet's resolve in dealing with some general problems, such as the deficit or unemployment, and they are important symbolic reminders to all Canadians of the power of organizations that have achieved such a level of institutionalized access. However, these annual briefings appear to be used less frequently in the 1990s than they were in previous decades.

### Bureaucracy and Group Access

While groups recognize the pivotal role of the Cabinet in the policy process, they are also aware of the fact that the bureaucracy provides multiple points of access to organized interests. Individual ministers come and go, but the bureaucracy goes on more or less forever and is more generally accessible than Cabinet ministers, whose schedules are too crowded to provide much time for interaction with groups. Moreover, organizations whose leaders do not enjoy the privileged access to ministers that is accorded certain elite groups are able to compete on a more level playing field when they interact with bureaucrats.

The close ties between the Canadian Federation of Agriculture and officials in the Department of Agriculture, between veterans' groups and the Department of Veterans Affairs, between consumers' groups and several departments, between the hospital and medical associations and the various departments of health, have already been noted. To these one could add the close relationships of industry and trade associations with various federal and provincial departments of trade and economic development, of financial and banking institutions with finance ministries, of mining associations with resource and mining ministries, and of the oil industry with the governments of the producing provinces. The list can be multiplied endlessly.

The reason for such close ties between major interest groups and government departments is that the latter are formally and explicitly mandated to serve the clientele represented by the former. As part of the same policy communities, clientele-oriented departments and pressure groups representing those clients develop very close symbiotic relationships. The interaction between the bureaucratic officials and the leadership of the interest groups concerned with the same policy areas often tends to be highly structured and maintained on an ongoing basis. The access afforded an organization that represents the clientele of a given department is thus permanent and virtually automatic, although the intensity of the interest-group–department relationship will vary according to whether there are important policy initiatives on the horizon.

In dealing with the bureaucracy, probably the major problem for an interest group operating in Ottawa or in one of the larger provincial capitals is trying to figure out who to talk to. The complexity of policy structures and the constantly shifting influence of different individuals in the policy community make it difficult for would-be lobbyists to "target" their campaigns. To a bureaucratic insider, the kaleidoscopic shifts can be dizzying, but to an outsider they are nearly unfathomable. No sooner might a group have succeeded in cultivating its relationship with a certain set of actors, than the system will be changed, eliminating some agencies completely and replacing current influential officials with a whole new cast of characters. It is little wonder that the past decade has seen a proliferation in Ottawa of lobbying and public-affairs consulting services, which, for a more than modest fee, will coach the bewildered outsider as to who to talk to and what to say.

In general, the most important targets of interest-group attention within the bureaucracy are not at the very top. The deputy minister is almost as busy as the minister, and almost certainly will not have time for the type of detail that may be very important to a group. It is the middle-level officials — assistant deputy ministers, directors, and senior policy advisors — who are most likely to be influential in shaping the details of policy and, unless the group is interested only in lofty issues far removed from the day-to-day concerns of most of its membership, it will often be better advised to deal with the middle than the top.

### Elite Interaction and Group Access

Likely the most important interaction between individual ministers and the leaders of interest groups is the result of common socio-economic background. The executives of large corporations and business associations enjoy a sort of automatic entrée to the elite circles of government because they, in all likelihood, attended the same types of schools, belong to the same country clubs, and have mutual acquaintances and interests. Moreover, so many Cabinet ministers were originally recruited from the ranks of business and professional elites that elites representing such groups can use the old-boy network to set up a private meeting with the appropriate minister.

One of the most effective routes of access to political decision-makers is the very direct one provided by the fact that the political elites themselves are often members of the interest groups that seek to influence decisions. Although conflict-of-interest guidelines limit the extent to which a minister can be an advocate of a special interest, it is not unusual for Cabinet ministers to continue to be at least nominal members of the Canadian Manufacturers' Association, the Canadian Medical Association, the Canadian Bar Association, or the Canadian Legion while they are sitting in Cabinet, and a search through the biographies in the *Parliamentary Guide* provides many such examples. In addition, many of the senators in Ottawa double as lobbyists, and particularly as unofficial industry representatives.

Finally, while it may not occur to the same degree as it does with Cabinet ministers, some groups enjoy a special relationship with the bureaucratic elites because of **overlapping memberships**. Many of the doctors who have been senior officials in federal and provincial departments of health have also been medical and hospital association members. An even more important potential type of interest-group access occurs as people move back and forth between the private sector and government. When a department is recruiting employees to regulate an industry, it naturally looks to people from that industry because their experience is useful. Later these same people may move back to a more or less grateful corporation.

Such **circulation of elites** is not necessarily harmful, and it is officially encouraged through *executive interchange*s. However, the close web that can be woven between those who regulate and those who are regulated, and between groups demanding certain policies and those who have the power to make the policies, does raise the possibility that the industry might, in effect, "capture" and hold hostage its own regulator.

### Advisory Committees

Advisory committees or advisory councils are committees of outside experts or representatives of various NGOs concerned with a particular issue area. They are formed to advise ministers or officials on policies, and virtually every federal department has hosted several such bodies at different times in the past. Organizations such as the Canadian Tax Foundation and the Canadian Bar Association act in many ways as advisory committees to the departments concerned with their areas of expertise. The Canadian Federation of Agriculture is asked to appoint representatives to advisory boards in the field of agricultural policy, and the head of the Alberta Wheat Pool holds a seat on the Canadian Wheat Board. At one time or another, the Canadian Manufacturers' Association has held positions on at least thirty-five different advisory boards and committees, and the Canadian Labour Congress must sometimes feel that its major *raison d'être* is to provide members for advisory committees.

## ▶ INDIRECT ACCESS TO GOVERNMENT

Up until now our discussion of group access to the policy process has focused upon direct contact, briefings, or lobbying of individuals within the system who themselves have varying degrees of influence over policy outcomes. Certainly these channels of access are preferred by organizations, and they are carefully nurtured and cared for by groups that have been able to establish them. However, not all interest groups have been able to successfully open up direct channels of access for reasons of inexperience, lack of legitimacy, or the marginal nature of the cause they are espousing. In order to get the attention of government, therefore, such marginalized groups must do so indirectly by influencing public opinion, by waging media campaigns or by working through other organizations that *do* have direct access.

### Public Opinion and the Media

Clearly, groups that enjoy privileged access to the Cabinet and the senior bureaucracy have a definite advantage in attempting to get their views heard. However, governments must still pay attention to grievances and demands that are not transmitted to them through the institutionalized process of interaction between the governmental elites and the important interest groups that operate at or near the core of the policy communities. Public support, or the appearance of it, can never be ignored by political decision-makers, and groups will from time to time launch large-scale public-relations offensives to supplement their other sources of access and influence.

At times, having been unsuccessful in direct lobbying efforts, a normally influential group may, as a last resort, engage in an advertising campaign directed at the general public. However, such campaigns by established interest groups are often looked upon in Canada with some disdain — not only by the authorities in the system, but by the cynical public as well. The recourse to these tactics is seen as indicative of weakness or failure in more traditional tactics or as a "sore-loser" response.

Hence, public-relations campaigns will often backfire if the public heart is unable to "bleed" much for "oppressed" groups such as the Canadian Petroleum Association, the Business Council on National Issues, or the Canadian Medical Association. However, successful groups seldom employ only one tactic at a time, and a full-scale campaign will usually involve several techniques, including appeals to public opinion, used simultaneously to back up the direct lobbying of key decision-makers.

**The "Media Event" Tactic** Groups on the fringe of the policy communities that have been unsuccessful in establishing direct institutionalized access to the decision-makers stand to gain the most by using public-relations campaigns as a tactic for getting the attention of the political movers and shakers. These same fringe groups are also chronically short of the funds necessary to launch an expensive advertising campaign in the media, so they must employ various techniques to attract the attention of the *news* media to gain free exposure for their cause. Because the general public and the political elites alike read the newspapers and watch the news on TV, a group that might otherwise be denied access to the policy process can get hearing indirectly through media reportage of its activities.

The commonest technique for eliciting free media coverage is through staging what have come to known as **media events**. These range from calling a press conference, which may or may not be attended by busy news reporters, to staging demonstrations, protest marches, or acts of civil disobedience, such as blockading public highways, which usually do get the attention of the media. While there are many examples of successful media events, aboriginal groups and environmental organizations have been extremely effective in utilizing such tactics. The opposition to the logging of old-growth timber in the Clayoquot Sound region of British Columbia through a demonstration and a blockade of the logging roads is a classic example of how a coalition of groups interested in environmental issues can swing first public opinion and then government policy in directions more favourable to a cause.

### Political Parties

For the sake of completeness, the role political parties play in this process should be mentioned, although in Canada it is generally not directly important. Much has been made of the interrelationship between parties and interest groups in other political systems. In Britain, most labour unions are directly affiliated with the Labour Party. In the United States, it has sometimes been suggested that the Democratic Party is little more than a coalition of interest groups. However, in both Britain and the United States, the groups that have been most successful — at least with respect to their political activities — tend to shy away from formal party affiliations. After all, the party might lose the election. And even if it wins, as many British unions have found to their chagrin, it may be easier to affect policy from outside the party hierarchy than from within.

Except for the direct affiliation of some union locals with the NDP, and the close ties between the NDP and the Canadian Labour Congress, Canadian interest groups have generally avoided formal connections with political parties. At any rate, organized labour in Ontario found little to cheer about after the NDP government of Bob Rae came to power in 1990. At election time, the parties themselves will attempt to incorporate the most important demands of the main groups in their platforms; but these platforms often mean little after the election is over, and the interest-group elites know it. Between elections, the interest group that wishes to approach a political party faces exactly the same problems as anyone else — it is nearly impossible to find a Canadian political party between elections. Even should the group succeed in that enterprise, the party structures have only very limited impact on government policy decisions.

**"Paid Access"** As we saw in Chapter 15, interest groups and large corporations donate significant amounts of money to political parties but they usually hedge their bets by giving a share to each of the major parties. While superficially these donations could be seen as bribes to buy the successful party's favours when it is in power, in reality nowadays no interest group really expects a specific policy — *quid pro quo* — in return for the cash donation to the party campaign chest, particularly since the size of their donation is a matter of public record. However, some would argue that by becoming a contributor to the party, particularly if the contribution is noticeably large, the donor organization may in fact buy access to the party bigwigs.

Such "paid access" to the elites of the party in power has become more institutionalized in recent years: corporate executives and interest-group elites pay big bucks to attend dinners or cocktail parties where they have a chance to rub shoulders with the party power brokers and celebrities. The PCs had their "Five Hundred Club" where individuals and organizations could "join up" for an annual contribution, and the Liberal Party has a similar if not as well-publicized arrangement. Moreover, both the Tories and the Liberals stage meet-the-leader events where the attendees are charged up to $1000 each for rubber chicken, a boring speech, and, most important, a chance to chat up the party influentials.

## ▶ THE DETERMINANTS OF GROUP INFLUENCE

Some groups are much more successful in influencing government than are others. Yet even the highly successful groups that enjoy direct institutionalized access to the policy process occasionally suffer significant reversals in their attempts to influence policy. Our look at the determinants of the success or failure of a group will examine the group's own structure, the existing policy orientations of the government, and the extent of conformity of the group's interest with those of the general public.

### The Resources of the Group

Access to the decision-makers of government is the *sine qua non* of interest-group influence on public policy, but in a way, that is *all* it is, for, having convinced decision-makers to listen to its case, the group must still be convincing about the substantive merits of its argument. Because a minister must ultimately seek re-election, he or she cannot always meet the demands of big business or other well-connected groups that have become cozy with the government. Even the interests of those powerful groups that have special access to the governmental decision-makers must often give way to the interests of broader, if less articulate and less organized, groups when the latter more closely coincide with the interests of the general public.

To be influential a group must make its case on the technical merit of its position, its impact on the broader policy agenda of the government, and ultimately on the number of votes that will be won and lost with the various policy options. Similarly, because the bureaucrat must ultimately sell a policy idea to the minister, he or she must not automatically accede to the demands of a close friend or client, unless those demands have at least some broad support in Canadian society and unless they make policy sense in objective terms. The political friends and elite cohorts of politicians and bureaucrats may have an easy time getting a hearing, but their policy preferences will not be implemented if to do so might cost the government the next election.

**Numerical Strength**   The number of members an interest group can boast is a less important determinant of success than one might expect. Decision-makers know that a person's membership in a group does not guarantee agreement with the group's views on a particular issue. If sheer numbers were the determining factor, labour organizations would be Canada's most important interest groups. In fact, a more important attribute of a group may be its organizational **cohesiveness** and the ability of the group leadership to actually deliver the vote of its membership at election time. If an organization's executive really does speak for its members, and if the members might be mobilized en masse in support of the group's ideas, any threats the group makes or implies will have considerable credibility.

It is also important here to recognize that the numerical strength of an interest group's membership is not as important as the number of non-members who are aware of the group's message and agree with it. For instance, many animal-rights groups seem to wield a great deal of influence over certain aspects of environmental policy because, acting as public-interest groups, they have been able to raise the consciousness of Canadians in general as to the plight of animals and the evils of "speciesism." In a similar way, aboriginal groups have been effective policy advocates because they have been able to enlist the support of many non-aboriginal Canadians who have become sympathetic to their cause.

**Financial Resources**   Plainly enough, one of the most important resources any group can have is money, and most interest groups, even those we might usually consider well-to-do, are chronically short of funds. The Canadian Federation of Agriculture is probably fairly typical in this respect for it receives widely varying amounts of money from year to year as farm fortunes rise and fall. Many industry associations suffer the same problem, for they are vulnerable to cut-backs whenever their industry hits a cyclical downturn. Promotional interest groups generally seem to suffer more difficulty in finding money than self-interest groups. The former have a very diffuse and indirectly interested clientele, whereas the latter directly represent the material interests of an identifiable membership, which is more likely to pay dues on a regular basis. Fledgling single-issue groups are unlikely to be able to get their supporters to put their money where their hearts are, particularly when the group cause does not involve the direct self-interest of its "congregation."

Nevertheless, some of the most powerful organizations are very well-financed. The Canadian Chamber of Commmerce likely has an annual budget greater than that of most national political parties. The Chamber's main source of funds is membership dues from thousands of firms. With its money, the Chamber is able to afford, among other things, a large permanent staff with experts in various fields related to the promotion of interests of businesses and industry. It is not surprising that the Chamber's briefs to governments are well presented, backed by solid data, and, hence, carefully considered in the formulation of regulations or the creation of new legislation that affects commerce in Canada. With its impressive organization and solid financing, it is hardly surprising that the Chamber of Commerce is so successful. But the wealth of the organization could not by itself "buy" the influence it has enjoyed as a result of its reputation.

**Economic Leverage**  The ability to have an effect on economic affairs can be an important source of influence for many interest groups. Interest groups whose influence is built largely on numerical strength, including most unions and consumer groups, can also have an impact by employing collective-action techniques, such as boycotts. Through strikes, slowdowns, and working to rule, labour unions can have huge impacts on specific industries and a consequent trickle-down effect on the national or regional economy. While unions do not possess a right to strike to further their *political* demands, it is always possible to subtly link a collective-bargaining dispute to non-bargainable political positions. Hence, the interest-group function of labour unions can never be completely "delinked" from its collective-bargaining function. What discourages unions from using tactics such as *general strikes* very often is that they are extremely blatant and visible to a public, which in Canada does not hold unions in very high regard to begin with. Using their economic clout to "hold a gun to the head" of the elected government is unacceptable to those that feel the general interest is more important than the special interest of any group of employees.

The economic leverage of large corporations is greater than that of unions because their message (or veiled threat!) can be delivered much more subtly to the government and remain invisible to the public. Because large corporations usually provide large numbers of jobs, they can always simply threaten to close down a plant if the government doesn't cooperate. For instance, the environmental movement would have much greater success in convincing governments to ban logging activities in ecologically sensitive areas or to enforce pollution-control measures more stringently if the affected companies couldn't counter with the threat of layoffs or plant closures. The company executives simply argue that the government's pollution-control policies or timber-cutting regulations make continued operation uneconomical, and the company therefore has no choice but to shut down its operation. Since such a shutdown represents a substantial cost to the company as well as to the local economy, all parties are anxious to avoid this happening.

Moreover, even if the public were to become aware that this sort of pressure is being put on the government by certain industries, it is unlikely it would cause much of a fuss. We are, after all, living in a capitalist society, and most Canadians accept the basic premise that it is acceptable or even laudable for companies to attempt to make a profit. Hence, if a big forest-products company says to government, "We will have to close down the mill that employs 2000 workers if we can't cut down trees in Clayoquot Sound," the public will not view it as blackmail but rather as a legitimate measure taken in the pursuit of profit.

**Reputation and Prestige**  The reputation and the prestige of a group is important because political and bureaucratic decision-makers are often impressed by the group's ideas in direct proportion to how impressed they are by its members as individuals. The Canadian Bar Association, for instance, is always listened to respectfully by government, not only because it is the national association of the already prestigious legal profession in Canada, but also because it has established a reputation for more reason and less emotion in its briefings than most other organizations. Similarly, policy-makers will always at least listen to the medical associations, and the Business Council on National Issues makes much of the fact that its members include the chief executive officers of Canada's 150 largest corporations. By contrast, the Canadian Piranha Breeders' Association, the National Institute of Motorcycle Buffs, or the Justice for Dew Worms Coalition might have more difficulty getting a sympathetic hearing.

Monopoly over a certain area of expertise is another potent factor in determining the prestige of a group. The power of knowledge, particularly legal knowledge, was recognized early on by John Bulloch in his struggle to make the Canadian Federation of Independent Businessmen into a significant political force. Said Bulloch:

> I began to see how the system is stacked in favour of those who own all the lawyers. I found out that the big corporations, without being conspiratorial, control the knowledge factory in the country; all the positions that government takes are the product of conversation, the chinwags, that go on between the experts who are owned by the major corporations and the trade unions and the experts who work for government. It's a mandarin to mandarin process.[3]

The power that flows from knowledge may also depend on how much the government mandarins need the expert resources of the interest-group mandarins at any given time.

Because the prestige and credibility of an interest group may depend on the socio-economic status of individual group members, it is not surprising that many of the public-interest and promotional-interest groups have great difficulty competing with their institutionalized and self-interested counterparts. On top of their relatively lower prestige, they lack funds, their leaders come and go and are mostly volunteers, and rank-and-file support is often sporadic. Moreover, the techniques that disempowered groups must resort to are often seen as *déclassé* or tasteless to elite policy-makers. Not only do sit-ins, demonstrations, and media events often receive negative media coverage, but the groups are seldom able to convince many supporters to turn out for demonstrations. Even when a media event does succeed in receiving the desired publicity, the group leaders are seldom able to keep the pressure on the government long enough to affect the policy process. Nevertheless, as pointed out earlier, a few groups on the fringes of the policy-community establishment *do* from time to time make the breakthrough and come to have considerable success in influencing policy.

---

3.  Quoted in Alexander Ross, "How to Join the March to New Politics," *Quest,* February 1977, p. 47.

**Cohesiveness and Group Solidarity** Many currently influential social movements began as loose coalitions of single-issue fringe groups that mobilized a broader base of support and forced government to pay attention, often by employing unconventional tactics. The successes of the women's movement, the environmental movement, the gay- and lesbian-rights movement, and the aboriginal-rights movement must be seen, at least in part, in terms of the integration of large numbers of single-issue groups that found they shared a similar world view and a similar experience of powerlessness. Their influence today flows from the fact that they are broadly based aggregations of many different but mutually supportive interests and from the fact that the leaders of the movements have been able to keep the coalitions cohesive. However, while the strength of social-movement groups and of interest-group coalitions lies in their broadly based and diverse support, herein also lurks their potential weakness. The very diversity and breadth that makes them influential also breeds internal strife and factionalism. Conflicts arise over the priorities that should be placed on various issues, over who should assume the leadership roles, and over group strategy and tactics. It is fortuitous for such organizations that there are always *core issues* upon which the leaders of the sub-groups within the movement all agree. These core issues can be used to rally the troops, to keep the movement united, and to keep the various factions generally pointed in the same direction.

### Group Strategy

While the most important determinant of the success of interest groups is the resources the group can bring to bear in its attempts to influence policy outcomes, it is also important how those resources are used. The group must be careful not to squander its bargaining capital on lost causes. It must be keenly sensitive to tactical and strategic considerations such as the timing of its pressure campaigns and the tone — aggressive or conciliatory — of its pitch to government. To be effective, the group must gather strategic intelligence about the commitment of the government to a given policy and about whether public opinion and government policy initiatives are in step. Above all, the group should ensure that its policy goals are not incompatible with current public sentiments or with the longer-term public interest.

**Government Commitment** Failure to recognize the overall direction of government policy, the intensity of the commitment to that policy, and the public opinion that underlies it, can be disastrous to even the most powerful pressure groups. The Canadian Petroleum Association and the multinational oil firms made such a mistake in the 1980s. The Liberal government of the day stated clearly that it was their intention to intervene in a major way in all aspects of the oil industry, but the industry's response was simply to refuse even to discuss such policy changes and walked out of the consultative process.

The industry misread public opinion, which at the time was both nationalistic and strongly against big oil companies, and refused to cooperate in any way with the government. The oil patch simply didn't believe the government would go ahead, which turned out to be a fatal error. The government introduced the National Energy Program in a raw and unmoderated form, which cut far more deeply into the petroleum sector than it might have done had the oil companies seen the writing on the wall and consented to become involved in the policy exercise with reduced expectations.

The president of one of Ottawa's largest executive consulting companies at the time was quoted as saying about the strategic error of the oil companies:

> This was a classic example of what can happen when you misread the political climate. The key to successful lobbying is realizing when a general objective has widespread public support, associating yourself with that objective, then trying to alter how it is eventually expressed as public policy.[4]

In other words, the lesson to interest groups is "if you can't beat 'em, join 'em!"

We see the same mistake being made in the nineties by interest groups who are opposed to social-program reforms in a time when governments are, by necessity, locked irrevocably into policies of deficit and debt reduction. Had the labour movement in Ontario understood the NDP government's commitment to reduce expenditures and gone along with the "Social Contract," they could have likely forced some compromises on the government. By simply walking out on the process, however, the unions guaranteed that the Ontario Social Contract would be imposed in an unbuffered form that was even more disadvantageous to their membership. If government policy-makers genuinely believe that they have no choice on a given matter, it is folly for an interest group to "swim upstream."

**Neutral Policy Issues**  Some groups are successful because there are no organized interests that oppose them. For instance, the Canadian Cancer Society, whose ultimate objective is to erradicate cancer through research, does not have to vie for government's attention with organizations that feel cancer is a good thing and should be protected, although it does have to compete for money with other deserving groups. Similarly, veteran's organizations, as long as they are advocating the well-being of war amputees, usually enjoy the entire stage when they are attempting to influence policy because nobody would openly oppose such a deserving cause.

On the other hand, even groups that operate unopposed in a given policy community must keep their activity focused on the goals that make them legitimate and not get sidetracked into secondary issues that are conflictual. For instance, if the Cancer Society were to campaign for physician-assisted suicide as a treatment for the disease, or if the Canadian Legion or the War Amps were to take positions on capital punishment or abortion, they would no longer operate unopposed. They would have moved, unwisely, into an entirely different policy community where their credibility and legitimacy would be dramatically reduced. However, the fact remains that if an interest group is advocating a position that 99 per cent of Canadians don't care a fig about, they may have success convincing government to do them a policy favour.

---

4.  Cited in David Hayes, "A Word to the Wise," *Toronto Globe and Mail,* February 12, 1983.

**The Public Interest**  While it is certainly useful for a group to be espousing goals that are either widely accepted or totally unopposed by competing groups, most groups do not operate in that sort of ideal context. Hence, it is critically important for all groups to couch their demands in terms that will minimize opposition if not maximize support. Interest groups obviously will be most successful in influencing government policy if their demands are in line with the basic values of the society within which they are operating. If a group is advocating a position to which most Canadians are opposed, they will almost never be successful. Hence (while it might receive secret funding from the sunscreen industry), a Canadian Coalition for the Elimination of the Ozone Layer would not likely have many members, it would not enjoy widespread public support, and government would not pay any attention to it.

Moreover, even if a group's ideas are intellectually sound, it will not generally succeed if it is espousing widely unpopular measures. Government must always be able to claim that it is acting in the public interest; therefore, special interests must always ensure that their demands are compatible with the general well-being of Canadians. Broadly based organizations such as the Assembly of First Nations have been successful because they have been able to convince many non-aboriginal Canadians not only that their goals are *compatible* with the public interest, but that measures such as aboriginal self-government are actually *in* the public interest.

## ▶ THE LEGITIMACY OF INTEREST-GROUP POLITICS

In Canada, the activities of interest groups are generally perceived, at least by government decision-makers and other elites, to be legitimate and worthwhile. Both opposition and government MPs do not regard the activities of lobbyists as a form of improper pressure, and most politicians in government believe that interest groups are necessary to make government aware of the needs of all the people. In fact, interest groups are such effective barometers of public opinion that it is not unusual, in a given policy area where there are no well-organized interest groups, for the government to help create them. The government needs interest groups as much as the interest groups need the government, and their relationship is mutually beneficial.

Interest groups are thus accepted as an integral part of our political process and since there are far more Canadians who participate in interest-group activities than in political parties, we might be tempted to view interest groups as the pre-eminent representative institutions in Canadian political life. There is no doubt that, if one wishes to influence government, the channels afforded by interest groups are the most effective ones to use. We have seen, too, that groups provide valuable information both to government and to their members, that they are prominent actors in the administration of government policy, and that they create a support structure for the regime upon which much of its legitimacy depends.

However, one must be careful not to go too far in eulogizing the interest-group system. One must recognize that there is a down side to too heavy a reliance upon interest groups as the *only* effective representative structures of society. For one thing, about 40 per cent of Canadians do not participate, in any way, in interest-group activities, and that excluded group is generally within the lower strata of society.[5] Thus, if the influence of interest groups is as significant as we have suggested, such groups may act to reinforce the powerlessness of certain segments of society. If political leaders react only to organized interests and disregard the unarticulated needs of disadvantaged members of our society, the existing inequities will be further entrenched.

As well, even for those Canadians who do participate in the activities of interest groups, the power of organized interests in this country is not equally distributed. The resources available to business and industry associations and to large corporations are so much greater than the resources available to all other groups that the balance of group power in the policy process is drastically asymmetrical. We could never realistically expect all groups to be equal nor should they all be equal. However, government should be sensitive to the asymmetrical distribution of power and influence among the various groups in a policy community and should make allowances for that imbalance so that the less powerful groups get a fair hearing.

### Limits to Interest-Group Power

There are, of course, limits to the power of interest groups. The Cabinet has a *collective* policy role, which may effectively counter group pressure on individual ministers. Similarily, the requirements of party solidarity in the parliamentary system limit the legislature as an arena for lobbyists. MPs, unlike US congressmen, are bound by party discipline and hence, even if they are sympathetic to a group's pleas, they are in no position to do anything about it if their party is taking a contrary line.

The public service, too, is by no means automatically sympathetic to interest-group demands. One should not underestimate the tenacity of the public servant in pursuing either the public good as he or she sees it or the aggrandizement of his or her own power, at some cost to specific interests. Thus, while all departments encourage their client groups, they may also act as an effective "brake," by imposing different priorities, financial constraints, and time lines. Moreover, departments often take the initiative to articulate the interests of segments of society that are not institutionalized. Departments and agencies of the bureaucracy are also more powerful in terms of expertise than the groups with which they interact. The largest and wealthiest interest group can in no way approach the research resources available to even small federal departments.

Another limitation on the power of interest groups is other interest groups. While, as we have stated earlier, a few groups are influential because their advocacy goes unopposed, this is a rare situation. The most powerful special-interest organizations — those representing industry, the professions, and labour — are all faced with equally powerful countergroups. Intergroup competition is a self-correcting mechanism that prevents any one interest group from becoming too powerful in the policy process.

---

5. Rick Van Loon and Mike Whittington, *The Canadian Political System: Environment, Structure and Process* (Toronto: McGraw-Hill Ryerson, 1987), p. 433.

## Lobbying and Public Scrutiny

Finally, because the most effective exercise of group power happens in the shadowy world of elite interaction, the greatest constraint on the abuse of elite power in a democracy is publicity. For instance, the legal requirement that the big contributors to political parties be identified inhibits any potential favouritism that cannot be justified by objective evidence. The quiet interaction among governmental elites and the elites of the most influential interests, however, was until recently carried on for the most part anonymously and invisibly. One response to this has been initiatives by government to provide some statutory regulation of the activities of lobbyists.

Lobbying is simply a tactic for influencing the governmental decision-makers that involves direct contact between political elites and representatives of an interest. Lobbying can be carried on by any individual, and in a sense it is simply a concomitant of democratic politics where politicians are expected to heed the wishes of the people that elect them. However, everybody does not enjoy equal access to the political decision-makers and there is a fear that those interests that can secure such privileged access will be able to make secret deals with government that are not necessarily in the general interest of Canadians.

The main targets for the critics of lobbying have been the so-called **professional lobbyists**. These include individuals who work for public-affairs consultancy firms, mostly located in Ottawa, and who have "insider status" in the corridors of power. These lobbyists can be hired to intervene at the highest levels of government on behalf of interests that can afford them — and they are usually very expensive indeed! As well, the very affluent groups and corporations can afford to hire their own lobbyists and set them up in Ottawa to "shmooze" the political elites on an ongoing basis.

The concerns of the critics are, first, that only very wealthy groups and organizations can afford such hired guns, and second, that these influence brokers operate essentially in secret. The first concern is more difficult to deal with. It is a legitimate part of the democratic process for groups and individuals to approach their elected representatives in order to express their concerns. The fact that the contact with the political elites might be indirect, through an intervenor or lobbyist, does not alter the fact that attempts to influence politicians are a necessary and fully legitimate concomitant of democratic government.

Where it is possible to attack the pervasive influence of professional lobbyists is with respect to the concern over the secrecy of the process. Legislation was passed in 1988 requiring professional lobbyists to be registered. The *Lobbyists Registration Act* identifies two types of lobbyists that must be registered. A "Tier I" lobbyist is defined as

> an individual who, for payment and on behalf of a client, undertakes to arrange a meeting with a public office-holder in an attempt to influence the development, making or amendment of any federal law, regulation or policy or program or the award of any federal monetary grant or the award of any federal contract.[6]

A "Tier II" lobbyist is an employee who lobbies on behalf of an employer. While close to a thousand lobbyists are currently registered, there is little to

---

6. *The Lobbyists Registration Act,* 1988.

indicate that the workings of the system have been altered at all. The publication of the names of registered lobbyists has not solved the secrecy problem: interaction between lobbyists and political elites still takes place out of the public eye. The *Lobbyists Registration Act* is currently being reviewed.

## ▶ CONCLUSION

Interest groups pervade the whole of the policy process in Canada, so much so that at least one analyst has been led to characterize the entire Canadian political process as *elite accommodation* between and among interest groups and governmental elites.[7] Moreover, although it is difficult to assess the relative strength of organized interests in different nations, Canada would not appear to be particularly unique. The *group-theory*[8] approach to government, whereby all of politics is reduced to different aspects of group interaction, was one early recognition of the pervasiveness of interest groups, particularly in the United States.

While group theory clearly overstates the case, the omnipresence and relative importance of interest groups to the political process in liberal democracies is recognized in Theodore Lowi's[9] description of the American system as *interest-group liberalism* or *liberal pluralism*. While the tactics of interest groups in Canada are different from those in the US because of our parliamentary system and our more decentralized form of federalism, liberalism and pluralism are pervasive components of our political culture as well.

7.  R. Presthus, *Elite Accommodation in Canadian Politics* (Toronto: Macmillan, 1973).
8.  A. F. Bentley, *The Governmental Process*, ed. Peter Odegard (Cambridge, Mass.: Harvard University Press, 1967); and D. B. Truman, *The Governmental Process* (New York: Alfred A. Knopf, 1965).
9.  T. Lowi, *The End of Liberalism* (Chicago: Norton, 1979).

► FURTHER READING: PART FOUR POLITICS

### Electoral System

Boyer, P. *The People's Mandate: Referendums and a More Democratic Canada.* Toronto: Dundurn Press, 1992.

Cairns, Alan. "The Electoral System and the Party System in Canada," *Canadian Journal of Political Science,* March 1968, pp. 675–97.

Canada. Elections Canada. *Report of the Chief Electoral Officer.* Ottawa: Supply and Services, published annually and after each election or referendum.

Canada. Royal Commission on Electoral Reform and Party Financing. *Reforming Electoral Democracy.* Ottawa: Supply and Services, 1992.

Canada. Royal Commission on Electoral Reform and Party Financing. *Research Studies* (23 separate collections of research papers prepared by the Royal Commission). Toronto: Dundurn Press, 1991.

Cassidy, Michael. *Democratic Rights and Electoral Reform in Canada.* Toronto: Dundurn Press, 1992.

Courtney, J., P. MacKinnon, and David Smith. *Drawing Boundaries: Legislatures, Courts and Electoral Values.* Saskatoon: Fifth House, 1992.

Fletcher, Fred. *Election Broadcasting in Canada.* Toronto: Dundurn Press, 1992.

Johnston, J. Paul, and H. Pasis. *Representation and Electoral Systems.* Scarborough: Prentice-Hall, 1990.

Small, D. *Drawing the Map: Equality and Efficacy of the Vote in Canadian Electoral Boundary Reform.* Toronto: Dundurn Press, 1991.


### Parties and Party Systems

Bakvis, H. *Canadian Political Parties: Leaders, Candidates and Organization.* Toronto: Dundurn Press, 1991.

Bradley, M. *Crisis of Clarity: The New Democratic Party and the Quest for the Holy Grail.* Toronto: Summerhill, 1985.

Brodie, Janine, and Jane Jenson. *Crisis, Challenge and Change: Party and Class in Canada Revisited.* Ottawa: Carleton University Press, 1988.

Brodie, Janine, and Jane Jenson. "The Party System," *in* M. S. Whittington and G. Williams, eds., *Canadian Politics in the 1990s.* Scarborough: Nelson, 1990, pp. 249–67.

Carty, K. *Canadian Political Systems.* Toronto: Broadview, 1992.

Christian, William, and Colin Campbell. *Political Parties and Ideologies in Canada,* 4th ed. Toronto: McGraw-Hill Ryerson, 1995.

Gagnon, Alain, and Brian Tanguay. *Canadian Parties in Transition.* Toronto: Nelson, 1989.

Martin, P., Alan Gregg, and G. Perlin. *Contenders: The Tory Quest for Power.* Scarborough: Prentice-Hall, 1983.

McCall-Newman, C. *Grits: An Intimate Portrait of the Liberal Party.* Toronto: Macmillan, 1982.

McDonald, Lynn. *The Party That Changed Canada: The New Democratic Party Then and Now.* Toronto: McClelland and Stewart, 1987.

Morton, Desmond. *The New Democrats 1981–1988.* Toronto: Copp Clark Pitman, 1986.

Perlin, George. *The Tory Syndrome: Leadership Politics in the Progressive Conservative Party*. Montreal: McGill-Queen's University Press, 1980.

Perlin, George. *Party Democracy in Canada: The Role of National Party Conventions*. Scarborough: Prentice-Hall, 1988.

Sharpe, S., and D. Braid. *Storming Babylon: Preston Manning and the Rise of the Reform Party*. Toronto: Key Porter, 1992.

Thorburn, H. G., ed. *Party Politics in Canada*. Scarborough: Prentice-Hall, 1991.

Wearing, Joseph. *The L-Shaped Party: The Liberal Party of Canada 1958–1980*. Toronto: McGraw-Hill Ryerson, 1981.

Wearing, Joseph. *Strained Relations: Canadian Parties and Voters*. Toronto: McClelland and Stewart, 1988.

Whitaker, Reg. *The Government Party: Organizing and Financing the Liberal Party of Canada 1930–1958*. Toronto: University of Toronto Press, 1977.

Whitehorn, Alan. *Canadian Socialism: Essays on the CCF and the NDP*. Toronto: Oxford University Press, 1992.

Wiseman, Nelson. "Political Parties," *in* M. S. Whittington and G. Williams, eds., *Canadian Politics in the 1990s*. Scarborough: Nelson, 1994. pp. 231–37.

## Electoral Behaviour

Archer, Keith. *Political Choices and Electoral Consequences*. Montreal: McGill-Queen's University Press, 1990.

Bakvis, H. *Voter Turnout in Canada*. Toronto: Dundurn Press, 1991.

Bashevkin, Sylvia. *Canadian Political Behaviour*. Toronto: Methuen, 1985.

Brook, Tom. *Getting Elected in Canada*. Stratford: Mercury Press, 1991.

Clarke, Harold, Jane Jenson, Larry Leduc, and Jon Pammett. *Political Choice in Canada*. Toronto: McGraw-Hill Ryerson, 1980.

Clarke Harold, Jane Jenson, Larry Leduc, and Jon Pammett. *Absent Mandate: The Politics of Discontent in Canada*. Toronto: Gage, 1984.

Frizzell, Alan, and Anthony Westell. *The Canadian General Election of 1984*. Ottawa: Carleton University Press, 1985.

Frizzell, Alan, and Anthony Westell. *The Canadian General Election of 1988*. Ottawa: Carleton University Press, 1989.

Frizzell, Alan, Jon Pammett, and Anthony Westell. *The Canadian General Election of 1993*. Ottawa: Carleton University Press, 1994.

Johnston, Richard, Andre Blais, and Henry Brady. *Letting the People Decide: Dynamics of a Canadian Election*. Montreal: McGill-Queen's University Press, 1992.

Leduc, Larry, and Jon Pammett. "Referendum Voting: Attitudes and Behaviour in the 1992 Constitutional Referendum," *Canadian Journal of Political Science*, March 1995, p. 34.

Mishler, William, and Harold Clarke. "Political Participation in Canada," *in* M. S. Whittington and G. Williams, *Canadian Politics in the 1990s*. Scarborough: Nelson, 1994, pp. 129–51.

Pammett, Jon. "Elections," *in* M. S. Whittington and G. Williams, *Canadian Politics in the 1990s*. Scarborough: Nelson, 1994, pp. 238–51.

Wearing, Joseph. *The Ballot and Its Message: Voting in Canada*. Toronto: Copp Clark Pitman, 1991.

## Interest Groups

Atkinson, Mike, and W. D. Coleman. *The State, Business and Industrial Change*. Toronto: University of Toronto Press, 1989.

Coleman, W. D. *Business and Politics: A Study of Collective Action*. Montreal: McGill-Queen's University Press, 1988.

Coleman, W. D., and Grace Skogstad, eds. *Policy Communities and Public Policy in Canada*. Toronto: Copp Clark Pitman, 1990.

Malvern, P. *Persuaders: Influence Peddling, Lobbying and Political Corruption in Canada*. Toronto: Methuen, 1985.

Pross, Paul. *Group Politics and Public Policy in Canada*. Toronto: Oxford University Press, 1986.

Pross, Paul. "Pressure Groups: Talking Chameleons," *in* M. S. Whittington and G. Williams, eds., *Canadian Politics in the 1990s*. Scarborough: Nelson, 1994. pp. 252–75.

Sawatsky, D. *The Insiders: Government, Business and the Lobbyists*. Toronto: McClelland and Stewart, 1987.

Seidle, Leslie. *Interest Groups and Elections in Canada*. Toronto: Dundurn Press, 1991.

Seidle, Leslie. *Equity and Community: The Charter, Interest Advocacy and Representation*. Montreal: IRPP, 1993.

Stanbury, William. *Business–Government Relations in Canada: Grappling with Leviathan*. Toronto: Methuen, 1986.

Thorburn, Hugh. *Interest Groups in the Canadian Federal System*. Toronto: University of Toronto Press, 1985.

# Government

*Chapter* **18**

# Parliamentary Government

The Canadian System of government can be described as a parliamentary democracy. It is a **democracy** because the people select their political leaders through the device of periodic elections, because the system operates on the principle of majoritarianism, and because, generally, the apparatus of the state or the government is responsive to the needs and desires of Canadian society. Our system of governance is a **parliamentary** democracy, because it is members of Parliament that we elect, it is Parliament that operates through the mechanism of majority rule, and it is the elected representatives of the people sitting in Parliament that are expected to respond to the needs and demands of society.

Parliament is thus the core institution of our constitutional framework. However, as we shall see, while Parliament is definitive of Canada's form of government, the role of Parliament in the policy and governmental processes is not exactly what the Constitution tells us it is. The aim of this chapter is to describe where Parliament fits in the day-to-day mêlée that is Canadian government and politics.

## ▶ THE FUNCTIONS OF PARLIAMENT

Parliament, the legislative branch of government in Canada, is constitutionally the supreme lawmaking authority for all matters falling within federal jurisdiction. Many of the legal implications of the constitutional principle of parliamentary supremacy have already been discussed in Chapter 4. In this section, our focus is upon the broader functions of Parliament in a governmental system where, while formally supreme, Parliament for the most part plays second fiddle to the prime minister and Cabinet.

### Formal Functions

The formal functions of Parliament are those established both explicitly and implicitly in our Constitution. In a formal or constitutional sense, Parliament, which is described in the *Constitution Act* of 1867 as including "the Queen, an Upper House styled the Senate, and the House of Commons," has the power to make laws for "the Peace, Order and Good Government of Canada." However, this tells us very little, even about the formal role of Parliament in the governmental process.

**Legislation** The principle of the rule of law means that all actions of the government must be sanctioned by law and only Parliament has the ultimate power to make law. While Parliament is formally composed of the Queen and a bicameral legislature, by constitutional practice and convention the Queen has no lawmaking role at all in Canada and the appointed Senate is a very minor player in a legislative process quite properly dominated by the popularly elected House of Commons.

There are three significant constitutional limits to the formal legislative authority of Parliament. First, Canadian sovereignty still technically resides in the Crown. The powers of the Crown include giving assent to bills passed by Parliament and other executive functions such as the spending of public moneys and order-in-council appointments. While the Queen no longer has any direct involvement in the governing of Canada, the authority of the Crown has come to be exercised *de facto* by the prime minister and Cabinet. The second constitutional limitation on the power of Parliament is our federal system. The Canadian legislature is not permitted to make laws in areas of jurisdiction reserved exclusively to the legislatures of the provinces. Finally, since 1982 the formal power of Parliament have been limited by the Charter of Rights and Freedoms and by the constitutional amendment provisions that provide for extensive participation by provincial legislatures.

**Responsible Government** The principle of responsible government, while not set down explicitly in our Constitution, is operationalized through constitutional conventions that we inherited from the English constitutional tradition. By this principle, the government of the day, embodied in the prime minister and Cabinet, is directly accountable to Parliament. In a formal way, Parliament is an "electoral college" from which our governmental elites are chosen to lead the country. Moreover, our governmental elites can only retain their power if they can continue to hold the support of a majority of the members of the House of Commons. However, the relationship between Cabinet and Parliament is much more predictable than the constitutional rules would suggest, and, as we shall see later in this chapter, the actual power of Parliament over the executive branch is significantly less than its formal power.

**Representation** Constitutionally, Parliament is the democratic link between the sovereign state, embodied in the Crown, and the Canadian people. MPs are elected by the people on a territorial basis and the individual MP is expected to represent the interests of his or her constitutents in the governmental processes. Even the much maligned Senate is set up in such a way that the senators are expected to represent the interests of the provinces from which they are selected. However, neither MPs nor senators are able today to perform the sort of representative role they were assigned in the Constitution. The representative function of Parliament has been reduced to a mere shadow of the proud role ascribed to it in classical democratic theory.

---

## ▶ CABINET GOVERNMENT: CONSTRAINTS ON PARLIAMENTARY SUPREMACY

The formal constitutional authority of Parliament appears enormous even when we take into account the constitutional limitations imposed by the federal division of powers and the Charter of Rights. However, most Canadians will recognize that, in reality, it is the prime minister and the Cabinet that carry the lion's share of governmental and policy-making muscle. There are serious *de facto* constraints on the formal power of Parliament, most of which flow from the way in which the relationship between Cabinet and Parliament has evolved. To understand this relationship we must begin with a few words about the constitutional and political role of the Cabinet.

### The Formal Powers of the Prime Minister and the Cabinet

As we saw in Chapter 6, the constitutional authority of the Cabinet derives far more from convention than it does from written provisions. The *Constitution Act*, 1867, provides, cryptically, that "there shall be a Council to aid and advise in the Government of Canada, to be styled the Queen's Privy Council for Canada." The formal role of the Cabinet, which is technically a committee of the Privy Council, is, thus, merely to *advise* the Queen or the governor-general and the Crown does not have to take that advice. Moreover, while the office of the prime minister is never even mentioned in the 1867 Act, the cornerstone of our system of government today is the constitutional convention that the **legislative powers** of the Crown are exercised *de facto* by the prime minister. Hence, for instance, royal assent to a bill is formally granted by the governor-general but only at the request of the prime minister, and no governor-general has ever refused such a request.

The **executive powers** of the Crown are also exercised almost exclusively by the prime minister and the Cabinet. The power to spend money and to introduce tax legislation is limited to ministers of the Crown and all of the royal prerogatives, such as the authority to summon, prorogue, and dissolve Parliament, are exercised exclusively by the prime minister. Finally, it is ministers of the Crown who are the formal heads of the various departments of government and who, conversely, are individually accountable to Parliament for the conduct of departmental business.

In sum, because the formal legislative and executive powers of the Crown are, in practice, exercised by the prime minister and Cabinet, there is a *prima facie* constraint on the supremacy of Parliament. However, the formal or constitutional limitations on the supremacy of Parliament tell only a small part of the story of the legislature's domination by the executive in Canada. To fully understand the functional subordination of Parliament in the governmental process we must look to the various tools of control that are employed by the prime minister and Cabinet.

### Party Discipline: Cabinet and Government Backbenchers

When a majority of MPs are from the government party, the ability to control the government side of the House is, naturally, all that is needed to control Parliament. In fact, there has never been a case of a **majority government** in Canada being defeated by a vote in the House of Commons, and the likelihood of that eventuality is virtually nil. The control by the prime minister and Cabinet over their own party's rank-and-file MPs (or **backbenchers**, because they sit in rows behind the Cabinet ministers in the House) is one aspect of what is usually known as **party discipline**. It is maintained by threat of various sanctions and by various inducements, although it is seldom, indeed, that the government is forced overtly to impose a sanction or withhold a promise in order to enforce discipline. Usually the authority of the governing party's parliamentary leadership is tacitly recognized and accepted by the government MPs so that party discipline is maintained without resort to specific sanctions.

### Party Leadership

Perhaps the most important single factor facilitating the Cabinet's control over its own backbenchers in the House of Commons is the simple fact that the prime minister and, to a lesser extent the other ministers, are the leaders of the party in the House. There is a natural willingness in government MPs to accept the leadership of the prime minister, who has been elected as party leader at a convention and who is responsible, to a large extent in this era of leadership politics, for the party's success at the polls. Besides this, the very fact that backbenchers and Cabinet ministers are members of the same political party provides a significant ideological common ground as a starting point for building a consensus.

This latter point should not be belaboured, however. As has been pointed out in Chapter 14, the major Canadian political parties tend not to be heavily ideological; they are omnibus or brokerage parties, which attempt to aggregate interests and tend to tolerate a fairly wide range of political views among their memberships. And while it is true that Canadian parties are often fraught with internal disagreements, once having achieved the Holy Grail of governmental power, most MPs on the government side of the House will willingly follow the political leaders that got them there (yuh dance with the one what brung yuh!). Certainly, the prime minister and the Cabinet find it infinitely easier to maintain the support of their own backbenchers than that of the opposition members.

**The Carrots and Sticks of Re-election** One set of sanctions and inducements for enforcing party discipline in both government and opposition parties flows from the influence the party can have on the chances of an MP's re-election. Fighting an election today, in the age of television campaigns and Madison-

Avenue techniques, is an expensive proposition, and most individual candidates will not be able to afford a winning campaign without some financial assistance from the party. Because it is the national party leadership that has control over the party purse strings, the prime minister and, to a certain extent, the leaders of the opposition parties, can control **maverick** backbenchers through either explicit or implicit threat of withdrawal of party financial support in the next election campaign.

There are non-financial elements of party support in an election that can be almost as important to the MP as assistance from the party treasurer. MPs who have been "good" and supported their parliamentary leaders will be assured of a visit to their constituencies by one of the party's notables to assist them in their campaigns. In an election campaign the visit to a constituency by the party leader might well enhance the prestige of the local candidate, thereby having an effect on the outcome of that riding's contest. Furthermore, while the party leaders must beware of overtly meddling with the autonomy of the constituency nominating process, if it is known that a sitting member is unlikely to get support from the national level of the party, or if it is made clear that the candidate is not in the good graces of the party leader, the local people might be influenced to ditch their sitting member.

Finally, as seen in Chapter 12, the *Canada Elections Act* gives to the leader of a political party the statutory right to refuse a candidate the privilege of having the name of the party appear beside his or her name on the ballot. While a constituency association could still choose to nominate such an individual, it would clearly be dissuaded from doing so if its candidate had to be listed as an "independent" on the ballot.

**Other Sanctions and Perks** Expulsion from the party caucus is another technique of control that can be exercised by the leadership of a parliamentary party over a rebellious MP. While both the Liberals and the Conservatives have used the device of expulsion from caucus, this technique cannot be used to control the opposition of large numbers of government MPs, for the simple reason that it publicizes the party's internal disunity and could, if party standings are close in the House, result in the government's defeat. For that reason, it is more often used to censure individual MPs who are far beyond the pale as far as the party is concerned, either in terms of ideology or in terms of personal conduct.

Other important inducements available to a government to control its backbenchers are perks such as committee memberships, appointments as parliamentary assistants to ministers, or even promotion to Cabinet. Conversely, if MPs oppose their party in the House, such perks can be removed — this happened to veteran MP Warren Allmand, who was removed as chair of the influential Justice Committee for voting against the budget legislation in 1995. In the extreme, the offer of a Cabinet post or other favours controlled by the leader of a rival party can sometimes even induce a disgruntled backbencher to switch parties. Not surprisingly however, members who have been induced into the traitorous act of "crossing the floor of the House" are usually rejected by their constituents in the next general election.

**Discipline and Opposition Parties** Party discipline is similarly applied in the relationship of the opposition leaders to their backbenchers. While the prime minister has a lot more goodies with which to reward the faithful, many of the sanctions and inducements available to the government party are also available to the leaders of non-government parties. For instance, the hope for a Cabinet post if and when the opposition party comes to power can keep dissident opposition backbenchers in line. But while party discipline is a factor in the relationship of the leaders of the opposition parties to their backbenchers, it is not quite as important as it is for the prime minister, whose government must maintain the confidence of the House to stay in power.

As well, the leaders of the opposition will tolerate a higher degree of dissension and disagreement among their MPs because they do not have to "deliver" their policy positions through legislation. In a majority-government situation, if a few opposition backbenchers split with the leaders of their party "on division" (a formal vote in the House of Commons), the result will be little more than embarrassment for the opposition leader, because the government bill would have passed anyway. Furthermore, when criticizing the government, an opposition MP can oppose in a number of ways. As long as the opposition MP is critical of the government, the leaders of the opposition will generally tolerate some deviation from the official party line.

**Caucus** It has been seen that party discipline prevents the government MP from either voting against the government or actively criticizing government policy on the floor of the House of Commons. In the privacy of the government **caucus** however, government backbenchers are permitted to candidly express their views on government policies and, through criticism and articulate dissent, to have an influence on policy. Each party's caucus consists of all that party's MPs and its function is to to establish and maintain a communication link between the party leaders and the rank-and-file MPs.

*Caucus and Government Policy* While all parties in the House have a caucus, the government party's caucus is the most potentially significant in the policy process. The meetings of government caucus occur weekly while the House is sitting. They are attended by the prime minister and the Cabinet ministers, and they are held *in camera*. The tradition of caucus procedure is that decisions are made not by a formal vote, but by a consensus achieved through dialogue and a willingness to seek mutually satisfactory agreement. Because the meetings are held behind closed doors, the MPs can speak their minds freely, with no fear of endangering the public image of party unity.

When there is widespread opposition in caucus to a government policy, it is possible for the other members to stall or even completely arrest legislative proposals put forward by the Cabinet, but this happens infrequently. The odds that a group as diverse in its interests as the caucus will ever be unanimous in opposition to the Cabinet are very slight. For the most part, the Cabinet can assume that divergences of opinion among the backbenchers themselves will be at least as wide as the gulf between the Cabinet and the rank and file. The greatest limitation on the power of the caucus, however, stems from the backbenchers' relative lack of information. The minister who is proposing and defending a given policy in caucus draws on a fund of facts and figures prepared by the bureaucracy, while the MP, having limited research facilities and limited personal expertise, cannot effectively challenge ministerial positions that are backed by a vast array of expert advice.

A secondary argument for the usefulness of the governing party's caucus as a policy organ of the party posits the role of the MP as a representative of constituency interests. The argument here is that the Cabinet can use caucus as a testing ground for its legislative proposals. In most cases today, however, the MP is not any better equipped than the prime minister to speak authoritatively about the wishes of "the average Canadian." This is, to a large extent, because the party elites have the advantage of advice from the political advisors in the PMO, who are able to assess the political feasibility of any policy proposal through the use of analytical techniques such as public-opinion polls. Again, the problem is not so much that the representative function has been taken away from the caucus, as that other institutions, such as the bureaucracy and the PMO, are usually more effective than the MP in guaging public opinion.

*The Structure of Caucus*  Before 1969, it was a fairly common practice in the Liberal Party to discuss the policy proposals in caucus after the legislation had actually been introduced and the government had already publicly committed to it. The function of the caucus was more to assist the government in scheduling the parliamentary speeches of its members, and to inform them what to expect in the upcoming parliamentary week, than to participate actively in policy deliberations. After a great deal of criticism from backbenchers, a new set of ground rules for caucus procedure and a major reorganization of the federal Liberal caucus itself was approved by the Cabinet and put into effect in the fall of 1969. Basically, those rules bound the ministers to introduce all legislative proposals in caucus before introducing them in the House. The Mulroney government, with its enormous majority, had to institute similar procedures to ensure that backbenchers did not become too discontented.

Both the Trudeau Liberals and the Mulroney Conservatives instituted a system of **caucus committees** in an attempt to regularize and institutionalize the role of the backbench MP in the policy process. This system divides the party caucus into functional committees roughly paralleling the standing committees of the House itself, in order to permit a higher degree of specialization in caucus deliberations. While, because of the secrecy of caucus deliberations, it is difficult to say to what extent these changes have made the caucus any more influential in the policy process, at least the government backbenchers are no longer the last to know when the Cabinet is about to introduce a new policy.

The MPs of the parties with a large number of seats in the House also organize themselves into informal **regional caucuses.** This, coupled with the fact that ministers with a particular regional interest are the informal leaders of the regional caucuses, has increased the influence of the caucus when an issue of special interest to one part of the country is being proposed by the party leadership. It would be rare for the sponsoring minister of a policy proposal not to run the idea past ministerial colleagues from the region affected and to attempt to bring the members of the regional caucus on side.

While there is no automatic veto by either a regional minister or the regional caucus, it is not unusual for a policy proposal to be delayed, altered, or even withdrawn in the face of strong regional opposition.

Each of the committees of the caucus is given some research assistance to enable it to develop a measure of expertise in a particular area of concern. While this is generally a good idea, the fact remains that one or two researchers working on a given policy area will not enable a caucus committee to compete with a minister who has an entire government department to provide research assistance. While these changes in caucus procedure have made the discussion in caucus marginally more meaningful, they cannot fundamentally alter the asymmetrical power relationship between the caucus and the Cabinet in the policy process.

### Majority Government and the Opposition

While party discipline can ensure the prime minister of the support of government backbenchers in the House, it certainly will not work with the MPs from other parties. A majority government can always use the brute force of its majority to override opposition to its legislative initiatives, but Parliament does not work very efficiently when every issue must be resolved by formal vote in the House. Thus, even with a solid majority, the government must make an effort to get along with the opposition.

**Government, Opposition, and House Procedure** In a majority-government situation, the basic strengths and weaknesses of the opposition parties in Parliament are determined by the procedures of the House of Commons. Since they are never going to be able to out-vote the government on any policy proposal, the opposition parties must content themselves with using procedural delaying tactics to influence government legislation.

*Filibuster and Obstruction* The basic power of the opposition in the House of Commons stems from its ability to control time through debate. The House rules of procedure are founded on a balance between two principles of parliamentary democracy. The first is that the government should be able to get on with the business of governing in an efficient and expeditious fashion, and the second is that the opposition should have ample time to criticize the government's proposals. In other words, the opposition should be able to oppose, but not to the extreme of **obstructionism**, and the government should be able to get its programs through the House of Commons efficiently, but not without permitting thorough and, to the government, tiresome debate.

Current House of Commons procedures are such that if every opposition member were to speak as long as the rules permitted on every stage of the debate, most legislation could be debated almost endlessly. Given this situation, the opposition, although unable to vote down the government's legislation, could achieve the same end by the technique of **filibuster**, or endless debate. However, in order to restrict filibustering, the procedures of the House of Commons also provide measures for the limitation or termination of debate by a majority vote of the House.

*Time Limitation on Debate*  **Closure** is a technique whereby the government party, on a simple motion by a minister, can unilaterally terminate a debate. It is not used very often because it is, in procedural terms, a "blunt instrument," and if the government were to resort to its use frequently the government would begin to appear to be dictatorial. A gentler instrument for countering the opposition's control over time is a procedure for **time allocation**. This can be done for all stages of debate on a bill with the agreement of all parties, which is obviously the preferable option, with the agreement of a majority of the parties in the House, or even by the government, unilaterally, if none of the opposition parties will go along with it, provided that the motion to impose the time limit is approved by a majority of the House.

The unilateral imposition of time allocation by a majority government is almost as blunt an instrument as closure, for its effect is to "gag" the opposition and to terminate obstructive tactics such as filibuster. Initially it was feared that this procedure would take away the fundamental source of opposition influence in the House of Commons, the control of time. However, it is as bad politically for the opposition to appear to be obstructionist, as it is for the government to apply closure and be branded dictatorial or heavy-handed, and up until the 1988 election neither the tactic of filibuster nor the countermeasures of time allocation and closure were used very often.

Unfortunately, the mood of government-opposition relations in the House took a distinctly nasty turn during the second Mulroney government. Opposition obstructiveness and government determination to ram unpopular legislation through the legislature resulted in a great number of bitter confrontations. During this blustery period, closure was invoked on fifteen separate occasions and unilateral time allocation was imposed by the government more than twenty times. Since the 1993 change in government, despite some testiness in interparty relations, the trend appears to have reversed or at least slowed down significantly.

*Interparty Negotiation*  It is in the interest of both the government and the opposition to seek some sort of mutually acceptable agreement on the limitation of debate. In practice, the government will usually make deals with the opposition regarding the specifics of the legislation being debated. In return for a minor change in the legislation, the opposition parties will often agree to limit their criticism to a set number of party spokespersons in order to speed up the passage of the bill in question. The government will seldom agree to major changes in the substance of legislation in return for this kind of agreement, and this fact is generally understood by the opposition parties.

Finally, one flaw in the argument that the opposition can influence policy through control over parliamentary time is that this power is a purely negative one. It is, indeed, possible to stall the government, and it is possible even to influence the government to make minor changes in its legislation. However, if a majority government is committed to any single piece of legislation, the substance of that legislation will be non-negotiable. The outcome is inevitable: the bill will pass ultimately and in the end the opposition has done little but waste time.

Perhaps the most important source of leverage that the government enjoys in its bargaining relationship with the opposition parties in Parliament is its control over the legislative agenda. One tactic the government can use is to stack the order paper with a number of bills, some of which it is not overly committed to. The government can place contentious "red herring" legislation on the order paper, along with less contentious legislation to which it is committed. The government House leader can then give way to the opposition on the red herring in return for concessions on the expeditious passage of the bills to which it is the most committed.

This tactic can also be used at later stages of the legislative process, where clever drafting can see to it that there are attackable but also non-essential, red-herring clauses deliberately written into government bills. This allows the opposition, or, conceivably, government backbenchers, to feel they are having an impact without compromising the overall integrity of a piece of legislation. The main limit to the effectiveness of this sort of tactic is that it is difficult to disguise. Savvy opposition House leaders, will be well aware that their opposite number on the government side is not above such puckish pranks.

**Government, Opposition, and Public Opinion**   Other than their control over the time to be used in the passage of government legislation, the opposition parties have only one fundamental strength in attempting to influence the government. This is the ability to criticize *publicly* the government's policy proposals. In debates in the House of Commons, and increasingly in the lobby of Parliament before the television cameras,[1] opposition MPs do their very best to make the government's policies appear foolhardy, irresponsible, dangerous, opportunistic, or just plain silly. The arguments that opposition parties present to back this up are designed to convince the voting public that a new government (naturally formed by themselves) should be put in power at the earliest opportunity.

Unfortunately for the opposition parties, their great weakness in endeavouring to convince the public that the government policy is bad is their lack of information and expertise. By the time the opposition parties are involved in the policy process, the legislation being debated in the House has already been the object of intensive research by innumerable experts in task forces, royal commissions, interdepartmental committees, government departments, and central agencies — all of which have probably taken into account the recommendations of interest groups and other stakeholders in that policy community.

While the *Freedom of Information Act* may appear to have increased the amount of technical information available to opposition MPs, the complexities of the process of accessing government documents, the significant exclusions

---

1.  Although the debates in the House are now televised in their entirety, very few television stations are willing to bump their own programming to pick up the Commons broadcasts. In fact, a few stations broadcast taped versions of the Oral Question Period and special events such as the budget speech, while cable services often devote one channel to House of Commons debates. But for the most part, very few Canadians actually watch Parliament on television. While of interest to political scientists and the relatives or friends of the MPs, for the most part the goings-on of the Canadian House of Commons cannot match the ratings of *Hockey Night in Canada* or the latest sitcom or cops-and-robbers show.

permitted by the Act, and the multiple competing demands on MPs' time make it very unlikely that they will be able to liberate the relevant information. Even if they do, the likelihood is still slim that a handful of MPs, with little time to spare for even cursory research, will ever be able to add much substantial criticism to such heavily studied proposals. Interest groups also feed opposition members all manner of information, and since many groups have significant resources at their disposal, the information is often quite effective. However, this source is tempered by the fact that because pressure groups are ultimately self-interested, their information is always slanted.

Finally, in the context of what we said in Chapter 10 about executive federalism, the backbench MP is effectively excluded from one of the key arenas of policy-making in Canada, federal-provincial relations. Many of the critical priority decisions in our system are taken by senior Cabinet ministers and their top officials at intergovernmental conferences behind closed doors. The backbencher is not privy to the machinery of elite accommodation that dominates intergovernmental decision-making and hence is unable to use publicity to force policy changes. As Robert Stanfield once said,

> The frustrations of Members of Parliament are increased by federal-provincial deals, agreements and resulting legislation which confront Parliament as *faits accomplis*. There may be no way to avoid this in contemporary Canada, but federal-provincial arrangements have significantly reduced the role of Parliament.[2]

Thus, while the opposition MPs can criticize government policy both publicly and in the House, the influence of this criticism is likely to be limited. Tasked with the responsibility for criticizing government policy, the opposition parties in the House of Commons are functionally disqualified from doing so through lack of expertise and exclusion from the *in camera* forums of policy decision-making in the Cabinet and in the intergovernmental committees. The really significant arguments will have been made and met already by competing experts in the various institutions vested with the responsibility for advising the government, and these arguments may never see the light of day.

### Minority Government and the Opposition

The relationship of the government to Parliament is significantly altered when there is **a minority-government** situation in the House of Commons. Minority government occurs when the government party does not have a majority of the seats in the House of Commons. Thus, to stay in power, it must at all times be able to secure the support not only of its own backbenchers but, as well, of enough MPs from other parties to give it a majority on division. The government, in a minority situation, is usually formed by the party that holds a plurality of seats, although it is conceivable that a party standing second in number of seats could form the government if it can secure the support of the third-place party. The third party or parties hold the balance of power in the House, and can choose either to defeat the government by voting against it, or to maintain

---

2. Robert Stanfield, "The Legislative Process: Myths and Realities," *in* W. A. W. Neilson and J. C. MacPherson, eds., *The Legislative Process in Canada: The Need for Reform* (Toronto: Butterworths, 1978), pp. 44–45.

the government by siding with it. The government can often be sustained at length in this situation.

**Power of Dissolution**   The power of dissolution is the basic constitutional control that the prime minister possesses over the "third" or minor parties in a minority situation in the Commons. According to this constitutional convention, the prime minister has the exclusive power to advise the governor-general to dissolve Parliament and call an election. In a general election, both government and opposition MPs must put their jobs on the line, and for most members this means a tough struggle. Not very many MPs have seats so safe that they can afford to campaign without great energy and large outlays of money, and the typical Canadian federal election will see some 30 to 40 per cent of MPs from all parties losing their jobs.

Moreover, the minor parties in the House must be mindful of public opinion and, unless the likelihood of improving their standing in an election is very high, they will be reluctant to help defeat the government and thereby be forced to face the verdict of the ballot box. While a government would never dissolve the House to whip its own backbenchers into line — this would show the public that there was a split in the party's ranks, and members of the Cabinet would have even more to lose than backbenchers — the threat of dissolution can be very important in influencing the behaviour of minority parties in the House of Commons in many minority-government situations.

**Non-Confidence and Dissolution**   While the power of dissolution is controlled by the PM, the government must be cautious in deciding when and how frequently it uses the power. The electorate enjoys a good election from time to time but can become peevish if there are too many elections in a short period. Hence, the issue of who is to blame for precipitating an election — the government or the opposition — is an important one when considering a dissolution. Clearly, if there is a majority government, or if, in a minority government, the PM calls an election without being defeated in the House, the blame lies with the government. On the other hand, it is a constitutional convention that, if the government is defeated on an explicit motion of non-confidence, the PM *must* resign and in most cases Parliament will be dissolved. In this latter instance, the PM has no choice in the matter, and the blame for the election can be laid squarely at the feet of the opposition parties.

However, the Constitution is not clear about whether a defeat of a government motion in the House necessarily constitutes a vote of non-confidence in the government. It is generally held that a defeat of a major government proposal, particularly one that involves the raising or spending of public money, is an indication of non-confidence and the government should step aside. The implication of this "rule" is that a minority government can press ahead with legislation that may be unpopular to the opposition parties, daring the House to defeat it, and in so doing take the responsibility for forcing an election.

In the spring of 1968, this issue arose and was settled in a manner that, at the time, appeared to have the potential for altering the status of minority governments. The Liberal government was defeated, quite by accident, because of a very high rate of absenteeism on the part of the government backbenchers. The vote was on the third reading of an important piece of financial legislation, and the Official Opposition argued that such a defeat of an important government bill required the resignation of the government and an immediate election.

At this time, the governing Liberals were embroiled in a leadership campaign and hence were unprepared for an election. The third parties were not prepared to fight an election so soon either. The solution was that the government introduced a motion of confidence in itself at the next sitting of the House, essentially asking the House of Commons if it really wanted an immediate election. The government was given a vote of confidence by the House and was permitted to stay in power. This helped to clarify the notion of non-confidence and confirmed that it is not always necessary for a government to resign if it is defeated on a motion other than an explicit non-confidence motion. The significance of this is that Parliament can defeat legislation it doesn't like without automatically forcing an election and if an election does ensue, the culpability for precipitating it must be shared by the government and opposition alike.

Partly as a result of the 1968 clarification of the confidence convention, during the 1972–1974 minority-government period, the Liberal government lost a total of eight recorded votes, and only the vote in May 1974, which precipitated the election, was viewed as indicating a want of confidence in the government. In assessing the historical evolution of the confidence convention, the Special Committee on the Reform of the House of Commons (the McGrath Committee) concluded that, clearly, not every vote involves confidence, and that governments in future should specify explicitly which votes are to be considered confidence matters.[3]

**Minority Governments: 1963–1995** The Liberals have been particularly successful in maintaining minority governments, most notably from 1963 to 1968 and again from 1972 to 1974. During both periods, they managed to stay in power with little difficulty, and when the subsequent elections were held, the Liberals were promoted to a majority government by the electorate. From 1963 to 1968, the minority Liberal government needed only a few opposition votes to retain control of the House of Commons, and, with thirty to fifty seats in the hands of the NDP, *Ralliement des créditistes*, and Social Credit, it was usually a simple matter to find them.

Part of the reason for the success of the Liberal government during this period was that it stood pretty much in the middle on most issues, with the NDP and *Créditistes* taking positions to the left and right of the government, respectively. Virtually all of the government's policy proposals were opposed by the Conservative Official Opposition "on principle," and by one or the other of the *Créditistes* and the NDP. However, the two minor parties were never able to vote on the same side because of their radically different points

---

3. Canada, *Report of the Special Committee on Reform of the House of Commons* (Ottawa: House of Commons, June, 1985), pp. 5–10.

of view, and also because through much of that period the third-party MPs and their parties feared an election at least as much as the Liberals did.

In the period from 1972 to 1974, the Liberals again formed a minority government and again successfully stayed in power by consistently acquiring support from the NDP. They were eventually defeated in a vote of non-confidence when the NDP finally abandoned them, but in the subsequent election the Liberals were swept to power with a majority, and the ranks of the NDP were seriously depleted, confirming a fear of third-party MPs that the forcing of elections in such circumstances is a bit of a crap shoot for third parties.

*The Effectiveness of Minority Governments*  The lesson of these two examples is not only that the problem of controlling the House of Commons in a minority-government situation is much more complicated and difficult than it is in the majority situation, but that it is still quite possible to govern effectively if some adjustments are made. From 1972 to 1974, for example, it was common practice for Cabinet ministers to consult opposition spokespeople before bringing bills forward, and ministers could be certain that they would have great difficulty in getting their bills on the order paper at all if they could not convince their Cabinet colleagues and the prime minister that sufficient discussions had taken place with the opposition to assure passage of the legislation. Meetings between government and opposition House leaders, weekly events in any case, became much more frequent, and the views of the opposition House leaders were given much more weight both in House scheduling and in Cabinet deliberations. With such efforts, a minority government can be made to work very successfully.

If the 1972–1974 Parliament provides us with an example of a fairly successful minority government, the 1979–1980 one demonstrated how fragile a minority can be if not properly managed. Prime Minister Joe Clark took the approach that he would govern "as though he had a majority," likely in the belief that, if defeated, his party would be returned with a majority, and likely in the belief that the Liberals, preoccupied with the initial labour pains of a leadership convention to replace Pierre Trudeau, would not permit the Tory government to fall. The result was that the Tories refused to accede to any of the demands of the other parties and were defeated on an NDP non-confidence motion. It is now part of the folklore of Canadian politics that Trudeau rose from the ashes, withdrew his resignation as leader of the party, and received a majority government from the same electorate that had turfed him out less than a year previously. The lesson of the Clark interlude is that minority government can work only if the prime minister is willing to seek compromise with the opposition parties.

To conclude this section, it can be re-emphasized that, while there is a potential for greater policy-making power in the hands of the opposition in the situation of minority government, there still remain limitations on the ability of the opposition to exercise this power. First, the fact remains that the opposition does not have the same access to expert advice as does the Cabinet and cannot therefore deal as meaningfully with policy issues. Second, procedure in the House of Commons is such that any control exercised by the opposition is largely negative in nature. Third, as we have pointed out, the ideological range of the minor parties in the House from 1963 to 1980 militated against unified opposition effort. Finally, since 1980, majority government seems once again to have become the norm in our system of government.

### Policy Functions

As pointed out in Chapter 2, Parliament dominates the policy process only at the legislative stage. However, it can and does have some influence at all stages of policy making, and we must comment briefly on that before proceeding to the more detailed discussion of Parliament as the core institution at the legislative stage.

**Policy Initiation**  As an initiator of policy ideas, Parliament has ample opportunity to influence policy decisions. Because the MPs can raise issues in the House of Commons during question period, through tabling petitions and through influencing their party leadership in caucus, they have institutionalized access to the priority-determination process. As was pointed out in Chapter 2, the basic problem of policy initiation is one of communication. It is necessary to communicate one's policy idea to the Cabinet, which functions as the main priority-setting institution in Canadian government.

Moreover, MPs function not only as a public-access point for the general public by transmitting information about the wants and needs of their constitutents to the Cabinet, but they can also use their institutionalized status in the House to pass on their own individual policy views to government. The Government Members' Lobby, just outside the Commons, and the weekly caucus meetings provide ample opportunities for backbenchers to buttonhole ministers, and the adroit minister is always very careful to be available to MPs on such occasions.

*MPs as a Channel of Public Access*  When people feel aggrieved or neglected by government, they often express their concerns by writing letters or speaking directly to their member of Parliament. This particular channel of access to government was especially important at an early period in Canadian political history, when other channels of access to the political decision-makers were not as well developed as they are now. As a point of access today, however, Parliament is in competition with many other institutions, such as interest groups, parties, the media, and the bureaucracy, all of which can communicate policy ideas to the Cabinet as well as, if not better than, Parliament.

Thus, because modern techniques of information gathering, such as public-opinion polling, and modern institutions, such as clientele-oriented bureaucratic agencies, have permitted the political executive and the bureaucracy to go out into the environment and actively seek out or promote new policy ideas, Parliament's role as a communicator of new policy ideas to the system's priority setters has been much diluted or proscribed. While parliamentarians can and do still pass on the concerns of their constituents to government, there are many other institutions and many other techniques that achieve the same end and can possibly achieve it more effectively.

*The MP as Policy Innovator* The MP can also function as a policy initiator in a very immediate way by communicating a personal idea in the House. One example of such direct policy innovation by an individual MP was the abolition of capital punishment. The idea was introduced in Parliament originally as a private member's bill, and was subsequently picked up by the Cabinet and re-introduced as government policy. Perhaps the classic example of innovation by an MP is the inception of an old-age security scheme in Canada. The introduction of that idea in 1927 was largely the work of the Independent Labour member of Parliament, J. S. Woodsworth.

Indeed, in the 1920s and 1930s, Woodsworth used Parliament as an effective platform to prompt Liberal governments into much of the social-welfare legislation that we have today. Certainly, during this period such radical policy options were not being generated by the relatively conservative general population. Occurrences such as these are not frequent. However, a Cabinet decision in 1973 to have all private members' bills examined with a view to allowing some that are in line with government priorities to pass may have gone some way to returning at least the potential for influencing policy initiation. Still more recently, procedures introduced by the Mulroney government in response to recommendations of the McGrath Committee on Parliamentary Reform have regularized a system of allowing a limited number of private members' bills to be fully debated and brought to a vote. We will discuss the importance of private members' business in greater detail in the next chapter.

**Priority Determination** While an MP's influence on the Cabinet should depend on his or her prestige and knowledge, in practical terms, it is often the regional base of support of the individual involved that determines influence. For instance, where a course of action being considered by the Cabinet is likely to affect a particular geographic region of Canada, there is a good chance that concerted opposition or support by the regional caucus will influence the Cabinet in setting its priorities. However, the Cabinet will probably have independent sources of information about the attitudes of the people in the affected region, and if the independent information contradicts the position of the MPs, the Cabinet is just as likely to heed the former.

The opposition MPs are likely to be even less influential than their counterparts in the government backbenches in influencing government priorities, for the simple fact that they don't have the direct access to the ministers in caucus. As we have seen in the preceding section, all of this can change in a minority government when the opposition parties may have some influence on the government's policy agenda. In sum, the role of Parliament at the priority-setting stage of policy making depends on the willingness of the Cabinet to be influenced by the MPs, on the availability and substance of competing advice, on the ability of the MPs or groups of MPs to sell their ideas, and on factors such as regional coalitions formed in caucus.

**The Legislative Stage: Refinement and Legitimation** Policy formulation, as we have seen in Chapter 2, is primarily the business of the bureaucracy, subject to the ultimate authority of the Cabinet. Parliament's role at this stage is very limited, because of the generally technical and complex nature of the problem of formulating policy alternatives. The pre-legislative use of parliamentary committees to conduct public hearings, review proposals, and make recommendations to Cabinet may influence the choice of governing instrument or options for implementation. Despite this, in terms of expertise and available time, the MP is still ill-equipped to add much at this stage of policy making.

However, Parliament is the core institution at the legislative stage of the process. While it is the legislative drafting branch of the Department of Justice that converts the raw policy, as formulated by the Cabinet and bureaucracy, into a bill, Parliament, through its committees, **refines** and polishes the draft so that it is a workable piece of legislation without unintended and perverse consequences. In the House of Commons, and more specifically in committees, the MPs go over government legislative proposals, tightening up the wording, criticizing any weaknesses, suggesting amendments, and, through public debate, publicizing the inherent advantages and disadvantages of the bill.

Finally, Parliament is one of the institutions involved in the ultimate conversion of government policy to statute law. In this sense the parliamentary phase of the process **legitimizes** the policy decision by giving it the symbolic sanction of the rule of law. As well, while the formal votes in the House of Commons and the Senate may appear to be merely *pro forma* or symbolic steps in the governmental process, akin to proclamation and the governor-general's assent, this formal ratification or rejection of government bills may, in fact, be the most significant function of Parliament. While it is true that the number of government proposals actually defeated in Parliament is very small, this is partially the result of parliamentary watchfulness, which discourages governments from introducing intemperate legislation in the first place. While its formal exercise has been extremely rare, it is the ultimate power to reject a government's legislative proposals in a formal vote and the ability to expose a foolhardy government to the glare of public scrutiny that is a fail-safe deterrent against dictatorial government.

### The Political Audit Function of Parliament

Perhaps, because of the *de facto* limitations on the role of Parliament in the policy process, the most important day-to-day function of Parliament today is keeping the government honest and accountable. This **political audit** role is to be distinguished from the **financial audit** function whereby, through the scrutiny of the estimates by the standing committees and through the work of the Public Accounts Committee and the auditor general, Parliament does audit the financial affairs of the government. The political audit function involves ongoing, broadly based, and open criticism of all activities of the government.

This process goes on almost constantly regardless of whether Parliament is actually sitting, and brings to the attention of the press and the public the real, alleged, and potential shortcomings of the government of the day. Because of party discipline and loyalty, this general surveillance and critique of the performance of the government is carried out primarily by the opposition parties, not by the government backbenchers. Furthermore, the thrust of this kind of criticism is not to offer up specific policy counterproposals but to publicly comment upon the state of the nation and the frailties of the government.

The effectiveness of the political audit function of Parliament is determined by two main factors. The first factor is that the *scope* of Parliament's criticism of government is virtually unlimited. Everything the government or an individual minister does is a potential target for a vigilant opposition, which, in turn, is motivated not only by its sense of civic duty, but also by the fact that its success at the next election may depend upon how effective it has been in discrediting the government in the eyes of the electorate. The second factor is simply that all of the critiques of government policies and all of the dirt, scandal, and dirty linen uncovered in the course of trying to discredit the government as a whole, or Cabinet ministers individually, are *open* and part of the public record.

Thus, given the essentially unlimited range of targets, the openness of the process, and the willing collaboration of the media in disseminating the opposition's criticism widely, this function of Parliament can be performed effectively. The specific procedural devices that assist Parliament in carrying out this responsibility such as Question Period will be discussed in the next chapter.

### The Representative Function: MPs and Constituents

Given the limits on Parliament's policy role, the most important aspects of the MP's representative role must be limited to non-policy matters. The MP today is acting more and more as a channel through which the individual constituent can register and seek redress for specific grievances. The types of problems being dealt with by MPs do not require large-scale policy decisions in order to effect a remedy; rather, they involve inequities in the application of existing policies to individual cases. These inequities can often be remedied by administrative action on instructions from the appropriate minister.

The means of redressing many individual grievances can be achieved through simple tactics such as a telephone call from the MP's office to the minister's office or, if that should fail, through a pointed question in the House of Commons. The latter has the effect of publicizing an injustice or inequity being perpetrated by the administration which might be embarrassing to the government or the specific minister reponsible. Hence, the MP has influence when seeking redress of a problem of a constituent simply because the minister concerned would rather solve the problem quickly, quietly, and apolitically than face public criticism.

**The MP as Ombudsman** This function of the MP can be likened to that of an **ombudsman**. An ombudsman is a senior government official who is responsible to a legislature rather than to a minister and who is empowered to hear complaints about the administration of the law, to mediate disputes, and to pursue legal remedies when all else fails. The concept of an ombudsman originated in the Scandinavian countries but most Canadian provinces now have created such a position to deal with administrative grievances. While there is no federal ombudsman, because the MP has official status in Ottawa, and because of the power to publicly assert the case in Parliament, the MP is in a good position to act as an ombudsman for individual constituents, or at least for those constituents who have the initiative to request assistance.

The ombudsman function of the MP is carried out mostly in a non-partisan context. MPs, in other words, represent all their constituents, and not just those who voted for them or for their parties. Similarly, ministers dealing with such issues pay equal attention to opposition and government MP interventions. The aim of the process is to deal with a concern of a citizen from a given constituency regardless of partisan factors.

This same concern with the "little hurts" — the inequities and injustices inevitably committed by large government administrations — probably also affects the individual MP's role in the policy-refining stage of the policy process, where Parliament can and does take a positive and active role. At this stage, potential administrative consequences of the manner of implementation of the legislation can be missed by the Cabinet and the bureaucracy and are sometimes picked up by MPs considering the bill in committee. Because of experience with the sorts of problems created for constituents by carelessly drafted legislation, the MP can make suggestions as to how to minimize the problems likely to arise during its implementation. Thus, the MP represents the interests of individual constituents not only in seeking to redress grievances, but also in attempting to prevent their occurrence in future.

The ombudsman function of the MP is important to the legitimacy of the government system, for it resolves problems among people who might otherwise feel that they have no access to the authorities. While many MPs still feel that their most important role is to represent the interests of their constituencies, their regions, or the country as a whole in the policy process, it is unlikely that backbench MPs will ever again be able to take a very positive policy role if, indeed, they ever did. However, as long as the MP remains alert to the injustices and inadequacies in the implementation of laws particularly as they affect individual Canadians, such unfortunate concomitants of big government can perhaps be minimized.

**The MP: "Of" the People?** Canadian members of Parliament today are intended to represent the people who elected them to power. We know that there are limitations on this role because of the nature of Cabinet government and the parliamentary system. However, while MPs are elected *by* us, they are not necessarily *of* us, and can be seen as junior members of our political elite.

Since MPs are elected from geographically based constituencies that are apportioned among the provinces roughly in accordance with population, there is no point in describing the provincial distribution of MPs. Nor is there much point in the 1990s in discussing the rural-urban distribution of federal MPs, since decennial redistributions of seats by impartial electoral-boundaries commissions has, to some extent, rectified the huge rural over-representation that persisted until the late 1950s. In any case, many constituencies mix rural and urban voters, and even in predominantly rural constituencies, the MPs still tend to be from the urban centres or "county seats."

The ethnic distribution of MPs still shows a heavy bias towards the two "charter" ethnic groups. The distribution between the English and French groups has been quite equitable, since French MPs normally represent French ridings. While elections since 1970 have shown significant increases in the number of non-charter-group candidates and MPs, the number of parliamentarians of French and British backgrounds is still disproportionately greater than the population. While the proportion of aboriginal MPs is still slightly less than their proportion of the population, in recent years aboriginal people have been more successful than many other ethnic groups in increasing their representation both in the House of Commons and in the Senate. This has occurred in part because aboriginal Canadians tend to be concentrated in more sparsely populated northern constituencies, where Indians, Métis, or Inuit are a significant percentage of the electorate.

The religious distribution of MPs parallels fairly closely that of the general public. Protestant/Catholic/"other" ratios of MPs are fairly proportional to population distribution. However, representation on the basis of religious background is not much to crow about given that religious issues are virtually non-existent on the agenda of national discourse in the modern era.

It is when we turn to the socio-economic backgrounds of MPs that we find the greatest discrepancies between the public and their representatives. The occupational status of MPs, though not as high as that of Cabinet ministers, is nonetheless quite high. In both level of income and occupation, MPs rank significantly higher than their constituents. Businessmen, lawyers, and other professionals make up more than two-thirds of the House of Commons, and the Senate is even more skewed in this direction in its composition. As one might expect, the educational level of MPs is also much higher than that of the average Canadian because of the correlation between higher education and higher-status occupations.

Finally, although women are more the 50 per cent of the Canadian population, they are still only 18 per cent of the MPs. While, as we have pointed out elsewhere, the representativeness of our political and governmental institutions by gender has improved significantly in recent years, there is still a very long way to go before we have anything approximating gender parity.

Thus, Canadian MPs are territorially but not socially representative. It is perhaps paradoxical, in view of the highly public nature of their jobs and the need to gain support from a broad spectrum of voters, that MPs can be so unlike the people they represent. They are representative of the French and English divisions in Canadian society, and they are quite representative with respect to religion and geography, but there the resemblance ends. MPs are not at all representative of whatever class differences exist in Canadian society, nor are they adequately representative of women, aboriginal people, or the growing populations of immigrant groups in our electorate.

▶ THE SENATE AND PARLIAMENTARY
DEMOCRACY

The Canadian Parliament is **bicameral** in structure, consisting of the House of Commons and the Senate. The House of Commons (or lower house) functions virtually exclusively as the effective legislative branch of the Canadian political system, while the Senate (or upper house) plays a relatively minor role in the legislative process.

### Functions of the Senate

It is clear that the Senate was always intended to play a lawmaking role complementary but secondary to the House. Many governmental systems around the world have bicameral legislatures, the justification being that laws should not be passed too hastily. Having bills passed by the lower house, subsequently reviewed and reconsidered by the upper house, allows an opportunity for a *sober second thought*. However, the Canadian Senate was originally intended to perform other functions in our system of government which go beyond second guessing the House of Commons.

**Representation** The Senate was originally viewed as the representative of various *regions* of the federation, with the Maritimes, Quebec, Ontario, and the West each allotted twenty-four senators. The entry of Newfoundland in 1949 added six more senators, and two more seats were added in 1975 to give representation to the Northwest Territories and the Yukon. This makes up today's normal[4] total of 104. The importance of the Senate today as a regional and provincial representative is not very significant because other institutions, such as the Cabinet and the federal-provincial conferences, which are more deeply involved in the policy process, are much better equipped to perform this function.

*Senate and Cabinet* Normally the Cabinet is composed of members of the House with a single senatorial minister to act as the **government leader** in the upper chamber. However, the Senate has also been used from time to time to provide regional representation in the Cabinet. The 1979 and 1980 elections left certain regions of the country under-represented in the government caucus in the House. To remedy this in the case of the short-lived Clark government, senators from Quebec were given key government portfolios, and in the case of the 1980–1984 Trudeau government, some Western senators were given Cabinet posts as well.

Although this practice considerably enlivened the daily question period in the Senate, it likely did not enhance the role of the Senate in the policy process as much as it simply reduced the credibility of the governments forced to place senators in important policy-related portfolios. Since 1984, the general elections have produced more balanced representation in the House and the tradition of having only one senator in the Cabinet has been restored.

*Age and Property* The second function of the Senate as perceived by the Fathers of Confederation was to act as a conservative "steadying hand" on the House of Commons. The fathers of Confederation, while clearly committed to the principle of popular sovereignty, were nonetheless elitists who were wary

---

4. Sections 26–28 of the *Constitution Act, 1867*, provide for the addition of four or eight senators, to a total of 112. This provision, once thought to be inoperative, has been used only once, by the Mulroney government in 1988.

of what they saw as a potentially overly youthful, impressionable, and impulsive lower chamber. To balance this scary side of democracy the Senate was to be composed of older, more experienced, and more cautious individuals. Hence, senators are required to be at least thirty years of age and to own property valued at a minimum of $4000 in the province they represent. Unlike the members of the lower house, who are elected, senators are appointed by the governor-general-in-council and enjoy permanent tenure until age seventy-five.[5]

**Policy Functions** Most of the factors that function to restrict the role of the House of Commons in the policy process apply also to the Senate. Specifically, the Senate cannot compete with the Cabinet as a priority setter, and it lacks the expertise to become deeply involved in policy formulation. Nevertheless, as with the House of Commons, the Senate does have a role to play in the consideration of policy issues before legislation is introduced.

*Committees and Task Forces* Committees of the Senate and joint Senate-Commons committees are frequently set up as task forces to conduct investigations of policy issues and to hold public hearings. An early example of the use of a Senate committee in such a pre-legislative or investigatory role was the 1970 landmark study done on the mass media in Canada. Similarly, senators have played a prominent role in joint committees on the Constitution in 1981 and in the post–Meech Lake period in 1992. A 1984 Senate report on legislation to create the Canadian Security Intelligence Service (the Pitfield Report) was extremely influential in securing an acceptable draft of the CSIS Act, and a Senate committee was established in 1995 to investigate the Pearson Airport affair.

It is because the Senate is usually less involved in the politics of the day that it can effectively provide pre-legislative investigatory services to the government. It can conduct such studies without the danger of sensationalism and grandstanding on the part of the committee members that might occur if the same investigation were undertaken by the more partisan House of Commons. Also, the House of Commons, because of its legislative responsibilities, has less time to conduct hearings in the leisurely fashion typical of the Senate. Thus, through Senate committees, the Canadian upper house can contribute some meaningful inputs to the policy process and simultaneously relieve some of the pressure on the House of Commons.

*Limits to the Policy Role of the Senate* There are, however, even more handicaps placed on the policy role of the Senate than on that of the House of Commons. In the first place, unlike MPs, senators are not elected to office but are appointed by the government whenever a vacancy occurs. Traditionally the prime minister appoints people who have shown themselves to be faithful to the party — Liberal governments have appointed Liberals and Conservative governments have appointed Conservatives, much to the annoyance of the NDP and the

---

5. Until 1965, tenure was for life. Senators appointed before that date have the option today of staying on or retiring at age seventy-five. Any senator appointed since 1965 must retire at seventy-five.

Reform Party, both of which are virtually unrepresented in the upper house. The effect of this partisan pattern of Senate appointments has been to deny the Senate both the legitimacy enjoyed by the House by virtue of popular election and also the respect that might accrue to a body that is appointed on merit rather than partisanship. In recent times, there has been somewhat less reluctance to appoint senators from non-government parties and from among people who have been basically non-partisan in their politics, but this has not been done often enough to give us a standard for evaluating its effect on the role or effectiveness of the upper chamber.

Another weakness of the Senate has been the tendency to offer Senate posts largely to people whose useful political lives have been terminated. As a reward for many years of faithful service to the party, an old politician is "retired" by being put in the Senate. Because of this tendency, the image of the Senate is that of an old-folks home for tired and retired party faithfuls, an image that severely restricts its prestige. Again, more recent trends may somewhat counter this opinion. The appointment to the Senate of people such as Michael Pitfield, Lowell Murray, Michael Kirby, Lorna Marsden, and Joyce Fairburn, whose useful lives are hardly at an end, has somewhat enhanced the prestige and credibility of the upper house in the eyes of both the public and public officials. However, we must still conclude that the Senate is not, nor should it be, a significant player in the policy process.

**Party Functions** The Senate also performs an important function for the Canadian party system in that it permits the party in power to retire party faithfuls without too seriously alienating them or imposing on them financial disaster. The Senate is, in this sense, a convenient place for stacking "over-age pols" who might cause political embarrassment if permitted to continue in the House of Commons, or who might be forced back into the private sector at a rather advanced age. The importance of this function of the Senate should not be minimized, for it provides some slight security for the politician. A politician, particularly a Cabinet minister, who manages to retire while his or her party is in office is likely to get either a Senate seat or some other patronage position. As a consequence, the politician need not constantly pander to private interests in the hope that they might be future employers when his or her days in politics are done.

The Senate has been used several times in recent years to provide a home base in Ottawa, an office on Parliament Hill, and a secure, if modest, income for important party backroom people. The foremost examples are Liberal Senators Keith Davey and Michael Kirby and Conservatives Norman Atkins and Lowell Murray, all of whom have been leading political strategists for their respective parties.

**Legislative Functions** Formally, the legislative role of the Senate is virtually equal to that of the House of Commons. Every bill passed by the House must go through three readings and a committee stage in the Senate, and the bill cannot become law until it has been passed by the Senate. While the Senate is legally empowered to make substantive amendments to or even to defeat government legislation passed by the House of Commons, the legitimacy of any significant interference by the Senate in the policy process is questionable in a system that values popular sovereignty.

Nevertheless, Senators occasionally brandish their formal power as a way to get ministerial attention or amendments. These exceptions to the rule of a passive upper house generally occur when a change in government follows a long period of one-party dominance during which all Senate appointments have gone to members of the government party. During the Mulroney years, for instance, the Liberal majority in the Senate, a legacy of twenty years of Liberal government, frequently delayed government bills and sometimes forced amendments. The Senate held up the passage of the free trade legislation in 1988, possibly helping to trigger an early election call, and the Senate also delayed the imposition of the GST. The latter blockage was resolved when Prime Minister Mulroney used an obscure provision of the *Constitution Act*, 1867, to appoint an additional eight Conservative senators, thus giving the government a majority in an upper house composed, for the first time, of 112 rather than 104 members.

With the Liberal victory in the 1993 general election, and the reduction of the PCs to a mere two seats in the Commons, the Conservative-dominated Senate became the only game in town for the Tories. As such, the Senate has become much more active than would normally be the case and the Conservative majority has forced more than one amendment to government legislation, perhaps most notably to a bill to reverse the privatization of Pearson International Airport.

The Senate is not permitted by the Constitution to introduce money bills, and in practice it cannot amend or defeat money bills either. (There is still some question as to the constitutionality of Senate amendments of money bills, but in practical terms the Senate does not even attempt to amend them today.) Bills can be introduced first either in the House of Commons or in the Senate. However, because of the normal absence of Cabinet ministers in the Senate, virtually all government bills are, by convention, introduced first in the House of Commons.

An adaptation of this procedure is the practice of having Senate committees study the subject matter of all government bills (including money bills) before they are introduced in the Senate, and while they are being considered in the House. The Senate can thus suggest amendments to the government, which, if accepted, can then be presented to the House of Commons for approval before the bill actually reaches the Senate. In this way, any wisdom to be found among the senators can be brought to bear profitably on government proposals without raising the spectre of an appointed body thwarting the wishes of the elected representatives of the people who sit in the lower house.

Also on the positive side of the ledger, the Senate does most of the parliamentary work involved in private bills, giving the overworked House of Commons more time for dealing with government legislation. As well, the detail work done in Senate committees on government bills already passed by the House serves as an important double check on the work of the committees of the lower chamber. Despite the partisan pall that periodically hangs over the deliberations on the floor of the upper house, there is a much less partisan spirit pervading in the committees. Hence, the experience of the committee members can be usefully brought to bear in the objective consideration of bills already approved by the House of Commons.

### Senate Reform

By way of conclusion to these brief remarks about the Senate, it should be mentioned that reform or abolition of the upper house has been considered continually since 1867. Some reforms have been implemented, such as compulsory retirement at age seventy-five and the provision that the Senate can delay a constitutional amendment motion passed by the House for no more than 180 days, after which it can be approved by the House unilaterally. While this latter provision means, in effect, that senators can no longer block amendments that would reform or abolish them, functionally, the Senate has not changed significantly since Confederation.

**Triple-"E" Proposals** Since the *Constitution Act*, 1982, which took away the Senate's veto on its own reform, there have been a number of proposals for reform but most of them focus on three concerns: the method of selection of senators, the distribution of seats among the provinces, and the powers of the upper house. These three concerns are adressed in a package of Senate-reform proposals developed in western Canada calling for a **triple-E Senate** — one that is *elected, effective*, and *equal*.

If it is made **elective**, it is argued, the Senate would have greater legitimacy and could therefore be given greater powers in the legislative process. The counter argument is that we already have an elected legislature, so why have two — why duplicate the House of Commons? While other countries, such as the United States, Australia, and Germany, have bicameral elective legislatures, there is no reason to assume that one is needed here. However, the more critical concern of would-be Senate reformers is to make the body more effective or more powerful than the exisiting upper house and to ensure that its responsibilities are different from those of the House of Commons.

Before 1982 there were a number of proposals for reform of the upper house, which would see it being converted into a more **effective** voice for provincial concerns in the federal Parliament. Here it was argued that a *House of the Federation* or a *House of the Provinces*, appointed by the provincial governments, would be more representative of regional interests than either the existing Senate or the House of Commons. The problem here, however, was that a more effective Senate — in terms of regional representation — would have to take power away from the elected House of Commons. The transfer of power from the House of Commons, which is, after all, representative of all parts of Canada, even if the government caucus might not be, to a non-elected body responsible to the provincial governments is a proposition that would require very careful scrutiny.

An *elected* Senate, however, that is also *effective* in representing provincial and regional interests would accomplish significantly more than simply duplicating the House of Commons. Such an upper house would provide an arena for the expression of *regional* interests in the national Parliament that the House of Commons, based on representation by population, could never achieve. While the power of the House would be reduced by such an institutional innovation, in all likelihood so would the power of the provincial goverments. If there were an elected legislative body in the national Parliament, it could claim to represent the interests of the people in the provinces as legitimately as the provincial governments. Thus, the process of elite accommodation, or executive federalism, that dominates intergovernmental relations in Canada today, and which gives so much power to the provincial political elites, could well be replaced, in part, by a mechanism of **intra-state federalism**.

Perhaps the most problematic "E" in the triple-E proposals is the notion of **equal** representation for the provinces. Naturally the smaller provinces like the idea and Ontario and Quebec don't. The Charlottetown Accord did include a proposal for a watered-down triple-E senate, which would have been either elected (in nine provinces) or appointed by the provincial government (in Quebec) and would have given each province six seats (plus two for the territories, for a total of sixty-two.) However, this new senate would not have had very much power relative to the House of Commons and could veto legislation only in matters of natural resources. In any event, as we all know, the Accord was rejected in a referendum and the Senate is still the same old Senate.

---

### ▶ SUMMARY AND CONCLUSION

One could conclude that Parliament is no longer of much significance in the Canadian governmental process, and that it functions primarily as an "electoral college" through which we indirectly elect a prime minister. It is clear, indeed, that on a day-to-day basis our constitutionally supreme lawmaking institution plays a supporting role to the Cabinet and the PM. However, Parliament does provide a sort of fail-safe mechanism that prevents governments from exceeding their authority. In extreme cases, if it were clear, for instance, that the prime minister was going insane or was attempting to govern without consulting either Cabinet colleagues or caucus, it is still open to the government members to say, "party discipline be damned," and to vote non-confidence. In the Canadian system there is no need of an impeachment process!

More routinely, at least, and, frequently important, it is through day-by-day criticism and comment by the opposition parties in the House of Commons, the publicizing of that criticism through the press, and the televising of debates that the government is kept on its toes. Cabinet ministers are constantly called upon publicly to justify the government's record through procedural devices such as Question Period, and we have seen that an important aspect of the role of the individual MP is the ombudsman function. The MP in this regard is both an elected watchdog and a communications link between the anonymous bureaucrat and the individual citizen.

We must also not forget that Parliament is a **symbol** of things we believe in, such as representative democracy and responsible government. The principle of parliamentary supremacy is not only an expression of the belief that ultimate lawmaking power *should* reside in the elected representatives of the people, but it is also a reflection of the continued commitment of our society to the basic value of popular sovereignty. It could be argued that the symbolic function of Parliament is as important as all the other functions combined, for it is Parliament around which most Canadians centre their perceptions of politics and government. Thus, despite the very real functional limitations on Parliament's ability to be truly "supreme," the institution remains significant both as an important part of the machinery of democratic government and as a symbol of our system of governance.

# Chapter 19

# The House of Commons: Structures and Processes

Having discussed the functions of Parliament and the power relationships between the political executive and the legislature, we must now look at the way in which Parliament is organized and the rules and procedures that govern the participation of parliamentarians in the governmental process. The focus here is almost exclusively on the House of Commons, for as we saw in the previous chapter, the Senate is a much less significant actor in both lawmaking and policy-making.

## ▶ THE STRUCTURES OF THE HOUSE

The organizational logic of the House of Commons is premised on the assumption of an **orderly** but largely **adversarial** relationship between the government and the opposition. This adversarial process is carried on through open debate, which is rendered orderly because there are clearly defined rules and procedures that govern the conduct of all members of the House. The organization of the House of Commons and the basic rules of procedure are set down in the Constitution, in the Standing Orders of the House of Commons, in the *Parliament of Canada Act*, and in innumerable practices and conventions of parliamentary debate that, for the most part, have been inherited from the Parliament of Westminster. To understand the organization of the House however, we must first take a look at the players and the roles that they are assigned in the parliamentary drama.

### The Players

The personnel involved in the activities of the House of Commons include the the formal officers of the House, the partisan captains and organizers of the adversarial process on the floor of the House, and the MPs themselves. Each of these classes of players and the roles that they are assigned must be identified and understood if we are to be able to assess the overall performance of the House of Commons.

**Officers of the House**  The authority and responsibilities of the formal officers of the House of Commons are defined by the Constitution and by the Standing Orders. They include the presiding officers of the lower chamber and the permanent staff of the House, who provide administrative support and keep the wheels of the parliamentary process turning efficiently.

*The Speaker*  The most important office of the House of Commons is the Speakership. The office of **Speaker of the House** was created by the BNA Act, Section 44, which states that

> the House of Commons on its first assembling after a General Election shall proceed with all practicable speed to elect one of its members to be speaker.

The main function of the Speaker, to **preside** over the debates in the House of Commons, is also defined by the BNA Act, although the elaboration of the duties of this role is left to the Standing Orders. The Speaker does not participate in debates except where necessary to defend the internal estimates of the House of Commons. Furthermore, Standing Orders explicitly state that the Speaker cannot vote on motions except to break a tie.

A secondary function of the office is to act as the administrative head of the House of Commons. Thus, in some ways, the Speaker is like a minister of a small department who is responsible in a formal way for the administrative policies of that department. The Speaker is responsible for the **internal economy** of the House, for the staffing of the House with permanent employees, and for preparing the estimates of internal costs and piloting them through the House of Commons. The Speaker is assisted in the financial management of the House by the Board of Internal Economy, which has both government and opposition members, and which acts as a sort of treasury board for the Commons.

*Election of the Speaker*  Constitutionally, it is clear that the Speaker is an officer of the House who is selected by the House itself and not by the Cabinet. In practice, however, because of the functional supremacy of the Cabinet in the parliamentary process, the Speaker was, until 1986, nominated by the prime minister and was usually elected without opposition. In 1986 House Speaker John Bosley resigned, and a new procedure for the election of the Speaker was instituted.

Today, the Standing Orders provide that the election of a Speaker is the first order of business when a new Parliament first meets after a general election. Technically, all MPs except ministers and party leaders are in the race for the job unless they notify the Clerk that they do not wish to stand. The vote is by secret ballot, and the Clerk acts as the chief electoral officer, bearing the responsibilty for counting the ballots. The results of the vote are not made known, but after each ballot, the names of members receiving fewer than 5 per cent of the vote are dropped from the list and another vote is taken. This procedure is followed for as many ballots as are necessary to give one candidate a clear majority.

Even with the new procedures, almost invariably, the Speaker will be a member from the government side of the House, although it is expected that he or she will function in a non-partisan and impartial manner. The tradition of impartiality was firmly established between 1963 and 1986. During this period it became the practice that the Speaker be nominated by the prime minister with the leader of the opposition as the seconder. In 1968, the Conservatives went one step further by indicating that they were willing to permit Lucien Lamoureux, a Liberal who had become a particularly astute and impartial presiding officer, to continue as the Speaker even if they won the election. To facilitate this, the Speaker ran as an independent and the Conservatives did not run a candidate against him in his own riding. This interparty cooperation paved the way for procedural changes that streamlined debate in the House by making most procedural rulings by the Speaker not subject to appeal to the House.

The response of Mr. Lamoureux to this grant of final authority in procedural matters was to take an extremely fair and impartial stand, often in opposition to the wishes of the government. Although Lamoureux did not contest the 1974 election, his successor, James Jerome, continued the practice of impartiality so effectively that he was retained as Speaker even when the Conservatives took power in the 1979 election. Since that time, the Speakership has always been filled by a government-party supporter, although for the most part the practice of an impartial presiding officer has been continued. By convention, the Speaker must be able to function in both official languages.

*Deputy Speaker and Deputy Chairmen of Committees of the Whole*  The **Deputy Speaker of the House**, who is also designated as the **chairman of Committees of the Whole**, is elected at the same time as the Speaker. The functions of this position are to take the place of the Speaker when the Speaker is not able to be present, and to preside over Committees of the Whole. Like the Speaker, the Deputy Speaker is elected for the duration of a Parliament and is expected to be proficient in whichever of the official languages is not the first language of the Speaker. The general practice is that the Deputy Speaker is selected from among the members of the government party.

Standing Orders provide for the temporary appointment, by the Speaker, of any member to chair the Committees of the Whole in the absence of the Deputy Speaker. However, it is more common today for a **deputy chairman of Committees** and an **assistant deputy chairman of Committees** to be appointed by the Speaker for the duration of the session to spell off the Deputy Speaker. These officers can also take over as Speaker in a situation where both the Speaker and the Deputy Speaker are absent. The officers are invariably members of the government party.

**The Clerk and Commons Staff**  The **Clerk of the House** is the permanent head of the House of Commons staff and is the most important non-elected officer of the House. The function of this position is to supervise all permanent officers and staff of the House of Commons, to ensure that the Orders of the Day are prepared and delivered to the Speaker, to print up documents in both official languages for the distribution to all members of the House, and to ensure that two copies of every bill presented in the House are forwarded to the minister of Justice.[1] In short, the Clerk of the House is a deputy minister of the House of Commons. His or her department is the permanent staff of the House, and the minister is the Speaker.

The Clerk of the House is expected, along with other officers of the House "at the table" to provide procedural advice to the Speaker when points of order are raised during Commons proceedings. The Clerk also acts as an intermediary between the House and the Senate, being responsible for delivering and receiving formal messages transmitted from one chamber to the other. Finally, the Clerk is responsible for safekeeping of all official documents and records and for the publication of *Hansard*, the verbatim record of debates in the House.

The **sergeant-at-arms** is the formal "peace officer" of the House of Commons. The position today is largely symbolic of the fact that the House is in charge of its own affairs, can bar entry to the chamber of any individual who is not an MP, and formally enforces the speaker's rulings. The sergeant-at-arms is the custodian of the **Mace**, which is the symbol of the House's power, and is also entrusted with the serving of warrants issued by the Speaker and the enforcement of orders of the House.

The House of Commons permanent staff of approximately three thousand persons, including the staff of the Library of Parliament, are not public servants according to the *Public Service Employment Act*, but are the direct employees of Parliament. They have a separate pension system and a separate system of employee-employer relations, and they are not subject to the regulations of the Public Service Commission. While this situation is merely a reflection of the need for Parliament to be independent from the whims of the government of the day in managing its own internal affairs, there has been some mild discontent among the employees themselves, who would like to have the collective-bargaining rights of public servants.

**Partisan Officials**  We have seen in earlier chapters that political parties have an important role to play in the organization and ordering of the business of the House of Commons. As one might expect, this does not occur through instinct or habit, but through the careful management of party affairs in the chamber by the parties themselves.

*Party Leaders*  The prime minister, as a member of Parliament, is the leader of his or her party in the House of Commons, and as such is responsible for the master legislative strategies of the party in the House. However, the PM is also very busy being the chief political executive and really doesn't have the luxury of actually leading the troops into battle on a day-to-day basis on the floor of the legislature. The leader of the party with the second largest number

---

1. This last provision was originally created to comply with the provision of the Canadian Bill of Rights; now the Justice minister makes sure that legislation is not repugnant to the Charter of Rights and Freedoms.

**Figure 19.1**
House of Commons schematic organization, 1994–1995.

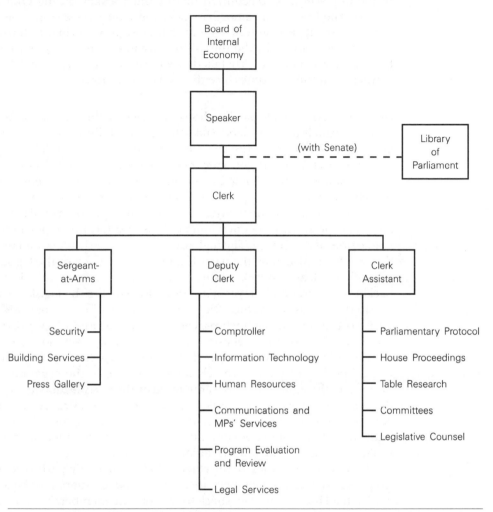

Source: Adapted from *The Hill Times*, Mar. 31, 1994, p. 5.

of seats in the House is given the formal title **Leader of of Her Majesty's Loyal Opposition**. The time constraints on the leader of the Official Opposition, as well as a multitude of party responsibilities outside the House, restrict his or her ability to be directly involved in the organization of the party's activities in the House much in the same way as the prime minister is restricted.

However, the office of opposition leader comes with a number of perks such as research assistance, a larger salary, and more office space. Similarly the Standing Orders provide that the leader of the Official Opposition has special privileges during debates such as being the first called to respond to the Speech from the Throne and being able to speak more often and longer in debating government bills. As well, it is a convention of House procedure that the leader of the opposition be recognized first by the Speaker during Oral Question Period. The leaders of minor parties in the House have some special status and some small perks as well, but only if their supporters in the House number at least twelve souls. In the thirty-fifth Parliament that commenced in 1994, both the Tories and the NDP failed to win twelve seats and as such lost all such privileges for the first time since they were introduced.

**House Leaders and Whips**  The **house leaders** of the various parties are appointed by their party leaders to take the responsibility for the overall in-House behaviour of their own MPs, and consequently for the overall flow of business through the House. The **government house leader** is a member of the Cabinet, and is responsible for seeing that the business of the government gets through the House as quickly as possible. Each opposition House leader, while not officially an officer of the House, acts as formal spokesman of his or her leader and negotiates, with the government House leader, the apportioning of the scarce time of the House. The high prestige of House leaders, and the fact that they are hand-picked by the party leaders to take much of the legislative load off the party leader's back, ensure that they have the power to instruct their backbenchers to do whatever is necessary to expedite the legislative process.

In this discussion of the officers of the House of Commons, we must also say a word about the **party whips**. Each party has a **chief whip** and, depending on its size, one or more assistant whips. The whips are not officers of the House; rather, they are MPs named by the various political parties represented there, but they play an extremely important role in the organization of the business of the House. They are appointed by the party leadership to represent their parties' respective interests in the **Committee on Procedure and House Affairs**. This standing committee functions as a "striking committee": it assigns individual MPs to all other committees and has a wide range of other responsibilities relating to the internal affairs of the House.

However, the key job of the chief whip is to maintain party discipline. The whips ensure that the members are all present when there is to be a recorded vote in the House, and they check to see that the members vote the right way on division. Finally, arrangements between parties, for instance, concerning the limitation of debate and the agenda for the sitting day, are sometimes worked out through the whips. Thus, while the whips are not formally House of Commons officers, they do have an integral part to play in the day-to-day workings of the House.

### Committees of the House of Commons

The basic organization of the House of Commons is based on the dichotomy of government and opposition. Virtually all of the procedural devices through which the political audit function of Parliament is performed are geared to the adversarial process of government-to-opposition debate on the floor of the House. However, most of the other functions of Parliament are performed in various types of committees. These bear further elaboration.

**The Committee of the Whole**  The **Committee of the Whole** is composed of all the members of the House sitting as a committee, with the Speaker out of the Chair and the Deputy Speaker presiding. Standing Orders generally apply when the House is sitting as a Committee of the Whole, with the exception that relevancy criteria are more strictly enforced and debate is less formalized. Traditionally, all legislation was referred to the Committee of the Whole after second reading, but now the clause-by-clause consideration of all bills is given in specialized legislative committees or standing committees.

Specialized Committees of the Whole — the Committee of Supply and the Committee of Ways and Means — were once required to give clause-by-clause consideration to all financial legislation. Up until very recently, the Committee of Ways and Means was required to deal separately with taxation proposals before introducing the actual bills in the House. However, in 1969, the Committee of Supply and the Committee of Ways and Means were abolished.

Thus, the function of the Committee of the Whole is today purely symbolic. Standing Order 73(4) states that "any Bill based on a Supply motion shall, after second reading, stand referred to a Committee of the Whole." However, this referral is done *pro forma* because the departmental estimates have already been scrutinized in detail by the standing committees before the supply bill is even introduced. The approval of a supply bill by the Committee of the Whole is accomplished without debate and without recorded vote.

**Standing, Joint, and Special Committees**  One of the first responsibilities of the House of Commons at the beginning of the first session of each Parliament is to appoint the Standing Committee on Procedure and House Affairs. The first task assigned to this committee, which usually includes the chief whips of the opposition parties, a representative of the ministry, and the chief government whip, who acts as the chair, is to convene as a **striking committee**. The function of the striking committee is to select the members of the Standing Committees of the House within ten days of the commencement of the session, and to ensure that all committees have a full complement of members throughout the session at all times.

At the time of writing, there are nineteen standing committees of the Canadian House of Commons, with between seven and fifteen members each. The committees are listed in Figure 19.2. The Committee on Procedure and House Affairs is also responsible for appointing the House members of the **Joint Standing Committees** of the Senate and House of Commons, on the Library of Parliament, Official Languages, and Scrutiny of Regulations.

The House of Commons may also set up **special committees** to conduct a prelegislative review or investigation of a particularly contentious policy issue. However, these seem to be a less-favoured option in recent years. If there is an issue of special concern, the standing committee that has the responsibility for the general subject area is empowered, by Standing Orders, to strike a sub-committee with a mandate to conduct hearings, receive briefs, and submit a report of findings and recommendations back to the parent standing committee. The sub-committee option is not available when the government wishes to set up a joint committee with the Senate. In this case, a special committee

**Figure 19.2**

Standing committees of the House of Commons, 1995.

Agriculture and Agri-Food
Canadian Heritage
Citizenship and Immigration
Environment and Sustainable Development
Finance
Fisheries and Oceans
Foreign Affairs and International Trade
Government Operations
Health
Human Resources Development
Human Rights and the Status of Disabled Persons
Aboriginal Affairs and Northern Development
Industry
Justice and Legal Affairs
National Defence and Veterans' Affairs
Natural Resources
Procedure and House Affairs
Public Accounts
Transport

Source: *Standing Orders of the House of Commons,* 1995.

such as the Special Joint Committee on the Constitution of 1991–1992, must be established *de novo.*

*Committee Membership* Membership on the standing committees is now limited to fifteen. The guiding principle for selection of committee members by the Procedure Committee is that the official parties should have representation proportional to their membership in the House. Chief party whips assign their parties' allotment of members to the various committees, usually according to the membership on the party caucus committees that correspond roughly to the standing committees of the House. Thus, a Liberal MP who is a member of the Caucus Committee on Agriculture is likely also to be a member of the House Standing Committee on Agriculture and Agri-Food. It is generally accepted that the selection of committee members is based entirely on the recommendation of the whips, and the Procedure Committee does not interfere with a party's wishes except with regard to the number of members allocated to each party for each committee.

Membership on committees used to be subject to change simply through notification of the Clerk of the House by the chief whip. However, since rule changes in 1982, the practice of frequent rotation of committee members has been discouraged. To maintain continuity and to accentuate the specialist role of the committees, it is intended that standing-committee membership carry over from session to session during the life of a Parliament. **Associate members** who are listed at the beginning of the session are permitted to sit as alternates for committee members who are absent.

Neither Cabinet ministers nor parliamentary secretaries are selected as members of the House committees. However, MPs who are not members of a committee may still attend and take part in the public proceedings of the committee, but they may not introduce motions, vote, or be counted as part of the quorum.

*Committee Chairmen*  The chairmen and two vice-chairmen of standing committees are elected by the committees themselves, and, because the government has a majority of the members of the committees, the chairmen are normally government MPs. However Standing Orders now provide that one of the vice-chairmen must be from an opposition party. The single exception to the rule of government domination of chairmanships is the Public Accounts Committee, which since the 1960s has always been chaired by a member of the opposition. From time to time, an opposition committee member with a unique interest or expertise in the area of the committee's responsibility might be elected chairman, but such occurrences are, as yet, relatively rare in Canada.

The function of the chairmen in Canadian committees is primarily to preside over the hearings of the committee, and not to assume the aggressive and dominant role of the chairs of US congressional committees. While this is a general rule, the practice of committees in this regard varies widely from committee to committee and from chairman to chairman. Joint committees often use the device of a co-chair, with a chairman named from each of the House and the Senate.

**Committee Procedure**  Procedure in the standing committees of the Canadian House of Commons is basically the same as that for the House itself, except that Standing Orders restricting the length of speeches and the number of times of speaking do not apply, in order to ensure a more relaxed discussion of the issues. However, the chair of the committee is still expected to maintain order and decorum in the conduct of the committee's deliberations. The committees hear witnesses, mainly from the public service but also from the private sector and the academic community, and they report back to the House of Commons.

Committees of the House are all staffed by clerks who are permanent employees of the House of Commons, and the research staff of the Library of Parliament can also give specialized assistance to the members. As well, the committees are empowered to hire technical advisors and clerical and research staff, subject to there being money available and the approval in advance of the Board of Internal Economy. All committee hearings are public in Canada, although neither the press nor the general public seems to pay very much attention to the proceedings of most committees, and Standing Orders provide that the committee proceedings may be televised with the consent of the House.

**Legislative Committees**

One of the changes introduced by the Mulroney government that came to power in 1984 was to create a new type of committee of the House of Commons. These are called **legislative committees** because their role is limited to the consideration of bills after they have been introduced and given first or second reading. Legislative committees last only for the period of time coinciding with the consideration of the specific legislation. The members are appointed pretty much in the same manner and format as the standing committees, and a legislative committee may be no larger than fifteen members. The logic of this system of legislative committees is that the composition of the committees doing clause-by-clause review of legislation can be based on the experience and specialization of the members — a "match" between the subject matter of the legislation and the specific aptitudes and interests of the MPs.

One significant difference between legislative committees and standing committees is that the former do not elect their own chairmen. Rather, Standing Orders provide that at the beginning of each session the Speaker is to appoint up to twelve members, selected proportionately from the official parties in the House, to act as chairmen for legislative committees. These appointees, along with the Deputy Speaker and the assistant deputy chairmen of Committees of the Whole, constitute a **panel of chairmen** to be drawn upon, as required, to chair legislative committees as they are struck. As well, while standing committees are empowered to conduct fairly wide-ranging investigations and to call a broad range of witnesses, the legislative committees are restricted to calling government officials as witnesses on "technical matters."

**Miscellaneous Committee Functions**  Finally, mention must be made of the fact that there are a number of standing committees whose functions are basically outside the realm of legislation or government policy. The Committee on Procedure and House Affairs, for instance, ensures that the other committees are all staffed, deals with matters of elections and electoral boundaries, and oversees the administration of the internal affairs of the House in concert with the Speaker and the Board of Internal Economy.

The **Liaison Committee** is composed of the chairman of each standing committee and is empowered to allocate among the committees the block of funds provided by the Board of Internal Economy for the expenses of committee activities. The role of the Joint Committee on the Library of Parliament, while important, is mundane and self-explanatory.

The **Joint Standing Committee on Scrutiny of Regulations**[2] was originally set up in 1972 pursuant to the *Statutory Instruments Act* of 1971. The function of this committee is to scrutinize all *subordinate legislation*[3] in much the same way that the Scrutiny Committee in Britain does. Given the amount of subordinate legislation and the general extent of delegation of legislative functions to executive and bureaucratic officers, such a committee performs a control function vis-à-vis the bureaucracy. Moreover, in some ways, it complements

---

2. Previously the name of this committee was the Joint Committee on Regulations and Other Statutory Instruments.

3. This is legislation that is passed by executive or administrative officials, pursuant to "enabling legislation," which is passed by Parliament, and which vests wide discretionary authority to make subordinate regulations that have the effect of law in officials and agencies other than the supreme lawmaking agency, Parliament.

the political audit process of Parliament and gives the Senate a substantive, if limited, role in that same process.

### The Parliamentary Process

While Parliament as a symbol and as an institutional abstraction may appear to be timeless, an individual Parliament is in fact a mortal entity with a finite life span. As with any living thing, a Parliament has certain life rhythms or patterns which, while unique to each individual Parliament, are also, in certain respects, common to all. In the widest time span, all Parliaments are "spawned" by the return of the election writs, and "born" in the executive prerogative act of being **summoned** by the governor-general. When a Parliament has reached the end of its life span, it is **dissolved**, again through the exercise of an executive prerogative by the governor-general, and the cycle begins anew with the calling of an election.

There are usually a number of smaller cycles within the life of a Parliament. We call these **sessions** and they begin with the summoning of Parliament, at which time a **speech from the throne** outlines the legislative goals of the government. The session ends with Parliament's being **prorogued** by the governor-general on the advice of the prime minister. Parliamentary sessions are generally expected to be annual, but some sessions have been only a few weeks and one in the early 1980s lasted nearly four years. Within sessions there will be a number of **recesses** when the House is **adjourned** for an extended period. Some recesses are predictable, for example, the Christmas Recess and the Summer Recess, but others can occur at almost any time, on the whim of the government.

The main focus of this section is to describe the processes in which a Parliament is engaged throughout its life span. We will discuss first the "master process" of **parliamentarism**, which is ordered public debate. Then we will look at the parliamentary role in the policy process, the political and financial audit processes, and the legislative process. However, before proceeding, it is important to say a few words about the daily rhythms of parliamentary life, which go on week after week, session after session, while the House of Commons is sitting.

**The Daily Routine**  While we are discussing the *daily* routine of the House, it is important to note that all days are not exactly the same on the weekly agenda. For instance, the hour set aside for private members' business is at different times on different days, and daily sittings begin and end at different times during the week. As well, there are cycles within a session, such as the business of supply, which has a cycle linked to the fiscal year and the imperatives of the expenditure budget. However, it is still possible to identify a fairly consistent order of business for the daily sittings of the House.

Table 19.1 shows the weekly agenda of House business. *Routine business* includes a wide range of formal activity and statements that, while not usually very exciting, are nevertheless a necessary part of the business of Parliament. These include, for instance, the tabling of documents, reports, and petitions; the introduction of bills before they are given first reading; ministerial state-

**TABLE 19.1**

Weekly Agenda of the House of Commons

| Time | Monday | Tuesday | Wednesday | Thursday | Friday |
|------|--------|---------|-----------|----------|--------|
| 10:00 | | Prayer | | Prayer | Prayer |
| | | RP and GO | | RP and GO | GO |
| 11:00 | Prayer | | | | MS |
| | PMB | | | | OQP |
| 12:00 | RP and GO | | | | RP and GO |
| 1:00 | | | | | |
| 1:30 | | | | | PMB |
| 2:00 | MS | MS | Prayer MS | MS | |
| 2:30 | OQP | OQP | OQP | OQP | |
| 3:00 | RP | GO | RP | GO | |
| 4:00 | and | | GO | | |
| 5:00 | | | | | |
| 5:30 | GO | PMB | PMB | PMB | |
| 6:00 | | | | | |
| 6:30 | Adjournment or Debate | | | | |

Abbreviations: GO: Government Orders; MS: Members' Statements; OQP: Oral Question Period; PMB: Private Members' Business; RP: Routine Procedures.

Source: Derived from *Standing Orders of the House of Commons*, 1995.

ments; motions; and replies to written questions. **Government orders** are the ongoing business of debating government legislation, and **private members' business** is the consideration of private members' bills. All of these will be discussed in more detail when we consider the legislative process.

### The Process of Debate: Order, Decorum, and Privilege

Some discussion has already been devoted to the basic functions of the Canadian Parliament. However, we have only briefly touched upon the fact that the general instrument or technique whereby Parliament performs all of these functions is **debate**. Above all else, the House of Commons and the Senate would appear, to an uninitiated observer, primarily as forums of debate. Even the root of the word *parliament* is derived from the French verb *parler* — 'to speak'. It is debate that occupies the bulk of time in the parliamentary day, and the rules of debate are therefore an important dimension of the parliamentary process. While the discussion below is focused on the House of Commons, for the most part, the rules are the same or very similar in the Senate.

**The Rules of Debate**  The rules of debate in the House, as already pointed out, are enforced by the Speaker or, in the Speaker's absence, by the Deputy Speaker or the deputy chairman of committees. The chair does not exercise control over debate in an arbitrary fashion; there are definite rules and procedures, which the chair is called upon to apply from time to time in the course of debate. It is a basic principle that every member who wishes to speak to a question should be permitted to do so. The problem faced by the Speaker is, therefore, not who should be permitted to speak, but who should speak first. The procedure for being recognized by the Speaker, or for catching the Speaker's eye, is for the member wishing to speak to rise in his or her place in the House. The Speaker attempts to switch back and forth from the government side of the House to the opposition side, to permit a fair alternation of speakers by party.

The Speaker's job has been greatly simplified through the practice of the party whips' supplying the Speaker with a daily list of members who wish to speak on that day. In the Question Period, it is traditional for the Speaker first to recognize a frontbencher from the Official Opposition, usually the leader, and then to turn to the leader of one of the minor opposition parties. In debates, however, the basic rule is that the parties themselves have worked out which of their members they wish to have heard and in which order, and the Speaker merely rotates from one party to another. If the whips have done their job, there will be only one person from a given party rising to address the House at any given time.

Speeches in the House have a time limit of twenty minutes when the Speaker is in the chair, and no member may speak more than once on any question. The exceptions to this rule are the prime minister, the leader of the Official Opposition, any minister moving a government order, and any member making a motion of non-confidence in the government, all of whom may speak more than once, and for longer than the normal time limit. A ten-minute time limit on speeches is specified for a number of debatable motions, special debates, private members' bills, and debates during the report stage of a government bill.

It is a convention of parliamentary debate that members should not read their speeches but should deliver them *extemporaneously*. This is not a written rule, however, and is difficult to enforce stringently. The result is that any member who so desires will read the speech, with some kidding and heckling from other members who observe the practice. The stock reply by a member who is chided for reading a speech is that he or she is merely following extensive notes very closely or that it couldn't be true because the member can't read.

There is a similar rule that the member may not repeat a point in a speech and that arguments made previously by other members may not be repeated. The former is applied infrequently by the Speaker, and the latter never; it defies enforcement. There are also rules requiring relevance in debate, which are similarly difficult to apply. The major impetus for relevance in speeches comes from the party whips, who try to ensure that time is not wasted during important debates (unless, of course, the tactic is to delay by filibuster). As we shall see, there are certain debates, such as the Throne Speech Debate and the Budget Debate, to which the requirement of relevance does not apply at all.

In addition to the more explicit rules of debate, there is a general rule that members should not use what is euphemistically called **unparliamentary language.** What this means is that the members should treat each other with politeness and should not revert to name-calling or *ad hominem* arguments in debate. The members generally abide by this rule, and it is seldom that the Speaker is called upon to rebuke a member for the use of unparliamentary language. However, the Speaker is charged with the responsibility for preserving order and decorum and may request that a member withdraw an unparliamentary remark, such as accusing a fellow member of lying. If the member refuses to withdraw the offensive comment, the Speaker will "name" the member and have the sergeant-at-arms escort him or her out of the chamber. It is to be noted that the truth or accuracy of the unparliamentary remark is not an acceptable defence!

Quite often there can be pretty heavy heckling and, often, rather bawdy exchanges among members who do not have the floor. Unparliamentary comments by members other than the member who has the floor usually go unrecognized formally by the chair, and, if recorded at all, appear in *Hansard* as "Some Hon. Members: 'Oh, Oh!' " The phrase "Oh, Oh!" is a cryptic euphemism for earthy comments ranging from those that cast aspersions on the honourable member's ancestry to harmless but quaint colloquialisms such as "yer mother wears army boots," "fuddle-duddle," "horsefeathers," or "bull-twaddle." It is not unheard of for frontbenchers on both sides of the House to contribute surreptitiously but enthusiastically to such ribaldry.

**Obligations of MPs**  The Standing Orders and the *Parliament of Canada Act* impose a fairly strict code of conduct on MPs. Members are expected to be present at all sittings of the House unless they are absent in order to be able to carry out other parliamentary or government responsibilities. However, it is impossible to prove that a member's truancy is due to sloth, indifference, or frivolity rather than to important constituency responsibilites; as a result, members are virtually never chastised for absences, many of which occur, not surprisingly, on Mondays and Fridays.

Members are also required to maintain a strict decorum in the House. Members must stand while speaking, and their speeches, remarks, and questions must be directed at the Speaker, not at a minister or other member. Fellow members of the House are always referred to in the third person, not by their names, but as "the Honourable Member" or "the Honourable Minister." MPs must not walk between the Speaker's chair and the member who has the floor, and when the House adjourns, the chair must leave the chamber before the rest of the House is permitted to rise. Finally, bribery and "influence peddling" are serious offences that are punishable by imprisonment and are naturally taken very seriously by all MPs.

**Parliamentary Privilege**  While MPs must abide by a strict code of conduct, the other side of the coin is that they are protected from frivolous or arbitrary interference while carrying out their parliamentary responsibilities. **Parliamentary privilege** is the sum of the rights and privileges of both the Senate and the House of Commons, and it functions to place Parliament in a position above all other institutions and individuals in the land. These rights are held by Parliament as a whole and by each individual MP and senator. They include such rights as freedom from arrest arising out of civil action while the House is in session, exemption from jury duty or from subpoena as a witness, and protection from libel actions for the content of speeches in the House and publications of the House. Among other things, these protections allow MPs to be candidly and bluntly critical of the behaviour of ministers of the Crown without fear of nuisance suits alleging libel or slander.

Another part of parliamentary privilege in Canada is the right of parliamentary committees to hear witnesses under oath. Breaches of privilege are considered to be analogous to contempt of court, and are punishable by imprisonment, fine, or censure by the House itself. For matters of privilege, the House can act as a court, calling witnesses "before the Bar of the House of Commons" and meting out punishments to both its own members and outsiders who have acted in contempt of Parliament.

While still important symbolically, the practical significance of parliamentary privilege has waned. Its significance today is primarily as a reminder to the public, the media, and the MPs themselves of the principles of freedom of speech and freedom from arrest, which were at one time not so widely accepted as they are today. Occasionally today, a member will rise in the House on a question of privilege to complain about statements made about him or her in the press, or to complain about the conduct of another member, but in many cases the question raised has very little to do with privilege. As W. F. Dawson has pointed out,

> at the root of the problem is the ignorance of the Canadian House of the true meaning of privilege, which is essentially the defensive weapon of a legislature which has been used to protect itself against interference. The Canadian House has never had to fear such trouble and has never bothered to develop a defence.[4]

Sporadic attempts to raise questions of privilege in the Canadian House of Commons have been motivated more by partisan needs and not by genuine threats to the security and freedom of the House.

**Decisions of the House**  Debates in the House of Commons that have been commenced by a motion inevitably end in a vote. The basic rule in a parliamentary system is that a majority of those present in the House decide the outcome of a motion. When debate on the motion has been concluded, the Speaker puts the question to the House by reading the main motion and any amendments. Those in agreement say "yea" and those against say "nay," and the Speaker announces which side has won — according to personal interpre-

---

4. W. F. Dawson, *Procedure in the Canadian House of Commons* (Toronto: University of Toronto Press, 1962), p. 54.

tation. If at least five members rise to demand a recorded vote or a **division**, the **division bells** are rung, to inform members not sitting in the House at the time that a division is about to occur.

*The Division Bells*  Traditionally the division bells could be rung for as long as necessary to allow the party whips to round up as many votes as are available. However, in the spring of 1982, the opposition whips simply refused to report to the Speaker that they had assembled their troops and were ready for the vote. As a result the bells rang for a full two weeks, during which period, the vote had to be delayed and, because of the grating noise of the bells, no other work could be carried out on Parliament Hill either.

To counter this tactic, Standing Orders were amended to set a fifteen-minute (thirty minutes for non-debatable motions) time limit for the whips to round up their supporters. This allows ample time to summon members from offices and other places within the Parliament Buildings. When the whips of all parties are content that they have as many as possible of their members present (or after fifteen or thirty minutes) the doors of the House are closed and the vote is taken. As well, in response to the bell-ringing incident, the grating fire-alarm-type bells were replaced throughout the Parliament Buildings with less intrusive, but nevertheless insistent, intermittent "bongs." (They are not, however, referred to as division bongs!) Members register their votes by standing in their places in the House of Commons to be counted by the Clerk of the House. When the vote is counted and recorded, the Speaker announces the outcome.

Recorded votes in the House are very time-consuming, so it is fortunate that many votes are settled without a formal division. In most circumstances, that is, in majority-government situations, it is obvious to all members that the government will be able to carry any motion. In recognition of this, when interparty relations are fairly cordial, a recorded vote will be taken only on very important motions such as non-confidence motions and second reading of government bills. For the most part, motions are carried by a voice vote, with the Speaker declaring the outcome.

*Pairing*  A member who is going to be absent from the House for a time will often arrange to **pair** with a member from the opposite side of the House. This means that both members agree not to vote on division if one of them is absent from the House. While the whips may register their paired members in a registry kept at the table, this practice is based only on gentleman's agreement. It is done because it means that, even if many members are absent from the House, there is no danger that the government will fall by mistake. The practice of pairing is obviously more important in the situation of a minority government, or when the government majority is very slim, than when the government has a healthy majority.

The supervision of pairing in the House is usually left to the whips, who organize pairs for members and who ensure that their own members who are paired honour their pair on division. While a paired member can still legally "break the pair" and vote anyway, if this happened deliberately, it would be viewed by the other members as a serious breach of parliamentary etiquette and the offending member would be severely reprimanded by his or her party. Pairing works only because all parties honour the practice. It is interesting to note that on one occasion in 1926, the government was actually defeated in the House by one vote because of an unintentional broken pair, and although everyone was embarrassed, the vote stood and the government was forced to resign.

*Free Votes* Rarely, decisions of the House are taken in a situation where the "whips are off" and members are not bound by party discipline. Issues such as divorce, abortion, and capital punishment are essentially issues of personal morality or ethics and sometimes the government will allow legislation in these areas to be decided without partisan interference. The motive of the government may be to duck an issue that might prove divisive at the next election, or the government may genuinely be either deeply divided internally or indifferent to the outcome.

In the situation of a free vote, while frontbenchers of all parties might try to sway their backbench colleagues, party loyalty is not usually a good predictor of the outcome. As well, in a free vote, the government's fate does not hang in the balance, because such votes are, by definition, not matters of confidence. While we will see free votes from time to time in the future, because they are not a part of the tradition of Cabinet government, they likely will continue to be the exception rather than the rule.

## ▶ PARLIAMENTARY PROCESSES

As we have seen earlier, the floor of the House itself is far more suited to the adversarial process of partisan debate than to creative modifications and improvements of government policy proposals. At most, the policy impact of the opposition on the floor of the House will be limited to obstruction, delaying tactics, and bargaining with the government whips and House leader for small concessions and compromises.

By contrast, committee proceedings are less formal, and in the case of legislative committees, less in the public eye than the proceedings on the floor of the legislature. This means that there is room for a more cooperative and conciliatory approach on the part of the committee members, regardless of party differences. Thus, the effective policy role of Parliament is almost exclusively carried out by the various standing, special, and joint committees that conduct prelegislative investigations and by the special, standing, or legislative committees that refine and polish legislation that is before the House.

### Committees and the Policy Process

It has become common in Canada for Parliamentary committees to be used as investigatory bodies to examine policy proposals before the legislative stage. In this way, the committees may be able to have some influence at both the priority-setting and the formulation stages of the policy process. A House committee or a joint committee can travel across the country, hearing testimony submitted by interested parties and gathering information that ultimately can be used by the Cabinet in setting priorities. The recommendations that the committee comes up with are often less important than the data it gathers about the attitudes of the public towards a particular issue, which are a signal to the prime minister as to the political viability of various policy options.

Parliamentary committees can also have an influence in the formulation stage of policy determination. Here committees act as information gatherers, often with respect to a specific set of policy options or instrument choices, such as those set down in government white papers, green papers, or other position papers of any colour at all. In such cases, the priority has already been set, and the task of the committee is to discover public attitudes to the various options for implementation before the government commits itself with draft legislation.

**Prelegislative Committees**  In their **prelegislative role**, as opposed to their legislative role, committees can take a more objective, problem-solving approach in their deliberations. Despite the fact that they must still formally report back to the highly adversarial floor of the House of Commons, investigative committees can afford to be less partisan than committees involved in the refining of government legislation. At the prelegislative phase, the government is not as locked into a policy, and if the findings of the committee differ from the government's position, the government can selectively heed the committee's recommendations without losing face.

Furthermore, whereas a legislative committee's report on a government bill is subject to debate and amendments on the floor of the House at the report stage, the reports of prelegislative committee investigations need not be debated at all. That is not to say that government and opposition members on an investigative committee will not differ. Indeed, they very often do, and members who disagree with the majority position often submit **minority reports**. As well, because the normal partisan lines are not so rigid in these committees, it is not unusual for minority reports to come even from government members.

*Public Participation*  Perhaps the most significant contribution that committees of the House of Commons can bring to the policy process at the prelegislative stage is the ability to conduct hearings and listen sympathetically to the submissions of the public. Here the committees can augment the government-sponsored task forces and royal commissions and the bureaucratic political advisory bodies in sounding public attitudes before any concrete policy commitments have been made. Thus, House committees can stimulate wider participation in the policy process and create feelings of efficacy among both the public and the MPs.

However, the extent to which investigatory committees will actually affect policy will depend entirely on the quality of the information they gather and how it compares with information gathered through other agencies. In short, there is a definite potential for additional input to the policy process through the use of parliamentary committees at the earlier stages of the process. The development of that potential will depend on the willingness of the government to utilize it fully, and on the recognition by the public and the committees themselves that such inputs can seldom be accepted without the double check of other sources of advice. There must be a realistic understanding that implementation of a committee recommendation is not automatically ensured, particularly if there exists a mass of technical advice that contradicts the committee findings.

*Committee Influence on Government* Prelegislative committees became more important after the introduction of procedural reforms in 1982. These committees, often sub-committees of a standing committee, are established by the House or the standing committee. The members remain with the committee for the duration of its work — usually about six months. The committees hear witnesses representing the stakeholders in the policy community and other interested Canadians and they may hire expert research support to assist in the development of their recommendations. Eventually, such investigatory committees table a report complete with recommendations.

The major sources of the influence of prelegislative committees lie in the experience the committee members develop, the research they conduct, and the broadly inclusive hearings they hold. As well, the fact that, in general, committee members from all parties often develop an in-group common view and often file a unanimous or consensus report, gives their recommendations credibility with the government. The committees have become still more influential because their reports are public and because the government is obliged to table an open reply to their recommendations within sixty sitting days of receipt of the report. They therefore cannot be merely ignored by government, and they often serve to influence the agenda of policy discussions in a way quite uncharacteristic of other parliamentary institutions.

Since changes in 1986, the standing committees have been given greater freedom to initiate investigations of the various policy concerns of the departments coming under their purview. While the standing committees always played this role with respect to the detailed scrutiny of departmental estimates, they now have more leeway to determine *what* they are going to investigate. This freeing-up of the standing committees to set their own agendas, coupled with the assignment, to a large extent, of the onerous responsibility for dealing with legislation after second reading to legislative committees, allows them to perform some of the investigative tasks previously assigned to special committees, or *ad hoc* parliamentary task forces.

**Refining Government Policy** The most important policy function of committees of the House of Commons is the detailed, clause-by-clause examination and refining of government bills. A bill is normally referred to a legislative committee after it has been given second reading, although, as we shall see when we consider the legislative process, the referral to committee can now happen before second reading as well. The committee studies the legislative proposal, hears witnesses from the public service and experts from other sectors, and proposes changes it feels would improve the quality or clarity of the end product. Legislative committees can perform this function much more effectively than the House itself, because their pattern of debate is procedurally less restrictive and the group dynamic is less partisan. It is possible for the committee members to informally discuss, rather than formally debate, the issues involved. Moreover, the members of legislative committees are also selected because they are generally more attuned to the specifics of the bill that is before them than are the rank-and-file members of the House.

Furthermore, if the committee is dealing with the bill after second reading, the principle of the legislation has already been accepted by the House. Consequently, having lost the main battle, the focus of the committee's deliberations can be brought to bear on improving the end product. While the opposition committee members may still try to sneak substantive changes into a bill under the guise of improving the wording, the emphasis in committee is upon "good-faith" negotiations and mutual respect rather than trickery.

**The Limits to Committee Influence** It is perhaps a paradox that, on second reading, opposition MPs perform the adversarial function of opposing the government's motion, and then, in committee, those same individuals will shift their role to positive and constructive criticism and often propose amendments to the bill that are accepted on merit by the government. This is partly because the matters the committees discuss — the details — are less likely to lend themselves to partisan disputes. However, it must be remembered that partisanship runs deep in the House of Commons. Many disagreements, even in committees, do follow party lines, and party discipline in committees has to be enforced by the whips much in the same way as it is in House. If an opposition committee member proposes an amendment to which the government is strongly opposed, the whips will be "on" and the amendment will be defeated by the government majority on the committee.

There are some other limitations and weaknesses in the committee system that must be considered to clarify its role in the policy process. The first and most obvious is that a committee considering a government bill reports back to the House of Commons. This means that all decisions made in committee are merely decisions to recommend something to the House, and have no final or binding effect by themselves. At the report stage, a recommendation of the committee can be simply reversed by a majority vote of the whole House. In sum, then, the basic tasks of committees in dealing with government bills are to attempt to refine the legislation, to attempt to foresee difficulties that might arise in the implementation or enforcement of the legislation, and to make such amendments as are necessary to achieve the desired improvements. Committees dealing with bills that have already passed second reading are precluded, by the rules of procedure, from making substantive changes in the legislation, and are precluded, by party discipline and the recommendatory nature of their decisions, from making even small changes with which the government does not agree.

### The Political Audit Process
While the parliamentary audit of the government's record goes on at all stages of government legislation and through opposition-party press releases, the bulk

of such criticism comes out through various procedural devices that are an institutionalized part of the parliamentary process. Each of these gives the opposition the opportunity to take pot shots at the government, to criticize its policy initiatives, and in general to keep the ministers honest and publicly accountable for their actions. Some of these mechanisms at the disposal of the opposition deserve more detailed mention.

**The Throne Speech Debate** The Standing Orders of the House of Commons provide for a debate on the Address in Reply to the Speech from the Throne. The **Speech from the Throne** is prepared by the closest advisors to the prime minister and read by the governor-general to a joint sitting of the House of Commons and the Senate. In this speech, which is delivered at the opening of each session of Parliament, there is a review of the "state of the nation" and a statement of the legislative program of the government in the coming session. Six days are set aside for opposition criticism and comment on the record of the government, and on these six days, which need not be held consecutively, the normal rules of relevancy that apply in debates in the House are suspended. Backbench members have the opportunity to speak their minds on anything that has been bothering them or any matter of special concern to their constituents, while government frontbenchers may use the occasion to defend aspects of proposed government policy and to tout past government accomplishments.

The tendency in the **Throne Speech Debate** is for the backbenchers to make special pleas for local needs and interests, and for the opposition frontbenchers to use the debate to introduce motions of non-confidence in the government. The subject matter of the Throne Speech Debate, while varied, does not usually involve specific policy proposals of the government, but tends to be devoted more to broad criticisms and defences of the record. To the extent that the speeches of the various MPs are reported in their home newspapers, this debate is helpful in showing the voters that their MP in Ottawa is working on their behalf. Similarly, to the extent that the frontbench speeches of the opposition parties are reported in the news media, the Throne Speech Debate functions to publicize the real and imagined shortcomings of the government as seen through opposition eyes.

**The Budget Debate** The second free-for-all debate that occurs during the parliamentary year (the first is the Throne Speech Debate) is the **Budget Debate**, during which the backbenchers are permitted to put on record their own comments on the government's overall financial policy for the benefit of their constituents and the nation. The Budget Debate begins after the minister of Finance has given the Budget Speech in the House of Commons, and it lasts for four days. As with the Throne Speech Debate, the relevancy rule for speeches is more relaxed and MPs can wander fairly far afield in seeking to embarrass the government or to make themselves look good, although they are encouraged to speak to the ways-and-means proposals set down in the Budget. This debate is, in fact, held on a government motion that "this House approves in general the budgetary policy of the government" and ends at the end of the fourth day of debate when the Speaker must put the question to the House. A defeat of this motion constitutes a vote of non-confidence and would force the prime minister to resign.

**Allotted Days**  A total of twenty days, spread over three separate supply periods, is allotted to the opposition. On these **allotted days**, also called **Opposition Days**, opposition motions take precedence over government business, and, with the exception of the mover and seconder of the motion, members' speeches are limited to twenty minutes. The function of these allotted days was traditionally to permit the opposition ample opportunity to criticize the government's spending policy. However, today the debates on allotted days cover a wide range of issues and constitute an important part of the political audit function of the House. These debates force the government to defend its policies publicly against tough opposition criticism, and in fact, five or six of these Opposition Days usually end in confidence votes. Their effectiveness, however, is considerably diminished by the fact that they rarely receive much media attention.

**Emergency Debates**  Standing Order (SO) 52 of the House of Commons provides for a motion to adjourn the House "for the purpose of discussing a specific and important matter requiring urgent consideration." If a matter has arisen suddenly and is not likely to be brought before the House of Commons in any other way, and if it is not a purely administrative matter, this standing order permits a special debate to consider it. The Speaker is given final say as to whether the matter is urgent and whether it is a matter for consideration under SO 52. If the Speaker decides the matter is not urgent or that it can be dealt with through more routine procedures, he or she is not required to give reasons for the decision, nor is the motion debatable.

If the Speaker decides that the matter is sufficiently urgent to require further consideration, the motion to adjourn is held over until an evening sitting of the House, at which time the matter is debated. The Speaker can declare the motion to adjourn carried when he or she "is satisfied that the debate has been concluded," and can forthwith adjourn the House until the next day. Otherwise, at midnight, Monday to Thursday, or at four p.m. on Friday the Speaker declares the motion carried and the House adjourns.

A time limit of twenty minutes is placed on speeches in an emergency debate. While such debates are not granted frequently, when they occur, emergency debates permit the opposition to raise issues with which the government is not dealing in the House, and to make public their opinion that the government should be doing something. While a debate under Standing Order 52 will not be granted to discuss something the government has already done but with which the opposition disagrees, it is an important means for pointing out something that the government should be doing but is not. Moreover, it is not necessary that the Speaker grant the request for a debate in order for this standing order to serve its purpose. Simply by requesting a debate, the opposition is suggesting that something is amiss and requires attention.

Another procedural device in the Standing Orders is a provision that allows members to make a sixty-second statement immediately before Question Period. This device functions to allow backbench MPs to put a point of view on the record or get something off their chests with a minimum of disruption to the routine business of the House of Commons. The time allotted for such **members' statements** is limited to fifteen minutes, after which the House moves directly into Oral Question Period.

**Questions in the House** Any backbencher, including those on the government side of the House, can ask a question of a minister, but, because of party discipline, because the government backbencher can usually get the desired information without a formal question, and because the Speaker traditionally recognizes opposition members in Question Period more often than government members, the Question Period has become a time almost exclusively for opposition questions.

*Written Questions* Questions simply seeking information from a minister of the Crown are normally written down and placed on the Order Paper. The answers to such **questions on the Order Paper** are simply handed to the Clerk of the House and subsequently printed in *Hansard*. The function of this form of question is to assist MPs in gathering information relevant to their interests and those of their constituents. However, in some cases the opposition will ask questions simply to get, on the record, information that might be embarrassing to the government in the future. Sometimes, if the answer is potentially embarrassing, an opposition member will ask for an oral answer. Oral answers are requested by placing an asterisk beside the written question. No member may have more than three such **starred questions** on the Order Paper at the same time.

*Oral Questions* More important, however, than either the written question or the starred questions, are those asked during the daily forty-five-minute **Oral Question Period**. Its purpose is to permit a member to ask a minister questions on matters of urgency, or questions that should be answered immediately rather than placed on the Order Paper. The Speaker is formally empowered to direct that an oral question is not urgent and therefore should be placed on the Order Paper, although in practice this stipulation is seldom invoked. Generally, the Oral Question Period, particularly since it is that part of the parliamentary day that is usually seen on our television sets and reported in the press, is an opportunity for the opposition to ask questions that could potentially embarrass the government.

An oral question must be very carefully phrased, in order to force the minister to answer it on the opposition's terms, for there is no debate permitted during Question Period. Sometimes a member will receive the permission of the Speaker to ask one or more **supplementary** questions if the minister has evaded the point of the main question. However, even then, it is difficult to pin down a minister who is determined to be evasive. Moreover, there is no requirement that a minister answer an oral quetion, only that he or she not mislead or lie to the House. Sometimes, if a minister is not well briefed on an issue that is the subject of an oral question, he or she will "take the question as 'notice'" and promise to provide the answer at some time in the future. However, this does not happen very much because it is taken as a sign of unpreparedness or incompetence.

One of the more entertaining features of the Oral Question Period is the seemingly random banter that is carried on by members who do not have the floor. Such heckling and wisecracking, which is often reported verbatim in *Hansard,* provides some opportunity for backbenchers on both sides of the House to put a few comments on the record on behalf of their side. What usually ensues is a verbal fencing match, with opposition members sparring with the ministers, attempting to bait them into saying something that will embarrass the government. The minister must keep cool and not be goaded into saying anything more than is necessary to provide factual information or, as is often the case, to gracefully and eloquently evade the question.

*The "Late Show"* A member who is not satisfied with the answer to a question may serve notice of an intention to raise the matter "on the adjournment" of the House. **Questions on the adjournment**, often referred to as the **"late show,"** provides for a thirty-minute debate at the termination of the daily sitting, wherein up to three members are recognized by the Speaker and are given seven minutes each to speak. Questions asked on the adjournment are more important in Britain than in Canada, but even here they provide an opportunity to debate a question that would not be debatable in Oral Question Period. Generally, adjournment debates are simply another opportunity for the opposition members to attempt to embarrass the government and for all members to raise questions involving the interests of their particular constituencies or regions.

*The Effectiveness of Questions* Questions in the House perform two functions. First, they can provide the MP with information. Second, they can give the opposition an opportunity to expose the shortcomings of the government. However, the limitations on questions as a device for parliamentary criticism of the government are many. In the first place, the minister may refuse to answer the question on the grounds that a government policy statement is forthcoming, or that to answer would be a breach of national security. Second, in the case of questions on the Order Paper, the minister can take a long time to answer the question, or may even choose not to answer at all. As well, as explained above, a minister can always take the question as "notice" and refuse to answer "at this time."

At the end of each session of Parliament, there is always a long list of unanswered questions left on the Order Paper that probably never will be answered. Finally, the minister can simply refuse to answer the question, even in Oral Question Period, without offering a reason. There is nothing that compels a minister to answer parliamentary questions, although for political reasons a minister cannot afford to treat Parliament with indifference or disdain. Furthermore, unanswered questions get asked over and over again, until either an answer is obtained or the public is made aware of the fact that a minister is covering up or withholding information from the Canadian people.

Perhaps the most important limitation of the Question Period as a tool to facilitate the political audit function of Parliament is the simple fact that most of the exchanges that occur between opposition members and ministers deteriorate to mere banter. Often this is a relatively friendly exchange of *bon mots* and "in" jokes and does not become elevated to the discussion of any matters of substance. The questions asked are loaded, and the answers given are usually evasive and designed to defuse the question rather than to answer it.

Once in a while, however, Question Period provides truly bitter exchanges between members, particularly if a member is alleging personal improprieties on the part of a minister. These "scandal-mongering" type of questions inevitably result in much name-calling by the principals and jeering by the rest. Sometimes such exchanges cause a minister to blurt out information the government would have preferred to keep quiet or to appear in a bad light because he or she is angry.

Thus, while at times Question Period does not accomplish anything of substance, it functions to keep the government alert. Corruption in high places is sometimes uncovered through the opposition's use of Question Period, and the threat of such public exposure perhaps serves as a conscience for the government. Despite its limitations, therefore, Question Period remains one of Parliament's most important procedural devices for criticizing the Cabinet and for auditing the record of the government.

**Conclusion: The Political Audit Process**  Opportunity for broad criticism of government policy comes up during the proceedings on public bills and at almost all stages of parliamentary debate, but on these occasions the debate is usually restricted to the specific legislation being considered. In other words, the Speaker will enforce the relevancy requirement for all speeches at all stages in the normal process of passing public bills. Thus, the best opportunity for broadly criticizing the Cabinet and publicly auditing the government's record occurs in the various special debates, Opposition Days, and Question Period.

The overall effectiveness of the opposition in Parliament as an auditor of the record of the government is lessened by that lack of information and expertise that is the Achilles' heel of all parliamentarians in the policy process. Nevertheless, there is still an important function to be performed here, and with the much broadened forum provided by the televising of Parliament, the opposition can function as an effective political auditor, even though parties that are not lucky enough to form the government can have only a limited role as policy makers.

**The Financial Audit Process**
The committees of the House of Commons have two main functions to perform in the financial audit process. They are delegated the responsibility for detailed scrutiny of the estimates before the supply bills are introduced formally and given first reading. In this sense they perform a sort of **pre-audit** of proposed government expenditures before the money is voted. As well, the Public Accounts Committee is responsible for performing a parliamentary **post-audit** of the Public Accounts and the Report of the Auditor General.

**Detailed Scrutiny of Estimates: The Business of Supply** Before the procedural changes of 1969 abolished the Committee of Supply, it was the responsibility of that committee of the whole to go over the annual expenditure estimates of each department in detail. Since then, in an effort to streamline the process and to allow individual MPs to become more specialized, the estimates for each department go instead to the appropriate standing committee for detailed scrutiny. Thus, for instance, the estimates of the Department of Health are reviewed by the Standing Committee on Health, the Department of National Defence estimates are reviewed by the Standing Committee on National Defence and Veterans Affairs, and so forth. While this has meant a large saving of time for the House of Commons, it has increased commensurately the amount of effort each individual member must spend in committee. Currently, by far the largest part of time MPs spend in committees is devoted to the consideration of the estimates before the supply bill is formally introduced in the House.[5]

The ability of a standing committee to effectively criticize the spending plans of a given department is limited, once again, by the lack of technical expertise in the committee. By the time the estimates reach Parliament, they have already run the gauntlet of criticism from the Treasury Board, the Treasury Board Secretariat, and departmental financial officers. Moreover, it is those very same departmental officials who are called as witnesses to back up or explain the estimates of the department to the committee.

Recent changes to procedures have made it possible for the standing committees to look at the departmental spending plans at an earlier stage of the expenditure-management cycle. This has been facilitated by changes to the executive side of the expenditure-management system. Now departments are required to submit "business plans" that set down the departmental management strategy and program priorities in a minimum three-year context. These business plans must be summarized in a departmental "outlook paper," which is given to the appropriate standing committee before it has to deal with the estimates. This has the advantage of allowing the committee members to acquire a sense of the bigger picture, by seeing the department's current-year estimates in the context of its longer-term priorities and management strategies. It is still too early to tell what effect this will have on the overall financial audit role of Parliament.

Despite these positive changes to the system, it is unlikely that the standing committee will be able to do much more than fine-tune the estimates, and, in fact, the department usually finds that getting the estimates through the Treasury Board Secretariat is far more difficult than getting them passed by the standing committee. However, the opposition parties can still, to some extent, use the consideration of the estimates in committee as an additional forum for open criticism of the government's programs and policy priorities. The fact that each department must publicly justify its estimated expenditures in committee probably prevents carelessness in the preparation of the estimates in

---

5. In fact, there is never enough time to consider the estimates thoroughly in committee. Standing Orders state that the estimates "shall be deemed to have been reported" by May 31 whether the committee is through with them or not.

the first place. It is in this sense that the committee stage of the estimates is at least as important for the audit function of Parliament as it is for improving the detailed estimates.

Finally, we should point out that the 1995 expenditure-mangement system is committed to making the budget-preparation process more **open**. Hence, Cabinet is now expected to develop a pre-Budget consultation strategy whereby Parliament and other interested groups and individuals may make suggestions to the minister of Finance before the Budget is finalized. To assist in this consultation process, the minister of Finance releases a series of budget-consultation papers that outline the basic projections and forecasts upon which the Budget will be based. While these are public documents, they are presented formally to the House Standing Committee on Finance, which goes over them in detail and makes formal recommendations to the minister before the final review of budget strategies in Cabinet. This consultation process was instituted for the first time in October 1994 (for the 1995 budget) and it is impossible to say yet whether the Standing Committee on Finance had any substantive impact on that very tough budget.

**The Public Accounts Committee: The Post-Audit Function**  The Public Accounts Committee is perhaps the most specialized of the standing committees. While, like other committees, it is controlled numerically by the government party, unlike the other standing committees, Public Accounts has had, since 1957, an opposition member as its chair. Furthermore, the auditor general, who is an independent officer of Parliament with a large and expert support staff, makes the job of the committee easier by providing it with expert assistance in scrutinizing the accounts of the government's expenditures. The functions of the Public Accounts Committee are to investigate the financial shortcomings of the government, as identified in the Report of the Auditor General, and as discovered through independent examination of the Public Accounts by the committee members themselves, and to make recommendations to the government as to how it might improve its spending practices.

The basic weakness of this procedure as a meaningful exercise of control over the financial affairs of the government is that the government is often unable to, or chooses not to, heed the recommendations. Each year, the auditor general lists a number of recommendations, made over the past years by the Public Accounts Committee, which have never been implemented by the government. Furthermore, the committee receives the Public Accounts late in the session, at which time the recommendations of the committee seem out of date. Because this review is a *post-audit*, many of the recommendations are analogous to telling the government to shut the barn door long after the horse has gone. However, the departments do pay attention to the recommendations of the auditor general and most are implemented. This acceptance of the AG's recommendations is made easier because it is normal practice for the department to be consulted before the AG's report is finalized.

To summarize, the Public Accounts Committee has considerable *potential* for investigating and publicizing the financial bungling and sleight-of-hand of the government and of government officials, but as yet it has been more a gadfly than a watchdog. The committee reports directly to the House, as do all standing committees, but the tabling of the committee report does not produce any debate. It is simply received by the House, has a short moment of glory in the media, and is quickly forgotten by the public and ignored by the government. This committee could be made more effective by making debate of its report mandatory, and by creating a greater public consciousness of the importance of its role and the relevance to the citizen of its recommendations. We will say more about the role of the auditor general and the post-audit function in our discussion of the bureaucracy.

### The Legislative Process

Once a policy has been formulated and a draft of the proposed legislation has been completed by the Department of Justice, it is then introduced in Parliament by the minister responsible for that particular policy area. All bills must be passed by both the House and the Senate, and while government bills, other than money bills, may be introduced first in either chamber, the practice is that this occurs almost exclusively in the lower house. The reasons for this are that the Senate is expected to be a sober *second* thought and that almost all of the ministers who introduce government bills are sitting in the House of Commons.

At the introductory stage of the legislative process, the policy proposal takes the form of a **bill**. When a bill has been passed by the House of Commons it is then passed by the Senate and at this time it becomes an **act** of Parliament. After formal assent by the governor-general, and after proclamation and publication in the *Canada Gazette*, the act becomes a **law** or more specifically a **statute** of Canada. Thus, although Parliament may have some influence on policy at any of several stages of the process, the *formal* or constitutional role of Parliament is to convert bills introduced by the government into acts. This role is carried out through the *legislative process*.

**Classes of Bills** All bills introduced in Parliament can be classed as either *public* or *private*, depending on whether their effect is intended to be general or specific. **Public bills**, in turn, are either **private members' bills** or **government bills**, depending on whether they are sponsored by a minister or a backbench MP. Because the procedures are different, government bills are broken down into either **money bills** or **non-money bills** and the former can be further dichotomized into **supply** (spending) or **ways-and-means** (taxation) measures. Figure 19.3 illustrates this classification of bills.

*Private Bills* **Private bills** are aimed at incorporating companies or altering the law only insofar as it affects an individual or a corporate individual. Examples of this kind of legislation are laws altering the charters of banks, railways, or other federal corporations. Every private bill must be introduced through a *petition* which must be signed and tabled by a member of the House or the Senate. Routine private bills are usually introduced in the Senate, where they are discussed and revised in detail by Senate committees. Passage by the House of Commons is usually more or less perfunctory, if the private bill has been approved already by the Senate.

**Figure 19.3**
Classes of bills.

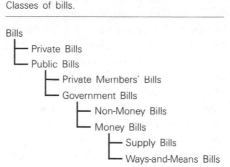

Often, if there are a number of routine private bills that have been passed by the Senate, they will be dealt with by the House of Commons in packages rather than individually, a practice that speeds up the process considerably. Much of the work to be done on private bills is simply to ensure that all of the appropriate procedural and technical hurdles have been cleared, and this chore is assigned to a House clerk designated the **Examiner of Private Bills.**

*Public Bills*   **Public bills** are intended to have a general effect and to alter the law as it affects all Canadians. Public bills take up by far the largest amount of parliamentary time, for it is by such measures that government policies are converted to statute law. Most of the legislation passed by Parliament can be classed as public; for example, the *Official Languages Act*, the *Income Tax Act*, the *Canada Pension Act*, the *Canadian Grain Act*, and the *Canada Health Act*. Because they generally involve the implementation of government policy, public bills are introduced in the House of Commons by the minister concerned. By contrast to the usually uncontentious private bills, public bills provide the focal points for heated partisan debate in the House of Commons.

**Private Members' Bills**   As we noted, most public bills originate with the government and, hence, are referred to as government bills. Before discussing how the House of Commons deals with such measures, however, we must say a few words about public bills introduced by individual MPs. This type of public bill is a private member's bill, signifying that it is the brain child of an individual MP and has nothing to do with the government or government policy. (Note here that **private members' bills** are completely different from **private bills**. The former term signifies the *originators* of the legislative proposals, while the latter signifies their *intent*.) Private members' bills, although procedurally a part of the parliamentary process, seldom go very far in the House of Commons. In fact, it has always been rare for a private member's bill to go beyond first reading, unless the government likes the idea and adopts it as its own.

However, rule changes adopted in 1985 provide that a few private members' bills per session will be debated and brought to a vote. At the beginning of the session, up to thirty bills or motions from private members are placed on the Order Paper and placed in an order of precedence by a lottery overseen by the Clerk. Five motions and five bills are then selected from the list of thirty by the Standing Committee on Procedure and House Affairs and are designated as "votable items." The lucky sponsors of these items will see their pet proposals debated for a limited time and then actually brought to a vote.

While this procedure guarantees that some non-government bills will be considered and brought to a decision, it does not, in any way, ensure that such bills will be passed. The high mortality rate of private members' bills and motions results from the fact that only five hours per week are set aside for private members' business. There is usually a long list of private members who wish to introduce bills or motions. Only thirty of these are placed on the Order Paper and only ten will come to a vote; these must share the allotted one-hour units of private members' time for debating their proposals. As well, if private members' business conflicts with other business of the House, the latter usually prevails. Hence, very few private members' bills are ever enacted into law, and such procedures can be said to have little impact on public policy.

It would be misleading, however, to limit our assessment of private members' bills or motions to their function in the policy process. The more important function of the private members' business in the House is that it permits the MP to state publicly the policy proposals he or she considers important and feels the government is ignoring. From time to time a private member's bill is passed down the line for consideration, on merit, by government officials, who may eventually incorporate some of the ideas in government bills.

Furthermore, by introducing a bill that favours a certain constituency's interests, the MP can publicize problems that exist there and are, perhaps, unique. In this way, the MP can use the private member's bill as a device to assist in the performance of the representative, or ombudsman, function, which we discussed earlier. Thus, it can be concluded that, although the private members' business is not important as a component of the legislative or policy processes, it is a useful device for criticizing the government's policy priorities and for publicizing special problems and needs within certain regions and constituencies of the country.

**Government Bills**   Government bills occupy the lion's share of the time available in the Canadian House of Commons, and the passage of these bills must be considered at greater length. The procedures for dealing with government bills differ slightly, depending on whether the legislation in question involves the spending or raising of public money. Money bills or tax amendments cannot be introduced in the Senate, and the procedures for dealing with money bills place a great deal of the debate in standing committees before first reading. Figure 19.4 illustrates the manner in which a government bill passes through Parliament.

Government bills are **introduced** by a minister in the House of Commons upon a **motion for leave**, which specifies the title of the bill and which may include a brief explanation of the provisions of the proposed legislation. After forty-eight hours, the bill may then be given **first reading**, which occurs through

**Figure 19.4**
The legislative process.

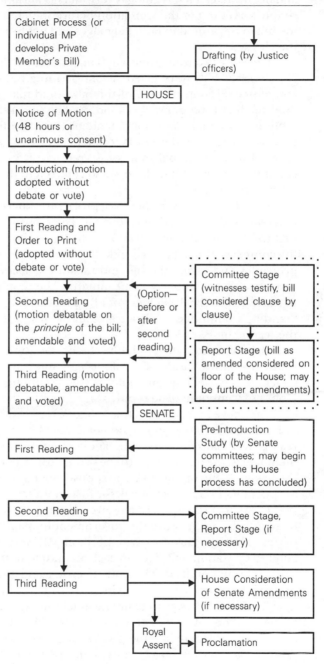

a non-debatable and non-amendable motion "that this bill be read a first time and be printed." First reading is very much a *pro forma* stage in the process and simply serves to get the legislation before the House. The Clerk then causes the bill to be printed in both languages and made available to the members of the House.

There are two routes that a bill can take after it has been given first reading. Traditionally bills were given **second reading** before being considerered in committee. Second reading of the bill would take place on a motion by the minister that it be granted second reading and referred to committee. The motion is debatable but not amendable, and the focus of second reading is upon the *principle* of the legislation. When the debate is concluded, the motion is voted on and the bill stands referred to a standing, special, or legislative committee. Supply bills, alone, stand referred to the Committee of the Whole after second reading.

Since 1995, however, there is a procedure whereby the bill can be referred to a committee *before* second reading. The reason for providing this option is that with some bills, the *principle* of the legislation can be understood only in the context of the details — the details, in other words, define the principle or principles underlying the bill and must be considered before the debate at second reading can become meaningful. The first legislation to be dealt with in this way was the 1995 Electoral Boundaries Bill, which was referred to the Standing Committee on Procedure and House Affairs before being read for the second time.

The committee stage, whether before or after second reading, involves a clause-by-clause consideration of the legislation, and when its deliberations are concluded, the bill, as amended by the committee, is reported back to the House of Commons. The **report stage** provides the members with the opportunity to move amendments to the bill. After giving twenty-four hours' notice of intentions to move an amendment, any MP may "amend, delete, insert or restore any clause" of the bill. These amendments are debatable and each member has the opportunity to speak once for ten minutes; the prime minister, the leader of the opposition, the sponsoring minister, and a member moving an amendment may each speak for forty minutes.

The report stage potentially gives the greatest opportunity to stall for time in an attempt to pressure the government to make changes. If there are a lot of amendments, and if each opposition MP were to speak for the full time allotted by Standing Orders on each amendment, the House could be tied up for a long time indeed. The only defence against this sort of procedural filibuster is for the government to invoke closure or impose time allocation. The Speaker has the power to combine amendments that are similar in intent or to declare "out of order" amendments that deal with issues already debated, in an effort to streamline the process at the report stage. However, even this does not always effectively restrict the power of the opposition to use up valuable time in an effort to force concessions on the government.

When the report stage is concluded, if the bill has still not been read for the second time, the minister moves "that the bill as amended be concurred in and be read a second time." This motion is not amendable or debatable. In the more common situation where a bill has been read for the second time before being considered in committee, the minister ends the report stage with a motion that "the bill (as amended) be concurred in." Again this motion is neither amendable nor debatable. Third reading is moved, usually at the next sitting of the House, and while the motion to read the bill for a third time is debatable, and general amendments are allowed, this stage of the process is normally perfunctory.

After third reading, the bill then goes to the Senate, where it is also given three readings and committee hearings. If the Senate amends the legislation, it must come back to the House for approval or rejection of its changes. In the case of a disagreement between Parliament and the Senate, there are provisions for a **conference** to attempt to resolve the dispute. While normally the Senate defers to the greater legitimacy of the elected House of Commons, if there is still a stalemate between the two chambers, the legislation could end up dying on the Order Paper and the government might be forced to call an election to legitimize its position.

## ▶ CONCLUSION

This concludes our discussion of the role of Parliament in the Canadian system. Parliament performs an important function in refining and legitimizing legislation that was usually dreamed up elsewhere and given priority by the Cabinet. As we have seen, the role of Parliament at other stages of the policy process is a sharply circumscribed one. Parliament is important as a constituency ombudsman and as an auditor of the government's record. Moreover, its symbolic position as the hub of the more active parts of the policy-making process is vital to the way Canadians relate to their political system, and can never be underestimated.

*Chapter* **20**

# The Political Executive:
# Function, Composition,
# and Structure

In an earlier chapter we stated that, to most Canadians, when they think of *politics* they think about political parties. However, when Canadians think about *government*, they think about the prime minister and the Cabinet. Indeed, we have seen that the *political executive*, composed of the prime minister and the Cabinet, is the effective core of our system of government, dominating even the operation of our constitutionally supreme Parliament. However, having dealt with the role of the political executive in the *legislative process* and the relationship of the PM and Cabinet to Parliament, we must now turn to an examination of the *executive functions* of Cabinet and its internal structure and composition. This will set the stage for a discussion of the processes of Cabinet government in the following chapter.

## ▶ THE FUNCTIONS OF THE EXECUTIVE BRANCH

The formal or constitutional functions of the executive branch in Canada were discussed in the the context of the operative principles of our Constitution in Chapter 5. As we have seen, the Crown is the symbolic embodiment of national sovereignty, and the powers of the Crown in Canada are exercised formally by the Queen's representatives, the governor-general and the lieutenant governors of the provinces. However, while Canada is technically a constitutional monarchy, we all know that the powers of the executive are exercised in reality by the prime minister, the provincial premiers, and their respective cabinets.

Afficionados of the constitutional niceties of our Constitution will still argue vehemently that the governor-general is more than a "rubber stamp" for decisions of the political executive, but to find an example of the independent exercise of power by the Queen's representative in Ottawa, they are forced to cite the King-Byng Affair that occurred seventy years ago. Hence, trivia buffs might find it interesting that, if the PM and the entire Cabinet were all killed simultaneously in an O-C Transpo accident, the governor-general (who is, fortunately, on another bus at the time) would, indeed, have to ask someone to form an interim government. However, for all practical purposes, it is safe to state that the executive powers of the government of Canada, including the royal prerogatives, are exercised by the political executive.

### Ceremonial and Honorific Duties

The role of the governor-general today is restricted to honorific and symbolic duties as the **head of state**. By contrast to the situation in the US, where the President is both the head of state and the **chief executive officer** of the government, in Canada the two roles are separate. On the positive side, this means that if the public comes to lose its respect for the chief executive in the person of the prime minister, the legitimacy of the regime itself as symbolized by the Crown and embodied in the office of the governor-general is not called into question. This allows Canadians to feel comfortable in venting their collective spleen against an unpopular government while remaining confident that the integrity and stability of the system is still intact.

In another context, the governor-general can perform a myriad of official duties such as honouring recipients of the Order of Canada, presiding over numerous ceremonial occasions, and hosting an annual New Year's Day levee. Canadians can attend such ceremonial events and feel good about Canada, despite the fact that they may despise the prime minister of the day. As well, by filling in for the chief executive in minor ceremonial affairs, the governor-general can leave the prime minister more time to do his or her real job of heading up the country.

However, this latter point should not be taken too far, for the political leaders of the country tend to like the idea of garnering public exposure in circumstances that are ceremonial and hence neutral to the political issues of the day. Thus, a wise PM will delegate only the less momentous ceremonial "happenings" to the formal head of state, reserving those that are more visible and that might cast the PM and the government in a "statesmanlike" role. For example, ceremonial kickoffs at Grey Cup games, appearances at Stanley Cup post-game celebrations, and throwing the first pitch on opening day are all potential "good news" stories; and besides, the PM usually gets a pretty good seat for the game!

### The Executive Functions of the Political Executive

We will discuss the role of the political executive in the policy process in the following section. While it is difficult to separate the Cabinet's performance of the executive and policy functions in the real world, we can make the distinction analytically. Thus, in this section, we will look at the "classic" executive **management responsibilities** of **directing** the officials that implement and enforce the laws of the land, **organizing** the bureaucracy, **staffing** the senior non-elective offices of the state, and **controlling** the financial affairs of the nation.[1]

**The Directing Function: The Minister as Department Head**   Each department of the government is headed up by a minister of the Crown. Formally, a minister is the "boss" or CEO of each department of government and is formally responsible to Parliament and the Cabinet as a whole for the goings on in his or her department. However, the bulk of the hands-on management is the job of senior bureaucrats. The top bureaucratic official in a department is the deputy-minister, who carries out the actual direction of the affairs of the department and acts as the link between the permanent employees and the political head.

*Limits to Ministerial Power over Departments*   The practical effectiveness of the minister in heading a department will depend, to a large extent, upon his or her competence and personality, and while there is a lot of room for the minister to provide encouragement and to generate excitement within the department about new policy initiatives, the minister is generally too busy with other things to become very involved in the administrative process. However, there are limitations on the minister's ability to actually **direct** the day-to-day affairs of the department that go beyond the simple fact that he or she is otherwise occupied.

In the first place, ministers are expected to be neither professional managers nor experts in the substantive concerns of the portfolio they are heading up. As we shall see in a later section, the selection of ministers is taken from the talent pool provided by the electoral process, and even then, the criteria for selection to Cabinet may involve a number of variables such as regional representation or party solidarity. While intelligence and ability certainly do not disqualify an MP from selection to the ministry, it is rare that ministers are selected because of their specialized knowledge related to a particular portfolio.

It is often said around Ottawa that the best minister is one who has "smarts" and influential stature in the Cabinet, but who knows relatively little about the line functions of the department itself. The minister can then represent the broad policy and budgetary interests of the department in Cabinet meetings, but is not motivated to meddle in the internal management of the department. But, then again, perhaps this theory is just the wishful thinking of public servants, who would prefer to keep the political head of the department involved in "political" priority decisions and out of their hair!

Another factor that may limit the involvement of the ministers in the direct management of departments is that they often do not stay very long in any one Cabinet post. Once named to the Cabinet, a minister will seldom remain in a portfolio for more than a few years. The pattern in recent years is for ministers to be shuffled from post to post in the government, partly to provide the

---

1.  As we will see in a later chapter, the basic sub-functions of *management* are planning, organizing, directing, staffing, and controlling. In the context of the the political executive, the planning function is subsumed in the policy role of the PM and Cabinet, which will be discussed separately.

individuals with a wider range of experience that will make them more effective priority decision-makers and partly because of the complex system of sanctions and inducements that sees the PM promoting and demoting ministers on the basis of overall performance and shifting political needs.

Finally, because they are, after all, politicians, ministers are impeded from making decisions about **staffing** within the bureaucracy. The ability to make decisions about rewarding and disciplining employees, which is critical in enabling a manager to motivate subordinates, should not be left to the discretion of individuals with partisan reponsibilities. The **merit principle**, which is the cornerstone of the personnel system in the public service, places the responsibility for recruitment, selection, promotion, and disciplinary action outside the control of politicians to prevent partisan patronage from creeping into the administrative process.

The merit principle was established to ensure that the criteria for rewarding or punishing public employees should be limited to an individual's abilities, performance, and objective suitability for the job. Hence, the management of human resources can be performed in the public-service context only by the professional senior managers of the departments, not by the political heads. As a result, it should not be surprising that the direction of the department on an ongoing basis is left to the experienced professionals who have made careers as public-service managers and who are the effective CEOs of the departments.

**The Cabinet as Government Employer** In spite of recent reductions in the size of the public service, the fact remains that the government as a whole is far and away the largest single employer in the economy. The federal Cabinet must perform a number of functions similar to those performed by the executives of large private corporations. The Cabinet is thus formally responsible for providing for the pay and benefits to its employees and for opportunities for skills-upgrading, management development, and bilingual training. For the most part these functions are performed by the bureaucracy, both within the human-resources branches of the individual departments and in the service-wide agencies such as the Public Service Commission and the Treasury Board Secretariat.

Where the Cabinet must play a more active role is in areas that involve the expenditure of large amounts of public moneys. Because the expenditure of money from the public purse is the collective responsibility of the political executive, the Cabinet must become involved in matters such as remuneration and pensions. Here, legislation delegates the reponsibility for being the employer to the **Treasury Board**, which is made up of six ministers, including the president of the Treasury Board, who is the chairman. Besides being formally responsible for overseeing matters of training, employee development, and classification, the Treasury Board has all of the responsibilities of management in the collective-bargaining process between the federal government and its public-service unions.

*Ministerial Accountability* While the minister is effectively precluded from acting as the hands-on manager of the department, it is perhaps a paradox that, in our system of government, the minister is still formally reponsible to

Parliament for the actions of both the department as a whole and the individual departmental officials. However, as a result of the growing complexity of departmental administrative affairs and the increased overall workload of Cabinet ministers, the once-sacred principle of **ministerial responsibility** has come to be watered down in practice. It is simply not realistic to hold the minister, who does not have hands-on responsibility for the department, personally responsible for the actions of thousands of departmental employees.

Even in the past, it was rare for a minister to be forced to resign because of indiscretions or incompetence on the part of departmental personnel. Since Confederation, although there have been over 150 ministerial resignations, only two could be clearly put down to the individual stepping down because of accepting responsibility for the indiscretions of subordinates.[2] Nevertheless, a minister whose department "blew it" would still have to face the gleeful attacks of the opposition in the House, who would characteristically demand his or her resignation and subject the unfortunate individual to a thorough roasting for several days or weeks in Question Period.

Now, however, it is becoming more difficult even to give the minister a rough ride in the House. More and more, ministers are getting away with the simple plea of ignorance — "I didn't know." While they are forced to take a generous measure of heat from the opposition, nobody really holds them personally responsible anymore, and certainly not even the most partisan opposition MPs actually expect the minister to resign. One, perhaps unfortunate, consequence of this is that, in many cases, in recent years, the blame is simply bumped down a notch or two into the departmental hierarchy, where a senior public servant may be fingered, with or without justification, as the scapegoat for departmental errors and indiscretions.

**Political Ethics and Conflict of Interest**  While it is difficult to hold ministers accountable for the behaviour of all of the people in a large government department, the same is not the case for the minister's own behaviour. Because they are in the public eye and because anything they do can reflect upon the Cabinet as a whole, ministers are expected to maintain standards of personal conduct and integrity that are above reproach. Offences such as **influence peddling** are clearly against the law for anybody, and a minister who breaches such rules might end up not only out of the Cabinet, but in *jail* as well. More difficult to deal with are questions of political ethics and morality, many of which come down to issues of **conflict of interest** between ministerial responsibilities and personal financial gain.

*Cabinet Ministers and Business Interests*  There have frequently been close connections between Cabinet ministers and the Canadian business community. The politics of the immediate post-Confederation era were largely concerned with railways, and Cabinet ministers were deeply involved: six of the original directors of the Grand Trunk Railway were Cabinet ministers. In 1885, while he was a Cabinet minister, Sir Charles Tupper had no qualms about accepting

---

2. S. Sutherland, "Responsible Government and Ministerial Responsibility," *Canadian Journal of Political Science,* March 1991.

$100,000 of CPR stock — a gift given in grateful appreciation of his help in selling CPR bonds.[3] Earlier, while acting as secretary of state, Sir Charles had simultaneously held three paid directorships; yet none of these activities precluded his serving as prime minister for a brief stretch in 1896, nor were they held against him at any time.

Wilfrid Laurier continued to be a director of Mutual Life Assurance during his term as prime minister,[4] and one of his ministers, Allen Bristol Aylesworth, carried on a private law practice at the same time as he held the Justice portfolio. Sir Robert Borden refused to permit his ministers to maintain outside business connections, but Mackenzie King had no such compunctions. His minister of Justice, Lomer Gouin, was simultaneously a director of the Bank of Montreal, the Cockshutt Plough Company, Montreal City and District Savings Bank, Royal Trust, and the Mount Royal and Mutual Life Assurance Companies.

In 1922, King stated: "In the long run we will gain more in virility in our public life by leaving some matters to conscience and honour rather than by seeking to enforce prohibitions that may be too severe and too drastic."[5] One of the major pillars of both King's and Louis St. Laurent's cabinets was C. D. Howe, who was, prior to his appointment in 1935, a highly successful construction engineer. The C. D. Howe Company, of which he "disposed" before taking office, continued to receive government business and to employ Howe's son and son-in-law. St. Laurent's cabinets also contained two ministers who retained private business practices after entering the Cabinet; George Prudham was one, and the other was J. J. McCann, who retained a directorship in Guaranty Trust even though his department, National Revenue, often engaged in negotiations with that company. St. Laurent may have been embarrassed, but the ministers remained unrepentant even under an opposition barrage.

*Conflict-of-Interest Guidelines* In more recent years, conflict-of-interest "codes" or guidelines have required ministers to divest themselves of directorships and holdings before taking office, a practice followed in more recent cabinets. The relationship between the private vocations and the public lives of ministers always raises the question of conflict of interest. As early as 1973, the issue was broached directly by the prime minister in the House of Commons, but no legislation was introduced. Instead, Trudeau said:

> Guidelines are preferable to additional legislation. . . . An element of discretion, to be exercised by a minister on the basis of discussion with the Prime Minister of the day, seems the best solution. . . . A minister will be expected in the future, as is the policy today, to resign any directorships in commercial or other profit-making corporations that he may have held before becoming a minister.[6]

---

3. E. M. Saunders, *The Life and Letters of the Rt. Hon. Sir Charles Tupper*, vol. 2 (Toronto: Carswell, 1916), pp. 60–61. See William A. Matheson, "The Canadian Cabinet and the Prime Minister: A Structural Study," Ph.D. diss. Carleton University, April 1973, pp. 249–58; and Rick Van Loon and Mike Whittington, *The Canadian Political System: Environment, Structure and Process* (Toronto: McGraw-Hill Ryerson, 1987), ch. 14.

4. Matheson, "The Canadian Cabinet," p. 252.

5. Ibid., p. 253.

6. Pierre Trudeau, *Statement on Conflict of Interest*, House of Commons, July 18, 1973.

Cabinet ministers are also covered by the provisions of the *Parliament of Canada Act*, which require disclosure of any pecuniary interest or benefit the member might have in any matter upon which he or she wishes to speak in Parliament.

Under the Trudeau administrations, ministers were required to place their assets either in a trust that would maintain the assets exactly as they were at the time the minister was appointed or in a blind trust, so that the minister could not know what transactions were taking place. Prime Minister Joe Clark issued a similar but more stringent code of conduct, which applied not just to ministers but to their immediate families. Assets could be placed only in blind trusts.[7]

As well, the Clark guidelines required that a minister's activities be sharply curtailed after he or she left the Cabinet. For a period of two years, ex-ministers could not serve on the boards of corporations with which they dealt as ministers; nor could they act on behalf of any such people or corporations, or act as lobbyists. For a period of one year, they could not accept jobs with companies with which they formerly dealt or act as a consultant for those companies. These guidelines were maintained when the Trudeau government returned to office in 1980, and were retained by the Mulroney government in 1984 until that government replaced them a year later with a new set of conflict guidelines.

After one of Mulroney's high-profile ministers, Sinclair Stevens, was caught out on several violations of the conflict code, the government introduced legislation to govern ministerial and senior bureaucratic behaviour but it died on the Order Paper on two separate occasions. The Chrétien government has not moved in the direction of legislated conflict rules but appointed Mitchell Sharp to be the PM's **personal advisor** on "integrity in government." Sharp's job was to screen all potential members of the ministry before their appointment to make sure there were no conflict disasters waiting to happen.

**The Organizing Function**  The actual structure of the bureaucracy is reflective of many variables. In the first place there are historical patterns to the manner in which the various portfolios are organized. Departments such as Finance, Justice, Agriculture, Defence, Foreign Affairs, and Transport have all been around for a century or more, and while the names may have changed over time the organizational *raison d'être* for these departments has not.

By contrast to such core departments, other parts of the bureaucracy have sprung up and disappeared, grown apace or faded away, according to political exigency as seen by successive cabinets. Even in recent decades we have seen departments such as Forestry and Regional Economic Expansion, or ministries of state such as Urban Affairs and Science and Technology spring up and fade away, with their remnant functions and personnel being absorbed into other departments. Because the bureaucracy must be adapted in order to be able to deliver new and changing programs and policies, the Cabinet, as the collective formal "manager" of the public service, is always involved in **organizing** and fine-tuning the departmental structures. It is impossible to be involved in policy

---

7.  Canada, "Conflict of Interest Guidelines for Ministers of the Crown" (Ottawa: Privy Council Office, August 1, 1979), mimeo.

innovation without also being involved in the bureaucratic restructuring that is required to effectuate the new policies.

In the 1990s, one of the main aims of reorganization has been to streamline and downsize the bureaucracy with a view to reducing costs. The imperatives of a policy of deficit reduction are such that it is necessary for the Cabinet to engage in a sort of **negative priority determination**. In an effort to cut costs, the government must spend a lot of its time deciding what programs can be eliminated and, hence, what departments and parts of departments can be declared redundant. The implications of this role of the political executive as reorganizers and rationalizers of the bureaucracy is that while they cannot fire, demote, or transfer individual employees, they can declare their positions to be redundant.

**The Staffing Function: Order-in-Council Appointments**  If we include military personnel, employees of crown corporations, and public servants, the government of Canada is "boss" to over 500,000 workers. In early 1995, over 225,000 of these work directly for the government in departments and agencies headed up by a minister, and even after the reductions of the 1995 budget, there are still around 200,000 federal public servants. The individual ministers do not have much say in staffing their departments. However, while the Cabinet has no authority at all with respect to the hiring of public servants, in the case of **order-in-council appointments** the political executive has both the formal and the actual discretionary authority.

Order-in-council (OIC) appointments are those made formally by the governor-general on the advice of the Cabinet. In practice, the governor-general only rubber stamps the decisions of the PM and the Cabinet. OIC appointments fill a myriad of positions within the governmental sphere. All federal judges and all superior, county, and district court judges in the provinces are appointed in this way, as are all senators, deputy ministers, ambassadors, royal commissioners, and boards of crown corporations and regulatory agencies.

*Political Appointments*  While OIC appointments are to a large extent made on the basis of competence, the Cabinet's choices for many of these positions are clearly influenced by partisan considerations as well. This is most obvious in the case of Senate appointments, which are almost always politically motivated because the government must be able to control the goings-on in the second chamber. In other cases, the government may select appointees on the basis of their ideological if not partisan compatibility with the government. This would seem to be the case with respect to the appointment of Supreme Court of Canada justices, the president of the Bank of Canada, and the heads of important regulatory agencies.

While such appointments are often dismissed by the media and the opposition as "patronage," we should learn to make a distinction between **political appointments** and **patronage appointments**. Political appointments are instrumental to the government, because people that the government feels comfortable working with are thereby placed in key positions. By contrast, patronage appointments are more instrumental to the appointee, who receives a reward for past loyalty to the party. Purely patronage appointments may be useful to the government, as well, because, for instance, they may allow the prime minister to offer an attractive early retirement package to a no longer useful colleague, but the main aim of patronage is to reward a partisan for services rendered.

*Patronage Appointments*  Thousands of appointments are made on the basis of patronage and while objections are made on the moral grounds that people should only get such jobs because they merit them or are otherwise deserving, the tendency is for parties in office to take full advantage of their patronage powers and for those out of office to act outraged. When a change of government occurs, the parties simply change places and the erstwhile government acts outraged while the erstwhile opposition goes on an orgy of patronage appointments. Such is political life in Canada.

There are a number of reasons why it probably doesn't matter a lot in the long run whether positions are filled by party stalwarts or ideological fellow travellers of the government. In the first place, many OIC appointments are for a permanent or set term. As a result, the appointees, once in office, cannot be given directions by the government that appointed them. As well, the competence of OIC appointees is still generally high. While the government may use party loyalty as a criterion, the government also wants fairly competent people in these jobs and will not usually name a dolt to an important position simply because he or she has the appropriate party credentials. Unfortunately, we can all think of at least a few exceptions to this statement!

*Deputy Ministers*  Deputy ministers (DMs) are all appointed by OIC. Significantly, they hold office only **at the pleasure** of the government and they can be fired at any time by the prime minister. It is with respect to the power of appointment and dismissal of DMs that the Cabinet can have a significant effect on the functioning of the executive branch of government. Because DMs have to work closely with the ministers of the departments, it has always been felt that the government of the day should be able to hire and fire these most senior bureaucrats whenever it seemed appropriate.

However, while wholesale turnovers of deputy ministers once occurred as a matter of course after each change in government, in recent years this practice has almost completely disappeared. Since the 1960s deputy ministers have tended to be recruited from the senior ranks of the career bureaucracy and not from outside of government. As a result the senior bureaucracy has become a cadre of non-partisan professionals who are comfortable serving whatever government is in power. Conversely, politicians have mostly come to appreciate and value the professionalism of the senior bureaucracy, and while changes in government may see some shuffling of DMs from one department to another, very few are ever actually fired by an incoming government.

**Financial Management and Control Functions**  Only the ministers of the Crown can spend money and introduce tax legislation. Hence, one of the key responsiblities of the Cabinet is to manage and **control** the financial affairs of the government, subject of course to the watchful scrutiny of Parliament. There are two main financial management sub-functions of the political executive:

the spending of money from the "public purse" and the raising of money to fill that purse through taxation. Each of these roles must be considered in more detail.

*The Spending Power* The principle that the executive may only spend money that is appropriated for it by Parliament is at the core of our system of reponsible government. However, while spending must be approved in advance by an **appropriation act**, only a minister of the Crown may introduce spending bills in the House of Commons. Moreover, Parliament itself is not empowered to *spend* money except for purposes of the internal economy of the legislature. The spending of public money is the exclusive prerogative of the Crown, which is also reponsible for keeping the **Public Accounts** which detail how, when, how much of, and for what purpose the money appropriated by Parliament is spent. As might be expected, given the complexity of the expenditure-management system of the government, it is public servants who do the actual preparation of the **estimates** and prepare the accounts, and the minister is merely the formal link between the bureaucracy and the legislature.

Thus, on the expenditure side of the ledger the Cabinet is ultimately reponsible for tabling the departmental estimates for the coming year, for seeing that the estimates are explained and justified to the satisfaction of Parliament, and for piloting the supply bills through the legislature. During the fiscal year, ministers are formally responsible for approving the expenditures of their departments and for seeing that the departmental accounts are kept in order. Finally, when the fiscal year is over, the Cabinet can be called upon to justify any irregularities in their financial affairs that are uncovered by the auditor general or the Public Accounts Committee.

*The Annual Budget* The government of Canada operates on an *annual* financial cycle that is based on the *fiscal year*. The key to managing the financial affairs of the government is the **Budget**, which is presented annually, and which outlines the federal government's current balance sheet, confirms the expenditure targets for the coming year, and indicates where the government is going to get the money. The Budget is prepared by officials in the Department of Finance under the broad direction of the minister. The 1995 Budget was the first one introduced under a new system of pre-budget consultation, wherein Cabinet and parliamentary committees are more deeply involved than under the previous regime.The substance of the Budget is presented in summary form in the **Budget Speech**, which is delivered in the House of Commons, usually in February, by the minister of Finance. Because the estimates are already being considered and the general spending targets are already known, the most important messages in the Budget Speech are what, if any, tax increases we will face in the coming fiscal year, and what the deficit is likely to be. If the Budget Speech announces significant cuts or significant tax increases, these are often not to take effect until two or three years down the road. This practice "softens up" the electorate by getting them used to the idea before they actually have to feel the pain. The Budget Speech may also be the major political event of the year (barring an election) and is used by the government to unveil new policy initiatives.

The Budget is also used in the overall management of the economy. It is the measures in the Budget that determine whether the economy is to be stimulated by expenditures or cooled down by restraint. The Budget certainly affects individual Canadians because it tells them what their tax bill is likely to be, but it also sends messages to banks, investors, and foreign governments, all of whom are extremely interested in the macro-economic implications of the government of Canada's financial policies. The Budget Speech is thus both a message about the financial state of the nation and a tool of fiscal and economic policy.

### The Policy Functions of the Political Executive

As we saw in Chapter 2, policy is never made in a single climactic act by any one actor or institution; rather, policies emerge over time through the complex actions and reactions of the large numbers of individuals, groups, and state institutions that make up a policy community. Policies are ultimately cast by the bureaucracy and polished and refined by Parliament, but it is Cabinet that is the "policy crucible," it is Cabinet that must decide whether there is to be a policy at all, and it is Cabinet that determines the order in which policy concerns should be tackled. Hence, while Cabinet has many functions, the policy function is far and away the most important one. Moreover, while many institutions play important supporting roles in the policy process, the *central* policy-making institution of government is the Cabinet.

**Priority Determination** It is at the priority-determination stage of the policy process that the Cabinet is the core institution, and as we have seen earlier, it is at this stage in the process that the most important determinations are made. In order to decide whether a policy idea should be developed further, the Cabinet must look at the technical, financial, and political pluses and minuses. The ultimate decision is taken in part on the basis of advice tendered by government departments, the party caucus, interest groups, the extra-parliamentary wing of the party, and the central agencies. The central agencies are particularly influential in the process of determining priorities and will be discussed in some detail in the next chapter.

However, despite all the help the Cabinet can draw upon in coming to a decision, the ultimate decision is in the hands of the prime minister and the Cabinet. A "yes" by the Cabinet means that the policy idea will be pursued further and likely ultimately given effect through legislation. A "no" means that the proposal is, for the time being at least, on the scrap heap of ideas ahead of their time politically.

**Policy Initiation** Policy initiation involves bringing a problem, issue, or policy idea to the attention of the priority setters of the policy process. Hence, when the prime minister or individual Cabinet ministers feel they have a good idea about a policy option, access is not a problem! Whenever the "policy muse" inspires a member of the Cabinet, he or she is in a position to get some of the departmental policy folks looking into the idea and ultimately the inspired minister can also begin to bend the ear of Cabinet colleagues and the PM.

As we saw in 1993, the Chrétien government took office with the Liberal "Red Book" promises to live up to, and the Cabinet indeed did proceed to initiate policies based on that very successful campaign brochure. However, after a government is in power for a while the business of policy making becomes more and more driven by the need to respond to new problems and demands that have arisen in society since the election. As a government's term in office unfolds, the Cabinet's job is increasingly focused upon responding to policy ideas generated elsewhere, and less on dreaming up new policy suggestions on its own.

**Formulation and Legislation**  The formulation of policy options after the Cabinet has established a priority is, for the most part, the responsibility of the bureaucracy. However, many issues that arise in the process of figuring out how a policy idea should be implemented are more than technical in nature. The choice of governing instrument, for instance, can be almost as important as the decision to put a policy in place. Whether to employ softer enforcement techniques such as persuasion or to implement a regulatory regime backed up by coercive measures is a question that can have a significant impact on the way in which the policy is received by the public. Hence, while the bureaucracy will propose alternative ways of "skinning the cat," it matters to the cat! The politicians wishing to woo the feline vote in the next election have to be involved in the choice of means as well as the choice of ends.

The role of the Cabinet in the legislative stage of the policy process has been discussed at length in the previous chapter. While it is the parliamentary committees that tidy up and refine the legislation, and ministers do not even participate in committee work in Parliament, the committees ultimately must report back to the House of Commons where the prime minister and the Cabinet are firmly in control. As a result, it can be said that the Cabinet has as much influence over the legislative stage of the policy process as it wishes, but that for the most part the work of the House committees in examining the details of legislation is genuinely appreciated by the government.

### The Representative Function of the Political Executive

In describing the representative function of the Cabinet in Canada, there are two possible approaches. We can examine the process through which a prime minister constructs a Cabinet, in order to see what groups the prime minister seeks to represent. Alternatively, we can examine the *results* of Cabinet formation — the types of people who end up in an elite group we call the Cabinet when the selection process has been completed.

**Cabinet Formation and Representation**  One can look at the people who have become Canadian ministers from a number of perspectives: their geographical distribution, their ethnic and social backgrounds, and their education, and their career patterns can all be examined. We shall see that this most important of our decision-making institutions in Canada is deliberately assembled in such a way that it represents some of the major categoric groups in Canadian society.[8]

*Province and Region*    In 1865, Christopher Dunkin, one of the most perceptive critics of the original Confederation settlement, stated:

> I think I may defy them to show that the cabinet can be formed on any other principle than that of a representation of the several provinces in that cabinet. Your federal problem will have to be worked out around the table of the Executive Council.[9]

Thus, from the very first days of Confederation, it was obvious that neither the Senate, which was intended to represent regions or provinces in Ottawa, nor the House of Commons would suffice as an arbiter of the regional cleavages of the federation. Yet four very different colonial communities had been brought together, and each was anxious to be able to continue to exercise influence over national political decisions. In the first Cabinet, Sir George-Étienne Cartier would accept no fewer than four positions for Quebec, of which three were to be held by French Canadians and one by an English-speaking, Protestant Quebecker. Ontario, because it had a larger population than Quebec, had to demand one more seat. If Nova Scotia and New Brunswick were to have an adequate say in the national political arena, they felt they would need two posts each. The principle of provincial representation in Cabinet was, thus, immediately established as a cornerstone of Cabinet composition, and there has been no substantial backing away from this principle in all the years since.

The regional composition of selected cabinets since Confederation is summarized in Table 20.1, which makes it clear that the patterns established at Confederation have generally survived the test of time. A few exceptions have turned out not to be trends but anomalies. In 1957 John Diefenbaker named eight ministers from the Atlantic Provinces, and in 1984 Mulroney had thirteen Western ministers as opposed to only eleven each from Ontario and Quebec. John Turner's brief government in 1984 had thirteen Ontarians and ten Quebeckers, but his successor Brian Mulroney returned to equal representation for the central provinces, despite the fact that his contingent of Quebec MPs was considerably less experienced in federal office than his Ontario caucus. Jean Chrétien appeared to have deviated still more from tradition in 1993 by selecting twelve Ontarians and only six Québécois out of a total of thirty-one (including both full ministers and secretaries of state). However, this is likely a reflection of the fact that the Liberals won all but one of the ninety-nine seats in Ontario, and only nineteen in Quebec, and with a more balanced representation in the House in the future, the ratio can be expected to return to "normal."

It has always been considered "normal" for each province to receive at least one Cabinet minister. However, the vagaries of election results sometimes make it difficult for a prime minister to comply with this practice. Prince

---

8. The major data sources for material on Cabinet ministers are parliamentary guides and biographies published by the Prime Minister's Office at the time appointments are made.
9. Christopher Dunkin, *Confederation Debates* (Ottawa: Queen's Printer, 1951), pp. 496, 513.

**TABLE 20.1**
Regional Representation in Cabinet (Selected Periods, 1867–1995)

| Year | Prime Minister | Number of Cabinet Ministers | | | | |
|------|----------------|------------------------------|--------|---------|------------------|-------|
| | | Atlantic Provinces | Quebec | Ontario | Western Provinces | Total |
| 1867 | Macdonald | 4 | 4 | 5 | 0 | 13 |
| 1873 | Mackenzie | 5 | 3 | 6 | 0 | 14 |
| 1896 | Laurier | 4 | 5 | 4 | 1 | 14 |
| 1911 | Borden | 4 | 5 | 7 | 2 | 18 |
| 1921 | King | 4 | 6 | 6 | 3 | 19 |
| 1930 | Bennett | 4 | 5 | 7 | 3 | 19 |
| 1957 | Diefenbaker | 8 | 3 | 6 | 4 | 21 |
| 1968 | Trudeau | 6 | 10 | 10 | 3 | 29 |
| 1979 | Clark | 5 | 5 | 11 | 9 | 30 |
| 1984 | Turner | 5 | 10 | 12 | 2 | 29 |
| 1984 | Mulroney | 5 | 11 | 11 | 13* | 40 |
| 1995 | Chrétien | 5 | 7 | 12 | 8 | 32 |

* Includes the Northwest Territories and the Yukon.
Source: Updated from Bill Matheson, *The Prime Minister and the Cabinet* (Toronto: Methuen, 1976).

Edward Island, with only four seats in the House of Commons and a population less than many suburbs of Toronto, Montreal, or Vancouver, has sometimes been left out of the Cabinet, and during the Trudeau years both Alberta and Saskatchewan habitually elected so few Liberals that those provinces were either unrepresented or represented by Liberal senators. Brian Mulroney had far more opportunity than his predecessors to provide adequate provincial representation in his Cabinet, since his parliamentary legions included an ample supply of MPs from every province. He responded by producing a Cabinet that, at forty members, was the largest in Canadian history. It was also roughly representative of the provinces on a basis proportional to their population. He chose to represent Ontario and Quebec equally, as had Trudeau. The 1993 Chrétien ministry has at least one appointee from each province and one from the Northwest Territories, and added one more minister from Quebec in 1994.

*Ethnicity and Language* The ethnic distribution of Cabinet ministers shows similar patterns. Since Confederation, the proportion of French-Canadian ministers has usually paralleled the proportion of French Canadians in the population. Because Joe Clark had only two members of his caucus from Quebec and one of those was an anglophone, his short-lived government under-represented francophones. Pierre Trudeau and John Turner both had more than 40 per cent francophone ministers, partially, again, a reflection of their lack of MPs from west of Ontario. Brian Mulroney's cabinets were between 25 and 30 per cent French-speaking, and Chrétien, with a Quebec caucus of only twenty-one, has only seven francophones out of a ministry of thirty-two.

As with provincial representation, the attempt to provide proportional representation by ethnic group, at least between the French and English segments of the population, has been deliberate. On the other hand, there was less evidence of a conscious effort on the part of prime ministers to represent "other" Canadians in the Cabinet. Occasionally, prior to 1960, someone such as J. T. Thorson, a man of Icelandic descent, or Michael Starr, who was of Ukrainian descent, did enter the Cabinet. Trudeau appointed Stanley Haidasz as minister of state for Multiculturalism and Herb Gray became the first Jewish Canadian to enter the Cabinet, but it is difficult to argue that these appointments were not simply based on merit or on regional factors.

Joe Clark's Cabinet contained more ministers with non-charter ethnicgroup backgrounds than any previous Cabinet, including Ray Hnatyshyn, Steve Paproski, Jake Epp, and Don Mazankowski. Again, however, it is doubtful that there was any conscious attempt to represent ethnic diversity. These individuals were almost certainly appointed on the basis of regional representation and merit rather than ethnic origin, and they all reappeared in Brian Mulroney's Cabinet along with several other ministers of non-charter-group background.

The 1993 Chrétien ministry may reflect a more conscious effort to represent ethnic minorities than has been the practice in the past. Although the ministry is small, six of the members are from non-French, non-English groups and represent aboriginals, Orientals, and non-Christian religions. As well, it is no accident that Sergio Marchi, an Italian Canadian, was given the Citizenship and Immigration portfolio. Chrétien has also carried on informal but longstanding practices such as giving the Agriculture portfolio to a Westerner, Fisheries to Atlantic Canada, and Finance to central Canada.

*Gender* The first woman to be appointed to the Cabinet was Ellen Fairclough in 1957. The number of females in Cabinet did not rise above three until 1984 when Brian Mulroney named six women to his rather large Cabinet. Chrétien has increased the number of female members of his ministry to eight out of thirty-two. While the Tories did give us the first female prime minister, Kim Campbell, and Chrétien gave us the first female deputy prime minister, Sheila Copps, in terms of their share of the total population of Canada, women remain as under-represented in the Cabinet as they are among the ranks of MPs.

*Occupation and Education* It is clear that the PM has always attempted to make the Cabinet regionally and ethnically representative. However, the Cabinet has never been representative of class or occupational groups. The Cabinet, in the final analysis, is made up of members of our social and economic elites. The poor, the uneducated, the unemployed, unskilled labourers, and even farmers have not been well represented in the Cabinet. Both by education and by occupation, Cabinet ministers have been distinctly unrepresentative of the general population since Confederation.

In Canada's first century fully 52 per cent of Canada's Cabinet ministers were lawyers, whereas the proportion of lawyers in the population was less than 1 per cent. Since 1970 the percentage of lawyers in Cabinet has dropped off to about 30 per cent and the number of ministers from the business community increased to about one-third of the total under Mulroney. The 1995

Liberal ministry has reduced this trend significantly, with only four ministers out of thirty-two that have a clear business background.

The three federal Cabinets that held office in 1984, as the government moved from the Liberal hands of Pierre Trudeau, through John Turner, to the Conservatives under Brian Mulroney, present an interesting contrast in business representation. Trudeau had only two ministers with significant business experience. Turner, who no doubt would have liked to have more, had only the same two, but Brian Mulroney had thirteen ministers whose primary occupational background was business and most of them were still around in 1992. The much higher proportion of business people in the Mulroney Cabinet may account in considerable part for the quite different orientation towards the processes and policies of government evidenced by the Liberal and Conservative governments.

A similar bias obtains if one looks at the educational background of Canada's ministers. Only one minister since the Second World War has not had at least highschool education. In the fairly typical Cabinet of the 1970s and 1980s, there might be one or two members with only highschool education but, at the other end of the scale, well more than half of the rest would have taken a second degree or some post-graduate studies. The Chrétien Cabinet has a dozen lawyers, three Ph.D.s, a medical doctor, and an engineer. More than two-thirds of the ministers have at least some education beyond an undergraduate degree. Thus, in terms of education, the Cabinet is still far from a microcosm of the Canadian social structure.

The elite composition of cabinets reflects, to some extent, upper-middle-class socialization patterns, which are more likely to give a person the skills and attitudes essential to the effective performance of political roles, and upper-middle-class occupations, which are more likely to provide the flexibility of careers necessary to politicians. While universities and law firms will cheerfully provide leaves of absence so that their faculty or partners can go into politics, and will generally welcome them back later, we are a long way yet from a situation where blue-collar workers are accorded the same privileges.

*Parliamentary Experience*  In the early years of Confederation, it was usual for ministers to serve a fairly long apprenticeship in Parliament before being appointed to the Cabinet. The relative importance of Parliament in a minister's activities has decreased steadily over the years, while the importance of administrative, departmental, federal-provincial, and general priority-setting duties has steadily increased. For this reason it has become increasingly the norm to choose ministers not on the basis of parliamentary experience or experience at another level of government, but on the basis of policy-making skills, administrative capabilities, or, occasionally, tactical skill in electioneering. This has sometimes led to the spectacle of a Cabinet that is administratively quite competent but that cannot defend its activities effectively under the scrutiny of the opposition in Parliament. This point requires some qualification.

The Pearson cabinets of 1963 to 1968 seemed particularly prone to parliamentary pratfalls caused by legislative inexperience. However, by the late 1970s, many members of those early Pearson cabinets were still in office, well experienced in the parliamentary game, and, hence, less liable to make the spectacular goofs that characterized Liberal cabinets in the 1960s. Most of the holders of major portfolios in the Clark Cabinet had previous parliamentary experience and therefore faced little difficulty in defending their policies in the House. Their collective tragic flaw was that none of them had any experience in governing. In attempting to apply the lessons they had learned in opposition to the problems of governing, they soon ended up back in opposition.

Some of the well-publicized problems of the first years of the Mulroney government undoubtedly resulted from such inexperience. Issues that could have been handled relatively easily by experienced ministers and staff were fumbled by parliamentary neophytes. The problem was particularly acute with respect to Quebec ministers, who, on average, had less than two years of experience in the House, and one of the most inexperienced, it must be remembered, was the prime minister himself. However, after eight years in power, the Mulroney Tories became quite effective in coping with the give and take of the parliamentary game.

The Chrétien Cabinet is an interesting mix of experience and fresh new faces. The PM himself is a seasoned veteran both on the floor of the House and in the Cabinet room. His support team is anchored by the thirty-year MP Herb Gray and veteran ministers from the Trudeau years such as André Ouellet, Lloyd Axworthy, and Roy Maclaren. David Anderson and Ralph Goodale were both leaders of provincial Liberal parties, and Art Eggleton was the longest-serving mayor in Toronto's history. Marcel Massé moved into the Cabinet after a distinguished career in the public service, and Paul Martin moved into government from the corporate sector. With this kind of experience in the Cabinet, the prime minister could afford to bring in a lot of new blood in 1993, making his one of the most diverse cabinets in recent times.

*Conclusion*   To conclude this discussion of the representative function of the Cabinet in Canada, we should enter a qualification as to the nature of representation *per se*. Overall, there may be a problem stemming from the well-educated, middle-class, professional, male composition of the highest decision-making body in the country. On the surface it may be difficult to understand how policy decision-makers can make equitable and sympathetic decisions affecting poverty, abortion, or discrimination if few of them have ever been poor, pregnant, or discriminated against.

However, it must also be pointed out that it is not necessary for a person to be "of" the people he or she represents to be a good representative. It is at least possible that ministers can represent people quite unlike themselves, because being a good representative is in part a learned skill, which, in theory at least, may be unconnected with one's personal background. One need not spend an afternoon in a hot oven to figure out how to roast a turkey!

## ▶ STRUCTURE OF THE MINISTRY

Having looked at the Cabinet in functional terms, it is now necessary to move to a consideration of the basic structure and organization of the institution.

We are referring to the political executive here collectively as the **ministry** because the Chrétien government has for the first time in Canadian history instituted two ministerial ranks. While it is new to Canada, this two-tier ministry system has long been used in the United Kingdom and it was introduced as a measure for cutting costs and streamlining the executive branch of government.

The **Cabinet** in the current system is composed of twenty-four "full" ministers. However, there are eight additional members of the ministry, who are **secretaries of state.** These are sworn in as privy councillors but sit in Cabinet meetings only on invitation from the PM. They receive 75 per cent of the pay of ministers and they do not have direct responsibility for a government department. Each of these secretaries of state is attached to a minister to assist that minister with specified areas within the portfolio. As we shall see in the next section, it can be argued that such a two-tier system may have existed implicitly in the Cabinet committee system of the past twenty-five years.

Finally, as has been the case since the 1960s, a number of **parliamentary secretaries** were appointed by the Chrétien government. Parliamentary secretaries are members of the government caucus assigned to ministers to assist them in dealings with the House of Commons and the House committees. They can fill in for the minister in case of an absence, and they can appear in committee to help explain and defend the government on questions arising over the estimates or legislative proposals. A position as a parliamentary secretary brings with it some additional financial perks, but more importantly, most MPs who are assigned to such positions view the experience they gain as a potential springboard to a Cabinet post some time down the road.

### Cabinet Committees

The Cabinet itself is formally a committee of the Queen's Privy Council for Canada, but since that august body has met only twice since 1867, it has no consequence beyond providing the names of its members with the prefix "the Honourable." The Cabinet is the *de facto* executive instrument in Canadian government and delegates some of the responsibility for priority determination to a number of committees drawn from its membership.

**The Evolution of the Cabinet Committee System**  The creation of a permanent committee structure for Cabinet is generally considered to have begun under Lester Pearson in the mid 1960s. However, well before that time, committees were used to expedite Cabinet business. John A. Macdonald and Wilfrid Laurier both used *ad hoc* committees, and during the First World War, most of the Borden Cabinet's business was carried out by a "war committee" and a "reconstruction committee." While there were as many as ten standing committees of Cabinet during the Second World War, one of them, the War Committee, to all intents and purposes displaced the parent body, the **plenary Cabinet**. In the postwar era, Mackenzie King, St. Laurent, and, to a lesser extent, Diefenbaker continued to use Cabinet committees on an *ad hoc* basis.

*Treasury Board*  The oldest formal committee made up of Cabinet ministers is the Treasury Board. This committee was established by the *Financial Administration Act* of 1875. Strictly speaking, the Treasury Board is a committee of the Privy Council and thus has equal status with the Cabinet. However, for all practical purposes the Treasury Board functions as a senior Cabinet committee but with a specialized statutory mandate. The Treasury Board was established to oversee the expenditure budget and to assist the departments in the preparation and submission of the estimates.

Since 1967, the Treasury Board has also been given the responsibility for all aspects of personnel management in the public service, except for those matters reserved exclusively to the Public Service Commission. Treasury Board functions as the government *employer* in union-management relations at the federal level. The Board is composed of six ministers, plus alternates, one of whom is always the minister of Finance and the rest normally from portfolios that are engaged in large expenditures or in the collection of taxes. The prime minister would be a member of Treasury Board only if he or she were also responsible for the Finance portfolio which has not happened in recent years. Since 1968, the Treasury Board has been chaired by a minister designated the **President of the Treasury Board** and who is also the head of the **Treasury Board Secretariat**, the department that supports the board in peforming its duties. The Treasury Board remains to this day one of the busiest and most influential of the Cabinet committees.

*Priorities and Planning*  Under Lester Pearson, the rather chaotic "non-procedures" of the Diefenbaker era were finally replaced by eleven special committees and ten permanent standing committees, which made "recommendations" to the *plenary* Cabinet. The committee structure was slowly developed and formalized during the Trudeau years. The Cabinet under Pierre Trudeau's first government had nine standing committees, including the **Cabinet Committee on Priorities and Planning** (P&P), which was chaired by the prime minister and was likened to a sort of inner cabinet similar to the British model. Its smaller size (usually no more than twelve), the eminence of its chairman, and the fact that its members included only the most influential ministers with the most important portfolios made P&P a better forum for important policy decisions than a full Cabinet meeting. Together with the Treasury Board, P&P became the dominant committee of Cabinet during the Trudeau years.

In 1979, the government of Joe Clark reduced the total number of Cabinet committees and replaced P&P with a smaller coordinating committee renamed the **inner Cabinet**. The inner Cabinet had complete and formal executive responsibility to act in Cabinet's name. The 1980 Trudeau government kept the reduced number of committees, but went back to calling the inner Cabinet the Committee on Priorities and Planning. John Turner, in his brief stint in office, eliminated one committee, and Brian Mulroney ultimately left the same system in place when he formed the government in 1984.

*"Ops and Chops"*  After the 1988 election Prime Minister Mulroney introduced a radical restructuring of the Cabinet committee system. The total number of committees was increased from ten to fourteen and membership on P&P was

increased to nineteen. Because P&P had grown so large, being composed of almost half of the ministers in the plenary Cabinet, an informal sub-committee of the most important ministers on P&P emerged and came to be formalized as the **Committee on Operations** (Ops). Ops became the "*inner* inner Cabinet," composed of the chairs of the other standing committees of Cabinet, and acted as the gatekeeper and agenda setter of the entire Cabinet process. It came to completely eclipse the once dominant Committee on Priorities and Planning and even restricted the influence of Treasury Board.

The emergence of Ops as the *de facto* power centre of the Mulroney government was complemented by the establishment of an Expenditure Review Committee (ERC). This committee bore the responsibility for a major ongoing review and cutback of government expenditures that had become a preoccupation of the deficit-plagued second-term Mulroney government. All policy proposals that involved expenditures had to be reviewed by ERC before going before any other committee of the Cabinet including Treasury Board. The "one-two punch" of Operations and Expenditure Review so dominated the executive process in the latter years of the Mulroney era that the Cabinet decision-making process was laconically dubbed "Ops and Chops."

**Figure 20.1**

Structure of the Cabinet (1988 Mulroney version).

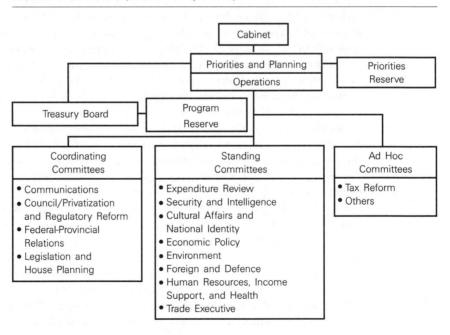

Source: R. VanLoon and M. S. Whittington, "Kaleidoscope in Grey: The Policy Process in Ottawa," *in* M. S. Whittington and G. Williams, eds., *Canadian Politics in the 1990s* (Scarborough: Nelson, 1990) p. 454.

**The Structure of Cabinet in 1995** With the unweildy size of the Cabinet and the dominant role played by the committees, the plenary Cabinet had virtually ceased to meet as a decision-making body by the end of the Mulroney era. When Kim Campbell won the Tory leadership in 1993 and became the new prime minister, she moved to pare down the size of Cabinet and to reduce the number of committees. While she never got the opportunity to try out the new system, the basic theme of a lean and mean Cabinet structure was carried on by her Liberal successor Jean Chrétien. The Chrétien Cabinet of 1993 was reduced to a "bare bones" twenty-three members and the number of Cabinet committees was reduced to four. The Chrétien reforms also eliminated the practice of having a core coordinating committee of the Cabinet such as P&P or an inner Cabinet and returned the agenda-setting and priority-determination role to the plenary Cabinet.

_The Ministry System_ As we mentioned earlier, the Chrétien model of Cabinet government made explicit the already implicit two-tier _ministry_. The pecking order within the Cabinet had previously been determined by a combination of the minister's portfolio and his or her committee memberships. Portfolios such as Finance, Justice, and External Affairs have always carried more status than Public Works, Indian Affairs, or Veterans Affairs. However, since the creation of the Cabinet committee system, the ministers who were members of the key committees such as P&P or Ops enjoyed a higher Cabinet rank than the more junior ministers who sat on the less influential standing committees. Hence, there have always been "senior" and "junior" ministers even though all were of equal status in a formal way.

In the current system, Cabinet ranking has been made more explicit with the creation of positions in the ministry called secretaries of state. The secretaries of state do not have portfolios, they do not sit on the plenary Cabinet, and they are paid less than the "full ministers" who head up departments. With only twenty-three ministers for the PM to assign to the various portfolios of the government it was necessary to reduce the total number of government departments as well. This process essentially involved a major reorganization of the bureaucracy by combining existing departments and eliminating a number of senior positions. This reorganization was begun by Kim Campbell and essentially retained by the Chrétien government.

_The Committee System Today_ As can be seen from Figure 20.2, there are now only four standing committees of Cabinet. Economic Development Policy and Social Development Policy are the "infield" of the Cabinet team, handling 80 per cent of the policy recommendations coming from the ministers. These **policy committees** then pass their recommendations on to the full Cabinet, including recommendations as to expenditure priorities in their respective policy "sectors." The plenary Cabinet once again has the final priority of determining responsibilities erstwhile handled by P&P, Ops, or the Expenditure Review Committee.

The estimates and management roles of Treasury Board are still defined by statute but the Board has also been delegated new responsibilities as a "budget office" that advises Cabinet on matters of efficient and effective man-

**Figure 20.2**
The Chrétien ministry (1995).

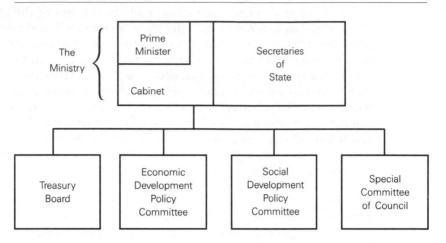

agement of resources. As well, the Board and its secretariat have been given the responsibility for reviewing the **Departmental Business Plans** that are a cornerstone of the new expenditure-management system. The fourth committee, the Special Committee of Council, is not a policy committee and deals with more routine matters such as order-in-council appointments. **Ad hoc committees** of the Cabinet can be established at any time by the prime minister to deal with important and usually fairly urgent matters; for instance, the Program Review Committee, chaired by Marcel Masse, was set up in 1993 to oversee the government-wide program-review exercise. This committee's mandate was completed with the presentation of the 1995 budget and was "decommissioned" at that time. We will say more about this program-review process in Chapter 23.

*Chapter* **21**

# PM, Cabinet, and Support Agencies: The Policy Process

The Cabinet is the most powerful aggregation of political elites in Canada and the ultimate source of its power is the fact that it is the dominant policy institution of our system of government. There are really two broad types of policy decisions that Cabinet must make. The first type is the establishing of substantive policy priorities, deciding what to do and how to get it done. This type of policy decision involves a process whereby individual ministers bring policy proposals from their departments to Cabinet through instruments called *memoranda to cabinet*. The Cabinet committees and, ultimately, the plenary Cabinet must then make a decision.

In the second type of policy decision the Cabinet must decide how the government's available resources are to be allocated among various programs and activities of government. This type of policy decision involves a much more complicated process called the *expenditure-management system*. Cabinet is involved in this process at various stages, including of course the critical final one, but the total process also involves many other institutional actors. Before dealing with each of these types of policy processes, however, it is necesary to discuss the nature of the power relationship between the PM and the Cabinet and the agencies that provide immediate policy support to the executive.

## ▶ THE POWER OF THE PRIME MINISTER

The nature of Cabinet decision-making very much reflects the way in which a prime minister wants to operate the Cabinet. The prime minister sits at the centre of the Cabinet decision-making system, is the architect of the Cabinet apparatus, and sets the tone and style of the government. A PM who enjoys a long period in office stamps his "era" of Canadian government and politics with his style. That we come to describe periods of Canadian history as the

"Trudeau era" or the "Mulroney years" is very much a symptom of the dominance of the PM in the process. There are a number of reasons for this dominance of the prime minister in the process of Cabinet government.

### Formal Power

We have already described the constitutional powers of the prime minister that flow from the fact that our formal head of state, the governor-general, makes decisions only on the advice of council, or "in council," and that it is the prime minister alone who transmits the "advice" of council to the representative of the Crown. It is the PM, therefore, who exercises all of the Crown prerogatives such as the power to summon, prorogue, and dissolve Parliament

**TABLE 21.1**

Canadian Prime Ministers, 1867–1995

| Prime Minister | Date | Party | Tenure |
|---|---|---|---|
| John A. Macdonald | 1867–1873 1878–1891 | Conservative | 19 years |
| Alexander Mackenzie | 1873–1878 | Liberal | 5 years |
| John Abbott | 1891–1892 | Conservative | 1 year |
| John Thompson | 1892–1894 | Conservative | 2 years |
| Mackenzie Bowell | 1894–1896 | Conservative | 1 year |
| Charles Tupper | 1896 | Conservative | 2 months |
| Wilfrid Laurier | 1896–1911 | Liberal | 15 years |
| Robert Borden | 1911–1920 | Conservative | 9 years |
| Arthur Meighen | 1920–1921 1926 | Conservative | 2 years |
| William Lyon Mackenzie King | 1921–1926 1926–1930 1935–1948 | Liberal | 22 years |
| R. B. Bennett | 1930–1935 | Conservative | 5 years |
| Louis St. Laurent | 1948–1957 | Liberal | 9 years |
| John Diefenbaker | 1957–1963 | PC | 6 years |
| Lester Pearson | 1963–1968 | Liberal | 5 years |
| Pierre Trudeau | 1968–1979 1980–1984 | Liberal | 15 years |
| Joe Clark | 1979–1980 | PC | 9 months |
| John Turner | 1984 | Liberal | 2 months |
| Brian Mulroney | 1984–1993 | PC | 9 years |
| Kim Campbell | 1993 | PC | 5 months |
| Jean Chrétien | 1993– | Liberal | current |

PC = Progressive Conservative. The Conservative Party changed its name to Progressive Conservative in 1941.

and to make order-in-council appointments. The PM appoints and dismisses ministers and distributes portfolio responsibilities among them as a necessary concomitant of "forming a government." The prime minister has a *prima facie* control over the rest of the Cabinet ministers because he or she has power over their jobs. The PM can implement a **Cabinet shuffle** at any time and can demote difficult ministers to lower-status portfolios or to the back benches or "reward" them with the obscurity of a Senate seat.

The prime minister also functions as the chair of the Cabinet, presiding over its deliberations and ultimately controlling its agenda. In this function, the PM has additional influence because it is the PM who is in charge of the key **central agencies**, the Prime Minister's Office (PMO) and the Privy Council Office (PCO). The PCO is tasked with advising the PM and committee chairs on policy matters, organizing the flow of paper, and providing the Cabinet and its committees with secretariat services. The PMO is a political advisory body complementing the substantive policy assistance of the PCO with hard partisan advice on which policies are best in terms of maximizing electoral support. By personally overseeing these agencies the PM has a a big edge over Cabinet colleagues when it comes to making informed policy decisions. (We will discuss these central agencies in the next section of this chapter.)

The PM is also the ultimate authority when it comes to determining the number, powers, and membership of Cabinet committees. Coupled with this control over the internal organization of the Cabinet, the PM also has the final say in the organization of the bureaucracy. He or she has the final say as to how many departments of government there will be and how the various functions of the non-political arm of the government will be bundled together into portfolios. While it would be rare for a prime minister to take any of these organizational decisions without listening to the advice of Cabinet colleagues, the central agencies, and specialists in the bureaucracy itself, the "buck stops" at the PM's desk when it comes to decision time.

### Political Leadership and Personal Style

Perhaps the greatest source of control a prime minister has over the Cabinet ministers is simply the fact that he or she is their affirmed **political leader**. The Cabinet colleagues all recognize that the PM is the elected leader of the party and that the individual in the top office got there because of a broader base of popular support in the party than any of the other candidates for the job. However, there are different **styles** of prime-ministerial leadership in Cabinet, depending on the personality and style of the individuals involved.

In earlier times, prime ministers such as Borden and Bennett often took decisions without much input from Cabinet colleagues. King took his own counsel much of the time, sometimes, it is said, with the assistance of the spirits of the deceased. Diefenbaker was a **charismatic leader** who inspired the troops on the basis of his personality and his enormous landslide victory in 1958. However, "Dief the Chief" ultimately had to stave off a "palace revolt" among Cabinet colleagues by going to caucus for a vote of confidence. By contrast, Lester Pearson was the consummate **collegial leader**, preferring to be the "honest broker" in mediating conflicts among his colleagues and "going with the flow" of Cabinet consensus.

Both Trudeau and Mulroney relied on their intial popularity with the electorate to impose their personal stamp on the Cabinet process and on the policy directions of the government. Their cabinets were fairly obedient, at first, because all ministers understood that they owed their jobs to the electoral performance of the party leader/PM. Neither ever became very tolerant of "heirs apparent" in the Cabinet ranks and limited "collegial" decision-making to small cabals of hand-picked Cabinet allies. Jean Chrétien, whether because he is, on principle, a "team player" or because he lacks the charismatic appeal of a Trudeau, appears to have returned to the "first among equals" approach of a Pearson and presides over a much more collegial decision-making process. The fact that he has chosen to reinstate the authority of the plenary Cabinet and eschew the P&P Committee approach is the best evidence of this different and more consensual style.

The personal power of the prime minister is enhanced with the Canadian public and within the Cabinet chamber because he is the leader of the country while in office. The PM is a high-profile *diplomat* representing the federal government in intergovernmental summit conferences and representing Canada in the international arena. The public exposure and media coverage that the PM receives in such contexts is usually quite positive and allows the statesman side of the job to overshadow the less flattering politician side. Singing "Irish Eyes Are Smiling" with the American president, however, may be an instance where the Canadian public got a mixed message!

### Limits to Prime Ministerial Power

While the power of the prime minister is very significant, being much greater than that of any other Cabinet minister, it is far from absolute. There are still many checks and limitations on how far a prime minister can go in unilaterally dictating the determination of priorities, the details of policy, and the choices of governing instruments.

**Collegiality and Collective Dissent**   While as their leader the prime minister can likely force ministers to accept any single policy initiative he or she chooses, no prime minister would be so foolhardy as to attempt to dictate the policy choice on *every* issue. Prime-ministerial power is very much like currency: invested judiciously, it multiplies, and spent profligately, it quickly disappears. Thus, a PM may on rare occasions over-rule even a majority of dissenting Cabinet colleagues if he or she has great personal commitment to a policy, but over the long haul the prime minister must be amenable to being convinced by the opinions of fellow ministers.

Cabinet colleagues collectively can constrain the prime minister's power to make unilateral policy decisions over the long run simply by virtue of their numbers. Cabinet decisions must be based on the principles of collegiality and solidarity, at least in public, and a prime minister can ill afford visible internal discord in the Cabinet. As well, individual ministers may have influence over the PM because of their access to information and sources in the bureaucracy, or because of the support they have marshalled either in caucus or in a particular region.

There will seldom be wholesale Cabinet revolt and only rarely are there individual resignations if the prime minister proceeds without a consensus on a few issues from time to time. However, Cabinet must, in the parliamentary system, at least appear to work as a team, and persistent internal discord cannot help but leak out to the ever-watchful media and the public. A prime minister therefore must walk a narrow line between allowing ministers too much leeway, which would create disarray, disunity, and bickering on the team, and allowing them too little, which might lead to defections, breaches of solidarity, and public airing of internal squabbles.

**Minister of Finance**  We have already alluded to the fact that different portfolios come with different levels of ministerial influence and prestige. The most important post in the Cabinet next to the PM is the Finance portfolio and it is generally the case that the minister of Finance is second only to the prime minister in influence. The major constraint on policy decison-making, particularly in this age of large deficits and alarming governmental debts, is a financial one. The realm of the possible for other ministers in setting policy priorities is therefore established by the budgetary framework set by the minister of Finance. It is the Finance minister's right, in consultation only with the prime minister, to bring down the Budget, and while he is obviously greatly constrained in his actions by the programs already in place, the economic climate, and the political situation, he still retains broad latitude to propose such things as the level at which total expenditures should be set or the nature and level of new tax measures.

The minister of Finance's influence is further enhanced by his role in preparing and delivering the Budget Speech. The speech is used as a vehicle for announcing major new initiatives in both tax and expenditure policy and it profoundly affects the psychological mood of the government, of the stock markets, and of the economy as a whole. Despite recent changes to make the process more open and to base it, in part, on consultation with Parliament and the public, the Budget is still prepared by officials in the Department of Finance, in secret, kept even from the Cabinet itself, and controlled directly by the minister of Finance. As such, the Budget constitutes a further source of power for whoever holds that portfolio. It is scarcely any wonder that other ministers await the Budget Speech with at least the same degree of anticipation and trepidation as all other Canadians, and that they sometimes view the minister of Finance with nearly the same awe with which they regard the prime minister.

There is another side of the coin to the Finance portfolio: it can also be a sentence of political death to its incumbent. Particularly when the economy is not healthy and when tough decisions to cut back popular programs or raise taxes must be made, it is the minister of Finance who must take a lot of the flak. It is not uncommon for prime ministers to assign defeated opponents in leadership contests or rising stars in the Cabinet who might be rivals for the party leadership to the Finance job. The PM can claim to be fostering party solidarity by magnanimously appointing would-be rivals to a prestigious portfolio. If the individual so rewarded does a good job and becomes popular with the public and the business community, the PM can take part of the credit for making such a wise appointment. If the individual should fail, the prime minister has a convenient scapegoat, and perhaps more importantly, can cut a would-be rival "bull" from the Cabinet "herd."

**Public Opinion** Undoubtedly, the most important of the checks on prime ministerial power is the inverse of the popularity with the electorate that can be such an important mechanism for controlling the Cabinet. By this we mean no more, and no less, than that the prime minister is subject to the same shifts in public opinion and public attitudinal vagaries as any politician. The fickle electorate can shift from blind adulation to unmitigated hatred in a very short time indeed, and often for reasons that have little to do with the performance of the individual in office. We have all seen landslide victories in one election become wholesale routs a mere four years later. The charming personal traits, quirks, and idiosyncracies that generated, for instance, the Diefenbaker landslide in 1958 and "Trudeaumania" in 1968, can become negative characteristics that are caricatured by the media and exploited by the opposition. Prime ministers, it seems, have a limited "shelf life" in the world of electronic media. Overexposure on TV turns our political leaders from heroes to objects of loathing, whereas the "real" prime minister is simply a human being with good and bad points and an extremely difficult job.

While some prime ministers survive the "end of the honeymoon" and go on to lead their parties and the country for multiple terms, many also succumb to the disenchantment of the electorate. Most recently we have seen the fairly rare situation of prime ministers in office in parliamentary systems who were not personally ready for retirement but who were forced out of office because of low public esteem in the polls. Both Margaret Thatcher in the UK and Brian Mulroney here in Canada were forced to depart public life in their prime because their parties became convinced that the next election would be a lost cause without a new leader. In the Canadian case, as we all know, Kim Campbell succeeded Mulroney and the party was still annihilated. In Britain, however, John Major succeeded Thatcher and the Tories were returned to power by the voters.

---

## ▶ EXECUTIVE SUPPORT TO PM AND CABINET

Cabinet receives considerable support in the performance of its core policy functions. We have seen in earlier chapters that the extra-parliamentary wing of the party and the government caucus both have the ability to tender advice to the government that might ultimately influence the decisions of the prime minister and Cabinet. However, these institutions provide advice to the Cabinet as only a part of their overall functions; their ability to influence Cabinet policy decisions is limited by the fact that they must compete with other agencies and individuals that are explicitly and exclusively tasked with the responsibility for supporting the prime minister and the Cabinet ministers in their policy deliberations.

This specialized policy support is provided by ministers' personal staffs, the central agencies, and the line departments of government. The policy role of the latter will be discussed in the next two chapters. However, before moving to a discussion of the key institutional actors in this role, the central agencies, we shoud say a few words about the political staff of the individual ministers.

### Ministerial Staff

The personal or *exempt* staff of the ministers — the executive assistants and the special assistants who work directly for the minister — can be influential in partisan political decisions. Cabinet ministers are busy people, and they require considerable administrative and advisory support. These functions are performed by the many, mostly young, men and women who stalk the corridors and antechambers adjacent to ministerial lairs, politely fending off most would-be visitors, quietly ushering in those deemed worthy of audience, controlling the flow of paper to their bosses, and acting as the minister's confidante when there are important issues to be chewed over. The secretaries of state also have personal support staff, but their offices are much smaller than those of the full ministers.

**The Gatekeeper Role**  In a somewhat similar way, **correspondence** units must filter the, literally, tons of incoming mail, bringing the most important correspondence (as they see it) to the minister's attention, and ensuring that appropriate replies are drafted for all letters. Ministerial **press secretaries** also must help to interpret and, they hope, to shape the opinions expressed by daily newspapers, particularly in the eyes of the department's client group. The press office of the minister also arranges press conferences and oversees the drafting of ministerial press releases.

The minister's staffers are referred to as **exempt staff** because as political appointees they are exempt from the rules and regulations of the *Public Service Employment Act* and the *Public Service Staff Relations Act* — in other words, they are not public servants and their tenure is at the pleasure of the minister who hired them. In the last few decades it has become increasingly common for individuals to be assigned or seconded to the minister's staff from within the department as well. These individuals are selected not for their partisan *bona-fides* but for their knowledge of the substantive policy concerns of the department, and for their familiarity with the client groups served by the portfolio. These **departmental assistants** retain the right to return to their department and the comfort of public-service tenure whenever they or the minister decide it is appropriate.

The power of a minister's senior staffers is that they are the gatekeepers controlling access to the minister. By determining who is important enough to get a personal hearing with the minister, by deciding which memoranda and briefing notes the minister needs to see, and often by having the last word with the minister before an important meeting, these people can have a major impact on what policy options ultimately get to the Cabinet level and what "spin" is put on the minister's message. They also sometimes attempt to play a role as intermediaries or communication links with the minister's department, often to the great displeasure of departmental officials. However, a good minister understands that "turf wars" between political staff and senior departmental officials are dysfunctional and will discourage such rivalries where they become evident.

**The Mulroney Years** During the Mulroney years ministerial staffs were enlarged and the senior staffer in the minister's office was given greater pay, the effective rank of an assistant deputy minister, and the title **Chief of Staff**. This was inspired by the fact that the Tory government did not trust the senior bureaucracy, which had long become accustomed to working closely with the outgoing Liberal Cabinet. By the end of the Mulroney era, some ministers' staffs had expanded from the normal complement of twenty to as many as seventy. The chiefs of staff, with a large support group and direct access to the minister, did indeed attempt to counter the advice flowing up from the department, revising briefing notes before the minister got them and briefing the minister before meetings with senior departmental officials.

While this system worked well in some instances, in others it worked very badly. Chiefs of staff and senior bureaucrats often ended up jousting for the attentions of the minister rather than working together to solve problems. As well, in some cases ministers appointed chiefs of staff who had been faithful parliamentary assistants while the party was in opposition but who were not talented enough to assume the responsibilities of chief of staff to a minister. Naturally, career bureaucrats resented the interference of such individuals in the interaction between the minister and the department. Besides, the system became not only fraught with redundancies but also too damned expensive.

**The Chrétien Reforms** Among the first things the Chrétien government did when it took power in 1993 was to abolish the post of Chief of Staff in ministers' offices and to impose significant reductions in the size of the exempt staffs. These measures were taken to save money but also because the new government recognized the inefficiency and duplication of effort that had befallen the old system. The stated goal of the Chrétien government was to re-establish the close working relationship between the minister and the senior officials of the department. The senior staffer in a minister's office today is an **executive assistant**, and only the prime minister has a chief of staff who is in charge of the central agency called the Prime Minister's Office.

### The Central Agencies

In the federal government, the **central agencies** include the **Prime Minister's Office**, the **Privy Council Office**, and the **Treasury Board Secretariat** (TBS). As well, although it appears, superficially, to be just another department, the Department of Finance functions as though it were a central agency. While it is not physically central in an organization chart of the government, Finance is a central actor in all policy deliberations because budgetary concerns are central to virtually all policy decisions. Similarly, the Department of Justice is often referred to as a central agency because all policy proposals must be vetted for legal and constitutional implications by officials of that department.

The central agencies must begin to consider policy issues well before their political masters are required to come to any decisions. They must do so because Cabinet must have adequate supporting information in order to make informed priority decisions. The central agencies are thus responsible either for generating relevant data themselves or for filtering, summarizing, and demystifying the mass of information from the departments for the already overloaded ministers. This **briefing function** — the preparation of briefing notes or the provision of oral briefings for ministers — is at the heart of the influence of the central agencies.

Since their function is to provide support for political leaders, political considerations colour all the advice tendered by the central agencies. It is important, however, to differentiate between **political considerations** and **partisan considerations**. The PMO is staffed by individuals who are expected to provide frankly partisan support to the PM and, indirectly, to the Cabinet as a whole. If another party comes to power, all of these people definitely lose their jobs. In fact, because the PMO personnel are expected to be loyal to the individual PM, a new PM of the *same* party may also do some serious house cleaning when he or she takes over.

By contrast to the PMO, all of the other central agencies provide support for the elected government of the day regardless of its partisan stripe. When one government is defeated, the PCO, TBS, and Finance all continue to provide support for the next Cabinet. Being human, they may have their personal preferences as to parties and incumbents, but they will generally be willing to serve regardless of their personal feelings, for they are, for the most part, professionals and careerists in the public service. While it is the prerogative of the incoming government to replace the most senior officials in the PCO and the deputy minister of Finance, any individuals so affected would normally only be rotated to other senior positions in the bureaucracy and would retain their rank and salary in the government. In recent years, it has not been uncommon for a new prime minister to leave these senior officers of the central agencies in place if they indicate a willingness to work for the incoming government.

**The Prime Minister's Office**   Since the prime minister bears the pre-eminent responsibility for the political fortunes of the government, it is the **Prime Minister's Office** that bears the largest responsibility for the provision of partisan political advice. The PMO is always staffed at the senior levels by close partisan loyalists and people whose advice is valued by the prime minister. Since the 1960s, it has been commonplace for many senior positions in the PMO to be filled by close personal friends and political associates of the incumbent PM. While it is quite rare for any of the staff of the PMO to be recruited from the public service, Brian Mulroney did recruit a few senior bureaucrats, such as Derek Birncy, to work in his staff.

The PMO was originally simply the small group of exempt political staff that served the prime minister personally. R. B. Bennett had a staff of about twelve during the 1930s, Mackenzie King, Louis St. Laurent, and John Diefenbaker each had about thirty staff members, and by the late 1960s, Lester Pearson's PMO rose to about forty employees. The PMO grew more rapidly during the Trudeau years and the office reached a high of almost 200 employees under Brian Mulroney. In keeping with the imperatives of reducing government expenditures across the board, Prime Minister Chrétien's office has been reduced to fewer than seventy individuals.

The uses a prime minister will make of the PMO will vary from time to time and from PM to PM. In the early Trudeau years, the PMO was avowedly a source of many major policy initiatives. Later, as an election approached and then as a minority government and another election followed, the PMO became much more devoted to partisan issues and electoral politics, providing advice to the prime minister on the relative partisan advantages of competing policy options. Brian Mulroney, who basically mistrusted the bureaucracy, sought a greater politicization of the policy process by expanding the PMO in both numbers and influence. Jean Chrétien, whose style of leadership leaves more authority in the hands of his individual ministers and who has publicly committed the government to working more closely with the senior bureaucracy, has reduced both the size and the ostensible power of the PMO.

While the absolute power of the PMO may wax and wane over time, the basic functions of the institution remain the same. Much of the total time and

**Figure 21.1**
Prime Minister's Office (PMO).

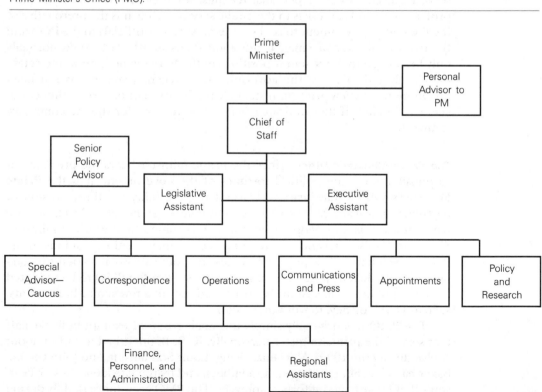

effort of the PMO is devoted to rather prosaic duties, such as screening and responding to the vast amount of **Correspondence** that crosses the PM's desk, and organizing the PM's agenda, arranging **Appointments**, and scheduling travel commitments. The **Communications** branch is reponsible for managing the flow of information to the media through the preparation of press releases and the organizing of press conferences and other media events. Other press officers in the Communications branch are responsible for scanning the national and regional media and regularly briefing the Cabinet on what issues appear to be politically "hot" in various parts of the country.

There are also several **regional assistants** in the PMO who are responsible for keeping tabs on important developments in the various regions, for fielding inquiries that come into the office from the regions, and for maintaining informal liaison with the regional caucuses as required. A precursor to these regional assistants was a system of **regional desks** established in the PMO by the Trudeau government. These were expected to keep the PM informed about the special political concerns of Canadians across the country, but were ultimately dismantled because of complaints from the regional caucuses that such a system centralized and usurped the legitmate representative role of the government MPs. The reinstitution of a capacity to assess regional concerns in the PMO will succeed only if it is done in close cooperation with the "regional ministers" and the regional caucuses.

The main policy mandate of the PMO is vested in the **Policy and Research** branch of the organization, headed up, in 1995, by the high-profile Chaviva Hosek, recently of the National Action Committee on the Status of Women. This unit has senior policy advisors on economic development, social development, and government operations who oversee policy research in their areas of specialization. However, all policy questions are reviewed by the senior officials in the PMO before they are placed on the agenda of Cabinet committees. The prime minister may also appoint, from time to time "special policy advisors" on specific areas of policy concern.

The highest level of policy advice to Prime Minister Chrétien comes from the **chief of staff**, Jean Pelletier, and the **senior policy advisor**, Eddie Goldenberg. These senior advisors in the PMO are likely closer to and more trusted by the prime minister than even his Cabinet colleagues. They act as his personal "brain trust" in whom he can confide and from whom he can seek advice, even on matters concerning the internal dynamics and problems of the Cabinet itself. Such individuals are obviously very powerful because they enjoy the absolute confidence and trust of the most powerful man in our governmental system.

**The Privy Council Office**  The non-partisan first cousin to the PMO, the **Privy Council Office**, shares office space in the immediate vicinity of Parliament Hill, space that symbolizes both the role of serving the Cabinet that meets there and the proximity to political and governmental power. Since the late 1960s, the role of the PCO has evolved from that of an agency almost entirely concerned with moving paper through Cabinet, through a brief and overly ambitious attempt to manage all aspects of government policy, to a position as architect of much of the machinery and process of government in Ottawa.

Today, the function of the PCO has receded again to the responsibility for providing major logistical and decision-making support for the Cabinet and its committees.

*Basic Structure* The PCO, which employs approximately 500 people, is headed by Canada's highest-ranking public servant, who holds the double-barrelled title, **Secretary to the Cabinet and Clerk of the Privy Council**. There are three major units in the PCO; two are headed up by a **deputy secretary to the Cabinet** and the third by the **deputy clerk of the Privy Council**. As indicated in Figure 21.2, each of these deputy secretaries is in charge of several secretariats. There is a fourth branch of the PCO, Intergovernmental Relations, that is headed up by a senior bureaucrat with another double-barrelled title, **Deputy Minister and Associate Secretary to the Cabinet**. This latter branch of the PCO, which will be discussed later, is composed of the remnants of the **Federal-Provincial Relations Office** (FPRO), which was at one time a separate central agency of the federal government. As well, the large **Corporate Services** branch is headed up by an ADM; it provides all of the administrative, personnel, and financial services for the PCO and is home to almost forty *legal advisors* provided by the Department of Justice.

The current organizational structure of the PCO is largely reflective of the Cabinet committee structure that evolved during the Trudeau and Mulroney years, with a specialized secretariat to support each committee. The PCO is still organized around numerous substantive policy areas, each of which had been assigned in the past to a separate Cabinet committee. Because the Chrétien Cabinet has only two policy committees, each is now served by more than one of the policy secretariats in the PCO. Each secretariat has six to twelve officers and a proportional support staff, and is headed by an **assistant secretary to the Cabinet**.

*Policy Secretariats* The **Operations** branch of the PCO contains the main policy secretariats. These include Economic and Regional Development, Social Development, Foreign and Defence Policy, and Government Operations. These are the working groups of professionals that provide the support for the Cabinet committees on Economic Development Policy and Social Development Policy. As well, Operations is responsible for managing the flow of paper in the organization, supporting the Special Committee of Council and operating the registry of orders-in-council and statutory instruments, called *The Canada Gazette*.

The most influential secretariat in the PCO has always been Priorities and Planning, which was responsible for backing up the Cabinet committee of the same name. Now that P&P has disappeared from the governmental map, its responsibilities assumed by the plenary Cabinet, the secretariat performs the same function it always did but for the prime minister and the full Cabinet. Along with the secretariat for Program Review, it is the Priorities and Planning secretariat of the PCO that has the main responsibility for briefing the PM, setting the Cabinet agenda, and organizing and managing the complex process of priority determination.

**Figure 21.2**
Privy Council Office (PCO).

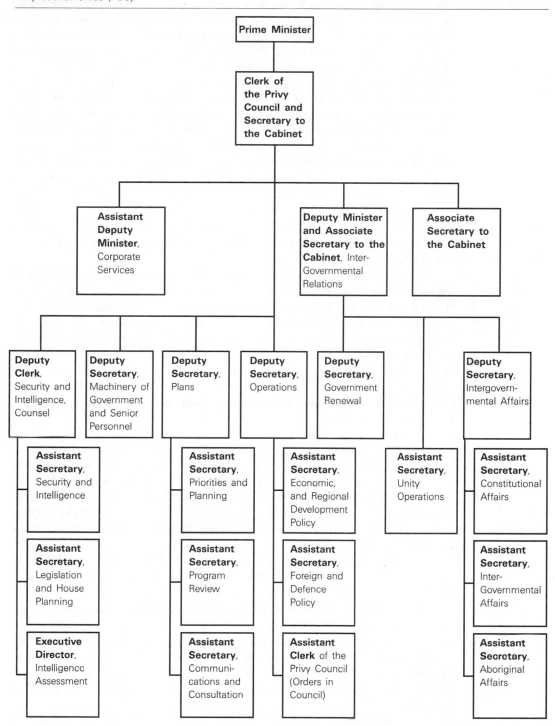

*Other Chores*  Besides the ones mentioned above, there are several other secretariats within the PCO. While they are all important, we will not deal with them in detail here because their involvement in the policy process is either limited or intermittent. The Communications and Consultation secretariat is responsible both for informing the public about government policy and for organizing the machinery for consultation with NGOs and individuals in a policy community affected by a pending Cabinet decision. The secretariat on the Machinery of Government, which is headed by its own deputy secretary, provides advice on government reorganization and can be very influential when the PM is in the mood to shuffle government departments and agencies.

There is also a secretariat that keeps track of the countless order-in-council positions that have to be filled. While the appointment of deputy ministers will be of interest to the prime minister and patronage plums that can be used to provide rewards and incur obligations in the future will be important to the party, there are many minor OIC appointments that must be made routinely. Most of these are not of great enough concern to require the personal involvement of the Cabinet and are made routinely by the government on the recommendation of the PCO.

The fairly large Security and Intelligence secretariat is supposed to assist the Cabinet in coming to strategic decisions about national security matters. While this secretariat is not quite as busy today as it was during the Cold War, it is also responsible for making recommendations about physical and personnel security matters of government-wide concern. Finally, there is the secretariat on Legislation and House Planning, which is responsible for assisting the prime minister and the House leader in organizing and scheduling the introduction of government bills in Parliament. The Cabinet Committee on Legislation and House Planning that this secretariat was intended exclusively to serve was abolished in 1993.

*Intergovernmental Affairs Branch*  In Chapter 10 we described the function of intergovernmental central agencies. The Intergovernmental Affairs branch of the PCO is such a central agency, recently a separate entity called the Federal-Provincial Relations Secretariat (FPRO), but currently in a period of institutional hibernation. The genealogy of the FPRO can be traced to the original reorganization of the Cabinet committee system by the newly elected Trudeau government of 1968.

The plan at that time was for a Committee of Cabinet on Federal-Provincial Relations to coordinate the federal side in all dealings with the provinces, and the staff support for this committee was to be a branch of the PCO under a deputy secretary to the Cabinet. The coordinative role of the Cabinet committee, however, never really blossomed, for the simple reason that relations with the provinces were either so all-encompassing in their scope that the prime minister himself and the Committee on Priorities and Planning had to carry the ball, or so narrow and portfolio-specific that the individual federal departments would organize things through their own federal-provincial relations branches.

In the meantime, the Federal-Provincial Relations secretariat in the PCO had evolved into a separate agency by 1975, under a full secretary to the

Cabinet. The FPRO went through a growth spurt, partly because the Canadian Unity Information Office was domiciled within it, and remained a separate bureaucratic agency presided over by a full secretary to the Cabinet under the administrations of Joe Clark, Pierre Trudeau, John Turner, and Brian Mulroney. In 1993 the FPRO was reabsorbed into the PCO under an associate secretary to the Cabinet.

Today, within the branch, the **Intergovernmental Affairs secretariat** retains the responsibility for organizing intergovernmental conferences, with the support of the **Canadian Intergovernmental Conference secretariat**, and its **Constitutional Affairs secretariat** maintains a special "watching brief" with respect to Quebec affairs. It is also the lead agency for briefing the minister most directly responsible for Quebec affairs and the PM on matters of provincial relations. As well, the **Aboriginal Affairs secretariat** is intended to coordinate relations betweeen aboriginal governments and the federal government,[1] but there are, as yet, not many aboriginal governments for Canada to have relations with. While this secretariat is also involved in the development and negotiation of options for implementing aboriginal self-government, it is a secondary player to the lead agency, Indian Affairs, and to Justice and Finance, which have very strong concerns about the legal and financial implications of self-government.

*Ministries of State and the PCO*   In the late 1970s the government experimented with alternative institutions for assisting the Cabinet in dealing with the complexities of allocating budgetary envelopes within policy sectors. The Cabinet committees had to be given technical backup in the determination of priorities within their general expenditure areas. Because this job would be most difficult on the economic-development and social-policy fronts, two new central agencies, the **Ministry of State for Social Development** (MSSD) and the **Ministry of State for Economic Development** (MSED)[2] were created.

These ministries of state were relatively small as Ottawa bureaucracies go, with MSSD ultimately containing approximately 100 staff members and MSED approximately twice that many. They engaged in long-range planning activities for their respective sectors. Each administered the forecast expenditures for new programs within its envelope, with the financing of existing programs being managed by the Treasury Board. Each ministry of state gained its power primarily by acting as a gatekeeper in the policy and expenditure-management systems.

Before any policy proposal went to the appropriate Cabinet committee, it would normally be discussed with ministry officials and considered by a committee of deputy ministers chaired by the secretary (deputy minister) of the ministry. The Cabinet committee was provided with written advice on the basis of these deliberations, and, in addition, the ministry was required to brief the chairman of the Cabinet committee, before the committee meeting, on the

---

1. The name of the secretariat was changed from *federal-provincial* relations to *intergovernmental* affairs to recognize the fact that the federal government today must deal with territorial governments and with aboriginal governments as well as with provinces.
2. The Ministry of State for Economic Development later became the Ministry of State for Economic and Regional Development (MSERD).

substance of proposals. Coordination and integration within the sector were to be achieved through the policy review functions of these agencies, and proposals did not normally proceed to Cabinet committees before a thorough examination by the ministries themselves.

The fatal flaw of the ministries of state may have been that they became too powerful, not only stepping on the toes of other central agencies but also challenging the power of the Cabinet committees themselves. Their main clients were their own Cabinet committees, but while their ministers may have appreciated the ministries' critiques of other ministers' proposals, they generally did not appreciate critiques of their own ideas. The ministries of state, therefore, became unpopular even with the ministers they were intended to support. This situation was exacerbated by the frustrations inevitably felt by ministers in the dying days of the Trudeau government, as they watched poll results steadily come to favour the opposition. As well, an environment already heavily cluttered with other central agencies generated expensive and unproductive competition for influence among policy-support institutions.

When John Turner took over from Pierre Trudeau in 1984, he was anxious to develop some distance between his government and its predecessor — to put a new face on his administration. One way in which he sought to do this was by eliminating ministries of state. This he accomplished as his first (and nearly his last) executive act. It will not have escaped the attention of some readers that, in many respects, the functions conducted by the latter-day ministries of state could have been carried out in the Privy Council Office. Indeed, around Ottawa, the ministries were often viewed either as PCO extensions or as PCO "wannabes" by another name. It was therefore anticipated, correctly, that the demise of the ministries would ultimately lead to an expansion of the Privy Council Office, particularly in the secretariats of committees formerly served by ministries. The ministry-of-state device has not reappeared since 1984.

*Summary: The Power of the PCO*   Since Cabinet and its policy committees are the key decision points for priority determination, control over the agendas of committees and over the wording of their decisions is a significant source of power. The writing of policy-committee recommendations to the full Cabinet is done by PCO officials after committee discussions. A decision is circulated in draft format before it is finalized, but there is always some latitude on the part of the officials to interpret what the ministers really decided, and, while a PCO officer cannot produce a committee recommendation that flies in the face of a firm decision, there is always the possibility of a bit of shaping.

Further influence accrues to the PCO because of its overall responsibility for making recommendations about the organization of the bureaucracy and because of its power to tender advice to the prime minister via the secretary to the Cabinet on all senior-personnel matters and key order-in-council appointments. However, perhaps the most significant source of PCO influence is its role in briefing the PM. Formally, these briefings are a joint PCO-PMO function, with the PCO having primary responsibility for all but the political aspects of the **briefing notes**.

In reality, the relative influence of these agencies, and the subject matter on which they tender advice, will depend on the relative degree of confidence the prime minister has in the personnel of each group. The source of material for PCO briefing notes is most often within operating departments, but it will also be gleaned from other central agencies such as the Finance ministry and the Treasury Board secretariat, and the responsible officer will often have had sufficient years of experience with the subject matter to add a personal "spin" to the material. While such PCO briefing notes are far from the only source of prime-ministerial information, next to the political briefings from the PMO, they are likely the most persuasive ones.

**Treasury Board Secretariat**   We have seen that the statutory committee of the Cabinet called the Treasury Board has two broad sets of responsibilities. The first of these relates to the management of the public service. In this regard, it attempts to improve the public service as an administrative system, offers more or less welcome advice to the line managers of government as to how they might improve their individual operations, acts as the employer for purposes of collective bargaining, and issues guidelines for administrative and financial procedures.

The second set of responsibilities of the Treasury Board relates to the budgetary process. The *Financial Administration Act*, which is the legislation governing the expenditure process, delegates to the Treasury Board the responsibility of overseeing the estimates process. As well, at an earlier phase of the budgetary cycle, the Treasury Board is responsible for evaluating and making recommendations to Cabinet on departmental program-expenditure targets, proposals for reallocation of funds from one program to another, and departmental business plans.

The secretary of the Treasury Board, a DM-rank public servant who heads up the Treasury Board secretariat, is also the comptroller general of Canada. The **Office of the Comptroller General** is responsible for developing financial-control procedures and for ensuring that they are implemented in all government programs. These financial-control measures and the evaluation procedures that accompany them have little direct bearing on the policy process. They could, in theory, be more influential in deciding where to impose cutbacks and reallocations of spending but most ministers, at least in the past, have tended to ignore them.

The key influence of the TBS stems from the fact that, unlike other Cabinet committees, the Treasury Board *per se* does not actually have to establish many priorites, but only to put in place priorities that have been approved by the full Cabinet. As a result, the permanent department that formally "supports" the board, the TBS, is the body that *actually* provides the advice to Cabinet on most matters within the mandate of the board. The ministers on the board, including the president, will have had their individual say on the priority issues in full Cabinet or on one of the policy committees, and they usually pass on the work of their secretariat without a lot of changes.

The main reason for the operational free rein given to the TBS is that its responsibilities are very well fenced in by statute, by explicit priorities and directions determined by Cabinet, and by the Department of Finance. Moreover, the bulk of its duties are highly technical and extremely detailed. No minister has either the time or the expertise to be able to evaluate programs and departmental business plans, conduct a detailed scrutiny of the estimates, or provide administrative support services to the entire bureaucracy. Hence, while within its defined sphere of responsibilities TBS has a fairly free rein, that sphere is very restricted. Neither the board nor its secretariat *determine* government priorities; rather, they *implement* and "ride herd" over priorities established elsewhere. We will say more about the overall job of the Treasury Board in the following chapter.

**Department of Finance**  The Department of Finance retains primary responsibility for advising the government on overall aspects of macro-economic policy, for setting the levels of transfer payments to the provinces, and for forecasting the potential effect of government policies on the economy. It is the Cabinet's primary advisor at the time when future-year expenditure allocations are made, setting out the fiscal framework for the coming fiscal year. The Department of Finance prepares the Budget and the Pre-Budget Consultation Papers and is responsible for making short- and long-term economic forecasts of government revenues. This information is a vital part of the data required to make priority decisions on all substantive policy issues if they will cost money — and they all do!

If the Department of Finance is forecasting declining government revenues, then the Cabinet will be extremely reluctant to take on a big new program, however desirable it may be politically. The Department of Finance is also responsible for all aspects of the raising of revenues and, hence, for all aspects of the taxation system, including those devices intended to provide financial inducements to people and corporations to behave in certain ways — the deductions, write-offs, loop-holes, and tax incentives that we call *tax expenditures*. If any policy proposal is to be carried out through the tax system, or if it will have a significant effect on the economy or government revenues, the role of the Department of Finance becomes paramount.

The great influence of this department as a "central agency" stems from its expertise and specialization. Since Cabinet ministers are not normally economists, and since they are too busy to be able to engage in extensive searches for alternative financial information, they are rather at the mercy of the Department of Finance when large economic questions are at issue. If any other department's policy designs appear to clash with those of the Department of Finance, the other department tends to emerge the loser. When the nation's economy is under financial pressure because of high interest rates, an unstable dollar, or a debt crisis, as it is in the 1990s, the Department of Finance's power is even greater. Needless to say, the great power of the department, and the attitude among many Finance "poobahs" that their authority is "as the divine right of kings" makes the department less than loved by officials in other departments.

### *Ad Hoc* Policy Support Mechanisms

Sometimes, areas of special concern to the government are dealt with by special task forces, study teams, or royal commissions, which are established and mandated by Cabinet. The use of task forces, and, to a lesser extent recently because of cost, royal commissions, has remained fairly popular at both federal and provincial levels of government as a way of combining private-sector and governmental expertise in a particularly complex or sensitive area.

**Royal Commissions** Royal commissions of inquiry have a long history in Canadian politics. At first, they were usually set up to investigate particularly sensitive areas where some wrongdoing in the governmental structure was suspected, and they were usually headed by a superior court judge. They had little real importance in the policy-making process, but lent legitimacy and objectivity to investigations that might have been lacking if politicians were given the job. The first major break with this predominantly investigative or quasi-judicial role was the Rowell-Sirois Commission of the late 1930s, which conducted massive research into all of the constitutional, financial, and political ills of the Depression-era federal system.

By the mid 1960s, royal commissions were being used increasingly to investigate areas of policy concern, such as public-service reform (Glassco), taxation (Carter), health services (Hall), or bilingualism and biculturalism (Dunton-Laurendeau). Today's typical royal commission is still small, has a relatively confined mandate, is headed by one to three commissioners, and has a staff of some ten or twelve. But there are occasional exceptions. In the late 1960s, the Carter Commission on Taxation, which led to major income-tax reforms, and the Hall Commission on Health Services, which still influences health policy-makers, had considerably larger staffs of experts. The Royal Commission on Bilingualism and Biculturalism (B&B) in the 1960s, featured nine commissioners with a staff of hundreds and managed, for a few brief years, to eliminate, almost completely, unemployment among Canadian social scientists.

The Royal Commission on the Economic Union and Development Prospects for Canada (the MacDonald Commission), was, in terms of size and hoopla, a worthy successor to the B&B commission. It featured thirteen commissioners, about the same size staff as the bilingualism and biculturalism commission, and provided a similar research-contract bonanza for a very substantial number of Canada's social scientists. The report of the MacDonald Commission was significant in moving Canada towards free trade agreements with the US. The most recent mega-commission has conducted a wide-ranging and multi-year study into aboriginal peoples' concerns; it reports in 1996.

The policy significance of royal commissions varies depending on the political circumstances of the times and on the extent to which the recommendations of the commission in question are in tune with governmental priorities and public opinion. A government is not formally bound by a royal commission report, but the very act of mandating the commission indicates substantial concern about a problem. Since most royal commissions publish most of their findings,[3] and since there has, presumably, been considerable public interest in the issue under study, governments usually move to implement at least a part of what is suggested in the reports.

It has often been suggested that governments will appoint a royal commission when they want to defuse a politically touchy issue or to buy themselves some time until public opinion gels. No doubt this is the intention behind the appointment of many commissions, but in following this route, a government must be aware that it is creating a ticking time bomb. Eventually the commission will report, and the report will be widely read or reported in the media. Since the commission, once appointed, cannot be controlled by government, and since it is viewed by the public as being expert, independent, and impartial, there may be very considerable pressure to implement its proposals. What can be very difficult for a government is to be handed a report from a royal commission established by its predecessor, and focused on problems that are not a high priority for the new government.

**Task Forces**  Task forces have the advantage to the government of providing input and advice on priorities, but in a more controllable and generally less publicly "hyped" format than a royal commission. Task forces vary in formality, size, and structure, but most commonly they have one overall director and a small staff of professionals, and typically they farm out many of their research responsibilities in the form of contracts. Many task forces, particularly those intended to give direction on the choice of policy options, report directly to Cabinet through a designated minister.

However, the term *task force* is not a precisely defined one and it is being used increasingly to describe lower-level bureaucratic working groups set up to investigate some area of concern within a specific portfolio. As well, at the other end of the spectrum, we now see ministerial "task forces," which are, in effect, no less than *ad hoc* committees of Cabinet. Whatever structure they take on, as far as governments are concerned, the great advantage of task forces is that their work and recommendations need not be released to the public. Certainly, if the recommendations of a task force coincide with the government's "druthers," it will release the report, usually with a few pious paeans about the public's right to know and the need for open government. However, if a government does not like what it is told, it simply fails to publish the task force's report and makes policy choices in another way.

Perhaps the most famous task force in Canadian political history had some of the characteristics described above, but it went considerably beyond what we normally think of when we use the term *task force*. The Ministerial Task Force on Program Review (the Nielsen Task Force) was actually a group of senior ministers, active from 1984 to 1986, under the chairmanship of the deputy prime minister, Erik Nielsen. It was intended to review the need for and the efficiency and effectiveness of delivery of a vast array of programs

---

3. The royal commission set up to look into alleged wrongdoings by the RCMP Security Service in the 1970s (McDonald Commission) withheld a significant amount of is findings because of either pending prosecutions or national security concerns. The commission's recommendations, however, led directly to the establishment of the "civilian" Canadian Security Intelligence Service (CSIS) in 1984.

covering nearly all aspects of government activity. The review work was actually conducted by study teams of public-sector and private-sector people who held hearings across the country and probed deeply into the conduct of government departments and agencies. Unlike many task-force activities, the study-team reports were published, in March 1986.

As a conclusion to this discussion of royal commissions and task forces, it is important to point out that, often, the impact of such studies comes as much from the process as it does from the report and recommendations. For example, the Neilson Task Force did not result directly in a great many changes to the structure of the bureaucracy, but it certainly got the attention of all public servants. The reports of the task force, which pointed the finger at every department of the government, led to a change in the "culture" of the Canadian bureaucracy and generated a universal consciousness of the need for greater efficiencies in government that made possible the reorganizations and cutbacks of the next decade.

In a similar, but also very different, way the greatest contribution of the Berger Commission on the Mackenzie Valley Pipeline was the extent to which it awakened the consciousness of the aboriginal people of the Mackenzie Valley to their own powerlessness and spurred them to mobilize politically. As well, the Berger Report was a very significant educative device: it made Canadians in general more aware of the plight of the people of the Mackenzie Valley and of aboriginal people elsewhere in Canada, and it made us all aware of the richness of their culture, traditions, and way of life. Thus, for some task forces and royal commissions, "the medium *is* the message."

---

## ▶ CABINET DECISION-MAKING

In an earlier chapter we said that the principle of responsible government is one of the constitutional cornerstones of Parliamentary democracy. One corollary of this principle is that ministers are *individually* accountable to Parliament for the management of their departments. A second corollary is that the government is *collectively* responsible to Parliament for the conduct of all of the affairs of the state, including the behaviour of individual ministers. Thus, because the Cabinet is collectively responsible, all ministers get tarred with the same brush if the government as a whole makes a mistake.

The decisions of the Cabinet are said to be taken by *consensus* and never by a formal vote. As a result, the public knows only that a decision has been taken but has no way of telling whether the issue was hotly contested or agreed upon unanimously by the ministers. There are certainly no dissenting opinions reported as is the case with judicial decisions. Even a minister who strongly disagrees with the collective decision must swallow the verdict of his or her colleagues, and the only recourse would be to resign from the Cabinet.

Because of collective responsibility and collegiality, it is accepted that, *within* Cabinet, ministers do have a right to express their views and to disagree with even a strong consensus within the collectivity. This system works only because the *secrecy* of the proceedings in the Cabinet chamber is a long-standing tradition of Cabinet government and one that is accepted by all ministers. A breach of **Cabinet secrecy** is one of the most serious transgressions that a minister can be accused of and would almost certainly result in the immediate dismissal of the offender from the Cabinet.

### Cabinet and the Policy Process

Obviously, it is very difficult to discuss the Cabinet decision-making process because Cabinet meetings are *in camera* and ministers are sworn to secrecy. However, even if we could be as a fly on the wall in the Cabinet chambers, we would still not really know the full story about how the decisions get made. By definition, "deciding" happens in the minds of individuals. Hence, because gaining access to peoples' minds is at least as difficult as gaining access to the Cabinet chamber, all we can actually observe is the outcome of the process. However, what we can say about policy decision-making in Cabinet is how a decision is triggered and how information about the issue is channelled to the ministers.

**Cabinet Documents**  In both Liberal and Conservative versions of the Cabinet structure, the main instrument that triggers a Cabinet decision is a document called a **Memorandum to the Cabinet** (MC) which must be signed by the minister. The MC consists of a three-page **ministerial recommendation** and its length and format are strictly limited by guidelines established by the PCO. The ministerial recommendation is backed up by a lengthier and more detailed *analysis* section. The ministerial recommendations are not made public, but the discussion papers, which contain most of the information of the memorandum, often amplified with considerable technical detail, are either released in an edited form for public consumption or become publicly available under the *Freedom of Information Act*.

By far the largest number of these **Cabinet documents** are written within the bureaucracy. They may express demands arising within the department, for example, when officials ask for a change in departmental terms of reference or programs, or they may result from ministerial initiatives. Whether they originate in the minister's office or within the bureaucracy, MCs can be inspired by political communication channels, such as caucus, the party organization, the PMO, or the minister's own contacts, or by demands from client groups, which have been communicated through bureaucratic channels. The sponsoring minister is responsible for piloting the recommendation through the Cabinet process.

Items appearing on the Cabinet agenda may also be written by individual ministers' offices. Memoranda produced personally by a minister may appear when ministers want to deal with sensitive political topics. Cabinet documents may also originate in the PCO and go forward to Cabinet over the signature of the PM. Those produced by the PCO are fairly rare and might deal with procedural or organizational matters in the system, security issues, or questions of the overall tone and direction of government priorities.

The former ministries of state also produced Cabinet memoranda when officials, supported by the committee chairman, felt that they had seen policy needs that departments missed because of the fragmented nature of departmental responsibilities. These MCs might appear when the subject was a major policy change cutting across the interests of several departments, when a major statement of priorities was required, or when financial issues dealing with a whole sector required Cabinet consideration. Since the abolition of the ministries of state, an option for triggering Cabinet discussion of multi-departmental policy concerns is an MC signed by two or more ministers, all of whom would share the responsibility for piloting the document through Cabinet.

Not every item dealt with in Cabinet requires a written document, however. Cabinet agendas usually have at the top of the list an item entitled, cryptically, *general discussion*. This may simply trigger a bit of chatter about current events and concerns, the results of a recent opinion poll, or comments about minor problems being faced in the portfolios. This item allows the heavy hitters in the Cabinet, the PM and the minister of Finance, to issue decrees from on high and to make announcements; regional ministers can wait to raise special issues of regional concern. While major policy decisions are not taken in this manner, sometimes a minister will attempt to "walk in" an especially urgent matter for decision that is ancillary to an MC already on the table, but such end runs around the central-agency gatekeepers are frowned on — especially by the central agencies.

**The Decision Flow** The normal trigger for Cabinet decision is, thus, a memorandum to the Cabinet whereby a sponsoring minister recommends a certain policy to his or her colleagues. The MC must be received by the PCO one week prior to the meeting in which it is to be discussed. If the paper work is deemed to be in order by the minions in the appropriate secretariat, the item is added to the agenda of the policy committee of Cabinet. The Cabinet committee discusses the issue and the policy proposal is defended by the sponsoring minister, often with the help of senior departmental officials who may be invited to attend the meeting.

After discussion and possible changes to the proposal by the Cabinet committee, the committee makes a recommendation to the full Cabinet. These recommendations are contained in a **committee report** (CR) written by the policy secretariat of the committee. Such CRs remain secret and are never made public. The full Cabinet will then address the issues raised by the CR with the recommendation being defended by the chairman of the committee. If the Cabinet ratifies the recommendation of a committee report, a **record of decision** (RD), written by the PCO, is issued, authorizing specific action such as the drafting of legislation. RDs are formal instructions to ministers as to what they should instruct their officials to do in order to put into effect the decision of Cabinet. The RDs remain secret documents and are intended only for internal use in the appropriate departments.

### Cabinet and the Expenditure-Management Process
While the decisions involving the establishment of major government policy priorities are the most exciting and the most newsworthy, we often forget that one of the most important kinds of decisions taken by the Cabinet involves the determination of budgetary priorities. Hence, one of the most important roles

of Cabinet and one of its most time-consuming responsibilities is the allocation of budgetary resources through the expenditure-management system. While much of the expenditure-management process happens within the line departments and in agencies such as the Treasury Board secretariat and the Department of Finance, the final determination of expenditure priorities must still be decided by the Cabinet. We will deal in more detail with the bureaucratic components of this process in the following chapters, but it is important to outline here the role of the Cabinet in the expenditure-mangement system and how that role has evolved.

**The Standard-Objects Budget** The expenditure-management system in Canada, as with most other countries, is based on the principle that the executive branch — the departments and agencies — of the government are funded by the legislature on the basis of estimates of expenditure needs for the coming fiscal year. This **estimates system** of financing departments is an upward and aggregative process whereby managers at the lower levels of the bureaucracy estimate the financial needs of their particular areas of responsibility and these specific estimates are bundled together at successively higher levels in the chain of command of the department until the entire estimates for the department can be approved by the deputy minister. The aggregate **departmental estimates** are then formally approved by the minister and passed on to the Treasury Board, whose secretariat reviews them in detail with an eye to improving efficiency and avoiding redundancies.

Before 1960 the preparation of the estimates was a routine procedure in the department, with next year's requirements calculated on the basis of the current-year expenditures projected into the future. This meant that the estimates were prepared without any real planning but were based on assumptions of **incremental growth** in expenses. Each department would simply ask for a certain percentage increase across the board in anticipation of increased costs of continuing existing programs. The organizational logic of the estimates was based on **standard objects** of expenditure such as the departmental establishment,[4] salaries, benefits, travel, and capital, and there was no requirement for the department to justify its expenditure needs in terms of programs or activities.

Under this system, the bulk of the government's annual expenditure needs for existing programs and activities would be calculated incrementally and submitted as the **main estimates.** If a new policy were to be put in place, Cabinet would approve it and introduce necessary legislation, and the funding would be arranged in a package of **supplementary estimates** ("Sups"). The justification for the extra money would be implicit in the legislation setting up the new program, and the actual supplementary estimates would simply reflect the anticipated additional requirements of the department in terms of the

---

4. The departmental *establishment* is the term once used to refer to the total employees in a department. A *person-year*, or PY, is a full-time position to which a department is entitled, regardless of whether there is someone actually working in the position. The PY concept is being replaced by the notion of a *full-time equivalent*, or FTE, which, in the view of some central-agency types, makes it somewhat easier to incorporate contract employees, casuals, indeterminates, and part-timers into a department's total human-resources establishment.

various standard objects. This system of budgeting was not fated to last through the 1960s; however, the estimates are still broken down into standard-objects categories to provide a "macro" perspective.

**The Planning, Programming, Budgeting System**  The change from the incremental, standard-objects-based system of expenditure management was triggered by two factors. First, the Glassco Commission recommended that the government adopt many of the practices of private-sector management. The dominant theme of the Glassco Report was to "let the managers manage" in the public sector as in the private sector. The most critical tool of management is the ability to plan, and hence it was recognized that senior managers in the public service must be able to budget on the basis of a longer time-frame than the annual estimates cycle.

The second factor that led to the abandonment of the incremental system of budgeting was the philosophical commitment of the Trudeau government to rationalist approaches to policy-making in general. We have seen that the structure of the Cabinet and the growth of the central agencies resulted from this new philosophy, and that the complexity of the policy process steadily increased throughout the Trudeau years. However, one of the most significant changes in the system was the adoption of a rationalist system of expenditure management called the **Planning, Programming, Budgeting System** (PPBS). This system attempted to link priority choices and expenditure decisions to programs and activities rather than to standard objects, and to do it all in a multi-year planning environment. The Treasury Board manual, *Planning Programming Budget Guide*, 1968, stated that the new expenditure and priority-management system would involve the following concepts:

(a) the setting of specific objectives;
(b) systematic analysis to clarify objectives and to assess alternative ways of meeting them;
(c) the framing of budgetary proposals in terms of programs directed towards the achievement of the objectives;
(d) the projection of the costs of these programs a number of years in the future;
(e) the formulation of plans of achievement year by year for each program; and
(f) an information system for each program to supply data for the monitoring of achievement of program objectives and the appropriateness of the program itself.[5]

The manual goes on to emphasize that this is a process for determining priorities through financial resource allocation:

The elements of the Canadian government PPB system have been developed . . . within the context of total resource allocation. By the latter phrase is meant that there is an explicit recognition that the total resources are limited in terms of the

5.  Canada, Treasury Board, *Planning, Programming, Budgeting Guide* (Ottawa: Queen's Printer, 1968), p. 4.

individual and collective demands of departments and there has to be a setting of priorities by the government itself in light of which departments can plan and budget. . . . Program budgeting is primarily concerned with resource allocation within the department.

The proponents of PPBS saw the system as a panacea for dealing with the increasingly complex decisions facing governments in a technological society. Its critics argued that the very system was itself so complicated that the process became more important than the substance — that PPBS was mostly just BS! Nevertheless, PPBS lived a long and healthy life in the government of Canada, and many of the core principles such as the need to plan, the need to plan in multi-year contexts, and the need to link expenditure management to policy priority decisions continue to influence governmental processes to this day.

**The Policy and Expenditure-Management System**  The structure and operations of Cabinet were changed considerably after the election of the Progressive Conservative government in May 1979. The major structural innovations were the creation of an inner Cabinet and two ministries of state. The major innovation in process was the creation of what came to be known as the **envelope system** of financial and policy management. The whole system was known formally as the **Policy and Expenditure Management System**, or PEMS.

In this system, the Committee on Priorities and Planning would establish the overall priorities for the government and set spending targets for each of the sectoral "envelopes" of the PEMS system. The ministries of state were eliminated in 1984, but the rest of the process remained essentially intact. Following Cabinet-committee discussion, a committee recommendation (CR) on the allocation of resources within the policy sector would be prepared and forwarded to the Committee on Priorities and Planning. The CRs were generally approved by P&P, for an important principle of the system was the delegation of real decision-making authority with respect to allocation of funds within the expenditure envelopes to the committees of Cabinet.

Under PEMS, the Committee on Priorities and Planning could also provide a policy committee with some money in excess of its requirements, to cover the needs of ongoing programs. This money, called a **policy reserve**, would then be available to the committee, to be allocated to new programs within its area of jurisdiction. Alternatively, a policy reserve could be created by the committee itself, if a minister would agree to cut programs and place the resultant savings at the disposition of the whole committee. For obvious reasons this sort of magnanimity on the part of individual ministers was a very rare occurrence indeed.

Creating a policy reserve by cutting old programs has never been easy. More than 90 per cent of expenditures are targeted to exisiting programs, the **A-Budget** or **A-Base**, of a department's funding, and there is a certain sanctity to the A-Base. Once a program is created, it is extremely difficult to eliminate it, for every program has both a clientele and a bureaucratic agency to deliver it, each of which will lose significantly if the program vanishes. For a minister concerned with avoiding the kind of conflict that can result in electoral defeat, the A-Base, which finances existing programs, therefore becomes a sacred cow, and to violate it requires extraordinary courage, extraordinary stubbornness, or extraordinary tendencies to self-destruction. The result, in a time of rising revenues, need not necessarily be a major problem, but in a time of declining revenues it can produce virtual paralysis.

The envelope system, although as complex as PPBS, survived several changes of prime minister and both Cabinet ministers and bureaucrats came to learn how to live with it. Its decline and fall, however, came as a result of government's need to respond to broader trends in the economy. The PEMS system of the 1980s was unfortunately premised on an assumption of continued economic growth, which led to an assumption that government expenditure would grow at least incrementally into the foreseeable future. Certainly, politicians and public-service managers assumed that the A-Base programs would be untouched even in periods that required fiscal restraint and austerity. Wrong!

**The Expenditure-Management System in the 1990s**  As with both PPBS and PEMS, the current system is still based on **planning**, it is still **multi-year**, and it is still **program centred**. However, a common feature of all expenditure-management practices up until the 1990s was that the systems were essentially **policy-driven.** By this we mean that the Cabinet would introduce new policies or expand existing ones and then try to find the money to fund them. The budgetary priorities in such a system are established by policy priorities. In the system that is evolving in 1995, this situation has been reversed so that the system is far more a **resources-driven** one. The policy priorities are being largely determined by the imperatives of the budget-planning process: if there isn't enough money available, no policy, however attractive politically, will see the light of day.

*Reserves*  Although, because of general budgetary restraint, the policy reserves, which were a formal feature of the envelope system, had long ceased to exist in practice, the Chrétien reforms to the system formally abolished them. While there will continue to be a **contingency reserve** to assist the government in meeting unexpected increases in forecast expenditures or decreases in forecast revenues, there will be no slush fund set aside for financing new policy initiatives. The Treasury Board also is to be allocated a small **operating reserve** that can provide loans to departments so that they can implement measures aimed at streamlining their program delivery, generating greater efficiency, or creating economies of scale. However, such grants from the operating reserve are simply advances that must be paid back to the board over time.

*Reallocation of Resources*  To ensure that innovation and creativity in government are not totally stifled, the current system of expenditure management does not absolutely preclude the possibility of implementing new policies and programs. Instead, the system focuses on the **reallocation** of exisiting funds to pay for new initiatives. Such reallocation can happen at the sectoral level or the departmental level.

At the sectoral level, this notion of reallocation harks back to the idea of policy committees of Cabinet allocating budgetary envelopes to the various departments and programs in the sector. While the envelopes are gone, it is still possible for a policy committee of Cabinet to decide to free up money in a low-priority program area and to reallocate it to a new higher-priority program. Such reallocative measures naturally must both be approved by the Treasury Board and ratified by the plenary Cabinet. Unfortunately, it is to be expected that this system will inherit the same flaws that plagued the PEMS idea of creating policy reserves by eliminating existing programs. Ministers can be expected to strongly resist and bitterly resent any reallocation of money from their departmental A-Base to some other minister's bailiwick.

This system also permits individual departments to reallocate resources to programs and activities that are entirely within the purview of a single minister. While this would require the approval of the appropriate policy committee of Cabinet, the device may signal a new flexibility for departmental managers to make adjustments and try out innovations without the strict regulation of Treasury Board. The longer-range intent of the evolving expenditure-management system is to reduce the amount of the Treasury Board's direct control over departmental managers by decentralizing authority, deregulating some aspects of the expenditure process, and reducing the reporting requirements of financial and administrative officers within the department.

*Opening Up the Process*  Finally, the expenditure-management system in the mid 1990s indicates a commitment to "opening up" the budgetary process to greater public scrutiny. It provides for the publication of **budget consultation papers** in the fall that will allow the House Committee on Finance to review the issues and offer suggestions to the minister of Finance before the Budget is brought down in February. As well, the departments are to prepare **business plans** in consultation with TBS which will outline the multi-year strategies for carrying on the department's "business."

These business plans will then be summarized by the spring in **departmental outlook statements.** These can then be used by the appropriate standing commmittees of the House of Commons in their pre-estimates review of departmental programs. It is hoped that these outlook papers, along with the business plans, will give the standing committees a multi-year perspective on the department's "job" when they come to review the annual departmental estimates in the following winter. The outlook statements are also used by Cabinet and its policy committees in determining budgetary priorities for the following fiscal year.

*Conclusion: An Evolving System*  At the time of writing, the new expenditure-management system is still evolving. As with any new system, it must be "debugged." It will not accomplish everything it is intended to accomplish and it will inevitably have unforeseen consequences. One thing is certain — the system will not remain static. It will evolve over time, adapting to new problems and developing its own internal practices and conventions to make the process predictable to those who must work within it. We have focused here primarily on the parts of the expenditure-management system that directly involve Cabinet. However, much of what makes up this new system happens outside the central executive arena; we will deal with these aspects of the system in the next two chapters, which focus on the bureacratic process.

## ▶ CONCLUSION: THE CABINET AND BUREAUCRATIC POWER

Paradoxically, the line departments of government, which provide Cabinet with the expert advice that ensures its dominance over Parliament, can also be viewed as one of its greatest rivals for ultimate control. The bureaucracy's near monopoly over many types of information has often served to ensure that the Cabinet is highly dependent upon its non-elected servants when priority decisions are made.

Despite attempts to alleviate this dependency by establishing independent royal commissions, by expanding the PMO, the PCO, and ministers' personal staffs, and sometimes simply by just trying to ignore the bureaucrats, Canadian Cabinets are still highly dependent on their bureaucracies. The "Yes, Minister" image of the well-intentioned but slightly naive Cabinet minister on his or her own against a sea of plotting, scheming, power-grabbing bureaucrats is a far-overstated caricature of reality. But in reality bureaucracies remain, among other things, large information-gathering networks that will continue both to serve their political masters and at the same time to profoundly influence their policy decisions.

However, as we said in the beginning of this discussion, the Cabinet is the "policy crucible." In the end, the establishment of new priorities for Canada and the allocation of resources among competing priority areas are still the ultimate responsibilities of the prime minister and the Cabinet. No matter how important the bureaucracy may be in priority determination, the final gate-keepers are and will continue to be the prime minister and the Cabinet.

# Chapter 22

# Bureaucracy: Function and Structure

In this chapter and the next our focus shifts from the political part of the government to the administrative arm of the executive branch, the **bureaucracy**. The bureaucracy, or the **public service**, is populated by a large number of non-elected full-time employees of the government whose twin responsibilities, in the most general terms, are to tender policy advice to the Cabinet and to put into effect or to *implement* the laws passed by Parliament. In this chapter we look first at the concept of bureaucracy and at the central process of bureaucracy, which is **management**; then we turn to the specific functions of the Canadian bureaucracy and the various institutional species that co-exist within it.

## ▶ BUREAUCRACY: EPITHET OR TERM OF ART?

Long used as an epithet by the media and the public, the word "bureaucracy" has come to be associated in common parlance with negative qualities such as inefficiency, "red tape," depersonalization, and slowness of execution. "Bureaucrats" are similarly stereotyped as lazy, unproductive, and insensitive to the needs of the individuals they are supposed to serve. There is, however, a more proper use of the term, which is derived from the literature of organization theory and which refers only to the objective structural characteristics of a certain type of organization. In this sense, bureaucracy is a purely descriptive "term of art" rather than an epithet. From the perspective of the pre-eminent bureaucratic theorist, Max Weber, bureaucracy is the **ideal-type** of legal-rational social organization.

### Routinization of Decision-Making

Before describing the bureaucratic structures in the Canadian government, we shall look briefly at the reasons for adopting a bureaucratic type of organization. Given all of its real or imagined malfunctions, what is good about the bureaucratic form? First, because equality is a value of our system of government, it is necessary, when applying the law to specific cases, to treat similar cases in a similar fashion. Bureaucratic organization permits a maximum of impartiality and rationality in dealing with the public by **routinizing** the decision-making process.

Second, the application of the law must be predictable, to be fair, and a bureaucratic system can be made highly predictable. The problem here is that, in applying the law equally and impartially, the person with the special case, who requires an *equitable* decision instead of an impartial one, is frequently penalized. How many times have we met with the standard bureaucratic answer: "If we do that for you we will have to do it for everyone else as well" or "We are sorry but our regulations do not permit any exceptions." Thus, while bureaucratic procedures are valid for perhaps 90 per cent of cases, for the 10 per cent that may be unusual or exceptional, the system can pose difficulties. The justification for such a system is that it is the only way we have of dealing fairly, and at reasonable cost, with the majority of the vast number of cases that come up.

Modern bureaucracies have, of course, developed some mechanisms for dealing with special cases. Many large programs dealing directly with the public have some form of appeal procedure, and individual bureaucrats at the operating levels of the government do have discretion in applying the law to individual cases. We have noted, too, in our discussions of the functions of Parliament, that one of the most important parts of the MP's role is helping constituents who have not been adequately dealt with by the bureaucracy.

Most provincial governments in Canada have supplemented the ombudsman role of members of provincial legislatures with the establishment of a special office of the legislature called the *Ombudsman*. The role of the Ombudsman is to ensure that special cases are fairly dealt with and that citizens have a complaints "window" through which they can express their grievances and seek redress. Nonetheless, in conclusion, we must return to the rather unsatisfactory comment that bureaucratic organization is the best way we know of to deal with "bigness" in government, and that some problems inevitably will arise.

### Structural Characteristics

A bureaucracy is a form of organization with certain structural characteristics, the most obvious of which is its large size. Most of the other characteristics have evolved to accommodate the pre-eminent one of "bigness." First of all, there is a well-developed **division of labour**, whereby the officials occupying roles within the organization perform clearly defined functions. Ideally, there is no duplication of effort and no overlapping of roles within a bureaucracy, although this is difficult to achieve in practice. Furthermore, a bureaucratic role or "job" is defined by the office or the formal "job description," not by the incumbent of the office. This is essential if bureaucratic behaviour is to be predictable in the short run and if there is to be continuity over time in the performance of the duties of that office.

Continuity over time is also facilitated by the keeping of detailed written records of all actions taken by the bureaucratic officers. In this way, every decision can be backed up by precedents established in the past, and in turn becomes part of the body of precedents for future decisions. There is no legal rule of precedent in bureaucratic decision-making, but the fact is that if someone else has made a certain decision in the past and has gotten away with it, the chances are that a similar decision today can be justified by the officer responsible. Hence, while a bureaucratic role is formally defined by the organization itself, it can still develop and evolve in orderly and predictable ways over time.

Also contributing to the continuity of bureaucratic decision-making is the fact that the holding of a bureaucratic office is a **full-time** occupation or a vocation. In recent years, bureaucratic officers have been tenured in the sense they do not hold office merely at the pleasure of their political employer. This means that being a public servant can be viewed as a **career**, and not simply as a temporary job. If he or she is interested, a faithful public servant can generally expect to spend a working lifetime in the same occupation, with periodic opportunities for career development and promotion. Even in a climate of restraint, wage freezes, cutbacks, buy-outs, and early retirement, employment in the public service is still essentially a career and not simply a way to "pick up a few bucks" while waiting for something better to come along.

Finally, although it is not unique to bureaucratic organizations, the basic mechanism of control within a bureaucracy is **hierarchy**. The principal of hierarchical authority, also called the **scalar principle**, means that authority is "top-down," flowing downward through the organization. Each level of the organization is responsible immediately to the level above and ultimately through a **chain of command** to a single "boss" at the top of the pyramid.

### Bureaucratic Maladies

While it is our intention to use *bureaucracy* here as a "term of art" that describes a certain type of organization characterized by identifiable features, it must also be recognized that, in the real world, bureaucracies don't always work as well as Max Weber might have expected. We have already explained that in seeking to treat all of its clients **equally**, a bureaucratic agency may not be able to treat them **equitably**. To apply the law more equitably would necessitate a lot more discretion in the hands of public servants, which might result in personal bias being allowed to compromise the impartiality built into the notion of the rule of law. The balance between administrative discretion and routinization of decision-making is a delicate one and it is easy for any bureaucratic system to lean too far one way or the other.

A second malady of bureaucracy is its inherent **conservatism**. Again this is the direct result of the routinization that is the *raison d'être* of such organizations but it also generates resistance to change. In the extreme, this conservatism may manifest itself as a **pathology of persistence** whereby governments never stop doing something once they have begun. Bureaucratic agencies quickly acquire an organizational "survival instinct," an imperative to live on at all cost. In a time of deep cutbacks to government they find it more difficult to survive, but examples abound in our recent past of government agencies that "soldier on" despite the fact that they have outlived their usefulness. One case in point is the Halifax Relief Commission, which was set up in 1917 to provide relief to victims of the Halifax harbour explosion, and was still in existence well into the 1970s!

A third common perversion of Weber's model is the tendency for bureaucratic officials to engage in **empire building**. While the conservative nature of bureaucratic organization inhibits change, the one form of change that always seems to be acceptable is growth. Hence there is a tendency for organizations to seek to expand their human-resources establishment and their jurisdiction, if necessary by raiding or absorbing other agencies. Such organizational imperialism can lead to bitter "turf wars" that are seriously dysfunctional in coordinating the efforts of departments of government that should be working together to serve the Canadian public.

Finally, it is often observed that the internal workings of government agencies are impaired by what we might call the **pathology of status**. While bureaucratic agencies are hierarchical, their positions in a hierarchy do not always allow career bureaucrats sufficient opportunities to differentiate themselves from their cohorts. Large numbers of people will find themselves at essentially the same levels of the hierarchy and will seek means of establishing relative status or prestige on the basis of criteria other than rank or salary. Hence, it is often possible to observe organizational snobbery, whereby agencies attempt to attain greater status for their employees on the basis of relative power and influence, relative size, or the relative luxuriousness of office accommodations. At the level of individual bureaucrats this can lead to jealousies over who gets a corner office, teak furniture, or a shag carpet. At one time in the 1970s, the importance of office carpeting in defining relative prestige came to be known as "rug ranking" in Ottawa bureaucratic circles.

### Conclusion

To conclude, while individual bureaucracies do suffer from some all too familiar maladies, *bureaucracy* is simply a form of organization with definitive structural characteristics. While the term *bureaucracy* can be used to apply to governmental and non-governmental organizations alike, in common usage in the discipline of political science the term refers specifically to the **public service** or to the **administrative branch** of government. The focus of this chapter is on the role of the non-elective officials of government, the bureaucrats, who work within the Canadian public service, the public services of the various provinces, municipalities, and territorial governments, and the multitude of public-sector agencies and corporations that are not formally a part of the "Public Service of Canada."

We will also see that bureaucratic structures in Canada, as in other parts of the world, do not perfectly mirror the "ideal-type" of Weber. There is considerably more flexibility and variability in bureaucratic structures than is implied in the classical descriptions. This is a desirable attribute of real-world bureaucracies, since it enables them to react more effectively to the multifaceted strains imposed on them by the modern world. However, Weber's ideal-type provides us with a conceptual benchmark against which to measure real bureaucracies and is, as a first approximation, still a useful guide to understanding administrative structures in Canada. We will return to a more detailed classification and description of bureaucratic structures after we have examined the core process of bureaucracy, which is **management**.

---

## ▶ THE FUNCTIONS OF MANAGEMENT

**Management** is a generic concept common to all organizations that are oriented to achieving goals through group effort. Management can be defined simply as **coordination**, or more explicitly as the *the coordination of individual effort to accomplish group or organizational goals*. The mechanisms whereby goal-directed coordination is achieved, whether applied to policy goals or administrative goals, can be broken down into a number of sub-functions or activities.

The sub-functions that are common to the process of management are **planning**, **organizing**, **controlling**, **directing**, and **staffing**. Each of these will be discussed separately, but first it is important to identify the characteristics that differentiate management in the private sector from management in the public sector.

### Public- and Private-Sector Management

The first and major difference is simply that private management is analytically less complex because the ultimate goal of private-sector organizations can, for the most part, be reduced to making a **profit**. This means that criteria for evaluating management systems, such as efficiency and economy, can be employed in their literal sense. The organization that survives and makes a profit for its shareholders is obviously blessed with "good management," and one that goes bankrupt or fails to make money is not. By contrast, for public management the criteria for being successful are not so clear. How, for instance, can one reduce the administration of a welfare program, the enforcement of the law, or the funding of medical research to profit?

**The Profit Motive**  The goals of government are regulatory, distributive, redistributive, and punitive, but seldom profit oriented or **capital accumulative**, as are the goals of most private-sector organizations. The ultimate measure of the worth of government is how effectively it has contributed to the happiness of its clients or to the general well-being of the citizenry. Although the emphasis in government has been changing in the era of large deficits and heavy tax burdens, the success of government activities has not traditionally been measured in terms of how frugally it has managed to run its operation, let alone in terms of how much wealth it has been able to accumulate for its "owners." Thus, public management is different in part because the ultimate goals of the organization are so diffuse and because individual happiness and societal well-being are difficult objectives to define and even more difficult to measure.

The public manager faces a second problem, which his or her counterpart in a private corporation is able to avoid: the goals of government are sometimes mutually exclusive. Redistributive programs, for instance, take money through taxation from those who have more, and give it in the form of transfer payments to those who have less. The latter will inevitably find this arrangement more pleasing than the former. Indeed, it is almost axiomatic that all government policies will please some people and displease others. In the process of seeking the utilitarian golden mean of satisfying as many Canadians as possible and alienating as few as possible, managers in one department may be in direct competition with managers in another, with obvious negative consequences for interagency or interdepartmental coordination.

**Control and Accountability** Management in the public sector is also distinguished by the extent to which one of the sub-processes, **control**, is emphasized. The need for responsibility and accountability of bureaucrats to Cabinet and Parliament is a given in a democracy. The consequence of this for the bureaucratic process is that the systems of financial and personnel administration are oriented more towards *controlling* the public-service managers than facilitating the line managerial function. Thus, for instance, the process of budgeting in the public service has seldom functioned as effectively as a tool of planning as it does in private corporations; instead, it is focused almost entirely on keeping the bureaucracy in check.

Finally, the bureaucratic process in the government of Canada, as we have seen in earlier chapters, is distinguished by the extent to which public servants are called upon to tender policy advice to the political arm of the government when it is determining priorities and choosing modes of policy implementation. We will say more about this later in the book, but first we must turn to a discussion of the functional components of management.

**Management: Functional Components**

We have already remarked that the core components of management involve planning, organizing, controlling, directing, and staffing. In this section we look at these processes in the public sector at the conceptual level to set the stage for looking at the public service of Canada's role in the administrative process and the policy process.

**Planning** Planning is at the core of any system of management, whether in the private or in the public sector. At the simplest level, all this means is that it is necessary to decide what to do and how best to do it before actually launching into the task. However, a manager must define and redefine operational goals and develop and adjust the means of accomplishing those goals on an ongoing basis. Thus, the planning component of the process of management is not a one-time task, but is a constant in effective management. Moreover, the planning process must focus on both ends and means, on the problems of both **goal determination** and **goal attainment**.

In the private sector, because the ultimate goal of making a profit is fairly well agreed upon, the manager's task as a planner is more focused. In government, however, the task is not so simple. Not only are the goals less clearly defined and less agreed upon, but the means of accomplishing them must fit within the particular norms of a liberal democratic polity. As well, both the program goals and the strategies or instruments of goal attainment must comply with the wishes of a set of decision-makers in Cabinet, whose main and quite legitimate motivation is to get themselves re-elected.

These constraints on the process of goal determination and on the choice of means have important implications for the planning process in the public sector. First, because one of the norms of a democratic system is that the activities of government should reflect the will of the public, the ultimate responsibility for goal determination falls to the political executive. Indeed, the Cabinet and its executive-support agencies take the major role not only in the determining of policy priorities, but also in approving the general means to be employed by the bureaucracy in implementing those priorities. The permanent officials of the government, who are *responsible* for administering programs and delivering services, do not have final control over what programs are put in place.

The politicians, as they sometimes are prone to do, can put policies in place against the advice of the bureaucrats, but the public-service managers are still responsible for trying to achieve those policy goals. In this sense the ultimate responsibility for setting goals is separated from the ultimate responsibility for accomplishing them, a situation all senior managers in the public service have found extremely frustrating at some point in their careers. This **bifurcation of planning** in government, where the responsibility for goal determination and goal attainment are split between different decision-making locales, is one of the key weaknesses of public-sector management.

A second limitation on effective planning in government is that there is a universal concern with keeping the bureaucracy *accountable* to the political branches of government. This has meant that managerial tools such as the expenditure budget, program review, and performance evaluation, which in the private sector are employed as tools of planning, in the public service have been geared almost single-mindedly to maintaining the accountability of the departmental managers to Parliament and the Cabinet. We will say more about this phenomenon when we discuss the administrative process in the next chapter.

**Organizing** In order for individuals to be able to work together effectively towards the attainment of organizational goals, a contrived structure of roles — an **organization** — must be designed and maintained. It is important to recognize, however, that the full story of an organization cannot be told by formal "org charts." Bureaucracies have both formal and informal organizational structures. The latter reflect unplanned patterns of personal interaction that develop within any group of people. Informal leaders will inevitably emerge in most work environments and these people sometimes rival the authority of the formal leaders or the "bosses" by virtue of their personal charisma, job competence, or long-time experience in the particular workplace.

The phenomenon of informal organization, which occurs in all formal social structures, has implications for the managerial function of *directing*, which will be elaborated upon later.

**Controlling** In this section we want to concentrate on the formal organizational aspects of bureaucracy and how the manager is responsible for defining the internal *span of control* and *chain of command* within government departments and agencies.

*Span of Control* The **span of control** in hierarchical organizations is defined by the number of individuals at any level who must report directly to a supervisor, senior manager, or boss. Thus, if a government department has six assistant deputy ministers (ADMs) who report directly to the deputy minister, the DM's span of control is six. Different textbooks on management have tried to define the optimum span of control, but without success, because the appropriate span of control will vary with the nature of the organization and the personalities of the people involved. Moreover, the most effective span of control will be affected by the extent to which informal organizational structures exist and the role they play in either facilitating or short-circuiting the vertical communication links. Generally, however, it is thought that a span of control of five to eight is optimum and that most managers cannot effectively direct or provide leadership to many more than eight immediate subordinates.

*Chain of Command* Where span of control defines the breadth of an organizational hierarchy, the concept of **chain of command** has to do with the length of the hierarchy. The length of the chain of command is the number of levels from top to bottom in the organization. Obviously, if the span of control is to remain manageable, as organizations grow, the chain of command must lengthen. While it is not possible to state that there is any universal optimum length of chain of command, generally, as the chain of command lengthens, the senior manager will be called upon increasingly to delegate authority and to trust subordinate managers. Thus, an important part of the managerial activity of organizing is to structure the formal organization in such a way that there is a balance between the span of control and the chain of command that permits delegation of responsibilities without sacrificing the ability of the top managers to "direct" the extremities of the operation.

Finally, closely related to the concept of chain of command is the concept of **unity of command**. What this means in a hierarchical organization is that there should be only one boss at the top. According to this principle, subordinate managers in a government department, for instance, must generally not have more than one superior, the chain of command must lead directly from top to bottom in the organization and it must be clear to managers at every level to whom they are responsible. It is difficult for a middle-level manager to function effectively if there is more than one boss giving orders.[1]

---

1. It should be noted that there is a mode of management known by the names *project management*, *matrix management*, or the *managerial grid*. This is a style of management sometimes applied to special projects requiring input from several departments or agencies. The "project manager" becomes the boss for purposes of the specific project assignment but the participants on the team from the various participating agencies still earn their pay and have their performance evaluations written by their superiors in their "home" department.

**Figure 22.1**
Span of control and chain of command in hierarchical organizations.

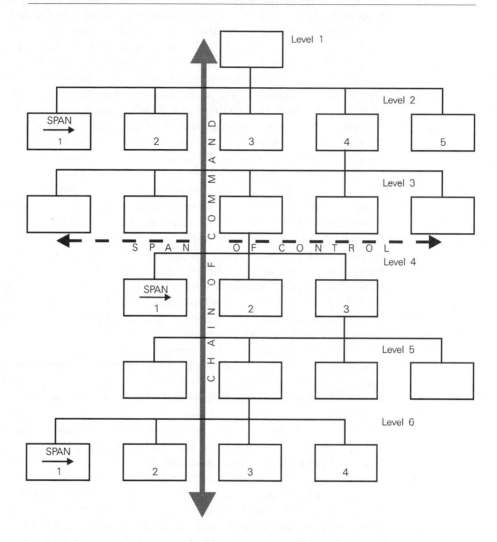

**Directing** In essence, **directing** means giving direction and providing leadership to subordinates in an organization. The key to the managerial activity of directing is to **motivate** the people within an organization so that they will be willing to put the goals of the group before their individual goals, at least while on the job. This can be achieved easily if the goals of the organization happen to be congruent with those of the individual, as is often the case with voluntary groups and associations. In bureaucracy, however, where employment is vocational and usually tied to a career, the organization motivates its workers by financial rewards (wages and salaries) and by incentives such as promotion, career enhancement, and oportunities for training and development.

In the private sector, the manager has considerable control over the relative material rewards (and penalties) to be allotted to his or her personnel. By influencing the processes of promotion, by parcelling out the opportunities for advancement through training programs, and by having the power to impose disciplinary sanctions, the manager in the private sector has the tools, the material sanctions, and the inducements to motivate subordinates. By contrast, the manager in the federal bureaucracy has only limited direct control over the salary, benefits, and career-development opportunities of employees. The deputy minister must continually work within the personnel policy directives of central agencies such as the Treasury Board, which is formally reponsible for personnel management in the public service, and the Public Service Commission, which oversees matters of promotion and job competitions. Thus, the DM is limited in the extent to which the managerial prerogatives, which are used as motivators in the private sector, can be exercised.

Lacking personal control over the material factors of motivation, the public-service manager must therefore resort to the more ethereal leadership skills in attempting to get the most out of subordinates. It is the qualities of the individual manager *per se*, such as charisma, professional expertise, and overall job competence, and not what the manager can do for the employee, that must be employed as motivators. If the manager is liked and respected by the employees, or if the employees believe in the kinds of goals the manager is trying to accomplish, they will work harder and more enthusiastically at their jobs; on the other hand, if they hold the manager in low regard and spend a lot of time figuring out how to avoid work, the manager has somewhat limited options with which to discipline them.

The other problem is that, lacking the formal authority to reward and punish subordinates, a manager in the public service may find it difficult to compete with **informal leaders** in the organization. The big edge the manager in the private sector has when dealing with informal organization is the possession of full authority within the formal organization. In the government, however, the ability of the manager to motivate underlings may hinge on the ability to become part of, or at least to figure out how to use, the informal authority patterns in the organization. Thus, managerial leadership or direction in government is not "command" to the same extent it tends to be in other hierarchical organizations, but a complex of personality resources, social and political skills, and a full awareness of the informal alliances, friendships, and personal animosities among the people employed. Directing in this sort of an organizational environment resembles more an art form than a professional skill.

**Staffing** The managerial activity referred to as **staffing** essentially involves "manning" the organization. This is achieved by **recruiting** candidates for positions in the organization, by **selecting** the best people from those recruited, by **training** the ones selected so they can do the job required of them, and by facilitating the development of their careers through **promotion** within the organization. In the private sector, the senior manager has control over virtually all aspects of the process of staffing and usually is assisted in this process by a fairly sizable personnel branch. However, ultimate decisions as to hiring and firing of employees, and decisions as to promotion, transfer, and discipline rest with senior line management within the organization.

In the public service, however, the authority of the senior manager is not as comprehensive. In the federal bureaucracy, as we have seen, the senior manager must share the staffing function with the Treasury Board and the Public Service Commission. The staffing function, however, does not cease with recruitment. As with any organization, it is necessary to train the people who are part of it, not only with respect to the technical skills of the specific occupation, but also with respect to the goals of the organization. The employee who has been thoroughly socialized into a bureaucratic organization will likely function more enthusiastically, and even more efficiently, than the person who looks on his or her occupation as "just a living." Hence, there is an almost constant process of training and development within the Canadian bureaucracy, which, by moulding the attitudes of public servants, can affect the **bureaucratic culture** that underlies decision-making.

The staffing function can also be seen as the **personnel administration** function of a large organization. Personnel administration must be distinguished from **personnel management**. The latter is, in effect, the core of the management activity we have referred to as directing: in other words, it means "managing people." Personnel *administration* is the provision of support services to the line managers by helping them recruit and select new employees, by assisting in the process of labour-management relations, and by providing employees with opportunities for training and development.

In private-sector organizations, the personnel administration function is performed entirely by units *within* the organization and subject to the directives of the CEO. In the Canadian Public Service, while there are personnel branches within each department, much of the personnel administration function is controlled centrally rather than departmentally. We will discuss the way in which this separation of many of the personnel functions from the line departments has affected the administrative process in the next chapter. Now we must turn to a discussion of the primary functions of the bureaucracy in Canada.

## ▶ THE FUNCTIONS OF THE CANADIAN BUREAUCRACY

The two most important classes of functions performed by the bureaucracy in Canada are **administrative functions** and **policy functions**. By far the largest numbers of public servants are engaged in the former, which involve delivering government programs and enforcing or applying the laws in Canadian society. The latter, by contrast, are the services that the bureaucracy performs in assisting the Cabinet in deciding what policies, programs, and laws should be put in place. While the policy role directly involves far fewer public servants, as we have seen in earlier chapters, policy-making is the central function of government. The bureaucracy also performs a range of **systemic functions** and **representative functions** that are incidental to the performance of its main duties but nonetheless important overall in our political community.

### The Policy Functions

That the bureaucracy in Canada has a significant role in the policy process is now accepted as fact, a point that is decried more than disputed. As we have indicated, this role is based largely on the concentration of expertise within the public service, making government departments and agencies the major sources of information about the technical and financial feasibility of policy options. As the technological complexity of our society increases, the reliance of political decision-makers on bureaucratic or technocratic specialists will tend to increase commensurately, and there is no indication that technological growth is slowing down.

**Initiation and Priority Determination**  It has been mentioned in previous chapters that the bureaucracy performs important functions both as an **initiator** of policy and as a **channel** of policy initiation to be used by other institutions and actors in the political process. Beyond this first-stage policy role, the bureaucracy continues to be deeply involved in the business of policy making. When policy **priorities** are being established, the Cabinet documents that form the basis of discussion in Cabinet committees are, for the most part, generated within the line departments. Although it is clear that, at the stage of priority determination, the Cabinet must ultimately decide, much of the information about the substantive issues comes from the bureaucracy.

Because all substantive policies involve the expenditure of public moneys, bureaucratic institutions such as the Treasury Board Secretariat and the Department of Finance have a great deal of control over priority determination. Obviously, this control is due to their expertise in the areas of public finance, the public purse, and macro-economics. The complexity of the expenditure-management system has tended to regularize, consolidate, and further aggrandize the influence of the bureaucrat in the Canadian policy process. If anything, the fiscal imperatives of budget cutting and deficit reduction in the 1990s have increased the power and influence of the financial technocrats of these central agencies.

Federal-provincial committees at the bureaucratic level also play an important role in the setting of policy priorities in Canada. Specifically, these intergovernmental bodies are usually concerned with coordination of federal-provincial programs. For example, in the process of considering the problems of fiscal relations, the intergovernmental meetings of finance and treasury officials have great influence on the spending priorities of both levels of government.

**Policy Formulation**  As we pointed out in Chapter 2, the bureaucracy is the core institution at the formulation stage of policy-making in Canada. Although Cabinet normally assigns the reponsibility for formulation in a certain policy area, more than one department, within an interdepartmental **steering committee**, may be involved in those policy decisions that affect more than one portfolio. The actual detailed formulation of specific policies is normally accomplished within the **sponsoring department** whose minister made the original recommendation to Cabinet.

Through ministerial briefing notes, discussion papers, white papers, and various "Cabinet documents," the department sets out the policy alternatives that are most feasible in technical, administrative, financial, and even political terms. The practical options for implementing a government policy priority are most frequently defined in this way, although Cabinet will not hesitate to come to a decision that runs counter to departmental advice if there is a consensus of the ministers that political considerations outweigh the advice of their officials. Similarly the choice of instrument for giving effect to a policy goal may be affected more by the financial and political concerns articulated by the central agencies than by the options presented by the line-department officials whose minister is sponsoring the proposal.

While policy formulation has been described here as a stage in the policy process that *follows* priority determination, it is, in fact, usually the case that the bureaucracy's formulation activity has begun long before any clear priority has been established. Indeed, the Cabinet often finds it impossible to make a clear priority decision in the absence of a good deal of detailed advice on policy formulation. The bureaucratic institutions are ever alert to indicators of future government priorities, and well before the priority decision has been taken, officials within the various line departments attempt to anticipate Cabinet-level decisions and begin to work on policy areas that are likely to be given priority.

One further reason for a department to begin looking at questions of formulation before a priority has been established by Cabinet is that the sponsoring department at the priority-determination stage will inevitably be given the responsibility for implementing the new program when it is legislated. As well, the administrative feasibility of a policy proposal may help to determine whether Cabinet will give it the go-ahead. Finally, the department may have played a role in the initiation of the policy in the first place, perhaps responding to the demands or complaints of a client group, and will have been thinking about the practical "doability" of the policy proposal from the outset.

**The Legislative Stage** The role of the bureaucracy at the legislative stage of the process is limited by the fact that, constitutionally, legislation must be put in place by Parliament and the political executive. However, even at this stage the bureaucracy does perform important functions. It is the Department of Justice that must not only give the final indication that the proposal is not inconsistent with the Constitution, but must also draft the bill. This translation of policy decisions from "policy-ese" to "legalese" is performed by specialized drafters in the Justice department and is based on "instructions" to the drafters prepared in the sponsoring department.

There should be very little discretion in the hands of public servants at this stage of the process, for the substance of the policy has already been determined by the preceding stages of the process. However, it is not uncommon for a bill, as drafted, to incorporate provisions that are not exactly what its sponsors intended. This happens more because of honest misinterpretations than from deliberate attempts to put a "spin" on the final product by the people who prepare the instructions to Justice or the Justice drafters themselves. The likelihood of such ambiguities or errors being written into a bill is increased by the fact that, in Canada, all bills must be passed in both official languages. The technical drafters must translate the final decision of Cabinet into both "French legalese" and "English legalese," which increases the chances that mistakes will happen.

Once the "adult" bill has been introduced into the house of Commons, the role of the bureaucrats who "reared" it is pretty much limited to explaining it, if asked, in parliamentary committees. The significance of this role is not to convince the opposition MPs that the policy is "good" in global terms, but to explain the intentions of the government. It is at this phase that ambiguities in the draft legislation can be clarified and corrected, and the potential flaws in the design of the implementation provisions can be tidied up. The MPs in the committees take centre stage in this refinement of legislation, and the public servants called upon to clarify and explain the intentions of the bill play a passive, supportive role in the deliberations.

### Administrative Functions

While the policy role of the Canadian bureaucracy may seem to place significant power in the hands of the bureaucrats and technocrats, we must recognize that, however pervasive this policy role may be, it is still, formally, only an **advisory** one. Although to a large extent the Cabinet does heed the counsel of its bureaucratic advisors, all policies are still subject to the ultimate approval of the elected officials of our government. However, there are many areas where even the formal power to convert policy to enforceable law is delegated directly to administrative, regulatory, supervisory, or quasi-judicial agencies of the government of Canada. In this sense, public servants become more than advisors — they become lawmakers, regulators, and adjudicators.

**Delegated Legislation**  The **delegation of legislative power** to the executive is not a new phenomenon in Canada. Canadian legislation has, for many years, granted very broad powers to the executive to make law by order-in-council. While this delegation of legislative power achieves a short cut of the normal procedures of lawmaking by the sovereign Parliament, the concerned citizen might take some solace in the fact that the *de facto* executive in this country is the Cabinet, which is ultimately responsible to Parliament. However, since the Cabinet is not an expert body, it often must **redelegate** the power to make law to non-elected officials in government departments, in police forces, and in administrative boards and tribunals. As policies become more technical and more complex, the power to work out the details will tend increasingly to be passed on to non-elected officials.

Part of the problem is that legislation today requires more detail than the non-expert elected actors in the policy process have time to deal with. For instance, legislation aimed at regulating the transportation industries in Canada sets down certain broad objectives, and then sets up the Canadian Transportation Commission (CTC) to which it delegates the power to make detailed regulations as to air traffic, railways, and freight rates. Similarly, the regulation of the broadcasting and telecommunications industries is delegated to the Canadian Radio-Television and Telecommunications Commission (CRTC), which has wide powers over both private- and public-sector enterprises.

To take another example, Canada Post, which is set up to provide a service to Canadians on a cost-recovery basis, also makes regulations regarding postal rates, contents of packages, the use of mails, and so on, which directly affect our postal privileges and the quality of service we receive. In the case both of purely regulatory agencies and of those that have a commercial role as well as a regulatory one, elected officials may publicly criticize but must not meddle. Thus, while politicians may express strong views about increases in postal rates, the reduction of passenger rail services, or the licensing of cable-TV networks, they are not supposed to interfere directly in the regulatory process.

The key point to be taken here is that the power to make regulations that have the effect of law, and that directly affect the rights and privileges of citizens, frequently rests directly with non-elected officials, and has been taken out of the hands of Parliament and the political executive. A most important bureaucratic function, therefore, is the power to make decisions in matters delegated to administrative bodies that constitute **legislative** outputs of the government.

**Internal Regulations**  Another important lawmaking or rule-making function of the bureaucracy is to make internal regulations regarding the administrative process itself. For instance, an agency such as the Public Service Commission is concerned directly and constantly with service-wide problems of staffing. The commission was created precisely to take matters of promotion, recruitment, and discipline out of the hands of the politicians. It was felt that public-service appointments should be based not on patronage but rather on the **merit** of the individual job applicant and the requirements of the position to be filled. It was felt that the logical way of removing such decisions from political interference was to create an independent central agency and delegate to it the power to make regulations necessary for bringing into effect a career public service based on the **merit principle**.

Each department and agency must also produce sets of rules outlining internal procedures and practices. The decisions as to what these rules should be are all made directly by administrative officials, and while they may be technically subject to ministerial approval, in practice they do not even come to the attention of the politicians. Although it is perhaps difficult to characterize these rules as "laws" of our government, such administrative regulations are very important because of their potential effect on the administrative side of the administrator-to-public relationship.

**Applying the Law**  It has been seen that the Canadian Constitution distinguishes between executive and judicial functions. Under closer scrutiny, however, one finds that the executive function and the judicial function are broadly similar, in that they both require the application of general rules to specific cases. Viewed in this way, the **rule-application function** of the bureaucracy includes both executive and judicial decision-making, and with respect to time, resources, and immediate impact on the public, it constitutes the central function of the Canadian bureaucracy.

*Administrative Discretion* While in theory the role of the administrator is simply to implement the laws of the land, the application of general laws to specific situations always involves some interpretive and judgemental decisions on the part of the public servant. In applying the law, administrators are called upon to make **discretionary** decisions all the time. As an example, public servants or committees set up by the public service have to make decisions as to which students are eligible for financial support or scholarships. Similarly, customs officers have the authority to decide whose luggage should be searched and who should be waved past with a "welcome to Canada," and Revenue Canada tax assessors can decide what expenses we declare are allowable tax deductions.

In cases such as these, the legislation itself does not provide very detailed guidelines as to the practical application of the principles involved. These sorts of decisions are left to the discretion of the administrative officers charged with carrying the act into effect, who are expected to act in the spirit of the intentions of the statute. In the extreme case, peace officers charged with the responsibility for enforcing the law possess discretionary powers up to and including the right to use force, and even in some circumstances to shoot to kill. The law cannot specify all of the situations where the use of such extreme force is necessary, and the decision is left to the discretion of the officer, who must make a judgement call in the field and on the spur of the moment. As we shall see in the next chapter, there are judicial controls over the abuse of discretionary powers by officials of the state, but the only practical safeguards against abuse ultimately lie in the training, experience, and good faith of the individuals involved.

*Adjudicative Functions* In many areas of administrative decision-making, the distinctions among the legislative, administrative, and judicial functions become blurred. For instance, administrative boards and inspectors under public-health acts and liquor-licensing legislation are called upon to decide who gets a licence and under what circumstances a licence should be revoked for non-compliance with the conditions established by the legislation.[2] A decision that involves the granting or revoking of a licence, or the imposition of a fine in lieu of revocation of a licence, is not only administrative; because the decision can have a punitive or compensatory effect on individuals, it is akin to the kind of decision we normally think of as being within the purview of a court. Hence, administrative officals and bodies often are delegated powers that are almost judicial or **quasi-judicial**.

It is significant that quasi-judicial decisions can become precedents that form guidelines for future applications of the legislation in future cases that have a similar fact situation. A body of administrative decisions thus formed can also have the effect of altering and even redefining the long-run meaning and impact of the law. This has resulted, in part, because of the increased role of the government in the regulation of our behaviour and its increased positive role in regulating and licensing individuals and corporations in the interest of

---

2. In this and similar cases, the law usually states that the ultimate decision rests with the responsible minister, but in fact most cases never reach the minister's notice, so the real power resides in the inspector.

securing public health and safety. We will say more about the quasi-judicial role of the administrative branch of government in the following chapter.

A sort of hybrid function of some bureaucratic agencies in Canada is the **investigative function**, which combines the roles of policy advisor and adjudicator. This function is distinguishable from the policy function because the focus of the investigation is a specific, rather than a generic, case or situation, and it can be differentiated from the adjudicative function because the findings of the board or commission are not binding, but are only recommendatory to the minister. For example, many regulatory agencies in Canada such as the Atomic Energy Control Board (AECB) or the National Energy Board (NEB) are required by law to investigate accidents that occur in the industries they are regulating, and to report the findings to the minister. In the case of the NEB, the regulatory agency is vested with the powers of a superior court of record when conducting hearings, which implies the right to subpoena witnesses, to require the presentation of documents, and to convict people for contempt of court.

### Systemic Functions

Beyond the policy and administrative functions we have described above, the Canadian bureaucracy also performs a number of ancillary or latent functions for the system as a whole. The main systemic **function** is **communication**; the incidental or latent functions include fostering of **support** and **stability** for the regime. We will look at each of these types of functions in turn.

**Communication**   Dissemination of information, the communication function of the public service, is not so much incidental to its main functions as it is *ancillary* to them. Educating the public as to how the law changes is a logical extension of the bureaucracy's role as the set of institutions responsible for applying the law in society. Hence, the basic agencies for the dissemination of information from government, for advertising or publicizing new laws and regulations as they are put into effect, are found predominantly within the bureaucracy.

In order to ensure that the public is aware of new legislation, the responsible department will publicize changes widely on radio and television and in the newspapers. All new legislation is published in the *Canada Gazette*, and the onus in law is on the individual citizen to find out what the law is and to obey it. However, it is also recognized by the government that a piece of legislation dealing with matters such as gun control, impaired driving, or smoking in government facilities is designed to modify human behaviour and will be effective only if everyone is aware of it.

Information outputs are produced by the bureaucracy, possibly at the urging and certainly with the acquiescence of the Cabinet. Superficially the dissemination of such information appears to be purely **educational** — the message is, in effect, that there is a new law or program that citizens should be aware of so that they can obey it or take advantage of it. However, such government advertising can sometimes be used as a device for the government of the day to blow its own horn about the nice things it is doing for the voters.

It is difficult to draw a distinct line between using communication funding for informing the public and using it to sell the government's case for getting re-elected.

It must not be forgotten that one governing instrument that can be used to put into effect a policy priority is persuasion. Thus, from time to time, the dissemination of information through ad campaigns is intended not just to tell people about what laws are "in effect" but directly to "give effect" to a policy by **exhorting** Canadians to do something good or desist from doing something bad. Anti-smoking campaigns, the advocacy of Participaction, and AIDS awareness advertising are all intended both to inform us that certain patterns of behaviour are better for us than others and to convince us to mend our ways.

Most departments have information-services or communications branches, and some agencies, such as Statistics Canada, are concerned primarily with the collection, compilation, and publication of information. While the politicians will inevitably attempt to put a favourable partisan slant on such government publications, the people in bureaucratic roles may also let a bias creep into their communications function. While information officers will likely try very hard to be impartial, they are only human, with personal biases, prejudices, and misconceptions of reality. Thus, what is virtually unavoidable is that government information may intentionally or unintentionally be coloured with the personal values of the public servants who prepare the information for publication. We can hope that those values are congruent with the values of society at large, but what is more important is that citizens recognize the potential for bias in all information and be able to evaluate all outputs in a critical light. Finally, the movement to a more open bureaucracy with the *Freedom of Information Act* has gone some of the way to ensuring that the public can get information directly, instead of waiting to see what the ministers and public servants are willing to divulge.

**Legitimacy and Stability** While it is in some ways an extension of its role in the dissemination of information, and while it would surprise those in the media who consider the term *bureaucratic* to be an unmitigated adjectival epithet, the bureaucracy likely plays a part in the fundamental process of creating public support for the regime itself. The accomplishments of Canadian government agencies in world affairs, scientific research, and the effective delivery of services to Canadian citizens can have a **legitimizing effect** for the system. When a career diplomat gains worldwide recognition and praise for efforts in a far-away embassy, or when a film produced by the National Film Board receives wide accolades (or even an Oscar!), it certainly brings credit to the government agency that achieved the recognition. However, such international acclaim may have a wider impact, by helping to generate a pride in Canadians about Canadian accomplishments and fostering support for our political community.

Another systemic role played by bureaucracy, and here we need not confine the discussion to Canada, is that of maintaining stability and continuity over time. For those who are committed to radical and rapid social change, this may well be viewed as a dysfunction of bureaucracy, but any system must have a static or conservative element, which enables it to persist over time. A constitution, a stable party system, or a stable economy may perform this function to varying degrees in different political systems. However, as we have seen, bureaucracies are by definition predictable, conservative, and, by empirical observation, sometimes pathologically inert; they provide continuity and stability even in a regime where other stabilizing institutions are failing.

### The Representative Function

While public servants might not be *elected* by us, they still may represent us quite well because of the structure of the bureaucracy. Most departments of government can identify a **client group** in the political community at large. The function of the department, in the administrative process, is to implement programs designed to benefit that clientele, and, in the policy process, to represent the interests of that clientele in policy initiation and priority determination. Thus, policy advisors within **clientele-oriented departments** press their political masters to adopt new policies or new programs, which will serve the interests of their clients.

We cannot pretend that the department fosters the interests of its clients for purely altruistic motives; rather, the motivation is that, if the department can invent and sell fancy new programs to the Cabinet, the department's share of the budgetary pie and the size of its person-year or "full-time equivalent" establishment will grow accordingly. Thus, serving the interests of a clientele is merely "good business" — a device for building or expanding a departmental empire. But whatever the motives, it may well be that the clientele-oriented departments of government represent the larger interests in Canadian society better and more consistently than the MPs, and perhaps even better than interest groups. While we should not go so far as to suggest that bureaucracy has "slain" democracy, we can certainly conclude that the representative role of Parliament is complemented by the representative role of the bureaucracy.

**The Meritocracy** Until the turn of the century the process of recruitment and selection for jobs in the bureaucracy was based to a large extent on partisan patronage. As a result, the bureaucracy was representative in the sense that the party with the majority of seats in the House of Commons also had a majority of the positions in the civil service. However, the bureaucracy was not representative of Canadians in that its members did not represent a cross-section of our population, and at the time this did not seem to be of great concern to the citizenry.

It is ironic that when recruitment and promotion in the civil service was removed from the patronage system and came to be based on merit, the bureaucracy became more competent but less representative. It became a **meritocracy**, where people lacking in skills and ability were effectively shut out of opportunities for public-service employment. While lower-level positions in the public service did not require very high levels of education or training, the senior officials of government constituted an **educational elite** in the same way that Cabinet ministers and judges can be placed in such a category.

Indeed, the public service appears to provide an important path of upward mobility in Canada, provided that somewhere along the way our potential Horatio Alger manages to obtain a university degree. Among the educational specializations of the senior bureaucracy, the largest number today have backgrounds in law, commerce or business, engineering, economics, political science, or public administration. The senior bureaucracy is an elite, based on merit, and merit is based to a large extent on educational achievement. Because education tends to correlate strongly with socio-economic status, this also means that the most influential bureaucrats tend to be drawn disproportionately from the upper middle class. As one might expect, the higher the rank in the bureaucracy, the higher the average level of educational achievement of the incumbents.

**TABLE 22.1**

Anglophones and Francophones in the Public Service

| Year | Anglophones | | Francophones | | Total |
| | Number | % | Number | % | |
|---|---|---|---|---|---|
| 1974 | 140,723 | 77 | 42,066 | 23 | 182,789 |
| 1978 | 158,479 | 75 | 53,406 | 25 | 211,885 |
| 1984 | 164,616 | 72 | 63,326 | 28 | 227,942 |
| 1993 | 155,904 | 72 | 60,751 | 28 | 216,655 |
| 1994 | 157,667 | 72 | 60,833 | 28 | 218,500 |

Source: *Official Languages in Federal Institutions, Annual Report,* 1993–1994.

*Language* In the case of language, it can be argued that the merit system was biased against francophones because literacy in English was assumed to be an important criterion of merit. Under the old patronage system, French-Canadian Cabinet ministers and members of Parliament were allowed to appoint their ethnic confrères to civil-service positions. Under the merit system, largely English-speaking boards tended to equate merit with facility in the English language, and French representation in the federal bureaucracy actually fell drastically as a result.

It was not until the 1960s that governments came to recognize that such biases in the public service did not reflect well on the image of the public service as the operational arm of a representative democracy. This was all the more obvious because the public sector in Canada had grown to become a significant proportion of the total labour force, and Canadians felt that there should be equal opportunity to compete for jobs in the government.While intelligence, competence, education, and training continued to be the main criteria for determining merit, it was recognized that in a bilingual country proficiency in both French and English was an important qualification for employment in the public service. The designation of many positions in government as **"bilingual imperative"** had the effect of greatly increasing the francophone component of the federal bureaucracy, largely because there were far fewer English Canadians who could speak French than French Canadians who could speak English. Today francophones are represented in the

**TABLE 22.2**
Executive-Category Public Servants by "Designated Group"

|  | 1993 | | 1994 | |
|---|---|---|---|---|
|  | **Number** | **%** | **Number** | **%** |
| Women | 731 | 17.6 | 708 | 18.3 |
| Aboriginal People | 44 | 1.1 | 44 | 1.1 |
| People with Disabilities | 81 | 1.9 | 77 | 2.0 |
| Members of Visible Minorities | 98 | 2.4 | 88 | 2.3 |
| Total Executive-Category Employees | 4155 | | 3875 | |

Source: *Employment Equity in the Public Service, Annual Reports,* 1992–1993, 1993–1994.

**TABLE 22.3**
All Public-Service Employees Classified by Age and Gender

| Age | March 1994 | | | | March 1995 | | | |
|---|---|---|---|---|---|---|---|---|
|  | **Men** | **Women** | **Total** | **% of Women** | **Men** | **Women** | **Total** | **% of Women** |
| 16–19 | 57 | 61 | 118 | 51.7 | 55 | 78 | 133 | 58.6 |
| 20–24 | 2,157 | 3,347 | 5,504 | 60.8 | 1,737 | 2,559 | 4,296 | 59.6 |
| 25–29 | 9,086 | 11,623 | 20,709 | 56.1 | 7,807 | 10,097 | 17,904 | 56.4 |
| 30–34 | 15,040 | 18,942 | 33,982 | 55.7 | 13,998 | 17,348 | 31,346 | 55.3 |
| 35–39 | 20,034 | 22,929 | 42,963 | 53.4 | 18,912 | 22,390 | 41,302 | 54.2 |
| 40–44 | 24,036 | 21,841 | 45,877 | 47.6 | 23,210 | 22,393 | 45,603 | 49.1 |
| 45–49 | 22,379 | 15,520 | 37,899 | 41.0 | 23,444 | 16,941 | 40,385 | 41.9 |
| 50–54 | 15,433 | 8,950 | 24,383 | 36.7 | 15,922 | 9,379 | 25,301 | 37.1 |
| 55–59 | 8,716 | 4,680 | 13,396 | 34.9 | 8,418 | 4,667 | 13,085 | 35.7 |
| 60–64 | 3,701 | 1,702 | 5,403 | 31.5 | 3,439 | 1,688 | 5,127 | 32.9 |
| 65–69 | 649 | 324 | 973 | 33.3 | 644 | 309 | 953 | 32.4 |
| 70+ | 123 | 61 | 184 | 33.2 | 128 | 56 | 184 | 30.4 |
| Total | 121,411 | 109,980 | 231,391 | 47.5 | 117,714 | 107,905 | 225,619 | 47.8 |

Source: Treasury Board Secretariat, *Employment Statistics for the Federal Public Service 1994–95.*

**TABLE 22.4**

Executive-Category Public-Service Employees Classified by Age and Gender

| Age | March 1994 | | | | March 1995 | | | |
|---|---|---|---|---|---|---|---|---|
| | Men | Women | Total | % of Women | Men | Women | Total | % of Women |
| 16–19 | 0 | 0 | 0 | 0.0 | 0 | 0 | 0 | 0.0 |
| 20–24 | 0 | 0 | 0 | 0.0 | 0 | 0 | 0 | 0.0 |
| 25–29 | 0 | 0 | 0 | 0.0 | 1 | 0 | 1 | 0.0 |
| 30–34 | 13 | 8 | 21 | 38.1 | 6 | 3 | 9 | 33.3 |
| 35–39 | 89 | 70 | 159 | 44.0 | 79 | 59 | 138 | 42.8 |
| 40–44 | 513 | 237 | 750 | 31.6 | 421 | 224 | 645 | 34.7 |
| 45–49 | 1,035 | 243 | 1,278 | 19.0 | 996 | 271 | 1,267 | 21.4 |
| 50–54 | 974 | 112 | 1,086 | 10.3 | 951 | 120 | 1,071 | 11.2 |
| 55–59 | 425 | 30 | 455 | 6.6 | 454 | 33 | 487 | 6.8 |
| 60–64 | 110 | 8 | 118 | 6.8 | 103 | 4 | 107 | 3.7 |
| 65–69 | 10 | 0 | 10 | 0.0 | 9 | 0 | 9 | 0.0 |
| 70+ | 1 | 0 | 1 | 0.0 | 1 | 0 | 1 | 0.0 |
| Total | 3,170 | 708 | 3,878 | 18.3 | 3,021 | 714 | 4,449 | 17.5 |

Source: Treasury Board Secretariat, *Employment Statistics for the Federal Public Service 1994–95.*

highest levels of the bureaucracy on roughly the same proportion as they are of the population as a whole (see Table 22.1).

*Affirmative Action and Employment Equity* The philosophy of recruitment practices in the federal public service changed in the 1970s and became based not simply on merit, but on the need to make the public service more representative of certain categoric groups. Hence, **affirmative action** policies were introduced to increase the presence of women at the higher levels of the bureaucracy, and these policies were extended to hire more people from the aboriginal communities, from among visible minorities, and from the ranks of individuals with disabilities. As indicated in Table 22.2, while we do not have proportional representation yet, aboriginal people, the physically disabled, and visible minorities are becoming better represented at all levels of the bureaucracy.

In 1995, it can be said that these policies have generally, if not completely, been successful in making the federal bureaucracy as a whole more representative of the **designated groups**. Although progress has been somewhat slower at the highest occupational levels, the relatively high percentages of representatives of the target groups as a proportion of the total *new* appointees to the executive category would indicate that the ultimate targets will eventually be met.

While women comprise 48 per cent of the total public service (Table 22.3), they are only about 18 per cent of the executive group (Table 22.4). However, the number of women in the bureaucratic elites has continued to grow, and when we take into account the relatively smaller number of women in the labour force, the inequities of representation by gender do not appear to be so severe. More importantly, perhaps, when we look at the age of our most senior bureaucrats, women are approximately one-third of those in the "up and coming" thirty-to-forty-five age bracket. As well, there are now seven female ministers out of a total of thirty-two and the Clerk of the Privy Council, who is also the "head" of the public service, is a woman. Hence, full gender parity is still in the future, but it is clearly possible.

To conclude this section on the functions of the bureaucracy, we have seen that, far from being only the passive instrument of the political executive, the modern bureaucracy has a very active role to play in government. Bureaucratic agencies not only implement law, they make law, they adjudicate, they have an enormous influence on policy, and they control much of the massive outflow of information to the general public. Moreover, because bureaucracy is such a pervasive force in the operation of our governmental system, it may well be performing broader systemic and representative functions, which heretofore have been considered the exclusive domain of other state institutions.

## ▶ THE STRUCTURE OF THE CANADIAN BUREAUCRACY

Before discussing the various structural types found in the bureaucracy we should say a few words about some of the terms used to describe the people who work in the government. The term **civil service** is no longer used with respect to the federal bureaucracy. "Civil servants" were full-time government employees, they worked in departments and agencies that reported directly to ministers, and they were eligible for pension benefits under the *Superannuation Act*. Civil servants became **public servants** under the 1967 *Public Service Employment Act* and the only difference in their status is that they have the right to bargain collectively with their employer. **Public-sector employees** at the federal level are a much larger group that includes the employees of crown corporations, the military, and other non-departmental agencies of the government, as well as the "true" public servants. At the provincial level, the "public-sector" category is very large indeed, including teachers, hospital employees, and municipal public servants.

The term *bureaucracy* is used here to describe the widest possible category, including the armed forces, the RCMP, government agencies of various types, and the public service. Clearly the key policy actors in the bureaucracy will be found in the public service and in the independent regulatory agencies, and while other public-sector actors can be included in one or more policy communities, they are definitely not at the core of the policy process. In Canada as a whole, all categories of public-sector employees, at all levels of government, make up over 40 per cent of the total labour force. In 1995, federal public-sector employees number about 500,000, and the public service itself has slipped from a high in 1975 of about 275,000 to just over 200,000.

There are several organizational types within the federal government. The main focus of our discussion here will be on the government **departments** and to a lesser extent on the **departmental corporations** and **crown corporations** that have an impact on the policy process. The Canadian Armed Forces and the RCMP are very large (115,000 and 20,000 employees, respectively) and have important roles to play but (thankfully in a liberal democracy!) have a very limited impact on the policy process.

### The Government Department

Departments, or **ministries** as they are sometimes known, are the core of the bureaucracy in Canada. They are key actors in the policy process and they are the direct administrative branch of the executive. They are best defined, however, in terms of their characteristics and *modus operandi*.

**Characteristics** Several characteristics distinguish the departmental form of organization from other types within the Canadian bureaucracy. First, a government department is answerable directly to a **Cabinet minister**, who functions as its formal head and who, conversely, is formally responsible to Parliament for the actions of both the department and the departmental officials. As we saw in Chapter 21, the practical effectiveness of the minister in heading a department is severely constrained and the administrative decisions will generally be left to the permanent officials.

The second distinguishing characteristic of the government department is that it is subject to the **estimates system** of budgeting, which means simply that the money appropriated for the department by Parliament is done on an annual basis and must be spent only in the manner directed by Parliament. The coming of the system of Planning Programming Budgeting (PPBS) in the 1960s, the adoption of a more centralized *envelope* system (PEMS) of budgetary apportionment in the 1970s, and the more recent trends to decentralization in the expenditure-mangement system have not changed the annual basis of the estimates. However, the various expenditure-management systems have all encouraged departments to *plan* their budgets over multi-year time frames through multi-year program forecasts, multi-year operational plans (MYOPs), or departmental business plans. We will say more about the current expenditure-management system in the next chapter.

The third characteristic of the government department is that personnel administration matters such as staffing, promotion, and discipline are subject to the *Public Service Employment Act*. This legislation places such matters under the supervision of the Public Service Commission, which is tasked with maintaining the integrity of the **merit principle** in the public service. With the exception of deputy ministers and associate deputy ministers, who are order-in-council appointments, and some temporary and part-time help, all the personnel of government departments are *public servants* under the *Public Service Employment Act*, and are recruited according to the principle of merit.

The fourth feature that distinguishes a government department is that, under the *Financial Administration Act*, it is subject to the Treasury Board's directives with respect to job classification, pay equity, pensions, and humanı esources development strategies. As well, under the *Public Service Staff Relations Act*, the Treasury Board is the departmental "employer" for purposes of collective bargaining and staff relations.

**The Deputy Minister**  Finally, one of the most important definitive characteristics of a government department is that the administrative head or CEO of the department is a **deputy minister.** The appointment of a DM is a prerogative, not of the department's minister, but of the prime minister, often on the advice of the secretary to the Cabinet. This process of appointment gives the prime minister some measure of control over individual departments, even if a minister becomes recalcitrant or remiss, but since the deputy minister usually works in very close contact with the minister and at arm's length from the prime minister, this power is more formal than real. The deputy minister, unlike a public servant, formally holds office only "at the pleasure" of the government, but as we saw in Chapter 21, the modern DM usually enjoys fairly secure tenure in practice. Experienced DMs are simply too valuable and too professional to be fired for partisan reasons.

In recent years, the position of **associate deputy minister** has evolved in the federal public service. Associate DMs are also order-in-council appointees, of deputy-ministerial rank, and their role is to take some of the responsibility off the shoulders of the DM. More than half of the federal departments today have an associate DM and there does not appear to be any sign of a reversal of this practice. Originally it may have been that the position was invented to provide a refuge for DMs who were either nearing retirement or whose departments had been reorganized out from underneath them. However, the associate DM position is evolving as an important component of departmental organization, and most of the individuals at this rank are future rather than former DMs, sharing the responsibilities for running the department while gaining valuable experience in the workings of the senior bureaucracy.

*The Management Function*  As the chief executive officer of a large organization called a government department the most obvious role of a deputy minister is a **managerial** one. As a senior manager he or she must plan and direct the operations of the department. The DM must set intra-departmental policy, participate in the selection of officers for senior positions within the organization (subject to the merit principle), and *coordinate* departmental activities through executive leadership. The function of coordination is in part facilitated through the delegation of managerial functions to subordinates. As well, in many departments, coordination occurs through a **management committee** or **executive committee**, chaired by the DM and consisting of the DM, the associate DM (if any), all of the ADMs, and other senior officials as required. The management committee sets the broad objectives and priorities of the department, examines any new proposals that may emerge from the bowels of the organization, and may deal, as well, with such vital management questions as the date of the departmental picnic or the colour of ink to be used for the departmental mission statement. However, properly operated, the committee can do much, together with the budget process, to rationalize intra-departmental priorities, and it can be used effectively by the deputy minister as a tool

**Figure 22.2**
Functions of the deputy-minister.

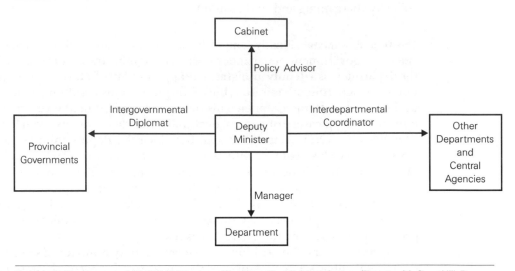

Source: R. Van Loon and M. S. Whittington, *The Canadian Political System* (Toronto: McGraw-Hill Ryerson, 1987), p. 345.

of internal planning, coordination, and liaison. The committee may also function as a **senior policy committee** in some departments.

*Interdepartmental Coordination*    The deputy minister is also formally responsible for the maintenance of liaison with people in other departments. This is necessary because each department must depend, to some extent, on service departments, such as the department of Public Works and Government Services, whose function it is to provide services for the rest. As well, it may be necessary to coordinate the efforts of two or more departments that are interested in similar policy objectives and whose portfolio boundaries overlap. Finally, in all cases, policy recommendations must be cleared with the central agencies before being submitted to the Cabinet, and the expenditure-mangement system requires almost constant interaction between the departments and the Treasury Board Secretariat.

Interdepartmental coordination is both extremely important to the department and a very delicate process. Much of it, being fairly routine, does not require the hands-on involvement of the busy DM, who delegates much of this responsibility to more specialized officals at lower levels in the hierarchy. All of this is achieved through a semi-institutionalized process of protocol and interdepartmental **diplomacy**, which has evolved to meet at least some of the needs of interdepartmental coordination and overall public-service efficiency.

*Intergovernmental Diplomacy*    Much the same can be said about the role of the DM in the **intergovernmental** arena. We explained in Chapter 10 how the process of **bureaucratic federalism** dominates the business of intergovernmental relations in the modern context. Next to the minister, the deputy minister bears the formal responsibility for ensuring that intergovernmental coordination is achieved expeditiously. There are extremely important omnilateral coordinating committees in the intergovernmental arena, such as the Coordinating Committee of Deputy Ministers of Finance and Provincial Treasurers, where the senior bureaucrats attend the meetings in the flesh. In fact, most departments with any significant relationships with provinces will have annual or semi-annual federal-provincial meetings at the deputy-ministerial level. However, for the most part, the process of intergovernmental coordination goes on at levels below that of the federal and provincial DMs.

*The Policy Mandarin*  In terms of the policy process in Canada, the most important function of the deputy minister is to act as the senior departmental **advisor** to the government. The DM has the key role in the transmission of policy information from administrative underlings with many types of expertise to the minister and through the minister to the Cabinet. The policy role of the deputy minister has changed over time, and in order to understand the current influence of the DM in the policy process, it will be helpful to look at the evolution of these senior bureaucratic **mandarins.**

The evolution of the DM from senior manager to policy mandarin happened because the number and complexity of policy decisions increased to a point where most Cabinet ministers were unable to make good decisions without considerable input from their departments. The influence of the mandarins over the determination of priorities grew because of a number of factors, some related to structural features of the system and others to the personal characteristics of the individuals involved. The most important of the **structural** factors was the deputy ministers' control over the flow of information upwards from the departmental technocracy and downwards from the Cabinet. A large vestige of this particular source of policy influence, the control over the vertical flow of information, still resides with the senior bureaucrats.

The most important *personal* factor contributing to the hegemony of the mandarins was the combination of **expertise** in a substantive field and long **experience** as a participant in the policy process. Because a mandarin's experience extended over a number of years, and frequently through a series of different governments, this senior bureaucrat often could possess a perspective that was much broader than that of the political boss. The deputy minister could have a profound influence on the minister, not only because the DM possessed a higher level of technical competence in the field, but also because, over the years, a feel for the political marketplace had been acquired as well. The discerning and experienced deputy minister would inevitably develop a **political acumen** or "savvy" that would prove invaluable to the minister in assessing what the political traffic would bear with a given client group at a given time. While the influence of the mandarins would naturally also be related to the willingness of the individual ministers and the government of the day to take their advice, for the most part they either became trusted and, therefore, influential, or they simply ceased to be mandarins.

*The Decline of the Mandarins*   Because John Diefenbaker deeply mistrusted the senior bureaucracy, during his era as PM, alternative advice was sought from the Conservative Party, from personal acquaintances, from the press, and from the mind of the leader himself. The somewhat strained relations between the PM and the bureaucracy during the Diefenbaker years ensured that there was a reduced chance of priorities being determined solely by the bureaucracy, and that more than normal attention was paid to alternate, if less expert, sources. Similar alternatives had been available during the Liberal years before 1957, and were available again under Lester Pearson, from 1963 to 1968. However, Liberal prime ministers, and in particular Mike Pearson, who was himself a "reformed mandarin," had shown little propensity to use them.

Prime Minister Trudeau and his advisors, on the other hand, appear to have believed that the most effective counter for one bureaucratic institution was other bureaucratic institutions with parallel responsibilities. The **political advisory power** of the mandarins was to be attenuated through the increase in size and influence of the PMO, and their **technical advice** was to be placed in competition with that coming from the departments and screened through a revamped and expanded PCO. As well, it was apparently the intention of the Trudeau government to temper the influence of the mandarins by moving deputy ministers about more rapidly, so that they were not in one position long enough to monopolize the field and, therefore, control their minister.

In fact, it can be argued that the eclipse of the traditional mandarins would have occurred even without the Trudeau reorganizations. The complexity of the technical aspects of policy determination increased to the extent that real "power as knowledge" came to be diffused among the myriad specialized public servants at lower levels of the departmental hierarchy. Moreover, with the size of departments growing so rapidly, the DMs were simply too busy being managers of large organizations to be able to develop either the political acumen or the technical know-how that had previously given them such influence over the ministers.

*The New Mandarins*   While the DM is only one person and therefore incapable of a total understanding of the specialist decisions made by his or her administrative underlings, as a professional manager, the DM is in a good position to decide which of several departmental technical advisors the government should put its faith in. It has been mentioned before that one of the important aspects of Cabinet decisions at the policy-formulation stage of the policy process is deciding which policy advice to convert into government action. In this respect, the deputy minister, as a **manager of expertise**, is invaluable to the Cabinet. These "new-style" mandarins can tell the minister which advice is likely to be better, not because the DM fully understands the **substance** of the advice, but because he or she knows the *people* generating the advice. We will revisit the evolution of the "new mandarins" in the context of our discussion of the policy process in the next chapter.

As we have seen, several PMs have attempted to counter the power of the senior bureaucracy by developing alternate sources of policy advice. The main success stories have been the PMO and the PCO. The PMO, being frankly partisan, does, indeed, provide a counter to the professional bureaucracy when it comes to political advice. The PMO is, in effect, a **political technocracy** whose advice may counter that of the "technical technocracy." The PCO, on the other hand, did cut into the exclusive power of the departmental mandarins. Thus, the departmental mandarins are limited by central-agency mandarins, and while competition between the two "mandarinates" is likely healthy, it is unlikely that cabinets today are, on the whole, any less dependent on senior public servants for the technical components of policy decisions.

_The DM: Conclusion_  In summary, the deputy minister of a Canadian government department plays the role of a manager of a very large organization. However, as we will see in the next chapter, the nature of government organization, with its emphasis on political accountability and control, places both unique powers and restrictions on the management function, and the extent to which the DM can exercise those unique powers and cope with those unique restrictions ultimately rests on personal ability. Deputy ministers, both in Ottawa and in the provinces, hold some of the most difficult and important jobs in Canada, and play a very central role in the overall working of the Canadian governmental process.

**The Internal Structure of Departments**  The internal functions of an organization can broadly be classed as **line** or **staff**. In Canada, this distinction is based on the type of relationship between various intra-departmental administrative structures and the goals of the department as a whole. To use the example of a specific department, the operational goal of the Department of National Revenue, simply stated, is tax collection. Those branches of the department involved directly in collecting tax revenues, departmental "operations," are said to be performing **line functions**. On the other hand, there are branches or divisions of the same department involved in matters such as personnel administration, financial administration, and communications, none of which directly involves the performance of the line function. These branches of the department are said to perform **staff functions** and they exist to assist the line managers, either in an administrative support capacity or through the performance of a specialized service. The staff components of the organization carry no direct authority over the line managers.

The basic structure of a government department is hierarchical, with the deputy minister at the top of the pyramid. Under the DM, there are a number of subordinate levels, each of which is, itself, hierarchical in structure and directly accountable to the level above. This is called the **chain of command** in an organization and is one of the defining characteristics of all bureaucratic structures. Figure 22.3 is a schematic representation of how a typical federal department might be organized. The DM is at the top, and the chain of command descends through associate DM, assistant deputy minister,[3] director general, director, and thence to lower supervisory levels (managers, chiefs, supervisors, heads, analysts, officers, etc.).

---

3.  The position of _Senior ADM_, while appearing on many departmental organization charts, is more an honorific title than a distinct level in the hierarchy. In fact, ADMs all report directly to the DM level.

**Figure 22.3**

Schematic departmental organization chart. Abbreviations: ADM: assistant deputy minister; D-G: director-general; DM: deputy minister. "Head" may also be called "chief," "supervisor," "manager," or other.

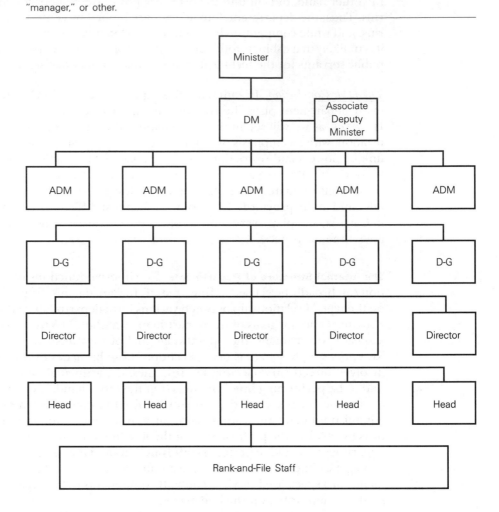

The reader will be relieved to know that a department-by-department analysis is beyond the scope of this text, so we must be satisfied with few generalizations and specific examples. However, it is useful first to look at how the various responsibilities of the government of Canada are parcelled out into discrete organizational entities called departments.

**The Principles of Departmentalization**  The largest number of government departments are what we can refer to as **line departments**. These are operational departments of government that are set up to look after the interests of specific **client groups** (Agriculture, Indian Affairs, Veterans' Affairs), to deal with issues of relevance to given **economic sectors** (Fisheries and Oceans, Natural Resources, Industry, Transport), to deliver certain categories of **service or protection** to the public (Human Resources, Health, Citizenship and Immigration, Defence, Solicitor General), or to **manage a national asset** or public good (Environment, Heritage). Most departments do not fit clearly into only one of these categories of departmentalization, instead spilling into more than one functional type. Thus, for instance, Agriculture Canada not only serves farmer-clients but also manages the agri-business industrial sector, Transport provides services as well as regulating an industry, and Fisheries and Oceans regulates an industry, serves a client group, and manages a national asset.

Other departments have a "horizontal" or **policy-service** rationale, being reponsible for coordinating a certain aspect of policy among a range of line departments. Thus, Justice provides legal services and coordinates constitutional matters for all departments, and Foreign Affairs and International Trade assists other departments in any matters within their portfolios that have international implications. Still other departments are set up to provide **administrative services**, not to the public, but to other government departments: Public Works and Government Services provides a wide range of services to the other departments; and Revenue Canada collects taxes on behalf of the government as a whole. Finally, there are the **central agencies**, which we discussed in the previous chapter, and which are exclusively concerned with policy development and coordination. All current federal departments and agencies are listed by category in Table 22.5. We will discuss the way in which government departments carry out their policy and administrative functions in the next chapter.

### Departmental Corporations

A **departmental corporation** is an agency of the government of Canada, established by act of Parliament, that is engaged in administrative, research, supervisory, or regulatory functions of a governmental nature. Schedule II of the *Financial Administration Act* (FAA) lists the departmental corporations:

> Atomic Energy Control Board
> Canada Employment and Immigration Commission
> Canadian Centre for Management Development
> Canadian Centre for Occupational Health and Safety
> Canadian Polar Commission
> Canadian Transportation Accident Investigation and Safety Board
> Director of Soldier Settlement
> The Director, The Veterans' Land Act
> Fisheries Prices Support Board
> Medical Research Council
> The National Battlefields Commission
> National Research Council of Canada
> National Round Table on the Environmant and the Economy
> Natural Sciences and Engineering Research Council
> Social Sciences and Humanities Research Council

**TABLE 22.5**
Federal Departments and Central Agencies by Category, 1995

| | |
|---|---|
| Line Departments | • Agriculture and Agri-Business<br>• Citizenship and Immigration<br>• Natural Resources<br>• Environment<br>• Fisheries and Oceans<br>• Indian Affairs and Northern Development<br>• Human Resources Development<br>• National Defence<br>• Health<br>• Industry<br>• Canadian Heritage<br>• Solicitor General<br>• Transport<br>• Veterans' Affairs |
| Policy Service Departments | • Foreign Affairs and International Trade<br>• Justice |
| Administrative Service Departments | • Public Works and Government Services<br>• National Revenue |
| Central Agencies | • Finance<br>• Treasury Board Secretariat<br>• Privy Council Office |

Basically, departmental corporations differ from government departments in the degree of direct political control exercised over them. As we noted above, a minister is the formal head of a department, and a deputy minister is the administrative head. However, a departmental corporation is expected to operate at arm's length from the government of the day. It would be inappropriate for partisan politicians to be in direct control of an organization which, for instance, awards research grants, regulates the nuclear industry, or investigates plane crashes. Hence, the departmental corporation is given a measure of independence from ministerial control and a freedom of action that line departments do not enjoy.

For purposes of the *Financial Administration Act*, departmental corporations have almost the same status as a line department. This is because departmental corporations do not have any significant revenue sources of their own and must be funded entirely out of the Consolidated Revenue Fund. A departmental corporation does not buy, sell, or own any assets in its own name, and all of its financial affairs are subject to the control of the Treasury Board and the auditor general.

However, while the money spent by a departmental corporation must be appropriated by Parliament and encumbered from the Consolidated Revenue Fund, there is a greater degree of independence than that exercised by a department in how the appropriated funds are actually spent. The estimates

**Figure 22.4**

Departmental corporation.

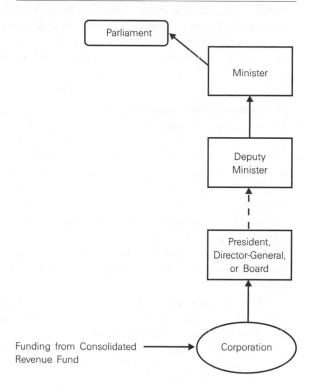

for a departmental corporation are usually put through Parliament in the form of one vote in the estimates of the department through whose minister the corporation must report to Parliament. Hence, the National Battlefields Commission reports to Parliament through the minister of Canadian Heritage and gets its money, for any given budgetary year, in the form of one item in the main estimates of the Department of Canadian Heritage.

By contrast to a government department, the budget for a departmental corporation is debated in parliamentary committee, if at all, as one item. However, the Treasury Board Secretariat *does* examine and approve the estimates for a departmental corporation before they are included in the departmental estimates. Hence, independence from parliamentary control may not mean very much when we consider that the Treasury Board, which exercises much of the real financial control over government expenditure, has as close a look at a Schedule II corporation's financial needs as it has at a department's.

A departmental corporation is usually headed by a president, director-general, or board appointed by the governor-general-in-council. The tenure of these positions varies from set ten-year periods to "the pleasure of Her Majesty." The corporation reports *through* but not directly *to* the DM. The employees of departmental corporations are, today, almost all public servants.

They come under the purview of the Public Service Commission and their tenure is the same as that of any departmental employee. Finally, all departmental corporations must submit an annual report, which must be tabled, by the minister responsible, in the House of Commons. This report is essentially to provide publicity for the activities of the organization and to ensure that such independent bodies are not above considerations of economy and efficiency.

### Semi-Independent Agencies of the Public Service

There are a great many commissions, agencies, councils, boards, and tribunals that have functions that might make them appropriate candidates for departmental corporation status, but which for various reasons have been kept within the public service proper. These bodies include regulatory, investigative, quasi-judicial, and even service-delivery institutions and are kept under closer control of the Cabinet because, in most cases, they have responsibilities that can be extremely significant in terms of public policy. They are listed in a separate schedule of the FAA and number more than fifty individual organizations. While there is no need to provide the entire list here, by mentioning a few of them, the reader will get a sense of the sorts of responsibilities these bodies have.

The **operational** or "service-provision" category includes the RCMP, the Canadian Security Intelligence Service (CSIS), Statistics Canada, the Public Service Commission, Elections Canada, and the National Archives. All of these government agencies are fairly large organizations, but because of the need for objectivity and non-partisanship in the performance of their duties, they report to a minister less directly than a line department does.

In the **quasi-judicial** or **investigative** category, agencies such as the Civil Aviation Tribunal, the Immigration and Refugee Board, the National Parole Board, the Public Service Staff Relations Board, and the Security Intelligence Review Board (SIRC) all have to be at arm's length from politics of the day in order to retain a modicum of impartiality. At the same time, because of the sensitivity of their decisions, the government has been reluctant to place them completely outside the purview of the Cabinet.

Finally, this *pot pourri* of organizational orphans also includes important **regulatory agencies** such as the CRTC, the National Energy Board, and the National Transportation Agency. While these agencies must operate in a semi-independent manner to keep raw partisan bias from sullying their deliberations, at the same time, their decisions are policy decisions of the government. Hence, the government of the day naturally wants to have them either close at hand or at a "short arm's length."

### Special Operating Agencies

Organizationally, the "newest kid on the block" in the federal public service is the **special operating agency** (SOA). One of the recommendations of *Public Service 2000*, which we will discuss in the next chapter, was to "achieve a new balance between the philosophy of control and risk avoidance and the desire

**Figure 22.5**
Special operating agency.

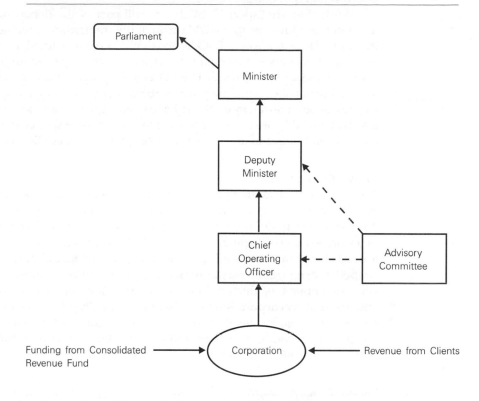

to encourage innovation and promote initiative."[4] The SOA is an institutional arrangement designed to accomplish that new balance.

The SOAs are set up through a framework agreement that defines an arm's-length relationship between a sponsoring department and a unit within the department. The special operating agency is given much greater autonomy within the department and, as well, is exempt from many of the government-wide administrative rules. Generally, the units that can be converted to SOAs are already self-contained within the department, they have a clear mandate or mission, and they have roles associated with the delivery of a specific service.

The first five SOAs started up in 1990 and four of these provide services to other departments and agencies in the government on a cost-recovery basis. The exception, the Passport Office, delivers its service directly to the public. While they don't actually "bill" their public-service clients, the SOAs are funded through a **revolving fund.** A revolving fund is a non-lapsing appropriation out of which the SOA pays its bills and into which it deposits its "revenues," in the form of paper transfers from the client departments. This allows the agency to

---

4.  Service-to-the-Public Task Force, *Report* (Ottawa: SSC, 1990) p. 16.

operate on a commercial basis and not to have to jump all of the accountability hoops set up by Treasury Board.

While they are "special," SOAs are still part of the department and are ultimately accountable to the DM through the framework agreement that sets them up. The employees of SOAs are public servants with all of the benefits and constraints associated with that status, and the organization is subject to review by the auditor general. The SOAs must prepare annual business plans as do all departments and they are expected to operate efficiently. At time of writing, about a dozen more SOAs have been approved and several are pending. None of this next wave of SOAs has an exclusive service-to-government function and in fact many of them deal only with a public clientele.

### Crown Corporations

A **crown corporation** is a government institution with a corporate form, created by act of Parliament to perform a public function. In 1995, the *Financial Administration Act* defines a crown corporation as a "parent Crown corporation or a wholly owned subsidiary." Historically, however, crown corporations were a much more inclusive category, including **departmental corporations**, described above; **agency corporations**, which carried on commercial activities with the public but which did not compete with private-sector corporations; and **proprietary corporations**, which were essentially private companies wholly owned by the government. The latter two categories of crown corporations are now all **parent crown corporations** and the distinction between agency corporations and proprietary corporations is no longer relevant.

**Parent Crown Corporations** A parent crown corporation is headed up by an independent board of directors, which is appointed for a set term by order-in-council. The members of the board usually include a full-time chairman or president, who may also function as the administrative head and chief executive of the corporation, and part-time members, who meet as a board only a few times each year. In the case of some crown corporations, members of the board may include public servants from other governmental agencies, but the trend is definitely away from this practice. The relationship of the chief executive of the corporation to the board will differ, depending on the nature of the corporation and the personalities involved. However, in some parent crown corporations the president is appointed by the government and in others is elected by the board itself.

The activities of parent crown corporations are not supervised directly by a Cabinet minister. Indeed, independence from direct political control is one of the major reasons for creating a crown corporation. Despite this, and mainly because it is felt that public enterprise financed by public money should be subjected to at least some parliamentary control, each crown corporation is assigned to a minister of the Crown, *through* which it must report to Parliament. The minister, however, does not in any way direct the activities of the corporation and is in no way personally responsible for the activities of the corporation.

A minister is assigned to act as a communication link, as necessary, between Parliament and the corporation, which is engaged in public enterprise and which, in many cases, is spending public money. The bulk of a minister's work on behalf of a crown corporation will entail justifying the corporation's funding to the House of Commons. Naturally, it may be possible for a minister to influence corporation policy informally, but this is difficult to document. All that can be said is that informal ministerial control over a crown corporation will depend largely on the personalities involved, on the extent to which the corporation requires government funds to stay in business, and on the policy implications of the corporation's activities.

**Part-I and Part-II Parent Crown Corporations**  Parent crown corporations are all listed in Parts I and II of Schedule III of the *Financial Administration Act*. Part-I corporations are generally responsible for "the management of trading or service operations on a quasi-commercial basis, or for the management of procurement, construction, or disposal activities on behalf of Her Majesty in right of Canada." These corporations deal directly with the public and with private corporations in the sense that they charge fees, tender contracts, or buy and sell assets and commodities in the open market. These corporations may act as the crown *parent* or holding company for any number of subsidiary corporations, but they are generally deemed to be in sufficiently sensitive or policy-relevant areas of enterprise to justify the government presence in the open marketplace. As well, Part-I corporations are generally expected to require at least some contribution from the Consolidated Revenue Fund in order to be able to survive. Part-I corporations are listed below.

Atlantic Pilotage Authority
Atomic Energy of Canada Limited
Canada Deposit Insurance Corporation
Canada Lands Company Limited
Canada Mortgage and Housing Corporation
Canadian Commercial Corporation
Canadian Dairy Commission
Canadian Museum of Civilization
Canadian Museum of Nature
Canadian Saltfish Corporation
Cape Breton Development Corporation
Defence Construction (1951) Limited
Enterprise Cape Breton Corporation
Export Development Corporation
Farm Credit Corporation
Federal Business Development Bank
Freshwater Fish Marketing Corporation
Great Lakes Pilotage Authority, Ltd.
Laurentian Pilotage Authority
Marine Atlantic Inc.
National Capital Commission
National Gallery of Canada

National Museum of Science and Technology
Pacific Pilotage Authority
The St. Lawrence Seaway Authority
Standards Council of Canada
VIA Rail Canada Inc.

Part-I parent corporations that have the word "Limited" or "Ltd." after their names were set up under the *Companies Act*; the rest were set up by separate legislation. The boards of directors of the limited corporations are named by the shareholders, but because the shares are held in trust for the Crown, the governor-general-in-council formally makes the actual appointments. Most of the other corporations are headed by a board of directors, which is appointed for a set term by the governor-general-in-council.

The employees of the Part I corporations are all appointed by the management of the corporation itself, and the salaries and conditions of work are also determined in a manner similar to private industry. While there are exceptions, generally these corporations are empowered to maintain accounts

**Figure 22.6**
Appropriation-dependent crown corporation (Part-I parent crown corporation).

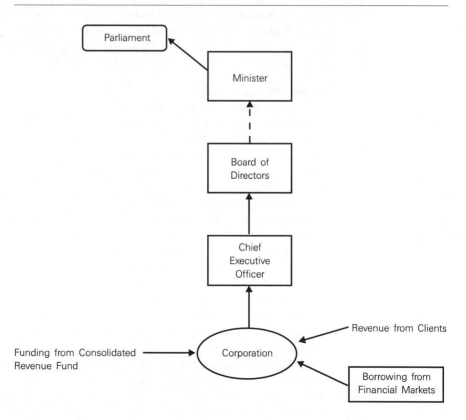

in their own names in any bank that is formally approved by the minister of Finance. The operating budget of the corporation is scrutinized by the minister through which the corporation reports to Parliament, but the actual estimates for operating costs are placed before Parliament in the form of one item in departmental estimates.

Capital budgets of Part-I parent corporations are subject to more detailed scrutiny by Parliament, and, as with departmental corporations, an annual report, including financial statements, must be presented to the minister responsible at the end of the fiscal year. These reports are then tabled in Parliament. All the financial statements of Part-I parent crown corporations are subject to the scrutiny of the auditor general.

The legal position of such corporations is much the same as that of any private corporation created under the *Corporations Act*. Most Part-I corporations can be sued in any court just as if they were not agents of the Crown. This is important in that it places them in much the same legal position vis-à-vis their clientele as any firm operating in the private sphere. By making them legally directly responsible for their activities, the government can also afford to grant them a great deal of independence from financial and political control.

The second category of parent crown corporation, listed in Part II of Schedule III, must operate in a competitive environment, must not normally be dependent upon appropriations for operating capital, must ordinarily earn a return on equity, and must have the potential of paying dividends. In effect, what distinguishes Part-II corporations from Part-I corporations is that the former are **"privatizable"** in terms of both their policy significance and their attractiveness to would-be private-sector buyers or shareholders. Past denizens of this schedule of the FAA include Air Canada, Eldorado Nuclear, Northern Transportation Company, Polymer Corporation, Teleglobe Canada, and PetroCanada. The current fairly short list includes eight port authorities, Canada Post, CNR, the Canada Development Investment Corporation (CDIC), and the Mint.

### Other Crown Agencies

There are many corporations wholly owned and operated by the government of Canada that are not listed in Schedules II and III of the *Financial Administration Act*. While these are not classed as departmental corporations or parent crown corporations, they perform mostly the same kinds of functions as those corporations listed in the FAA, and therefore should be considered briefly at this point.

Most of these unclassified crown corporations are set up by separate federal legislation to perform functions that require a degree of independence of action but, often for unstated reasons, they have been excluded in the schedules of the *Financial Administration Act*. The most notable examples of this sort of bureaucratic agency are the Bank of Canada and the Canadian Wheat Board, each of which has been set up by its own special legislation. Recent additions to this list include the CBC, which was originally classified as a proprietary crown corporation, and the Canada Council.

These unclassified corporations, because they display many varieties of internal organization and procedures for control, do not lend themselves to

**Figure 22.7**
Commercial crown corporation (Part-II parent crown corporation).

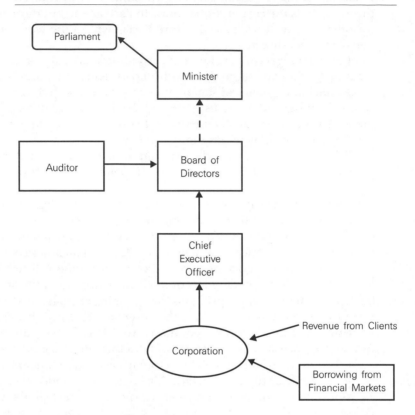

description here. It should also be mentioned, at this point, that there are many government corporations at the provincial level that function in approximately the same way their federal counterparts do. Because of their organizational diversity and great numbers, we can do no more in this study than mention the fact of their existence.

There are a number of government corporations and commissions in existence that are unique not because of their line functions but because their structure, composition, and legislative mandates are *intergovernmental*. Examples of these are federal-provincial agencies such as the interprovincial and territorial boundary commissions, which are set up as required. Each consists of a commissioner from the provinces concerned and the surveyor-general of Canada as the federal representative. Another example of joint federal-provincial enterprise is Syncrude, in which federal and provincial governments as well as the private sector were joint participants in an oil-sands development.

**Figure 22.8**
Organizational forms in the Government of Canada: summary chart.

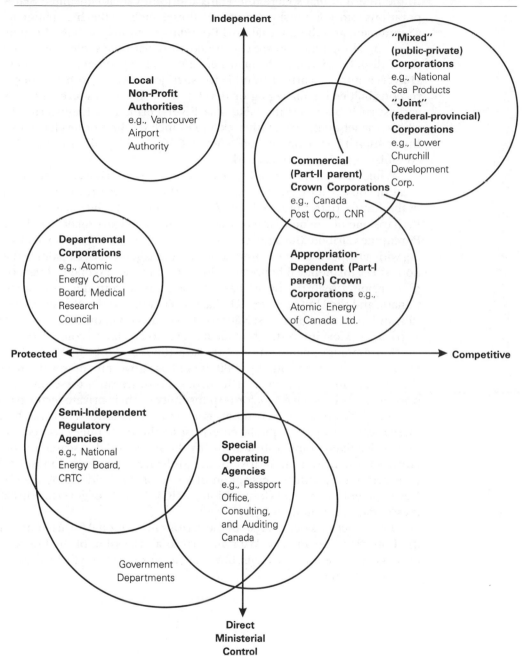

### Miscellaneous Government Structures

In the international sphere, there are also joint Canadian-United States corporations and commissions. Some of these, such as the International Joint Commission and the International Boundary Commission, have been in existence for a long time and are concerned more with the settlement of international disputes than with the management of some genuinely joint enterprise. However, a more current trend is for such joint bodies to have operational responsibilities for managing or developing a shared resource. Perhaps the earliest such body was the Columbia River Permanent Engineering Board, which was set up in 1964. Other examples include the Roosevelt Campobello International Park Commission, where a Canada—United States board jointly administers an international park.

While such bodies are still the exception, it seems likely, particularly in the areas of conservation and recreation, that there will be greater need for them in the future, both in the federal-provincial and in the international context. Perhaps one of the more interesting of these mixed-jurisdiction bodies is the Porcupine Caribou Management Board, which has the responsibility for dealing with all aspects of the conservation and management of a resource that has no respect for political boundaries in its wanderings. While it does not give the caribou a seat, the board has representatives from the governments of Canada and the United States, Alaska, the Yukon, and the Northwest Territories, and from aboriginal First Nations of Alaska, the Yukon, and the Northwest Territories. Most interestingly of all, it seems to be able to come to decisions!

A prominent phenomenon of the late 1960s and the 1970s was the *mixed public-private enterprise*, and by 1980 the federal government was the majority shareholder in about fifteen such corporations. Because these mixed-enterprise corporations have a major responsibility to their private-sector partners and shareholders, a major corporate goal is to make money. However, because these are at least partly "public enterprises," there are policy-related goals as well, which likely complicate and qualify the single-minded search for profits. However, the privatization drive of the Mulroney years ended most of these enterprises and, with the exception of some of the holdings of the Canada Development Investment Corporation (CDIC), this type of government activity is essentially moribund today.

This concludes our analysis of the various institutional forms found within the Canadian bureaucracy. We now turn to a discussion of the bureaucratic process and attempt to explain how the various bureaucratic institutions actually fit into the governmental process.

# Chapter 23

# The Bureaucratic Process: Policy-Making, Public Administration, and Control

This chapter is concerned with how the bureaucracy goes about performing its primary functions of tendering policy advice to the Cabinet and administering programs and services. As we have seen, the bureaucracy's **policy role** is to provide information to the political leaders of the country that will assist them in deciding what to do and how to do it. The bureaucracy's **administrative role** is to actually do what the politicians have decided should be done, that is, to carry out the business of delivering programs and services to the public.

## ▶ BUREAUCRACY AND THE POLICY PROCESS

Elsewhere in the text we have many times alluded to the role of the Canadian bureaucracy in the policy process. However, these discussions were incidental to explaining the role of other institutions such as interest groups, the Cabinet, and the central agencies. It is the aim of this section of the chapter to zero in on the policy-related processes internal to the government departments and to explain the responsibilities of the senior bureaucrats as managers of policy-relevant information.

### Policy Initiation: Advocacy and Innovation

At the policy-initiation stage, we see the bureaucracy acting as a **channel** through which information about the policy needs of groups and individuals in Canadian society can be brought to the attention of the "policy centre" — the Cabinet. However, this "channel of access" role is seldom a purely passive one, for the departmental officials also act as **gatekeepers.** They pass on only information that is deemed sufficiently critical to merit bothering the busy minister and any information that does make it through the "gate" is usually transmitted with a positive or negative "spin."

As well, government departments sometimes take the initiative themselves: they actively **advocate** policy options even before there is much stirring from the client group. In the advocacy role, the departmental officials will generate their own policy innovations and attempt to convince their minister and ultimately the Cabinet that there is a policy need in the real world that should be addressed. Each of these departmental roles in policy initiation deserves further elaboration.

**Policy Gatekeepers**  To act as an effective channel of information input, the departmental manager must maintain open lines of communication and establish a close working relationship with the key interest groups in the appropriate policy community. This means that the department is functioning as a representative institution, usually in direct competition for limited resources with other clientele-oriented departments. Such activity often puts the department directly in competition with other institutions, such as Parliament, the political parties, and the electoral system, which also function as channels of access to the Cabinet.

*Bureaucratic Activism*  In the process of channelling policy ideas into the system, the most effective bureaucratic agencies are those that take more than a passive role in the process. It is not always necessary to simply wait for a policy need to gradually evolve out of the activities of a client group; the department, through what amounts to intelligence gathering, can often discover policy needs even before the non-governmental actors in the policy community. In this fashion, the department can both anticipate the needs of existing client groups and, often, discover new groups of potential clients. Having discovered such latent policy needs, it is not uncommon for government officials to become involved as "social animators," helping to organize and politicize the affected group.

This activist role of the bureaucracy emerged because, no matter how clever the policy idea may be intrinsically, the politicians in the Cabinet will be unlikely to take any action unless it becomes clear that there is a growing political demand for action. Hence, beginning in the 1970s, the departmental policy managers became increasingly involved in the process of "educating" their clients as to what options might be available and even in assisting the affected groups to organize themselves as pressure groups, by providing core funding. In effect, in the 1970s and early 1980s, clientele-oriented agencies of government, at both federal and provincial levels, not only helped to articulate the policy demands of their clients to the Cabinet, but they also may have helped to create, fund, and organize the very interest groups that ended up making demands on them and on the minister.

*A Symbiotic Relationship*  The interest group–department relationship, thus, often served the interests of both the bureaucracy and the client group. The relationship became *symbiotic* because a successful campaign for the initiation of a new policy benefits both the department and the interest group. The latter benefits directly in that the membership it represents gets an immediate payoff or benefit from the new program. The former benefits through the increased jurisdictional "turf," budgetary allocation, and person-years it receives in order to be able to implement the new policy. However, the result of such tactics was almost always beneficial to the political executive as well. The party in power will also be able to bask in the reflected kudos and, hopefully, reap increased electoral support as a reward for being such a "sympathetic and understanding government."

In sum, government departments, in functioning as channels of input for demands from interest groups, have often gone far beyond the passive gate-keeper role to become active advocates of client interests. Moreover, in some cases the department would actually enter into a sort of "collusion" with the interest groups in the relevant policy community, in attempting to generate and articulate policy demands to the Cabinet and the central agencies. As we shall see later, however, this activist advocacy style of bureaucratic politics is far easier when there are lots of funds available for new policy initiatives.

In the situation of severe restraint we have experienced since the mid 1980s, departmental officials and their client groups alike are learning that they are lucky if they can avoid program cutbacks, let alone win new policy concessions. To the extent that there is still a mutually supportive relationship between government departments and organized stakeholders within a policy community, we can conclude that the policy goals are, for the most part, focused on defending existing programs from the onslaught of deficit-reduction initiatives.

**Policy Innovation**  While the bureaucracy may function not only as a facilitator but also as an active manipulator of the flow of information from the environment to the system, such an activist advocacy role requires the departmental managers to foster creativity and **policy innovation**. The basic problem for the senior bureaucratic manager in organizing the department to act as an agency of innovation stems from the very nature of bureaucratic organization. As we have seen, the *raison d'être* of bureaucracy is to make administrative behaviour rational and predictable. This is accomplished largely through a process described as the *"routinization* of decision making." However, in an organization geared to predictability and routinization, creativity and innovation can be negative or dysfunctional traits. Hence, the challenge of the public-service manager is to find organizational devices that will permit innovative activity and at the same time not compromise the basic organizational goal of routinization, in other words, to integrate creativity and predictability.

*Organizing for Innovation*  One organizational device that has been employed in an attempt to resolve the inherent contradiction between the goals of innovation and routinization in federal bureaucratic structures is to organize the department so that there are policy officers, policy branches, sectors, secretariats, or "strategic" policy units that are to some extent insulated from the line operations of the department. The aim here was to foster creative thinking and experimentation within specialized policy units without "infecting" the line managers and creating "loose cannons" where what is required is predictability and routine.

Two problems emerged with this "ghettoization" of policy innovation. First, after a period of time, policy units, being staffed with bureaucrats, naturally tend to become regularized and predictable in their operations. If this tendency is not checked, we end up with the somewhat paradoxical situation where the creativity and imagination within these units becomes routinized. *Routinized innovation* is obviously an oxymoron! The second problem is that being insulated from the line operations of the department can result in the policy officers' recommending impractical pie-in-the-sky policy options.

A partial solution to both of these problems was to rotate officers from managerial positions in the operational side of the department into policy roles and vice versa. These periodic "personnel transfusions" function to keep the policy units both "keen" to be creative yet sensitive to the realities of actually administering programs. Periodic exposure to the less routine business of policy development also keeps the line managers from becoming stale and resistant to change.

*Innovation and Reallocation*  The tendency in the 1990s with respect to fostering innovation in the bureaucracy is very much reflective of the fact that there is not very much money available to embark on major new policy initiatives. Because the only new funds available to a departmental manager have to be found through **reallocation** of existing budgets within the department, there has been a need to integrate the program-review and evaluation process of the expenditure-management system with the policy-development process. The result has been a closer integration of the operational and policy functions of the bureaucracy, often to the point of combining policy analysis and program review in a single organizational unit.

A second tendency, which is directly related to the emphasis on integrating the program review and policy-development functions, has been the trend away from highly centralized policy branches within the department. Instead, because the deficit precludes many department-wide "mega policy" initiatives, the policy units tend to be smaller, decentralized bodies reporting to an ADM or even to a director-general. These more specialized policy units, dispersed throughout the department, are more effective in policy development because they are closer to the day-to-day operations in a given branch and, hence, are able to discern the much more "local" and more modest policy initiatives that are possible in the current fiscal regime.

To the extent that departments still have centralized "departmental" policy branches — and some do — they focus more on providing "policy services" to the decentralized policy units, on coordinating policy initiatives coming from below, and on developing "strategic policy" options for the department as a whole. Thus, the role of sitting around brainstorming and thinking up neat new things to do that was once ascribed to the policy branches in the good ole days has basically been put on hold until the current budgetary malaise passes. Until that time, ironically, there is perhaps even more need for creativity and innovation in government if the public sector is to continue to do its job with drastically reduced funds.

**Innovation and Reverse Incrementalism** Despite attempts throughout the 1970s and 1980s to make the bureaucratic dimensions of the policy and expenditure-management process planning-oriented, innovative, and comprehensive, none of these experiments with rationalist techniques of decision-making ever completely succeeded. In fact, not only the spending decisions about existing programs but also most new policies that came to the surface at the priority-determination phase of the policy process could be seen as simply **incremental**, linear extensions of existing policies — as logical outgrowths of current practice, rather than genuinely new policy initiatives. But, with so much effort devoted to making the system more rational, why did real policy innovation in government meet with only limited success, and why did even the process of new-policy development remain so relentlessly incremental?

Incrementalism prevailed, in part, because it was safe. In a decision-making environment characterized by *uncertainty* — the inability to predict the future accurately — it is always easier for the policy makers either to decide to do nothing or to opt for small adjustments to the status quo. In a situation of incomplete information, it is risky to attempt great leaps forward with radical policy options, for the great leap may precipitate unforeseen consequences more serious than the problem the policy is designed to solve in the first place.

Finally, the persistence of incrementalism in the policy process during the past two decades may reflect the fact that during this period the kinds of real-world changes to which policy makers were forced to react appeared to be, themselves, incremental. Thus, although we were faced with serious problems such as economic stagnation, energy shortfalls or gluts, and ethnic conflict, these were thought to be chronic rather than acute ills. Hence, the approach of constant but incremental policy adjustments as new information became available was often felt to be the best approach for the times. The tragic flaw in this approach was analogous to the optimistic adventurer who, after jumping off a very tall building, was heard to say, halfway to the ground, "So far so good!" The "so far, so good," or incrementalist, approach of expanding programs through deficit financing ultimately led us into the fiscal crisis of the nineties.

In the 1990s, it is interesting that very few critics of incrementalism can be found either in academia or in the bureaucracy. The reason is that incremental change in the past, however unimaginative, was still *growth*. By contrast, the only predictable change in government policy in the 1990s is that all departments and agencies, most programs, and the role of government as a whole will shrink in size. Hence, it can be argued that the dominant force in the policy process today is still incrementalism, but that it is **reverse incrementalism**, which is even less conducive to creativity and innovation than its predecessor.

It is clear that the driving motivational dynamic of public-service managers in the last few years has been the defence of turf. The best that senior bureaucrats can hope for is to limit the inevitable cutbacks to their programs, activities, and personnel to gradual and incremental ones. However, the most recent expenditure-management system in the federal government indicates a move away from across-the-board cutbacks and places the emphasis on reallocation as a means of freeing up funds for policy innovation. At time of writing, this new system has not yet been fully road-tested, but it is clearly structured in such a way that it will discourage the negative, defensive, and inward-looking psychology of reverse incrementalism.

### Priority Determination: Submissions to Cabinet

For the bureaucracy to be able to influence the determination of priorities, the core problem is getting the attention of the ultimate priority decision-makers in the Cabinet. The instrument for achieving this is a formal **submission to Cabinet** signed by a minister. There are different forms of Cabinet submissions but, for the most part, these documents are all generated within the bureaucracy. If the intention is merely to provide the Cabinet with information but with no request for a specific decision, the submission may be in the form of an **aide-mémoire** or **memorandum to Cabinet "For Information."** While such submissions must still be signed by the minister, and while their ultimate goal may be to soften the ministers up for a **recommendation for decision** (RD) at some time in the future, they do not directly result in any policy deliberations.

When the intention is to get a decision out of Cabinet, as we saw in an earlier chapter, the process is triggered by a **memorandum to Cabinet** (MC) that includes a recommendation for decision. Because it is memoranda to Cabinet that actually influence the priority-determination part of the policy process, our focus in this section will be upon the manner in which a department prepares MCs for the minister's signature. While there are variations from department to department in how this actually works, it is possible to speak generically about how such submissions to Cabinet are prepared and approved in most departments.

### Preparation of Cabinet Documents

While an idea that forms the core of a policy recommendation can be generated at any level of a government department, the actual **sponsor** of a Cabinet document will normally be an assistant deputy minister. The first step for the ADM is to get the approval of the deputy minister to initiate the preparation of a submission to Cabinet. The ADM is required to indicate briefly what the proposed policy change is, why it is necessary to have Cabinet consider it, and what the target date is for a decision by Cabinet. The request for approval from the DM must also indicate what plans there are for consultation, both within the department and externally, and what the financial resource implications are likely to be. As well, the ADM must indicate whether legislation will be required to give effect to the policy, if Cabinet gives its approval.

*Preparation of the Draft* If the deputy minister gives the go-ahead, the ADM will normally assign the task of shepherding the actual preparation of the document to a director general. The DG, in turn, will assign the task of preparing the draft submission to one or more policy officers from his or her sector of the department. Even in the preparation of the first draft, there will be extensive **internal consultation** with other branches or sectors of the department. The drafters must ensure that they have taken into account financial, environmental, constitutional, and legal implications and that the communications branch of the department is "up to speed" on what will be required as a **communications strategy**.

The minister's office will normally be consulted at this stage on broader strategies for getting the proposal approved and may instruct the DG to consult with affected client groups. The Policy Services and Legislation sections of the department will be consulted on technical matters and on the formatting of the draft submission. Finally, the drafters will be wise to consult the administrative heads of the various sectors and branches of the department to ensure nobody is working at cross purposes. This latter process may occur in the context of a general discussion by the **departmental policy committee** (if the particular department has one).

*Internal Review and Revision*  Once the first draft of the Cabinet submission is completed, the DG will circulate it within the department for **internal review**. All involved operational sectors of the department will be asked to make their comments at this stage, and administrative support units, including Financial Services, Legal Services, Communications and Information Services, Policy Sevices, and the legislative-initiatives coordinators will all have a second "kick at the can." The drafters of the Cabinet document will then attempt to incorporate the comments generated by the internal review process into a second draft.

At this stage the revised draft is circulated among the senior officials that make up the departmental policy committee. After giving the members of the policy committee some time to read the document, the sponsoring ADM will convene the policy committee to discuss the draft. Changes recommended by the committee will then be incorporated into what will be the third and penultimate draft of the Cabinet submission.

*External Review and Final Submission*  The draft, having been thoroughly vetted within the sponsoring department, must then be circulated to other concerned departments and to the central agencies. Comments can inevitably be expected from the Privy Council Office, the Treasury Board Secretariat, the Department of Finance, and the Department of Justice. All of the comments from this process of **external review** must be taken into account and, if possible, incorporated into the draft submission if the document is to get easy passage to the Cabinet agenda.

If the proposal has gotten this far (and it may by this time be only vaguely recognizable to the original drafters!), it must be translated into the second official language. Because it is, by now, fairly certain that the document will actually get to the Cabinet, briefing notes must be prepared for the minister. The briefing notes, often prepared by the officials who drafted the submission, are meant to provide the minister with **"talking points"** and answers to likely questions that can be used in defending the proposal in Cabinet committee. The DM and the sponsoring ADM will then brief the minister on the whole package before he or she "signs off" on the memorandum to Cabinet.

Depending on the time between sign off and Cabinet committee consideration, and depending on how experienced (and smart) the minister is, there may be a subsequent briefing for the minister immediately before the proposal is discussed in Cabinet committee. By this time, the bureaucracy has contributed all it can. The fate of the policy proposal is in the hands of the Cabinet, and its success or failure may depend as much on the persuasive skills of the sponsoring minister as on the quality of the document before the committee.

### Policy Formulation: the Management of Expertise

As we have explained elsewhere, policy formulation involves developing a policy idea into a detailed set of proposals for implementation. While, analytically, this part of the process occurs after a priority has been established, in fact the proposals for implementation are being developed at the initiation and priority stages. What distinguishes the formulation stage is that the process is more exclusively internal to the department. At the stage of policy initiation, the focus is upon generating new policy ideas that can be sold to the priority setters, but once a priority has been established, the department must concern itself with developing the means of achieving the desired goals.

**Process Expertise and Operational Technology**  The stuff of policy formulation is ultimately specialized information and technical data, which must be brought to bear on the problems of how to achieve the policy goals defined by the priority setters. The activity of policy formulation is basically problem solving, and the role of the senior manager in this process is in the first instance to coordinate the efforts of the technical staff of the department. The line officers of the department may play a more significant role in policy formulation than they do in earlier stages of the process because they will ultimately bear the responsibility for delivering the proposed program or service.

Because "implementability" is a concern at this stage, there is a much greater need to integrate the efforts of the **"process" technocrats** with the **operational expertise** that resides in the line managers. While the branch policy units or the departmental policy-services unit may assist in technical formatting and coordination of the proposals for ultimate Cabinet approval, they will not have as significant a role at the formulation stage as they do at the priority-determination stage. The coordination of the process expertise and the operational experience is, thus, a major challenge to the senior managers in the department. The problem of integrating process considerations and operational considerations may be made more difficult by the isolation of the policy units from the line functions in the department. While the isolation or ghettoization of the policy advisors, which we discussed earlier, is preferable if innovation is to be reconciled with routine, even the most brilliant policy ideas must be ultimately reformulated so that they can be put into effect.

Beyond the problems of blending the creative juices of the policy advisors with the more pedestrian concerns and operational "savvy" of the line administrators, the senior manager must also ensure that the policy proposal, once formulated, is acceptable to the central agencies and to the Cabinet. This means that the central agencies must be brought into the process almost from the start, to ensure that the means or the governing instruments being proposed are financially feasible and practically acceptable.

**Technocracy and Democracy**  In terms of time and numbers of people directly involved, policy formulation is not the largest role played by the Canadian bureaucracy, but it is certainly the largest *policy* role. And, because policy formulation involves greater utilization of technical expertise than do other stages of policy-making, this function of the bureaucracy is the most difficult to control. The department must normally offer more than one option for accomplishing the policy goals defined by the priority setters and, superficially, this means that the Cabinet, with the help of advice from the central agencies, gets to choose one of the options.

However, in many cases the "choice" will be an illusion. Inevitably one alternative, the one preferred by the department, will be painted with far more attractive colours than its competition. Furthermore, by the time a large team of highly specialized public servants has spent as much as several months putting together a set of proposals, it is unlikely that their non-expert political masters will be able to mount much effective criticism of the detailed substance of their recommendations. While the bureaucratic choice may, indeed, be the best one most of the time, one might be concerned that both Cabinet and Parliament are effectively shut out of the process.

At another level, however, it can be argued that one of the important results of the increased use of policy-consultation documents such as white papers or green papers is the enhancement of the participation of parliamentary committees and non-governmental stakeholders in the policy communities. While such documents are prepared by departmental officials, and while the content may be quite technical in nature, by making them public, the government is encouraging wider participation in policy deliberations.

**"Throwaways" and "Red Herrings"**  It is often the case that policy-consultation papers are used by the bureaucracy and by the Cabinet to focus and, thereby, moderate anticipated public and parliamentary criticism. As a tactical measure, it is always possible to include a few throwaway items or red herrings in the published proposals to draw the fire of opponents, whether they be in Parliament, the media, interest groups, or even Cabinet. The intention is to create a confrontation, in which oponents can express outrage even to the point of holding demonstrations marches and sit-ins. Then, when the smoke has cleared, and, usually, after a subsequent period of rational debate, the proponents of the policy can allow themselves to be convinced and graciously agree to excise the troublesome provisions.

Through this tactic it is sometimes possible to retain, intact, the basic substance of a policy option while giving the critics a sense of efficacy. The 1994 paper on Social Policy Review was full of suggestions that the government clearly had no intention of implementing, and the gun-control proposals originally released for public consultation in 1994 obviously went further than necessary to achieve the core objectives of the policy. In each case the public outrage was palpable and in each case the government was able to make concessions and still get the policy accepted.

While it is difficult to prove any deliberate intent to "fool" us in such cases, taking a position that allows some room for compromise is the oldest negotiating tactic of them all. Thus, whether it involves bureaucrats trying to manipulate ministers, Cabinet trying to manipulate Parliament, or government trying to influence the public, we have to conclude that it is a tried and true tactic, and however cynical it may appear, it still works. Ultimately the only thing that prevents people from being manipulated is the knowledge that they can be.

### Technology and Policy: A Dilemma

It may be an irony of technocracy that the degree of specialization of technical policy advisors is at once their source of strength and their greatest weakness. In this sense, the specialized policy advisor can become so expert in a narrow field that the substance of the advice given is virtually unassailable by the non-expert Cabinet, and difficult to challenge even for the general-manager type of senior bureaucrat to whom the technocrat reports. On the other side of the coin, the technocrats may become so specialized that they lack perspective on the overall policy implications of their advice, and end up being erudite but irrelevant. This *dilemma* is possibly the most troubling dimension of the policy role of the bureaucracy.

**The Dilemma** At the broadest level of speculation, we can hypothesize that this phenomenon may be symptomatic of a fundamental weakness in the policy process in many modern industrialized systems. The experts are too specialized to see or understand the significance of their knowledge in terms of the big picture or even in relationship to the knowledge of their equally specialized peers in different areas of expertise. The senior bureaucratic generalists in the government, in whom we vest the responsibility for integrating and coordinating the process of policy formulation, cannot challenge the substance of the highly technical information being generated from their subordinates. One might ask, therefore, if there is anybody with a philosopher king's combination of skills to actually pilot the ship of state.

While not all policy decisions require the same levels of technical advice, and while some departments need more specialized policy advisors than others, this dilemma (which is admittedly painted in the extreme here to make the point) may partly explain the only limited success of experiments with rationalist decision-making in the 1970s and 1980s. Perhaps the easing of the dilemma lies not in changing the system but in changing the philosophy or ethos of management in both federal and provincial bureaucracies. Where management in traditional bureaucratic structures is viewed as the coordination of people and the allocation of material resources, in organizations mandated to produce policy advice perhaps the management philosophy has to be different.

**A New Managment Ethos?** There are some indications in the government of Canada that there may be a new breed of hard-headed senior bureaucrats emerging who are less concerned with being "warm and cuddly" and "loved by their troops" and who see their relevant skills as **intellectual** rather than **interpersonal**. This approach, which is likely only appropriate in large policy-relevant departments, is that the public-service manager, as a senior policy advisor, has to manage, not people, but expertise. He or she must zero in on organizing the *knowledge* of subordinates in such a way that it can be directed to the attainment of predetermined policy goals and to the determination of the goals as well.

These **new mandarins** must concentrate their efforts on integrating the policy knowledge at their disposal into a comprehensive world view. As the bosses of the people who possess the relevant policy knowledge, these managers should be primarily concerned with figuring out which of their subordinates are the "smartest" and, hence, should be listened to most closely when making policy decisions. One obvious problem with this style of management is that executive job satisfaction must come from being *right* and not from being popular.

Moreover, while it may have a positive effect on the quality of policy advice tendered to our political leadership, it is likely that our current bureaucratic culture will tolerate this style of management in only a few of the most policy-relevant portfolios. Certainly, in the line or operational parts of the bureaucracy, the gentler, friendlier style of management is still more effective in motivating subordinates and maintaining a day-to-day environment in which employees are comfortable working.

### Public Policy and Public Administrative

This concludes what is admittedly a fairly cursory look at the process of bureaucratic policy-making. We must now look at the way the Canadian bureaucracy carries out its second major function, the administration of programs and services. Other than its role in the policy process, the main function of the bureaucracy is simply to *apply* the policies of the government as reflected in legislation. Public servants provide services, deliver programs, and enforce regulatory regimes. They also collect taxes, levy fines, and issue loans and grants. There is nothing very complicated conceptually about any of this — it is simply people doing jobs. The primary mechanism that makes the administrative process work is management, and as we have seen earlier, management is an activity common to all human endeavours that involve more than one person.

When discussing the role that uses up most of the bureaucracy's resources and occupies most of its time, there is nothing very sophisticated that can be said. However, there are two sets of activities that, while ancillary to the main function of implementing the government's programs, are very important to the success of the whole process. These ancillary sets of activities are the personnel administration process and the budgetary process and they are of critical importance because they determine the allocation of human resources and financial resources, respectively, to the line departments. We shall consider each of these in some detail in the next two sections.

▶ STAFF RELATIONS AND THE PERSONNEL
PROCESS

The *Public Service Employment Act* and the *Public Service Staff Relations Act*, passed in 1967, had as one of their underlying goals the implementation of the Glassco

Commission's admonition to "let the managers manage." The legislation purported to give the deputy minister flexibility in managing human resources within the department, and at the same time to ensure uniform standards and procedures across the public service through the Treasury Board and the Public Service Commission (PSC). The former is responsible for staff relations and collective bargaining and the latter oversees the staffing process. As it has turned out the DM is still forced to operate within parameters defined by these two agencies and a DM's independent authority over either the staffing process or over staff relations within the department remains quite constrained.

According to the *Financial Administration Act*, the Treasury Board, as the central management agency of the government, has the responsibility for the management of all personnel functions in the public service. These include the allocation of human resources throughout the public service, classification of positions and pay, and the establishment of standards of discipline. The Treasury Board also has the formal responsibilty for training and development, although most of these functions are delegated out to the departments and the Public Service Commission. Finally, the FAA has given the board the responsibility for implementing the government's employment-equity program whereby designated groups such as women, the handicapped, aboriginal people, and visible minorities are given special employment opportunities.

### Staff Relations: Collective Bargaining in the Bureaucracy

Staff relations is an important aspect of managing any organization, public or private. Hence, perhaps most significant among the Treasury Board's public-service manager functions is the responsibility to act as the "employer" in all collective negotiations with employee unions.

**The Evolution of Collective Bargaining** Until 1966, the public servant, as an employee, had very little in the way of true bargaining rights vis-à-vis the government-as-employer. The attitude was that the government, being a **sovereign employer**, could not constitutionally or morally be coerced in any way by the public-service unions, or "staff associations" as they were then euphemistically called. This meant essentially that public servants could organize in much the same way that any union in the private sector could, but that their relationship with the government employer was a consultative one only, and in no way a true bargaining one.

In any true bargaining relationship, after all, the parties involved each have certain inducements and sanctions with which to threaten or entice the other side into meeting their demands. In private industry, the employer holds the power to raise or reduce wages, alter working conditions, and lay off or lock out the employees. The employees, on the other hand, have the threat of strike action as an ultimate bargaining weapon. In such a situation, there is a tacitly understood balance of power that keeps the relationship between the two sides in equilibrium.

Up until 1966, therefore, while there was a **National Joint Council** (NJC) that facilitated the consultation of the government-as-employer with the staff associations, and while the relationship was filled with good intentions, it was not collective bargaining because the staff side had no bargaining power. The National Joint Council still exists today and has become a useful forum for discussion of matters that are not formally bargainable. The NJC is also useful for consultations between the employer and the employee organizations where a service-wide approach is more useful than piecemeal bargaining.

However, despite the denial of true collective bargaining, a very special kind of "quasi-collective bargaining" relationship emerged with respect to staff relations. Given the fact that they had no economic sanctions to bring to bear against the sovereign employer, the staff associations very slowly began to realize that politically — in terms of the number of votes they represented in certain constituencies — they did have a real bargaining power. It was not the direct economic sanction of the labour union, but the subtler political sanction of the pressure group.

Thus, the implied threat of the public-service "union" was not "meet our demands or we will strike," but "meet our demands or our members will all vote against you in the next election." While this sort of bargaining clout did not in any way give the staff associations the power of labour unions in the private sector, it did permit them to speak with some authority when discussing wages and working conditions in the National Joint Council. Often, MPs in constituencies with large numbers of public servants would speak out on behalf of the staff associations, realizing that if they were not supportive, it could very well spell a defeat at the next election.

**The *Public Service Staff Relations Act*** In 1967, the *Public Service Staff Relations Act* (PSSRA) established a system of collective bargaining for federal public servants that included the right to strike. The Act also set up the **Public Service Staff Relations Board** (PSSRB), which is responsible for certification of the bargaining units, conciliation, arbitration, and dispute adjudication. Excluded from the collective-bargaining system are employees in managerial positions, those acting in confidential, policy-related capacities, part-time and casual workers, and those declared by the government to be "essential workers." Any disputes over exclusionary decisions are settled by the PSSRB, and its decisions are final and binding.

There are at present approximately ninety certified bargaining units in the federal public service, and many of them are affiliated with either the Public Service Alliance of Canada (PSAC) or the Professional Institute of the Public Service (PIPS). As we pointed out earlier in this chapter, the Treasury Board is the bargaining agent for the government in all of its negotiations with the employee associations, although in a few cases, particularly with respect to working conditions, the senior managers in the department may be invited to participate at the table on the management side.

*Bargainable Matters* While generally "terms and conditions of employment and related matters" can be the subject of a collective agreement, there are several matters explicitly excluded from the process by the PSSRA. For instance, because the Act cannot be interpreted so as to interfere with the supremacy of Parliament, any matter that requires legislative implementation is not bargainable, nor are matters dealt with in legislation such as the *Public Service Employment Act* or the *Superannuation Act*.

Perhaps the most contentious exclusions from negotiations are the matters of the "merit system," under the jurisdiction of the Public Service Commission. These include such things as recruitment, promotions, transfers, discharge for incompetence, layoffs, and pension benefits. As well, the unions do not like the fact that matters having to do with the organization of the government such as job evaluation and classification are not bargainable in the public service, although all of these matters are normally bargainable in the private sector.

*Dispute Settlement*　As with any collective-bargaining system, the PSSRA provides for settlement of disputes. In the case of disputes that arise in the negotiation of a collective agreement, or **interest disputes**, the PSSRA provides for two distinct and separate methods of dispute resolution: **compulsory arbitration** and **conciliation** (with the right to strike). The bargaining agent has the right to decide which route to take, but the decision must be made before bargaining begins, and the union is bound to stick to the method chosen until the settlement is reached.

In the first years of the PSSRA, the tendency was for bargaining agents to opt for the arbitration method of settlement. By this system, either a single arbitrator or a three-person arbitration tribunal is set up by the PSSRB. Both sides present their cases and the arbitrator reaches a decision that is binding on both sides. In the 1970s, however, the trend was for more and more of the bargaining units to opt for the conciliation route. Here the PSSRB names a conciliation board or a single conciliator who attempts to assist the parties to come to an agreement that is mutually acceptable. The recommendations of a conciliation board are not binding, however, and if the union is not satisfied, its next step is to strike.

In the 1980s and 1990s, it became more common for governments, both federal and provincial, to pass special legislation to break strikes, so that the employee side was always at some risk if it took the strike route. Still more recently, the fiscal constraints of the government have induced governments to legislate wage freezes or even cutbacks that have rendered the collective-bargaining system inoperative in practical terms. For a public-service union to strike in the current climate of layoffs and cutbacks is obviously a very risky tactic. Moreover, with large private-sector unemployment and a public mood that is not sympathetic to what is perceived as an underworked and overpaid public service, a tough stance by the government would be applauded.

*Grievances and Appeals*　The PSSRA provides for the settlement of grievances as well. By contrast to the private sector, the right to grieve under the PSSRA is extended not only to employees who are members of bargaining units but to those excluded by the Act. Moreover, there are even matters that do not come within a collective agreement that are nevertheless grievable. There are two methods of resolving grievances, depending on the circumstances of the complaint. In the case of grievances arising out of the interpretation of a collective agreement or out of disciplinary actions that involve severe penalties such as dismissal or financial penalty, the procedure involves four internal hearings up to the deputy-minister level and thence, if no settlement is reached, to adjudication.

The second type of grievance is that involving the job-evaluation system. This is one of the matters generally excluded from the collective-bargaining system and is generally viewed as a prerogative of the employer in the federal public service. As a result, the grievance is heard by government **classification officers** and their decisions are binding and not appealable. As well, there is a right to *appeal* a number of non-grievable decisions involving recruitment and promotion matters to the PSC **Appeal Board.** Such decisions are final and binding on the parties.

### The Merit System: Personnel Administration

The creation of the first Civil Service Commission in Canada in 1908 was precipitated by changes that occurred in the functions of the bureaucracy and in the attitudes of Canadians concerning the nature of the public service. At one time there was a general acceptance that appointment to bureaucratic office should be based not on the qualifications of the applicant and the requirements of the job but on partisan considerations. Liberal governments rewarded the party faithful by granting them jobs in the public service, and Conservative governments did the same. The **spoils** of public office were distributed among the victors and the losers lost their jobs.

**The Fall of the "Spoils System"**  The short-run effect of this practice was to aid the political parties in building strong party organizations in most of the country's constituencies. As the parties built up bases of support, however, they no longer needed the promise of patronage appointments to entice people into working for the party; by then, the administrative problem of distributing the patronage had become a great headache to the party leader. As well, people began to consider such tactics morally and ethically improper, and movements sprang up to reform the civil service.

Perhaps the most important factor leading to the demise of the patronage system was that the role of government expanded. With this expansion, the jobs to be done in the public service began to require a degree of expertise that was often sadly lacking in a person who was appointed for reasons of political preference. The upshot of all of these changes was that the underlying principle of the recruitment process in the civil service was changed from *patronage* to *merit*. Applicants for public-service positions were now to be selected on the basis of the match between their qualifications and the requirements of the position. If more than one applicant was found to be suitable for a single position, the choice between them was to be made on the basis of a **competition** overseen by the newly established civil service commission. The original Civil Service Commission was set up in 1918 to supervise all aspects of the implementation of the merit system of recruitment in the public service.

**The Public Service Commission**  Today, the **Public Service Commission** (PSC) is made up of three commissioners, appointed for a set term by the governor-general-in-council, with salaries set by Parliament and a large permanent staff. The functions of the PSC include the overseeing of the merit system and other responsibilities related to staffing the public service of Canada, as well as certain types of appeals concerned with staffing. In short, because of its large measure of control over the people who get into the Canadian public service, the Public Service Commission is an important independent agency in the staffing process. In practice, however, while the PSC controls the rules within which the process of staffing must be carried on, the responsibility for staffing, with the exception of the most senior levels of the bureaucracy, has been delegated to the line managers.

*Training and Development*  An important component of the staffing function of management is the provision of opportunities for training and career development. The formal responsibility for training and development is divided between the senior managers in the departments and the Treasury Board. However, the board has, to a large extent, delegated its share of the responsibility in this area to the Public Service Commission. Thus, training and development programs within the federal bureaucracy are run by the managers in the departments, by the Public Service Commission, and, when things are working as they should, through the cooperation of both.

The PSC offers special entry courses to managers being promoted to the executive category and provides a number of specialized career-development courses for middle managers. The PSC also does second-language training as a part of the government's bilingualism program and administers an executive interchange program that allows private- and public-sector managers to "see how the other half lives." A special operating agency within the commission called Training and Development Canada conducts a wide range of specialized courses on areas such as human-resources management, financial management, and internal audit and information management.

**The Obligations of Public Employment**  Public servants have traditionally been viewed as different from employees in the private sector. In part, this is because they are "servants of the public" and should therefore take a highly responsible attitude to their jobs. However, by far the greatest justification for treating public servants differently from their counterparts in private industry is simply their proximity to politics. Because they have access to information that the general public does not, and because they are involved in the process of policy formulation, public servants could potentially do a great deal of damage to the government of the day.

By leaking information to the opposition parties or by sabotaging government projects, the public servant could potentially bring down the government. Thus a tradition has evolved: while the public servant must be cognizant of a personal responsibility to the public, if duty to the public conflicts with the interests of the government, the public servant must look to the government first, since it is the government — not the bureaucracy — which must ultimately face the public. For instance, one public servant felt in the 1970s that it was his responsibility to the public to tell them, through the media, that the government's metrication program was unwise. That public servant was summarily dismissed.

To protect the government from this kind of "betrayal," there are clauses in the *Official Secrets Act* providing for severe penalties for public servants who make unauthorized statements based on official information. However, this Act is generally thought to be too severe and is rarely used except in cases of outright espionage. Furthermore, upon entering the federal public service, public servants must take an oath of office in which each swears not to "disclose or make known any matter that comes to my knowledge by reason of such employment." Violation of this principle can mean immediate dismissal.

There are also restrictions on the extent to which a public servant can become involved in politics. He or she can vote, contribute money to parties, and attend political meetings while a public servant, but cannot actively campaign on behalf of a candidate or run for elected office. Since the passage of the most recent *Public Service Employment Act*, public servants have been permitted to request a leave of absence without pay from their jobs to seek election at the federal, provincial, or municipal levels. The restrictions on the political activities of provincial public servants are generally similar to those at the federal level.

Senior public servants also must comply with conflict-of-interest guidelines established by the Cabinet. Basically the same rules apply for deputy ministers as for Cabinet ministers in that investments must be registered and placed in a blind trust, and there is a prohibition on carrying on a private business "on the side." The latter provision is likely not particularly onerous for senior public servants because they are far to busy doing their government jobs to be able to find the time for extra-curricular activities. Finally, when they leave the public service, senior public servants are prohibited for a year from taking on jobs or contracts in the private sector that relate to the matters the individual dealt with while in government. There is an **Ethics Counsellor**, located in the Industry department, who is available to advise senior bureaucrats as to what is and is not acceptable within the conflict guidelines.

## ▶ FINANCIAL ADMINISTRATION: THE BUDGETARY PROCESS

There are two major components of the **budgetary process** in Canada. The first is the **revenue process** whereby the government must find the money to pay for its operations through taxation and borrowing. At the political level this process is referred to as the business of **ways and means**. The second process is the **expenditure process** whereby the moneys are allocated to the various programs of the government and ultimately spent by the various agencies tasked with delivering them. This process at the political level is known as the business of **supply**.

Our main focus in this section is upon the bureaucratic part of the budgetary process and on the administrative mechanisms that govern the bureaucracy's role therein. We will not deal with the revenue process in this section, except in passing, because we have already considered it in earlier chapters. The business of ways and means is the soul of the process of political priority determination in a democracy and, in the final analysis, the decisions are taken by the Cabinet on the advice of the Department of Finance and the other central agencies.

## The Expenditure Process

The expenditure process itself has two discrete components, the *appropiation* of funds and the actual *spending* of the money that is appropriated. The former is an integral part of the overall planning and priority-determination process of the government, and the latter is a much more formalized set of mechanisms that are overwhelmingly focused on maintaining control over the public purse. Each will be discussed below.

**The Budgetary Cycle**  The function of the expenditure-management process is to establish the expenditure budget of the the government. It is difficult to talk about this process starting or finishing at any time during the year because it happens in a multi-year cycle. By the time money is being appropriated by Parliament for the current fiscal year, the process of preparing the budget for the next year is already well underway within the departments. Moreover, the entire planning and priority-determination component of the budgetary process is carried out in the context of multi-year time frames, and at any point in the cycle at least some of the institutional actors will be looking four or five years down the road and others will be looking at current-year considerations.

While the process cannot be said to ever begin or end in terms of the calendar, it is possible to identify *analytically* two distinct parts of the cycle. The first is the **planning and forecasting** exercise and it logically precedes the second exercise, which is the more routine and more structured process of **preparing the estimates**. We will discuss the estimates process in the next section. Here our focus is upon the **expenditure-management system** and the role of the bureaucracy in that process.

**The Expenditure-Management System**  We have already looked at the way the expenditure-management system has evolved from a purely **standard-objects** focus to a program-based, multi-year planning process. The current system is very much reflective of its precursors but has many differences in emphasis for reasons of the unique constraints imposed on governments in the difficult fiscal context of the 1990s. We have described how the system works at the level of the Cabinet and the central agencies, but it is now necessary to discuss how the system works at the level of the line "spending departments" of government.

*The Incredible Shrinking A-Base*  With the introduction of the "PPB" system of expenditure management, government departments came to expect that a certain component of their budgets could be counted on as inviolable and sacrosanct from one year to the next. This component, which covered the allocation of funds to the department's ongoing core programs and activities,

**Figure 23.1**

The expenditure-management cycle. Abbreviations: PCO, Privy Council Office; TBS, Treasury Board Secretariat.

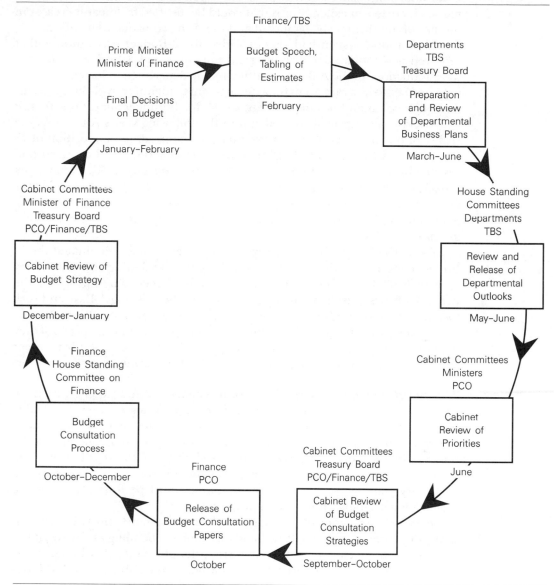

Source: Canada, Department of Supply and Services, *The Expenditure Management System of the Government of Canada*, 1995, p. 8. Cat. BT 22-23/1995.

came to be called the **A-Base**. The A-Base was a department's "turf" and while it did not countenance any new program expenditures, it did allow for incremental increases in expenditures that could be justified by linear increases in the size of the clientele being served and the rising costs due to inflation.

The original system had also provided for **B-Budget** expenditures that required new moneys for new program initiatives and **X-Budget** items that were reductions to the A-Base identified by the department. Not surprisingly, it turned out to be a rare event for a department to identify any X-Budget items and quite common for a department to ask for B-Budget allocations that, if approved, would normally be rolled into the following year's A-Base. As the reality of our fiscal problems was gradually recognized, the imposition of X-Budget items by the central agencies became something to be feared and resisted by the departments and the PEMS system during the Mulroney years introduced the still scarier spectre of **Z-Budget** items. The "Z" likely stood for *zero*, because such items were imposed by the Cabinet and the central agencies, generating reductions in the department's A-Base by eliminating entire programs or activities.

As we shall see below, the current system has virtually eliminated the B-Budget concept, and the possibility of a department's getting any new money is virtually nil. If the Cabinet should decide to implement a new program, the necessary funds must be found by reductions in the exisiting A-Base and reallocation of those funds to the new initiative. Moreover, the A-Base of every department is now fair game for reductions, and departmental managers, if they manage to keep their own jobs, have to get used to the fact that, for the near future, their expenditure turf is much more likely to shrink from year to year.

*The Budget Planning Process* The core mechanism of the expenditure-management system in the mid 1990s is the **budget planning process**. While this has always been the case to some extent, the current system is intended to integrate more completely the traditional economic planning functions of the budget with the more specific policy and expenditure initiatives of the government. The key here is that any new policy initiatives must be driven by the budgetary planning process and the resources must be found through the reallocation of funds from existing programs.

Because the function of the budget has been expanded to provide direction to the departments as to the thrust and direction of spending initiatives, it has become less the exclusive fiefdom of the minister of Finance. The budget must incorporate sectoral policy priorities established by the Cabinet as well as intra-sectoral strategic priorities identified by the policy committees. As well, the new system acknowledges that all ministers are a part of the process and have the opportunity to bring their own portfolio's priorities forward in the course of developing budget strategies.

*The Budget Consultation Process* The budget planning process implemented in 1995 is also designed to make the system more transparent and accessible to the public and to involve the committees of Parliament more directly in the process. To facilitate this new departure, the minister of Finance is mandated to release **budget consultation papers** outlining the fiscal framework, the

**Figure 23.2**

Roles in the expenditure-management system.

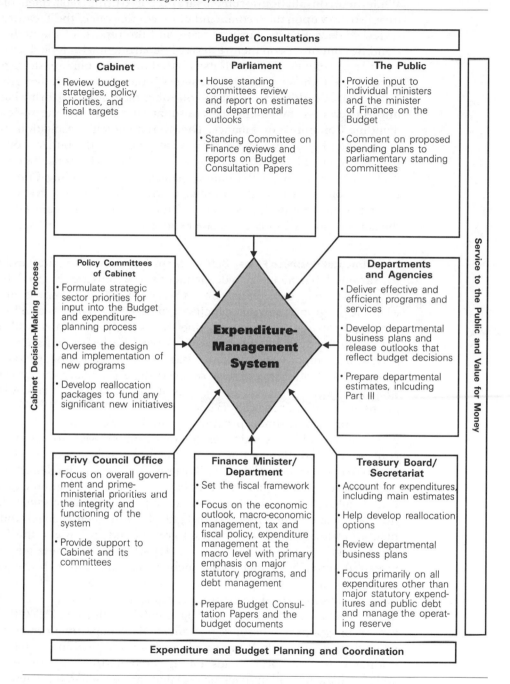

Source: Canada, Department of Supply and Services, *The Expenditure Management System of the Government of Canada*, 1995, p. 10. Cat. BT 22-37/1995.

economic outlook, fiscal targets, and the options for achieving these targets. While these consultation documents are prepared in the Department of Finance they also draw upon the recommendations coming out of the Treasury Board's review of departmental business plans and the reports of the parliamentary standing committees on their reviews of departmental outlook documents.

The consultation process is itself based on a consultation strategy formulated by the Cabinet. This process allows inputs from interested groups and individuals outside government, but one of its main goals is to bring Parliament into the process, by tabling the consultation papers for the review of the Standing Committee on Finance. The overall budget consultation strategy is reviewed and approved by Cabinet in early fall and the budget consultation papers are tabled in Parliament by mid October. The consultation process itself and the review of the budget papers by the Standing Committee on Finance continues through to January, when the Cabinet reviews the final budget plans. The Budget Speech and the tabling of the main estimates for the coming fiscal year occurs in late February.

**Departmental Business Plans** Before the preparation of the draft estimates by the various departments each department's programs are reviewed, first internally, and then by the Treasury Board Secretariat. This exercise is intended to examine programs in terms of their continued importance and to look at any proposals for expanding or reducing the activities associated with the programs. During the era of the sacrosanct A-Base the departments used **program review** to attempt to expand their A-Base. While Treasury Board was aware of this ploy, and often rejected or reduced departmental requests for higher spending targets for existing programs, it almost never cut back A-Base programs as a result of program review.

The process of annual program review, however, remained a useful exercise because, unlike the estimates, the program reviews were set in multi-year contexts and forced departments to plan ahead. This system evolved into the **Multi-Year Operational Plan** (MYOP) system wherein the department is required to submit an updated three-year projection of program expenditures with detailed justifications. MYOPs were required to be submitted twice a year (to make adjustments necessary in light of unforeseen changes and supplementary estimates) and were subject to review and approval by the TBS.

The successor to the MYOP is the **departmental business plan**, which is prepared annually by each department in consultation with the TBS. The business plans must be consistent with the directives brought down in the budget, and should be sited in three-year time frames. Unlike the departmental MYOP which was essentially a stapling together of individual MYOPs from the various programs, the business plan must take a department-wide integrated management approach. It must address resourcing within budget targets by finding ways to reallocate funds among the department's existing programs and (fat chance!) by identifying savings that can be used to fund new initiatives by other departments within the policy sector.

The business-plan approach is also intended to foster a **"service-to-clients"** perspective among line managers and to encourage departments to plan internally in terms of discrete "service lines." The departmental business plan must identify goals and targets that can form the basis for evaluating "strategic results." This approach also requires the development and implementation of evaluation measures that will allow the managers to judge the department's performance in terms of service to the client.

Business plans are subject to review and approval by the Treasury Board, and once approved, the department is required to produce what amounts to an executive summary of the plan, called a **departmental outlook document**. The outlook documents are brief, summarizing the main thrusts of the business plan, and are to be used by the Cabinet committees in determining sectoral priorities that might be identified in the budget. As well, the outlook papers are reviewed by the standing committees of the House of Commons to give the MPs a multi-year perspective when they have to scrutinize the next year's estimates.

*Ministerial Flexibility* The current expenditure-management system is also designed to give departments, and by implication, individual ministers, greater flexibility and discretion in the internal affairs of the portfolio. It anticipates that departments will have greater freedom to reallocate resources among programs entirely within a single department. While such initiatives would still be subject to review by the appropriate Cabinet committee, such freedom to organize and restructure programs and budgets makes it possible for the senior managers to operate more like private business executives do.

Other initiatives to increase the internal flexibility within departments are logical extensions of the **Increased Ministerial Accountability and Authority** (IMAA) program that was already in effect. The current system proposes to move towards less control by central agencies, particularly the TBS, by loosening up the reporting and accounting requirements and by decentralization, to the department, of some of the control functions curently exercised by TBS. Down the road, it is anticipated that multi-year spending authorization might be possible through devices such as the revolving funds now used for funding special operating agencies.

It is also possible that with amendments to the *Financial Administration Act* departments could carry forward funds to the next fiscal year rather than having them lapse if they are not spent by March 31. This would offset the unseemly spectacle of departments letting consulting contracts or redoing the washrooms in March, whether needed or not, in order to avoid forfeiting some unspent appropriations. However, these proposals are still just proposals.

The current expenditure-management system is brand new and it is impossible to even speculate about how successful it might be. Perhaps its most important impact will be to reinforce the message that the era of growth in the public service is over for the time being at least and that public servants and their clients alike must bite the bullet and learn to live with less. As for the stated goal of providing greater flexibility to departments and reducing centralized control, it is likely long overdue in a system that has been committed to letting the managers manage since the 1960s. But from the perspective of the seasoned senior bureaucrat, it will be small consolation to have a lot of flexibility over almost no resources!

**The Main Estimates** The *Financial Administration Act* vests formal responsibility for the preparation of the estimates in the hands of the Treasury Board. The main estimates are tabled in the House of Commons by the president of the Treasury Board, who bears the responsibility for piloting supply bills through the House. In late summer or early fall, the Treasury Board president formally notifies the departments of the spending guidelines established by the budget process and asks the departments to prepare their **main estimates** within those guidelines.

*Preparation of the "Mains"* The departments are not surprised by this request; in fact, they have already been preparing information since they did their business plans. By late September the deputy minister (and in some cases the departmental policy committee) reviews the total estimates of the department. In late fall, the minister reviews the departmental estimates and gives them formal approval, usually without making any significant changes. The main estimates are the basic or "main" forecasts by the departments as to how much money they will need to finance all of their activities in the coming fiscal year.

For the most part the **mains**, as they are often referred to, form the current-year A-Base for a department. The main estimates are formatted in three parts. Part I is an overview summary of total government expenditures and is prepared by the TBS without any input from the departments. Part II, which is known as the **Blue Book**, is the most important part of the estimates as it contains the actual votes that become the *Appropriation Act* after approval by Parliament. This part is prepared by the TBS on the basis of the information tendered by the departments. Part III includes the supporting details of the spending plans of the departments broken down into specific activities, which are, for the most part, developed by the departments and only reviewed and approved by the TBS. The estimates explain each program in terms of its objectives and break down each program into various activities, specifying the "sub-objectives" of each activity.

*Pre-Legislative Approval* In discussing this process as a series of distinct stages, to some extent we distort the true picture. In fact, senior departmental officials, in particular the financial officers, are in periodic but more or less continuous contact with officials in the TBS throughout the preparation of the estimates in the department. Often this contact is informal, characterized by a phone call from one person to another, but its effect is to keep the people involved in the preparation of the estimates aware of what to expect from the next stage of the process.

Once the estimates have been approved by the minister, they are sent to the Treasury Board Secretariat, which goes over them in great detail, with an eye to cutting down on expenses. The concern of the TBS at this point is with economy and frugality — not with the overall advisability of the various departmental programs that have already been approved in principle in the business plans. Once again, because there has been considerable consultation between the TBS and individual departments at earlier stages, there shouldn't be too many surprises at this stage. In fact, it is a stated aim of the new system of expenditure management that departments should have greater flexibility with respect to the detailed expenditure plans. It is proposed that the structure of Part III of the estimates and the process by which it is reviewed and approved be changed to reflect this policy of intra-governmental "deregulation."

Having passed the approval of Treasury Board Secretariat, the main estimates are then reviewed and approved by the Treasury Board itself, whose responsibility it is to put all the estimates of all the departments in some kind of perspective. If the spending priorities set at earlier stages of the expenditure process have been reasonably accurate, and if in preparing the estimates the departments have adhered to the original targets and guidelines, there should be relatively few significant changes at this stage.

*The Appropriation Act*  Having survived the scrutiny of the Treasury Board, the formal approval of the Cabinet as a whole is not usually difficult, or even of much interest. After Cabinet approval, the main estimates are then printed up and tabled in the House of Commons by the president of the Treasury Board in late February. Part II of the "mains" lists the actual **votes** that ultimately will be passed in Parliament, and these are backed up by supporting details, in Part III. At one time, there was just one *blue book* but today there is a series of them, including one for each major department or agency and summary volumes that, among other things, outline the overall expenditure plans of the government and break the votes down into standard-objects categories.

The estimates of the various departments are then passed on to the appropriate standing committees of the House of Commons. These committees go over the estimates item by item, calling upon officials of the department whose estimates are being discussed to defend its programs and estimated expenditures. The committees then report back to the House of Commons, and the estimates of all the departments are bundled together as the **main supply bill**. The main supply bill is usually passed in a matter of hours, with little comment or debate and with unanimous waiving of the forty-eight-hour "notice" provisions at each reading.

The main supply bill must be passed by Parliament by the end of June. When it has passed through both Houses of Parliament and has been assented to by the governor-general, it becomes the *Appropriation Act*. The *Appropriation Act*, which essentially comprises Part II of the approved estimates, becomes part of the law of the land, and the supporting details, in Part III, are appended merely for the information of the public and as guidelines for the spending of funds by the department.

**Additional Supply Instruments**  The discussion up until now has centred on the preparation of the *main* estimates and the *main* supply bill, which indeed involves the most important and the most substantial appropriation of public funds in any year. However, there are a few additional supply measures that can occur at other times of the year and are in fact intended to deal with exigencies not anticipated in the main estimates.

*Supplementary Estimates*  The **supplementary estimates** or **"sups,"** which are intended to meet new expenditure requirements that were unforeseen at the time of the preparation of the main estimates, are voted late in the parliamentary session. It is expected that these will not be large in terms of the amount appropriated. However, they are sometimes used tactically to fund new and possibly contentious program initiatives without compromising or delaying the routine process of approving the A-Base items in the mains. The new expenditure needs may have been known at the time of the preparation of the main estimates and deliberately omitted.

**Further supplementary estimates** are sometimes introduced just before the close of the fiscal year to look after any additional items not covered by the main or supplementary estimates. These are sometimes voted near the end of the parliamentary session, and as a result they are passed without too much fuss by MPs who want to get on with the summer recess. However, for the time being, there is so little *new* spending going on that the supplementary estimates may end up being used as originally intended, for covering unanticipated expenditures.

*Interim Supply and Warrants* **Interim supply** is a measure passed after the current fiscal year has begun in April, but before the main estimates are approved at the end of June. A vote of interim supply merely assumes that the main supply bill will pass successfully, and it approves expenditures "in the interim" in amounts such as one-twelfth or one-sixth of the main estimates. This permits the departments to continue to carry out their programs and pay their bills, even while Parliament is theoretically still only pondering the advisability of voting them the money to do so.

An interesting situation would arise if a main supply bill were actually defeated or if Parliament were to be dissolved before the main supply bill is passed. While such a defeat is highly unlikely, when Parliament is not in session the government can spend money through the use of **governor-general's warrants**. These are expected to be used only for emergencies, when it is not possible to summon Parliament to do the job. Warrants must be approved retroactively by Parliament in the normal way as part of the next supplementary estimates. Students are requested not to ask what would happen if Parliament refused such retroactive approval!

### Spending the Appropriations

Once the money has been appropriated by Parliament, it can be spent only by the executive and (with the exception of the moneys voted to the Speaker to fund the internal affairs of Parliament) never by the legislature. Parliament does not spend money, it merely appropriates it, and it can vote appropriations only on the basis of bills introduced by a minister. Finally, if Parliament has voted the money for a specific program, there is no way it can *force* the government to actually spend it, if the government should change its mind.

**The Consolidated Revenue Fund** The actual spending of money by the executive is governed by the provisions of the *Financial Administration Act*. Every expenditure requires an **encumbrance** of funds from the revenue pool of the government of Canada, called the **Consolidated Revenue Fund** (CRF). The CRF is best conceived of as the government's bank account into which all tax revenues are deposited and out of which all cheques and payments are withdrawn. The Crown officer responsible for the CRF is the **receiver general for Canada**, who is normally the minister of Public Works and Government Service (PWGS). The CRF contains only enough cash to pay current expenditures and the remainder is invested wisely by the minister of Finance so that it will generate revenue until such time as it is needed.

Funds are drawn by the departments as needed only for purposes specified in the *Appropriation Act*. The deputy minister of Public Works and Government Services is the **deputy receiver general for Canada** and acts as the custodian of the Consolidated Revenue Fund. The deputy receiver general is responsible for ensuring that the expenditure for which the money is being encumbered is within the terms of the *Appropriation Act*, and that the appropriate paperwork specified in the FAA has been done. Only then is a cheque issued.

When it comes time to spend money, a department must spend it for the exact purposes stated in the *Appropriation Act*. With the approval of the Treasury Board, the department is permitted to deviate somewhat from the more detailed presentation of the estimates in Part III. Normally, however, it is expected that the department will closely adhere even to the supporting details of the mains as well as to the votes of the *Appropriation Act* itself. The flexibilty of the department to reallocate moneys within programs on its own initiative was increased under the IMAA program and is further enhanced by the new expenditure-management system. However, all departments are still bound by the *Appropriation Act* and are not permitted to use funds voted to one program on another program. Furthermore, money is still voted for one year only and if the money is not spent by the end of the fiscal year, it lapses.

**The Public Accounts** The function of the deputy receiver general is, in effect, a **pre-audit** function. He or she is assisted in this overall responsibility by internal or **operational auditors** located in the departments and agencies throughout the public service. These officers are responsible not only for balancing their department's books on a day-to-day basis, but also for the preparation of the accounts of the departments. Originally, this internal audit function was performed by "treasury officers" who were seconded to the departments. Today, largely because of the recommendations of the Glassco Commission in the 1960s, the internal-audit or operational-audit function is performed not by treasury officers seconded to the department but by departmental officials.

In the case of some of the smaller departments or agencies of the government of Canada, audit advice and audit services can be contracted out to Consulting and Audit Canada, which is a special operating agency located in PWGS. The **Office of the Comptroller General**, located in the Treasury Board, is responsible for developing and overseeing the implementation of sound financial accounting and operational audit procedures. The FAA assigns the responsibility for preparing and keeping the consolidated **Public Accounts** to the receiver general. The Public Accounts must show the expenditures made under each appropriation, the revenues paid into the CRF, and the assets and liabilities of Canada.

This concludes our discussion of the administrative process in the Canadian bureaucracy. While we can conclude that the manager in the public sector generally works within extremely severe constraints imposed by the environment of government, the central agencies, and the requirements for political accountability, the Canadian bureaucracy does get managed somehow. It is easy to be critical of management in the bureaucracy, but before attempting any overall verdict, it is necessary first to look at the mechanisms whereby the bureaucracy and individual bureaucrats are controlled.

## ▶ THE PROCESS OF CONTROL

We have seen in this and the previous chapter that one of the functional components of the human activity called management is the maintenance of control over the behaviour of individuals in the organization. This control is achieved by the line managers over their subordinates through the obvious mechanism of a chain of command, through some control over promotion and discipline, and through indirect mechanisms such as performance evaluations that become a part of an employee's employment record.

As well, we have seen that management is different in the public sector from what it is in the private sector because public service managers must share the responsibility for controlling their subordinates with central agencies that are tasked with overseeing the entire process. As examples, legislation such as the *Financial Administration Act*, the *Public Service Employment Act*, and the *Public Service Staff Relations Act* vest significant control over management in the public service in centralized agencies and functionaries such as the Treasury Board, the Public Service Commission, the Public Service Staff Relations Board, the receiver general, the comptroller general, and many others.

With all of this internal oversight, scrutiny, and evaluation going on, the Public Service of Canada is certainly not a very good breeding ground for individual "loose cannons." However, there is still the problem of controlling the bureaucracy as a collective beast. Thus, the focus of this last section of the chapter is on the modes of control or the constraints placed on bureaucratic decision-making by non-bureaucratic institutions. We will look at political control of bureaucracy in terms of the relationship between the Cabinet and the line managers, at the role of Parliament, at the financial control established by the audit process, and at judicial review of administrative decisions.

### Control by Cabinet

We have said many times in this book that bureaucratic power derives to a significant extent from the concentration of various kinds of expertise within the bureaucracy and from the degree of control over the flow of information to the Cabinet. The bureaucracy significantly influences priority determination and dominates policy formulation because it is expected to advise the Cabinet on the basis of the information it possesses. However, while the bureaucracy occupies a position of great importance in the policy process, ultimate political power still rests with the Cabinet and the prime minister. Whether on whim or political exigency, whether wisely or unwisely, the Cabinet and the prime minister can and do periodically choose to disregard bureaucratic advice, even when that advice was requested by the government in the first place.

The actual exercise of this ultimate control by the Cabinet is usually limited to situations in which the action demanded by political expedience is not congruent with the course of action indicated by technical or administrative considerations. When this happens, the political advisors to the Cabinet such as those in the Prime Minister's Office, the Cabinet ministers and the prime minister tend to be in a position of competition vis-à-vis the bureaucracy proper. If the prime minister or the Cabinet as a whole should become convinced that the political considerations are more important than the technical, financial, or administrative ones, the regular bureaucrats will, at least for the moment, lose out.

This situation of competing advice from the political advisors and the bureaucratic advisors can exist at all stages of the decision-making process, although in many cases it is likely that political and other considerations will in fact coincide. The point that must be emphasized in this regard is simply that the political advisors, particularly in the PMO or among the staff of Cabinet ministers, may function as an alternate source of information, which can place major restrictions on the power of the bureaucracy.

When it comes to the process of management in the public service, the presence of political control is more difficult to demonstrate. Naturally, in the case of policy decisions relating to organization and reorganization of the departmental structure of the bureaucracy, the planning apparatus that includes the Cabinet and the central agencies will supersede the line managers, and political considerations will tend to hold more weight than administrative ones. Nevertheless, the mechanisms of control here tend to be dominated by central-agency types rather than by the politicians themselves; so, for the most part, what appears to be "political" control over the bureaucracy is in fact central-agency control over the line managers in the departments.

### Parliament and the Public Purse

Additional control over the bureaucracy is exercised through the traditional processes of public finance. According to Norman Ward, there are two basic principles of public finance in Canada. First, the executive should have no money that is not granted to it or otherwise sanctioned by Parliament and, second, the executive should make no expenditures except those authorized specifically by Parliament.[1] In brief, therefore, the executive branch and its operational arm, the bureaucracy, can get funds only through parliamentary appropriation, and they can spend those funds only for purposes specified by Parliament. The implementation of these two basic principles is facilitated by a complicated set of practices and procedures.

As we have seen, there must be a budget, which is a clear enunciation of the present financial needs of the government, the plans for the upcoming year, and a general statement of the financial state of the nation. In a formal way, all of the measures included in the budget must be approved by Parlia-

---

1.  N. Ward, *The Public Purse* (Toronto: University of Toronto Press, 1955).

ment. While Parliament's *de facto* power is constrained by a number of factors, the most important implication of this exercise is that, by requiring formal approval of Parliament, the entire process is made public and, hence, subject to the scrutiny of everybody.

### Post Audit: The Auditor General

The **auditor general** (AG) also performs a significant control function. The AG is an officer of Parliament, not of the government, and is responsible only to Parliament. The AG's salary is set by statute and the AG can be removed from office only through a joint address by the House of Commons and the Senate. The office was created in 1878, and its functions today are defined in the *Financial Administration Act*. Basically, the role of the auditor general is to check up on all expenditures in the public service, to confirm that money has been spent efficiently and according to law, and to bring any matter involving the financial affairs of the government to the attention of Parliament.

**The Powers of the Auditor General**  The auditor general has the power to access all the government's financial books and to make public any indiscretions found therein. The report of the auditor general comes out annually and is tabled in the House of Commons. The normal procedure at this stage is for the auditor's report to be handed over immediately to the House of Commons Public Accounts Committee for more detailed study. The AG, besides conducting a **post-audit** of the Public Accounts, is also empowered to undertake "spot audits" of all departments and programs.

One weakness inherent in the **Office of the Auditor General** (OAG) is that the staff consists of public servants rather than parliamentary officials like the AG. This means that the establishment of the Office of the Auditor General depends on recommendations of the Cabinet and the TBS. There is nothing in law to prevent the government of the day from cutting back on the staff of the OAG and in this way weakening its effectiveness as a financial watchdog for Parliament. In fact, however, no government can politically afford to go too far in this regard, for the auditor general has become an important symbol of the financial authority of Parliament. Any attempt to limit the OAG's independence from the government of the day, although quite "legal," would definitely be seen as a breach of convention and might do political damage to the party that so dared. Indeed, it has not been unusual over the past several years for the Office of the Auditor General to actually expand more rapidly than the rest of the bureaucracy.

**An Expanding Role?**  Following the passage of legislation in 1977, auditors general have attempted, with considerable success, to expand their role from a purely financial-audit function to include responsibility for **comprehensive** or *value-for-money* auditing. Comprehensive auditing means, to the auditor general, the right to consider not merely whether Parliament's appropriations have been spent prudently and in accordance with the estimates, but also to consider whether the executive arm of government has been prudent in the policies it has adopted.[2] This expanded definition of the auditor general's watchdog role can be wide-ranging indeed, and has been extended, in the recent past, to include such matters as whether the government's capital expenditures give due regard to the effect of the purchase on the country's balance of payments, the value of the dollar, tax revenues, and future capital spending requirements.[3]

Such issues are not merely issues of financial rectitude, but impugn the wisdom of government policy as well. It is hardly surprising, therefore, that recent governments have been distinctly unenthusiastic about the auditor general's proclivity to snoop beyond what the government has considered the AG's proper mandate. The government argues that it has been elected to govern, and that its accountability for policy is directly to Parliament and ultimately to the voters of Canada. The auditor general, by contrast, is unelected, and not directly responsible to the people.

The auditors general counter that they are officers of Parliament, appointed to be guardians of the rectitude of public expenditures. This, they argue, must include not merely the efficiency with which funds are spent, but also the appropriateness of what they are spent on. The disagreements at one point became sufficiently rancorous that the courts were asked to determine the nature of material to which the auditor should have access. The court ruled that the auditor does have the right to see documents providing policy advice to Cabinet, but not actual recommendations made to Cabinet by ministers.

This presumption of a "policy review" role by the auditor may have very considerable consequences. Sharon Sutherland and Bruce Doern, in their study for the Macdonald Commission, argued that

> the new OAG [Office of the Auditor General] is, in essence, an entrenched autonomously led force at the heart of both policy and management in the federal public sector. . . . For, while the OAG has no share in ongoing executive decision-making, . . . the new scope of its activity (the inclusion of a review of policy advice and of the revenue budget in its self-ascribed mandate) creates an environment where the parameters for action by a cabinet may be seriously limited.[4]

We can anticipate continued tension in the future between the government of the day and auditors general, since, by its very nature, the watchdog role is bound to be contentious, and since modern auditors general have adopted a very aggressive approach to the job. However, in the short term, the government is so concerned with streamlining and reducing its own affairs to combat the fiscal problems we face in the nineties, that Cabinet may even outdo its most visible critic in parsimony and efficiency.

2. Sharon L. Sutherland, "On the Audit Trail of the Auditor General: Parliament's Servant 1973–1980," *Canadian Public Administration*, vol. 23, no. 4, Winter, 1980; and Sharon Sutherland and Bruce Doern, *Bureaucracy in Canada: Control and Reform* (Ottawa: Royal Commission on the Economic Union and Development Prospects for Canada, Research Volume 43, 1985), particularly pp. 49–51.
3. See Doern and Sutherland, *Bureaucracy in Canada*, for further elaboration.
4. Doern and Sutherland, *Bureaucracy in Canada*, p. 50.

### Judicial Review of Administrative Decisions

Judicial control over the Canadian bureaucracy is exercised not with respect to policy decisions or advice from public servants, but rather with respect to administrative jurisdiction and procedures. In the case of most administrative functions, public officials are granted fairly wide discretionary powers with which to carry out their responsibilities. Within the area of discretion granted them by law, public servants enjoy a significant degree of independence from judicial control. However, the courts review the administrative decisions of public officials to determine whether these decisions are within the jurisdiction granted to the official by law.

**The Doctrine of *Ultra Vires*** If a public official has made a discretionary decision that is lacking in good judgement but that is within the jurisdiction granted by law, the courts will usually take no action. However, if an official makes a decision or takes administrative action beyond his or her competence, or ***ultra vires*** his or her discretionary powers, the courts will step in to quash the decision. Note that this can occur only with respect to *administrative* decisions that have a direct impact on individuals in society. In the case of *policy* decisions the bureaucratic official is formally only making a recommendation to the political decision-makers in the process. A policy recommendation has no immediate or necessary impact on citizens, for it does not become legally binding until implemented by Cabinet and Parliament.

<u>*Natural Justice*</u> If administrative decisions are judicial or quasi-judicial in nature, the courts will act to control the bureaucracy in another way. Here the courts question not only the jurisdiction of the administrative official or board, but the procedures followed in coming to the decision. Basically, judicial control over bureaucratic decisions exists if an individual is affected by that decision and if the administrative official or board, in making the decision, has not adhered to the principles of **natural justice**. The principles of natural justice define the standards for fair procedures in coming to decisions that affect the rights and privileges of individuals.

The first principle of natural justice is *nemo judex in sua causa*, roughly translated as "no man should be a judge in his own cause." In other words, the administrative officials on the board or tribunal making the decision must be impartial and not directly affected themselves by the outcome of the hearing. The second principle, *audi alteram partem*, is that all parties to a dispute have a right to be heard. Each party's position must be aired and considered by the board before a decision is made. If either of these principles has been ignored by a bureaucratic agency or by an individual bureaucrat in coming to a judicial or quasi-judicial decision, the court will deem the decision to be *ultra vires* and order that the decision be **quashed**.

**Limits to Judicial Review** It is important to emphasize the nature of judicial remedies as mechanisms of control over the bureaucracy. In the case of many decisions by bureaucratic agencies or officers, the decisions are not **appealable**. However, they are **reviewable**, which means that the court, while not empowered to reconsider the case on its substantive merits, is empowered to look at the procedures of the bureaucratic decision. If the court decides that the board, tribunal, or administrative officer acted either *ultra vires*, or *intra vires* but improperly, the result is that the original decision is nullified or quashed. The problem, particularly where the court quashes a decision because it was taken improperly, is that the tribunal of first instance can go back, implement the correct procedures, and bring down exactly the same decision. Thus, judicial review, while ensuring fairness in administrative decisions, does not permit the court actually to *replace* the administrative decision with its own decision in the manner of appeal.

At a practical level, the effectiveness of judicial remedies in curbing abuses of bureaucratic power is limited by the number of cases that emerge. Not only are the courts unable to deal with misuses of discretionary power unless the administrative act is also *ultra vires*, but, even in cases where judicial action is appropriate, the backlog of cases means that litigants must often wait years for satisfaction. One solution at the federal level was to create a specialized administrative court, the **Federal Court of Canada**, which has jurisdiction to hear appeals from federal boards and tribunals. We will discuss the Federal Court further in the next chapter.

A partial solution to the backlog of administrative law cases in some of the provinces has been to appoint an *ombudsman*, whose function is to investigate complaints by individuals who feel they have been wronged by a bureaucratic decision. As an independent official of the legislature whose salary is set by statute, the ombudsman has broad powers of access to most public files and a modest staff to aid in investigations. Unlike the courts, an ombudsman can investigate cases in which the bureaucratic decision has been *intra vires*, but, in terms of equity, a bad decision.

However, an ombudsman has the power only to investigate, to publicize abuses of bureaucratic power, and, in some cases, to initiate legal action, much as a private citizen would. An ombudsman alone cannot order a decision to be quashed. In the final analysis, an ombudsman can be an effective check on bureaucratic excesses only if the bureaucrats themselves respect or fear the office. Much of the work has to be done by phone calls to the official about whom there has been a complaint. The official might agree to reconsider the decision, to change it somewhat, or to rehear the case, and will, at least, offer reasons for the decision. There are ombudsmen in a majority of the provinces, but, although the concept was actively considered by the federal government in the 1970s, it is not currently under consideration in Ottawa.

### Management and Control: A Conclusion

Likely the most effective mechanisms of control over the bureaucracy as a whole are those related to the budgetary process and the systems of financial accountability. However, too much attention to accountability can tie the hands of the senior managers and severely hamper their ability to get the job done. Thus, reforms in this area must proceed on the middle ground. It is necessary to try to develop controls that make the bureaucracy as a whole accountable to the Cabinet, but which, at the same time, recognize the need to let the managers do their jobs without excessive meddling on the part of the central agencies.

**Public Access to Information**   Control over the policy role of the bureaucracy is more problematical. With the exception of the obvious power of the Cabinet to decide to disregard its bureaucratic advisors, there are very few direct checks over the policy advice provided by bureaucrats. The press, academics, interest groups, the parliamentary opposition, and even the provincial governments are, to a large extent, prevented from evaluating the policies formulated by federal bureaucrats by the strong control over information and technical expertise possessed by the large numbers of federal policy advisors.

Moreover, much of this process is hidden from the public by a veil of secrecy. Outsiders can only rarely find out what bureaucratic advice has been offered and, by then, it is usually too late, for the government has already acted on that advice. It is clear that the Canadian public is not always well served by this situation. One of the more important reforms in recent years has been the passage of the *Freedom of Information Act*, which guarantees freer access for the public to the information necessary to criticize the bureaucratic policy-makers. But then again, this is possible only after the advice has either been taken or ignored by the Cabinet.

**Control and the Management Corps**   Finally, given the role of the senior bureaucrats as managers of the information-generating and -disseminating machinery that produces policy advice in Canada, it is possible that one medium of control over the technocrats is to ensure that we have a skilled corps of senior policy managers. These individuals must possess the standard managerial skills needed in both the public sector and the private sector, and must know, as well, the baroque patterns of the adversarial process of bureaucratic politics. On top of this, public-sector managers must be able to function as coordinators of expertise in the process of initiation and formulation of public policy — a role largely alien to their counterparts in the private sector.

The overall quality of management in the Canadian public service has always been extremely high. Despite the carping and bureaucrat bashing that characterizes so much of the media commentary on the public service, and despite the openly hostile and derogatory approach of the Mulroney government to the government sector in much of the 1980s, the conclusion must still be that the quality of senior personnel is quite high. However, the several waves of cutbacks, layoffs, buyouts, and declared redundancies since 1985 have created a situation of declining morale in the public service. Being a senior public servant in Canada today is not as attractive a career as it once was, and it may be harder and harder to recruit the best-quality executives in the future. We will revisit this point in our conclusion.

### The Canadian Bureaucracy in Flux: A Conclusion

There has probably never been a time when the bureaucracy was not the subject of at least some criticism and some form of ongoing review. However, since the early 1980s there has been virtually constant criticism, demands for reform and for reductions in size, and "big bang" initiatives for radical restructuring. As a conclusion to this chapter we will look at some of these initiatives and their impact on the federal public service.

**The Mulroney Reform Initiatives: 1984–1988**  In September 1984, the newly elected Mulroney government initiated the first "big bang" initiative for restructuring the bureaucracy by establishing the Ministerial Task Force on Program Review (the Nielsen Task Force), whose mandate it was to evaluate a wide range of government programs with a view to improving the overall performance of the federal government. The main thrust of this review was to improve efficiency and eliminate waste and duplication.

*Public-Sector Efficiency*  The basic philosophy applied was instructed by the experience of the private sector but the task force and its various sectoral working groups explicitly recognized from the start that government is indeed different from private enterprise. Thus, the task force took the position that

> government should be as efficient as possible while providing all essential programs and services. In this context, outdated regulations, waste, duplication, and conflicting program objectives can add to federal spending without meeting national goals. In fact, by rendering the economy more rigid and unadaptive, they can, and do, hinder the achievement of both economic and social goals.[5]

Thus, while the Ministerial Task Force addressed the problem of inefficiency and ineffectiveness in government, the study teams involved, which included people from the private sector as well as public servants, did not necessarily attempt to apply the oft-cited panacea of making government more like business. It was recognized that government is simply different, and public-sector efficiency must be evaluated according to a separate set of criteria and measurements.

*Privatization, Cutbacks, and Deregulation*  The principles of seeking greater efficiency and less waste, however, turned out to be only a small component of the Mulroney government's drive to "reform" the public sector. It was also committed to reducing the deficit by cutting programs and reducing the size of the public service. It is unfortunate that the underlying spirit of this exercise was an unmitigated mistrust and even outright hostility to the public service and to public servants. There was a sense among public servants that the government felt cutbacks were desirable not only because the government could not afford to do as much as it had in the past, but, as well, because there was something almost immoral about the way the public sector operated. Whatever its morality, the public sector certainly went through a decline in *morale* during this era of bureaucrat-bashing.

A third principle embraced by the early Mulroney reforms was that it was not only inefficient and costly, but also immoral, for government to be involved in the private sector either as regulators or as state entrepreneurs. As a result,

---

5.  Canada, Task Force on Program Review. *An Introduction to the Process of Program Review* (Ottawa: Supply and Services Canada, 1986), p. 1.

crown corporations that made a profit were sold to the private sector, or **privatized**, usually at bargain prices, and many of those that were not profitable were simply shut down and dismantled. Coupled with the drive to privatize was the drive to **deregulate**. However, neither selling off only the crown corporations that generated income to the federal government nor deregulating industries saved any money. The motive, again, seemed to be driven by the notions that it is unseemly for government to be making money in competition with honest private-sector entrepreneurs and that it is inefficient to allow bonehead public servants to regulate the private sector in the public interest.

The results of this first phase of public-sector reform under the Tories were not very impressive when we have the advantage of hindsight. The Nielson Task Force recommendations were generally forgotten or ingnored, and did not significantly improve the internal efficiencies of the bureaucracy. The program cutbacks, privatizations, and deregulation did not save any money to speak of and the deficits at the end of this era were higher than ever. Finally, the cost to Canada might have to be assessed ultimately in terms of the number of dedicated and competent public servants, particularly at the middle management levels, who left the government at this time to seek greener pastures in industry and the universities. As we shall see later, this unfortunate trend has not been reversed to any extent since.

**Public Service 2000**   The second Mulroney government took a different and more moderate approach to the public sevice than the first one had. Under the direction of the Clerk of the Privy Council, Paul Tellier, the government launched an initiative called *Public Service 2000* (PS 2000). Ten task forces, entirely internal to the bureaucracy, were set up to look into a range of issues such as staffing, classification, training, staff relations, pay and benefits, resource management, administrative policies, and service to the public. The resulting reports generated thousands of words and over 300 recommendations.

**Reinventing Government**   The thrust of this exercise was ultimately to change the prevailing attitudes in the public service and to alter permanently the *culture* of the federal bureaucracy. The three core objectives of the program were first to make the public service actually "serve" the public better by decentralization of service delivery and by giving the line managers a greater say in how those services are delivered in the field. The second objective was to free the line managers from the oppressive control by central agencies and complicated systems of accountability. Finally, the review exercise was to find ways of making the system more flexible and to enable it to adapt to outside forces quickly and effectively.

While this sounds a lot like "letting the managers manage" revisited, the PS 2000 initiative did have a positive effect overall:

> With the introduction of PS 2000, public sector reorganization took on a calmer and more nuanced tone. Now the purpose was to take a battered and abused public

service and revitalize it with a new corporate culture of empowerment, client service and flexibility.[6]

However, the next phase of what has come to be called **"reinventing government,"**[7] which was instituted in 1993 during Kim Campbell's brief tenure as prime minister, tended to undermine many of the positive effects of the PS 2000 exercise.

The "Campbell reforms" (which were actually drawn up by Robert de Cotret during the last months of Mulroney's reign) were supposed to go hand in hand with the PS 2000 initiatives, by reducing the total number of departments, reducing the size of the Cabinet, and in general streamlining the federal bureaucracy. The problem was in the way it was done by the successor to Paul Tellier, Glen Shortliffe. The thrust of changes appeared to be a return to the slash and burn approach of the early Mulroney years. Right off the top, forty ADMs were summarily given pink slips and several departments disappeared completely, being absorbed into new "mega-departments."

**Public Service Renewal: The Chrétien Public Service**  Not many of the specific recommendations of the PS 2000 task forces were ever implemented, and the process, which was supposed to be ongoing, has sort of fizzled out. However, the Chrétien government left in place the basic restructuring of the bureaucracy that was introduced by Kim Campbell and embarked on yet another government-wide review of programs. Under the direction of Marcel Massé who is the minister responsible for **Public Service Renewal**, the Liberal version of reinventing government was begun almost immediately in 1993. The incoming Liberal government initiated a program-review exercise that was to be carried out by the departments themselves. It is clear that one of the ultimate goals was and is to reduce government expenditures by eliminating some programs, reducing the costs of other programs, and laying off or "buying off" forty to fifty thousand public servants.

The program-review exercise has required departments to assess their programs and activities, or "program comoponents," in terms of six "tests." The first test is the **public interest test**: does the program component provide goods or services to the public that are needed by the public? The second test is the **role of government test**, which asks if the program is an appropriate activity for government and what would happen if the government got out of the area entirely. The **federalism test** or level of government test, asks if the federal government should be delivering a program component or if it should more properly be left to the provinces. The **partnership test** asks whether the program should more properly be delivered by the private sector or the voluntary sector instead of government. The **efficiency test** asks if the program could be delivered effectively at lower cost, and the sixth test, which likely underlies all of the rest, is the **affordability test**, which asks if the program component is affordable in a time of fiscal restraint.

---

6. Leslie Pal, "The Federal Bureaucracy: Reinventing the Links Between State and Society," *in* Whittington and Williams, eds. *Canadian Politics in the 1990s* (Toronto: Nelson, 1994), p. 286.
7. D. Osborne and Ted Gaebler, *Reinventing Government: How the Entrepreneurial Spirit is Transforming the Public Sector* (Reading, Mass.: Addison-Wesley, 1992).

The review process required the departments to apply all of the tests and then to provide a summary narrative about the feasibilty of five options:

maintenance of the status quo
improvement of efficiency only
expansion of the program
devolution of the program, in part or completely to the private sector, provinces, or municipalities
elimination of the program entirely

One does not have to be all that sophisticated to realize that the ultimate goal of this exercise is not so much to renew the public service as to "bonsai" it!

However, the other side of the coin is that all governments in Canada have to bite the bullet and attempt to balance their budgets. Tax increases can go only so far in eliminating the deficit, for both political and economic reasons; hence, even some programs that meet the "tests" will likely have to be cut back or eliminated. It would appear that the current government is taking a slightly more nuanced approach to cutting back than the Tories did in 1993, but there is no question that the cuts will be deep, further damaging the already bruised morale of our public service.

**The Decline of the Management Corps** One phenomenon, likely in part the result of the overall decline in public-service morale, has been that a large number of individuals in the executive (EX) category simply quit in order to seek greener pastures in industry, consulting, or academia. In 1993 and 1994, almost one-quarter of the EX level employees who left the government did so voluntarily, and it is almost certain that they left because they had better offers elsewhere.

Conversely, in the same two-year period, of the 1636 people appointed to the EX group, only 47 were brought in from outside government. The rest were either promoted from lower levels in the hierarchy or transferred in

**TABLE 23.1**

Reasons for Leaving Public Service (Executive Category)

| Reason | 1992–1993 | | 1993–1994 | |
|---|---|---|---|---|
| | Number | % | Number | % |
| Lay off | 58 | 20.1 | 49 | 16.6 |
| Voluntary Resignation | 71 | 24.6 | 64 | 21.7 |
| Retirement | 131 | 45.3 | 131 | 44.4 |
| Other or Unknown | 29 | 10.0 | 50 | 17.3 |
| Total | 289 | 100.0 | 294 | 100.0 |

Source: Adapted from Treasury Board Secretariat, *Employment Statistics for the Federal Public Service 1993–94.*

laterally from the "priority lists" of people whose positions elsewhere in government had been declared redundant. If people who are employable outside government are leaving, and if there is little new blood coming into the senior bureaucracy from outside, one might begin to despair about the inevitable dilution of the aggregate quality of the folks who remain.

**TABLE 23.2**

Appointments to the Executive Category

| Type | 1992–1993 | | 1993–1994 | |
|---|---|---|---|---|
| | Number | % | Number | % |
| Outside Appointment | 27 | 2.3 | 20 | 4.4 |
| Lateral Transfer | 596 | 50.3 | 75 | 16.7 |
| Promotion | 349 | 29.4 | 193 | 42.9 |
| Acting Appointment | 214 | 18.0 | 162 | 36.0 |
| Total | 1,186 | 100.0 | 450 | 100.0 |

Source: Adapted from *Public Service of Canada Annual Report,* 1993–1994.

Nor can we be much more optimistic about the way in which cutbacks to the management corps are being achieved. People who accept buyouts or early retirement are more likely to be those who have an alternative to go to outside the government. As well, layoffs that occur because a position disappears are not based on **"negative merit"** but simply hit the current incumbent, regardless of the individual's ability or potential as a public-service manager. When all of these trends are added together, the prospects for attracting and keeping the brightest and the best in government service are not high. Even the excellent, dedicated senior bureaucrats who still soldier on, despite the harsh times, can be expected to think seriously about private-sector options when faced with the declining quality of the people they must work with.

Sadly, there is no indication that current trends will change very much in the near future. Cutbacks, buyouts, early retirement, and defections to the private sector will continue to dilute the quality of management that is left behind. To be sure, many of the very best people will stay out of loyalty, commitment to public service, or the fascinating, if daunting, challenges they face in the public sector today. However, under the current regimen their jobs will become more difficult before they get better, and the quality of service to the public can only be expected to slip, unless the government takes creative measures to make a public-sector career as attractive and aspired to as it once was.

This concludes our discussion of the Canadian bureaucracy. The reader will have to look further into other sources listed in the recommended readings for more detailed information about the structures and processes of this country's public service. We have attempted to give a perspective on the bureaucracy in the political and governmental process and to demonstrate that, while the bureaucracy is crucial to the processes of policy determination and public administration, it is also an important actor in many other aspects of political life in Canada.

# Chapter 24

# The Judicial Process: Judges, Courts, and the Law

In Chapter 5, the concept of the **rule of law** was introduced as a basic operational principle of the Canadian Constitution, but little was said about the nature of the positive law or about the origins and characteristics of the Canadian judicial system. In this chapter, it is our intention to describe the structure of the Canadian judiciary and the manner in which the judicial process relates to the governmental process as a whole. Because it is *law* that is the subject matter of judicial decision-making, and because, formally, it is law that constitutes, limits, and authorizes all governmental activity, a brief discussion of the law, its nature, and its origins is an appropriate introduction to this chapter.

## ▶ LAW IN CANADA

The relationship of the individual to the state in a nation built upon the principle of the rule of law is determined, as one might expect, by law. Moreover, that relationship is a reciprocal one. As we have seen in earlier chapters, the Constitution defines the structures of government and sets the basic limits of legitimate governmental interference with the rights of Canadians. The **positive law**, on the other hand, is intended to limit and regulate the behaviour of individuals in the interests of the society as a whole. The latter is a process whereby general rules of behaviour are set down in statutes and regulations and applied to individuals in society by administrative officials, by law-enforcement agencies, and by judges.

### The Nature of Law

The function of law is to regulate human behaviour. The Constitution regulates the behaviour of people in government and the positive law regulates the behaviour of people in society. In its broadest context, the law could be viewed as including all rules of human behaviour, whether customary, moral, ethical, or religious, which have application in a given society. However, when one speaks of the law in a modern society, what is usually implied is the *positive* embodiment of the customary, ethical, moral, and religious values of a society in the form of its constitution, statutes, and judicial decisions.

In this more formal and positive sense, law is concrete and explicit in a way that a code of behaviour, implicit in "natural law," customs, or moral standards, can never be. In a more concrete sense, law can be distinguished from custom and morality by the existence of explicit sanctions and positive means for enforcement: "What distinguishes law from customs and morality is the additional sanction of sheriffs, bailiffs, police, jails, and armed forces to be called into operation if needed to coerce the stubborn."[1]

**Categories of Law** The term *law* is used in a wide variety of contexts and is a much broader notion than what we are focusing on here. We speak of laws of nature, laws of physics, the law of averages, and Murphy's Law, and with the possible exception of the latter, none of these has much to do with Canadian government. Clearly, it would be silly, even for a Reform Party national convention, to decide to "repeal" the law of gravity or the law of averages, for such laws are beyond the reach even of our supreme Parliament. Hence, when we speak of law in the context of the discipline of political science, we mean, for the most part, the **positive law**.

Despite the fact that political philosophers have flirted with the notion of a law of nature, or a **natural law** that takes precedent over the laws made by human political institutions, there has never been a consensus as to what the principles of natural law are or how they can practically be applied to the positive law. Whether there *is* a body of laws that is made by God or nature is a conundrum too esoteric for a textbook on Canadian government, but what we must acknowledge is that individual judges, when determining the constitutionality of positive-law enactments, may be influenced by their own moral, ethical, or religious beliefs. The written court decision may be couched in the strictest of positive-law principles, but the underlying reasons for the decision may lie in the judges' beliefs as to what is intrinsically "right" or "wrong" in terms of their perceptions of natural law.

Leaving aside the category of natural law, the positive law with respect to Canada can be broken down into **international law** and **Canadian law**. International law is composed of a broad set of principles governing the relationships among nations in the international community. Although international law is at least partly codified in international treaties, declarations, and conventions, it is for the most part unenforceable, unlike domestic law. The relations among nations are generally governed only by the relative military and economic might of the members of the international community, and the decisions of bodies such as the international tribunal at The Hague are only binding to the extent that the sovereign nations agree to be bound.

---

1. J. A. Corry and J. E. Hodgetts, *Democratic Government and Politics* (Toronto: University of Toronto Press, 1959), p. 424.

The domestic law of Canada is composed of the laws enacted by the legislatures of the provinces and by Parliament. Canadian law can be broken down into **public law** and **private law**. The latter is the law governing the relations among private individuals and corporations in Canadian society and includes, among other matters, contracts, property, torts, wills, patents, family law, and company law. While statutes may establish the rules and procedures of private law, any private-law cases to be decided by the courts involve litigation between private individuals or corporations. A government or "the Crown" becomes directly engaged in private-law litigation only when the issue involves a question of constitutionality, in which case various interested provinces and the government of Canada may "intervene" on appeal.

The largest branch of public law is **criminal law**. Criminal cases involve prosecutions by the Crown of individuals who have committed crimes as defined in the Criminal Code and in other statutes aimed at prohibiting certain classes of human behaviour that are deemed to be unacceptable in our society. Strictly speaking, crimes can be defined only by the federal Parliament, under section 91(27) of the *Constitution Act*, 1867, although offences are sometimes created pursuant to provincial statutes that are essentially "criminal" in that the sanctions are equivalent to those imposed for offences under the Criminal

**Figure 24.1**
Categories of law.

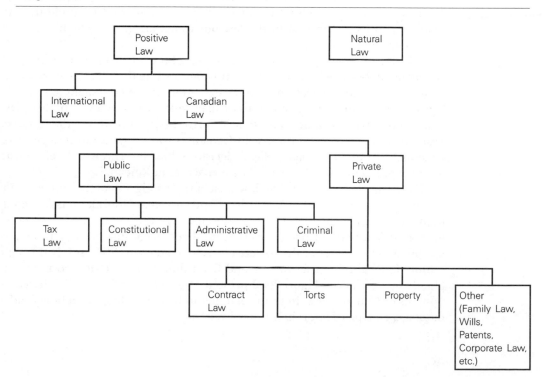

Code of Canada. While the criminal law is a federal power, **criminal prosecutions** are made by provincial crown attorneys, and in provincially administered courts, because of the provinces' authority over the "administration of justice" in section 92(14) of the *Constitution Act*, 1867.

The other branches of public law in Canada include tax law, administrative law, and constitutional law. **Tax law** is a very specialized branch of public law dealing with disputes between the taxing government and the taxpayer at both the federal and provincial levels. **Administrative law**, which we dealt with in our chapters on the bureaucracy, concerns disputes between citizens and the implementation and enforcement agencies and officials of the government. **Constitutional law** is perhaps the most important branch of public law in that it involves disputes not only between individuals and the Canadian state, but between and among federal and provincial governments. We have already considered Canadian constitutional law in the context of both the Charter of Rights and Freedoms and the federal distribution of powers, so the topic does not require further elaboration here.

**The Hierarchy of Laws**  The law in Canada can be said to consist of the Constitution, statutes, regulations, and judicial decisions or precedents. The Constitution is the fundamental law of the land and all other categories of law must be consistent with it. **Statutes** are the creatures of our legislatures — the Canadian Parliament and the assemblies of the provinces. **Regulations** are "subordinate" laws in the sense that they are *executive* orders passed pursuant to legislation that delegates powers to ministers and government officials. The executive branch of the government also issues ministerial "interpretations," "directives," and procedural manuals, which are intended to guide the bureaucracy in its application of the law but which are not legally binding on either citizens or the courts.

All of the above types of law are products of the lawmaking institutions of government, both legislative and executive. But while there has always been a large annual output of statute law and regulations passed pursuant to statutes, legislatures do no more than add to or make alterations to a vast body of law that is already in existence, and that is derived largely from another source. Much of what constitutes the law in Canada is to be found not in legislative enactments, but in myriad judicial decisions that interpret and refine our understanding of what those legislative enactments "mean."

This huge body of **common law**, case law, or judge-made law reflects our society's overall moral, ethical, religious, and customary foundations far better than the specific enactments of any legislature. In this sense, the law is incremental. It is a body of principles that has been accumulated over time and modified as the values of the society have changed — modified subtly through minute judicial reinterpretations, and from time to time modified more explicitly by legislation. Figure 24.2 presents a graphic illustration of the components of Canadian law in terms of a hierarchy depending upon how fundamental each type of law is in our legal system.

**Figure 24.2**
The hierarchy of law.

Common Law and the Civil Law The Canadian legal system stems from two quite distinct legal traditions and is consequently a unique reflection of the duality of Canadian political culture. One tradition is rooted in the **Roman law** tradition and the other in the **English common law.** Roman law is codified in the form of general rules and principles, which must be applied to each case individually. It is Roman law that was adopted in varying forms throughout western Europe at the time of the Renaissance. The settlers of New France naturally brought with them the legal system of their mother country, so in the Province of Quebec the Roman legal tradition is still to some extent reflected.

The English common law is based on "the common custom of the realm"[2] as interpreted by judges, and is derived from judicial precedents that build on earlier precedents and so on. It is not codified; rather, it is a set of principles merely implicit in the judicial decisions of England and of the courts in systems that have adopted the English legal system. The common law came to Canada via the early English settlers, and was even partially introduced into Quebec through the conquest. Today in Quebec, **private law** (or **civil law**) is based on the *Code civil du Québec*, which is derived from the French *Code Napoléon*, whereas in the other Canadian provinces, private law is based on the English common law. **Criminal law** in Canada is uniform across the country, being based on the Canadian Criminal Code, which, in turn, is derived almost exclusively from the principles of English criminal jurisprudence.

### Legal Practices and Principles in Canada

The basic principles that underly procedure in criminal cases, such as the presumption of innocence and the right not to be forced to testify against

---

2. Ibid., p. 428.

oneself, are now entrenched in the Charter and need not be revisited at this juncture. As well, there are principles, such as trial by jury, which were incorporated into our system from the English common law and are so well understood that they need not be discussed at length in a political-science text. However, underlying the Canadian legal system is a range of practices, principles, and procedures, which, in the aggregate, make up what we might call our **legal culture**. While entire books could be written on Canada's legal culture, a few of the more important, if essentially unwritten, principles should be summarized before attempting to explain the role of the judiciary and the structure of our court system.

**"Knowability"** It is a cliché among amateur afficionados of the law that "ignorance of the law" is not an acceptable defence. As citizens we are obliged to know what the law is and to behave in a manner consistent with it. However, the assumption underlying one's obligation to know what the law *is* is that the law must, indeed, be **knowable**. If a society is effectively performing the function of providing guidelines for human behaviour in a society, people obviously must be able to find out what standards of behaviour their society is imposing on them.

As well as being knowable to us, the law also must be applied in a way that is **predictable** to us. If we are to be capable of adjusting our behaviour so that it conforms to the requirements of the law, not only must we be aware of the broad principles embodied in the law, but we must also be able to predict the way in which the officials of the government will go about applying and enforcing it, and what the penalties for disobeying are likely to be.

**Public Proceedings** An important characteristic of the Canadian system of justice is that court proceedings must generally be *open* or public. The aim of this practice is to ensure that injustices are not committed against individuals through the device of secret trials. It is felt that an open legal process allows the scrutiny of the public and the press and discourages unfair practices on the part of the government, particularly in criminal proceedings.

However, there are a number of exceptions to the **rule of openness** in Canadian court proceedings. For example, under the *Young Offender's Act* of 1985, there are provisions for the judge in a Youth Court to close the proceedings if there is reason to believe that the publicity would be harmful to the victim, the accused, or an underage witness. Similarly, even in situations where the court proceedings are open, there can be statutory limitations on the publication of certain evidence. For instance, the Criminal Code provides that the names of the victims of sexual assault cannot be published.

Finally, apart from the explicit statutory provisions that go against the principle of openness, superior court judges possess the authority to close their courts or to ban the publication of proceedings in the media.[3] A 1993–1995 example of the use of this power was in the notorious Bernardo/Homolka trials, where the publication ban was imposed, in part, in the vain hope of finding some jurors who were not completely biased by the grisly evidence

---

3. G. Gall, *The Canadian Legal System* (Toronto: Carswell, 1990), p. 130.

produced at the first trial. As well, in cases such as this, a judge may simply decide that the evidence is so salacious that publication would be inappropriate. However, the discretionary power of a judge to close the court proceedings to the public and the media is by no means automatically accepted. A 1994 decision of the Supreme Court of Canada concluded that the Charter provisions of the right to a fair trial and freedom of the press must be read together and balanced. In this case, a judge's order to ban the media from the courtroom was overturned on appeal.

Despite the exceptions cited above, open proceedings are still the rule in Canada, and where there are restrictions on publicity, they are imposed for the most part to protect the victim and the accused, and not to enable the Crown to abuse human rights by meting out justice behind closed doors. Naturally, the media are never all that happy about such measures as publication bans, but one cannot help wondering whether the media mavens are more concerned about being able to publish the sensational stuff that will sell newspapers than with the principle of fairness in the courtroom.

**The Adversarial System**  It is the aim of the judicial process to arrive at some sort of objective truth in its deliberations. In the English legal tradition it has been determined that the best way to achieve this aim is through a process in which the judge remains neutral in the proceedings and the parties or **litigants**, represented by counsel, each attempt to convince the court that their position is more worthy. This method of discovering the truth and, hence, of achieving justice is referred to as the **adversarial system**. The role of the judge is to render the decison on the basis of the evidence presented and not on any first-hand knowledge of the case or personal convictions.

The system works because the judge is forced to be unbiased. In writing the decision, the judge must base his or her arguments on evidence that was presented during the trial. If the reasons for the judgement include information not presented by counsel during the trial, the judge's decision may be thrown out on appeal. The down side of the adversarial process, however, is that not all lawyers are equal in ability. It may be that a case is won or lost because the lawyer for one side failed to bring forward pertinent evidence or failed to see and rebut the flaws and weaknesses in the evidence presented by the other side.

*Stare Decisis*  While the law is a growing thing, its growth is controlled rather than random. The element of control in Canada is injected, in part, through the **rule of precedent**, the principle of *stare decisis*. The basic principle of the rule of precedent is that judges, when making a decision today, take into account the decisions of previous courts in similar cases in the past. Precedents can be of two types: *binding* or *persuasive*. **Binding precedent** exists where "within any particular system of judicature the lower courts in the hierarchy are bound to follow the rules previously used to decide sufficiently similar cases in the higher court or courts of the hierarchy."[4] Thus, in the Canadian system, decisions by higher courts are binding on lower courts in the same judicial

---

4.  W. R. Lederman, "The Common Law System in Canada," *in* E. McWhinney, ed., *Canadian Jurisprudence: The Civil Law and Common Law in Canada* (Toronto: Carswell, 1958), p. 36.

hierarchy. However, the question as to whether a court is bound by its *own* precedents is dependent mainly on the court itself. A court can choose to consider itself bound by its own precedents, or it can choose not to be so bound. The Supreme Court of Canada and, before 1949, the Judicial Committee of the Privy Council have stated that they were *not* strictly bound by their own precedents. The record of both these courts of final appeal, however, indicates that a previous decision has a great deal of persuasive force in helping them to decide current cases, and it is seldom indeed that the Supreme Court of Canada reverses the stand it took in a previous case: "Even though a court regards its own previous decisions as persuasive only, they turn out to be so highly persuasive that the distinction from a binding precedent becomes rather dim."[5]

One of the differences between the common-law system and the Quebec *Code civil* system is supposed to be that the rule of precedent does not bind judges in the latter. The theory here is that the judge in the Quebec system is expected to apply the Code to the fact situation at hand in each case as it arises, and not to depend on the arguments raised by previous judges in previous cases which may have had similar circumstances. However, the fact that the Canadian judicial system is an integrated one with appeals from private-law decisions in Quebec courts going to the Supreme Court of Canada on appeal, has meant that the rule of *stare decisis* has been brought into the jurisprudence of the **Code civil du Québec**. In actuality, the practice of private law in the Province of Quebec today is hardly distinguishable from the common-law tradition of private law practised in the rest of Canada.

## ▶ THE LEGAL COMMUNITY: JUDGES, LAWYERS, AND JUDICIAL SUPPORT STAFF

Before beginning our examination of the Canadian judicial system, which is comprised of both federal and provincial courts, it is perhaps useful to say a few words about the people who make up the legal community. Obviously the judges who preside over the courts at all levels are the most important actors in this complex set of institutions, but, as well, the courts are peopled by many lesser beings who nevertheless play important roles in our judicial system. We will start by discussing the legal profession as a whole in Canada; then, we will consider the various individuals who provide professional and administrative support to the system; and finally, we will examine the judiciary itself.

### The Legal Profession in Canada

Legal professionals in Canada — lawyers — are prominent among the elites of our society. They are the largest single profession in legislatures across the country, they are prominent among the business elites and on the boards of major corporations, and most of our prime ministers have been lawyers, including the last five. In the judiciary, however, everyone is a lawyer; a person

---

5. Ibid., p. 37.

must be a member of the bar of a province in order to be appointed to the bench. Hence, before we move to our discussion of the judiciary, it is useful to look at the profession from which all Canadian judges are selected.

**Joining the Club**   The basic requirement for becoming a lawyer is a degree from an accredited law school. Once that degree is earned, the aspiring lawyer must then article or apprentice with a practising lawyer or law firm to learn the practical and often prosaic skills that a practising lawyer needs. Finally, the would-be lawyer must then take the provincial bar admission course, which is usually about six months long, and pass the rigorous bar admission examinations. After jumping all of these hurdles the lucky individual is admitted to the bar of the province. When one takes into account how relatively few Canadians complete a first university degree, how few graduates who apply to law school are ultimately admitted, and the drop-out rate in law school itself, it is not difficult to understand why members of the legal profession are considered an elite group in Canadian society.

When we consider the sorts of people who get to law school in the first place, as one might expect, the recruitment for these institutions is disproportionately from the upper and middle classes of Canadian society. Dennis Olson has pointed out that "lawyers in Canada are certainly not drawn from a representative cross section of the population. . . . The class and ethnic biases that will ultimately find their expression in the composition of the high courts have their beginning in the selection for law school."[6]

While many law schools in recent years have been attempting to recruit more students from visible minorities, from the aboriginal communities, from working class or farm backgrounds — in essence, people other than the sons and daughters of lawyers, the subsequent career patterns of lawyers still reflect ethnic and socio-economic biases. The plum legal positions, such as partnerships in large firms and specialization in the more lucrative sub-disciplines of the profession, tend to be dominated by "charter-group" and upper-middle-class Canadians. The only significant exceptions to these generalizations would seem to be women and Jews, who have made definite inroads into the legal profession in Canada.[7]

The legal profession can be considered an elite group for other reasons as well. The gatekeepers of the legal fraternity are the provincially established **law societies**, which have the authority to admit individuals to the bar of that province, to enforce codes of discipline, and ultimately to discipline or disbar members of the club who have broken its rules. However, while the law societies of the provinces are established and mandated by provincial legislation, the **benchers** of the law society are all lawyers and, hence, the legal profession is almost entirely self-regulating.

Finally, as a profession, the legal community is represented nationally by the Canadian Bar Association (CBA), which is one of the most powerful interest groups in the country. The CBA functions as a sort of legal conscience of the nation, passing judgement on all manner of subjects and lobbying with re-

---

6.   D. Olson, *The State Elite* (Toronto: McClelland and Stewart, 1980), p. 44.
7.   Ibid.

markable success for changes in the law and for improvements in the working environment of the members of the profession. The influence of the CBA is profound, and while it clearly functions to further the interests of the people it represents, the level of professionalism it brings to its advocacy role usually makes its recommendations worthy of consideration "on merit" by whatever government is in power.

**Club Rules** While becoming a member of the legal profession is a daunting challenge, many seem to accomplish the feat — there are approximately fifty thousand lawyers in Canada. However, many people who become lawyers never actually practice law, choosing instead to become involved in business, politics, legal education, or legal research. All governments in Canada hire a large number of legal professionals to provide policy advice, conduct research into legal issues, and function as agents of the government in its dealings with other governments, groups, and individuals. However, those who do follow the law as a profession are required to adhere to a strict code of conduct defined by the legislation and policed by the vigilant benchers of the provincial law society.

At the broadest level of generalization the conduct of a lawyer must be guided by two broad roles that he or she must play simultaneously. In the first instance, the lawyer is bound to act in a manner that is consistent with the best interests of his or her client. The **lawyer-client relationship** is one of complete trust and the onus is upon the lawyer to ensure that the trust is never breached. This trust relationship is sanctified by common-law principles such as the **privilege** or complete secrecy granted to information exchanged between the lawyer and the client.

Second, the lawyer is also an **officer of the court** and, as such, has an obligation to respect the rules and procedures of the court and to ensure that justice is done in a fair and impartial manner. The lawyer must also be aware of the symbolic importance of the judicial process, and must not act in a manner detrimental to the decorum and dignity of the court proceedings. Not unexpectedly, particularly in criminal cases, the obligations as an officer of the court, serving Canadian society as a whole, and the obligations as counsel for the defence to an obviously guilty client, can often present dilemmas to a conscientious lawyer.

**The Perks of Membership** While some people who become lawyers end up only with a "pot" (the legacy of a sedentary occupation) but not the one at the end of the rainbow, it is a statistical fact that the profession of law can be a springboard to power, social status, influence, and wealth. Certainly the standards of professional and personal conduct are high, but so are the "perks" of the job. Significantly, the key qualification to become a superior, district, or county court judge, according to section 96 of the BNA Act, is to be a member of the bar of one of the provinces. Similarly, the minimum qualifications to become a judge of any provincial court in Canada include being a member of the bar of the province where the vacancy occurs. Thus, for the successful legal professional, one of the ultimate rewards in an already rewarding career is the possibility of a judgeship.

### The Judiciary

When we refer to the **judiciary** what we mean is the almost two thousand real people who, as judges, preside over the courts of the land. There are many different courts in Canada and we will consider them in the next section. At this point however, we must look at the way in which judges are selected and appointed and the manner in which their *independence* is secured.

**Judicial Appointments**  As we have seen in Chapter 6, the judges of all federal courts and all superior, county, and district courts in the provinces are appointed and remunerated by the federal government, and the lower provincial court judges are appointed and paid by the provincial governments. We have also seen that the legal profession forms the human-resources pool from which judges are exclusively selected. Thus, the already heavily selective process of recruitment to the legal profession in Canada is reinforced by the even more selective process whereby the almost eight hundred federally appointed and more than one thousand provincially appointed judgeships are filled.

*Partisanship*  It is members of the political elite who formally select the members of the judiciary, and it seems likely that even the best-intentioned ministers of Justice will be biased by a personal view of what constitutes a good judge. However, the largest amount of criticism has been levelled at the putatively **partisan** taint of judicial appointment processes. Historically, the members of the bench were selected unabashedly from the ranks of those faithful to the party in power. Likely, ministers of Justice who recommended judicial nominees would attempt to select good legal minds for the judgeships, but, all things being equal, a Liberal government would select a good Liberal legal mind over a good Conservative legal mind, almost every time.

However, the partisan component of the criteria for selection of judges has clearly declined in the past thirty years. Since the late 1960s until 1988, the practice was for the federal Justice minister to submit the names of potential judicial appointees to a committee of the Canadian Bar Association. The aim of this practice was to ensure that legal rather than political qualifications would be the critical determinants of who might become a judge in the Canadian courts. This procedure likely worked fairly well, for in fact there were increasing numbers of non-partisan or even "wrong-party" appointments to the bench.

The critics of this practice, however, argued that the political elites in government and the elites of the legal profession, in the Canadian Bar Association, are virtually identical in terms of their class and ethnic origins. It was argued that the end result of the procedure is that the control over judicial appointments has simply shifted "from lawyers wearing political garb to lawyers wearing legal garb."[8] However, it is clear that such a procedure did reduce,

---

8.  Ibid., p. 47.

quite drastically, the extent to which the power of judicial appointment was used simply as a partisan **patronage** power.

*Nomination Committees*  A new process for the appointment of section 96 judges was introduced in 1988. Although the power of appointment still rests with the federal minister of Justice, the manner in which the names of would-be judges are submitted to the minister has changed. The Judicial Appointments Committee of the Canadian Bar Association has been replaced by provincial and territorial **nomination committees**. These committees are each composed of five people including one nominee each of the provincial government, the local branch of the CBA, the law society, and the federal minister of Justice, and a puisne judge of a section 96 court in the province who is named by the provincial chief justice, and the appointee of the federal minister must be a lay person, not a lawyer.

The aspirants to judicial office can be nominated by anyone, including themselves, and the provincial or territorial committee must then determine whether the individuals so nominated are "qualified" for the job. The minister of Justice must then make the appointment from the names on the list of qualified applicants. The benefits of this sort of system are that partisanship is virtually eliminated as a criterion for appointment, and, because the committees include at least one member who is not a lawyer, the dominance of the legal profession that flawed the CBA appointments committee is less of a problem. Most of the provinces, including Ontario, have now introduced a similar system for screening applicants for provincial judgeships.

*Supreme Court of Canada Appointments*  There is no formal nomination or screening mechanism for appointments to the federal judiciary. In appointments to the Federal Court of Canada or the Tax Court, the minister of Justice may take the counsel of anyone he or she chooses, but in the end the appointment decision is completely discretionary. The appointment procedure for the Supreme Court of Canada is not even left entirely in the hands of the minister of Justice, but is usually controlled by the prime minister.

While up until 1949 appointments to the Supreme Court of Canada were usually frankly partisan, after appeals to the Judicial Committee of the Privy Council were abolished, prime ministers appear to have recognized that the primary criterion for such appointments should be the quality of the legal mind. It is impossible to prove even that prime ministers select Supreme Court judges on the basis of an ideological compatibility with the government, although there has never been a "socialist" on the highest court. It could be argued that this is prime-ministerial bias at work, or simply that the legal profession itself is not heavily representative of dyed-in-the-wool radical political thought!

There have been a number of suggestions and proposals for introducing reforms to the appointment process for the Supreme Court of Canada, most of which come from individuals and groups who believe *they* should be involved. Not surprisingly, the Canadian Bar Association argues that it should have a role, and the provincial law societies believe that they should at least be consulted. However, the proposals that have been taken the most seriously have argued that, because the Supreme Court has such a critical role as the "umpire" of the federal system, the provincial governments should have a say. The Meech Lake proposals would have put in place a system whereby the provinces would nominate prospective candidates, and the prime minister and minister of Justice would have to choose from the list of provincial nominees. However, when the Accord gasped its last, so did this proposal, and it has not been revived since the onset of our post-Charlottetown constitutional hangover.

**Operationalizing Judicial Independence**  In Chapter 6 we discussed at some length the principle of the independence of the judiciary. However, while we looked at the concept of an independent judiciary as a cornerstone principle of our Constitution, we did not elaborate upon the mechanisms employed to make it work in the real world. These mechanisms fall into two main categories. First, there are provisions that **insulate** and protect the judge from interference by other branches of government; second, there are **standards of behaviour** that require the judge to act, both professionally and personally, in a manner consistent with the impartiality, dignity, and trust inherent in the office.

*Protecting the Judges*  The procedures for appointing judges, as we have seen, leaves open the possibility that the ministers making the appointments may exhibit some bias in the exercise of their discretion. However, once in office, a judge is placed in a position where he or she cannot be coerced into making judgements favourable to the government that made the appointment. This is achieved because judges are appointed until age seventy-five, have fixed salaries set by statute, and can be removed from office only after a joint address by the House of Commons and the Senate.

Judges are also protected from being openly criticized for their decisons while on the bench. An individual may be fined or imprisoned for **contempt of court** for making derogatory remarks about a judge or about a judicial decision. Even if the critic is a minister of the Crown, open criticism of a member of the judiciary might bring a conviction for contempt, as happened in 1976 to a federal minister. Judges also enjoy immunity from both civil and criminal prosecutions for acts committed in the course of carrying out their duties. Finally, while it is not something that can be legislated, another end product of placing judges above the normal fray of day-to-day life is that they enjoy enormous prestige.

*Standards of Conduct*  Except for mandatory retirement at age seventy-five, judges hold office **during good behaviour**. What constitutes "good behaviour" for a judge has never been clearly defined, but it is generally agreed that it allows the individual member of the judiciary a fairly wide scope. In the past it was held that the only ground for removing a judge from office was the commission of a serious crime. However, more recently, the opinion seems to have evolved so that the grounds for dismissal could include such things as persistent neglect of duties, inability to perform duties because of excessive drink, or conflict of interest. As well, a life of profligacy or debauchery might be deemed to be incompatible with the decorum of the job.

Until 1971, allegations of judicial wrongdoing were dealt with by *ad hoc* judicial inquiries that were set up to investigate and make recommendations as to appropriate disciplinary action. In 1971 the **Canadian Judicial Council** was created. This body, composed of the chief justices and the associate chief justices of all the provincial superior courts, is chaired by the chief justice of the Supreme Court of Canada. The role of the council is to investigate complaints about alleged judicial misconduct. If the council concludes that there has, indeed, been serious misconduct, it has the power to remove county or district court judges directly, and to recommend such action to Parliament when the impugned judge is from a superior court. While judges have been forced to resign for sundry alleged indiscretions or misdemeanours, both professional and personal, no judge has ever actually been fired in Canada.

*Judges and Freedom of Expression*  While we place our judges in an enviable position of public esteem and power, the privileged position of the judge has its price. Judges are expected to live exemplary lives both on and off the bench. The judge must, at all times, behave in a manner consistent with the dignity and decorum of the court to ensure that the administration of justice is not brought into disrepute and is expected to remain above the political and social conflicts that occupy the thoughts and words of other Canadians. Judges are expected, above all, to refrain from expressing strong political views, which might compromise the image of objectivity that is so important in maintaining the credibility of our independent judicial system.

The issue of the freedom of speech of a judge versus his or her obligation to remain totally above the fray of public discourse was tested in 1982, when Mr. Justice Thomas Berger spoke out against certain provisions in the patriation package of 1982. In effect he criticized the Government of Canada for the contents of the *Constitution Act, 1982*. The matter was referred to the Canadian Judicial Council after a complaint by another superior court judge, and the council concluded that "a judge's conscience is not an acceptable excuse for contravening a fundamental rule so important to the existence of parliamentary democracy and judicial independence."[9] However, the council did not feel that Mr. Justice Berger's comments warranted any disciplinary action.

Not long after this incident, Berger resigned from the bench, stating that he was not comfortable in a job where he was not able to comment critically on the important issues of the day. In commenting on the case, Bora Laskin, then chief justice of the Supreme Court of Canada, stated:

> It was said that the pursuit of the complaint against Justice Berger was an interference with his freedom of speech. Plain nonsense! A judge has no freedom of speech to address political issues which have nothing to do with his judicial duties. His abstention from political involvement is one of the guarantees of his impartiality, his integrity, his *independence*.[10]

---

9.  Cited in Rick Van Loon and Mike Whittington, *The Canadian Political System: Environment, Structure and Process* (Toronto: McGraw-Hill Ryerson, 1987), p. 184.

10.  F. L Morton, *Law, Politics and the Judicial Process in Canada* (Calgary: University of Calgary Press, 1984), p. 118.

While Chief Justice Laskin may have been overly cranky in his comments, there are many that share the basic view that judges should not become embroiled in public debates about political issues. It is held that while publicly expressing strong opinions does not necesssarily compromise the objectivity of a judge, it does compromise the *appearance* of objectivity that is so important in maintaining the legitimacy of the judicial process.

## Judicial System Support

While lawyers and judges dominate the courtroom drama, there are many other people working in the background who are critical to the smooth running of our legal and judicial system. These include individuals who provide technical and para-legal services to the legal professionals, and the "justice bureaucracies" that provide policy, research, and litigation services to governments. However, before discussing the sources of backup support to the judges and the lawyers, it is important to explain the role of justices of the peace in the judicial process.

## Justices of the Peace

The lowest level of the judicial hierarchy in most provinces and in the Yukon and the Northwest Territories is the **justice of the peace** (JP). A justice of the peace is appointed by the province or territory and holds office **at pleasure**, which means he or she can be fired summarily at any time without cause. There are few specific qualifications for the office, and while, rarely, JPs may have legal training, for the most part they are lay persons. The jurisdiction of a JP is usually territorially limited to the municipality or judicial district where the appointment takes place.

In Ontario, there are approximately a hundred full-time JPs, half of whom are in Toronto. As well, there are hundreds more individuals who have been given many of the minor powers of JPs and who operate on a part-time basis. Some of these part-time JPs are already employed by the government of Ontario in other capacities and perform their JP functions as a part of their jobs. Other part-time JPs are **"fee JPs"** who charge user fees for their services.

Within their territories, full-time justices of the peace have a surprisingly wide range of powers and responsibilities. The use of JPs varies quite a bit from province to province, but in Ontario, particularly, they are assuming a growing share of the routine duties of provincial court judges. The traditional functions of JPs are mostly related to routine legal process matters such as issuing summonses, warrants, search warrants, and subpoenas. As well, they can perform marriages, swear affidavits and statutory declarations, and conduct certain kinds of bail hearings.

In some provincial jurisdictions the role of the JP has been expanded to include many **adjudicative** responsibilities as well as the traditional and pretrial functions. Particularly in large centres such as Toronto, Vancouver, and Montreal, the JPs preside over traffic courts, settling cases involving minor provincial and municipal offences. There are some federal summary conviction offences that may also be dealt with by a JP, sometimes working under the supervision of a provincial court judge, and there are a few provisions of the

Criminal Code that still permit two or more JPs sitting together to fill in for a provincial court judge. Perhaps the most extensive use of JPs in the Canadian experience is in Ontario, where JPs preside over the **Provincial Offences Court**, which is a court of record having jurisdiction over minor provincial and municipal by-law offences. Quebec also has instituted a **Justice of the Peace Court**, which is used not in the urban centres but in the more remote regions of the province that do not have access to a regular provincial court.

It is interesting that the role of JPs in Canada has been expanding both in large urban centres and in remote communities. In the former case the JPs take some of the burden off the provincial court judges, and in the latter case JPs are able to provide local justice services in communities where access to the normal court system is limited or difficult. In the two northern territories JPs play an important role in bringing justice "closer to the people." Most of these appointees are local people in the remotest settlements of the territories, and many of them are of aboriginal origins, so that minor offences can be dealt with by judicial officials who, while lacking in formal legal training, will have a sensitivity to local problems and to the cultural idiosyncracies of the specific community. This system is, however, under an ongoing review, and the role of the JP may end up being integrated into proposed tribal justice or aboriginal court systems that are currently being explored as a part of overall aboriginal self-government initiatives.

**Technical and Para-Legal Support** The lawyers are backed up not only by colleagues in the profession, and, in particular, in their law firms but, as well, by numerous technical personnel who assist them in their professional activities. More and more these technical people have formal training as **para-legals** and include title searchers, legal secretaries, and law clerks, all of whom do much of the routine work so that the lawyers can concentrate their efforts on the bigger questions of law, legal interpretation, and litigation. Judges, too, have a lot of backup in the form of **officers of the court**. These include court reporters, bailiffs, sheriffs, and registrars, who together keep the wheels of justice turning.

**Justice Bureaucracies** Beyond the law office and the courtroom, there exists a very large justice-related bureaucracy that provides overall administrative and policy support to the judicial system. The governments of Canada and of all of the provinces and territories have large justice departments. These bureaucracies provide policy advice and legal research services for their cabinets and for other departments. As well, the justice departments in the provinces, because they are the support units for the offices of the provincial attorneys-general, are reponsible for criminal prosecutions and for cases that involve the province as one of the litigants. All provinces and the federal government also have **law reform commissions** whose job it is to examine existing laws and procedures with an eye to recommending improvements to the system as a whole.

The **Office of the Commissioner for Federal Judicial Affairs**, created in 1977, has the responsibility for overseeing the personnel administration of all federally appointed judges. Up until 1977, this role was performed within the

Department of Justice, but it was felt that such matters should be conducted at arm's length from the federal minister in order to better ensure the independence of section 96 judges. The Office of the Commissioner and the support staff are thus separate from the department, although the commissioner reports through the minister of Justice. Although the commissioner is responsible for the personnel administration of the Federal Court of Canada as well as the federally appointed judges in the provincial superior courts, the Supreme Court of Canada runs as a totally separate operation under the direction of the **registrar** of the court.

## ▶ THE JUDICIAL SYSTEM

The function of the judicial system in Canada, as in all countries, is to **adjudicate** disputes arising among individuals in society, between individuals and government, and between governments. It is in this sense that the judicary plays a role in the overall function of government, which is to manage or peacefully resolve conflict. As well, the judicial system, built upon and embodying important regime values such as fairness, equity, and impartiality, plays a role in **legitimizing** our system of government as a whole. Finally, the judicial system performs an important **educative** function by dramatizing certain kinds of conflicts and by making clear to citizens what is right and wrong or acceptable and unacceptable in terms of both individual and governmental behaviour. Our courts teach governments to be better governments and citizens to be better citizens in the course of resolving specific disputes.

Before moving to a consideration of the structure of the courts in Canada, two caveats should be entered with respect to the adjudicative function. First, courts are not the exclusive instruments of dispute resolution, and second, judges are not exclusively preoccupied with courts. There are other mechanisms of dispute resolution, such as negotiation, conciliation, mediation, and arbitration, which are cheaper and often more effective than the formal legal apparatus of courts, judges, and lawyers. On the other hand, Canadian judges are often called upon to assume non-adjudicative roles as, for instance, royal commissioners. By taking on such non-judicial responsibilities, members of the judiciary perform important services for the system as a whole; at the same time, however, they can be exposed to political controversy that could compromise both the independence of the individual judge and the dignity and decorum of the judicial process in general.

### The Canadian Court System

Because Canada is a federal political system, it would be natural to expect that our judicial system would also be federal in nature. Indeed, there are both federal and provincial courts in Canada, and the powers and the responsibilities with respect to the administration of justice are divided up between the two levels of government. In contrast to the United States, where the federal and state courts exist separately from each other in *vertically* parallel hierarchies, each with its distinct jurisdiction, the Canadian system of courts divides provincial and federal court jurisdiction *horizontally*.

In the United States, the federal courts decide cases involving federal laws and jurisdiction while the state courts deal with matters of state law and jurisidiction. When a decision of a trial court is appealed, it is appealed to a higher court in the same hierarchy. For example, in the United States, criminal law is primarily a state matter;[11] hence, criminal cases arc tried and appealed only in state courts. For such cases, the final court of appeal is the supreme court of the state, and there is no appeal from the supreme court of the state to the Supreme Court of the United States except on constitutional issues.

In Canada, however, while there are separate provincial and federal courts, the eventual course of appeal may move from provincial courts to the Supreme Court of Canada. Thus, while criminal law is enacted by the federal government, all criminal cases are tried in provincial courts, and what determines whether a case can be appealed from the highest court of the province to the Supreme Court of Canada is not what government has legislative jurisdiction over the subject matter, but the seriousness of the issues being raised.

### The Hierarchy of Courts

Not only are the various provincial and federal courts integrated in terms of jurisdiction; they are also integrated, to some extent, through the process of appointment set down in the BNA Act. Sections 96–100 provide for the appointment, removal, and salaries of all "superior, county, and district" court judges in the provinces. These highest of provincial courts are set up and administered by the provinces pursuant to section 92(14) of the *Constitution Act*, 1867, which states that the provinces are responsible for the administration of justice. However, the judges are appointed and remunerated by the federal government.

Section 101 of the 1867 Act provides that the Parliament of Canada can set up its own courts, and it has done so. The most important federal courts are the Supreme Court of Canada, the Federal Court of Canada, and the Tax Court. As one would expect, the judges of the various federal courts are all appointed and paid for by the Government of Canada. Finally, there are also provincial courts. These are "lower courts" established by the province pursuant to section 92(14) and are presided over by **provincial court judges** who are appointed and remunerated by the provincial governments.

### The Provincial Courts

There is a significant variation from province to province in the nomenclature applied to the provincial court system, but the functions that are performed by the various levels of the provincial judiciary are remarkably similar. We will attempt here to make some generalizations about the provincial courts, and in the final section of the chapter we will say a bit more about the new trends emerging in Ontario and elsewhere with respect to the increasing amalgamation of the provincial courts into a single judiciary.

---

11. There are, as well, in the United States, "federal crimes," which are tried in federal courts.

**TABLE 24.1**

The Judicial Hierarchy in Canada

|  | Description | Examples |
|---|---|---|
| Federal Courts | • established pursuant to Section 101, *Constitution Act,* 1867<br>• judges federally appointed<br>• judges remunerated by federal government | • Supreme Court of Canada<br>• Federal Court of Canada<br>• Tax Court<br>• Citizenship Courts |
| "Section 96" Courts | • established pursuant to Section 96, *Constitution Act,* 1867<br>• judges federally appointed<br>• judges remunerated by federal government<br>• courts created by provincial statute | • Provincial Trial Courts<br>  • Superior Courts<br>  • County and District Courts<br>  • Surrogate Courts<br>• Court of Appeal |
| Provincial Courts | • established pursuant to Section 92(14), *Constitution Act,* 1867<br>• judges provincially appointed<br>• judges remunerated by provincial governments | • Lower Trial Courts<br>  • Criminal Courts<br>  • Civil Courts<br>  • Family Courts<br>  • Youth Courts |
| Justices of the Peace | • established pursuant to Section 92(14), *Constitution Act,* 1867<br>• appointed by provinces *at pleasure* | • Provincial Offences Court<br>• Traffic Court |

**The Lower Provincial Courts** While the practice varies a lot from province to province, the jurisdiction of provincial judges includes presiding over the provincial criminal, civil, and family courts, as well as presiding over the youth court in criminal matters under the *Young Offenders Act.* Some provinces maintain separate courts for each of these functions, while others have set up a single provincial court but with different *divisions* for each of the four main areas of jurisdiction. The tendency across Canada, however, is for a greater integration of the provincial trial-court systems.

The **criminal jurisdiction** of the provincial courts extends to all summary conviction offences, certain indictable offences specified in the Criminal Code, indictable offences where the accused has opted for the speedier lower court process, preliminary hearings, and all provincial offences. The civil or **small-claims jurisdiction** of the provincial courts is primarily concerned with claims for debts up to a monetary maximum, which varies from province to province and ranges from $1000 to as high as $4000. The aim in small-claims courts is to make the process speedy, affordable, and simple, and while litigants may choose to be represented by counsel, it is not necessary in a growing number of provinces.

The **family-court jurisdiction** of the lower provincial courts includes issues of maintenance, child custody, adoption, and guardianship, and a few criminal matters such as spousal assault. The family court jurisdiction at one time included juvenile offences, but since the passage of the *Young Offenders Act* in 1985, many provinces have set up separate **youth courts** that deal with both young offenders and matters under the *Child Welfare Act.* Several provinces, including Ontario, have opted to set up a **unified family court** in which both family and youth court cases are heard by superior court judges.

**Section 96 Courts** The organization of superior, county, and district courts varies a great deal from province to province, but in functional terms the jurisdiction of section 96 judges is very similar across the country. The county or district courts have jurisdiction over indictable offences if the accused *elects* to be tried in this court, and the trial can be before a judge sitting alone or with a jury. The civil jurisdiction of these courts is limited monetarily and kicks in at the lower end at the *ceiling* for small-claims court jurisdiction. The county or district court judge also hears appeals from summary-conviction criminal cases and from provincial civil or small-claims courts. The jurisdiction of county and district courts has also normally been limited territorially, with the judge presiding over cases within a set geographical area.

There is also a **surrogate court**, which has a geographically limited jurisdiction (in most provinces) and deals with most testamentary matters, determination of minor financial claims against an estate, the appointment of guardians for the children of the deceased, and, generally, all such probate matters except interpretation of wills, administration of estates, and determination of actions for legacies. In most cases, the judge acting as **surrogate court judge** is the local county or district court judge.

The highest courts of first instance with general jurisdiction are the superior or supreme courts in each of the provinces. The **trial division** or **Court of Queen's Bench** functions with judges sitting singly, with or without jury, and has general jurisdiction unlimited as to monetary value in all civil matters. The criminal jurisdiction of these courts includes concurrent jurisdiction with lower courts for most indictable offences, and in the case of the most serious indictable offences, such as murder, the superior courts have exclusive jurisdiction. The superior courts also have jurisdiction over **administrative law** disputes emanating from provincial boards and tribunals, and judges of the highest provincial trial courts also hear *appeals* of summary convictions and decisions of the family courts.

The highest court in the province is the **court of appeal**, which functions as a general court of appeal for the province, hearing appeals from the lower courts, and delivering opinions on references by the lieutenant-governor-in-council. The provincial court of appeal hears cases from the superior court trial division, from the county or district courts, from surrogate courts if the issue is above a certain monetary amount, and from *Young Offenders Act* indictable offences.

### Federal Courts

The most important federal courts in Canada are the Supreme Court of Canada and the Federal Court of Canada. The Tax Court of Canada is also a federal court but is very limited in jurisdiction. The Tax Court, composed of fifteen judges, was set up to replace the Tax Review Board in 1983, and has appeal jurisdiction in respect of assessments under the *Income Tax Act* and the *Canada*

*Pension Plan.* The Federal Court and the Supreme Court of Canada, however, have much broader jurisdiction and bear further discussion.

**The Federal Court of Canada** The **Federal Court of Canada**, which replaced the Exchequer Court, was set up by the *Federal Court Act*, 1970. The Federal Court consists of a court of original jurisdiction, known as the **Trial Division**, and a court of appeal, known as the **Appeal Division**. The Federal Court is composed of a chief justice, who functions as the president of the Appeal Division, an associate chief justice, who functions as the president of the Trial Division, and up to twenty-nine *puisne* judges. Ten of the judges must be appointed to the Appeal Division and the rest are trial judges, although both trial and appeal judges are *ex officio* members of the other division as well. There is an additional requirement that at least four of the Federal Court judges must be appointed from among members of the bar or bench of the Province of Quebec. The basic requirements for appointment to the Federal Court are the same as for the Supreme Court of Canada, and tenure is during good behaviour until age seventy.

*Review and Appeal* In order to understand the jurisdiction of the Trial and Appeal divisions of the Federal Court it is necessary to remind the reader of the difference between **appeals** and judicial **review.** The right of appeal is a statutory right to have a higher court reconsider a decision of a lower court. In an appeal situation, the higher court may examine the *substance* of the lower court's decision and may *change* it. The result of the appeal can be that the appeal is denied and the decision of the lower court affirmed, or that the decision of the lower court is altered or reversed.

By contrast, judicial review is a power vested in superior courts that originated in the common law but which in most cases is now defined and clarified in statute. In the situation of review, the court is concerned not with the substance of the decision but with the manner in which the decision was taken by the lower court or tribunal. The remedies under judicial review permit the higher court to invalidate or quash the decision but not to replace the decision of the lower court with its own. In other words, in a situation of judicial review, the higher court tells the lower court not that its *decision* was incorrect but that it was taken in an unfair or inappropriate *manner* and must be decided over again, using the correct procedures.

*Trial Division* When the Federal Court was originally set up it was intended to have exclusive juridsdiction over a wide range of disputes involving the Crown as a litigant. However, in 1992 the *Federal Court Act* was amended to make *exclusive* jurisdiction the exception and *concurrent* jurisdiction with the provincial courts the more common rule. Today the Trial Division has exclusive jurisdiction only in matters such as the *review* and provision of equitable relief against the decisions of federal boards, tribunals, or commissions; issues of copyright, trademark, and patents; and some matters involving applications from members of the armed forces.

Where once matters of **Crown liability** were intended to be exclusively within the jurisdiction of the Trial Division, now such matters are shared with the provincial courts, a situation that makes the Government of Canada much more readily "sue-able" than it was previously. Other areas of concurrent jurisdiction with other courts include aeronautics, interprovincial public works, claims by the Crown, and bills of exchange and promissory notes. The Act also provides that the Trial Division retains **residuary** jurisdiction where no other Canadian court has jurisdiction, and that it may adjudicate federal-provincial disputes where the governments concerned agree.

As we discussed in the previous chapter, likely the most important role of the Trial Division of the Federal Court is in the general area of administrative law, where it can provide remedies against decisions of all federal administrative agencies, boards, and commissions with the exception of a few very important ones that are explicitly put under the scrutiny of the Appeal Division. Since 1993, the Trial Division has also assumed responsibility for applications in respect of immigration and refugee matters, and it hears appeals from citizenship courts.

*Appeal Division*  The jurisdiction of the Appeal Division of the Federal Court of Canada includes hearing appeals from the Trial Division of the Federal Court and appeals under a range of federal statutes. It also has the responsibility for the review of the decisions of specified federal boards, commissions, and tribunals. This latter *review* jurisdiction of the Federal Court is limited, by section 28 of the *Federal Court Act*, to specified bodies such as the Pension Appeals Board, the National Energy Board, the Public Service Staff Relations Board, the Canada Labour Relations Board, and the CRTC. The power of review here is vested in the Appeal Division rather than the Trial Division because not only are the bodies being overseen very important substantively, but they also function as though they were, themselves, courts.

The Appeal Division may quash a decision in which the federal board or tribunal has failed to observe the principles of natural justice, has gone beyond its jurisdiction, has made an error in law, or has based its decision on erroneous findings of fact. The Act provides, however, that there is no right of review if other legislation already provides for a statutory appeal to the Treasury Board, the governor-general-in-council, or the Supreme Court of Canada.

**The Supreme Court of Canada**  The **Supreme Court of Canada** is a superior court of common law and equity in and for Canada, and was established by the *Supreme Court Act* in 1875. The Supreme Court is composed of a chief justice and eight puisne judges, all appointed by the governor-general-in-council. An appointee must be a judge of a provincial superior court or a barrister of at least ten years' experience, and must take up residence within 40 kilometres of the National Capital Region. Justices hold office during good behaviour until age seventy-five and are removable by the governor-general-in-council on joint address of the Senate and the House of Commons. The Supreme Court sits only in Ottawa and has three sessions per annum.

An additional requirement set down explicitly in the *Supreme Court Act* and now protected by the *Constitution Act* of 1982 is that three of the nine judges must be appointed from the Quebec bench or bar in order to provide some expertise on the Supreme Court in the *Code civil* system. On appeal in civil cases from the province of Quebec, it is customary that at least two of the sitting judges be from that province but this is not mandatory.

The Supreme Court of Canada is a general court of appeal and does not have original jurisdiction except when a question of constitutional law is referred to the court by the governor-general-in-council. Five judges normally constitute a quorum, except that four judges may sit with the consent of the parties. The court hears criminal appeals **by leave** (with its own "permission") with the exception that if a decision of a provincial court of appeal was not unanimous there is a *right* of appeal. In civil matters, there is an appeal to the Supreme Court of Canada only by leave. Applications for *leave* to appeal in civil matters may be heard by as few as three justices. The Supreme Court of Canada also hears appeals from the highest provincial courts on constitutional references submitted by the provincial governments. In sum, the Supreme Court of Canada has all the powers of a superior court, and also, since the abolition of appeals to the Judicial Committee of the Privy Council in 1949, it functions as the final court of appeal for Canada.

Unlike the Judicial Committee of the Privy Council, which made its decisions by consensus, with a single law lord writing the judgement, decisions of the Supreme Court, and of the courts of appeal in the provinces, are now taken by a simple majority of the judges hearing the case. If the court is unanimous, usually one judge will be delegated the reponsibility for writing the judgement for the court. However, when the court is not unanimous, any judges who disagree with the majority decision may write a **dissenting opinion**, which is reported along with the majority judgement. As well, if a judge agrees with the majority decision, but for different reasons, he or she may include a **concurring judgement**, which outlines the different *ratio* or reasons for concurring with the majority. Only the majority decision of the court can establish a binding precedent, but, frequently, well-argued dissents may become persuasive to future courts.

▶ THE JUDICIAL SYSTEM: PROBLEMS, ISSUES, AND REFORM

All institutions of society are subject to the ebb and flow of social change and the unpredictable if inexorable whims of history, and the judicial system is no exception. The role of the courts in Canada has changed over time and the functions of the judiciary today are quite different from what the founders of our nation expected them to be. One of the most pronounced and most problematic changes identified in recent times has been the tendency for the courts to be less and less the **passive arbiters** of disputes over the meaning and application of laws passed by our elected representatives in legislatures and to be more and more drawn into the position where the judges must themselves become **active policy makers.**

This alleged new role for the judiciary has emerged in part because the judges themselves have come to approach the business of adjudication with a more *activist* judicial philosophy. However, more important than any activist "revolution" in judicial thinking in Canada has been the new roles thrust upon the judicial system by increased litigiousness in our society, greater involvement of the state in the day-to-day activities of its citizenry, and the introduction of vague new legal-moral frameworks for society such as the Charter of Rights and Freedoms. Certainly the caseload of the courts and the "job of judge" have changed radically and the ensuing problems have generated demands for reforms of the system. Some of the problems and some of the proposals for reform bear more detailed consideration.

### Accessibility and Efficiency

While one of the long-standing and ongoing criticisms of the judiciary has been its elite nature, in recent years there has been growing concern with the elitist nature of the legal process itself. The problem here is, in part, that it costs money to use our court systems. Lawyers' fees alone are beyond the means of many Canadians, and the legal process, especially in higher-level courts, is dominated exclusively by members of the legal profession. This means that lower-class Canadians and the non-charter ethnic-group Canadians tend to dominate the docket in the lower courts, and middle-class Canadians tend to dominate the business of the higher courts.

This stratification exists, in part, because the jurisdiction in civil matters is often determined by the amount of money involved. It is therefore to be expected that middle-class Canadians will appear before the higher courts more often simply because they, by definition, have more money. Similarly, there are definite correlations between certain criminal offences, which are dealt with by lower courts, and certain categoric groups in society such as aboriginal people and the lower socio-economic strata.

As well, when we turn to **appeal cases**, we find that such use of the courts, except in serious criminal offences, is almost exclusively restricted to more privileged Canadians. Here the legal system *can* be blamed, for the access to the avenues of appeal in our system is virtually closed to all but affluent Canadians by reasons of cost. Even **legal-aid** programs, which are in operation in all provinces, and which are aimed at providing free access to legal advice to those who cannot afford it, only begin to solve the problem. Many potential users of the legal-aid system don't even know of its existence, and those that have discovered the program often find that they end up being represented by a green, if earnest and well-meaning, recent graduate of the bar-admissions course. Legal aid, therefore, is a step in the right direction, but it is only a step, and the existing legal-aid system likely could be improved both in terms of accessibility and in terms of the quality of legal advice available to its clients.

The other area of difficulty faced by the judicial system is the rapidly increasing caseload that must be dealt with. The number of cases waiting to be heard is expanding much more quickly than the number of judges available to hear them. This has created enormous backlogs and very long waiting periods that are unfair, particularly to those cooling their heels in jail while they wait for their criminal cases to be heard. In some provinces significant numbers of cases have been thrown out without coming to trial at all on the grounds that the delay in bringing the defendants to trial constituted a denial of a *fair* trial under the provisions of the Charter.

The responses to this overload on the system at the level of the trial court have included obvious solutions such as increasing the number of judges and streamlining criminal procedure in non-indictable offences. As well, however, most provinces have begun to overhaul their entire court systems in order to make them more efficient. Because Ontario has gone as far as any province in this respect, we will look briefly at the nature of the changes already undertaken and those planned for in the future in that province.

**The Ontario Court Reforms** In 1984, the *Judicature Act* of Ontario was replaced by the *Courts of Justice Act*, which, with the significant amendments in 1989, is today the statutory basis of the current court system in Ontario. There are two core principles of the new Ontario justice system. The first is that all of the province's courts except for the **Court of Appeal** are *amalgamated* or merged into a single **Ontario Court of Justice**, which is divided into a **General Division**, made up of all of the section 96 judges in the province, and a **Provincial Division**, composed of all of the provincially appointed judges. The reason for this amalgamation is that while judges can, as in the past, specialize in certain kinds of cases, if a family-law specialist, for instance, is not busy, he or she can be reassigned to hear cases in an area where there is a significant backlog.

**Figure 24.3**
The Ontario court system.

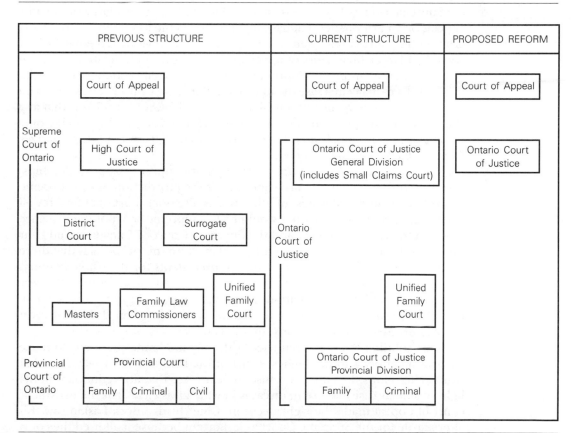

Source: Adapted from G. Gall, *The Canadian Legal System* (Toronto: Carswell, 1990), p. 159.

The second core principle of the new Ontario system is that the courts are now decentralized so that the administration of the courts and the assignment of cases to judges is done regionally. Again this is beneficial because it allows the **senior judge** and the **chief administrator** of the region to allocate the available judges and court resources in such a way as to fit the special needs of the region. On the whole, the combination of amalgamation of the courts and decentralization of the judicial process has helped to make the Ontario system more accessible and more efficient than in the past.

The ultimate plan in Ontario is to amalgamate the system totally so that there is a court of appeal and a single, unified Ontario Court of Justice that includes both section 96 and provincially appointed judges. While there would continue to be specialized court proceedings within the system, and while judges would continue individually to specialize in certain types of proceedings, any judge would be able to fill in on any court if the docket pressures in any region should shift from one type of proceeding to another. However, to fully implement this totally amalgamated court system, it is likely that the Constitution would have to be amended to allow provincially appointed judges to take on the responsibilities of section 96 courts.

**Supreme Court of Canada**   The caseload at the top of our judicial hierarchy has also become virtually unmanageable. The reason for the backlog of cases in the Supreme Court of Canada is, in part, that there are a very large number of appeals on Charter issues that have emerged from the lower courts. The Government of Canada has been hesitant to take the obvious remedial step of creating a larger final court of appeal, in part because the legitimacy of the system depends upon the Supreme Court being seen to be a very special tribunal. To casually increase the number of Supreme Court justices would be seen as *diluting* the quality of our highest jurists. However, it is likely that any change in the composition of the court, would, in any event, be possible only through a constitutional amendment because of the guarantee of three judges from the bar or bench of Quebec.

Given the difficulty of simply creating more Supreme Court judgeships, another proferred solution has been to limit the jurisdiction of the Supreme Court to constitutional issues. In other words, the final court of appeal for all cases except constitutional ones would be the supreme court of the province in which the case originated, and the Supreme Court of Canada would hear only constitutional issues. One of the problems with this proposal is that there would cease to be a unified set of judicial precedents for the whole country, which, particularly in areas such as criminal law, would run contrary to the very idea of a single integrated nation. Moreover, this would not go very far in reducing the heavy caseload of the Supreme Court, given that the largest number of cases it hears are constitutional anyway.

One solution that has been tried with only moderate success is to make virtually all appeals to the highest court of the land to be "by leave" of that court. This allows the court to refuse to hear cases that are redundant in the light of similar cases before it, or cases in which it is clear that the provincial court of appeal made the right decision. Chief Justice Bora Laskin saw this altered role for the Supreme Court as important because it allowed the court to have greater control over its own docket. At the same time, Laskin was pleased that the changes "blunted the case that could be made for *limiting* the Supreme Court of Canada to federal and constitutional issues."[12] Instead, the court's role has changed, according to Laskin, from a "general appellate tribunal in the traditional sense" to a **supervisory tribunal**, mandated to grant leave to appeal only where

> any question involved therein is, by reason of its public importance, or the importance of any issue of law, or any issue of mixed law and fact involved in such question, one that ought to be decided by the Supreme Court.[13]

One down side of this has proven to be the amount of time the Supreme Court has had to spend hearing **motions for leave**, and the other has been that the judges of the highest court seem to be reluctant *not* to hear a case if there is any doubt about the answers to questions of law in the provincial courts of appeal. They tend to err, perhaps wisely, on the side of granting rather than refusing leave if there is any doubt. The end result is that the docket of the Supreme Court is no less full today than it has been in the recent past.

### Democracy and the Judicial Process

The involvement of provincial nomination committees in the appointment of section 96 judges has helped to reduce the amount of partisan bias in the selection process, and any further evolution in this direction can only improve the independence and credibility, if not the operational effectiveness, of the courts. Beyond the claims of partisanship in the appointment process, what the critics of the Canadian judiciary also claim is that the judiciary is an elite group and unrepresentative of the society over which it has so much power.

Judges are naturally an elite group, because of the relatively few judgeships that are available in Canada, and because of the special qualifications one must have to become a judge. Because judges must be lawyers first, the socio-economic and ethnic composition of the judiciary is reflective of the biases in the legal profession itself. Hence, the judiciary in Canada is, indeed, dominated by ethnic charter-group and middle-class Canadians. Despite the gains that have been made by women in the legal profession generally in the past two decades, they are still under-represented in appointments to the bench. While women comprise about 25 per cent of the legal profession in Canada and are over 40 per cent of those registered in Canadian law schools, of the nearly two thousand judgeships in Canada, fewer than two hundred are female. Two of the nine judges of the Supreme Court of Canada in 1995 are women.

That the judiciary in Canada is an **educational elite** is incontrovertible. However, to have a non-elite judiciary in a system built on the premise of judicial independence is likely impossible. Most Canadians would agree that it is better to be judged by a well-trained professional who is paid to be an *objective* arbiter of disputes and not an advocate or representative of any particular ethnic group, social stratum, region, or point of view. This means that judgeships will continue to be limited to members of the legal profession, and that

12.  Bora Laskin, cited in Morton, *Law, Politics and the Judicial Process,* p. 50.
13.  Ibid.

any significant improvement in the ethnic and class representativeness of the Canadian judiciary will depend upon democratizing the law schools and the legal profession in general, and not upon making structural changes to the legal system.

**Judicial Independence and the Supreme Court of Canada**  The Supreme Court of Canada has been subjected to criticism since its creation in 1875, and it narrowly escaped abolition at several points in its history. However, since the abolition of appeals to the Judicial Committee of the Privy Council in 1949, when the Supreme Court of Canada became our final court of appeal, its position has been secure. The question now is not whether Canada needs a supreme court, but rather how the existing one can be improved.

*Partisanship and Appointments*  Much of the criticism of the Supreme Court has been levelled at the method of appointment of the judges, which is done exclusively by the federal government and often appears to be based, at least in part, on partisan considerations. That is not to say that a government will appoint a bad lawyer to the bench just because he or she is a loyal supporter, but rather that the government will find a good lawyer who is sympathetic to the government's approach and give that person the appointment. Basically, the argument against appointments to the bench that take such variables into account is that it may compromise the principle of a truly independent judiciary.

Being human, of course, no judge is ever really independent in an absolute way. The judge is influenced by all sorts of personal preferences and biases, and will tend to interpret the law in such a way that the decision made is congruent with personal values. A few exploratory studies of judicial behaviour have indicated that judges often take characteristic and predictable stands when particular issues are involved.[14] However, none of these studies has indicated that there is a positive correlation in Canada between the stand a judge takes on issues and the tenets of the political party that appointed the judge to the bench.

Most legal experts feel that Supreme Court judges should be selected with some formal participation on the part of the existing bench, the Canadian Bar Association, or both. The arguments in favour of participation by the existing bench or the Canadian Bar Association contend that in order to get the best judges, the selection should be made not so much by a non-partisan body as by, or with the advice of, a body of experts who have some knowledge about the requirements and qualifications of a good judge. Such reform could be achieved informally, by simply co-opting the Canadian Bar Association into the selection process while continuing to make the formal appointment as provided in sections 96–101 of the BNA Act.

14. D. E. Fouts, "Policy Making in the Supreme Court of Canada, 1950–60," and S. R. Peck, "A Scalogram Analysis of the Supreme Court of Canada, 1958–67," both *in* G. Schubert and D. J. Danelski, eds., *Comparative Behaviour* (Toronto: Oxford University Press, 1969), pp. 257–334. A study was also done for the Royal Commission on the Economic Union and Development Prospects for Canada (Macdonald Commission) entitled, "The Social Attitudes of Judges of the Supreme Court of Canada," by Robert Martin, 1985.

*Provincial Representation* The question being raised by many critics of the current practice is not so much about *partisan* bias, but whether Supreme Court judges should be appointed in a manner that is more responsive to the dominant social forces in the society rather than leaving the decision either to the party in power or to an advisory nominating committee that is over-representative of the legal profession. It *is* possible, of course, to make a case for a democratically *representative* Supreme Court. In some democratic regimes, judges are even popularly elected. While most Canadians would not go so far as to suggest that our highest court judges should be elected, there seems to be a sense that non-elite Canadians' opinions should be brought to bear on the appointment decision.

One suggestion has been that, because they are "closer" to the people, and certainly more representative of the people in given regions, the provincial governments or legislatures should be given some control over the appointment of Supreme Court judges. The utility of provincial participation in the process of appointing justices to a court that so significantly affects their interests has been recognized in the constitutional reform proposals of the late 1980s and early 1990s. Here it was proposed that Supreme Court judges be appointed only from lists submitted to the attorney-general of Canada by the provincial governments.

Proponents of specific regional or provincial quotas on the Supreme Court argue that the court is *already* regionally representative in that three of the nine judges must be appointed from the bar or bench of Quebec. Providing for the representation of other regions on the highest court, it is argued, is simply an extension of the principle that already applies with respect to Quebec. However, the aim of the *Supreme Court Act* is not to represent *Quebec* in constitutional cases, but to ensure that there are judges sitting on the highest court of the land who have the legal training to be able to effectively cope with civil appeals from Quebec courts.

Finally, the point can be made that, by custom, the Supreme Court of Canada *is* representative of the various regions of the country in terms of the province of origin of the nine judges. Three judges must be from Quebec and, by convention, three are normally from Ontario (although Brian Mulroney recently replaced an Ontario female judge with an Alberta male), and there is one each from the Atlantic region, the prairie provinces, and British Columbia. Moreover, the *practice* of filling vacancies by this sort of informal formula is born out by evidence marshalled by Peter Russell and by MacKay and Bauman.[15]

What is implicit in proposals that the justices be selected proportionally from the various regions of Canada is the principle of a **representative judiciary**. The inherent flaw in these sorts of proposals is that they would effectively scuttle the constitutional principle of judicial independence, for there is no way that a representative judiciary can function *independently* — the justices would be expected, quite naturally, to reflect the interests of the region from

---

15. P. H. Russell, *The Supreme Court of Canada as a Bilingual and Bicultural Institution* (Ottawa: Queen's Printer, 1969), p. 64; MacKay and Bauman, "The Supreme Court of Canada . . ." *in* Beckton and MacKay, eds., *The Courts and the Charter*, (Toronto: University of Toronto Press, 1985), p. 72.

**TABLE 24.2**

Regional Representation of Supreme Court Judges at Selected Dates, 1875–1995

| Date | Atlantic Provinces | Western Provinces | Quebec | Ontario | Total |
|------|-------------------|-------------------|--------|---------|-------|
| 1875 | 2 | 0 | 2 | 2 | 6 |
| 1888 | 1 | 0 | 2 | 3 | 6 |
| 1893 | 2 | 0 | 2 | 2 | 6 |
| 1903 | 2 | 1 | 2 | 1 | 6 |
| 1905 | 2 | 0 | 2 | 2 | 6 |
| 1906 | 1 | 1 | 2 | 2 | 6 |
| 1924 | 0 | 1 | 2 | 3 | 6 |
| 1927 | 0 | 2 | 2 | 3 | 7 |
| 1932 | 1 | 2 | 2 | 2 | 7 |
| 1949 | 1 | 2 | 3 | 3 | 9 |
| 1979 | 1 | 3 | 3 | 2 | 9 |
| 1982 | 1 | 2 | 3 | 3 | 9 |
| 1986 | 1 | 2 | 3 | 3 | 9 |
| 1995 | 1 | 3 | 3 | 2 | 9 |

Source: Adapted from P. H. Russell, *The Supreme Court of Canada as a Bilingual and Bicultural Institution* (Ottawa: Queen's Printer, 1969), and MacKay and Bauman, "Reform Implications," in Beckton and MacKay, eds., *The Courts and the Charter* (Toronto: University of Toronto Press, 1985).

which they were appointed. Through what, on the surface, is mere institutional "fiddling" with the Supreme Court, we could end up with a judicial process that replaces impartiality with advocacy as the *modus operandi* of judicial decision-making.

### The Supreme Court and Judicial Policy-Making

An important theme that has emerged in critical writings on the role of the Supreme Court is that it is less a passive arbitrator of legal disputes and more and more engaged in what can only be described as policy-making. This has been described by Michael Mandel as the "legalization of politics," and by Peter Russell as the politicization of the judiciary.[16] Whichever way we look at it, the point is that the role of the judiciary *is* changing qualitatively as well as in terms of an enlarged caseload, and we must ask why this is happening.

**The Changing Role of the Judiciary**  Mandel sees the trend towards the legalization of politics as inexorably linked to the enactment of the Charter of Rights and Freedoms in 1982. Russell, on the other hand, states that while the Charter clearly "deals the judiciary into a wider range of political issues,"[17] the political or policy role of the judiciary in Canada is not new:

16. Michael Mandel, *The Charter of Rights and the Legalization of Politics in Canada* (Toronto: Thompson, 1994); and P. H. Russell, *The Judiciary in Canada* (Toronto: McGraw-Hill Ryerson, 1987).
17. Russell, *The Judiciary in Canada*, p. 5.

While it is undoubtedly true that a constitutional Charter of Rights will expand the policy-making role of Canadian courts, it is misleading to imply that the Canadian courts have had no significant policy-making role in the past.[18]

Canada has inherited from the English legal tradition the principle that the courts should interpret only the *words* written down in statutes and not attempt to divine the intentions of the legislators. As well, the Canadian courts have tended to look at the law literally as it was originally written instead of interpreting it in such a way that it makes sense in a contemporary context. Despite this avowed **literalist** or *structuralist* mode of interpretation, however, both the Judicial Committee of the Privy Council and the Supreme Court of Canada have from time to time used considerable imagination in rationalizing decisions that, on the surface, do not appear consistent with either the letter of the law or the stated intentions of the lawmakers.

It is in this sense that Peter Russell's view that the courts to some extent have always had an active policy role in Canada is more accurate than the notion that judicial policy-making began with the Charter. In a 1982 article, Russell argued, convincingly, that a trend towards the admission of extrinsic evidence in deciding constitutional issues in the late 1970s and early 1980s formed a clear message, and that the Supreme Court is beginning to recognize that it has a social-policy responsibility, as well as its more traditional responsibility as a passive adjudicator of legal disputes.[19]

**The Courts and the Charter** On the other hand, we must agree with Mandel to the extent that our *awareness* of this policy role of judges was awakened with the series of Charter cases that have been decided since 1982. It is true that the courts, before 1982, transformed our federal system and built our common law by engaging in more than merely passive interpretation of words in statutes, but it was the Charter that allowed us to "unmask"[20] the true face of judicial decision-making in Canada. Up until the Charter it was possible for our courts to put a spin on their interpretations and still maintain the veil of objectivity and judicial independence, but because the Charter provisions are so broad and so vague, and because there was no body of precedent to work from, the courts were forced to make it up as they went along in arriving at many important decisions. It is obvious from reading these judgements that they contain *normative* as well as *objective* components.

The experiences of the first four years of cases involving the Charter of Rights and Freedoms indicated that the judiciary was willing to take a more activist role, particularly with respect to procedural rights in criminal matters and the determination of "reasonableness" under section 1. In its initial decisions, the Supreme Court justices gave notice that "they would interpret this constitutional Charter much more liberally and sympathetically than their predecessors had interpreted the statutory Bill of Rights."[21] This prediction by

18. Peter Russell,"The Effect of a Charter of Rights on the Policy-Making Role of Canadian Courts," *Canadian Public Administration,* vol. 25, no. 1, Spring 1982, p. 2.
19. Ibid., p. 5.
20. Russell, *The Judiciary in Canada,* p. 4.
21. P. Russell, "The First Three Years in Charterland," *Canadian Public Administration,* vol. 28, no. 3, Fall 1985, p. 385.

Peter Russell has been borne out in the decisions of the Supreme Court in Charter cases since. The justices have been willing to take the bull by the horns and demonstrate that they indeed are putting current issues into current political and social contexts.

**Judicial Philosophies** While there is clear evidence that the Charter has resulted in the transfer of some policy decision-making from the legislative and executive arena to the adjudicative, the extent of that transfer has been limited. One possible explanation of this residual hesitancy to move abruptly to a more American style of "activist-socially conscious" judicial decision-making is that the judges of the Supreme Court have by no means been in total agreement as to the wisdom of this shift in role.

In fact, the battle lines in this debate were being drawn up several years ago, when Chief Justice Bora Laskin (dissenting) and his successor, Brian Dickson, set down their different philosophies with respect to the role of the Supreme Court. Laskin chose the more activist role, decrying the "mechanical deference to *stare decisis*." Dickson was hesitant about the court's being more "creative," and opted for a more conservative role for the court. He thought the court should "proceed in the discharge of its adjudicative functions in a reasoned way from principled decisions and established concepts."[22]

As confirmation of the possibility of a philosophical split among members of the Supreme Court of Canada, we can cite some very candid observations by Bertha Wilson, a Supreme Court justice at the time, which were made in a series of lectures at the University of Toronto Law School. As reported by Southam News, Justice Wilson stated: "You have judges who think it is more important to be consistent than to be correct, those who see caution as a virtue and denigrate 'much speaking.' "[23] According to the Southam News report,

> Wilson used rhetorical devices to let her sophisticated audience know that a real intellectual donnybrook is raging in the inner chambers of the Supreme Court. Listeners winced when she described "pruning shears" taken to the decisions of activist judges.[24]

While the use of the term "donnybrook" may have reflected a bit of journalistic licence, and the "wincing" may have had Freudian explanations, it seems clear that there were and are differences among our Supreme Court justices as to the appropriate role of the court.

In the 1995 Supreme Court, only the chief justice, Antonio Lamer, was appointed by someone other than Brian Mulroney, and it is likely fair to say that the current crop of judges are, on the whole, a tad to the conservative side of an already conservative vocational group. Nevertheless, the court's docket is large and the backlog of cases is daunting, so we are guaranteed that the *amount* of judicial output will continue to be prolific. Moreover, the court may not be "conservative" in terms of judicial philosophy. It is possible that the contemporary Supreme Court may turn out to be *activist* in incorporating socially and economically conservative values into its Charter decisions.

---

22. *Harrison v. Carswell* (1976) 2 SCR 200.
23. Peter Calamai, *Ottawa Citizen,* November 30, 1985.
24. Ibid.

It is clear that a combination of new issues in federal-provincial relations and the advent of the Charter of Rights and Freedoms have forced both the judges themselves and academic analysts of the judicial process to rethink the traditional model of Canadian judicial decision-making. What is perhaps still more important is the possibility that our political leaders see the Supreme Court as a handy mechanism for avoiding difficult decisions in highly divisive policy issues such as abortion, spousal benefits for gay couples, and the right to physician-assisted suicides. The jury is still out (get it?!) with respect to coming to a definite conclusion as to the changing role of the Supreme Court in the Canadian political process — passive adjudicator or activist policy-maker. Only time will tell.

► FURTHER READING: PART FIVE
GOVERNMENT

### Parliament

Atkinson, Mike. "Parliamentary Government in Canada," *in* M. S. Whittington and G. Williams, *Canadian Politics in the 1990s*. Scarborough: Nelson, 1994, pp. 360–81.

Campbell, Colin. *The Canadian Senate: A Lobby from Within*. Toronto: Macmillan, 1978.

Canada. House of Commons. *Standing Orders*. September 1994.

Clarke, Harold, F. Q. Quo, and A. Goddard. *Parliament, Policy and Representation*. Toronto: Methuen, 1980.

Courtney, John, ed. *The Canadian House of Commons: Essays in Honour of Norman Ward*. Calgary: University of Calgary Press, 1985.

d'Aquino, Thomas, Bruce Doern, and Cassandra Blair. *Parliamentary Democracy in Canada: Issues for Reform*. Toronto: Methuen, 1983.

Fleming, R. J. *Canadian Legislatures*. Ottawa: Ampersand, 1988.

Franks, C. E. S. *The Parliament of Canada*. Toronto: University of Toronto Press, 1987.

Fraser, Alistair, W. F. Dawson, and J. Holtby. *Beauchesne's Rules and Forms of the House of Commons of Canada*. Toronto: Carswell, 1989.

Frazer, John. *The House of Commons at Work*. Montreal: Les Éditions de la Chenelière, 1993.

Jackson, Bob, and Michael Atkinson. *The Canadian Legislative System*. Toronto: Macmillan, 1980.

Kornberg, Alan, and William Mishler. *Influence in Parliament*. Durham: Duke Press, 1976.

Kunz, F. A. *The Modern Senate of Canada*. Toronto: University of Toronto Press, 1965.

Stewart, J. *The Canadian House of Commons*. Montreal: McGill-Queen's University Press, 1977.


### Cabinet

Aucoin, Peter. "Organizational Change in the Machinery of Government: From Rational Management to Brokerage Politics," *Canadian Journal of Political Science*, March 1986, pp. 3–15.

Axworthy, Tom. "Of Secretaries to Princes," *Canadian Public Administration*, Summer 1988, pp. 247–64.

Bakvis, H. *Regional Ministers: Power and Influence in the Canadian Cabinet*. Toronto, University of Toronto Press, 1991.

French, Richard. *How Ottawa Decides*. Toronto: Lorimer, 1984.

Canada. *Guide to Canadian Ministries Since Confederation: July 1, 1887–February 1, 1982*. Ottawa: Supply and Services, 1982.

Mancuso, Maureen, R. Price, and R. Wagenberg. *Leaders and Leadership in Canada*. Toronto, Oxford University Press, 1994.

Matheson, William. *The Prime Minister and the Cabinet*. Toronto: Methuen, 1976.

Ondaatje, Christopher. *The Prime Ministers of Canada: Macdonald to Mulroney*. Toronto: Pagurian, 1985.

Pal, Leslie, and David Taras. *Prime Ministers and Premiers: Political Leadership and Public Policy in Canada*. Toronto: Prentice-Hall, 1988.

Punnett, R. M. *The Prime Minister in Canadian Government and Politics*. Toronto: Macmillan, 1977.

Smith, David. "The Federal Cabinet in Canadian Politics," *in* M. S. Whittington and
G. Williams, *Canadian Politics in the 1990s*. Scarborough: Nelson, 1994, pp. 382–401.

Sutherland, Sharon. "Responsible Government and Ministerial Responsibility: Every
Reform Is Its Own Problem," *Canadian Journal of Political Science*, March 1991, pp.
91–120.

Van Loon, Richard, and Mike Whittington. "Kaleidoscope in Grey: The Policy Process
in Ottawa," *in* M. S. Whittington and G. Williams, *Canadian Politics in the 1990s*.
Scarborough: Nelson, 1990, pp. 448–67.

Weller, Patrick. *First Among Equals: Prime Ministers in Westminster Systems*. London: Allen
and Unwin, 1985.

## Bureaucracy

Adie, R., and Paul Thomas. *Canadian Public Administration*. Scarborough: Prentice-Hall,
1987.

Bernier, I., and A. Lajoie. *Regulations, Crown Corporations and Administrative Tribunals*.
Toronto: University of Toronto Press, 1985.

Bourgault, J., and S. Dion. *The Changing Profile of Federal Deputy Ministers, 1887–1988*.
Ottawa: Centre for Management Development, 1990.

Brooks, Stephen. *Who's in Charge? The Mixed Ownership Corporation in Canada*. Halifax:
IRPP, 1987.

Brown-John, L. *Canadian Regulatory Agencies*. Toronto: Butterworths, 1981.

Canada. *Public Service 2000: The Renewal of the Public Service of Canada*. Ottawa: Supply
and Services, 1990.

Canada. *Public Service 2000: A Report on Progress*. Ottawa: Supply and Services, 1992.

Carleton University, School of Public Administration. *How Ottawa Spends*. Ottawa: Carleton University Press, Annual. (Edited by different scholars in different years).

Clark, J. D. *Getting the Incentives Right: Toward a Productivity-Oriented Management Framework for the Public Service*. Ottawa: Treasury Board, 1993.

Doern, Bruce, Allan Maslove, and Michael Prince. *Public Budgeting in Canada: Politics,
Economics and Management*. Ottawa: Carleton University Press, 1988.

Doerr, Audrey. *The Machinery of Government in Canada*. Toronto: Methuen, 1981.

Granatstein, J. L. *The Ottawa Men: Civil Service Mandarins 1935–57*. Toronto: Oxford
University Press, 1982.

Hardin, H. *The Privatization Putsch*. Halifax: IRPP, 1989.

Holland, D., and J. P. McGowan. *Delegated Legislation in Canada*. Toronto: Carswell,
1989.

Kernaghan, K., and John Langford. *The Responsible Public Servant*. Halifax: IRPP, 1990.

Kernaghan, K., and David Siegal. *Public Administration in Canada: A Text*. Scarborough:
Nelson, 1991.

Laux, Jeanne, and Maureen Molot. *State Capitalism: Public Enterprise in Canada*. Ithaca:
Cornell Press, 1988.

Osbaldeston, Gordon. *Keeping Deputy Ministers Accountable*. Toronto: McGraw-Hill Ryerson, 1989.

Osbaldeston, Gordon. *Organizing to Govern*. Toronto: McGraw-Hill Ryerson, 1992.

Pal, Leslie. "The Federal Bureaucracy: Reinventing the Links Between State and Society," *in* M. S. Whittington and G. Williams, *Canadian Politics in the 1990s*. Scarborough: Nelson, 1994, pp. 276–91.

Savoie, Donald. *The Politics of Public Spending in Canada*. Toronto: University of Toronto Press, 1990.

Sutherland, Sharon, and Bruce Doern. *Bureaucracy in Canada: Control and Reform*. Toronto: University of Toronto Press, 1985.

Whitaker, Reg. "Politicians and Bureaucrats in the Policy Process," *in* M. S. Whittington and G. Williams, *Canadian Politics in the 1990s*. Scarborough: Nelson, 1994, pp. 424–40.

## Judiciary

Gall, Gerald. *The Canadian Legal System*. Toronto: Carswell, 1990.

Mandel, Michael. *The Charter of Rights and the Legalization of Politics*. Toronto: Thompson, 1994.

Morton, F. L. *Law, Politics and the Judicial Process in Canada*. Calgary: University of Calgary Press, 1984.

Russell, Peter. *The Judiciary in Canada: The Third Branch of Government*. Toronto: McGraw-Hill Ryerson, 1987.

Snell, J. G., and Frederick Vaughan. *The Supreme Court of Canada: History of the Institution*. Toronto: The Osgoode Society, 1985.

# Constitution Acts, 1867 to 1982*

FOREWORD

This consolidation contains the text of the *Constitution Act, 1867* (formerly the *British North America Act, 1867*), together with amendments made to it since its enactment, and the text of the *Constitution Act, 1982*, as amended by the *Constitution Amendment Proclamation, 1983*. The *Constitution Act, 1982* contains the *Canadian Charter of Rights and Freedoms* and other new provisions, including the procedure for amending the Constitution of Canada.

The *Constitution Act, 1982* also contains a Schedule of repeals of certain constitutional enactments and provides for the renaming of others. The *British North America Act, 1949*, for example, is renamed in the Schedule, the *Newfoundland Act*. The new names of these enactments are used in this consolidation, but their former names may be found in the Schedule.

The *Constitution Act, 1982*, was enacted as Schedule B to the *Canada Act 1982* (U.K.) 1982, c. 11. It is set out in this consolidation as a separate Act after the *Constitution Act, 1867*, and the *Canada Act 1982* is contained in the first footnote thereto.

The law embodied in the *Constitution Act, 1867* has been altered many times otherwise than by direct amendment, not only by the Parliament of the United Kingdom, but also by the Parliament of Canada and the legislatures of the provinces in those cases where provisions of that Act are expressed to be subject to alteration by Parliament or the legislatures. A consolidation of the Constitution Acts with only such subsequent enactments as directly alter the text of the Act would therefore not produce a true statement of the law. In preparing this consolidation an attempt has been made to reflect accurately the substance of the law contained in enactments modifying the provisions of the *Constitution Act, 1867*.

The various classes of enactments modifying the text of the *Constitution Act, 1867*, have been dealt with as follows:

---

* Reproduced with permission of the Minister of Supply and Services Canada.

## I.  DIRECT AMENDMENTS

**1.** *Repeals*

Repealed provisions (e.g. section 2) have been deleted from the text and quoted in a footnote.

Amended provisions (e.g. section 4) are reproduced in the text in their amended form and the original provisions are quoted in a footnote.

**3.** *Additions*

Added provisions (e.g. section 51(A) are included in the text.

**4.** *Substitutions*

Substituted provisions (e.g. section 18) are included in the text, and the former provision is quoted in a footnote.

## II.  INDIRECT AMENDMENTS

**1.** *Alterations by United Kingdom Parliament*

Provisions altered by the United Kingdom Parliament otherwise than by direct amendment (e.g. section 21) are included in the text in their altered form, and the original provision is quoted in a footnote.

**2.** *Additions by United Kingdom Parliament*

Constitutional provisions added otherwise than by the insertion of additional provisions in the *Constitution Act, 1867* (e.g. provisions of the *Constitution Act, 1871* authorizing Parliament to legislate for any territory not included in a province) are not incorporated in the text, but the additional provisions are quoted in an appropriate footnote.

**3.** *Alterations by Parliament of Canada*

Provisions subject to alteration by the Parliament of Canada (e.g. section 37) have been included in the text in their altered form, wherever possible, but where this was not feasible (e.g. section 40) the original section has been retained in the text and a footnote reference made to the Act of the Parliament of Canada effecting the alteration.

**4.** *Alterations by the Legislatures*

Provisions subject to alteration by legislatures of the provinces, either by virtue of specific authority (e.g. sections 83, 84) or by virtue of head 1 of section 92 (e.g. sections 70, 72), have been included in the text in their original form, but the footnotes refer to the provincial enactments effecting the alteration. Amendments to provincial enactments are not referred to; these may be readily found by consulting the indexes to provincial statutes. The enactments of the original provinces only are referred to; there are corresponding enactments by the provinces created at a later date.

## III.  SPENT PROVISIONS

Footnote references are made to those sections that are spent or are probably spent. For example, section 119 became spent by lapse of time and the footnote reference so indicates; on the other hand, section 140 is probably spent, but short of examining all statutes passed before Confederation there would be no way of ascertaining definitely whether or not the section is spent; the footnote reference therefore indicates the section as being probably spent.

The enactments of the United Kingdom Parliament or the Parliament of Canada, the Orders in Council admitting territories, referred to in the footnotes, may be found in Appendix II to the

Revised Statutes of Canada, 1970, and in the subsequent sessional volumes of the statutes of Canada.

The reader will notice inconsistencies in the capitalization of nouns. It was originally the practice to capitalize the first letter of all nouns in British statutes and the *Constitution Act, 1867*, was so written, but this practice was discontinued and was never followed in Canadian statutes. In the original provisions included in this consolidation nouns are written as they were enacted.

**********

This consolidation contains material prepared by the late Dr. E. A. Driedger, Q.C., which was last published by the Department of Justice in 1982 under the title *The Constitution Acts, 1867 to 1982*. The material has been updated where necessary but the Department gratefully acknowledges Dr. Driedger's earlier work.

## THE CONSTITUTION ACT, 1867

30 & 31 Victoria, c. 3.

(Consolidated with amendments)

An Act for the Union of Canada, Nova Scotia, and New Brunswick, and the Government thereof; and for Purposes connected therewith.

*(29th March, 1867.)*

Whereas the Provinces of Canada, Nova Scotia and New Brunswick have expressed their Desire to be federally united into One Dominion under the Crown of the United Kingdom of Great Britain and Ireland, with a Constitution similar in Principle to that of the United Kingdom:

And whereas such a Union would conduce to the Welfare of the Provinces and promote the Interests of the British Empire:

And whereas on the Establishment of the Union by Authority of Parliament it is expedient, not only that the Constitution of the Legislative Authority in the Dominion be provided for, but also that the Nature of the Executive Government therein be declared:

And whereas it is expedient that Provision be made for the eventual Admission into the Union of other Parts of British North America: (1)

### 1.—PRELIMINARY.

Short title.

**1.** This Act may be cited as the *Constitution Act, 1867*. (2)

**2.** Repealed. (3)

---

(1) The enacting clause was repealed by the *Statute Law Revision Act, 1893*, 56-57 Vict., c. 14 (U.K.). It read as follows:

Be it therefore enacted and declared by the Queen's Most Excellent Majesty, by and with the Advice and Consent of the Lords Spiritual and Temporal, and Commons, in this present Parliament assembled, and by the Authority of the same, as follows:

(2) As enacted by the *Constitution Act, 1982*, which came into force on April 17, 1982. The section, as originally enacted, read as follows:

1. This Act may be cited as The British North America Act, 1867.

(3) Section 2, repealed by the *Statute Law Revision Act, 1893*, 56-57 Vict., c. 14 (U.K.), read as follows.

2. The Provisions of this Act referring to Her Majesty the Queen extend also to the Heirs and Successors of Her Majesty, Kings and Queens of the United Kingdom of Great Britain and Ireland.

## II.–UNION.

Declaration
of Union.

**3.** It shall be lawful for the Queen, by and with the Advice of Her Majesty's Most Honourable Privy Council, to declare by Proclamation that, on and after a Day therein appointed, not being more than Six Months after the passing of this Act, the Provinces of Canada, Nova Scotia, and New Brunswick shall form and be One Dominion under the Name of Canada; and on and after that Day those Three Provinces shall form and be One Dominion under that Name accordingly. (4)

Construction
of subsequent
Provisions of
Act.

**4.** Unless it is otherwise expressed or implied, the Name Canada shall be taken to mean Canada as constituted under this Act. (5)

Four
Provinces.

**5.** Canada shall be divided into Four Provinces, named Ontario, Quebec, Nova Scotia, and New Brunswick. (6)

---

(4) The first day of July, 1867, was fixed by proclamation dated May 22, 1867.

(5) Partially repealed by the *Statute Law Revision Act, 1893*, 56-57 Vict., c. 14 (U.K.). As originally enacted the section read as follows:

> **4.** The subsequent Provisions of this Act, shall, unless it is otherwise expressed or implied, commence and have effect on and after the Union, that is to say, on and after the Day appointed for the Union taking effect in the Queen's Proclamation; and in the same Provisions, unless it is otherwise expressed or impled, the Name Canada shall be taken to mean Canada as constituted under this Act.

(6) Canada now consists of ten provinces (Ontario, Quebec, Nova Scotia, New Brunswick, Manitoba, British Columbia, Prince Edward Island, Alberta, Saskatchewan and Newfoundland) and two territories (the Yukon Territory and the Northwest Territories).

The first territories added to the Union were Rupert's Land and the North-Western Territory, (subsequently designated the Northwest Territories), which were admitted pursuant to section 146 of the *Constitution Act, 1867* and the *Rupert's Land Act, 1868*, 31-32 Vict., c. 105 (U.K.), by the *Rupert's Land and North-Western Territory Order* of June 23, 1870, effective July 15, 1870. Prior to the admission of those territories the Parliament of Canada enacted *An Act for the temporary Government of Rupert's Land and the North-Western Territory when united with Canada* (32-33 Vict., c. 3), and the *Manitoba Act, 1870*, (33 Vict., c. 3), which provided for the formation of the Province of Manitoba.

British Columbia was admitted into the Union pursuant to section 146 of the *Constitution Act, 1867*, by the *British Columbia Terms of Union*, being Order in Council of May 16, 1871, effective July 20, 1871.

Prince Edward Island was admitted pursuant to section 146 of the *Constitution Act, 1867*, by the *Prince Edward Island Terms of Union*, being Order in Council of June 26, 1873, effective July 1, 1873.

On June 29, 1871, the United Kingdom Parliament enacted the *Constitution Act, 1871* (34-35 Vict., c. 28) authorizing the creation of additional provinces out of territories not included in any province. Pursuant to this statute, the Parliament of Canada enacted the *Alberta Act*, (July 20, 1905, 4-5 Edw. VII, c. 3) and the *Saskatchewan Act*, (July 20, 1905, 4-5 Edw. VII, c. 42), providing for the creation of the provinces of Alberta and Saskatchewan, respectively. Both these Acts came into force on Sept. 1, 1905.

Meanwhile, all remaining British possessions and territories in North America and the islands adjacent thereto, except the colony of Newfoundland and its dependencies, were admitted into the Canadian Confederation by the *Adjacent Territories Order*, dated July 31, 1880.

The Parliament of Canada added portions of the Northwest Territories to the adjoining provinces in 1912 by *The Ontario Boundaries Extension Act, 1912*, 2 Geo. V, c. 40, *The Quebec Boundaries Extension Act, 1912*, 2 Geo. V, c. 45 and *The Manitoba Boundaries Extension Act, 1912*, 2 Geo. V, c. 32, and further additions were made to Manitoba by *The Manitoba Boundaries Exentsion Act, 1930*, 20-21 Geo. V, c. 28.

The Yukon Territory was created out of the Northwest Territories in 1898 by *The Yukon Territory Act*, 61 Vict., c. 6, (Canada).

Newfoundland was added on March 31, 1949, by the *Newfoundland Act*, (U.K.), 12-13 Geo. VI, c. 22, which ratified the Terms of Union between Canada and Newfoundland.

Provinces of
Ontario and
Quebec.

**6.** The Parts of the Province of Canada (as it exists at the passing of this Act) which formerly constituted respectively the Provinces of Upper Canada and Lower Canada shall be deemed to be severed, and shall form Two separate Provinces. The Part which formerly constituted the Province of Upper Canada shall constitute the Province of Ontario; and the Part which formerly constituted the Province of Lower Canada shall constitute the Province of Quebec.

Provinces of
Nova Scotia
and New
Brunswick.

**7.** The Provinces of Nova Scotia and New Brunswick shall have the same Limits as at the passing of this Act.

Decennial
Census.

**8.** In the general Census of the Population of Canada which is hereby required to be taken in the Year One thousand eight hundred and seventy-one, and in every Tenth Year thereafter, the respective Populations of the Four Provinces shall be distinguished.

### III.–EXECUTIVE POWER.

Declaration
of Executive
Power in the
Queen.

**9.** The Executive Government and Authority of and over Canada is hereby declared to continue and be vested in the Queen.

Application
of Provisions
referring to
Governor
General.

**10.** The Provisions of this Act referring to the Governor General extend and apply to the Governor General for the Time being of Canada, or other the Chief Executive Officer or Administrator for the Time being carrying on the Government of Canada on behalf and in the Name of the Queen, by whatever Title he is designated.

Constitution
of Privy
Council for
Canada.

**11.** There shall be a Council to aid and advise in the Government of Canada, to be styled the Queen's Privy Council for Canada; and the Persons who are to be Members of that Council shall be from Time to Time chosen and summoned by the Governor General and sworn in as Privy Councillors, and Members thereof may be from Time to Time removed by the Governor General.

All Powers
under Acts to
be exercised
by Governor
General with
Advice of
Privy Council,
or alone.

**12.** All Powers, Authorities, and Functions which under any Act of the Parliament of Great Britain, or of the Parliament of the United Kingdom of Great Britain and Ireland, or of the Legislature of Upper Canada, Lower Canada, Canada, Nova Scotia, or New Brunswick, are at the Union vested in or exerciseable by the respective Governors or Lieutenant Governors of those Provinces, with the Advice, or with the Advice and Consent, of the respective Executive Councils thereof, or in conjunction with those Councils, or with any Number of Members thereof, or by those Governors or Lieutenant Governors individually, shall, as far as the same continue in existence and capable of being exercised after the Union in relation to the Government of Canada, be vested in and exerciseable by the Governor General, with the Advice or with the Advice and Consent of or in conjunction with the Queen's Privy Council for Canada, or any Member thereof, or by the Governor General individually, as the Case requires, subject nevertheless (except with respect to such as exist under Acts of the Parliament of Great Britain or of the Parliament of the United Kingdom of Great Britain and Ireland) to be abolished or altered by the Parliament of Canada. (7)

Application
of Provisions
referring to
Governor
General in
Council.

**13.** The Provisions of this Act referring to the Governor General in Council shall be construed as referring to the Governor General acting by and with the Advice of the Queen's Privy Council for Canada.

Power to Her
Majesty to
authorize
Governor
General to
appoint
Deputies.

**14.** It shall be lawful for the Queen, if Her Majesty thinks fit, to authorize the Governor General from Time to Time to appoint any Person or any Persons jointly or severally to be his Deputy or Deputies within any Part or Parts of Canada, and in that Capacity to exercise during

(7) See the notes to section 129, *infra*.

the Pleasure of the Governor General such of the Powers, Authorities, and Functions of the Governor General as the Governor General deems it necessary or expedient to assign to him or them, subject to any Limitations or Directions expressed or given by the Queen; but the Appointment of such a Deputy or Deputies shall not affect the Exercise by the Governor General himself of any Power, Authority or Function.

**Command of armed Forces to continue to be vested in the Queen.**

**15.** The Command-in-Chief of the Land and Naval Militia, and of all Naval and Military Forces, of and in Canada, is hereby declared to continue and be vested in the Queen.

**Seat of Government of Canada.**

**16.** Until the Queen otherwise directs, the Seat of Government of Canada shall be Ottawa.

### IV.—LEGISLATIVE POWER.

**Constitution of Parliament of Canada.**

**17.** There shall be One Parliament for Canada, consisting of the Queen, an Upper House styled the Senate, and the House of Commons.

**Privileges, etc. of Houses.**

**18.** The privileges, immunities, and powers to be held, enjoyed, and exercised by the Senate and by the House of Commons, and by the Members thereof respectively, shall be such as are from time to time defined by Act of the Parliament of Canada, but so that any Act of the Parliament of Canada defining such privileges, immunities, and powers shall not confer any privileges, immunities, or powers exceeding those at the passing of such Act held, enjoyed, and exercised by the Commons House of Parliament of the United Kingdom of Great Britain and Ireland, and by the Members thereof. (8)

**First Session of the Parliament of Canada.**

**19.** The Parliament of Canada shall be called together not later than Six Months after the Union. (9)

**20.** Repealed. (10)

*The Senate.*

**Number of Senators.**

**21.** The Senate shall, subject to the Provisions of this Act, consist of One Hundred and four Members, who shall be styled Senators. (11)

---

(8)  Repealed and re-enacted by the *Parliament of Canada Act, 1875*, 38-39 Vict., c. 38 (U.K.). The original section read as follows:

18.  The Privileges, Immunities, and Powers to be held, enjoyed, and exercised by the Senate and by the House of Commons and by the Members thereof respectively shall be such as are from Time to Time defined by Act of the Parliament of Canada, but so that the same shall never exceed those at the passing of this Act held, enjoyed, and exercised by the Commons House of Parliament of the United Kingdom of Great Britain and Ireland and by the Members thereof.

(9)  Spent. The first session of the first Parliament began on November 6, 1867.

(10)  Section 20, repealed by the Schedule to the *Constitution Act, 1982*, read as follows:

20.  There shall be a Session of the Parliament of Canada once at least in every Year, so that Twelve Months shall not intervene between the last Sitting of the Parliament in one Session and its first Sitting in the next Session.

Section 20 has been replaced by section 5 of the *Constitution Act, 1982*, which provides that there shall be a sitting of Parliament at least once every twelve months.

(11)  As amended by the *Constitution Act, 1915*, 5-6 Geo. V, c. 45 (U.K.) and modified by the *Newfoundland Act*, 12-13 Geo. VI, c. 22 (U.K.), and the *Constitution Act (No. 2), 1975*, S.C. 1974-75-76, c. 53.

Representation
of Provinces in
Senate.

**22.** In relation to the Constitution of the Senate Canada shall be deemed to consist of Four Divisions:—

1. Ontario;
2. Quebec;
3. The Maritime Provinces, Nova Scotia and New Brunswick, and Prince Edward Island;
4. The Western Provinces of Manitoba, British Columbia, Saskatchewan, and Alberta;

which Four Divisions shall (subject to the Provisions of this Act) be equally represented in the Senate as follows: Ontario by twenty-four senators; Quebec by twenty-four senators; the Maritime Provinces and Prince Edward Island by twenty-four senators, ten thereof representing Nova Scotia, ten thereof representing New Brunswick, and four thereof representing Prince Edward Island; the Western Provinces by twenty-four senators, six thereof representing Manitoba, six thereof representing British Columbia, six thereof representing Saskatchewan, and six thereof representing Alberta; Newfoundland shall be entitled to be represented in the Senate by six members; the Yukon Territory and the Northwest Territories shall be entitled to be represented in the Senate by one member each.

In the Case of Quebec each of the Twenty-four Senators representing that Province shall be appointed for One of the Twenty-four Electoral Divisions of Lower Canada specified in Schedule A. to Chapter One of the Consolidated Statutes of Canada. (12)

Qualifications
of Senator.

**23.** The Qualification of a Senator shall be as follows:

(1) He shall be of the full age of Thirty Years:
(2) he shall be either a natural-born Subject of the Queen, or a Subject of the Queen naturalized by an Act of the Parliament of Great Britain, or of the Parliament of the United Kingdom of Great Britain and Ireland, or of the Legislature of One of the Provinces of Upper Canada, Lower Canada, Canada, Nova Scotia, or New Brunswick, before the Union, or of the Parliament of Canada, after the Union:
(3) He shall be legally or equitably seised as of Freehold for his own Use and Benefit of Lands or Tenements held in Free and Common Socage, or seised or possessed for his own Use and Benefit of Lands or Tenements held in Franc-alleu or in Roture, within the Province for which he is appointed, of the Value of Four thousand Dollars, over and above all Rents, Dues, Debts,

---

The original section read as follows:

**21.** The Senate shall, subject to the Provisions of this Act, consist of Seventy-two Members, who shall be styled Senators.

The *Manitoba Act, 1870,* added two for Manitoba; the *British Columbia Terms of Union* added three; upon admission of Prince Edward Island four more were provided by section 147 of the *Constitution Act, 1867;* the *Alberta Act* and the *Saskatchewan Act* each added four. The Senate was reconstituted at 96 by the *Constitution Act, 1915.* Six more Senators were added upon union with Newfoundland, and one Senator each was added for the Yukon Territory and the Northwest Territories by the *Constitution Act (No. 2), 1975.*

(12) As amended by the *Constitution Act, 1915,* the *Newfoundand Act,* 12-13 Geo. VI, c. 22 (U.K.), and the *Constitution Act (No. 2), 1975,* S.C. 1974-75-76, c. 53. The original section read as follows:

**22.** In relation to the Constitution of the Senate, Canada shall be deemed to consist of Three Divisions:

1. Ontario;

2. Quebec;

3. The Maritime Provinces, Nova Scotia and New Brunswick;
which Three Divisions shall (subject to the Provisions of this Act) be equally represented in the Senate as follows: Ontario by Twenty-four Senators; Quebec by Twenty-four Senators; and the Maritime Provinces by Twenty-four Senators, Twelve thereof representing Nova Scotia, and Twelve thereof representing New Brunswick.

In the case of Quebec each of the Twenty-four Senators representing that Province shall be appointed for One of the Twenty-four Electoral Divisions of Lower Canada specified in Schedule A. to Chapter One of the Consolidated Statutes of Canada.

Charges, Mortgages, and Incumbrances due or payable out of or charged on or affecting the same:

(4) His Real and Personal Property shall be together worth Four thousand Dollars over and above his Debts and Liabilities:

(5) He shall be resident in the Province for which he is appointed:

(6) In the Case of Quebec he shall have his Real Property Qualification in the Electoral Division for which he is appointed, or shall be resident in that Division. (13)

**Summons of Senator.**

**24.** The Governor General shall from Time to Time, in the Queen's Name, by Instrument under the Great Seal of Canada, summon qualified Persons to the Senate; and, subject to the Provisions of this Act, every Person so summoned shall become and be a Member of the Senate and a Senator.

**25.** Repealed. (14)

**Addition of Senators in certain cases.**

**26.** If at any Time on the Recommendation of the Governor General the Queen thinks fit to direct that Four or Eight Members be added to the Senate, the Governor General may by Summons to Four or Eight qualified Persons (as the Case may be), representing equally the Four Divisions of Canada, add to the Senate accordingly. (15)

**Reduction of Senate to normal Number.**

**27.** In case of such Addition being at any Time made, the Governor General shall not summon any Person to the Senate, except upon a further like Direction by the Queen on the like Recommendation, to represent one of the Four Divisions until such Division is represented by Twenty-four Senators and no more. (16)

**Maximum Number of Senators.**

**28.** The Number of Senators shall not at any Time exceed One Hundred and twelve. (17)

---

(13) Section 2 of the *Constitution Act (No. 2), 1975*, S.C. 1974-75-76, c. 53 provided that for the purposes of that Act (which added one Senator each for the Yukon Territory and the Northwest Territories) the term "Province" in section 23 of the *Constitution Act, 1867*, has the same meaning as is assigned to the term "province" by section 28 of the *Interpretation Act*, R.S.C. 1970, c. I-23, which provides that the term "province" means "a province of Canada, and includes the Yukon Territory and the Northwest Territories."

(14) Repealed by the *Statute Law Revision Act, 1893*, 56-57 Vict., c. 14 (U.K.). The section read as follows:

**25.** Such Persons shall be first summoned to the Senate as the Queen by Warrant under Her Majesty's Royal Sign Manual thinks fit to approve, and their Names shall be inserted in the Queen's Proclamation of Union.

(15) As amended by the *Constitution Act, 1915*, 5-6 Geo. V, c. 45 (U.K.). The original section read as follows:

**26.** If at any Time on the Recommendation of the Governor General the Queen thinks fit to direct that Three or Six Members be added to the Senate, the Governor General may by Summons to Three or Six qualified Persons (as the Case may be), representing equally the Three Divisions of Canada, add to the Senate accordingly.

(16) As amended by the *Constitution Act, 1915*, 5-6 Geo. V, c. 45 (U.K.). The original section read as follows:

**27.** In case of such Addition being at any Time made the Governor General shall not summon any Person to the Senate except on a further like Direction by the Queen on the like Recommendation, until each of the Three Divisions of Canada is represented by Twenty-four Senators and no more.

(17) As amended by the *Constitution Act, 1915*, 5-6 Geo. V, c. 45 (U.K.), and the *Constitution Act (No. 2), 1975*, S.C. 1974-75-76, c. 53. The original section read as follows:

**28.** The Number of Senators shall not at any Time exceed Seventy-eight.

Tenure of
Place in
Senate.

**29.** (1) Subject to subsection (2), a Senator shall, subject to the provisions of this Act, hold his place in the Senate for life.

Retirement upon
attaining age of
seventy-five years.

(2) A Senator who is summoned to the Senate after the coming into force of this subsection shall, subject to this Act, hold his place in the Senate until he attains the age of seventy-five years. (18)

Resignation
of Place in
Senate.

**30.** A Senator may by Writing under his Hand addressed to the Governor General resign his Place in the Senate, and thereupon the same shall be vacant.

Disqualification
of Senators.

**31.** The Place of a Senator shall become vacant in any of the following Cases:

(1) If for Two consecutive Sessions of the Parliament he fails to give his Attendance in the Senate:

(2) If he takes an Oath or makes a Declaration or Acknowledgement of Allegiance, Obedience, or Adherence to a Foreign Power, or does an Act whereby he becomes a Subject or Citizen, or entitled to the Rights or Privileges of a Subject or Citizen, of a Foreign Power:

(3) If he is adjudged Bankrupt or Insolvent, or applies for the Benefit of any Law relating to Insolvent Debtors, or becomes a public Defaulter:

(4) If he is attainted of Treason or convicted of Felony or of any infamous Crime:

(5) If he ceases to be qualified in respect of Property or of Residence; provided, that a Senator shall not be deemed to have ceased to be qualified in respect of Residence by reason only of his residing at the Seat of the Government of Canada while holding an Office under that Government requiring his Presence there.

Summons on
Vacancy in
Senate.

**32.** When a Vacancy happens in the Senate by Resignation, Death or otherwise, the Governor General shall by Summons to a fit and qualified Person fill the Vacancy.

Questions as to
Qualifications and
Vacancies in Senate.

**33.** If any Question arises respecting the Qualification of a Senator or a Vacancy in the Senate the same shall be heard and determined by the Senate.

Appointment of
Speaker of Senate.

**34.** The Governor General may from Time to Time, by Instrument under the Great Seal of Canada, appoint a Senator to be Speaker of the Senate, and may remove him and appoint another in his Stead. (19)

Quorum of Senate.

**35.** Until the Parliament of Canada otherwise provides, the Presence of at least Fifteen Senators, including the Speaker, shall be necessary to constitute a Meeting of the Senate for the Exercise of its Powers.

Voting in Senate.

**36.** Questions arising in the Senate shall be decided by a Majority of Voices, and the Speaker shall in all Cases have a Vote, and when the Voices are equal the Decision shall be deemed to be in the Negative.

*The House of Commons.*

Constitution of
House of Commons
in Canada.

**37.** The House of Commons shall, subject to the Provisions of this Act, consist of two hundred and eighty-two members of whom ninety-five shall be elected for Ontario, seventy-five for Quebec,

---

(18) As enacted by the *Constitution Act, 1965*, Statutes of Canada, 1965, c. 4 which came into force on the 1st of June, 1965. The original section read as follows:

**29.** A Senator shall, subject to the Provisions of this Act, hold his Place in the Senate for Life.

(19) Provision for exercising the functions of Speaker during his absence is made by the *Speaker of the Senate Act*, R.S.C. 1970, c. S-14. Doubts as to the power of Parliament to enact such an Act were removed by the *Canadian Speaker (Appointment of Deputy) Act, 1895*, 59 Vict., c. 3 (U.K.) which was repealed by the *Constitution Act, 1982*.

eleven for Nova Scotia, ten for New Brunswick, fourteen for Manitoba, twenty-eight for British Columbia, four for Prince Edward Island, twenty-one for Alberta, fourteen for Saskatchewan, seven for Newfoundland, one for the Yukon Territory and two for the Northwest Territories. (20)

Summoning of House of Commons.

**38.** The Governor General shall from Time to Time, in the Queen's Name, by Instrument under the Great Seal of Canada, summon and call together the House of Commons.

Senators not to sit in House of Commons.

**39.** A Senator shall not be capable of being elected or of sitting or voting as a Member of the House of Commons.

Electoral districts of the four Provinces.

**40.** Until the Parliament of Canada otherwise provides, Ontario, Quebec, Nova Scotia and New Brunswick shall, for the Purposes of the Election of Members to serve in the House of Commons, be divided into Electoral districts as follows:

### 1.—ONTARIO.

Ontario shall be divided into the Counties, Ridings of Counties, Cities, Parts of Cities, and Towns enumerated in the First Schedule to this Act, each whereof shall be an Electoral District, each such District as numbered in that Schedule being entitled to return One Member.

### 2.—QUEBEC.

Quebec shall be divided into Sixty-five Electoral Districts, composed of the Sixty-five Electoral Divisions into which Lower Canada is at the passing of this Act divided under Chapter Two of the Consolidated Statutes of Canada, Chapter Seventy-five of the Consolidated Statutes for Lower Canada, and the Act of the Province of Canada of the Twenty-third Year of the Queen, Chapter One, or any other Act amending the same in force at the Union, so that each such Electoral Division shall be for the Purposes of this Act an Electoral District entitled to return One Member.

### 3.—NOVA SCOTIA.

Each of the Eighteen Counties of Nova Scotia shall be an Electoral District. The County of Halifax shall be entitled to return Two Members, and each of the other Counties One Member.

### 4.—NEW BRUNSWICK.

Each of the Fourteen Counties into which New Brunswick is divided, including the City and County of St. John, shall be an Electoral District. The City of St. John shall also be a separate Electoral District. Each of those Fifteen Electoral Districts shall be entitled to return One Member. (21)

Continuance of existing Election Laws until Parliament of Canada otherwise provides.

**41.** Until the Parliament of Canada otherwise provides, all Laws in force in the several Provinces at the Union relative to the following Matters or any of them, namely, — the Qualifications and Disqualifications of Persons to be elected or to sit or vote as Members of the House of Assembly or Legislative Assembly in the several Provinces, the Voters at Elections of such Members, the Oaths to be taken by Voters, the Returning Officers, their Powers and Duties, the Proceedings at

---

(20) The figures given here result from the application of section 51, as enacted by the *Constitution Act, 1974*, S.C. 1974-75-76, c. 13, amended by the *Constitution Act (No. 1), 1975*, S.C. 1974-75-76, c. 28 and readjusted pursuant to the *Electoral Boundaries Readjustment Act*, R.S.C. 1970, c. E-2. The original section (which was altered from time to time as the result of the addition of new provinces and changes in population) read as follows:

**37.** The House of Commons shall, subject to the Provisions of this Act, consist of one hundred and eighty-one members, of whom Eighty-two shall be elected for Ontario, Sixty-five for Quebec, Nineteen for Nova Scotia, and Fifteen for New Brunswick.

(21) Spent. The electoral districts are now established by Proclamations issued from time to time under the *Electoral Boundaries Readjustment Act*, R.S.C. 1970, c. E-2, as amended for particular districts by Acts of Parliament, for which see the most recent Table of Public Statutes.

Elections, the Periods during which Elections may be continued, the Trial of controverted Elections, and Proceedings incident thereto, the vacating of Seats of Members, and the Execution of new Writs in case of Seats vacated otherwise than by Dissolution,—shall respectively apply to Elections of Members to serve in the House of Commons for the same several Provinces.

Provided that, until the Parliament of Canada otherwise provides, at any Election for a Member of the House of Commons for the District of Algoma, in addition to Persons qualified by the Law of the Province of Canada to vote, every Male British Subject, aged Twenty-one Years or upwards, being a Householder, shall have a Vote. (22)

**42.** Repealed. (23)

**43.** Repealed. (24)

As to Election of Speaker of House of Commons.

**44.** The House of Commons on its first assembling after a General Election shall proceed with all practicable Speed to elect One of its Members to be Speaker.

As to filling up Vacancy in Office of Speaker.

**45.** In case of a Vacancy happening in the Office of Speaker by Death, Resignation, or otherwise, the House of Commons shall with all practicable Speed proceed to elect another of its Members to be Speaker.

Speaker to preside.

**46.** The Speaker shall preside at all Meetings of the House of Commons.

Provision in case of Absence of Speaker.

**47.** Until the Parliament of Canada otherwise provides, in case of the Absence for any Reason of the Speaker from the Chair of the House of Commons for a Period of Forty-eight consecutive Hours, the House may elect another of its Members to act as Speaker, and the Member so elected shall during the Continuance of such Absence of the Speaker have and execute all the Powers, Privileges, and Duties of Speaker. (25)

---

(22)  Spent. Elections are now provided for by the *Canada Elections Act,* R.S.C. 1970 (1st Supp.), c. 14; controverted elections by the *Dominion Controverted Elections Act,* R.S.C. 1970, c. C-28; qualifications and disqualifications of members by the *House of Commons Act,* R.S.C. 1970, c. H-9 and the *Senate and House of Commons Act,* R.S.C. 1970, c. S-8. The right of citizens to vote and hold office is provided for in section 3 of the *Constitution Act, 1982.*

(23)  Repealed by the *Statute Law Revision Act, 1893,* 56-57 Vict., c. 14 (U.K.). The section read as follows:

**42.**  For the First Election of Members to serve in the House of Commons the Governor General shall cause Writs to be issued by such Person, in such Form, and addressed to such Returning Officers as he thinks fit.

The person issuing Writs under this Section shall have the like Powers as are possessed at the Union by the Officers charged with the issuing of Writs for the Election of Members to serve in the respective House of Assembly or Legislative Assembly of the Province of Canada, Nova Scotia, or New Brunswick; and the Returning Officers to whom Writs are directed under this Section shall have the like Powers as are possessed at the Union by the Officers charged with the returning of Writs for the Election of Members to serve in the same respective House of Assembly or Legislative Assembly.

(24)  Repealed by the *Statute Law Revision Act, 1893,* 56-57 Vict., c. 14 (U.K.). The section read as follows:

**43.**  In case a Vacancy in the Representation in the House of Commons of any Electoral District happens before the Meeting of the Parliament, or after the Meeting of the Parliament before Provision is made by the Parliament in this Behalf, the Provisions of the last foregoing Section of this Act shall extend and apply to the issuing and returning of a Writ in respect of such vacant District.

(25)  Provision for exercising the functions of Speaker during his absence is now made by the *Speaker of the House of Commons Act,* R.S.C. 1970, c. S-13.

Quorum of House
of Commons.

**48.** The Presence of at least Twenty Members of the House of Commons shall be necessary to constitute a Meeting of the House for the Exercise of its Powers, and for that Purpose the Speaker shall be reckoned as a Member.

Voting in House of
Commons.

**49.** Questions arising in the House of Commons shall be decided by a Majority of Voices other than that of the Speaker, and when the Voices are equal, but not otherwise, the Speaker shall have a Vote.

Duration of House
of Commons.

**50.** Every House of Commons shall continue for Five Years from the Day of the Return of the Writs for choosing the House (subject to be sooner dissolved by the Governor General), and no longer. (26)

Readjustment
of representation
in Commons.

**51.** (1) The number of members of the House of Commons and the representation of the provinces therein shall upon the coming into force of this subsection and thereafter on the completion of each decennial census be readjusted by such authority, in such manner, and from such time as the Parliament of Canada from time to time provides, subject and according to the following Rules:

Rules.

**1.** There shall be assigned to Quebec seventy-five members in the readjustment following the completion of the decennial census taken in the year 1971, and thereafter four additional members in each subsequent readjustment.

**2.** Subject to Rules 5(2) and (3), there shall be assigned to a large province a number of members equal to the number obtained by dividing the population of the large province by the electoral quotient of Quebec.

**3.** Subject to Rules 5(2) and (3), there shall be assigned to a small province a number of members equal to the number obtained by dividing

(*a*) the sum of the populations, determined according to the results of the penultimate decennial census, of the provinces (other than Quebec) having populations of less than one and a half million, determined according to the results of that census, by the sum of the numbers of members assigned to those provinces in the readjustment following the completion of that census; and

(*b*) the population of the small province by the quotient obtained under paragraph (*a*).

**4.** Subject to Rules 5(1)(*a*), (2) and (3), there shall be assigned to an intermediate province a number of members equal to the number obtained

(*a*) by dividing the sum of the populations of the provinces (other than Quebec) having populations of less than one and a half million by the sum of the number of members assigned to those provinces under any of Rules 3, 5(1)(*b*), (2) and (3);

(*b*) by dividing the population of the intermediate province by the quotient obtained under paragraph (*a*); and

(*c*) by adding to the number of members assigned to the intermediate province in the readjustment following the completion of the penultimate decennial census one-half of the difference resulting from the subtraction of that number from the quotient obtained under paragraph (*b*).

**5.** (1) On any readjustment,

(*a*) if no province (other than Quebec) has a population of less than one and a half million, Rule 4 shall not be applied and, subject to Rules 5(2) and (3), there shall be assigned to an intermediate province a number of members equal to the number obtained by dividing

(i) the sum of the populations, determined according to the results of the penultimate decennial census, of the provinces (other than Quebec) having populations of not less than one and a half million and not more than two and a half million,

---

(26)  The term of the twelfth Parliament was extended by the *British North America Act, 1916*, 6-7 Geo. V, c. 19 (U.K.), which Act was repealed by the *Statute Law Revision Act, 1927*, 17-18 Geo. V, c. 42 (U.K.). See also subsection 4(1) of the *Constitution Act, 1982*, which provides that no House of Commons shall continue for longer than five years from the date fixed for the return of the writs at a general election of its members, and subsection 4(2) thereof, which provides for continuation of the House of Commons in special circumstances.

determined according to the results of that census, by the sum of the numbers of members assigned to those provinces in the readjustment following the completion of that census, and

(ii) the population of the intermediate province by the quotient obtained under subparagraph (i);

(*b*) if a province (other than Quebec) having a population of

(i) less than one and a half million, or

(ii) not less than one and a half million and not more than two and a half million

does not have a population greater than its population determined according to the results of the penultimate decennial census, it shall, subject to Rules 5(2) and (3), be assigned the number of members assigned to it in the readjustment following the completion of that census.

(2) On any readjustment,

(*a*) if, under any of Rules 2 to 5(1), the number of members to be assigned to a province (in this paragraph referred to as "the first province") is smaller than the number of members to be assigned to any other province not having a population greater than that of the first province, those Rules shall not be applied to the first province and it shall be assigned a number of members equal to the largest number of members to be assigned to any other province not having a population greater than that of the first province;

(*b*) if, under any of Rules 2 to 5(1)(*a*), the number of members to be assigned to a province is smaller than the number of members assigned to it in the readjustment following the completion of the penultimate decennial census, those Rules shall not be applied to it and it shall be assigned the latter number of members;

(*c*) if both paragraphs (*a*) and (*b*) apply to a province, it shall be assigned a number of members equal to the greater of the numbers produced under those paragraphs.

(3) On any readjustment,

(*a*) if the electoral quotient of a province (in this paragraph referred to as "the first province") obtained by dividing its population by the number of members to be assigned to it under any of Rules 2 to 5(2) is greater than the electoral quotient of Quebec, those Rules shall not be applied to the first province and it shall be assigned a number of members equal to the number obtained by dividing its population by the electoral quotient of Quebec;

(*b*) if, as a result of the application of Rule 6(2)(*a*), the number of members assigned to a province under paragraph (*a*) equals the number of members to be assigned to it under any of Rules 2 to 5(2), it shall be assigned that number of members and paragraph (*a*) shall cease to apply to that province.

**6.** (1) In these Rules,

"electoral quotient" means, in respect of a province, the quotient obtained by dividing its population, determined according to the results of the then most recent decennial census, by the number of members to be assigned to it under any of Rules 1 to 5(3) in the readjustment following the completion of that census;

"intermediate province" means a province (other than Quebec) having a population greater than its population determined according to the results of the penultimate decennial census but not more than two and a half million and not less than one and a half million;

"large province" means a province (other than Quebec) having a population greater than two and a half million;

"penultimate decennial census" means the decennial census that preceded the then most recent decennial census;

"population" means, except where otherwise specified, the population determined according to the results of the then most recent decennial census;

"small province" means a province (other than Quebec) having a population greater than its population determined according to the results of the penultimate decennial census and less than one and half million.

(2) For the purposes of these Rules,

(*a*) if any fraction less than one remains upon completion of the final calculation that produces the number of members to be assigned to a province, that number of members shall equal the number so produced disregarding the fraction;

(*b*) if more than one readjustment follows the completion of a decennial census, the most recent of those readjustments shall, upon taking effect, be deemed to be the only readjustment following the completion of that census;

(*c*) a readjustment shall not take effect until the termination of the then existing Parliament. (27)

---

(27) As enacted by the *Constitution Act, 1974*, S.C. 1974-75-76, c. 13, which came into force on December 31, 1974. The section, as originally enacted, read as follows:

**51.** On the Completion of the Census in the Year One Thousand eight hundred and seventy-one, and of each subsequent decennial Census, the Representation of the Four Provinces shall be readjusted by such Authority, in such Manner, and from such Time, as the Parliament of Canada from Time to Time provides, subject and according to the following Rules:

(1) Quebec shall have the fixed Number of Sixty-five Members.

(2) There shall be assigned to each of the other Provinces such a Number of Members as will bear the same Proportion to the Number of its Population (ascertained at such Census) as the Number Sixty-five bears to the Number of the Population of Quebec (so ascertained):

(3) In the Computation of the Number of Members for a Province a fractional Part not exceeding One Half of the whole Number requisite for entitling the Province to a Member shall be disregarded; but a fractional Part exceeding One Half of that Number shall be equivalent to the whole Number:

(4) On any such Re-adjustment the Number of Members for a Province shall not be reduced unless the Proportion which the Number of the Population of the Province bore to the Number of the aggregate Population of Canada at the then last preceding Re-adjustment of the Number of Members for the Province is ascertained at the then latest Census to be diminished by One Twentieth Part or upwards:

(5) Such Re-adjustment shall not take effect until the Termination of the then existing Parliament.

The section was amended by the *Statute Law Revision Act, 1893*, 56-57 Vict., c. 14 (U.K.) by repealing the words from "of the census" to "seventy-one and" and the word "subsequent".

By the *British North America Act, 1943*, 6-7 Geo. VI, c. 30 (U.K.), which Act was repealed by the *Constitution Act, 1982*, redistribution of seats following the 1941 census was postponed until the first session of Parliament after the war. The section was re-enacted by the *British North America Act, 1946*, 9-10 Geo. VI, c. 63 (U.K.), which Act was also repealed by the *Constitution Act, 1982*, to read as follows:

**51.** (1) The number of members of the House of Commons shall be two hundred and fifty-five and the representation of the provinces therein shall forthwith upon the coming into force of this section and thereafter on the completion of each decennial census be readjusted by such authority, in such manner, and from such time as the Parliament of Canada from time to time provides, subject and according to the following rules:

(1) Subject as hereinafter provided there shall be assigned to each of the provinces a number of members computed by dividing the total population of the provinces by two hundred and fifty-four and by dividing the population of each province by the quotient so obtained, disregarding, except as hereinafter in this section provided, the remainder, if any, after the said process of division.

(2) If the total number of members assigned to all the provinces pursuant to rule one is less than two hundred and fifty-four, additional members shall be assigned to the provinces (one to a province) having remainders in the computation under rule one commencing with the province having the largest remainder and continuing with the other provinces in the order of the magnitude of their respective remainders until the total number of members assigned is two hundred and fifty-four.

(3) Notwithstanding anything in this section, if upon completion of a computation under rules one and two, the number of members to be assigned to a province is less than the number of senators representing the said province, rules one and two shall cease to apply in respect of the said province, and there shall be assigned to the said province a number of members equal to the said number of senators.

(4) In the event that rules one and two cease to apply in respect of a province then, for the purpose of computing the number of members to be assigned to the provinces in respect of which

Yukon Territory and
Northwest
Territories.

(2) The Yukon Territory as bounded and described in the schedule to chapter Y-2 of the Revised Statutes of Canada, 1970, shall be entitled to one member, and the Northwest

rules one and two continue to apply, the total population of the provinces shall be reduced by the number of the population of the province in respect of which rules one and two have ceased to apply and the number two hundred and fifty-four shall be reduced by the number of members assigned to such province pursuant to rule three.

(5) Such readjustments shall not take effect until the termination of the then existing Parliament.

(2) The Yukon Territory as constituted by Chapter forty-one of the Statutes of Canada, 1901, together with any Part of Canada not comprised within a province which may from time to time be included therein by the Parliament of Canada for the purposes of representation in Parliament, shall be entitled to one member.

The section was re-enacted by the *British North America Act, 1952,* S.C. 1952, c. 15, which Act was also repealed by the *Constitution Act, 1982,* as follows:

**51.** (1) Subject as hereinafter provided, the number of members of the House of Commons shall be two hundred and sixty-three and the representation of the provinces therein shall forthwith upon the coming into force of this section and thereafter on the completion of each decennial census be readjusted by such authority, in such manner, and from such time as the Parliament of Canada from time to time provides, subject and according to the following rules:

1. There shall be assigned to each of the provinces a number of members computed by dividing the total population of the provinces by two hundred and sixty-one and by dividing the population of each province by the quotient so obtained, disregarding, except as hereinafter in this section provided, the remainder, if any, after the said process of division.

2. If the total number of members assigned to all the provinces pursuant to rule one is less than two hundred and sixty-one, additional members shall be assigned to the provinces (one to a province) having remainders in the computation under rule one commencing with the province having the largest remainder and continuing with the other provinces in the order of the magnitude of their respective remainders until the total number of members assigned is two hundred and sixty-one.

3. Notwithstanding anything in this section, if upon completion of a computation under rules one and two the number of members to be assigned to a province is less than the number of senators representing the said province, rules one and two shall cease to apply in respect of the said province, and there shall be assigned to the said province a number of members equal to the said number of senators.

4. In the event that rules one and two cease to apply in respect of a province then, for the purpose of computing the number of members to be assigned to the provinces in respect of which rules one and two continue to apply, the total population of the provinces shall be reduced by the number of the population of the province in respect of which rules one and two have ceased to apply and the number two hundred and sixty-one shall be reduced by the number of members assigned to such province pursuant to rule three.

5. On any such readjustment the number of members for any province shall not be reduced by more than fifteen per cent below the representation to which such province was entitled under rules one to four of the subsection at the last preceding readjustment of the representation of that province, and there shall be no reduction in the representation of any province as a result of which that province would have a smaller number of members than any other province that according to the results of the then last decennial census did not have a larger population; but for the purposes of any subsequent readjustment of representation under this section any increase in the number of members of the House of Commons resulting from the application of this rule shall not be included in the divisor mentioned in rules one to four of this subsection.

6. Such readjustment shall not take effect until the termination of the then existing Parliament.

(2) The Yukon Territory as constituted by chapter forty-one of the statutes of Canada, 1901, shall be entitled to one member, and such other part of Canada not comprised within a province as may from time to time be defined by the Parliament of Canada shall be entitled to one member.

Territories as bounded and described in section 2 of chapter N-22 of the Revised Statutes of Canada, 1970, shall be entitled to two members. (28)

Constitution of
House of
Commons.

**51A.** Notwithstanding anything in this Act a province shall always be entitled to a number of members in the House of Commons not less than the number of senators representing such province. (29)

Increase of Number
of House of
Commons.

**52.** The Number of Members of the House of Commons may be from Time to Time increased by the Parliament of Canada, provided the proportionate Representation of the Provinces prescribed by this Act is not thereby disturbed.

*Money Votes; Royal Assent.*

Appropriation
and Tax Bills.

**53.** Bills for appropriating any Part of the Public Revenue, or for imposing any Tax or Impost, shall originate in the House of Commons.

Recommendation
of Money Votes.

**54.** It shall not be lawful for the House of Commons to adopt or pass any Vote, Resolution, Address, or Bill for the Appropriation of any Part of the Public Revenue, or of any Tax or Impost, to any Purpose that has not been first recommended to that House by Message of the Governor General in the Session in which such Vote, Resolution, Address, or Bill is proposed.

Royal Assent to
Bills, etc.

**55.** Where a Bill passed by the Houses of the Parliament is presented to the Governor General for the Queen's Assent, he shall declare, according to his Discretion, but subject to the Provisions of this Act and to Her Majesty's Instructions, either that he assents thereto in the Queen's Name, or that he withholds the Queen's Assent, or that he reserves the Bill for the Signification of the Queen's Pleasure.

Disallowance by
Order in Council of
Act assented to by
Governor General.

**56.** Where the Governor General assents to a Bill in the Queen's Name, he shall by the first convenient Opportunity send an authentic Copy of the Act to one of Her Majesty's Principal Secretaries of State, and if the Queen in Council within Two Years after Receipt thereof by the Secretary of State thinks fit to disallow the Act, such Disallowance (with a Certificate of the Secretary of State of the Day on which the Act was received by him) being signified by the Governor General, by Speech or Message to each of the Houses of the Parliament or by Proclamation, shall annul the Act from and after the Day of such Signification.

Signification of
Queen's Pleasure on
Bill reserved.

**57.** A Bill reserved for the Signification of the Queen's Pleasure shall not have any Force unless and until, within Two Years from the Day on which it was presented to the Governor General for the Queen's Assent, the Governor General signifies, by Speech or Message to each of the Houses of the Parliament or by Proclamation, that it has received the Assent of the Queen in Council.

An Entry of every such Speech, Message, or Proclamation shall be made in the Journal of each House, and a Duplicate thereof duly attested shall be delivered to the proper Officer to be kept among the Records of Canada.

## V.–PROVINCIAL CONSTITUTIONS.

*Executive Power.*

Appointment of
Lieutenant
Governors of
Provinces.

**58.** For each Province there shall be an Officer, styled the Lieutenant Governor, appointed by the Governor General in Council by Instrument under the Great Seal of Canada.

---

(28) As enacted by the *Constitution Act (No. 1), 1975,* S.C. 1974-75-76, c. 28.

(29) As enacted by the *Constitution Act, 1915,* 5-6 Geo. V, c. 45 (U.K.).

**Tenure of Office of Lieutenant Governor.**

**59.** A Lieutenant Governor shall hold Office during the Pleasure of the Governor General; but any Lieutenant Governor appointed after the Commencement of the First Session of the Parliament of Canada shall not be removeable within Five Years from his Appointment, except for Cause assigned, which shall be communicated to him in Writing within One Month after the Order for his Removal is made, and shall be communicated by Message to the Senate and to the House of Commons within One Week thereafter if the Parliament is then sitting, and if not then within One Week after the Commencement of the next Session of the Parliament.

**Salaries of Lieutenant Governors.**

**60.** The Salaries of the Lieutenant Governors shall be fixed and provided by the Parliament of Canada. (30)

**Oaths, etc., of Lieutenant Governor.**

**61.** Every Lieutenant Governor shall, before assuming the Duties of his Office, make and subscribe before the Governor General or some Person authorized by him Oaths of Allegiance and Office similar to those taken by the Governor General.

**Application of provisions referring to Lieutenant Governor.**

**62.** The Provisions of this Act referring to the Lieutenant Governor extend and apply to the Lieutenant Governor for the Time being of each Province, or other the Chief Executive Officer or Administrator for the Time being carrying on the Government of the Province, by whatever Title he is designated.

**Appointment of Executive Officers for Ontario and Quebec.**

**63.** The Executive Council of Ontario and of Quebec shall be composed of such Persons as the Lieutenant Governor from Time to Time thinks fit, and in the first instance of the following Officers, namely, — the Attorney General, the Secretary and Registrar of the Province, the Treasurer of the Province, the Commissioner of Crown Lands, and the Commissioner of Agriculture and Public Works, with in Quebec, the Speaker of the Legislative Council and the Solicitor General. (31)

**Executive Government of Nova Scotia and New Brunswick.**

**64.** The Constitution of the Executive Authority in each of the Provinces of Nova Scotia and New Brunswick shall, subject to the Provisions of this Act, continue as it exists at the Union until altered under the Authority of this Act. (32)

**Powers to be exercised by Lieutenant Governor of Ontario or Quebec with Advice, or alone.**

**65.** All Powers, Authorities, and Functions which under any Act of the Parliament of Great Britain, or of the Parliament of the United Kingdom of Great Britain and Ireland, or of the Legislature of Upper Canada, Lower Canada, or Canada, were or are before or at the Union vested in or exerciseable by the respective Governors or Lieutenant Governors of those Provinces, with the Advice or with the Advice and Consent of the respective Executive Councils thereof, or in conjunction with those Councils, or with any Number of Members thereof, or by those Governors or Lieutenant Governors individually, shall, as far as the same are capable of being exercised after the Union in relation to the Government of Ontario and Quebec respectively, be vested in and shall or may be exercised by the Lieutenant Governor of Ontario and Quebec respectively, with the Advice or with the Advice and consent of or in conjunction with the respective Executive Councils, or any Members thereof, or by the Lieutenant Governor individually, as the Case requires, subject nevertheless (except with respect to such as exist under Acts of the Parliament of Great Britain, or of the Parliament of the United Kingdom of Great Britain and Ireland,) to be abolished or altered by the respective Legislatures of Ontario and Quebec. (33)

---

(30) Provided for by the *Salaries Act*, R.S.C. 1970, c. S-2.

(31) Now provided for in Ontario by the *Executive Council Act*, R.S.O. 1980, c. 147, and in Quebec by the *Executive Power Act*, R.S.Q. 1977, c. E-18.

(32) A similar provision was included in each of the instruments admitting British Columbia, Prince Edward Island, and Newfoundland. The Executive Authorities for Manitoba, Alberta and Saskatchewan were established by the statutes creating those provinces. See the notes to section 5, *supra*.

(33) See the notes to section 129, *infra*.

Application of Provisions referring to Lieutenant Governor in Council.

**66.** The Provisions of this Act referring to the Lieutenant Governor in Council shall be construed as referring to the Lieutenant Governor of the Province acting by and with the Advice of the Executive Council thereof.

Administration in Absence, etc., of Lieutenant Governor.

**67.** The Governor General in Council may from Time to Time appoint an Administrator to execute the office and Functions of Lieutenant Governor during his Absence, Illness, or other Inability.

Seats of Provincial Governments.

**68.** Unless and until the Executive Government of any Province otherwise directs with respect to that Province, the Seats of Government of the Provinces shall be as follows, namely,—of Ontario, the City of Toronto; of Quebec, the City of Quebec; of Nova Scotia, the City of Halifax; and of New Brunswick, the City of Fredericton.

*Legislative Power.*

## 1.—ONTARIO.

Legislature for Ontario.

**69.** There shall be a Legislature for Ontario consisting of the Lieutenant Governor and of One House, styled the Legislative Assembly of Ontario.

Electoral districts.

**70.** The Legislative Assembly of Ontario shall be composed of Eighty-two Members, to be elected to represent the Eighty-two Electoral Districts set forth in the First Schedule to this Act. (34)

## 2.—QUEBEC.

Legislature for Quebec.

**71.** There shall be a Legislature for Quebec consisting of the Lieutenant Governor and of Two Houses, styled the Legislative Council of Quebec and the Legislative Assembly of Quebec. (35)

Constitution of Legislative Council.

**72.** The Legislative Council of Quebec shall be composed of Twenty-four Members, to be appointed by the Lieutenant Governor, in the Queen's Name, by Instrument under the Great Seal of Quebec, One being appointed to represent each of the Twenty-four Electoral Divisions of Lower Canada in this Act referred to, and each holding Office for the Term of his Life, unless the Legislature of Quebec otherwise provides under the Provisions of this Act.

Qualifications of Legislative Councillors.

**73.** The Qualifications of the Legislative Councillors of Quebec shall be the same as those of the Senators for Quebec.

Resignation, Disqualification etc.

**74.** The Place of a Legislative Councillor of Quebec shall become vacant in the Cases, *mutatis mutandis*, in which the Place of Senator becomes vacant.

Vacancies.

**75.** When a Vacancy happens in the Legislative Council of Quebec by Resignation, Death, or otherwise, the Lieutenant Governor, in the Queen's Name, by Instrument under the Great Seal of Quebec, shall appoint a fit and qualified Person to fill the Vacancy.

Question as to Vacancies, etc.

**76.** If any Question arises respecting the Qualification of a Legislative Councillor of Quebec, or a Vacancy in the Legislative Council of Quebec, the same shall be heard and determined by the Legislative Council.

---

(34) Spent. Now covered by the *Representation Act*, R.S.O. 1980, c. 450.

(35) The Act respecting the Legislative Council of Quebec, S.Q. 9168, c. 9, provided that the Legislature for Quebec shall consist of the Lieutenant Governor and the National Assembly of Quebec, and repealed the provisions of the *Legislature Act*, R.S.Q. 1964, c. 6, relating to the Legislative Council of Quebec. Sections 72 to 79 following are therefore completely spent.

Speaker of
Legislative Council.

**77.** The Lieutenant Governor may from Time to Time, by Instrument under the Great Seal of Quebec, appoint a Member of the Legislative Council of Quebec to be Speaker thereof, and may remove him and appoint another in his Stead.

Quorum of
Legislative Council.

**78.** Until the Legislature of Quebec otherwise provides, the Presence of at least Ten Members of the Legislative Council, including the Speaker, shall be necessary to constitute a Meeting for the Exercise of its Powers.

Voting in Legislative
Council.

**79.** Questions arising in the Legislative Council of Quebec shall be decided by a Majority of Voices, and the Speaker shall in all Cases have a Vote, and when the Voices are equal the Decision shall be deemed to be in the Negative.

Constitution of
Legislative Assembly
of Quebec.

**80.** The Legislative Assembly of Quebec shall be composed of Sixty-five Members, to be elected to represent the Sixty-five Electoral Divisions or Districts of Lower Canada in this Act referred to, subject to Alteration thereof by the Legislature of Quebec: Provided that it shall not be lawful to present to the Lieutenant Governor of Quebec for Assent any Bill for altering the Limits of any of the Electoral Divisions or Districts mentioned in the Second Schedule to this Act, unless the Second and Third Readings of such Bill have been passed in the Legislative Assembly with the Concurrence of the Majority of the Members representing all those Electoral Divisions or Districts, and the Assent shall not be given to such Bill unless an Address has been presented by the Legislative Assembly to the Lieutenant Governor stating that it has been so passed. (36)

### 3.–ONTARIO AND QUEBEC.

**81.** Repealed. (37)

Summoning of
Legislative
Assemblies.

**82.** The Lieutenant Governor of Ontario and of Quebec shall from Time to Time, in the Queen's Name, by Instrument under the Great Seal of the Province, summon and call together the Legislative Assembly of the Province.

Restriction on
election of Holders
of offices.

**83.** Until the Legislature of Ontario or of Quebec otherwise provides, a Person accepting or holding in Ontario or in Quebec any Office, Commission, or Employment, permanent or temporary, at the Nomination of the Lieutenant Governor, to which an annual Salary, or any Fee, Allowance, Emolument, or Profit of any Kind or Amount whatever from the Province is attached, shall not be eligible as a Member of the Legislative Assembly of the respective Province, nor shall he sit or vote as such; but nothing in this Section shall make ineligible any Person being a member of the Executive Council of the respective Province, or holding any of the following Offices, that is to say, the Offices of Attorney General, Secretary and Registrar of the Province, Treasurer of the Province, Commissioner of Crown Lands, and Commissioner of Agriculture and Public Works, and in Quebec Solicitor General, or shall disqualify him to sit or vote in the House for which he is elected, provided he is elected while holding such Office. (38)

Continuance of
existing Election
Laws.

**84.** Until the legislatures of Ontario and Quebec respectively otherwise provide, all Laws which at the Union are in force in those Provinces respectively, relative to the following Matters, or any of them, namely, — the Qualifications and Disqualifications of Persons to be elected or to sit or vote as Members of the Assembly of Canada, the Qualifications or Disqualifications of Voters, the Oaths to be taken by Voters, the Returning Officers, their Powers and Duties, the Proceedings

---

(36)  The Act respecting electoral districts, S.Q. 1970, c. 7, s. 1, provides that this section no longer has effect.

(37)  Repealed by the *Statute Law Revision Act, 1893*, 56-57 Vict., c. 14 (U.K.). The section read as follows:

> **81.** The Legislatures of Ontario and Quebec respectively shall be called together not later than Six Months after the Union.

(38)  Probably spent. The subject-matter of this section is now covered in Ontario by the *Legislative Assembly Act*, R.S.O. 1980, c. 235, and in Quebec by the *Legislature Act*, R.S.Q. 1977, c. L-1.

at Elections, the Periods during which such Elections may be continued, and the Trial of controverted Elections and the Proceedings incident thereto, the vacating of the Seats of Members and the issuing and execution of new Writs in case of Seats vacated otherwise than by Dissolution, — shall respectively apply to Elections of Members to serve in the respective Legislative Assemblies of Ontario and Quebec.

Provided that, until the Legislature of Ontario otherwise provides, at any Election for a Member of the Legislative Assembly of Ontario for the District of Algoma, in addition to Persons qualified by the Law of the Province of Canada to vote, every male British Subject, aged Twenty-one Years or upwards, being a Householder, shall have a vote. (39)

Duration of Legislative Assemblies.

**85.** Every Legislative Assembly of Ontario and every Legislative Assembly of Quebec shall continue for Four Years from the Day of the Return of the Writs for choosing the same (subject nevertheless to either the Legislative Assembly of Ontario or the Legislative Assembly of Quebec being sooner dissolved by the Lieutenant Governor of the Province), and no longer. (40)

Yearly Session of Legislature.

**86.** There shall be a Session of the Legislature of Ontario and of that of Quebec once at least in every Year, so that Twelve Months shall not intervene between the last Sitting of the Legislature in each Province in one Session and its first Sitting in the next Session. (41)

Speaker, Quorum, etc.

**87.** The following Provisions of this Act respecting the House of Commons of Canada shall extend and apply to the Legislative Assemblies of Ontario and Quebec, that is to say, — the Provisions relating to the Election of a Speaker originally and on Vacancies, the Duties of the Speaker, the Absence of the Speaker, the Quorum, and the Mode of voting, as if those Provisions were here re-enacted and made applicable in Terms to each such Legislative Assembly.

### 4.–NOVA SCOTIA AND NEW BRUNSWICK.

Constitutions of Legislatures of Nova Scotia and New Brunswick.

**88.** The Constitution of the Legislature of each of the Provinces of Nova Scotia and New Brunswick shall, subject to the Provisions of this Act, continue as it exists at the Union until altered under the Authority of this Act. (42)

---

(39) Probably spent. The subject-matter of this section is now covered in Ontario by the *Election Act*, R.S.O. 1980, c. 133, and the *Legislative Assembly Act*, R.S.O. 1980, c. 235, in Quebec by the *Elections Act*, R.S.Q. 1977, c. E-3, the *Provincial Controverted Elections Act*, R.S.Q. 1977, c. C-65, and the *Legislature Act*, R.S.Q. 1977, c. L-1.

(40) The maximum duration of the Legislative Assemblies of Ontario and Quebec has been changed to five years. See the *Legislative Assembly Act*, R.S.O. 1980, c. 235, and the *Legislature Act*, R.S.Q. 1977, c. L-1, respectively. See also section 4 of the *Constitution Act, 1982*, which provides a maximum duration for a legislative assembly of five years but also authorizes continuation in special circumstances.

(41) See also section 5 of the *Constitution Act, 1982*, which provides that there shall be a sitting of each legislature at least once every twelve months.

(42) Partially repealed by the *Statute Law Revision Act, 1893*, 56-57 Vict., c. 14 (U.K.), which deleted the following concluding words of the original enactment:

and the House of Assembly of New Brunswick existing at the passing of this Act shall, unless sooner dissolved, continue for the Period for which it was elected.

A similar provision was included in each of the instruments admitting British Columbia, Prince Edward Island and Newfoundland. The Legislatures of Manitoba, Alberta and Saskatchewan were established by the statutes creating those provinces. See the footnotes to section 5, *supra*.

See also sections 3 to 5 of the *Constitution Act, 1982*, which prescribe democratic rights applicable to all provinces, and subitem 2(2) of the Schedule to that Act, which sets out the repeal of section 20 of the *Manitoba Act, 1870*. Section 20 of the *Manitoba Act, 1870*, has been replaced by section 5 of the *Constitution Act, 1982*.

Section 20 reads as follows:

**20.** There shall be a Session of the Legislature once at least in every year, so that twelve months

**89.** Repealed. (43)

## 6.—THE FOUR PROVINCES.

Applications to
Legislatures of
Provisions
respecting Money
Votes, etc.

**90.** The following Provisions of this Act respecting the Parliament of Canada, namely, — the Provisions relating to Appropriation and Tax Bills, the Recommendation of Money Votes, the Assent to Bills, the Disallowance of Acts, and the Signification of Pleasure on Bills reserved, — shall extend and apply to the Legislatures of the several Provinces as if those Provisions were here re-enacted and made applicable in Terms to the respective Provinces and the Legislatures thereof, with the Substitution of the Lieutenant Governor of the Province for the Governor General, of the Governor General for the Queen and for a Secretary of State, of One Year for Two Years, and of the Province for Canada.

## VI.—DISTRIBUTION OF LEGISLATIVE POWERS.

### Powers of the Parliament.

Legislative
Authority of
Parliament of
Canada.

**91.** It shall be lawful for the Queen, by and with the Advice and Consent of the Senate and House of Commons, to make Laws for the Peace, Order, and good Government of Canada, in relation to all Matters not coming within the Classes of Subjects by this Act assigned exclusively to the Legislatures of the Provinces; and for greater Certainty, but not so as to restrict the Generality of the foregoing Terms of this Section, it is hereby declared that (notwithstanding anything in this Act) the exclusive Legislative Authority of the Parliament of Canada extends to all Matters coming within the Classes of Subjects next hereinafter enumerated; that is to say, —

1. Repealed. (44)
1A. The Public Debt and Property. (45)
2. The Regulation of Trade and Commerce.

---

shall not intervene between the last sitting of the Legislature in one Session and its first sitting in the next Session.

(43) Repealed by the *Statute Law Revision Act, 1893*, 56-57 Vict., c. 14 (U.K.). The section read as follows:

5.—Ontario, Quebec, and Nova Scotia.

**89.** Each of the Lieutenant Governors of Ontario, Quebec and Nova Scotia shall cause Writs to be issued for the First Election of Members of the Legislative Assembly thereof in such Form and by such Person as he thinks fit, and at such Time and addressed to such Returning Officer as the Governor General directs, and so that the First Election of Member of Assembly for any Electoral District or any Subdivision thereof shall be held at the same Time and at the same Places as the Election for a Member to serve in the House of Commons of Canada for the Electoral District.

(44) Class 1 was added by the *British North America (No. 2) Act, 1949*, 13 Geo. VI, c. 8 (U.K.). That Act and class 1 were repealed by the *Constitution Act, 1982*. The matters referred to in class 1 are provided for in subsection 4(2) and Part V of the *Constitution Act, 1982*. As enacted, class 1 read as follows:

1. The amendment from time to time of the Constitution of Canada, except as regards matters coming within the classes of subjects by this Act assigned exclusively to the Legislatures of the provinces, or as regards rights or privileges by this or any other Constitutional Act granted or secured to the Legislature or the Government of a province, or to any class of persons with respect to schools or as regards the use of the English or the French language or as regards the requirements that there shall be a session of the Parliament of Canada at least once each year, and that no House of Commons shall continue for more than five years from the day of the return of the Writs for choosing the House: provided, however, that a House of Commons may in time of real or apprehended war, invasion or insurrection be continued by the Parliament of Canada if such continuation is not opposed by the votes of more than one-third of the members of such House.

(45) Re-numbered by the *British North America (No. 2) Act, 1949*.

2A. Unemployment insurance. (46)

3. The raising of Money by any Mode or System of Taxation.

4. The borrowing of Money on the Public Credit.

5. Postal Service.

6. The Census and Statistics.

7. Militia, Military and Naval Service, and Defence.

8. The fixing of and providing for the Salaries and Allowances of Civil and other Officers of the Government of Canada.

9. Beacons, Buoys, Lighthouses, and Sable Island.

10. Navigation and Shipping.

11. Quarantine and the Establishment and Maintenance of Marine Hospitals.

12. Sea Coast and Inland Fisheries.

13. Ferries between a Province and any British or Foreign Country or between Two Provinces.

14. Currency and Coinage.

15. Banking, Incorporation of Banks, and the Issue of Paper Money.

16. Savings Banks.

17. Weights and Measures.

18. Bills of Exchange and Promissory Notes.

19. Interest.

20. Legal Tender.

21. Bankruptcy and Insolvency.

22. Patents of Invention and Discovery.

23. Copyrights.

24. Indians, and Lands reserved for the Indians.

25. Naturalization and Aliens.

26. Marriage and Divorce.

27. The Criminal Law, except the Constitution of Courts of Criminal Jurisdiction, but including the Procedure in Criminal Matters.

28. The Establishment, Maintenance, and Management of Penitentiaries.

29. Such Classes of Subjects as are expressly excepted in the Enumeration of the Classes of Subjects by this Act assigned exclusively to the Legislatures of the Provinces.

And any Matter coming within any of the Classes of Subjects enumerated in this Section shall not be deemed to come within the Class of Matters of a local or private Nature comprised in the Enumeration of the Classes of Subjects by this Act assigned exclusively to the Legislatures of the Provinces. (47)

---

(46)  Added by the *Constitution Act, 1940*, 3-4 Geo. VI, c. 36 (U.K.).

(47)  Legislative authority has been conferred on Parliament by other Acts as follows:

1. The *Constitution Act, 1871*, 34-35 Vict., c. 28 (U.K.).

2. The Parliament of Canada may from time to time establish new Provinces in any territories forming for the time being part of the Dominion of Canada, but not included in any Province thereof, and may, at the time of such establishment, make provision of the constitution and administration of any such Province, and for the passing of laws for the peace, order, and good government of such Province, and for its representation in the said Parliament.

3. The Parliament of Canada may from time to time, with the consent of the Legislature of any province of the said Dominion, increase, diminish, or otherwise alter the limits of such Province, upon such terms and conditions as may be agreed to by the said Legislature, and may, with the like consent, make provision respecting the effect and operation of any such increase or diminution or alteration of territory in relation to any Province affected thereby.

4. The Parliament of Canada may from time to time make provision for the administration, peace, order, and good government of any territory not for the time being included in any Province.

5. The following Acts passed by the said Parliament of Canada, and intituled respectively, — "An Act for the temporary government of Rupert's Land and the North Western Territory when united with Canada"; and "An Act to amend and continue the Act thirty-two and thirty-three Victoria, chapter

*Exclusive Powers of Provincial Legislatures.*

Subjects of exclusive
Provincial
Legislation.

**92.** In each Province the Legislature may exclusively make Laws in relation to Matters coming within the Classes of Subject next hereinafter enumerated; that is to say, —

1. Repealed. (48)
2. Direct Taxation within the Province in order to the raising of a Revenue for Provincial Purposes.
3. The borrowing of Money on the sole Credit of the Province.
4. The Establishment and Tenure of Provincial Offices and the Appointment and Payment of Provincial Officers.
5. The Management and Sale of the Public Lands belonging to the Province and of the Timber and Wood thereon.
6. The Establishment, Maintenance, and Management of Public and Reformatory Prisons in and for the Province.
7. The Establishment, Maintenance, and Management of Hospitals, Asylums, Charities, and Eleemosynary Institutions in and for the Province, other than Marine Hospitals.
8. Municipal Institutions in the Province.
9. Shop, Saloon, Tavern, Auctioneer, and other Licences in order to the raising of a Revenue for Provincial, Local, or Municipal Purposes.

---

three, and to establish and provide for the government of "the Province of Manitoba", shall be and be deemed to have been valid and effectual for all purposes whatsoever from the date at which they respectively received the assent, in the Queen's name, of the Governor General of the said Dominion of Canada.

6. Except as provided by the third section of this Act, it shall not be competent for the Parliament of Canada to alter the provisions of the last-mentioned Act of the said Parliament in so far as it relates to the Province of Manitoba, or of any other Act hereafter establishing new Provinces in the said Dominion, subject always to the right of the Legislature of the Province of Manitoba to alter from time to time the provisions of any law respecting the qualification of electors and members of the Legislative Assembly, and to make laws respecting elections in the said Province.

The *Rupert's Land Act, 1868*, 31-32 Vict., c. 105 (U.K.) (repealed by the *Statute Law Revision Act, 1893*, 56-57 Vict., c. 14 (U.K.) had previously conferred similar authority in relation to Rupert's Land and the North Western Territory upon admission of those areas.
2. The *Constitution Act, 1886*, 49-50 Vict., c. 35, (U.K.).

1. The Parliament of Canada may from time to time make provision for the representation in the Senate and House of Commons of Canada, or in either of them, of any territories which for the time being form part of the Dominion of Canada, but are not included in any province thereof.

3. The *Statute of Westminster, 1931*, 22 Geo. V, c. 4 (U.K.).

3. It is hereby declared and enacted that the Parliament of a Dominion has full power to make laws having extra-territorial operation.

4. Section 44 of the *Constitution Act, 1982*, authorizes Parliament to amend the Constitution of Canada in relation to the executive government of Canada or the Senate and House of Commons. Sections 38, 41, 42, and 43 of that Act authorize the Senate and House of Commons to give their approval to certain other constitutional amendments by resolution.

(48) Class I was repealed by the *Constitution Act, 1982*. As enacted, it read as follows:

1. The Amendment from Time to Time, notwithstanding anything in this Act, of the Constitution of the province, except as regards the Office of the Lieutenant Governor.

Section 45 of the *Constitution Act, 1982*, now authorizes legislatures to make laws amending the constitution of the province. Sections 38, 41, 42, and 43 of that Act authorize legislative assemblies to give their approval by resolution to certain other amendments to the Constitution of Canada.

10. Local Works and Undertakings other than such as are of the following Classes:—
   (*a*) Lines of Steam or other Ships, Railways, Canals, Telegraphs, and other Works and Undertakings connecting the Province with any other or others of the Provinces, or extending beyond the Limits of the Province;
   (*b*) Lines of Steam Ships between the Province and any British or Foreign Country;
   (*c*) Such Works as, although wholly situate within the Province, are before or after their Execution declared by the Parliament of Canada to be for the general Advantage of Canada or for the Advantage of Two or more of the Provinces.
11. The Incorporation of Companies with Provincial Objects.
12. The Solemnization of Marriage in the Province.
13. Property and Civil Rights in the Province.
14. The Administration of Justice in the Province, including the Constitution, Maintenance, and Organization of Provincial Courts, both of Civil and of Criminal Jurisdiction, and including Procedure in Civil Matters in those Courts.
15. The Imposition of Punishment by Fine, Penalty, or Imprisonment for enforcing any Law of the Province made in relation to any Matter coming within any of the Classes of Subjects enumerated in this Section.
16. Generally all Matters of a merely local or private Nature in the Province.

*Non-Renewable Natural Resources, Forestry Resources and Electrical Energy.*

Laws respecting non-renewable natural resources, forestry resources and electrical energy.

**92A.** (1) In each province, the legislature may exclusively make laws in relation to
   (*a*) exploration for non-renewable natural resources in the province;
   (*b*) development, conservation and management of non-renewable natural resources and forestry resources in the province, including laws in relation to the rate of primary production therefrom; and
   (*c*) development, conservation and management of sites and facilities in the province for the generation and production of electrical energy.

Export from provinces of resources.

(2) In each province, the legislature may make laws in relation to the export from the province to another part of Canada of the primary production from non-renewable natural resources and forestry resources in the province and the production from facilities in the province for the generation of electrical energy, but such laws may not authorize or provide for discrimination in prices or in supplies exported to another part of Canada.

Authority of Parliament.

(3) Nothing in subsection (2) derogates from the authority of Parliament to enact laws in relation to the matters referred to in that subsection and, where such a law of Parliament and a law of a province conflict, the law of Parliament prevails to the extent of the conflict.

Taxation of resources.

(4) In each province, the legislature may make laws in relation to the raising of money by any mode or system of taxation in respect of
   (*a*) non-renewable natural resources and forestry resources in the province and the primary production therefrom, and
   (*b*) sites and facilities in the province for the generation of electrical energy and the production therefrom.
whether or not such production is exported in whole or in part from the province, but such laws may not authorize or provide for taxation that differentiates between production exported to another part of Canada and production not exported from the province.

"Primary production."

(5) The expression "primary production" has the meaning assigned by the Sixth Schedule.

Existing powers or rights.

(6) Nothing in subsections (1) to (5) derogates from any powers or rights that a legislature or government of a province had immediately before the coming into force of this section. (49)

(49) Added by the *Constitution Act, 1982.*

*Education.*

Legislation
respecting
Education.

**93.** In and for each Province the Legislature may exclusively make Laws in relation to Education, subject and according to the following Provisions:—

(1) Nothing in any such Law shall prejudicially affect any Right or Privilege with respect to Denominational Schools which any Class of Persons have by Law in the Province at the Union:

(2) All the Powers, Privileges, and Duties at the Union by Law conferred and imposed in Upper Canada on the Separate Schools and School Trustees of the Queen's Roman Catholic Subjects shall be and the same are hereby extended to the Dissentient Schools of the Queen's Protestant and Roman Catholic Subjects in Quebec:

(3) Where in any Province a System of Separate or Dissentient Schools exists by Law at the Union or is thereafter established by the Legislature of the Province, an Appeal shall lie to the Governor General in Council from any Act or Decision of any Provincial Authority affecting any Right or Privilege of the Protestant or Roman Catholic Minority of the Queen's Subjects in relation to Education:

(4) In case any such Provincial Law as from Time to Time seems to the Governor General in Council requisite for the due Execution of the Provisions of this Section is not made, or in case any Decision of the Governor General in Council on any Appeal under this Section is not duly executed by the proper Provincial Authority in that Behalf, then and in every such Case, and as far only as the Circumstances of each Case require, the Parliament of Canada may make remedial Laws for the due Execution of the Provisions of this Section and of any Decision of the Governor General in Council under this Section. (50)

---

(50) Altered for Manitoba by section 22 of the *Manitoba Act, 1870*, 33 Vict., c. 3 (Canada), (confirmed by the *Constitution Act, 1871*), which read as follows:

**22.** In and for the Province, the said Legislature may exclusively make Laws in relation to Education, subject and according to the following provisions:—

(1) Nothing in any such Law shall prejudicially affect any right or privilege with respect to Denominational Schools which any class of persons have by Law or practice in the Province at the Union:

(2) An appeal shall lie to the Governor General in Council from any Act or decision of the Legislature of the Province, or of any Provincial Authority, affecting any right or privilege, of the Protestant or Roman Catholic minority of the Queen's subjects in relation to Eduction:

(3) In case any such Provincial Law, as from time to time seems to the Governor General in Council requisite for the due execution of the provisions of this section, is not made, or in case any decision of the Governor General in Council on any appeal under this section is not duly executed by the proper Provincial Authority in that behalf, then, and in every such case, and as far only as the circumstances of each case require, the Parliament of Canada may make remedial Laws for the due execution of the provisions of this section, and of any decision of the Governor General in Council under this section.

Altered for Alberta by section 17 of the *Alberta Act*, 4-5 Edw. VII, c. 3, 1905 (Canada), which reads as follows:

**17.** Section 93 of the *Constitution Act, 1867*, shall apply to the said province, with the substitution for paragraph (1) of the said section 93 of the following paragraph: —

(1) Nothing in any such law shall prejudicially affect any right or privilege with respect to separate schools which any class of persons have at the date of the passing of this Act, under the terms of chapters 29 and 30 of the Ordinances of the Northwest Territories, passed in the year 1901, or with respect to religious instruction in any public or separate school as provided for in the said ordinances.

**2.** In the appropriation by the Legislature or distribution by the Government of the province of any moneys for the support of schools organized and carried on in accordance with the said chapter 29 or any Act passed in amendment thereof, or in substitution therefor, there shall be no discrimination against schools of any class described in the said chapter 29.

**3.** Where the expression "by law" is employed in paragraph 3 of the said section 93, it shall be held to mean the law as set out in the said chapters 29 and 30, and where the expression "at the Union"

*Uniformity of Laws in Ontario, Nova Scotia and New Brunswick.*

Legislation for
Uniformity of Laws
in Three Provinces.

**94.** Notwithstanding anything in this Act, the Parliament of Canada may make Provision for the Uniformity of all or any of the Laws relative to Property and Civil Rights in Ontario, Nova Scotia, and New Brunswick, and of the Procedure of all or any of the Courts in Those Three Provinces, and from and after the passing of any Act in that Behalf the Power of the Parliament of Canada to make Laws in relation to any Matter comprised in any such Act shall, notwithstanding anything in this Act, be unrestricted; but any Act of the Parliament of Canada making Provision for such Uniformity shall not have effect in any Province unless and until it is adopted and enacted as Law by the Legislature thereof.

*Old Age Pensions.*

Legislation
respecting old age
pensions and
supplementary
benefits.

**94A.** The Parliament of Canada may make laws in relation to old age pensions and supplementary benefits, including survivors, and disability benefits irrespective of age, but no such law

---

is employed, in the said paragraph 3, it shall be held to mean the date at which this Act comes into force.

Altered for Saskatchewan by section 17 of the *Saskatchewan Act*, 4-5 Edw. VII, c. 42, 1905 (Canada), which read as follows:

**17.** Section 93 of the *Constitution Act, 1867*, shall apply to the said province, with the substitution for paragraph (1) of the said section 93, of the following paragraph: —

(1) Nothing in any such law shall prejudicially affect any right or privilege with respect to separate schools which any class of persons have at the date of the passing of this Act, under the terms of chapters 29 and 30 of the Ordinances of the Northwest Territories, passed in the year 1901, or with respect to religious instruction in any public or separate school as provided for in the said ordinances.

2. In the appropriation by the Legislature or distribution by the Government of the province of any moneys for the support of schools organized and carried on in accordance with the said chapter 29, or any Act passed in amendment thereof or in substitution therefor, there shall be no discrimination against schools of any class described in the said chapter 29.

3. Where the expression "by law" is employed in paragraph (3) of the said section 93, it shall be held to mean the law as set out in the said chapters 29 and 30; and where the expression "at the Union" is employed in the said paragraph (3), it shall be held to mean the date at which this Act comes into force.

Altered by Term 17 of the Terms of Union of Newfoundland with Canada (confirmed by the *Newfoundland Act*, 12-13 Geo. VI, c. 22 (U.K.)), which read as follows:

**17.** In lieu of section ninety-three of the *Constitution Act, 1867*, the following term shall apply in respect of the Province of Newfoundland:

In and for the Province of Newfoundland the Legislature shall have exclusive authority to make laws in relation to education, but the Legislature will not have authority to make laws prejudicially affecting any right or privilege with respect to denominational schools, common (amalgamated) schools, or denominational colleges, that any class or classes of persons have by law in Newfoundland at the date of Union, and out of public funds of the Province of Newfoundland, provided for education,

(*a*) all such schools shall receive their share of such funds in accordance with scales determined on a non-discriminatory basis from time to time by the Legislature for all schools then being conducted under authority of the Legislature; and

(*b*) all such colleges shall receive their share of any grant from time to time voted for all colleges then being conducted under authority of the Legislature, such grant being distributed on a non-discriminatory basis.

See also sections 23, 29, and 59 of the *Constitution Act, 1982*. Section 23 provides for new minority language educational rights and section 59 permits a delay in respect of the coming into force in Quebec of one aspect of those rights. Section 29 provides that nothing in the *Canadian Charter of Rights and Freedoms* abrogates or derogates from any rights or privileges guaranteed by or under the Constitution of Canada in respect of denominational, separate or dissentient schools.

shall affect the operation of any law present or future of a provincial legislature in relation to any such matter. (51)

*Agriculture and Immigration.*

Concurrent Powers of Legislation respecting Agriculture, etc.

**95.** In each Province the Legislature may make Laws in relation to Agriculture in the Province, and to Immigration into the Province; and it is hereby declared that the Parliament of Canada may from Time to Time make Laws in relation to Agriculture in all or any of the Provinces, and to Immigration into all or any of the Provinces; and any Law of the Legislature of a Province relative to Agriculture or to Immigration shall have effect in and for the Province as long and as far only as it is not repugnant to any Act of the Parliament of Canada.

## VII.—JUDICATURE.

Appointment of Judges.

**96.** The Governor General shall appoint the Judges of the Superior, District, and County Courts in each Province, except those of the Courts of Probate in Nova Scotia and New Brunswick.

Selection of Judges in Ontario, etc.

**97.** Until the laws relative to Property and Civil Rights in Ontario, Nova Scotia, and New Brunswick, and the Procedure of the Courts in those Provinces, are made uniform, the Judges of the Courts of those Provinces appointed by the Governor General shall be selected from the respective Bars of those Provinces.

Selections of Judges in Quebec.

**98.** The Judges of the Courts of Quebec shall be selected from the Bar of that Province.

Tenure of office of Judges.

**99.** (1) Subject to subsection two of this section, the Judges of the Superior Courts shall hold office during good behaviour, but shall be removable by the Governor General on Address of the Senate and House of Commons.

Termination at age 75.

(2) A Judge of a Superior Court, whether appointed before or after the coming into force of this section, shall cease to hold office upon attaining the age of seventy-five years, or upon the coming into force of this section if at that time he has already attained that age. (52)

Salaries etc., of Judges.

**100.** The Salaries, Allowances, and Pensions of the Judges of the Superior, District, and County Courts (except the Courts of Probate in Nova Scotia and New Brunswick), and of the Admiralty Courts in Cases where the Judges thereof are for the Time being being paid by Salary, shall be fixed and provided by the Parliament of Canada. (53)

General Court of Appeal, etc.

**101.** The Parliament of Canada may, notwithstanding anything in this Act, from Time to Time provide for the Constitution, Maintenance, and Organization of a General Court of Appeal

---

(51) Added by the *Constitution Act, 1964*, 12-13 Eliz. II, c. 73 (U.K.). As originally enacted by the *British North America Act, 1951*, 14-15 Geo. VI, c. 32 (U.K.), which was repealed by the *Constitution Act, 1982*, section 92A read as follows:

**94A.** It is hereby declared that the Parliament of Canada may from time to time make laws in relation to old age pensions in Canada, but no law made by the Parliament of Canada in relation to old age pensions shall affect the operation of any law present or future of a Provincial Legislature in relation to old age pensions.

(52) Repealed and re-enacted by the *Constitution Act, 1960*, 9 Eliz. II, c. 2 (U.K.), which came into force on the 1st day of March, 1961. The original section read as follows:

**99.** The Judges of the Superior Courts shall hold Office during good Behaviour, but shall be removable by the Governor General on Address of the Senate and House of Commons.

(53) Now provided for in the *Judges Act*, R.S.C. 1970, c. J-1.

for Canada, and for the Establishment of any additional Courts for the better Administration of the Laws of Canada. (54)

VIII.—REVENUES; DEBTS; ASSETS; TAXATION.

Creation of Consolidated Revenue Fund.

**102.** All Duties and Revenues over which the respective Legislatures of Canada, Nova Scotia, and New Brunswick before and at the Union had and have Power of Appropriation, except such Portions thereof as are by this Act reserved to the respective Legislatures of the Provinces, or are raised by them in accordance with the special Powers conferred on them by this Act, shall form One Consolidated Revenue Fund, to be appropriated for the Public Service of Canada in the Manner and subject to the Charges of this Act provided.

Expenses of Collection, etc.

**103.** The Consolidated Revenue Fund of Canada shall be permanently charged with the Costs, Charges, and Expenses incident to the Collection, Management, and Receipt thereof, and the same shall form the First Charge thereon, subject to be reviewed and audited in such Manner as shall be ordered by the Governor General in Council until the Parliament otherwise provides.

Interest of Provincial Public Debts.

**104.** The annual Interest of the Public Debts of the several Provinces of Canada, Nova Scotia, and New Brunswick at the Union shall form the Second Charge on the Consolidated Revenue Fund of Canada.

Salary of Governor General.

**105.** Unless altered by the Parliament of Canada, the Salary of the Governor General shall be Ten thousand Pounds Sterling Money of the United Kingdom of Great Britain and Ireland, payable out of the Consolidated Revenue Fund of Canada, and the same shall form the Third Charge thereon. (55)

Appropriation from Time to Time.

**106.** Subject to the several Payments by this Act charged on the Consolidated Revenue Fund of Canada, the same shall be appropriated by the Parliament of Canada for the Public Service.

Transfer of Stocks, etc.

**107.** All Stocks, Cash, Banker's Balances, and Securities for Money belonging to each Province at the Time of the Union, except as in this Act mentioned, shall be the Property of Canada, and shall be taken in Reduction of the Amount of the respective Debts of the Provinces at the Union.

Transfer of Property in Schedule.

**108.** The Public Works and Property of each Province, enumerated in the Third Schedule to this Act, shall be the Property of Canada.

Property in Lands, Mines, etc.

**109.** All Lands, Mines, Minerals, and Royalties belonging to the several Provinces of Canada, Nova Scotia, and New Brunswick at the Union, and all Sums then due or payable for such Lands, Mines, Minerals, or Royalties, shall belong to the several Provinces of Ontario, Quebec, Nova Scotia, and New Brunswick in which the same are situate or arise, subject to any Trusts existing in respect thereof, and to any Interest other than that of the Province in the same. (56)

Assets connected with Provincial Debts.

**110.** All Assets connected with such Portions of the Public Debt of each Province as are assumed by that Province shall belong to that Province.

Canada to be liable for Provincial Debts.

**111.** Canada shall be liable for the Debts and Liabilities of each Province existing at the Union.

Debts of Ontario and Quebec.

**112.** Ontario and Quebec conjointly shall be liable to Canada for the Amount (if any) by which the Debt of the Province of Canada exceeds at the Union Sixty-two million five hundred

---

(54) See the *Supreme Court Act*, R.S.C. 1970, c. S-19, and the *Federal Court Act*, R.S.C. 1970, (2nd Supp.) c. 10.

(55) Now covered by the *Governor General's Act*, R.S.C. 1970, c. G-14.

(56) The three prairie provinces were placed in the same position as the original provinces by the *Constitution Act, 1930*, 21 Geo. V, c. 26 (U.K.).

thousand Dollars, and shall be charged with Interest at the Rate of Five Per Centum per Annum thereon.

Assets of Ontario and Quebec.

**113.** The Assets enumerated in the Fourth Schedule to this Act belonging at the Union to the Province of Canada shall be the Property of Ontario and Quebec conjointly.

Debt of Nova Scotia.

**114.** Nova Scotia shall be liable to Canada for the Amount (if any) by which its Public Debt exceeds at the Union Eight million Dollars, and shall be charged with Interest at the Rate of Five per Centum per Annum thereon. (57)

Debt of New Brunswick.

**115.** New Brunswick shall be liable to Canada for the Amount (if any) by which its Public Debt exceeds at the Union Seven million Dollars, and shall be charged with Interest at the Rate of Five per Centum per Annum thereon.

Payment of Interest to Nova Scotia and New Brunswick.

**116.** In case the Public Debts of Nova Scotia and New Brunswick do not at the Union amount to Eight million and Seven million Dollars respectively, they shall respectively receive by half-yearly Payments in advance from the Government of Canada Interest at Five per Centum per Annum on the Difference between the actual Amounts of their respective Debts and such stipulated Amounts.

Provincial Public Property.

**117.** The several Provinces shall retain all their respective Public Property not otherwise disposed of in this Act, subject to the Right of Canada to assume any Lands or Public Property required for Fortifications or for the Defence of the Country.

**118.** Repealed. (58)

---

(57) The obligations imposed by this section, sections 115 and 116, and similar obligations under the instruments creating or admitting other provinces, have been carried into legislation of the Parliament of Canada and are now to be found in the *Provincial Subsidies Act*, R.S.C. 1970, c. P-26.

(58) Repealed by the *Statute Law Revision Act, 1950*, 14 Geo. VI, c. 6 (U.K.). As originally enacted the section read as follows:

**118.** The following Sums shall be paid yearly by Canada to the several Provinces for the Support of their Governments and Legislatures:

|  | Dollars |
|---|---|
| Ontario | Eighty thousand. |
| Quebec | Seventy thousand. |
| Nova Scotia | Sixty thousand. |
| New Brunswick | Fifty thousand. |

Two hundred and sixty thousand;

and an annual Grant in aid of each Province shall be made, equal to Eighty Cents per Head of the Population as ascertained by the Census of One thousand eight hundred and sixty-one, and in the Case of Nova Scotia and New Brunswick, by each subsequent Decennial Census until the Population of each of those two Provinces amounts to Four hundred thousand Souls, at which Rate such Grant shall thereafter remain. Such Grants shall be in full Settlement of all future Demands on Canada, and shall be paid half-yearly in advance to each Province; but the Government of Canada shall deduct from such Grants, as against any Province, all Sums chargeable as Interest on the Public Debt of that Province in excess of the several Amounts stipulated in this Act.

The section was made obsolete by the *Constitution Act, 1907*, 7 Edw. VII, c. 11 (U.K.) which provided:

1. (1) The following grants shall be made yearly by Canada to every province, which at the commencement of this Act is a province of the Dominion, for its local purposes and the support of its Government and Legislature:—

(a) A fixed grant—

where the population of the province is under one hundred and fifty thousand, of one hundred

Further Grant to
New Brunswick.

**119.** New Brunswick shall receive by half-yearly Payments in advance from Canada for the period of Ten years from the Union an additional Allowance of Sixty-three thousand Dollars per Annum; but as long as the Public Debt of that Province remains under Seven million Dollars, a

---

thousand dollars;

where the population of the province is one hundred and fifty thousand, but does not exceed two hundred thousand, of one hundred and fifty thousand dollars;

where the population of the province is two hundred thousand, but does not exceed four hundred thousand, of one hundred and eighty thousand dollars;

where the population of the province is four hundred thousand, but does not exceed eight hundred thousand, of one hundred and ninety thousand dollars;

where the population of the province is eight hundred thousand, but does not exceed one million five hundred thousand, of two hundred and twenty thousand dollars;)

where the population of the province exceeds one million five hundred thousand, of two hundred and forty thousand dollars; and

(*b*) Subject to the special provisions of this Act as to the provinces of British Columbia and Prince Edward Island, a grant at the rate of eighty cents per head of the population of the province up to the number of two million five hundred thousand, and at the rate of sixty cents per head of so much of the population as exceeds that number.

(2) An additional grant of one hundred thousand dollars shall be made yearly to the province of British Columbia for a period of ten years from the commencement of this Act.

(3) The population of a province shall be ascertained from time to time in the case of the provinces of Manitoba, Saskatchewan, and Alberta respectively by the last quinquennial census or statutory estimate of population made under the Acts establishing those provinces or any other Act of the Parliament of Canada making provision for the purpose, and in the case of any other province by the last decennial census for the time being.

(4) The grants payable under this Act shall be paid half-yearly in advance to each province.

(5) The grants payable under this Act shall be substituted for the grants or subsidies (in this Act referred to as existing grants) payable for the like purposes at the commencement of this Act to the several provinces of the Dominion under the provisions of section one hundred and eighteen of the *Constitution Act, 1867*, or of any Order in Council establishing a province, or of any Act of the Parliament of Canada containing directions for the payment of any such grant or subsidy, and those provisions shall cease to have effect.

(6) The Government of Canada shall have the same power of deducting sums charged against a province on account of the interest on public debt in the case of the grant payable under this Act to the province as they have in the case of the existing grant.

(7) Nothing in this Act shall affect the obligation of the Government of Canada to pay to any province any grant which is payable to that province, other than the existing grant for which the grant under this Act is substituted.

(8) In the case of the provinces of British Columbia and Prince Edward Island, the amount paid on account of the grant payable per head of the population to the provinces under this Act shall not at any time be less than the amount of the corresponding grant payable at the commencement of this Act, and if it is found on any decennial census that the population of the province has decreased since the last decennial census, the amount paid on account of the grant shall not be decreased below the amount then payable, notwithstanding the decrease of the population.

See the *Provincial Statutes Act*, R.S.C. 1970, c. P-26, *The Maritime Provinces Additional Subsidies Act*, 1942-43, c. 14, and the Terms of Union of Newfoundland with Canada, appended to the *Newfoundland Act*, and also to *An Act to approve the Terms of Union of Newfoundland with Canada*, chapter 1 of the Statutes of Canada, 1949.

See also Part III of the *Constitution Act, 1982*, which sets out commitments by Parliament and the provincial legislatures respecting equal opportunities, economic development and the provision of essential public services and a commitment by Parliament and the government of Canada to the principle of making equalization payments.

Deduction equal to the Interest at Five per Centum per Annum on such Deficiency shall be made from that Allowance of Sixty-three thousand Dollars. (59)

**Form of Payments.**

**120.** All Payments to be made under this Act, or in discharge of Liabilities created under any Act of the Provinces of Canada, Nova Scotia, and New Brunswick respectively, and assumed by Canada, shall, until the Parliament of Canada otherwise directs, be made in such Form and Manner as may from Time to Time be ordered by the Governor General in Council.

**Canadian Manufactures, etc.**

**121.** All Articles of the Growth, Produce, or Manufacture of any one of the Provinces shall, from and after the Union, be admitted free into each of the other Provinces.

**Continuance of Customs and Excise Laws.**

**122.** The Customs and Excise Laws of each Province shall, subject to the Provisions of this Act, continue in force until altered by the Parliament of Canada. (60)

**Exportation and Importation as between Two Provinces.**

**123.** Where Customs Duties are, at the Union, leviable on any Goods, Wares, or Merchandises in any Two Provinces, those Goods, Wares, and Merchandises may, from and after the Union, be imported from one of those Provinces into the other of them on Proof of Payment of the Customs Duty leviable thereon in the Province of Exportation, and on Payment of such further Amount (if any) of Customs Duty as is leviable thereon in the Province of Importation. (61)

**Lumber Dues in New Brunswick.**

**124.** Nothing in this Act shall affect the Right of New Brunswick to levy the Lumber Dues provided in Chapter Fifteen of Title Three of the Revised Statutes of New Brunswick, or in any Act amending that Act before or after the Union, and not increasing the Amount of such Dues; but the Lumber of any of the Provinces other than New Brunswick shall not be subject to such Dues. (62)

**Exemption of Public Lands, etc.**

**125.** No Lands or Property belonging to Canada or any Province shall be liable to Taxation.

**Provincial Consolidated Revenue Fund.**

**126.** Such Portions of the Duties and Revenues over which the respective Legislatures of Canada, Nova Scotia, and New Brunswick had before the Union Power of Appropriation as are by this Act reserved to the respective Governments or Legislatures of the Provinces, and all Duties and Revenues raised by them in accordance with the special Powers conferred upon them by this Act, shall in each Province form One Consolidated Revenue Fund to be appropriated for the Public Service of the Province.

## IX.—MISCELLANEOUS PROVISIONS.

*General.*

**127.** Repealed. (63)

**Oath of Allegiance, etc.**

**128.** Every Member of the Senate or House of Commons of Canada shall before taking his Seat therein take and subscribe before the Governor General or some Person authorized by him,

---

(59) Spent.

(60) Spent. Now covered by the *Customs Act*, R.S.C. 1970, c. C-40, the *Customs Tariff*, R.S.C. 1970, c. C-41, the *Excise Act*, R.S.C. 1970, c. E-12 and the *Excise Tax Act*, R.S.C. 1970, c. E-13.

(61) Spent.

(62) Those dues were repealed in 1873 by 36 Vict., c. 16 (N.B.). And see *An Act respecting the Export Duties imposed on Lumber*, etc. (1873) 36 Vict., c. 41 (Canada), and section 2 of the *Provincial Statutes Act*, R.S.C. 1970, c. P-26.

(63) Repealed by the *Statute Law Revision Act, 1893*, 56-57 Vict., c. 14 (U.K.). The section read as follows:

  **127.** If any Person being at the passing of this Act a Member of the Legislative Council of Canada,

and every Member of a Legislative Council or Legislative Assembly of any Province shall before taking his Seat therein take and subscribe before the Lieutenant Governor of the Province or some Person authorized by him, the Oath of Allegiance contained in the Fifth Schedule to this Act; and every Member of the Senate of Canada and every Member of the Legislative Council of Quebec shall also, before taking his Seat therein, take and subscribe before the Governor General, or some Person authorized by him, the Declaration of Qualification contained in the same Schedule.

Continuance of existing Laws, Courts, Officers, etc.

**129.** Except as otherwise provided by this Act, all Laws in force in Canada, Nova Scotia, or New Brunswick at the Union, and all Courts of Civil and Criminal Jurisdiction, and all legal Commissions, Powers, and Authorities, and all Officers, Judicial, Administrative, and Ministerial, existing therein at the Union, shall continue in Ontario, Quebec, Nova Scotia, and New Brunswick respectively, as if the Union had not been made; subject nevertheless (except with respect to such as are enacted by or exist under Acts of the Parliament of Great Britain or of the Parliament of the United Kingdom of Great Britain and Ireland), to be repealed, abolished, or altered by the Parliament of Canada, or by the Legislature of the respective Province, according to the Authority of the Parliament or of that Legislature under this Act. (64)

Transfer of Officers to Canada.

**130.** Until the Parliament of Canada otherwise provides, all Officers of the several Provinces having Duties to discharge in relation to Matters other than those coming within the Classes of Subjects by this Act assigned exclusively to the Legislature of the Provinces shall be Officers of Canada, and shall continue to discharge the Duties of their respective Offices under the same Liabilities, Responsibilities, and Penalties as if the Union had not been made. (65)

Appointment of new Officers.

**131.** Until the Parliament of Canada otherwise provides, the Governor General in Council may from Time to Time appoint such Officers as the Governor General in Council deems necessary or proper for the effectual Execution of this Act.

Treaty Obligations.

**132.** The Parliament and Government of Canada shall have all Powers necessary or proper for performing the Obligations of Canada or of any Province thereof, as Part of the British Empire, towards Foreign Countries, arising under Treaties between the Empire and such Foreign Countries.

Use of English and French languages.

**133.** Either the English or the French Language may be used by any Person in the Debates of the Houses of the Parliament of Canada and of the Houses of the Legislature of Quebec; and both those Languages shall be used in the respective Records and Journals of those Houses; and either of those Languages may be used by any Person or in any Pleading or Process in or issuing from any Court of Canada established under this Act, and in or from all or any of the Courts of Quebec.

The Acts of the Parliament of Canada and of the Legislature of Quebec shall be printed and published in both those Languages. (66)

---

Nova Scotia, or New Brunswick to whom a Place in the Senate is offered, does not within Thirty Days thereafter, by Writing under his Hand addressed to the Governor General of the Province of Canada or to the Lieutenant Governor of Nova Scotia or New Brunswick (as the Case may be), accept the same, he shall be deemed to have declined the same, and any Person who, being at the passing of this Act a Member of the Legislative Council of Nova Scotia or New Brunswick, accepts a Place in the Senate, shall thereby vacate his Seat in such Legislative Council.

(64) The restriction against altering or repealing laws enacted by or existing under statutes of the United Kingdom was removed by the *Statute of Westminster, 1931,* 22 Geo. V, c. 4 (U.K.) except in respect of certain constitutional documents. Comprehensive procedures for amending enactments forming part of the Constitution of Canada were provided by Part V of the *Constitution Act, 1982,* (U.K.) 1982, c. 11.

(65) Spent.

(66) A similar provision was enacted for Manitoba by Section 23 of the *Manitoba Act, 1870,* 33 Vict., c. 3 (Canada) (confirmed by the *Constitution Act, 1871*). Section 23 read as follows:

23. Either the English or the French language may be used by any person in the debates of the Houses of the Legislature, and both these languages shall be used in the respective Records and

*Ontario and Quebec.*

Appointment of Executive Officers for Ontario and Quebec.

**134.** Until the Legislature of Ontario or of Quebec otherwise provides, the Lieutenant Governors of Ontario and Quebec may each appoint under the Great Seal of the Province the following Officers, to hold Office during Pleasure, that is to say, — the Attorney General, the Secretary and Registrar of the Province, the Treasurer of the Province, the Commissioner of Crown Lands, and the Commissioner of Agriculture and Public Works, and in the Case of Quebec the Solicitor General, and may, by Order of the Lieutenant Governor in Council, from Time to Time prescribe the Duties of those Officers, and of the several Departments over which they shall preside or to which they shall belong, and of the Officers and Clerks thereof, and may also appoint other and additional Officers to hold Office during Pleasure, and may from Time to Time prescribe the Duties of those Officers, and of the several Departments over which they shall preside or to which they shall belong, and of the Officers and Clerks thereof. (67)

Powers, Duties, etc. of Executive Officers.

**135.** Until the Legislature of Ontario or Quebec otherwise provides, all Rights, Powers, Duties, Functions, Responsibilities, or Authorities at the passing of this Act vested in or imposed on the Attorney General, Solicitor General, Secretary and Registrar of the Province of Canada, Minister of Finance, Commissioner of Crown Lands, Commissioner of Public Works, and Minister of Agriculture and Receiver General, by any Law, Statute, or Ordinance of Upper Canada, Lower Canada, or Canada, and not repugnant to this Act, shall be vested in or imposed on any Officer to be appointed by the Lieutenant Governor for the discharge of the same or any of them; and the Commissioner of Agriculture and Public Works shall perform the Duties and Functions of the Office of Minister of Agriculture at the passing of this Act imposed by the Law of the Province of Canada, as well as those of the Commissioner of Public Works. (68)

Great Seals.

**136.** Until altered by the Lieutenant Governor in Council, the Great Seals of Ontario and Quebec respectively shall be the same, or of the same Design, as those used in the Provinces of Upper Canada and Lower Canada respectively before their Union as the Province of Canada.

Construction of temporary Acts.

**137.** The words "and from thence to the End of the then next ensuing Session of the Legislature," or Words to the same Effect, used in any temporary Act of the Province of Canada not expired before the Union, shall be construed to extend and apply to the next Session of the Parliament of Canada if the Subject Matter of the Act is within the Powers of the same as defined by this Act, or to the next Sessions of the Legislatures of Ontario and Quebec respectively if the Subject Matter of the Act is within the Powers of the same as defined by this Act.

As to Errors in Names.

**138.** From and after the Union the Use of the Words Upper Canada", instead of "Ontario," or "Lower Canada" instead of "Quebec," in any Deed, Writ, Process, Pleading, Document, Matter, or Thing shall not invalidate the same.

As to issue of Proclamations before Union, to commence after Union.

**139.** Any Proclamation under the Great Seal of the Province of Canada issued before the Union to take effect at a Time which is subsequent to the Union, whether relating to that Province,

---

Journals of those Houses; and either of those languages may be used by any person, or in any Pleading or Process, in or issuing from any Court of Canada established under the British North America Act, 1007, or in or from all or any of the Courts of the Province. The Acts of the Legislature shall be printed and published in both those languages.

Sections 17 to 19 of the *Constitution Act, 1982,* restate the language rights set out in section 133 in respect of Parliament and the courts established under the *Constitution Act, 1867,* and also guarantees those rights in respect of the legislature of New Brunswick and the courts of that province.

Section 16 and sections 20, 21 and 23 of the *Constitution Act, 1982,* recognize additional language rights in respect of the English and French languages. Section 22 preserves language rights and privileges of languages other than English or French.

(67)  Spent. Now covered in Ontario by the *Executive Council Act,* R.S.O. 1980, c. 147 and in Quebec by the *Executive Power Act,* R.S.Q. 1977, c. E-18.

(68)  Probably spent.

or to Upper Canada, or to Lower Canada, and the several Matters and Things therein proclaimed, shall be and continue of like Force and Effect as if the Union had not been made. (69)

As to issue of Proclamations after Union.

**140.** Any Proclamation which is authorized by any Act of the Legislature of the Province of Canada to be issued under the Great Seal of the Province of Canada, whether relating to that Province, or to Upper Canada, or to Lower Canada, and which is not issued before the Union, may be issued by the Lieutenant Governor of Ontario or Quebec, as its Subject Matter requires, under the Great Seal thereof; and from and after the Issue of such Proclamation the same and the several Matters and Things therein proclaimed shall be and continue of the like Force and Effect in Ontario or Quebec as if the Union had not been made. (70)

Penitentiary.

**141.** The Penitentiary of the Province of Canada shall, until the Parliament of Canada otherwise provides, be and continue the Penitentiary of Ontario and of Quebec. (71)

Arbitration respecting Debts, etc.

**142.** The Division and Adjustment of the Debts, Credits, Liabilities, Properties, and Assets of Upper Canada and Lower Canada shall be referred to the Arbitrament of Three Arbitrators, One chosen by the Government of Ontario, One by the Government of Quebec, and One by the Government of Canada; and the Selection of the Arbitrators shall not be made until the Parliament of Canada and the Legislatures of Ontario and Quebec have met; and the Arbitrator chosen by the Government of Canada shall not be a Resident either in Ontario or Quebec. (72)

Division of Records.

**143.** The Governor General in Council may from Time to Time order that such and so many of the Records, Books, and Documents of the Province of Canada as he thinks fit shall be appropriated and delivered either to Ontario or to Quebec, and the same shall thenceforth be the Property of that Province; and any Copy thereof or Extract therefrom, duly certified by the Officer having charge of the Original thereof, shall be admitted as Evidence. (73)

Constitution of Townships in Quebec.

**144.** The Lieutenant Governor of Quebec may from Time to Time, by Proclamation under the Great Seal of the Province, to take effect from a Day to be appointed therein, constitute Townships in those Parts of the Province of Quebec in which Townships are not then already constituted, and fix the Metes and Bounds thereof.

**145.** Repealed. (74)

---

(69) Probably spent.

(70) Probably spent.

(71) Spent. Penitentiaries are now provided for by the *Penitentiary Act*, R.S.C. 1970, c. P-6.

(72) Spent. See pages (xi) and (xii) of the Public Accounts, 1902-03.

(73) Probably spent. Two orders were made under this section on the 24th of January, 1868.

(74) Repealed by the *Statute Law Revision Act, 1893*, 56-57 Vict., c. 14, (U.K.). The section read as follows:

X.—Intercolonial Railway.

**145.** Inasmuch as the Provinces of Canada, Nova Scotia, and New Brunswick have joined in a Declaration that the Construction of the Intercolonial Railway is essential to the Consolidation of the Union of British North America, and to the Assent thereto of Nova Scotia and New Brunswick, and have consequently agreed that Provision should be made for its immediate Construction by the Government of Canada; Therefore, in order to give effect to that Agreement, it shall be the Duty of the Government and Parliament of Canada to provide for the Commencement, within Six Months after the Union, of a Railway connecting the River St. Lawrence with the City of Halifax in Nova Scotia, and for the Construction thereof without Intermission, and the Completion thereof with all practicable Speed.

## XI.—ADMISSION OF OTHER COLONIES.

Power to admit Newfoundland etc., into the Union.

**146.** It shall be lawful for the Queen, by and with the Advice of Her Majesty's Most Honourable Privy Council, on Addresses from the Houses of the Parliament of Canada, and from the Houses of the respective Legislatures of the Colonies or Provinces of Newfoundland, Prince Edward Island, and British Columbia, to admit those Colonies or Provinces, or any of them, into the Union, and on Address from the Houses of the Parliament of Canada to admit Rupert's Land and the North-western Territory, or either of them, into the Union, on such Terms and Conditions in each Case as are in the Addresses expressed and as the Queen thinks fit to approve, subject to the Provisions of this Act; and the Provisions of any Order in Council in that Behalf shall have effect as if they had been enacted by the Parliament of the United Kingdom of Great Britain and Ireland. (75)

As to Representation of Newfoundland and Prince Edward Island in Senate.

**147.** In case of the Admission of Newfoundland and Prince Edward Island, or either of them, each shall be entitled to a Representation in the Senate of Canada of Four Members, and (notwithstanding anything in this Act) in case of the Admission of Newfoundland the normal Number of Senators shall be Seventy-six and their maximum Number shall be Eighty-two; but Prince Edward Island when admitted shall be deemed to be comprised in the Third of Three Divisions into which Canada is, in relation to the Constitution of the Senate, divided by this Act, and accordingly, after the Admission of Prince Edward Island, whether Newfoundland is admitted or not, the Representation of Nova Scotia and New Brunswick in the Senate shall, as Vacancies occur, be reduced from Twelve to Ten Members respectively, and the Representation of each of those Provinces shall not be increased at any Time beyond Ten, except under the Provisions of this Act for the Appointment of Three or Six additional Senators under the Direction of the Queen. (76)

## SCHEDULES

## THE FIRST SCHEDULE. (77)

*Electoral Districts of Ontario.*

### A.

## EXISTING ELECTORAL DIVISIONS.

### COUNTIES.

1. Prescott.
2. Glengarry.
3. Stormont.
4. Dundas.
5. Russell

6. Carleton.
7. Prince Edward.
8. Halton.
9. Essex.

RIDINGS OF COUNTIES.

10. North Riding of Lanark.
11. South Riding of Lanark.
12. North Riding of Leeds and North Riding of Grenville.
13. South Riding of Leeds.
14. South Riding of Grenville.
15. East Riding of Northumberland.

---

(75) All territories mentioned in this section are now part of Canada. See the notes to section 5, *supra*.

(76) Spent. See the notes to sections 21, 22, 26, 27 and 28, *supra*.

(77) Spent. *Representation Act,* R.S.O. 1970, c. 413.

16. West Riding of Northumberland (excepting therefrom the Township of South Monaghan).
17. East Riding of Durham.
18. West Riding of Durham.
19. North Riding of Ontario.
20. South Riding of Ontario.
21. East Riding of York.
22. West Riding of York.
23. North Riding of York.
24. North Riding of Wentworth.
25. South Riding of Wentworth.
26. East Riding of Elgin.
27. West Riding of Elgin.
28. North Riding of Waterloo.
29. South Riding of Waterloo.
30. North Riding of Brant.
31. South Riding of Brant.
32. North Riding of Oxford.
33. South Riding of Oxford.
34. East Riding of Middlesex.

CITIES, PARTS OF CITIES, AND TOWNS.

35. West Toronto.
36. East Toronto.
37. Hamilton.
38. Ottawa.
39. Kingston.
40. London.
41. Town of Brockville, with the Township of Elizabethtown thereto attached.
42. Town of Niagara, with the Township of Niagara thereto attached.
43. Town of Cornwall, with the Township of Cornwall thereto attached.

B.

NEW ELECTORAL DISTRICTS.

44. The Provisional Judicial District of ALGOMA.

The County of BRUCE, divided into Two Ridings, to be called respectively the North and South Ridings:—
45. The North Riding of Bruce to consist of the Townships of Bury, Lindsay, Eastnor, Albermarle, Amable, Arran, Bruce, Elderslie, and Saugeen, and the Village of Southampton.
46. The South Riding of Bruce to consist of the Townships of Kincardine (including the Village of Kincardine), Greenock, Brant, Huron, Kinloss, Culross, and Carrick.

The County of HURON, divided into Two Ridings, to be called respectively the North and South Ridings:—
47. The North Riding to consist of the Townships of Ashfield, Wawanosh, Turnberry, Howick, Morris, Grey, Colborne, Hullett, including the Village of Clinton, and McKillop.
48. The South Riding to consist of the Town of Goderich and the Townships of Goderich, Tuckersmith, Stanley, Hay, Usborne, and Stephen.

The County of MIDDLESEX, divided into Three Ridings, to be called respectively the North, West, and East Ridings:—
49. The North Riding to consist of the Townships of McGillivray and Biddulph (taken from the County of Huron), and Williams East, Williams West, Adelaide, and Lobo.
50. The West Riding to consist of the Townships of Delaware, Carradoc, Metcalfe, Mosa and Ekfrid, and the Village of Strathroy.

[The East Riding to consist of the Townships now embraced therein, and be bounded as it is at present.]

51. The County of LAMBTON to consist of the Townships of Bosanquet, Warwick, Plympton, Sarnia, Moore, Enniskillen, and Brooke, and the Town of Sarnia.

52. The County of KENT to consist of the Townships of Chatham, Dover, East Tilbury, Romney, Raleigh, and Harwich, and the town of Chatham.

53. The County of BOTHWELL to consist of the Townships of Sombra, Dawn, and Euphemia (taken from the County of Lambton), and the Townships of Zone, Camden with the Gore thereof, Orford, and Howard (taken from the County of Kent).

The County of GREY divided into Two Ridings to be called respectively the South and North Ridings:—

54. The South Riding to consist of the Townships of Bentinck, Glenelg, Artemesia, Osprey, Normanby, Egremont, Proton, and Melancthon.

55. The North Riding to consist of the Townships of Collingwood, Euphrasia, Holland, Saint-Vincent, Sydenham, Sullivan, Derby, and Keppel, Sarawak and Brooke, and the Town of Owen Sound.

The County of PERTH divided into Two Ridings, to be called respectively the South and North Ridings:—

56. The North Riding to consist of the Townships of Wallace, Elma, Logan, Ellice, Mornington, and North Easthope, and the Town of Stratford.

57. The South Riding to consist of the Townships of Blanchard, Downie, South Easthope, Fullarton, Hibbert, and the Villages of Mitchell and Ste. Marys.

The County of WELLINGTON divided into Three Ridings to be called respectively North, South and Centre Ridings:—

58. The North Riding to consist of the Townships of Amaranth, Arthur, Luther, Minto, Maryborough, Peel, and the Village of Mount Forest.

59. The Centre Riding to consist of the Townships of Garafraxa, Erin, Eramosa, Nichol, and Pilkington, and the Villages of Fergus and Elora.

60. The South Riding to consist of the Town of Guelph, and the Townships of Guelph and Puslinch.

The County of NORFOLK, divided into Two Ridings, to be called respectively the South and North Ridings:—

61. The South Riding to consist of the Townships of Charlotteville, Houghton, Walsingham, and Woodhouse, and with the Gore thereof.

62. The North Riding to consist of the Townships of Middleton, Townsend, and Windham, and the Town of Simcoe.

63. The County of HALDIMAND to consist of the Townships of Oneida, Seneca, Cayuga North, Cayuga South, Rainham, Walpole, and Dunn.

64. The County of MONCK to consist of the Townships of Canborough and Moulton, and Sherbrooke, and the Village of Dunnville (taken from the County of Haldimand), the Townships of Caister and Gainsborough (taken from the County of Lincoln), and the Townships of Pelham and Wainfleet (taken from the County of Welland).

65. The County of LINCOLN to consist of the Townships of Clinton, Grantham, Grimsby, and Louth, and the Town of St. Catherines.

66. The County of WELLAND to consist of the Townships of Bertie, Crowland, Humberstone, Stamford, Thorold, and Willoughby, and the Villages of Chippewa, Clifton, Fort Erie, Thorold, and Welland.

67. The County of PEEL to consist of the Townships of Chinguacousy, Toronto, and the Gore of Toronto, and the Villages of Brampton and Streetsville.

68. The County of CARDWELL to consist of the Townships of Albion and Caledon (taken from the County of Peel), and the Townships of Adjala and Mono (taken from the County of Simcoe).

The County of SIMCOE, divided into Two Ridings, to be called respectively the South and North Ridings:—

69. The South Riding to consist of the Townships of West Gwillimbury, Tecumseth, Innisfil, Essa, Tossorontio, Mulmur, and the Village of Bradford.

70. The North Riding to consist of the Townships of Nottawasaga, Sunnidale, Vespra, Flos, Oro, Medonte, Orillia and Matchedash, Tiny and Tay, Balaklava and Robinson, and the Towns of Barrie and Collingwood.

The County of VICTORIA, divided into Two Ridings, to be called respectively the South and North Ridings:—

71. The South Riding to consist of the Township of Ops, Mariposa, Emily, Verulam, and the Town of Lindsay.

72. The North Riding to consist of the Townships of Anson, Bexley, Carden, Dalton, Digby, Eldon, Fenelon, Hindon, Laxton, Lutterworth, Macaulay and Draper, Sommerville, and Morrison, Muskoka, Monck and Watt (taken from the County of Simcoe), and any other surveyed Townships lying to the North of the said North Riding.

The County of PETERBOROUGH, divided into Two Ridings, to be called respectively the West and East Ridings:—

73. The West Riding to consist of the Townships of South Monaghan (taken from the County of Northumberland), North Monaghan, Smith, and Ennismore, and the Town of Peterborough.

74. The East Riding to consist of the Townships of Asphodel, Belmont and Methuen, Douro, Dummer, Galway, Harvey, Minden, Stanhope and Dysart, Otonabee, and Snowden, and the Village of Ashburnham, and any other surveyed Townships lying to the North of the said East Riding.

The County of HASTINGS, divided into Three Ridings, to be called respectively the West, East, and North Ridings:—

75. The West Riding to consist of the Town of Belleville, the Township of Sydney, and the Village of Trenton.

76. The East Riding to consist of the Townships of Thurlow, Tyendinaga, and Hungerford.

77. The North Riding to consist of the Townships of Rawdon, Huntingdon, Madoc, Elzevir, Tudor, Marmora, and Lake, and the Village of Stirling, and any other surveyed Townships lying to the North of the said North Riding.

78. The County of LENNOX, to consist of the Townships of Richmond, Adolphustown, North Fredericksburgh, South Fredericksburgh, Ernest Town, and Amherst Island, and the Village of Napanee.

79. The County of ADDINGTON to consist of the Townships of Camden, Portland, Sheffield, Hinchinbrooke, Kaladar, Kennebec, Olden, Oso, Anglesea, Barrie, Clarendon, Palmerston, Effingham, Abinger, Miller, Canonto, Denbigh, Loughborough, and Bedford.

80. The County of FRONTENAC to consist of the Townships of Kingston, Wolfe Island, Pittsburgh and Howe Island, and Storrington.

The County of RENFREW, divided into Two Ridings, to be called respectively the South and North Ridings:—

81. The South Riding to consist of the Townships of McNab, Bagot, Blithfield, Brougham, Horton, Admaston, Grattan, Matawatchan, Griffith, Lyndoch, Raglan, Radcliffe, Brudenell, Sebastopol, and the Villages of Arnprior and Renfrew.

82. The North Riding to consist of the Townships of Ross, Bromley, Westmeath, Stafford, Pembroke, Wilberforce, Alice, Petawawa, Buchanan, South Algoma, North Algoma, Fraser, McKay, Wylie, Rolph, Head, Maria, Clara, Haggerty, Sherwood, Burns, and Richards, and any other surveyed Townships lying Northwesterly of the said North Riding.

---

Every Town and incorporated Village existing at the Union, not specially mentioned in this Schedule, is to be taken as Part of the County or Riding within which it is locally situate.

---

## THE SECOND SCHEDULE.

*Electoral Districts of Quebec specially fixed.*

COUNTIES OF—

| | | |
|---|---|---|
| Pontiac. | Missisquoi. | Compton. |
| Ottawa. | Brome. | Wolfe and |
| Argenteuil. | Shefford. | Richmond. |
| Huntingdon. | Stanstead. | Megantic. |

Town of Sherbrooke

## THE THIRD SCHEDULE.

*Provincial Public Works and Property to be the Property of Canada.*

1. Canals, with Lands and Water Power connected therewith.
2. Public Harbours.
3. Lighthouses and Piers, and Sable Island.
4. Steamboats, Dredges, and public Vessels.
5. Rivers and Lake Improvements.
6. Railways and Railway Stocks, Mortgages, and other Debts due by Railway Companies.
7. Military Roads.
8. Custom Houses, Post Offices, and all other Public Buildings, except such as the Government of Canada appropriate for the Use of the Provincial Legislature and Governments.
9. Property transferred by the Imperial Government, and known as Ordinance Property.
10. Armouries, Drill Sheds, Military Clothing, and Munitions of War, and Lands set apart for general Public Purposes.

## THE FOURTH SCHEDULE.

*Assets to be the Property of Ontario and Quebec conjointly.*

Upper Canada Building Fund.
Lunatic Asylums.
Normal School.
Court
Houses,
    in
Aylmer.                    } Lower Canada
Montreal.
Kamouraska.
Law Society, Upper Canada.
Montreal Turnpike Trust.
University Permanent Fund.
Royal Institution.
Consolidated Municipal Loan Fund, Upper Canada.
Consolidated Municipal Loan Fund, Lower Canada.

Agricultural Society, Upper Canada.
Lower Canada Legislative Grant.
Quebec Fire Loan.
Temiscouata Advance Account.
Quebec Turnpike Trust.
Education—East.
Building and Jury Fund, Lower Canada.
Municipalities Fund.
Lower Canada Superior Education Income Fund.

---

---

## THE FIFTH SCHEDULE.

---

### OATH OF ALLEGIANCE.

I, *A.B.* do swear, That I will be faithful and bear true Allegiance to Her Majesty Queen Victoria.

*Note.—The Name of the King or Queen of the United Kingdom of Great Britain and Ireland for the Time being is to be substituted from Time to Time, with Proper Terms of Reference thereto.*

### DECLARATION OF QUALIFICATION.

I, *A.B.* do declare and testify, That I am by Law duly qualified to be appointed a Member of the Senate of Canada [*or as the Case may be*], and that I am legally or equitably seised as of Freehold for my own Use and Benefit of Lands or Tenements held in Free and Common Socage [*or seised or possessed for my own Use and Benefit of Lands or Tenements held in Franc-alleu or in Roture (as the Case may be*),] in the Province of Nova Scotia [*or as the Case may be*] of the Value of Four thousand Dollars over and above all Rents, Dues, Debts, Mortgages, Charges, and Incumbrances due or payable out of or charged on or affecting the same, and that I have not collusively or colourably obtained a Title to or become possessed of the said Lands and Tenements or any Part thereof for the Purpose of enabling me to become a Member of the Senate of Canada [*or a the Case may be*,] and that my Real and Personal Property are together worth Four thousand Dollars over and above my Debts and Liabilities.

---

---

## THE SIXTH SCHEDULE. (78)

---

*Primary Production from Non-Renewable Natural
Resources and Forestry Resources*

1. For the purposes of section 92A of this Act,
   (*a*) production from a non-renewable natural resource is primary production therefrom if
       (i) it is in the form in which it exists upon its recovery or severance from its natural state, or
       (ii) it is a product resulting from processing or refining the resource, and is not a manufactured product or a product resulting from refining crude oil, refining upgraded heavy crude oil, refining gases or liquids derived from coal or refining a synthetic equivalent or crude oil; and
   (*b*) production from a forestry resource is primary production therefrom if it consists of sawlogs, poles, lumber, wood chips, sawdust or any other primary wood product, or wood pulp, and is not a product manufactured from wood.

---

(78)  As enacted by the *Constitution Act, 1982.*

## THE CONSTITUTION ACT, 1982*

### PART I

### CANADIAN CHARTER OF RIGHTS AND FREEDOMS

Whereas Canada is founded upon principles that recognize the supremacy of God and the rule of law:

*Guarantee of Rights and Freedoms*

1. The *Canadian Charter of Rights and Freedoms* guarantees the rights and freedoms set out in it subject only to such reasonable limits prescribed by law as can be demonstrably justified in a free and democratic society.

*Fundamental Freedoms*

2. Everyone has the following fundamental freedoms:
   (*a*) freedom of conscience and religion;
   (*b*) freedom of thought, belief, opinion and expression, including freedom of the press and other media of communication;
   (*c*) freedom of peaceful assembly; and
   (*d*) freedom of association.

*Democratic Rights*

3. Every citizen of Canada has the right to vote in an election of members of the House of Commons or of a legislative assembly and to be qualified for membership therein.

4. (1) No House of Commons and no legislative assembly shall continue for longer than five years from the date fixed for the return of the writs at a general election of its members.
   (2) In time of real or apprehended war, invasion or insurrection, a House of Commons may be continued by Parliament and a legislative assembly may be continued by the legislature beyond five years if such continuation is not opposed by the votes of more than one-third of the members of the House of Commons or the legislative assembly, as the case may be.

5. There shall be a sitting of Parliament and of each legislature at least once every twelve months.

*Mobility Rights*

6. (1) Every citizen of Canada has the right to enter, remain in and leave Canada.
   (2) Every citizen of Canada and every person who has the status of a permanent resident of Canada has the right
   (*a*) to move to and take up residence in any province; and
   (*b*) to pursue the gaining of a livelihood in any province.
   (3) The rights specified in subsection (2) are subject to
   (a) any laws or practices of general application in force in a province other than those that discriminate among persons primarily on the basis of province of present or previous residence; and
   (b) any laws providing for reasonable residency requirements as a qualification for the receipt of publicly provided social services.
   (4) Subsections (2) and (3) do not preclude any law, program or activity that has as its object the amelioration in a province of conditions of individuals in that province who are socially or economically disadvantaged if the rate of employment in that province is below the rate of employment in Canada.

---

* Enacted as Schedule B to the *Canada Act 1982* (U.K.) 1982, c. 11, which came into force on April 17, 1982.

*Legal Rights*

7. Everyone has the right to life, liberty and security of the person and the right not to be deprived thereof except in accordance with the principles of fundamental justice.

8. Everyone has the right to be secure against unreasonable search or seizure.

9. Everyone has the right not to be arbitrarily detained or imprisoned.

10. Everyone has the right on arrest or detention
    (*a*) to be informed promptly of the reasons therefor;
    (*b*) to retain and instruct counsel without delay and to be informed of that right; and
    (*c*) to have the validity of the detention determined by way of *habeas corpus* and to be released if the detention is not lawful.

11. Any person charged with an offence has the right
    (*a*) to be informed without unreasonable delay of the specific offence;
    (*b*) to be tried within a reasonable time;
    (*c*) not to be compelled to be a witness in proceedings against that person in respect of the offence;
    (*d*) to be presumed innocent until proven guilty according to law in a fair and public hearing by an independent and impartial tribunal;
    (*e*) not to be denied reasonable bail without just cause;
    (*f*) except in the case of an offence under military law tried before a military tribunal, to the benefit of trial by jury where the maximum punishment for the offence is imprisonment for five years or a more severe punishment;
    (*g*) not to be found guilty on account of any act or omission unless, at the time of the act or omission, it constituted an offence under Canadian or international law or was criminal according to the general principles of law recognized by the community of nations;
    (*h*) if finally acquitted of the offence, not to be tried for it again and, if finally found guilty and punished for the offence, not to be tried or punished for it again; and
    (*i*) if found guilty of the offence and if the punishment for the offence has been varied between the time of commission and the time of sentencing, to the benefit of the lesser punishment.

12. Everyone has the right not to be subjected to any cruel and unusual treatment or punishment.

13. A witness who testifies in any proceedings has the right not to have any incriminating evidence so given used to incriminate that witness in any other proceedings, except in a prosecution for perjury or for the giving of contradictory evidence.

14. A party or witness in any proceedings who does not understand or speak the language in which the proceedings are conducted or who is deaf has the right to the assistance of an interpreter.

*Equality Rights*

15. (1) Every individual is equal before and under the law and has the right to the equal protection and equal benefit of the law without discrimination and, in particular, without discrimination based on race, national or ethnic origin, colour, religion, sex, age or mental or physical disability.
    (2) Subsection (1) does not preclude any law, program or activity that has as its object the amelioration of conditions of disadvantaged individuals or groups including those that are disadvantaged because of race, national or ethnic origin, colour, religion, sex, age or mental or physical disability.

*Official Languages of Canada*

**16.** (1) English and French are the official languages of Canada and have equality of status and equal rights and privileges as to their use in all institutions of the Parliament and government of Canada.

(2) English and French are the official languages of New Brunswick and have equality of status and equal rights and privileges as to their use in all institutions of the legislature and government of New Brunswick.

(3) Nothing in this Charter limits the authority of Parliament or a legislature to advance the equality of status or use of English and French.

**17.** (1) Everyone has the right to use English or French in any debates and other proceedings of Parliament.

(2) Everyone has the right to use English or French in any debates and other proceedings of the legislature of New Brunswick.

**18.** (1) The statutes, records and journals of Parliament shall be printed and published in English and French and both language versions are equally authoritative.

(2) The statutes, records and journals of the legislature of New Brunswick shall be printed and published in English and French and both language versions are equally authoritative.

**19.** (1) Either English or French may be used by any person in, or in any pleading in or process issuing from, any court established by Parliament.

(2) Either English or French may be used by any person in, or in any pleading in or process issuing from, any court of New Brunswick.

**20.** (1) Any member of the public in Canada has the right to communicate with, and to receive available services from, any head or central office of an institution of the Parliament or government of Canada in English or French, and has the same right with respect to any other office of any such institution where

(*a*) there is a significant demand for communications with and services from that office in such language; or

(*b*) due to the nature of the office, it is reasonable that communications with and services from that office be available in both English and French.

(2) Any member of the public in New Brunswick has the right to communicate with, and to receive available services from, any office of an institution of the legislature or government of New Brunswick in English or French.

**21.** Nothing in sections 16 to 20 abrogates or derogates from any right, privilege or obligation with respect to the English and French languages, or either of them, that exists or is continued by virtue of any other provision of the Constitution of Canada.

**22.** Nothing in sections 16 to 20 abrogates or derogates from any legal or customary right or privilege acquired or enjoyed either before or after the coming into force of this Charter with respect to any language that is not English or French.

*Minority Language Educational Rights*

**23.** (1) Citizens of Canada

(*a*) whose first language learned and still understood is that of the English or French linguistic minority population of the province in which they reside, or

(*b*) who have received their primary school instruction in Canada in English or French and reside in a province where the language in which they received that instruction is the language of the English or French linguistic minority population of the province,

have the right to have their children receive primary and secondary school instruction in that language in that province.

(2) Citizens of Canada of whom any child has received or is receiving primary or secondary school instruction in English or French in Canada, have the right to have all their children receive primary and secondary school instruction in the same language.

(3) The right of citizens of Canada under subsections (1) and (2) to have their children receive primary and secondary school instruction in the language of the English or French linguistic minority population of a province

(a) applies wherever in the province the number of children of citizens who have such a right is sufficient to warrant the provision to them out of public funds of minority language instruction; and

(b) includes, where the number of children so warrants, the right to have them receive that instruction in minority language educational facilities provided out of public funds.

*Enforcement*

**24.** (1) Anyone whose rights or freedoms, as guaranteed by this Charter, have been infringed or denied may apply to a court of competent jurisdiction to obtain such remedy as the court considers appropriate and just in the circumstances.

(2) Where, in proceedings under subsection (1), a court concludes that evidence was obtained in a manner that infringed or denied any rights or freedoms guaranteed by this Charter, the evidence shall be excluded if it is established that, having regard to all the circumstances, the admission of it in the proceedings would bring the administration of justice into disrepute.

*General*

**25.** The guarantee in this Charter of certain rights and freedoms shall not be construed so as to abrogate or derogate from any aboriginal, treaty or other rights or freedoms that pertain to the aboriginal peoples of Canada including

(a) any rights or freedoms that have been recognized by the Royal Proclamation of October 7, 1763; and

(b) any rights or freedoms that now exist by way of land claims agreements or may be so acquired.*

**26.** The guarantee in this Charter of certain rights and freedoms shall not be construed as denying the existence of any other rights or freedoms that exist in Canada.

**27.** This Charter shall be interpreted in a manner consistent with the preservation and enhancement of the multicultural heritage of Canadians.

**28.** Notwithstanding anything in this Charter, the rights and freedoms referred to in it are guaranteed equally to male and female persons.

**29.** Nothing in this Charter abrogates or derogates from any rights or privileges guaranteed by or under the Constitution of Canada in respect of denominational, separate or dissentient schools.

**30.** A reference in this Charter to a province or to the legislative assembly or legislature of a province shall be deemed to include a reference to the Yukon Territory and the Northwest Territories, or to the appropriate legislative authority thereof, as the case may be.

**31.** Nothing in this Charter extends the legislative powers of any body or authority.

*Application of Charter*

**32.** (1) This Charter applies

(a) to the Parliament and government of Canada in respect of all matters within the

---

* As amended June 21, 1984.

authority of Parliament including all matters relating to the Yukon Territory and North-west Territories; and

(b) to the legislature and government of each province in respect of all matters within the authority of the legislature of each province.

(2) Notwithstanding subsection (1), section 15 shall not have effect until three years after this section comes into force.

33. (1) Parliament or the legislature of a province may expressly declare in an Act of Parliament or of the legislature, as the case may be, that the Act or a provision thereof shall operate notwithstanding a provision included in section 2 or sections 7 to 15 of this Charter.

(2) An Act or provision of an Act in respect of which a declaration made under this section is in effect shall have such operation as it would have but for the provision of this Charter referred to in the declaration.

(3) A declaration made under subsection (1) shall cease to have effect five years after it comes into force or on such earlier date as may be specified in the declaration.

(4) Parliament or a legislature of a province may re-enact a declaration made under subsection (1).

(5) Subsection (3) applies in respect of a re-enactment made under subsection (4).

*Citation*

34. This Part may be cited as the *Canadian Charter of Rights and Freedoms*.

## PART II

## RIGHTS OF THE ABORIGINAL PEOPLES OF CANADA

35. (1) The existing aboriginal and treaty rights of the aboriginal peoples of Canada are hereby recognized and affirmed.

(2) In this Act, "aboriginal peoples of Canada" includes the Indian, Inuit and Métis peoples of Canada.

(3) For greater certainty, in subsection (1) "treaty rights" includes rights that now exist by way of land claims agreements or may be so acquired.*

(4) Notwithstanding any other provision of this Act, the aboriginal and treaty rights referred to in subsection (1) are guaranteed equally to male and female persons.*

35.1 The government of Canada and the provincial governments are committed to the principle that, before any amendment is made to Class 24 of section 91 of the *Constitution Act, 1867*, to section 25 of this Act or to this Part,

(a) a constitutional conference that includes in its agenda an item relating to the proposed amendment, composed of the Prime Minister of Canada and the first ministers of the provinces, will be convened by the Prime Minister of Canada; and

(b) the Prime Minister of Canada will invite representatives of the aboriginal peoples of Canada to participate in the discussions on that item.*

## PART III

## EQUALIZATION AND REGIONAL DISPARITIES

36. (1) Without altering the legislative authority of Parliament or of the provincial legislatures, or the rights of any of them with respect to the exercise of their legislative authority, Parliament and the legislatures, together with the government of Canada and the provincial governments, are committed to

(a) promoting equal opportunities for the well-being of Canadians;

---

* Subsections 35(3) and 35(4) and section 35.1 were added to the original *Constitution Act, 1982* by amendments proclaimed on June 21, 1984.

(*b*) furthering economic development to reduce disparity in opportunities; and

(*c*) providing essential public services of reasonable quality to all Canadians.

(2) Parliament and the government of Canada are committed to the principle of making equalization payments to ensure that provincial governments have sufficient revenues to provide reasonably comparable levels of public services at reasonably comparable levels of taxation.

## PART IV.1**

### CONSTITUTIONAL CONFERENCES

**37.1** (1) In addition to the conference convened in March 1983, at least two constitutional conferences composed of the Prime Minister of Canada and the first ministers of the provinces shall be convened by the Prime Minister of Canada, the first within three years after April 17, 1982 and the second within five years after that date.

(2) Each conference convened under subsection (1) shall have included in its agenda constitutional matters that directly affect the aboriginal peoples of Canada, and the Prime Minister of Canada shall invite representatives of those peoples to participate in the discussions on those matters.

(3) The Prime Minister of Canada shall invite elected representatives of the governments of the Yukon Territory and the Northwest Territories to participate in the discussions on any item on the agenda of a conference convened under subsection (1) that, in the opinion of the Prime Minister, directly affects the Yukon Territory and the Northwest Territories.

(4) Nothing in this section shall be construed so as to derogate from subsection 35(1).

## PART V

### PROCEDURE FOR AMENDING CONSTITUTION OF CANADA

**38.** (1) An amendment to the Constitution of Canada may be made by proclamation issued by the Governor General under the Great Seal of Canada where so authorized by

(*a*) resolutions of the Senate and House of Commons; and

(*b*) resolutions of the legislative assemblies of at least two-thirds of the provinces that have, in the aggregate, according to the then latest general census, at least fifty per cent of the population of all the provinces.

(2) An amendment made under subsection (1) that derogates from the legislative powers, the proprietary rights or any other rights or privileges of the legislature or government of a province shall require a resolution supported by a majority of the members of each of the Senate, the House of Commons and the legislative assemblies required under subsection (1).

(3) An amendment referred to in subsection (2) shall not have effect in a province the legislative assembly of which has expressed its dissent thereto by resolution supported by a majority of its members prior to the issue of the proclamation to which the amendment relates unless that legislative assembly, subsequently, by resolution supported by a majority of its members, revokes its dissent and authorizes the amendment.

(4) A resolution of dissent made for the purposes of subsection (3) may be revoked at any time before or after the issue of the proclamation to which it relates.

**39.** (1) A proclamation shall not be issued under subsection 38(1) before the expiration of one year from the adoption of the resolution initiating the amendment procedure thereunder, unless the legislative assembly of each province has previously adopted a resolution of assent or dissent.

---

** Part IV.1 was added by amendment on June 21, 1984. The former Part IV, which provided for the 1983 constitutional conference, was automatically repealed on April 17, 1983.

(2) A proclamation shall not be issued under subsection 38(1) after the expiration of three years from the adoption of the resolution initiating the amendment procedure thereunder.

**40.** Where an amendment is made under subsection 38(1) that transfers provincial legislative powers relating to education or other cultural matters from provincial legislatures to Parliament, Canada shall provide reasonable compensation to any province to which the amendment does not apply.

**41.** An amendment to the Constitution of Canada in relation to the following matters may be made by proclamation issued by the Governor General under the Great Seal of Canada only where authorized by resolutions of the Senate and House of Commons and of the legislative assembly of each province:
(*a*) the office of the Queen, the Governor General and the Lieutenant Governor of a province;
(*b*) the right of a province to a number of members in the House of Commons not less than the number of Senators by which the province is entitled to be represented at the time this Part comes into force;
(*c*) subject to section 43, the use of the English or the French language;
(*d*) the composition of the Supreme Court of Canada;
(*e*) an amendment to this Part.

**42.** (1) An amendment to the Constitution of Canada in relation to the following matters may be made only in accordance with subsection 38(1):
(*a*) the principle of proportionate representation of the provinces in the House of Commons prescribed by the Constitution of Canada;
(*b*) the powers of the Senate and the method of selecting Senators;
(*c*) the number of members by which a province is entitled to be represented in the Senate and the residence qualifications of Senators;
(*d*) subject to paragraph 41(*d*), the Supreme Court of Canada;
(*e*) the extension of existing provinces into the territories; and
(*f*) notwithstanding any other law or practice, the establishment of new provinces.
(2) Subsections 38(2) to (4) do not apply in respect of amendments in relation to matters referred to in subsection (1).

**43.** An amendment to the Constitution of Canada in relation to any provision that applies to one or more, but not all, provinces, including
(*a*) any alteration to boundaries between provinces, and
(*b*) any amendment to any provision that relates to the use of the English or the French language within a province,
may be made by proclamation issued by the Governor General under the Great Seal of Canada only where so authorized by resolutions of the Senate and House of Commons and of the legislative assembly of each province to which the amendment applies.

**44.** Subject to sections 41 and 42, Parliament may exclusively make laws amending the Constitution of Canada in relation to the executive government of Canada or the Senate and House of Commons.

**45.** Subject to section 41, the legislature of each province may exclusively make laws amending the constitution of the province.

**46.** (1) The procedures for amendment under sections 38, 41, 42 and 43 may be initiated either by the Senate or House of Commons or by the legislative assembly of a province.
(2) A resolution of assent made for the purposes of this Part may be revoked at any time before the issue of a proclamation authorized by it.

**47.** (1) An amendment to the Constitution of Canada made by proclamation under section 38, 41, 42 or 43 may be made without a resolution of the Senate authorizing the issue of the proclamation if, within one hundred and eighty days after the adoption by the House of

Commons of a resolution authorizing its issue, the Senate has not adopted such a resolution and if, at any time after the expiration of that period, the House of Commons again adopts the resolution.

(2) Any period when Parliament is prorogued or dissolved shall not be counted in computing the one hundred and eighty day period referred to in subsection (1).

**48.** The Queen's Privy Council for Canada shall advise the Governor General to issue a proclamation under this Part forthwith on the adoption of the resolutions required for an amendment made by proclamation under this Part.

**49.** A constitutional conference composed of the Prime Minister of Canada and the first ministers of the provinces shall be convened by the Prime Minister of Canada within fifteen years after this Part comes into force to review the provisions of this Part.

PART VI

AMENDMENT TO THE CONSTITUTION ACT, 1867

**50.** The *Constitution Act, 1867* (formerly named the *British North America Act, 1867*) is amended by adding thereto, immediately after section 92 thereof, the following heading and section:

*"Non-Renewable Natural Resources, Forestry Resources and Electrical Energy*

**92A.**(1) In each province, the legislature may exclusively make laws in relation to
(a) exploration for non-renewable natural resources in the province;
(b) development, conservation and management of non-renewable natural resources and forestry resources in the province, including laws in relation to the rate of primary production therefrom; and
(c) development, conservation and management of sites and facilities in the province for the generation and production of electrical energy.

(2) In each province, the legislature may make laws in relation to the export from the province to another part of Canada of the primary production from non-renewable natural resources and forestry resources in the province and the production from facilities in the province for the generation of electrical energy, but such laws may not authorize or provide for discrimination in prices or in supplies exported to another part of Canada.

(3) Nothing in subsection (2) derogates from the authority of Parliament to enact laws in relation to the matters referred to in that subsection and, where such a law of Parliament and a law of a province conflict, the law of Parliament prevails to the extent of the conflict.

(4) In each province, the legislature may make laws in relation to the raising of money by any mode or system of taxation in respect of
(a) non-renewable natural resources and forestry resources in the province and the primary production therefrom, and
(b) sites and facilities in the province for the generation of electrical energy and the production therefrom,
whether or not such production is exported in whole or in part from the province, but such laws may not authorize or provide for taxation that differentiates between production exported to another part of Canada and production not exported from the province.

(5) The expression "primary production" has the meaning assigned by the Sixth Schedule.

(6) Nothing in subsections (1) to (5) derogates from any powers or rights that a legislature or government of a province had immediately before the coming into force of this section."

**51.** The said Act is further amended by adding thereto the following Schedule:

"THE SIXTH SCHEDULE

*Primary Production from Non-Renewable Natural Resources and Forestry Resources*

1. For the purposes of section 92A of this Act,
    (*a*) production from a non-renewable resource is a primary production therefrom if
        (i) it is in the form in which it exists upon its recovery or severance from its natural state, or
        (ii) it is a product resulting from processing or refining the resource, and is not a manufactured product or a product resulting from refining crude oil, refining upgraded heavy crude oil, refining gases or liquids derived from coal or refining a synthetic equivalent of crude oil; and
    (*b*) production from a forestry resource is primary production therefrom if it consists of sawlogs, poles, lumber, wood chips, sawdust or any other primary wood product, or wood pulp, and is not a product manufactured from wood."

PART VII

GENERAL

**52.** (1) The Constitution of Canada is the supreme law of Canada, and any law that is inconsistent with the provisions of the Constitution is, to the extent of the inconsistency, of no force or effect.
    (2) The Constitution of Canada includes
        (*a*) the *Canada Act*, including this Act;
        (*b*) the Acts and orders referred to in Schedule I; and
        (*c*) any amendment to any Act or order referred to in paragraph (a) or (b).
    (3) Amendments to the Constitution of Canada shall be made only in accordance with the authority contained in the Constitution of Canada.

**53.** (1) The enactments referred to in Column I of Schedule I are hereby repealed or amended to the extent indicated in Column II thereof and, unless repealed, shall continue as law in Canada under the names set out in Column III thereof.
    (2) Every enactment, except the *Canada Act*, that refers to an enactment referred to in Schedule I by the name in Column I thereof is hereby amended by substituting for that name the corresponding name in Column III thereof, and any British North America Act not referred to in Schedule I may be cited as the *Constitution Act* followed by the year and number, if any, of its enactment.

**54.** Part IV is repealed on the day that is one year after this Part comes into force and this section may be repealed and this Act renumbered, consequential upon the repeal of Part IV and this section, by proclamation issued by the Governor General under the Great Seal of Canada.

**54.1** Part IV.1 and this section are repealed on April 18, 1987.*

**55.** A French version of the portions of the Constitution of Canada referred to in Schedule I shall be prepared by the Minister of Justice of Canada as expeditiously as possible and, when any portion thereof sufficient to warrant action being taken has been so prepared, it shall be put forward for enactment by proclamation issued by the Governor General under the Great Seal of Canada pursuant to the procedure then applicable to an amendment of the same provisions of the Constitution of Canada.

**56.** Where any portion of the Constitution of Canada has been or is enacted in English and French or where a French version of any portion of the Constitution is enacted pursuant to section 55, the English and French versions of that portion of the Constitution are equally authoritative.

---

* Section 54.1 was added by amendment on June 21, 1984.

**57.** The English and French versions of this Act are equally authoritative.

**58.** Subject to section 59, this Act shall come into force on a day to be fixed by proclamation issued by the Queen or the Governor General under the Great Seal of Canada.

**59.** (1) Paragraph 23(1)(*a*) shall come into force in respect of Quebec on a day to be fixed by proclamation issued by the Queen or the Governor General under the Great Seal of Canada.

   (2) A proclamation under subsection (1) shall be issued only where authorized by the legislative assembly or government of Quebec.

   (3) This section may be repealed on the day paragraph 23(1) (a) comes into force in respect of Quebec and this Act amended and renumbered, consequential upon the repeal of this section, by proclamation issued by the Queen or the Governor General under the Great Seal of Canada.

**60.** This Act may be cited as the *Constitution Act, 1982,* and the Constitution Acts 1867 to 1975 (No. 2) and this Act may be cited together as the *Constitution Acts, 1867 to 1982.*

**61.** A reference to the *Constitution Acts, 1867 to 1982* shall be deemed to include a reference to the *Constitution Amendment Proclamation, 1983.*\*\*

---

---

**SCHEDULE 1**

to the

CONSTITUTION ACT, 1982

---

*Modernization of the Constitution*

| Item | Column I<br>Act Affected | Column II<br>Amendment | Column III<br>New Name |
|------|--------------------------|------------------------|------------------------|
| 1. | British North America Act, 1867, 30-31 Vict., C. 3 (U.K.) | (1) Section 1 is repealed and the following substituted therefor: "1. This Act may be cited as the *Constitution Act, 1867.*" (2) Section 20 is repealed. (3) Class 1 of section 91 is repealed. (4) Class 1 of section 92 is repealed. | Constitution Act, 1867 |
| 2. | An Act to amend and continue the Act 32-33 Victoria chapter 3; and to establish and provide for the Government of the Province of Manitoba, 1870, 33 Vict. c. 3 (Can.) | (1) The long title is repealed and the following substituted therefor: "*Manitoba Act, 1870.*" (2) Section 20 is repealed. | Manitoba Act, 1870 |

---

\*\* Section 61 was added by amendment on June 21, 1984.

| | | | |
|---|---|---|---|
| 3. | Order of Her Majesty in Council admitting Rupert's Land and the North-Western Territory into the Union, dated the 23rd day of June, 1870 | | Rupert's Land and North-Western Territory Order |
| 4. | Order of Her Majesty in Council admitting British Columbia into the Union, dated the 16th day of May, 1871 | | British Columbia Terms of Union |
| 5. | British North America Act 1871, 34-35 Vict., C. 28 (U.K.) | Section 1 is repealed and the following substituted therefor: "1. This Act may be cited as the *Constitution Act, 1871*." | Constitution Act, 1871 |
| 6. | Order of Her Majesty in Council admitting Prince Edward Island into the Union, dated the 26th day of June, 1873 | | Prince Edward Island Terms of Union |
| 7. | Parliament of Canada Act, 1875, 38-39 Vict., c. 38 (U.K.) | | Parliament of Canada Act, 1875 |
| 8. | Order of Her Majesty in Council admitting all British possessions and Territories in North America and islands adjacent thereto into the Union, dated the 31st day of July, 1880 | | Adjacent Territories Order |
| 9. | British North America Act, 1886, 49-50 Vict., c. 35 (U.K.) | Section 3 is repealed and the following substituted therefor: "3. This Act may be cited as the *Constitution Act, 1886*." | Constitution Act, 1886 |
| 10. | Canada (Ontario Boundary) Act, 1889, 52-53 Vict., c. 28 (U.K.) | | Canada (Ontario Boundary) Act, 1889 |
| 11. | Canadian Speaker (Appointment of Deputy) Act, 1895, 2nd Sess., 59 Vict., c. 3 (U.K.) | The Act is repealed. | |
| 12. | The Alberta Act, 1905, 4-5 Edw. VII, c. 3 (Can.) | | Alberta Act |
| 13. | The Saskatchewan Act, 1905, 4-5 Edw. VII, c. 42 (Can.) | | Saskatchewan Act |
| 14. | British North America Act, 1907, 7 Edw. VII, c. 11 (U.K.) | Section 2 is repealed and the following substituted therefor: "2. This Act may be cited as the *Constitution Act, 1907*." | Constitution Act, 1907 |

| | | | |
|---|---|---|---|
| 15. | British North America Act, 1915, 5-6 Geo. V, c. 45 (U.K.) | Section 3 is repealed and the following substituted therefor:<br>"3. This Act may be cited as the *Constitution Act, 1915*." | Constitution Act, 1915 |
| 16. | British North America Act, 1930, 20-21 Geo. V, c. 26 (U.K.) | Section 3 is repealed and the following substituted therefor:<br>"3. This Act may be cited as the *Constitution Act, 1930*." | Constitution Act, 1930 |
| 17. | Statute of Westminster, 1931, 22 Geo. V, c. 4 (U.K.) | In so far as they apply to Canada,<br>(a) section 4 is repealed; and<br>(b) subsection 7(1) is repealed. | Statute of Westminster, 1931 |
| 18. | British North America Act, 1940, 3-4 Geo. VI, c. 36 (U.K.) | Section 2 is repealed and the following substituted therefor:<br>"2. This Act may be cited as the *Constitution Act, 1940*." | Constitution Act, 1940 |
| 19. | British North America Act, 1943, 6-7 Geo. VI, c. 30 (U.K.) | The Act is repealed. | |
| 20. | British North America Act, 1946, 9-10 Geo. VI, c. 63 (U.K.) | The Act is repealed. | |
| 21. | British North America Act, 1949, 12-13 Geo. VI, c. 22 (U.K.) | Section 3 is repealed and the following substituted therefor:<br>"3. This Act may be cited as the *Newfoundland Act*." | Newfoundland Act |
| 22. | British North America (No. 2) Act, 1949, 13 Geo. VI, c.81 (U.K.) | The Act is repealed. | |
| 23. | British North America Act, 1951, 14-15 Geo. VI, c. 32 (U.K.) | The Act is repealed. | |
| 24. | British North America Act, 1952, 1 Eliz. II, c. 15 (Can.) | The Act is repealed. | |
| 25. | British North America Act, 1960, 9 Eliz. II, c. 2 (U.K.) | Section 2 is repealed and the following substituted therefor:<br>"2. This Act may be cited as the *Constitution Act, 1960*." | Constitution Act, 1960 |
| 26. | British North America Act, 1964, 12-13 Eliz. II, c. 73 (U.K.) | Section 2 is repealed and the following substituted therefor:<br>"2. This Act may be cited as the *Constitution Act, 1964*." | Constitution Act, 1964 |

| | | | |
|---|---|---|---|
| 27. | British North America Act, 1965, 14 Eliz. II, c. 4, Part I (Can.) | Section 2 is repealed and the following substituted therefor:<br>"2. This Part may be cited as the *Constitution Act, 1965*." | Constitution Act, 1965 |
| 28. | British North America Act, 1974, 23 Eliz. II, c. 13, Part I (Can.) | Section 3, as amended by 25-26 Eliz. II, c. 28, s. 38(1) (Can.), is repealed and the following substituted therefor:<br>"3. This Part may be cited as the *Constitution Act, 1974*." | Constitution Act, 1974 |
| 29. | British North America Act, 1975, 23-24 Eliz. II, c. 28, Part I (Can.) | Section 3, as amended by 25-26 Eliz. II, c. 28, s. 31 (Can.), is repealed and the following substituted therefor:<br>"3. This Part may be cited as the *Constitution Act (No. 1), 1975*." | Constitution Act (No. 1), 1975 |
| 30. | British North America Act, (No. 2), 1975, 23-24 Eliz. II, c. 53 (Can.) | Section 3 is repealed and the following substituted therefor:<br>"3. This Act may be cited as the *Constitution Act (No. 2), 1975*." | Constitution Act (No. 2), 1975 |

# Index

# STUDENT REPLY CARD

In order to improve future editions, we are seeking your comments on
*Canadian Government and Politics: Institutions and Processes*
by Whittington and Van Loon. After you have read this text, please answer the
following questions and return this form via Business Reply Mail. *Your opinions
matter! Thank you in advance for your feedback!*

Name of your college or university: _____ _____

Major program of study: _____

Course title: _____

Were you required to buy this book?     ———— yes ———— no

Did you buy this book new or used?     ———— new ———— used ($ ——— )

Do you plan to keep or sell this book?     ———— keep ——— sell

Is the order of topic coverage consistent with what was taught in your course?

Are there chapters or sections of this text that were not assigned for your course?
Please specify:

Were there topics covered in your course that are not included in this text?
Please specify:

What did you like most about this text?

What did you like least?

If you would like to say more, we'd love to hear from you. Please write to us at the
address shown on the reverse of this card.

- - - - - - - - - - - - - - - - *cut here* - - - - - - - - - - - - - -

- - - - - - - - - - - - - - *fold here* - - - - - - - - - -

**Postage will be paid by**

MAIL ➤ POSTE

Canada Post Corporation / Société canadienne des postes

**Postage paid**
if mailed in Canada

**Port payé**
si posté au Canada

**Business
Reply**

**Réponse
d'affaires**

0183560299          01

0183560299-L1N9B6-BR01

Attn.: Sponsoring Editor
College Division

MCGRAW-HILL RYERSON LIMITED
300 WATER ST
WHITBY ON   L1N 9Z9